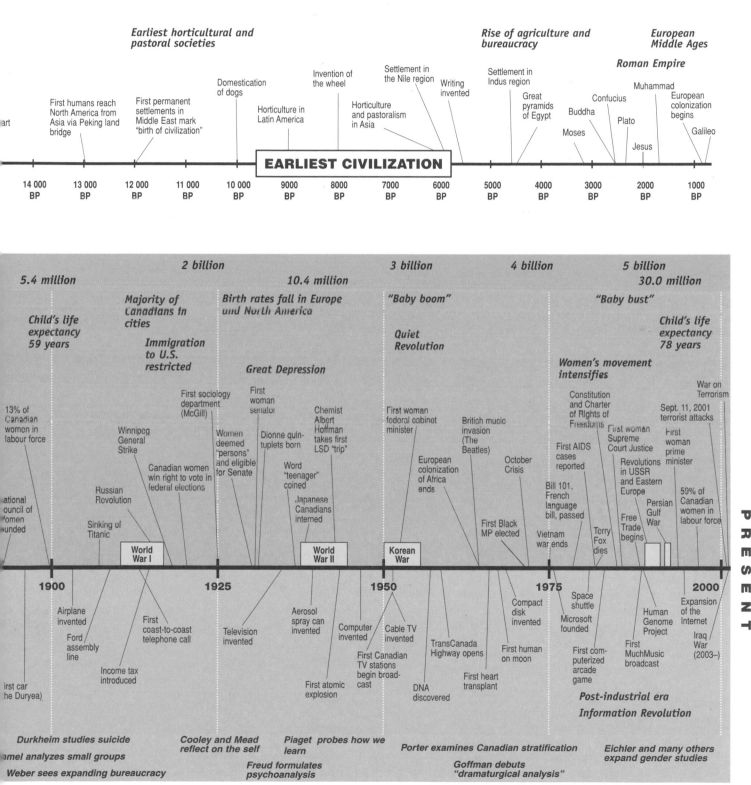

cent, indeed, with the first permanent settlements occurring in the Middle East a scant 12 000 years ago. But the written record of our species' existence extends back only half this long, to the time humans invented writing and first farmed with animal-driven plows some 5000 years BP.

Sociology came into being in the wake of the many changes to society wrought by the Industrial Revolution over the last few centuries—just the blink of an eye in evolutionary perspective. The lower timeline provides a close-up look at the events and trends that have defined **The Modern Era**, most of which are discussed in this text. Innovations in technology are charted in the beige panel below the line and provide a useful backdrop for viewing the milestones of social progress highlighted in the blue panel above the line. Major contributions to the development of sociological thought are traced along the very bottom of this timeline.

SOCIOLOGY

This book is offered to teachers of sociology in the hope that it will help our students understand their place in today's society and in tomorrow's world.

—*John J. Macionis & Linda M. Gerber*

Sixth Canadian Edition

SOCIOLOGY

JOHN J. MACIONIS
Kenyon College

LINDA M. GERBER
University of Guelph

PEARSON

Prentice
Hall

Toronto

Library and Archives Canada Cataloguing in Publication

Macionis, John J.
    Sociology / John J. Macionis, Linda M. Gerber. — 6th Canadian ed.

Includes bibliographical references and index.
ISBN-13: 978-0-13-236759-2

    1. Sociology—Textbooks. I. Gerber, Linda M. (Linda Marie), 1944– II. Title.

HM586.M325 2008   301   C2006-906967-0

ISBN-13: 978-0-13-236759-2
ISBN-10: 0-13-236759-9

Editor-in-Chief, Vice-President of Sales: Kelly Shaw
Acquisitions Editors: Ky Pruesse, Laura Forbes
Executive Marketing Manager: Judith Allen
Developmental Editor: Charlotte Morrison-Reed
Production Editor: Richard di Santo
Copy Editor: Susan Quirk
Proofreader: Camille Isaacs
Permissions Research: Bree Seeley, Amanda McCormick
Production Coordinator: Janis Raisen
Composition: Joan M. Wilson
Art Director: Julia Hall
Interior Design: Anthony Leung
Cover Design: Kerrin Hands
Cover Image: Getty Images/Michael Kelley

1 2 3 4 5   12 11 10 09 08

Printed and bound in the United States of America.

BRIEF CONTENTS

CONTENTS

PART II
The Foundations of Society

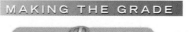

CHAPTER

Social Class in Canada   264

DIMENSIONS OF SOCIAL INEQUALITY   266

CANADIAN STRATIFICATION: MERIT AND CASTE   271

SOCIAL CLASSES IN CANADA   272

THE DIFFERENCE CLASS MAKES   278

SOCIAL MOBILITY   279

POVERTY IN CANADA   280

MAKING THE GRADE

CHAPTER

Global Stratification   290

GLOBAL STRATIFICATION: AN OVERVIEW   292

GLOBAL WEALTH AND POVERTY   296

GLOBAL STRATIFICATION: THEORETICAL ANALYSIS   305

GLOBAL STRATIFICATION: LOOKING AHEAD   311

MAKING THE GRADE

CHAPTER

Gender Stratification   316

GENDER AND INEQUALITY   319

CHAPTER

Race and Ethnicity   348

CHAPTER

Aging and the Elderly   378

PART IV
Social Institutions

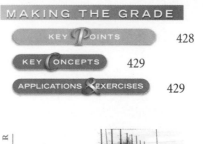

CHAPTER 16

The Economy and Work   402

CHAPTER 17

Politics and Government   430

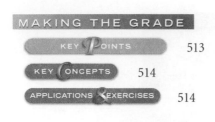

PART V
Social Change

CHAPTER

24

Social Change: Traditional, Modern, and Postmodern Societies   624

BOXES

APPLYING SOCIOLOGY

MEDIA PERSPECTIVES

THINKING CRITICALLY

THINKING ABOUT DIVERSITY:
RACE, CLASS, & GENDER

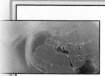

THINKING GLOBALLY

THINKING IT THROUGH

MAPS

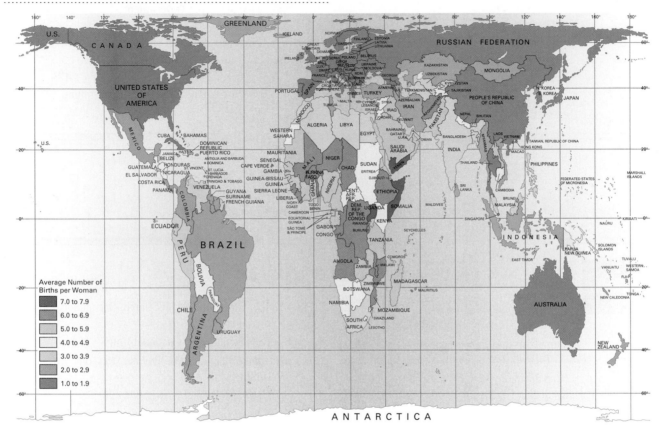

NATIONAL MAPS:
SEEING OURSELVES

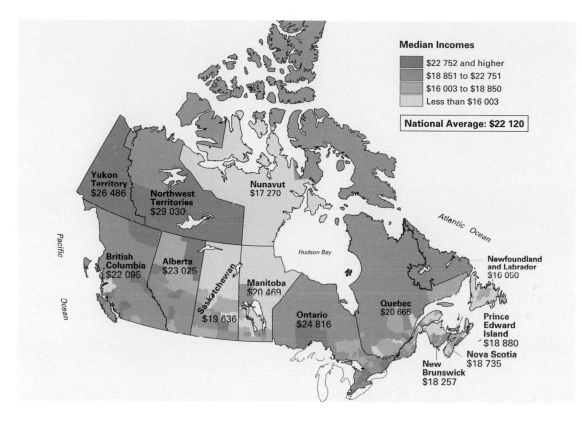

Median Incomes

- $22 752 and higher
- $18 851 to $22 751
- $16 003 to $18 850
- Less than $16 003

National Average: $22 120

Yukon Territory $26 486

Northwest Territories $29 030

Nunavut $17 270

Atlantic Ocean

Pacific Ocean

British Columbia $22 095

Alberta $23 025

Saskatchewan $19 636

Manitoba $20 469

Hudson Bay

Ontario $24 816

Quebec $20 665

Newfoundland and Labrador $16 050

Prince Edward Island $18 880

Nova Scotia $18 735

New Brunswick $18 257

It's here!
MySocLab™

to accompany Macionis and Gerber,
Sociology, *Sixth Canadian Edition*

This exciting new learning and teaching tool is designed to increase student success in the classroom *and* provide instructors with every resource needed to teach and administer an introductory sociology course!

WATCH

LISTEN

EXPLORE

PRE-TEST

MySocLab is an interactive and instructive multimedia resource that can be used as a supplement to a traditional lecture course, or to completely administer an online course. Its power lies in its design as an all-inclusive tool, combining an online version of the textbook plus multimedia, tutorials, audio, video, animations, and controlled assessments to completely engage students and reinforce learning.

PRENTICE HALL
mysoclab™
Where learning & the sociological imagination intersect.

PRACTICE

POST-TEST

Fully customizable, **MySocLab** meets the individual teaching and learning needs of *every* instructor and *every* student. It saves you and your students time, and it helps increase success in your course. What's more, it's EASY! Discover the benefits of using MySocLab for your sociology course today!

EXAM

BIOGRAPHY

PREFACE

The daily email we receive from students in Canada, the United States, and around the world stands as testimony to the power of sociology to help people understand their world and, often, to transform people's lives. All instructors know well the deep satisfaction that comes from making a difference in the lives of our students. Indeed, there is no greater reward for our work, and no better reason for constantly striving to improve each new edition of *Sociology*, the discipline's most popular text. We hope you will find *Sociology* to be authoritative, comprehensive, stimulating, and—as so many students testify—plain fun to read.

In addition to the book, every new copy of the sixth Canadian edition of *Sociology* comes with other learning tools. The package includes a student access kit for MySocLab, a state-of-the-art, interactive, and instructive online solution for introductory sociology. MySocLab combines multimedia, tutorials, video, audio, tests, and quizzes to make teaching and learning fun. MySocLab also gives students access to three exclusive online databases of high-quality source material: the ContentSelect™ Academic Journal Database, *The New York Times* Search-by-Subject™ Archive, and Link Library, a collection of editorially selected websites for sociology, through Pearson's Research Navigator™.

The *Sociology* learning package is completed with a full-featured, open-access website at **www.pearsoned.ca/macionis**. From the main page, users simply click on the cover of the text and select a chapter to find chapter summaries, learning objectives, critical-thinking and applying sociology exercises, links to additional online resources, and self-test quizzes that the server will immediately grade. Faculty will find a full complement of resources as well, including the syllabus manager that allows posting a course syllabus to the Internet.

The textbook, MySocLab with Research Navigator™, and the Companion Website form a comprehensive multimedia package that is the foundation for sound learning in this new information age. We invite you to examine all of these elements.

Organization of This Text

Part I of the textbook introduces the foundations of sociology. Underlying the discipline is the *sociological perspective*—the focus of Chapter 1, which explains how this exciting point of view brings the world to life in a new and instructive way. Chapter 2 spotlights *sociological investigation*, or the "doing of sociology." This chapter explains the scientific, interpretive, and critical orientations of the discipline, and illustrates major research strategies with actual, well-known sociological work.

Part II surveys the foundations of social life. Chapter 3 focuses on the central concept of *culture*, emphasizing the cultural diversity that makes up our society and world. The focus of Chapter 4 is the concept of *society*, presenting four time-honoured models for understanding the structure and dynamics of social organization. This unique chapter provides introductory students with the background to understand the ideas of important thinkers—including Karl Marx, Max Weber, Emile Durkheim, and Gerhard Lenski—that appear in subsequent chapters. Chapter 5 turns to *socialization*, exploring how we gain our humanity as we learn to participate in society. Chapter 6 provides a micro-level look at the patterns of *social interaction* that make up our everyday lives. Chapter 7 offers full-chapter coverage of *groups and organizations*, explaining the importance of group life and investigating how and why large organizations have come to dominate our way of life. Chapter 8 explains the social foundations of *human sexuality*. This chapter surveys sexual patterns in Canada and also explores variations in sexual practices through history and around the world today. Chapter 9 explains how the operation of society generates both *deviance and conformity*, and also surveys the operation of the criminal justice system.

Part III offers unparalleled discussion of social inequality, beginning with three chapters on *social stratification*. Chapter 10 introduces major concepts and presents theoretical explanations of social inequality. This chapter richly illustrates historical changes in stratification and how patterns of inequality vary in today's world. Chapter 11 surveys *social inequality in Canada*, confronting common perceptions of inequality and assessing how well they square with research findings. Chapter 12 extends analysis with a look at *global stratification*, revealing the disparities in wealth and power that separate rich and poor nations. Both Chapters 11 and 12 pay special attention to how global developments affect stratification in Canada just as they explore our society's role in global inequality. Chapter 13, *Gender Stratification*, explains how gender is a central element in social stratification in Canada, as it is worldwide. *Race and ethnicity*, additional important dimensions of social inequality that often intersect with differences based on class and gender, are detailed in Chapter 14. *Aging and the elderly*, a topic of increasing concern to "greying" societies such as our own, is addressed in Chapter 15.

Part IV includes a full chapter on each social institution. Leading off is Chapter 16, *The Economy and Work*, because most sociologists recognize the economy as having the greatest impact on all other institutions. This chapter traces the rise and fall of industrial production and the emergence of a global economy, and explains what such transformations mean for the Canadian labour force.

Chapter 17, *Politics and Government*, analyzes the distribution of power in Canadian society as well as surveying political systems around the world. In addition, this chapter includes a new discussion of terrorism and its impact on global social structures. Chapter 18, *Family*, explains the central importance of families to social organization, and underscores the diversity of family life both here and in other societies. Chapter 19, *Religion*, addresses the timeless human search for ultimate purpose and meaning, introduces major world religions, and explains how religious beliefs are linked to other dimensions of social life. Chapter 20, *Education*, analyzes the expansion of schooling in industrial societies. Here again, schooling in Canada comes to life through contrasts with educational patterns in other countries. Chapter 21, *Health and Medicine*, reveals health to be a social issue just as much as it is a matter of biological processes. This chapter traces the historical emergence of medicine, analyzes current medical issues, and compares Canadian patterns in health care to those found in other countries.

Part **V** examines important dimensions of global social change. Chapter 22 highlights the impact of *population growth and urbanization* in Canada and throughout the world with special attention to the *natural environment*. Chapter 23 explores forms of *collective behaviour* and explains how people seek or resist social change by joining *social movements*. Chapter 24 concludes the text with an overview of *social change* that contrasts *traditional, modern, and postmodern societies*. This chapter rounds out the text by explaining how and why world societies change and by critically analyzing the benefits and liabilities of traditional, modern, and postmodern ways of life.

Continuity: Established Features of Sociology

Everyone knows that introductory sociology texts have some things in common, but differences run deep. The extraordinary success of *Sociology*—far and away the most widely adopted text of its kind—results from a combination of the following distinctive features.

The best writing style   Most important, this text offers a writing style widely praised by students and faculty alike as elegant and inviting. *Sociology* is an enjoyable text that encourages students to read—even beyond their assignments.

A global perspective   *Sociology* has taken a leading role in expanding the horizons of our discipline beyond Canada. *Sociology* was the first text to mainstream global content, introduce global maps, and offer coverage of global topics such as stratification and the environment. Each chapter explores global social diversity as well as explaining why social trends in Canada—from musical tastes, to the price of wheat, to Quebec separatism—are influenced by what happens elsewhere. Furthermore, students will learn ways in which social patterns and policies in Canada affect poor nations around the world.

A focus on social diversity   *Sociology* invites students from all social backgrounds to discover fresh and exciting ways to see the world and understand themselves. Readers will find in the text the diversity of Canadian society—people of African, Asian, European, and Aboriginal ancestry, as well as women and men of various classes—in all parts of the country, and at all points in life. Just as importantly, without flinching from the problems that marginalized people confront, this text does not treat minorities as social problems but notes their achievements.

Emphasis on critical thinking   Critical-thinking skills include the ability to challenge common assumptions by formulating questions, identify and weigh appropriate evidence, and reach reasoned conclusions. This text not only teaches but encourages students to discover on their own.

The broadest coverage so that instructors have a choice   No other text matches *Sociology*'s twenty-four-chapter coverage of the field. We offer such breadth—at no greater cost—knowing that few instructors will assign every chapter, but with the goal of supporting instructors as they choose exactly what they wish to teach.

Engaging and instructive chapter openings   One of the most popular features of earlier editions of *Sociology* has been the inviting vignettes that begin each chapter. These openings—for instance, using the tragic sinking of the *Titanic* to illustrate the life-and-death consequences of social inequality, or beginning the discussion of global inequality by describing how a fire in a Pakistani sweatshop that manufactures clothing for sale in North America left dozens of low-paid workers dead—spark the interest of readers as they introduce important themes. This revision retains this engrossing feature.

Inclusive focus on women and men   Beyond devoting two full chapters to the important concepts of sex and gender, *Sociology* mainstreams gender into *every* chapter, showing how the topic at hand affects women and men differently and explaining how gender operates as a basic dimension of social organization.

Theoretically clear and balanced   *Sociology* makes theory easy. Chapter 1 introduces the discipline's major theoretical approaches, which are used in all the chapters that follow. The text highlights not only the social-conflict, structural-functional, and symbolic-interaction paradigms, but incorporates feminist theory, postmodernist theory, social-exchange analysis, ethnomethodology, cultural ecology, and sociobiology.

Chapter 4—unique to this text—provides students with an easy-to-understand introduction to important social theorists *before* they encounter their work in later chapters. The ideas of Max Weber, Karl Marx, and Emile Durkheim, as well as Gerhard Lenski's historical overview of human societies, appear in distinct sections that instructors may assign together or refer to separately at different points in the course.

Learning aids   This text has many features to help students learn. In each chapter, **Key Concepts** are identified by bold-faced type; following each is *a precise, italicized definition.* A complete **Glossary** is found at the end of the book. At the end of each chapter, students will find **Making the Grade,** a new active learning system designed to help students succeed in this course. A **Key Points** summary covers all the important issues, and a **Key Concepts** section provides *precise, italicized definitions of glossary terms.* Three **Applications & Exercises** help students move beyond the text to learn on their own on or near the campus, and the chapters close with a reminder to students to use **MySocLab** to its full potential.

Outstanding images: Photography and fine art   This book offers the finest and most extensive program of photography and artwork available in a sociology textbook. The Sixth Canadian Edition of *Sociology* displays many examples of fine art as well as hundreds of colour photographs. Each of these images has been carefully selected by the authors and appears with an insightful caption. Moreover, both photographs and artwork present people of various social backgrounds and historical periods.

Thought-provoking theme boxes   Although boxed material is common to introductory texts, *Sociology* provides a wealth of uncommonly good boxes. Each chapter typically contains a variety of boxes, which fall into six types that amplify central themes of the text. **Media Perspectives** boxes present new and exciting voices in sociology and explore sociology through a modern viewpoint. **Applying Sociology** boxes show readers how to apply the perspective, theory, and methods of sociology to greatest advantage. **Thinking About Diversity: Race, Class, and Gender** boxes focus on multicultural issues and present the voices of women and people of colour. **Thinking Critically** boxes teach students to ask sociological questions about their surroundings and help them evaluate important, controversial issues. **Thinking It Through** boxes present several points of view on hotly debated issues. **Thinking Globally** boxes provoke readers to think about their own way of life by examining the fascinating social diversity that characterizes our world. All boxes are followed by three "What do you think?" questions.

Sociology, Sixth Canadian Edition, contains over ninety boxes, many of which are brand new to this edition or have been heavily updated and revised. A complete list of the boxes in this text can be found following the table of contents.

An unparalleled program of global and national maps   This is the text that pioneered the use of global and national maps.

Window on the World Global Maps—twenty-two in all and many updated for this edition—are truly sociological maps offering a comparative look at income disparity, favoured languages, the extent of prostitution, permitted marriage forms, the degree of political freedom, the incidence of HIV/AIDS infection, and a host of other issues. The global maps use the non-Eurocentric projection devised by cartographer Arno Peters that accurately portrays the relative size of all the continents. A complete listing of the *Window on the World Global Maps* can be found on page xxii.

Seeing Ourselves National Maps help illuminate the social diversity of Canada. These maps highlight homicide rates, household income, foreign-born populations, birth rates, unemployment rates, and other measures of Canada's population. A complete listing of the *Seeing Ourselves National Maps* can be found on page xxiii.

Innovation: Changes in the Sixth Canadian Edition

Each new edition of *Sociology* has broken new ground, one reason that the popularity of this text and its brief version keep rising. Now, having reached the sixth Canadian edition, we energize the book once again, with many fresh ideas, new features, and innovative teaching tools. Here is a brief overview of what's new in *Sociology, Sixth Canadian Edition.*

A new look   As instructors understand, today's students are very visually oriented—in a world of rapid-fire images, they respond to what they see. Just as important, the photographs that we see in newspapers, on television, and online are more sociological than ever before. As a result, this new edition of *Sociology* offers more and better images, and the text has an exciting new look that is clear, attractive, and sure to boost student interest.

Sociology encourages students to use images to learn. Bold, vibrant, and colourful photos on the chapter-opening spreads pull students into the chapter material and become teaching opportunities. Together with the chapter-opening stories that follow, these images will inspire students to want to learn.

A new feel   A new look also calls for a new feel to the text. Our goal in this edition can be stated in the form of a promise: Every student in every class will be able to immediately understand the material on every page of the text. This promise does not come at the cost of any of the content you expect. What it means is that the authors have prepared this revision with the greatest care and with an eye toward making language and arguments as clear as they can be. Student tested—student friendly!

New chapter-opening questions   Each chapter of this edition begins with three questions that alert students to key themes discussed in the chapter.

Interactive "Your Turn" questions   To make this edition of *Sociology* more engaging and interactive, we have placed at least four or five "Your Turn" questions at different points in every chapter. "Your Turn" questions ask the student to apply the ideas being discussed to some other issue or link the ideas to their personal lives.

A greater focus on careers   Most students who enroll in a sociology course hope to find something useful for their future careers. Students using *Sociology* surely will. This text reflects the discipline's *career relevance* more than ever before. Chapter 1 ("The Sociological Perspective") includes a major new discussion of sociology and student careers. Many of the chapters that follow apply sociological insights to careers, for example, by explaining how today's corporate marketing is becoming more multicultural (Chapter 3, "Culture") and why physicians need to understand the social dynamics of an office visit or a medical examination (Chapter 6, "Social Interaction in Everyday Life"). In addition, there is greatly expanded coverage of the criminal justice system (Chapter 9, "Deviance"), as well as a discussion of the medical establishment, including the work of both physicians and nurses (Chapter 21, "Health and Medicine").

For additional connections between sociology and careers, look for the **Sociology@Work** icon. Found in all chapters, these icons draw student attention to discussions that have particular importance to the world of work. These icons help students to apply what they read to their consideration of future careers.

Applying sociology to students' everyday lives   The value of sociology depends on students' ability to apply what they learn to their own lives. This revision illustrates concepts in ways that encourage students to see these connections. In addition, the Applying Sociology series of boxes shows how to put sociology to work in people's everyday lives, on the job, at home, and on the campus.

Encouraging active reading   This book encourages students to be active readers. Of course, the lively, easy-to-understand writing style and use of current examples are important. In addition, all of the boxes in this revision now include three follow-up questions that invite students to think critically and to apply what they have learned to new situations.

A better way to teach theory   Sociological theory is important, but it is sometimes challenging for students. To ensure that students learn the important lessons, theoretical discussions are followed by "Critical Review" sections. In this revision, we have added new Applying Theory tables, which summarize, at a glance, how the various theoretical approaches view the topic at hand.

More popular culture   Today's students live in a world largely defined by North American popular culture. To more directly link the content of *Sociology* to the lives of readers, this revision integrates more popular culture into topic discussions. In particular, we draw many examples of important issues from the mass media, including popular films and television programming.

Making the Grade   At the end of each chapter of this text, students will find **Making the Grade,** a new active learning system designed to help students succeed in this course. A **Key Points** summary covers all the important issues, and a **Key Concepts** section provides precise definitions of glossary terms. Three **Applications & Exercises** help students move beyond the text to learn on their own on or near the campus, and the chapters close with a reminder to students to use **MySocLab** to its full potential.

Both students and faculty benefit from the following innovations:

New chapter-opening vignettes   This revision keeps the best of the popular chapter-opening vignettes and adds some to address new priorities in our changing world.

New and updated boxes   New boxes represent six themes of the text: Media Perspectives, Thinking About Diversity: Race, Class, and Gender; Thinking Critically; Thinking Globally; Thinking It Through; and Applying Sociology. A number of these boxes are new, and many more have been revised and updated for this revision.

Canadian Content

Canadian references and examples appear throughout the sixth Canadian edition of *Sociology*, and for some chapters—especially Chapter 11: Social Class in Canada, Chapter 14: Race and Ethnicity, and Chapter 17: Politics and Government—substantial parts are entirely Canadian. In addition, to Canadian content throughout the body of the text, most of the chapter openers, boxes, figures, and tables are unique to the Canadian edition. Extensive updating of references, statistics (including tables and figures), boxes, and examples has been undertaken for this edition, and new tables and graphs have been added. Major additions to this edition are labelled below as *New*. Maps of Canada appear in a number of chapters and Canadian authors and researchers are featured prominently throughout. Below we have listed just a few of the unique Canadian elements found in the sixth Canadian edition of Macionis/Gerber, *Sociology*.

HIGHLIGHTS FROM THE SIXTH CANADIAN EDITION

Chapter 1
- Suicide rates and trends in Canada
- Applying Sociology: Female Canadian astronaut spends 100 days in simulated space station
- *New* Media Perspectives: McLuhan on media theory
- Canadian sociology—distinctive touches (Harold Innis, John Porter, Marshall McLuhan, Erving Goffman)

Chapter 2
- Women (including Florence Nightingale) as methodologists
- Applying Sociology: Feminist research
- Thinking about Diversity: Conducting research with Aboriginal peoples
- *New* Thinking Critically: Reading tables—Aboriginal employment and income
- Media Perspectives: data collection, analysis, and publication—from card-punching to cyberspace

Chapter 3
- Thinking about Diversity: Aboriginal languages in danger of extinction
- *New* Media Perspectives: A lesson in values from cyberspace
- Thinking It Through: Canadians and Americans—what makes us different?
- Media Perspectives: Princess Diana and the paparazzi

Chapter 4
- Thinking It Through: Designing a better society
- Thinking Critically: Is Canadian society getting better or worse?

Chapter 5
- *New* Thinking about Diversity: Ethnic and racial identities (census-based research for this edition)
- Media Perspectives: Media portrayal of minorities
- Thinking It Through: Ontario's first boot camp (1997–2003)

Chapter 6
- Common-law unions in Canada
- *New* Media Perspectives: Disease and disability in Hollywood film
- Applying Sociology: Working online

Chapter 7
- *New* Applying Sociology: The club DJ from a symbolic-interactionist perspective
- Thinking It Through: Networks in cyberspace
- Thinking Globally: The Japanese business model in Canada
- Thinking Critically: Large organizations, identity, files, and privacy

Chapter 8
- Chapter opening vignette: Sex change surgery in Canada's military and police force

- Media Perspectives: The Canadian boy who was raised as a girl
- Thinking about Diversity: Same sex marriage in Canada
- Applying Sociology: Date rape
- Thinking It Through: The abortion controversy in Canada

Chapter 9
- Thinking about Diversity: Suicide among Aboriginal people
- *New* Media Perspectives: Crime in high places (Bre-X to Adscam)
- *New* Thinking It Through: Dangerous masculinity—violence in hockey (Michael Atkinson)
- Canadian, American, and global perspectives on crime
- The Canadian criminal justice system

Chapter 10
- Thinking about Diversity: Titanic, unknown child in Halifax cemetery (a relative of co-author Linda Gerber)
- Applying Sociology: Salaries of Canadians—average workers to celebrities and CEOs

Chapter 11
- *New* Occupational ranking in Waterloo, Ontario
- Thinking about Diversity: Social class and Aboriginal peoples
- Thinking It Through: Computers and social class
- Applying Sociology: The Calgary Stampede
- *New* Media Perspectives: The Homeless census in Toronto
- Thinking Critically: The welfare dilemma

Chapter 12
- Canada and low-income countries
- Thinking It Through: Sustainable development for Yucatan farmers

Chapter 13
- *New* Chapter opening vignette: The Famous Five; Women as persons (1929); Women and the Charter of Rights and Freedoms (1982)
- *New* Thinking It Through: The gender gap in occupation and income (new census-based research by Linda Gerber—a four-page box)
- *New* Media Perspectives: Powerful Canadian women
- Thinking about Diversity: Canadian women in hockey

Chapter 14
- Thinking about Diversity: Black history in Canada
- Ethnic identification—the growth of Canadian/ *Canadien* identity
- *New* A comparison of English, French, Chinese, Japanese, Black and Aboriginal Canadians on education, employment and income
- *New* Applying Sociology: Visible minorities in Toronto, Vancouver, and Montreal
- *New* Media Perspectives: The Aboriginal Peoples Television Network

- Thinking It Through: Distinct societies and national unity

Chapter 15

- *New* Chapter opening vignette: BC centenarian: 107 years young and she loves to dance
- Applying Sociology: Aboriginal elders
- *New* Media Perspectives: Aging in retirement residences and nursing homes; Gay/grey couples

Chapter 16

- Thinking about Diversity: The French Canadians of Manchester, New Hampshire
- Thinking It Through: Regional economic disparities
- Media Perspectives: Brain drain, brain gain
- *New* Employment patterns (including self-employment) for English, French, Chinese, Japanese, Black and Aboriginal Canadians (research for this edition)
- Thinking Globally: Working through cyberspace
- Thinking Globally: Free market and government intervention—a Canada/US comparison

Chapter 17

- Thinking about Diversity: Aboriginal self-government
- Parties, the political spectrum, and Canadian elections (1988 to 2006)
- *New* Media Perspectives: Who decides? (Politicians, polls, the media, the Gomery report, and Sheila Fraser)
- Thinking Critically: Managing our relationship with the United States
- Thinking It Through: Reforming Canada's political system

Chapter 18

- Chapter opening vignette: Families with lesbian parents
- Thinking about Diversity: International adoption
- *New* Thinking It Through: Spousal violence in Canada
- Applying Sociology: Cohabitation among Canadians
- *New* Media Perspectives: The controversy over child care

Chapter 19

- *New* Chapter opening vignette: Evangelical megachurches in Canada
- *New* Applying Sociology: Religion in Canada: Decline or renaissance
- *New* Media Perspectives: Check the media—religion is hot

Chapter 20

- *New* Chapter opening vignette: Educational outcomes on reserves
- Thinking It Through: Functional illiteracy in Canada
- *New* Educational attainment for English, French, Chinese, Japanese, Black and Aboriginal Canadians (research for this edition)
- Thinking about Diversity: The legacy of Canada's residential schools
- *New* Applying Sociology: Explaining educational attainment

- Media Perspectives: Welcome to cyberschool
- Thinking Critically: Is political correctness undermining education?

Chapter 21

- Thinking It Through: SARS, West Nile, Mad Cow, and Bird Flu
- *New* AIDS cases by ethnicity and sexual orientation in Canada
- Media Perspectives: Two-tiered health care: threat, fact, or fiction?

Chapter 22

- Chapter opening vignette: Intensive livestock operations and water contamination
- *New* Thinking about Diversity: Minorities in Canada's metropolitan areas (new research for this edition)
- Media Perspectives: Environmentally friendly Canada, eh?

Chapter 23

- Chapter opening vignette: Oka and the people of Kahnawake
- *New* Public opinion: It's all in the wording of the question
- *New* Media Perspectives: Car phone danger
- Thinking It Through: Taking a stand—the No rally in Montreal (October 1995)

Chapter 24

- Media Perspectives: The Canadian revolution—from deference to defiance
- *New* Thinking Critically: We're different, eh?

Supplements

Sociology, Sixth Canadian Edition, is the heart of a learning package that includes a wide range of proven instructional aids. As the authors of the text, we maintain a keen interest in all of the supplements to ensure their quality and integration with the text. Supplements for this revision have been thoroughly updated, improved, and expanded.

FOR THE INSTRUCTOR

Instructor's Resource Manual The *Instructor's Resource Manual* provides more than detailed chapter outlines and discussion questions; it contains statistical profiles of Canada and other nations, summaries of important developments and significant research, and supplemental lecture material for every chapter of the text.

Test Item File A completely revised *Test Item File* is available in both Word and MyTest versions. The file contains 2400 items—100 per chapter—in multiple-choice, true/false, and essay formats. Questions are identified as simple "recall" items or as more complex "inferential" issues. The answers to all questions are page-referenced to the text. MyTest is a highly flexible testing program that allows for the creation of personalized exams and is compatible with both Windows and Mac platforms.

Introductory Sociology PowerPoint Slides This PowerPoint presentation set combines graphics and text in a colourful format to help you convey sociological principles in a new and exciting way. This set contains more than 300 slides that cover the entire text and can be incorporated into lecture-specific PowerPoint presentations.

Instructor's Resource CD-ROM Digital files of all of the above instructor supplements are now available on one convenient CD-ROM.

Instructor Central Website This website provides password-protected access to all of the instructor supplements described above. Your Pearson representative can provide a password, or you can register online at **www.pearsoned.ca/instructor** to receive your password within a few hours, and download the supplements.

Pearson Education Canada's Sociology Video Library Few will dispute that video is the most dynamic supplement you can use to enhance a class. However, the quality of the video material and how well it relates to your course still make all the difference. Paul Lamy (University of Ottawa) and Vicki Nygaard (University of Victoria) have put together a fantastic video library and guide. The Pearson Education Sociology Video Library offers four VHS cassettes or four DVDs with over six hours of video clips, ranging in length from 10 to 25 minutes each. The clips offer a wealth of exciting material to use in the classroom. For adopters only; contact your Pearson Education Canada sales representative for more information.

Media and Society DVD This new DVD supplement contains eight video segments selected by Mark Belanger of Vanier College to support instructors who wish to include material on the influence of the media, journalism, and advertising on individuals and institutions. Professor Belanger has also written an accompanying Faculty Guide with a synopsis of each segment, teaching ideas, and discussion questions.

MEDIA SUPPLEMENTS

MySocLab

combines a complete electronic version of the sixth Canadian edition of *Sociology*, with video, audio, animations, research support, practice tests, exams, and more. MySocLab is a state-of-the-art interactive solution for introductory sociology. A Student Starter Kit for MySocLab is available with the purchase of every new text. MySocLab engages students and gives them the opportunities and tools

they need to extend their learning experience and enhance their performance. Visit **www.pearsoned.ca/mysoclab/** to find out more.

Research Navigator™

The goal of Research Navigator™ is to help students understand the steps in the research process so they can more confidently and efficiently complete research assignments. In addition, Research Navigator™ offers students three exclusive databases of credible and reliable source content to help focus their research efforts and get the research process started.

Students and faculty can access Research Navigator™ through MySocLab. Research Navigator™ includes three databases of credible and reliable source material:

- **EBSCO's ContentSelect™ Academic Journal Database**, organized by subject, contains 50 to 100 of the leading academic journals for each discipline. Instructors and students can search these online journals by keyword, topic, or multiple topics. Articles come complete with abstract and citation information and can be cut, pasted, emailed, or saved for later use.

- **The *New York Times* Search-by-Subject™** Archive, specific to sociology, is searchable by single or multiple keywords. Instructors and students can view full-text articles from the world's leading journalists at the *New York Times*.

- **Link Library** offers editorially selected "Best of the Web" sites for sociology. Link Libraries are continually scanned and updated in order to provide the most relevant and accurate links for research assignments.

Companion Website In tandem with the text, students and professors can now take full advantage of the Internet to enrich their study of sociology. The *Sociology* Companion Website continues to lead the way in providing students with avenues for delving deeper into topics covered in the text. Features of the Companion Website include chapter objectives, study questions, and faculty resources, as well as links to interesting material and information from other websites that will reinforce and enhance the content of each chapter. To enter, simply visit the site at **www.pearsoned.ca/macionis** and click on the cover of the Sixth Canadian Edition.

Online Learning Solutions Pearson Education Canada supports instructors interested in using online course management systems. We provide text-related content in WebCT, Blackboard, and CourseCompass, our own private-label version of Blackboard. To find out more about creating an online course using Pearson content in one of these platforms, contact your local Pearson Education Canada representative.

FOR THE STUDENT

In addition to the media supplements mentioned above, students can also make use of the following learning aids.

Study Guide   This complete guide helps students review and reflect on the material presented in *Sociology*. Each of the twenty-four chapters in the *Study Guide* provides an overview of the corresponding chapter in the text, summarizes its major topics and concepts, offers applied exercises, and features end-of-chapter tests with solutions.

VangoNotes

 Study on the go with VangoNotes. Just download chapter reviews from your text and listen to them on any mp3 player. Now, wherever you are—whatever you're doing—you can study by listening to the following for each chapter of your textbook:

- **Big Ideas**: Your "need to know" for each chapter

- **Practice Test**: A gut check for the Big Ideas—tells you if you need to keep studying

- **Key Terms**: Audio "flashcards" to help you review key concepts and terms

- **Rapid Review**: A quick drill session—use it right before your test

VangoNotes are *flexible*; download all the material directly to your player, or only the chapters you need. And they're *efficient*. Use them in your car, at the gym, walking to class, wherever. So get yours today. And get studying.

In Appreciation

The conventional practice of designating just two authors obscures the efforts of dozens of women and men that have resulted in *Sociology*, Sixth Canadian Edition. We would like to express our thanks to the Pearson Education Canada edi-

torial team, including Ky Pruesse, Laura Forbes, Charlotte Morrison-Reed, John Polanszky, and Richard di Santo.

We are grateful to the authors of the supplements for this edition.

We also have a large debt to Judith Allen for directing our marketing campaign, and the members of the sales staff, the men and women who have given this text such remarkable support over the years.

It goes without saying that every colleague knows more about some topics covered in this book than the authors do. For that reason, we are grateful to the hundreds of faculty and students who have written to offer comments and suggestions. More formally, we are grateful to the following people, who have given feedback on our revision plans or reviewed the Sixth Canadian Edition manuscript:

Siobhan Ashe, Douglas College

Michelle Coleman, Acadia University

Frank Cormier, University of Manitoba

David Dwyer, Fanshawe College

Raymond Foui, University of Manitoba

Bernie Hammond, University of Western Ontario

Melody Hessing, Douglas College

Nicole Jacobs, Okanagan University College

Linda McDevitt, Algonquin College

Cyndy Parker, New Brunswick Community College

Harry Rosenbaum, University of Winnipeg

Reuben N. Roth, Laurentian University

Isher-Paul Sahni, Concordia University

John Steckley, Humber College

Ed Thompson, Conestoga College

Without the support, encouragement, and patience of Linda Gerber's family—Gerhard and Martin Gerber, Laura Gerber and Glen Herbert, and Elsie Kojola—the Canadian revisions would not have been possible.

John Macionis
Linda Gerber

ABOUT THE AUTHORS

John J. Macionis (pronounced ma-SHOW-nis) was born and raised in Philadelphia, Pennsylvania. He earned a bachelor's degree from Cornell University and a doctorate in sociology from the University of Pennsylvania.

His publications are wide-ranging, focusing on community life in the United States, interpersonal intimacy in families, effective teaching, humour, new information technology, and the importance of global education. He and Nijole V. Benokraitis have edited the anthology *Seeing Ourselves: Classic, Contemporary, and Cross-Cultural Readings in Sociology.* Macionis has also authored *Society: The Basics,* the leading brief text in the field, and he collaborates on international editions of the texts *Sociology,* Canadian Edition, *Society: The Basics,* Canadian Edition, *Seeing Ourselves,* Canadian Edition, and *Sociology: A Global Introduction* (published by Prentice Hall Europe). *Sociology* is also available for high school students and in various foreign language editions. In addition, Macionis and Vincent Parrillo have written the urban studies text: *Cities and Urban Life* (Prentice Hall). Finally, Macionis has authored *Social Problems* (Prentice Hall), which is now the leading text in that course. The latest on all the Macionis textbooks, as well as information and dozens of Internet links of interest to students and faculty in sociology, are found at the author's personal website: **www.macionis.com** or **www.TheSociologyPage.com**.

John Macionis is Professor and Distinguished Scholar of Sociology at Kenyon College in Gambier, Ohio. In 2003, he received the Philander Chase Medal for completing 25 years of teaching at Kenyon. During that time, he has chaired the Sociology Department, directed the college's multidisciplinary program in human studies, presided over the campus senate and the college's faculty, and, most importantly, taught sociology to thousands of students.

In 2002, the American Sociological Association named Macionis recipient of the Award for Distinguished Contributions to Teaching, citing his innovative use of global material as well as introduction of new teaching technology in the development of his textbooks.

Professor Macionis has been active in academic programs in other countries, having traveled to some 50 nations. During his last study tour, he directed the global education course for the University of Pittsburgh's Semester at Sea program, teaching 400 students on a floating campus that visited 12 countries as it circled the globe.

Macionis writes, "I am an ambitious traveller, eager to learn and, through the texts, to share much of what I discover with students, many of whom know little about the rest of the world. For me, travelling and writing are all dimensions of teaching. First, and foremost, I am a teacher—a passion for teaching animates everything I do." At Kenyon, Macionis offers a wide range of upper-level courses, but his favorite course is Introduction to Sociology, which he teaches every year. He enjoys extensive contact with students and each term invites members of his classes to enjoy a home-cooked meal.

The Macionis family—John, Amy, and children McLean and Whitney (along with Braveheart the dog and six very independent cats)—live on a farm in rural Ohio. In his free time, John plays tennis, swims, and bicycles through the Ohio countryside. During the summer, he is a competitive sailor and, year-round, he enjoys performing oldies rock and roll and playing the Scottish bagpipes.

Professor Macionis welcomes (and responds to) comments and suggestions about this book from faculty and students. Write to the Sociology Department, Palme House, Kenyon College, Gambier, Ohio 43022, or direct email to macionis@kenyon.edu.

Linda M. Gerber was born in Toronto (to Finnish parents) and raised in Thornhill (just north of Toronto). Finnish was her first language and she remains sufficiently fluent to speak the language with roughly one hundred relatives on regular trips to Finland.

After graduating from the Nightingale School of Nursing (in Toronto), she toured Europe on a Eurailpass over the summer—and spent the next year nursing in Helsinki, Finland. Upon her return, she completed a nursing degree at the University of Toronto—before switching to sociology at the MA and PhD levels.

While still an undergraduate in nursing, she married Gerhard Gerber, whose family (pictured below) had escaped from East Germany when he was 10 years old. Contact with his parents and extended family meant that she would come to understand German conversation quite well.

As a graduate student, she was a consultant in highway planning, doing socio-impact assessment for a range of highway planning projects in southern and central Ontario. She also taught a course on Canadian Native peoples at York University's Glendon campus.

On completion of their PhDs in sociology and in biochemistry (and three weeks after the birth of their daughter), the Gerbers moved to Boston, Massachusetts for continued study. Dr Gerber spent three years there as a research associate at Harvard's Centre for Population Studies before accepting a position in the Department of Sociology and Anthropology at the University of Guelph. In over 29 years at Guelph, she has taught a wide range of courses at the undergraduate and graduate levels. Most recently, she has been teaching courses in introductory sociology, political sociology, contemporary Native peoples and Canadian society.

Professor Gerber's research has focused on Canada's Aboriginal peoples, politics, and ethnic relations, but she has a broader interest in Canadian society (its demographics, its identity and its regional tensions). Her publications are in the areas of Aboriginal studies, voting behaviour, ethnic relations, and Quebec separatism.

The Gerber family includes Gerhard and Linda, Martin (an engineering student at the University of Toronto), Laura (a pediatrician), Glen Herbert (a writer and editor), and Grace (2 years old). A brother for Grace is expected in early February, 2007.

On October 12, 2006, when other Canadians were celebrating Thanksgiving, the Gerber family met for its own special reunion marking 50 years since Maria and Herbert Gerber arrived in Canada—with four of their children—after escaping from East Germany. Two sons had gone ahead separately (each at about 19 years of age) with no assurances that they would see the rest of the family again. The escape, which was meticulously planned and executed, took place just before the Berlin Wall was erected.

The family has grown and prospered over the past fifty years. Maria and Herbert Gerber (now deceased) are responsible for adding 6 children, 19 grandchildren and 31 great-grandchildren to the Canadian population. With spouses, the Gerber clan now boasts 75 members, 47 of whom were at the reunion. The rest are scattered as far afield as Germany, Vancouver, Chicago, and the southeastern United States. Interestingly, four of the six children (Gerhard's generation) married Germans, but only two of the 19 grandchildren married German-Canadians.

1

CHAPTER ONE

The Sociological Perspective

How does the sociological perspective change the way you see the world?

What is a global perspective?

Can sociology help you in your future career?

Imagine that you are walking along and have taken the hand of a member of the opposite sex. Now stop and take a close look at what has just happened. If you are a man, it is almost certain that you will be holding your partner's hand from the front; if you are a woman, you will be holding hands from behind. Was this hypothesis supported in your case?

If you want to do a little experiment, try this. As you are about to clasp hands, stop, reconsider, and take your partner's hand opposite to the way you normally would. Now check for reactions in each of you. Are there any signs that this feels unnatural? Both of you are likely to feel uncomfortable with the new arrangement, and signs of this discomfort will be obvious.

So what does this reaction mean? Why does holding hands this way feel awkward? Since holding hands is a highly personal or individual act, people should be able to hold hands one way or the other, as a matter of choice. Surely there are no unwritten rules about how males and females are to hold hands. Assuming an absence of hand-holding rules, it is worth noting that the vast majority of us *conform* to predictable patterns of behaviour. If, on the other hand, there *are* rules underlying this conformity, how do we learn about them? And why is it the man's hand that is in front? Is it a matter of height differences, leadership, or power and dominance?

Understanding *society* is a much more difficult task than understanding hand-holding behaviour, but this example suggests that people act in highly predictable ways; life does not unfold on the basis of sheer chance or complete free will. The essential wisdom of sociology is that society guides our actions and shapes our values; knowledge of the social forces at work allows sociologists to understand and predict the behaviour of individuals, groups, or categories of people.

When it comes to holding hands, or even falling in love, the decisions people make do not simply result from the process philosophers call "free will." Sociology teaches us that the social world guides all our life choices in much the same way that the seasons influence our clothing and activities.

The authors' website is a great resource for new sociologists: www.TheSociologyPage.com

The Sociological Perspective

Sociology is *the systematic study of human society*. At the heart of sociology is a special point of view called the *sociological perspective*.

SEEING THE GENERAL IN THE PARTICULAR

Years ago, Peter Berger (1963) described the **sociological perspective** as *seeing the general in the particular*. By this he meant that sociologists identify general patterns in the behaviour of particular individuals. While acknowledging that each individual is unique, sociologists recognize that society acts differently on various *categories* of people (say, children compared to adults, women versus men, the rich as opposed to the poor). We think sociologically when we realize how the general categories into which we happen to fall shape our particular life experiences.

At a 1997 Toronto conference, sociology professor Donna Winslow illustrated this perspective in her report on a study commissioned by the federal government. Her four-hundred-page tome, *The Canadian Airborne Regiment: A Socio-Cultural Inquiry*, attempts to explain the atrocities committed by Canadian peacekeepers in Somalia—not in terms of the characteristics of the individual soldiers who brutally murdered a Somali civilian, but in terms of the combat or warrior culture within which they functioned. The culture of the Airborne regiment, which focused on war making, was enhanced by recruitment, the chain of command, training, and even the nature of weapons at hand. Training for the peacekeeping role, in the areas of ethics and

We can easily see the power of society over the individual by imagining how different our lives would be had we been born in place of any of these children from, respectively, Bolivia, Ethiopia, Thailand, Botswana, South Korea, and El Salvador.

technique, was minimal: soldiers were unprepared in terms of recruitment, attitude, skill, or equipment to engage in problem solving, negotiation, or dealing with high-stress civilian situations with milder force (perhaps riot gear and dogs) (Winslow, 1997). Despite Canada's commitment to peacekeeping, its military has continued to prepare soldiers for war instead of peace, thereby setting the scene for violence towards civilians (Skelton, 1997). The explanation lies in the position of Canadian soldiers within a structural and cultural environment—not in individual personality.

We begin to think sociologically when we realize that our individual life experiences are shaped by the society in which we live—as well as by the general categories into which we fall.

YOUR TURN

How do you think your social class background shapes the kind of job you expect to have after you graduate? What effect did your background have on your decision to go to college or university?

SEEING THE STRANGE IN THE FAMILIAR

At first, using the sociological perspective is *seeing the strange in the familiar*. Imagine a young woman walking up to a young male friend and saying, "You fit all the right social categories, which means you would make a wonderful husband for me!" We are used to thinking that people fall in love and decide to marry based on personal feelings. But the sociological perspective reveals the initially strange idea that society shapes what we think and do.

Because we live in an individualistic society, learning to see how society affects us may take a bit of practice. Asked why you chose to enrol at your particular university or college, you might offer any of the following reasons: to stay near home, to ensure a good job, to be with old friends on campus, or because you were not accepted in a preferred program elsewhere. Such responses are certainly grounded in reality for the people expressing them. But do they tell the whole story? The sociological perspective provides additional insights that may not be readily apparent.

Thinking sociologically about university and college attendance, we should understand that, for young people throughout most of the world, postsecondary education is out of reach. Moreover, had we lived a century ago, the

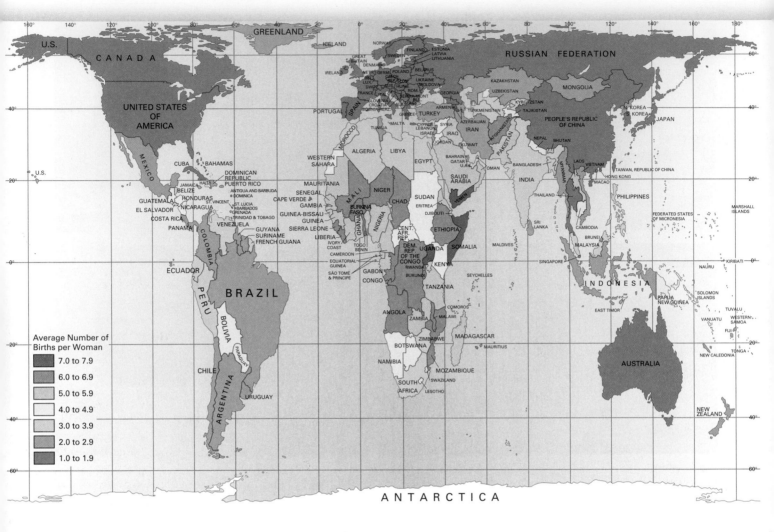

Average Number of Births per Woman	
■	7.0 to 7.9
■	6.0 to 6.9
■	5.0 to 5.9
□	4.0 to 4.9
■	3.0 to 3.9
■	2.0 to 2.9
■	1.0 to 1.9

WINDOW ON THE WORLD

GLOBAL MAP 1–1   Women's Childbearing in Global Perspective

Is childbearing simply a matter of personal choice? A look around the world shows that it is not. In general, women living in poor countries have many more children than women in rich nations. Can you point to some of the reasons for this global disparity? In simple terms, such differences mean that, if you had been born into another society (whether you are female or male), your life might be quite different from what it is now.

Source: Data from United Nations (2000) and U.S. Census Bureau (2003). Map projection from *Peters Atlas of the World* (1990).

choice to go to university or college would not have been an option. Even now, a look around your classroom suggests that social forces determine whether one pursues higher education. Typically, university and college students are young—between 18 and 24 years of age. Why? Because in our society university and college attendance is associated with this period of life. But more than age is involved, because the majority of Canadians in their late teens or early twenties are not enrolled.

For a look at how society has shaped celebrity names, click on the "Play 'The Name Game'" link at www.The SociologyPage.com

Other factors include socio-economic background—higher education is expensive—race or ethnicity, and region. Is it reasonable, in light of these facts, to say that attending college or university is simply a matter of personal choice?

SEEING PERSONAL CHOICE IN SOCIAL CONTEXT

To see how society shapes personal choices, consider the number of children women have. In Canada and the United States, as shown in Global Map 1–1, the average woman has slightly fewer than two children during her lifetime. In India, however, the average is about three; in Cambodia, four; in

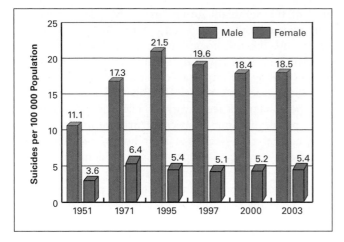

FIGURE 1-1   Suicide Rates for Canada by Sex:
1951–2003

Suicide rates are consistently higher for men than for women. The
number of suicides per 100 000 men and women increased
substantially between 1951 and 1971 and remained relatively high
thereafter.

Compiled by L.M. Gerber from Colombo (1992-01) and Statistics Canada: Health
Statistics Division (2005a).

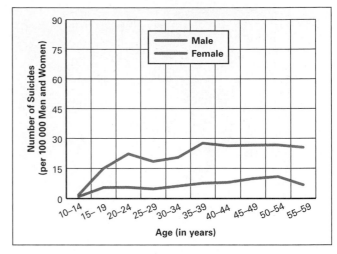

FIGURE 1-2   Suicide Rates for Canada by Age and
Sex: 2003

In each of the above age categories, suicide rates for males are 2.5
to 6.5 times higher than for females. The number of suicides per
100 000 men and women is highest among those between 35 and
54 years of age.

Source: Compiled by L.M. Gerber from Statistics Canada (2005a).

Saudi Arabia, five; in Niger, six; and in Yemen, seven. Why
these striking differences? As later chapters explain, women in
poor countries have less schooling and fewer economic
opportunities, are more likely to remain in the home, and are
less likely to use contraception. Clearly, society has much to do
with the decisions women and men make about childbearing.

Another illustration of the power of society to shape
even our most private choices comes from the study of suicide. What choice could be more personal than the decision
to end your own life? But Emile Durkheim (1858–1917),
one of sociology's pioneers, showed that, even here, social
forces are at work.

Examining official records in France, his own country,
Durkheim (1966; orig. 1897) found that some categories of
people were more likely than others to take their own lives.
Men, Protestants, wealthy people, and the unmarried had
much higher suicide rates than women, Catholics and Jews,
the poor, and married people. Durkheim explained the differences in terms of *social integration*: categories of people
with strong social ties had low suicide rates, and more individualistic categories of people had high suicide rates.

In Durkheim's time, men had much more freedom
than women. But despite its advantages, freedom weakens
social ties and thereby increases the risk of suicide. Likewise,
more individualistic Protestants were more likely to commit
suicide than more tradition-bound Catholics and Jews,
whose rituals encourage stronger social ties. The wealthy
have much more freedom than the poor but, once again, at
the cost of a higher suicide rate.

A century later, statistical evidence continues to support
Durkheim's analysis. Figure 1–1 reveals changes in suicide
rates for males and females from 1951 to 2003 in Canada: the

rates are consistently higher for men than for women. This
male/female difference is apparent across all age groups, as
shown in Figure 1–2; it is also apparent throughout each
province and territory of Canada and throughout the United
States. Observe the suicide rates for males and females in
1997—19.6 and 5.1 (Figure 1–1)—and note that the American rates for White men and women, in 2002, were 19.9 and
4.8, respectively (Kochanek, *et al.*, 2004). Our similar societies have similar suicide rates for men and women.

Following Durkheim's argument, we might conclude
that the higher suicide rate among men is a result of their
greater affluence and autonomy in Canadian society. Interestingly, male suicide rates are highest (30 per 100 000 population) in Quebec and the Northwest Territories, where
marriage rates are the lowest, as well as in the Yukon (62 per
100 000 population), where the divorce rate is the highest.
In addition, these areas are still undergoing substantial
social change. Over the past decade or so, young people in
Canada's First Nation communities have had suicide rates
five or more times higher than those of other Canadians
(Canada, 2003a). Aboriginal communities are still experiencing massive social change and upheaval, which,
Durkheim would have argued, affect levels of social integration by putting norms and values into a state of flux. In contrast to the situation of Aboriginal peoples in Canada,
suicide rates among African-American men and women are
substantially *lower* than those for White men and women.
This suggests lower levels of affluence and autonomy, more
limited social choices, as well as stronger social ties and
greater social cohesion or solidarity.

Thus, we observe general social patterns in even the
most personal actions of individuals. Social forces are

People with the greatest privileges tend to see individuals as responsible for their own lives. Those at the margins of society, by contrast, are quick to see how race, class, and gender can create disadvantages. Before his death in 1996, Tupac Shakur expressed in his music the frustration felt by many inner-city African Americans.

complex, of course, but we can see that linked to gender, they produce patterns with regard to suicide. Gender operates consistently: men are more prone to suicide than are women. The rates may change over time and across space, but even in the case of suicide we are able to see the impact of social conditions.

YOUR TURN

Single people are at greater risk of suicide than married people. Can you explain why?

SEEING SOCIOLOGICALLY: MARGINALITY AND CRISIS

Anyone can learn to see the world using the sociological perspective. But two situations help people see clearly how society shapes individual lives: living on the margins of society and living through a social crisis.

From time to time, everyone feels like an "outsider." For some categories of people, however, being an *outsider*—not

part of the dominant group—is an everyday experience. The greater people's social marginality, the better able they are to use the sociological perspective. For example, no African American grows up in the United States without understanding the importance of race in shaping people's lives. Songs such as "Trapped" by Tupac Shakur, in which he says he sometimes feels worked "like a slave," show that some people of colour—especially African Americans living in the inner city—feel as if their hopes and dreams are crushed by society. But people in the dominant White majority—in Canada as much as in the United States—think less often about their race and the privileges it provides, believing that race affects only people from visible minorities and not themselves. People at the margins of social life, including women, gay people, people with disabilities, and the very old, are aware of social patterns that others rarely think about. To become better at using the sociological perspective, we must step back from our familiar routines and look at our lives with new curiosity.

Periods of change or crisis make everyone feel a little off balance, encouraging us to use the sociological perspective. The sociologist C. Wright Mills (1916–62) illustrated this idea using the Great Depression of the 1930s. As the unemployment rate soared to 25 percent, people out of work could not help but see general social forces at work in their particular lives. Rather than saying, "Something is wrong with me; I can't find a job," they took a sociological approach and realized, "The economy has collapsed; there are no jobs to be found!" Mills (1959) believed that using what he called the "sociological imagination" in this way helps people understand not only their society but their own lives, because the two are closely related. The Thinking Critically box (p. 7) takes a closer look.

Just as social change encourages sociological thinking, sociological thinking can bring about social change. The more we learn about how "the system" operates, the more we may want to change it in some way. Becoming aware of the power of gender, for example, has caused many women and men to try to reduce gender inequality.

The Importance of a Global Perspective

As new information technology draws the farthest reaches of Earth closer together, many academic disciplines are taking a **global perspective,** *the study of the larger world and our society's place in it.* What is the importance of a global perspective for sociology?

First, global awareness is a logical extension of the sociological perspective. Since sociology shows us that our place in society shapes our life experiences, it stands to reason that the position of our society in the larger world system affects everyone in Canada. Consider Canada's ambivalent relationship to the United States—the destination of

THINKING CRITICALLY

The Sociological Imagination: Turning Personal Problems into Public Issues

The power of the sociological perspective lies not just in changing individual lives but in transforming society. As C. Wright Mills saw it,

To find out more about C. Wright Mills, visit the Gallery of Sociologists at www. TheSociologyPage. com

society, not people's personal failings, is the cause of poverty and other social problems. The sociological imagination brings people together to create change by transforming personal *problems* into public *issues*.

In the following excerpt,[1] Mills explains the need for a sociological imagination:

When a society becomes industrialized, a peasant becomes a worker; a feudal lord is liquidated or becomes a businessman. When classes rise or fall, a man is employed or unemployed; when the rate of investment goes up or down, a man takes new heart or goes broke. When wars happen, an insurance salesman becomes a rocket launcher; a store clerk, a radar man; a wife lives alone; a child grows up without a father. Neither the life of an individual nor the history of a society can be understood without understanding both.

Yet men do not usually define the troubles they endure in terms of historical change.... The well-being they enjoy, they do not usually impute to the big ups and downs of the society in which they live. Seldom aware of the intricate connection between the patterns of their own lives and the course of world history, ordinary men do not usually know what this connection means for the kind of men they are becoming and for the kinds of history-making in which they might take part. They do not possess the quality of mind essential to grasp the interplay of men and society, of biography and history, of self and world....

What they need... is a quality of mind that will help them to [see] what is going on in the world and... what may be happening within themselves. It is this quality... that... may be called the sociological imagination. (1959:3–5)

---

[1] In this excerpt, Mills uses "man" and male pronouns to apply to all people. Note that even an outspoken critic of society such as Mills reflected the conventional writing practices of his time as far as gender was concerned.

WHAT DO YOU THINK?

1. As Mills sees it, how are personal troubles different from public issues?
2. Why do we blame ourselves for the personal problems we face?
3. How are we empowered by using the sociological imagination?

---

85 percent of our exports—and our nation's attempts to come to terms with the emerging economic powers of China and India. For another perspective on our place in the "global village," see the Thinking Globally box (on p. 9).

The world's 192 nations can be divided into three broad categories according to their level of economic development (see Global Map 12–1, on p. 297). **High-income countries** are the *nations with the highest overall standards of living.* The roughly fifty countries in this category include Canada and the United States, Argentina, Chile, the nations of Western Europe, South Africa, Israel, Saudi Arabia, Japan, South Korea, Australia, and New Zealand. Taken together, these nations produce most of the world's goods and services, and the people who live there own most of the planet's wealth. Economically speaking, people in these countries are very well off, not because they are smarter or work harder than anyone else, but because they were lucky enough to be born in a rich region of the world.

A second category is **middle-income countries,** *nations with a standard of living about average for the world as a whole.* People in any of these eighty nations—many in Eastern Europe, seven in Africa, and almost all of Asia and Central and South America—are as likely to live in rural villages as in cities and to walk or ride tractors, scooters, bicycles, or animals as to drive automobiles. On average, they receive six to eight years of schooling. Most middle-income countries also have considerable social inequality within their borders, so that some people are extremely rich (members of the business elite in nations across North Africa, for example), but many more lack safe housing and adequate nutrition (e.g., people living in the shanty settlements that surround Mexico City or Lima, Peru).

The remaining sixty nations of the world are **low-income countries,** *nations with a low standard of living in which most people are poor.* Most of the poorest countries in the world are in Africa, and a few are in Asia (Afghanistan,

Two websites that provide maps showing patterns of interest to sociologists can be found at http://atlas.gc/ca and www.nationalgeographic.com.

Pakistan, Nepal, Bangladesh, Mongolia, Myanmar, Laos, Cambodia, and Vietnam); Haiti is the only such country in the Americas. Here, again, a few people are very rich, but the majority struggle to get by with poor housing, unsafe water, too little food, and, perhaps most seriously of all, little chance to improve their lives.

The disparity between the "haves" and "have-nots" in the world is presented in another way in Table 1–1, which lists the ten best countries in which to live when ranked according to the United Nations' Human Development Index. This index determines quality of life by combining measures of income, life expectancy, literacy, and school enrolment. Canada ranked at the top of the list for many years before dropping to third place in 2001 and fifth place in 2003.

Chapter 12 ("Global Stratification") explains the causes and consequences of global wealth and poverty. But every chapter of this text makes comparisons between North America and other world regions for four reasons:

1. **Where we live shapes the lives we lead.** As we saw in Global Map 1–1, women living in rich and poor countries have different size families, in part determined by the very different lives they lead. To understand ourselves and appreciate how others live, we must understand something about how countries differ, which is one good reason to pay attention to the global maps found throughout this text.

For a website that offers a range of data about all 192 nations in the world, see www.countrywatch.com.

2. **Societies throughout the world are increasingly interconnected.** Although, in the past, we may have paid little attention to the countries beyond our borders, in recent decades Canadians have become linked as never before to people in the rest of the world. Electronic technology now transmits sounds, pictures, and written documents around the globe in seconds. E-mail and internet chat groups have freed social interaction from the constraints of geography.

One effect of new technology is that people the world over now share many tastes in food, clothing, and music. Rich countries such as the United States influence other nations, whose people are ever more likely to gobble up its Big Macs and Whoppers, dance to the latest popular American music, and speak the English language. Living next door makes Canadians especially sensitive to American cultural influence. As the North American way of life is projected onto much of the world, the larger world, too, has its impact here. In all but two years since 1990, more than 200 000 immigrants have arrived here, adding to the historical flow of immigration that has built our country (Canadian Global Almanac 2005: 61). In response, Canada

has adopted many of the favourite sights, sounds, and tastes of its new members. The enhanced ethnic and cultural diversity of this country is apparent in our streets, our festivals, our grocery stores, and the media.

Trade across national borders has created a global economy. Large corporations manufacture and market goods worldwide, just as global financial markets linked by satellite now operate around the clock. Today, no stock trader in Toronto dares to ignore what happens in the financial markets in New York, Tokyo, and Hong Kong, just as no wheat farmer in Manitoba can afford to overlook the price of grain in the former Soviet republic of Georgia. When you receive routine calls from "Canadian" corporations, they may well come from call centres in India—and many familiar North American products (clothing, shoes, or electronics) may be made, entirely or in part, in low-wage countries halfway around the world. Because many new Canadian jobs involve international trade, gaining greater global understanding has never been more critical.

3. **Many social problems that we face in Canada are far more serious elsewhere.** Poverty is a serious problem in Canada but, as Chapter 12 ("Global Stratification") explains, poverty in Latin America, Africa, and Asia is both more common and more severe. Moreover, although Canadian women have lower social standing than men, gender inequality is even greater in the world's poor countries.

4. **Thinking globally helps us learn more about ourselves.** We cannot walk the streets of a distant city without thinking about what it means to live in Canada. Comparing life in various settings also leads to unexpected lessons. For instance, a squatter settlement in Madras, India, reveals people who thrive in the love and support of family members—despite desperate poverty. Why, in contrast, are so many of our own poor angry and alone? Are material things—so central to our definition of the "good life"—the best way to measure human well-being?

In sum, in an increasingly interconnected world, we can understand ourselves only to the extent that we understand others. Sociology is an invitation to learn a new way of looking at the world around us. But is this invitation worth accepting? What are the benefits of applying the sociological perspective?

→ **YOUR TURN** ←

How would your life be different if you had been born into an impoverished family in an Asian farming village? What might you be doing right now instead of reading this textbook?

The Global Village: A Social Snapshot of Our World

The Earth is home to 6.5 billion people who live in the cities and villages of 192 nations. To grasp the social shape of the world, imagine shrinking the planet's population to a "global village" of just 1000 people. In this "village," more than half (610) of the inhabitants are Asian, of whom 200 are citizens of China. Next, in terms of numbers, we would find 140 Africans, 110 Europeans, 85 people from Latin America and the Caribbean, 5 from Australia and the South Pacific—and just 45 Americans and 5 Canadians.

A close look at this settlement would reveal some startling facts. The village is a rich place, with a spectacular range of goods and services for sale; yet most of the villagers can only dream about such treasures, because they are so poor: 80 percent of the village's total

income is earned by just 200 people. For most, the greatest problem is getting enough food. Every year, village workers produce more than enough to feed everyone; even so, half the villagers, including most of the children, do not get enough to eat, and many must go to sleep hungry every night. The worst-off 200 residents—who, together, have less money than the richest person in the village—lack both clean drinking water and safe shelter. Weak and unable to work, their lives are at risk from life-threatening diseases.

The village has many schools, including a fine university. About 50 inhabitants have completed a college degree, but about one-third of the village's people are not able even to read or write.

Canadians, on average, would be among the village's richest people.

Although we may think that our comfortable lives are the result of our own talent and hard work, the sociological perspective reminds us that our achievements also result from our nation's privileged position in the worldwide social system.

WHAT DO YOU THINK?

1. Do any of the statistics in this reading surprise you? Which ones? Why?
2. How do the lives of poor people in a lower-income country differ from those of Canadians or Americans?
3. Was your decision to attend college or university affected by where you live? How?

Sources: Calculations by John J. Macionis based on data from Population Reference Bureau (2005) and United Nations Development Programme (2005).

Applying the Sociological Perspective

Applying the sociological perspective is useful in many ways. First, sociology is at work guiding many of the laws and policies that shape our lives. Second, on an individual level, making use of the sociological perspective leads to important personal growth and expanded awareness. Third, for anyone, studying sociology is excellent preparation for the world of work. We will look briefly at these different ways of putting sociology to work.

SOCIOLOGY AND PUBLIC POLICY

Sociology has played an important role in the development of Canadian social policy. For example, sociological research strongly influenced the Royal Commission on Health Services (1964–65), from which Canada's medicare system arose. The findings of sociologists also underpinned the Royal Commission on Bilingualism and Biculturalism (1963–69) and the Royal Commission on the Status of Women in Canada (1967–70), which brought far-reaching policy changes. In Quebec, La Commission d'enquête sur l'enseignement au Québec (1963–66) drastically altered the educational system in that province. Aboriginal peoples are still waiting for research

results for the Royal Commission on Aboriginal Peoples (1993–96) to have positive effects on public policy. Many sociologists have done policy-relevant work outside the context of royal commissions. Raymond Breton—University of Toronto professor emeritus and former director of Montreal's Institute for Research on Public Policy—has done influential work in the areas of ethnicity, cultural boundaries, Quebec nationalism, regionalism, and constitutional change. Hundreds of people with sociological training, who are employed by government, polling agencies, the media and universities, have impacts on Canadian public policy and response in general to social issues.

 For research and analysis that focuses on social and economic trends and their effects on the lives of Canadians, see work by the not-for-profit organization, the Canadian Council on Social Development at www.ccsd.ca.

SOCIOLOGY AND PERSONAL GROWTH

By applying the sociological perspective, we become more active, aware, and critical in our thinking. Using sociology benefits us in four ways:

1. **The sociological perspective helps us assess the truth of "common sense."** We all take many things for granted, but that does not make them true. Take the

One important reason to gain global understanding is that, living in a high-income nation, we fail to appreciate the suffering that goes on in much of the world. This family, living in the African nation of Zambia, has none of the security most of us take for granted. In poor nations, children have only a 50/50 chance of surviving to adulthood.

idea that we are free individuals, personally responsible for our own lives. Assuming you decide your own fate, you might praise very successful people as superior and less successful ones as personally deficient. A sociological approach, in contrast, encourages us to ask whether such common beliefs are true and, to the extent that they are not, why they are so widely held.

2. **The sociological perspective helps us see the opportunities and constraints in our lives.** Sociological thinking leads us to see that, in the game of life, we have a say in how to play our cards, but it is society that deals us the hand. The more we understand the game, the better players we will be. Sociology helps us

 To view maps showing patterns of interest to sociologists, go to www.nationalatlas.gov.

"size up" our world so that we can pursue our goals more effectively.

3. **The sociological perspective empowers us to be active participants in our society.** The more we understand about how society works, the more active citizens we become. As C. Wright Mills (1959) explained (see Thinking Critically box on p. 7), it is the sociological perspective that turns a "personal problem" (such as being out of work) into a "public issue" (a lack of good jobs). As we come to see how society affects us, we may support society as it is, or we may set out with others to change it.

TABLE 1–1
The Ten Best Places To Live in the World According to the United Nations' Human Development Index

1997	2001	2005
Canada	Norway	Norway
Norway	Australia	Iceland
United States	Canada	Australia
Australia	Sweden	Luxembourg
Iceland	Belgium	Canada
Sweden	United States	Sweden
Belgium	Iceland	Switzerland
Netherlands	Netherlands	Ireland
Japan	Japan	Belgium
United Kingdom	Finland	United States

Source: United Nations Development Program, Human Development Index from Human Development Report 1997, 2001, 2003, 2005 available at www.undp.org

---

4. **The sociological perspective helps us live in a diverse world.** North Americans represent just 5 percent of the world's people; Canadians alone represent only 0.5 percent. As the remaining chapters of this book explain, many of the other 95 percent of people live lives very different from ours. The Applying Sociology box (on p. 12) notes how contrasting behaviour can even affect professional sociologists in space. Still, like people everywhere, we tend to define our own way of life as "right," "natural," and "better." The sociological perspective encourages us to think critically about the rel-

 In a short video, John Macionis offers a personal response to the question "Why would someone want to be a sociologist?" See the Video Gallery at www.The SociologyPage.com.

ative strengths and weaknesses of all ways of life, including our own.

CAREERS: THE "SOCIOLOGY ADVANTAGE"

Most post-secondary students are interested in getting a good job. A background in sociology is excellent preparation for the working world. Of course, completing a bachelor's degree in sociology is the right choice for people who decide they would like to go on to graduate work to eventually become a

 professor or researcher in the field. Throughout Canada, thousands of men and women teach sociology in universities, colleges, and high schools. But just as many professional sociologists work as researchers for government agencies or private foundations and businesses, gathering important information on social behaviour and carrying out evaluation research. In today's cost-conscious world, agencies and companies want to be sure that the programs and policies they set in place can get the job done at the lowest cost. Sociologists, especially those

Living in a society that stresses individual freedom and responsibility, we grow up thinking that people are entirely responsible for their lives. The sociological perspective helps us to see that the operation of society, including the way the economy works, can shape the fate of millions of people.

with advanced research skills, are in high demand for this kind of work (Deutscher, 1999).

But sociology is not just for people who want to be sociologists. People who work in criminal justice—including jobs in police departments, probation offices, and corrections facilities—gain the "sociology advantage" by learning which categories of people are most at risk of becoming criminals or victims, how effective various policies and programs are at preventing crime, and why people turn to crime in the first place. Similarly, people who work in health care—including doctors, nurses, and technicians—also gain a "sociology advantage" by learning about patterns of health and illness, as well as the effects of race, gender, and social class on human health and attitudes towards health care providers. Social work is a field chosen by many young people with a solid foundation in sociology.

Sociology is also excellent preparation for jobs in dozens of additional fields, including advertising, banking, business, education, government, journalism, law, public relations, and personnel management. In almost any type of work, success depends on understanding how various categories of people differ in beliefs, family patterns, and other ways of life. Unless you plan to have a job that never involves dealing with people, you should consider the workplace benefits of learning more about sociology.

YOUR TURN

Write down five jobs that appeal to you, and then identify ways in which sociological thinking would increase your chances of success in each one.

The Origins of Sociology

Like the "choices" made by individuals, major historical events rarely just "happen." The birth of sociology was itself the result of powerful social forces.

SOCIAL CHANGE AND SOCIOLOGY

Striking changes took place in Europe during the eighteenth and nineteenth centuries. Three kinds of change were especially important in the development of sociology: the rise of a factory-based industrial economy, the explosive growth of cities, and the spread of new ideas about democracy and political rights.

A New Industrial Economy

During the Middle Ages in Europe, most people plowed fields near their homes or worked in small-scale *manufacturing* (a word derived from Latin words meaning "to make by hand"). By the end of the eighteenth century, inventors used new sources of energy—the power of moving water and then steam—to operate large machines in mills and factories. Instead of labouring at home, workers became part of a large and anonymous labour force, under the control of strangers who owned the factories. This change in the system of production took people out of their homes, weakening the traditions that had guided community life for centuries.

The Growth of Cities

Across Europe, landowners took part in what historians call the *enclosure movement*: they fenced off more and more farmland to create grazing areas for sheep, the source of

APPLYING SOCIOLOGY
Reining in the Cowboys in Outer Space

Dr. Judith Lapierre wants to be an astronaut. This Canadian nurse has earned a Ph.D. in public health and social medicine, and has studied space sociology as well: as a scientist and social scientist, she seems to be the ideal candidate for the job.

Under the sponsorship of the Canadian Space Agency, Dr. Lapierre participated in a simulated space mission at the Institute for Biomedical Problems in Moscow, spending 110 days in a mock space station that consisted of two linked capsules, each the size of a railway car. The space program mixed a "potent human cocktail," combining one woman, seven men, five cultures, and copious amounts of vodka for the duration of the mission. The results included frequent conflict, bloody fist-fights, and, for Judith Lapierre, sexual harassment when she was forcibly kissed by an amorous Russian colleague emboldened by the vodka.

Not surprisingly, the sexual harassment codes of Canadian workplaces fail to apply in this international setting, but surely the highly trained and dedicated scientists who were carefully screened for the mission should have known how to behave—whatever the context. Not so! There are no accepted guidelines for intercultural and gender relations within a mock space station—and it takes considerable time for sustained interaction to bring about the emergence of norms and shared understandings.

In the absence of naturally emergent rules for behaviour, the agencies preparing for the actual International Space Station must resort to a strict, bureaucratically devised code of conduct—but creating a code that is acceptable to the different nations involved will not be easy. They will also have to spend more than the six hours that were allotted for Dr. Lapierre's colleagues to discuss topics such as team

building, cultural and sensitivity awareness, and conflict resolution. In her article about the incident, Martin remarks: "Space may be the last frontier, but it's clearly time to set aside the old cowboy stereotypes of the rugged individual, and remember there's a place out there behind the beyond for social science as well as science" (2000:R2).

WHAT DO YOU THINK?

1. Why did the highly trained astronauts in the mock space station not know how to conduct themselves?
2. Is a code of conduct required in such contrived settings? What if there are no women involved?
3. Who is responsible for devising a code of conduct in novel settings like a mock space station with international personnel? Whose values are to be reflected in the code?

---

wool for the thriving textile mills. Without land, countless tenant farmers had little choice but to head to the cities in search of work in the new factories. As cities grew larger, these urban migrants faced many social problems, including pollution, crime, and homelessness. Moving through streets crowded with strangers, they faced a new, impersonal social world.

Political Change

Europeans in the Middle Ages viewed society as an expression of God's will: from royalty to serf, each person on the social ladder played a part in the holy plan. This view of society is captured in lines from the old Anglican hymn "All Things Bright and Beautiful":

> The rich man in his castle,
> The poor man at his gate,
> God made them high and lowly
> And ordered their estate.

But as cities grew, traditional thinking like this came under spirited attack. In the writings of Thomas Hobbes (1588–1679), John Locke (1632–1704), and Adam Smith (1723–90), we see a shift in focus from a moral obligation to God and monarch to the pursuit of self-interest. In the

new political climate, philosophers spoke of *individual liberty* and *individual rights*. The French Revolution, which began in 1789, was an even greater break with political and social tradition. The French social analyst Alexis de Tocqueville (1805–59) thought the changes in society brought about by the French Revolution were so great that they amounted to "nothing short of the regeneration of the whole human race" (1955:13; orig. 1856).

We hear an echo of these sentiments today in the Canadian constitution, which asserts that each individual has certain rights, freedoms, and protections. Section 2, "Fundamental Freedoms," of the Canadian Charter of Rights and Freedoms states:

To view an extensive collection of Canadian constitutional documents before and since confederation, see *Canadian Constitutional Documents: A Legal History* at www.solon.org.

Everyone has the following fundamental freedoms:

(a) freedom of conscience and religion;

(b) freedom of thought, belief, opinion and expression, including freedom of the press and other media of communication;

(c) freedom of peaceful assembly; and

(d) freedom of association. (Canada, 1982)

A New Awareness of Society

Huge factories, exploding cities, a new spirit of individualism—these changes combined to make people aware of their surroundings. The new discipline of sociology was born in England, France, and Germany—precisely where the changes were greatest.

SCIENCE AND SOCIOLOGY

It was the French social thinker Auguste Comte (1798–1857) who coined the term *sociology* in 1838 to describe a new way of looking at society. This makes sociology one of the youngest academic disciplines—far newer than history, physics, or economics, for example. Of course, Comte was not the first person to think about the nature of society. Such questions fascinated the brilliant thinkers of ancient civilizations,

 For a biographical sketch of Comte, visit the Gallery of Sociologists at www.TheSociologyPage.com.

including the Chinese philosopher K'ung fu-tzu (Confucius, 551–479 B.C.E.), and the Greek philosophers Plato (c. 427–347 B.C.E.) and Aristotle (384–322 B.C.E.).[1] Centuries later, the Roman emperor Marcus Aurelius (121–180), the mediaeval thinkers Saint Thomas Aquinas (c. 1225–1274) and Christine de Pisan (c. 1363–1431), and the English playwright William Shakespeare (1564–1616) wrote about the workings of society. Yet these thinkers were more interested in imagining the ideal society than looking at reality.

Comte and other pioneers of sociology all cared about how society could be improved, but their major goal was to understand how society actually operates. Comte (1975; orig. 1851–54) saw sociology as the product of a three-stage historical development:

- During the earliest, the *theological stage*, from the beginning of human history to the end of the European Middle Ages (about 1350 C.E.), people took a religious view that society expressed God's will.
- With the dawn of the Renaissance in the fifteenth century, the theological approach gave way to a *metaphysical stage* of history in which people saw society as a natural rather than a supernatural system. Thomas Hobbes (1588–1679), for example, suggested that society reflected not the perfection of God so much as the failings of a selfish human nature.
- What Comte called the *scientific stage* of history began with the work of early scientists such as the Polish astronomer Copernicus (1473–1543), the Italian astronomer and physicist Galileo (1564–1642), and the English physicist and mathematician Isaac Newton (1642–1727). Comte's contribution came in applying the scientific approach—first used to study the physical world—to the study of society.[2]

Comte's approach is called **positivism,** *a way of understanding based on science.* As a positivist, Comte believed that society operates according to its own laws, much as the physical world operates according to gravity and other laws of nature.

By the beginning of the twentieth century, sociology had spread to North America and showed the influence of Comte's ideas. Today, most sociologists still consider science a crucial part of sociology. But as Chapter 2 ("Sociological Investigation") explains, we now realize that human behaviour is far more complex than the movement of planets or even the actions of other living things. We are creatures of imagination and spontaneity, so human behaviour can never fully be explained by rigid "laws of society." In addition, early sociologists such as Karl Marx (1818–83), whose ideas are discussed in Chapter 4 ("Society"), were troubled by the striking inequality of industrial society. They wanted the new discipline of sociology not just to understand society but to bring about change towards social justice.

CANADIAN SOCIOLOGY: DISTINCTIVE TOUCHES

Canadian sociology arose from different traditions and continues to be, in many ways, distinct from American sociology. As a discipline that reflects a country with two major cultures and linguistic communities, Canadian sociology includes a unique francophone component. Sociology began in Canada, as in the United States, in the early part of the twentieth century. By 1920, sociology courses were being offered in a number of disciplines, including theology. During this period the Canadian Political Science Association, formed in 1913, accepted sociologists as members. Teaching and research in sociology were undertaken earlier in Quebec—at Laval, l'Université de Montréal, and then later at l'Université de Québec—than in the rest of the country. French-Canadian sociology was influenced, initially, by the Roman Catholic Church and, in the longer term, by developments in Europe and France, where sociologists tended to investigate and compare economic and political trends. English-Canadian sociology began both at McGill, following the U.S. tradition, and at the University of Toronto, following the British tradition.

Sociology did not have its own department at the University of Toronto until the 1960s. Before that time, social thinkers of sociological cast worked out of the department of political economy. Sociology at the University of Toronto differed from the American-influenced social issues and the community study approach that characterized studies at McGill. The University of Toronto approach—modelled on British sociology and influenced by Harold Innis

---

[1] The abbreviation B.C.E. means "before the common era." To reflect the religious diversity of our society, we use this throughout the text instead of the traditional B.C. ("before Christ"). Similarly, in place of the traditional A.D. (*anno Domini*, or "in the year of our Lord"), we use the abbreviation C.E. ("common era").

[2] Illustrating Comte's stages, the ancient Greeks and Romans viewed the planets as gods; Renaissance metaphysical thinkers saw them as astral influences (giving rise to astrology); by the time of Galileo, scientists understood planets as natural objects moving according to natural laws.

Here we see Galileo, one of the great pioneers of the scientific revolution, defending himself before church officials, who were greatly threatened by his claims that science could explain the operation of the universe. Just as Galileo challenged the common sense of his day, pioneering sociologists such as Auguste Comte later argued that society is neither rigidly fixed by God's will nor set by human nature. On the contrary, Comte claimed, society is a system we can study scientifically and, based on what we learn, we can act intentionally to improve our lives.

Source: North Wind Picture Archives

(1894–1962)—tackled questions of political and economic history. Innis's argument that Canadian economic development depended on resource extraction and exportation (known as the staples thesis) formed the backdrop to the development of the sociological perspective in Canada. This perspective focused on economic developments such as the branch-plant nature of the Canadian economy. Innis also noted the role of communications and communications technology in the development of Canadian society.

Marshall McLuhan (1911–80) gained world renown for his insight into the impact of electronic communication on culture, politics, and personal identities. In reality a social theorist, he provoked Canadians with his musings on the interplay of the media—the electronic media in particular—with human thought, human behaviour, and the shape of society. He had Canadians chew on tidbits such as "the medium is the message" and "global village," while his thinking laid the groundwork for our understanding of the current concepts of cyberspace and virtual reality and their impact on social cohesion and identity (Benedetti and DeHart, 1996; Goyder, 1997). Thirty years ahead of his time, McLuhan would have been very comfortable with the concepts of "cyberspace," "virtual reality," and "real time." See the Media Perspectives box (on p. 16) for further insight into his work.

John Porter (1921–79), in many minds, is Canada's leading sociologist. His book *The Vertical Mosaic* (1965) laid the groundwork for the focus on Canadian society in the context of development and underdevelopment (particularly as compared to the United States), ethnic inequality and inequity, elites, French/English relations, and bureaucratic structures.

Canada's massive size, its sparse but diverse population, its proximity to the United States, and its global situation (economic, cultural, and political) ensure that Canadian sociology will be concerned with questions of unity, political movements, economic development and inequality, regionalism, environment, identity, communications, and diversity, as well as cultural expression and survival (Helmes-Hayes, 1988; Whyte and Vallee, 1988; and Brym and Fox, 1989).

Sociological Theory

Weaving observations into understanding brings us to another aspect of sociology: theory. A **theory** is *a statement of how and why specific facts are related*. The job of sociological theory is to explain social behaviour in the real world. For example, recall Emile Durkheim's theory that categories of people with low social integration (men, Protestants, the wealthy, and the unmarried) are at higher risk of suicide. As the next chapter ("Sociological Investigation") explains, sociologists test their theories by gathering evidence using various research methods. Durkheim did exactly this, finding out which categories of people were more likely to commit suicide and which were less likely, and then devising a theory that best squared with all available evidence.

In building theory, sociologists face two fundamental questions: What issues should we study? How should we connect the facts? In the process of answering these questions, sociologists look to one or more theoretical paradigms, or approaches, as "road maps." Think of a **theoretical approach** as *a basic image of society that guides thinking and research*. Sociologists make use of three major theoretical approaches: the structural-functional approach, the social-conflict approach, and the symbolic-interaction approach, each of which will be explored in the remainder of this chapter. We also discuss two more recent paradigms, feminism and postmodernism.

Harold A. Innis (*left*) was best known as a political economist and a pioneer in communication studies—analyzing the impact of modes of communication on social development. He was a member of the University of Toronto's political economy department from 1920 to his death in 1952. His first major work, *The Fur Trade in Canada* (1930), introduced the staples thesis of development and established his reputation.

John Porter (*centre left*), a graduate of the London School of Economics, spent most of his career in Ottawa at Carleton University, as a faculty member, department chair, dean, and academic vice-president. He profoundly influenced his students, many of whom are important sociologists today (Vallee, 1988).

Marshall McLuhan (*centre right*) was a controversial figure who achieved international recognition in the 1960s and 1970s. His work was ignored for a while, but it is being revisited as social scientists acknowledge the revolutionary impact of the electronic media. Trained in literature at Cambridge, McLuhan became an unconventional professor of English at the University of Toronto, where he simultaneously enthralled and enraged his students.

Erving Goffman (*right*), born in Alberta in 1922, received his bachelor's degree from the University of Toronto before going on to his master's and doctorate at the University of Chicago. His immensely influential books include *The Presentation of Self in Everyday Life* (1959), *Asylums: Essays on the Social Situation of Mental Patients and Other Inmates* (1961), and *Stigma: Notes on the Management of Spoiled Identity* (1963). He taught at the University of California at Berkeley and at the University of Pennsylvania, and was the president of the American Sociological Association prior to his death in 1982.

THE STRUCTURAL-FUNCTIONAL APPROACH

The **structural-functional approach** is *a framework for building theory that sees society as a complex system whose parts work together to promote solidarity and stability.* As its name suggests, this approach points to **social structure,** *any relatively stable pattern of social behaviour.* Social structure gives our lives shape—in families, the workplace, the classroom, and the community. This approach also looks for a structure's **social functions,** *the consequences of any social pattern for the operation of society as a whole.* All social structure, from a simple handshake to complex religious rituals, functions to keep society going, at least in its present form.

The structural-functional approach owes much to Auguste Comte, who pointed out the need to keep society unified when many traditions were breaking down. Emile

Find biographical sketches of Durkheim and Spencer in the Gallery of Sociologists at www.TheSociologyPage.com.

Durkheim, who helped establish the study of sociology in French universities, also based his work on this approach. A third structural-functional pioneer was the English sociologist Herbert Spencer (1820–1903). Spencer compared society to the human body. Just as the structural parts of the human body—the skeleton, muscles, and various internal organs —function interdependently to help the entire organism survive, social structures work together to preserve society. The structural-functional approach, then, leads sociologists to identify various structures of society and investigate their functions.

Robert K. Merton (1910–2003) expanded our understanding of the concept of social function by pointing out that any social structure probably has many functions, some more obvious than others. He distinguished between **manifest functions,** *the recognized and intended consequences of any social pattern,* and **latent functions,** *the unrecognized and unintended consequences of any social pattern.* For example, the manifest function of our system of higher education is to provide young people with the information and skills they need to perform jobs after graduation. Less often acknowledged is its latent function as a "marriage broker," bringing together people of similar social backgrounds. Higher education also limits unemployment by keeping young people out of the labour market, where many of them would have difficulty finding jobs.

But Merton also recognized that the effects of social structure are not all good, and certainly not good for everybody. Consequently, a **social dysfunction** is *any social pattern that may disrupt the operation of society.* People often disagree about what is helpful and what is harmful to society as a whole. In addition, what is functional for one category of people (say, high profits for factory owners) may well be dysfunctional for another category of people (say, low wages for factory workers).

MEDIA PERSPECTIVES
Marshall McLuhan: Media Theorist

When, in the 1960s, Marshall McLuhan (1911–80) claimed that the electronic media would transform the world as we knew it, he captured the attention of the world, achieving a fame that would fade by the late 1970s. Then, personal computers, laptops, and the Canadian BlackBerry were decades away. McLuhan was a renegade, too far ahead of everyone else. He spoke of running a factory, or indeed the world, from a cottage computer—at a time when computers, mostly operated by universities or large institutions, were the size of a small room. McLuhan's students at the University of Toronto struggled to understand his science fiction. Today, you might have difficulty comprehending the revolutionary impact of his thought, because—like fish oblivious to water—you are totally immersed in the very world he foresaw. Now that we live in the information age, scholars are revisiting McLuhan's thought and reviving his fame two decades after his death.

McLuhan taught us that "the instantaneous world of electronic information media involves all of us, all at once" in a "global village" or "instantaneous happening" (cited in Benedetti and DeHart (1996)). The instant movement of electronic information involves anyone connected to it in the business of others. Electronic communication extends our nervous systems so that we can be aware, immediately, of things that are happening in the global village. This instant awareness explodes local or even national boundaries—which cease to exist—making each of us part of the global village: recall our experience of the December 2004 tsunami and the phenomenal generosity of Canadian donors. At the same time, the world implodes or collapses in on us as instantaneous communication can come at us from everywhere. Explosion and implosion occur simultaneously.

"The medium is the message": this enigmatic or contradictory statement is typical of those with which McLuhan would tease his students. Because he wanted to teach rather than inform or entertain, he sought to engage his students in the process of discovery or puzzle solving. In observing that the *medium* is the message, he is saying that content is not everything. The book, the television, the cell phone, the camera, or the computer—in and of itself—changes the way we interact with the world around us. The bits of information we acquire may be of less importance than the media through which we obtain them. Think about the death of Princess Diana or New Orleans after hurricane Katrina. How differently did you absorb the news from the television and from the newspaper? Each medium covered the same "news," but the impacts on the recipients have little in common. Instantaneous coverage via satellite television makes us feel part of the "global village" in a way that the newspaper cannot.

Take a look at the following aphorisms or brief statements of principle to get a sense of McLuhan's approach to teaching—making you a puzzle solver rather than a passive recipient of information as you come to grips with his intent.

> The telephone: speech without walls.
> The phonograph: music hall without walls.
> The photograph: museum without walls.
> The electric light: space without walls.
> The movie, radio, and TV: classroom without walls (cited in Benedetti and DeHart (1996):102).

WHAT DO YOU THINK?

1. Does instantaneous electronic communication make *you* feel like a part of the "global village"?
2. *Is* the "medium" the "message"?
3. Do McLuhan's aphorisms make sense to you?

Critical Review The main idea of the structural-functional approach is its vision of society as stable and orderly. The main goal of the sociologists who use this approach, then, is to figure out "what makes society tick."

In the mid-1900s, most sociologists favoured the structural-functional approach. In recent decades, however, its influence has declined. By focusing on social stability and unity, critics say, structural-functionalism ignores inequalities of social class, race, and gender, which cause tension and conflict. In general, its focus on stability at the expense of conflict makes this approach somewhat conservative. As a critical response, sociologists developed the social-conflict approach.

THE SOCIAL-CONFLICT APPROACH

The **social-conflict approach** is *a framework for building theory that sees society as an arena of inequality that generates conflict and change.* Unlike the structural-functional emphasis on solidarity and stability, this approach highlights inequality and change. Guided by this approach, sociologists investigate how factors such as social class, race, ethnicity, gender, sexual orientation, and age are linked to a society's unequal distribution of money, power, education, and social prestige. A conflict analysis rejects the idea that social structure promotes the operation of society as a whole, focusing instead on how social patterns benefit some people while hurting others.

The approach of the structural-functional paradigm is conveyed by the painting *St. Regis Indian Reservation* by Amy Jones (1937). Here we see society composed of major rounds of life, each serving a particular purpose that contributes to the operation of the entire system.

Source: Amy Jones, *St. Regis Indian Reservation*, 1937. Photo courtesy Janet Marqusee Fine Arts Ltd.

Sociologists using the social-conflict approach look at ongoing conflict between dominant and disadvantaged categories of people—the rich in relation to the poor, White people in relation to people of colour, and men in relation to women. Typically, people in a dominant position try to protect their privileges while the disadvantaged try to gain more for themselves.

To illustrate, conflict analysis of our educational system might highlight the ways in which schooling perpetuates inequality by helping to reproduce the class structure in every new generation. The process begins as secondary schools assign some students to university preparatory programs while assigning others to vocational training. From a functional point of view, such "streaming" may benefit all of society because, ideally, students receive the training appropriate to their academic abilities. Conflict analysis counters that streaming has less to do with talent than social background—well-to-do students are placed in higher streams and poor students end up in the lower ones. Through streaming, privileged families gain favoured treatment for their children from schools and, subsequently, universities. With the best schooling behind them, these young people leave university to pursue occupations that confer both prestige and high income. In comparison, children from poor families and communities are unprepared for university or college; like their parents before them, these young people typically move from high school into low-paying jobs. In each case, the social standing of one generation is passed on to another, with schools justifying the practice in terms of individual merit, not privilege.

Many sociologists use the social-conflict approach not just to understand society but to bring about societal change that would reduce inequality. Karl Marx, whose ideas are discussed at length in Chapter 4 ("Society"), championed the cause of the workers in what he saw as their battle against factory owners. In a well-known statement, Marx asserted: "The philosophers have only interpreted the world, in various ways; the point, however, is to change it" (inscribed on his monument in London's Highgate Cemetery).

Feminism and the Gender-Conflict Approach

One important type of conflict analysis is the **gender-conflict approach,** *a point of view that focuses on inequality and conflict between women and men.* The gender-conflict approach is closely linked to *feminism,* the advocacy of social equality for women and men. The importance of the gender-conflict approach lies in making us aware of the many ways in which our way of life places men in positions of power over women: in the home (where men are usually considered the "head of household"), in the workplace (where men earn more and hold most positions of power), and in the mass media (where few executives are women).

Another contribution of the gender-conflict approach is making us aware of the importance of women to the development of sociology. Harriet Martineau (1802–1876) is regarded as the first woman sociologist. Martineau, who was born to a wealthy English family, made her mark in 1853 by translating the writings of Auguste Comte from French into English. Martineau established her reputation as a sociologist with studies that documented the evils of slavery and argued for laws to protect factory workers, defending workers' right to unionize. She was particularly concerned about the position of women in society and fought for changes in education policy, so that women could look forward to more in life than marriage and raising children. She also found time to write novels, travel widely, and pursue a full-time career as a journalist, in spite of recurrent ill health and deafness.

In the United States, Jane Addams (1860–1935) was a sociological pioneer whose contributions began in 1889 when she helped found Hull House, a Chicago settlement house that provided assistance to immigrant families. Although widely published (she wrote eleven books and hundreds of articles), Addams chose the life of a public activist over that of a university sociologist, speaking out on issues involving immigration and the pursuit of peace. Despite the controversy caused by her pacifism during World War I, she was awarded the Nobel Peace Prize in 1931.

We can use the sociological perspective to look at sociology itself. All of the most widely recognized pioneers of the discipline were men. This is because, in the nineteenth century, it was all but unheard of for women to be college professors, and few women took a central role in public life. But Harriet Martineau in England (*left*), Jane Addams in the United States (*right*) are among the women who made contributions to sociology that we now recognize as important and lasting.

In the past several decades, feminist sociology has been challenging the male-dominated discipline with critiques of methodology, theory, and all the substantive areas of the field. Feminist sociology, along with feminist analysis in other areas of academic life, has established a new field called *women's studies*. There are now women's studies programs in universities and colleges across Canada. All chapters of this book consider the importance of gender and gender inequality. For a detailed look at feminism and the social standing of women and men, see Chapter 13 ("Gender Stratification").

The Race-Conflict Approach

Another important type of social-conflict analysis is the **race-conflict approach,** *a point of view that focuses on inequality and conflict between people of different racial and ethnic categories.* Just as men have power over women, White people have numerous social advantages over people from visible minorities including, on average, higher incomes, more schooling, better health, and longer life. An important contribution to understanding race in the United States was made by William Edward Burghardt Du Bois (1868–1963). Born to a poor Massachusetts family, Du Bois eventually enrolled at Harvard University, where he earned the first doctorate awarded by that university to a person from a visible minority. Like most people who follow the social-conflict approach—whether focusing on class, gender, or race, Du Bois believed that sociologists should try to solve society's problems. He therefore studied the Black community (1967; orig. 1899), spoke out against racial inequality, and served as a founding member of the National Association for the Advancement of Colored People.

Ethnic and racial diversity have long been important themes in Canadian sociology. John Porter, in *The Vertical Mosaic* (1965), argued that class and power were functions of ethnicity and race, with people of British descent at the top of the hierarchy. Canada's Aboriginal peoples, who are still at the bottom of that hierarchy, are the subject of extensive research in sociology departments throughout the country. Trent University (in Peterborough, Ontario) is known for its special programs in Native Studies, while other universities have programs designed for Aboriginal students. The existence of a journal, *Canadian Ethnic Studies*, reflects the importance of issues related to diversity in Canadian society.

Critical Review   The various social-conflict approaches have gained a large following in recent decades but, like other approaches, they have met with criticism. Because any conflict analysis focuses on inequality, it largely ignores how shared values and interdependence unify members of a society. In addition, to the extent that the conflict approach pursues political goals, it cannot claim scientific objectivity. Supporters of social-conflict approaches respond that *all* theoretical approaches have political consequences.

A final criticism of both the structural-functional and the social-conflict approaches is that they paint society in broad strokes—in terms of "family," "social class," "race," and so on. A third theoretical approach views society in terms of the everyday experience of individual people.

THE SYMBOLIC-INTERACTION APPROACH

The structural-functional and social-conflict approaches share a **macro-level orientation,** *a broad focus on social structures that shape society as a whole.* Macro-level sociology takes in the big picture, rather like observing a city from high above in a helicopter and seeing how highways help people move from place to place or how housing differs from rich to poor neighbourhoods. Sociology also uses a **micro-level orientation,** *a close-up focus on social interaction in specific situations.* Exploring urban life in this way occurs at street level, where you might watch how children invent games on a school playground or observe how pedestrians respond to homeless people they pass on the street. The **symbolic-interaction approach,** then, is *a framework for building theory that sees society as the product of the everyday interactions of individuals.*

How does "society" result from the ongoing experiences of tens of millions of people? One answer, explained in Chapter 6 ("Social Interaction in Everyday Life"), is that society is nothing more than the shared reality that people construct as they interact with one another. That is, human beings live in a world of symbols, attaching *meaning* to

The social-conflict approach points out patterns of inequality. In general, students are relatively privileged women and men who routinely come into contact with other people who have far fewer opportunities for success. What patterns of social inequality do you see in your everyday life?

virtually everything, from the words on this page to the wink of an eye. "Reality," therefore, is simply how we define our surroundings, our obligations towards others, and even our own identities.

The symbolic-interaction approach has roots in the thinking of Max Weber (1864–1920), a German sociologist who emphasized the need to understand a setting from the point of view of the people in it. Weber's approach is discussed in detail in Chapter 4 ("Society"). Since Weber's time, sociologists have taken micro-level sociology in a number of directions. Chapter 5 ("Socialization") discusses the ideas of George Herbert Mead (1863–1931), who explored how our personalities develop as a result of social experience. Chapter 6 ("Social Interaction in Everyday Life") presents the work of Erving Goffman (1922–82), whose *dramaturgical analysis* describes how we resemble actors on a stage as we play out our various roles. Other contemporary sociologists, including George Homans and Peter Blau, have developed *social-exchange analysis*. In their view, social interaction is guided by what each person stands to gain and lose from others. In the ritual of courtship, for example, people seek mates who offer at least as much—in terms of physical attractiveness, intelligence, and social standing—as they offer in return.

Critical Review Without denying the existence of macro-level social structures such as "the family" and "social class," the symbolic-interaction approach reminds us that society basically amounts to *people interacting*. That is, micro-level sociology tries to show how individuals actually experience society. But on the other side of the coin, by focusing on what is unique in each social scene, this approach risks overlooking the widespread influence of culture, as well as factors such as class, gender, and race.

THE POSTMODERN PARADIGM

Postmodernism is *an approach that is critical of modernism, with a mistrust of grand theories and ideologies,* that can have either a micro or a macro orientation. As applied by the social sciences, postmodernism is at its core both anti theory and anti methods: human sciences, it proposes, cannot be scientific because of human subjectivity, which makes discovering objective truth impossible. Proponents argue that they are not trying to create systematic new knowledge but are writing to permit multiple interpretations by their readers. Postmodernists seek to observe other societies without applying the conceptual baggage of their own. They observe with the goal of achieving understanding and a vision rather than data collection. Through deconstruction (taking apart) of existing text, postmodernists can demystify (uncover or identify) the assumptions, hierarchies of knowledge, and ideological motivation of the social sciences.

Michel Foucault (1926–84), a French philosopher and one of the most influential postmodernists, would agree with Weber that scientific rationality is a means to an end that tells us nothing about the values that should guide our lives. Furthermore, his treatment of power, which for him permeates all of society, takes it out of the exclusive hands of capitalists, males, or any other category of people (Foucault, 1980).

The Applying Theory table (on p. 21) summarizes the main characteristics of the classical paradigms—structural functionalism, social conflict, and symbolic interactionism—as well as the feminist and postmodernist paradigms. Each approach deals with specific kinds of questions about society. However, the fullest understanding of our social world comes from combining approaches, as we show with the following analysis of sport in North America.

The basic insight of the symbolic-interaction approach is that people create the reality they experience as they interact. In other words, as these three students engage one another in conversation, they are literally deciding "what's going on."

APPLYING THE APPROACHES: THE SOCIOLOGY OF SPORTS

Who among us doesn't enjoy sports? Children as young as six or seven may play as many as two or three organized sports at a time.[1] Almost everyone has engaged in some type of sport: in Canada, about 45 percent of those aged 15 and over indicate regular participation in some kind of sport; the number reaches a high of 53 percent in British Columbia and dips to 36 percent in Newfoundland (Corbeil, 2000a). For adults, weekend television is filled with sporting events, and whole sections of our newspapers report the scores. Wayne Gretzky and Hayley Wickenheiser (hockey), Eric Gagné and David Ortiz (baseball), David Pelletier and Jamie Salé (pair's figure skating), Mike Weir and Tiger Woods (golf), and Serena Williams and Roger Federer (tennis) are all top athletes who are famous celebrities—even after they retire from active participation. Sports, amateur and professional, have become a multibillion-dollar industry. What sociological insights can our three major theoretical approaches give us into this familiar part of everyday life?

The Functions of Sports

A structural-functional approach directs our attention to the ways in which sports help society operate. The manifest functions of sports include providing recreation, a means of getting in physical shape, and a relatively harmless way to let off steam. Sports have important latent functions as well, from building social relationships to creating tens of thousands of jobs. Sports encourage competition and the pursuit of success, both of which are central to our society's way of life.

Sports also have dysfunctional consequences. For example, colleges and universities sometimes recruit students for athletic skill rather than academic ability. This practice, which is more common in the United Sates than in Canada, not only lowers the academic standards of a school but also shortchanges athletes who spend little time doing the academic work that will prepare them for later careers (Upthegrove, *et al.*, 1999).

Sports and Conflict

A social-conflict analysis of sports begins by pointing out that the games people play reflect their social standing. Some sports—including tennis, polo, golf, sailing, and skiing—are expensive, so taking part is largely limited to the affluent. Football, baseball, and basketball, however, are accessible to people of almost all income levels. In Canada and the United States, sports are oriented primarily towards males. The first modern Olympic Games held in 1896 excluded women from competition; until recently, moreover, even little league teams in most parts of Canada barred girls from the playing field. Such male-only practices have been defended by unfounded notions that girls and women lack the ability to engage in sports or risk losing their femininity if they do so. Thus, our society encourages men to be athletes and expects women to be attentive observers and cheerleaders. (The Thinking It Through box on pp. 226–27 in Chapter 9 ponders whether men's hockey fosters masculinity that is dangerous.)

More women now play competitive sports than ever before—in women's hockey, Canada won gold at the 2002 Winter Olympics at Salt Lake City, Utah—yet they continued to take a back seat to men, particularly in sports that yield the greatest earnings, media coverage, and prestige. Canada's women's hockey team won gold again in 2006 (Turin, Italy): furthermore, women won five of our seven gold medals and sixteen (two-thirds) of our twenty-four medals overall. With that kind of performance by women—including speed skater, Cindy Klassen, who won five of Canada's Olympic medals and alpine skier, Lauren Woolstencroft, who won four

---

[1] Recognizing the importance of involvement in sports for Canada's children, Prime Minister Harper promised tax credits in 2006 to help parents cover the expenses of organized sport.

APPLYING THEORY
THEORETICAL PARADIGMS

	Classical Paradigms			Recent Paradigms	
	Structural-Functional Approach	**Social-Conflict Approach**	**Symbolic-Interaction Approach**	**Feminist Paradigm**	**Postmodernist Paradigm**
What is the level of analysis?	Macro level	Macro level	Micro level	Micro and macro levels	Micro and macro levels
What image of society does the approach have?	Society is a system of inter-related parts that is relatively stable. Each part works to keep society operating in an orderly way. Members have general agreement about what is morally right.	Society is a system of social inequality. Society operates to benefit some categories of people and to harm others. Social inequality causes conflict that leads to social change.	Society is an ongoing process. People interact in countless settings using symbolic communications. The reality that people experience is variable and changing.	A gender-based hierarchy where men dominate women in all realms of social life (including the family, religion, the polity, the economy, and education)	Shifting patterns of social order, institutions, and personal relations, about which truths and assumptions are subject to change
What core questions does the approach ask?	How is society held together? What are the major parts of society? How are these parts linked? What does each part do to help society work?	What factors give rise to social inequality? How do advantaged people protect their privileges? How do disadvantaged people challenge the system to seek change?	How do people experience society? How do people shape the reality they experience? How do behaviour and meaning change from person to person and from one situation to another?	What factors give rise to gender-based inequality? What are the effects of male domination on men and on women? How can such a structure be overturned?	How does power permeate social relations or society, and change with circumstances? How do we understand societies or interpersonal relations, while rejecting the theories and methods of the social sciences, and our assumptions about human nature?

of Canada's thirteen Paralympic medals—we *should* see women moving onto the front seat with men. (The Thinking about Diversity box on p. 346 of Chapter 13 discusses the evolution of women's hockey in Canada.)

While North American society long excluded people from visible minorities from big league sports, the opportunity to earn high incomes in professional sports has expanded in recent decades. Professional baseball first admitted African-American players when Jackie Robinson broke the "colour bar" in 1946, playing for the Montreal Royals before moving to Major League Baseball in the United States. Willie O'Ree, originally from Fredericton, New Brunswick, was the first Black player in the National Hockey League, when he was brought up from the minor leagues to play for the Boston Bruins in 1958. By 1993, African Americans—12 percent of the U.S. population— accounted for 17 percent of players in the Major League

Some concern has been expressed recently about the dramatic *decrease* in African-American youngsters entering college and professional baseball. See www.blackathlete.com/ Collegesports/062304.shtml.

Baseball, 68 percent of players in the National Football League, and 77 percent of players in the National Basketball Association (Center for the Study of Sport in Society, 1998). Figure 1–3 reveals, however, that the placement of White and Black players in professional football may still not be fair.

One reason for the increasing proportion of Black people in professional sports is the fact that precisely measured athletic performances cannot be diminished by prejudice. There's no disputing the gold-medal Olympic performances of Canada's Donovan Bailey and the men's 4 × 100 metre relay team (1996), Daniel Igali in wrestling (2000), or Jarome Iginla as a dominant member of the 2002 men's Olympic hockey team, which won gold. Recently in North America, Black athletes have earned higher salaries,

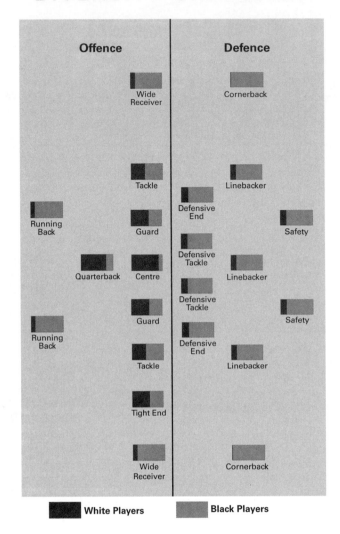

FIGURE 1-3 Race and Sport: "Stacking" in Professional Football

Does race play a part in professional sports? Looking at the various positions in American professional football, we see that White players are more likely to play the central and offensive positions. What do you make of this pattern?

Source: Lapchick (2005).

Taking a wider view, who gains the greatest benefits from professional sports? While millions of fans follow their teams, the vast amounts of money teams take in are controlled by the small number of people (predominantly White men) for whom teams are income-generating property. In sum, sport in North America is bound up with inequalities based on gender, race, and class.

Sports as Interaction

At a micro level, a sporting event is a complex, face-to-face interaction. In part, play is guided by the players' assigned positions and the rules of the game. But players are also spontaneous and unpredictable. Following the symbolic-interaction approach, we see sports less as a system than as an ongoing process. From this point of view, we expect each player to understand the game a little differently. Some players enjoy a setting of stiff competition; for others, love of the game may be greater than the need to win. In addition, the behaviour of any single player may change over time. A rookie in professional baseball, for example, may feel self-conscious during the first few games in the big leagues but go on to develop a comfortable sense of fitting in with the team. Feeling at home on the field came slowly and painfully to Jackie Robinson, who knew that many White players, and millions of White fans, resented his presence. In time, however, his outstanding ability and his confident and co-operative manner won him the respect of team mates and fans alike.

The three major theoretical approaches—the structural—functional approach, the social-conflict approach, and the symbolic-interaction approach—provide different insights into sports, and none is more correct than the others. Applied to any issue, each approach generates its own interpretations. To appreciate fully the power of the sociological perspective, you should become familiar with all three.

The Thinking it Through box (on p. 23) discusses the use of the sociological perspective and reviews many of the ideas presented in this chapter. This box raises a number of questions that will help you understand how sociological generalizations differ from the common stereotypes we encounter every day.

on average, than White players; Tiger Woods and V.J. Singh, and Venus and Serena Williams have achieved outstanding success in the traditionally elitist sports of professional golf and tennis, respectively. But racial discrimination still taints professional sports: Black athletes figure prominently in only a handful of sports (baseball, basketball, football, boxing, and track), and almost all managers, head coaches, and owners are White.

YOUR TURN

Apply the three theoretical approaches to the issues of love and marriage. Consider questions such as these: What categories of people are you most likely to date? Why? Why do young people put off marriage longer than they did twenty years ago?

THINKING IT THROUGH
Is Sociology Nothing More than Stereotypes?

"Protestants are the ones who commit suicide!"

"Americans are violent; Canadians are not!"

"Everyone knows that you have to be Black to play professional basketball!"

Everyone, including the sociologist, tends to generalize. Recognizing this fact, some students who begin the study of sociology may wonder whether statements like those above are sociological insights or simply stereotypes. What, exactly, is the difference between the two?

All three statements above illustrate the *stereotype*, an exaggerated description that one applies to all people in a given category. Rather than describing averages, each statement paints every individual in a category with the same brush. Further, each ignores facts and distorts reality (even though each contains some element of truth), and each sounds more like a put down than an unbiased assertion.

Crafting a sociological insight, by contrast, does involve making generalizations, but with these important conditions. Instead of indiscriminately applying these generalizations to individuals, we ensure that a generalization squares with available facts. We also offer a generalization fair-mindedly, with an interest in getting at the truth.

Recall that the sociological perspective reveals "the general in the particular"; therefore, a sociological insight is a generalization about some category of people. An example is the assertion, made earlier in this chapter, that the suicide rate among Protestants is higher than that among Catholics or Jews. However, the way the statement above is phrased—"Protestants are the ones who commit suicide!"—is false, because the vast majority of Protestants do no such thing.

Sociologists base their generalizations on available facts. A more factual and accurate version of the second statement above might be that American cities tend to have higher rates of violent crime than do Canadian cities.

It is a gross exaggeration to imply that all Americans are violent while Canadians are not.

Lastly, sociologists strive to be fair-minded; that is, they are motivated by a passion for learning and for truth. The third statement above about Black athletes and basketball fails as good sociology not only because it doesn't square with the facts, but because it seems motivated by bias rather than truth seeking or understanding.

Good sociology, then, stands apart from stereotyping. One of the most valuable aspects of a sociology course is that, through it, we learn how to collect the factual information that we need in order to assess the truth of popular wisdom.

WHAT DO YOU THINK?

1. Why do people generate stereotypes?
2. Do you think taking a sociology course erodes stereotypes or generates new ones?
3. Can you cite a stereotype that could be challenged by sociology?

MAKING THE GRADE

The following learning tools will help you to see what you know, identify what you still need to learn, and expand your understanding beyond the text. You can also visit this text's Companion Website™ at www.pearsoned.ca/macionis to find useful practice tests.

KEY POINTS

The Sociological Perspective

The sociological perspective shows "the general in the particular," or the effect of society on individual lives. Because our culture emphasizes individual choice, recognizing the power of society in our lives may seem, at first, like "seeing the strange in the familiar." C. Wright Mills called this point of view the "sociological imagination," claiming it turns private troubles into public issues. The chapter explained that differences in the number of children born to women around the world, as well as Emile Durkheim's research on suicide rates among some categories of people, show that society affects even our most personal choices and actions. Categories of people who experience social marginality—for example, visible minorities or people with disabilities—are more likely to see the world sociologically. For everyone, social crises encourage sociological thinking.

The Importance of a Global Perspective

Global awareness is an important part of the sociological perspective for four major reasons. First, people in high- and low-income countries live very differently. Second, all the world's societies are becoming more closely linked. Third, many social problems are more serious in other countries. Fourth, global awareness helps us better understand ourselves.

Applying the Sociological Perspective

Sociology has an impact on our everyday lives because it plays an important part in shaping public policy. On an individual level, sociology promotes personal growth in four major ways. First, it helps us assess common beliefs. Second, it helps us appreciate the opportunities and limits in our lives. Third, sociology encourages more active participation in society. Fourth, it increases our awareness of social diversity in the world around us. In addition, sociology is excellent preparation for a number of important careers and increases the chances for success in almost any job.

The Origins of Sociology

Sociology was born in response to important changes in Europe during the eighteenth and nineteenth centuries. Three changes—the rise of an industrial economy, the explosive growth of cities, and the emergence of new political ideas—made people pay attention to the operation of society. Auguste Comte gave sociology its name in 1838. Earlier social thinkers had focused on what society ought to be, but Comte's new discipline used scientific methods to understand society as it is.

Sociological Theory

A theory states how facts are related, weaving observations into insight and understanding. Sociologists use three classical theoretical paradigms to create theories about the operation of society. The structural-functional approach, which focuses on how patterns of behaviour help society operate, highlights society's stability and integration. The social-conflict approach, which emphasizes social inequality, sees conflict as a cause of change. The gender-conflict approach (feminist paradigm) highlights how men have power over women. The race-conflict approach focuses on how White people have power over visible minorities. In contrast to these broad, macro-level approaches, the symbolic-interaction approach is a micro-level framework that focuses on people's face-to-face interaction. The postmodernist paradigm seeks to understand society without the theories and methods of the social sciences.

Applying the Approaches: The Sociology of Sports

Applied to sports, the structural-functional approach looks at how sports contribute to the operation of society. The social-conflict approach examines the links between sports and social inequality. The symbolic-interaction approach highlights the different meanings and understandings people have of sports.

KEY CONCEPTS

sociology (p. 2) the systematic study of human society

sociological perspective (p. 2) the special point of view of sociology that sees general patterns of society in the lives of particular people

global perspective (p. 6) the study of the larger world and our society's place in it

high-income countries (p. 7) nations with the highest overall standards of living

middle-income countries (p. 7) nations with a standard of living about average for the world as a whole

low-income countries (p. 7) nations with a low standard of living in which most people are poor

positivism (p. 13) a way of understanding based on science

theory (p. 14) a statement of how and why specific facts are related

theoretical approach (theoretical paradigm) (p. 14) a basic image of society that guides thinking and research

structural-functional approach (p. 15) a framework for building theory that sees society as a complex system whose parts work together to promote solidarity and stability

social structure (p. 15) any relatively stable pattern of social behaviour

social functions (p. 15) the consequences of any social pattern for the operation of society as a whole

manifest functions (p. 15) the recognized and intended consequences of any social pattern

latent functions (p. 15) the unrecognized and unintended consequences of any social pattern

social dysfunction (p. 15) any social pattern that may disrupt the operation of society

social-conflict approach (p. 16) a framework for building theory that sees society as an arena of inequality that generates conflict and change

gender-conflict approach (p. 17) a point of view that focuses on inequality and conflict between women and men

race-conflict approach (p. 18) a point of view that focuses on inequality and conflict between people of different racial and ethnic categories

macro-level orientation (p. 18) a broad focus on social structures that shape society as a whole

micro-level orientation (p. 18) a close-up focus on social interaction in specific situations

symbolic-interaction approach (p. 18) a framework for building theory that sees society as the product of the everyday interactions of individuals

postmodernism (p. 19) an approach that is critical of modernism, with a mistrust of grand theories and ideologies

APPLICATIONS & EXERCISES

1. Explore your local area, and draw a sociological map. Include the types of buildings (e.g., "big single-family homes," "warehouses," "new office buildings," "apartments") found in various places, and guess at the categories of people who live or work there. What patterns do you see?

2. Observe students in a campus cafeteria. Can you see any stable patterns in the seating arrangements at the tables? Do race and gender contribute to these patterns?

3. What are the functions of the Olympic Games for Canada and for the international community? Can you apply the structural-functional, social-conflict, and symbolic-interaction theoretical approaches to the Olympic Games?

PRENTICE HALL
mysoclab™
Where learning & the sociological imagination intersect.

To reinforce your understanding of this chapter, and to identify topics for further study, visit MySocLab at **www.pearsoned.ca/mysoclab/** for diagnostic tests and a multimedia ebook.

2

CHAPTER TWO

Sociological Investigation

How does sociological research challenge common sense?

Why do sociologists use different methods to do research?

What part do gender and cultural differences play in sociological research?

S tudents in Professor Gerber's political sociology course are busily engaged in *real* research. Each student is responsible for collecting census and election data for 10 of Canada's 308 federal electoral districts (ridings). By comparing notes on socioeconomic characteristics and 2004 or 2006 election outcomes, these students are trying to explain voting behaviour in their assigned ridings. What riding characteristics, they ask, are associated with more or less support for the candidates of the major federal parties—Conservative, Liberal, Bloc Québécois, and New Democratic?

Each student, armed with a coding sheet, collects specific items of information from the census (on CD-ROM) and the Report of the Chief Electoral Officer for each of his or her 10 electoral districts. The census data are then converted into percentages so that the students know, for example, how much of each riding's population is immigrant, university educated, francophone, bilingual, or employed full-time. The students can then compare findings, asking if largely francophone Quebec ridings are the ones most likely to vote for the Bloc Québécois—or if the proportion of immigrants within Canada's ridings is related to the proportion of the vote going to the Liberals.

By looking separately at patterns in specific regions, the class begins to understand the impact of riding characteristics and region on support for specific parties. In Election 2006, the Conservatives had their greatest support in the prairie provinces and, more generally, outside the major cities of Montreal, Toronto, and Vancouver, while the Bloc Québécois continue to dominate in Quebec. What kinds of ridings were responsible for these patterns? And what do we know about the 10 Quebec ridings that surprised everyone by electing Conservatives? Students come out of this process with a clear understanding of the ways in which 308 mini-elections, at the riding level, determine the outcome of a Canadian federal election.

Many people think that scientists work only in laboratories, carefully taking measurements using complex equipment. But, as this chapter explains, sociologists also conduct scientific research in the familiar terrain of neighbourhood streets, in homes, at workplaces, and in prisons, as well as in unfamiliar locales throughout the world—in short, wherever people can be found. The opening example illustrates the basics of scientific analysis—existing data or official statistics are used to determine the characteristics and actions of people.

There are, of course, many other approaches to sociological research, as illustrated by the work of Reginald Bibby, a professor of sociology at the University of Lethbridge. For almost thirty years, Bibby measured changes in Canadians' attitudes towards a wide range of issues. Every five years from 1975 to 1995, Bibby mailed out a self-administered questionnaire to a representative sample of about 1100 adult Canadians. These questionnaires measured changes in attitudes towards a wide range of variables, including religion, sex, family, career, the economy, intergroup relations (and intermarriage), health, and happiness.

Along with his surveys of adult Canadians, Bibby has conducted a series dealing specifically with teenagers. His most recent teen survey, in the fall of 2000, involved 3500 young people, aged 15 to 19, from 150 high school classes chosen randomly throughout the country. One of his reasons for studying young people is that parents worry and fret about their attitudes and behaviours. His research shows that many—though not all—of those parental fears are unfounded. For example, Table 2–1 reveals that teens with body piercings and tattoos are similar to their peers in some respects, while differing in others. Bibby finds minor differences in self-image among teens with and without piercings or tattoos: regardless of body ornamentation, the teens are almost equally likely to feel that they are well-liked, good people, good-looking, capable, and confident. When he turns to behaviours and values, he finds that pierc-

TABLE 2–1

Correlates of Piercings and Tattoos

	Piercings		Tattoos	
	Yes	No	Yes	No
Self-image				
I am well liked	94%	93%	94%	93%
I am a good person	93	96	92	96
I am good-looking	79	76	80	76
I can do most things very well	78	83	82	83
I have lots of confidence	67	71	69	71
Behaviour/Values				
Engage in sex	71	45	82	45
Highly value concern for others	68	62	61	62
Use marijuana	61	33	65	33
Would return $10 in erroneous change	29	37	23	37
Attend services weekly-plus	12	23	10	23

Source: Bibby (2001):73.

ings and tattoos are associated with no difference in "concern for others"; but those *with* these ornamentations are more likely to engage in sex and use marijuana—and are less likely to attend religious services regularly. While this may suggest that you *can* judge a book by its cover, Bibby is careful to point out that there are many young people with piercings or tattoos who do *not* engage in sex or smoke marijuana (29% and 39%, respectively, compared to 49% and 63% of the national sample [Bibby (2001)]).

In this case, the individual teenager is the unit of analysis, as opposed to the electoral district in the opening example. The latter illustrates analysis at the aggregate level; Bibby's analysis is carried out at the individual level.

This chapter highlights the range of methods that sociologists use to conduct research. Along the way, we shall see that sociological research involves not just procedures for gathering information but controversies about whether that research should strive to be objective or to offer a bold prescription for change. After all, some sociological research has important policy implications. We shall tackle questions of values after addressing the basics of sociological investigation.

 A menu of worldwide resources is provided by Intute: Social Studies, including an array of mailing lists, journals, associations, organizations, and archives at www.intute.ac.uk.

Basics of Sociological Investigation

Sociological investigation starts with two simple requirements. The first is the focus of Chapter 1: *Apply the sociological perspective.* This point of view reveals curious patterns of behaviour all around us that call for further study and leads to the second requirement: *Be curious and ask questions.* These two requirements—seeing the world socio-

logically and asking questions—are fundamental to sociological investigation. Yet they are only the beginning. They draw us into the social world, stimulating our curiosity. But then we face the challenging task of finding answers to our questions. To understand the kind of insights sociology offers, we need to realize that there are various kinds of "truth."

SCIENCE AS ONE FORM OF TRUTH

Saying that we "know" something can mean many things. Most members of our society, a substantial 81 percent in fact, claim to believe in the existence of God (Bibby, 1995). Few would assert that they have direct contact with God, but they are believers all the same. We call this kind of knowing "belief" or "faith." A second kind of truth rests on the pronouncement of some recognized expert. Parents with questions about raising their children, for example, often consult child psychologists or their pediatricians about which practices are "right." A third type of truth is based on simple agreement among ordinary people. Everyone "knows" that littering is wrong.

People's "truths" differ the world over, and we often encounter "facts" at odds with our own. Imagine being a CUSO[1] volunteer just arriving in a small, traditional village in Latin America. With the job of helping the local people to grow more food, you take to the fields, observing a curious practice: farmers carefully plant seeds and then place a dead fish directly on top of each one. In response to your question, they reply that the fish is a gift to the god of the

---

[1] CUSO began at the University of Toronto in 1960 as Canadian University Services Overseas. Its website suggests that it is now a large international organization, with roots firmly in Canada, that is called simply CUSO.

harvest. A local elder adds sternly that the harvest was poor one year when no fish were offered as gifts. From that society's point of view, using fish as gifts to the harvest god makes sense. The people believe in it, their experts endorse it, and everyone seems to agree that the system works. But, with scientific training in agriculture, you have to shake your head and wonder. The scientific "truth" in this situation is something entirely different: the decomposing fish fertilize the ground, producing a better crop.

Science, then, represents a fourth way of knowing. **Science** is *a logical system that bases knowledge on direct, systematic observation.* Standing apart from faith, the wisdom of experts, and general agreement, scientific knowledge rests on **empirical evidence,** meaning *information we can verify with our senses.*

Our CUSO example does not mean that people in traditional villages ignore what their senses tell them, or that members of technologically advanced societies reject nonscientific ways of knowing. A medical researcher using science to seek an effective treatment for cancer, for example, may still practice her religion as a matter of faith. She may turn to experts when making financial decisions, and she may derive political opinions from family and friends. In short, we all embrace various kinds of truths at the same time.

COMMON SENSE VERSUS SCIENTIFIC EVIDENCE

Like the sociological perspective, scientific evidence sometimes challenges our common sense. Here are six statements that many North Americans assume are true:

1. **"Poor people are far more likely than rich people to break the law."** Not true. If you regularly watch television shows like *Cops*, you might think that police arrest only people from "bad" neighbourhoods. Chapter 9 ("Deviance") explains that poor people do stand out in the official arrest statistics. But research also shows that police and prosecutors treat the wealthy and powerful more leniently, as when politicians are accused of shoplifting or drunk driving.

2. **"Canada is a middle-class society in which people are more or less equal."** False. In 2000, 4.8 million Canadians or 16 percent of the population had incomes below the poverty line (or what Statistics Canada calls the "low-income cut-off"). In 2004, about 842 000 Canadians used the 250 food banks that are members of the Canadian Association of Food Banks to feed themselves and their children (CAFB, 2004). Some people are clearly much better off than others.

3. **"Poor people don't want to work."** Wrong. Research included in Chapter 11 ("Social Class in Canada") suggests that this is true of some but certainly not all or even most of the poor. Substantial majorities of unattached people over 65 and single parents with children are poor. *Employed* people who work for low

or minimum wages (the working poor) are clearly not people who are avoiding work.

4. **"Differences in the behaviour of females and males are just 'human nature.'"** Wrong again. Much of what we call "human nature" is constructed by the society in which we live, as Chapter 3 ("Culture") explains. Further, as argued in Chapter 8 ("Sexuality") and Chapter 13 ("Gender Stratification"), societies define "feminine" and "masculine" very differently.

5. **"People change as they grow old, losing many interests as they focus on their health."** Not really. Chapter 15 ("Aging and the Elderly") reports that aging does little to change one's personality. Problems of health increase in old age but, by and large, elderly people retain their distinctive personalities and interests.

6. **"Most people marry because they are in love."** Not always. To members of our society, few statements are so obvious. Surprisingly, however, in many societies marriage has little to do with love. Chapter 18 ("Family") explains why.

These examples confirm the old saying "It's not what we don't know that gets us into trouble as much as things we *do* know that *just aren't so.*" We all have been brought up believing widely accepted "truths," being bombarded by expert advice, and feeling pressure to accept the opinions of people around us. As adults, we need to evaluate more critically what we see, read, and hear. Sociology can help us do just that.

↦ **YOUR TURN** ↤

Think of several "common sense" ideas you were brought up to believe that you later learned were not true.

Three Ways To Do Sociology

"Doing" sociology means learning more about the social world. There is more than one way to do this. Just as sociologists can use one or more theoretical approaches (described in Chapter 1, "The Sociological Perspective"), they may also use different methodological orientations. The following sections describe three ways to do research: scientific sociology, interpretive sociology, and critical sociology.

SCIENTIFIC SOCIOLOGY

In Chapter 1, we explained how early sociologists such as Auguste Comte and Emile Durkheim applied science to the study of society just as natural scientists investigate the physical world. **Scientific sociology,** then, is *the study of society based on systematic observation of social behaviour.* The scientific orientation to knowing, called *positivism,* assumes that an objective reality exists "out there." The student research into federal electoral districts and Bibby's findings about teenagers, discussed earlier, are both studies in the positivist approach. The job of the scientist is to discover this reality by gathering empirical evidence, facts we can verify with our senses by "seeing," "hearing," or "touching."

Concepts, Variables, and Measurement

A basic element of science is the **concept,** *a mental construct that represents some part of the world in a simplified form.* "Society" is a concept, as are the structural parts of societies, such as "the family" and "the economy." Sociologists also use concepts to describe people, as when we speak of someone's "race" or "social class."

A **variable** is *a concept whose value changes from case to case.* The familiar variable "price," for example, changes from item to item in a supermarket. Similarly, we use the concept "social class" to identify people as "upper-class," "middle-class," "working-class," or "lower-class."

The use of variables depends on **measurement,** *a procedure for determining the value of a variable in a specific case.* Some variables are easy to measure, as when you step on a scale to see how much you weigh. But measuring sociological variables can be far more difficult. For example, how would you measure a person's "social class"? You might look at clothing, listen to patterns of speech, or note a home address. Or, in an attempt to be more precise, you might ask about income, occupation, and education.

Because almost any variable can be measured in more than one way, sociologists often have to decide which factors to consider. For example, having a very high income might qualify a person as "upper-class." But what if the income comes from selling automobiles, an occupation most people think of as "middle-class"? Would having only a grade 8 education make the person "lower-class"? In a case like this, sociologists usually combine three measures—income, occupation, and education—to assign social class, as described in Chapter 10 ("Social Stratification") and Chapter 11 ("Social Class in Canada").

Sociologists face another interesting problem in measuring variables: dealing with huge numbers of people. How, for instance, do you describe the income of all Canadian families? Reporting millions of numbers carries little meaning and tells us nothing about the people as a whole. Therefore, sociologists use *statistical measures*—like mode, mean and median—to describe people or communities.

Defining Concepts Measurement is always somewhat arbitrary because the value of any variable partly depends on how it is defined. In addition, deciding how to measure abstract concepts such as "love," "family," or "intelligence" can lead to lengthy debates. Good research, therefore, requires that sociologists **operationalize a variable,** which means *specifying exactly what is to be measured before assigning a value to a variable.* Before measuring the concept of social class, for example, we would have to decide exactly what we were going to measure: say, income level, years of schooling, or occupational prestige. Sometimes sociologists measure several of these things; in such cases, they need to specify exactly how they plan to combine these variables into one overall score. The next time you read the results of a study, notice the way the researchers operationalize each variable. How they define terms can greatly affect the results.

The definition (or operationalization) of race and ethnicity in the Canadian census has taken some interesting turns. Until the 1980s, people were asked to note the country from which their first ancestor (on the paternal side) came to Canada. Over time, this became an inadequate measure of our multicultural and multiracial society, where individuals often have multiple origins. The census questions gradually evolved to allow for multiple responses—up to four—which respondents could identify. (One might indicate German, Italian, Chinese and Lithuanian ancestry.) People can identify themselves as Black, North American Indian, or Inuit and, in general terms, as a visible minority. A complicating factor in achieving an accurate description of Canada's ethnic and racial diversity is the increasing choice of "Canadian/*Canadien*"—and *only* Canadian/*Canadien*—to describe one's background. (This is discussed further in Chapter 14 "Race and Ethnicity.")

Reliability and Validity For a measurement to be useful, it must be reliable and valid. **Reliability** refers to *consistency in measurement.* A measurement is reliable if repeated measurements give the same result time after time. But consistency does not guarantee **validity,** which means *actually measuring exactly what you intend to measure.* Getting a valid measurement is sometimes tricky. For example, if you want to study how "religious" people are, you might ask the people you are studying how often they attend services. But is going to a church, temple, or mosque really the same thing as being religious? People may attend religious services because of deep personal beliefs, but they may also do so out of habit or because others pressure them to go. And what about spiritual people who avoid organized religion altogether? Even when a measurement yields consistent results (making it reliable), it still may not measure what we want it to (and therefore lack validity). In Chapter 19 ("Religion"), we suggest that measuring religiosity should take account of not only service attendance but also a person's beliefs and the degree to which a person lives by religious convictions. In sum, careful measurement is important, but it is also often a challenge.

YOUR TURN

What specific questions would you ask to measure a person's social class?

FIGURE 2-1   Correlation and Cause: An Example

Correlation is not the same as cause. Here's why.

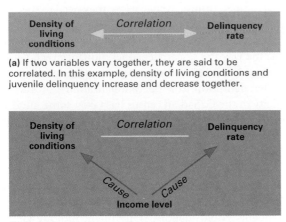

(a) If two variables vary together, they are said to be correlated. In this example, density of living conditions and juvenile delinquency increase and decrease together.

(b) Here we consider the effect of a third variable: income level. Low income level may cause *both* high-density living conditions *and* a high delinquency rate. In other words, as income level decreases, both the density of living conditions and the delinquency rate increase.

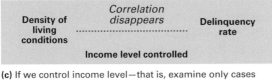

(c) If we control income level—that is, examine only cases with the same income level—do those with higher-density living conditions still have a higher delinquency rate? The answer is no. There is no longer a correlation between these two variables.

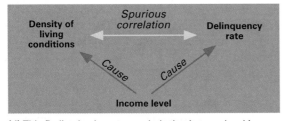

(d) This finding leads us to conclude that income level is a cause of both density of living conditions and delinquency rate. The original two variables (density of living conditions and delinquency rate) are thus correlated, but neither one causes the other. Their correlation is therefore *spurious*.

Relationships among Variables Once measurements are made, investigators can pursue the real payoff: seeing how variables are related. The scientific ideal is **cause and effect,** *a relationship in which change in one variable causes change in another.* Cause-and-effect relationships occur around us every day, such as when studying hard for an exam results in a high grade. *The variable that causes the change* (in this case, how much you study) is called the **independent variable.** *The variable that changes* (the exam grade) is called the **dependent variable.** The value of one variable, in other words, depends on the value of another. Why is linking variables in terms of cause and effect important? Because this kind of relationship allows us to *predict* the

outcome of future events—if we know one thing, we can accurately predict another. For example, knowing that studying hard results in a better exam grade, we can predict with confidence that, if you do study hard for the next exam, you will receive a high grade and, if you do not study hard, your grade will suffer.

But just because two variables change together does not mean that they are linked in a cause-and-effect relationship. For example, sociologists recognize that juvenile delinquency is more common among young people who live in crowded housing. Say we operationalize the variable "juvenile delinquency" as the number of times a person under the age of eighteen has been arrested, and we define "crowded housing" by a home's number of square feet of living space per person. It turns out that these variables are related: delinquency rates are high in densely populated neighbourhoods. But should we conclude that crowding in the home (in this case, the independent variable) causes delinquency (the dependent variable)? Not necessarily. **Correlation** is *a relationship in which two (or more) variables change together.* We know that density and delinquency are correlated because they change together, as shown in part (a) of Figure 2–1. This relationship *may* mean that crowding causes more delinquency, but it could also mean that some third factor is at work causing change in *both* of the variables under observation.

To identify a third variable, think about who lives in crowded housing: people with less money and few choices—the poor. Poor youngsters are also more likely to end up with police records. In reality, crowded housing and juvenile delinquency are found together because *both* are caused by a third factor—poverty—as shown in part (b) of Figure 2–1. In short, the apparent connection between crowding and delinquency is "explained away" by a third variable—low income—that causes them both to change. So our original connection turns out to be a **spurious correlation,** *an apparent but false relationship between two (or more) variables that is caused by some other variable.*

Exposing a correlation as spurious requires a bit of detective work, assisted by a technique called **control,** *holding constant all variables except one in order to see clearly the effect of that variable.* In our example, we suspect that income level may be causing a spurious link between housing density and delinquency. To check whether the correlation between delinquency and crowding is spurious, we control for income—that is, we hold income constant by looking at only young people of one income level. If the correlation between density and delinquency remains— that is, if young people of the same income level living in more crowded housing show higher rates of arrest than young people in less crowded housing—we have more reason to think that crowding does, in fact, cause delinquency. But if the relationship disappears when we control for income, as shown in part (c) of Figure 2–1, then we know we were dealing with a spurious correlation. In fact, research shows that the correlation between crowding and

Cigarette smoking is more common among people of lower social position. But knowing this correlation does not establish cause and effect. In your opinion, why would factory workers be more likely to smoke than people working as corporate executives?

delinquency just about disappears if income is controlled (Fischer, 1984). So we have now sorted out the relationship among the three variables, as illustrated in part (d) of the figure. Housing density and juvenile delinquency have a spurious correlation; evidence shows that both variables rise or fall according to income.

To sum up, correlation means only that two (or more) variables change together. To establish cause and effect, three requirements must be met:

1. a demonstrated correlation

2. an independent (or causal) variable that occurs before the dependent variable, and

3. no evidence that a third variable could be causing a spurious correlation between the two

Natural scientists usually have an easier time than social scientists in identifying cause-and-effect relationships because they work in laboratories, where they can control other variables. Carrying out research in a workplace or on the streets, however, makes control very difficult, so sociologists often have to settle for demonstrating only correlation. Also, human behaviour is highly complex, involving dozens of causal variables at any one time, so establishing all the cause-and-effect relationships in any situation is extremely difficult.

The Ideal of Objectivity

Ten students are sitting around a dorm lounge discussing the dream vacation spot for the upcoming spring break. Will one place end up being everyone's clear favourite? That seems unlikely. In scientific terms, each of the ten people probably operationalizes the concept "dream vacation" differently. For one, it might be a deserted, sunny beach in Mexico; for another, Vancouver, a lively city with a very active social scene; for still another, hiking or skiing in the Rocky Mountains. Like so many other "bests" in life, the best vacations turn out to be a matter of individual taste.

Personal values are fine when it comes to choosing travel destinations, but they pose a challenge to scientific research. Remember, science assumes that reality is "out there." Social scientists need to study this reality without changing it in any way, and so they strive for **objectivity**, *personal neutrality in conducting research.* Objectivity means that researchers carefully hold to scientific procedures, not letting their own attitudes and beliefs influence the results. Scientific objectivity is an ideal rather than a reality, of course, because no one can be completely neutral. Even the topic someone chooses to study reflects a personal interest of one sort or another. But the scientific ideal is to keep a professional sense of distance or detachment from the results. When conducting research, sociologists do their best to see that conscious or unconscious biases do not distort their findings. As an extra precaution, many researchers openly state their personal leanings in research reports so that readers can interpret conclusions with them in mind.

The influential German sociologist Max Weber expected people to select their research topics according to personal beliefs and interests. Why else, after all, would one person study world hunger, another investigate the effects of racism, and still another study children in one-parent families? Knowing that people select topics that are *value-relevant*, Weber cautioned researchers to be *value-free* in their investigations. Only by controlling their personal feelings and opinions—as every professional should—can researchers study the world *as it is* rather than tell us *how they think it should be.* This detachment, for Weber, is a crucial element of science that sets it apart from politics. Politicians are committed to particular outcomes; scientists maintain open minds about the results of their investigations, whatever they may turn out to be. Weber's argument still carries much weight in sociology, although most sociologists admit that we can never be completely value-free

One principle of scientific research is that sociologists and other investigators should try to be objective in their work, so that their personal values and beliefs do not distort their findings. But such a detached attitude may discourage the relationship needed in order for people to open up and share information. Thus, as sociologists study human relationships, they have to be especially mindful of their own—when it comes to their subjects.

or even aware of all our biases. Keep in mind, however, that sociologists are not "average" people: most are White, highly educated, and more politically liberal than the population as a whole (Klein and Stern, 2004). Remember that sociologists, like everyone else, are influenced by their social backgrounds.

One way to limit distortion caused by personal values is **replication,** *repetition of research by other investigators.* If other researchers repeat a study using the same procedures and obtain the same results, we gain confidence that the results are accurate (both reliable and valid). The need for replication in scientific investigation probably explains why the search for knowledge is called "*re*-search" in the first place.

The *Electronic Journal of Sociology,* which publishes full-text articles online, provides a search function to help researchers locate references to specific topics. See its website at www.sociology.org.

Keep in mind that the logic of science does not guarantee objective, absolute truth. What science offers is an approach to knowledge that is *self-correcting* so that, in the long run, researchers stand a good chance of limiting their biases. Objectivity and truth lie, then, not in any one study but in the scientific process itself as it continues over time.

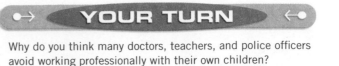

Why do you think many doctors, teachers, and police officers avoid working professionally with their own children?

Some Limitations of Scientific Sociology

Science is one important way of knowing. Yet, applied to social life, science has several important limitations.

1. **Human behaviour is too complex for sociologists to predict any individual's actions precisely.** Astronomers calculate the movement of objects in the skies with remarkable precision, but comets and planets are unthinking objects. Humans have minds of their own, so no two people react to any event, whether a sports victory or a natural disaster, in exactly the same way. Sociologists, therefore, must be satisfied with showing that *categories* of people *typically* act in one way or another. This is not a failing of sociology. It simply reflects the fact that sociologists study creative, spontaneous people.

2. **Because humans respond to their surroundings, the mere presence of a researcher may affect the behaviour being studied.** An astronomer's gaze has no effect whatever on a distant comet. But most people react to being observed. Try staring at someone for a few minutes and see for yourself. In effect, we can change people just by studying them.

3. **Social patterns change; what is true in one time or place may not hold true in another.** The same laws of physics will apply tomorrow as today, and they hold true all around the world. But human behaviour is so variable that there are no universal sociological laws.

4. **Because sociologists are part of the social world they study, being value-free when conducting social research is difficult.** Barring a laboratory mishap, chemists are rarely personally affected by what goes on in test tubes. But sociologists live in their "test tube," the society they study. Therefore, social scientists may find it difficult to control—or even to recognize— personal values that may distort their work.

INTERPRETIVE SOCIOLOGY

All sociologists agree that studying social behaviour scientifically presents some real challenges; others go further, suggesting that science as it is used to study the natural world misses a vital part of the social world—and that is *meaning.* Human beings do not simply act: they engage in meaningful action. Max Weber, who pioneered this framework, incorporated that insight, arguing that the proper focus of sociology is *interpretation,* or understanding the meanings involved in everyday life. **Interpretive sociology**

A basic lesson of social research is that being observed affects how people behave. Researchers can never be certain precisely how this will occur; some people resent public attention, but others become highly animated when they think they have an audience.

is *the study of society that focuses on the meanings people attach to their social world.*

Interpretive sociology differs from scientific, or positivist, sociology in three ways. First, scientific sociology focuses on action, or what people do, whereas interpretive sociology deals with the meaning attached to behaviour. Second, while scientific sociology sees an objective reality "out there," interpretive sociology sees reality as being constructed by people themselves in the course of their everyday lives. Third, while scientific sociology tends to make use of *quantitative data*, interpretive sociology relies on *qualitative data.*

In sum, the scientific or positivist approach is well suited to research in a laboratory, where investigators observe while taking careful measurements. The interpretive approach is better suited to research in a natural setting where investigators interact with people, learning how they make sense of their everyday lives.

Max Weber combined the best of both the scientific and interpretive approaches—the positivism of Auguste Comte and the interpretive emphasis of Wilhelm Dilthey (1833–1911), who might accurately be called the founder of interpretive sociology (Bakker, 1999). Weber believed that one of the keys to the interpretive component lay in *Verstehen*—the German word for "understanding." That concept, in turn, can be attributed to Dilthey.

It is the interpretive sociologist's job not just to observe *what* people do but to share in their world of meaning and come to appreciate *why* they act as they do. Subjective thoughts and feelings—which science tends to dismiss as "bias"—now become the focus of the researcher (Berger and Kellner, 1981; Neuman, 2000).

Robert Prus of the University of Waterloo argues that George Herbert Mead forged the unique interpretive tradi-

tion of *symbolic interaction.* For Mead, *language* is absolutely fundamental to the human experience, to shared symbols and understandings, and to social life and interaction. To understand group life, one must get inside the minds of the individual actors through close and sustained contact. One must achieve intimate familiarity by relying on "three sources of data: *observation, participant-observation,* and *interviews*" (Prus, 1994:21).

In an attempt to understand how Canadian university students approach studying in preparation for exams, Albas and Albas (1994) relied on interviews, observations, and logs that, over their twenty years of teaching, they had students keep. Students, they found, came to identify themselves as *aces, moderates,* or *bombers* (the terminology may differ from year to year). Their identities determined their approaches to studying, their relationships with other students in each of the categories, their friendship choices, their leisure activities, their levels of procrastination, and their expectations with respect to grades. Shared perspectives and patterns of behaviour were apparent within each of the categories, but almost all students sought to wear "the cloak of coolness"—the appearance of getting good grades with the minimum of effort. Since it is uncool to "work your butt off," serious studying—even among aces—was done out of sight or behind closed doors. Clearly, this type of interpretive understanding requires systematic analysis based on sustained personal contact with students themselves.

CRITICAL SOCIOLOGY

There is a third methodological orientation in sociology. Like the interpretive orientation, critical sociology developed in reaction to the limitations of scientific sociology. This time, however, the problem was the foremost principle of scientific research: objectivity. Scientific sociology holds that reality is

SUMMING UP

Three Methodological Orientations in Sociology

	Scientific	Interpretive	Critical
What is reality?	Society is an orderly system. There is an objective reality "out there."	Society is ongoing interaction. People construct reality as they attach meanings to their behaviour.	Society is patterns of inequality. Reality is that some categories of people dominate others.
How do we conduct research?	Researcher gathers empirical, ideally quantitative, data. Researcher tries to be a neutral observer.	Researcher develops a qualitative account of the subjective sense people make of their world. Researcher is a participant.	Research is a strategy to bring about desired social change. Researcher is an activist.
Corresponding theoretical approach	Structural-functional approach	Symbolic-interaction approach	Social-conflict approach

"out there," and the researcher's task is to study and document this reality. But Karl Marx, who founded the critical orientation, rejected the idea that society exists as a "natural" system with a fixed order. To assume this, he claimed, is the same as saying that society cannot be changed. Scientific sociology, from this point of view, ends up supporting the status quo. **Critical sociology,** by contrast, is *the study of society that focuses on the need for social change.*

The Importance of Change

Rather than asking the scientific question "How does society work?" critical sociologists ask moral and political questions, such as "Should society exist in its present form?" Their answer to this question, typically, is that it should not. One recent account of this orientation, echoing Marx, claims that the point of sociology is "not just to research the social world but to change it in the direction of democracy and social justice" (Feagin and Hernán, 2001:1). In making value judgments about how society should be improved, critical sociology rejects Weber's goal that researchers be value-free and emphasizes instead that they should be social activists in pursuit of desirable change.

Sociologists using the critical orientation seek to change not just society but the character of research itself. They often identify personally with their research subjects and encourage them to help decide what to study and how to do the work. Typically, researchers and subjects use their findings to provide a voice for less powerful people and to advance the political goal of a more equal society (Hess, 1999; Feagin and Hernán, 2001; Perrucci, 2001).

Sociology As Politics

Scientific sociologists object to taking sides in this way, charging that critical sociology—whether feminist, Marxist,

or postmodern—becomes political, lacks objectivity, and cannot correct for its own biases. Critical sociologists reply that *all* research is political or biased—either it calls for change or it does not. Sociologists, they continue, have no choice about their work being political, but they can choose *which* positions to support. Critical sociology is an activist orientation tying knowledge to action, seeking not just to understand the world but also to improve it. Generally speaking, scientific sociology tends to appeal to researchers with nonpolitical or conservative political views; critical sociology appeals to those whose politics range from liberal to radical left.

METHODS AND THEORY

Is there a link between methodological orientations and sociological theory? There is no precise connection, but each of the three methodological orientations—scientific, interpretive, and critical—does stand closer to one of the theoretical approaches presented in Chapter 1 ("The Sociological Perspective"). Scientific sociology corresponds to the structural-functional approach, interpretive sociology is related to the symbolic-interaction approach, and critical sociology is linked to the social-conflict approach. The Summing Up table (above) provides a quick review of the differences among the three methodological orientations. Many sociologists favour one orientation over another; however, because each provides useful insights, it is a good idea to become familiar with all three (Gamson, 1999).

GENDER AND RESEARCH

In recent years, sociologists have become aware that research is affected by **gender,** *the personal traits and social positions that members of a society attach to being female or male.* The Applying Sociology box (p. 38) offers three examples of sociology studies in which gender is integral to the research. Margrit Eichler (1988) identifies five ways in which gender can shape research:

1. **Androcentricity.** *Androcentricity* (*andro-* in Greek means "male"; *centricity* means "being centered on") refers to approaching an issue from a male perspective. Sometimes researchers act as if only men's activities are important, ignoring what women do. For years, researchers studying occupations focused on the paid work of men and overlooked the housework and child care traditionally performed by women. When Matthews (1976) sought to understand the attitudes and values of three small Newfoundland communities that were being considered for relocation, he limited his interviews to a random sample of male household heads and all of the community leaders (who were also male). Needless to say, research that seeks to understand full range of human behaviour cannot ignore half of humanity.

   Gynocentricity—seeing the world from a female perspective—can also limit good sociological investigation. While, in our male-dominated society, this problem arises less often, there are those who would argue that this is the main drawback of much feminist research. Feminists, in turn, would argue that gynocentricity in their work is essential to counter generations of androcentricity—in society, the media, and research.

2. **Overgeneralizing.** This problem occurs when researchers use data drawn from people of only one sex to support conclusions about "humanity" or "society." For example, in an investigation of child-rearing practices, collecting data only from women would allow researchers to draw conclusions about "motherhood" but not about the more general issue of "parenthood."

3. **Gender blindness.** Failing to consider the variable of gender at all is called "gender blindness." As is evident throughout this book, the lives of men and women differ in countless ways. A study of growing old in Canada might suffer from gender blindness if it overlooked the fact that most elderly men live with their wives while elderly women typically live alone.

4. **Double standards.** Researchers must be careful not to distort what they study by judging men and women differently. For example, a family researcher who labels a couple as "man and wife" may define the man as the "head of household" and treat him accordingly, and may assume that the woman simply engages in family "support work."

5. **Interference.** Another way gender can distort a study is if a subject reacts to the sex of the researcher, interfering with the research operation. While studying a small community in Sicily, for instance, Maureen Giovannini (1992) found that many men treated her as a woman rather than as a researcher. Some thought it was wrong for any single woman to speak privately with a man. Others denied Giovannini access to places they considered off-limits to women.

There is nothing wrong with focusing research on one sex or the other. But all sociologists, as well as people who read their work, should be aware of the importance of gender in any investigation.

YOUR TURN

Think of three research topics in Canadian society that might be affected by the gender of the researcher. In each case, explain why.

WOMEN AS METHODOLOGISTS

Sociology's attention to men in the past has prompted some contemporary researchers to make special efforts to investigate the lives of women. Feminist researchers embrace two key tenets: (1) their research should focus on the condition of women in society, and (2) their research must be grounded in the assumption that women generally experience subordination. Thus, feminist research rejects Weber's value-free orientation in favour of being overtly political—doing research in pursuit of gender equality.

There is no single feminist research strategy. On the contrary, feminists employ any and all conventional scientific techniques, including all of those described in this chapter. But some go further, claiming that feminist research must transform science itself, which they see as a masculine form of knowledge. Mainstream methodology, in the eyes of many modern feminists, is simply "malestream" methodology that supports patriarchy and the status quo (McDonald, 1994:4). Whereas traditional notions about science demand detachment, feminists seek connections: a sympathetic understanding between investigator and subject. Moreover, conventional scientists take charge of the research agenda, deciding in advance what issues to raise and how to study them. Feminist researchers, in contrast, favour a more egalitarian approach that allows participants a chance to voice their needs and interests in their own words (Nelson and Robinson, 1999).

University of Guelph professor Lynn McDonald shook up mainstream sociologists and feminists alike with her analysis of the role of women in the early development of sociology—and social science methodology in particular. McDonald argues that the feminists who reject empirical or scientific research and quantitative analysis—as serving the

Feminist Research: Critical and Interpretive Examples

How are women's lives affected by a capitalist and patriarchal social order? Canadian sociologists Dorothy Smith, Meg Luxton, and Susan Wendell have done sociological research to describe and analyze this question.

In a series of essays (1977, 1979, 1983), Dorothy Smith notes the ways in which relations between men and women depend on economic conditions. Her argument begins with the idea that, in the early homesteading period, the division of labour between the sexes was fairly evenly split. Men and women depended on one another for house building, clearing land, growing and harvesting gardens, caring for livestock, and preserving food for winter. This situation of approximate equality changed as farmers moved towards cash production. As land speculation led to increased prices and expensive mortgages on houses and machinery, families had to produce more than they themselves needed for their own subsistence. They needed profits to pay off bank loans and to buy equipment and other goods. But, legally, only men could own property and borrow money at the bank. The labour of wives earned them nothing: the benefits went to their husbands. The result was drudgery and a loss of power for the women. As late as 1973, the powerlessness of the farm wife was underscored in court decisions regarding Irene Murdoch. She worked on the family farm for twenty-five years, but, when she and her husband divorced, a court decided that Murdoch had no right to any of the farm property. Women's organizations rallied to protest this injustice. Murdoch took her case to the Supreme Court of Canada—and lost. Her case, however, was important for social policy. During the 1970s, province after province began

to define marriage as a partnership of equals whose assets should be divided equally upon divorce (Anderson, 1991). By the late 1980s, Rosa Becker won the right to the financial assets of a twenty-five–year common-law partnership.

Women's work is still undervalued, and women continue to play a subservient role to men in their homes and in corporations. Their services maintain the labour power of their husbands and children. Meg Luxton's book *More Than a Labour of Love* (1980) describes the process whereby women work to "re-produce" labour power for a corporation in a single-industry mining town in Flin Flon, Manitoba. She describes the way in which the lives of the women are constrained by the requirements of the corporations. The rhythms of the lives of the women and their children revolve around the husbands' need for sleep, food, rest, and relaxation, all in the interest of maintaining their employment. Luxton also documents the ways in which the husbands' frustrations at work are carried home to be vented on the wives. In extreme cases, wives contend not only with surplus anger and frustration but become the victims of violence, as their husbands act out their frustrations with the corporation.

Susan Wendell (1995), a woman who was suddenly stricken with a disabling chronic illness, uses her own experience, along with those of other disabled individuals, to develop what she calls a "feminist theory of disability." Central to her interpretation is the assumption that disabled women are oppressed both as women in male-dominated societies and as disabled people in a world dominated by able-bodied people. But, she argues, "much of what is *disabling* about our physical conditions is also a consequence of

social arrangements" (p. 457). Because North American society idealizes the human body—in terms of appearance, strength, energy, and control—disabled people are marginalized. Furthermore, in a society that values independence, dependence on others is humiliating and damaging to one's self-esteem; as a result, a disabled person may experience a profound alienation from his or her own body. The physical limitations imposed by disabilities are made more problematic by the social arrangements that designate disabled persons as "other," or as marginal to normal human life; being a disabled *woman* compounds the difficulties.

Smith, Luxton, and Wendell are not concerned with the operationalization of concepts into quantitative variables. Causality is not determined mathematically on the basis of numerical measurements of variables, but instead is elicited from a subjective or interpretive analysis of the situation each is studying. In their view, exploitation and injustice in power, gender, class, and race characterize social relations, and changes in these relations over time and place need to be explained. Since change towards justice is the ultimate goal, in this approach, interpretive sociology differs greatly from positivist sociology.

WHAT DO YOU THINK?

1. Should men and women share assets equally when marriages or common-law relationships fail? Why?
2. Has the relationship between women and corporations changed since Luxton wrote *More than a Labour of Love*? If so, how?
3. In your experience, are the consequences of disability different for men and for women? How?

interests of men—are rejecting methodologies that women helped to develop in order to further their causes. Among the many women whose contributions are outlined in *The Women Founders of the Social Sciences* (McDonald, 1994) are Harriet Martineau (1802–76) and Florence Nightingale (1820–1910).

Martineau made her living as a writer and an investigative journalist, producing more than 50 books and 1600 feature articles on a wide range of issues. She also dealt with methodology in "Essays on the Art of Thinking" and an 1838 book entitled *How to Observe Morals and Manners*. Her *Society in America*, which appeared in 1837, made her the first to tackle comparative analysis, applying an explicitly sociological approach. Martineau, an activist, supported the anti-slavery movement and worked for women's rights to education, divorce, occupations, the right to vote, and freedom from violence.

The name Florence Nightingale is familiar to all of us. She was "the lady with the lamp," the woman from a wealthy background who ministered to the needs of soldiers wounded in Crimea. McDonald (1994) reveals a Nightingale of such methodological and theoretical sophistication that

 For details about a Canadian project to publish the complete works of Florence Nightingale, go to www.sociology.uoguelph.ca/fnightingale/.

one wonders if Durkheim was intellectually indebted to her. She was a "passionate statistician" who gathered data—often presented in pie charts that simultaneously compared data cross-sectionally and over time. She used her statistics to show that improved sanitation would reduce mortality in Crimean hospitals, in childbirth, and in British hospitals and would be cost-effective at the same time. Nightingale's application of statistics to more general issues of public administration led her to "describe the laws of social science as God's laws for the right operation of the world" (p. 186). She noted that crime, suicide, mortality, accident, marriage, and poverty levels could be predicted with exact precision, despite individual free will. As an activist who believed that social and individual conditions could be changed, Nightingale sought to improve a wide range of laws, policies, and administrative practices.

RESEARCH ETHICS

Like all investigators, sociologists must be aware that research can harm as well as help subjects or communities. For this reason, the American Sociological Association (1997) and Canada's Social Sciences and Humanities Research Council (Canada, 2003b) have established formal guidelines for the

 Read about ethics guidelines from Canada's Social Sciences and Humanities Research Council at and www.sshrc.ca/web/about/policies/policy_list_e.asp, and those of the American Sociological Association at www.asanet.org/.

ethical conduct of research. The prime directive is that sociologists strive to be both technically competent

and fair-minded in conducting their research. Sociologists must disclose all their findings, without omitting significant

Florence Nightingale not only revolutionized the practice of nursing in the nineteenth century, but was also one of the first to use statistics and probability theory to reform public health laws.

data, and they are ethically bound to make their results available to other sociologists, some of whom may wish to replicate the research.

Sociologists also must strive to ensure the safety of their subjects. Should research develop in a manner that threatens the well-being of participants, investigators must terminate their work immediately. Furthermore, professional guidelines direct researchers to protect the privacy of anyone involved in a research project. Yet this is a promise that may be difficult to keep, since researchers sometimes come under pressure (say, from the police or courts) to disclose information. Therefore, researchers must think carefully about their responsibility to protect subjects, and they should discuss this issue with those who take part in research. An important principle in ethical research is obtaining the informed consent of participants, which means that subjects understand the responsibilities and risks that the research involves and agree to take part.

Another important guideline concerns funding. Sociologists must include in their published results the sources of any and all financial support. Furthermore, sociologists must seek to avoid any conflicts of interest (or even the appearance of such conflicts) that may compromise the integrity of their work. For example, researchers must never accept funding from any organization that seeks to influence the research results for its own purposes.

THINKING ABOUT DIVERSITY:
RACE, CLASS, & GENDER
Conducting Research with Aboriginal Peoples

A Royal Commission on Aboriginal Peoples was announced in 1991 with a mandate to do extensive research and provide baseline data on the lives of Aboriginal peoples living in Canada.[1] The ethical guidelines for the conduct of this research were published in the *Northern Health Research Bulletin* (Canada, 1993a). As well as the standard principles for the conduct of ethical research, the royal commission established new guidelines with respect to the benefits of research to the community—as stated under the heading "Community Benefit":

- In setting research priorities and objectives for community-based research, the Commission and the researchers it engages shall give serious and due consideration to the benefit of the community concerned.
- In assessing community benefit, regard shall be given to the widest possible range of community interest, whether the groups in question be Aboriginal or non-Aboriginal, and also to the impact of research at the local, regional, or national level. Wherever possible, conflicts between interests within the community should be identified and resolved in advance of commencing the project. Researchers should be equipped to draw on a range of

problem-solving strategies to resolve such conflicts as may arise in the course of research.
- Whenever possible, research should support the transfer of skills to individuals and increase the capacity of the community to manage its own research.

The final, five-volume report of the royal commission covers every conceivable issue related to Aboriginal peoples—constitutional, political, social, medical, economic, demographic, and cultural (Canada, 1996). The report was based on the information acquired by the commission in meetings and hearings across the country, as well as from more than four hundred reports prepared by various organizations and individuals (Aboriginal and non-Aboriginal); sociologists and other social scientists were among those who submitted these reports. The report is also available on

CD-ROM under the title *For Seven Generations: An Information Legacy of the Royal Commission on Aboriginal Peoples*. The CD-ROM has an elaborate search capacity (by subject, for example) that greatly increases access to the contents of the report. Thus, social scientists, politicians, and Aboriginal communities can do research on the report itself.

---

[1]Aboriginal peoples in Canada include Status and non-Status Indians, Inuit, and Métis. Status (or Treaty) Indians are registered under the *Indian Act* and now usually call themselves First Nations. Non-status Indians, who would also identify themselves as "North American Indian" in the census, are not subject to the *Indian Act*; in that sense, they are more like Inuit and Métis. Inuit (in the eastern Arctic) includes Inuvialuit (in the western Arctic). Indian, Inuit, and Métis are recognised in the Canadian constitution (Canada, 1982).

WHAT DO YOU THINK?

1. Should Aboriginal people have the final word on research involving their communities? Why?
2. Can non-Indigenous researchers do a credible job of "studying" Aboriginal communities?
3. To what extent should the report of the 1996 Royal Commission shape public policy?

Ethical concerns extend well beyond the issues raised here and address the role of sociologists as teachers, administrators, and clinical practitioners. At the broadest level, there are also global dimensions to research ethics. Before beginning research in other countries, investigators must become familiar enough with those societies to understand what people there are likely to perceive as a violation of privacy or as a source of personal danger. In a multicultural society such as ours, the same rule applies to studying people whose cultural backgrounds differ from our own. The Thinking about

Diversity box (above) offers some tips about how outsiders can effectively and sensitively study Aboriginal communities.

Methods of Sociological Research

A **research method** is *a systematic plan for doing research.* The remainder of this chapter introduces four commonly used methods of sociological investigation: experiments, surveys, participant observation, and the use of existing

Doing Research in Sociology contains links for, among other helpful advice, how to search CD-ROM databases, cite electronic resources, and do effective library research at www.lib. uwaterloo/discipline/sociology/ index.html.

data. None is better or worse than any other. Rather, in the same way that a carpenter selects a particular tool for a specific task, researchers choose a method—or mix several methods—according to whom they plan to study and what they wish to learn.

TESTING A HYPOTHESIS: THE EXPERIMENT

The logic of science is most clearly found in the **experiment**, *a research method for investigating cause and effect under highly controlled conditions*. Experimental research is *explanatory;* that is, it asks not just what happens but why. Typically, researchers devise an experiment to test a **hypothesis**, *a statement of a possible relationship between two (or more) variables*. A hypothesis typically takes the form of an *if–then* statement: *If* one thing were to happen, *then* something else will result.

The ideal experiment consists of four steps:

- First, the researcher specifies the variable that is assumed to cause the change (the independent variable, or the "cause") as well as the variable that is changed (the dependent variable, or the "effect").
- Second, the researcher measures the initial value of the dependent variable.
- Third, the researcher exposes the dependent variable to the independent variable (the "treatment").
- Fourth, the researcher again measures the dependent variable to see what change took place.

If the expected change did occur, the experiment supports the hypothesis; if not, the hypothesis must be modified.

But a change in the dependent variable could be due to something other than the supposed cause. (Think back to our discussion of spurious correlations.) To be certain that they identify the correct cause, researchers carefully control other factors that might affect the outcome of the experiment. Such control is easiest in a laboratory, a setting specially constructed to neutralize outside influences.

Another strategy to gain control is dividing research subjects into an *experimental group* and a *control group*. Early in the study, the researcher measures the dependent variable for subjects in both groups but later exposes only the experimental group to the independent variable or treatment. (The control group typically gets a "placebo," a treatment that the members of the group think is the same but really has no effect on the experiment.) Then the investigator measures the subjects in both groups again. Any factor occurring during the course of the research that influences people in the experimental group (say, a news event) would do the same to those in the control group, thus controlling or "washing out" the factor. By comparing the before and after measurements of the two groups, a researcher can learn how much of the change is caused by the independent variable.

The Hawthorne Effect

Researchers need to be aware that behaviour may change because subjects are getting special attention, as one classic experiment revealed. In the late 1930s, the Western Electric Company hired researchers to investigate worker productivity in its Hawthorne factory near Chicago (Roethlisberger and Dickson, 1939). One experiment tested the hypothesis that increasing the available lighting would raise worker output. First, researchers measured worker productivity (the dependent variable). Then they increased the lighting (the independent variable) and measured output a second time. The resulting increased productivity supported the hypothesis. But when the research team later turned the lighting back down, productivity increased again. What was going on? In time, the researchers realized that the employees were working harder—even if they could not see as well—simply because people were paying attention to them and measuring their output. From this research, social scientists coined the term **Hawthorne effect** to refer to *a change in a subject's behaviour caused simply by the awareness of being studied*.

Illustration of an Experiment: The Stanford County Prison

Prisons can be violent settings, but is this simply because of the "bad" people who end up there? Or, as Philip Zimbardo suspected, does the prison itself somehow generate violent behaviour? This question led Zimbardo to devise a fascinating experiment, which he called the "Stanford County Prison" (Zimbardo, 1972; Haney, *et al.*, 1973). Zimbardo thought that, once inside a prison, even emotionally healthy people are prone to violence. Therefore, Zimbardo treated the *prison setting* as the independent variable capable of causing *violence*, the dependent variable.

To test this hypothesis, Zimbardo's research team constructed a realistic-looking "prison" in the basement of the psychology building on the campus of California's Stanford University. Then they placed an ad in the local newspaper, offering to pay young men to help with a two-week research project. To each of the seventy who responded they administered a series of physical and psychological tests and then selected the healthiest twenty-four. The next step was to assign randomly half the men to be "prisoners" and half to be "guards." The plan called for the guards and prisoners to spend the next two weeks in the mock prison. The prisoners began their part of the experiment soon afterwards when the city police "arrested" them at their homes. After searching and handcuffing the men, the police drove them to the local police station, where they were fingerprinted. Then police transported their captives to the Stanford prison, where the guards locked them up.

On April 22, 1994, six inmates of the Prison for Women in Kingston, Ontario, turned on their guards in what became four days of violence. They were finally subdued by a male riot squad, which strip-searched the female inmates. A federal inquiry investigating the incident heard inmates' rights activists criticize the repressive, brutal actions of the male riot squad. The women's prison was closed in 2000.

Zimbardo started his video camera rolling and watched to see what would happen next.

The experiment turned into more than anyone had bargained for. Both guards and prisoners soon became embittered and hostile towards one another. Guards humiliated the prisoners by assigning them tasks such as cleaning out toilets with their bare hands. The prisoners, for their part, resisted and insulted the guards. Within four days, the researchers removed five prisoners who displayed "extreme emotional depression, crying, rage and acute anxiety" (Haney, *et al.*, 1973:81). Before the end of the first week, the situation had become so bad that the researchers had to cancel the experiment. Zimbardo explains:

> The ugliest, most base, pathological side of human nature surfaced. We were horrified because we saw some boys (guards) treat others as if they were despicable animals, taking pleasure in cruelty, while other boys (prisoners) became servile, dehumanized robots who thought only of escape, of their own individual survival and of their mounting hatred for the guards. (Zimbardo, 1972:4)

The events that unfolded at the "Stanford County Prison" supported Zimbardo's hypothesis that prison violence is rooted in the social character of jails themselves, not in the personalities of guards and prisoners. This finding raises questions about our society's prisons, suggesting the need for basic reform. Notice, too, that this experiment shows the potential of research to threaten the physical and mental well-being of subjects. Such dangers are not always as obvious as they were in this case. Therefore, researchers must consider carefully the potential harm to subjects at all stages of their work and end any study, as Zimbardo did, if subjects may suffer harm of any kind.

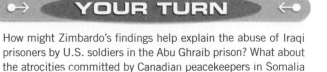

YOUR TURN

How might Zimbardo's findings help explain the abuse of Iraqi prisoners by U.S. soldiers in the Abu Ghraib prison? What about the atrocities committed by Canadian peacekeepers in Somalia (see Chapter 1 "Seeing the General in the Particular")?

ASKING QUESTIONS: SURVEY RESEARCH

A **survey** is *a research method in which subjects respond to a series of statements or questions in a questionnaire or an interview.* The most widely used of all research methods, surveys are especially good for studying attitudes—such as beliefs about politics, religion, or race—since there is no way to observe directly what people think. Sometimes surveys provide clues about cause and effect, but typically they yield *descriptive* findings, painting a picture of people's views on some issue.

Population and Sample

A survey targets some **population,** *the people who are the focus of research.* Lois Benjamin, in a study of racism (1991), studied a select population: talented African Americans. Other surveys such as political polls that predict election results treat every adult in the country as the population.

Obviously, contacting millions of people is impossible for even the best-funded and most patient researcher. Fortunately, there is an easier way that yields accurate results. Researchers collect data from a **sample,** *a part of a population that represents the whole.* National polls typically survey a sample of about one thousand people.

How can we be sure a sample really represents the entire population? One way is *random sampling*, in which researchers draw a sample from the population randomly so that every person in the population has an equal chance to be selected. The mathematical laws of probability dictate that a random sample is likely to represent the population as a whole. Selecting a random sample usually means listing everyone in the population and using a computer to make a random selection. Beginning researchers sometimes make the mistake of assuming that "randomly" walking up to people on a street produces a sample that is representative of the entire city. Unfortunately, this technique does not give every person an equal chance to be included in the sample. For one thing, any setting—whether a rich neighbourhood, ethnic enclave, or college campus—contains more of some kinds of people than others. The fact that some people are more approachable than others introduces another source of bias.

While good sampling is no simple task, it offers considerable savings in time and expense. We are spared the tedious work of contacting everyone in a population; yet we can obtain essentially the same results.

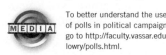

To better understand the use of polls in political campaigns, go to http://faculty.vassar.edu/lowry/polls.html.

Using Questionnaires

Selecting subjects is just the first step in carrying out a survey. Also needed is a plan for asking questions and recording answers. Most surveys use a questionnaire for this purpose. A **questionnaire** is *a series of written questions a researcher presents to subjects.* One type of questionnaire provides not only the questions but also a selection of fixed responses (similar to a multiple-choice examination). This *closed-ended format* makes it fairly easy to analyze the results, but, by narrowing the range of responses, it can also distort the findings. For example, Frederick Lorenz and Brent Bruton (1996) found that the number of hours per week students say they study for a college course depends on the options offered to them. When the researchers presented students with options ranging from one hour or less to nine hours or more, 75 percent said that they studied four hours or less per week. But when subjects in a comparable group were given choices ranging from four hours or less to twelve hours or longer (a higher figure that suggests students should study more), they suddenly became more studious; only 34 percent reported that they studied four hours or less each week.

A second type of questionnaire, using an *open-ended format,* allows subjects to respond freely, expressing various shades of opinion. The drawback of this approach is that the researcher has to make sense out of what can be a very wide range of answers.

The researcher must also decide how to present questions to subjects. Most often, researchers use a *self-administered survey,* mailing or e-mailing questionnaires to respondents and asking them to complete the form and send it back. Since no researcher is present when subjects read the questionnaire, it must be both inviting and clearly written. *Pretesting* a self-administered questionnaire with a small number of people before sending it to the entire sample can prevent the costly problem of finding out—too late—that instructions or questions were confusing.

Using the mail or e-mail allows a researcher to contact a large number of people over a wide geographic area at minimal expense. But many people treat such questionnaires as junk mail, so typically no more than half are completed and returned. Often, researchers must send follow-up mailings to urge reluctant subjects to respond.

Finally, keep in mind that many people are not capable of completing a questionnaire on their own. Young children obviously cannot, nor can many hospital patients or a surprising number of adults who simply lack the required reading and writing skills.

 For a website on surveys conducted by computer-based methods, see www.isurveys.com.au/resources.html.

Conducting Interviews

An **interview** is *a series of questions a researcher asks respondents in person.* In a closed-format design, researchers read a question or statement and then ask the subject to select a response from several that are presented. More commonly,

Most census data are obtained from questionnaires that officials send and receive back through the mail, or deliver and pick up by hand. Although this strategy is generally quite efficient, it is likely to undercount the homeless or others who lack a customary street address. Olaf Solheim (*above*) was evicted from a rooming house in Vancouver's West End to make room for tourist housing for Expo '86. Less than six weeks later, Solheim was dead. While some sociologists do research using government statistics, others are committed to research that allows voices like Solheim's to be heard.

however, interviews are open ended, so that subjects can respond as they choose and researchers can probe with follow-up questions. In either case, the researcher must guard against influencing a subject, which is as easy as raising an eyebrow when a person begins to answer.

While subjects are more likely to complete a survey if contacted personally by the researcher, interviews have some disadvantages. Tracking people down is costly and takes time, especially if subjects do not live in the same area. Telephone interviews allow far greater "reach," but the impersonality of cold calls by telephone—and reaching answering machines—can lower the response rate.

In both questionnaires and interviews, the wording of questions may significantly affect answers. For instance, emotionally loaded language can easily sway subjects: the term "welfare mothers," as opposed to "mothers on social assistance," injects an emotional element into a survey and encourages respondents to answer more negatively. In still other cases, the wording of questions may hint at what other people think, thereby steering subjects. For example, people are more likely to respond positively to the question "Do you *agree* that the police force is doing a good job?" than to the similar question "Do you *think* that the police force is doing a good job?" Similarly, respondents are more likely to endorse a statement to "not allow" something (say, public speeches against the government) than a statement to "forbid" the same activity (Rademacher, 1992).

Conducting a good interview means standardizing the technique—treating all subjects in the same way. But this, too, can lead to problems. Drawing people out requires establishing rapport, which in turn depends on responding naturally to the particular person being interviewed, as you would in a normal conversation. In the end, researchers have to decide where to strike the balance between uniformity and rapport (Lavin and Maynard, 2001).

Illustration of Survey Research: The Case of Anti-Semitism in Quebec

On September 17, 1991, Mordecai Richler, a prominent Canadian novelist with an international reputation and a Jew, wrote an article on French-Canadian nationalism in *The New Yorker*, in which he alleged that French Canadians are anti-Semitic. His statements were the beginning of passionately felt and argued controversy. Are French Canadians anti-Semitic? If so, are they more anti-Semitic than English Canadians? If they are more anti-Semitic, what is the explanation? A team of sociologists headed by Paul Sniderman attempted to answer these questions.

Sniderman used the data from an existing survey entitled the *Charter of Rights Study Survey*, carried out in 1993 (Sniderman, *et al.*, 1993). The study used random digit dialling (RDD) of a random sample (2084 people) of the 97 percent of Canadian households that have telephones. The Quebec sampling strategy was specifically designed to yield a representative sample of the province. The survey was designed to include the right proportions of male and female, older and younger, urban dwellers and rural dwellers, and so on, in order to reflect the total population of both the country and Quebec.

The questionnaire was designed to identify not only whether French-speaking Quebecers held more anti-Semitic views than English-speaking Canadians (the dependent variable), but also which of these factors was the underlying cause of those views (the independent variable). The five questions used to measure anti-Semitism were as follows:

> We realize no statement is true of all people in a group, but generally speaking, please tell me whether you agree or disagree with the following statements. Would you say you agree strongly, agree somewhat, disagree somewhat or disagree with this statement?
>
> Most Jews don't care what happens to people who aren't Jewish.
>
> Most Jews are pushy.
>
> Jews have made an important contribution to the cultural life of Canada.
>
> Jews are more willing than others to use shady practices to get ahead.
>
> Most Jews are warm and friendly people. (Sniderman, *et al.*, 1993:247)

Note the carefully worded introduction, which was designed to make respondents feel comfortable expressing their views candidly by qualifying the responses. Given the sensitive nature of the topic, this qualification was deemed necessary in order to combat what sociologists refer to as the *social desirability effect*, whereby respondents are unwilling to commit themselves to an opinion that might place

them outside the "normal" range. By acknowledging that the statements could not be applied to all Jews, the researchers allowed respondents freer rein in expressing their attitudes. Even if respondents agreed strongly with one of the negative statements, they could rest assured that they fell within "acceptable norms," since the response was not going to be taken as a blanket condemnation of all Jews.

Findings   The researchers found that French-speaking Quebecers were, in fact, more anti-Semitic than English-speaking Canadians. While the personality basis for anti-Semitism was conspicuously weak, the cultural basis for anti-Semitism was strong and related more to the high value placed on conformity in Quebec (normative conformity) than on nationalist sentiment, as had been suggested by some commentators. French-speaking Quebecers were significantly more likely than English-speaking Canadians to express support for conformity as a value: "They place a greater priority on people learning to fit in and get along with others" and on the larger society being "a unified body pursuing a common goal" (Sniderman, *et al.*, 1993:264). They are therefore more likely to distrust and dislike those whom they perceive as different or for whom cultural diversity is a more important value than cultural conformity.

Conclusions   The authors make the point that, while francophone Quebecers overall, are more anti-Semitic than other Canadians, most are not anti-Semitic at all. Moreover, on every test but one, a majority expressed positive sentiments regarding Jews: "Quebeckers differ from other Canadians not so much in their readiness to submit to the full syndrome of anti-Semitic ideas but rather in their willingness to accept one or two negative characterizations of Jews" (Sniderman, *et al.*, 1993:265). Québécois were as tolerant as English-speaking Canadians and were as willing as anglophones to support such things as the rights of groups with unpopular points of view to hold public rallies, and the need for restrictions on the rights of Canada's security service to wiretap. Lastly, recognition of slightly more anti-Semitism in Quebec does nothing to negate its existence in the rest of Canada.

IN THE FIELD: PARTICIPANT OBSERVATION

Sociological investigation takes place not only in laboratories but also "in the field," that is, where people carry on their everyday lives. The most widely used strategy for field study is **participant observation,** *a research method in which investigators systematically observe people while joining them in their routine activities.* Participant observation allows researchers an inside look at social life in settings ranging from nightclubs to religious seminaries. Cultural anthropologists commonly use participant observation (which they call *fieldwork*) to study communities in other societies. They term their descriptions of unfamiliar cultures *ethnographies.* Sociologists prefer to call their accounts of people in particular settings *case studies.*

At the beginning of a field study, most investigators do not have a specific hypothesis in mind. In fact, they may not yet realize what the important questions will turn out to be. Therefore, most field research is *exploratory* and *descriptive.*

As its name suggests, participant observation has two sides. On one hand, getting an insider's look depends on becoming a participant in the setting—hanging out with the research subjects, trying to act, think, and even feel the way they do. Compared to experiments and survey research, participant observation has fewer hard-and-fast rules. But it is precisely this flexibility that allows investigators to explore the unfamiliar and adapt to the unexpected.

Unlike other research methods, participant observation may require that the researcher enter the setting not just for a week or two but for months or even years. At the same time, however, the researcher must maintain some distance as an "observer," mentally stepping back to record field notes and, later, to interpret them. Because the investigator must both "play the participant" to win acceptance and gain access to people's lives and "play the observer" to maintain the distance needed for thoughtful analysis, there is an inherent tension in this method. Carrying out the twin roles of insider participant and outsider observer often comes down to a series of careful compromises.

Most sociologists carry out participant observation alone, so they—and readers, too—must remember that the results depend on the work of a single person. Participant observation usually falls within interpretive sociology, yielding mostly qualitative data—the researcher's accounts of people's lives and what they think of themselves and the world around them—although researchers sometimes collect some quantitative (numerical) data. From a scientific point of view, participant observation is a "soft" method that relies heavily on personal judgment and lacks scientific rigour. Yet its personal approach is also a strength. A highly visible team of sociologists attempting to administer formal surveys would disrupt many social settings, but a single skilful participant-observer can gain a lot of insight into people's natural behaviour.

Illustration of Participant Observation: *Street Corner Society*

In the late 1930s, a young graduate student at Harvard University named William Foote Whyte (1914–2000) was fascinated by the lively street life of a nearby, rather rundown section of Boston. His curiosity led him to carry out four years of participant observation in this neighbourhood, which he called "Cornerville," and in the process to produce a sociological classic. At the time, Cornerville was home to first- and second-generation Italian immigrants. Many were poor, and many people living in the rest of Boston considered Cornerville a place to avoid: a poor slum that was home to racketeers. Unwilling to accept easy stereotypes, Whyte set out to discover for himself exactly what kind of life went on in this community. His celebrated

Sociologists can carry out research in almost any setting. They can, for example, visit night spots in order to understand how and why young people participate in raves.
Tammy L. Anderson, Ph.D.

book, *Street Corner Society* (1981; orig. 1943), describes Cornerville as a complex community with a distinctive code of values and its own social conflicts.

In beginning his investigation, Whyte considered a range of research methods. Should he take questionnaires to one of Cornerville's community centres and ask local people to fill them out? Should he invite members of the community to come to his Harvard office for interviews? It is easy to see that such formal strategies would have gained little co-operation from the local people. Whyte decided, therefore, to set out on his own, working his way into Cornerville life in the hope of coming to understand this rather mysterious place.

Right away, Whyte discovered the challenges of even getting started in field research. After all, an upper-middle-class WASP graduate student from Harvard did not exactly fit into Cornerville life. Even a friendly overture from an outsider could seem pushy and rude. One night, Whyte dropped in at a local bar, hoping to buy a woman a drink and encourage her to talk about Cornerville. Looking around the room, he could find no woman alone. But then he saw a man sitting down with two women. He walked up to them and asked, "Pardon me. Would you mind if I joined you?" Instantly, he realized his mistake:

> There was a moment of silence while the man stared at me. Then he offered to throw me down the stairs. I assured him that this would not be necessary, and demonstrated as much by walking right out of there without any assistance. (1981:289)

As this incident suggests, gaining entry to a community is the difficult (and sometimes hazardous) first step in field research. "Breaking in" requires patience, quick thinking, and a little luck. Whyte's big break came when he met a young man named "Doc" at a local social service agency. Whyte explained to Doc how hard it was to make friends in Cornerville. Doc responded by taking Whyte under his wing and introducing him to others in the community. With Doc's help, Whyte soon became a neighbourhood regular.

Whyte's friendship with Doc illustrates the importance of a *key informant* in field research. Such people not only introduce a researcher to a community but often remain a source of information and help. But using a key informant also has its risks. Because any person has a particular circle of friends, a key informant's guidance is certain to "spin" or bias the study in one way or another. In addition, in the eyes of others, the reputation of the key informant—good or bad—usually rubs off on the investigator. So although a key informant is helpful early on, a participant-observer must soon seek a broader range of contacts.

Having entered the Cornerville world, Whyte quickly learned another lesson: a field researcher needs to know when to speak up and when to shut up. One evening, he joined a group discussing neighbourhood gambling. Wanting to get the facts straight, Whyte asked innocently, "I suppose the cops were all paid off?" In a heartbeat, Whyte reported,

> the gambler's jaw dropped. He glared at me. Then he denied vehemently that any policeman had been paid off and immediately switched the conversation to another subject. For the rest of that evening I felt very uncomfortable. The next day, Doc offered some sound advice: "Go easy on that 'who,' 'what,' 'why,' 'when,' 'where' stuff, Bill. You ask those questions and people will clam up on you. If people accept you, you can just hang around, and you'll learn the answers in the long run without even having to ask the questions." (1981:303)

In the months and years that followed, Whyte became familiar with life in Cornerville and even married a local woman with whom he would spend the rest of his life. In the process, he learned that the common stereotypes were wrong. In Cornerville, most people worked hard, many were quite successful, and some even boasted of sending children to college. Even today, Whyte's book is a fascinating story of the deeds, dreams, and disappointments of immigrants and their children living in one ethnic community, and it contains the kind of rich details that come only from years of participant observation.

USING AVAILABLE DATA: SECONDARY AND HISTORICAL ANALYSIS

Not all research requires investigators to collect their own data. In many cases, sociologists engage in **secondary analysis,** *a research method in which a researcher utilizes data collected by others.* The most widely used statistics in social science are gathered by government agencies. Statistics Canada continually updates information about the Canadian population and offers much of interest to sociologists. Comparable data on the United States are available from the Bureau of the Census, a branch of the U.S. government. Global investigations benefit from various publications of the United Nations and the World Bank. In short, a wide range of data about the whole world is as close as the internet. Since using available data—whether government statistics or the findings of individual researchers—saves researchers time and money, this approach holds special appeal to sociologists with low budgets. The quality of government data is generally better than that of any data even well-funded researchers could hope to obtain on their own.

The Thinking Critically and Media Perspectives boxes in this chapter (pp. 47 and 48, respectively) are based on secondary analysis of existing data collected by Statistics Canada and Indian and Northern Affairs Canada.

Still, despite its usefulness, secondary analysis has inherent problems. For one thing, available data may not exist in precisely the form one might wish; further, there are always questions about the meaning and accuracy of work done by others. For example, in his classic study of suicide, Emile Durkheim realized that he could not be sure that a death classified as an "accident" was not, in reality, a "suicide," and vice versa. He also knew that various agencies used different procedures and categories in collecting data, making comparisons difficult. Using second-hand data is a little like shopping for a used car: bargains are plentiful, but you have to be careful to avoid being stuck with a lemon.

Content Analysis

Another type of secondary analysis is called *content analysis.* This entails the counting or coding of the content of written, aural, or visual materials, such as television and radio programming, novels, magazines, and advertisements. Content analysis has a long tradition in sociology. One of the best-known early content analyses of this century in North America is *The Polish Peasant in Europe and America* by Thomas and Znaniecki (1971; orig. 1919), which used diaries and letters written to and from Polish immigrants in America to describe the adjustment processes of new American immigrants. A 1977 study by the Montreal YWCA Women's Centre of gender roles in 38 grade 1 readers used in Montreal's anglophone schools is another example of the use of content research; this study found that gender stereotypes were mirrored in the books. Males were portrayed as central characters and as active, competitive problem solvers. Females were less often included and, when they were, they tended to be portrayed in passive, domestic roles and occupations. Males were shown in 78 different occupations; most females were housewives, and those who were not were described as nurses, librarians, teachers, or cooks (Mackie, 1983). Research by Nancarrow Clarke (1991) on media "treatment" of cancer, heart

THINKING CRITICALLY
Reading Tables: An Important Skill

A table provides a lot of information in a small amount of space, so learning to read tables can increase your reading efficiency. When you spot a table, look first at the title to see what information it contains. The title of Table 2–2 below tells you that it deals with labour-force participation and income of Aboriginal men and women in 1986. Reading across the top of the table, you see that data are presented for men and women in four categories: Indian (i.e., First Nation members and non-Status persons), Métis, Inuit, and Canadian. The research summarized here makes use of existing data—specifically census data—for people who identify themselves as "North American Indian," "Métis," or "Inuit" as well as for Canadians as a whole. The full article (Gerber, 1995) is entitled "Indian, Métis, and Inuit Women and Men: Multiple Jeopardy in a Canadian Context." The data in that paper come from 1986 census documents—specifically, Statistics Canada catalogues 93–154 and 93–155.

Reading down the left-hand side of the table, you learn that it provides, for each category (men and women), data on labour-force participation rates, unemployment rates, full-time all-year employment, and income over $35 000 per year. Superscript letters refer you to the notes below the table, where explanations of each measure are provided.

As you move from left to right across the first row of the table, you see how Aboriginal men and women compare on labour-force participation with all men and women in Canada. You will notice that Aboriginal men have lower participation rates than those of Canadian men in general. The same is true of Aboriginal women. Among all three Aboriginal categories, men have *higher* participation rates than Canadian women as a whole—while Indian women have the lowest rates and Métis men the highest.

The second row reveals that, in each Aboriginal category, unemployment rates are higher for men than for women. Among Canadians in general, men have *lower* levels of unemployment than women. Note that unemployment rates are based on the active labour force (those employed or looking for work) rather than on the population 15 years of age and over as a whole. Sometimes unemployment rates go *up* when the economy improves or the school year ends, and new people enter the labour market and look for work.

Row three indicates the percentage in each category that is employed full time, all year. You might be surprised to learn that throughout Canada in 1986, 37.2 percent of men and 23.3 percent of women were fully employed. Other people 15 years of age and over may have been working part time or out of the labour force entirely as a result of retirement, disability, home-making, being in school, or being on welfare. In any case, full employment figures are lower for all Aboriginal categories than for either Canadian men or Canadian women. Among the Aboriginal categories, Indian women are least likely and Inuit men most likely to be employed full time, all year.

When you look at the income data, keep in mind that we are dealing with 1985—a time when a $35 000 annual income was considered to be high. Women are much less likely than men to earn $35 000 or more per year. Among the Aboriginal categories, Indian women are least likely and Métis men are most likely to earn over $35 000. Once again, on this measure, the men in each Aboriginal category fare *better* than Canadian women in general.

Now that you know how to read the table, you can start thinking about what the data tell you about gender and racial or ethnic inequality in Canada.

WHAT DO YOU THINK?

1. Why are statistical data, such as those in this table, an efficient way to convey lots of information?
2. Looking at the table, can you determine how one is disadvantaged by being female *and* Aboriginal?
3. Do you have an explanation for the discrepancies that appear in this table? Are there identifiable social forces in play here?

TABLE 2–2   Labour-Force Participation and Income of Aboriginal Men and Women, 1986

	Indian*		Métis		Inuit		Canadian	
	Men	**Women**	**Men**	**Women**	**Men**	**Women**	**Men**	**Women**
Participation rate[a]	59.5	39.0	66.4	44.5	59.5	43.7	77.5	55.9
Unemployment rate[b]	32.7	28.7	30.3	27.0	28.9	26.0	9.6	11.2
Employment[c]	17.9	11.6	18.7	12.3	22.0	12.5	37.2	23.3
Income[d]	4.6	0.7	6.2	0.9	5.2	1.1	16.1	3.4

* In the Canadian census, "North American Indian" or "Indian" includes First Nation (i.e., Status Indian) and non-Status Indian persons (i.e., those who are not registered under the *Indian Act*).
[a] Percentage of population in the labour force (i.e. employed or looking for work).
[b] Percentage of labour force unemployed.
[c] Percentage of population, 15 years of age and older, employed full time, all year.
[d] Percentage of population, 15 years of age and older, with annual income of $35 000 or more.
   (1985 income, as 1986 census asked for income earned in the previous year).

MEDIA PERSPECTIVES

From Card Punching to Cyberspace: Evolution in the Media of Research

How have technological advances changed research? One of the authors of this text, Linda Gerber, began the research for her Ph.D. thesis—dealing with out-migration from First Nations communities (Gerber, 1976)—around 1970, which in techno-logical terms was the dinosaur era. Her data collection involved the laborious coding of about 80 variables for each of 600 First Nation communities. Using a keypunch machine, the data were then punched onto several thousand cards that had to be manually fed into the University of Toronto's huge mainframe computers—every time she wanted to carry out a new piece of analysis.

Towards the end of the research period, these cards were read onto magnetic tape, which made the final analyses—"one more run, just one more run"—considerably less labour-intensive. Several drafts of that thesis were hammered out on a manual type-writer; since whiteout was not allowed, a mistake on any of the 313 pages of the final document required that the entire page in question be retyped. Subsequent papers submitted to jour-nals in hopes of publication were produced in the same plodding way.

By the mid–1980s, the Canadian census was arriving at the University of Guelph's library on paper *and* on magnetic tape. This new medium made secondary analysis infinitely easier for anyone who analyzed census data. In

Familiarity with computers is far more common among younger members of our society than older generations. Today's young people will find computers a natural and indispensable part of day-to-day living.

addition, the development and improvement of word processors made "keyboarding" (males do not "type") of manuscripts a breeze. Journal articles were submitted on paper for considera-tion by reviewers; by the early 1990s, the final copy of an "accepted" paper would be sent to most of the major journals on a disk.

Today, data must still be coded, but the process is a lot less labour-intensive. Those who analyze the census pull the data directly off the internet or a CD-ROM. The data are transferred onto microcomputer or mainframe files, where they can be recoded and subjected to all kinds of sophisticated analysis using statistical software packages. Word processing produces "papers," which might never see anything but electronic form until they appear in the journals destined for our libraries.

Increasingly, established journals are making the arti-cles from their paper-based publications available on the internet as well, with members paying for the right to read and print copies of the various papers. By 1996, a number of new sociology jour-nals started appearing on the internet and on the internet alone. These journals have no paper copy available anywhere! Submission of scholarly articles to these jour-nals is done electronically.

Just think of the implications for a moment. It is now possible to "collect" data, conduct sophis-ticated analysis, write a scholarly article, submit it, and have it "published" with instantaneous access around the world. All of this is accom-plished electronically without ever putting ink or laser imprint to paper. Media theorist Marshall McLuhan would have been quick to point out the revolutionary impact of these develop-ments.

WHAT DO YOU THINK?

1. Did you experience some of this evolution or change in the way you produced papers during your high school years?
2. Do the new media of research and publication make cheating or plagiarism easier? How should colleges and universities respond?
3. Will the electronic media eventually eliminate hard-copy books and jour-nals altogether? Why?

disease, and AIDS (see Chapter 3, "Culture") provides another example of content analysis.

TECHNOLOGY AND RESEARCH

In recent decades, new information technology has changed our lives considerably, and this applies to the practice of research as well. Personal computers—which have only been on the scene since the early 1980s—now give individual sociologists remarkable technical ability to randomly select samples, perform complex statistical analysis, and prepare written reports efficiently. Today's average office computer is far more powerful than even the massive mainframe devices that filled entire rooms on university campuses a generation ago. See the Media Perspectives box (on p. 48) for further detail.

The development of the internet (the so-called electronic superhighway) is certain to further enhance our research capabilities in the years to come. The internet now links some 670 million people throughout the world, allowing for an unprecedented level of communication. Contemporary sociologists are capable of building networks throughout the country and around the globe, which will facilitate collaboration and prompt comparative research. Statistics Canada opened its website on the internet in 1994. Such developments—and other as-yet-unimagined forms of technological change—promise to transform sociological investigation throughout the current century.

THE INTERPLAY OF THEORY AND METHOD

No matter how sociologists collect their data, they have to turn facts into meaning by building theory. They do this in two ways: inductive logical thought and deductive logical thought.

Inductive logical thought is *reasoning that transforms specific observations into general theory.* In this mode, a researcher's thinking runs from the specific to the general and goes something like this: "I have some interesting data here; I wonder what they mean?" When you take Table 2–2 (on p. 47) and try to determine what the data are saying, you are engaged in inductive reasoning.

A second type of logical thought moves "downwards," in the opposite direction: **deductive logical thought** is *reasoning that transforms general theory into specific hypotheses suitable for testing.* The researcher's thinking runs from the general to the specific: "I have this hunch about human behaviour; let's collect some data and put it to the test." Working deductively, the researcher first states the theory in the form of a hypothesis and then selects a method by which to test it. To the extent that the data support the hypothesis, we conclude that the theory is correct; if the data refute the hypothesis, we know that the theory needs to be revised or maybe rejected entirely.

Philip Zimbardo's Stanford County Prison experiment illustrates deductive logic. Zimbardo began with the general

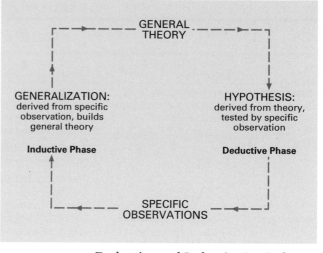

FIGURE 2-2   Deductive and Inductive Logical Thought

Sociologists link theory and method through both inductive and deductive logic.

theory that a social environment can change human behaviour. He then developed a specific, testable hypothesis: placed in a prison setting, even emotionally well-balanced young men will behave violently. The violence that erupted soon after his experiment began supported Zimbardo's hypothesis. Had his experiment produced friendly behaviour between prisoners and guards, his hypothesis clearly would have been wrong.

Just as researchers often employ several methods over the course of one study, they typically use *both* kinds of logical thought. Figure 2–2 illustrates both types of reasoning: inductively building theory from observations and deductively making observations to test a theory.

Often we conclude that an argument must be true simply because there are statistics to back it up. However, we must look at statistics with a cautious eye. After all, researchers choose the data to present, interpret their statistics, and use tables and graphs to steer readers towards particular conclusions. The Thinking it Through box (p. 00) considers truth telling and statistics.

The Summing Up table (on p. 50) provides a quick review of the four major methods of sociological investigation.

Putting it All Together: Ten Steps in Sociological Investigation

We can summarize this chapter by outlining ten steps in the process of carrying out sociological investigation. Each step takes the form of an important question.

SUMMING UP

Four Research Methods

	Experiment	Survey	Participant Observation	Existing Sources
Application	For explanatory research that specifies relationships between variables Generates quantitative data	For gathering information about issues that cannot be directly observed, such as attitudes and values Useful for descriptive and explanatory research Generates quantitative or qualitative data	For exploratory and descriptive study of people in a "natural" setting Generates qualitative data	For exploratory, descriptive, or explanatory research whenever suitable data are available
Advantages	Provides the greatest opportunity to specify cause-and-effect relationships Replication of research is relatively easy	Sampling, using questionnaires, allows surveys of large populations Interviews provide detailed responses	Allows study of "natural" behaviour Usually inexpensive	Saves time and expense of data collection Makes historical research possible
Limitations	Laboratory settings have an artificial quality Unless the research environment is carefully controlled, results may be biased	Questionnaires must be carefully prepared and may yield a low return rate Interviews are expensive and time-consuming	Time-consuming Replication of research is difficult Researcher must balance roles of participant and observer	Researcher has no control over possible biases in data Data may only partially fit current research needs

1. **What is your topic?** Being curious and applying the sociological perspective can generate ideas for social research at any time and in any place. Pick a topic you find important to study.

2. **What have others already learned?** You are probably not the first person with an interest in the issue you have selected. Visit the library to see what theories and methods other researchers have applied to your topic. In reviewing the existing research, note problems that have come up to avoid repeating past mistakes.

3. **What, exactly, are your questions?** Are you seeking to explore an unfamiliar social setting? to describe some category of people? to investigate cause and effect among variables? If your study is exploratory or descriptive, identify *whom* you wish to study, *where* the research will take place, and *what* kinds of issues you want to explore. If it is explanatory, you also must formulate the hypothesis to be tested and operationalize each variable.

4. **What will you need to carry out research?** How much time and money are available to you? Is special equipment or training necessary? Can you do the work

yourself? You should answer all these questions as you plan the research project.

5. **Are there ethical concerns?** Not all research raises serious ethical questions, but you must be sensitive to this possibility. Can the research cause harm or threaten anyone's privacy? How might you design the study to minimize the chances for injury? Will you promise anonymity to the people who are your subjects? If so, how will you ensure that anonymity is maintained?

6. **What method will you use?** Consider all major research strategies, as well as combinations of approaches. Keep in mind that the best method depends on the kinds of questions you are asking as well as the resources available to you.

7. **How will you record the data?** Your research method is a plan for data collection. Record all information accurately and in a way that will make sense later. (It may be some time before you actually write up the results of your work.) Be alert for any bias that may creep into the research.

THINKING IT THROUGH
Can People Lie with Statistics?

Is scientific research always as objective and factual as we think? Not according to the great English politician Benjamin Disraeli, who once noted wryly: "There are three kinds of lies: lies, damned lies, and statistics!" In a world that bombards us with numbers—often in the form of "scientific facts" and "official figures"—it is well worth pausing to consider that "statistical evidence" is not synonymous with truth. Every method of data collection is prone to error; furthermore, since data do not speak for themselves, someone has to interpret them to provide meaning. Some analysts may dress up their data almost the way politicians whip up a campaign speech—with an eye more to winning you over than to getting at the truth. The best way to ferret out statistical manipulation is to understand how these tricks are performed. Here are three ways people can lie with statistics.

1. **People select their data.** Many times, the data we confront are not wrong—they just do not tell the whole story. Let's say someone claims that television is ruining our way of life and, as evidence, offers statistics indicating that we watch more television today than a generation ago, and that standard mathematics and reading scores have fallen during that time. Such data are actually correct, but they are selectively chosen. Another person could just as correctly counter that Canadians spend much more on books today than we did a generation ago, suggesting that there is no cultural crisis at all. In short, people on all sides of a political debate can find statistics to bolster their arguments.

2. **People interpret their data.** Another way people manipulate statistics is to package them inside a ready-made interpretation, as if to say, "Here are the numbers, and this is what they mean." Usually several different slants can be put on any particular set of data. For example, using average income as a measure, one can show irrefutably that Aboriginal peoples are poor relative to other Canadians. Looking at distribution across income categories reveals, just as truthfully, that there are many Aboriginal individuals in the upper income categories. The inferences based on these two measures of income are very different.

3. **People use graphs to "spin" the "truth."** Especially in newspapers and other popular media, we find graphic representations of statistical data. While graphs make comprehending data easy (showing, for example, an upward or downward trend), they also provide the designer with the opportunity to "spin" data in various ways. One common technique for casting data in a particular light involves compressing or expanding the graph's time frame. A graph of the crime rate over the last several years would reveal a downward trend: shifting the time frame to the last few decades would show a sharp increase.

WHAT DO YOU THINK?

1. Why do you think people are so quick to accept "statistics" as true?
2. Can you find a newspaper article that present biased data or conclusions? What are the biases?
3. From a scientific point of view, is spinning the truth acceptable? Is this practice okay when someone—with a critical approach—is trying to advance social change?

---

8. **What do the data tell you?** Study the data in terms of your initial questions and decide how to interpret the data you have collected. If your study involves a specific hypothesis, you must decide whether to confirm, reject, or modify the hypothesis. Keep in mind that there may be several ways to look at your data, depending on which theoretical approach you use, and you should consider all interpretations.

9. **What are your conclusions?** Prepare a final report stating your conclusions. How does your work advance sociological theory? Does it suggest ways to improve research methods? Does your study have policy implications? What would the general public find interesting in your work? Finally, evaluate your own work, noting problems that arose and questions that were left unanswered.

10. **How can you share what you've learned?** Consider sending your research paper to a campus newspaper or magazine or making a presentation to a class, a campus gathering, or perhaps a meeting of professional sociologists. The point is to share what you have learned with others and to let them respond to your work.

2 MAKING THE GRADE

The following learning tools will help you see what you know, identify what you still need to learn, and expand your understanding beyond the text. You can also visit this text's Companion Website™ at www.pearsoned.ca/macionis to find useful practice tests.

KEY POINTS

Basics of Sociological Investigation

There are two basic requirements for sociological investigation. First, we should know how to apply the sociological perspective. Second, we should be curious and ready to ask questions about the world around us.

Three Ways To Do Sociology

Scientific sociology studies society by systematically observing social behaviour. This methodological orientation requires carefully operationalizing concepts and ensuring that measurement is both reliable and valid. A goal of science is to discover how variables are related. Correlation means that two or more variables change value together. A cause-and-effect relationship means that change in one variable actually causes change in another variable. When a cause-and-effect relationship exists, a researcher who knows the value of an independent variable can predict the value of some dependent variable. Researchers typically select topics according to their personal interests. But the scientific ideal of objectivity demands that they try to suspend personal values and biases as they conduct research.

Interpretive sociology is a methodological orientation that focuses on the meaning people attach to their behaviour. Reality is not "out there" but is constructed by people in their everyday interactions.

Critical sociology is a methodological orientation that uses research as a means of bringing about social change. Critical sociology rejects the scientific principle of objectivity; those who follow this orientation claim that all research has a political character.

Scientific sociology stands closest to the structural-functional approach, interpretive sociology is closest to the symbolic-interaction approach, and critical sociology is linked to the social-conflict approach. Because research has the ability to harm subjects and communities, sociologists must remain aware of research ethics.

Methods of Sociological Research

The logic of science is most clearly expressed in the experiment, which is performed under controlled conditions and tries to specify causal relationships between two (or more) variables. Surveys measure people's attitudes or behaviour using questionnaires or interviews. Participant observation is a method in which a researcher directly observes a social setting while participating in it for an extended period of time. Sociologists often use existing data; using available data is easier and often more efficient than collecting data at first hand, and it allows the study of historical issues.

Theory and research are linked in two ways. Deductive logical thought starts with general theories and generates specific hypotheses suitable for testing. Inductive logical thought starts with specific observations and builds general theories.

KEY CONCEPTS

science (p. 30) a logical system that bases knowledge on direct, systematic observation

empirical evidence (p. 30) information we can verify with our senses

scientific sociology (p. 30) the study of society based on systematic observation of social behaviour

concept (p. 31) a mental construct that represents some part of the world in a simplified form

variable (p. 31) a concept whose value changes from case to case

measurement (p. 31) a procedure for determining the value of a variable in a specific case

operationalize a variable (p. 31) specifying exactly what is to be measured before assigning a value to a variable

reliability (p. 31) consistency in measurement

validity (p. 31) actually measuring exactly what you intend to measure

cause and effect (p. 32) a relationship in which change in one variable (the independent variable) causes change in another (the dependent variable)

independent variable (p. 32) a variable that causes change in another (dependent) variable

dependent variable (p. 32) a variable that is changed by another (independent) variable

correlation (p. 32) a relationship in which two (or more) variables change together

spurious correlation (p. 32) an apparent but false relationship between two (or more) variables that is caused by some other variable

control (p. 32) holding constant all variables except one in order to see clearly the effect of that variable

objectivity (p. 33) personal neutrality in conducting research

replication (p. 34) repetition of research by other investigators

interpretive sociology (p. 34) the study of society that focuses on the meanings people attach to their social world

critical sociology (p. 36) the study of society that focuses on the need for social change

gender (p. 36) the personal traits and social positions that members of a society attach to being female or male

research method (p. 40) a systematic plan for doing research

experiment (p. 41) a research method for investigating cause and effect under highly controlled conditions

hypothesis (p. 41) a statement of a possible relationship between two (or more) variables

Hawthorne effect (p. 41) a change in a subject's behaviour caused simply by the awareness of being studied

survey (p. 42) a research method in which subjects respond to a series of statements or questions in a questionnaire or an interview

population (p. 42) the people who are the focus of research

sample (p. 42) a part of a population that represents the whole

questionnaire (p. 43) a series of written questions a researcher presents to subjects

interview (p. 43) a series of questions a researcher asks respondents in person

participant observation (p. 44) a research method in which investigators systematically observe people while joining them in their routine activities

secondary analysis (p. 46) a research method in which a researcher utilizes data collected by others

inductive logical thought (p. 49) reasoning that transforms specific observations into general theory

deductive logical thought (p. 49) reasoning that transforms general theory into specific hypotheses suitable for testing

---

APPLICATIONS & EXERCISES

1. Observe your instructor in class one day to grade his or her teaching skills. Operationalize the concept "good teaching" in terms of specific traits you can measure. How easy is it to measure "good teaching"?

2. Visit three sociology instructors (or other social science instructors) during their office hours. Ask each whether they think sociology is an objective science. Do they agree? Why?

3. Select a number of prime time television shows, and note the race of major characters. You will have to decide what "prime time" means, what a "major" character is, how to gauge someone's "race," and other issues before you begin. Sketch out a research plan to evaluate the hypothesis that visible minorities seldom appear on prime time television.

CHAPTER 3

Culture

What is culture?

Why is it so important to understand people's
cultural differences?

How does culture support social inequality?

M ush!" the hunter cried into the wind. Through the rising vapour of a northern Manitoba February, so crisp, so dry, the snow creaked underfoot, the caribou hunter Abraham Okimasis drove his sled and team of eight grey huskies through the orange-rose–tinted dusk. His left hand gripping handlebar of sled, his right snapping moose-hide whip above his head, Abraham Okimasis was urging his huskies forward....

He had sworn to his dear wife, Mariesis Okimasis, on pain of separation and divorce, unthinkable for a Roman Catholic in the year of our Lord 1951, that he would win the world championship just for her: the silver cup, that holy chalice was to be his twenty-first–anniversary gift to her....

"Please, please, God in heaven, let me win this race, and I will thank you with every deed, every touch, every breath for the rest of my long life, for hallowed be thy name"...

"Boom," the voice went, "boom, boom." Something about "Abraham Okimasis, forty-three years old, caribou hunter, fur trapper, fisherman, boom, boom." Something about "Abraham Okimasis, musher from the Eemanapiteepitat Indian reserve, northwestern Manitoba, boom." Something having to do with "Abraham Okimasis, first Indian to win this gruelling race in its twenty-eight–year history... " The syllables became one vast, rolling rumble.

Source: Extracted from *Kiss of the Fur Queen* by Tomson Highway. Copyright © Tomson Highway 1998. Reprinted by permission of Doubleday Canada.

The 6.5 billion people on Earth today are members of a single biological species: Homo sapiens. Even so, the differences among people the world over can delight, puzzle, disturb, and sometimes overwhelm us. Some differences in lifestyles are simply matters of convention: the Chinese, for example, wear white at funerals, while Canadians prefer black. Similarly, Chinese people associate the number four with bad luck, just as we think of the number thirteen. Or take the practice of kissing: most Canadians kiss in public at times, whereas most Chinese kiss only in private; the French kiss publicly twice, once on each cheek, while Belgians kiss three times, starting on either cheek. Most Nigerians don't kiss at all. At weddings, moreover, Canadian couples kiss, Koreans bow, and a Cambodian groom touches his nose to the bride's cheek.

Other cultural differences, however, are more profound. The world over, people wear much or little clothing, have many or few children, venerate or shunt aside the elderly, are peaceful or warlike, embrace different religious beliefs, and enjoy different kinds of art and music. In short, although we are all the same biological creature, we have developed strikingly different ideas about what is pleasant and repulsive, polite and rude, beautiful and ugly, right and wrong. These sometimes startling differences are the expression of human culture.

What Is Culture?

Culture refers to *the values, beliefs, behaviour, and material objects that together form a people's way of life.* Culture includes what we think, how we act, and what we own—in effect, everything we create with our hands and our minds. It is both our link to the past and our guide to the future. To understand culture, we must consider both thoughts and things. **Nonmaterial culture** is *the ideas created by members of a society,* ideas that range from art to Zen. **Material culture,** in contrast, refers to *the physical things created by members of a society*—everything from zippers to our homes and satellites in space. Culture shapes not only what we do but also what we think and how we feel—elements of what we commonly, but wrongly, describe as "human nature." The warlike Yąnomamö of the Brazilian rain forest think aggression is natural, while, halfway around the world, the Semai of Malaysia live peacefully. The cultures of the United States and Japan both stress achievement and hard work, but Americans typically put a higher value on individualism than do the Japanese, who value collective harmony.

Given the extent of cultural differences in the world and people's tendency to view their own way of life as "natural," it is no wonder that travellers often find themselves feeling uneasy as they encounter an unfamiliar

Human beings around the globe create diverse ways of life. Such differences begin with outward appearance: contrast the women shown here (*top, from left*) from Brazil, Kenya, New Guinea, and South Yemen, and the men from Taiwan, India, Canada, and New Guinea. Less obvious, but of even greater importance, are internal differences, since culture also shapes our goals in life, our sense of justice, and even our innermost personal feelings.

culture. This uneasiness is **culture shock,** *personal disorientation when experiencing an unfamiliar way of life.* People experience such disorientation when they immigrate to or visit a new country or, to a lesser extent, when they move between social environments within their own country. A young person moving from rural Newfoundland to attend university in Vancouver or Toronto knows the feeling of culture shock. More surprisingly, those who teach English in Japan for a year or more experience culture shock on their return to Canada.

No way of life is "natural" to humanity, even though most people around the world view their own behaviour that way. The co-operation that comes naturally to people in the Andes Mountains of Peru is very different from the competitive living that comes naturally to people in Toronto or New York. Such variation arises when human beings join together to create distinctive ways of life. Every other animal—from ant to zebra—behaves the same way around the world, because animal behaviour is guided by *instinct,* or biological programming over which the species

CULTURE AND HUMAN INTELLIGENCE

Scientists estimate that this planet is 4.5 billion years old (see the timeline inside the front cover of this text). Life appeared about 1 billion years later; fast-forward another 2 to 3 billion years and dinosaurs rule. It was when these giant creatures disappeared—some 65 million years ago—that primates appeared. The importance of primates is that they have the largest brains relative to body size of all living creatures.

About 12 million years ago, primates began to evolve along two different lines, setting humans apart from the great apes. Then, some 3 million years ago, our distant human ancestors climbed down from the trees of central Africa to move about in the tall grasses. There, walking upright, they learned the advantages of hunting in groups and made use of fire, tools, and weapons; they built simple shelters and fashioned basic clothing. These Stone Age achievements may seem modest, but they mark the point at which our ancestors set off on a distinct evolutionary course, making culture their primary strategy for survival. By about 250 000 years ago, our own species—*Homo sapiens* (derived from the Latin meaning "thinking person")—finally emerged. Humans continued to evolve so that, by about 40 000 years ago, people who looked more or less like us roamed the Earth. With larger brains, these "modern" *Homo sapiens* developed cultures rapidly, as suggested by the wide range of tools and cave art from this period.

By about 12 000 years ago, the founding of permanent settlements and the creation of specialized occupations in what is now Iraq and Egypt marked the "birth of civilization." At this point, humans no longer lived by biological instincts but by a more efficient survival scheme: *changing the natural environment to benefit themselves.* Ever since, humans have made and remade their world in countless ways, resulting in today's fascinating cultural diversity.

CULTURE, NATION, STATE, AND SOCIETY

At this point, we pause to clarify the proper use of several similar terms: "culture," "nation," "state," and "society." Culture refers to the ideas, values, and artifacts that make up a shared way of life. Nation is commonly used to refer to a political entity—a state or country; it also refers to a people who share a culture (including language), ancestry, and history. A state is a political entity in a territory with designated borders, such as Argentina or Zimbabwe. Society refers to organized interaction of people within a nation, state, or other boundary who share a culture. While it is a controversial idea, Canada can be said to encompass several nations—including francophone Quebec, First Nations (the term by which most Status Indian communities describe themselves), and Inuit. When Canadians talk of nation building, they refer to the attempt to create a sense of nationhood—at the federal or state level—that supersedes multicultural and regional loyalties.

All societies contain cultural differences that can provoke a mild case of culture shock. This woman traveling on a French bus looks with disapproval at another woman wearing the Muslim *hijab* to cover the head. France has banned the wearing of religious apparel, such as the *hijab*, in schools.

has no control. A few animals—notably chimpanzees and related primates—have the capacity for limited culture, as researchers have noted by observing them using tools and teaching simple skills to their offspring. But the creative power of humans is far greater than that of any other form of life and has resulted in countless ways of being "human." In short, *only humans rely on culture rather than instinct to create a way of life and ensure survival* (Harris, 1987). To understand how human culture came to be, we need to look back at the history of our species.

YOUR TURN

Can you describe specific practices or social patterns familiar to Canadians that would shock people from another society?

THINKING ABOUT DIVERSITY:
RACE, CLASS, & GENDER
Aboriginal Languages in Danger of Extinction

Of the sixty Aboriginal languages spoken throughout Canada a century ago, only four—namely, Cree, Inuktitut, Ojibwa, and Dakota—are not on the brink of extinction today. Some of Canada's Aboriginal languages are already extinct, and six others have fewer than ten known speakers. So serious is the linguistic haemorrhage that, in 1996, 71 percent of Aboriginal children had never spoken their native languages.

According to Ron Ignace, Canada should be declaring a state of emergency, introducing legislation, and setting aside more than $100 million to fund Aboriginal language immersion programs throughout the country. Ron Ignace is the chief of the Skeetchestn Reserve in British Columbia and chair of the Committee on Aboriginal Languages (of the Assembly of First Nations). His wife, Marianne Ignace, is an associate professor of First Nations Studies at Simon Fraser University. Mr. Ignace worries because he and his wife are the only parents in their community of 400 who are still speaking Shuswap to their children. When so few people commit themselves to speaking the language of their culture, languages disappear.

"Canada is on the verge of losing precious jewels of its cultural heritage," says Mr. Ignace. "These languages represent vast reservoirs of intellectual knowledge stretching back thousands of years. The English language is an infant relative to our languages." The loss of these ancient languages, he says, is one of the world's great ecological disasters (Philp, 2000). According to Abley (2006), Canada has up to sixty-one Indigenous languages, many of which are so radically different that they have as much in common as English and Tibetan. Each of these indigenous tongues "embodies a unique way of understanding and responding to the world" and may have embedded in them ancient knowledge valuable to us today. An example is from southwestern British Columbia, where the Halkomelem word *th'alátel*, which refers to wild ginger but also means "a device for the heart." Only recently have medical studies revealed that, in addition to aiding digestion and reducing nausea, ginger reduces cholesterol and prevents blood clots. Science is now learning something that this indigenous community has known for thousands of years, knowledge which is built into its language.

Another important component of language is the definition of spirituality and one's relationship to a deity. A Squamish speaker (also from southwestern British Columbia) told Abley that, "Language and culture are an umbilical cord to the Creator." Clearly, language shapes our experience of life, in the most simple and most profound ways. In short, it gives meaning to our lives. Abley asks if the loss of language helps to explain "why so many indigenous communities are now in such evident distress." The loss of Aboriginal languages in Canada can be attributed to residential schooling, English-language television and radio, migration to urban areas, and even intermarriage. The most secure languages are those spoken in the largest or most isolated communities.

The extinction of any language is a serious loss to world culture in terms of diversity and vital knowledge. North America loses irreplaceable parts of its culture when the languages that evolved on this continent and embody its rich cultural heritage disappear.

WHAT DO YOU THINK?

1. Does it really matter if Aboriginal languages disappear? Why?
2. What does it take to preserve these languages?
3. Is it important for people—all of us —to speak more than one language?

Source: Based on Philp (2000) and Abley (2006).

HOW MANY CULTURES?

To learn more about how anthropologists study other cultures, go to www.aaanet.org.

Globally, experts document almost 7000 languages, suggesting the existence of at least that many distinct cultures. Yet the number of languages spoken around the world is declining, and roughly half now are spoken by fewer than 10 000 people. Experts expect that the coming decades may see the disappearance of hundreds of these languages, from Gullah, Pennsylvania German, and Pawnee (in the United States) to Shuswap and Algonquian (in Canada), Oro (in the Amazon region of Brazil), Sardinian (on the European island of Sardinia), Aramaic (in the Middle East), Nu Shu (in southern China, the only language known to be used exclusively by women), and Wakka Wakka and several other Aboriginal tongues spoken in Australia. What accounts for the decline? Likely causes include high-technology communication, increasing international migration, and an expanding global economy (UNESCO, 2001; Barovick, 2002; Hayden, 2003). See the Thinking about Diversity box (above) to learn more about Aboriginal languages in Canada that are facing extinction.

People throughout the world communicate not just with spoken words but also with gestures. Because gestures vary from culture to culture, they can be the cause of misunderstandings. For instance, the commonplace "thumbs up" gesture that we use to express "Good job!" can get a Canadian into trouble in Australia, where people take it to mean "Up yours!" Prime Minister Stephen Harper used the gesture as he spoke to Canadian troops in Afghanistan. While our soldiers understand, might "thumbs up" have an entirely different meaning for the local people?

Behaviour that people in one society consider routine can be chilling to members of another culture. In the Russian city of St. Petersburg, this young mother and her six-week-old son brave the −27°C temperature for a dip in a nearby lake. To Russians, this is normal—to us, cruel or even dangerous.

The Elements of Culture

Explore elements of Canadian cultures, visit the Museum of Civilization (designed by Métis architect Douglas Cardinal) online at www.civilization.ca.

Although cultures vary greatly, they all have common elements, including symbols, language, values, and norms. We begin with the one that is the basis for all the others: symbols.

SYMBOLS

Human beings not only sense the surrounding world as other creatures do, we build a reality of meaning. Thus, humans transform elements of the world into **symbols,** *anything that carries a particular meaning recognized by people who share culture.* A whistle, a wall of graffiti, a flashing red light, and a fist raised in the air all serve as symbols. The human capacity to create and manipulate symbols is reflected in the very different meanings associated with the simple act of

Read from 1600 articles about symbols and to learn more about symbols from ideograms to graffiti, including 2500 signs from Western cultures, go to www.symbols.com/.

winking the eye: in some settings this action conveys interest; in others, understanding; in still others, insult. We are so dependent on our culture's symbols that we take them for granted. Occasionally, however, we become keenly aware of a symbol when someone uses it in an unconventional way—as when political protesters in Brockville, Ontario, stomped on a Quebec flag in 1989. Entering an unfamiliar society also reminds us of the power of symbols: the resulting culture shock involves the inability to "read" meaning into one's surroundings. We feel lost and isolated, unsure of how to act, and sometimes frightened—a consequence of being outside the symbolic web of culture that joins individuals in meaningful social life.

Culture shock is a two-way process: it is something the traveller experiences when encountering people whose way of life is unfamiliar, and it is also what the traveller inflicts on others by acting in ways that might offend them. For example, because North Americans consider dogs to be beloved household pets, travellers to northern regions of China may be appalled to find people roasting dogs for dinner. On the other hand, travellers may inflict culture shock on others by acting in ways that offend them (e.g., kissing in public). Indeed, travel abroad provides endless opportunities for misunderstanding.

APPLYING SOCIOLOGY
New Symbols in the World of Instant Messaging

Soc was Gr8!
   What happened?
I was :'-D
   Y?
The prof looks like =(_8^(1)
   Maybe his wife looks like
      >@@@@8^)
GMTA
   See you B4 class. B4N
BCNU

The world of symbols changes all the time. Often, people create new symbols in response to new information technology. Today, almost 50 million North Americans—most of them young and many of them students—communicate using an instant messaging (IM) program. All you need is a computer and a connection to the internet. About 100 million people stay connected using a cellular phone, with or without text messaging, or a BlackBerry, a Canadian invention.

The exchange above starts with one friend telling the other how much she enjoyed her new sociology class. It makes use of some of the new shorthand symbols that have emerged in the IM world. Here is a sampling of IM symbols. (To appreciate the "emoticon" faces, rotate the page 90° to the right.)

:'-D laughing so hard I cried
:-(I am sad.
:-() I am shocked.
:-) I am smiling.
:-O Wow!
:-ll I am angry with you.
:- P I'm sticking my tongue out at you!
%-} I think I've had too much to drink.
:-x My lips are sealed!
@}———>——— Here's a rose for you!
=(_8^(1) Homer Simpson
@@@@8^) Marge Simpson
AFAIK As far as I know
AWHFY Are we having fun yet?
B4 Before
B4N Bye for now!
BBL Be back later!
BCNU Be seeing you!
BRB Be right back!
CU See you!
GAL Get a life!
GMTA Great minds think alike.
Gr8 Great!
GTG Got to go.
HAGN Have a good night.

H&K Hugs and kisses
J4F Just for fun
KC Keep cool.
L8r Later
LOL Laughing out loud
LTNC Long time no see
MYOB Mind your own business.
ROFL Rolling on the floor laughing
U You
U R You are
UR Your/you're
TTFN Ta ta for now
Y Why
2L8 Too late

WHAT DO YOU THINK?

1. What does the creation of symbols such as these suggest about culture?
2. Do you think that using such symbols is a good way to communicate? Does it lead to confusion or misunderstanding? Why?
3. What other kinds of symbols can you think of that are new to your generation?

Sources: J. Rubin (2003), Berteau (2005), and Martin Gerber and friends (2006).

Symbolic meanings vary even within a single society. A fur coat, prized by one person as a luxurious symbol of success, may represent to another the inhumane treatment of animals. Similarly, the Canadian flag, which to many Canadians embodies national pride, to separatists may symbolize oppression of the Québécois. Cultural symbols also change over time. Blue jeans were created more than a century ago as sturdy, inexpensive clothing for people engaged in physical labour. In the liberal political climate of the 1960s, this working-class aura made jeans popular among affluent students—many of whom wore them simply to look "different" or to identify with working people. In the late 1970s, "designer jeans" emerged as high-priced status symbols that conveyed quite a different message. Today, everyday jeans remain as popular as ever, simply as comfortable apparel.

In sum, symbols allow people to make sense of their lives, and without them human existence would be meaningless. Manipulating symbols correctly allows us to engage others within our own cultural system. Societies create new symbols all the time. The Applying Sociology box (above) describes some of the cyber-symbols that have developed along with our increasing use of computers for communication.

LANGUAGE

In infancy, an illness left Helen Keller (1880–1968) blind and deaf. Without these two senses, she was cut off from the

 To learn more about the life of Helen Keller, go to www.helen-keller.freeservers.com/ or www.hki.org/.

symbolic world, and her social development was greatly limited. Only when

اقْرَوْا	**Read**	독서
Arabic	English	Korean
ԿարԴա	διαβαζω	بخوانیه
Armenian	Greek	Persian
෮ᧄᦤᦰ	אֲקרָא	читать
Cambodian	Hebrew	Russian
閱讀	पढ़नाⁿ	Aaniin
Chinese	Hindi	Ojibway

FIGURE 3–1   Human Languages: A Variety of Symbols

Here the single English word "Read" is written in twelve of the hundreds of languages humans use to communicate with one another.

her teacher, Anne Mansfield Sullivan, broke through Keller's isolation using sign language did Helen Keller begin to realize her human potential. This remarkable woman, who later became a famous educator herself, recalls the moment she first understood the concept of language:

> We walked down the path to the well-house, attracted by the smell of honeysuckle with which it was covered. Someone was drawing water, and my teacher placed my hand under the spout. As the cool stream gushed over one hand, she spelled into the other the word *water*, first slowly, then rapidly. I stood still, my whole attention fixed upon the motions of her fingers. Suddenly I felt a misty consciousness as of something forgotten—a thrill of returning thought; and somehow the mystery of language was revealed to me. I knew then that "w-a-t-e-r" meant the wonderful cool something that was flowing over my hand. That living word awakened my soul; gave it light, hope, joy, set it free! (1903:24)

Language, the key to the world of culture, is *a system of symbols that allows people to communicate with one another.* Humans have created many sounds and alphabets to express the hundreds of languages we speak. Several examples are shown in Figure 3–1. Even rules for writing differ; most people in Western societies write from left to right, but people in northern Africa and western Asia write from right to left, and people in eastern Asia write from top to bottom. Global Map 3–1 shows where we find the world's three most widely spoken languages.

Language not only allows communication but is also the key to **cultural transmission,** *the process by which one generation passes culture to the next.* Just as our bodies contain the genes of our ancestors, our culture contains countless symbols of those who came before us. Language is the key that unlocks centuries of accumulated wisdom. The Thinking about Diversity box (on page 59) makes just such an argument with respect to Canada's Aboriginal languages, most of which are threatened with extinction.

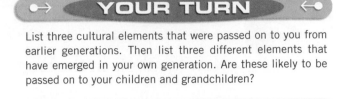

YOUR TURN

List three cultural elements that were passed on to you from earlier generations. Then list three different elements that have emerged in your own generation. Are these likely to be passed on to your children and grandchildren?

Canadians are very familiar with the importance of language to culture. Although Canada is officially bilingual, in practice it is geographically unilingual, with French-speaking majorities in Quebec and northern New Brunswick, and English predominant elsewhere. Bill 101, which regulates the use of English in Quebec and made French the only official language of the province, was an attempt to preserve the distinctive Québécois culture. To many French-speaking Quebecers, Bill 101 is essential to their survival as a nation; to some English-speaking Canadians, the law seems to be an infringement of the rights of the minority English-speaking Quebecers. The heated debates over language that characterize Canadian—and especially Quebec—politics are evidence of how strongly people feel about their languages.

Throughout human history, people have transmitted culture through speech—or the oral cultural tradition. Only as recently as five thousand years ago did humans invent writing and, even then, just a favoured few ever learned to read and write. It was not until this century that industrial, high-income countries claimed nearly universal literacy. Nevertheless, the International Adult Literacy Survey of 2003 revealed that 42 percent of Canadians aged 16 to 65 do not have "the 'desired level' of competence for coping with the increasing skill demands of the emerging knowledge and information economy" (Statistics Canada, 2003b); furthermore, the situation has not changed since the previous literacy survey in 1994. Data on selected categories reveal that literacy levels are lower among those over 65 years of age, francophones, Aboriginal peoples, and immigrants. Among immigrants, those with French or English as their mother tongue fared better than those with other mother tongues; and there is little improvement for those who have been in this country for more than ten years. Clearly, many Canadians face almost insurmountable barriers to opportunity in a society that increasingly demands symbolic skills.

For information about literacy in Canada, go to www.hrsdc. gc.ca/en/gateways/nav/top_nav/program/nls.shtml.

Language skills may link us with the past, but they also spark the human imagination to connect symbols in new ways, creating an almost limitless range of future possibilities. Language sets humans apart as the only creatures who are self-conscious, aware of our limitations and ultimate mortality, yet able to dream and to hope for a future better than the present.

WINDOW ON THE WORLD

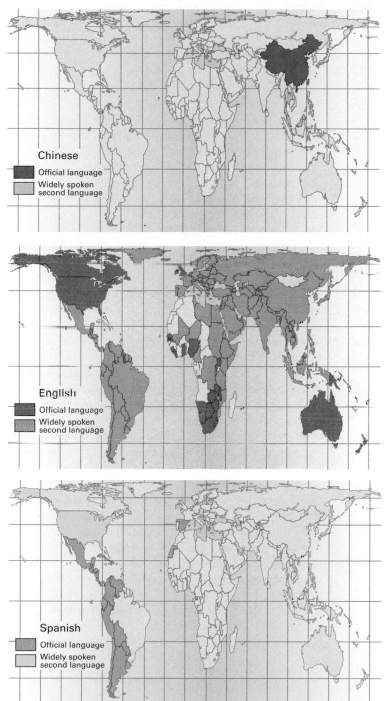

Language in Global Perspective

Chinese (including Mandarin, Cantonese, and dozens of other dialects) is the native tongue of one-fifth of the world's people, almost all of whom live in Asia. Although all Chinese people read and write with the same characters, they use several dozen dialects. The "official" dialect, taught in schools throughout China and Taiwan, is Mandarin (the dialect of Beijing, China's historic capital city). Cantonese, the language of Canton, is the second most common Chinese dialect; it differs in sound from Mandarin roughly the way French differs from Spanish.

English is the native tongue or official language in several world regions (spoken by one-tenth of humanity) and has become the preferred second language in most of the world.

The largest concentration of Spanish speakers is in Latin America and, of course, Spain. Spanish is also the second most widely spoken language in the United States.

Source: *Peters Atlas of the World* (1990); updated by John J. Macionis.

Does Language Shape Reality?

Do the Japanese, who think in one language, experience the world differently from others who think in English, French, or Estonian? The answer is yes, since each language has its own distinct symbols serving as the building blocks of reality.

Edward Sapir (1929, 1949) and Benjamin Whorf (1956; orig. 1941), two anthropologists who specialized in linguistic studies, noted that each language has words or expressions with no precise counterparts in others. Further, all languages fuse symbols with distinctive emotions. Thus, as multilingual people can attest, a single idea often "feels" different if

Australian artist and feminist Sally Swain alters famous artists' paintings to make fun of our culture's tendency to ignore the everyday lives of women. This spoof is entitled *Mrs. Matisse Polishes the Goldfish*.

Mrs. Matisse Polishes the Goldfish from *Great Housewives of Art* by Sally Swain, copyright © 1988, 1989 by Sally Swain. Used by permission of Viking Penguin, a division of Penguin Group (USA) Inc.

spoken in, say, French rather than in English or Chinese (Falk, 1987). For many of these reasons, jokes do not translate well from one language or culture to another. Formally, then, what we call the **Sapir-Whorf hypothesis** states that *people perceive the world through the cultural lens of language.* Using different symbolic systems, a Filipino, a Turk, a Brazilian, and, indeed, anglophone and francophone Canadians actually experience "distinct worlds, not merely the same world with different labels attached" (Sapir, 1949:162). More recently, scholars have taken issue with this thesis, arguing that, although we do fashion reality from our symbols, evidence does not support the notion that language *determines* reality the way Sapir and Whorf claimed. For example, children understand the *idea* of "family" long before they learn the word; adults can imagine new ideas or things before naming them (Kay and Kempton, 1984; Pinker, 1994). Nonetheless, language has major impacts on the ways in which we experience the world.

The capacity to create and manipulate language gives humans everywhere the power to alter their experience. For example, the use of "Ms." rather than "Mrs." or "Miss" means that a woman can be introduced as a woman rather than as the holder of a marital status. A system of language guides how we understand the world but does not preclude change—or choice.

VALUES AND BELIEFS

What accounts for the popularity of Hollywood film characters such as James Bond, Neo, Erin Brockovich, and Lara Croft? Each is ruggedly individualistic, going it alone and relying on personal skill and savvy to challenge "the system." In admiring such characters, we are supporting certain **values,** *culturally defined standards that people use to decide what is desirable, good, and beautiful, and that serve as broad guidelines for social living.* Values are standards that people who share a culture use to make choices about how to live. (See the Media Perspectives box (on p. 65) for some insight into the choices we make.)

Values are broad principles that support **beliefs,** *specific statements that people hold to be true.* In other words, values are abstract standards of goodness, and beliefs are particular matters that individuals consider to be true or false. Cultural values and beliefs not only colour how we perceive our surroundings but also form the core of our personalities. We learn from families, schools, and religious organizations to think and act according to approved principles, to pursue worthy goals, and to believe a host of cultural truths while rejecting alternatives as false. Particular values and beliefs thus operate as a form of "cultural capital" that can spark in some people the optimistic determination to pursue success and, in others, a sense of hopelessness that little will ever change (Sowell, 1996).

In a nation as large and diverse as Canada, of course, few cultural values and beliefs are shared by everyone. In fact, with a long history of immigration, Canada has become a cultural mosaic. In this regard, we stand apart from many countries, such as China or Japan, that have more homogeneous cultural values. Even so, there is a broad shape to our national life that suggests Canadians share certain "key values." The Thinking It Through box (on p. 66) paints pictures of North American society by comparing Canadian and American values.

← → YOUR TURN ← →

Think about the games you played when you were growing up, such as tag, or board games, such as Monopoly. You might think about the fact that, before the 1970s, boys and girls alike played "cowboys and Indians"; the game became discouraged because of sensitivity about guns and Aboriginal peoples and, now, is "politically incorrect." What cultural values did your childhood games teach? How do they differ from the values taught by today's video games?

MEDIA PERSPECTIVES
A Lesson in Values from Cyberspace

This message was received by email. When things in your life seem almost too much to handle, when twenty-four hours in a day just aren't enough, remember the mayonnaise jar and the two cups of coffee.

A professor stood before his philosophy class and had some items in front of him. When the class began, he wordlessly picked up a very large and empty mayonnaise jar and proceeded to fill it with golf balls. He then asked the students if the jar was full. They agreed that it was. The professor then picked up a box of pebbles and poured them into the jar. He shook the jar lightly. The pebbles rolled into the open areas between the golf balls. He then asked the students again if the jar was full. They agreed it was.

The professor next picked up a box of sand and poured it into the jar. Of course, the sand filled up everything else. He asked once more if the jar was full. The students responded with a unanimous "yes."

The professor then produced two cups of coffee from under the table and poured the entire contents into the jar, effectively filling the empty space between the grains of sand. The students laughed.

"Now," said the professor as the laughter subsided, "I want you to recognize that this jar represents your life. The golf balls are the important things—your family, your children, your health, your friends and your favourite passions—and if everything else was lost and only they remained, your life would still be full. The pebbles are the other things that matter like your job, your house and your car. The sand is everything else—the small stuff. "If you put the sand into the jar first," he continued, "there is no room for the pebbles or the golf balls. The same goes for life. If you spend all your time and energy on the small stuff you will never have room for the things that are important to you. Pay attention to the things that are critical to your happiness. Play with your children. Take time to get medical checkups. Take your spouse out to lunch or dinner. Play another 18. Take that vacation you've been thinking about for years. Visit your parents if you're lucky enough to still have them. There will always be time to clean the house and fix the disposal. Take care of the golf balls first—the things that really matter. Set your priorities. The rest is just sand."

One of the students raised her hand and inquired what the coffee represented. The professor smiled. "I'm glad you asked. It just goes to show you that no matter how full your life may seem, there's always room for a couple of cups of coffee with a friend."

WHAT DO YOU THINK?

1. Can you think of a better way to illustrate the importance of evaluating and setting your priorities?
2. How often do you receive gems like this one among your e-mail messages?
3. Will this e-mail message make you stop to think about what you value most in life?

Source: This story exists elsewhere in cyberspace, with attributions as diverse as Moses and Dr. Phil. Should the original author be discovered, the author will happily seek formal permission and provide proper credit.

Values: Inconsistency and Conflict

Cultural values can be inconsistent and even contradictory (Lynd, 1967; Bellah, *et al.*, 1985). Living in Canada, we sometimes find ourselves torn between the "me first" attitude of an individualistic, success-at-all-costs way of life and the opposing need to belong and contribute to some larger community. Similarly, we affirm our belief in equality of opportunity only to turn around and promote or degrade others because of their race or gender. Value inconsistency reflects the cultural diversity of Canadian society and the process of cultural change by which new trends supplant older traditions. One tradition that continues to be central to the Canadian winter and that elusive Canadian identity is hockey. Yet the traditional hockey scene in Canada is being transformed by the arrival of women's hockey at the international level: young girls now have women hockey players as role models. So central to our identity is hockey, that Canada's failure to win gold at the 1998 Winter Olympics in Nagano, Japan (a silver medal for the women and no medal at all for the men) unleashed anger, despair, and depressive slumps throughout the country. The double gold in men's and women's hockey in Salt Lake City (2002) restored our dignity and pride, but they were dashed again when, in Turin, Italy (2006), the women won gold but the men were shut out of the medals again. Canadians think of themselves as co-operative rather than competitive and gentler or placid rather than violent. But, when it comes to hockey, we like it rough and aggressive—and we like to win, just as much as the Americans do. The fact that Canadian women are excelling in hockey—at world and Olympic levels—points to value inconsistencies regarding aggressiveness, competitiveness, and even femininity.

THINKING IT THROUGH
Canadians and Americans: What Makes Us Different?

When asked about what it means to be Canadian or what factors contribute to a Canadian identity, the average person will shrug and say, "I don't really know." When pushed a little harder we might admit that we know we are Canadians because we are "not American." We share many attributes and attitudes with Americans, but there are significant differences, some of which are intriguing.

Seymour Martin Lipset (1985) argued in the 1950s that the traditional differences between Canadian and American values are rooted in the past. A central feature of U.S. history was the war of independence from Great Britain. In a sense, Canada separated formally from Britain only in 1982 with the patriation of the constitution. This difference is pivotal, Lipset argues, for cultural distinctions between the United States and Canada. Canada, in Lipset's view, sits somewhere between the United States and Great Britain with respect to values. Americans place great value on freedom, individual initiative, achievement, and success; Canadians, on the other hand, stress conformity and obedience to the law. In the American West, outlaws such as Jesse James and Billy the Kid were lionized; in Canada it was the Mountie—the lawman—who was admired.

Practically speaking, the Canadian tendency to emphasize the good of the collectivity over the good of the individual has resulted in social programs such as universal medical care. Until now, Americans have cherished the individual right to choose (and pay for) medical care as desired—with various sorts and levels of medical coverage for people with varying abilities to pay.

Roger Sauvé, a futurist and former journalist, gathered comparable data for the early 1990s on American and Canadian characteristics and attitudes (1994), providing us with the following insights:

- Americans believe in hell and in the devil (60% and 52%) more than Canadians do (34% and 30%).
- Canadians are more likely than Americans to say that premarital sex is okay (70% versus 54%).
- Canadians are slightly more in favour than Americans of restrictive gun laws (77% and 70%).
- Americans are more likely than Canadians to own handguns (24% versus 3%).
- The birth rate among 15- to 19-year-old girls is higher in the United States than in Canada (62 American births per 1000, compared to 27 Canadian births per 1000).
- American marriages are more likely than Canadian marriages to end in divorce (43% versus 28%).
- Americans aged 25 to 64 are more likely than Canadians of equivalent age to be university graduates (25% and 17%).

More recently, Ipsos-Reid pollsters Bricker and Wright (2005) asked Americans and Canadians a few questions of their own—once again revealing interesting differences:

- Americans are more likely than Canadians to claim that "my religious faith is very important to me in my day-to-day life" (82% versus 64%).
- Americans are more likely than Canadians to believe that same-sex marriage is "wrong and should never be lawful" (47% versus 27%).
- Americans are more likely than Canadians to support the death penalty (71% versus 42%).
- Canadians are more likely than Americans to think that decriminalizing marijuana is "a sound idea" (51% versus 36%).

- Canadians are more likely than Americans to think that Canada is a major player in world affairs (76% versus 52%).
- Canadians are much more likely than Americans to see our two countries as closest friends and allies (60% versus 18%).

Sauvé (1994) reported that 66 percent of Americans and 14 percent of Canadians are in favour of Canada becoming part of the United States. A decade later, Bricker and Wright report that 23 percent of Canadians and 32 percent of Quebecers are in favour of a formal economic union (free trade and a common currency), while 4 percent of Canadians and 7 percent of Quebecers think we should become part of the United States. The apparent decline in the latter measure over ten years is complicated by the fact that two levels of union are being discussed within Canada. At either level, a quarter of us are willing to forge closer formal ties with the United States.

Bricker and Wright (2005:258) provide us with an amusing anecdote to ponder. Mavis Gallant, the famous Canadian writer who lives in France, asked Robertson Davies, the famous English author who lived in Canada: "Why don't Canadians love Canada the way the Americans love America?" His answer was: "It's not a country you love; it's a country you worry about."

WHAT DO YOU THINK?

1. Taking everything into account, are there more similarities or differences between Canadians and Americans?
2. Are you surprised that Canadians' attitudes towards gun laws are so similar?
3. How do people in your extended family feel about closer economic ties between Canada and the United States?

Whether based on the ethnic mix of Canadian society or changes in our way of life, today's value inconsistencies can lead to strain and awkward balancing acts. Sometimes we pursue one value at the expense of another, supporting the principle of equal opportunity, say, while opposing the acceptance of gay people as elementary school teachers.

Values: A Global Perspective

Each of the thousands of cultures in the world has its own values. In general, the values that are important in higher-income countries differ somewhat from those in lower-income countries.

Societies in lower-income nations have cultures that value survival: people who are desperately poor give priority to physical safety and economic security. They worry about having enough to eat and a safe place to sleep at night. In general, lower-income societies tend to be traditional, with values that celebrate the past, and emphasize the importance of family and religious beliefs, obedience to authority, and conformity. These nations, dominated by men, typically discourage or forbid practices such as divorce and abortion.

Societies in higher-income countries, where people take survival for granted, have cultures that value individualism and self-expression, and focus on quality of life. People in these countries think about lifestyle and personal happiness. In general, these countries tend to be secular-rational, placing less emphasis on family ties and religious beliefs, and more on independence and tolerance of diversity. In higher-income countries, women have social standing more equal to men, and there is widespread support for practices such as divorce and abortion (*World Values Survey*, 2004). Figure 3–2 compares selected countries in terms of their cultural values.

NORMS

Most Canadians are eager to gossip about "who's hot" and "who's not." North American Aboriginal communities, however, typically condemn such behaviour as rude and divisive. Both patterns illustrate the operation of **norms,** *rules and expectations by which a society guides the behaviour of its members.* Some norms are *proscriptive,* stating what we *should not* do, as when health officials warn us to avoid casual sex. *Prescriptive* norms, on the other hand, state what we *should* do, as when our schools teach "safe sex" practices. The most important norms in a culture apply everywhere and at all times. For example, parents expect obedience from young children regardless of the setting. Other norms depend on the situation: in Canada, we expect the audience to applaud after a musical performance; we may applaud, although it is not expected, at the end of a classroom lecture; we do not applaud at the end of a religious sermon.

What does the popularity of the television show *The Apprentice* tell you about the values at the heart of U.S. culture? Do Canadians share those values, along with their fascination with the show?

YOUR TURN

If you agree that Figure 3–2 deals with fundamental values, what do you make of the fact that Canada and the United States appear at almost exactly the same location?

Mores and Folkways

William Graham Sumner (1959, orig. 1906), an early U.S. sociologist, recognized that some norms are more important to our lives than others. Sumner coined the term **mores** (pronounced "more-rays") to refer to *norms that are widely observed and have great moral significance.* Mores, or *taboos,* include our society's insistence that adults not engage in sexual relations with children. People pay less attention to **folkways,** *norms for routine or casual interaction.* Examples include ideas about appropriate greetings and proper dress. In short, mores distinguish between right and wrong, and folkways draw a line between right and *rude.* A man who does not wear a tie to a formal dinner party may raise eyebrows for violating folkways: were he to arrive wearing *only* a tie, he would violate cultural mores and invite a more serious response.

Social Control

Mores and folkways are the basic rules of everyday life. Although we sometimes resist pressures to conform, we can see that norms make our dealings with others more orderly and predictable. Observing or breaking the rules of social life prompts a response from others, in the form of reward or

GLOBAL SNAPSHOT

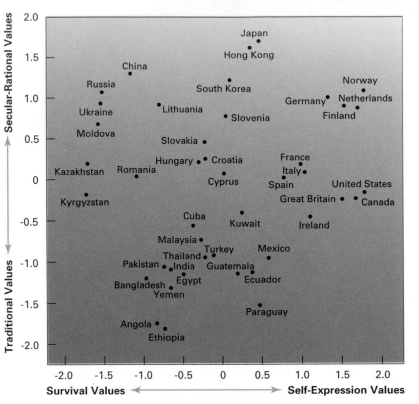

FIGURE 3-2   Cultural Values of Selected Countries

Higher-income countries are secular/rational and favour self-expression. The cultures of lower-income countries are more traditional and concerned with economic survival.

Source: Inglehart and Welzel (2005).

punishment. Sanctions—whether an approving smile or a raised eyebrow—operate as a system of **social control,** *attempts by society to regulate people's thoughts and behaviour.*

As we learn cultural norms, we gain the capacity to evaluate our own behaviour. Doing wrong (say, downloading a term paper from the internet) can cause both *shame* (the painful sense that others disapprove of our actions) and *guilt* (a negative judgment we make of ourselves). Only cultural creatures can experience shame and guilt. This is probably what Mark Twain had in mind when he remarked that people "are the only animals that blush—or need to."

IDEAL AND REAL CULTURE

Societies devise values and norms as moral guidelines for their members. As such, these cultural elements do not describe actual behaviour as much as they tell us how we should behave. We must remember, then, that **ideal culture,** *social patterns mandated by cultural values and norms,* is not the same as **real culture,** *actual social patterns that only approximate cultural expectations.* To illustrate, most of us acknowledge the importance of sexual fidelity in marriage. Even so, a 1994 *Maclean's* poll indicated that about 14 percent of married men and 7 percent of married women reported being sexually unfaithful to their spouses at some point in the marriage (*Maclean's*/CTV, 1994). Such discrepancies occur in all societies, since no one lives up to ideal standards all the time.

YOUR TURN

Give two examples of violating campus folkways and two examples of violating campus mores. What are the likely consequences of each type of violation?

MATERIAL CULTURE AND TECHNOLOGY

In addition to symbolic elements such as values and norms, every culture includes a wide range of physical human creations, which sociologists call *artifacts.* The Chinese eat with chopsticks rather than knives and forks, the Japanese put mats rather than rugs on the floor, and many men and women in India prefer flowing robes to the close-fitting clothing common in North America. The material culture of a people may seem as strange to outsiders as their language, values, and norms.

Visit the website of the National Geographic Society for information on world cultures at www.nationalgeographic.com.

A society's artifacts partly reflect underlying cultural values. The warlike Yǎnomamö of Venezuela and Brazil carefully craft their weapons and prize the poison tips on their arrows, while the emphasis of North Americans on individualism and independence helps to explain our love of the automobile. In Canada, there are more than 13 million motor vehicles—1 for every 2 people (men, women, and children). In recent years, more than half of all cars sold in the United States were the large sports utility vehicles that we might expect rugged, individualistic people to like. Canadians were buying SUVs in greater numbers—before the rise in fuel prices, a trend that suggests that we, too, value rugged individualism.

In addition to reflecting values, material culture also reflects a society's **technology,** *knowledge that people use to make a way of life in their surroundings.* The more complex a society's technology, the more its members are able—for better or worse—to shape the world for themselves. Advanced technology has allowed North Americans to criss-cross the continent with highways and to fill them with auto-mobiles. At the same time, the internal-combustion engines in those vehicles release carbon dioxide into the atmosphere, which contributes to air pollution and global warming. The values that push us to purchase those SUVs—or any car for that matter—are at odds with our environmental values.

Because North Americans attach great importance to science and sophisticated technology, we tend to judge societies with simpler technology as less advanced than our own. Some facts support such an assessment. For example, life expectancy for children born in Canada today is about 80 years; the life-span of the Yanomamö in Brazil is about 40 years (Chagnon, 1992). However, we must be careful not to make self-serving judgments about cultures that differ from our own. While our powerful and complex technology has produced work-reducing devices and seemingly miraculous forms of medical treatment, it has also contributed to unhealthy levels of stress, eroded the quality of the natural environment, and created weapons capable of destroying in a blinding flash everything that humankind has managed to achieve.

Finally, technology is another cultural element that varies substantially within Canada. Although many of us cannot imagine life without CD players, televisions, and the latest personal computers, many members of our society cannot afford such items, and others reject them on principle.

The Old Order Mennonites, many of whom live in small farming communities across southwestern Ontario, shun most modern conveniences as a matter of religious conviction. With their traditional black garb and horse-drawn buggies, the Old

For more information about Old Order Mennonites, go to the Mennonite Archives of Ontario at http://grebel.uwaterloo.ca/mao/.

Order Mennonites may seem like a curious relic of the past. Yet their communities flourish, grounded in vibrant families and individuals with a strong sense of identity and purpose. Outsiders who observe them come away with the suspicion that these simple, stable communities suggest an attractive alternative to modern materialism and competitiveness.

NEW INFORMATION TECHNOLOGY AND CULTURE

Many rich nations, such as Canada, have entered a post-industrial phase based on computers and new information technology. Industrial production is centred on factories and

Standards of beauty—including the colour and design of everyday surroundings—vary significantly from one culture to another. These two Nankani women put the finishing touches on their lavishly decorated homes. Housing in North America and Europe appears much more subdued.

machinery that generate material goods. In contrast, post-industrial production is based on computers and other electronic devices that create, process, store, and apply information. In this new information economy, workers need symbolic skills in place of the mechanical skills of the industrial age. Symbolic skills include the ability to speak, write, compute, design, and create images in such fields as art, advertising, entertainment, and education. In today's computer-based economy, people with creative jobs are generating new cultural ideas, images, and products all the time.

SOCIOLOGY *@* WORK

YOUR TURN

If archaeologists dig up our civilization 50 000 years from now, what kind of people will they think we were, based on the artifacts they might find? Point to specific artifacts (such as SUVs, cell phones, and credit cards) and what they say about us.

Any society exhibits countless different cultural patterns, some of which may seem strange to others. What cultural values are evident in the pierced noses and tattoos of these two men? Are these values consistent with or completely at odds with the highly individualistic way of life in North America?

Cultural Diversity in Canada

Canada exhibits striking cultural diversity, compared with Japan, whose historic isolation made it the most monocultural of industrial nations. Heavy immigration over two centuries and especially the last thirty years, has made Canada the world's most multicultural country.

Figure 3–3 gives some indication of Canada's cultural diversity, and reveals that patterns of immigration have changed over time. Before 1961, about 90 percent of immigrants to Canada came from Europe, especially the United Kingdom, and less than 5 percent came from countries in Asia and the Middle East. Since 1961, more and more immigrants have come from Asia and the Middle East. Between 1991 and 2001, European immigrants made up only 20 percent of total immigration, while those from Asia and the Middle East made up 58 percent. This change in pattern, which has greatly increased the cultural diversity of our country, is the result of deliberate change in our immigration policy. Given this diversity, sociologists call Canada a *cultural mosaic.*

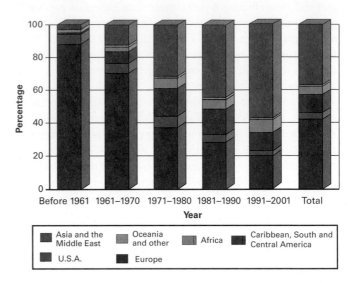

FIGURE 3-3 Immigrant Population by Place of Birth and Period of Immigration, 2001

Source: Calculations by L.M. Gerber based on Statistics Canada, catalogue 11–008E and 2001 census tables, catalogue no. 95F0359XCB2001004.

HIGH CULTURE AND POPULAR CULTURE

To this point cultural diversity has been linked to ethnicity and multiculturalism, but there other dimensions of diversity: one of them is rooted in social class. In everyday conversation, we may reserve the term "culture" for sophisticated art forms such as classical literature, opera, ballet, and painting. We praise symphony conductors, Shakespearean actors, and dance choreographers as "cultured" because they presumably appreciate the "finer things in life." The term "culture" itself has the same Latin root as the word "cultivate," suggesting that the "cultured" individual has refined tastes. In contrast, we speak less glowingly of the tastes of ordinary people, assuming that everyday cultural patterns are somehow less worthy. In more concrete terms, we are tempted to judge the music of Mozart as more "cultured" than Motown's, fine cuisine as better than fish sticks, and polo as more polished than ping-pong.

Such judgments imply that many cultural patterns are readily accessible to some but not all members of a society (Hall and Neitz, 1993). Sociologists use the shorthand term **high culture** to refer to *cultural patterns that distinguish a society's elite;* **popular culture,** then, designates *cultural patterns that are widespread throughout society.* The publication of *Mondo Canuck: A Canadian Pop Culture Odyssey* (Pevere and Dymond, 1996) is a refreshing celebration of Canada's cultural creativity: the book itself is pop culture. Common sense may suggest that high culture is superior to popular culture. After all, history chronicles the lives of elites much more than those of ordinary people. But sociologists use the term "culture" to refer to all elements of a society's way of life, even as they recognize that cultural patterns vary throughout a population.

We should resist quick judgments about the merits of high culture as opposed to popular culture for two key reasons. First, neither elites nor ordinary people have uniform tastes and interests. Second, we praise high culture not because it is inherently better than popular culture, but because its supporters have more money, power, and prestige. For example, there is no difference between a violin and a fiddle; however, we refer to the instrument as a violin when it is used to produce a type of music enjoyed by the elite, and as a fiddle when the musician is playing for ordinary folk.

SUBCULTURE

The term **subculture** refers to *cultural patterns that set apart some segment of a society's population.* Teenagers, First Nations on reserves, homeless people, race-car drivers, jazz musicians, hockey fans, the police, and even sociologists all display subcultural patterns. It is easy—but often inaccurate—to place people in subcultural categories. Almost everyone participates simultaneously in numerous subcultures, to which we have various levels of commitment.

In some cases, important cultural traits such as ethnicity or religion do divide people—sometimes with tragic results. Consider the former nation of Yugoslavia in southeastern Europe (now the five nations of Slovenia, Croatia, Macedonia, Bosnia and Herzegovina, and Serbia and Montenegro). The ongoing turmoil there is fuelled by astounding cultural diversity. Before its breakup, the former Yugoslavia, was about the size of the Atlantic provinces, but with a population of 25 million. This one small country made use of two alphabets, professed three religions, spoke four languages, was home to five major nationalities, was divided into six political republics, and absorbed the cultural influences of seven surrounding countries.

Sociologists see Canada as a mosaic, with many nationalities contributing to a larger "Canadian" culture. But, considering the extent of our cultural diversity, how accurate is the "mosaic" description? One factor complicates this idealistic notion: cultural diversity involves not just variety but also hierarchy. Too often, what we view as dominant cultural patterns are those favoured by powerful segments of the population, while we relegate the lives of the disadvantaged to the realm of "subculture." Those subcultures underlie our new policy of multiculturalism.

Many subcultures that develop involve young people. One recent example is the skateboarding subculture that includes not only the sport but a distinctive style of dress.

MULTICULTURALISM

As well as being bilingual, Canadian society is officially multicultural. **Multiculturalism** is embodied in *social policy designed to encourage ethnic or cultural heterogeneity.* Historically, our society downplayed cultural diversity, defining our way of life primarily in terms familiar to the English or French immigrants who dominated Canada socially. Historians highlighted the role of descendants of the English and French and described events from their point of view, pushing aside the perspectives and accomplishments of other immigrants and Aboriginal peoples. The European way of life was set up as an ideal to which all should aspire and by which all should be judged. Multiculturalists describe this singular pattern in Canada as **Eurocentrism,** *the dominance of European cultural patterns.* The legacy of this practice is a spirited debate over whether we should continue to stress Western European, especially French and English, cultural contributions to the exclusion of those made by Chinese, Caribbean, Ukrainian, and Indian immigrants. An interesting example of the continued presence of Eurocentric ideas in Canada was the widespread opposition to the 1990 decision to allow a Sikh, Baltej Singh Dhillon, to wear a turban as part of his RCMP uniform.

While few deny that our culture has multiple roots, multiculturalism generates controversy because it requires rethinking of core norms and values. One area of debate involves language. Although Canada is officially bilingual, the Canadian population is actually composed of people with

YOUR TURN

List five subcultures that are part of your life. Which are the most important?

TABLE 3–1
Mother Tongues in Canada, 1996 and 2001

Mother Tongue	Percent of Population	
	1996	2001
English	59.2	58.5
French	23.2	22.6
Chinese	2.5	2.8
Italian	1.7	1.6
German	1.6	1.5
Polish	0.7	0.7
Spanish	0.7	0.8
Portuguese	0.7	0.7
Punjabi	0.7	0.9
Ukrainian	0.6	0.5
Arabic	0.5	0.7
Dutch	0.5	0.4
Tagalog (Filipino)	0.5	0.6
Greek	0.4	0.4
Vietnamese	0.4	0.4
Cree	0.3	0.2
Inuktitut	0.1	0.1
Other nonofficial languages	4.2	5.1
Multiple languages	1.4	1.3

Source: Calculations by L.M. Gerber based on Statistics Canada, catalogue no. 97F0007XCB2001009.

many different mother tongues. Table 3–1 provides the distribution of Canadians by mother tongue. Despite the significant number of different languages spoken in this country, minority languages are not officially recognized by federal law. As a result, critics charge that multiculturalism has only symbolic significance in Canada—meaning that multiculturalism allows people belonging to minorities to maintain their culture within their home while forcing them to speak either French or English outside. Gradually, such people will lose the use of their mother tongue and, with it, many of their distinctive cultural practices. On the other hand, some observers point out that each minority actually makes a very small part of the total population of Canada. Accommodating each of the many minorities in Canada would lead to a fractured society, one with no sense of commonality or cohesiveness.

The debate rages, and important questions are left unresolved. To what extent should Canada encourage those who speak languages other than French or English to maintain their mother tongue? Should Canadian taxpayers support heritage language schools and courses? How should our schools—from the early grades through university— teach about culture? It is among educators that the clash over multiculturalism has been most intense. Four basic positions have emerged from this discussion:

- First, proponents defend multiculturalism as a way to capture a more accurate picture of our past. Proposed

educational reforms seek, for example, to temper the simplistic praise directed at European explorers by realistically assessing the tragic impact of the European conquest on the Indigenous peoples of this hemisphere. From the point of view of North American Aboriginal peoples, contact with Europeans unleashed centuries of subordination and death from war and disease. Furthermore, a multicultural approach would recognize the achievements of many women and men whose cultural backgrounds have kept them on the sidelines of history.

- Second, multiculturalism allows us to come to terms with our current diversity. Children born today can expect to see immigration from African, Asian, and Hispanic countries increase even more.

- Third, proponents assert that multiculturalism is a way to strengthen the academic achievement of children of immigrants, most of whom are from visible minorities, and others who find little personal relevance in traditional educational programs.

- Fourth, proponents see multiculturalism as worthwhile preparation for all people in Canada to live in a world that is increasingly interdependent. As various chapters of this book explain, social patterns in this country are becoming more closely linked to issues and events elsewhere in the world. Multiculturalism undermines nationalistic prejudices by pointing out global connectedness; it also makes Canadians more flexible in their international political and business dealings.

The argument most commonly voiced by opponents of multiculturalism is that any society remains cohesive only to the extent that its cultural patterns are widely shared. Multiculturalism, say critics, fuels the "politics of difference," encouraging divisiveness as individuals identify with their subcultures rather than with Canada as a whole. Opponents also charge that multiculturalism erodes the claim to common truth by maintaining that ideas should be evaluated according to the race (and gender) of those who present them. Furthermore, some ask if multiculturalism actually benefits minorities as claimed, since multiculturalism demands precisely the kind of segregation that we deplore. For example, a heritage-centred curriculum denies children a wide range of knowledge and skills by encouraging study from a more limited point of view.

COUNTERCULTURE

Cultural diversity also includes outright rejection of conventional ideas or behaviour. **Counterculture** refers to *cultural patterns that strongly oppose those widely accepted within a society.* During the 1960s, a youth-oriented counterculture rejected mainstream culture as overly competitive, self-centred, and materialistic. Instead, hippies and other counterculturalists favoured a co-operative lifestyle in which "being" took precedence over "doing," and the capacity for personal growth—or "expanded consciousness"—

was prized over material possessions such as homes and cars. They drew personal identity from long hair, headbands, and blue jeans, from peace signs instead of handshakes, from drugs, and from the energy of rock-and-roll music. Such differences, in values, behaviour, and music led some to "drop out" of the larger society.

Some countercultures, flourishing in North America, Europe, and beyond, seek to disrupt their societies. These highly significant countercultures may involve militaristic bands of men and women who are deeply suspicious of government and willing to resort to violence. In Canada, the Front de libération du Québec, active through the 1960s and early 1970s, resorted to bombings, kidnapping, and murder in its quest for an independent socialist Quebec. More recently, in California, counterculture extremists from the Earth Liberation Front torched Hummer dealerships and new construction sites (Madigan, 2003).

CULTURAL CHANGE

Cultural change is not only continuous, but change in one dimension is usually associated with other transformations. For example, increased labour force participation among women occurs along with changing family patterns, including a later age at first marriage, fewer births, more divorce, and more children being raised in households without fathers. Such connections illustrate the principle of **cultural integration,** *the close relationship among various elements of a cultural system.* But all elements of a cultural system do not change at the same speed.

William Ogburn (1964) observed that technology moves quickly, generating new elements of material culture (such as test-tube babies) faster than nonmaterial culture (such as ideas about parenthood) can keep up with them. Ogburn called this inconsistency **cultural lag,** *cultural elements changing at different rates, causing various degrees of disruption in cultural systems.* In a culture with the technical ability to allow one woman to give birth to a child by using another woman's egg that has been fertilized in a laboratory with the sperm of a total stranger, how are we to apply the traditional notions of motherhood and fatherhood? What if an infertile woman has her own mother conceive by artificial insemination with her husband's sperm? The "grandmother" who bears the child would be the biological mother, and the "mother" would be a half-sister to the child. What if a man has himself cloned and implants the embryo in his wife's womb? His own parents—the child's "grandparents"—would be the biological mother and father. It will be decades before the social, psychological, and legal elements of our culture catch up with this technological change.

Causes of Cultural Change

Cultural change is set in motion in three ways. The first is invention, the process of creating new cultural elements. Invention has given us the telephone (1876), the airplane (1903), and the aerosol spray can (1941), all of which have had a tremendous impact on our way of life. The process of invention goes on constantly, as indicated by the numbers of applications submitted annually to the Canadian Patent Office.

Discovery, a second cause of cultural change, involves recognizing and understanding something not fully understood before—from a distant star, to the foods of another culture, to the athletic excellence of the Olympic team that brought home a record number of medals in 2006. Many discoveries result from scientific research—such as the Canadian BlackBerry. Yet discovery can also happen quite by accident, as when Marie Curie left a rock on a piece of photographic paper in 1898 and serendipitously discovered radium.

The third cause of cultural change is diffusion, the spread of cultural traits from one society to another. For example, insulin—developed first by Frederick Banting and Charles Best at the University of Toronto in the 1920s— and the telephone—conceived by Alexander Graham Bell in Brantford, Ontario, in 1874—have spread around the world. The technological ability to send information around the globe in seconds by means of radio, television, facsimile, and computer means that the level of cultural diffusion has never been greater than it is today. Certainly our own society has contributed many significant cultural elements to the world, but diffusion works the other way as well, so that much of what we assume is inherently "Canadian" actually comes from other cultures. Ralph Linton (1937) explained that many commonplace elements of our way of life—clothing and furniture, clocks, newspapers, money, and even the English language—are all derived from other cultures.

ETHNOCENTRISM AND CULTURAL RELATIVISM

We think of childhood as a time of innocence and freedom from adult burdens like regular work. In poor countries throughout the world, however, families depend on income earned by children. So what people in one society think of as right and natural, people elsewhere find puzzling and even immoral. Perhaps the Chinese philosopher K'ung fu-tzu (Confucius) had it right when he noted that "all people are the same; it's only their habits that are different."

Just about every imaginable idea or behaviour is commonplace somewhere in the world, and this cultural variation causes travellers both excitement and distress. Australians flip light switches down to turn them on; North Americans flip them up. Japanese name city blocks; North Americans name streets. Egyptians move very close to others when in conversation; North Americans are used to maintaining considerable interpersonal space. Given that a particular culture is the basis for each person's reality, it is no wonder that people everywhere exhibit **ethnocentrism,** *the practice of judging another culture by the standards of one's own culture.* Some degree of ethnocentrism is necessary for people to be emotionally attached to their way of life, but ethnocentrism also generates misunderstanding and conflict.

In the world's low-income countries, most children must work to provide their families with needed income. This young child in Dhaka, Bangladesh, is sorting discarded materials in a factory that makes recycled lead batteries. Is it ethnocentric for people living in high-income nations to condemn the practice of child labour because we think youngsters belong in school? Explain your reasoning.

Even terminology is culturally biased. Centuries ago, people in Europe and North America referred to China as the "Far East." But this term, unknown to the Chinese, is an ethnocentric expression for a region that is far to the east *of us.* The Chinese name for their country translates as "Central Kingdom," suggesting that they, like us, see their own society as the centre of the world. The map (on p. 75) challenges our own ethnocentrism by presenting a "down under" view of the western hemisphere.

The logical alternative to ethnocentrism is **cultural relativism,** *the practice of judging a culture by its own standards.* Cultural relativism can be difficult for travellers to adopt. It requires not only openness to unfamiliar values and norms but also the ability to put aside cultural standards we have known all our lives. Even so, as people of the world come into increasing contact with one another, the importance of understanding other cultures increases. North American businesses are learning the value of marketing to culturally diverse populations. Similarly, businesses are learning that success in the global economy depends on awareness of cultural patterns around the world. For example, IBM now provides technical support for its products using websites in twenty-two languages (Fonda, 2001).

This trend is a change from the past, when many corporations used marketing strategies that lacked sensitivity to cultural diversity. The Coors phrase "Turn it Loose" startled Spanish-speaking customers by proclaiming that the beer would cause diarrhoea. Braniff Airlines translated its slogan "Fly in Leather" so carelessly into Spanish that it read "Fly Naked." Similarly, Eastern Airlines' slogan "We Earn Our Wings Daily" became "We Fly Every Day to Heaven." Even poultry giant Frank Purdue fell victim to poor marketing when his pitch "It Takes a Tough Man To Make a Tender Chicken" was transformed into the Spanish

words reading "A Sexually Excited Man Will Make a Chicken Affectionate" (Helin, 1992).

But cultural relativism introduces problems of its own. If almost any kind of behaviour is the norm *somewhere* in the world, does that mean everything is equally right? Does the fact that some Indian and Moroccan families benefit from having their children work long hours justify child labour?

Since we are all members of a single species, surely there must be some universal standards of proper conduct. But what are they? And in trying to develop them, how can we avoid imposing our own standards on others? There are no simple answers. But when confronting an unfamiliar cultural practice, we should not make judgments before grasping the perspective of the others; at the same time, we should look at our own way of life. After all, what we gain most from studying others is better insight into ourselves.

 Two brief videos present issues of cultural relativism at www.TheSociologyPage.com.

A GLOBAL CULTURE?

Today more than ever before, we can observe many of the same cultural practices the world over. Walking the streets of Seoul, South Korea; Kuala Lumpur, Malaysia; Madras, India; Cairo, Egypt; and Casablanca, Morocco, we see people wearing jeans, hear familiar pop music, and read ads for many of the same products we use in this country. Recall, too, from Global Map 3–1 that English is rapidly emerging as the preferred second language around the world. Are we, therefore, witnessing the birth of a single global culture?

Societies now have more contact with one another than ever before, involving the flow of goods, information, and people:

1. **Global economy: the flow of goods.** International trade has never been greater. The global economy has

spread many of the same consumer goods—from cars and television shows to music and fashions—throughout the world. Canada's $717 billion ($2 billion each day) in imports and exports (Canadian Global Almanac, 2005:224–25) represents tremendous movement of goods and services across our borders.

2. **Global communications: the flow of information**. Satellite-based communications enable people to experience the sights and sounds of events taking place thousands of kilometres away—often as they happen. In Marshall McLuhan's words, this has made us part of an "instantaneous happening," the "global village."

3. **Global migration: the flow of people**. Knowing about the rest of the world motivates people to move to where they imagine life will be better. In addition, today's transportation technology, especially air travel, makes relocating easier than ever before. As a result, in most countries, significant numbers of people were born elsewhere (including about 6 million people in Canada, or 18% of our population [Statistics Canada, 2001 Census, catalogue no. 95F0358XCB2001004]).

These global links make the cultures of the world more similar. But there are three important limitations to the global culture thesis.

• First, the global flow of goods, information, and people is uneven. Generally speaking, urban areas (centres of commerce, communication, and people) have stronger ties to one another, while many rural villages remain unaffected by global movements. In addition, the greater economic and military power of North America and Western Europe means that these regions influence the rest of the world more than the rest of the world influences them.

• Second, the global culture thesis assumes that people everywhere are able to *afford* various new goods and services. As Chapter 12 ("Global Stratification") explains, desperate poverty in much of the world deprives people of even the basic necessities of a safe and secure life.

• Third, while many cultural practices are now found throughout the world, people everywhere do not attach the same meanings to them. Do children in Tokyo draw the same insights from reading the Harry Potter books as their counterparts in Vancouver or Edinburgh? Similarly, we enjoy foods from around the world while knowing little about the lives of the people who created them.

In short, people everywhere still see the world through their own cultural lenses.

Theoretical Analysis of Culture

Sociologists have the special task of understanding how culture helps people make sense of themselves and the

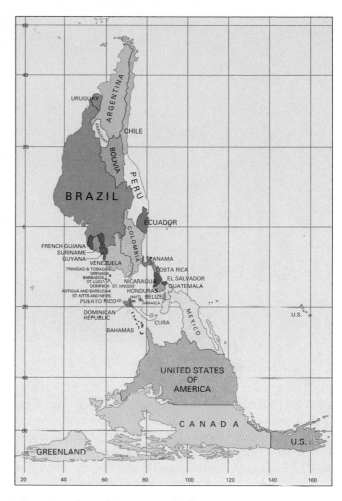

The View from "Down Under"
North America should be "up" and South America "down," right? But because we live on a globe, "up" and "down" have no meaning at all. The reason this map of the western hemisphere looks wrong to us is not that it is geographically inaccurate; it simply violates our ethnocentric assumption that Canada and the United States should be "above" the rest of the Americas.

surrounding world. Here we will examine several macro-level theoretical approaches to understanding culture; a micro-level approach to the personal experience of culture is the focus of Chapter 6 ("Social Interaction in Everyday Life").

THE FUNCTIONS OF CULTURE: STRUCTURAL-FUNCTIONAL ANALYSIS

The structural-functional approach explains culture as a complex strategy for meeting human needs. Borrowing from the philosophical doctrine of *idealism*, this approach considers values to be the core of a culture (Parsons, 1966; Williams, 1970). In other words, cultural values direct our lives, give meaning to what we do, and bind people together. Countless other cultural traits have various functions that support the operation of society.

Following the structural-functional approach, what do you make of the practice of "barn raising," by Amish, Mennonite, or Hutterite communities, in which everyone joins together to raise a family's new barn in a day?

Using a structural-functional approach, let us reconsider the Old Order Mennonite farmer plowing his farm with a team of horses. Within the Mennonite cultural system, rejecting tractors, automobiles, and electricity makes sense because it ensures that there is plenty of hard work. Continuous labour—usually outside the home for men, inside for women—maintains the Mennonite value of discipline, which shapes their way of life. Long days of work, along with meals and recreation at home, define Old Order Mennonite culture and bind family members together. Their rejection of modern technology also has the functions of making them self-sufficient (Fretz, 1989) and minimizing the need to engage with mainstream society. Of course, cultural traits have both functional and dysfunctional consequences. The Old Order Mennonite trait of "shunning," by which people cease social contact with anyone judged to have violated Mennonite mores, generates conformity but also provokes tension and, at the extreme, can cause a serious rift in the community.

If cultures are strategies for meeting human needs, we would expect to find many common patterns around the world. The term **cultural universals** refers to *traits that are part of every known culture*. Comparing hundreds of cultures, George Murdock (1945) identified dozens of cultural universals. One common element is the family, which functions everywhere to control sexual reproduction and to oversee the care of children. Funeral rites, too, are found everywhere, because all human communities cope with the reality of death. Jokes are another cultural universal, serving as a safe means of releasing social tensions.

Critical Review The strength of the structural-functional approach is that it shows how culture operates to meet human needs. Yet by emphasizing a society's dominant cultural patterns, this approach largely ignores cultural diversity. Also, because this approach emphasizes cultural stability, it downplays the importance of change. In short, cultural systems are not as stable or subject to as much agreement as structural functionalism leads us to believe.

INEQUALITY AND CULTURE: SOCIAL-CONFLICT ANALYSIS

The social-conflict approach stresses the link between culture and inequality. Any cultural trait, from this theoretical point of view, benefits some members of society at the expense of others. Why do certain values dominate a society in the first place? Many conflict theorists, especially Marxists, argue that culture is shaped by a society's system of economic production. "It is not the consciousness of men that determines their being," Karl Marx proclaimed; "it is their social being that determines their consciousness" (Marx and Engels, 1978 [orig. 1859]:4). Social-conflict theory, then, is rooted in the philosophical doctrine of *materialism*, which holds that a society's system of material production (such as our own capitalist economy) has a powerful effect on the rest of a culture. This materialist approach contrasts with the idealist leanings of structural functionalism.

Social-conflict analysis ties our cultural values of competitiveness and material success to our country's capitalist economy, which serves the interests of the nation's wealthy elite. The culture of capitalism further teaches us to think that rich and powerful people work harder or longer than others and, therefore, deserve their wealth and privileges. It also encourages us to view capitalism as somehow "natural," discouraging us from trying to reduce economic inequality. Eventually, however, the strains of inequality

Using an evolutionary perspective, sociobiologists explain that different reproductive strategies give rise to a double standard. Men treat women as sexual objects more than women treat men that way. While this may be so, many sociologists counter that behaviour—such as that shown in Ruth Orkin's photograph, *American Girl in Italy*—is more correctly understood as resulting from a culture of male domination.

Copyright 1952, 1980 Ruth Orkin.

erupt into movements for social change. Two examples in Canada are the women's and gay right's movements. Both seek greater equality, and both encounter opposition from defenders of the status quo.

Critical Review The social-conflict approach suggests that cultural systems do not address human needs equally, allowing some people to dominate others. This inequity in turn generates pressure towards change. Yet by stressing the divisiveness of culture, this approach understates the ways that cultural patterns integrate members of society. Therefore, we should consider both social-conflict and structural-functional insights for a fuller understanding of culture.

EVOLUTION AND CULTURE: SOCIOBIOLOGY

We know that culture is a human creation, but does human biology influence how this process unfolds? A third theoretical approach, standing with one leg in biology and one in sociology, is **sociobiology,** *a theoretical approach that explores ways in which human biology affects how we create culture.* Sociobiology rests on the theory of evolution proposed by Charles Darwin in his book *On the Origin of Species* (1968; orig. 1859). Darwin asserted that living organisms change over long periods of time as a result of *natural selection*, a matter of four principles. First, all living things live to reproduce themselves. Second, the blueprint for reproduction is in the genes, which carry traits of one generation into the next. Third, some random variation in genes allows a species to try out new life patterns in a particular environment—allowing some organisms to survive better than others and to pass on their advantageous genes to their offspring. Finally, over thousands of generations, a species *adapts* to its environment, and dominant traits emerge as the "nature" of the organism.

Sociobiologists claim that the existence of a large number of cultural universals reflects the fact that all humans are members of a single biological species. It is our common biology that underlies, for example, the apparently universal "double standard" of sexual behaviour. Sex researcher Alfred Kinsey put it this way: "Among all people everywhere in the world, the male is more likely than the female to desire sex with a variety of partners" (quoted in Barash, 1981:49). But why?

We all know that children result from joining a woman's egg with a man's sperm. But the biological importance of a single sperm and of a single egg is quite different. For a healthy man, sperm represent a "renewable resource" produced by the testes throughout most of his life. A man releases hundreds of millions of sperm in a single ejaculation—technically, enough to fertilize every woman in North America (Barash, 1981:47). A newborn female's ovaries, however, contain her entire lifetime supply of immature eggs. A woman generally releases a single egg cell from her ovaries each month. So, while a man is biologically capable of fathering thousands, a woman can bear only a few children. Given this biological difference, men reproduce their genes most efficiently by being promiscuous—readily engaging in sex. This scheme, however, opposes the reproductive interests of women. Each of a woman's relatively few pregnancies demands that she carry the child for nine months, give birth, and provide care for some time afterwards. Thus, efficient reproduction on the part of the woman depends on carefully selecting a mate whose qualities—beginning with the likelihood that he will stay around—will contribute to their child's survival and, later, successful reproduction.

The double standard certainly involves more than biology and is tangled up with the historical domination of women by men. But sociobiology suggests that this cultural

APPLYING THEORY

CULTURE

	Structural-Functional Approach	Social-Conflict Approach	Sociobiology Approach
What is the level of analysis?	Macro level	Macro level	Macro level
What is culture?	Culture is a system of behaviour by which members of societies co-operate to meet their needs.	Culture is a system that benefits some people and disadvantages others.	Culture is a system of behaviour that is partly shaped by human biology.
What is the foundation of culture?	Cultural patterns are rooted in a society's core values and beliefs.	Cultural patterns are rooted in a society's system of economic production.	Cultural patterns are rooted in humanity's biological evolution.
What core questions does the approach ask?	How does a cultural pattern help society to operate? What cultural patterns are found in all societies?	How does a cultural pattern benefit some people and harm others? How does a cultural pattern support social inequality?	How does a cultural pattern help a species adapt to its environment?

pattern, like many others, has an underlying "bio-logic." Simply put, the double standard exists around the world because biological differences lead women and men everywhere to favour distinctive reproductive strategies.

Critical Review Sociobiology has generated intriguing theories about the biological roots of some cultural patterns. But the approach remains controversial for two main reasons. First, some critics fear that sociobiology may revive biological arguments from a century ago that claimed the superiority of one race or gender. But defenders counter that sociobiology rejects the past pseudoscience of racial superiority; in fact, they say, sociobiology unites all of humanity because all people share a single evolutionary history. Sociobiology does assert that men and women differ biologically in some ways that culture cannot overcome. But far from claiming that males are somehow more important than females, sociobiology emphasizes that both sexes are vital to human reproduction.

Second, say the critics, sociobiologists have little evidence to support their theories. Research to date suggests that biological forces do not determine human behaviour in any rigid sense. Rather, humans *learn* behaviour within a cultural system. The contribution of sociobiology, then, lies in explaining why some cultural patterns seem easier to learn than others (Barash, 1981).

The Applying Theory table (on p. 78) summarizes the main lessons of each theoretical approach about culture. Because any analysis of culture requires a broad focus on the workings of society, these are all macro-level approaches. The symbolic-interaction approach, with its micro-level focus on behaviour in everyday situations, is explored in Chapter 6 ("Social Interaction in Everyday Life").

Culture and Human Freedom

This entire chapter leads us to wonder about an important question: To what extent are human beings, as cultural creatures, free? Does culture bind us to each other and to the past? Or does culture enhance our capacity for individual thought and independent choices?

As symbolic creatures, humans cannot live without culture. But the capacity for culture does have some drawbacks. We may be the only animals who name ourselves, but living in a symbolic world means that we are also the only creatures who experience alienation. In addition, culture is largely a matter of habit, which limits our choices and drives us to repeat troubling patterns, such as racial prejudice and sex discrimination, in each new generation. Our society's emphasis on competitive achievement urges us towards excellence, yet this same pattern also isolates us from one another. Material things comfort us in some ways but divert us from the security and satisfaction that come from close relationships and spiritual strength.

For better or worse, human beings are cultural creatures, just as ants and bees are prisoners of their biology. But there is a crucial difference. Biological instincts create a ready-made world; culture, in contrast, forces us to choose as we make and remake a world for ourselves. No better evidence of this freedom exists than the cultural diversity of our own society and the even greater human diversity around the world.

Princess Diana—free because the world was at her feet and because she transcended any specific culture—was also no stranger to cultural constraints. The Media Perspectives box (p. 79) deals with the death of Princess Diana, who was a cultural icon, in turn constrained or even imprisoned by her own newsworthiness.

MEDIA PERSPECTIVES

The Paparazzi: Villains or Our Eyes to the World?

Paparazzi! The word, which we heard repeatedly in the months following the tragic death of Princess Diana in 1997, is one that only then became part of our active vocabularies. The term comes from the classic film *La Dolce Vita* (1959), directed by Federico Fellini, in which the main character, a journalist, was named Paparazzo.

The paparazzi are freelance photo-journalists who indulge our passion for intimate glimpses into the lives of celebrities by relentlessly stalking them. their goal is to capture private moments on camera. Many celebrities are pursued by the paparazzi, but Diana—the most photographed woman in the world—had experienced more than her share of their attentions. Some of the paparazzi had devoted their whole careers to "doing Di": taking rapid-fire pictures of her was referred to as "banging," "blitzing," "smudging," or "ripping" Di (Lyall and Pogrebin, 1997). The desperate quest for photos of Diana is understood better, perhaps, if one realizes that the right photo could be worth as much as a million dollars.

Princess Diana reached the heights of celebrity partly because of her ambivalent relationship with the media, and the paparazzi in particular. The media propelled Diana—the beautiful, the vulnerable, the good, the irreverent—into the public eye, an outcome that she sometimes seemed to invite. For example, she used the media to present her own point of view, particularly concerning her relationship with her husband Prince Charles and with the rest of the royal family.

But, at the same time, the media made her life a living hell. The cost of celebrity was the loss of her freedom and her privacy. She was stalked by the paparazzi,

You can find a comprehensive Princess Diana site at www.great dreams.com/ princess.htm.

Dr. Esther Konigsberg, a family physician in Burlington, Ontario, responded to the death of Princess Diana with a crusade to get merchants to stop selling the tabloids that publish pictures taken by the paparazzi. She circulated a petition asking consumers, merchants, and advertisers to stop buying, selling, and advertising in the tabloids. Dr. Konigsberg found it personally unsettling to realize that she is "part of a society whose curiosity and fascination with public figures have contributed to the unfortunate events" that led to Diana's death (Whitnell, 1997).

but it was through their work that we came to know her so well. When she died, mourner after mourner would say, "I really felt that I knew her!" This is the kind of intimacy that was predicted by media theorist Marshall McLuhan.

Shortly after Diana's death, the British tabloids collectively suggested their own code of ethics regarding the purchase of paparazzi photos. Her sons, princes William and Harry, were to be off limits until they were adults, and other photos of the private lives of celebrities were to be obtained only with the permission of the subjects. As Prince William approached his eighteenth birthday, *Maclean's* made this event its cover story (Came, 2000). Now he is known as "the reluctant prince" for his aversion to media attention and the perks of royalty.

The terrible accident that killed Princess Diana was the result of speed, alcohol, another car, bad judgment, and the actions of the pursuing paparazzi. There are many who would add that the mass media as a whole and the general public, worldwide, must share responsibility for creating the circumstances that hastened Diana's death. The collective appetite for information about celebrities—the more personal the information, the better—is voracious. To some extent, the paparazzi were merely convenient scapegoats, soon forgotten when the public recovered from the initial shock over Diana's death.

There's a postmodernist explanation for the way in which a British royal was embraced as part of Canada's popular culture—as our "people's princess." Because she went public with her pain and vulnerability and resisted the domination of the royal family, she remained at the margins of royal and aristocratic privilege. Diana's story is an "allegory of post-colonialism" in that her identity is compatible with English Canada's "post-colonial sense of itself as a nation that has emerged from the legacy of its inheritance from Britain and is now an autonomous player on the international stage" (Wilson, 1999:163).

It could be argued that celebrities need media exposure, and perhaps even the paparazzi, to keep them in the spotlight. If "the medium is the message," as Marshall McLuhan suggested, what does the existence of the paparazzi, and the media that support them, say about our culture?

Postscript June 2, 2003, marked fifty years since the coronation of Queen Elizabeth. Since live transatlantic broadcasting was impossible at the time of her coronation, the CBC flew a crew of three to London on a Royal Canadian Air Force jet—with the equipment to develop its film on the flight home. The CBC actually won the race to air its coronation footage against the

continued

better-funded American networks, NBC, ABC, and CBS. Meanwhile, thousands of Canadians were buying their first television just so that they could watch the coronation. This experience allowed them to see, up close, a monarch who previously had been remote. Canadians formed a warm bond with their queen as a result of this new and intimate involvement (Muhtadie, 2003).

In 2006, close to ten years after her death, Princess Diana is still in the news. She is compared to Camilla, the new wife of Prince Charles. Conspiracy theories persist, with various people including members of the royal family allegedly arranging the accident. Stories of cover-ups and botched investigations abound and the results of the French official investigation have been forwarded to Britain's high court.

WHAT DO YOU THINK?

1. Should governments take steps to restrain the activities of paparazzi? What impact could this have on freedom of speech?
2. Why do we buy the magazines and tabloids that publish the paparazzi's pictures? Do we share responsibility for their intrusive activities?
3. Celebrities (North American, European, and Asian) have also experienced harassment at the hands of the paparazzi. Is it fair to encourage intrusion into a star's life—intimate stories and photos—by buying tabloids?

3 MAKING THE GRADE

The following learning tools will help you to see what you know, identify what you still need to learn, and expand your understanding beyond the text. You can also visit this text's Companion Website™ at www.pearsoned.ca/macionis to find useful practice tests.

KEY POINTS

What Is Culture?

Culture is a way of life shared by members of a society. Several species display a limited capacity for culture, but only human beings rely on culture for survival. As the human brain evolved, the first elements of culture appeared some 3 million years ago; culture eventually replaced biological instincts as our species' primary strategy for survival.

The Elements of Culture

Culture relies on symbols to express meaning. Language is the symbolic system by which one generation transmits culture to the next. Values are culturally defined standards of what ought to be; beliefs are statements that people who share a culture hold to be true. Norms, which guide human behaviour, are of two kinds: mores, which have great moral significance, and folkways, which are norms for everyday interaction.

Cultural Diversity

In terms of the cultural backgrounds of its population, Canada is one of the most culturally diverse societies in the world. "High culture" refers to patterns that distinguish a society's elite; "popular culture" refers to widespread social patterns. "Subculture" refers to distinctive cultural patterns supported by some part of a population and "counterculture" to patterns strongly opposed to a conventional way of life. Multiculturalism is an educational effort to encourage an awareness and appreciation of cultural diversity.

Invention, discovery, and diffusion all generate cultural change and cultural diversity. Cultural lag results as some parts of a cultural system change faster than others. Ethnocentrism involves judging others by the standards of one's own culture. By contrast, "cultural relativism" means evaluating another culture according to its own standards. Global cultural patterns result from the worldwide flow of goods, information, and people.

Theoretical Analysis of Culture

Structural-functional analysis views culture as a relatively stable system built on core values; all cultural patterns function to maintain the overall system. The social-conflict approach envisions culture as a dynamic arena of inequality and conflict; cultural patterns benefit some categories of people more than others. Sociobiology studies how humanity's evolutionary past shapes cultural patterns.

Culture and Human Freedom

Culture can limit the choices we make; yet, as cultural creatures, we have the capacity to shape and reshape our world to meet our needs and pursue our dreams.

KEY CONCEPTS

culture (p. 56) the values, beliefs, behaviour, and material objects that together form a people's way of life

nonmaterial culture (p. 56) the ideas created by members of a society

material culture (p. 56) the physical things created by members of a society

culture shock (p. 57) personal disorientation when experiencing an unfamiliar way of life

symbol (p. 60) anything that carries a particular meaning recognized by people who share a culture

language (p. 62) a system of symbols that allows people to communicate with one another

cultural transmission (p. 62) the process by which one generation passes culture to the next

Sapir-Whorf hypothesis (p. 64) the idea that people see and understand the world through the cultural lens of language

values (p. 64) culturally defined standards that people use to decide what is desirable, good, and beautiful, and that serve as broad guidelines for social living

beliefs (p. 64) specific statements that people hold to be true

norms (p. 67) rules and expectations by which a society guides the behaviour of its members

mores (p. 67) norms that are widely observed and have great moral significance

folkways (p. 67) norms for routine or casual interaction

social control (p. 68) attempts by society to regulate people's thoughts and behaviour

ideal culture (p. 68) social patterns mandated by cultural values and norms

real culture (p. 68) actual social patterns that only approximate cultural expectations

technology (p. 69) knowledge that people use to make a way of life in their surroundings

high culture (p. 70) cultural patterns that distinguish a society's elite

popular culture (p. 70) cultural patterns that are widespread among a society's population

subculture (p. 71) cultural patterns that set apart some segment of a society's population

multiculturalism (p. 71) an educational program recognizing the cultural diversity of the United States and promoting the equality of all cultural traditions

Eurocentrism (p. 71) the dominance of European (especially English) cultural patterns

counterculture (p. 72) cultural patterns that strongly oppose those widely accepted within a society

cultural integration (p. 73) the close relationships among various elements of a cultural system

cultural lag (p. 73 the fact that some cultural elements change more quickly than others, disrupting a cultural system

ethnocentrism (p. 73) the practice of judging another culture by the standards of one's own culture

cultural relativism (p. 74) the practice of judging a culture by its own standards

cultural universals (p. 76) traits that are part of every known culture

sociobiology (p. 77) a theoretical approach that explores ways in which human biology affects how we create culture

APPLICATIONS & EXERCISES

1. New words are created all the time. What was going on in North America that helps explain the creation of the following new words (Herzog, 2004): sweatshop (1892), motel (1925), supermarket (1933), teenager (1938), workaholic (1971), couch potato (1976), and soccer mom (1996)?

2. Find someone on campus who has lived in another country, and ask how the culture of that society differs from ours. How does the perspective of your informant differ from those who have lived here all their lives?

3. Watch an animated Disney film, such as *Finding Nemo*, *The Lion King*, *The Little Mermaid*, *Aladdin*, or *Pocahontas*. One reason for the popularity of these films is that they all share cultural themes. How does the film you selected reflect Canadian cultural values?

PRENTICE HALL
mysoclab
Where learning & the sociological imagination intersect.

To reinforce your understanding of this chapter, and to identify topics for further study, visit MySocLab at **www.pearsoned.ca/mysoclab/** for diagnostic tests and a multimedia ebook.

CHAPTER FOUR

Society

What factors shape society?

Why do societies change?

How have Karl Marx, Max Weber, and
Emile Durkheim increased our understanding
of modern societies?

What is it about Canadian society that is so intriguing? Is it the dilemmas and problems of a society created by wide open spaces? Is it the reality of being a relatively young society in spite of some longevity? Is it the search for common ground among a far-flung, diverse, and changing population? Is it the sense of belonging together that persists in spite of crises that threaten to tear the society apart?

It may seem ironic indeed that even though the Canadian state is over 130 years old, the precise nature of Canadian society and its existence as an entity are still in question. In fact, the stormy years after the centennial birthday in 1967 suggested more than ever that the concept of a Canadian society could not be taken for granted. While Quebec was contemplating what degree of distance from the rest of Canadian society was most appropriate, the Symons Report was concluding that Canadians knew little about their own society, and a federal Task Force on Canadian Unity was scouring the country for clues about ways to create a more integrated and cohesive society. More recently, the failure of the Meech Lake accord and the Charlottetown accord with their "distinct Quebec society" ideas, as well as the anxieties produced by two Quebec referendums (and now the threat of a third referendum), continued to point out the fragility of national unity. What kind of society is this that has been problematic for so long?

Source: Excerpted from Hiller (1996):1–2.

The societies that exist around the world can be quite different from our own. But what is a society? What makes societies different? How and why do they change over time? **Society** refers to *people who interact in a defined territory and share a culture*. In this chapter, we discuss human societies with the help of four important sociologists. We begin with the approach of Gerhard Lenski, who describes how societies have changed over the past 10 000 years. Lenski points to the importance of technology in shaping any society. Then we turn to three of sociology's founders. Karl Marx, like Lenski, took a long historical view of societies. But Marx's story of society is all about social conflict that arises from how people work within an economic system to produce material goods. Max Weber tells a different tale, showing that the power of *ideas* shapes society. Weber contrasted the traditional thinking of simple societies with the rational thought that dominates complex societies today. Finally, Emile Durkheim helps us see the different ways that traditional and modern societies hang together.

All four visions of society answer a number of important questions: What makes the way of life of people such as the Tuareg of the Sahara so different from your life as a college student in Canada? How and why do all societies change? What forces divide a society? What forces hold a society together? This chapter will provide answers to all of these questions as we look at the work of important sociologists.

Gerhard Lenski: Society and Technology

Members of our society—who take instant messaging and television, as well as schools and hospitals, for granted—

To learn more about Lenski's work, visit www.faculty.rsu.edu/~felwell/Theorists/Lenski/Index.htm.

must wonder at the nomads of the Sahara, who live more or less the same simple life their ancestors did centuries ago. The work of Gerhard Lenski (Nolan and Lenski, 2004) helps us understand the great differences among societies that have existed throughout human history.

Lenski uses the term **sociocultural evolution** to mean *changes that occur as a society gains new technology*. Societies with the simplest technology have little control over nature, so they can support only a small number of people. Societies with complex technology such as cars and cell phones, while not necessarily better, support hundreds of millions of people in far more affluent ways of life.

Inventing or adopting new technology sends ripples of change throughout a society. When our ancestors first discovered how to use wind to move a boat using a sail, they created a device that would take them to new lands, greatly expand their economy, and increase their military power. In

→ **YOUR TURN** ←

Which of the items mentioned below would most amaze your great-grandmother? Why do you think so?

In technologically simple societies, successful hunting of large game wins men great praise. However, foraging by women is a more dependable and easily available source of nutrition.

addition, the more technology a society has, the faster it changes. Technologically simple societies change very slowly; so that even today their members live more or less the life of their ancestors. How many Canadians can say that they live the way their grandparents or great-grandparents did? Modern, high-technology societies, such as our own, change so fast that individuals will experience major social changes during their lives. Imagine how surprised your great-grandmother would be to hear about beepers and instant messaging, computer matchmaking and telephone sex, artificial hearts and test-tube babies, space shuttles and smart bombs.

Drawing on Lenski's work, we will describe five types of societies, defined by their technology: hunter/gatherer, horticultural and pastoral, agrarian, industrial, and post-industrial societies.

HUNTER/GATHERER SOCIETIES

In the simplest of all societies, people live by **hunting and gathering,** *the use of simple tools to hunt animals and gather vegetation.* From the time that our species appeared three million years ago until about 12 000 years ago, all humans were hunters and gatherers. Even in 1800, many hunter/gatherer societies could be found around the world. But today just a few remain, such as the Aka and Baka of Central Africa, the Basarwa (or San) of Botswana, and the Batek and Semai of Malaysia. Many Aboriginal peoples in Canada, and the Aborigines of Australia, retain their hunter/gatherer traditions, although they no longer rely solely on subsistence as a way of life.

With little ability to control their environment, hunters and gatherers spend most of their time looking for game and collecting plants to eat. Only in lush areas with lots of food do hunters and gatherers have much free time. Because it takes a large amount of land to support even a few people, hunter/gatherer societies tend to stay together in extended family groups of just a few dozen members. They must also be nomadic, moving on to find new sources of vegetation or to follow migrating animals. Although they may return to favoured sites, they rarely form permanent settlements.

Hunter/gatherer societies depend on the family to do many things. The family must get and distribute food, protect its members, and teach the children. Everyone's life is much the same; people spend most of their time getting their next meal. Age and gender have some effect on what individuals do. Healthy adults do most of the work, leaving the very young and the very old to help out as they can. Women gather vegetation as well as fish, small mammals, and birds—which provides most of the food, while men take on the less certain job of hunting large game. While men and women perform different tasks, most hunters and gatherers probably see the sexes as having about the same socioeconomic importance (Leacock, 1978). Hunter/gatherer societies usually have a shaman, or spiritual leader, who enjoys high prestige but has to work to find food like everyone else. In short, people in hunter/gatherer societies come close to being socially equal.

Hunters and gatherers use simple tools—the spear, the bow and arrow, and the bone or stone knife—but rarely as weapons to wage war. Their real enemy is the forces of nature: storms and droughts can kill off their food supply, and there is little they can do for someone who has a serious accident or illness. Being at risk in this way encourages people to co-operate and share, a strategy that raises everyone's chances of survival. But the truth is that many die in childhood, and no more than half reach the age of twenty (Lenski, et al., 1995:104).

During the past century, societies with more powerful technology have closed in on the few remaining hunters and gatherers, using their lands for other purposes and reducing their food supply. As a result, hunter/gatherer societies are disappearing from Earth. However, study of this way of life has given us valuable information about human history and our basic ties to the natural world.

What would it be like to live in a society with simple technology? That's the premise of the television show *Survivor*. What advantages do societies with simple technology afford their members? What disadvantages do you see?

YOUR TURN

What are some of the important lessons we can learn from studying hunter/gatherer societies?

HORTICULTURAL AND PASTORAL SOCIETIES

About 10 000 to 12 000 years ago, as the timeline inside the front cover shows, a new technology began to change the lives of human beings. People discovered **horticulture,** *the use of hand tools to raise crops.* Using a hoe to work the soil and a digging stick to punch holes in the ground to plant seeds may not seem like something that would change the world, but these inventions allowed people to give up gathering in favour of growing their own food. The first humans to plant gardens lived in fertile regions of the Middle East. Soon after, cultural diffusion spread this knowledge to Latin America and Asia and eventually all over the world.

Not all societies were quick to give up hunting and gathering for horticulture. Hunters and gatherers living where food was plentiful probably saw little reason to change their ways. People living in dry regions (such as the Sahara in western Africa) or mountainous areas found little use for horticulture because they could not grow much anyway. Such people, including the Saharan Tuareg, were more likely to adopt **pastoralism,** *the domestication of animals.* Today, societies that mix horticulture and pastoralism can be found throughout South America, Africa, and Asia.

Growing plants and raising animals greatly increased food production, so populations expanded to hundreds of people in one location. Pastoralists remained nomadic, leading their herds to fresh grazing lands, but horticulturists formed settlements, moving only when the soil gave out. Joined by trade, these settlements formed societies with populations reaching into the thousands.

Once a society is capable of producing a *material surplus*—more resources than are needed to support the population—not everyone has to work at providing food. Greater specialization results: some people make crafts, while others engage in trade, cut hair, apply tattoos, or serve as priests. Compared to hunter/gatherer societies, horticultural and pastoral societies are more socially diverse. But being more productive does not make a society better. As some families produce more than others, they become richer and more powerful. Horticultural and pastoral societies have greater inequality, with elites using government power—and military force—to serve their own interests. But leaders do not have the ability to communicate or to travel over large distances, so they can control only a small number of people, rather than vast empires.

Religion also differs among types of societies. Hunters and gatherers are likely to believe that many spirits inhabit the world. Horticulturists, however, are more likely to think of one God as Creator. Pastoral societies carry this belief further, seeing God as directly involved in the well-being of the entire world. This view of God (in, for example, "The Lord is my shepherd" [Psalm 23]) is common among members of our own society because Christianity, Islam, and Judaism all began in pastoral societies of the Middle East.

AGRARIAN SOCIETIES

About 5000 years ago, another revolution in technology was taking place in the Middle East, one that would change the entire world. This was the development of **agriculture,** *large-scale cultivation using plows harnessed to animals or more powerful energy sources.* So important was the invention of the animal-drawn plow, along with other breakthroughs of the period—including irrigation, the wheel, writing, numbers, and the use of various metals—that this moment in history is often called "the dawn of civilization."

Using animal-drawn plows, farmers could cultivate fields far bigger than the garden-sized plots planted by horticulturists. Plows have the added advantage of turning and aerating the soil, making it more fertile. As a result, farmers could work the same land for generations, encouraging the development of permanent settlements. With the ability to grow a surplus of food and to transport goods using animal-powered wagons, agrarian societies greatly expanded in size and population. About 100 C.E., for example, the agrarian Roman Empire contained some 70 million people spread throughout 5.2 million square kilometres (2 million square miles) (Nolan and Lenski, 2004).

Greater production meant even more specialization. Now there are dozens and dozens of distinct occupations, from farmers to builders to metalworkers. With so many people producing so many different things, people invented money as a common standard of exchange, and the old barter system—by which people traded one thing for another—was abandoned.

Agrarian societies have extreme social inequality, typically more than modern societies such as our own. In most cases, a large share of the people are peasants or slaves, who do most of the work. Elites therefore have time for more refined activities, including the study of philosophy, art, and literature. (This explains the historical link between high culture and social privilege noted in Chapter 3.)

Among hunter/gatherers and also among horticulturists, women provide most of the food, which gives them socioeconomic importance. Agriculture, however, raises men to a position of social dominance. Using the metal plow pulled by large animals, men take charge of food production in agrarian societies. Women are left with the support tasks, such as weeding and carrying water to the fields (Boulding, 1976; Fisher, 1979).

In agrarian societies, religion reinforces the power of elites by defining both loyalty and hard work as moral obligations. Many of the "wonders" of the ancient world, such as the Great Walls of China and the Great Pyramids of Egypt, were possible only because emperors and pharaohs had almost absolute power and were able to control a large political system and order their people to work for a lifetime without pay. By comparison with hunter/gatherer, pastoralist, and horticulturist societies, agrarian societies have the most social inequality. Agrarian technology also gives people a greater range of life choices, which is the reason that agrarian societies differ more from one another than horticultural and pastoral societies do.

Learn more about the wonders of ancient Mediterranean societies at http://ce.eng.usf.edu/pharos/wonders/list.html.

INDUSTRIAL SOCIETIES

Industrialism, which first took hold in the rich nations of today's world, is *the production of goods using advanced sources of energy to drive large machinery.* Until the industrial era began, the major source of energy had been the muscles of humans and the animals they tended. Around the year 1750, people used water power, then steam boilers to operate mills and factories filled with larger and larger machines. Industrial technology gave people such power over their environment that change took place faster than ever before. It is probably correct to say that the new indus-

Of Egypt's 130 pyramids, the Great Pyramids at Giza are the largest. Each of the three major structures stands more than 40 storeys high and is composed of 3 million massive stone blocks. Some 4500 years ago, tens of thousands of people laboured to construct these pyramids so that the pharaoh might have a godlike monument for his tomb. Clearly social inequality in this agrarian society was striking.

trial societies changed more in one century than they had over the course of the previous thousand years. As explained in Chapter 1 ("The Sociological Perspective"), change was so rapid that it sparked the birth of sociology itself. By 1900, railways crossed the land, steamships travelled the seas, and steel-framed skyscrapers reached far higher than any of the old cathedrals that symbolized the agrarian age.

But that was only the beginning. Soon after, automobiles allowed people to move quickly almost anywhere, and electricity powered homes full of such modern conveniences as refrigerators, washing machines, air conditioners, and audio-visual entertainment centres. Electronic communication—beginning with the telegraph and the telephone and followed by radio and television—gave people the ability to reach others instantly, all over the world.

SUMMING UP

Sociocultural Evolution

Type of Society	Historical Period	Productive Technology	Population Size
Hunter/Gatherer Societies	Only type of society until about 12 000 years ago; still common several centuries ago; the few examples remaining today are threatened with extinction.	Primitive tools	25–40 people (scattered extended families)
Horticultural and Pastoral Societies	From about 12 000 years ago, with decreasing numbers after about 3000 B.C.E.	Horticultural societies use hand tools for cultivating plants; pastoral societies are based on the domestication of animals.	Settlements of several hundred people, connected through trading ties to form societies of several thousand people.
Agrarian Societies	From about 5000 years ago, with large but decreasing numbers today	Animal-drawn plow	Millions of people
Industrial Societies	From about 1750 to the present	Advanced sources of energy; mechanized production	Millions of people
Post-industrial Societies	Emerging in recent decades	Computers that support an information-based economy	Millions of people

Work also changed. In agrarian communities, most men and women worked in the home or in the fields nearby. Industrialization drew people away from home to factories situated near energy sources (such as coalfields) that power their machinery. The result is that workers lost close working relationships, strong family ties, and many of the traditional values, beliefs, and customs that guide agrarian life. With industrialization, occupational specialization became greater than ever. Today, the kind of work people do has a lot to do with their standard of living, so people now often size up one another in terms of their jobs rather than according to their family ties, as historically earlier people did. Rapid change and people's tendency to move for employment also make social life more anonymous, increase cultural diversity, and promote subcultures and countercultures, as described in Chapter 3 ("Culture").

Industrial technology changes the family, too, reducing its traditional importance as the centre of social life. No longer does the family serve as the main setting for work, learning, and religious worship. As Chapter 18 ("Family") explains, technological change also plays a part in making families more diverse, with a greater share of single people, divorced people, single-parent families, and stepfamilies.

Perhaps the greatest effect of industrialization has been to raise living standards, which increased fivefold in North America over the past century. Although at first it only benefits the elite few, industrial technology is so much more productive that incomes in general rise over time, and people throughout society have longer and more comfortable lives. Even social inequality decreases slightly, as explained in Chapter 10 ("Social Stratification"), because industrial societies provide extended schooling and greater political rights. Around the world, industrialization has had the effect of increasing the demand for a greater political voice—a pattern evident in South Korea, Taiwan, China, the nations of Eastern Europe, and the former Soviet Union.

POST-INDUSTRIAL SOCIETIES

Many industrial societies, including Canada, have now entered another phase of technological development, and we can extend Lenski's analysis to take account of recent trends. A generation ago, the sociologist Daniel Bell (1973) coined the term **post-industrialism** to refer to *technology that supports an information-based economy*. As noted in Chapter 3 ("Culture"), production in industrial societies centres on factories and machinery generating material goods; today, post-industrial production relies on computers and other electronic devices that create, process, store, and apply information. Just as people in industrial

SOCIOLOGY @ WORK

Settlement Pattern	Social Organization	Examples
Nomadic	Family-centred; specialization limited to age and sex; little social inequality	Baka of Central Africa Basarwa (San) of Botswana Semai of Malaysia
Horticulturalists form small permanent settlements; pastoralists are nomadic	Family-centred; religious system begins to develop; moderate specialization; increased social inequality	Middle Eastern societies about 5000 B.C.E Various societies today in New Guinea and other Pacific islands Yąnomamö today in Brazil
Cities become common, but they generally contain only a small proportion of the population.	Family loses significance as distinct religious, political, and economic systems emerge; extensive specialization; increased social inequality	Egypt during construction of the Great Pyramids Mediaeval Europe Numerous predominantly agrarian societies of the world today
Cities contain most of the population	Distinct religious, political, economic, educational, and family systems; highly specialized; marked social inequality persists, lessening somewhat over time	Societies today in Europe and North America, Australia, and Asia, which generate most of the world's industrial production
Population remains concentrated in cities	Similar to industrial societies, with information processing and other service work gradually replacing industrial production	Industrial societies noted above are now entering the post-industrial stage

societies learn mechanical skills, people in post-industrial societies develop information-based skills and carry out their work using computers and other forms of high-technology communication. As Chapter 16 ("The Economy and Work") explains, a post-industrial society uses less and less of its labour force for industrial production. At the same time, more jobs become available for clerical workers, teachers, writers, sales managers, and marketing representatives, all of whom process information.

The information revolution, which is at the heart of post-industrial society, is most evident in rich nations, yet new information technology affects the whole world. As discussed in Chapter 3 ("Culture"), a worldwide flow of goods, people, and information now links societies and has advanced a global culture. In this sense, the post-industrial society is at the heart of globalization.

The Summing Up table (on pp. 88–89) reviews how technology shapes societies at different stages of sociocultural evolution.

THE LIMITS OF TECHNOLOGY

More complex technology has made life better by raising productivity, reducing infectious disease, and sometimes just relieving boredom. But technology provides no quick fix for social problems. Poverty, for example, remains a reality for millions of women and men in Canada (detailed in Chapter 11, "Social Class in Canada" and a billion people worldwide (see Chapter 12, "Global Stratification").

Technology also creates new problems that our ancestors could hardly imagine. Industrial and post-industrial societies give us more personal freedom, but often we lack the sense of community that was part of pre-industrial life. Further, while technology can be used for good, the most powerful nations in the world today have stockpiles of nuclear weapons that could send the world back to the Stone Age—if anyone survived at all. Advancing technology has also threatened the physical environment. Each stage in sociocultural evolution has introduced more powerful sources of energy and increased the appetite for Earth's resources. Ask yourself whether we can continue to pursue material prosperity without permanently damaging our planet. (See Chapter 22, "Population, Urbanization, and Environment.")

In some ways, technological advances have improved life and brought the world's people closer. But establishing peace, ensuring justice, and protecting the environment are problems that technology alone cannot solve. Take a look at one author's attempt to envision an ideal but modern society in the Thinking It Through box (on p. 91).

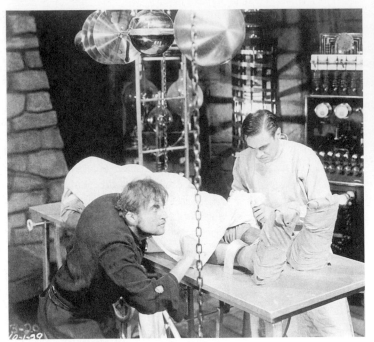

Does advancing technology make society better? In some ways, perhaps. However, many films—as far back as *Frankenstein* in 1931 (*left*) and as recently as *Minority Report* in 2002 (*right*)—have expressed the concern that new technology not only solves old problems but creates new ones. All the sociological theorists discussed in this chapter shared this ambivalent view of the modern world.

YOUR TURN

Why do you think many people are quick to see the advantages of advancing technology but slow to see its negative consequences? Take the cellphone as an example.

Karl Marx: Society and Conflict

The first of our classic visions of society comes from Karl Marx (1818–83), an early giant in the field of sociology whose influence continues even today. A keen observer of how the Industrial Revolution changed Europe, Marx spent most of his adult life in London, the capital of what was then the vast British Empire. He was awed by the size and productive power of the new factories going up all over Britain. Along with other industrial nations, Great Britain was producing more goods than ever before, drawing resources from around the world and churning out products at a dizzying rate.

 Visit the Dead Sociologists' Society to learn more about Marx: www2.pfeiffer.edu/~lridener/DSS/index.html.

What astounded Marx even more was how the riches produced by this new technology ended up in the hands of only a few people. As he walked around the city of London, he could see for himself how a handful of aristocrats and industrialists lived in fabulous mansions staffed by servants, where they enjoyed both luxury and privilege. At the same time, most people laboured long hours for low wages and lived in slums. Some even slept in the streets, where they were likely to die young from diseases brought on by cold and poor nutrition. Marx saw his society in terms of a basic contradiction: In a country so rich, how could so many people be so poor? Just as important, he asked, how can this situation be changed? Many people think Karl Marx set out to tear societies apart. But he was motivated by compassion and wanted to help a badly divided society create a new and just social order.

At the heart of Marx's thinking is the idea of **social conflict,** *the struggle between segments of society over valued resources.* Social conflict can, of course, take many forms: individuals quarrel, colleges have long-standing sports rivalries, and nations go to war. For Marx, however, the most important type of social conflict was class conflict arising from the way a society produces material goods.

SOCIETY AND PRODUCTION

Living in the nineteenth century, Marx observed the early decades of industrial capitalism in Europe. This economic system, Marx explained, turned a small part of the population into **capitalists,** *people who own and operate factories and other businesses in pursuit of profits.* A capitalist tries to make a profit by selling a product for more than it costs to produce. Capitalism turns most of the population into industrial workers, whom Marx called **proletarians,** *people who sell their labour for wages.* To Marx, a system of capitalist production always ends up creating conflict between capitalists and workers. To keep profits high, capitalists keep wages low. But workers want higher wages. Since profits and wages come from the same pool of funds, the result is conflict. As Marx saw it, this conflict could end only with the end of capitalism itself.

THINKING IT THROUGH
Can Sociology Help Us To Design a Better Society?

If sociology is of any value, it should help us to deal with social problems. Taking that thought further, sociology should allow us to design a better society. Karl Marx thought he knew how to create a classless society; various utopians have offered their versions of perfect societies. According to University of Guelph professor Ken Menzies, the trick is designing a better society that will work—one that ultimately can reproduce or perpetuate itself without losing sight of its core values.

Applying theoretical and empirical knowledge of societal dynamics, Menzies is writing a book entitled *The People-Serving Society*. The result of a "thought experiment," the book fleshes out the design of a society based on liberal, social democratic values. The result is not a perfect society, because creating a society that *works* requires making compromises that detract from perfection. Also, one of the underlying values is that of providing freedom of choice—and, wherever there is choice, some people will choose evil or wrongdoing. Of course, the political and legal framework of the society will have to discourage or prohibit some behaviours.

Within the context of a liberal, social democratic society, the people-serving society will attempt to deliver freedom, equality, and justice to all citizens. To achieve this goal, the society's political, legal, educational and economic institutions must work together in relative harmony and equilibrium. This kind of total system approach is necessary because spot reduction of social problems does not work.

Menzies' society is based on an innovating or rapidly changing market economy that embraces technology. The goal of his society is to make sure that everyone, on the basis of his or her skills or aptitudes, has access to appropriate opportunities. The educational institutions need to be flexible enough to provide access to initial education and training as well as regular upgrading for people who want to move up the occupational hierarchy.

Underlying this thought experiment is the assumption that only by making use of the theories and findings of modern social science—with its wide scope and complexity—can one come up with a credible vision of where we should be as a society.

WHAT DO YOU THINK?

1. Is it possible to create a classless society as Marx believed? Can there be social classes in a society that values equality?
2. Once you've designed a better society, what's the next step in turning your dream into reality?
3. Given geographic space and people "imported" from elsewhere, what does it take to create your better society?

Source: Based on Menzies ([n.d.])

All societies are composed of **social institutions,** *the major spheres of social life, or societal subsystems, organized to meet human needs.* Examples of social institutions include the economy, political system, family, religion, and education. In his analysis of society, Marx argued that one institution—the economy—dominates all the others and defines the true nature of a society. Drawing on the philosophical approach called *materialism*, which says that how humans produce material goods shapes their experiences, Marx believed that the other social institutions all operate in a way that supports a society's economy. Lenski focused on how technology moulds a society, but Marx argued that the economy is a society's "real foundation" (1959 [orig. 1859]:43).

Marx viewed the economic system as society's *infrastructure* (*infra* is Latin, meaning "below"). Other social institutions, including the family, the political system, and religion, are built on this foundation, form society's *superstructure*, and support the economy. Marx's theory is illustrated in Figure 4–1. For example, under capitalism, the legal system protects capitalists' wealth just as the family allows capitalists to pass their property from one generation to the next.

Marx was well aware that most people living in industrial/capitalist societies do not see how capitalism shapes the entire operation of their society. Most people, in fact, see the right to own private property or pass it on to children as natural. In the same way, many of us tend to see rich people as having earned their money through long years of schooling and hard work; we might see the poor, on the other hand, as lacking skills and the personal drive to make more of themselves. Marx rejected this type of thinking, calling it **false consciousness,** *explanations of social problems as the shortcomings of individuals rather than as the flaws of society.* Marx was saying, in effect, that it is the system of capitalist production and not people who make society so unequal. False consciousness, he continued, hurts people by hiding the real cause of their problems.

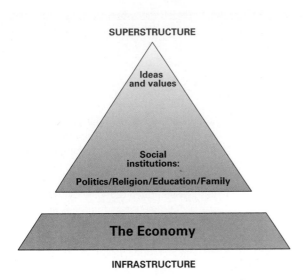

SUPERSTRUCTURE

Ideas
and values

Social
institutions:

Politics/Religion/Education/Family

The Economy

INFRASTRUCTURE

FIGURE 4-1 Karl Marx's Model of Society

This diagram illustrates Marx's materialist view that the system of economic production shapes the entire society. Economic production involves both technology and social relationships—for capitalism, the relationships involve the capitalists, who own the factories and businesses, and the workers, who are the source of labour. On this infrastructure, or foundation, rests society's superstructure, which includes its major social institutions as well as core cultural values and ideas. Marx maintained that every part of a society supports the economic system.

CONFLICT AND HISTORY

For Marx, conflict is the engine that drives social change. Sometimes societies change at a slow, *evolutionary* rate, but they may erupt in rapid, *revolutionary change*. To Marx, early hunters and gatherers formed primitive communist societies. *Communism* is a system by which people commonly own and equally share the food and other things they produce. People in hunter/gatherer societies do not have much, but they share what they have. In addition, because everyone does the same kind of work, there is little chance of social conflict.

With technological advance comes social inequality. Among horticultural, pastoral, and early agrarian societies—which Marx lumped together as the "ancient world"—warfare was frequent, and the victors made their captives slaves. Agriculture brings still more wealth to a society's elite but does little for most other people, who labour as serfs and are barely better off than slaves. As Marx saw it, the state supported the feudal system, in which the elite or nobility had all the power, assisted by the church, which claimed that this arrangement was God's will. This is why Marx thought that feudalism was simply "exploitation,

veiled by religious and political illusions" (Marx and Engels, 1972 [orig. 1848]:337).

Gradually, new productive forces started to break down the feudal order. As trade steadily increased, cities grew, and merchants and skilled craftspeople formed the new capitalist class or *bourgeoisie* (a French word meaning "people of the town"). After 1800, the bourgeoisie also controlled factories, becoming richer and richer so that they soon rivalled the ancient landowning nobility. For their part, the nobles looked down their noses at this upstart commercial class, but, in time, these capitalists took control of European societies. To Marx's way of thinking, then, new technology was only part of the Industrial Revolution; it also served as a class revolution in which capitalists overthrew the old agrarian elite.

Industrialization also led to the growth of the proletariat. English landowners converted fields once plowed by serfs into grazing land for sheep to produce wool for the textile mills. Forced from the land, millions of people migrated to cities to work in factories. Marx envisioned these workers one day joining together to form a revolutionary class that would overthrow the capitalist system.

CAPITALISM AND CLASS CONFLICT

"The history of all hitherto existing society is the history of class struggles": with these words, Marx and his collaborator Friedrich Engels began their best-known statement, the *Manifesto of the Communist Party* (1972 [1848]:335). Industrial capitalism, like earlier types of society, contains two major social classes—the ruling class, whose members (capitalists or bourgeoisie) own productive property, and the oppressed (proletarians), who sell their labour—reflecting the two basic positions in the productive system. Like masters and slaves in the ancient world, and like nobles and serfs in feudal systems, capitalists and proletarians are engaged in class conflict today. Currently, as in the past, one class controls the other as productive property. Marx used the term **class conflict** (and sometimes class struggle) to refer to *conflict between entire classes over the distribution of a society's wealth and power.*

Class conflict is nothing new. What distinguishes the conflict in capitalist society, Marx pointed out, is how out in the open it is. Agrarian nobles and serfs, for all their differences, were bound together by traditions and mutual obligations. Industrial capitalism dissolved those ties so that loyalty and honour were replaced by naked self-interest. Because the proletarians had no personal ties to the capitalists, Marx saw no reason for them to put up with their oppression. Marx knew that revolution still would not come easily. First, workers must become aware of their oppression and see capitalism as its true cause. Second, they must organize and act to address their problems. This means that false consciousness must be replaced with **class consciousness,** *workers' recognition of themselves as a class unified in* *opposition to capitalists and ultimately to capitalism itself.* Because the inhumanity of early capitalism was plain for him to see, Marx concluded that industrial workers would soon rise up to destroy this economic system.

How would the capitalists react? Their wealth made them strong. But Marx saw a weakness in the capitalist armour. Motivated by a desire for personal gain, capitalists feared competition with other capitalists. Marx predicted, therefore, that capitalists would be slow to band together despite their common interests. In addition, he reasoned, capitalists kept employees' wages low in order to maximize profits, which made the workers' misery grow ever greater. In the long run, Marx believed, capitalists would bring about their own undoing.

CAPITALISM AND ALIENATION

Marx also condemned capitalist society for producing **alienation,** *the experience of isolation and misery resulting from powerlessness.* To the capitalists, workers are nothing more than a source of labour, to be hired and fired at will. Dehumanized by their jobs (i.e., repetitive factory work in the past and processing orders on a computer today), workers find little satisfaction and feel unable to improve their situation. Here we see another contradiction of capitalist society: as people develop technology to gain power over the world, the capitalist economy gains more control over people.

Marx noted four ways in which capitalism alienates workers:

1. *Alienation from the act of working.* Ideally, people work to meet their needs and to develop their personal potential. Capitalism, however, denies workers a say in what they make or how they make it. Further, much of the work is a constant repetition of routine tasks. The fact that today we replace workers with machines whenever possible would not have surprised Marx. As far as he was concerned, capitalism had turned human beings into machines long ago.

2. *Alienation from the products of work.* The product of work belongs not to workers but to capitalists, who sell it for profit. Thus, Marx reasoned, the more of themselves workers invest in their work, the more they lose.

3. *Alienation from other workers.* Through work, Marx claimed, people build bonds of community. Industrial capitalism, however, makes work competitive rather than co-operative, setting each person apart from everyone else and offering little chance for human companionship.

4. *Alienation from human potential.* Industrial capitalism alienates workers from their human potential. Marx argued that a worker "does not fulfil himself in his work but denies himself, has a feeling of misery rather

Karl Marx—shown here at work on the *Manifesto of the Communist Party* with his friend, benefactor, and collaborator Friedrich Engels—was surely the pioneering sociologist who had the greatest influence on the world as a whole. Through the second half of the last century, one billion people—nearly one-fifth of humanity—lived in societies organized on Marxist principles.

than well-being, does not freely develop his physical and mental energies, but is physically exhausted and mentally debased. The worker, therefore, feels himself to be at home only during his leisure time, whereas at work he feels homeless" (1964a [orig. 1844]:124–25). In short, industrial capitalism turns an activity that should express the best qualities in human beings into a dull and dehumanizing experience.

Marx viewed alienation, in its various forms, as a barrier to social change. But he hoped that industrial workers would overcome their alienation by uniting into a true social class, aware of the cause of their problems and ready to change society.

⟶   YOUR TURN   ⟵

Can you think of workplace settings that do not produce alienation? What are they, and what makes them better?

The 2004 film, *The Motorcycle Diaries*, tells the story of the motorcycle journey through South America of Che Guevara. Seeing such desperate poverty inspired Guevara to become a Marxist and fight for revolutionary change. He went on to play an important role in the Cuban Revolution.

YOUR TURN

Sociologists sometimes say that Weber's work is "a debate with the ghost of Karl Marx." Thinking of their basic approaches, can you explain why?

REVOLUTION

The only way out of the trap of capitalism, argued Marx, is to remake society. He imagined a system of production that could provide for the social needs of all. He called this system *socialism*. Although Marx knew that such a dramatic change would not come easily, he must have been disappointed that he did not live to see workers in England rise up. Still, convinced that capitalism was a social evil, he believed that in time the working majority would realize they held the key to a better future. This change would certainly be revolutionary and perhaps even violent. Marx believed a socialist society would bring class conflict to an end. Chapter 10 ("Social Stratification") explains more about changes in industrial-capitalist societies since Marx's time and why the revolution he wanted never took place. In addition, as Chapter 17 ("Politics and Government") explains, Marx failed to foresee that the revolution he imagined could take the form of repressive regimes—such as Stalin's government in the Soviet Union—that would end up killing tens of millions of people (Hamilton, 2001). But in his own time, Marx looked towards the future with hope: "The proletarians have nothing to lose but their chains. They have a world to win" (Marx and Engels, 1972 [orig. 1848]:362).

Max Weber: The Rationalization of Society

With a wide knowledge of law, economics, religion, and history, Max Weber (1864–1920) produced what many

To learn more about Weber, go to www.faculty.rsu.edu/~felwell/ Theorists/Weber/Whome.htm.

experts regard as the greatest individual contribution to sociology. This scholar, born to a prosperous family in Germany, had much to say about how modern society differs from earlier types of social organization.

Weber understood the power of technology, and he shared many of Marx's ideas about social conflict. But he disagreed with Marx's philosophy of materialism. Weber's philosophical approach, called *idealism*, emphasized how human ideas—especially beliefs and values—shape society. He argued that societies differ not in terms of how people produce things but in how people think about the world. In Weber's view, modern society was the product of a new way of thinking.

Weber compared societies in different times and places. To make the comparisons, he relied on the **ideal type,** *an abstract statement of the essential characteristics of any social phenomenon.* Following Weber's approach, for example, we might speak of pre-industrial and industrial societies as ideal types. The use of the word "ideal" does not mean that one or the other is good or better. Nor does an ideal type refer to any actual society. Rather, think of an "ideal" type as a way of defining a type of society in its pure form. We have already used ideal types in comparing hunter/gatherer societies with industrial societies, and capitalism with socialism.

TWO WORLD VIEWS: TRADITION AND RATIONALITY

Rather than categorizing societies according to their technology or productive systems, Weber focused on ways people think about their world: members of pre-industrial societies are bound by tradition, and people in industrial-capitalist societies are guided by *rationality*. By **tradition,** Weber meant *values and beliefs passed from generation to generation.* In other words, traditional people are guided by the past. They consider particular actions right and proper mostly because they have been accepted for so long. People in modern societies, however, favour **rationality,** *a way of thinking that emphasizes deliberate, matter-of-fact calculation of the most efficient way to accomplish a particular task.* Sentimental ties to the past have no place in a rational world view, and tradition becomes simply one kind of information. Typically, modern people think and act on the basis of what they see as the present and future consequences of their choices. They evaluate jobs, schooling, and even relationships in terms of what they put into them and what they expect to receive in return.

Weber viewed both the Industrial Revolution and the development of capitalism as evidence of modern rationality. Such changes are all part of the **rationalization of society,** *the historical change from tradition to rationality as the main mode of human thought.* Weber went on to describe modern society as "disenchanted" because scientific thinking has swept away most of people's sentimental ties to the past.

The willingness to adopt the latest technology is one strong indicator of how rationalized a society is. To illustrate the global pattern of rationalization, Global Map 4–1 (on p. 96) shows where personal computers are found in the world. In general, computer use in the high-income countries of North America and Europe is highest, and it is rare in low-income nations. Why are some societies more eager than others to adopt new technology, such as personal computers? Those with a more rational world view might consider new computer or medical technology a breakthrough, but those with a very traditional culture might reject such devices as a threat to their way of life. The Tuareg nomads of northern Mali shrug off the idea of using telephones: Why would anyone in the Sahara want a cell phone? Similarly, Canada's Old Order Mennonites do not embrace the telephone because of its potential to disrupt their traditional way of life. In Weber's view, the amount of technological innovation depends on how a society's people understand their world. Many people throughout history have had the opportunity to adopt new technology, but only in the rational cultural climate of Western Europe did people exploit scientific discoveries to spark the Industrial Revolution (Weber, 1958a; orig. 1904–05).

IS CAPITALISM RATIONAL?

Is industrial capitalism a rational economic system? Here again, Weber and Marx came down on different sides. Weber considered industrial capitalism to be highly rational, because capitalists try to make money in any way they can. Marx, however, thought capitalism irrational because it fails to meet the basic needs of most of the people (Gerth and Mills, 1946:49).

WEBER'S GREAT THESIS: PROTESTANTISM AND CAPITALISM

Weber spent many years considering how and why industrial capitalism developed in the first place. Why did it emerge in parts of Western Europe during the eighteenth and nineteenth centuries? Weber claimed that the key to the birth of industrial capitalism lay in the Protestant Reformation. Specifically, he saw industrial capitalism as the major outcome of Calvinism, a Christian religious movement founded by John Calvin (1509–64).

Calvinists approached life in a highly disciplined and rational way. One of Calvin's most important ideas was *predestination,* the belief that an all-knowing and all-powerful God had predestined some people for salvation and others for damnation. Believing that everyone's fate was set before

A common fear among thinkers in the early industrial era was that people—now slaves to the new machines—would be stripped of their humanity. No one better captured this idea than the comic actor Charlie Chaplin, who starred in the 1936 film *Modern Times.*

birth, early Calvinists thought people could do nothing to change their destiny and, even worse, did not know what their destiny was. So Calvinists swung between hopeful visions of spiritual salvation and anxious fears of eternal damnation. Not knowing their fate was intolerable, so Calvinists gradually came to a resolution of sorts. Why shouldn't those chosen for glory in the next world, they reasoned, see signs of divine favour in *this* world? In this way, Calvinists came to see worldly prosperity as a sign of God's grace. Eager to gain this reassurance, Calvinists threw themselves into a quest for success, applying rationality, discipline, and hard work to their tasks. They did not pursue wealth for its own sake because spending on themselves would be self-indulgent and sinful. Neither were Calvinists likely to share their wealth with the poor, because they viewed poverty as a sign of God's rejection. Their duty was to press forward in what they saw as their personal *calling* from God, reinvesting profits for still greater success. It is easy to see how such activity—saving money, using wealth to create more wealth, and adopting new technology—became the foundation of capitalism.

Other world religions did not encourage the rational pursuit of wealth the way Calvinism did. Catholicism, the traditional religion in most of Europe, taught a passive otherworldly view, that good deeds performed humbly on Earth would bring rewards in heaven. For Catholics, making money had none of the spiritual significance it had for Calvinists. Weber concluded that this was the reason that industrial capitalism developed primarily in areas of Europe where Calvinism was strong.

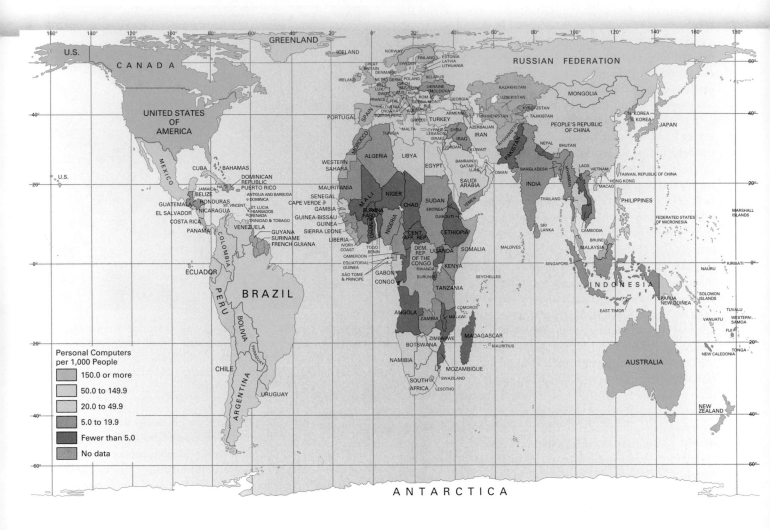

WINDOW ON THE WORLD

GLOBAL MAP 4–1   High Technology in Global Perspective

People with traditional cultures cannot afford, ignore, or sometimes even resist new technology, which people with a highly rationalized way of life quickly embrace. Personal computers, central to today's high technology, are commonplace in high-income countries with post-industrial societies. In low-income nations, by contrast, they are unknown to most people.

Source: International Telecommunication Union (2005).

Weber's study of Calvinism provides striking evidence of the power of ideas to shape society. Not one to accept simple explanations, Weber knew that industrial capitalism had many causes. But by stressing the importance of ideas, Weber tried to counter Marx's strictly economic explanation of modern society.

As the decades passed, later generations of Calvinists lost much of their early religious enthusiasm. But their drive for success and personal discipline remained, and slowly a religious ethic was transformed into a work ethic.

In this sense, industrial capitalism can be seen as disenchanted religion, with wealth now valued for its own sake. This trend is seen in the fact that the practice of accounting—which, to early Calvinists, meant keeping a daily record of moral deeds—before long came to mean simply keeping track of money.

RATIONAL SOCIAL ORGANIZATION

According to Weber, rationality is the basis of modern society, giving rise to both the Industrial Revolution and capitalism. He went on to identify seven characteristics of rational social organization:

1. *Distinctive social institutions.* In hunter/gatherer societies, the family is the centre of all activity. Gradually, however, religious, political, and economic systems develop as separate social institutions. In modern societies, new institutions—including education and health care—also appear. Specialized social institutions are a rational strategy to meet human needs efficiently.

2. *Large-scale organizations.* Modern rationality can be seen in the spread of large-scale organizations. As early as the horticultural era, small groups of political officials made decisions concerning religious observances, public works, and warfare. By the time Europe developed agrarian societies, the Catholic church had grown into a much larger organization with thousands of officials. In today's modern, rational society, almost everyone works for large formal organizations, and governments employ millions of workers.

3. *Specialized tasks.* Unlike members of traditional societies, people in modern societies are likely to have very specialized jobs. The Yellow Pages of any city's telephone directory suggest just how many different occupations there are today.

4. *Personal discipline.* Modern societies put a premium on self-discipline. Most business and government organizations expect their workers to be disciplined, and discipline is also encouraged by our cultural values of achievement and success.

5. *Awareness of time.* In traditional societies, people measure time according to the rhythm of sun and seasons. Modern people, by contrast, schedule events precisely by the hour and even the minute. Clocks began appearing in European cities some 500 years ago, about the same time commerce began to expand. Soon people began to think (to borrow Benjamin Franklin's phrase) that "time is money."

6. *Technical competence.* Members of traditional societies size up one another on the basis of who they are— their family ties. Modern rationality leads us to judge people according to what they are, with an eye towards their education, skills, and abilities. Most workers have to keep up with the latest skills and knowledge in their field to be successful.

7. *Impersonality.* In a rational society, technical competence is the basis for hiring, so the world becomes impersonal. People interact as specialists concerned with particular tasks, rather than as individuals concerned with one another as people. Because showing your feelings can threaten personal discipline, modern people tend to devalue emotion.

Max Weber agreed with Karl Marx that modern society is alienating to the individual, but they identified different causes of this problem. For Marx, economic inequality is the reason; for Weber, the issue is widespread and dehumanizing bureaucracy. George Tooker's painting *Landscape with Figures* echoes Weber's sentiments.

George Tooker, *Landscape with Figures*, 1963, egg tempera on gesso panel, 26 × 3 × 30 in. Private collection. Reproduction courtesy D.C. Moore Gallery, New York.

All these characteristics can be found in one important expression of modern rationality: bureaucracy.

Rationality, Bureaucracy, and Science

Weber considered the growth of large, rational organizations to be one of the defining traits of modern societies. Another term for this type of organization is *bureaucracy*. Weber believed that bureaucracy has much in common with capitalism—another key factor in modern social life:

> Today, it is primarily the capitalist market economy which demands that the official business of public administration be discharged precisely, unambiguously, continuously, and with as much speed as possible. Normally, the very large capitalist enterprises are themselves unequalled models of strict bureaucratic organization. (1978 [orig. 1921]:974)

As Chapter 7 ("Groups and Organizations") explains, we find aspects of bureaucracy in today's businesses, government agencies, labour unions, and universities. Weber considered bureaucracy highly rational because its elements—offices, duties, and policies—help achieve specific goals as efficiently as possible. Weber saw that capitalism, bureaucracy, and also science—the highly disciplined pursuit of knowledge—are all expressions of the same underlying factor: rationality.

Rationality and Alienation

Max Weber agreed with Karl Marx that industrial capitalism was highly productive. Weber also agreed with Marx that modern society generates widespread alienation, although his reasons were different. Marx thought alienation was caused by economic inequality. Weber blamed alienation on bureaucracy's countless rules and regulations. Bureaucracies, Weber warned, treat a human being as a "number" or a "case" rather than as a unique individual. In addition, working for large organizations demands highly specialized and often tedious routines. In the end, Weber saw modern society as a vast and growing system of rules trying to regulate everything, and he feared that modern society would end up crushing the human spirit.

Like Marx, Weber found it ironic that modern society—meant to serve humanity—turns on its creators and enslaves them. Just as Marx described the dehumanizing effects of industrial capitalism, Weber portrayed the modern individual as "only a small cog in a ceaselessly moving mechanism that prescribes to him an endlessly fixed routine of march" (1978 [orig. 1921]:988). Although Weber could see the advantages of modern society, he was deeply pessimistic about the future. He feared that, in the end, the rationalization of society would reduce human beings to robots.

YOUR TURN

Marx saw revolution as the way to overcome the problems of capitalism. Would the creation of a socialist government solve the problem of excessive rationality that worried Weber? Why? Explain your reasons.

Emile Durkheim: Society and Function

"To love society is to love something beyond us and something in ourselves" (1974 [orig. 1924]:55). These are the words of the French soci-

For a closer look at the life and work of Durkheim, visit www.hewett.norfolk.sch.uk/curric/soc/durkheim/durk.htm.

ologist Emile Durkheim (1858–1917), another of the discipline's founders. In Durkheim's ideas we find another important vision of human society.

STRUCTURE: SOCIETY BEYOND OURSELVES

Emile Durkheim's great insight was recognizing that society exists beyond ourselves. Society is more than the individuals who compose it. Society was here long before we were born, it shapes us while we live, and it will remain long after we are gone. Patterns of human behaviour—cultural norms, values,

and beliefs—exist as established structures, or *social facts*, that have an objective reality beyond the lives of individuals.

Because society is bigger than any one of us, it has the power to guide our thoughts and actions. This is why studying individuals alone (as psychologists or biologists do) can never capture the heart of the social experience. A classroom of college students taking a math exam, a family gathered around a table sharing a meal, people quietly waiting their turn in a doctor's office—all are examples of the countless situations that have a familiar organization apart from any particular individual who has ever been part of them.

Once created by people, Durkheim claimed, society takes on a life of its own and demands a measure of obedience from its creators. We experience the reality of society in the order of our lives, or as we face temptation and feel the tug of morality.

FUNCTION: SOCIETY AS SYSTEM

Having established that society has structure, Durkheim turned to the concept of *function*. The significance of any social fact, he explained, is more than what individuals see in their immediate lives; social facts help society as a whole to operate. As an illustration, consider crime. Of course, as victims of crime, individuals experience pain and loss. But, taking a broader view, Durkheim saw that crime is vital to the ongoing life of society itself. As Chapter 9 ("Deviance") explains, only by defining acts as wrong do people construct and defend morality, which gives direction and meaning to our collective lives. For this reason, Durkheim rejected the common view of crime as abnormal; on the contrary, he concluded, crime is "normal" for the most basic of reasons: a society could not exist without it (1964; orig. 1893, 1964; orig. 1895).

PERSONALITY: SOCIETY IN OURSELVES

Durkheim said that society is not only "beyond ourselves" but also "in ourselves," helping to form our personalities. How we act, think, and feel is drawn from the society that nurtures us. Society shapes us in another way as well—by providing the moral discipline that guides our behaviour and controls our desires. Durkheim believed that human beings need the restraint of society because, as creatures who can want more and more, we are in constant danger of being overpowered by our own desires: "The more one has, the more one wants, since satisfactions received only stimulate instead of filling needs" (1966 [orig. 1897]:248).

Nowhere is the need for societal regulation better illustrated than in Durkheim's study of suicide (1966; orig. 1897), which was described in Chapter 1 ("The Sociological Perspective"). Why is it that rock stars—from Janis Joplin to Jimi Hendrix and Kurt Cobain—seem so prone to self-destruction? Durkheim had the answer long before the invention of the electric guitar: now as then, the *highest* suicide rates are found among categories of people with the lowest level of societal integration. In short, the enormous

Durkheim's observation that people with weak social bonds are prone to self-destructive behaviour stands as stark evidence of the power of society to shape individual lives. When rock singers become famous, they are wrenched out of familiar life patterns and existing relationships, sometimes with deadly results. The history of rock and roll contains many tragic stories of this kind, including (*from left*) Janis Joplin's and Jimi Hendrix's deaths by drug overdose (both 1970) and Kurt Cobain's suicide (1994).

freedom of the young, rich, and famous carries a high price in terms of the risk of suicide.

MODERNITY AND ANOMIE

Compared to traditional societies, modern societies impose fewer restrictions on everyone. Durkheim acknowledged the advantages of modern-day freedom, but he warned of increased **anomie,** *a condition in which society provides little moral guidance to individuals.* The pattern by which many celebrities are "destroyed by fame" well illustrates the destructive effects of anomie. Sudden fame tears people from their families and familiar routines, disrupts established values and norms, and breaks down society's support and regulation of an individual—sometimes with fatal results. Thus, Durkheim explained, an individual's desires must be balanced by the claims and guidance of society—a balance that is sometimes difficult to achieve in the modern world. Durkheim would not have been surprised to see a rising suicide rate in modern societies such as Canada.

EVOLVING SOCIETIES: THE DIVISION OF LABOUR

Like Marx and Weber, Durkheim lived through rapid social change in Europe during the nineteenth century. But Durkheim offered different reasons for this change. In pre-industrial societies, he explained, tradition operates as the social cement that binds people together. In fact, what he termed the *collective conscience* is so strong that the community moves quickly to punish anyone who dares to challenge conventional ways of life. Durkheim used the term **mechanical solidarity** to refer to *social bonds, based on common sentiments and shared moral values, that are strong among members of pre-industrial societies.* In practice, mechanical solidarity is based on *likeness.* Durkheim called these bonds "mechanical" because people are linked together in lockstep, with a more or less automatic sense of belonging together and acting alike.

With industrialization, Durkheim continued, mechanical solidarity becomes weaker and weaker, and people are much less bound by tradition. But this does not mean that society dissolves. Modern life creates a new type of solidarity. Durkheim called this new social integration **organic solidarity,** defined as *social bonds, based on specialization and interdependence, that are strong among members of industrial societies.* The solidarity that was once rooted in likeness is now based on *differences* among people who find that their specialized work— as plumbers, college students, midwives, or sociology instructors—makes them rely on other people for most of their daily needs.

For Durkheim, then, the key to change in a society is an expanding **division of labour,** or *specialized economic activity.* Weber said that modern societies specialize in order to become more efficient, and Durkheim filled out the picture by showing that members of modern societies count on tens of thousands of others—most of them strangers— for the goods and services needed every day. As members of modern societies, we depend more and more on people we trust less and less. Why do we look to people we hardly know and whose beliefs may well differ from our own? Durkheim's answer was "because we can't live without them." So, for Durkheim, modern society rests far less on *moral consensus* and far more on *functional interdependence.* Herein lies what we might call "Durkheim's dilemma": the technological power and greater personal freedom of modern society come at the cost of declining morality and the rising risk of anomie.

Like Marx and Weber, Durkheim worried about the direction society was taking. But of the three, Durkheim was the most optimistic. He saw that large, anonymous societies—despite their impersonality—had the positive effect of giving people more freedom and privacy than small towns did. Anomie remains a danger, but Durkheim hoped we would be able to create laws and other norms to regulate our behaviour.

In traditional societies, such as communities of Old Order Mennonites (in Ontario) and Hutterites (in Alberta), everyone does much the same work (*left*). These societies are held together by strong moral beliefs. Modern societies, illustrated by urban areas in this country (*right*), are held together by a system of production in which people perform specialized work and rely on one another through large organizations.

Compare Durkheim's concept of anomie with the two concepts of alienation developed by Marx and Weber.

How can we apply Durkheim's views to the Information Revolution? The Applying Sociology box (on p. 102) suggests that Durkheim, Weber, and Marx would have had much to say about today's new computer technology.

Critical Review: Four Visions of Society

This chapter opened with several important questions about society. We will conclude by summarizing how each of the four visions of society answers these questions.

WHAT HOLDS SOCIETIES TOGETHER?

How is something as complex as society possible? Lenski claims that members of a society are united by a shared culture, and that cultural patterns become more diverse as a society gains more complex technology. He also points out that, as technology becomes more complex, inequality divides a society more and more, although industrialization reduces inequality somewhat.

Marx saw in society not unity but social division based on class. From his point of view, elites may force an uneasy peace, but true social unity can occur only if production becomes a co-operative process. To Weber, the members of a society share a world view. Just as tradition joined people together in the past, so modern societies have created rational, large-scale organizations that connect people's lives. Finally, Durkheim made solidarity the focus of his work. He contrasted the mechanical solidarity of pre-industrial societies, which is based on shared morality, with modern society's organic solidarity, which is based on specialization.

HOW HAVE SOCIETIES CHANGED?

According to Lenski's model of sociocultural evolution, societies differ mostly in terms of changing technology. Modern society stands out from past societies in terms of its enormous productive power. Marx, too, noted historical differences in productivity, yet pointed to continuing social conflict, except perhaps among egalitarian hunter/gatherers; for Marx, modern society is distinctive mostly because it brings that conflict out into the open. Weber considered the question of change from the perspective of how people look at the world. Members of pre-industrial societies have a traditional outlook; modern people have a rational world view. Finally, for Durkheim, traditional societies are characterized by mechanical solidarity based on moral cohesion. In industrial societies, mechanical solidarity gives way to organic solidarity based on productive specialization.

THINKING CRITICALLY

Is Our Society Getting Better or Worse?

Optimism has been a defining trait of Canadian society. As time goes on, life gets better—or so it is thought. But a survey by Alberta sociologist Reginald Bibby suggests that optimism may be waning. Between 1975 and 1995, the proportion of people who believed that the "lot of the average person" is getting worse rose from 45 to 70 percent; the proportion who believed that racial and visible minorities are experiencing discrimination increased from 55 percent in 1980 to 67 percent in 1995; and, in one decade (1985 to 1995), the proportion of respondents who agreed that "values in Canada have been changing for the worse" rose from 54 to 74 percent. In addition, when asked to identify their major concerns, Canadians placed the national debt, unemployment, and the economy at the top of their list—followed by crime, government incompetence, child abuse, AIDS, delinquency, family breakdown, and violence (Bibby, 1995). Clearly, in 1995, with the economy in a slump and Quebec coming close to voting Yes on breaking up our country, Canadians were worried.

What's going on here? After all, there are good reasons for optimism about Canada. Since the beginning of this century, educational attainment has increased dramatically so that, proportionately, more of us are university and college graduates. After taking inflation into account, average Canadians have enjoyed higher incomes and greater buying power. Almost every household has a telephone, television, and refrigerator, and more than 80 percent have automobiles, DVDs, and microwaves. Most importantly, while people born in 1900 lived an average of 47 years, children born today can expect to live about 30 years longer.

But some trends of the last decade or two are troubling. Canadians are less certain that hard work pays off in higher incomes. Divorce rates are climbing while marriage rates are decreasing, and a perception of rising crime rates has undermined people's sense of personal safety, even in their own homes. For 46 percent of Canadians, crime is a "very serious" concern, and 87 percent think the courts should be tougher on law breakers. Our relative affluence, coupled with our capacity to move farther and faster than ever before, seems to have eroded our sense of responsibility for others, unleashing a wave of individualism accompanied by a dramatic move to the right of the political spectrum.

Despite recent trends, a large and slightly increasing majority of Canadians claim to be "very happy" or "pretty happy" (87% and 92% in 1975 and 1995) and even more—among the married—claim to have marriages in the two "happy" categories (92% and 94% in 1975 and 1995). And since the terrorist attacks in the United States on September 11, 2001, Canada's economy has outperformed that of the United States: we have created hundreds of thousands of jobs, while the Americans have lost ground. Even our loonie has soared to unaccustomed heights. The stock market has recovered from the dot.com crash and real estate is booming throughout the country.

Ipsos-Reid pollsters, Bricker and Wright (2005), have been tracking change in Canadian attitudes as well—finding that 73 percent feel we are taxed too highly for the value we get in social services, that 62 percent are afraid of being in debt, and two-thirds of parents with children under 18 fear that costs are putting college or university education out of reach for their children. Concerns about health care are such that 82 percent of Canadians polled agree that the federal government should spend $15 billion more on health care as recommended by the Romanow Report—while, at the same time, 56 percent feel that we should be able to pay out of pocket for private delivery if the public health care system cannot meet our needs. We do not trust politicians, but we *do* trust firefighters, pharmacists, nurses, and doctors. Among major retailers, Wal-Mart and Sears tie for first on our trust ranking. When informed that automotive emissions from passenger vehicles are responsible for half our production of greenhouse gases, 62 percent *oppose* increasing taxes to improve public transit—and 42 percent are *strongly* opposed. While 84 percent of Canadians believe in God, only 20 percent attend services weekly. People feel stressed by work (43%) and managing finances (39%)—and feel that they have less free time than they did five years previously (41%). To top it off, parents are terrified that their children will hang out with the wrong crowd and not go on to college or university.

So, which is it? Is Canadian society getting better or worse? The theorists highlighted in this chapter shed some light on this question. It is easy to equate "high tech" with progress but, the Lenskis maintain, we should make such assumptions cautiously; history shows us that although advancing technology does offer real advantages, it is no guarantee of a better life. Marx, Weber, and Durkheim also acknowledged the growing affluence of societies over time, yet each offered a pointed criticism of modern society's dangerous tendency towards individualism. For Marx, capitalism is the culprit, elevating money to godlike status and fostering a culture of selfishness. Weber's analysis claims that the modern spirit of rationality wears away traditional ties of kinship and neighbourhood while expanding bureaucracy, which both manipulates and isolates people. In Durkheim's view, functional interdependence joins members of modern societies, who are less and less able to establish a common moral framework within which to judge right and wrong. Technological advances, it seems, are offset by the loss of human community. How well, one might ask, do the insights of these theorists describe Canadian society?

WHAT DO YOU THINK?

1. Do you think life in Canada is getting better or worse? How?
2. What are your major worries or concerns?
3. Are you and your peers optimistic about the future?

APPLYING SOCIOLOGY

The Information Revolution: What Would Durkheim, Weber, and Marx Have Thought?

New technology is changing our society at a dizzying pace. Were they alive today, the three founding sociologists would be eager observers of the current scene. Imagine for a moment the kinds of questions Emile Durkheim, Max Weber, and Karl Marx might ask about the effects of computer technology on society.

Durkheim, who emphasized the increasing division of labour in modern society, would probably wonder if new information technology is pushing specialization even further. There is good reason to think that it is. Because electronic communication (say, a website) gives anyone a vast market (already, several billion people use the internet), people can specialize far more than if they were trying to make a living in a small geographic area.

For example, while most small-town lawyers have a general practice, an attorney in the information age living anywhere can provide specialized guidance on, say, prenuptial agreements or electronic copyright law. As we move into the electronic age, the number of highly specialized small businesses—some of which become very large—in all fields is increasing rapidly.

Durkheim might also point out that the internet threatens to increase the problem of anomie. Using computers

has a tendency to isolate people from personal relationships with others. In addition, although the internet offers a flood of information, it provides little in the way of moral guidance about what is wise or good or worth knowing.

Weber believed that modern societies are distinctive because their members share a rational world view, and nothing illustrates this world view better than bureaucracy. But will bureaucracy be as important during the twenty-first century? Here is one reason to think it may not: while organizations will probably continue to regulate workers performing the kinds of routine tasks that were common in the industrial era, much work in the post-industrial era involves imagination. Consider such the work of creating animation sequences for film, designing ergonomic furniture, or writing software; such creative work cannot be regulated in the same way as putting together automobiles as they move down an assembly line. Perhaps this is the reason many high-technology companies have done away with dress codes and time clocks.

Finally, what might Marx make of the Information Revolution? Since Marx considered the earlier Industrial Revolution a *class* revolution that allowed the owners of industry to domi-

nate society, he would probably be concerned about the emergence of a new symbolic elite. Some analysts point out that film and television writers, producers, and performers now enjoy vast wealth, international prestige, and enormous power (Lichter, *et al.*, 1990). Just as people without industrial skills stayed at the bottom of the class system in past decades, so people without symbolic skills may well become the "underclass" of the twenty-first century.

Durkheim, Weber, and Marx greatly improved our understanding of industrial societies. As we continue into the post-industrial age, there is plenty of room for new generations of sociologists to carry on.

WHAT DO YOU THINK?

1. Is computer technology likely to continue to increase specialization? Why?
2. Can you think of examples of creative businesses that are less bureaucratic than industrial companies are? Why would you expect this to be the case?
3. What effect will the increased importance of symbolic skills have on the earning power of college or university education?

Change can have positive and negative consequences: the Thinking Critically box (on p. 101) looks at change—for better or worse—in Canadian society.

WHY DO SOCIETIES CHANGE?

As Lenski sees it, social change comes about through technological innovation that, over time, transforms an entire society. Marx's materialist approach highlights the struggle between classes as the engine of change, pushing societies towards revolution. Weber, by contrast, pointed out

that ideas contribute to social change. He demonstrated how a particular world view—Calvinism—set in motion the Industrial Revolution, which ended up reshaping many societies. Finally, Durkheim pointed to an expanding division of labour as the key dimension of social change.

The fact that these four approaches are so different does not mean that any one of them is right or wrong. Society is exceedingly complex, and our understanding of society benefits from applying all four visions.

4 MAKING THE GRADE

The following learning tools will help you see what you know, identify what you still need to learn, and expand your understanding beyond the text. You can also visit this text's Companion Website™ at www.pearsoned.ca/macionis to find useful practice tests.

KEY POINTS

Gerhard Lenski: Society and Technology

Lenski's sociocultural evolution explores how technological advances change societies. The earliest societies, which lived by hunting and gathering, were composed of a small number of family-centred nomads. Horticulture began some 12 000 years ago as people used hand tools for cultivation; at about the same time, pastoral societies domesticated animals and created networks of trade. Agriculture, large-scale cultivation using animal-drawn plows, developed about 5000 years ago. This more productive technology allowed societies to expand into vast empires, and it also created more inequality. Industrialization began just over 250 years ago in Europe as people used new energy sources to operate large machinery. In today's post-industrial societies, production has shifted from heavy machinery making material things to computers and related technology processing information.

Karl Marx: Society and Conflict

Marx's materialist approach claims that societies are defined by their economic systems. He traced conflict between social classes, from ancient societies (with masters and slaves) to agrarian societies (with nobles and serfs) to industrial/capitalist societies (with capitalists and proletarians). Industrial capitalism alienates workers in four ways: from the act of working, from the products of work, from other workers, and from their own potential. Marx believed that once workers overcame their false consciousness, they would overthrow the industrial/capitalist system.

Max Weber: The Rationalization of Society

Weber's idealist approach claims that ideas have a powerful effect on society. Weber contrasted the tradition of pre-industrial societies with the rationality of modern, industrial societies. He traced the origins of capitalism to Calvinist religious beliefs. Today's rational societies are marked not only by capitalism and science but also by bureaucratic organizations. Weber feared that this rationality would stifle human creativity.

Emile Durkheim: Society and Function

Durkheim explained that society has an objective existence apart from individuals. He understood that social elements (such as crime) have functions that help society operate. Society also shapes our personalities, guiding how we act, think, and feel. Societies require solidarity. Traditional societies have mechanical solidarity, which is based on a shared morality; modern societies depend on organic solidarity, which is based on specialization, or a division of labour.

KEY CONCEPTS

society (p. 84) people who interact in a defined territory and share a culture

sociocultural evolution (p. 84) Lenski's term for the changes that occur as a society gains new technology

hunting and gathering (p. 85) the use of simple tools to hunt animals and gather vegetation

horticulture (p. 86) the use of hand tools to raise crops

pastoralism (p. 86) the domestication of animals

agriculture (p. 86) large-scale cultivation using plows harnessed to animals or more powerful energy sources

industrialism (p. 87) the production of goods using advanced sources of energy to drive large machinery

post-industrialism (p. 88) technology that supports an information-based economy

social conflict (p. 90) the struggle between segments of society over valued resources

capitalists (p. 90) people who own and operate factories and other businesses in pursuit of profits

proletarians (p. 90) people who sell their labour for wages

social institutions (p. 91) the major spheres of social life, or societal subsystems, organized to meet human needs

false consciousness (p. 91) Marx's term for explanations of social problems as the shortcomings of individuals rather than as the flaws of society

class conflict (or struggle) (p. 92) conflict between entire classes over the distribution of a society's wealth and power

class consciousness (p. 92) Marx's term for workers' recognition of themselves as a class unified in opposition to capitalists and ultimately to capitalism itself

alienation (p. 93) the experience of isolation and misery resulting from powerlessness

ideal type (p. 94) an abstract statement of the essential characteristics of any social phenomenon

tradition (p. 94) values and beliefs passed from generation to generation

rationality (p. 94) a way of thinking that emphasizes deliberate, matter-of-fact calculation of the most efficient way to accomplish a particular task

rationalization of society (p. 95) Weber's term for the historical change from tradition to rationality as the main mode of human thought

anomie (p. 99) Durkheim's term for a condition in which society provides little moral guidance to individuals

mechanical solidarity (p. 99) Durkheim's term for social bonds, based on common sentiments and shared moral values, that are strong among members of pre-industrial societies

organic solidarity (p. 99) Durkheim's term for social bonds, based on specialization and interdependence, that are strong among members of industrial societies

division of labour (p. 99) specialized economic activity

APPLICATIONS & EXERCISES

1. Hunter/gatherers gazed at the stars and named the constellations in terms that reflected their way of life—mostly the names of animals and hunters. As a way of revealing what is important to our way of life, write a short paper imagining the meanings we would give to clusters of stars if people in post-industrial societies were naming them, starting from scratch.

2. Spend an hour in your home trying to identify every device that has a computer chip in it. How many did you find? Were you surprised by the number?

3. Do some research on a past civilization such as the Inca society of Peru. Learn about the people's skills in agriculture, weaving, pottery, and architecture. (Some Inca buildings have withstood earthquakes that have destroyed much newer construction.) See if what you learn makes you think twice before assuming that modern societies are always superior to past societies.

PRENTICE HALL
mysoclab™
Where learning & the sociological imagination intersect.

To reinforce your understanding of this chapter, and to identify topics for further study, visit MySocLab at **www.pearsoned.ca/mysoclab/** for diagnostic tests and a multimedia ebook.

5

Socialization

Why is social experience the key to
human personality?

What familiar social settings have special
importance to human development?

How do people's experiences change
over the life course?

On a cold winter day in 1938, a social worker walked quickly to the door of a rural Pennsylvania farmhouse. Investigating a case of possible child abuse, the social worker entered the home and soon discovered a five-year-old girl hidden in a second-floor storage room. The child, whose name was Anna, was wedged into an old chair with her arms tied above her head so that she couldn't move. She was wearing filthy clothes, and her arms and legs were as thin as matchsticks (Davis, 1940).

Anna's situation was tragic. She had been born in 1932 to an unmarried and mentally impaired woman of twenty-six who lived with her strict father. Angry about his daughter's "illegitimate" motherhood, the grandfather did not even want the child in his house; for the first six months of her life, Anna was passed among several welfare agencies. But her mother could not afford to pay for her care, and Anna was returned to the hostile home of her grandfather. To lessen the grandfather's anger, Anna's mother kept Anna in the storage room and gave her just enough milk to keep her alive. There she stayed—day after day, month after month, with almost no human contact—enduring for five years.

Learning of the discovery of Anna, the sociologist Kingsley Davis (1940, 1947) immediately went to see her. He found her with local officials at a county home. Davis was stunned by the emaciated child, who could not laugh, speak, or even smile. Anna was completely unresponsive, as if alone in an empty world.

Social Experience: The Key to Our Humanity

Socialization is so basic to human development that we sometimes overlook its importance. But here, in the terrible case of an isolated child, we can see what humans would be like without social contact. Although physically alive, Anna hardly seems to have been human. We can see that, without social experience, a child is not able to act or communicate in a meaningful way and seems to be as much an *object* as a *person*.

Sociologists use the term **socialization** to refer to *the lifelong social experience by which people develop their human potential and learn culture.* Unlike other living species, whose behaviour is biologically set, humans need social experience to learn their culture and to survive. Social experience is also the foundation of **personality,** *a person's fairly consistent patterns of acting, thinking, and feeling.* We build a personality by internalizing (taking in) our surroundings. But without social experience, as Anna's case shows, personality hardly develops at all.

HUMAN DEVELOPMENT: NATURE AND NURTURE

Anna's case makes clear that humans depend on others to provide the care and nurture needed not only for physical growth but also for personality to develop. A century ago, however, people mistakenly believed that humans were born with instincts that determined their personality and behaviour.

The Biological Sciences: The Role of Nature

Charles Darwin's 1859 groundbreaking study of evolution, described in Chapter 3 ("Culture"), led people to think that human behaviour was instinctive, simply our *nature*. Such ideas led to claims that the North American economic system reflects "instinctive human competitiveness," that some people are "born criminals," or that women are "naturally" emotional while men are "naturally" rational.

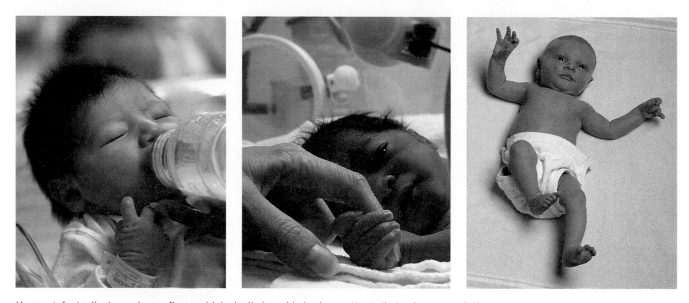

Human infants display various reflexes—biologically based behaviour patterns that enhance survival. The sucking reflex, which actually begins before birth, enables the infant to obtain nourishment. The grasping reflex, triggered by placing a finger on the infant's palm causing the hand to close, helps the infant to maintain contact with a parent and, later on, to grasp objects. The Moro reflex, activated by startling the infant, has the infant swinging both arms outwards and then bringing them together across the chest. This action, which disappears after several months of life, probably developed among our evolutionary ancestors so that a falling infant could grasp the body of a parent.

People trying to understand cultural diversity also misunderstood Darwin's thinking. From centuries of world exploration, Western Europeans knew that people around the world behaved quite differently from one another. But Europeans linked these differences to biology rather than to culture. It was an easy, although incorrect and very damaging, step to claim that members of technologically simple societies were biologically less evolved and therefore less human. This ethnocentric view helped to justify colonialism: why not take advantage of those who do not seem to be human?

 You can read and search for specific topics in Darwin's *On the Origin of Species* (1859), *The Descent of Man* (1871), and *The Voyage of the Beagle* (1909) at www.infidel.org.

The Social Sciences: The Role of Nurture

In the twentieth century, biological explanations of human behaviour came under fire. The psychologist John B. Watson (1878–1958) developed a theory called *behaviourism*, which holds that behaviour is not instinctive but learned. Thus, people everywhere are equally human, differing only in their cultural patterns. In short, Watson rooted human behaviour not in nature but in *nurture*.

While social scientists today are cautious about describing *any* human behaviour as instinctive, this does not mean that biology plays no part. Human life, after all, depends on the functioning of the body. We also know that children often share biological traits (like height and hair colour) with their parents and that heredity plays a part in intelligence, musical and artistic talent, and personality (such as how you react to frustration). However, whether you develop your inherited potential depends on how you are raised. For example, unless children are stimulated to use their brains early in life, the brain does not fully develop. Therefore, the ability to realize any inherited potential depends on having the opportunity to develop it (Goldsmith, 1983; Begley, 1995).

Without denying the importance of nature, then, we can correctly say that nurture matters more in shaping human behaviour. More precisely, *nurture is our nature.*

SOCIAL ISOLATION

As the story of Anna shows, cutting people off from the social world is very harmful. For ethical reasons, researchers can never place human beings in total isolation to study what happens. But in the past, they have studied the effects of social isolation on nonhuman primates.

Studies of Nonhuman Primates

In a classic study, the psychologists Harry and Margaret Harlow (1962) placed rhesus monkeys—whose behaviour is in some ways surprisingly similar to human behaviour—in various conditions of social isolation. They found that complete isolation with adequate nutrition for even six months seriously disturbed the monkeys' development. When returned to their group, these monkeys were passive, anxious, and fearful.

The Harlows then placed infant rhesus monkeys in cages with an artificial "mother" made of wire mesh with a wooden head and the nipple of a feeding tube where the breast would be. These monkeys also survived but were unable to interact with others when placed in a group. But monkeys in a third category, isolated with an artificial wire mesh "mother" covered with soft terry cloth, did better. Each of these monkeys would cling to its "mother" closely. Because these monkeys showed less developmental damage than earlier groups, the Harlows concluded that the monkeys benefitted from this closeness. The experiment confirmed how important it is that adults cradle infants affectionately.

Finally, the Harlows discovered that infant monkeys could recover from about three months of isolation. But, by about six months, isolation caused irreversible emotional and behavioural damage.

YOUR TURN

What new understanding of the ad campaign "Have you hugged your child today?" do you gain from the Harlow studies?

Studies of Isolated Children

Tragic cases of children isolated by abusive family members show the damage caused by depriving human beings of social experience. We will review three such cases.

Anna: The Rest of the Story The rest of Anna's story squares with the Harlows' findings. After her discovery, Anna received extensive medical attention and soon showed improvement. When Kingsley Davis visited her after ten days, he found her more alert and even smiling—perhaps for the first time in her life! Over the next year, Anna made slow but steady progress, showing more interest in other people and gradually learning to walk. After a year and a half, she could feed herself and play with toys. But, as the Harlows might have predicted, five years of social isolation had caused permanent damage. At age eight, her mental development was less than that of a two-year-old. Not until she was almost ten did she begin to use words. Because Anna's mother was mentally impaired, perhaps Anna was also. The riddle was never solved, because Anna died at age ten from a blood disorder, possibly related to the years of abuse she suffered (Davis, 1940, 1947).

Isabelle: Another Case A second case involves another girl, Isabelle, found at about the same time as Anna and under similar circumstances. After more than six years of virtual isolation, this girl displayed the same lack of responsiveness as Anna. But Isabelle had the benefit of an intensive learning program directed by psychologists. Within a week,

Isabelle was trying to speak and, a year and a half later, she knew some 2000 words. The psychologists concluded that intensive effort had pushed Isabelle through six years of normal development in only two years. By the time she was fourteen, Isabelle was attending sixth-grade classes, damaged by her early ordeal but on her way to a relatively normal life (Davis, 1947).

Genie: A Third Case A more recent case of childhood isolation involves a California girl abused by her parents (Curtiss, 1977; Rymer, 1994). From the time she was two, Genie was tied to a potty chair in a dark garage. In 1970,

 More about the life of Genie at www.pbs.org/wgbh/nova/transcripts/2112gchild.html.

when she was rescued at age thirteen, Genie weighed only 27 kilograms (59 pounds) and had the mental development of a one-year-old. With intensive treatment, she became physically healthy, but her language ability remains that of a young child. Today, Genie lives in a home for developmentally impaired adults.

Critical Review All evidence points to the crucial importance of social experience in personality development. Human beings can recover from abuse and short-term isolation. But there is a point—precisely when is unclear from the small number of cases studied—at which isolation in early childhood causes permanent developmental damage.

YOUR TURN

What ethical issues prevent the isolation of humans for research purposes? Do these same issues arise when conducting this type of research with animals? Do you think the Harlow studies would be allowed today?

Understanding Socialization

Socialization is a complex, lifelong process. The following discussions highlight the work of six researchers who have made lasting contributions to our understanding of human development.

SIGMUND FREUD'S ELEMENTS OF PERSONALITY

Sigmund Freud (1856–1939) lived in Vienna at a time when most Europeans considered human behaviour to be biolog-

 Visit the Sigmund Freud Museum of Vienna, Austria, at www.freud-museum.at.

ically fixed. Trained as a physician, Freud gradually turned to the study of personality and mental disorders and eventually developed the celebrated theory of psychoanalysis.

Basic Human Needs

Freud claimed that biology plays a major part in human development, although not in terms of specific instincts, as is the case in other species. Rather, he theorized that humans have two basic needs or drives that are present at birth. First is a need for sexual and emotional bonding, which he called the "life instinct" or *eros* (from the Greek god of love). Second, we share an aggressive drive he called the "death instinct" or *thanatos* (from the Greek, meaning "death"). These opposing forces, operating at an unconscious level, create deep inner tension.

Freud's Model of Personality

Freud combined basic needs and the influence of society into a model of personality with three parts: id, ego, and superego. The **id** (the Latin word for "it") represents *the human being's basic drives*, which are unconscious and demand immediate satisfaction. Rooted in biology, the id is present at birth, making a newborn a bundle of demands for attention, touching, and food. But society opposes the self-centred id, which is why one of the first words a child typically learns is "no."

To avoid frustration, a child must learn to approach the world realistically. This is done through the **ego** (Latin for "I"), which is *a person's conscious efforts to balance innate pleasure-seeking drives with the demands of society*. The ego develops as we become aware of ourselves and at the same time realize that we cannot have everything we want.

In the human personality, **superego** (Latin meaning "above" or "beyond" the ego) is *the cultural values and norms internalized by an individual*. The superego operates as our conscience, telling us *why* we cannot have everything we want. The superego begins to form as a child becomes aware of parental demands, and it matures as the child comes to understand that everyone's behaviour should take account of cultural norms.

Personality Development

To the id-centred child, the world is a bewildering assortment of physical sensations that bring either pleasure or pain. As the superego develops, however, the child learns the moral concepts of right and wrong. Initially, in other words, children can feel good only in a physical way (such as by being held and cuddled), but after three or four years, they feel good or bad according to how they judge their behaviour against cultural norms (doing the right thing). The id and superego remain in conflict, but, in a well-adjusted person, the ego manages these two opposing forces. If conflicts are not resolved during childhood, Freud claimed, they may surface as personality disorders later on.

Culture, in the form of the superego, *represses* selfish demands, forcing people to look beyond their own desires. Often the competing demands of self and society result in a compromise that Freud called *sublimation*. Sublimation

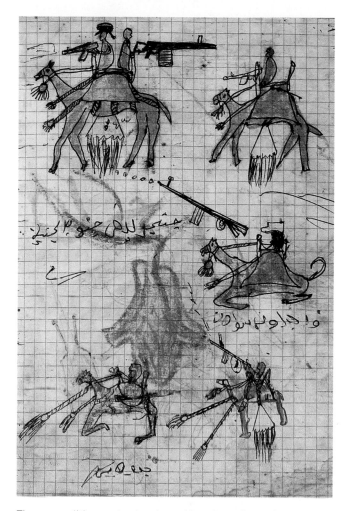

The personalities we develop depend largely on the environment in which we live. When a child's world is shredded by violence, the damage can be profound and lasting. This drawing was made by thirteen-year-old Rahid in the Darfur region of Sudan, where armed militia have killed more than 150 000 people since 2003. What are the likely effects of such experiences on a young person's self-confidence and capacity to trust others?

Courtesy of Dr. Annie Sparrow, Human Rights Watch

redirects selfish drives into socially acceptable behaviour: marriage makes the satisfaction of sexual urges socially acceptable, for example, and competitive sports are an outlet for aggression.

Critical Review In Freud's time, few people were ready to accept sex as a basic human drive. More recent critics have charged that Freud's work presents humans in male terms and devalues women (Donovan and Littenberg, 1982). Freud's theories are also difficult to test scientifically. But Freud influenced everyone who later studied human personality. Of special importance to sociology are his ideas that we internalize social norms and that childhood experiences have a lasting impact on our personalities.

JEAN PIAGET'S THEORY OF COGNITIVE DEVELOPMENT

The Swiss psychologist Jean Piaget (1896–1980) studied human *cognition*, how people think and understand. As

 To learn more about Piaget and his work, visit www.piaget.org.

Piaget watched his own three children grow, he wondered not just *what* they knew but *how* they made sense of the world. Piaget went on to identify four stages of cognitive development.

The Sensorimotor Stage

Stage one is the **sensorimotor stage,** *the level of human development at which individuals experience the world only through their senses.* For about the first two years of life, the infant knows the world only through the five senses: touching, tasting, smelling, looking, and listening. "Knowing" to young children amounts to what their senses tell them.

The Pre-operational Stage

At about age two, children enter the **pre-operational stage,** *the level of human development at which individuals first use language and other symbols.* Here, children begin to think about the world mentally and use imagination. But "pre-op" children between about two and six still attach meaning only to specific experiences and objects. They can identify a toy as their favourite but cannot explain what *kinds* of toys they like.

Lacking abstract concepts, a child also cannot judge size, weight, or volume. In one of his best-known experiments, Piaget placed two identical glasses containing equal amounts of water on a table. He asked several children aged five and six if the amount in each glass was the same. They nodded that it was. The children then watched Piaget take one of the glasses and pour its contents into a taller, narrower glass so that the level of the water in the glass was higher. Asked again if each glass held the same amount, the five- or six-year-olds insisted that the taller glass held more water. By about age seven, children are able to think abstractly and realize that the amount of water stays the same.

The Concrete Operational Stage

Next comes the **concrete operational stage,** *the level of human development at which individuals first see causal connections in their surroundings.* Between the ages of seven and eleven, children focus on how and why things happen. In addition, children attach more than one symbol to a particular event or object. If, for example, you say to a child of five, "Today is Wednesday," she might respond, "No, it's my birthday!" indicating that she can use just one symbol at a time. But a ten-year-old at the concrete operational stage would be able to respond, "Yes, and it's also my birthday!"

The Formal Operational Stage

The last stage in Piaget's model is the **formal operational stage,** *the level of human development at which individuals think abstractly and critically.* At about age twelve, young people begin to reason abstractly rather than thinking only of concrete situations. If, for example, you were to ask a seven-year-old, "What would you like to be when you grow up?" you might receive a concrete response such as "a teacher." But most teenagers can think more abstractly and might reply, "I would like a job that helps others." As they gain the capacity for abstract thought, young people also learn to understand metaphors. Hearing the phrase "A penny for your thoughts" might lead a child to ask for a coin, but a teenager will recognize a gentle invitation to confide.

Critical Review Freud saw human beings torn by opposing forces of biology and culture. Piaget saw the mind as active and creative. He saw an ability to engage the world unfolding in stages as the result of both biological maturation and social experience. But do people in all societies pass through all four of Piaget's stages? Living in a traditional society that changes slowly probably limits a person's capacity for abstract and critical thought. Even in North America, perhaps 30 percent of people never reach the formal operational stage (Kohlberg and Gilligan, 1971).

LAWRENCE KOHLBERG'S THEORY OF MORAL DEVELOPMENT

Lawrence Kohlberg (1981) built on Piaget's work to study *moral reasoning*, how individuals judge situations as right or wrong. Here again, development occurs in stages. Young children who experience the world in terms of pain and pleasure (Piaget's sensorimotor stage) are at the *preconventional* level of moral development. At this early stage, in other words, "rightness" amounts to "what feels good to me." For example, a young child may simply reach for something on a table that looks shiny, which is the reason parents of young children have to childproof their homes.

The *conventional* level, Kohlberg's second stage, appears by the teen years (corresponding to Piaget's final, formal operational stage). At this point, young people lose some of their selfishness as they learn to define right and wrong in terms of what pleases parents and conforms to cultural norms. Individuals at this stage also begin to assess intention in reaching moral judgments instead of simply looking at what people do. For example, they understand that stealing in order to give food to hungry children is not the same as stealing an iPod to sell for profit.

In Kohlberg's final stage of moral development, the *postconventional* level, people move beyond their society's norms to consider abstract ethical principles. Here, they think about liberty, freedom, or justice, perhaps arguing that what is legal still may not be right. When the African

Childhood is a time to learn principles of right and wrong. According to Carol Gilligan, however, boys and girls define what is "right" in different ways. After reading about her theory, can you suggest what these two might be arguing about?

American activist Rosa Parks refused to give up her seat on a bus in Montgomery, Alabama, in 1955, she violated that city's segregation laws in order to call attention to the racial injustice of the law.

Critical Review Like the work of Piaget, Kohlberg's model explains moral development in terms of distinct stages. But whether this model applies to people in all societies remains unclear. Further, many Americans apparently never reach the postconventional level of moral reasoning, although exactly why is still an open question. Another problem with Kohlberg's research is that his subjects were all boys. He committed a common research error, described in Chapter 2 ("Sociological Investigation"), by generalizing the results of male subjects to all people. This problem led a colleague, Carol Gilligan, to investigate how gender affects moral reasoning.

CAROL GILLIGAN'S THEORY OF GENDER AND MORAL DEVELOPMENT

Carol Gilligan, whose approach is highlighted in the Thinking about Diversity box (on p. 114), compared the moral development of girls and boys, and concluded that the two genders use different standards of rightness. Gilligan (1982, 1990) claims that boys have a *justice perspective*, meaning that they rely on formal rules to define right and wrong. Girls, in contrast, have a *care and responsibility perspective*, judging a situation with an eye towards personal relationships. For example, as boys see it, stealing is wrong because it breaks the law. Girls are more likely to wonder why someone would steal and to be sympathetic towards a poor person who steals to feed her family.

Kohlberg treats rule-based male reasoning as superior to the person-based female approach. Gilligan notes that impersonal rules dominate men's lives in the workplace, but personal relationships are more relevant to women's lives as mothers and caregivers. Why, then, Gilligan asks, should our society accept male standards as the norms by which we judge everyone?

Critical Review Gilligan's work sharpens our understanding of both human development and gender issues in research. Yet the question remains: Does *nature* or *nurture* account for the differences between females and males? In Gilligan's view, cultural conditioning is at work. If so, the moral reasoning of women and men will probably become more similar as more women organize their lives around the workplace.

GEORGE HERBERT MEAD'S THEORY OF THE SOCIAL SELF

George Herbert Mead (1863–1931) developed a theory of *social behaviourism* to explain how social experience develops an individual's personality (1962; orig. 1934).

The Self

Mead's central concept is the **self**, *the part of an individual's personality composed of self-awareness and self-image.* Mead's genius was in seeing the self as the product of social experience.

First, said Mead, *the self develops only with social experience.* The self is not part of the body, and it does not exist at birth. Mead rejected the idea that personality is guided by biological drives (as Freud asserted) or biological maturation (as Piaget claimed). For Mead, the self develops only as the individual

THINKING ABOUT DIVERSITY:
RACE, CLASS, & GENDER
The Importance of Gender in Research

Carol Gilligan (1990) has shown how gender guides social behaviour. Her early work exposed the gender bias in studies by Kohlberg and others who had used only male subjects. But as her research progressed, Gilligan made a major discovery: boys and girls actually use different standards in making moral decisions. By ignoring gender, we end up with an incomplete view of human behaviour.

Gilligan has also looked at the effect of gender on self-esteem. Her research team interviewed more than 2000 girls, aged six to eighteen, over a five-year period. She found a clear pattern: young girls start out eager and

confident, but their self-esteem slips away as they pass through adolescence. Why? Gilligan claims that the answer lies in our society's socialization of females: the ideal woman is calm, controlled, and eager to please. Then, too, as girls move from the elementary grades to secondary school, they have fewer women teachers and find that most authority figures are men. As a result, by their late teens, girls struggle to regain the personal strength they had a decade earlier.

When their research was finished, Gilligan and her colleagues returned to a private girls' school where they had interviewed their subjects to share the

results of their work. As their conclusions led them to expect, most younger girls who had been interviewed were eager to have their names appear in the forthcoming book. But the older girls were hesitant—many were fearful that they would be talked about.

WHAT DO YOU THINK?

1. How does Gilligan's research show the importance of gender in the socialization process?
2. Are boys subject to some of the same pressures and difficulties as girls? Explain your answer.
3. How has your gender shaped your personality?

interacts with others. Without interaction, as we see from cases of isolated children, the body grows, but no self emerges.

Second, Mead explained, *social experience is the exchange of symbols.* Only people use words, a wave of the hand, or a smile to create meaning. We can train a dog using reward and praise, but the dog attaches no meaning to its actions. Human beings, by contrast, find meaning in action by imagining people's underlying intentions. In short, a dog responds to *what you do;* a human responds to *what you have in mind* as you do it. You can train a dog to go to the hallway and bring back an umbrella. But because it doesn't understand intention, if the dog cannot find the umbrella, it is incapable of the *human* response: to look for a raincoat instead.

Third, Mead continued, *understanding intention requires imagining the situation from the other's point of view.* Using symbols, we imagine ourselves in another person's shoes and see ourselves as that person does. We can therefore anticipate how others will respond to us even before we act. A simple toss of a ball requires stepping outside ourselves to imagine how another will catch our throw. All social interaction involves seeing ourselves as others see us—a process that Mead termed *taking the role of the other.*

The Looking-Glass Self

In effect, others are a mirror (which people used to call a "looking glass") in which we can see ourselves. What we

think of ourselves, then, depends on how we think others see us. For example, if we think others see us as clever, we will think of ourselves in the same way. But if we feel they think of us as clumsy, then that is how we will see ourselves. Charles Horton Cooley (1864–1929) used the phrase **looking-glass self** to mean *a self-image based on how we think others see us* (1964; orig. 1902).

The I and the Me

Mead's fourth point is that, *by taking the role of the other, we become self-aware.* Another way of saying this is that the self has two parts. One part of the self operates as subject, being active and spontaneous. Mead called the active side of the self the *I* (the subjective form of the personal pronoun). The

 Mead is featured in the Gallery of Sociologists at www.TheSociologyPage.com.

other part of the self works as an object, the way we imagine others see us. Mead called the objective side of the self the *me* (the objective form of the personal pronoun). All social experience has both components: we initiate an action (the I–phase, or subject side, of self) and then we continue the action based on how others respond to us (the me–phase, or object side, of self).

Development of the Self

According to Mead, the key to developing the self is learning to take the role of the other. With limited social experience,

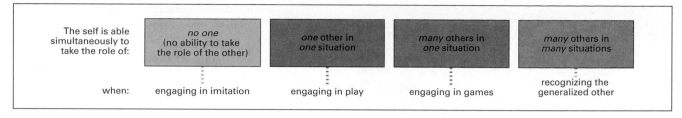

The self is able simultaneously to take the role of:	*no one* (no ability to take the role of the other)	*one* other in *one* situation	*many* others in *one* situation	*many* others in *many* situations
when:	engaging in imitation	engaging in play	engaging in games	recognizing the generalized other

FIGURE 5–1   Building on Social Experience

George Herbert Mead described the development of the self as a process of gaining social experience. That is, the self develops as we expand our capacity to take the role of the other.

infants can do this only through *imitation.* They mimic behaviour without understanding underlying intentions and so, at this point, they have no self. As children learn to use language and other symbols, the self emerges in the form of *play.* Play involves assuming roles modelled on **significant others,** *people, such as parents, who have special importance for socialization.* Playing "mommy and daddy"—often putting themselves literally in the shoes of a parent—helps young children imagine the world from a parent's point of view. Gradually, children learn to take the roles of several others at once. This skill lets them move from simple play (say, playing catch) with one other person to complex *games* (such as baseball) involving many others. By about age seven, most children have the social experience needed to engage in team sports. Figure 5–1 charts the progression from imitation to play to games.

But there is a final stage in the development of the self. A game involves taking the role of specific people in just one situation. Everyday life demands that we see ourselves in terms of cultural norms as *any* member of our society might. Mead used the term **generalized other** to refer to *widespread cultural norms and values we use as a reference in evaluating ourselves.*

As life goes on, the self continues to change along with our social experiences. But no matter how much the world shapes us, we always remain creative beings, able to act back towards the world. Thus, Mead concluded, we play a key role in our own socialization.

Critical Review   Mead's work explores the character of social experience itself. In the symbolic interaction of human beings, he believed he had found the root of both self and society. Mead's view is completely social, allowing no biological element at all. This is a problem for critics who stand with Freud (who said our general drives are rooted in the body) and Piaget (whose stages of development are tied to biological maturity).

Be careful not to confuse Mead's concepts of the I and the me with Freud's id and superego. For Freud, the id originates in our biology, but Mead rejected any biological element of the self, although he never clearly spelled out the origin of the I. In addition, the id and the superego are locked in continual combat, but the I and the me work cooperatively together (Meltzer, 1978).

YOUR TURN

Have you ever seen young children put their hands in front of their faces and exclaim, "You can't see me!"? They assume that if they can't see you, you can't see them. What does this suggest about a young child's ability to "take the role of the other"?

ERIK H. ERIKSON'S EIGHT STAGES OF DEVELOPMENT

While some analysts, including Freud, point to childhood as the crucial time when personality takes shape, Erik H. Erikson (1902–94) took a broader view of socialization. He explained that we face challenges throughout the life course (1963; orig. 1950).

Stage 1—Infancy: the challenge of trust (versus mistrust). Between birth and about eighteen months, infants face the first of life's challenges: to establish a sense of trust that their world is a safe place. Family members play a key part in how any infant meets this challenge.

Stage 2—Toddlerhood: the challenge of autonomy (versus doubt and shame). The next challenge, up to age three, is to learn skills to cope with the world in a confident way. Failing to gain self-control leads children to doubt their abilities.

Stage 3—Preschool: the challenge of initiative (versus guilt). Four- and five-year-olds must learn to engage their surroundings, including people outside the family, or experience guilt at failing to meet the expectations of parents and others.

Stage 4—Pre-adolescence: the challenge of industriousness (versus inferiority). Between ages six and thirteen, children enter school, make friends, and strike out on their own more and more. They either feel proud of their accomplishments or fear that they do not measure up.

George Herbert Mead wrote: "No hard-and-fast line can be drawn between our own selves and the selves of others." The painting *Manyness* by Rimma Gerlovina and Valeriy Gerlovin conveys this important truth. While we tend to think of ourselves as unique individuals, each person's characteristics develop in an ongoing process of interaction with others.

Rimma Gerlovina and Valeriy Gerlovin, *Manyness*, 1990. © the artists, New City, New York.

Stage 5—Adolescence: the challenge of gaining identity (versus confusion). During the teen years, young people struggle to establish their own identity. In part, teenagers identify with others, but they also want to be unique. Almost all teens experience some confusion as they struggle to establish an identity.

Stage 6—Young adulthood: the challenge of intimacy (versus isolation). The challenge for young adults is to form and maintain intimate relationships with others. Falling in love or making close friends involves balancing the need to bond with the need to have a separate identity.

Stage 7—Middle adulthood: the challenge of making a difference (versus self-absorption). The challenge of middle age is contributing to the lives of others in the family, at work, and in the larger world. Failing at this, people become self-centred, caught up in their own limited concerns.

Stage 8—Old age: the challenge of integrity (versus despair). Near the end of our lives, Erikson explains, people hope to look back on what they have accomplished with a sense of integrity and satisfaction. For those who have been self-

absorbed, old age brings only a sense of despair over missed opportunities.

Critical Review Erikson's theory views personality formation as a lifelong process, with success at one stage (say, as an infant gaining trust) preparing us to meet the next challenge. However, not everyone faces these challenges in the exact order presented by Erikson. Nor is it clear that failure to meet the challenge of one stage of life means that a person is doomed to fail later on. A broader question, raised earlier in our discussion of Piaget's ideas, is whether people in other cultures and in other times in history would define a successful life in Erikson's terms. In sum, Erikson's model points out how many factors—including the family and school—shape our personalities. We now take a close look at these important agents of socialization.

Agents of Socialization

Every social experience we have affects us in at least a small way. However, several familiar settings have special importance in the socialization process.

THE FAMILY

The family is the most important agent of socialization because it is the centre of the child's life. As we have seen, infants are almost totally dependent on others, and the responsibility of meeting their needs almost always falls on parents and other family members. At least until the onset of schooling, the family also shoulders the task of teaching children cultural values and attitudes about themselves and others. Overall, research suggests that nothing is more likely to produce a happy well-adjusted child than being in a loving family (Gibbs, 2001). Family-based socialization is not all intentional. Children learn continuously from the kind of environment that adults create. Whether children learn to think of themselves as strong or weak, smart or stupid, loved or simply tolerated, and—as Erikson suggests, whether they believe the world to be trustworthy or dangerous—depends largely on the quality of the surroundings provided by parents and other caregivers.

The family also confers social position on children— that is, parents not only bring children into the physical world but they also place them in society in terms of race, ethnicity, religion, and class. In time, all these elements become part of a child's self-concept. Of course, some aspects of social position may change later on, but social standing at birth affects us throughout our lives.

Interestingly, children are aware from a very early age of the accessories of class. Canadian sociologists Bernd Baldus and Verna Tribe (1978) presented children in grades 1, 3, and 6 with sets of pictures of two men (one who was well dressed and one who was casually dressed), two houses (one from a high-income area of the city), two dining rooms, and two cars (both reflecting expensive taste and less expensive taste). Regardless of gender, school environment, or class background, the children's ability to match person and appropriate taste level increased with grade level. Furthermore, the children were able to give "character" descriptions of the two men: the well-dressed man was described as cheerful, nice, smart, and likeable, while the casually dressed man was described as tough, lazy, and likely to swear, steal, drink, or be uncaring about his family. Clearly, when children learn about class, they are actually learning to assign different values to different people. This ability, in return, can have an effect on how they value themselves—in short, on their self-esteem.

In addition, research shows that class position affects not just how much money parents spend on their children but also what parents expect of them (Ellison, *et al.*, 1996). When asked to pick from a list of traits most desirable in a child, those with lower social standing favoured obedience and conformity; in contrast, affluent people chose good judgment and creativity (NORC, 2003). Why the difference? Melvin Kohn (1977) explains that people of lower social standing usually have limited education and perform routine jobs under close supervision. Expecting that their children will hold similar positions, they encourage obedience and may even use physical punishment like spanking to get it. Because well-off parents have had more schooling, they usually have jobs that demand imagination and creativity, so they try to inspire the same qualities in their children. Consciously or not, all parents act in ways that encourage their children to follow in their footsteps.

Affluent parents typically provide their children with an extensive program of leisure activities, including sports, travel, and music or dance lessons. These enrichment activities—far less available to children growing up in low-income families—represent important *cultural capital* that advances learning and creates a sense of confidence in these children that they will succeed later in life (Lareau, 2002).

The ethnic or racial background of families also contributes to the development of social identity, placing individuals within the cultural mosaic or the rainbow class structure—as visible minorities increasingly find themselves unemployed and poor (Frideres, 2005). Clearly, one's ethnic or racial background has profound effects on the development of self and identity, particularly if one is an immigrant, or the child of immigrants, and lives in a cohesive ethnic community. The Thinking about Diversity box (on p. 118) reveals the complexity of ethnic or racial socialization resulting from the arrival of new immigrants (renewal of diversity) and ethnic or racial intermarriage (dilution of diversity).

THE SCHOOL

Schooling enlarges children's social world to include people with backgrounds different from their own. It is only as they

Sociological research indicates that affluent parents tend to encourage creativity in their children while poor parents foster conformity. While this general difference may be valid, parents at all class levels can and do provide loving support and guidance by simply involving themselves in their children's lives. Here father and daughter add a little fun to a practice session at a week-long Suzuki Institute workshop.

encounter people who differ from themselves that children come to understand the importance of factors such as race and social class. As they do, they are likely to cluster in play-groups made up of one class, race, and gender (Lever, 1978; Finkelstein and Haskins, 1983).

GENDER

Schools join with families in socializing children into gender roles. Studies show that at school, boys engage in more physical activities and spend more time outdoors, and girls are more likely to help teachers with various house-keeping chores. Boys also engage in more aggressive behav-

THINKING ABOUT DIVERSITY:
RACE, CLASS, & GENDER
Ethnic and Racial Identities: Evidence of Renewal and Dilution

The government of Canada developed its multiculturalism policy to frame its response to the diversity created by a history of immigration, as discussed in Chapter 3 ("Culture"). We are to celebrate diversity rather than force assimilation—and encourage each ethnic community to pass its heritage and values on to generations of Canadian-born members. Nonetheless, the colourful cultural mosaic has developed blurred boundaries over time, as a result of interethnic and interracial marriages. Over time, an ever-larger proportion of Canadians claim multiple origins, thereby diluting the impacts of ethnic socialization. This dilution process is less advanced in the communities that experience renewal in the form of continuing immigration.

The 2001 census provides us with wonderful data that illustrate these processes, by asking about the ethnic group(s)—up to four—to which one's ancestors belonged and one's racial identity—White, Black, Chinese, South Asian, Latin American, and so forth. A census respondent who did not indicate "Aboriginal" or "White" on this question was considered to be a member of a visible minority. Thus, for each individual, we know ethnic background (up to four identities) and visible minority status.

Table 5–1 reveals the number of people with selected ethnic backgrounds. For example, four million people claim some Scottish ancestry: among them are those who are Scottish on both paternal and maternal sides

and those who have one Scottish ancestor out of four; the first are single-origin, the latter multiple-origin. The left column indicates that 85 percent of the four million people claiming Scottish heritage have multiple origins and, therefore, might be only one-quarter Scottish—or less if there are more than four ancestral origins.

The third column indicates the percentage of foreign-born among those claiming each ethnic heritage: the more recent the ethnic community (e.g., Filipino) the higher the proportion of immigrants. The older communities (e.g., French or English) are comprised of few immigrants. It is this variable, the percentage of immigrant, that is used to rank the ethnic categories from Aboriginal "North American Indian" to relatively recent East Indian, Filipino, and Chinese. Thus, in Table 5–1, the proportion of immigrants increases from top to bottom.

The fourth column indicates the percentage of people in each ethnic category who identify themselves as belonging to a visible minority. Looking back at Figure 3–3 (on p. 70) you will see that, increasingly since 1970, immigrants to Canada have come not from Europe but from Asia, Africa, and the Caribbean. Relatively recent waves of immigration from these countries mean that relatively few are Canadian-born, most belong to a visible minority, and intermarriage has not yet increased the multiple-origin components. In other words, in Table 5–1, where the percentage of immigrants is large, so

too is the percentage of visible minority; in contrast, the proportion with multiple origins is small.

Among the more established categories of Canadians of European origin (French to Finnish), Table 5–1 shows very large multiple-origin components (above 70%), indicating a great deal of interethnic marriage. The Italian and Japanese communities have slightly larger immigrant components and smaller multiple-origin components. From the Japanese to the Chinese, we see larger immigrant components—meaning that these communities experience continuing cultural renewal. While people who report Haitian or East Indian ancestry are unlikely to report multiple origins (14% and 19%, respectively), this is especially true of Somalis or the Chinese (9% and 1%, respectively). Bringing the percentage of Canadians belonging to a visible minority into our observations allows us to draw conclusions about both interethnic and interracial marriage: they lead to dilution of distinctive cultural characteristics or blur racial and ethnic boundaries. Imagine being part of Vancouver's Chinese community and compare that to having *some* Scottish ancestry. In which case would ethnic background frame one's life and shape one's identity?

You may have noticed the "Canadian" ethnic category. This is used mainly by people whose ancestors came to Canada many generations ago and who probably have very complicated—and possibly unknown—ancestral histories. The speed at which one's ancestral record can become unman-

iour in the classroom, while girls are typically quieter and better behaved (Best, 1983; Jordan and Cowan, 1995). Schools also contribute to the gender stereotyping that affects course choices and, ultimately, career aspirations—so that fewer girls prepare for advanced study in mathematics, engineering, or the physical sciences.

YOUR TURN

Point to ways in which campus life accentuates or minimizes the differences between women and men.

ageable is illustrated by the family history of author Linda Gerber. Her mother was born near Winnipeg of Finnish immigrant parents; Elsie married another immigrant from Finland and had three children who would describe themselves on the census as single-origin Finnish. Linda then married a German immigrant, so her children would report Finnish and German origins—and appear in four places in Table 5–1 (i.e., Finnish origin, German origin, Finnish multiple-origin, and German multiple-origin). Her daughter married a man of English and Irish ancestry—so their daughter,

Grace, would fill in all four spaces in the census with Finnish, German, English, and Irish, thereby appearing in eight places in the table. If Grace were to marry a man—with an equally diverse ancestry (perhaps Italian, Jamaican, Scottish, and Japanese)—her son would have too many distinct ancestries to report. How would he decide which ancestries to include in the four allotted spaces? His surname and inherited racial characteristics might help him choose. On the other hand, if his parents and grandparents were all Canadian-born, he might report—despite eight distinct ances-

tries and diverse cultural influences—that he belongs to a visible minority and is a single-origin Canadian.

WHAT DO YOU THINK?

1. How does a family get from such diversity to "Canadian" identities (or values), as described here?
2. If you were filling in the census, how would you report your own ancestry?
3. Are there cultural influences from the country (or countries) you or your ancestors came from that shape your life and identity?

TABLE 5–1   Ethnicity and Race in Canada: Immigration, Visible Minority Status, and Multiple Origins, 2001

Ethnic or Racial Category	Population	Immigrant (%)	Visible Minority (%)	Multiple Origins (%)
North American Indian[a]	1 000 890	0.01	0.01	54.45
Canadian	11 682 680	0.04	0.02	42.22
French	4 668 410	3.02	0.01	77.29
Irish	3 822 660	5.07	1.20	86.99
Scottish	4 157 210	5.87	1.25	85.39
English	5 978 875	9.14	1.81	75.25
German	2 742 770	11.55	1.17	74.26
Finnish	114 690	13.91	0.01	72.17
Italian	1 270 365	28.43	1.73	42.83
Japanese	85 255	34.39	89.44	37.68
Lebanese	143 635	48.75	50.30	34.61
Jamaican	211 725	53.09	90.08	34.72
Haitian	82 405	56.79	95.75	14.19
Somali	33 725	61.42	98.81	8.61
Egyptian	41 310	63.92	62.95	36.80
East Indian	713 330	66.62	96.91	18.51
Filipino	327 550	69.89	96.97	18.75
Chinese	1 094 700	71.96	97.89	1.44

[a] "North American Indian" includes First Nation (Status Indian) and non-Status Indian persons (i.e., those who are not registered under the *Indian Act*). In the census, North American Indians, Métis, and Inuit are instructed to bypass the question on visible minority status since they are not included in that category.

Source: Calculations by L.M. Gerber based on Statistics Canada, 2001 Census, Selected Demographic and Cultural Characteristics, catalogue number 97F0010XCB2001040.

What Children Learn

Schooling is not the same for children living in rich and poor communities. As Chapter 20 ("Education") explains, children from well-off families typically have a far better experience in school than those whose families are poor. For

all children, the lessons learned in school include more than the formal lesson plans. Schools informally teach many things, which together might be called the *hidden curriculum*. Activities such as spelling bees teach children not only how to spell but how society divides people into "winners"

Concern with violence and the mass media extends to the world of video games, especially those popular with young boys. Among the most controversial games, which include high levels of violence, is *Grand Theft Auto*. Do you think the current rating codes are sufficient to guide parents and children who buy video games, or would you support greater restrictions on game content?

and "losers." Moving beyond the personal web of family life, children soon discover that evaluation of skills, such as in reading and arithmetic, is based on impersonal standardized tests. Here, the emphasis shifts from *who* they are to *how* they perform. In addition, team sports help students develop strength and skills, while teaching them important lessons in co-operation and competition.

School is also the first experience with bureaucracy for most children. The school day is based on impersonal rules and a strict time schedule. Not surprisingly, these are also the traits of the large organizations that will employ most of them later in life.

THE PEER GROUP

By the time they enter school, children have discovered the **peer group,** *a social group whose members have interests, social position, and age in common.* Unlike the family and the school, the peer group lets children escape the direct supervision of adults. Among peers, children learn to form relationships on their own. Peer groups also offer the chance to discuss interests that adults may not share with their children (such as clothing and popular music) or permit (such as drugs and sex).

Not surprisingly, parents express concern about their children's friends. In a rapidly changing society, peer groups have tremendous influence and contribute to the generation gap. Peer group influence typically peaks during adolescence, when young people begin to break away from their families and think of themselves as adults. Even during adolescence, however, parental influence on children remains strong. Peers may affect short-term interests, such as music or films, but parents have greater influence on long-term goals, such as going to college (Davies and Kandel, 1981).

Finally, any neighbourhood or school is made up of many peer groups. As Chapter 7 ("Groups and Organizations")

explains, individuals tend to view their own groups in positive terms and put down others. In addition, people are influenced by peer groups they would like to join, a process sociologists call **anticipatory socialization,** *learning that helps a person achieve a desired position.* In school, for example, young people may copy the styles and slang of a group they hope will accept them. Later in life, a young lawyer who hopes to become a partner in the law firm may conform to the attitudes and behaviour of the firm's partners in order to be accepted.

THE MASS MEDIA

The **mass media** are *impersonal communications directed to a vast audience.* The term *media* comes from Latin meaning "middle," suggesting that the media function to connect people. The development of mass media occurs as communications technologies—first newspapers, then radio and television, and now the internet—disseminate information on a broad scale. See Figure 5–2 for the extent of television ownership worldwide.

Since the mass media have enormous effects on our attitudes and behaviour, they are important contributors to the socialization process. Television, broadcast on a regular basis in North America since the 1950s, has rapidly become the dominant medium in Canada. By 2001, 99.2 percent of Canadian households had colour televisions, 91.5 percent had VCRs, 19.8 had DVD players, and 68.3 had cable television (Statistics Canada, 2002d). Furthermore, rental spending on videos and DVDs is expected to reach $1.7 billion by 2007 (PricewaterhouseCoopers, 2003). Unfortunately, the vast majority of these expenditures will be on non-Canadian cultural products.

Just how "glued" to the television are we? The average Canadian watches 21 hours of television per week (Statistics Canada, 2002e). Years before children learn to read, watching television becomes a regular routine—as they grow up, young girls and boys spend about 14 hours per week in front of a television (Statistics Canada, 2002c). Indeed, television consumes as much of a child's time as interacting with parents.

 Parents and educators can find information about effects on children of exposure to various media, as well as strategies for reducing negative effects at www.media-awareness.ca/english/.

The extent of television viewing during childhood concerns researchers, who have found that television renders children more passive and less likely to use their imaginations (American Psychological Association, 1993; Fellman, 1995).

Television and Bias

Comedian Fred Allen once quipped that we call television a "medium" because it is rarely well done. For a variety of reasons, television—as well as all mass media—has provoked plenty of criticism. Some cite biases in television programming: liberal (or left-leaning) critics maintain that television shows mirror our society's patterns of inequality and rarely challenge the status quo. That is, television shows have traditionally portrayed men and women according to cultural stereotypes, placing men in positions of power and relegating women to the roles of mothers or subordinates. Moreover, television shows have long portrayed well-to-do people favourably, while depicting less affluent individuals—Archie Bunker of *All in the Family* is the classic example—as ignorant and wrongheaded. And, although visible minorities in the United States tend to watch more television than the White majority, until recent decades minorities have been all but absent from American programming (Gans, 1980; Cantor and Pingree, 1983; Ang, 1985; Parenti, 1986; Brown, 1990). The Media Perspectives box (on p. 122) discusses the characterization of minorities in the television programming we see here in Canada. In 2001, 61 percent of the television programs watched by Canadians were of foreign, mostly U.S., origin, which means, conversely, that only 39 percent originated in Canada (Statistics Canada, 2002c). The Canadian Radio-television Telecommunications Council (CRTC) requires that 60 percent of the programming on television, between 6 A.M. and midnight, is Canadian. Of course, television producers can provide Canadian content, but the viewer operates the remote control.

On the other side of the fence, conservative critics charge that the television and film industries are dominated by a cultural elite that is far more liberal than the population as a whole. Especially in recent years, they maintain, the media have become increasingly "politically correct," advancing various socially liberal causes, including feminism and gay rights (Rothman, *et al.*, 1993; Goldberg, 2002).

 An online chapter on the mass media is available at www.prenticehall.ca/macionis/massmedia.html.

The increasing popularity of Fox News—home to Sean Hannity, Bill O'Reilly, Brit Hume, and other more conservative commentators—suggests that Americans can now find programming with "spin" from both sides of the political

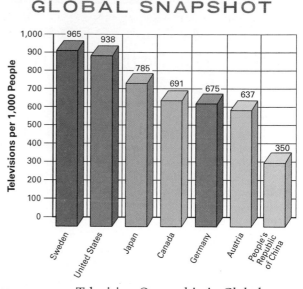

GLOBAL SNAPSHOT

FIGURE 5-2   Television Ownership in Global Perspective

Television is popular in all high-income countries, especially in Sweden and the United States where there is one television set for almost every person

Source: International Telecommunication Union (2005).

spectrum. Fox News was approved for digital cable in Canada by the CRTC in November 2004.

Television and Violence

In 1996, the American Medical Association issued the startling statement that violence in television and film had reached such a high level that it posed a hazard to health. For example, there is a strong link between aggressive behaviour and the amount of time elementary schoolchildren spend watching television and using video games. The public is concerned about this issue: three-quarters of American adults report having walked out of a movie or turned off the television because of too much violence. Almost two-thirds of television programs contain violence and, in most such scenes, violent characters show no remorse and are not punished (Wilson, 1998). Canadians have the same concerns and their own measures for dealing with media violence.

Two similar neighbouring towns in British Columbia provided a unique opportunity to study the impact of television violence, as one of the towns had received television before the other. By measuring the level of aggressive behaviour in children in both communities, initially and two years after the arrival of television in the second town, Williams (1986) was able to demonstrate that, after the arrival of television, the children caught up—in terms of aggressiveness—to those in the neighbouring community with longer exposure.

MEDIA PERSPECTIVES
How Do the Media Portray Minorities?

In an old *Saturday Night Live* sketch, Ron Howard tells comedian Eddie Murphy about a new film, *Night Shift*, in which two mortuary workers decide to open their own sideline business, a prostitution ring. Murphy asks whether any Black actors are in the film; Howard shakes his head for No. Murphy then thunders: "A story about two pimps and there wasn't no brothers in it? I don't know whether to thank you or punch you in the mouth, man!"

Murphy's ambivalence points up twin criticisms of the mass media. The first is that films and television portray minorities in stereotypical fashion, the second, that they are excluded altogether (Press, 1993). Certainly, in the 1950s, minorities were almost nowhere to be found on television and in films. Even the wildly successful 1950s comedy *I Love Lucy* was originally turned down by every major television studio because it featured Desi Arnaz, a Cuban, in a starring role. While the early Westerns presented stereotypical images of cowboys and "Indians," at least one of them starred an authentic Canadian Aboriginal actor: Six Nations' Jay Silverheels as Tonto, loyal sidekick of the Lone Ranger. Since then, the media have steadily included more minorities, so that the issue of exclusion has declined in importance. Since a majority of the programming watched by Canadians is of U.S. origin, changes there have immediate impact here.

But the second issue—*how* the media portray minorities—is just as important. The few African Americans who managed to break into television in the 1950s (for example, the infamous Amos and Andy, and Jack Benny's butler, Rochester) were confined to stereotypical roles portraying uneducated people of lowly status. More recently, many television shows feature Black stars: some are situation comedies replete with crude humour and bumbling characters; others, though humorous, depict upper-status

Black families. Several soap operas (*The Young and the Restless*, *As the World Turns*) reveal Blacks as young professionals—among them, physicians, hospital administrators, lawyers, fashion photographers, successful models, and corporate vice presidents. Oprah Winfrey, host of her own talk show, is very successful, very wealthy, and in a position of power or authority relative to that of her guests.

The portrayal of Aboriginal peoples has changed from the days when made-up White actors played "Indians" to American cowboys. Two Aboriginal performers from Canada, Chief Dan George (British Columbia) and Graham Greene (Ontario), helped redefine the role of the "Indian" in the major U.S. films *Little Big Man* and *Dances with Wolves*. Greene continues to appear in a wide range of film and television roles. In the meantime, singer/actor Buffy Sainte-Marie (Saskatchewan) provided early exposure to youngsters through her long-term involvement with *Sesame Street*. The popular Canadian production *North of 60* depicts Aboriginal peoples in the whole range of roles common to northern communities. Inuit singer Susan Aglukark (Nunavut) has changed the sound of Canadian music, just as Shania Twain (whose name means "on my way" in Ojibwa and who was raised for a time by an Ojibwa stepfather) has changed the sound of country music.

Perhaps the best indicator of the stature of Aboriginal programming is the creation of the Aboriginal Peoples Television Network, which is broadcast to Canadian homes via cable or satellite (Richards, 2006). (See the Media Perspectives box on p. 369 in Chapter 14.) At the same time, Carla Robinson (British Columbia), an Aboriginal woman with university degrees in mass communication and journalism, anchors the weekly CBC show, *Absolutely Canadian*, which is devoted to First Peoples' news and hosts the

monthly education program, *News in Review* (CBC, 2006).

Significant change has taken place in news reporting on the CBC and other television channels. Representation of social diversity today is greater than it was even a decade ago. In large measure, this stems from deliberate personnel policies responding to demands for greater minority representation and the need to appeal to diverse audiences. Increasingly, the news is conveyed to us by women, by members of visible minorities, and, in Canada, by people with names that are neither English nor French. Even such exclusively "White male" areas as sports, stock market coverage, business analysis, and war zone activity increasingly are reported by women and visible minorities.

Certainly, the mass media in Canada and the United States can boast of improvement in the portrayal of minorities: the perpetuation of former stereotypes has given way to depiction of minority individuals in a wide range of occupations and social classes. Some critics argue that depiction of minorities in high-status positions is unrealistic, as it masks the fact that minorities continue to face major barriers to full participation. On the other hand, such representation does reflect the fact that visible minorities, as well as women, are found in the *real* world in all social class categories.

WHAT DO YOU THINK?

1. Do you think that the mass media still present stereotypical images based on race, ethnicity, and gender?
2. What images of Aboriginal peoples have you acquired from the mass media?
3. Is Oprah Winfrey a token African-American woman placed in the spotlight in the interests of political correctness? or is hers a genuine success story?

Visit the website of the CRTC, which provides for Canadians a detailed chronology of reports, regulations, and actions taken on television violence at www.crtc.gc.ca/.

The federal government turned its attention to the impact of television violence on the behaviour of children through a House of Commons committee. The committee concluded that the evidence of a link was inconclusive and contradictory; nonetheless, it recommended implementation of legislation to control extremely violent forms of entertainment and a classification system to help parents protect their children from exposure to television violence (Canada, 1993b). The 1990s witnessed sustained activity on the part of the CRTC regarding television violence. Two studies commissioned by the CRTC, reported in 1992, concluded that there is a link between violence on television and violence in society, though it is not one of direct cause and effect. The Action Group for Violence on Television was set up with representatives from advertisers, producers, broadcasters, and cable companies. This committee developed classification guidelines and worked with other groups to regulate programming and broadcasting. They have worked closely with American legislators and producers on regulation and in the development of the V-chip, which allows parents to block unduly violent programming from their televisions. The Canadian Association of Broadcasters, deciding that *Mighty Morphin Power Rangers* violated its violence code, was instrumental in getting YTV and Global to remove the program from their schedules in 1994.

Television and other mass media have enriched our lives, generating a wide range of entertaining and educational programming. Moreover, the media increase our understanding of diverse cultures and provoke discussion of current issues. Note that television and radio have become highly interactive in recent years, asking people to call or email with their responses and reactions to current events or a range of issues. Even children participate. At the same time, the power of the media—especially television—to shape how we think continues to fuel controversy on many fronts. Computers and the internet complicate the picture further because governments cannot censor or otherwise effectively control the flow of information into or out of their countries.

Finally, many other spheres of life also play a part in social learning. For most people in Canada, these include religious organizations, the workplace, social clubs, neighbourhoods, and even ethnic communities. In the end, socialization proves to be not a simple matter of learning but a complex balancing act, as we absorb information from different sources. In the process of sorting, weighing, and internalizing all the information we receive, we shape our own distinctive personalities.

In recent decades, some people have become concerned that North American society is shortening childhood, pushing children to grow up faster and faster. Do films such as *Thirteen*, which show young girls dressing and behaving as if they were much older, encourage a "hurried childhood"? Do you see this as a problem? Why?

Socialization and the Life Course

While childhood has special importance in the socialization process, learning continues throughout our lives. An overview of the life course reveals that our society organizes human experience according to age: childhood, adolescence, adulthood, and, finally, old age.

CHILDHOOD

A few years ago, the maker of popular athletic shoes Nike Corporation came under attack. Its shoes are made in Taiwan and Indonesia—in many cases by children who work in factories instead of going to school. Some 250 million of the world's children work, half of them full time, earning about $0.50 an hour (Human Rights Watch, 2004). Criticism of Nike springs from the fact that most North Americans think of *childhood*—roughly the first 12 years of life—as a carefree time for learning and play. Yet, as the historian Philippe Ariès (1965) explains, that notion of childhood is fairly new. During the Middle Ages, children of four or five were treated like adults, expected to fend for themselves.

Today we defend our idea of childhood because children are biologically immature. But a look back in time and around the world shows that the concept of childhood is grounded not in biology but in culture (LaRossa and Reitzes, 2001). In rich countries, not everyone has to work, so childhood can be extended to allow time for young people to learn the skills they will need in a high-technology workplace. Because childhood in North America lasts such a long time, some people worry when children seem to be growing up too fast. In part, this "hurried child" syndrome results from changes in the family—including high divorce rates and both parents in the labour force—that leave children with less supervision. In addition, adult programming on television, in films, and on the internet carries grown-up concerns such as sex, drugs, and violence into young lives. Today's ten- to twelve-year-olds, says one executive of a children's television channel, have interests and experiences typical of twelve- to fourteen-year-olds a generation ago (Hymowitz, 1998). Perhaps this is why today's children, compared to kids fifty years ago, have higher levels of stress and anxiety (Gorman, 2000).

 Human Rights Watch reports on child soldiers around the world at www.hrw.org/campaigns/crp/index.htm.

ADOLESCENCE

At the same time that industrialization created childhood as a distinct stage of life, adolescence emerged as a buffer between childhood and adulthood. We generally link *adolescence*, or the teenage years, with emotional and social turmoil as young people struggle to develop their own identities. Again, we are tempted to attribute teenage rebelliousness and confusion to the biological changes of puberty. But it correctly reflects cultural inconsistency; for example, the mass media glorify sex, and schools hand out condoms, even as parents urge restraint. Consider, too, that an eighteen-year-old can go off to war but lacks the adult right to drink a beer. In short, adolescence is a time of social contradictions, when people are no longer children but not yet adults.

As is true of all stages of life, adolescence varies according to social background. Most young people from working-class families move directly from high school into the adult world of work and parenting. Teens from wealthier families, however, have the resources to attend college or university and perhaps graduate school, stretching adolescence into the late twenties and even the thirties.

ADULTHOOD

If stages of life were based on biological stages, it would be easy to define *adulthood*. However, deciding when someone

← → **YOUR TURN** ← →

What do you think marks the transition to adulthood? When will you consider yourself to be an adult?

is an adult turns out to be more complicated than it may seem. The term "adultescent" was coined in 1996 to describe people who are marrying, on average, four years later than in 1970, or not marrying at all, and who are living with their parents until they are 30 years of age or older—so that in effect "30 is the new 20" and "40 is the new 30" (Tierney, 2004). Regardless of its age of onset, adulthood is the time when life's major tasks, such as establishing a career and raising a family, are accomplished. Personalities are largely formed by then, although marked changes in one's circumstances—such as marriage, parenthood, unemployment, divorce, disability, or serious illness—cause significant changes to the self.

During early adulthood—until about age forty—young adults learn to manage day-to-day affairs for themselves, often juggling conflicting priorities: parents, partner, children, schooling, and work. Women are especially likely to try to do it all, because our culture gives them the major responsibility for child rearing and housework even if they have demanding jobs outside the home.

In middle adulthood—roughly ages forty to sixty—one's life circumstances are pretty well set. People become more aware of the fragility of health, which the young typically take for granted. Women who have spent many years raising a family find middle adulthood emotionally trying. Children grow up and require less attention, and husbands become absorbed in their careers, leaving some women with spaces in their life that are difficult to fill. Many women who divorce also face serious financial problems (Weitzman, 1985, 1996). For all these reasons, an increasing number of women in middle adulthood return to school and seek new careers.

For everyone, growing older means facing physical decline, a prospect our culture makes especially painful for women. Because good looks are considered more important for women, wrinkles and greying hair can be traumatic. Men have their own particular difficulties as they get older, perhaps worrying about the loss of hair or virility. Some women and men must admit that they are never going to reach earlier career goals or that the price of career success has been neglect of family or personal health.

OLD AGE

Old age comprises the later years of adulthood and the final stage of life itself, beginning in about the mid-sixties. Here again, societies attach different meanings to a time of life. Pre-industrial people typically grant elders great influence and prestige. As explained in Chapter 15 ("Aging and the

Elderly"), traditional societies confer on older people control of most of the land and other wealth; moreover, since their societies change slowly, older people amass a lifetime of wisdom, which earns them great respect (Sheehan, 1976; Hareven, 1982). In industrial societies, however, younger people work apart from the family, becoming more independent of their elders. Rapid change and our society's youth orientation combine to define anyone older as obsolete or even unimportant. To younger people, then, elderly people may be dismissed as old-fashioned and irrelevant. No doubt, however, this anti-elderly bias will diminish as the proportion of older people increases. The proportion of our population older than 65 has almost tripled since the beginning of the twentieth century and life expectancy is still increasing. Most men and women in their mid-sixties (the "young" elderly) can look forward to decades more of life. Statistics Canada expects the population aged 80 years old or more to reach an estimated 1.3 million by 2011, representing an increase of 43 percent from 2001 (Statistics Canada, 2002a).

This final phase of the life course differs in an important way from earlier stages. Growing up typically means entering new roles and assuming new responsibilities; growing old, in contrast, involves leaving roles that provided both satisfaction and social identity. Retirement may turn out to be restful or rewarding, but it may mean the loss of valued activity, sometimes resulting in outright boredom. As another life transition, retirement demands learning new and different patterns while unlearning familiar routines, such as those associated with work.

DEATH AND DYING

Through most of human history, death caused by disease or accident came at any age because of low living standards and primitive medical technology. In Canada today, however, the average life span is 79 years (76 for males, 83 for females). Therefore, while most senior citizens can look forward to more than another decade of life, growing old cannot be separated from eventual physical decline and, ultimately, death.

After observing many dying people, the psychologist Elisabeth Kübler-Ross (1969) described death as an orderly transition involving five distinct stages. Typically, a person first faces death with *denial*, perhaps out of fear and perhaps because our culture largely ignores the reality of death. The second phase is *anger*, when a person facing death sees it as a gross injustice. Third, anger gives way to *negotiation* as the person imagines avoiding death by striking a bargain with God. The fourth response, *resignation*, is often accompanied by psychological depression. Finally, a complete adjustment to death requires *acceptance*. At this point, no longer paralyzed by fear and anxiety, the person whose life is ending finds peace and makes the most of whatever time remains.

As the proportion of older women and men increases in our society, we can expect our culture to become more

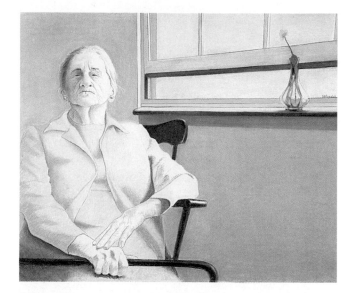

Various categories of people experience the stages of life in distinctive ways. Most men, for example, pass through old age with the support of a partner. Women, who typically outlive men, endure much of their old age alone, a reality poignantly captured in G.G. Kopliak's painting *Still Life*.

G.G. Kopliak, *Still Life*, private collection, Superstock, Inc.

comfortable with the idea of death. In recent years, we have started talking about death more openly and, increasingly, viewing dying as natural—and better than painful or prolonged suffering. More married couples now prepare for death with legal and financial planning. This openness may ease somewhat the pain of the surviving spouse who, more often than not, is a woman.

THE LIFE COURSE: PATTERNS AND VARIATIONS

This brief look at the life course points to two major conclusions. While each stage of life is linked to the biological process of aging, the life course is largely a social construction. For this reason, people in other societies may experience a stage of life quite differently or, for that matter, not at all. Next, in any society, the stages of the life course present certain problems and transitions that involve learning new and unlearning established routines.

Societies organize the life course according to age, but other forces—such as class, race, ethnicity, religion, and gender—also shape people's lives. This means that the general patterns described in this chapter apply differently to various categories of people within any society. Life experiences also vary depending on when, in the history of the society, people are born. A **cohort** is *a category of people with something in common, usually their age*. Because age cohorts are generally influenced by the same economic and cultural trends, they tend to have similar attitudes and values. Women and men born in the 1940s and 1950s, for example,

Prisons are one example of a total institution in which inmates dress alike and carry out daily routines under the direct supervision and control of the institutional staff.

grew up during a time of economic expansion that gave them a sense of optimism. Today's young people, who have grown up in an age of economic uncertainty, are less confident of the future.

YOUR TURN

Can you identify the influences—of family, peers, school (or teachers), religion, or the mass media—that have shaped your sense of self, attitudes, and values?

Resocialization: Total Institutions

A final type of socialization involves being confined—usually against one's will—in prisons or psychiatric hospitals. This is the **total institution,** *a setting in which people are isolated from the rest of society and manipulated by an administrative staff.* According to Erving Goffman (1961), total institutions have three important characteristics. First, staff members supervise all aspects of daily life, including where residents (or inmates) eat, sleep, and work. Second, life in a total institution is controlled and standardized, with the same food, uniforms, and activities for everyone. And lastly, formal rules dictate when, where, and how inmates perform their daily routines.

The purpose of such rigid routines is **resocialization,** *efforts to effect radical change in an inmate's personality by carefully controlling the environment.* Prisons and psychiatric hospitals physically isolate inmates behind fences, barred windows, and locked doors and limit their access to the telephone, mail, and visitors. The institution becomes their entire world, making it easier for the staff to bring about personality change—or at least obedience—in the inmate.

Resocialization is a two-part process. The staff breaks down the new inmate's existing identity: for example, an inmate must give up personal possessions, including clothing and grooming articles used to maintain a distinctive appearance; instead, the staff provides standard-issue clothes so that everyone looks alike. In prisons, the staff subjects new inmates to "mortifications of the self," which can include searches, head shaving, medical examinations, fingerprinting, and assignment of a serial number. Once inside the walls of a prison or psychiatric hospital, individuals also give up their privacy as guards or staff routinely inspect their living quarters.

In the second part of the resocialization process, the staff tries to build a new self in the inmate through a system of rewards and punishments. Having a book to read, watching television, or making a telephone call may seem like minor pleasures to the outsider, but, in the rigid environment of the total institution, gaining such simple privileges as these can be a powerful motivation to conform. The length of confinement or the condition of the patient typically depends on how well the inmate co-operates with the staff.

Total institutions affect people in different ways. Some inmates end up "rehabilitated" or "recovered," but others change little, and still others become hostile and bitter or increasingly withdrawn. Over a long period of time, living in a rigidly controlled environment can leave some *institutionalized,* without the capacity for independent living. The Thinking It Through box (on p. 127) takes a look at the effects on young offenders of short-term confinement in a strict discipline facility or boot camp.

THINKING IT THROUGH

Ontario's First Boot Camp as a Total Institution: 1997–2003

Newly arrived cadets, in black, march in front of their guards at Project Turnaround, a strict discipline facility in cottage country near Orillia, Ontario. The staff hopes that, by the time inmates leave in four to six months, they will have learned to respect discipline and structure. In theory, the thirty-two repeat offenders will leave the facility with greater self-esteem, new attitudes and values, and a reduced likelihood of returning to crime.

Resocialization in a total institution actually can change one's personality, or so the theory goes. The rebuilding of the self is extremely difficult, however, and no two people are likely to respond to any program in precisely the same way. Resocialization is the goal of prisons, psychiatric hospitals, and, in this case, Project Turnaround (1997–2003)—otherwise known as boot camp. The key to the operation of a total institution such as a boot camp is complete control of the environment so that only desired behaviours are permitted.

Staff members with a background in the military or social work maintain discipline but are expected to treat inmates (called cadets) with respect. In return, the cadets are expected to refer to staff as "Sir" or "Ma'am"—and are made do push-ups if they forget. The atmosphere is stern but not brutal: cadets do not experience physical punishment or abuse.

On arrival, young offenders get military-style brush cuts and learn to make their beds and tie their shoes the required way. They are introduced to discipline and plenty of it! Up at 6 A.M., lights out at 10 P.M., tidiness in austere surroundings, and lots of marching to wherever they otherwise might have sauntered. Other detention centres may allow inmates to watch television, play ping-pong, pool or video games, and even select their own food; idle moments are also part of an inmate's day. However, none of these is on the agenda at Project Turnaround. Instead, plenty of marching on the tarmac, more marching to and from various activities, calisthenics and some outdoor basketball and volleyball, three hours of school plus homework, and meals fill up the typical day. Towards the end of their term, the cadets build cedar canoes—no mean achievement—and take them, under staff supervision, on a wilderness adventure.

The program is designed, ultimately, to change cadet behaviour, attitudes, and values as well as to foster respect for themselves and for others. "Chins up. Look proud," they are told, in hopes that looking proud will make them feel proud. Those running the program believe that young people who respect themselves will be less inclined to return to a life of crime.

Postscript   Project Turnaround was created in 1997, during the period when Premier Mike Harris privatized a number of public services, in part to achieve cost reductions. This new facility cost 33 percent less per inmate per day to run and achieved a recidivism (reoffending) rate that was 17 percent lower than other youth detention facilities. Nonetheless, when

Dalton McGuinty's Liberals defeated the Conservative government, his government cancelled Project Turnaround (in 2003)—partly in response to union demands. The local MPP, Garfield Dunlop, brought the project story into the Ontario legislature (2006:236), pointing to its achievements (in cost and recidivism) and to the loss of jobs in the Orillia area resulting from its cancellation.

WHAT DO YOU THINK?

1. Why did incarceration at Project Turnaround result in 17 percent lower recidivism rates? What is it about their experience that made the inmates less likely to reoffend?
2. Does the "punishment fit the crime" or is boot camp "cruel and unusual punishment"?
3. If you were to be convicted of a crime, would you prefer to be sent to boot camp or to a conventional youth detention centre (or secure-custody facility)? Why?

Source: Based on Edwards (1997).

5 MAKING THE GRADE

The following learning tools will help you see what you know, identify what you still need to learn, and expand your understanding beyond the text. You can also visit this text's Companion Website™ at www.pearsoned.ca/macionis to find useful practice tests.

KEY POINTS

Social Experience: The Key to Our Humanity

Socialization is the lifelong process by which we develop our humanity and our particular personalities. A century ago, people thought that most human behaviour was guided by biological instinct. Today, we know that human behaviour is mostly a result of nurture rather than nature. The importance of social experience to human development is seen in the fact that social isolation can lead to permanent damage.

Understanding Socialization

Sigmund Freud's model of the human personality has three parts. The id represents innate human drives (the life and death instincts), the superego is internalized cultural values and norms, and the ego is our ability to resolve competition between the demands of the id and the restraints of the superego.

Jean Piaget believed that human development involves both biological maturation and social experience. He identified four stages of cognitive development: sensorimotor, preoperational, concrete operational, and formal operational.

Lawrence Kohlberg applied Piaget's approach to moral development. We first judge rightness in preconventional terms, according to our individual needs. Next, conventional moral reasoning takes account of parental attitudes and cultural norms. Finally, postconventional reasoning allows us to criticize society itself.

Carol Gilligan studied the effect of gender on moral development and found that males rely on abstract standards of rightness while females look at the effect of decisions on relationships.

To George Herbert Mead, the self comes from social experience and is partly self-directed (the I) and partly guided by society (the me). Infants yet to form the self can only imitate others; later, the self develops through play and games and eventually includes the generalized other. Charles Horton Cooley used the term "looking-glass self" to explain that we see ourselves as we imagine others see us.

Erik H. Erikson identified challenges that individuals face at each stage of life from infancy to old age.

Agents of Socialization

Usually the first setting of socialization, the family has the greatest influence on a child's attitudes and behaviour. Schools expose children to greater social diversity and introduce them to impersonal bureaucracy. Peer groups free children from adult supervision and take on great significance during adolescence. The mass media, especially television, have great impact on the socialization process; the average child spends as much time watching television as attending school or interacting with parents—with negative consequences.

Socialization and the Life Course

Each stage of the life course—childhood, adolescence, adulthood, and old age—is socially constructed in ways that vary from society to society. People in high-income countries typically fend off death until old age. Accepting death is part of socialization for the elderly.

Resocialization: Total Institutions

Total institutions, such as prisons and psychiatric hospitals, try to resocialize inmates, that is, to effect radical change in their personalities.

KEY CONCEPTS

socialization (p. 108) the lifelong social experience by which people develop their human potential and learn culture

personality (p. 108) a person's fairly consistent patterns of acting, thinking, and feeling

id (p. 111) Freud's term for the human being's basic drives

ego (p. 111) Freud's term for a person's conscious efforts to balance innate pleasure-seeking drives with the demands of society

superego (p. 111) Freud's term for the cultural values and norms internalized by an individual

sensorimotor stage (p. 112) Piaget's term for the level of human development at which individuals experience the world only through their senses

preoperational stage (p. 112) Piaget's term for the level of human development at which individuals first use language and other symbols

concrete operational stage (p. 112) Piaget's term for the level of human development at which individuals first see causal connections in their surroundings

formal operational stage (p. 112) Piaget's term for the level of human development at which individuals think abstractly and critically

self (p. 113) George Herbert Mead's term for the part of an individual's personality composed of self-awareness and self-image

looking-glass self (p. 114) Cooley's term for a self-image based on how we think others see us

significant others (p. 115) people, such as parents, who have special importance for socialization

generalized other (p. 115) George Herbert Mead's term for widespread cultural norms and values we use as a reference in evaluating ourselves

peer group (p. 120) a social group whose members have interests, social position, and age in common

anticipatory socialization (p. 120) learning that helps a person achieve a desired position

mass media (p. 120) the means for delivering impersonal communications to a vast audience

cohort (p. 125) a category of people with something in common, usually their age

total institution (p. 126) a setting in which people are isolated from the rest of society and manipulated by an administrative staff

resocialization (p. 126) efforts to effect radical change in an inmate's personality by carefully controlling the environment

APPLICATIONS & EXERCISES

1. Gather data by asking classmates and friends to name traits they consider to be part of "human nature." Then get them to discuss the extent to which these traits come from nature or nurture.

2. Find a copy of the book or 1963 film *Lord of the Flies*, a tale based on a Freudian model of personality. Do you agree with author William Golding's belief that violence is part of human nature?

3. Watch several hours of prime time programming on television, keeping track of any element of violence that is shown. On the basis of observing this small (and unrepresentative) sample of programs, what are your conclusions?

PRENTICE HALL
mysoclab™
Where learning & the sociological imagination intersect.

To reinforce your understanding of this chapter, and to identify topics for further study, visit MySocLab at **www.pearsoned.ca/mysoclab/** for diagnostic tests and a multimedia ebook.

CHAPTER SIX

Social Interaction in Everyday Life

How do we create reality in our
face-to-face interactions?

Why do employers try to control their workers'
feelings as well as their on-the-job behaviour?

What makes something funny?

att and Dianne are on their way to visit friends in an unfamiliar section of Calgary. They are now late because, for the last twenty minutes, they have been going in circles looking for Creek View Drive. Matt, gripping the wheel ever more tightly, is doing a slow burn. Dianne, sitting next to him, looks straight ahead, afraid to utter a word. Both realize the evening is off to a bad start.

Here we have a simple case of two people unable to locate the home of some friends. But Matt and Dianne are lost in more ways than one, since they fail to grasp why they are growing more and more angry with their situation and each other.

Consider the predicament from the man's point of view. Matt cannot tolerate getting lost—the longer he drives around, the more incompetent he feels. Dianne is seething, too, but for a different reason. She does not understand why Matt refuses to pull over and ask for directions to Creek View Drive. If she were driving, she fumes to herself, they already would have arrived and would be comfortably settled with their friends.

Why don't men ask for directions? Because men value their independence, they are uncomfortable asking for help—and are also reluctant to accept it. To men, asking for assistance is an admission of inadequacy, a sure sign that others know something they don't. If it takes Matt a few more minutes to find Creek View Drive on his own—and to keep his self-respect in the process—he thinks that's the way to go.

Women are more in tune with others and strive for connectedness. From Dianne's point of view, asking for help is right because sharing information builds social bonds and gets the job done. Asking for directions seems as natural to her as searching on his own is to Matt. Obviously, getting lost is sure to result in conflict as long as neither understands the other's point of view.

Such everyday experiences are the focus of this chapter. The central concept is **social interaction**, *the process by which people act and react in relation to others.* We begin by presenting several important sociological concepts that describe the building blocks of common experience and then explore the almost magical way that face-to-face interaction creates the reality in which we live.

Social Structure: A Guide to Everyday Living

For a short video ("Sociology and Cultural Relativity") on the difficulty of travelling to unfamiliar places, go to www.TheSociologyPage.com. Members of every society rely on social structure to make sense out of everyday situations and frame their lives. The world can be confusing—even frightening—when society's rules are unclear. We now take a closer look at the ways societies set the rules of everyday life.

Status

In every society, one of the building blocks of everyday life is **status,** *a social position that a person holds.* In general use, the word *status* generally means "prestige," in the sense that a university president has more status than a newly hired assistant professor. But sociologically speaking, both "president" and "professor" are statuses within the university organization. Status is part of social identity and helps define our relationships to others. As Georg Simmel (1950; orig. 1902), one of the founders of sociology, once pointed out, before we can deal with anyone, we need to know *who* the person is.

STATUS SET

Each of us holds many statuses at once. The term **status set** refers to *all the statuses a person holds at a given time.* A teenage girl is a daughter to her parents, a sister to her brother, a student at school, and a goalie on her hockey team. Status sets change over the life course. A child grows

Governor General Michaëlle Jean who is Commander-in-Chief of Canadian forces, is reviewing troops in this photo. In any rigidly ranked setting, no interaction can proceed until people assess each other's social standing; thus, military personnel wear clear insignia to designate their level of authority. Don't we size up one another in much the same way in routine interaction, noting a person's rough age, quality of clothing, and manner for clues about social position?

Mike Myers poses with Lorne Michaels after the two unveiled their stars on the Canadian Walk of Fame in Toronto in 2003. Which qualities do you think make Mike Myers a role model for young people?

up to become a parent, a student graduates to become a lawyer, and a single person marries to become a husband or wife, sometimes becoming single again as a result of death or divorce. Joining an organization or finding a job enlarges our status set; withdrawing from activities makes it smaller. Over a lifetime, people gain and lose dozens of statuses.

ASCRIBED AND ACHIEVED STATUS

Sociologists classify statuses in terms of how people obtain them. An **ascribed status** is *a social position that someone receives at birth or assumes involuntarily later in life.* Examples of statuses that are generally ascribed include being a daughter, an Aboriginal person, a teenager, or a widower. Ascribed statuses are matters about which people have little or no choice. In contrast, an **achieved status** refers to *a social position that someone assumes voluntarily and that reflects personal ability and effort.* Among achieved statuses are being an honour student, an Olympic athlete, a spouse, a computer programmer, a Rhodes Scholar, or a thief. In each case, the individual has at least some choice in the matter.

In practice, of course, most statuses involve some combination of ascription and achievement. That is, ascribed status affects achieved status. Adults who achieve the status of lawyer, for example, are likely to share the ascribed trait of being born into relatively privileged families. And any person of privileged sex, race, ethnicity, or age has far more opportunity to realize desirable achieved statuses than does someone without such advantages. In contrast, less desirable statuses such as criminal, drug addict, or welfare recipient are more easily acquired by people born into poverty.

YOUR TURN

Make a list of ten important statuses in your own life. Indicate whether each one is ascribed or achieved. Is this difficult to do? Explain your answer.

MASTER STATUS

Some statuses matter more than others. A **master status** is *a status that has exceptional importance for social identity, often shaping a person's entire life.* For many people, occupation is a master status since it conveys a great deal about social background, education, and income. Family of birth or marriage can function this way, too. Being an Eaton, a McCain, a Trudeau, a Mulroney, or a Stronach is enough by itself to push an individual into the limelight. Most societies of the world also limit the opportunities of women, whatever their abilities, making gender, too, a master status.

In a negative sense, serious disease also operates as a master status. Sometimes even lifelong friends avoid people with cancer, AIDS, or mental illness—simply because of the illness. In part, this is because we do not know what to say or how to act. Finally, we sometimes dehumanize people with physical disabilities by perceiving them only in terms of their disability. In the Thinking It Through box (on p. 134), three people with a physical disability describe this problem.

THINKING IT THROUGH
Physical Disability as a Master Status

In the following interviews, three women explain how a physical disability can become a master status—a trait that overshadows everything else about them. The first voice is that of twenty-nine–year-old Donna, who lives with her husband and son, and holds a master's degree in social work. She is blind:

> Most people don't expect handicapped people to grow up; they are always supposed to be children.... You aren't supposed to date, you aren't supposed to have a job, somehow you're just supposed to disappear. I'm not saying this is true of anyone else, but in my own case I think I was more intellectually mature than most children, and more emotionally immature. I'd say that not until the last four or five years have I felt really whole.

Rose is a retired elderly woman who suffers from spinal meningitis and is also blind:

> You ask me if people are really different today than in the '20s and '30s. Not too much. They are still fearful of the handicapped. I don't know if "fearful" is the right word, but uncomfortable at least. But I can understand it somewhat; it happened to me. I once asked a man to tell me which staircase to

use to get from the subway out to the street. He started giving me directions that were confusing, and I said, "Do you mind taking me?" He said, "Not at all." He grabbed me on the side with my dog on it, so I asked him to take my other arm. And he said, "I'm sorry, I have no other arm." And I said, "That's all right, I'll hold onto the jacket." It felt funny hanging onto the sleeve without the arm in it.

The third person suffers from chronic fatigue syndrome (CFS) or myalgic encephalomyelitis (ME):

> Well, when I first got diagnosed because there was such a stigma... you know, like it's a psychological thing, and I felt embarrassed. I didn't really tell anybody other than my immediate family and my very closest friends, whereas now when I'm talking I'll just say what I have because how are people going to learn if they don't know what it is and how it affects us? So in the beginning, I felt embarrassed. I cried... I mean I didn't cry when I had the growth as much as I cried when I got diagnosed with CFS because it was such a negative.... I felt... you know, and I went to a support group, and I said why do I feel like we're a group that has... you know, where we should be

shipped on an island all by ourself.... I mean I wouldn't even say half of my complaints because they were so weird... like my fingers hurt, my joints hurt or I feel like I have arthritis but I'm too young to have arthritis. You know, half the time you didn't even tell them because you felt like you were a hypochondriac.

Notice here how the disease is seen as a threat to the very self of the sufferer. She experiences social isolation, embarrassment, and stigma. There is continuing debate about whether CFS is just an excuse for a break among hard-driving, ambitious young people—hence its early nickname, the "Yuppie flu," a psychosomatic disorder, or a biologically based and therefore real disease. Those with the disease suffer from the current lack of clarity as to its cause and treatment.

WHAT DO YOU THINK?

1. Have you or a member of your family ever had a disease or disability that became a master status? If so, how did others react?
2. How might such a master status affect one's personality?
3. Can being very fat or very thin serve as a master status? Why?

Sources: Nancarrow Clarke (1985) and Orlansky and Heward (1981).

Role

A second important social structure is **role,** *behaviour expected of someone who holds a particular status.* A person *holds* a status and *performs* a role (Linton, 1937a). For example, holding the status of student leads you to perform the role of attending classes and completing assignments. Both statuses and roles vary by culture. In North America, the status of "uncle" refers to the brother of either your mother or your father, and the role of your maternal and paternal uncles might be much the same. In Vietnam,

however, the word for "uncle" is different on the mother's and father's sides of the family, and maternal and paternal uncles have different responsibilities. In every society, actual role performance varies according to an individual's unique personality, although some societies permit more individual expression of a role than others.

ROLE SET

Because we hold many statuses at once—a status set—everyday life is a mix of multiple roles. Robert Merton

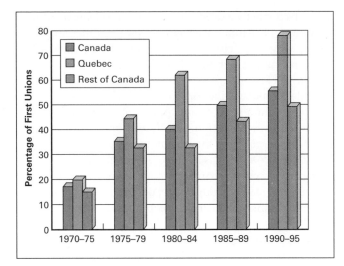

FIGURE 6–2   Common-Law Unions as a Proportion of First Unions: Canada, Quebec, and the Rest of Canada

Source: Adapted by L.M. Gerber from the article "Moving in Together: The Formation of First Common-Law Unions," published in the Statistics Canada publication *Canadian Social Trends*, Catalogue 11-008, Summer 1997, No. 47.

Flirting is an everyday experience in reality construction. Each person offers information to the other, and hints at romantic interest. Yet the interaction proceeds with a tentative and often humorous air so that either individual can withdraw at any time without further obligation.

couples negotiate the terms of their unions, eight out of ten choose to cohabit rather than marry. The collective impact of these common-law unions, negotiated one at a time, on the institution of marriage is far greater than that of the gays and lesbians who benefit from the redefinition of marriage to include same-sex couples. For the symbolic interactionist, the important elements in this restructuring of social life are the personal decisions made, in private, by individuals choosing cohabitation.

For another example of the social construction of reality, consider how this short excerpt from "True Trash," a short story by Margaret Atwood, illustrates one way that names and clothing styles construct a certain type of person.

> Eleven years later Donny is walking along Yorkville Avenue, in Toronto, in the summer heat. He's no longer Donny. At some point, which even he can't remember exactly, he has changed into Don. He's wearing sandals, and a white Indian-style shirt over his cut-off jeans. He has longish hair and a beard. The beard has come out yellow, whereas the hair is brown. He likes the effect: WASP Jesus or Hollywood Viking, depending on his mood. He has a string of wooden beads around his neck.
>
> This is how he dresses on Saturdays, to go to Yorkville; to go there and just hang around, with the crowds of others who are doing the same. Sometimes he gets high, on the pot that circulates as freely as cigarettes did once. He thinks he should be enjoying this experience more than he actually does.
>
> During the rest of the week he has a job in his father's law office. He can get away with the beard there, just barely, as long as he balances it with a suit. (But even the older guys are growing their sideburns and wearing coloured shirts, and using words like "creative" more than they used to.) He doesn't tell the people he meets in Yorkville about this job,

> just as he doesn't tell the law office about his friends' acid trips. He's leading a double life. It feels precarious, and brave. (1991:30–31)

This situation reveals the drama by which human beings create reality. Of course, not everyone enters a negotiation with equal standing. The fact that Donny was the son of the lawyer in whose office he was working likely helped him bridge the two realities.

THE THOMAS THEOREM

Donny's impression management allowed him to be part of the Yorkville scene and his father's law office. W.I. Thomas (1966 [orig. 1931]:301) succinctly expressed this insight in what has come to be known as the **Thomas theorem:** *situations we define as real become real in their consequences.* Applied to social interaction, Thomas's insight means that although reality is initially "soft" as it is fashioned, it can become "hard" in its effects. In the case of Donny, having succeeded as a member in two very different groups, he is able to lead a double life.

ETHNOMETHODOLOGY

Most of the time, we take social reality for granted. To become more aware of the world we help create, Harold Garfinkel (1967) devised **ethnomethodology,** *the study of the way people make sense of their everyday surroundings.* This approach begins by pointing out that everyday behaviour rests on a number of assumptions. When you ask someone the simple question "How are you?" you usually want to know how the person is doing in general, but you might really be wondering how the person is dealing with a specific physical, mental, spiritual, or financial challenge.

People build reality from their surrounding culture. Yet, because cultural systems are marked by diversity and even outright conflict, reality construction always involves tensions and choices. Turkey is a nation with a mostly Muslim population, but it is also a country that has embraced Western culture. Here, women confront starkly different definitions of what is "feminine."

Staton R. Winter, *The New York Times.*

However, the person being asked probably assumes that you are not really interested in details about any of these things, that you are just being polite.

One good way to uncover the assumptions we make about reality is to purposely *break the rules*. For example, the next time someone greets you by saying "How're you doing?" offer details from your last physical examination, or explain all the good and bad things that have happened since you woke up that morning, and see how the person reacts. To test assumptions about how close people should stand to each other while talking, slowly move closer to another person during a conversation. What happens if you face the back of the elevator, or—if you are a woman—you take your boyfriend or partner's hand from the front?

The results are predictable, because we all have some idea of what the "rules" of everyday interaction are. Witnesses to your rule breaking will most likely become confused or irritated by your unexpected behaviour—a reaction that helps us see not only what the "rules" are but also how important they are to everyday reality.

REALITY BUILDING: CLASS AND CULTURE

People do not build everyday experience out of thin air. In part, how we act or what we see in our surroundings depends on our interests. Gazing at the sky on a starry night, for example, lovers discover romance, and scientists see hydrogen atoms fusing into helium. Social background

also affects what we see: for this reason, residents of affluent Westmount in Montreal experience the city differently from those living in the city's east end, where the unemployment rate is one of the highest in Canada.

In global perspective, reality construction is even more variable. People waiting for a bus in London, England, typically queue in a straight line; people in Montreal wait in a much less orderly fashion. Constraints on women in Saudi Arabia—for example, they are not allowed to drive cars—would be incomprehensible here. Although the birth rate is rising in Moscow, where women perceive increased economic security, it remains low in the rest of Russia, where economic turmoil persists. In Canada, people assume that "a short walk" means a few blocks or a few minutes; in the Andes Mountains of Peru, this same phrase means a few kilometres.

The point is that people build reality from the surrounding culture. Chapter 3 ("Culture") explains how people the world over find different meanings in specific gestures, so inexperienced travelers can find themselves building an unexpected and unwelcome reality. Similarly, in a study of popular culture, Shively (1992) screened "westerns" to men of European descent and to Aboriginal men. The men in both categories claimed to enjoy the films, but for very different reasons. The men of European descent interpreted the films as praising rugged people striking out for the West and conquering the forces of nature. The Aboriginal men saw in the same films a celebration of land and nature. It is as if people in the two groups saw two different films.

Films also have an effect on the reality we all experience. The recent film *Ray*, about the life of the musician Ray Charles, who overcame the challenge of blindness, is only the latest in a series of films that have changed the public's awareness of disabilities. (See the Media Perspectives box on p. 140.)

Dramaturgical Analysis: "The Presentation of Self"

Erving Goffman was another sociologist who studied social interaction, explaining how people live their lives much like actors performing on a stage. If we imagine ourselves as directors observing what goes on in the theatre of everyday life, we are doing what Goffman called **dramaturgical analysis,** *the study of social interaction in terms of theatrical performance.*

Dramaturgical analysis offers a fresh look at the concepts of status and role. A status is like a part in a play, and a role serves as a script, supplying dialogue and action for the characters. Goffman described each individual's "performance" as the **presentation of self,** *a person's efforts to create specific impressions in the minds of others.* This process, sometimes called *impression management,* begins with the idea of personal performance (Goffman, 1959, 1967). The Media

Read Goffman's paper "The Presentation of the Self in Electronic Life: Goffman on the Internet" at www.ess.ntu.ac.uk/miller/cyberpsych/goffman.htm.

Perspectives box (on p. 140) invites you to try your hand at dramaturgical analysis, by taking a look at presentation of self and performance in the context of master status based on disability—in the context of major Hollywood films.

PERFORMANCES

As we present ourselves in everyday situations, we reveal information—consciously and unconsciously—to others. Our performance includes the way we dress (costume), the objects we carry (props), and our tone of voice and gestures (manner). In addition, we vary our performances according to where we are (the set). We may joke loudly in a restaurant, for example, but lower our voices when entering a church or other place of worship. People also design settings, such as homes or offices, to bring about desired reactions in others.

An Application: The Doctor's Office

Consider how a physician uses an office to convey particular information to the audience of patients. The fact that physicians enjoy high prestige and power is clear on entering a doctor's office. First, the doctor is nowhere to be seen. Instead, in what Goffman describes as the "front region" of the setting, each patient encounters a receptionist, or gatekeeper, who decides whether and when the patient can meet the doctor. A simple glance around the doctor's waiting room, with patients—often impatiently—waiting to be invited into the inner sanctum, leaves little doubt that the doctor and the staff are in charge.

The "back region" of the setting is composed of the examination room plus the doctor's private office. Once inside the office, a patient can see a wide range of props, such as medical books and framed degrees, that give the impression that the doctor has the specialized knowledge necessary to call the shots. The doctor is often seated behind a desk—the larger the desk, the greater the statement of power—and a patient is given only a chair.

The doctor's appearance and manner offer still more information. The white lab coat (costume) may have the practical function of keeping clothes from becoming dirty, but its social function is to let others know at a glance the physician's status. A stethoscope around the neck, and a medical chart in hand (more props), have the same purpose. A doctor uses highly technical language that is often mystifying to a patient, again emphasizing that the doctor is in charge. Finally, a patient usually uses the title "doctor," but the doctor often addresses a patient by his or her first name, which further shows the doctor's dominant position. The overall message of a doctor's performance is clear: "I will help you, but you must allow me to take charge."

YOUR TURN

Try doing a similar analysis of the offices of several faculty members on your campus. What differences do you notice? How do you explain the patterns?

NONVERBAL COMMUNICATION

The novelist William Sansom describes a fictional Mr. Preedy, an English vacationer on a beach in Spain:

> He took care to avoid catching anyone's eye. First, he had to make it clear to those potential companions of his holiday that they were of no concern to him whatsoever. He stared through them, round them, over them—eyes lost in space. The beach might have been empty. If by chance a ball was thrown his way, he looked surprised; then let a smile of amusement light his face (Kindly Preedy), looked around dazed to see that there were people on the beach, tossed it back with a smile to himself and not a smile *at* the people....
>
> [He] then gathered together his beach-wrap and bag into a neat sand-resistant pile (Methodical and Sensible Preedy), rose slowly to stretch his huge frame (Big-Cat Preedy), and tossed aside his sandals (Carefree Preedy, after all). (1956:230–31)

Without saying a single word, Mr. Preedy offers a great deal of information about himself to anyone watching him. This is the process of **nonverbal communication,** *communication using body movements, gestures, and facial expressions rather than speech.*

People use many parts of the body to convey information to others through *body language.* Facial expressions are the most important type of body language. Smiling, for instance, shows pleasure, although we distinguish among the deliberate smile of Kindly Preedy on the beach, a spontaneous smile of joy at seeing a friend, a pained smile of embarrassment after spilling a cup of coffee, and the full unrestrained smile of self-satisfaction we often associate with winning some important contest.

MEDIA PERSPECTIVES
Disease and Disability in Hollywood Film: Twenty Years of Change

Jamie Foxx won an Oscar (for best actor) for his brilliant portrayal of the blind musician, Ray Charles. This film, *Ray*, is the latest in a series that has raised public awareness of the challenges faced—and frequently overcome—by people with disabilities. This is good news for people with disabilities as well as for the people who help them. Most importantly, people with disabilities are being portrayed with greater accuracy and realism, so that the public learns what it means to live with a specific illness or disability. These films give human faces to various conditions and remove some of the fear that comes with lack of knowledge or unfamiliarity. They also illustrate the powerful grip of a master status defined by disability as well as the consequences of these disabilities for presentation of self and the performances of everyday life.

The first of these influential movies, *The Miracle Worker*, came out in 1962, telling the story of Helen Keller who, though both deaf and blind, was taught to communicate by her persistent tutor, Annie Sullivan. The Helen Keller National Center for Deaf-Blind Youths and Adults is still reaping the benefits of that film forty years later.

In the last two decades, people with a wide range of disabilities have been the subjects of perhaps fifteen major motion pictures. So important are these films that it seems one cannot win an Oscar or nomination for best actor without playing a severely troubled or challenged character.

Dustin Hoffman portrays a man with autism in *Rain Man*, Anthony Hopkins, in *The Silence of the Lambs*, plays a man who is criminally insane, and Al Pacino portrays blindness in *Scent of a Woman*. Tom Hanks has AIDS in *Philadelphia* and is developmentally challenged in *Forrest Gump*. In *Leaving Las Vegas*, Nicholas Cage portrays an alcoholic; Jack Nicholson plays someone with obsessive-compulsive disorder in *As Good as It Gets*. Leonardo DiCaprio portrays a developmentally challenged younger bother, Arnie, in *What's Eating Gilbert Grape*—and follows that with *The Aviator*, as the disturbed and reclusive Howard Hughes.

Each of these powerful films takes us into a previously unknown world and allows us to identify with someone who faces seemingly insurmountable physical and psychological challenges. These films destigmatize the disabilities and encourage donations to meaningful causes. At the very least, after viewing them, we should be more sensitive to and empathetic with the disabled people we encounter. In addition, we might be more willing to donate time or money to the organizations that do research and provide services for people with a range of disabilities. Often the actors themselves take up the cause, using their clout to raise funds, as did Tom Hanks after portraying a man with AIDS in *Philadelphia*.

Among the films that depict the triumph of talent or genius over the adversity of physical or psychological

disability are: *My Left Foot*, in which Daniel Day-Lewis portrays Irish writer/artist, Christy Brown, whose cerebral palsy leaves him in total control of only his left foot; *Shine*, in which Geoffrey Rush portrays Australian concert pianist, David Helfgott, whose early career is ruined by a nervous breakdown; *A Beautiful Mind*, in which Russell Crowe assumes the role of John Nash, mathematical genius and Nobel Laureate, who suffers from paranoid schizophrenia; and *Ray*, in which Jamie Foxx plays Ray Charles whose musical talent prevails despite blindness and drug addiction. Each story, embellished though it is by Hollywood, is based on a true story and the life of a real—and inspiring—individual. In each case, the individual achieves greatness despite the overarching master status defined by his disability. In these films, we see performances—or presentation of self—at two levels: those of the characters portrayed in the films and those of the brilliant actors who portray them.

WHAT DO YOU THINK?

1. Can you point to specific lessons about disabilities that we can learn from films?
2. Have you seen any of the films mentioned in this box? Why did you choose to see them and what were your reactions?
3. Can you apply dramaturgical analysis to these films? Can you do so at the two levels noted above?

Source: Based, in part, on Haberman (2005).

Eye contact is another key element of nonverbal communication. Generally, we use eye contact to invite social interaction. Someone across the room "catches your eye," sparking a conversation. Avoiding another's eyes, in contrast, discourages communication. Hands, too, speak for us. Common hand gestures in our society convey, among other things, an insult, a request for a ride, an invitation for someone to join us, or a demand that others stop in their tracks. Gestures also supplement spoken words; for example, pointing at someone in a threatening way gives greater emphasis to a word of warning, just as shrugging the shoulders adds an air of indifference to the phrase "I don't know," and rapidly waving the arms adds urgency to the single word "Hurry!"

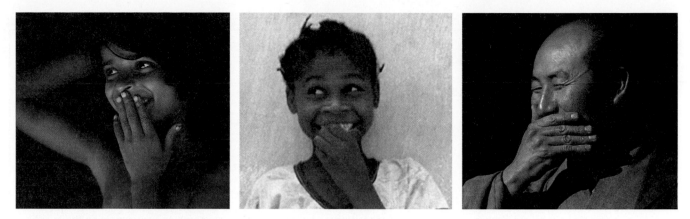

Hand gestures vary widely from one culture to another. Yet people everywhere chuckle, grin, or smirk to indicate that they don't take another person's performance seriously. Therefore, the world over, people who cannot restrain their mirth tactfully cover their faces.

Body Language and Deception

As any actor knows, it is very difficult to pull off a perfect performance. In everyday performances, unintended body language can contradict our planned meaning: a teenage boy offers an explanation for getting home late, for example, but his mother doubts his words because he avoids looking her in the eye. The movie star on a television talk show claims that her recent flop at the box office is "no big deal," but the nervous swing of her leg suggests otherwise. Because nonverbal communication is hard to control, it offers clues to deception, in much the same way that changes in breathing, pulse rate, perspiration, and blood pressure recorded on a lie detector indicate that a person is lying.

Can you tell an honest smile from a phoney one? Detecting phoney performances is difficult, because no one bodily gesture tells us that someone is lying. But because any performance involves so much body language, few people can lie without some slip-up, raising the suspicions of a careful observer. The key to detecting lies is to view the whole performance with an eye for inconsistencies.

GENDER AND PERFORMANCES

Because women are socialized to respond to others, they tend to be more sensitive than men to nonverbal communication. In fact, gender is a central element in personal performances, particularly with regard to demeanour, personal space, facial expression, and touching.

Demeanour—the way we act and carry ourselves—is a clue to social power. Simply put, powerful people enjoy more freedom in how they act. Off-colour remarks, swearing, or putting your feet on the desk may be acceptable for the boss but rarely for employees. Similarly, powerful people can interrupt others; less powerful people are expected to show respect through silence (Smith-Lovin and Brody, 1989; Henley, *et al.*, 1992; Johnson, 1994). Because women generally occupy positions of lesser power, demeanour is a gender issue as well. As Chapter 13 ("Gender Stratification")

explains, close to half of all working women in Canada hold clerical or service jobs under the control of supervisors who are usually men. Women, then, learn to craft their personal performances more carefully than men and to defer to men more often in everyday interaction.

How much space does a personal performance require? Power plays a key role here; the more power you have, the more space you use. Men typically command more space than women, whether pacing back and forth before an audience or casually sitting on a bench. Why? Our culture traditionally has measured femininity by how *little* space women occupy with the standard of "daintiness"—and masculinity by how *much* territory a man controls with the standard of "turf" (Henley, *et al.*, 1992).

For both sexes, the concept of **personal space** refers to *the surrounding area over which a person makes some claim to privacy*. In Canada, people typically position themselves some distance apart when speaking, though this distance varies depending on how well the speakers know each other; throughout the Middle East, in contrast, people stand much closer when conversing. Just about everywhere, men—with their greater social power—often intrude into women's personal space. If a woman moves into a man's personal space, however, her movement is likely to be interpreted as a sign of sexual interest.

For most North Americans, eye contact encourages interaction. In conversations, women hold eye contact more than men. But men have their own brand of eye contact: staring. When men stare at women, they are claiming social dominance and defining women as sexual objects. While it often shows pleasure, smiling can also be a sign of trying to please someone or of submission. In a male-dominated world, it is not surprising that women smile more than men (Henley, *et al.*, 1992). Note, however, that most Aboriginal cultures have quite different patterns of eye contact; for men and women, staring is discourteous and eye contact is made only fleetingly, perhaps in greeting or to check to see if someone else has finished speaking.

APPLYING SOCIOLOGY
Social Interaction: Working Online

Whereas technology traditionally merely sustained human relationships already formed from face-to-face contact, an internet relationship can be initiated technologically. Because they are so disembodied, so devoid of physical presence... divisions between man and woman, old and young, strong and weak, sick and healthy, cool dude and nerd begin to be bridged as in few other ways. (Goyder, 1997:186)

Social interaction based on electronic communication, and the internet in particular, has become an increasingly important part of the experience of Canadians. While providing an innovative basis of interaction in ongoing relationships, this new medium has put us in contact with people around the world and given new meaning to the concept of social network. We are, in McLuhan's terms, disembodied and unconstrained in time and space to the point where we lose our former identities and become part of the world or global village (Benedetti and DeHart, 1996).

At the University of Guelph, Professor Gerber has students in second- and fourth-year Canadian society courses involved in computer conferencing. Students meet face-to-face in the classroom, but they also communicate electronically with the class as a whole and with smaller working groups as they report on their research activities, respond to current events, debate various issues, react to contributions by other group members, and prepare for class presentations.

Since the conferencing begins early in each semester, most students *first* become acquainted with their classmates and study group members via computer. Initially, one hears—and reads on the computer screen—rumblings of resistance and discontent as students complain about the impersonality of computer contact and, instead, try to arrange group meetings "in the flesh." Later, these same students are involved in intensive electronic communication—effective communication that reaches all group members without the need to juggle schedules for face-to-face meetings restricted by time and place.

Their task at hand might be rewriting the Canadian constitution by groups representing Canada's provinces or regions, designing social or economic policies and programs as "ministers" of government departments, researching special topics and preparing for group presentations—or simply sharing reactions to current events. The conferencing system allows students to reach the whole class or their research group by simply logging on, from home or the computer lab, at any time of the day or night.

Over the course of the semester, discussion—and sometimes argument—can become quite intense. Differences of opinion and interpersonal conflict are sorted out through conferencing as well as face-to-face contact. Some of the conference group members admit to becoming "addicted," logging on several times a day with comments, references, or suggestions for areas to explore; others do the bare minimum. Comments on

the conferences and in-course evaluations reveal that some students thoroughly enjoy the experience while others remain frustrated and unenthusiastic. Inevitably, at the end of the semester, conference messages turn to goodbyes and comments on the quality and emotional impact of the group work: "Let's keep in touch"; "I'm going to miss this"; "Hey, we really accomplished a lot!" One student noted, "I never thought I'd get emotionally attached to you all. This has been the best group experience I've had at university."

This experience with electronic communication is increasingly relevant to the world of work. Many people who work as teams through this medium may meet in person rarely or not at all. More and more people, including those highly placed in various corporations, are doing some or all of their work from home offices—electronically linked to their head offices and the rest of the world. Disembodied and unconstrained by time or place, students and workers alike are engaged in productive activity through cyberspace.

WHAT DO YOU THINK?

1. Is it possible to form meaningful relationships over the internet? Do you know of individuals who met online, went on to date, and possibly married or plan to marry?
2. Can work, for an employer, be done effectively and efficiently using mainly online communication? Will more of us be working from home offices?
3. Does electronic communication empower or diminish you? Why?

Finally, mutual touching suggests intimacy and caring. Apart from close relationships, touching is generally something men do to women but, rarely in North American culture, to other men. A male physician touches the shoulder of his female nurse as they examine a report, a young man touches the back of his woman friend as he guides her across the street, or a male

skiing instructor touches young women as he teaches them to ski. In such examples, the intent of touching may be harmless and may bring little response, but it amounts to a subtle ritual by which men claim dominance over women.

None of the senses help us to communicate online, however, as the Applying Sociology box (above) explores.

YOUR TURN

As you watch people in elevators, can you see patterns of behaviour? Why do people in elevators behave in these highly predictable ways?

IDEALIZATION

People behave the way they do for many, often complex, reasons. Even so, Goffman suggests, we construct performances to *idealize* our intentions. That is, we try to convince others, and perhaps ourselves, that what we do reflects ideal cultural standards rather than selfish motives. Idealization is easily illustrated by returning to the world of doctors and patients. In a hospital, doctors engage in a performance commonly described as "making rounds." Entering the room of a patient, the doctor often stops at the foot of the bed and silently reads the patient's chart. Afterwards, doctor and patient talk briefly. In ideal terms, this routine involves a doctor making a personal visit to check on a patient's condition. In reality, the picture is not so perfect. A doctor may see several dozen patients a day and remember little about many of them. Reading the chart is a chance to recall the patient's name and medical problems, but revealing the impersonality of medical care would undermine the cultural ideal of the doctor as deeply concerned about the welfare of others.

Doctors, college professors, and other professionals typically idealize their motives for entering their chosen careers. They describe their work as "making a contribution to science," "helping others," "serving the community," or even "answering a calling from God." Rarely do they admit the more common, less honourable, motives: the income, power, prestige, and leisure time that these occupations provide.

We all use idealization to some degree. When was the last time you smiled and spoke politely to someone you do not like? Such little deceptions help us get through everyday life. Even when we suspect others are putting on an act, we are unlikely to challenge their performances, for reasons we shall examine next.

EMBARRASSMENT AND TACT

The famous speaker keeps mispronouncing the dean's name; the visiting ambassador rises from the table to speak, unaware of the napkin still hanging from her neck; the president becomes ill at a state dinner. As carefully as individuals may craft their performances, slip-ups of all kinds occur. The result is *embarrassment*, discomfort following a spoiled performance. Goffman describes embarrassment as "losing face," that is, temporarily losing some of the prestige associated with a status. Embarrassment is an ever-present danger because idealized performances usually contain some deception. In addition, most performances involve juggling so many elements that one thoughtless moment can shatter the intended impression.

A curious fact is that an audience often overlooks flaws in a performance, allowing an actor to avoid embarrassment. If we do point out a misstep—"Excuse me, but your fly is open"—we do it quietly and only to help someone avoid even greater loss of face. In Hans Christian Andersen's classic fable "The Emperor's New Clothes," the child who blurts out the truth—that the emperor is parading about naked—is scolded for being rude.

Often members of an audience actually help the performer recover a flawed performance. *Tact*, then, amounts to helping someone "save face." After hearing a supposed expert make an embarrassingly inaccurate remark, for example, people may tactfully ignore the comment, as if it had never been spoken, or treat what was said as a joke, perhaps with mild laughter. Or they may simply respond "I'm sure you didn't mean that," hearing the statement but not allowing it to destroy the actor's performance. With this in mind, we can understand Abraham Lincoln's comment, "Tact is the ability to describe others the way they see themselves." Tact is so common because embarrassment creates discomfort for the actor *and* for everyone else. Just as a theatre audience feels uneasy when an actor forgets a line, people who observe awkward behaviour are reminded of how fragile their own performances are. Socially constructed reality thus functions like a dam holding back a sea of chaos. When one person's performance springs a leak, others tactfully help make repairs. Everyone, after all, lends a hand in building reality, and no one wants it suddenly swept away.

In sum, Goffman's research shows that, although behaviour is spontaneous in some respects, it is more patterned than appears on the surface. Four centuries ago, Shakespeare captured this idea in memorable lines that still ring true:

> All the world's a stage,
> And all the men and women merely players:
> They have their exits and their entrances;
> And one man in his time plays many parts.
> (*As You Like It*, act 2, scene 7)

Interaction in Everyday Life: Three Applications

Is it possible to build a machine capable of human interaction? Check out www.ai.mit.edu/projects/humanoid-robotics-group/.

The final sections of this chapter illustrate the major elements of social interaction by focusing on three dimensions of everyday life: emotions, language, and humour.

EMOTIONS: THE SOCIAL CONSTRUCTION OF FEELING

Emotions, more commonly called *feelings*, are an important element of human social life. In truth, what we *do* often matters less than how we *feel* about it. Emotions seem very personal because they are private. Even so, just as society guides our behaviour, it guides our emotional life.

To most of us, these expressions convey (*from top left*) anger, fear, disgust, happiness, surprise, and sadness. But do people around the world define them in the same way? Research suggests that most human beings experience the same basic emotions and display them to others in the same basic ways. Culture plays a part by specifying the situations that trigger one emotion or another.

Adapted from Ekman and Friesen (1975).

The Biological Side of Emotions

Studying people all over the world, Paul Ekman (1980a, 1980b) reports that people everywhere recognize and express six basic emotions: happiness, sadness, anger, fear, disgust, and surprise. In addition, he found that people everywhere use the same facial expressions to show these emotions. Some emotional responses are "wired" into human beings, that is, they are biologically programmed in our facial features, muscles, and central nervous system. Why? From an evolutionary perspective, emotions have biological roots, but they also serve a social purpose: supporting group life. Emotions are powerful forces that allow us to overcome our self-centredness and build connections with others. Thus, the capacity for emotion arose in our ancestors along with the capacity for culture (Turner, 2000).

 Discover more about Paul Ekman's research on human emotions at ww.paulekman.com/.

The Cultural Side of Emotions

Culture, however, does play an important role in guiding human emotions. As Ekman explains, culture determines the *trigger* for emotion. Whether a specific event is defined as joyous (causing happiness), insulting (arousing anger), a loss (producing sadness), or mystical (provoking surprise and awe) is a function of culture. Culture also provides rules or contexts for the *display* of emotions. For example, most of us express emotions more freely with family members than with workplace colleagues. Similarly, we expect children to express emotions to parents, but parents to hide their emotions from their children. Furthermore, culture guides how we *value* emotions. Some societies encourage the expression of emotion; others expect members to control their feelings and maintain a "stiff upper lip." Gender also plays a part; traditionally, many cultures expect women to show emotions, but consider emotional expression by men to be a sign of weakness. In some cultures, of course, this pattern is less pronounced or even reversed.

Emotions on the Job

Most people are freer to express their feelings at home than on the job. The reason, as Hochschild (1979, 1983) explains, is that the typical company tries to regulate the behaviour and the emotions of its employees. Take the case of an airline flight attendant who offers passengers a meal and a smile. While this smile may convey real pleasure at serving the customer, Hochschild's study points to a different conclusion: the smile is an emotional script demanded by the airline as the right way to do the job. Therefore, we see that the "presentation of self" described by Erving Goffman can involve not just surface acting but also the "deep acting" of emotions. Thus, we socially construct our emotions as part of everyday reality, a process sociologists call *emotion management*.

LANGUAGE: THE SOCIAL CONSTRUCTION OF GENDER

As Chapter 3 ("Culture") explains, language is the thread that weaves members of a society into the symbolic web we call culture. Language communicates not only a surface reality but also deeper levels of meaning. One such level involves gender. Language defines men and women differently in terms of both power and value (Henley, *et al.*, 1992; Thorne, *et al.*, 1983).

Language and Power

A young man proudly rides his new motorcycle up his friend's driveway and boasts, "Isn't she a beauty?" On the surface, the question has little to do with gender. Yet why does he use the pronoun *she* to refer to his prized possession? The answer is that men often use language to establish control over their surroundings. In Roman and mediaeval Europe, a woman was legally the possession of a man (her father, brother, spouse, or guardian)—a situation that has changed in law only in recent years. But everyday language retains this concept when a man attaches a female pronoun to a motorcycle or boat or car, *because* it reflects the power of ownership.

Perhaps this is also why, in North America and elsewhere, a woman who marries usually takes the last name of her husband. When Joe Clark became Canada's prime minister in 1979, he encountered hostility and resistance from some quarters because his wife, Maureen Mc'leer, retained her birth name; the attitude seemed to reflect the idea that if a man can't control his wife, how can he possibly run the country? Stephen Harper, leader of Canada's current Conservative Party, is married to Laureen Teskey who also kept her unmarried name; on her husband becoming prime minister, she seems to have become Laureen Harper. On the other hand, in Quebec, women are not merely encouraged to retain their original names: the law actually requires them to do so.

YOUR TURN

When you see or hear references to Canada's prime minister and his wife in the media, is she called Laureen Teskey, Mrs. Harper, Ms. Harper, Laureen Harper, or Stephen Harper's wife Laureen? What do your observations reveal about gender equality in Canada today?

Language and Value

Typically, the English language treats as masculine whatever has great value, force, or significance. For instance, the word "virtuous" (meaning "morally worthy" or "excellent") comes from the Latin word *vir*, meaning "man." On the other hand, the adjective "hysterical" (meaning "emotionally out of control") is taken from the Greek word *hystera*, meaning "uterus." In many familiar ways, language also confers different value on the two sexes. Traditional masculine terms such as "king" and "lord" have a positive meaning, and comparable terms, such as "queen," "madam," and "dame," can have negative meanings. Similarly, use of the suffixes "-ette" and "-ess" to denote femininity usually devalues the words to which they are added: for example, a "major" has higher standing than a "majorette," as does a "host" in relation to a "hostess," or a "master" in relation to a "mistress." Language both mirrors social attitudes and helps perpetuate them.

Language and Attention

Language also shapes reality by directing greater attention to masculine endeavours. Consider our use of personal pronouns. In the English language, the plural pronoun "they" is neutral, as it refers to both sexes. But the corresponding singular pronouns "he" and "she" specify gender. Formerly, it was grammatical practice to use "he," "his," and "him" to refer to all people. As such, readers were to assume that the bit of wisdom "He who hesitates is lost" refers to women as well as to men. But this practice also reflected the traditional cultural pattern of ignoring the lives of women. This factual statement is a classic: "Man, like other mammals, breast-feeds his young."

The English language has no gender-neutral, third-person-singular personal pronoun. Recently, however, the

A general information source for gender-free alternatives to gendered pronouns is available at www.aetherlumina.com/gnp/.

plural pronouns "they" and "them" have gained currency as singular pronouns in speech (e.g., "A person should do as they please"). This usage remains controversial—it violates grammatical rules—but spoken English is now evolving to accept such gender-neutral constructions.

Even as the English language changes in response to social imperatives, gender is likely to remain a source of miscommunication between women and men. A booklet entitled *Words that Count Women Out/In* (Ontario Women's Directorate, 1992) examines some of the most common assumptions and barriers that have made the transition to gender-inclusive language troublesome. The authors point out that sexist language can even be found in the one piece of music that all Canadians hear and sing so frequently:

> O Canada! Our home and native land!
> True patriot love in all thy sons command.

Our national anthem, the symbol of our democratic spirit, excludes half the population—women, as well as immigrants who are not native to Canada.

YOUR TURN

Which team is (or was) likely to earn the most interest and respect—the Saskatchewan Roughriders (a football team) or the Preston Rivulettes (a phenomenally successful Ontario women's hockey team of the 1930s)? Explain your reasons.

REALITY PLAY: THE SOCIAL CONSTRUCTION OF HUMOUR

Humour plays an important part in everyday life. Everyone laughs at a joke, but few people think about what makes something funny. We can apply many of the ideas developed in this chapter to explain how, by using humour, we "play with reality" (Macionis, 1987).

The Foundation of Humour

Humour is produced by the social construction of reality; it arises as people create and contrast two different realities. Generally, one reality is *conventional*, that is, what people in a specific situation expect. The other reality is *unconventional*, an unexpected violation of cultural patterns. Humour therefore arises from contradiction, ambiguity, and double meanings found in differing definitions of the same situation.

There are countless ways to mix realities and generate humour. Contrasting realities are found in statements that contradict themselves, such as "Nostalgia is not what it used to be"; statements that repeat themselves, such as Yogi Berra's line "It's *déjà vu* all over again"; or statements that mix up words, such as Oscar Wilde's quip "Work is the curse of the drinking class." Even switching around syllables does the trick, as in the case of the country song "I'd Rather Have a Bottle in Front of Me than a Frontal Lobotomy."

Of course, a joke can be built the other way around, so that the audience is led to expect an unconventional answer and then receives a very ordinary one. When a reporter asked the famous criminal Willy Sutton why he robbed banks, for example, he replied dryly, "Because that's where the money is." However a joke is constructed, the greater the opposition or difference between the two definitions of reality, the greater the humour.

When telling jokes, a comedian uses various strategies to strengthen this opposition and make the joke funnier. One common technique is to present the first, or conventional, remark in conversation with another actor, then to turn towards the audience (or the camera) to deliver the second, unexpected line. In a Marx Brothers film, Groucho remarks, "Outside of a dog, a book is a man's best friend"; then, raising his voice and turning to the camera, he adds, "And *inside* of a dog, it's too dark to read!" Such "changing channels" emphasizes the difference between the two realities. Following the same logic, stand-up comedians may "reset" the audience to conventional expectations by interjecting the phrase, "But seriously, folks" between jokes.

People who like to tell jokes pay careful attention to their performance—the precise words they use and the timing of their delivery. A joke is well told if the teller creates the sharpest possible opposition between the realities; in a careless performance, the joke falls flat. Because the key to humour lies in the collision of realities, we can see why the climax of a joke is termed the *punch* line. See the Media Perspectives box (on p. 147) and be prepared to chuckle.

The Dynamics of Humour: "Getting It"

After someone tells you a joke, have you ever had to say, "I don't get it"? To "get" humour, you must understand both the conventional and the unconventional realities well enough to appreciate their difference. Someone telling a joke may make getting it harder by leaving out some important information. In such cases, listeners must pay attention to the stated elements of the joke and then fill in the missing pieces on their own. A simple example is the comment of the movie producer Hal Roach on his one hundredth birthday: "If I had known I would live to be one hundred, I would have taken better care of myself!" Here, getting the joke depends on realizing that Roach must have taken pretty good care of himself in order to make it to one hundred. Or take one of W.C. Fields' lines: "Some weasel took the cork out of my lunch." Here is an even more complex joke: "What do you get if you cross an insomniac, a dyslexic, and an agnostic? Answer: A person who stays up all night wondering if there is a dog." To get this one, you must know that insomnia is an inability to sleep, that dyslexia can cause a person to reverse the letters in words, and that an agnostic doubts the existence of God.

The Globe and Mail, under "Your Morning Smile," published a submission by Torontonian Poly O'Keefe: "What was the name of the first sociologist to study the impact of new communications technology on society? Answer: E-mail Durkheim" (August 2, 1997:A1). Getting it requires some knowledge of sociology. Needless to say, your recognition chuckle would have been more spontaneous had you encountered this tidbit out of context in the newspaper.

Why would someone telling a joke want the hearer to make this sort of effort to understand a joke? Our enjoyment of a joke is increased by the pleasure of figuring out all the pieces needed to "get it." In addition, getting the joke makes you an "insider" compared to those who don't "get it." We have all experienced the frustration of *not* getting a joke: fear of being judged stupid, along with a sense of being excluded from shared pleasure. People may tactfully explain a joke so that no one feels left out, but, as the old saying goes, if a joke has to be explained, it isn't very funny.

The Topics of Humour

All over the world, people smile and laugh, making humour a universal element of human culture. But, because people live in different cultures, humour rarely travels well. This travel journal entry provides an illustration:

October 1, Kobe, Japan. Can you share a joke with people who live halfway around the world? At dinner, I ask two Japanese college women to tell me a joke. "You know 'crayon'?" Asako asks. I nod. "How do you ask for a crayon in

MEDIA PERSPECTIVES
Double Take: Real Headlines That Make People Laugh

Humour is generated by mixing two distinct and opposing realities. Here are several actual headlines from newspaper stories. Read each one and identify the conventional meaning intended by the writer as well as the unconventional interpretation that generates humour.

"Police Begin Campaign To Run Down Jaywalkers"

"Iraqi Head Seeks Arms"

"Panda Mating Fails: Veterinarian Takes Over"

"Squad Helps Dog Bite Victim"

"War Dims Hope for Peace"

"Drunk Gets Nine Months in Violin Case"

"Stud Tires Out"

"Soviet Virgin Lands Short of Goal Again"

"Miners Refuse To Work after Death"

"British Left Waffles on Falkland Islands"

"Survivor of Siamese Twins Joins Parents"

"Prostitutes Appeal to Pope"

"Teacher Strikes Idle Kids"

"Killer Sentenced To Die for Second Time in Ten Years"

"Stolen Painting Found by Tree"

WHAT DO YOU THINK?

1. How would you "fix" these titles to make them straightforward newspaper headlines?
2. Why do headline writers print such bloopers?
3. Can you explain, in your own words, why these headlines are funny?

Source: Thanks to Kay Fletcher.

Japanese?" I respond that I have no idea. She laughs out loud as she says what sounds like "crayon crayon." Her companion Mayumi laughs too. My wife and I sit awkwardly, straight-faced. Asako relieves some of our embarrassment by explaining that the Japanese word for "give me" is kureyo, which sounds like "crayon." I force a smile. [John J. Macionis]

What is humorous to the Japanese may be lost on the Chinese, Iraqis, or Canadians. Even the social diversity of this country means that different types of people will find humour in different situations. Newfoundlanders, Québécois, Inuit, and Albertans have their own brands of humour, as do Canadians of Italian or Jamaican origin. Teenage girls, middle-aged men, Bay Street brokers, and rodeo riders will have specific kinds of jokes that they find funny. But for everyone, topics that lend themselves to double meanings or controversy generate humour. The first jokes many of us learned as children concerned bodily functions kids are not supposed to talk about. The mere mention of "unmentionable acts" or even certain parts of the body can dissolve young faces in laughter.

Are there jokes that do break through the culture barrier? Yes, but they must touch on universal human experiences such as, for example, turning on a friend:

I think of a number of jokes, but none seems likely to work in this cross-cultural setting. Is there something more universal? Inspiration: "Two fellows are walking in the woods and come upon a huge bear. One guy leans over and tightens up the laces on his running shoes. 'Jake,' says the other, 'what are you doing? You can't outrun this bear!' 'I don't have to outrun the bear,' responds Jake. 'I just have to outrun you!'" Smiles all around. [John J. Macionis]

The controversy found in humour often walks a fine line between what is funny and what is "sick." Before and during the Middle Ages, people used the word "humours" (derived from the Latin *humidus*, meaning "moist") to refer to four bodily fluids that were thought to regulate a person's temperament and, therefore, their health. Researchers today document the power of humour to reduce stress and improve health, confirming the old saying that "Laughter is the best medicine" (Haig, 1988; Bakalar, 2005).

Then too, every social group considers certain topics too sensitive for humorous treatment. Of course, you can still joke about them, but doing so risks criticism for telling a "sick" joke, or being labelled "sick" yourself. People's religious beliefs, tragic accidents, or appalling crimes are the stuff of jokes that are "sick" jokes or without humour. So close to the event, there have been no jokes about the victims of the terrorist attacks of September 11, 2001: that would be going too far.

The Functions of Humour

Humour is found everywhere because it works as a safety valve for potentially disruptive sentiments. Put another way, it provides an acceptable way to discuss sensitive topics without appearing to be serious. Having said something controversial, people can use humour to defuse the situation by simply stating, "I didn't mean anything—it was just a joke!" People also use humour to relieve tension in uncomfortable situations. One study of medical examinations found that most patients try to joke with doctors to ease their own nervousness (Baker, *et al.*, 1997).

As Canadians, we use humour to express our common identity. By laughing at ourselves or putting ourselves down, we reinforce a sense of our common bond. In a recent panel discussion called "Why Are Canadians So Funny?" moderator Michael J. Fox noted that *Maclean's* asked its readers to fill in the blank at the end of the phrase, "As Canadian as..." to counterbalance the motto "As American as apple pie." According to Fox, the winning entry was "As Canadian as possible under the circumstances" (Vowell, 1999).

Or Canada's idea of a joke is debating a constitutional accord as a matter of life and death, then changing the subject. "Canada is a nation without a punch line." These jokes play on Canadian insecurity about who we are. In the midst of the deep divisions caused by the constitutional discussions of the 1980s and 1990s, the second joke reminds us that we have a common national identity. We are "insiders" to the joke, not only because we are familiar with the debate but also because we recognize a pattern that characterizes our country. Because anglophones share constitutional angst with the Québécois, this joke should be funny in French. Would Americans find the joke funny?

Humour and Conflict

Humour may be a source of pleasure, but it can also be used to put down others. Men who tell jokes about women, for example, typically are expressing some measure of hostility towards them (Powell and Paton, 1988; Benokraitis and Feagin, 1995). Similarly, jokes about gay people reveal tensions about sexual orientation. Real conflict can be masked by humour in situations where one or both parties choose not to bring the conflict out into the open (Primeggia and Varacalli, 1990).

"Put-down" jokes make one category of people feel good at the expense of another. After collecting and analyzing jokes from many societies, Christie Davies (1990) confirmed that ethnic conflict is one driving force behind humour in most of the world. The typical ethnic joke makes fun of some disadvantaged category of people, at the same time making the joke teller feel superior. Given the Anglo-Saxon and French traditions of Canadian society, ethnic and racial minorities have long been the butt of jokes, as have Newfoundlanders ("Newfies") in eastern Canada, Irish in England, Sikhs in India, Turks in Germany, and Kurds in Iraq.

At times, people belonging to cultural minorities turn the joke on themselves. Peter Berger (1997) points out that Jews are so good at this that their jokes have become part of the larger American repertoire. This kind of humour illustrates that "jokes can summarize an often complex situation in wondrously economical ways, simplifying and illuminating and definitely providing some cognitive benefit" (p. 137). One of Berger's examples reveals the feelings of the Québécois, who believe that theirs is an island of French in an English-speaking ocean:

> In a village in Quebec a little girl goes out to collect mushrooms when the Virgin Mary appears to her. The little girl sinks to her knees and says: "*Ah, vous êtes Notre Dame! Vous êtes si belle. Vous êtes magnifique. Je vous adore. Je vous aime.*"
>
> And the Virgin Mary replies: "I'm sorry. I don't speak French."

Aboriginal Canadians also create this kind of humour. Many Aboriginal comedians have become popular with Aboriginal and non-Aboriginal audiences. Actor Graham Greene has been featured often on the CBC's *Air Farce*. And the CBC radio program *Dead Dog Café* had the effect of illuminating Aboriginal culture—it is corny, satirical, and right on!

Disadvantaged people, of course, also make fun of the powerful, as well as themselves, although they usually do so discreetly. Women in North America have long joked about men, and poor people poke fun at the rich. Throughout the world, people target their leaders with humour, and officials in some countries take such jokes seriously enough to vigorously repress them. Political jokes are "subversive by definition" (Berger, 1997).

In sum, the significance of humour is much greater than first impressions suggest. Humour amounts to a means of mental escape from a conventional world that is not entirely to our liking (Flaherty, 1984, 1990; Yoels and Clair, 1995). With that in mind, it makes sense that a disproportionate number of North America's comedians come from among the ranks of oppressed people, including Jews and African

⟷ YOUR TURN ⟵

Humour is most common among people with roughly the same social standing. Why is it risky to joke with people who have more power than you do? What about joking with people who have less power?

THINKING CRITICALLY
Is Technology Changing Our Reality?

Any technology tends to create a new human environment.... Technological environments are not merely passive containers of people but are active processes that reshape people and other technologies alike. In our time the sudden shift from the mechanical technology of the wheel to the technology of electric circuitry represents one of the major shifts of all historical time. (Marshall McLuhan, *The Gutenberg Galaxy*, 1969)

When Alexander Graham Bell invented the telephone in 1874 and made the first long-distance call between Brantford and Paris, Ontario, people were amazed that he had the ability to talk to others who were far away. People were just as astounded when Guglielmo Marconi received the first transatlantic wireless (radio) message on a hilltop at St. John's, Newfoundland (1901), or when the first airplane left the ground (1903), or when the first television signal was broadcast (1928).

Is today's new information technology once again restructuring reality? Absolutely. Computers and other information technologies have already altered the Canadian economy: the production of material goods (paper, steel, and cars) that defined the Industrial Age is steadily being replaced by the creation of ideas and images. This changes not only the nature of work, but also the skills needed for employment and even our legal definition of property.

Furthermore, new information technology erodes the importance of place in our lives. Bell's telephone was able to "reshape people"—to borrow McLuhan's phrase—by greatly extending their ears' "reach"; because sound travelled along wires, Bell knew exactly where the call was going. Telephones remained basically unchanged for a century after that. Today, cellular technology allows one to reach someone who could be anywhere on Earth—or even in flight. Similarly, technological advances are reconstructing the workplace so that "the new factory" is now any place with a computer terminal or fax machine, including one's home. Even the centuries-old concepts of national boundaries and citizenship have grown fuzzy under the influence of recent technology. Consider an employee who logs on to a computer terminal in Vancouver and connects to a U.S. bank in Manhattan (her employer) where she processes transactions throughout the day. Is this "electronic migrant" part of the workforce of Canada or the United States?

There is no more basic foundation of our sense of reality than the timeless adage, "Seeing is believing." But digital imagery now allows photographers to combine and manipulate pictures to show anything; computer animation enables movie producers to have humans interact with lifelike dinosaurs, and the technology of "virtual reality" means that, connected to computers, we can see, hear, and even feel the "touch" of another person thousands of kilometres away.

Finally, new information technology is reshaping the university and college scene. Historically, publishers have produced textbooks that augment the instruction of a classroom teacher. But books are becoming a smaller and smaller part of publishers' offerings, as we witness a proliferation of images on tape, film, and computer disk. In the years to come, textbooks themselves gradually will be replaced by CD-ROMs. In a world of interactive computer-based instruction, will students still need to travel to classrooms to learn? Will the university or college campus eventually be obsolete?

WHAT DO YOU THINK?

1. More than thirty years ago, Canadian media theorist Marshall McLuhan predicted that nations and their boundaries would be unable to survive the new electronic technologies, with their power of "totally involving all people in all other people." Under the influence of border-jumping technologies such as the internet, will Canada survive as a separate country? What is your own prediction?

2. As the "electronic age" unfolds further, what changes would you predict in everyday routines involving school, recreation, entertainment, shopping, employment, and the economy?

3. If the university or college campus were to disappear—if we were to do our teaching and learning online—would the university or college as an institution disappear as well?

Americans. They also come, disproportionately, from Canada. As long as we maintain a sense of humour, we assert our freedom and are no longer prisoners of reality—in doing so, we change the world and ourselves just a little.

We ended this chapter with a look (in the Thinking Critically box above) at the way technology has changed our everyday world, ourselves, and the ways in which we experience the world.

6 MAKING THE GRADE

The following learning tools will help you see what you know, identify what you still need to learn, and expand your understanding beyond the text. You can also visit this text's Companion Website™ at www.pearsoned.ca/macionis to find useful practice tests.

KEY POINTS

Social Structure: A Guide to Everyday Living

Social structure provides guidelines for behaviour, making everyday life understandable and predictable.

Status

A major component of social structure is status. Within an entire status set, a master status has special importance for a person's identity. Ascribed statuses are involuntary; achieved statuses are earned. Many statuses we hold are both ascribed and achieved.

Role

Role is the active expression of a status. Tension among the roles linked to two or more statuses causes role conflict; tension among the roles linked to a single status causes role strain.

The Social Construction of Reality

The social construction of reality is the idea that we build the social world through our interactions with others. The Thomas theorem states that situations defined as real are real in their consequences. Ethnomethodology is a strategy to reveal the assumptions and understandings people have of their social world. The social realities people build reflect both their culture and their social standing.

Dramaturgical Analysis: "The Presentation of Self"

Dramaturgical analysis views everyday life as theatrical performance, noting that people try to create particular impressions in the minds of others. Social power affects performances, which is one reason that men's behaviour typically differs from women's. Everyday behaviour carries the ever-present danger of embarrassment, or "loss of face." People use tact to prevent others' performances from breaking down.

Interaction in Everyday Life: Three Applications

The first application involves emotions. While the same basic emotions seem to be biologically programmed into all human beings, culture guides what triggers emotions, how we display emotions, and what value we attach to emotion. In everyday life, presentations of self involve managing emotions as well as behaviour.

The second application involves gender and language. In various ways, language defines women and men differently, generally to the advantage of men.

The third application involves humour, which stems from creating a difference between conventional and unconventional definitions of a situation. Because humour is an element of culture, people throughout the world find different situations funny.

KEY CONCEPTS

social interaction (p. 132) the process by which people act and react in relation to others

status (p. 132) a social position that a person holds

status set (p. 132) all the statuses a person holds at a given time

ascribed status (p. 133) a social position a person receives at birth or takes on involuntarily later in life

achieved status (p. 133) a social position a person takes on voluntarily that reflects personal ability and effort

master status (p. 133) a status that has special importance for social identity, often shaping a person's entire life

role (p. 134) behaviour expected of someone who holds a particular status

role set (p. 135) a number of roles attached to a single status

role conflict (p. 135) conflict among the roles connected to two or more statuses

role strain (p. 135) tension among the roles connected to a single status

social construction of reality (p. 136) the process by which people creatively shape reality through social interaction

Thomas theorem (p. 137) W.I. Thomas's statement that situations that are defined as real are real in their consequences

ethnomethodology (p. 137) Harold Garfinkel's term for the study of the way people make sense of their everyday surroundings

dramaturgical analysis (p. 138) Erving Goffman's term for the study of social interaction in terms of theatrical performance

presentation of self (p. 138) Erving Goffman's term for a person's efforts to create specific impressions in the minds of others

nonverbal communication (p. 139) communication using body movements, gestures, and facial expressions rather than speech

personal space (p. 141) the surrounding area over which a person makes some claim to privacy

APPLICATIONS & EXERCISES

1. Sketch out your own status set and the role set that goes with it. Identify any master statuses and any sources of role conflict or role strain.

2. During the next twenty-four hours, every time somebody asks, "How are you?" stop and actually give a complete, truthful answer. What happens when you respond to a polite question in an honest way? Listen to how people respond and watch their body language. What can you conclude?

3. Stroll around downtown or at a local mall. Pay attention to how many women and men you find at each location. From your observations, would you conclude that such places are "gendered" so that there are "female spaces" and "male spaces"?

PRENTICE HALL
mysoclab™
Where learning & the sociological imagination intersect.

To reinforce your understanding of this chapter, and to identify topics for further study, visit MySocLab at **www.pearsoned.ca/mysoclab/** for diagnostic tests and a multimedia ebook.

7

Groups and Organizations

How do groups affect the behaviour of members?

Why can "who you know" be as important as "what you know"?

In what ways have large business organizations changed in recent decades?

Seventy years ago, the opening of a new restaurant in California attracted little attention from the local community and went unnoticed by the nation as a whole. Yet this seemingly insignificant small business, owned and operated by Mac and Dick McDonald, would eventually spark a revolution in the restaurant industry and provide an organizational model that would be copied by countless other businesses of all kinds.

The McDonald brothers prospered; in 1940, they moved their single restaurant to San Bernardino and focused on serving hamburgers. The basic formula they put into place—which they called the "Speedee Service System" and we now call "fast food"—was to serve good quality food quickly and inexpensively to large numbers of people. They trained employees to perform specialized jobs, so that one person grilled hamburgers while others dressed them, made French fries, whipped up milkshakes, or presented the food to the customers. In 1953, the brothers began to franchise their hamburger restaurant.

In 1954, events took an unexpected turn when Ray Kroc, a travelling blender and mixer merchant, paid a visit to a McDonald's restaurant. Kroc was fascinated by the brothers' efficient system and, almost immediately, saw the potential for a greatly expanded system of fast-food restaurants. Kroc launched his plans in partnership with the McDonald brothers. Soon, he bought out their interests and set out on his own to become one of the greatest success stories of all time. Today, about 31 000 McDonald's restaurants serve people in 120 countries around the world.

The success of McDonald's is evidence of more than just the popularity of hamburgers and French fries. The organizational principles that guide this company are coming to dominate social life throughout North America and elsewhere. We begin this chapter with an examination of *social groups*, the clusters of people with whom we interact in our daily lives. As you will learn, the scope of group life in Canada expanded greatly during the twentieth century. From a world of families, local neighbourhoods, and small businesses, our society now turns on the operation of huge corporations and other bureaucracies (e.g., government) that sociologists describe as *formal organizations*. Understanding this expanding scale of social life and appreciating what it means for us as individuals are the main objectives of this chapter.

Social Groups

Almost everyone wants a sense of belonging, which is the essence of group life. A **social group** is *two or more people who identify and interact with one another*. Human beings come together in couples, families, circles of friends, churches, clubs, businesses, neighbourhoods, and large organizations. Whatever its form, a group is made up of people with shared experiences, loyalties, and interests. In short, while keeping their individuality, members of social groups also think of themselves as a special "us."

Not every collection of individuals forms a group. People all over the country with a status in common, such as women, homeowners, soldiers, millionaires, university graduates, and Roman Catholics, are not a group but a

Volunteers help during the massive blackout that hit Ontario in August 2003. Extraordinary circumstances such as storms, floods, tornadoes, or accidents can turn a crowd into a group, and strangers into neighbours.

Around the world, families are the most important primary group. In industrial societies, however, numerous friendship groups stand alongside families, joining individuals on the basis of shared interests rather than kinship.

category. While they know that others hold the same status, most are strangers to one another. Similarly, students sitting in a large lecture hall interact to a very limited extent. Such a loosely formed collection of people in one place is a *crowd* rather than a group.

However, the right circumstances can quickly turn a crowd into a group. Unexpected events, from power failures to terrorist attacks, can make strangers bond quickly. As Ontarians learned during the massive power failure that occurred in August 2003, people rapidly become keenly aware of their common plight and begin to help one another. Such extraordinary experiences sometimes become the basis for lasting relationships.

PRIMARY AND SECONDARY GROUPS

People often greet one another with a smile and the simple phrase, "Hi! How are you?" The response usually is, "Fine, thanks. How about you?" This answer is often more scripted than truthful. Explaining how one is *really* doing would make most strangers or casual acquaintances feel so awkward that they beat a hasty retreat. Friends, however, might genuinely want to hear a fuller response.

Social groups fall into one of two types, depending on their members' degree of personal concern for one another. According to Charles Horton Cooley (1864–1929), a **primary group** is *a small social group whose members share personal and lasting relationships*. Joined by *primary relationships*, people spend a great deal of time

To learn more about Cooley, visit the Gallery of Sociologists at www.TheSociologyPage.com.

together, engage in a wide range of activities, and feel that they know one another pretty well. In short, they show real concern for one another. The family is every society's most important primary group.

Cooley called personal and tightly integrated groups "primary" because they are among the first groups we experience in life. In addition, the family and early play groups have primary importance in the socialization process, shaping attitudes, behaviour, and social identity. Members of primary groups help one another in many ways, but they generally think of the group as an end in itself rather than as a means to some goal. In other words, we prefer to think that family and friendship link people who belong together. Members of a primary group also tend to view each other as unique and irreplaceable. Especially in the family, we are bound to others by emotion and loyalty. Brothers and sisters may not always get along, but they always remain siblings.

In contrast to the primary group, the **secondary group** is *a large and impersonal social group whose members pursue a specific goal or activity*. In most respects, secondary groups have characteristics opposite to those of primary groups. *Secondary relationships* involve weak emotional ties and little personal knowledge of one another. Most secondary groups are short-term, beginning and ending without particular significance. Students in a college course, who

SUMMING UP

Primary Groups and Secondary Groups

	Primary Groups ⟷	Secondary Groups
Quality of relationships	Personal orientation	Goal orientation
Duration of relationships	Usually long-term	Variable; often short-term
Breadth of relationships	Broad; usually involving many activities	Narrow; usually involving few activities
Perception of relationships	As ends in themselves	As means to an end
Examples	Families, circles of friends	Co-workers, political organizations

interact but may not see one another after the semester ends, are one example of a secondary group.

Secondary groups include many more people than primary groups. For example, dozens or even hundreds of people may work together in the same company, yet most of them pay only passing attention to one another. In some cases, time may transform a group from secondary to primary, as with co-workers who share an office for many years and develop closer relationships. But, generally, members of a secondary group do not think of themselves as "us." Secondary ties need not be hostile or cold, of course. Interactions among students, co-workers, and business associates are often quite pleasant, even if they are impersonal.

Unlike members of primary groups, who display a *personal orientation*, people in secondary groups have a *goal orientation*. Primary group members define each other according to *who* they are in terms of family ties or personal qualities, but people in secondary groups look to one another for *what* they are, that is, what they can do for each other. In secondary groups, we tend to "keep score," aware of what we give others and what we receive in return. This goal orientation means that secondary-group members usually remain formal and polite. In a secondary relationship, therefore, we ask the question "How are you?" without expecting a truthful answer.

The Summing Up table (above) reviews the characteristics of primary and secondary groups. Keep in mind that these traits define two types of groups in general terms; most real groups contain elements of both. For example, a women's group on a university campus may be quite large (and therefore secondary), but its members may identify strongly with one another and provide lots of mutual support (making it seem primary).

 Become a member of a virtual group at http://groups.yahoo.com.

Many people think that small towns and rural areas have mostly primary relationships and that large cities are characterized by more secondary ties. This generalization is partly true, but some urban neighbourhoods—especially those populated by people of a single ethnic or religious category, or long-time residents—can be very tightly knit.

YOUR TURN

List five social groups that are important in your life. In each case, is the group more primary or more secondary?

GROUP LEADERSHIP

One important element of group dynamics, or behaviour, is leadership. While a small circle of friends may have no leader at all, most large secondary groups place leaders in a formal chain of command.

Two Leadership Roles

Groups typically benefit from two kinds of leadership. **Instrumental leadership** refers to *group leadership that focuses on the completion of tasks.* Members look to instrumental leaders to make plans, give orders, and get things done. **Expressive leadership,** by contrast, is *group leadership that focuses on the group's well-being.* Expressive leaders take less interest in achieving goals than in raising group morale, and minimizing tension and conflict among members. Because they concentrate on performance, instrumental leaders usually have formal secondary relationships with other members; these leaders give orders, and reward or punish members according to how much the members contribute to the group's efforts. Expressive leaders build more personal primary ties; they offer sympathy to a member going through tough times, keep the group united, and lighten serious moments with humour. Typically, successful instrumental leaders enjoy more *respect* from members, and expressive leaders generally receive more personal *affection*.

In the traditional Canadian family, the two types of leadership are linked to gender. Historically, cultural norms have given instrumental leadership to men, who, as fathers and husbands, assumed primary responsibility for earning income and making major family decisions. Traditionally, expressive leadership belonged to women: mothers and

APPLYING SOCIOLOGY

The Club DJ: Local Musician, Global Ties

A father/son team set out to understand the social world of club DJs from a symbolic-inter-actionist perspective—using the interpretive approach discussed in Chapter 2 ("Sociological Investigation"). The father is University of Guelph professor, Hans Bakker: the son is Theo Bakker, otherwise known as DJ Krinjah of Montreal. Together they set out to make sense of the DJ scene. The father provided the analytical framework, while the son acted as participant observer and informant. They recently published a paper entitled, "The Club DJ: A Semiotic and Interactionist Analysis." You already know that we are dealing here with micro-level analysis, the everyday social interaction of individuals, the *social construction of reality*, and *meaning*.

In determining "meaningful signs in the world of popular music," the Bakkers identified the most important as the beat and the turntable. Variation of the beat from one song to the next is "the real thing": the ability to do this requires "listening to music of one tempo in one ear and then adjusting another song until it is the right tempo in the other ear" in a process called "beat matching." The turntablist techniques of scratching and juggling constitute the "grammar of dubbing." When reggae DJs spin records (and

that's old-tech vinyl record albums), they don't just play them: "they are dubbing, adding another layer of inter-pretation, the additional 'dub' of meaning." The reputation of DJs among their peers is determined by their skills in this fine art.

The roots of club DJing lie in the reggae music of Jamaica and are reflected in the continued use of Jamaican patois by DJs. While DJ Krinjah did most of his empirical work in Montreal, he also had extensive discussions with about three hundred DJs, over a six-year period, throughout North America and Europe. Because of the spatial or geographic scope of the study, the Bakker team argues that some of its claims can apply "to club DJs throughout the Western world." The network of reggae club DJs is far reaching. Obviously, no individual has contact with all of the others in the network, but the ties that bind them are strong because of their shared techniques and meanings. When they do meet, they speak the same international language.

Changes in technology have given rise to a rift within the DJ world— between club DJs and radio DJs. The former continue to perfect their skills on the turntable, while the latter have turned to the digital media, which are cheaper and allow new options, without

the requirement of learning turntablist techniques. One of the measures of prestige—in this world of turntables, the beat and dubbing—is the DJ's collection of records, which is so important that the collector may forgo eating in order to purchase them. Without vinyl, the DJ cannot display the valued skill: "Ability to manipulate vinyl is a technical skill that is highly respected and that differentiates DJs among themselves."

Once again, we come back to the beat, and beat-matching. It is through the beat of the music—more than the melody—that club DJs "speak" to the audience and earn the respect of their peers. Engaged in symbolic communication and meaning-making, they shape the social world of the reggae DJ, and the audiences who understand and respond to the language and grammar of the beat.

WHAT DO YOU THINK?

1. To what extent are club DJs and their audiences in a world of their own making?
2. Do you understand the world of the club DJ? How?
3. Why did the researchers use symbolic-interactionism to frame this study?

Source: Bakker and Bakker (2006).

---

wives encouraged supportive and peaceful relationships between or among family members. One result of this division of labour was that many children had greater respect for their fathers but closer personal ties with their mothers (Parsons and Bales, 1955; Macionis, 1978). Greater equality between men and women has blurred this gender-based distinction. In family life, as in other settings, women and men now take on both leadership roles.

Three Leadership Styles

Sociologists also describe leadership in terms of decision-making style. *Authoritarian leadership* focuses on instrumen-

tal concerns, takes personal charge of decision making, and demands that group members obey orders. While this leadership style may win little affection from the group, a fast-acting authoritarian leader is appreciated in a crisis. *Democratic leadership* is more expressive and makes a point of including everyone in the decision-making process. Although less successful in a crisis situation, democratic leaders generally draw on the ideas of all members to develop creative solutions to problems. *Laissez-faire leadership* allows the group to function more or less on its own. (*Laissez-faire* is French for "leave it alone.") Typically, this style is the least effective in promoting group goals (White and Lippitt, 1953; Ridgeway, 1983).

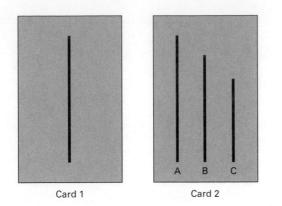

FIGURE 7-1 Cards Used in Asch's Experiment in Group Conformity

In Asch's experiment, subjects were asked to match the line on Card 1 to one of the lines on Card 2. Most subjects agreed with the wrong answers given by others in their group.

Source: Asch (1952).

Take a look at the Applying Sociology box (on p. 157) and ask yourself what kind of leadership is most likely to emerge in the DJ subculture.

GROUP CONFORMITY

Canadians throughout the country were shocked by news from Vancouver Island in November 1997. A group of teenagers on a river bank had brutally beaten fourteen-year-old Reena Virk, whose body was found in the water a week later. Perhaps the most shocking element in this story was the fact that the teenagers who viciously attacked their classmate were, with one exception, *girls*. An incident that began with accusations that Reena had been spreading rumours about one of the girls escalated into brutal violence after the girl stubbed a cigarette out on Reena's forehead. Seven girls and one boy proceeded to assault Reena, while ten others watched and did nothing to intervene; the boy and one girl returned after the others left, and pushed the unconscious Reena into the river. Actions that would not have been contemplated by the individuals involved became possible in the group context—in fact, the actions became part of the process of belonging to the group or conforming to group expectations.

The fact that teens are anxious to fit in surprises no one, although many people might be amazed at the lengths to which some will go to gain acceptance. Social scientists confirm the power of group pressure to shape human behaviour and report that it remains strong into adulthood. Thus, groups influence the behaviour of their members by promoting conformity. Fitting in provides a secure feeling of belonging but, in the extreme, group pressure can be unpleasant and even dangerous. As experiments by Solomon Asch and Stanley Milgram showed, even strangers can encourage conformity.

Asch's Research

Solomon Asch (1952) recruited students, supposedly to study visual perception. Before the experiment began, he explained to all but one member of a small group that their real purpose was to put pressure on the remaining person. Arranging six to eight students around a table, Asch showed them a standard line, as drawn on Card 1 in Figure 7–1, and asked them to match it to one of three lines on Card 2. Anyone with normal vision could easily see that the line marked "A" on Card 2 is the correct choice.

At the beginning of the experiment, everyone made the matches correctly. But then Asch's secret accomplices began answering incorrectly, leaving the naive subject—seated at the table so as to answer next to last—bewildered and uncomfortable. What happened? Asch found that one-third of all subjects chose to conform by answering incorrectly. Apparently, many of us are willing to compromise our own judgment to avoid the discomfort of being different, even from people we do not know.

Milgram's Research

Stanley Milgram, a former student of Solomon Asch's, conducted conformity experiments of his own (1963, 1965; Miller, 1986). In Milgram's controversial study (1963), a researcher explained to male recruits that they would be taking part in a study of how punishment affects learning. One by one, he assigned the subjects to the role of "teacher" and placed another person—actually an accomplice of Milgram's—in a connecting room to pose as a "learner." The "teacher" watched as the "learner" was seated in what looked like an electric chair. The researcher applied electrode paste to one of the wrists of the "learner," explaining that this would "prevent blisters and burns." The researcher then attached an electrode to the wrist and secured the leather straps, explaining that these would "prevent excessive movement while the learner was being shocked." The researcher assured the "teacher" that, although the shocks would be painful, they would cause "no permanent tissue damage."

The researcher then led the "teacher" back to the next room, explaining that the "electric chair" was connected to a "shock generator"—actually a phoney but realistic-looking piece of equipment with a label that read "Shock Generator, Type ZLB, Dyson Instrument Company, Waltham, Mass." On the front was a dial that appeared to regulate electric current from 15 volts (labelled "Slight Shock") to 300 volts (marked "Intense Shock") to 450 volts (marked "Danger: Severe Shock"). Seated in front of the "shock generator," the "teacher" was told to read aloud pairs of words. Then the "teacher" was to repeat the first word of each pair and wait for the "learner" to recall the second word. Whenever the "learner" failed to answer correctly, the "teacher" was told to apply an electric shock.

The researcher, dressed in the white lab coat of a scientist, directed the "teacher" to begin at the lowest level (15 volts) and to increase the shock by another 15 volts every time the learner made a mistake. And so the "teacher" did. At 75, 90, and 105 volts, the "teacher" heard moans from the "learner"; at 120 volts, shouts of pain; at 270 volts, screams; at 315 volts, pounding on the wall; after that, deadly silence. None of forty subjects assigned to the role of "teacher" during the initial research even questioned the procedure before reaching 300 volts, and twenty-six of the subjects—almost two-thirds—went all the way to 450 volts. Even Milgram was surprised at how readily people obeyed authority figures.

YOUR TURN

Was Milgram's research ethical, according to the guidelines you read about in Chapter 2, ("Sociological Investigation")? Explain your answer.

Milgram (1964) then modified his research to see if groups of ordinary people—not authority figures—could pressure people to administer electrical shocks, as Asch's groups had pressured individuals to match lines incorrectly.

This time, Milgram formed a group of three "teachers," two of whom were his accomplices. Each of the three "teachers" was to suggest a shock level when the "learner" made an error; the rule was that the group would then administer the *lowest* of the three suggested levels. This arrangement gave the naive subject the power to deliver a lesser shock regardless of what the others said.

The accomplices suggested increasing the shock level with each error, putting pressure on the third member to do the same. The subjects in these groups applied voltages three to four times higher than the levels applied by subjects  acting alone. Thus, Milgram's research suggests that people are likely to follow the lead of not only legitimate authority figures but also groups of ordinary individuals, even when it means harming another person. Recall that Canadian *peacekeepers* tortured and brutally murdered a Somali civilian under the influence of their peers.

Janis's "Groupthink"

Experts also cave in to group pressure, says Irving L. Janis (1972, 1989). Janis argues that a number of U.S. foreign policy errors—including the failure to foresee Japan's attack on Pearl Harbor during World War II and the ill-fated involvement in the Vietnam War—resulted from group conformity among the highest-ranking political leaders.

Common sense tells us that group discussion improves decision making. Janis counters that group members often seek agreement that closes off other points of view. Janis called this process **groupthink,** *the tendency of group members to conform, resulting in a narrow view of some issue.*

A Canadian illustration of the groupthink phenomenon was the inability of the federal supporters against the 1995 Quebec sovereignty referendum to see that they were in difficulty. Assuming that Quebecers would vote against sovereignty, Prime Minister Chrétien and his strategists appeared to have no plan for dealing with a victory by the Yes supporters. The dramatic takeover of the Yes supporters by Bloc Québécois leader Lucien Bouchard, which took federal strategists by surprise, contributed to a razor-thin No victory (50.4%). Embarrassment and discomfort in the wake of the referendum led to attempts to assign or apportion blame. The Quebec Liberal leader and head of the provincial No supporters, Daniel Johnson, became the convenient scapegoat. By implication, federalist leaders and strategists were not at fault.

REFERENCE GROUPS

How do we assess our own attitudes and behaviour? Frequently, we use a **reference group,** *a social group that serves as a point of reference in making evaluations and decisions.* A young man who imagines his family's response to a woman he is dating is using his family as a reference group. A supervisor who tries to predict her employees' reaction to a new vacation policy is using them in the same way. As these examples suggest, reference groups can be primary or secondary. In either case, our need to conform shows how others' attitudes affect us. We also use groups that we do *not* belong to for reference. Being well prepared for a job interview means showing up dressed the way people in that company dress for work. Conforming to groups we do not belong to is a strategy to win acceptance and illustrates the process of *anticipatory socialization,* described in Chapter 5 ("Socialization").

Stouffer's Research

Samuel A. Stouffer and his colleagues (1949) conducted a classic study of reference group dynamics during World War II. Among many other things, the researchers asked soldiers to rate their own or any competent soldier's chances of promotion in their army unit.  You might guess that soldiers serving in outfits with a high promotion rate would be optimistic about advancement. Yet the Stouffer research pointed to the opposite conclusion: soldiers in army units with low promotion rates were actually more positive about their chances to move ahead.

The key to understanding the Stouffer results lies in the groups against which soldiers measured themselves. Those assigned to units with lower promotion rates looked around them and saw people making no more headway than they

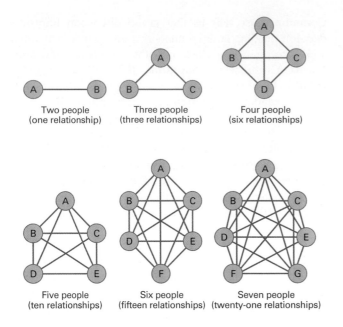

Two people
(one relationship)

Three people
(three relationships)

Four people
(six relationships)

Five people
(ten relationships)

Six people
(fifteen relationships)

Seven people
(twenty-one relationships)

FIGURE 7-2   Group Size and Relationships

As the number of people in a group increases, the number of
relationships that link them increases even faster. By the time six or
seven people share a conversation, the group usually divides into two.

Source: Created by John J. Macionis.

were. That is, although they had not been promoted, neither
had many others, so they did not feel deprived. However,
soldiers in units with a higher promotion rate could easily
think of people who had been promoted sooner or more
often than they. With such people in mind, even soldiers
who had been promoted were likely to feel shortchanged.

The point is that we do not make judgments about
ourselves in isolation, nor do we compare ourselves with
just anyone. Regardless of our situation in *absolute* terms,
we form a subjective sense of our well-being by looking at
ourselves in relation to specific reference groups.

IN-GROUPS AND OUT-GROUPS

Each of us favours some groups over others, because of
political outlook, social prestige, or just manner of dress.
On campus, for example, left-leaning student activists may
look down on fraternity members, whom they consider too
conservative; fraternity members, in turn, may snub the
computer nerds who work too hard. People in just about
every social setting make positive and negative evaluations
of members of other groups.

Such judgments illustrate another important element of
group dynamics: the opposition of in-groups and out-
groups. An **in-group** is *a social group towards which a member
feels respect and loyalty.* An in-group exists in relation to an
out-group, *a social group towards which a person feels a sense
of competition or opposition.* Many social groups follow this
pattern. A sports team, the Montreal Canadiens, for example,

is both an in-group to its members and an out-group for
members of opposing teams, such as the Calgary Flames. A
town's active New Democrats are likely to think of themselves
as an in-group in relation to the local Tories. Pairs of universities, such as the Universities of Guelph and Western
Ontario, may have long-standing rivalries. Whatever the
boundaries, in-groups and out-groups work on the principle
that "we" have valued characteristics that "they" lack.

Tensions between groups sharpen the groups' boundaries and give people a clearer social identity. However,
members of in-groups generally hold overly positive views of
themselves and unfairly negative views of various out-groups.

Power also plays a part in intergroup relations. A
powerful in-group can define others as a lower-status out-
group. Historically, in countless U.S. towns and cities, many
White people viewed people belonging to visible minorities
as an out-group and subordinated them socially, politically,
and economically. Internalizing these negative attitudes,
minorities often struggle to overcome negative self-images.
In this way, in-groups and out-groups foster loyalty but also
generate conflict (Tajfel, 1982; Bobo and Hutchings, 1996).

YOUR TURN

Identify five in-groups and five out-groups on campus.
Explain why you define each group as "in" or "out." Would
others agree with your choices?

GROUP SIZE

The next time you go to a party, try to arrive first. If you do,
you will be able to watch some fascinating group dynamics.
Until about six people enter the room, every person who
arrives shares a single conversation. As more people arrive,
the group divides into two clusters, and it divides again and
again as the party grows. Size plays an important role in
how group members interact.

To understand why, note the mathematical number of
relationships among two to seven people. As shown in
Figure 7–2, two people form a single relationship; adding a
third person results in three relationships; adding a fourth
person yields six. Increasing the number of people one at a
time, then, expands the number of relationships much
more rapidly since every new individual can interact with
everyone already there. Thus, by the time seven people join
one conversation, twenty-one potential channels connect
them. With so many open channels, some people begin to
feel left out, and the group usually divides.

The Dyad

The German sociologist Georg Simmel (1858–1918) studied
social dynamics in the smallest groups. Simmel (1950; orig.
1902) used the term **dyad** to designate *a social group with two*

members. Simmel explained that social interaction in a dyad is typically more intense than in larger groups because neither member shares the other's attention with anyone else. In North America, love affairs, marriages, and the closest friendships are dyadic. But like a stool with only two legs, dyads are unstable. Both members of a dyad must work to keep the relationship going; if either withdraws, the group collapses. Because the stability of marriages is important to society, the marital dyad is supported by legal, economic, and often religious ties.

 Read about the *Fifth Estate*'s investigation into a controversial polygamous community in British Columbia at www.cbc.ca/fifth/bustupinbountiful/

The Triad

Simmel also studied the **triad,** *a social group with three members,* which contains three relationships, each uniting two of the three people. A triad is more stable than a dyad because one member can act as a mediator should the relationship between the other two become strained. Such group dynamics help explain why members of a dyad (say, a married couple) might seek out a third person (such as a counsellor) to discuss tensions between them. On the other hand, two of the three can pair up to press their views on the third, or two may intensify their relationship, leaving the other feeling left out. For example, when two of the three develop a romantic interest in each other, they will come to understand the old saying, "Two's company, three's a crowd." The potential for romance within a triad was the basis for much of the humour in the 1977–84 television sitcom, *Three's Company.*

As groups grow beyond three people, they become more stable and capable of withstanding the loss of one or more members. At the same time, increases in group size reduce the intense personal interaction possible only in the smallest groups. This is why larger groups are based less on personal attachment and more on formal rules and regulations.

SOCIAL DIVERSITY: RACE, CLASS, AND GENDER

Race, ethnicity, class, and gender each play a part in group dynamics. Peter Blau (1977; Blau, *et al.*, 1982; South and Messner, 1986) points out three ways in which social diversity influences intergroup contact:

- **Large groups turn inwards**. Extending Simmel's analysis of group size, Blau explains that the larger a group, the more likely its members are to maintain relationships exclusively among themselves. University of Toronto sociologist Raymond Breton (1964) studied this phenomenon among urban minorities, coining the term *institutional completeness* to account for the abilities of larger groups to meet their members' needs from within their own boundaries. In contrast, members of smaller groups reach beyond their immediate social circles. Generations ago, when the Montreal Jewish community was very small, young people could not find marriage

The triad, illustrated by Jonathan Green's painting *Friends,* includes three people. A triad is more stable than a dyad because conflict between any two persons can be mediated by the third member. Even so, should the relationship between any two become more intense in a positive sense, those two are likely to exclude the third.

Jonathan Green, *Friends,* 1992. Oil on masonite, 14 in. × 11 in. © Jonathan Green, Naples, Florida. Collection of Patric McCoy.

partners from within; therefore, many migrated to centres with larger Jewish populations (New York, for example) or married non-Jews, thereby threatening the viability of the Montreal community.

- **Heterogeneous groups turn outwards**. The more internally diverse the group, the more likely its members are to interact with outsiders. Members of campus groups that recruit people of both sexes and various social backgrounds typically have more intergroup contact than those with members of one social category.

- **Physical boundaries create social boundaries**. To the extent that a social group is physically segregated from others (by having its own residence or dining area, for example), its members are less likely to interact with other people.

NETWORKS

A **network** is *a web of weak social ties.* Think of a network as a "fuzzy" group containing people who come into occasional contact but who lack a sense of boundaries and belonging. If a group is a circle of friends, then a network might be

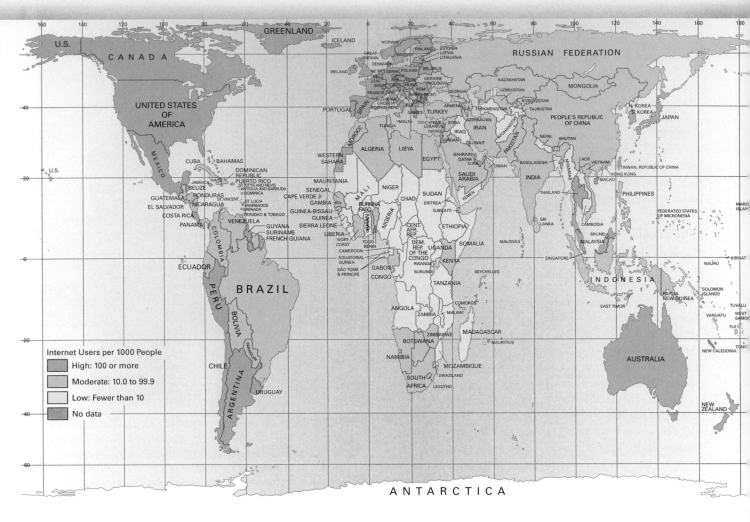

WINDOW ON THE WORLD

GLOBAL MAP 7–1 Internet Users in Global Perspective

This map shows how the Information Revolution has affected countries around the world. In most high-income nations, at least one-third of the population uses the internet. By contrast, only a small proportion of people in low-income nations does so. What effect does this have on people's access to information? What does this mean for the future in terms of global inequality?

Sources: International Telecommunication Union (2005) and United Nations Development Programme (2005).

described as a "social web" expanding outwards, often reaching great distances and including large numbers of people. Some networks come close to being groups, as is the case with college classmates who stay in touch after graduation through class newsletters and reunions. More commonly, however, a network includes people we *know of*—or who *know of us*—but with whom we interact rarely, if at all. One woman with a widespread reputation as a community organizer explains, "I get calls at home, someone says, 'Are you Roseann Navarro? Somebody told me to call you. I have this problem...'" (quoted in Kaminer, 1984:94).

Network ties often give us the sense that we live in a "small" world. In a classic experiment, Stanley Milgram (1967; Watts, 1999) gave letters to subjects in Kansas and Nebraska intended for a few specific people in Boston who were unknown to the original subjects. No addresses were supplied, and the subjects in the study were told to send the letters to others they knew personally who might know the target people. Milgram found that the target people received the letters with, on average, six subjects passing them on. This result led Milgram to conclude that just about everyone is connected to everyone else by "six degrees of separation." Later

Today's colleges and universities encourage social diversity. One of the resulting challenges is ensuring that all categories of students are fully integrated into campus life. This is not always easy. Following Blau's theory of group dynamics, as students from minorities increase in numbers, they tend to form groups of their own and interact less with others.

of being "well" connected. The networks of more privileged categories of people—such as the members of an expensive country club—are a valuable form of social "capital," which is more likely to lead people to higher-paying jobs (Green, *et al.*, 1999; Lin, *et al.*, 2001).

Some people also have denser networks than others; that is, they are connected to more people. Typically, the largest social networks include people who are young, well educated, and living in large cities (Fernandez and Weinberg, 1997; Podolny and Baron, 1997).

Gender also shapes networks. While the networks of men and women are typically the same size, women include more relatives (and more women) in their networks, and men include more co-workers (and more men). Research suggests that women's ties do not carry quite the same clout as typical "old boy" networks. Even so, research suggests that, as gender equality increases, the networks of women and men are becoming more alike (Reskin and McBrier, 2000; Torres and Huffman, 2002).

In a study of "intimate networks," Wellman (1979) found that almost everyone could name one to six intimates outside the home, only half of whom were kin. While most of their intimate contacts lived within Metropolitan Toronto, only 13 percent lived in their neighbourhood; in other words, Wellman's respondents felt close to people who were widely dispersed. Neither weak-tie networks nor the intimate variety are geographically bound. More recently, Wellman has turned his attention to internet-based social networks—as revealed in the Thinking It Through box (on p. 164). In fact, new information technology has generated a global network of unprecedented size in the form of the internet. But the World Wide Web has not yet linked the entire world. Global Map 7–1 (on p. 162) shows that internet use is high in rich countries and far less common in poor nations.

Formal Organizations

A century ago, most people lived in small groups of family, friends, and neighbours. Today, most North Americans' lives revolve more and more around **formal organizations,** *large secondary groups organized to achieve their goals efficiently.* Formal organizations, such as business corporations and government agencies, differ from families and neighbourhoods in their impersonal and formally planned atmosphere.

research, however, has cast doubt on Milgram's conclusions. Examining Milgram's original data, Judith Kleinfeld (Wildavsky, 2002) points out that most of Milgram's letters (240 out of 300) never arrived at all. Those that did were typically given to subjects who were wealthy, a fact that led Kleinfeld to conclude that rich people are far better connected throughout the United States than ordinary women and men.

Network ties may be weak, but they can be a powerful resource. For immigrants trying to become established in a new community, businesspeople seeking to expand their operations, or anyone looking for a job, *who you know* is often as important as *what you know* (Hagan, 1998; Petersen, *et al.*, 2000).

Networks are based on one's schools, clubs, neighbourhoods, political parties, and personal interests. Obviously, some networks contain people with considerably more wealth, power, and prestige than others; that explains the importance

 To learn more about new internet-based social networks, visit www.friendster.com.

YOUR TURN

Today's world has so many large organizations that we identify many of them just by initials: APEC, CBC, CNN, CFL, EU, IBM, NATO, NDP, OHIP, LPGA, and so on. How many more can you think of?

THINKING IT THROUGH
Virtual Community: Building Networks through Cyberspace

Recently, young people have been turning to ICQ or MSN for intensive "conversation" with classmates with whom they were involved in face-to-face communication hours, or minutes, earlier. Outside school hours, one can easily find ten or more of the members of this network (of perhaps seventy-five in total) sharing information about some topic—or just chatting.

Barry Wellman, a University of Toronto sociologist, and other prominent scholars have dedicated their careers to studying social networks and their role in the creation of community. Sociologists have long been concerned about the impact of urbanization and industrialization on traditional community bonds or solidarity. Every new technology—such as the telegraph, telephone, automobile, and airplane—that has lifted the individual from a geographically defined community or neighbourhood has raised concerns about the demise of community. When social ties extend beyond the neighbourhood, sociologists have

argued, surely they will be less meaningful and supportive.

In a book entitled *Networks in the Global Village*, Wellman has collected a number of articles on social networks in various settings around the world. Among these is an article by Wellman and Gulia entitled "Net-Surfers Don't Ride Alone: Virtual Communities as Communities" (1999). The authors argue that, instead of being "lost in cyberspace," people who establish contact over the internet are able to build meaningful relationships and a sense of community. While communicating solely online can easily result in misunderstandings—and be more difficult to repair them, online relationships mimic those of the face-to-face world in many ways. Some relationships are weak; others are strong and broadly supportive. Some are short lived; others become more personal and intimate over time. While some online bonds are based on specialized interests, others are multifaceted. In many cases, online contact complements and enhances face-to-face relationships, or maintains ties among relatives or long-time friends separated by distance.

The authors conclude that, while the internet does not *preclude* intimacy, the lack of social and physical cues allows individuals "to control the timing and content of self-disclosure" (p. 352) and, thus, the development of intimacy. Further, the internet fosters community diversity across the boundaries of geography, social class, gender, and race or ethnicity, so that: "cyber-

links between people become social links between groups that otherwise would be socially and physically dispersed" (p. 356).

On the basis of recent research into e-mail use, reported by Mahoney (2006) in *The Globe and Mail*, Wellman points out that the sky hasn't fallen as predicted. Rather than destroying community, the internet and e-mail actually expand and strengthen relationships. E-mail *supplements* communication with others—while we continue to have telephone and face-to-face contact—rather than replacing it. As with ICQ and MSN, the bulk of e-mail contact appears to be with people in the local area. As a medium that is more convenient and cheaper than letters or long-distance telephone calls, e-mail helps to make us part of McLuhan's global village.

WHAT DO YOU THINK?

1. Why would anyone send e-mail, or an MSN message, to someone a few blocks—or three offices—away?
2. Do you and your family keep in touch with distant friends and relatives through e-mail? Are some of these people in other countries, and is contact more frequent than it would be by mail or telephone?
3. Are you part of a network that is sustained by the internet? If so, how would you describe the relationships in sociological terms?

Source: Based on Wellman and Gulia (1999), Mahoney (2006).

Organizing a society with 32 million members is a remarkable feat. Countless tasks are involved, from collecting taxes to delivering the mail. To meet most of these responsibilities, we rely on large, formal organizations. Government, Canada's largest formal organization, employs about 1 million people in federal, provincial/territorial, regional, and municipal administration, and in police, military, and intelligence services. Such vast organizations develop lives and cultures of their own, so that, as members come and go, the statuses they fill and the roles they perform remain relatively unchanged.

TYPES OF FORMAL ORGANIZATIONS

Amitai Etzioni (1975) identified three types of formal organizations, distinguished by the reasons people participate in them: utilitarian organizations, normative organizations, and coercive organizations.

Utilitarian Organizations

Just about everyone who works for a regular paycheque belongs to a *utilitarian organization*, one that pays people for their efforts. Large businesses, for example, generate profits for their owners and income for their employees. Joining a utilitarian organization is usually a matter of individual choice, although most people must join one or another such organization to make a living. As noted above, government is Canada's largest employer.

Normative Organizations

People join *normative organizations* not for income but to pursue some goal they think is morally worthwhile. Sometimes called *voluntary associations*, these include community service groups (such as the Lions Club or Kiwanis, and the Red Cross), as well as political parties and religious organizations. In global perspective, people living in Canada and other high-income nations with relatively democratic political systems are likely to join voluntary associations. Recent studies have found that 82 percent of first-year college students in the United States claimed to have participated in some volunteer activity within the past year (Curtis, *et al.*, 2001; Schofer and Fourcade-Gourinchas, 2001; Hurtado, *et al.*, 2004). Canadian students are increasingly involved in volunteering, at high school and postsecondary levels, and can join people of all ages in matching themselves with appropriate volunteering opportunities through Volunteer Canada.

 You can find out more about volunteering in Canada at www.volunteer.ca.

Coercive Organizations

Coercive organizations have involuntary memberships. People are forced to join these organizations as a form of punishment (i.e., prisons) or treatment (i.e., some psychiatric hospitals). Coercive organizations have special physical features, such as locked doors and barred windows, and are supervised by security personnel. They isolate people, whom they label "inmates" or "patients," for a period of time in order to effect a radical change their attitudes and behaviour. Recall from Chapter 5 ("Socialization") the power of a total institution to change a person's overall sense of self.

It is possible for a single organization to fall into *all* of these categories. For example, a psychiatric hospital serves as a coercive organization for the patient, a utilitarian organiza-tion for the psychiatrist, and a normative organization for the hospital volunteer.

ORIGINS OF FORMAL ORGANIZATIONS

Formal organizations date back thousands of years. Elites that controlled early empires relied on government officials to collect taxes, undertake military campaigns, and build monumental structures, from the Great Walls of China to the pyramids of Egypt. However, early organizations had two limitations. They lacked the technology to let people travel over large distances, to communicate quickly, and to collect and store information. In addition, these pre-industrial societies had traditional cultures, so for the most part ruling organizations tried to preserve cultural systems, not to change them. But during the last few centuries, what Max Weber called a "rational" world view emerged in parts of the world, a process described in Chapter 4 ("Society"). In Europe and North America, the Industrial Revolution ushered in a new structure for formal organizations concerned with efficiency that Weber called "bureaucracy."

CHARACTERISTICS OF BUREAUCRACY

Bureaucracy is *an organizational model rationally designed to perform tasks efficiently.* Bureaucratic officials regularly create and revise policy to increase efficiency. To appreciate the power and scope of bureaucratic organization, consider that any one of more than 300 million telephones in North America can connect you within seconds to any other phone in a home, business, automobile, or even a hiker's backpack on a remote mountain trail in the Rockies. Such instant communication was inconceivable in the early to mid–1900s.

Our telephone system depends on technology such as electricity, fibre optics, and computers. But the system could not exist without the bureaucracy that keeps track of every telephone call—noting which telephone calls which other telephone, when, and for how long—and then presents only the relevant bits of this information to each of millions of telephone users in the form of a monthly bill.

What specific traits promote organizational efficiency? Max Weber (1978; orig. 1921) identified six key elements of the ideal bureaucratic organization:

1. *Specialization.* Our ancestors spent most of their time looking for food and shelter. Bureaucracy, by contrast, assigns individuals highly specialized jobs and compensates them so that they can pay other people for food and shelter.

2. *Hierarchy of offices.* Bureaucracies arrange personnel in a vertical ranking of offices. Each person is supervised by higher-ups in the organization, while in turn supervising others in lower positions. Usually, with few people at the top and many at the bottom, bureaucratic organizations take the form of a pyramid.

Although formal organization is vital to modern, industrial societies, it is far from new. Twenty-five centuries ago, the Chinese philosopher and teacher K'ung fu-tzu ("Master Kong," also known as Confucius) endorsed the idea that government offices should be filled by the most talented young men. This led to what was probably the world's first system of civil service examinations. Here, would-be bureaucrats compose essays to demonstrate their knowledge of Confucian texts.

3. *Rules and regulations.* Cultural tradition counts for little in a bureaucracy. Instead, rationally enacted rules and regulations guide a bureaucracy's operation. Ideally, a bureaucracy operates in a completely predictable way.

4. *Technical competence.* Bureaucratic officials and staff have the technical competence to carry out their duties. Bureaucracies typically hire new members according to set standards and regularly monitor their performance. Such impersonal evaluation contrasts with the custom of *nepotism*, favouring relatives, whatever their talents, over strangers.

5. *Impersonality.* Bureaucracy puts rules ahead of personal whim, so that both clients and workers are treated in the same way. From this impersonal approach comes the idea of the "faceless" bureaucrat.

6. *Formal, written communications.* Someone once said that the heart of bureaucracy is not people but paperwork. Rather than casual, face-to-face talk, bureaucracy relies on formal, written memos and reports, which accumulate in vast files.

Bureaucratic organization promotes efficiency by carefully hiring workers and limiting the unpredictable effects of personal taste and opinion. The Summing Up table (on p. 167) reviews the differences between small social groups and large bureaucratic organizations.

In some ways, the internet mimics formal organization or bureaucracy, but at the same time it negates (or escapes) bureaucracy entirely. For a discussion of the unregulated medium, go to the Media Perspectives box (on p. 168).

ORGANIZATIONAL ENVIRONMENT

No organization operates in a vacuum. The performance of any organization depends not only on its own goals and policies but also on the **organizational environment,** *factors outside an organization that affect its operation.* These factors include technology, economic and political trends, current events, the available workforce, and other organizations.

- Modern organizations are shaped by the *technology* of computers, telephone systems, and personal digital assistants. Computers give employees access to more information and people than ever before. At the same time,

SUMMING UP

Small Groups and Formal Organizations

	Small Groups	Formal Organizations
Activities	Much the same for all members	Distinct and highly specialized
Hierarchy	Often informal or nonexistent	Clearly defined, corresponding to offices
Norms	General norms, informally applied	Clearly defined rules and regulations
Membership criteria	Variable; often based on personal affection or kinship	Technical competence to carry out assigned tasks
Relationships	Variable and typically primary	Typically secondary, with selective primary ties
Communications	Typically casual and face to face	Typically formal and in writing
Focus	Person-oriented	Task-oriented

computer technology allows managers to monitor closely the activities of workers (Markoff, 1991).

- *Economic and political trends* affect organizations. All organizations are helped or hurt by periodic economic growth or recession. Most industries also face competition as well as changes in laws, such as new environmental standards.

- *Current events* can have significant effects on organizations that are far removed from the location of the events themselves. The terrorist attacks in the United States on September 11, 2001, for example, were followed by an economic slowdown and an increase in security at the U.S./Canadian border that affected many businesses in Canada.

- *Population patterns,* such as the size and composition of the surrounding population, also affect organizations. The average age, typical education, and social diversity of a local community determine the available workforce and sometimes the market for an organization's products or services.

- *Other organizations* also contribute to the organizational environment. To be competitive, a hospital must be responsive to the insurance industry and to organizations representing doctors, nurses, and other health care workers. It must also be aware of the equipment and procedures available at nearby facilities, as well as their prices.

THE INFORMAL SIDE OF BUREAUCRACY

Weber's ideal bureaucracy deliberately regulates every activity. In actual organizations, however, human beings are creative—and stubborn—enough to resist bureaucratic regulation. Informality may amount to simply cutting corners on your job, but it can also provide the flexibility needed to adapt and prosper.

In part, informality comes from the personalities of organizational leaders. Studies of U.S. corporations document that the qualities and quirks of individuals—including personal charisma, interpersonal skills, and the willingness to recognize problems—can have a great effect on organizational outcomes (Halberstam, 1986; Baron, *et al.,* 1999). Authoritarian, democratic, and laissez-faire types of leadership (described earlier in this chapter) reflect individual personality as much as any organizational plan. In actual organizations, leaders sometimes seek to benefit personally by abusing organizational power. Recent high-profile examples include corporate scandals in such companies as Enron, Conrad Black's Hollinger International, and Bernard Ebbers' Worldcom. More commonly, leaders take credit for the efforts of the people who work for them; for example, the authority and responsibilities of many secretaries are far greater than their official job titles and salaries suggest.

Communication offers another example of organizational informality. Memos and other written communications are the formal way to spread information throughout an organization. Typically, however, individuals also create informal networks, or grapevines, that spread information quickly, if not always accurately. Grapevines, using both word of mouth and e-mail, are particularly important to rank-and-file workers because higher-ups often try to keep important information from them. The spread of e-mail has flattened organizations somewhat, allowing even the lowest-ranking employee to bypass immediate superiors and communicate directly with the organization's leader or with all fellow employees at once. Some organizations object to open-channel communication and, therefore, limit the use of e-mail. Microsoft Corporation—whose founder, Bill Gates, has an unlisted e-mail address that helps him limit his mail to hundreds of messages each day—has developed screens that filter out messages from everyone except certain approved people (Gwynne and Dickerson, 1997).

MEDIA PERSPECTIVES

The Internet: The Unregulated Medium

Its origins seem right out of the 1963 Cold War film *Dr. Strangelove*. Four decades ago, government officials and scientists in the United States worried about running the country after an atomic attack—which, they assumed, would instantaneously eliminate telephones and television. The brilliant solution was to devise a communication system with no central headquarters, no one in charge, and no main power switch—in short, an electronic web that would link the country in one vast network.

The brain behind it all belongs to Tim Berners-Lee, who created the internet in Europe in1980 and the first website (for the European Organization for Nuclear Research) in 1990. He ran the not-for-profit World Wide Web Consortium from a small barren office at the Massachusetts Institute of Technology (1994 to 2004), where he helped maintain technical standards and the freedom of the internet. Unlike his associates, such as the founders of Microsoft and Netscape, Berners-Lee maintains a very low profile.

By 1985, the U.S. government was installing high-speed data lines around the country in time for the internet to be born. Today, thousands of government offices, as well as universities and businesses around the world, are joined by the internet. Many millions of other individuals connect their home computers to this information super-highway through a telephone-line or cable modem, or use wireless devices to gain access to the internet from classrooms, coffee shops, or trains.

Approximately 16 percent of the world's population has access to the internet (Internet World Stats, 2006)—though the figures vary from 0.1 percent in Afghanistan to 88 percent in the Falkland Islands (a tiny British colony of 2700 people near the southern tip of South America), or 2.6

"On the Internet, nobody knows you're a dog."

percent in Africa to 68.6 percent in North America (excluding Mexico). In 1997, Finland—where 60 percent of the population had access to the internet—took over from Canada as the world's most "wired" country. Since then, both countries have been left in the dust. Canada and Finland currently have 67.9 and 62.5 percent access to the internet. In New Zealand, Iceland, and Sweden, about 75 percent of the population uses the internet; in Denmark and Hong Kong this is the case for about 70 percent. The United States and Canada currently rank eighth and ninth on internet penetration, with Finland (the home of Nokia) in eighteenth place.

What is available on the internet? There are now millions of sites—far more than anyone could ever list in a single directory. But popular search engines such as Yahoo! Canada (**www.yahoo.ca**) and metasearch engines such as Mr. Sapo (**www.mrsapo.com**) provide site listings for just about any topic you can imagine. And of course

there's e-mail. Through the internet, you can also participate in discussion groups, create your own blog, visit museums, hotels, or homes for sale (by virtual tour), locate data from a host of government agencies (e.g. Statistics Canada at **www.statcan.ca**), and search libraries across your campus and around the world for books or other information. The excitement of the internet lies in the fact that, given the lack of formal rules for its use, its potential defies the imagination.

Ironically, it is precisely this chaotic quality that has many people up in arms. Pundits warn that "electronic democracy" may undermine established political practices, autocratic countries fear the subversive effect of uncontrolled communication among their citizens, parents fear that their technologically sophisticated children will access sites that offer sexually explicit content, and purists bristle at the flood of advertising and commercial enterprise. Censorship and copyright protection prove to be extremely difficult, if not impossible. In effect, the "anything goes" character of the internet makes it a virtual image of the real world. Not surprisingly, therefore, more and more users are now employing passwords, fees, and other "gates" to restrict access to networks limited to people like themselves. As a result, a host of smaller social groups is emerging from the one vast network.

WHAT DO YOU THINK?

1. What are the implications of the fact that *anyone* can publish on the internet?
2. Do you think governments should find the internet threatening?
3. How has the internet changed the way you learn or seek information?

Sources: Elmer–DeWitt (1993, 1994), Hafner (1994), Ibrahim (1997), and Wright (1997).

George Tooker's painting *Government Bureau* is a powerful statement about the human costs of bureaucracy. The artist paints members of the public in a drab sameness—reduced from human beings to mere "cases" to be disposed of as quickly as possible. Set apart from others by their positions, officials are "faceless bureaucrats" concerned more with numbers than with providing genuine assistance (notice that the artist places the fingers of the officials on calculators).

George Tooker, *Government Bureau*, 1956. Egg tempera on gesso panel, 19 × 29 inches. The Metropolitan Museum of Art, George A. Hearn Fund, 1956 (56.78). Photograph © 1984 The Metropolitan Museum of Art.

Using new information technology as well as age-old human ingenuity, members of organizations often try to break free of rigid rules in order to personalize procedures and surroundings. Such efforts suggest that we should now take a closer look at some of the problems of bureaucracy.

PROBLEMS OF BUREAUCRACY

We rely on bureaucracy to manage everyday life efficiently, but many people are uneasy about large organizations. Bureaucracy can dehumanize and manipulate us, and some say it poses a threat to political democracy.

Bureaucratic Alienation

Max Weber held up bureaucracy as a model of productivity. However, Weber was keenly aware of bureaucracy's ability to *dehumanize* the people it is supposed to serve. The same impersonality that fosters efficiency also keeps officials and clients from responding to one another's unique personal needs. Far from it: officials at large government and corporate agencies must treat each client impersonally, as a standard case.

Formal organizations cause *alienation*, according to Weber, by reducing the human being to "a small cog in a ceaselessly moving mechanism" (1978 [orig. 1921]:988). While formal organizations are intended to benefit humanity, Weber feared that humanity might well end up serving formal organizations.

Bureaucratic Inefficiency and Ritualism

Inefficiency, the failure of an organization to carry out the work that it exists to perform, is a familiar problem. According to one report, the U.S. General Services Administration—the U.S. government agency that buys equipment for federal workers—took up to three years to process a request for a new computer; this delay ensured that, by the time the computer arrived, it was already obsolete (Gwynne and Dickerson, 1997). In Canada, we are aware of the many years that refugees wait to have their claims considered; by the time their cases are heard, many of them have married and had children here in Canada. Once refugees have settled, it is much more difficult to justify sending them back to their country of origin.

The problem of inefficiency is captured in the concept of *red tape*, a term that refers to the red tape used by eighteenth-century English administrators to wrap official parcels and records (Shipley, 1985). To Robert Merton (1968), red tape amounts to a new twist on the already familiar concept of group conformity. He coined the term **bureaucratic ritualism** to describe *a focus on rules and regulations to the point of undermining an organization's goals.* After the terrorist attacks of September 11, 2001, for example, the U.S. Postal Service continued to help deliver mail addressed to Osama bin Laden to a post office in Afghanistan, despite the objections of the FBI. It took an act of Congress to change the policy (Bedard, 2002).

Bureaucratic Inertia

If bureaucrats sometimes have little reason to work especially hard, they have every reason to protect their jobs. Officials typically work to keep an organization going, as Weber observed, even after its original goal has been realized: "Once fully established, bureaucracy is among the social structures which are hardest to destroy" (1978 [orig.1921]:987). **Bureaucratic inertia** refers to *the tendency*

According to Max Weber, bureaucracy is an organizational strategy that promotes efficiency. Impersonality, however, also fosters alienation among employees, who may become indifferent to the formal goals of the organization. The behaviour of this municipal employee in Bombay, India, is understandable to members of formal organizations almost anywhere in the world.

of bureaucratic organizations to perpetuate themselves. Formal organizations tend to take on a life of their own beyond their formal objectives; for example, as the need for service to veterans declined, Canadian War Amputations turned its attention to the needs of child amputees. Bureaucratic inertia usually leads formal organizations to devise new justifications for themselves after they have outlived their original purpose.

OLIGARCHY

Early in the twentieth century, Robert Michels (1876–1936) pointed out the link between bureaucracy and political **oligarchy,** *the rule of the many by the few* (1949; orig. 1911). According to what Michels called "the iron law of oligarchy," the pyramidal shape of bureaucracy places a few leaders in charge of the resources of the entire organization.

Max Weber credited a strict hierarchy of responsibility with high organizational efficiency. But Michels countered that this hierarchical structure also concentrates power and, thus, threatens democracy because executives can and often do use their access to information, resources, and the media to promote their personal interests.

Furthermore, bureaucracy helps distance executives from the public, as in the case of the corporate president or public official who is "unavailable for comment" to the local press or the U.S. president who withholds documents from Congress claiming executive privilege. Oligarchy, then,

thrives in the hierarchical structure of bureaucracy and reduces the accountability of leaders to other personnel or citizens (Tolson, 1995).

Canada Map 7–1 illustrates the extent to which government bureaucracy permeates Canadian society. While 6.2 percent of Canada's labour force is employed in public administration (federal, provincial, and municipal), regional variation is clearly evident—with levels ranging from 4.8 percent in Alberta to 27.4 percent in Nunavut.

The Evolution of Formal Organizations

The problems of bureaucracy—especially the alienation it produces and its tendency towards oligarchy—stem from two organizational traits: hierarchy and rigidity. To Weber, bureaucracy was a top-down system: rules and regulations made at the top guide every facet of people's lives down the chain of command. A century ago, Weber's ideas took hold in an organizational model called *scientific management*. We begin with a look at this model, then examine three challenges over the course of the twentieth century that gradually led to a new model, the *flexible organization*.

SCIENTIFIC MANAGEMENT

Frederick Winslow Taylor (1911) had a simple message: most businesses in the United States were sadly inefficient. Managers had little idea of how to increase their business's output, and workers relied on the same tired skills of earlier generations. To increase efficiency, Taylor explained, business should apply the principles of science. **Scientific management,** then, is *the application of scientific principles to the operation of a business or other large organization.* Scientific management involves three steps:

* First, managers carefully observe the task performed by each worker, identifying all the operations involved and measuring the time needed for each.
* Second, managers analyze their data, trying to discover ways for workers to perform each job more efficiently. For example, managers might decide to give the worker different tools or to reposition various work operations within the factory.
* Third, management provides guidance and incentives for workers to do their jobs more quickly. If a factory worker moves 20 tonnes of pig iron in one day, for example, management shows the worker how to do the job more efficiently and then provides higher wages as the worker's productivity rises.

Taylor concluded that, if scientific principles were applied in this way, companies would become more profitable, workers would earn higher wages, and consumers would

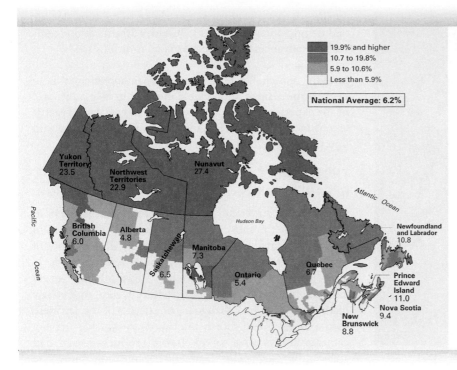

CANADA MAP 7–1

Employment in Government Service, 2001: Percentage by Province and Territory*

*Employment in federal, provincial/territorial, and municipal government is shown as a percentage of all employment. Note that employment in government service increases with distance from major urban centres and is highest in the territories

Source: Calculations by L.M. Gerber based on data retrieved from the Statistics Canada CANSIM database http://cansim2.statcan.ca, Table 183-0003.

Legend: 19.9% and higher; 10.7 to 19.8%; 5.9 to 10.6%; Less than 5.9%. National Average: 6.2%

Yukon Territory 23.5; Northwest Territories 22.9; Nunavut 27.4; British Columbia 6.0; Alberta 4.8; Saskatchewan 6.5; Manitoba 7.3; Ontario 5.4; Quebec 6.7; Newfoundland and Labrador 10.8; Prince Edward Island 11.0; Nova Scotia 9.4; New Brunswick 8.8

pay lower prices. A century ago, the auto pioneer Henry Ford asserted: "Save ten steps a day for each of 12 000 employees, and you will have saved fifty miles of wasted motion and misspent energy" (Allen and Hyman, 1999:209). In the early 1900s, the Ford Motor Company and many other businesses followed Taylor's lead and made improvements in efficiency.

The principles of scientific management suggested that workplace power should reside with owners and executives, who paid little attention to the ideas of their workers. As the decades passed, formal organizations faced important challenges, involving race and gender, rising competition, and the changing nature of work. We now take a brief look at each of these challenges.

THE FIRST CHALLENGE: RACE AND GENDER

In the 1960s, critics pointed out that big businesses and other organizations engaged in unfair hiring practices. Rather than hiring on the basis of competence as Weber had proposed, they excluded women and minorities, especially from positions of power. Hiring on the basis of competence is partly a matter of fairness; it is also a matter of increasing the source of talent to promote efficiency.

Patterns of Privilege and Exclusion

Rosabeth Moss Kanter (1977; Kanter and Stein, 1979) points out that excluding women and minorities from the

workplace ignores the talents of more than half the population. Furthermore, underrepresented people in an organization often feel like socially isolated out-groups— uncomfortably visible, taken less seriously, and given fewer chances for promotion. A smaller representation in the workplace, argues Kanter, may leave women, visible minorities, and those from economically disadvantaged backgrounds feeling like members of socially isolated out-groups. Understandably, minority individuals may conclude that they must work twice as hard as those in dominant categories to maintain their present positions, let alone advance to higher ones (Kanter, 1977; Kanter and Stein, 1979). Bassett (1985) found a similar belief among Canadian career women and refers to this requirement as one of society's double standards.[1]

Kanter (1977) finds that providing a structure of unequal opportunities has important consequences for everyone's on-the-job performance. A company with many dead-end jobs, she explains, only encourages workers to become "zombies" with little aspiration, poor self-concept, and little loyalty to the organization. Widespread opportunity, in contrast, motivates employees, turning them into "fast-trackers" with higher aspirations, greater self-esteem,

[1] Charlotte Whitton, the late mayor of Ottawa, put it as follows: "A woman has to be twice as good as a man to get ahead—fortunately, it's not difficult" (cited in Bassett, 1985:45).

The ideas of scientific management were most successfully applied by Henry Ford, who pioneered the automobile assembly line. As shown in this 1928 photograph of the Dearborn, Michigan, plant, Ford divided up the job of building cars into hundreds of different tasks, each performed by a worker as the cars moved along an assembly line. The result was that new cars could be produced so cheaply that most of these autoworkers could afford to buy one.

and stronger commitment to the organization. In a corporate environment with wide-open opportunity for advancement, leaders value the input of subordinates and seek to bolster their morale and well-being. It is officials with no real power, Kanter maintains, who jealously guard their own privileges and rigidly ride herd over subordinates.

The "Female Advantage"

Some organizational researchers argue that women bring special management skills that strengthen an organization. According to Deborah Tannen (1994), women have a greater "information focus" and more readily ask questions in order to understand an issue. Men, on the other hand, have an "image focus" that makes them wonder how asking questions in a particular situation will affect their reputation.

In another study of women executives, Sally Helgesen (1990) found three other gender-linked patterns. First, women place greater value on communication skills than men and share information more than men do. Second, women are more flexible leaders who typically give their employees greater freedom. Third, compared to men, women tend to emphasize the interconnectedness of all organizational operations. In these ways, women bring a

female advantage to companies striving to be more flexible and democratic. (Chapter 13, "Gender Stratification" deals with the advances women have made in various fields.)

In sum, one challenge to conventional bureaucracy is to become more open and flexible in order to take advantage of the experience, ideas, and creativity of everyone, regardless of race or gender. The result goes right to the bottom line: greater profits.

THE SECOND CHALLENGE: THE JAPANESE WORK ORGANIZATION

In 1980, the American corporate world was shaken to discover that the most popular automobile model sold in the United States was not a Chevrolet, Ford, or Plymouth built in North America but the Honda Accord, made in Japan. As late as the 1950s, the label "Made in Japan" generally was found on products that were cheap and poorly made. But times had changed. The success of the Japanese auto industry—and shortly afterwards, companies making cameras and a range of electronic products—soon had analysts buzzing about Japanese organization. How else could so small a country challenge the world's economic powerhouse?

Japanese organizations reflect that country's strong collective spirit. In contrast to the North American emphasis on individualism, the Japanese value co-operation. In effect, formal organizations in Japan are more like large primary groups. A generation ago, William Ouchi (1981) highlighted five differences between formal organizations in Japan and those in North America:

*   First, Japanese companies hired new workers in groups, giving everyone the same salary and responsibilities.
*   Second, many Japanese companies hired workers for life, fostering a strong sense of loyalty.
*   Third, with the idea that employees would spend their entire careers there, many Japanese companies trained workers in all phases of their operations.
*   Fourth, although Japanese corporate leaders took final responsibility for their organization's performance, they involved workers in "quality circles" to discuss decisions that affected them.
*   Fifth, Japanese companies played a large role in the lives of workers, providing home mortgages, sponsoring recreational activities, and scheduling social events.

Together, such policies encourage much more loyalty among members of Japanese organizations than is typically the case in their North American counterparts.

For decades, people around the world marvelled at the economic turnaround of Japanese organizations. But the praise was premature. Around 1990, the Japanese economy entered a trend downwards that is only now showing signs

The best of today's information age jobs—including working at the popular search-engine website Google—allow people lots of personal freedom as long as they produce good ideas. At the same time, many other jobs—such as working the counter at McDonald's—involve the same routines and strict supervision found in factories a century ago.

of ending. As a result of this downturn, most Japanese companies no longer offer workers jobs for life or many of the other benefits noted by Ouchi. Check out the Thinking Globally box (on p. 174) to learn how Canadian companies have adopted aspects of Japan's organizational model.

THE THIRD CHALLENGE: THE CHANGING NATURE OF WORK

Beyond rising global competition and the need to provide equal opportunity for all, pressure to modify conventional organizations is coming from changes in the nature of work itself. Chapter 4 ("Society") described the shift from industrial to post-industrial production. Rather than working in factories using heavy machinery to make *things*, more and more people are using computers and other electronic technology to create or process *information*. The post-industrial society, then, is characterized by information-based organizations.

Frederick Taylor developed his concept of scientific management at a time when jobs involved tasks that, often backbreaking as well, were routine. Workers shovelled coal, poured liquid iron into moulds, welded body panels to automobiles on an assembly line, or shot hot rivets into steel girders to build skyscrapers. In addition, many of the industrial workers in Taylor's day were immigrants, most of whom had little schooling and many of whom knew little English. The routine nature of industrial jobs, coupled with the limited skills of the labour force, led Taylor to treat work

as a series of fixed tasks, set down by management and followed by employees.

Many of today's information age jobs are very different: the work of designers, artists, writers, composers, and programmers now demands individual creativity and imagination. Here are several ways in which today's organizations differ from those of a century ago:

- *Creative autonomy.* One Hewlett-Packard executive remarked that: "From their first day of work here, people are given important responsibilities and are encouraged to grow" (cited in Brooks, 2000:128). Today's organizations now treat employees with Information Age skills as a vital resource. Executives can set production goals but cannot dictate how a worker is to accomplish tasks that require imagination and discovery. This gives highly skilled workers *creative freedom*, which means less day-to-day supervision as long as they generate good ideas in the long run.

- *Competitive work teams.* Organizations typically give several groups of employees the freedom to work on a problem, offering the greatest rewards to those who come up with the best solution. Competitive work teams, a strategy first used by Japanese organizations, draw out the creative contributions of everyone and at the same time reduce the alienation often found in conventional organizations (Maddox, 1994; Yeatts, 1994).

- *A flatter organization.* By spreading responsibility for creative problem solving throughout the workforce,

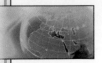

THINKING GLOBALLY

The Japanese Model: Does it Work in North America?

Economic competition from Asia, and increasingly from Europe, is forcing North American companies to reconsider long-held notions about how corporate organizations should operate. While the Japanese economy has suffered setbacks in recent years, Canadian and American companies have continued to incorporate Japanese business principles. Among the most interesting examples of new organizations are Japanese manufacturing plants built in North America. By and large, these transplants have been quite successful in terms of productivity, demonstrating the adaptive ability of organizations. Yet some Canadians—workers, union leaders, and managers—speak as bitterly about transplanting Japanese organizational techniques as they do about importing Japanese cars.

Manufacturing plants operated in Canada by Honda and Toyota (in Alliston, Ontario, and Cambridge, Ontario, respectively) and in the United States by Honda, Nissan, and Toyota have achieved the same degree of efficiency and quality that have won these companies praise in Japan. However, these organizations have had to struggle to win the support of many North Americans for some traditional Japanese practices, especially the idea of broad worker participation. Our corporate culture, with its rigid hierarchy, its heritage of individualism, and its history of labour/management conflict makes proposals to enhance worker participation highly controversial. Many workers here dislike the concept of worker participation because they see it as increasing their workload. While still responsible for building cars, for instance, workers are now asked to be responsible for quality control, unit costs, and overall company efficiency—concerns usually shouldered by management. Some

employees see the broad training favoured by the Japanese as a demanding routine of moving from job to job, always having to learn new skills. Many union leaders are also suspicious of new plans formulated by management, fearing that an alliance between workers and managers may undermine union strength. Some managers, too, look cautiously on worker-participation programs. Sharing with employees the power to direct production and even to schedule their own vacations does not come easily in light of past practices. Finally, North American corporations have a short-term outlook on profits, which discourages investing time and money in organizational restructuring.

Primarily owing to rising global competition, however, worker-participation programs are slowly changing the North American workplace. While the Honda and Toyota plants here brought with them the Japanese organizational and management package, many other firms are adopting components of that package and using them to modify their organizations. One of these approaches, Total Quality Management (TQM), has been adopted at Culinar (Montreal), Cadet Uniform Services (Toronto), Reimer Express Lines (Winnipeg), and General Electric (Bromont, Quebec). Culinar, the Canadian pioneer of TQM, has discontinued its effort, but the other three companies are very enthusiastic about the results in terms of worker involvement and morale, customer satisfaction, and profits. The second approach, called Continuous Improvement or CI (*kaizen* in Japanese), has been responsible for a major comeback at a Schneider food-processing plant in Kitchener, Ontario; the plant experienced improved efficiency, reduced waste, less absenteeism, and a dramatic increase in profits.

The successful implementation of either TQM or CI requires real commitment from senior management, a friendly or receptive corporate culture, highly motivated workers, willingness to change at all levels of the organization, and patience. The advantages go right to the bottom line: productivity and profits are usually higher when workers have a say in decision making. And most employees in worker-participation programs seem significantly happier with their jobs. Workers who have long used only their bodies are now enjoying the opportunity to use their minds as well.

While Canadian businesses have adopted Japanese management principles to their benefit, Japan has been reeling from the effects of a prolonged recession, reduced competitiveness and efficiency, downsizing, unprecedented levels of unemployment, and currency devaluation. The notion of lifelong bonds and loyalty between corporations and their employees suffered strain in some organizations and was abandoned in others. Despite what seemed to be superior business practices, Japan has joined the rest of the industrialized world in undergoing economic restructuring.

WHAT DO YOU THINK?

1. Do you know anyone who has worked under Japanese management principles? What were his or her reactions?
2. What factors would make it difficult for a Canadian company to adopt the Japanese management model?
3. Would you consider working for a company that had adopted Japanese management techniques? Do you think you would be happiest in that kind of setting?

Sources: Hoerr (1989), Florida and Kenny (1991), Scott (1992), and Fife (1992).

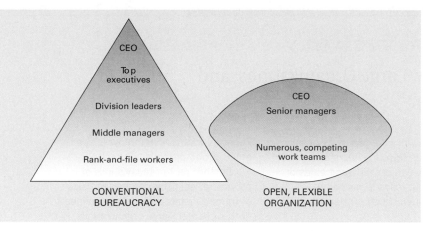

FIGURE 7-3 Two Organizational Models

The conventional model of bureaucratic organizations has a pyramidal shape (*left*), with a clear chain of command. Orders flow from the top down, and reports of performance flow from the base up. Such organizations have extensive rules and regulations, and their workers have highly specialized jobs. More open and flexible organizations have a flatter shape (*right*), more like a football. With fewer levels in the hierarchy, responsibility for generating ideas and making decisions is shared throughout the organization. Many workers do their jobs in teams and have a broad knowledge of the entire organization's operation.

Source: John J. Macionis.

 Find out about the Saturn car company's flatter organizational structure at www.saturn.com.

organizations take on a flatter shape. That is, the pyramidal shape of conventional bureaucracy is replaced by an organizational form with fewer levels in the chain of command, as shown in Figure 7–3.

- *Greater flexibility.* The typical industrial organization was a rigid structure guided from the top. Such organizations may accomplish a large amount of work, but they are not especially creative or able to respond quickly to changes in the larger environment. The ideal model in the Information Age is a more open, *flexible* organization that both generates new ideas and, in a rapidly changing global marketplace, adapts quickly.

What does all this mean for formal organizations? David Brooks comments: "The machine is no longer held up as the standard that healthy organizations should emulate. Now it's the ecosystem" (2000:128). Today's "smart" companies seek out intelligent, creative people—America Online's main building is called "Creative Centre One"—and nurture the growth of their talents.

Keep in mind, however, that many of today's jobs do not involve creative work at all. More correctly, the post-industrial economy has created two very different types of work: high-skill creative work and low-skill service work. Work in the fast-

 SOCIOLOGY WORK

food industry, for example, is routine and highly supervised and, thus, has much more in common with the factory work of a century ago than with the creative teamwork typical of today's information organizations. Therefore, at the same time that some organizations have taken on a flexible, flatter form, others continue to use the rigid chain of command.

Whatever the shape, there is little doubt that organizations have grown in power and intrusiveness. See the Thinking Critically box (on p. 176) for a discussion of the potential impacts of large-scale organizations and computers on personal privacy.

YOUR TURN

Have you ever had a dead-end job? What about a job that demands creativity? Which would you prefer and why?

THE "MCDONALDIZATION" OF SOCIETY

McDonald's has enjoyed enormous success. From a single restaurant in 1940, McDonald's now operates more than 31 000 restaurants in 119 countries, serving more than 46 million customers a day. Japan has more than 2400 Golden Arches, and the world's largest McDonald's is located in Beijing. By 2003, McDonald's Restaurants of Canada operated more than 1300 outlets in Canada. It was the Canadian branch that ventured into Moscow just as the Soviet Union crumbled, and its restaurant in Pushkin Square is the busiest McDonald's restaurant in the world.

The appeal of the burger has placed McDonald's Restaurants of Canada near the top of Canadian companies ranked by revenues—number 102 in 2002 (*The Financial Post 500*, 2003) with $2.3 billion in revenues and 77 000 employees. It is worth noting, however, that the value of McDonald's stock in Canada—but also in the United States—dropped precipitously when "mad cow" disease was found in one Alberta cow in May 2003. That financial setback, coupled with growing public concern about the relationship between fast-food consumption and obesity, led the company to initiate a worldwide marketing blitz to win back younger customers.

McDonald's has become a symbol of the North American way of life. When you consider that children are exposed to him daily or weekly, the gleeful clown Ronald McDonald is as much a celebrity as Santa Claus, who is relevant to children only once a year. More importantly, the organizational principles that underlie McDonald's are beginning to dominate our entire society. Our culture is

THINKING CRITICALLY

Computer Technology, Large Organizations, and the Assault on Privacy

Late for a meeting with a new client, Sarah drives her car through a yellow light as it turns red at a main intersection. A computer linked to a pair of cameras notes the violation and takes one picture of her licence plate and another of her sitting in the driver's seat. In seven days, she receives a summons to appear in traffic court.

Joe calls a toll-free number to check the pollen count. As he listens to a recorded message, caller ID identifies Joe, records the call, and pulls up his profile from a public database. The computer adds to the profile the fact that Joe suffers from allergies. Several weeks later, tens of thousands of profiles are sold to a drug company, which sends Joe and others a free sample of its new allergy medication.

Julio looks through his mail and finds a letter from a data services company in Vancouver, British Columbia, telling him that he is one of about 145 000 people whose name, address, Social Security number, and credit file have recently been sold to crimi-

nals in Toronto, posing as business-people. With this information, other people can obtain credit cards or take out loans in his name. (Hamilton, 2001; O'Harrow, 2005)

These are all cases showing that today's organizations—which know more about us than ever before, and more than most of us realize—pose a growing threat to personal privacy. Large organizations are necessary for today's society to operate. In some cases, organizations using information about us may actually be helpful, but cases of identity theft are on the rise and personal privacy is on the decline.

In the past, small-town life gave people little privacy. But at least, if people knew something about you, you were just as likely to know some-thing about them. Today, unknown people can access information about each of us all the time. In part, the loss of privacy is a result of more and more complex computer technology. Are you aware that every e-mail you send and every website you visit leaves a record in one or more computers? Most of these records can be retrieved by people you don't

know, as well as by employers and other public officials.

Another part of today's loss of privacy reflects the number and size of formal organizations. As explained in this chapter, large organizations treat people impersonally and have huge appetites for information. Mix large organizations with ever more complex computer technology, and it is no wonder that most of us are concerned about who knows what about us—and what they are doing with this information.

Consider some of the obvious ways in which organizations compile personal information. As they issue driver's licences, for example, provincial/territo-rial departments generate files that they can dispatch to police or other officials at the touch of a button. In Canada, driver's licences—and address changes on those licences—are used to create and modify permanent voters' lists in provincial/territorial and federal ridings. Similarly, our customs and tax depart-ments, health, welfare, and government programs that benefit veterans, students, the poor, and the unemployed all collect extensive information.

Businesses in the private sector compile information on our tastes and

heavily influenced by "McDonaldization"[1]—meaning that we model many aspects of our lives on the famous restau-rant chain. Canadians, who love doughnuts more than Americans do, indulge their cravings at Tim Hortons or Country Style Donuts, where they know exactly what they'll get because those outlets follow the McDonald's model. We buy our household and automotive supplies at Canadian Tire, where inventory is continuously monitored for just-

in-time replacement. More vacations take the form of resort and tour packages, television presents news in ten-second sound bites, and medical school applicants are screened on the basis of their MCAT results. The list goes on.

McDonaldization: Three Principles

What do all these developments have in common? According to George Ritzer (1993), the McDonaldization of society rests on three organizational principles:

- *Efficiency*. Ray Kroc, the marketing genius behind the expansion of McDonald's, set out to serve a hamburger,

---

[1] The term "McDonaldization" was coined by Jim Hightower (1975); much of this discussion is based on Ritzer (1993, 1998, 2000) and Schlosser (2002).

preferences—and our whereabouts—every time we use a credit card or purchase something online. Most people find the use of credit cards a great convenience—North Americans now average more than five per adult. But few people stop to think that credit card purchases automatically generate electronic records that can end up almost anywhere.

We also experience the erosion of privacy in the surveillance cameras that monitor more and more public places: along main streets, in the shopping malls, and even across campuses. And then there is the escalating amount of junk mail. Mailing lists for this material grow exponentially as one company sells names and addresses to others. If you ever rent an X-rated video, recognize that many video stores keep records of the movie preferences of customers and pass them along to other businesses, whose advertising soon arrives in their mailbox.

Of particular concern to Canadians is the information stored in connection with our Social Insurance Numbers (SINs). The amount of personal information associated with one's SIN, the multiple uses of the number, and the possibility of merging massive files are particularly sensitive issues. Access by one government department or agency, such as the Canada Customs and Revenue Agency or the RCMP, to SIN-related data or Statistics Canada files would also be a worrisome invasion of privacy. It is possible, as well, for unauthorized users—from anywhere in the world, in fact—to gain access to and link the various files containing personal information about us. Identity theft based on such personal files can have incalculable consequences. In the spring of 2000, Human Resources Development Canada came under fire for compiling, into single files, data on individual Canadians from a variety of sources. The department was storing up to 2000 items of information about every adult Canadian. So extreme was the public's reaction to the discovery that the department was forced to destroy the files.

Similar concerns arise from the proliferation of multipurpose smart cards. Simpler ones, debit cards, for example, act as cash and allow access to all of our accounts. Potentially, a single card—with a fingerprint—could act as driver's licence, cash card, health card, insurance record, and so on. The potential for information abuse here is high. Now that Canadians and Americans require passports—or some other secure identification—in order to enter or return to the United States, Canada is considering the possibility of creating cards with biometric data (i.e., fingerprints or iris scans) that can take the place of costly passports.

Concern about the erosion of privacy runs high. In response, privacy legislation has been enacted in Canada by the provinces and territories, and the federal government. The federal *Privacy Act* (1978; amended in 1982) permits citizens to examine and correct information contained about them in government files. Canadians also have access to information (e.g., consultants' reports) that contributes to the making of government decisions and policy. The *Personal Information Protection and Electronic Documents Act* (2001) outlines corporate responsibilities and consumer rights when companies and other organizations collect information about individuals. But so many organizations now have information about us that current laws simply can't address the scope of the problem.

WHAT DO YOU THINK?

1. Which do you think represents a larger threat to personal privacy—government or business? Why?
2. Internet search engines such as Yahoo! Canada have "people search" programs that let you locate almost anyone. Do you think such programs are, on balance, helpful or threatening to the public?
3. Have you checked your credit history recently? Do you know how to reduce the chances of someone stealing your identity?

Sources: R.E. Smith (1979), Rubin (1988), Miller (1991), and Bornstein (1997).

French fries, and a milkshake to a customer in fifty seconds. Today, one of the company's most popular items is the Egg McMuffin, an entire breakfast in a single sandwich. In the restaurant, customers dispose of their trash and stack their own trays as they walk out the door or, better still, drive away from the pickup window taking whatever mess they make with them. Such efficiency is now central to our way of life. We tend to think that anything done quickly is, for that reason alone, good.

- *Uniformity*. The first McDonald's operating manual set the weight of a regular raw hamburger at 1.6 ounces (45.36 grams), its size at 3.875 inches (9.84 centimetres) across, and its fat content at 19 percent. A slice of cheese weighs exactly half an ounce (14.2 grams). Fries are cut precisely $9/_{32}$ of an inch (7 millimetres) thick. Think about how many objects around your home, the workplace, and the campus are designed and mass-produced according to a standard plan. Not just our environment but our life experiences—from travelling the nation's highways to sitting at home viewing television—are more standardized than ever before. Almost anywhere in the world, a person can walk into a McDonald's restaurant and receive the same sandwiches, drinks, and desserts prepared in precisely the same way. Uniformity results from a highly rational system that specifies every action and leaves nothing to chance.[1]

- *Control.* The most unreliable element in the McDonald's system is human beings. After all, people have good and bad days, sometimes let their minds wander, or simply decide to try something a different way. To minimize the unpredictable human element, McDonald's has automated its equipment to cook food at a fixed temperature for a set length of time. Even the cash register at McDonald's is keyed to pictures of the items so that ringing up a customer's order is as simple as possible. Similarly, automatic teller machines are replacing banks, highly automated bakeries now produce bread while people stand back and watch, and chickens and eggs (or is it eggs and chickens?) emerge from automated hatcheries. In some supermarkets, laser scanners at self-checkouts are phasing out human checkers. We do most of our shopping in malls, where everything from temperature and humidity to the kinds of stores and products is carefully controlled and supervised (Ide and Cordell, 1994).

Can Rationality Be Irrational?

There is no doubt about the popularity or efficiency of McDonald's. But there is another side to the story. Max Weber was alarmed at the increasing rationalization of the world, fearing that formal organizations would cage our imaginations and crush the human spirit. As Weber saw it, rational systems were efficient but dehumanizing. "McDonaldization" bears him out. Each of the three principles just discussed limits human creativity, choice, and freedom. Echoing Weber, Ritzer states that "the ultimate irrationality of McDonaldization is that people could lose control over the system and it would come to control us"

(1993:145). Perhaps even McDonald's understands this: the company has now expanded into more upscale, less McDonaldized restaurants such as Chipotle's and Pret-à-Manger that offer food that is more sophisticated, fresh, and healthful (Philadelphia, 2002).

The Future of Organizations: Opposing Trends

Early in the twentieth century, ever-larger organizations arose in North America, most taking on the bureaucratic form described by Max Weber. In many respects, these organizations resembled armies led by powerful generals who issued orders to their captains and lieutenants. Foot soldiers, working in the factories, did what they were told.

With the emergence of a post-industrial economy about 1950, as well as rising competition, many organizations evolved a flatter, more flexible model that prizes communication and creativity. Such "intelligent organizations" (Pinchot and Pinchot, 1993; Brooks, 2000) have become more productive than ever. Just as importantly, for highly skilled people who now enjoy creative freedom, these organizations cause less of the alienation that so worried Max Weber.

But this is only half the story. Although the post-industrial economy has created many highly skilled jobs, it has created even more routine service jobs, such as those offered by McDonald's. Fast-food companies now represent the largest pool of low-wage labour, aside from migrant workers (Schlosser, 2002). Work of this kind, which Ritzer terms "McJobs," offers few of the benefits that today's highly skilled workers enjoy. On the contrary, the automated routines that define work in the fast-food industry, telemarketing, and similar fields are very much the same as those that Frederick Taylor described a century ago.

Today, the organizational flexibility that gives better-off workers more freedom carries, for rank-and-file employees, the ever-present threat of "downsizing" (Sennett, 1998). Organizations facing global competition are eager to have creative employees, but they are just as eager to cut costs by eliminating as many routine jobs as possible. The net result is that some people are better off than ever, while others worry about holding their jobs and struggle to make ends meet—a trend that Chapter 11 ("Social Class in Canada") explores in detail.

---

[1]As McDonald's has "gone global," a few products have been added or changed according to local tastes. For example, in Uruguay, customers enjoy the McHuevo (hamburger with poached egg on top); Norwegians can buy McLaks (grilled salmon sandwiches); the Dutch favour the Groenteburger (vegetable burger); in Thailand, McDonald's serves Samurai pork burgers (pork burgers with teriyaki sauce); the Japanese can purchase a Chicken Tatsuta Sandwich (chicken seasoned with soy and ginger); Filipinos eat McSpaghetti (spaghetti with tomato sauce and bits of hot dogs); and in India, where Hindus eat no beef, McDonald's sells a vegetarian Maharaja Mac (Sullivan, 1995). And in Canada, mainly in Quebec, McDonald's serves poutine.

7 MAKING THE GRADE

The following learning tools will help you see what you know, identify what you still need to learn, and expand your understanding beyond the text. You can also visit this text's Companion Website™ at www.pearsoned.ca/macionis to find useful practice tests.

KEY POINTS

Social Groups

Social groups are building blocks of society that join members as well as perform various tasks. Primary groups tend to be small and person-oriented; secondary groups are typically large and goal-oriented.

Leadership is one key dimension of group dynamics. Instrumental leadership is concerned with realizing a group's goals; expressive leadership focuses on members' morale and well-being.

The Asch, Milgram, and Janis studies all show that group members often seek agreement and may pressure one another towards conformity. Individuals use reference groups—both in-groups and out-groups—to form attitudes and make evaluations.

Georg Simmel described the dyad as intense but unstable; a triad, he added, can easily turn into a dyad by excluding one member.

Peter Blau explored how group size, social diversity, and the physical segregation of groups affect members' behaviour.

Social networks are relational webs that link people with little common identity and limited interaction. The internet is a vast electronic network linking millions of people worldwide.

Formal Organizations

Formal organizations are large secondary groups that try to carry out complex tasks efficiently. They are classified as utilitarian, normative, or coercive, depending on their members' reasons for joining. Bureaucracy, which expands in modern societies, is based on specialization, hierarchy, rules and regulations, technical competence, impersonal interaction, and formal written communication. All formal organizations operate in an environment influenced by technology, political and economic trends, population patterns, and other organizations.

Ideally, bureaucracy promotes efficiency. But Max Weber claimed that bureaucracy can also lead to alienation. Robert Michels linked bureaucracy to the problem of oligarchy.

The Evolution of Formal Organizations

Frederick Taylor's concept of scientific management shaped U.S. organizations a century ago. Since then, organizations have evolved a more open and flexible form as they have included larger numbers of women and minorities, responded to global competition, and shifted their focus from industrial production to post-industrial information processing.

The "McDonaldization" of society refers not just to the spread of fast food but also to the expansion of the principles of efficiency, uniformity, and control.

The Future of Organizations: Opposing Trends

The future of organizations is likely to involve opposing trends: towards more creative freedom for highly skilled information workers, and towards increased supervision and discipline for less skilled service workers.

KEY CONCEPTS

social group (p. 154) two or more people who identify and interact with one another

primary group (p. 155) a small social group whose members share personal and lasting relationships

secondary group (p. 155) a large and impersonal social group whose members pursue a specific goal or activity

instrumental leadership (p. 156) group leadership that focuses on the completion of tasks

expressive leadership (p. 156) group leadership that focuses on the group's well-being

groupthink (p. 159) the tendency of group members to conform, resulting in a narrow view of some issue

reference group (p. 159) a social group that serves as a point of reference in making evaluations and decisions

in-group (p. 160) a social group towards which a member feels respect and loyalty

out-group (p. 160) a social group towards which a person feels a sense of competition or opposition

dyad (p. 160) a social group with two members

triad (p. 161) a social group with three members

network (p. 161) a web of weak social ties

formal organization (p. 163) a large secondary group organized to achieve its goals efficiently

bureaucracy (p. 165) an organizational model rationally designed to perform tasks efficiently

organizational environment (p. 166) factors outside an organization that affect its operation

bureaucratic ritualism (p. 169) a focus on rules and regulations to the point of undermining an organization's goals

bureaucratic inertia (p. 169) the tendency of bureaucratic organizations to perpetuate themselves

oligarchy (p. 170) the rule of the many by the few

scientific management (p. 170) Frederick Taylor's term for the application of scientific principles to the operation of a business or other large organization

APPLICATIONS & EXERCISES

1. The next time you are eating at a fast-food restaurant, watch to see how not just employees but also customers are expected to behave in certain ways. For example, many such restaurants expect customers to line up to order. What other norms are at work?

2. Visit any large public building with an elevator. Observe groups of people as they approach the elevator, then enter the elevator with them. Watch their behaviour. What happens to conversations as the elevator doors close? Where do people fix their eyes? Can you explain these patterns?

3. Using campus publications or your school's webpage (and some assistance from an instructor), try to draw an organizational pyramid for your college or university. Show the key academic and administrative positions, and how they supervise and report to one another.

PRENTICE HALL
mysoclab™
Where learning & the sociological imagination intersect.

To reinforce your understanding of this chapter, and to identify topics for further study, visit MySocLab at **www.pearsoned.ca/mysoclab/** for diagnostic tests and a multimedia ebook.

CHAPTER EIGHT

Sexuality and Society

How did the sexual revolution change our society?

Why do societies control people's
sexual behaviour?

What part does sexuality play in social inequality?

Sergeant Sylvia Durand, in leopard-skin jacket and long auburn hair, is an example of recent profound change in the Canadian military: until recently she was Sergeant Sylvain Durand, a male communications specialist at the Department of National Defence in Ottawa. Her sex-change operation is significant enough in itself, but it has also become a historic event: the military was not just tolerant of the sex change, it actually paid the bill, at a Quebec clinic that draws clients from throughout North America.

Durand's partner, Cynthia Cousens, is a former police officer. As Peter Cousens, he put in twenty-eight years of service in downtown Toronto's tough 14 Division—only to go to his retirement party dressed as a woman. Cousens had been a married man who loved his wife deeply and had two children; yet, because, he felt compelled to deal with this deeply rooted yearning within him, he too underwent a sex-change operation.

Durand and Cousens met while they were undergoing counselling and treatment prior to their operations, and went on to form a relationship that defies easy classification. They are not, as Sergeant Durand explains, in a traditional lesbian relationship. Nor are they gay. They are two transsexuals in transition who are very much in love.

Both Durand and Cousens realized, at about age five, that they were not like other little boys—and felt they were in the wrong bodies. The surgery, for Durand, was a miracle that left her feeling at peace with herself. Her "metamorphosis from he to she is a shining example of Canadian open-mindedness. She is the only soldier in the world to undergo a sex-change operation while serving in the military." That her transformation was accepted by her colleagues, with no ridicule or discrimination, speaks volumes about the change that has occurred in Canadian society and its military.

Source: Adapted from Peritz (2000).

This chapter examines the importance of sex to society and presents what researchers have learned about patterns of sexual behaviour. As you will see, sexual attitudes are quite diverse around the world and, in North America, beliefs about sex have changed dramatically over the past century. Today, we continue to debate a number of social issues involving sexuality, including gay rights, teen pregnancy, prostitution, date rape, and abortion.

Understanding Sexuality

How much of your day does *not* involve thoughts about sexuality? If you are like most people, the answer is "not very much," because sexuality is not just about having sex. Sexuality is found almost everywhere—on campus, in the workplace, in advertising, and especially in the mass media. The sex industry, including pornography and prostitution, is a multibillion-dollar business. Sexuality is an important part of how we think about ourselves as well as how others think about us. In truth, there are few areas of life in which sexuality does not play some part.

Nevertheless, North American culture has long treated sex as taboo; even today, many people avoid talking about it. As a result, although sex can produce much pleasure, it also causes confusion, anxiety, and sometimes outright fear. Even scientists long considered sex off limits as a topic of research. It was not until the middle of the twentieth century that researchers turned their attention to this vital dimension of social life. Since then, we have discovered a great deal about human sexuality.

Sex: A Biological Issue

Sex refers *to the biological distinction between females and males.* From a biological point of view, sex is the way humans reproduce. A female ovum and a male sperm— each containing twenty-three pairs of chromosomes (that is, biological codes that guide physical development)— combine to form a fertilized embryo. To one of these pairs, which determines the child's sex, the mother contributes an X chromosome and the father contributes either an X or a Y. An X from the father produces a female (XX) embryo; a Y from the father produces a male (XY) embryo. In this way, a child's sex is determined biologically at the moment of conception.

Within weeks, the sex of an embryo starts to guide its development. If the embryo is male, testicular tissue starts to produce large amounts of testosterone, a hormone that triggers the development of male genitals, or sex organs. If little testosterone is present, the embryo develops female genitals. Interestingly, about 105 boys are born for every 100 girls, but a higher death rate among males makes females a slight majority by the time people reach their mid-thirties (Mathews and Hamilton, 2005).

SEX AND THE BODY

Some differences in the body set males and females apart. Right from birth, the two sexes have different **primary sex characteristics,** namely, *the genitals, organs used for reproduction.* At puberty, as people reach sexual maturity, additional sex differentiation takes place. At this point, people develop **secondary sex characteristics,** *bodily development, apart from the genitals, that distinguishes biologically mature females and males.* Mature females have wider hips for giving birth, milk-producing breasts for nurturing infants, and deposits of soft, fatty tissue that provides a reserve supply of nutrition during pregnancy and breast-feeding. Mature males typically develop more muscle in the upper body, more extensive body hair, and deeper voices. Of course, these are general differences; some males are smaller and have less body hair and higher voices than some females.

Keep in mind that sex is not the same thing as gender. *Gender* is an element of culture that refers to the personal traits and patterns of behaviour, including responsibilities, opportunities, and privileges, that a culture attaches to being female or male. Chapter 13 ("Gender Stratification") describes the importance of gender in social life.

Intersexual People

Sex is not always as clear-cut as we have just described. The term **intersexual people** refers to *people whose bodies, including genitals, have both female and male characteristics.* Another term for intersexual people is *hermaphrodites* (derived from Hermaphroditus, the child of the mythologi-cal Greek gods Hermes and Aphrodite, who embodied both sexes). A true hermaphrodite has both a female ovary and a male testis. However, our culture demands sex to be clear-cut, a fact evident in the requirement that parents record the sex of their new child at birth as either female or male. In North America, some people respond to hermaphrodites with confusion or even disgust. But attitudes in other cultures are quite different: Pokot people in eastern Africa, for example, pay little attention to what they consider a simple biological error, and Dinee (or Navajo) look on intersexual people with awe, seeing in them the full potential of both the female and the male (Geertz, 1975).

Transsexuals

Transsexuals are *people who feel they are one sex even though biologically they are the other.* Tens of thousands of people in North America have experienced the feeling of being trapped in a body of the wrong sex and a desire to be the other sex. Most become *transgendered,* meaning that they begin to disregard conventional ideas about how females or males should look and behave. Many, like Sylvain and Peter in the chapter opener, go one step further and undergo *gender reassignment,* surgical alteration of their genitals, usually with hormone treatments. This medical procedure is complex and takes months or even years, but it helps many people gain a joyful sense of finally matching the outside with how they feel on the inside (Tewksbury and Gagné, 1996; Gagné, *et al.,* 1997).

The Media Perspectives box (on p. 186) deals with a unique and involuntary case of gender reassignment and eventual reversal. This case tests the assumption that gender identity—the social construct—is infinitely malleable.

YOUR TURN

In the opener, you learned that the military paid for the gender reassignment of Sylvain/Sylvia Durand. Should our provincial/territorial health care programs cover the cost of gender reassignment? Why?

SEX: A CULTURAL ISSUE

Sexuality has a biological foundation. But like all elements of human behaviour, sexuality is also very much a cultural issue. Biology may explain some animals' mating rituals, but humans have no similar biological program. While there is a biological "sex drive" in the sense that people find sex pleasurable and may want to engage in sexual activity, our biology does not dictate any specific ways of being sexual any more than our desire to eat dictates any particular foods or table manners.

MEDIA PERSPECTIVES
The Boy Who Was Raised as a Girl

In 1963, a physician in a Canadian prairie town was performing a routine penis circumcision on seven-month–old identical twin boys. While using electrocautery (surgery with a heated needle), the physician accidentally burned off the penis of one boy. Understandably, the parents were horrified. After consulting with Dr. John Money of Johns Hopkins University, they decided to surgically change the boy's sex and to raise him as a girl.

The parents dressed "Joan" as a girl, let her hair grow long, and treated her according to cultural definitions of femininity. Meanwhile, the twin brother was raised as a boy. In the initial reports, the researchers reported that, because of their different socialization, each child adopted a distinctive **gender identity,** *traits that females and males, guided by their culture, incorporate into their personality.* In this extraordinary case, it was reported, one child learned to think of himself in masculine terms, while the other child— despite beginning life as a male—soon began to think of herself as feminine.

The girl's development did not proceed smoothly, however, suggesting that some biological forces were coming into play. While feminine in some respects, later researchers reported that she began to display some masculine traits, including a desire to gain dominance among her peers. As she reached adolescence, she was showing signs of resisting her feminine gender identity (Diamond,

David Reimer is the man in the book, *As Nature Made Him: The Boy Who Was Raised as a Girl* (2000). Author John Colapinto convinced Reimer that his story needed to be told.

1982). By the spring of 1997, the gender reassignment appeared much less successful than previously reported. By age fourteen, "Joan," who had been teased mercilessly by other children for her boyish looks and behaviour, was suicidal and refused to continue living as a girl. When the father broke down and told "Joan" the truth, she was relieved to finally understand herself. "Joan" became "John," undergoing a mastectomy, hormone treatment, and surgical reconstruction of male genitalia. Happy as a man, John married and adopted his wife's children (Angier, 1997). This complex case reveals that, while gender, a social construct, is the product of the social

environment, cultural conditioning is limited by biology.

Joan/John (whose real name was David Reimer) was featured in a *Fifth Estate* documentary on gender reassignment, in which he talked about the painful childhood he had endured because of rejection by his peers. His mother, who was interviewed as well, told of their experience from her perspective and, essentially, contradicted the researchers concerning the "feminine" qualities of her child. Several years later, reporter John Colapinto came to Winnipeg to learn more about David Reimer. He convinced Reimer that it was time to put his experience into book form—but only if he was ready to reveal his true identity. The book, written by Colapinto with Reimer's co-operation, tells the story of David's struggle against his imposed girlhood, challenging Money's contention that gender identity is determined by cultural conditioning rather than by genes.

Sadly, David Reimer took his own life in 2004.

WHAT DO YOU THINK?

1. What should his parents have done when Reimer's penis was destroyed through a botched circumcision?
2. Who has the right to "choose" the gender of a baby with damaged sex organs or indeterminate sex characteristics?
3. To what extent is gender identity the function of nature or nurture?

Cultural Variation

Almost every sexual practice shows considerable variation from one society to another. In his pioneering study of sexuality in the United States, Alfred Kinsey (1948) found that most heterosexual couples reported having intercourse in a single position—face to face, with the woman under the man. Halfway around the world, in the South Seas, most couples *never* have sex in this way. In fact, when the people of the South Seas learned of this practice from Western missionaries, they poked fun at it as the strange "missionary position." Even the simple practice of showing affection varies from society to society. Most of us kiss in public, but

We claim that "beauty is in the eye of the beholder," which suggests the importance of culture in setting standards of attractiveness. All of the people pictured here (*from top left*)—from Morocco, South Africa, Nigeria, Myanmar, Japan, and Ecuador—are beautiful to members of their own society. At the same time, sociobiologists point out that, in every society on Earth, people are attracted to youthfulness. The reason is that, as sociobiologists see it, attractiveness underlies our choices about reproduction, which is most readily accomplished in early adulthood.

the Chinese kiss only in private. The French kiss publicly (once on each cheek) and the Belgians kiss three times (starting on either cheek). The Maoris of New Zealand rub noses, and most people in Nigeria don't kiss at all.

Modesty, too, is culturally variable. If a woman stepping into a bath is interrupted, what body parts do you think she would cover? Helen Colton (1983) reports that an Islamic woman covers her face, a Laotian woman covers her breasts, a Samoan woman covers her navel, a Sumatran woman covers her knees, and a European woman covers her breasts with one hand and her genital area with the other.

Around the world, some societies restrict sexuality, and others are more permissive. In China, for example, norms closely regulate sexuality so that few people have sexual intercourse before they marry. In Canada—at least in recent decades—intercourse prior to marriage has become the norm, and many choose to have sex without strong commitment.

The Incest Taboo

When it comes to sex, do all societies agree on anything? The answer is Yes. One *cultural universal*—an element found in every society the world over—is the **incest taboo**, *a norm forbidding sexual relations or marriage between certain relatives.* In Canada, both law and cultural mores prohibit close relatives—including brothers and sisters, parents and children—from having sex or marrying. The incest taboo varies from state to state in the United States, where twenty-four outlaw marriage between first cousins; twenty-six do not. In Canada, first-cousin marriage is permitted.

Some societies, such as the Dinee (or Navajo), apply incest taboos only to the mother and others on her side of the family. There are also societies on record, including ancient Peru and Egypt, that have approved brother/sister marriages among the nobility to keep power within a single family (Murdock, 1965; orig. 1949).

TABLE 8–1

Canadian Attitudes towards Nonmarital Sex, Extramarital Sex, and Homosexuality, 1975–95

	Distribution of Responses (%)				
	1975	**1980**	**1985**	**1990**	**1995**
Nonmarital sex					
Not wrong at all	39	46	50	55	57
Sometimes wrong	29	28	27	25	23
Almost always wrong	13	10	8	7	7
Always wrong	19	16	15	13	13
Extramarital sex					
Not wrong at all	5	4	3	3	3
Sometimes wrong	17	17	16	13	12
Almost always wrong	28	26	26	22	25
Always wrong	50	53	55	62	60
Homosexuality					
Not wrong at all	14	16	16	21	32
Sometimes wrong	14	14	13	13	16
Almost always wrong	10	8	9	7	7
Always wrong	62	62	62	59	45

Source: Adapted by L.M. Gerber from Bibby (1995:69, 72, 75).

Why does some form of incest taboo exist everywhere? Part of the reason is biology: reproduction between close relatives of any species raises the odds of producing offspring with mental or physical problems. But why, of all living species, do only humans observe an incest taboo? This fact suggests that controlling sexuality among close relatives is a necessary element of *social* organization. For one thing, the incest taboo limits sexual competition in families by restricting sex to spouses—ruling out, for example, sex between parent and child. Because family ties define people's rights and obligations towards one another, reproduction between close relatives would hopelessly confuse kinship; if a mother and son had a daughter, would the child consider the male a father or a brother? Requiring marriage outside immediate families, the incest taboo integrates the larger society as people look beyond their close kin to form new families.

Sexual Attitudes

What do North Americans think about sex? Our cultural orientation towards sexuality has always been something of a contradiction. Most European immigrants arrived with rigid ideas about "correct" sexuality, typically limiting sex to reproduction within marriage. The early Puritan settlers of New England demanded strict conformity in attitudes and behaviour, and imposed severe penalties for what they perceived as sexual misconduct. Regulation of sexuality has continued ever since. As late as the 1960s in the United States, several states legally banned the sale of condoms in stores; until 2003, thirteen states had laws forbidding sexual acts between partners of the same sex; and "fornication" laws, which are still on the books in eleven states, can be used to punish heterosexual intercourse by unmarried couples. In Canada, it was not until 1969 that birth control and homosexual acts, in private between consenting adults, were removed from the *Criminal Code of Canada.*

On the other hand, since our culture is individualistic, many of us believe we should be free to do what we wish as long as we cause no direct harm to others. The idea that actions in the privacy of our homes are our own business makes sex a matter of individual freedom and personal choice.

When it comes to sexuality, are Canadians restrictive or permissive? The answer is both. Many of us still see sexual conduct in terms of personal morality. But sex is strongly promoted by the mass media—even to children as young as ten or twelve—as if to say that "anything goes." Table 8–1 reveals change from 1975 to 1995 in our attitudes towards nonmarital sex (sex outside marriage), extramarital sex (adultery), and homosexuality. Bibby asked respondents to classify each as "not wrong at all," "sometimes wrong," "almost always wrong," or "always wrong." He found that Canadians became more accepting of nonmarital sex and homosexuality over time; conversely, we increasingly viewed extramarital sex as "always wrong" (from 50% to 60%). Thus, we are more permissive with respect to nonmarital sex and homosexuality, but more restrictive with respect to extramarital sex. Take a look at the table itself, making sure you understand how these conclusions are supported by the data.

In December 1967, Prime Minister Pierre Elliott Trudeau shocked conservative Canada with the radical statement that "the state has no place in the bedrooms of the nation." As justice minister, he had proposed the decriminalization of homosexual acts carried out in private by two consenting adults—at a time when police actions and public opinion were still highly punitive of homosexuality (Kinsman, 1996).

THE SEXUAL REVOLUTION

During the twentieth century, we saw profound changes in sexual attitudes and practices. The first indications of change came in the 1920s as people left farms and small towns for rapidly growing cities. There, away from their families and meeting new friends, young people enjoyed considerable sexual freedom, in the "Roaring Twenties." In the 1930s and 1940s, the Great Depression and World War II slowed the rate of change. But in the postwar period, Alfred Kinsey set the stage for the *sexual revolution*. Kinsey and his colleagues published their first study of sexuality in the United States in 1948, and it raised eyebrows everywhere. While he presented startling results, the national uproar resulted not so much from what he said as from the fact that scientists were actually studying sex. Kinsey's two books (1948, 1953) became best-sellers partly because they revealed that Americans, on average, were far less conventional in sexual matters than most had thought. These books encouraged a new openness towards sexuality.

DIVERSITY SNAPSHOT

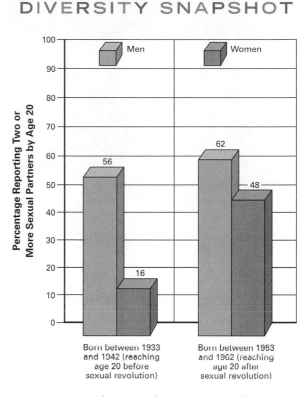

FIGURE 8-1   The Sexual Revolution: Closing the Double Standard

A larger share of men than women report having had two or more sexual partners by age twenty. But the sexual revolution greatly reduced the gender gap.

Source: Laumann, *et al.* (1994:198).

In the late 1960s, the Sexual Revolution truly came of age. Youth culture dominated public life, and such expressions as "if it feels good, do it" and "sex, drugs, and rock 'n' roll" summed up a new, freer attitude towards sex. The baby boom generation, born between 1946 and 1964, became the first cohort to grow up with the idea that sex was part of life—with or without marriage. Technology also played a part in the Sexual Revolution. The birth control pill, introduced in 1960, not only prevented pregnancy but also made sex more convenient. Unlike a condom or a diaphragm, which must be applied before or at the time of intercourse, the pill could be taken at any time during the day. With it, women could engage in sex spontaneously without specific preparation.

Historically, women were subject to greater sexual regulation than men, so the Sexual Revolution had special significance for them. Society's sexual "double standard" allows—and even encourages—men to be sexually active but expects women to be virgins until marriage and faithful to their husbands afterwards. The survey data in Figure 8–1 show the narrowing of the double standard. Among people

Over the course of the last century, social attitudes have become more accepting of human sexuality. What do you see as some of the benefits of this greater openness? What are some of the negative consequences?

born between 1933 and 1942 (that is, people who are in their sixties and seventies today), 56 percent of men but just 16 percent of women report having had two or more sexual partners by the time they reached age twenty. Compare this wide gap to the pattern among the baby boomers born between 1953 and 1962 (people now in their forties and fifties), who came of age after the Sexual Revolution; in this category, 62 percent of men and 48 percent of women say they had two or more sexual partners by age twenty (Laumann, *et al.*, 1994:198). The Sexual Revolution increased sexual activity overall, but it changed women's behaviour much more than men's.

Greater openness about sexuality develops as societies become richer and the opportunities for women increase. With these facts in mind, look for a pattern in the global use of birth control shown in Global Map 8–1.

THE SEXUAL COUNTERREVOLUTION

The Sexual Revolution made sex a topic of everyday discussion and sexual activity more a matter of individual choice. However, by 1980, the climate of sexual freedom that had marked the late 1960s and 1970s was criticized by some as evidence of moral decline, and the *sexual counterrevolution* began. Politically speaking, this was a conservative call for a return to "family values" and a change from sexual freedom back towards what critics saw as the sexual responsibility valued by earlier generations. Critics of the Sexual Revolution objected not just to the idea of free love but to trends such as cohabitation (living together) and unmarried couples having children.

Looking back, the sexual counterrevolution did little to change the notion of sexual freedom. But, whether for

moral reasons or concerns about sexually transmitted diseases, more people began choosing to limit their number of sexual partners or not to have sex at all.

PREMARITAL SEX

In light of the sexual revolution and the sexual counterrevolution, how much has sexual behaviour in North America really changed? One interesting trend involves premarital sex—the likelihood that young people will have sexual intercourse before marriage.

YOUR TURN

Are there many among your peers who have decided on complete abstinence from sex until marriage? What is the reaction of other young people to their decision?

Table 8–2 shows attitudes towards premarital sex in Canada for 1975 and 1995, and in the United States for 1998. In Canada, attitudes towards premarital sex changed dramatically between 1975 and 1995—in step with the Sexual Revolution. The proportion of Canadians who felt that premarital sex is "not wrong at all" increased from 39 to 57 percent, while the belief that it is "always wrong" decreased from 19 to 13 percent. Premarital sex, within Canada, has clearly gained in approval over this twenty-year period (Bibby, 1995:69). Americans in 1998 were less liberal than their Canadian counterparts: in fact, the U.S. figures for 1998 are similar to those for Canadians in 1975.

WINDOW ON THE WORLD

GLOBAL MAP 8–1   Contraceptive Use in Global Perspective

The map shows the percentage of married women using modern contraception methods (such as barrier methods, contraceptive pill, implants, injectables, intrauterine contraceptive devices, or sterilization). In general, how do high-income nations differ from low-income nations? Can you explain this difference?

Source: Data from United Nations Development Programme (2005).

Now consider what people *do* regarding premarital intercourse. For women, there has been marked change over time. The Kinsey studies (1948, 1953) report that, for people born in the early 1900s, about 50 percent of men but 6 percent of women had premarital sexual intercourse before age nineteen. Studies of baby boomers born after World War II show a slight increase in premarital intercourse among men but a large increase—to about one-third—among women. Recent studies, targeting men and women born in the 1970s, show that 76 percent of men and 66 percent of women had premarital sexual intercourse by their senior year in high school (Laumann, *et al.*, 1994:323–24). Thus, while general public attitudes remain divided on premarital sex, it is widely practised among young people.

While the sexual double standard (guys should, gals shouldn't) has been largely eliminated, male/female differences in the meaning attached to sex persist among Canadian university students. Among anglophone students, males are more likely than females (36.4% and 19.7%, respectively) to endorse the recreational or fun aspect of sex. Women, in contrast, adhere to a love aspect more than men do (48.9% and 39.1%, respectively). While the gender difference persists, francophone men and women are more

TABLE 8–2

How Canadians and Americans View Premarital Sex

	Canada 1975	Canada 1995	United States 1998
"Always wrong"	19%	13%	25%
"Not wrong at all"	39%	57%	42%

Sources: Bibby (1995) and NORC (1999, 2003).

sexuality in the second half of life is "quite an achievement" and is the result of a revitalized attitude towards sexuality among aging baby boomers (reported in Mahoney, 2006).

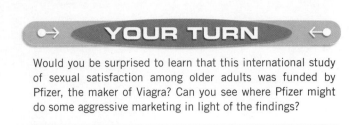

likely to endorse the fun aspect (51.9% and 37.1%, respectively) than are their anglophone peers; at the same time francophone men are slightly less likely (33.9%) to embrace the love aspect (Nelson and Robinson, 1999:354).

SEX BETWEEN ADULTS

Judging from the media, Americans are very active sexually. But do popular images reflect reality? The study by Laumann and his colleagues (1994), the largest study of sexuality since Kinsey's groundbreaking research, found that frequency of sexual activity varies widely among Americans. One-third of adults have sex with a partner a few times a year or not at all, another third once or several times a month, and the remainder two or more times a week.

And how do Canadians compare? Bibby (1995:65–67) found considerable variation in the frequency of sexual activity in Canada as well. The pattern breaks down as follows: 24 percent report sexual activity rarely or never; 23 percent are active one to three times per month; and 53 percent of Canadians have sex at least once a week. Quebecers report higher levels of sexual activity than Canadians on the whole, and activity peaks among 30- to 39-year-olds for both men and women, decreasing gradually into old age. It appears that Canadians are more active sexually than Americans.

More recently, Laumann was involved in a study of subjective sexual well-being in 29 countries (Mahoney, 2006)—which reveals that Canadians claim to be more sexually satisfied than Americans, though not by much. This study is the first of its kind—since it looks at sexual behaviour and satisfaction among people over 40 years of age—finding greater contentment in countries with gender equality. A ranking of countries, by the percentage of people reporting sexual satisfaction, reveals the following: Austria ranks first at 71.4 percent, Canada ranks third at 66.1 percent, the United States is fifth at 64.2 percent, and Sweden ranks ninth at 60.5 percent. Among the lowest five are Thailand, China, and Japan at 35.9 percent, 34.9 percent, and 25.8 percent, respectively. Professor Edward Herold, at the University of Guelph, notes that this study of

Extramarital Sex

What about sex outside marriage? Adultery, or extramarital sex, is widely condemned: more than 85 percent and 90 percent, respectively, of Canadian and American adults consider extramarital sex to be "almost always wrong" or "always wrong." Thus, the norm of sexual fidelity within marriage has been and remains strongly supported in North American culture. In fact, this is one area in which we have become less liberal over the past few decades: the proportion of Canadians saying that extramarital sex is "always wrong" *increased* from 50 percent to 60 percent between 1975 and 1995 (see Table 8–1).

Cultural ideals often differ from real life—so that, predictably, extramarital sex is more common than it *should* be. Among Americans, about 25 percent of married men and 10 percent of married women have had at least one extramarital sexual experience (Laumann, *et al.*, 1994:214, NORC, 2003:1227).

Bricker and Wright (2005: 214–17), of the polling firm Ipsos-Reid, report some interesting findings regarding cheating on one's partner (married or not): 10 percent of men and 5 percent of women say they would cheat on their partners if there was no chance of getting caught—with those in British Columbia and Ontario being slightly more likely to stray, while 33 percent and 35 percent of men and women have been cheated on by a partner. Once again, note the discrepancy between the ideal and real. Somewhat surprisingly, 39 percent of Canadians believe that even "happily married people" have affairs," and 53 percent of married people would forgive an affair. On the other hand, 63 percent of divorces can be attributed to affairs.

Sexual Orientation

In recent decades, public opinion about sexual orientation has shown a remarkable change. **Sexual orientation** is *a person's romantic and emotional attraction to another person.* The norm in all human societies is **heterosexuality** (*hetero* is a Greek word meaning "the other of two"), meaning *sexual attraction to someone of the other sex.* Yet in every society, a significant share of people experience **homosexuality** (*homo* is the Greek word for "the same"), *sexual attraction to someone of the same sex.* Keep in mind that people do not necessarily fall into just one of these categories; they may have varying degrees of attraction to both sexes. The idea that sexual orientation is not clear-cut is confirmed by the existence of a third category: **bisexuality,** *sexual attraction to people of both sexes.* Some bisexual people are equally attracted to males and females; many others are more attracted to one sex than the other. Finally, **asexuality** refers to *a lack of sexual attraction to people of either sex.* Figure 8–2 describes each of these sexual orientations in relation to the others.

It is important to remember that sexual *attraction* is not the same thing as sexual *behaviour.* Many people, perhaps even most people, have experienced attraction to someone of the same sex, but far fewer ever engage in same-sex behaviour. This is in large part because our culture discourages such actions.

Around the world, heterosexuality is the norm because, biologically speaking, heterosexual relations permit human reproduction. Even so, most societies tolerate homosexuality. Among the ancient Greeks, upper-class men considered homosexuality the highest form of relationship, partly because they looked down on women as intellectually inferior; as these men saw it, heterosexuality was necessary only so they could have children, and "real" men preferred homosexual relations (Kluckhohn, 1948; Ford and Beach, 1951; Greenberg, 1988).

WHAT GIVES US A SEXUAL ORIENTATION?

For a summary of recent research on sexual orientation, go to www.davidmyers.org/Brix?pageID=62.

The question of *how* people develop sexual orientation in the first place is strongly debated. The arguments cluster into two general positions: sexual orientation as a product of society and sexual orientation as a product of biology.

Sexual Orientation: A Product of Society

This approach argues that people in any society attach meanings to sexual activity, and these meanings differ from place to place and over time. Michel Foucault (1990; orig. 1978) points out, for example, that there was no distinct category of people called "homosexuals" until a century ago, when scientists and eventually the public as a whole began defining people that way. Throughout history, many

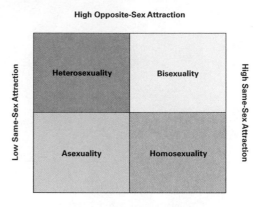

High Opposite-Sex Attraction

Heterosexuality	Bisexuality
Asexuality	Homosexuality

Low Same-Sex Attraction — High Same-Sex Attraction

Low Opposite-Sex Attraction

FIGURE 8–2   Four Sexual Orientations

A person's level of same-sex attraction and opposite-sex attraction are two distinct dimensions that combine in various ways to produce four major sexual orientations.

Source: Adapted from Storms (1980).

people no doubt had what we would call "homosexual experiences," but neither they nor others saw in this behaviour the basis for any special identity.

Anthropological studies show that patterns of homosexuality differ from one society to another. In Siberia, for example, Chukchee homosexual males have a practice in which one man dresses like a female and does a woman's work. Sambia, who dwell in the Eastern Highlands of New Guinea, have a ritual in which young boys perform oral sex on older men in the belief that ingesting semen will enhance their masculinity. The existence of such diverse patterns in societies around the world indicates that human sexual expression is socially constructed (Murray and Roscoe, 1998; Blackwood and Wieringa, 1999).

Sexual Orientation: A Product of Biology

A growing body of evidence suggests that sexual orientation is innate or biological. Arguing this position, LeVay (1993)

The American Psychological Association posts answers to commonly asked questions about sexual orientation at www.apa.org/pubinfo/answers.html.

links sexual orientation to the structure of a person's brain, finding a small but important difference in the size of the hypothalamus, a part of the brain that regulates hormones. This anatomical difference may play a part in shaping sexual orientation.

Genetics may also influence sexual orientation. One study of forty-four pairs of brothers, all homosexual, found that thirty-three pairs had a distinctive genetic pattern involving the X chromosome. The gay brothers also had an unusually high number of gay male relatives—but only on

Halifax, Toronto, and Vancouver are among the North American and European cities that hold annual Gay Pride parades, like the one attended by this gay couple.

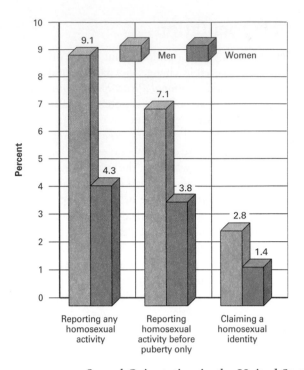

FIGURE 8-3 Sexual Orientation in the United States: Survey Data

The percentage of people who are classified as having a homosexual orientation depends on how this concept is operationalized. Research suggests that 2.8 percent of adult men and 1.4 percent of adult women claim a homosexual identity.

Source: Adapted from Laumann, *et al.* (1994).

their mother's side. Such evidence leads some researchers to think there may be a "gay" gene located on the X chromosome (Hamer and Copeland, 1994).

Critical Review Mounting evidence supports the conclusion that sexual orientation is rooted in biology, although the best guess at present is that both nature and nurture play a part. Remember that sexual orientation is not a matter of neat categories. Many who think of themselves as homosexual have had heterosexual experience, just as many heterosexuals have had homosexual experience. Some homosexuals "come out" after marrying and raising children to adulthood. There is also a political issue here with great importance for gay men and lesbians. To the extent that sexual orientation is based in biology, homosexuals have no more choice about their sexual orientation than they do about their skin colour. If this is so, shouldn't gay men and lesbians expect the same rights and legal protection as visible minorities?

HOW MANY GAY PEOPLE ARE THERE?

What share of our population is homosexual, or gay? This is a difficult question to answer because, as we have explained, sexual orientation is not a matter of neat categories. In addition, not all people are willing to reveal their sexuality to strangers or even to family members. The pioneering sex researcher Alfred Kinsey (1948, 1953) estimated that about 4 percent of males and 2 percent of

females have an exclusively same-sex orientation, although he pointed out that most people experience same-sex attraction at some point in their life.

Some social scientists put the gay share of the population at 10 percent. But the research by Laumann and his colleagues (1994) shows that the specific definition of homosexuality greatly affects research results. As Figure 8–3 shows, about 9 percent and 4 percent, respectively, of American men and women (aged 18 to 59) reported homosexual activity *at some time in their lives.* In Canada, estimates of the gay and lesbian or homosexual population range from 1 to 10 percent. As with the American data, everything depends on the definition.

Kinsey treated sexual orientation as an either/or trait: but same-sex and other-sex attractions can operate independently. Bisexual people (less than 1 percent of adults) feel a strong attraction to people of both sexes, and asexual people experience little sexual attraction to those of either sex.

In 2001, the Canadian census asked individuals in a common-law relationship to indicate if they are same-sex couples, because same-sex couples are entitled to the same benefits as heterosexual common-law partners. The 2001 census counted 34 200 same-sex common-law couples, representing 0.5 percent of all couples (Statistics Canada, 2002b).

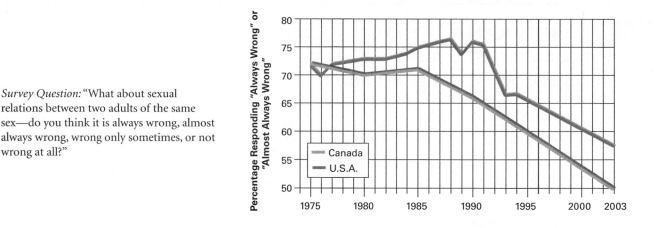

Survey Question: "What about sexual relations between two adults of the same sex—do you think it is always wrong, almost always wrong, wrong only sometimes, or not wrong at all?"

FIGURE 8-4   Canadian and American Attitudes towards Homosexual Relations, 1975–2003

Between 1975 and 2003, the proportions of Canadians and Americans claiming that homosexual relations are wrong—always or almost always—have declined dramatically.

Source: Bibby (1995), NORC (2003), and NFO Cfgroup, (2003).

THE GAY RIGHTS MOVEMENT

In recent decades, the public has become increasingly accepting of homosexuality. In 1975, as shown in Figure 8–4, 72 percent of Americans and Canadians felt that homosexual relations were "always wrong" or "almost always wrong." From 1975 to 1990, Americans became slightly more intolerant before rapidly changing their attitudes, to the point where, in 1995, only 64 percent strongly disapproved of homosexuality. In Canada, the proportion of people who disapproved of homosexuality dropped off sooner. By 1995, only 52 percent of Canadians were strongly disapproving, with 45 percent saying that homosexuality is "always wrong" (Bibby, 1995:72). By 2003, 48 percent of Canadians and 57 percent of Americans felt homosexuality is wrong (NFO Cfgroup, 2003).

In large measure, this change came about through the gay rights movement that arose in the 1960s (Chauncey, 1994). At that time, most people did not discuss homosexuality, and it was common for companies—including the federal government and the military—to fire anyone who was thought to be gay. Mental health professionals, too, took a hard line, describing homosexuals as "sick" and sometimes placing them in mental hospitals, where, presumably, they might be cured.

In this climate of intolerance, most lesbians and gay men remained "in the closet"—closely guarding their secret. The gay rights movement strengthened during the 1960s and, in 1969, Canada removed homosexual activity in private between consenting adults (aged 21 or older) from the Criminal Code. This limited reform passed in the context of heated debate, including talk of "gross indecency," "horror," and "sickness" (Kinsman, 1996). In 1974, the American Psychological Association declared that homosexuality was

not an illness but simply a form of "sexual behaviour." By 1998, Canada had extended such benefits to partners in same-sex relationships as pensions but was careful to reiterate that *marriage* is defined as the union of a man and a woman; this definition was affirmed in Bill C-23, which, in June 2000, extended to same-sex couples in committed relationships both the *benefits* and the *obligations* of other unions. But, in June 2003, after the marriage laws were struck down by courts in Ontario, British Columbia, and Quebec, the federal government announced it would submit legislation allowing same-sex marriages to the Supreme Court for review. On July 20, 2005, the *Civil Marriage Act*—passed by Paul Martin's Liberal government—made same sex marriage legal throughout the country. See the Thinking about Diversity box (on p. 196) for details.

The United States is also dealing with pressure to recognize "gay marriage" in law: in 2004, a number of cities and towns allowed gay couples to marry; now gay marriage is legal in the state of Massachusetts, and gay civil unions (marriage without the name) are legal in Vermont and Connecticut. At the same time, seventeen states have enacted laws that forbid gay marriage and prohibit recognizing such marriages performed elsewhere.

The gay rights movement began using the term **homophobia** to describe *the dread of close personal interaction with people thought to be gay, lesbian, or bisexual* (Weinberg, 1973). The concept of homophobia (literally, "fear of sameness") turns the tables on society: instead of asking "What's wrong with gay people?" the question becomes "What's wrong with people who can't accept a different sexual orientation?" Can you see the tension between these two approaches in the political manoeuvrings regarding same-sex marriage?

THINKING ABOUT DIVERSITY:
RACE, CLASS, & GENDER
Same-Sex Marriage in Canada

In August 2002, friends and family gathered on Algonquin Island against the Toronto skyline for a commitment ceremony celebrating the love of this same-sex couple. On the first anniversary of this ceremony, the couple was able to marry legally, as the Court of Appeal had made same-sex marriage legal in Ontario.

On January 14, 2001, Toronto made history, witnessing the world's first legal homosexual marriages since the Middle Ages—an event that attracted reporters from around the world. In Canada, legal marriage can be arranged through two routes: the first is through application for a marriage licence; the second involves the Christian tradition of the publication of banns on three Sundays prior to the marriage. Applications for marriage licences by homosexual couples had been refused throughout Canada, but Toronto's Metropolitan Community Church published banns for Joe Varnell and Kevin Bourassa and for Anne and Elaine Vantour. Even though the Ontario government refused to register these marriages at that time, the marriages were legal (Humphreys, 2001).

In a judgment in June 2003 making same-sex marriage legal in Ontario, the province's Court of Appeal said that the "exclusion of gays from the institution of marriage is illogical, offensive, and unjustifiable" (Makin, 2003). In doing so, the Ontario court joined those of British Columbia and Quebec in striking down marriage laws. But, unlike the courts in British Columbia and Quebec, the Ontario court did not give the province a grace period to bring its laws into conformity with the Canadian Charter of Rights and Freedoms. As a result, Ontario acted immediately to give out marriage licences to gays and lesbians: the first among them being Joe Varnell and Kevin Bourassa, one of the two couples married by the Metropolitan Community Church in 2001.

Over the past decade or two, Canadians have become more tolerant and supportive of the alternative lifestyles of lesbians and gays. The extension of spousal rights—similar to those of heterosexual common-law couples—to same-sex couples was accepted by a majority of Canadians as just. A poll reported in *The Globe and Mail* (Makin, 2003) suggests that young adults 18 to 24 years of age are most supportive of same-sex marriage (61.2% of males, 69.2% of females); among those 35 to 54 years old, support comes in at 55 percent among males and 62.2 percent of females; while among those over 55 years of age, support limps along at 24.6 percent among males and 37.6 percent among females. Thus, a majority of Canadians—especially among younger adults—is in favour of extending the right to marry to same-sex couples.

While these figures reveal substantial support for same-sex marriage in principle, they do not reveal the extent of support for changing the *definition* of marriage. As recently as 1999, a motion to reaffirm the definition of marriage "as a union of one man and one woman to the exclusion of all others" was passed in Parliament with 216 votes for and 55 against (Lunman, 2003). A repeat motion to that effect, in the fall of 2003, was defeated by a very narrow margin. Whatever the values and beliefs of our parliamentarians, court rulings that existing laws were discriminatory meant that the government could no longer avoid dealing with this issue. Justice Canada presented draft legislation defining marriage as a union of two persons—rather than one man and one woman—to the Supreme Court of Canada for its opinion. It was then presented to the House of Commons for debate and approval, and was passed on July 20, 2005.

Canada joined the Netherlands (in 2001) and Belgium (in 2002) as the first countries to allow same-sex marriage. Joe Varnell and Kevin Bourassa, because they rushed to have their marriage of January 2001 registered "legally" on June 11, 2003, became the first gays to marry—not just in Canada but in the world.

WHAT DO YOU THINK?

1. Were you aware that a number of American states have legalized same-sex marriage?
2. Are there gays or lesbians in your family? If so, did your family adjust easily or with difficulty?
3. What proportion of gay and lesbian couples do you think will take advantage of the right to marry?

Sexual Issues and Controversies

Sexuality lies at the heart of a number of controversies in North America today. Here we take a look at four key issues: teen pregnancy, pornography, prostitution, and sexual violence.

TEEN PREGNANCY

Sexual activity—especially intercourse—demands a high level of responsibility, since pregnancy can result. Teenagers who may be biologically, but not socially, mature, might fail to appreciate the consequences of their actions. Indeed, surveys indicate that, while 1 million American teens become pregnant each year—at rates of more than 100 pregnancies per 1000 teenage women—most of the pregnancies are unplanned. The U.S. rate of births to teens is higher than that of all other high-income countries and twice that of Canada (Darroch, *et al.*, 2001).

Concern about high rates of teenage pregnancy has led to sex education in the schools, but to some extent the focus in Canada has changed to concern about the problems of female-headed single-parent families—including those of

Visit www.canadian-health-network.ca for information about teen pregnancies and other health matters, or the U.S. National Campaign to Prevent Teen Pregnancy at www.teenpregnancy.org.

teenage mothers. This is largely because Canada's rate of teen pregnancy dropped from 50 pregnancies per 1000 women (aged fifteen to nineteen) in the early 1990s to 43 by 1997. In 1995, there were 19 724 babies born to teenage mothers and an additional 21 233 pregnancies that ended in **abortion,** *the deliberate termination of a pregnancy*; in other words, more than half of Canada's teen pregnancies end in abortion. (The Thinking it Through box (on p. 204) looks at the issue of abortion generally.)

Interestingly, between 1961 and 1991, the proportion of births to *unmarried* mothers that involved teens dropped from 38 to 19 percent because *older* women, in growing numbers, began to have children out of wedlock (Belle and McQuillan, 2000; Dryburgh, 2003). The teen pregnancy rate has continued to drop in recent years so that, by 2002, there were 34 pregnancies per 1000 women aged 15 to 19 (Society of Obstetricians and Gynaecologists of Canada, 2006). In other words, within a single decade, Canada's teen pregnancy rate had dropped from 50 to 34 per 1000 teenage women.

PORNOGRAPHY

In general terms, **pornography** refers to *sexually explicit material that causes sexual arousal*. But what, exactly, is or is not pornographic has long been a matter of debate. In Canada pornography is legal, while *obscenity*, which involves undue exploitation of sex and violation of community standards, is illegal. Much of the debate about material featuring adults deals with the point at which pornography crosses the line from erotica to obscenity. Sex, combined with bestiality, the degradation or humiliation of women, and/or violence—even murder (i.e., in "snuff" films) qualifies as obscenity. But where, in the continuum from *Playboy* to *snuff*, is that line crossed? Child pornography, especially pictures transmitted over the internet, has elicited a lot of reaction recently: this is one area where the line is *not* fuzzy.

Definitions aside, pornography is popular in North America: X-rated videos, 1–900 telephone numbers for sexual conversations, and a host of sexually explicit movies and magazines together constitute an industry that generates US$10 billion a year. The figure is rising as people buy more and more pornography from thousands of sites on the internet.

Traditionally, people have criticized pornography on *moral* grounds. U.S. surveys confirm that 60 percent of adults are concerned that "sexual materials lead to a breakdown of morals" (NORC, 1999:237). Today, however, pornography is also seen as a *power* issue because it depicts women as the sexual playthings of men (Nelson and Fleras, 1998). Pornography may also cause violence against women. While it is difficult to document a scientific cause-and-effect relationship between viewing and acting, research does support the idea that pornography makes men think of women as objects rather than as people. The public shares a concern about pornography and violence, with almost half believing that pornography encourages people to commit sexual assault, or rape (NORC, 1999:237). In fact, these concerns inform Canada's obscenity legislation.

While people everywhere object to sexual material they find offensive, many also value free speech and want to protect artistic expression. Therefore, when we propose censorship of pornography in Canada, we need to balance our demands against the constitutionally protected rights of free expression.

PROSTITUTION

Prostitution is *the selling of sexual services*. Often called the "oldest profession," prostitution has always been widespread. Even so, since people think of sex as interpersonal intimacy, many find the idea of sex performed for money disturbing. As a result, prostitution is against the law in the United States. In Canada, prostitution itself is not a crime; instead, the Criminal Code prohibits "those activities related to prostitution that are considered threatening to public order or offensive to public decency"—activities such as soliciting or communicating for the purposes of prostitution in a public place (Wolff and Geissel, 2000).

Around the world, prostitution prevails in poor countries where patriarchy is strong and traditional cultural norms limit women's ability to earn a living. Global Map 8–2 shows where prostitution is most widespread.

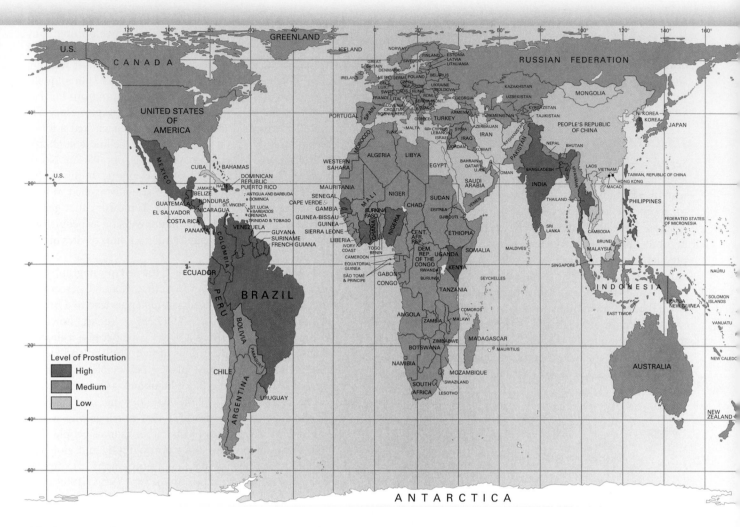

WINDOW ON THE WORLD

GLOBAL MAP 8–2 Prostitution in Global Perspective

Generally speaking, prostitution is widespread in societies where women have low standing. Officially, at least, China boasts of gender equality, including the elimination of vices such as prostitution, which oppresses women. By contrast, in much of Latin America, where patriarchy is strong, prostitution is common. In many Islamic societies, where patriarchy is also strong, religion is a counterbalance, so prostitution is limited. Western high-income nations have a moderate amount of prostitution.

Sources: *Peters Atlas of the World* (1990) and Mackay (2000).

Types of Prostitution

Most—but not all—prostitutes are women. Prostitutes (or "sex workers") fall into different categories. *Call girls* are elite prostitutes, typically women who are young, attractive, and well educated, and who arrange to meet clients by telephone. The classified pages of any large city newspaper contain numerous ads for escort services, by which women (and sometimes men) offer both companionship and sex for a fee.

Members of a middle category of prostitutes work in massage parlours or brothels under the control of managers. These sex workers have less choice in clients, receive less money for their services, and keep only half of their earnings.

At the bottom of the sex-worker hierarchy are *street walkers*, women and men who "work the streets" of large cities. Female street walkers are often under the control of

Experts agree that one factor contributing to the problem of sexual violence on campus is the widespread use of alcohol. What policies are in force on your campus to discourage the kind of drinking that leads to one person imposing sex on another?

male managers, or pimps, who take most of their earnings. Many street prostitutes fall victim to violence from pimps and clients (Gordon and Snyder, 1989; Davidson, 1998; Estes, 2001).

A Victimless Crime?

Communicating for the purposes of prostitution is against the law in Canada, but many people consider it a victimless crime. Thus, instead of enforcing prostitution laws all the time, police stage occasional crackdowns—suggesting that our society wants to control prostitution rather than to eliminate it.

Is selling sex a victimless crime that hurts no one? Certainly, those who assume a "live and let live" attitude to prostitution think so. But they ignore the fact that prostitutes are subjected to abuse and violence and play a part in spreading sexually transmitted diseases, including AIDS. Also, many poor women, trapped in a life of selling sex, put their own lives at risk. Canadian homicide statistics highlight the dangers associated with prostitution. In 1991 and 1992, 22 prostitutes were murdered, 5 percent of all the female murder victims 16 or older; four of the murdered women were 16 and 17 years of age (Wolff and Geissel, 2000).

Through 2002 and 2003, the most extensive murder probe in Canadian history looked into the disappearance since the mid–1990s of 63 women from Vancouver's skid row, most of whom were drug-addicted prostitutes. Hundreds of investigators, including fifty-two forensic anthropologists, searched every part of the pig farm of Robert Pickton and a nearby piece of land along a highway near Mission, British Columbia. As a result, evidence of 15 of the missing women was initially found and identified,

and Pickton was charged with 15 counts of first-degree murder (Armstrong, 2003). By 2006, Pickton stood charged with the murder of at least 22 women. He is to be tried first for the murder of 6, as there are too many victims to be considered at a single trial. Unfortunately, it took the disappearance of many prostitutes and pressure by their families and social activists before the police would investigate the possibility of serial murder.

SEXUAL ASSAULT

Ideally, sexual activity occurs within a loving relationship. In reality, sex can be twisted by hate and violence. In Canada, rape is officially recorded as *sexual assault.* From 2000 to 2004, there were, on average, 76 *reported* incidents per 100 000 population (Statistics Canada, 2006a), but be aware that the number of reported incidents is much higher.

 For information about studies and statistics dealing with sexual assault and date rape, go to Women Against Violence Against Women at www.wavaw.ca/informed_stats.php.

Victimization surveys in Canada lead to tremendous variation in estimates of sexual assault rates—for example, estimates vary from 600 to 2900 per 100 000 women, with only a fraction of cases showing up in official statistics (Johnson, 1996). Sexual assault statistics include only victims who are women, but men too are raped, in perhaps 10 percent of all cases. Most men who rape men are heterosexuals, motivated not by a desire for sex but by the urge to dominate. Keep in mind, too, that sexual assault is not necessarily perpetrated by strangers: often, it occurs in situations characterized by trust, including marriage. For a detailed discussion of date, or acquaintance, rape, see the Applying Sociology box (on p. 200).

APPLYING SOCIOLOGY
Date Rape: Exposing Dangerous Myths

When is it appropriate to have sexual intercourse? How well should you know the other person? If you do have sex, are you obliged to see each other again? If your date says No, and you press on with your sexual advances, are you simply persistent or guilty of sexual assault? If you are both drunk, is your behaviour justified?

Sexual activity must involve clear statements of consent by both participants and no one should knowingly expose another person to a sexually transmitted disease. Giving consent differentiates "having sex" from being raped by a date or casual acquaintance.

In recent years, the issue of date rape has been widely discussed at colleges and universities. While the open environment on campus encourages trust and communication, it also invites an alarming level of sexual violence. While 12 percent of Canadian women (18 and older) have experienced sexual assault by a date or boyfriend, this is true of 17 percent of female students (Johnson, 1996). Thus, being a student *increases* the likelihood of sexual violence. American research suggests that 1 in 6 female students will be raped before graduation: 1 in 6 translates to 17 percent, the comparable Canadian figure. General violence rates (e.g., murder rates) may be much higher in the United States but, when it comes to rape on campus, Canadian and American rates are identical. Equally disturbing is the observation that university men who abuse their dates do so, quite often, with the support of male friends who encourage and legitimize female victimization (DeKeseredy and Hinch, 1991).

If you *have* been raped and file a report, will the authorities take you seriously? Can you prosecute in the absence of such evidence as bruises, a medical examination, and torn clothes? Is it worth filing a report?

In most incidences of sexual assault, the victim files no police report, and no offender is arrested. So reluctant are the victims of such attacks to come forward that, in Canada, "somewhere between 60 and 90 percent of rapes go unreported" (DeKeseredy and Hinch, 1991:94).

When women do report sexual attacks, police judgment as to whether a criminal act has occurred often depends on the victim's reputation. When females referred to by the Canadian police as "women who can't be raped" or "open territory victims" filed complaints, 98 percent of the claims were dismissed as unfounded. Police claimed that "these women were prostitutes, known alcoholics, women who were drinking at the time of the offence, drug users, women on welfare, and unemployed women as well as women noted in police reports as 'idle'" (DeKeseredy and Hinch, 1991:66–67). Small wonder that women are reluctant to report a sexual assault, particularly if their attacker is known to them or if they had been partying before the assault took place.

In order to clear up confusion about sexual assault, or rape, we look at three false notions that are so common they qualify as "rape myths":

Myth #1: *Rape involves strangers*. A sexual attack brings to mind men lurking in the shadows who suddenly spring on unsuspecting victims. But this pattern is the exception rather than the rule: experts report that only one in five sexual assaults involves a stranger. Most sexual assaults, in fact, are *acquaintance rape* or, more simply, *date rape*.

Myth #2: *Women provoke their attackers*. Surely, a woman claiming sexual assault must have done *something* to encourage the man, to lead him on, to make him think that she really wanted to have sex. Didn't the young woman agree to have dinner with him and willingly admit him to her room? These questions may paralyze victims, but having dinner with a man—or inviting him into her room—is no more a woman's statement of consent to have sex than it is an invitation to have him beat her with a club.

Myth #3: *Rape is simply sex*. If there is no knife held to a woman's throat, or if she is not bound and gagged, then how can sex be a crime? The answer is that, under the law, forcing a woman to have sex without her consent is a *violent crime*. To accept the idea that sexual assault is sex, we would also have to see no difference between brutal combat and playful wrestling. "Having sex" implies intimacy, caring, and communication—none of which is present in cases of sexual assault.

The more people believe these myths, the more women will become victims of sexual violence.

To eliminate sexual violence, we must begin by exposing the myths about rape. In addition, the campus must be transformed so that women and men interact with dignity and equality. Serious questions also surround the role of alcohol on campus and the effects of cultural patterns that define sex as a sport. To address the crisis of date rape, everyone needs to understand two simple truths: forcing sex without a woman's consent is sexual assault (a crime), and when a woman says No, she means just that.

WHAT DO YOU THINK?

1. Is sexual assault a serious problem on your campus? Is there a program to walk students safely to a car or bus from late night classes or events?
2. Have you heard of cases of date rape among your peers? How did the victim handle the situation? Was it reported and, if so, what was the outcome?
3. Do you think the boundary between consensual sex and date rape is confusing? Why?

APPLYING THEORY

SEXUALITY

	Structural-Functional Approach	Symbolic-Interaction Approach	Social-Conflict Approach
What is the level of analysis?	Macro level	Micro level	Macro level
What is the importance of sexuality for society?	Society depends on sexuality for reproduction. Society uses the incest taboo and other norms to control sexuality in order to maintain social order.	Sexual practices vary among the many cultures of the world. Some societies allow individuals more freedom than others in matters of sexual behaviour.	Sexuality is linked to social inequality. Society regulates women's sexuality more than men's, which is part of the larger pattern of men dominating women.
Has sexuality changed over time? How?	Yes. As advances in birth control technology separate sex from reproduction, societies relax some controls on sexuality.	Yes. The meanings people attach to virginity and other sexual matters are all socially constructed and subject to change.	Yes and no. Some sexual standards have relaxed, but society still defines women in sexual terms, just as homosexual people are harmed by society's heterosexual bias.

Theoretical Analysis of Sexuality

Applying sociology's various theoretical approaches gives us a better understanding of human sexuality. The following sections discuss the three major approaches, and the Applying Theory table (above) highlights the key insights of each approach.

STRUCTURAL-FUNCTIONAL ANALYSIS

The structural-functional approach highlights the contribution of any social pattern to the overall operation of society. Because sexuality can have such important consequences, it is regulated by society.

The Need To Regulate Sexuality

From a biological point of view, sex allows our species to reproduce. But culture and social institutions regulate *with whom* and *when* people reproduce. For example, most societies condemn people for extramarital sex. To allow sexual passion to go unchecked would threaten family life, especially the raising of children. The fact that the incest taboo exists everywhere shows that no society permits completely free choice in sexual partners. Reproduction by family members other than married partners would break down the system of kinship and hopelessly confuse human relationships.

Historically, the social control of sexuality was strong because sex led to childbirth. We see these controls at work in the traditional distinction between legitimate reproduction (i.e., within marriage) and illegitimate reproduction (i.e., outside marriage). Once a society develops birth control, it becomes more permissive—to the point where sex

moves beyond its basic reproductive function and becomes accepted as a form of intimacy and even recreation (Giddens, 1992).

Latent Functions: The Case of Prostitution

It is easy to see that prostitution is harmful because it spreads disease and exploits women, but it takes latent functions to explain why prostitution is so widespread. According to Kingsley Davis (1971), prostitution performs several useful functions. It is one way to meet the sexual needs of a large number of people who may not have ready access to sex, including soldiers, travellers, people who are not physically attractive, or people who are too poor to attract a marriage partner. Some people favour prostitutes because they want sex without the "trouble" of a relationship: "Men don't pay for sex; they pay so they can leave" (Miracle, *et al.*, 2003:421).

Critical Review The structural-functional approach helps us see the important part sexuality plays in the organization of society. The incest taboo and other cultural norms also suggest that society has always paid attention to who has sex with whom and, especially, who reproduces with whom. But functionalist analysis sometimes ignores gender; when Kingsley Davis wrote of the benefits of prostitution for society, he was really talking about the benefits to some *men*. In addition, the fact that sexual patterns change over time and differ in remarkable ways around the world gets little attention using the functionalist approach.

The control of women's sexuality is a common theme in human history. During the Middle Ages, wealthy European men devised the "chastity belt"—a metal device locked about a woman's groin that prevented sexual intercourse and probably interfered with other bodily functions as well. While such devices are all but unknown today, the social control of sexuality continues. Can you point to examples?

SYMBOLIC-INTERACTION ANALYSIS

The symbolic-interaction approach highlights the construction of everyday reality. Because people construct very different realities regarding sexuality, they vary from context to context and change over time.

The Social Construction of Sexuality

Social patterns involving sexuality changed considerably during the twentieth century. Take virginity as an example. A century ago, women were to be virgins until marriage, mainly because there was no effective birth control and virginity was a man's only assurance that his bride-to-be was not carrying another's child. Today, with sex largely separated from reproduction, the virginity norm has weakened. Not surprisingly, premarital sex has increased dramatically in Canada—revealing a doubling of sexual activity levels among youth since the 1970s (Nelson and Robinson, 1999:354). Among single adults who have never been married, 87 percent say that they engage in sex—half of them at least weekly (Bibby, 1995:66). Very few, it seems adhere to the norm of virginity until marriage.

Another example of our society's construction of sexuality involves children. A century ago, childhood was a time of innocence in sexual matters. In recent decades, however, our thinking has changed. Though we expect them to refrain from sex, we believe they should be educated about sex so that they can make intelligent choices as they grow older.

Global Comparisons

Around the world, different meanings are attached to sexuality. Ruth Benedict (1938), who spent years learning the ways of life of the Melanesian peoples of southeastern New Guinea, reported that adults paid little attention when young children engaged in sexual experimentation with one another. Parents shrugged off such activity because, before puberty, sex cannot lead to reproduction. Sexual practices vary from culture to culture. *Male circumcision* of infant boys (the practice of removing all or part of the foreskin of the penis) is common in North America but rare in many other parts of the world. A practice sometimes referred to incorrectly as *female circumcision* (the removal of the clitoris) is prohibited here but is common in parts of Africa and the Middle East (Crossette, 1995; Huffman, 2000).

Critical Review The strength of the symbolic-interaction approach lies in revealing the constructed character of familiar social patterns. Knowing that people "construct" sexuality, helps us understand the variety of sexual practices found over time and in different societies. One limitation of this approach, however, is that not all sexual practices are so variable. Throughout our own history—and around the world—men are more likely to see women in sexual terms than the other way around. Some broader social structure must be at work in a pattern that is this widespread.

SOCIAL-CONFLICT ANALYSIS

As you have seen in earlier chapters, the social-conflict approach—particularly the gender-conflict or feminist approach—highlights dimensions of inequality. This approach shows how sexuality both reflects patterns of social inequality and helps to perpetuate them.

Sexuality: Reflecting Social Inequality

Societal response to prostitution varies considerably throughout North America, but, whatever the nature of prostitution laws, enforcement is uneven at best—especially when it comes to who is and is not likely to be arrested. While two people are involved, the record shows that police are far more likely to arrest (less powerful) female prostitutes than (more powerful) male clients. Similarly, of all women engaged in prostitution, it is streetwalkers—women with the least income and those most likely to be visible minorities—who face the highest risk of arrest. And, of course, it is poverty that drives many women into prostitution in the first place.

YOUR TURN

Are women defined in terms of sexuality? What effect does being defined in sexual terms have on women's economic opportunities?

Sexuality: Creating Social Inequality

Social-conflict theorists, especially feminists, point to sexuality as the root of inequality between women and men. Defining women in sexual terms amounts to devaluing them from full human beings into objects of men's interest and attention. Is it any wonder that the word *pornography* comes from the Greek word *porne*, meaning "a man's sexual slave"? If men define women in sexual terms, it is easy to see pornography—almost all of which is consumed by males—as a power issue. Because it typically shows women pleasing men, it supports the idea that men have power over women.

Some radical critics doubt that the element of power can ever be removed from heterosexual relations (Dworkin, 1987). Our culture often describes sexuality in terms of sport (men "scoring" with women) and violence ("slamming," "banging," and "hitting on"). Most social-conflict theorists do not reject heterosexuality but do agree that sexuality can and does degrade women.

Queer Theory

Finally, social-conflict theory has taken aim not only at the domination of women by men but also at heterosexuals dominating homosexuals. In recent years, as many lesbians

 The Queer Resources Directory looks at a wide range of issues from a queer theory perspective: www.qrd.org/qrd/.

and gay men have sought public acceptance, a gay voice has arisen in sociology. The term **queer theory** refers to *a growing body of research findings that challenges the heterosexual bias in Western society.* Queer theory begins with the claim that our society is characterized by **heterosexism,** *a view that labels anyone who is not heterosexual as "queer."* Our heterosexual culture victimizes a wide range of people, including gay men, lesbians, and bisexual, intersexual, transsexual, and even asexual people. While most people agree that bias against women (sexism) and visible minorities (racism) is wrong, heterosexism is widely tolerated and often well within the law.

From a social-conflict point of view, sexuality is not so much a "natural" part of our humanity as it is a socially constructed pattern of behaviour. Sexuality plays an important part in social inequality: by defining women in sexual terms, men devalue them as objects. Would you consider the behaviour shown here to be "natural" or socially directed? Why?

↔ YOUR TURN ↔

Can you think of three attitudes or social patterns that are examples of heterosexism?

Critical Review The social-conflict approach shows that sexuality is both a cause and an effect of inequality. In particular, it helps us understand men's power over women and the domination of heterosexual people over homosexual people. At the same time, this approach overlooks the fact that many people do not see sexuality as a power issue; on the contrary, many couples enjoy a vital sexual relationship that deepens their commitment to one another. In addition, the social-conflict approach pays little attention to steps taken, by society, to reduce inequality, the treatment of women as sex objects, and sexual harassment in the workplace—or the success of the gay rights movement in securing greater opportunities and social acceptance for gays and lesbians.

This chapter closes with a Thinking It Through box (on p. 204) on what is perhaps the most divisive issue involving sexuality: abortion. There seems to be no middle ground in this controversial issue.

THINKING IT THROUGH
The Abortion Controversy

A van pulls up in front of a storefront in a busy section of the city. Two women get out of the front seat and cautiously scan the sidewalk. After a moment, one nods to the other and opens the rear door to let a third woman out of the van. Standing to the right and left of their charge, the two quickly whisk her inside the building. They are escorting a woman who has decided to have an abortion. Why should they be so cautious? There have been heated confrontations at abortion clinics across North America, and some doctors who perform abortions have been targeted and killed.

There are about 850 000 abortions performed in the United States each year compared to 105 000 in Canada. A quick calculation reveals that in both countries the rate is 3 abortions per 1000 population. Most therapeutic abortions in Canada are performed in hospitals, while others take place in doctors' offices or in clinics like those run by Dr. Henry Morgentaler, an advocate who performed abortions long before the liberalization of Canada's laws.

Abortion was illegal until the mid–1900s, driving abortion underground, where many women, especially the poor, had little choice but to seek help from unlicensed abortionists, sometimes with tragic results.

In 1969, under the Trudeau Liberal government, Canada's laws were liberalized to allow abortion in cases where three physicians certified that the mother's life or health was endangered. The law was not applied evenly across provinces or between large cities and rural areas—because the definition of "danger" to the mother's life or health was not specified. If hospitals, many of them Catholic, simply refused to perform abortions, women were forced to turn elsewhere. In 1973, the U.S.

Supreme Court rendered a landmark decision, striking down all state laws banning abortion—in effect, establishing a woman's legal access to abortion. In 1988, the Supreme Court of Canada left Canadians *without* an abortion law by declaring the existing legislation unconstitutional.

While North American women now have legal access to abortion, the controversy has not abated. On one side are people, describing themselves as "pro-choice," who support a woman's right to choose; some of them are feminists who argue that women should have complete control of their sexuality and their bodies. On the other side are those, calling themselves "pro-life," who oppose abortion as morally wrong and defend life from the very moment of conception. Because of his support of the pro-life perspective, Stephen Harper in the 2006 election campaign and as prime minister, has had to assure Canadians that his government will not reopen the abortion debate.

How strong is the support for each side of the abortion controversy? About 40 percent of Canadians and Americans feel that women should have access to abortion, whatever their reasons. A vast majority of Americans and Canadians are in favour of abortion if a woman's health is in danger. The vast majority of Americans and Canadians would allow abortion if there were a strong chance of a serious defect in the baby or if the pregnancy were the result of sexual assault. Only about 5 percent would prohibit abortion under any circumstances. Anti-abortionists feel that abortion amounts to killing unborn children. Pro-choice advocates see the abortion debate in terms of the standing of women in society, arguing that women must control their own sexuality. If preg-

nancy dictates the course of women's lives, they will never be able to compete with men on equal terms. For pro-choice supporters, legal and safe abortion is a necessary condition for the full participation of women in society.

Canada may be the only country in the developed world with no abortion law whatsoever. Some European countries, for example, limit abortions to the first two trimesters to avoid the termination of pregnancies involving a viable fetus. In theory, an abortion can take place in Canada at any time during a normal pregnancy. Many of the people who are pressing for some kind of abortion law in Canada are concerned, not with abortions that take place in the first few weeks of pregnancy but with later-stage abortions where the fetus would be able to survive outside the womb. Considering the grey areas involving very sensitive issues, you may understand why our parliamentarians—even the Conservatives—are not anxious to revisit the contentious and divisive debate.

WHAT DO YOU THINK?

1. The more conservative people who do not support abortion see it as a moral issue, while more liberal people who do support abortion see it as a power issue. How does this relate to the way conservatives and liberals view the issue of pornography?
2. Surveys show that men and women have almost the same opinions about abortion. Does this surprise you? Why?
3. Why is the abortion controversy is so bitter that Canadians have been unable to find middle ground?

Sources: Luker (1984), MacKenzie (1990), Tannahill (1992), Bibby (1995), Nelson and Robinson (1999).

8 MAKING THE GRADE

The following learning tools will help you see what you know, identify what you still need to learn, and expand your understanding beyond the text. You can also visit this text's Companion Website™ at www.pearsoned.ca/macionis to find useful practice tests.

KEY POINTS

Understanding Sexuality

North American culture has long defined sex as a taboo topic. The Kinsey research was one of the first to study human sexuality.

Sex refers to the biological distinction between females and males, which is determined at conception as a male sperm joins a female ovum. *Gender* is a cultural concept referring to the personal traits and social positions that members of a society attach to being female or male.

Males and females are distinguished not only by their genitals (primary sex characteristics) but also by bodily development as they mature (secondary sex characteristics). Intersexual people (also called *hermaphrodites*) have some combination of both male and female genitalia. Transsexuals are people who feel they are one sex even though, biologically, they are the other.

For most species, sex is rigidly directed by biology; for human beings, sex is a matter of cultural definition as well as personal choice. Patterns of kissing, modesty, and standards of beauty all vary around the world, revealing the cultural foundation of sexual practices.

Sexual Attitudes

Over the course of history, social attitudes towards sexuality have become more permissive. The Sexual Revolution in the 1960s and 1970s brought discussion of sexuality into the open. Research shows that changes in sexuality were greater for women than for men. By 1980, a sexual counterrevolution was taking form, condemning permissiveness and urging a return to more conservative "family values."

The proportion of North Americans who have premarital sexual intercourse increased during the twentieth century. Today, research shows that about three-quarters of young men and two-thirds of young women have intercourse by their senior year in high school.

Among adults, the level of sexual activity varies: one-third report having sex with a partner a few times a year or not at all; another one-third have sex once or several times a month; the remaining one-third have sex two or more times a week. While extramarital sex is widely condemned, about 25 percent of married men and 10 percent of married women report being sexually unfaithful to their spouses at some time.

Sexual Orientation

Sexual orientation refers to a person's romantic and emotional attraction to another person. Four major orientations are heterosexuality, homosexuality, bisexuality, and asexuality. Sexual orientation reflects both biological and cultural factors.

The share of the population that is homosexual depends on how researchers define "homosexuality." About 9 percent of adult men and 4 percent of adult women report engaging in some homosexual activity; 2.8 percent of men and 1.4 percent of women consider themselves as homosexual.

The gay rights movement has gained greater acceptance for gay people in recent decades. Largely because of this movement, the share of the North American population condemning homosexuality as morally wrong has decreased steadily to about 55 percent.

Sexual Issues and Controversies

Nearly 1 million teenagers become pregnant each year in North America. The rate of teenage pregnancy has dropped since 1950, when many teens married and had children. In recent years, the proportion of births to *unmarried* mothers that involved teens declined because *older* women, in growing numbers, began to have children out of wedlock.

In Canada, pornography is legal whereas obscenity is not. Much of the debate in Canada centres on the question of when pornography crosses the line into obscenity. While many people are offended by sexually explicit material, Canadians also value free speech and artistic freedom.

Prostitution, the selling of sexual services, is against the law almost everywhere in North America. While many people think of prostitution as a victimless crime, others point out that it victimizes women and spreads sexually transmitted diseases.

In Canada, rape is officially recorded as *sexual assault*. Since only a fraction of cases show up in official statistics, the real sexual assault rate is many times higher. Rape is a violent crime in which victims and offenders typically know one another. Date rape is a serious problem for women students.

Theoretical Analysis of Sexuality

The structural-functional approach highlights society's need to regulate sexual activity. One universal norm is the incest taboo, which keeps family relations clear.

The symbolic-interaction approach emphasizes the various meanings people attach to sexuality. Societies differ from one another in terms of sexual attitudes and practices, and sexual patterns can change in a society over time.

According to the social-conflict approach, one way men dominate women is by devaluing them to the level of sexual objects. *Queer theory* points to the norm of heterosexism that defines anything different as "queer."

KEY CONCEPTS

sex (p. 185) the biological distinction between females and males

primary sex characteristics (p. 185) the genitals, organs used for reproduction

secondary sex characteristics (p. 185) bodily development, apart from the genitals, that distinguishes biologically mature females and males

intersexual people (p. 185) people whose bodies, including genitals, have both female and male characteristics

transsexuals (p. 185) people who feel they are one sex even though biologically they are the other

gender identity (p. 186) traits that females and males, guided by their culture, incorporate into their personality

incest taboo (p. 187) a norm forbidding sexual relations or marriage between certain relatives

sexual orientation (p. 193) a person's romantic and emotional attraction to another person

heterosexuality (p. 193) sexual attraction to someone of the other sex

homosexuality (p. 193) sexual attraction to someone of the same sex

bisexuality (p. 193) sexual attraction to people of both sexes

asexuality (p. 193) a lack of sexual attraction to people of either sex

homophobia (p. 195) discomfort over close personal interaction with people thought to be gay, lesbian, or bisexual

abortion (p. 197) the deliberate termination of a pregnancy

pornography (p. 197) sexually explicit material intended to cause sexual arousal

prostitution (p. 197) the selling of sexual services

queer theory (p. 203) a growing body of research findings that challenges the heterosexual bias in Western society

heterosexism (p. 203) a view that labels anyone who is not heterosexual as "queer"

APPLICATIONS & EXERCISES

1. Do a content analysis of ads on television and in magazines. To what extent do they rely on sexuality to sell products? Note the gender of people portrayed as sex objects or in submissive roles.

2. Contact your school's student services office, and ask for information about the extent of sexual violence on your campus. Do people typically report such crimes? What policies and procedures does your school have to respond to sexual violence?

3. Use the campus library and internet sources to learn more about the experiences of women and men involved in prostitution. As you learn more, decide whether you think prostitution should be considered a "victimless crime."

PRENTICE HALL
mysoclab™
Where learning & the sociological imagination intersect.

To reinforce your understanding of this chapter, and to identify topics for further study, visit MySocLab at **www.pearsoned.ca/mysoclab/** for diagnostic tests and a multimedia ebook.

CHAPTER NINE

Deviance

Why is deviance found in all societies?

How does *who* and *what* are defined as deviant
reflect social inequality?

What effect does punishment have in
reducing crime?

The black SUV rolled through the gates of the federal women's prison in Alderson, West Virginia, threading its way among the sea of news reporters, many of whom leaned towards the vehicle to catch a glimpse of the famous woman sitting in the back. Martha Stewart had just been released from jail. Stewart was sent to prison in 2004 after being convicted of lying about an improper stock deal. After five months behind bars, she was eager to get home. Soon after leaving the prison, the woman who made a fortune explaining how to live well boarded a private jet that whisked her to her 62-hectare (153-acre) ranch in Katonah, New York. Within three days, she reported to her probation officer who placed an electronic monitor on her ankle and explained that she would have to spend the next five months at home under house arrest.

The day after her release, Wes Smith, who is a postal carrier in Katonah, smiled at reporters. As he delivered mail to Stewart's home, he noted: "She's served her time. She's probably a changed person. Maybe she learned her lesson" (Fitzgerald, 2005).

This chapter explores deviance, crime, criminals, and punishment. One important lesson is that individuals convicted of wrongdoing—like Martha Stewart—do not always fit the common stereotype of the street criminal. This chapter also tackles the larger question of why societies develop standards of right and wrong in the first place. As we shall see, law is simply one part of a complex system of social control. We begin our investigation by defining several basic concepts.

What Is Deviance?

Deviance is *the recognized violation of cultural norms.* Norms guide almost all human activities, so the concept of deviance is quite broad. One category of deviance is **crime**, *the violation of a society's formally enacted criminal law.* Even criminal deviance spans a wide range of behaviour, from minor traffic violations to sexual assault to murder. Most familiar examples of nonconformity are negative instances of rule breaking, such as stealing from a campus bookstore, assaulting a fellow student, or driving while intoxicated. But we also define especially righteous people—students who speak up too much in class, or people who are overly enthusiastic about new computer technology—as deviant, even if we give them a measure of respect. What deviant actions or attitudes, whether negative or positive, have in common is some element of *difference* that causes us to think of another person as an "outsider" (Becker, 1966).

SOCIAL CONTROL

All of us are subject to **social control**, *attempts by society to regulate people's thoughts and behaviour.* Often this process is informal, as when parents praise or scold their children, or when friends make fun of a classmate's unusual choice of music. Cases of serious deviance, however, may involve the **criminal justice system**, *a formal response by police, courts, and prison officials to alleged violations of the law.*

How a society defines deviance, *who* is branded as deviant, and *what* people decide to do about deviance all have to do with the way society is organized. Only gradually, however, have people recognized that deviance is much more than a matter of individual choice, as this chapter now explains.

 Visit the bilingual Access to Justice site for information on Canadian justice and legal issues in plain language at www.acjnet.org.

THE BIOLOGICAL CONTEXT

Chapter 5 ("Socialization") explained that, a century ago, most people understood—or more correctly, misunderstood—human behaviour to be the result of biological instincts. Early interest in criminality therefore focused on biological causes. In 1876, Cesare Lombroso (1835–1909), for example, theorized that criminals stand out physically, with low foreheads, prominent jaws and cheekbones, hairiness, and unusually long arms. Had he looked more carefully, he would have found the physical features he linked to criminality throughout the entire population. No physical traits distinguish criminals from noncriminals.

In the middle of the twentieth century, William Sheldon took a different approach, suggesting that body structure might predict criminality (Sheldon, *et al.*, 1949). Checking hundreds of young men for body type and criminal history, he linked criminality to muscular, athletic builds. Glueck and Glueck (1950) cautioned that a powerful build does not necessarily *cause* criminality: parents tend to be distant from powerfully built sons, and general expectations about muscular boys may lead to self-fulfilling prophecies.

Today, genetics research seeks possible links between biology and crime. In 2003, scientists reported results of a 25-year study of crime among 400 boys. They collected DNA samples and noted any trouble with the law. The researchers concluded that genetic factors (i.e., defective genes) *together with* environmental factors (e.g., abuse early in life) were strong predictors of adult crime and violence (Lemonick, 2003; Pinker, 2003).

Critical Review Biological theories offer a limited explanation of crime. The best guess at present is that biological traits in combination with environmental factors explain some serious crime. Furthermore, a biological approach looks at the individual and offers no insight into the process by which certain behaviours are defined as deviant in the first place.

PERSONALITY FACTORS

Like biological theories, psychological explanations of deviance focus on abnormality in the individual personality. Some personality traits are inherited, but most psychologists think that personality is shaped primarily by social experience. Deviance, then, is viewed as the result of "unsuccessful" socialization.

Classic research by Reckless and Dinitz (1967) illustrates the psychological approach. They asked a number of teachers to categorize twelve-year-old male students as likely or unlikely to get into trouble with the law: the "good" boy displayed a strong conscience (what Freud called *super-ego*), could handle frustration, and identified with cultural norms and values; the "bad" boy had a weaker conscience, displayed little tolerance of frustration, and felt out of step with conventional culture. As we might expect, the "good" boys went on to have fewer run-ins with the police than the "bad" boys. Assuming that staying out of trouble meant control of deviant impulses, the authors called their analysis *containment theory*.

Critical Review Psychologists have shown that personality patterns have some connection to deviance. Some serious criminals are psychopaths who do not feel guilt or shame, have no fear of punishment, and have little sympathy for the people they harm (Herpertz and Sass, 2000). However, most serious crimes are committed by people whose psychological profiles are normal.

Deviance is always a matter of difference. Deviance emerges in everyday life as we encounter people whose appearance or behaviour differs from what we consider to be "right." Who is the "deviant" in this photograph? from whose point of view?

Both the biological and psychological approaches view deviance as a trait of individuals, but wrongdoing is largely a function of society. We now turn to a sociological approach, to look at the source of ideas of right and wrong, the labelling of some rule breakers as deviant, and the role of power in this process.

THE SOCIAL FOUNDATIONS OF DEVIANCE

While we view deviance as the free choice or personal failing of individuals, all behaviour—deviance as well as conformity—is shaped by society. Three social foundations of deviance identified here will be discussed later in this chapter:

1. **Deviance varies according to cultural norms**. No thought or action is inherently deviant; it becomes deviant only in relation to particular norms. The life patterns of rural Albertans, residents of Newfoundland fishing villages, and West Vancouverites differ in highly significant ways: as a result, their values and behavioural standards are different. Laws, too, differ from place to place. Quebecers can drink at a younger age than Ontarians, and are able to purchase wine and

beer at corner stores, whereas only beer with 0.5 percent alcohol can be found in Ontario grocery stores. Casinos are now legal in Ontario and Saskatchewan, even for First Nations; they are also legal in Manitoba—but definitely not on reserves.[1] In other words, what is deviant or even criminal is not uniform throughout the country. Around the world, deviance is even more diverse: Albania outlaws any public display of religious faith (such as crossing oneself); Cuba and Vietnam can prosecute citizens for meeting with foreigners; Malaysia prohibits tight-fitting jeans on women; Iran outlaws women wearing makeup; and Saudi Arabia bans the sale of red flowers on Valentine's Day.

2. **People become deviant as others define them that way.** Everyone violates cultural norms at one time or another. Have you ever laughed in public by yourself, or taken a pen from your workplace without intending to return it? Whether such behaviour defines you as mentally ill or criminal depends on how others perceive, define, and respond to it.

3. **Both norms and the way people define rule breaking involve social power.** The law, declared Karl Marx, is the means by which powerful people protect their interests. A homeless person who stands on a street corner speaking out against the government risks arrest for disturbing the peace; a mayoral candidate during an election campaign does exactly the same thing and gets police protection. In short, norms and their application reflect social inequality.

The Functions of Deviance: Structural-Functional Analysis

The key insight of the structural-functional approach is that deviance is a necessary part of social organization. This point was made a century ago by Emile Durkheim.

DURKHEIM'S BASIC INSIGHT

In his pioneering study of deviance, Emile Durkheim (1964; orig. 1893, 1964; orig. 1895) made the surprising statement that there is nothing abnormal about deviance. In fact, it performs four essential functions:

1. **Deviance affirms cultural values and norms.** Any definition of virtue rests on an opposing idea of vice: there can be no good without evil and no justice with-

out crime. Deviance draws the boundaries of acceptable behaviour.

2. **Responding to deviance clarifies moral boundaries.** By defining some individuals as deviant, people draw a boundary between right and wrong. For example, a college marks the line between academic honesty and cheating, and punishes students who cross it.

3. **Responding to serious deviance brings people together.** People typically react to serious deviance with shared outrage. In doing so, Durkheim explained, they reaffirm the moral ties that bind them. For example, the murder of fourteen female engineering students at Montreal's École Polytechnique on December 6, 1989, was met with reactions of horror and profound grief throughout Canada. The fact that anniversaries of the massacre are still commemorated indicates the depth of its impact.

4. **Deviance encourages social change.** Deviant people push a society's moral boundaries, suggesting alternatives to the status quo and encouraging change. Today's deviance, declared Durkheim, can become tomorrow's morality (1964 [orig. 1893]:71). For example, rock 'n' roll, condemned as immoral in the 1950s, is now a multibillion-dollar mainstream industry, and other types of popular music are considered deviant.

YOUR TURN

Keeping in mind Durkheim's social functions of deviance, why do you think we often define people only in terms of their deviance, as when we call someone "an addict" or "a thief"?

Aboriginal suicide has been attributed to the effects of rapid social change and damages to social solidarity (see the discussion in Chapter 1, p. 5). The Thinking about Diversity box (on p. 213) looks more closely at the social context of suicide among Aboriginal peoples in Canada.

An Illustration: The Puritans of Massachusetts Bay

Kai Erikson's (2005a; orig. 1966) classic study of the Puritans of Massachusetts Bay brings Durkheim's theory to life. Even the Puritans, a disciplined and highly religious group, created deviance to clarify their moral boundaries. In fact, Durkheim might well have had the Puritans in mind when he wrote:

Imagine a society of saints, a perfect cloister of exemplary individuals. Crimes, properly so called, will there be unknown; but faults which appear [insignificant] to the layman will create there the same scandal that the ordinary offence does in ordinary consciousness.... For the same

---

[1] In the 1990s, several reserve communities attempted to establish casinos, in part as a test of their sovereignty. While Manitoba closed down casinos that were opened illegally, Ontario gave its blessing to a casino on the Rama reserve near Orillia. Proceeds are shared with the other Bands of Ontario and with the government of Ontario. There are five First Nation casinos in Saskatchewan, regulated through Saskatchewan Indian Gaming Authority.

THINKING ABOUT DIVERSITY: RACE, CLASS, & GENDER
Suicide among Aboriginal People

So serious is the problem of suicide among Aboriginal people—among youth in particular—that the Royal Commission on Aboriginal Peoples felt compelled to conduct a study of the problem (Canada, 1995). The commission felt that suicide is a crucial issue not only because it is a matter of life and death, but also because it is an expression of collective anguish based on "the cumulative effect of three hundred years of colonial history: lands occupied, resources

Read the report *Choosing Life: Special Report on Suicide among Aboriginal People* at www.turtleisland.org/healing/healing-suicide1.htm.

seized, beliefs and cultures ridiculed, children taken away, power concentrated in distant capitals, hopes for honourable coexistence dashed over and over again." Note the emphasis on social conditions as causes of suicide.

The report points out that, year after year, Aboriginal suicide rates are two to three times higher than those of non-Aboriginal Canadians; rates among Aboriginal *youth* are five to six times

higher than among their non-Aboriginal peers. The problem is compounded by the ripple effect, whereby copycat suicides occur in related families and communities.

Looking for causes, the commission identifies four contributors: (1) psychobiological factors; (2) life history or situational factors; (3) socioeconomic factors; and (4) cultural stress. Once again, social conditions loom large, particularly with respect to the last two categories. Cultural stress applies to "societies that have undergone massive, imposed or uncontrollable change."

The solutions suggested by the commission are varied. But among them are a number that relate to community solidarity or social integration: community development, self-government or community control, cultural and spiritual revitalization, strengthened bonds of family and community, holistic health and healing programs, and involvement of the whole community.

If you think back to the discussion of Emile Durkheim's analysis of suicide (in Chapter 1, p. 5) you will recall his

conclusion that degree of *social integration* is the key to understanding suicide. High suicide rates are found among people who are more socially isolated and individualistic. The cultural and social dislocation experienced by Aboriginal people is the result of their colonial history—a history based on government paternalism and compulsory residential schooling. A compounding factor contributing to weaker social ties is the phenomenal rate of social and economic change in recent decades. This report contains insights that mirror those of Durkheim's pioneering sociological analysis a century ago.

WHAT DO YOU THINK?

1. How would Durkheim account for the high rates of suicide among Aboriginal people?
2. Can you think of ways to encourage Aboriginal people, especially youth, to want to live?
3. In school, what did you learn about the history of Aboriginal/non-Aboriginal relations in Canada?

---

reason, the perfect and upright man judges his smallest failings with a severity that the majority reserve for acts more truly in the nature of an offence. (1964 [orig. 1983]:68–69)

Deviance is not a matter of a few "bad apples" but a necessary condition of "good" social living.

Deviance may be found in every society, but the *kind* of deviance people generate depends on the moral issues they seek to clarify. The Puritans, for example, experienced a number of crime waves, including the infamous outbreak of witchcraft in 1692. With each response, the Puritans answered questions about the range of proper beliefs by condemning some of their members as deviant. While the offences changed, the proportion of people the Puritans defined as deviant remained steady over time—confirming Durkheim's claim that society creates deviants to mark its changing moral boundaries.

MERTON'S STRAIN THEORY

Robert Merton (1938, 1968) argued that deviance depends on the extent to which society provides the *means* (i.e., schooling and jobs) to achieve cultural *goals* (i.e., financial success). Conformity lies in pursuing cultural goals through approved means. Thus, the North American success story is someone who gains wealth and prestige through talent, schooling, and hard work. But not everyone who wants conventional success has the opportunity to attain it. According to Merton, the strain generated by our culture's emphasis on wealth and the lack of opportunities to get rich encourage some people to engage in stealing, drug dealing, or other forms of crime. Merton called this type of deviance *innovation*—using unconventional means (i.e., street crime) to achieve a culturally approved goal (e.g., wealth).

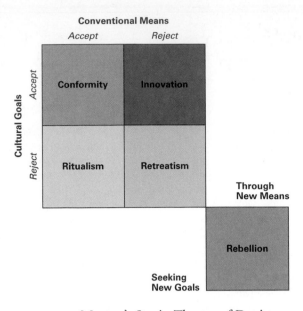

FIGURE 9-1 Merton's Strain Theory of Deviance

Combining a person's view of cultural goals and the conventional means to obtain them allowed Robert Merton to identify various types of deviants.

Source: Merton (1968).

In some respects, a notorious gangster such as Al Capone was quite conventional: he pursued the fame and fortune at the heart of the American dream; but, finding the usual doors to success closed to members of a minority, he blazed his own trail to the top. A Canadian with close ties to Capone established a parallel career. In 1918, when Prohibition outlawed the sale of liquor in Canada, Rocco Perri saw an opportunity to augment his income by selling bootleg liquor at the back of his grocery store in Hamilton, Ontario. By the time Prohibition was adopted in the United States, in 1920, Perri had "the organization and experience to take quick advantage of the opportunity.... Before long, he was a major supplier to gangsters like Al Capone" (Carrigan, 1991:174). Perri had become "King of the Bootleggers." In the wake of Prohibition, Rocco Perri's "formidable criminal organization" expanded its links to U.S. gangs through a wide range of activities, including gambling, prostitution, and extortion. Like Capone, Canada's innovator acquired wealth and power but never attained prestige in the larger society.

Figure 9–1 shows that innovation involves accepting a cultural goal, financial success, but rejecting the conventional means—hard work at a legal job—in favour of unconventional means, street crime.

The inability to reach a cultural goal may also prompt another type of deviance that Merton calls *ritualism* (see Figure 9–1). For example, many people believe that they cannot achieve the cultural goal of becoming rich; therefore, they rigidly stick to the conventional means (the rules) in order to at least feel respectable. In essence, they embrace

the rules to the point where they lose sight of their larger goals. Thus, lower-level bureaucrats may succumb to ritualism to maintain their self-respect.

A third response to the inability to succeed is *retreatism*—the rejection of both cultural goals and means, so that a person in effect "drops out." Some alcoholics, drug addicts, and street people are retreatists. The deviance of retreatists lies in their unconventional lifestyle and in what seems to be their willingness to live this way.

The fourth response to failure is *rebellion*. Like retreatists, rebels (such as radical "survivalists") reject both the cultural definition of success and the conventional means of achieving it, but they go one step further by forming a counterculture supporting alternatives to the existing social order. Many of us applaud rebels, whom we might admire—but do not emulate in their breaking of rules or laws. The popularity of rebellion is evident from the number of movies and novels about it.

DEVIANT SUBCULTURES

Richard Cloward and Lloyd Ohlin (1966) extended Merton's theory, proposing that crime results not simply from limited legitimate (legal) opportunity but also from readily accessible illegitimate (illegal) opportunity. In short, deviance or conformity arises from the *relative opportunity structure* that frames a person's life.

The lives of Al Capone and Rocco Perri show how an ambitious person denied legitimate opportunity by the barriers of poverty and ethnic prejudice can organize a criminal empire to meet the demand for alcohol during Prohibition. In other words, illegal opportunities foster the development of *criminal subcultures* that offer the knowledge, skills, and other resources needed to succeed in unconventional ways. Indeed, gangs such as Hell's Angels specialize in one or another form of criminality according to available opportunities and resources (Carrigan, 1991; Sheley, *et al.*, 1995).

But what happens when people cannot identify *any* kind of opportunity, legal or illegal? Then deviance may take the form of *conflict subcultures* (e.g., armed street gangs), where violence is ignited by frustration and a desire for respect, or *retreatist subcultures* (e.g., skid rows), in which deviants drop out and perhaps abuse alcohol or other drugs.

Albert Cohen (1971; orig. 1955) suggests that *delinquency* (minor crime) is most common among lower-class youths because they have the least opportunity to achieve conventional success. Neglected by society, they seek self-respect by creating a delinquent subculture that defines as worthy the traits these youths do have. Being feared on the street may satisfy a young person's desire to be "somebody" in the local neighbourhood.

Finally, Elijah Anderson (1994, 2002) explains that, in poor urban neighbourhoods, most people manage to conform to conventional values. Yet faced with neighbourhood crime and violence, indifference or even hostility from police, and sometimes even neglect by their own parents, some young men decide to live by the "street code." To show

Young people cut off from legitimate opportunity often form subcultures that many people view as deviant. Gang subcultures, including tattoos on the fingers, are one way young people gain the sense of belonging and respect denied to them by the larger culture.

that they can survive on the street, a young man displays nerve, a willingness to stand up to any threat. The risk of ending up in jail—or worse—is very high for these young men, who have been pushed to the margins of our society.

Critical Review Durkheim made an important contribution by pointing out the functions of deviance. However, there is evidence that a community does not always come together in reaction to crime; sometimes fear of crime causes people to withdraw from public life (Liska and Warner, 1991; Warr and Ellison, 2000).

Merton's strain theory has been criticized for explaining some kinds of deviance (stealing, for example) better than others (such as crimes of passion or mental illness). In addition, not everyone seeks success in the conventional terms of wealth, as strain theory suggests.

The general argument—that deviance reflects the opportunity structure of society—has been confirmed by subsequent research (Allan and Steffensmeier, 1989; Uggen, 1999). However, these theories fall short by assuming that everyone shares the same cultural standards for judging right and wrong. If we define crime as not just burglary and auto theft but the type of illegal stock deals that sent Martha Stewart to prison, then more high-income people will be counted among criminals. The sponsorship scandal that brought down the Liberal government in the 2006 election involved the illegal transfer of funds to the federal Liberal Party. The media and, as a result the public, now define this kind of behaviour as criminal.

Labelling Deviance: Symbolic-Interaction Analysis

The symbolic-interaction approach explains how people define deviance in everyday situations. From this point of

Many gangs constitute a peer group in which violence, drug use, and trafficking are "normal." Here, members of the Hell's Angels, identifiable by their motorcycles and clothing, attend a funeral of one of their compatriots.

view, definitions of deviance and conformity are surprisingly flexible.

LABELLING THEORY

The main contribution of symbolic-interaction analysis is **labelling theory,** *the idea that deviance and conformity result not so much from what people do as from how others respond to those actions.* Labelling theory stresses the relativity of deviance, the idea that people may define the same behaviour in any number of ways. Consider these situations: a university student takes an article of clothing from a roommate's drawer, a married woman at a convention has sex with a former boyfriend, a mayor gives a big city contract to a major campaign contributor. The consequences in each case depends on detection and labelling as deviant or criminal.

YOUR TURN

Explain in your own words Howard Becker's (1966) statement that deviance is nothing more than behaviour that people define as deviant.

In Winnipeg, a born-again Christian gives visible expression to his faith. When city council warned that his signs violated civic by-laws, the man vowed to challenge any charges in court.

Primary and Secondary Deviance

Edwin Lemert (1951, 1972) observed that some norm violations—say, skipping school or underage drinking—provoke slight reaction from others and have little effect on a person's self-concept. Lemert calls such passing episodes *primary deviance*. But what happens if other people notice someone's deviance and make something of it? For example, if friends describe a young man as an "alcohol abuser" and exclude him from their group, he may become bitter, drink even more, and seek the company of others who approve of his behaviour. The response to primary deviance sets in motion *secondary deviance*, by which a person repeatedly violates a norm and begins to take on a deviant identity. Thus, a situation that is defined as real becomes real in its consequences.

Stigma

Secondary deviance marks the start of what Erving Goffman (1963) calls a *deviant career*. As people develop a stronger commitment to deviant behaviour, they typically acquire a **stigma,** *a powerfully negative label that greatly changes a person's self-concept and social identity.* A stigma operates as a master status (see Chapter 6), overpowering other aspects of social identity, so that a person is discredited in the minds of others and becomes socially isolated. Cigarette smokers, for example, have become stigmatized in North America. Sometimes an entire community formally stigmatizes an individual through what Harold Garfinkel (1956) calls a *degradation ceremony*; a criminal trial is an example.

Retrospective and Projective Labelling

Once people stigmatize an individual, they may engage in *retrospective labelling*, interpreting someone's past in light of present deviance (Scheff, 1984). For example, after discovering that a priest has sexually molested a child, others rethink his past, noting that he liked to be around children. In *projective labelling*, a deviant identity is used to predict future action, such as repeated molestation. Either type of labelling increases the likelihood of further deviance.

Labelling Difference as Deviance

Is a homeless man who refuses to allow police to take him to a city shelter on a cold night behaving independently or "crazily"? Behaviour that irritates or threatens us is not labelled just as "different" but as deviance or mental illness. The psychiatrist Thomas Szasz (1961, 1970; orig. 1961, 2003, 2004) charges that people are too quick to apply the label of mental illness to conditions that simply amount to a difference we don't like. The only way to avoid this troubling practice, Szasz continues, is to abandon the idea of mental illness entirely. The world is full of people whose differences in thought or action may annoy us, but such differences are no grounds for defining them as mentally ill.

Most mental health care professionals cling to the idea that mental illness exists, but they agree that it is important to think critically about how we define difference. People who are mentally ill are no more to blame for their condition than people who suffer from cancer or arthritis. Therefore, neither mental nor physical illness is grounds for being labelled deviant. Such labelling, Szasz claims, is merely the exercise of power by those in a position to enforce conformity.

THE MEDICALIZATION OF DEVIANCE

Labelling theory helps to explain an important shift in the way our society understands deviance. Over the past fifty years, the growing influence of psychiatry and medicine has led to the **medicalization of deviance,** *the transformation of moral and legal deviance into a medical condition.* Medicalization amounts to swapping one set of labels for another. In moral terms, we evaluate people or their behaviour as "bad" or "good." However, the scientific objectivity of medicine passes no moral judgment, instead using clinical diagnoses such as "sick" or "well." To illustrate, until the mid-twentieth century, people generally viewed alcoholics as morally weak people easily tempted by the pleasure of drink. Gradually, however, medical specialists redefined alcoholism so that most people now consider it a condition that renders people "sick" rather than "bad." In the same way, obesity, drug addiction, child abuse, sexual promiscuity, and other behaviours that used to be strictly moral matters are widely defined today as illnesses for which people need help rather than punishment.

Every once in a while, people commit a crime so shocking that we wonder if they are "crazy." Here is security camera photo of Eric Harris and Dylan Klebold as they stalked and killed twelve students and one teacher in Colorado's Columbine High School in 1999. Were these boys "evil," "sick," or "misguided"?

The Difference Labels Make

Whether we define deviance as a moral or a medical issue has three consequences. First, it affects *who responds* to deviance. An offence against common morality usually brings about a reaction from members of the community or the police. A medical label, however, places the situation under the control of clinical specialists, including counsellors, psychiatrists, and doctors. A second difference is *how people respond* to deviance. A moral approach defines deviants as offenders subject to punishment; medically, they are patients who need treatment. Punishment is designed to fit the crime, treatment to fit the patient.

Most importantly, the two labels differ on *personal competence of the deviant person.* From a moral standpoint, whether we are right or wrong, at least we take responsibility for our own behaviour. Once defined as sick, however, a deviant is seen as unable to control—(or, if "mentally ill," even understand—his or her actions. People who are labelled incompetent are in turn subjected to treatment, often against their will. Therefore, defining deviance in medical terms should be done with caution.

YOUR TURN

An old saying goes, "Sticks and stones can break my bones, but names can never hurt me." What might labelling theory have to say about this idea?

SUTHERLAND'S DIFFERENTIAL ASSOCIATION THEORY

Learning any behavioural pattern, whether conventional or deviant, is a process that takes place in groups. According to Edwin Sutherland (1940), a person's tendency towards conformity or deviance depends on the amount of contact with others who encourage—or reject—conventional behaviour. This is Sutherland's theory of *differential association.*

Several studies confirm the idea that young people are more likely to engage in delinquency if they believe members of their peer groups encourage such activity (Akers, *et al.*, 1979; Miller and Matthews, 2001). One recent investigation focused on sexual activity among eighth-grade students: two strong predictors of such behaviour for young girls was having a boyfriend who encouraged sexual relations and having girlfriends they believed would approve. Similarly, boys were encouraged to become sexually active by friends who rewarded them with high status in the peer group (Little and Rankin, 2001).

HIRSCHI'S CONTROL THEORY

The sociologist Travis Hirschi (1969; Gottfredson and Hirschi, 1995) developed *control theory*—which states that social control depends on people anticipating the consequences of their behaviour. Hirschi assumes that everyone finds at least some deviance tempting. But the thought of a ruined career keeps most people from breaking the rules; for some, just imagining the reactions of family and friends is enough. On the other hand, individuals who feel they have little to lose by deviance are likely to become rule breakers.

Specifically, Hirschi links conformity to four different types of social control:

1. *Attachment.* Strong social attachments encourage conformity. Weak family, peer, and school relationships leave people freer to engage in deviance.
2. *Opportunity.* The greater a person's access to legitimate opportunity, the greater the advantages of conformity. Conversely, someone with little confidence in future success is more likely to drift towards deviance.
3. *Involvement.* Extensive involvement in legitimate activities—such as holding a job, going to school, or playing sports—inhibits deviance (Langbein and Bess, 2002). In contrast, people who simply "hang out" waiting for something to happen have time and energy to engage in deviant activity.
4. *Belief.* Strong belief in conventional morality and respect for authority figures restrain tendencies towards deviance. Someone with a weak conscience (i.e., left unsupervised) is more open to temptation (Stack, *et al.*, 2004).

Hirschi's analysis combines a number of earlier ideas about the causes of deviant behaviour. Note that social privilege, as well as family and community environment, affect the risk of deviant behaviour (Hope, *et al.*, 2003).

Our society's definition of crime leads us to consider both the criminal act and the intention of the person committing the act. People cannot be prosecuted simply because others think they look suspicious or believe they are likely to commit crimes at some later point in time. In the recent film *Minority Report*, Tom Cruise plays a character named Anderson who is fleeing from the Precrime police because they are trying to arrest him for a crime they believe he will commit in the future.

Critical Review The various symbolic-interaction theories all see deviance as process. Labelling theory links deviance not to *action* but to the *reaction* of others. Thus, some people are defined as deviant and others who think or behave in the same way are not. The concepts of secondary deviance, deviant career, and stigma show how being labelled deviant can become a lasting self-concept.

Yet labelling theory has several limitations. Because it takes a relative view of deviance, it ignores the fact that some kinds of behaviour—such as murder or having sex with one's child—are condemned just about everywhere. Therefore, labelling theory is most usefully applied to less serious issues, such as sexual promiscuity or theft. Also, research reveals that deviant labelling may encourage *or* discourage further deviance (Smith and Gartin, 1989; Sherman and Smith, 1992). Lastly, not everyone resists being labelled deviant; some people actively seek it out (Vold and Bernard, 1986); for example, people take part in civil disobedience and willingly subject themselves to arrest in order to call attention to social or environmental injustice.

Sociologists consider Sutherland's differential association theory and Hirschi's control theory to be important contributions to our understanding of deviance. We now turn to social-conflict theory to address the question of why society defines certain activities as deviant.

Deviance and Inequality: Social-Conflict Analysis

The social-conflict approach links deviance to social inequality: that is, *who* or *what* is labelled "deviant" depends on who holds power.

DEVIANCE AND POWER

Alexander Liazos (1972) points out that the people we call deviant—those we dismiss as "nuts" and "sluts"—are typically powerless. Bag ladies—not corporate polluters—and unemployed men on street corners—not international arms dealers—carry the stigma of deviance.

Social-conflict theory explains this pattern in three ways. First, all norms and especially the laws of any society generally reflect the interests of the rich and powerful. Those who threaten the wealthy, either by taking their property or by advocating a more egalitarian society, are defined as "common thieves" or "political radicals." As noted in Chapter 4 ("Society"), Karl Marx argued that the law and all other social institutions support the interests of the rich. Richard Quinney observed that: "Capitalist justice is by the capitalist class, for the capitalist class, and against the working class" (1977:3).

Second, even if their behaviour is called into question, the powerful have the resources to resist deviant labels. The majority of the executives involved in recent corporate scandals have yet to be arrested; very few have gone to jail.

Third, the widespread belief that norms and laws are natural and good masks their political character. For this reason, although we may condemn the *unequal application* of the law, we give little thought to whether the *laws themselves* are really fair or not.

DEVIANCE AND CAPITALISM

In the Marxist tradition, Steven Spitzer (1980) argues that deviant labels are applied to people who interfere with the operation of capitalism. Since capitalism is based on private control of wealth, people who threaten the property of others—especially the poor who steal from the rich—are prime candidates for being labelled deviant. Conversely, the rich who take advantage of the poor are less likely to be labelled deviant. For example, landlords who charge poor tenants high rents and evict those who cannot pay are not considered criminals; they are simply doing business.

Capitalism depends on productive labour: people who cannot or will not work risk being labelled deviant. Many members of our society think people who are out of work, through no fault of their own, are somehow deviant.

Also, capitalism depends on respect for authority figures, so people who resist authority are called deviant. Examples are children who skip school or talk back to teachers, and adults who play Solitaire on the computer at work. Those who directly challenge the capitalist status quo—labour organizers, radical environmentalists, and antiwar activists—are likely to be defined as deviant.

On the other side of the coin, society labels positively behaviour that supports the operation of capitalism. For example, winning athletes enjoy celebrity status because they express the values of individual achievement and competition, both vital to capitalism. Also, Spitzer notes, we condemn using drugs of escape as deviant (such as marijuana, psychedelics, heroin, and crack) but encourage drugs that promote adjustment to the status quo (such as alcohol and caffeine). The capitalist system also tries to control people who don't fit into the system. The elderly, people with mental or physical disabilities, and Robert Merton's retreatists (people addicted to alcohol or other drugs) are a "costly yet relatively harmless burden" on society. Such people, claims Spitzer, are subject to control by social welfare agencies. But people who openly challenge the capitalist system, including the inner-city underclass and revolutionaries—Merton's innovators and rebels—are controlled by the criminal justice system.

Note that both the social welfare and criminal justice systems blame individuals, not the system, for social problems. Welfare recipients are considered unworthy freeloaders, poor people who express rage at their plight are labelled rioters, anyone who challenges the government is branded a radical, and those who try to gain illegally what they will never get legally are rounded up as criminals.

WHITE-COLLAR CRIME

Reputable Canadians have long been known to circumvent the law when doing so is likely to be immensely profitable (Carrigan, 1991:113–65). For example, during World War II, when consumer goods were rationed, big and small businesses and government officials were caught up in wartime racketeering, supplying illegal goods through the black market. More recently, Canada has had its share of stock and real estate fraud, bid-rigging, and tax evasion—activities that have cost taxpayers and consumers billions of dollars. Many of these perpetrators are never charged or convicted of their crimes.

The cases described in the Media Perspectives box (on pp. 220–21) exemplify **white-collar crime,** defined by Edwin Sutherland in 1940, *as crimes committed by persons of high social position in the course of their occupation* (Sutherland and Cressey, 1978:44). White-collar crime rarely involves uniformed police converging on a scene with drawn guns; thus, it does not refer to such crimes as murder, assault, or sexual assault (rape) that happen to be carried out by people of high social position. Instead, white-collar crimes are acts by powerful people making use of their occupational position to enrich themselves or others illegally, often causing significant public harm in the process (Hagan and Parker, 1985; Vold and Bernard, 1986). Crime in government offices and corporate boardrooms is *crime in the suites* rather than *crime in the streets*.

The public harm wreaked by false advertising, marketing of unsafe products, embezzlement, and bribery of public officials is more extensive than most people realize—possibly greater than the more visible street crime (Reiman, 1990). The marketing of unsafe products and the failure to implement workplace safety regulations are responsible for many deaths. Immeasurable sums of money are stolen every year through fraud. Since much of it goes undetected, and overburdened fraud units are unable to prosecute all known cases, it is difficult to estimate the dollar value of white-collar crime.

Until recently, such deviance rarely resulted in criminal labelling of powerful people. Even when their actions lead to extensive public harm, officials are rarely prosecuted. And in the event that white-collar criminals do face the music, the odds are they will not go to jail. One of the Adscam trials from the Sponsorship scandal resulted in house arrest—excluding evenings and weekends! The public is less concerned about white-collar crime than street crime, because corporate crime victimizes everyone and no one.

CORPORATE CRIME

Sometimes whole companies, not just individuals, break the law. **Corporate crime** refers to *the illegal actions of a corporation or people acting on its behalf.* Corporate crime ranges from knowingly selling faulty or dangerous products to deliberately polluting the environment (Derber, 2004). The collapse of the Enron Corporation in 2001 followed extensive violations of business and accounting laws, and resulted in the losses to stockholders and others exceeding US$50 billion (Lavelle, 2002). Keep in mind that stockholders of Canadian and American companies can be anywhere in the world: when they collectively lose more than billions of dollars to corporate crime, Canadians, Canadian pension plans, and perhaps your own family are among those affected.

As with white-collar crime, most cases of corporate crime go unpunished, and many are never even known to the public. In addition, the cost of corporate crime goes beyond dollars. The collapse of Enron, Global Crossing, and other corporations in recent years has cost tens of thousands of people their jobs and their pensions. Even more seriously, for decades, coal-mining companies have knowingly put miners at risk from inhaling coal dust, and hundreds of people die annually of "black lung" disease; miners only realized recently that their cancers are related to decades of work in the mines. Canadian uranium mines are even more deadly: effluent from the uranium processing plants contaminates large areas, often devastating Aboriginal lands and communities. The U.S. death toll from all job-related hazards that are known to companies probably exceeds 100 000 annually (Carroll, 1999; Jones, 1999). The proportionate figure for Canada, with its smaller population base, would be about 11 000.

MEDIA PERSPECTIVES
Crime in High Places

Over the past decade, Canada and the United States have witnessed an escalating wave of scandals involving politicians, corporate executives, and other powerful individuals who have bent the rules and broken the law. In some cases, the scandals are made public first by the media, forcing governments or the police and the law to take action. Thereafter, the media keep us informed of investigations, inquiries, arrests, and trials involving influential people, political parties and corporations. Without the media—and the help of whistle-blowers, anonymous sources, and access-to-information legislation—these crimes would have escaped our attention.

One notorious Canadian example of 1997, the Bre-X case, may be the greatest gold hoax of all time (Francis, 1997). Investors, big and small alike, were scammed to the tune of more than $3 billion by an upstart company that "salted" (tampered with) ore

Conrad Black

samples to fake a massive gold find in Indonesia. The apparent suicide of the chief geologist and the complete collapse of Bre-X share prices brought the scam to an end.

More recent American examples—Enron, WorldCom, and ImClone—brought corporate and white-collar crime into the limelight in a way that the justice system could not ignore. The energy trading company, Enron, deceived its investors and employees by playing fast-and-loose with its

accounts in order to enhance the value of its shares. The investigations and trials that followed Enron's bankruptcy were played out in public mass media. Its accounting firm, Arthur Andersen, one of the largest in the United States, was put out of business. Among other banks, Canada's CIBC aided Enron with its deception by loaning it money (US$205 million) while aware that Enron was concealing US$22 billion in debt (Howlett, et al., 2003). Executives at telecommunications giant WorldCom, including Canadian-born CEO Bernard Ebbers, were accused of securities fraud when the company fell US$41 billion in debt. Because of the scale of their financial fraud, WorldCom and Enron rank first and second as the biggest companies to seek bankruptcy protection in American history (Waldie and Howlett, 2003). ImClone was a simpler case of insider trading: company executives and friends sold their shares before bad news—failure to gain FDA approval

---

YOUR TURN

Why do you think the public seems less concerned with white-collar crime and corporate crime than with street crime? In light of recent corporate scandals, do you think this pattern is changing?

ORGANIZED CRIME

Organized crime is *a business supplying illegal goods or services.* Sometimes criminal organizations force people to do business with them, as when a gang extorts money from shopkeepers for "protection." In most cases, however, organized crime involves the sale of illegal goods and services—including sex, drugs, and gambling—to willing buyers. Organized crime has flourished in North America, as it has elsewhere in the world, for more than a century. The scope of its operations expanded among immigrants,

who found that society was not always willing to share its opportunities with them. Some ambitious individuals (such as Capone and Perri) made their own success, especially during Prohibition, as described earlier. The Italian Mafia is a well-known example of organized crime. But other criminal organizations in North America involve Blacks, Chinese, Colombians, Cubans, Haitians, Nigerians, Russians, and others of almost every racial and ethnic category—and motorcycle gangs, like Hell's Angels and Vagabonds. Today, organized crime involves a wide range of activities: selling illegal drugs; prostitution; credit card fraud; and selling false identification papers to illegal immigrants (Valdez, 1997).

Critical Review   According to social-conflict theory, a capitalist society's inequality in wealth and power shapes its laws and their application. The criminal justice and social welfare systems act as political agents, controlling categories of people who are a threat to the capitalist system.

Like other approaches to deviance, social-conflict theory has its critics. It implies that laws and other cultural norms

of a drug—became common knowledge. ImClone's CEO was jailed. The trial of his friend Martha Stewart, for obstruction of justice by lying about a timely stock trade, resulted in a prison sentence followed by a lengthy period of house arrest.

Financial scandals in the Canadian political system have been with us since the days of Sir John A. MacDonald, who solicited money from businesspeople in exchange for contracts to build the Canadian National Railway. Nonetheless, no previous incident had the public exposure of our recent sponsorship scandal, or Adscam. After almost losing the Quebec sovereignty referendum of 1995, Prime Minister Jean Chrétien created the sponsorship program with the intention of promoting Canada in a variety of Quebec venues. Millions of dollars went to Liberal-friendly ad agencies; in some cases, the money was accepted but no work was done; in another, the money found its way—via brown paper envelope—into the coffers of the Quebec wing of the federal Liberal Party.

When Paul Martin took over as prime minister in December 2003, he created the Gomery inquiry to look into the mismanagement of public funds—and decided that the proceedings of the inquiry would be televised. He had no way of knowing what Justice Gomery would reveal or that the public, especially Quebecers, would be mesmerized by the television coverage, which showed how "every rule in the book" had been broken. Heads rolled: senior civil servants and executives lost their jobs, and several people went on to trials and convictions. But the most significant result was the fall of the Martin Liberal government in January 2006. When Quebecers realized that the sponsorship program was an attempt to "buy" their loyalty and their votes, they were furious. Stephen Harper's Conservatives won an astounding ten seats in Quebec, as a direct result of Adscam and the television coverage of the Gomery inquiry.

Over the same period, Canadians watched the downfall of Conrad Black, former CEO of newspaper conglomerate Hollinger International. Black was born in Toronto, made his fortune in the newspaper business, assumed a lavish lifestyle, and gave up his Canadian citizenship in 2001 in order to become a baron, Lord Black of Crossharbour. In November 2004, the U.S. Securities and Exchange Commission filed a civil fraud lawsuit against Black, alleging that he diverted, to himself and others, some US$85 million that belonged to Hollinger International shareholders and, in a suit filed in the summer of 2006, that he and other company officials failed to pay millions that Hollinger owed in taxes, owing to under-reporting of corporate earnings. Black vehemently denies any wrongdoing and has countersued.

The rich and well-connected still retain their influence and prestige when they break the rules, but—in large part because of the media—infractions by the powerful are now in our radar.

WHAT DO YOU THINK?

1. Does the average Canadian suffer from white-collar crime? If so, how?
2. Are the affluent and powerful more likely to be caught and punished for their crimes today than in the past?
3. How have the media inadvertently turned investigative journalism into investigative policing?

Sources: CBC (2004), CBC (2005a), CTV (2005), Green Party (2005).

are created directly by the rich and powerful to promote their own interests. This is oversimplification, as laws also protect human rights, workers, consumers, and the environment—often at the expense of corporations and the rich.

Social-conflict analysis argues that criminality is the result of inequality. However, as Durkheim noted, deviance exists in all societies, whatever the economic system. It also appears in all social strata, as white-collar crime so clearly reveals.

The sociological explanations for crime and other types of deviance that we have discussed are summarized in the Applying Theory table (on p. 222).

Deviance, Race, Ethnicity, and Gender

What people consider deviant reflects the relative power and privilege of different categories of people. The following sections offer two examples: hate crime motivated by race or ethnicity, and the link between gender and deviance.

HATE CRIMES

A **hate crime** is *a criminal act against a person or a person's property by an offender motivated by racial or other bias.* Hate crimes, which may refer to race, religion, ancestry, sexual orientation, or physical disability, are common in all societies, but rates vary dramatically across countries, over time, and in response to crises like war or recession.

A recent Canadian survey of 12 major Canadian police forces collected data on hate crimes for 2001 and 2002, finding 928 reported hate crimes over the two years. Figure 9–2 reveals that a full quarter of these hate crimes is directed against Jewish people or institutions. Anti-Semitism, it appears, is firmly embedded in our apparently tolerant Canadian culture. Overall, 57 percent of hate crimes is motivated by ethnicity and race, targeting mainly Blacks and Asians, while 43 percent targets religion, mainly Jewish and Muslim. A relatively small 9 percent, motivated by sexual orientation, targets gays and lesbians.

APPLYING THEORY
DEVIANCE

	Structural-Functional Approach	Symbolic-Interaction Approach	Social-Conflict Approach
What is the level of analysis?	Macro level	Micro level	Macro level
What is deviance? What part does it play in society?	Deviance is a basic part of social organization. By defining deviance, society sets its moral boundaries.	Deviance is part of socially constructed reality that emerges in interaction. Deviance comes into being as individuals label something deviant.	Deviance results from social inequality. Norms, including laws, reflect the interests of powerful members of society.
What is important about deviance?	Deviance is universal: all societies contain deviance.	Deviance is variable: any act or person may or may not be labelled as deviant.	Deviance is political: people with little power are at high risk for becoming deviant.

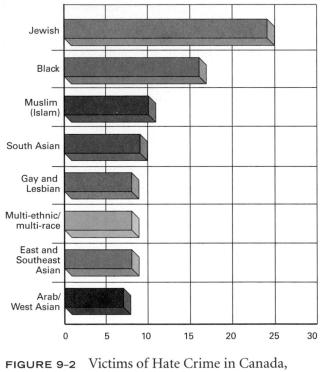

FIGURE 9-2 Victims of Hate Crime in Canada, 2001–02*

---

*Jewish most likely targets of hate crime in twelve major police forces in Canada.

Source: Adapted from the Statistics Canada publication *The Daily* (2004). http://www.statcan.ca/english/040601/d040601a.htm.

Both Canada and the United States have hate crime laws protecting multiple categories of people: in each case a given crime (e.g., arson or homicide) is treated more harshly if it is motivated by hatred.

DEVIANCE AND GENDER

Virtually every society in the world applies stricter normative controls to women than to men, usually centring the lives of women on the home. Women's opportunities in the workplace, in politics, in athletics, and in the military are more limited than those of men: those who test the limits are deviants. In Saudi Arabia, women cannot vote or drive; in Iran, women who dare to expose their hair in public can be whipped; in 2002, a Nigerian court convicted a divorced woman of bearing a child out of wedlock and sentenced her to death by stoning (Eboh, 2002).

Gender also figures in the theories of deviance discussed earlier. Robert Merton's strain theory, for example, defines cultural goals in terms of financial success. Traditionally, at least, this goal has had more to do with the lives of men because women have been taught to define success in terms of relationships, particularly marriage and motherhood (Leonard, 1982). A more woman-focused theory might recognize the strain that results from the cultural ideal of equality clashing with the reality of gender-based inequality.

According to labelling theory, gender's influence on the definition of deviance derives from the different standards applied to women and men. Further, because society puts men in positions of power over women, men often escape direct responsibility for actions that victimize women. In the past, at least, men who sexually harassed or assaulted women were labelled as only mildly deviant and escaped punishment entirely. In contrast, women who are victimized may have to convince others—even members of a jury—that they were not to blame for having been sexual assaulted. Research confirms an important truth: whether people define a situation as deviance—and, if so, who the deviant is—depends on the gender of audience and actor (King and Clayson, 1988).

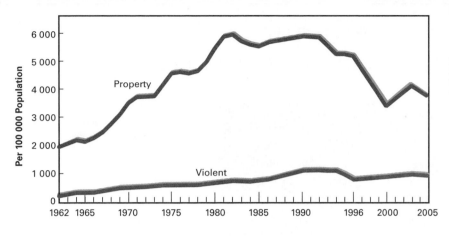

FIGURE 9-3   Violent and Property
Crime Rates in Canada,
1962–2004

Source: Based on data from Statistics Canada, catalogue nos. 85-205 and 85-002-SPE, Vol. 17, No. 8, and Vol. 19, No. 9, Canadian Statistics, Justice and Crime, available at www.statcan.ca/202/csto1/legal.htm.

Despite its focus on social inequality, much social-conflict analysis fails to address the issue of gender. If economic disadvantage is a primary cause of crime, as conflict theory suggests, why do women commit far *fewer* crimes than men? Why are men more violent in general? The Thinking it Through box (on pp. 224–225), takes a look at the link between masculinity and violence in hockey.

Crime

Crime is the violation of criminal law enacted by the federal government: nonetheless, implementation of Canada's Criminal Code may vary among provincial and territorial jurisdictions. All crimes are composed of two elements: the *act* itself (or, in some cases, the failure to do what the law requires) and *criminal intent*, in legal terminology, the *mens rea* ("guilty mind"). Intent is a matter of degree, ranging from negligence to wilful conduct; someone who is negligent does not deliberately

Selected data on crime in Canada are published by Statistics Canada at www40. statcan.ca/l01/ind01/l3_2693_2102.htm?hili_none.

set out to hurt anyone but acts, or fails to act, in a way that results in harm. Prosecutors weigh the degree of intent in deciding whether, for example, to charge someone with first-degree murder, second-degree murder, or manslaughter. Alternatively, they may consider a killing justifiable, as in self-defence.

TYPES OF CRIME

In Canada, information on criminal offences is obtained from the Uniform Crime Reporting system and reported in a Statistics Canada publication called *Canadian Crime Statistics.* Violent crime and property crime are recorded separately. **Violent crimes,** *crimes against people that involve violence or the threat of violence,* include murder, manslaughter, infanticide, assault, sexual assault, abduction, and robbery. **Property crimes,** *crimes that involve theft of property belonging to others,* include breaking and entering, motor vehicle theft, theft over $5000, theft of $5000 and under, possession of stolen goods, and fraud.

A third category of offences includes **victimless crimes,** *violations of law in which there are no readily apparent victims*—such as prostitution and gambling. There is also a separate category of offences under the *Narcotic Control Act,* regarding the use of illegal drugs, including cannabis or marijuana. However, "victimless crime" is often a misnomer. How victimless is a crime when a young runaway is lured into prostitution? or if a young pregnant woman using crack causes death or permanent injury to her baby? or if one spouse spends a family's savings on gambling losses? Generally, a person who commits such a crime is both offender and victim.

CRIMINAL STATISTICS

Canada's crime statistics show steady increases in both violent and property crime rates from 1962 to the early 1990s, followed by clear declines sustained through to 2004. Figure 9–3 illustrates these trends in violent and property crimes over the period in question. Note that violent and property crime rates in the United States also peaked in the early 1990s and then declined.

Canada Map 9–1 suggests that homicide rates differ not only between countries, but also among our own provinces and territories. Note that the variation within Canada is greater than that between Canada and the United States. Nunavut's homicide rate is 17 times that of Newfoundland and Labrador, while the American rate is 3 to 4 times that of Canada. Homicide rates in Canada increase from east to west and again to the north. For the country as a whole, homicide rates have dropped from a high of 2.7 per 100 000 population in 1992 to 2.1 in 1996, and to 1.8 in 2001 and 2004. Comparing provincial statistics (five-year averages) for the 1997–2001 period with those of 2000–2004 reveals lower rates in Quebec, Ontario, Alberta, and British Columbia—the most populated provinces—coupled with higher rates in other parts of the country, such as Manitoba, Saskatchewan, and the territories.

Always read crime statistics with caution, since they include only crimes known to the police. The police learn about almost all homicides, but assaults—especially among

THINKING IT THROUGH
Dangerous Masculinity: Violence and Crime in Hockey

When is assault criminal and when is it just part of the game? To what extent is violence in men's hockey part of the culture of the game—that is, normal and therefore not criminal? And what about the victims of violence? How do the law, the NHL, the players, the media, and the fans react in the face of serious on-ice assault?

Professor Michael Atkinson immersed himself in the hockey world in an attempt to understand the responses of various parties when, in a game on February 21, 2000, Marty McSorely "viciously slashed opposing player Donald Brashear across the side of his head." Atkinson's approach is interpretive and therefore consistent with the symbolic-interaction paradigm and participant observation methodology. Atkinson recounts that, when McSorely clipped Brashear from behind "with a two-handed stick slash to the right temple...,

Professor Michael Atkinson of the Department of Sociology at McMaster University conducts research on violence and aggression in sports cultures (e.g., ice hockey, animal blood sports, triathlon), radical body modification (e.g., tattooing, cosmetic surgery), and youth subcultures like Straightedge. He prefers to engage his sociological interests through participant observation, by becoming a full member of the groups he explores. As a result, he has participated in the social world as a ticket scalper, endurance athlete, hockey player, tattoo enthusiast, cosmetic surgery patient, and Straightedge practitioner. Through these projects and others, Dr. Atkinson believes that one should actively experience the world sociologically rather than just imagine it theoretically.

Brashear went tumbling backwards to the ice in a state of unconsciousness. Brashear's head bounced off the ice and blood started pouring from his nose. He laid prone and motionless on the ice, save for the periodic twitching of his feet and rolling of his eyes [as he had a seizure]." Clearly, what Atkinson calls the *dangerous masculinity* of ice hockey had impelled McSorely into a vicious assault that would be judged as criminal had the incident occurred *off* the ice.

The police got involved in this case, and McSorely was found guilty of assault with a weapon under the Criminal Code. He was sentenced to an "eighteen-month conditional discharge (essentially probation), and ordered that he not play in any future NHL games involving Brashear." As a result, McSorely has no criminal record and is able to cross international boundaries freely. The NHL suspended him for the Bruins' remaining twenty-three games of the 1999–2000 season, costing him more than

---

acquaintances—are far less likely to be reported. The police record an even smaller proportion of property crimes, especially when losses are minor. And reported sexual assault—which includes date rape—still grossly understates the extent of these crimes.

One way to evaluate official crime statistics is through a *victimization survey*, in which a researcher asks a representative sample of people about their experience with crime. People do not always respond fully or truthfully to such surveys, but the results of these surveys indicate that actual crime occurs at substantially higher rates than suggested by official reports. Canada's first national survey on violence

against women, in 1993, found that half of Canadian women have experienced physical or sexual violence at least once since turning 16. Among those who have been married or lived common-law, 29 percent have been physically or sexually assaulted by their partners. Victimization remained stable between 1988 and 1993, with 24 percent of the female population experiencing at least one instance of criminal victimization (Statistics Canada, 1994a).

The analysis above was based on a "single-gender victimization survey" (Lupri, 2002), which implies that only women are subject to domestic abuse and ignores the fact that more than thirty studies in the 1970s and 1980s found "equal rates of assault by men *and* women." While more women report physical injury, both abused men and women suffer low

Cdn$100 000 in lost wages. This then was the extent of McSorely's punishment. In the background was "the faint memory of the player who had been injured."

This incident, Atkinson argues, illustrates the embedding of social constructions of masculinity in the interpretation of on-ice violence—or viewing "player violence in ice hockey through the lens of dangerous masculinity." While the larger discipline of sociology has turned to gender studies, and often the feminist perspective, the sociology of sport is, for Atkinson, unique in its "critical, *empirical* investigation of masculinity." Through the lens of dangerous masculinity, we see hockey as a game that includes fights and violence—with rules or limits, of course—and explicit consent, on the part of the players, to the risk of on-ice contact and injury. In effect, Brashear, by being a hockey player, had given his consent to the assault. Atkinson observes that the ability to "intimidate and dominate opponents, play through pain and injury, [and] carefully manage emotion [are] established benchmarks of one's ability to participate in dangerous masculinity." Since this is central to hockey and hockey culture, which Brashear embraced, he was *not* the victim of a random vicious attack or subject to criminal victimization.

Brashear's situation was complicated by an underlying dynamic through that particular game: he was asking for it, by taunting McSorely and refusing to fight. Media commentator Don Cherry's assessment of the situation was "You should never ridicule and humiliate a warrior.... You play with the bull, and you're gonna get the horns" (quoted in Atkinson [forthcoming]). The general public was horrified but the media, the fans, and the justice system—like Don Cherry—were sympathetic and even protective of McSorely. The hockey league was on the defensive about its authority to deal with on-ice behaviour without intervention by the police or courts: "NHL players and executives claimed themselves to be the most appropriate judges and juries of violence within the game... on the grounds that outsiders cannot conceptualize the mindset (vis-à-vis the socialization) of the *men* committing violence in the game." Even the judge in McSorely's trial, Mr. Justice Kitchen, felt the impact of dangerous masculine ideologies, writing that he was impressed with McSorely's dedication to the game, diligence, and bravery—and that his inability to admit his guilt is understandable. He was almost apologetic as he "sentenced" him to probation and acknowledged that the league's punishment and criminal prosecution constituted a "blow to his masculinity."

The culture of violence in hockey contributes to the excitement of the game, for players and fans alike.

Players are considered to be masculine warriors whose inevitable wounds will heal. Since hockey players consent to pain and injury, there is no such thing as a victim in hockey violence. Therefore, we blame the victim, implying that Brashear brought the attack on himself. NHL players and executives, the media, and the fans effectively condone and welcome hockey violence. A fan named Matt put it well in a web posting: "the fans love violence, players need the freedom to vent frustration, and we don't want laws that will change the face of the game to the point where hockey is no longer hockey. After all, this is a game for MEN" (quoted in Atkinson, [forthcoming]). In the end, Atkinson concludes, "the message is perhaps most clear to ice hockey players; the philosophy of dangerous masculinity is a privileging but brutalizing code of conduct within the world of professional sport."

WHAT DO YOU THINK?

1. Is the level of violence in hockey acceptable or out of control?
2. Why was Brashear, the victim, ignored through the uproar about the treatment of McSorely?
3. What does the concept of hockey as a display of dangerous masculinity mean for women's hockey in Canada? Do those Olympic gold medals make a difference?

Source: Michael Atkinson (2007).

---

levels of self-esteem, embarrassment, and shame. Whatever the direction of the abuse, Lupri argues, the impacts on children in the home are the same—behavioural effects such as "aggression and delinquency," or psychological effects including "anxiety, depression, and low self-esteem." By focusing on the abuse of women and ignoring the abuse of men, society acknowledges only part of the problem.

THE STREET CRIMINAL: A PROFILE

Official statistics paint a broad-brush picture of people arrested for violent and property crimes. Here we examine the breakdown of these arrest statistics by age, gender, social class, race, and ethnicity.

Age

Official crime rates rise sharply during adolescence, peak in the late teens, and then fall as people get older. People between the ages of 15 and 24 represent just 14 percent of the U.S. population, but in 2003 they accounted for 39.3 percent of all arrests for violent crimes and 46.8 percent of arrests for property crimes. Not surprisingly, 20- to 34-year-olds make up 25 percent of the Canadian population and 62 percent of prison inmates.

Gender

While each sex constitutes roughly half of our population, about 85 to 90 percent of arrests involve males, and about

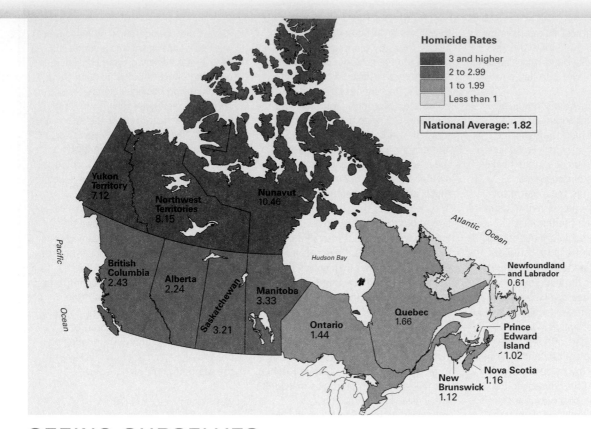

SEEING OURSELVES

CANADA MAP 9–1   Homicide Rates for Canada, Provinces, and Territories, 2000–2004 (Five-Year Averages, Rates per 100 000 People)*

*Averages are compiled to even out the impacts of an unusual number of homicides in one year in a relatively small population (e.g., in the Yukon, rates were 6.5, 3.3, 0.0, 3.3, and 22.4 per 100 000 people in the years 2000 to 2004).

Source: Calculations by L.M. Gerber from the Statistics Canada website http://www.statcan.ca/english/Pgdb/legal12a.htm.

97 percent of prison inmates are male. The proportion of females arrested is always low but varies considerably from one country to another: one study found Finland registered a low of 6.7 percent, Canada 9.8, the United States 13.7, and New Zealand 20.5 (Simon and Sharma, 1979).

Alberta sociologist Helen Boritch (1997), in one of the first comprehensive analyses of female criminality in Canada, asks if the changing position of women has led to increased rates and new patterns of crime. She finds that "while women's participation in crime is increasing, the overall pattern of female criminality has not changed dramatically... women's crimes continue to be primarily non-violent in nature, economically motivated, or victimless crimes" (1997:20). Very few women are charged with homicide in Canada, and there is no discernible change in the rate of homicides by women over recent decades.

Some of this gender gap stems from the reluctance of law enforcement officials to define women as criminals (Scott, 1992; Cluff, *et al.*, 1998). Canada witnessed this reluctance to assume the worst about women as it watched the Bernardo-Homolka murder case unfold. Initially, the justice system and the public were ready to believe that Karla Homolka was an unwilling accomplice—a victim, in effect—forced to participate in abduction, rape, and murder by a husband she feared. Before the incriminating videotapes, which revealed her as an enthusiastic participant, were found, Homolka was allowed to **plea bargain,** *a legal negotiation in which the prosecution reduces a defendant's charge in exchange for a guilty plea.* She received a manslaughter conviction and a twelve-year sentence, in exchange for giving evidence against Paul Bernardo.

Social Class

While people commonly associate criminality with poverty, sociological research suggests that rich and poor alike commit crimes, albeit somewhat different kinds of offences. People arrested for violent and property crimes in North America and elsewhere disproportionately have low social standing (Thornberry and Farnsworth, 1982; Wolfgang, *et al.*, 1987). In part, this pattern reflects the historical tendency to view poor people as less worthy than those whose wealth and power confer apparent respectability (Tittle, *et al.*, 1978; Elias, 1986). Strain theory, discussed above, contributes to the expectation that law breakers will come from less affluent neighbourhoods. Police officers are conditioned to focus their search for crime and its perpetrators in the poor sections of town rather than in the pristine office towers of business and government—where embezzlement, insider trading, and bid-rigging occur.

The evidence also suggests that street crime disproportionately victimizes people of lower social position. Violent crime in particular is commonplace among the small number of chronically poor people living in inner-city neighbourhoods—or in isolated Aboriginal communities. But only a small proportion of less advantaged people are ever convicted of crimes; most crimes are committed by a relatively few hard-core offenders. Moreover, the connection between social standing and criminality depends entirely on the kind of crime under consideration. If the definition of crime is expanded beyond street crime to include white-collar and corporate crime, the "average" criminal has a much higher social position.

Race and Ethnicity

In Canada, Black people and, particularly, Aboriginal people are arrested in disproportionate numbers. The effect is apparent in the racial composition of our prison inmates: in 1991, Black people represented roughly 1 percent of Canada's population but made up 3.8 percent of federal inmates; Aboriginal people made up about 2 percent of the population but 11.3 percent of inmates. This pattern was even more pronounced among female prisoners, where 8.8 percent were Black and 15.4 percent were Aboriginal. More disturbing is the fact that in the Prairie provinces, where Aboriginal people made up about 6 percent of the population, but 36 percent of male inmates and 47 percent of female inmates in federal prisons. By 1999, despite programs designed to divert them from prison, the proportion of Aboriginal inmates in federal prisons had increased to 17.2 percent (Canada, 2006a): the figures for Aboriginal women and men were 21 and 17 percent, respectively.

The report of the Commission on Systemic Racism in the Ontario Criminal Justice System (Ontario, 1996) reveals that the imprisonment of Black people increased by 204 percent between 1986 and 1994, while the comparable figure for White people was 23 percent. The report argues that, at every stage of their contact with the justice system—

from arrest through trial to imprisonment, Black people are treated more harshly. Frideres and Gadacz declare that: "In Canada, members of minority groups are 7 to 16 times more likely than Whites to be imprisoned" (2001:129).

To the degree that prejudice related to race prompts police to arrest Aboriginal and Black people more readily than White people, these two groups are overly criminalized. In similar situations, Aboriginal people are more likely than non-Aboriginal people to be arrested, charged with an offence, and denied bail. Once involved in the criminal justice system, they find themselves in the "revolving door syndrome": many are "admitted to a prison several times a year and it is estimated that 90 percent of all adult male Indians" have been in jail at least once (Frideres and Gadacz, 2001:131).

Race in Canada closely relates to social standing (Kallen, 2003:46–47; Li, 2003:104–14), which, as we have already shown, affects the likelihood of engaging in street crimes.

Read a U.S. report on violent victimization and race at www.ojp.usdoj.gov/bjs/pub/pdf/vvr98.pdf and a report on Aboriginal people and the justice system by the Canadian Criminal Justice Association at www.ccja-acjp.ca/en/abori4.html.

Several researchers claim that membership in lower-class gangs promotes criminality. American sociologists Judith and Peter Blau (1982) take a different tack, suggesting that criminality—especially violent crime—is promoted by the sting of poverty in the midst of affluence. Suffering the hardships of poverty in a rich society encourages some people to perceive society as unjust and to disregard its laws.

CRIME: CANADIAN, AMERICAN, AND GLOBAL PERSPECTIVES

By world standards, the United States has a lot of crime. The U.S. homicide rate stands 4 times higher than Canada's and 5 times higher than Europe's, while its rape (sexual assault) rate is 2.6 times higher than Canada's and 7 times higher than Europe's (Kalish, 1988). New York City led American cities with 1182 murders in 1995—dropping to 575 in 2002. In comparison, Canada (with almost 4 times the population of New York City), had 732 murders in 1995, 582 in 2002, and 622 in 2004 (Messing, 2003; Statistics Canada, 2003a).

Why are U.S. crime rates so high? Elliot Currie (1985) blames its cultural emphasis on personal economic success—at the expense of family and community. Unlike European nations, the United States does not guarantee minimum income, medical care, or other social services—and has high levels of unemployment and underemployment. The key to reducing crime, then, lies in social change, not in hiring more police and building more prisons. Canada falls between Europe and the United States in the provision of social services and income support but, in recent years, our "safety nets" have become increasingly frayed. According to Currie's reasoning, we should have experienced rising crime rates. Instead, crime rates—in particular, violent crime rates—have declined in Canada, *and* in the United States.

TABLE 9–1
Homicide by Method for Canada, 2000 to 2004

Method	2000 (%)	2001 (%)	2002 (%)	2003 (%)	2004 (%)
Shooting	33.7	30.9	26.1	29.3	27.7
Stabbing	27.3	30.9	31.3	25.9	33.0
Beating	23.4	22.1	21.6	22.0	21.9
Strangulation	7.1	8.5	11.3	11.7	10.1
Other methods	8.5	7.6	9.7	11.1	7.3
Number of homicides	546	553	582	549	622

Source: Calculations by L.M. Gerber based on Statistics Canada data, available at www40.statcan.ca/l01/cst01/legal01.htm.

Another factor contributing to the relatively high level of violence in the United States is the widespread private ownership of guns. In any given year, roughly two-thirds of murder victims die from shootings. (In Canada, fewer than one-third of murder victims die in this way.) The fact that the number of guns in the United States is equal to the American population helps to account for its runaway leadership in handgun deaths among industrial nations: see Figure 9–4.

Table 9–1 provides statistics for Canadian homicide, by method, for 2000 to 2004. Note that the proportion of murders by stabbing increases from 27.3 to 33.0 percent, but the proportion of murders by shooting declines slightly during that period: from 33.7 to 27.7 percent. Gun control legislation was enacted in Canada in the fall of 1995. Public interest groups, such as Canadians Against Violence Everywhere Advocating its Termination, were instrumental in persuading the government to prohibit certain kinds of weapons and require the registration of others. As of 2000, all guns must be registered, and licences must be shown in order to purchase ammunition. Collectors and rural people—including Aboriginal people—mounted significant resistance to the new regulations. Costs for the gun registry have ballooned to well over $1 billion as a result of technical problems and public resistance. Registration "deadlines" have been moved several times and, a decade later, Canadians are still debating the merits of gun control.

Figure 9–5 shows Canadian firearm homicide rates, by type of firearm, from 1988 to 1998. Note the sharp decline in the rates since 1991 by all types of firearms except the "other" category. Interestingly, homicide rates declined in the United States over the same period.

As noted in earlier chapters, globalization is increasing on many fronts, including crime. Some types of crime have always been multinational, including terrorism, espionage, and arms dealing (Martin and Romano, 1992). Since the terrorist attacks on New York's World Trade Center and the Pentagon on September 11, 2001, the United States and

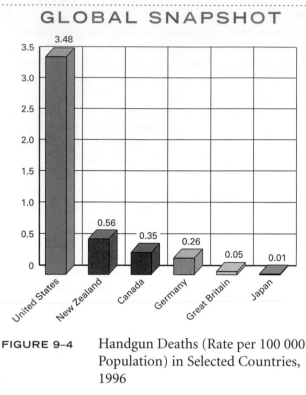

GLOBAL SNAPSHOT

FIGURE 9–4   Handgun Deaths (Rate per 100 000 Population) in Selected Countries, 1996

Source: Adapted by L.M. Gerber from Handgun Control Inc. (1998).

Canada have become partners in the war on terror. However reluctantly, Canada has modified its approach to border and airport security in response to American fears. We even toyed, temporarily, with national identity cards including biometric data, like fingerprints or iris scans but have held off on implementation because of privacy concerns.

Another multinational crime is the illegal drug trade. In part, the proliferation of illegal drugs in North America stems from demand: there is a very profitable market— Hell's Angels, or "Les Hells," are involved in murderous wars with other gangs as they manoeuvre for international domination of the illegal drug trade—much of which passes through Canada on its way to the United States. Furthermore, the Americans are concerned about the flow from Canada of marijuana—which organized crime grows in large amounts here, often in empty houses or warehouses in rural areas with power tapped illegally from hydro lines.

The Criminal Justice System

The criminal justice system is a society's formal response to crime. In some countries, military police keep a tight rein on everyone; in others, including Canada, police have more limited powers to respond to specific violations of criminal law. We shall briefly introduce the key elements of this scheme: police, the courts, and punishment.

POLICE

The police are the primary point of contact between society and the criminal justice system. In principle, the police maintain public order by uniformly enforcing the law. Since Canada's police officers (1 per 523 people in 1995) cannot effectively monitor the activities of 30 million people, the police exercise considerable discretion about which situations warrant their attention and how to handle them.

How, then, do police carry out their duties? A study of police behaviour in five U.S. cities (Smith and Visher, 1981; Smith, Douglas A., 1987) concluded that, because they must respond swiftly, police make several quick assessments that guide their actions. They are more likely to make an arrest if the crime is serious, if the suspect is unco-operative, if the suspect has been arrested before, if there are bystanders present, and if the suspect is of a visible minority.

Factors affecting police discretion have been examined in Ontario as well (Schellenberg, 1995). Police officers are more likely to apply the rules regarding traffic offences, leaving less room for leniency, when their actions are being recorded by mobile video camera. More generally, when the police are considering arrests, they are less likely to check an individual's record—even when they have computer access in their patrol cars—if they know the person or feel that he or she is trustworthy. Race and class can easily enter into the decision-making process at this point, raising the issue of racial profiling.

In Canada, to visible minorities are arrested and imprisoned in disproportionate numbers, but this observation does not apply equally to all visible minorities. While Black and Aboriginal people, respectively, are imprisoned at 5 and 3 times the rate for White people, people of Arabic, East Indian, and Asian origin are imprisoned at two-thirds to half the rate for White people (Ontario, 1996).

Finally, the greater numbers of police relative to population are found in areas with two key characteristics: high concentrations of minorities and large income disparities between rich and poor (Jacobs, 1979). As a result, the Northwest Territories and the Yukon have both the highest rates of violent crime, as indicated by homicide rates and the largest numbers of police officers relative to population (1 officer per 275 and 266 residents, respectively, in 1995). See Canada Map 9–1 (on p. 231). The higher crime rates in these areas may be related, in part, to alcohol consumption and poverty or social disruption; they may also reflect bias in police surveillance, arrests, and convictions, as well as an emphasis on crime control and law enforcement rather than crime prevention (LaPrairie, 1988; Depew, 1992).

COURTS

After arrest, a court determines guilt or innocence. In principle, courts in Canada rely on an adversarial process involving

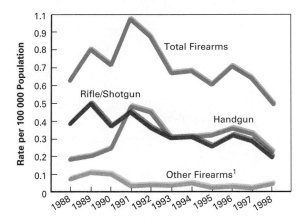

FIGURE 9-5   Firearm Homicide Rates by Type of Firearm, Canada 1988–98

[1]"Other firearms" includes sawed-off rifles/shotguns, fully automatic firearms, and other firearm–like weapons.

Source: Adapted from the Statistics Canada publication "Juristat", Catalogue 85-002 Vol. 19, No.10, October 1999.

attorneys in the presence of a judge who ensures adherence to legal procedures. In practice, however, a large percentage of criminal cases are resolved prior to court appearance through plea bargaining. Getting a reduced sentence by pleading guilty is a widespread practice, because it spares the judicial system the time and expense of a court trial. Also, a trial is unnecessary if there is little disagreement about the facts of the case. By selectively trying only a small proportion of the cases, the courts can channel resources into the most important cases (Reid, 1991).

But this process pressures defendants, who are presumed innocent, to plead guilty, thereby undercutting their rights. Defendants who have little understanding of the criminal justice system, as well as those unable to afford a good lawyer, are likely to suffer from what has been called 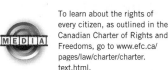 To learn about the rights of every citizen, as outlined in the Canadian Charter of Rights and Freedoms, go to www.efc.ca/pages/law/charter/charter.text.html. "bargain-counter justice" (Blumberg, 1970). On the other hand, Canadians who felt that Karla Homolka got off too lightly asked to have her plea bargain reassessed. Her case was not reopened because doing so would have threatened the plea-bargaining system.

PUNISHMENT

Ever since differences in power and authority began to emerge in human groups, punishment has been a means of discipline or control. Punishment may range from a "time out" or the spanking of children to imprisonment or capital punishment for the most serious of crimes.

The use of the death penalty differs across time and countries. In 1831, the officials in an English town hanged a nine-

Police must be allowed discretion if they are to handle effectively the many different situations they face every day. At the same time, it is important that the police treat people fairly. Here we see a police officer deciding whether or not to charge a young woman for driving while intoxicated.

year-old boy who was found guilty of setting fire to a house (Kittrie, 1971:103). Canadians today would be appalled by this outcome for several reasons. As shown on Global Map 9–1,

Learn more about the death penalty in the United States, including a database of characteristics for people who have been executed, at www.deathpenalty.org.

the global trend now is towards abolition of the death penalty. According to Amnesty International (2005a), since 1980, more than thirty nations have ended this practice. The United States still has the death penalty, though several states have abolished it. Canada last conducted an execution in 1962 and abolished the death penalty in 1976.

Canadians have also decided that young people have a lower capacity for crime and deserve the special protections of the *Youth Criminal Justice Act.* Clearly, approaches to

The history of Canadian legislation regarding youth crime is discussed at www.mapleleafweb.com/features/crime/youth-act/.

punishment have changed over time and vary from country to country. Debate about the appropriateness

of specific punishments as applied to adults and juvenile offenders raises the question of how and why society should punish its wrongdoers. This leads us to consider four justifications for punishment.

Retribution

The oldest justification for punishment is to satisfy people's need for **retribution,** *an act of moral vengeance by which society makes the offender suffer as much as the suffering caused*

by the crime. Retribution assumes that society maintains a moral order, supported by punishment in equal measure.

A Toronto case illustrates the importance of the perceived appropriateness of the judicial response. In October 1997, Gordon Stuckless, the equipment manager of Maple Leaf Gardens, was sentenced to two years less a day for the sexual abuse of young boys over a period of more than twenty years. Stuckless had traded sexual favours for tickets to hockey games or opportunities to meet players. After Martin Kruse came forward with allegations of sexual abuse, police received calls from many other men who had had similar experiences. Shortly after Stuckless was sentenced, Kruse committed suicide. His family felt the light sentence—which did not fit the crime—was one of the reasons for his suicide.

Deterrence

A second justification for punishment, **deterrence,** amounts to *the attempt to discourage criminality through punishment.* Deterrence reflects the notion from the eighteenth-century Enlightenment that, as calculating and rational creatures, humans will forgo deviance if they perceive that the pain of punishment outweighs the pleasure of mischief.

Deterrence emerged as an alternative to harsh punishment based on retribution. Why put someone to death for stealing, critics asked, if theft can be discouraged with a prison sentence? Punishment may deter crime in two ways: *specific deterrence* demonstrates to an offender that crime does not pay; and through *general deterrence*, the punishment of one person serves as an example to others.

Rehabilitation

The third justification for punishment is **rehabilitation,** *a program for reforming the offender to preclude subsequent offences.* If people learn deviance in environments marked by poverty or a lack of parental supervision, they can also learn to obey the rules—the key being control of the environment. *Reformatories* or *houses of correction* served as a controlled setting to help people learn proper behaviour. (Recall the description of total institutions and boot camp in Chapter 5.) Rehabilitation resembles deterrence in that both motivate the offender towards conformity. But rehabilitation emphasizes constructive improvement, while deterrence, like retribution, inflicts suffering on an offender. Whereas retribution demands that the punishment fit the crime, rehabilitation tailors treatment to the offender.

Societal Protection

A final justification for punishment, **social protection,** refers to *rendering an offender incapable of further offences either temporarily through incarceration or permanently by execution.* One of the concerns expressed by the Canadian public is that dangerous offenders are given "life" sentences and then released on parole. After the murder of her daughter Nina in Burlington, Ontario, Priscilla DeVilliers founded Canadians Against Violence Everywhere Advocating its Termination; she involved herself in a massive campaign to

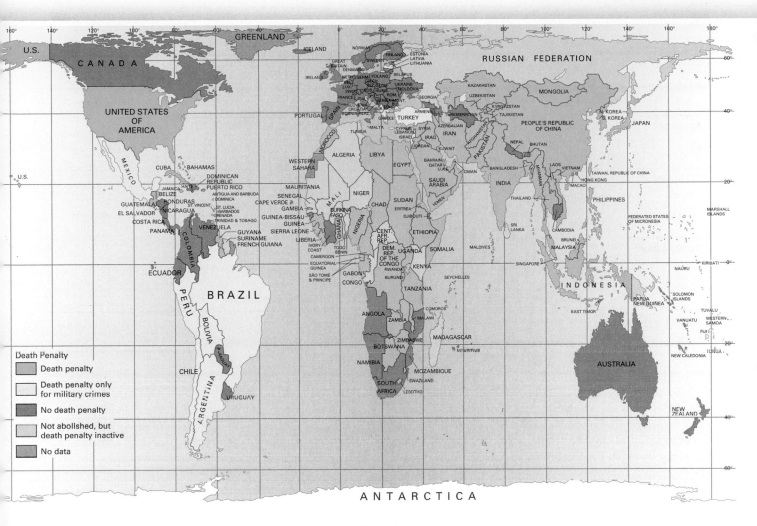

WINDOW ON THE WORLD

GLOBAL MAP 9-1   Capital Punishment in Global Perspective

The map identifies 76 countries and territories in which the law allows the death penalty for ordinary crimes; in 11 more, the death penalty is reserved for exceptional crimes under military law or during times of war. The death penalty does not exist in 85 countries and territories; in 24 more, the death penalty remains in law, but no execution has taken place in more than ten years. Compare rich and poor nations: what general pattern do you see? In what way are the United States and Japan exceptions to this pattern?

Source: Amnesty International (2005a).

restrict parole and bail for dangerous offenders. Her campaign touched a responsive cord in an apprehensive public that feels inadequately protected at present. When a dangerous man such as Clifford Olson is granted early release and kills eleven young people, as he did in British Columbia in 1980–81, people question the level of protection afforded them.[1]

The Summing Up table (on p. 232) summarizes these four justifications for punishment.

Critical Review Retribution reminds us of Durkheim's contention that punishing the deviant bolsters the moral consciousness of others. To accomplish this objective,

---

[1]At the time of Olson's release in 1980, he was serving a prison sentence for murder. He is now serving the maximum sentence of 25 years *without* the possibility of parole. He can expect to be released in 2007, when he will be 67 years old. Peter Worthington (1993) wrote about the 1980–81 murders of which Olson was convicted, as well as about many others he claims to have committed.

SUMMING UP

Four Justifications for Punishment

Retribution	The oldest justification for punishment. Punishment is society's revenge for a moral wrong. In principle, punishment should be equal in severity to the deviance itself.
Deterrence	An early modern approach. Deviance is considered social disruption which society acts to control. People are viewed as rational and self-interested; deterrence works because the pain of punishment outweighs the pleasure of deviance.
Rehabilitation	A modern strategy linked to the development of social sciences. Deviance is viewed as the result of social problems (such as poverty) or personal problems (such as mental illness). Social conditions are improved; treatment is tailored to the offender's condition.
Societal protection	A modern approach easier to carry out than rehabilitation. If society is unable or unwilling to rehabilitate offenders or reform social conditions, people are protected by the imprisonment or execution of the offender.

punishment was traditionally a public event. Public executions occurred in England until 1868, whereas the last public execution in the United States took place in Kentucky in 1937. Even today, the American mass media ensure public awareness of executions carried out inside prison walls (Kittrie, 1971). Though executions no longer occur in Canada, we have television coverage when criminals convicted of sensational crimes, such as Paul Bernardo, are taken away to prison.

North Americans can agree that punishment deters some crime (Wright, 1994), yet our society also has a high rate of **criminal recidivism,** *subsequent offences by people previously convicted of crimes.* Various studies of people released from prison show that substantial percentages are rearrested and returned to prison within a few years, raising questions about the extent to which punishment actually deters crime. Then, too, only about one-third of all crimes are known to police and, of these, only about 1 in 5 results in an arrest. The old adage that "crime doesn't pay" rings hollow when such a small proportion of offences results in punishment.

General deterrence is even more difficult to investigate scientifically, since we have no way of knowing how people might act if they were unaware of punishments meted out to others. In the debate over capital punishment, critics argue that the death penalty has limited value as a general deterrent in the United States. Furthermore, an examination of the Canadian homicide rates from 1954 to 1986 compiled by Lenton (1989) reveals no sudden increase in homicide rates after 1962, when the last execution occurred, or after 1976, when capital punishment was abolished; in fact, the homicide rate went down for a few years after 1976.

Prisons accomplish short-term societal protection by keeping offenders off the streets, but they do little to reshape attitudes or behaviour (Wright, 1994). Rehabilitation may be an unrealistic expectation, since, according to Sutherland's theory of differential association, locking someone up among criminals for months or years strengthens criminal attitudes and skills. And, according to Hirschi's control theory, incarceration severs whatever social ties inmates may have, making them prone to further crime on release.

Which of the four reasons for punishment do you think is most important in Canadian society? Why?

COMMUNITY-BASED CORRECTIONS

Prisons keep convicted criminals off the streets. But the evidence suggests that they do little to rehabilitate most offenders. Furthermore, prisons are expensive, because of the annual cost of supporting each inmate and the initial costs of building the facilities. One alternative to traditional prison is **community-based corrections,** *correctional programs operating within society at large rather than behind prison walls.* Community-based corrections have three main advantages: reducing costs, reducing overcrowding in prisons, and allowing for supervision of convicts—while eliminating the hardships and stigma of imprisonment. Since the aim of community-based corrections is not to punish but to reform, such programs are usually offered to those who have committed less serious offences (Inciardi, 2000).

Probation

One form of community-based corrections is *probation*, a policy permitting a convicted offender to remain in the community under the regular supervision of a probation officer. Courts may require, for example, that a probationer receive counselling, attend a drug treatment program, hold a job, or avoid associating with known criminals. Should the probationer commit a new offence or fail to live up to the conditions set, the court may revoke probation in favour of imprisonment.

Parole

Parole is a policy of releasing inmates from prison to serve the remainder of their sentence in the local community under the supervision of a parole officer. While some sentences specifically deny the possibility of parole, most inmates become eligible for parole after serving a certain portion of their sentence. At that time, a parole board evaluates the risks and benefits of each inmate's early release from prison. If parole is granted, the parole board monitors the parolee's conduct until the sentence is completed. Should the offender be arrested for another crime or not comply with the conditions of parole, the board can revoke parole and return the offender to prison to complete the sentence.

Sentencing Circles

Learn more about sentencing circles at www.usask.ca/nativelaw/publications/jah/circle.html.

Canada has been experimenting with a unique form of community-based corrections for Aboriginal offenders, who may choose to submit to a *sentencing circle* to determine a suitable punishment. Sentencing circles—which may include the accused, the victim, their families, and other community members—are intended to start the healing process in the accused, the victim and the community at large.

Critical Review Evaluations of probation and parole are mixed. There is little question that these programs are much less expensive than conventional imprisonment and that they free up room in prisons for individuals who commit more serious crimes. Yet research suggests that, although probation does seem to work for some people, it does not significantly reduce recidivism. Parole is also useful to prison officials as a means to encourage good behaviour among inmates. It is too early to evaluate the impacts of sentencing circles on recidivism rates but, if Hirshi is to be believed, they should be effective.

In the end, the criminal justice system cannot eliminate crime, since crime and other forms of deviance are not just the acts of "bad" people, but reflect the operation of society itself. This raises the question of what can be done about crime—which is the subject of the Thinking Critically box (below).

YOUR TURN

Would Emile Durkheim be surprised that the criminal justice system cannot eliminate crime? What about Karl Marx? Explain your answers.

THINKING CRITICALLY
What Can Be Done about Crime?

People throughout Canada are fearful of and fed up with crime. Guard dogs, special locks, and electronic security systems have never been more popular. By 1991, private security guards outnumbered police officers by more than 2 to 1, and Canadians have begun, though slowly, to copy the American practice of building gated communities. While crime rates have gone down, many people perceive increases in their neighbourhoods and women are afraid to walk alone at night near their homes. The perception that we are more vulnerable to crime leads to questions of what we can do about it.

Travis Hirschi, sociologist and author of the well-known *control theory*, has offered his own version of a "community approach" to crime. He begins by pointing out two key traits that define today's criminals:

• The first is age: most offenders are young; crime rates are high among those in the late teens and early twenties, and they fall quickly thereafter.

• The second factor is that most offenders take a short-term view of their lives; law breakers, in Hirschi's words, are people "relatively unable to sustain a course of action towards some distant goal, whether that goal be education, friendship, employment, or criminal gain. In fact, the defining characteristic of offenders appears to be *low self-control*." (Gottfredson and Hirschi, 1995)

These two factors, for Hirschi, are clues that suggest why the criminal

continued

justice system, on its own, can never control crime. For one thing, going to jail is too uncertain and too far removed in time to deter the typical offender. Therefore, calls for "stiffer" sentences actually have little effect. Moreover, by the time many offenders get to prison, they are already moving beyond the "crime years" simply because *they are growing older*. Statistically speaking, then, the offenders aging in prison represent a shrinking crime threat.

Therefore, Hirschi argues that, rather than locking up adults, society needs to focus resources on younger people *before* they commit crimes. He calls for closer attention to teenagers—those at highest risk of criminal behaviour. Effective crime control, he explains, depends on keeping teens away from not only guns and drugs, but also alcohol, cars and even each other when peer influences tend to deviance.

The most effective way to control crime, Hirschi concludes, is for us to teach our children the key trait of *self-control*. This is a job ill-suited to government, and so the responsibility

falls on parents. But government can help by targeting seriously dysfunctional families for assistance and through any other strategy that fosters strong—preferably two-parent—families. Simply "delaying pregnancy among teenage girls," he predicts, "would probably do more to affect long-term crime rates than all the criminal justice programs combined."

The question of what can be done about crime is particularly salient at this time. On Boxing Day, 2005, ten to fifteen young people from rival gangs went on a shooting spree just north of the Eaton Centre on Yonge Street, which was crowded with shoppers. A fifteen-year-old bargain hunter, Jane Creba, was killed by a shot to the head, and six others were injured. Toronto was already reeling from an escalation in gun violence over the past year, and many residents were saying that the city had lost its innocence.

As it happened, Canada was in the middle of a federal election at the time and all of the political parties and leaders weighed in on the subject of

guns and violent crime. Minimum sentencing for people committing crimes with guns generated heated debate. But there were also people arguing that better social programs, rather than stiffer sentences, were the solution. After the election, Prime Minister Stephen Harper announced a two-pronged approach to gun crime: both stiffer minimum sentences for crimes involving guns *and* better social programs to alleviate the conditions that give rise to crime.

WHAT DO YOU THINK?

1. How effective are minimum sentences—say ten years for gun-related crime—in reducing levels of gun crime?
2. Would strengthening two-parent households cut the crime rate? Realistically, can society shape families in this way?
3. Would social programs directed at reducing poverty help to eliminate crime? What specific programs would you suggest?

9 MAKING THE GRADE

The following learning tools will help you see what you know, identify what you still need to learn, and expand your understanding beyond the text. You can also visit this text's Companion Website™ at www.pearsoned.ca/macionis to find useful practice tests.

KEY POINTS

What Is Deviance?

Deviance refers to norm violations ranging from bad manners to serious violence. Research suggests that biological factors, in combination with environmental factors, provide a limited explanation of crime. Psychological studies link deviance to abnormal personality resulting from either biological or environmental causes. Psychological theories help explain some types of deviance.

The root of deviance lies in society rather than individuals, because deviance varies according to cultural norms, is socially defined, and reflects patterns of social power.

The Functions of Deviance: Structural-Functional Analysis

Taking the structural-functional approach, Durkheim explained that deviance affirms norms and values, clarifies moral boundaries, brings people together, and encourages social change. Merton's strain theory explains deviance in terms of a society's cultural goals and the means available to achieve them.

Labelling Deviance: Symbolic-Interaction Analysis

The symbolic-interaction approach is the basis of labelling theory, which holds that deviance lies in people's reaction to someone's behaviour, not in the behaviour itself. Acquiring a stigma of deviance can lead to secondary deviance and a deviant career.

The medicalization of deviance is the transformation of moral and legal deviance into a medical condition. In practice, this means a change from thinking about deviance as "good" or "bad" to thinking in terms of people being "sick" or "well."

Sutherland's differential association theory links deviance to how much others encourage or discourage such behaviour. Hirschi's control theory states that people who are well integrated into society are less likely to engage in deviant behaviour.

Deviance and Inequality: Social-Conflict Analysis

Based on Karl Marx's ideas, social-conflict theory holds that laws and other norms reflect the interests of powerful members of society. While white-collar and corporate crimes cause extensive social harm, offenders are rarely branded as criminals.

White-collar offences are crimes committed by people of high social position as part of their job. Corporate crime refers to illegal action by a company or people acting on its behalf. Organized crime has a long history in North America, especially among people with fewer legitimate opportunities.

Deviance, Race, and Gender

Hate crimes are motivated by racial or other bias. In North America and elsewhere, societies control the behaviour of women more closely than that of men.

Crime

Official statistics show that arrest rates peak in late adolescence and then drop steadily with advancing age. People arrested for property crimes and violent crimes are overwhelmingly male. Poorer people commit more street crime than people with greater wealth. When white-collar and corporate crimes are included among criminal offences, however, the socioeconomic difference in criminal activity becomes smaller. While more White than Black people are arrested for street crime, Black people are arrested more often than their numbers warrant— meaning that their arrest *rate* is high. People of Asian ancestry have low arrest rates, while Aboriginal people are over-represented in arrests, court convictions, and imprisonment.

The Criminal Justice System

Police use a great deal of personal judgment in their work. Arrest is more likely if the offence is serious, bystanders are present, or the accused is of visible minority status.

While the court system is set up as to be adversarial, courts resolve most cases through plea bargaining. Though efficient, this method puts less powerful people at a disadvantage.

Justifications of punishment include retribution, deterrence, rehabilitation, and societal protection. Because its consequences are difficult to evaluate scientifically, punishment—like deviance itself—sparks controversy.

Community-based corrections include probation and parole. Such policies lower the cost of supervising people convicted of crimes and reduce prison overcrowding but have not been shown to reduce recidivism. Canada is experimenting with sentencing circles for Aboriginal inmates.

KEY CONCEPTS

deviance (p. 210) the recognized violation of cultural norms

crime (p. 210) the violation of a society's formally enacted criminal law

social control (p. 210) attempts by society to regulate people's thoughts and behaviour

criminal justice system (p. 210) a formal response by police, courts, and prison officials to alleged violations of the law

labelling theory (p. 215) the idea that deviance and conformity result not so much from what people do as from how others respond to those actions

stigma (p. 216) a powerfully negative label that greatly changes a person's self-concept and social identity

medicalization of deviance (p. 216) the transformation of moral and legal deviance into a medical condition

white-collar crime (p. 219) crime committed by people of high social position in the course of their occupation

corporate crime (p. 219) the illegal actions of a corporation or people acting on its behalf

organized crime (p. 220) a business supplying illegal goods or services

hate crime (p. 221) a criminal act against a person or a person's property by an offender motivated by racial or other bias

violent crimes (p. 223) crimes against people that involve violence or the threat of violence

crimes against property (property crimes) (p. 223) crimes that involve theft of property belonging to others

victimless crimes (p. 223) violations of law in which there are no obvious victims

plea bargaining (p. 226) a legal negotiation in which a prosecutor reduces a charge in exchange for a defendant's guilty plea

retribution (p. 230) an act of moral vengeance by which society makes the offender suffer as much as the suffering caused by the crime

deterrence (p. 230) the attempt to discourage criminality through the use of punishment

rehabilitation (p. 230) a program for reforming the offender to prevent later offences

societal protection (p. 230) rendering an offender incapable of further offences temporarily through imprisonment or permanently by execution

criminal recidivism (p. 232) later offences committed by people previously convicted of crimes

community-based corrections (p. 232) correctional programs operating within society at large rather than behind prison walls

APPLICATIONS & EXERCISES

1. Take a look at the figures in this chapter depicting change in crime rates. What factors explain the changing levels of crime in Canada?

2. Rent a wheelchair for a day or two (check with a local pharmacy or medical supply store), and use it as much as possible. What barriers did you encounter and how did people react to you?

3. Watch an episode of the real-action police show *Cops*. Based on what you see, how would you profile the people who commit crimes?

To reinforce your understanding of this chapter, and to identify topics for further study, visit MySocLab at **www.pearsoned.ca/mysoclab/** for diagnostic tests and a multimedia ebook.

CHAPTER TEN

Social Stratification

What is social stratification?

Why does social inequality exist?

How does social stratification differ in societies
around the world?

On April 10, 1912, the ocean liner *Titanic* slipped away from the docks of Southampton, England, on its first voyage. After stops in France and Ireland, it would cross the northern Atlantic to New York. A proud symbol of the new Industrial Age, the towering ship carried 2300 passengers, some enjoying more luxury than most travellers today could imagine. By contrast, poor immigrants crowded the lower decks, journeying to what they hoped would be a better life in North America.

Two days out, the crew received radio warnings of icebergs in the area but paid little notice. Then, near midnight, as the ship steamed swiftly westwards, a lookout was stunned to see a massive shape rising out of the dark ocean directly ahead. Moments later, the *Titanic* collided with a huge iceberg, its tip almost as tall as the ship itself, which split open its starboard side as if the grand vessel were nothing more than a giant tin can.

Sea water surged into the ship's lower levels, and within 25 minutes people were rushing for the lifeboats. By 2 A.M., the bow of the *Titanic* was submerged and the stern reared high above the water. Clinging to the deck, observed by those in the lifeboats, hundreds of helpless passengers solemnly passed their final minutes before the ship disappeared into the frigid Atlantic Ocean (Lord, 1976).

The tragic loss of more than 1600 lives made news around the world. Looking back dispassionately at this terrible accident with a sociological eye, however, we see that some categories of passengers had much better odds of survival than others. In an age of conventional gallantry, women and children boarded the boats first, so that 80 percent of the casualties were men. Class, too, was at work. Of people holding first-class tickets, more than 60 percent were saved, primarily because they were on the upper decks, where warnings were sounded first and lifeboats were available. Only 36 percent of the second-class passengers survived and, of the third-class passengers on the lower decks, only 24 percent escaped drowning. On board the *Titanic*, class turned out to mean much more than the quality of accommodations—it was a matter of life or death.

The fate of those aboard the *Titanic* dramatically illustrates how social inequality affects the way people live and sometimes whether they live at all. This chapter explores the important concept of social stratification. Chapter 11 ("Social Class in Canada") continues the story by examining social inequality in Canada, and Chapter 12 ("Global Stratification") takes a broader look at how our country fits into a global system of wealth and poverty.

What Is Social Stratification?

For tens of thousands of years, humans the world over lived in small societies of hunter/gatherers. While members of these bands might single out one person as swifter, stronger, or more skilful in collecting food, everyone had roughly the same social standing. As societies became more complex—a process detailed in Chapter 4 ("Society")—a major change

The personal experience of poverty is clear in this photograph of a homeless couple spending the night in a low-cost rooming house. The main sociological insight is that, while we feel the effects of social stratification personally, our social standing is largely the result of the way society—or a world of societies—structures opportunity and reward. To the core of our being, we are all products of social stratification.

came about. Societies began to elevate specific categories of people above others, giving some parts of the population more wealth, power, and prestige than others. **Social stratification**, *a system by which a society ranks categories of people in a hierarchy,* is based on four basic principles:

1. **Social stratification is a trait of society, not simply a reflection of individual differences**. Many of us think of social standing in terms of personal talent and effort and, as a result, we often exaggerate the extent to which we control our own fate. Did a higher percentage of the first-class passengers on the *Titanic* survive because they were better swimmers than second- and third-class passengers? Hardly. They did better because of their privileged position on the ship, which gave them first access to the lifeboats. Similarly, children born into wealthy families are more likely than children born into poverty to enjoy good health, do well in school, succeed in a career, and live a long life. Neither the rich nor the poor created social stratification, yet this system shapes the lives of us all.

2. **Social stratification carries over from generation to generation**. We have only to look at how parents pass their social position on to their children to see that stratification is a trait of societies rather than individuals.

   Some individuals, especially in high-income societies, do experience **social mobility,** *a change in position within the social hierarchy*. Social mobility may be upwards or downwards. Our society celebrates the achievements of a Jean Chrétien, a Céline Dion, a Jim Carrey, or a Wayne Gretzky, all of whom rose to prominence from modest beginnings. But we also acknowledge that people move downwards as a result of business setbacks, unemployment, or illness. More often, people move *horizontally*, exchanging one occupation for another at a comparable level. The social standing of most people remains much the same over their individual lifetime.

3. **Social stratification is universal but variable**. Social stratification is found everywhere. Yet *what* is unequal, and *how* unequal it is, varies from one society to another. In some societies, inequality is mostly a matter of prestige; in others, wealth or power is the key element of difference. In addition, some societies contain more inequality than others. The Thinking about Diversity box (on p. 242) picks up the theme of the *Titanic* tragedy opener—that social class can be a matter of life and death.

4. **Social stratification involves not just inequality but beliefs as well**. Any system of inequality not only gives some people more than others but also defines these arrangements as fair. Like the *what* of inequality, the explanation of *why* people should be unequal differs from society to society.

Caste and Class Systems

Sociologists distinguish between *closed systems*, which allow for little change in social position, and *open systems*, which permit much more social mobility (Tumin, 1985). The *caste system* is closed, and the *class system* is more open.

THE CASTE SYSTEM

A **caste system** is *social stratification based on ascription, or birth*. A pure caste system is closed because birth alone determines a person's entire future, allowing little or no social mobility based on individual effort. People live out their lives in the rigid categories assigned to them, without the possibility of change for the better or worse. Many of the world's societies, most of them agrarian, are caste systems. In India, for example, much of the population still lives in traditional villages where the caste system persists more than sixty years after being formally outlawed.

THINKING ABOUT DIVERSITY:
RACE, CLASS, & GENDER
The *Titanic*: Personal and Canadian Connections

In the spring of 1912, Maria Panula set off from Lapua, Finland, with five sons aged thirteen months to sixteen years. They boarded the magnificent new ship *Titanic* on its maiden voyage to the United States, where they were to join Juha Panula, who had gone on ahead to get established in America. Before leaving, Maria Panula had given an American silver dollar to her five-year-old godson and cousin Viljo Kojola—the father of author Linda Gerber. The Panulas were among the third-class passengers, 76 percent of whom perished in the icy waters of the northern Atlantic. They must have been on the upper decks at the time disaster struck, for Maria made it onto a lifeboat with her infant son Eino. Survivors told her husband that, when she realized her other children did not have places in the lifeboat, she got out again with Eino in her arms to face certain death with the rest of her children.

After the shipwreck, the crew of the *Mackay-Bennett*, a Canadian ship, spotted a number of bodies floating in the water. Among them was "a young child, his blond hair and blue eyes poking through a grey coat trimmed with fur" (Humphreys, 2001). When no one claimed the child's body, the sailors resolved that he would have a proper burial. As a result, in a Halifax cemetery, you can find a tombstone that reads:

> Erected to the memory of an unknown child whose remains were

The grave of the Unknown Child in Halifax, recently identified as Eino Panula of Finland (second cousin of author L.M. Gerber).

recovered after the disaster to the 'Titanic' April 15th 1912.

Thereafter, the grave was known, simply, as that of the Unknown Child.

In the mid–1990s, Ryan Parr, a professor at Lakehead University in Thunder Bay, and Alan Ruffman, a Halifax oceanographer and historian, pulled together an international team of researchers who would use archives, genealogy, and cutting-edge DNA testing to determine the identity of the Unknown Child. Since there were six children of approximately the right age who went down with the *Titanic*, their task—still immensely complex—was limited to tracking down the families of

those six children, getting blood samples from relatives on the maternal side of each family, and matching the mitochondrial DNA from the women with that of the tiny exhumed body. By early November 2002, the researchers had identified the child as Eino Panula.

The news hit the papers all over the world, but nowhere with as much impact as in Finland and Canada. Relatives had lived for ninety years with the story of Maria Panula, her children, and the *Titanic* tucked away in their memory banks. No one could have imagined that one day a nameless child buried in Halifax would be identified as one of our own kin. Had the Paleo-DNA laboratory of Lakehead University not been capable of extracting and analyzing the DNA from tiny bone fragments, and had Parr and Ruffman not dared to dream, none of this would have happened.

WHAT DO YOU THINK?

1. How do life and death on the *Titanic* reflect the class structure of modern societies?
2. Were you aware of the power of modern genealogical research?
3. Are you curious about your family history and genealogy? Does your family keep records? Are there rags-to-riches stories, major achievements, or fascinating tales in your background?

Source: Based on Humphreys (2002) and personal knowledge of Linda Gerber.

An Illustration: India

The Indian system identifies four major castes (or *varna*, a Sanskrit word that means "colour"): Brahman, Kshatriya, Vaishya, and Shudra. On the local level, each of these is composed of hundreds of subcaste groups (or *jati*). From birth, a caste system determines the direction of a person's life:

- First, with the exception of farming, which is open to everyone, families in each caste perform one type of

THINKING GLOBALLY

Race as Caste: A Report from South Africa

At the southern tip of the African continent lies South Africa, a country with a land area slightly larger than Ontario's with a population, in 2005, of about 47 million. For 300 years the Indigenous Africans were ruled by White people, first by the Dutch traders and farmers who settled there in the mid–seventeenth century, then by the British, who colonized the area early in the nineteenth century. By the early 1900s, the British had taken over the entire country, naming it the Union of South Africa. In 1961, the nation declared its independence from Britain, calling itself the Republic of South Africa, but freedom for the majority—the Indigenous Africans, referred to as "Blacks"—was still decades away.

To ensure their political control over the population of Black Africans as well as people of mixed race and Asian ancestry, the British colonial administrators created a policy of *apartheid*, or racial separation. Apartheid, written into law in 1948, denied Blacks national citizenship, ownership of land, and any voice in the government; Blacks had to live on Bantustans, which were similar to reserves set aside for Indians in Canada. As the lowest caste, Blacks received little schooling and performed menial, low-paying jobs. White people with even average wealth had at least one Black household servant. The White minority claimed that apartheid protected their cultural traditions from the influence of people they believed to be inferior beings. When Black South Africans resisted apartheid, the White government used brutal military repression to maintain its power.

Even so, steady resistance—especially from younger Black South Africans, who demanded a political voice and economic opportunity—gradually forced change. Criticism from other industrial nations added to the pressure. By the mid–1980s, the tide began to turn as the South African government granted limited political rights to people of mixed race and Asian ancestry. Next came the right of all people to form labour unions, to enter occupations once limited to Whites, and to own property. Officials also repealed

To view the findings of the Truth and Reconciliation Commission established by the government of Nelson Mandela in an attempt for South Africa to heal from apartheid, visit www.doj.gov.za/trc.

laws that separated the races in public places. The pace of change increased in 1990 with the release from prison of Nelson Mandela, who led the final assault against apartheid. In 1994, the first national election open to all races made Mandela president—an event that finally ended centuries of White minority rule.

Despite this dramatic political change, social stratification in South Africa is still based on race. Even with the right to own property, one-third of Black South Africans have no work, and the majority remain dirt poor. The worst off are some 7 million *ukuhleleleka* ("marginal people" in the Xhosa language). Soweto-by-the-Sea may sound like a summer getaway, but it is home to thousands of people who live crammed into shacks made of packing cases, corrugated metal, card-

board, and other discarded materials. There is no electricity for lights or refrigeration. Without plumbing, people use buckets to haul sewage; women line up to take a turn at a single water tap that serves more than a thousand people. Jobs are hard to come by, and those who do find work are lucky to earn $250 a month.

South Africa's current president, Thabo Mbeki, who was elected in 1999, leads a nation still crippled by its history of racial caste. Tourism is up and holds the promise of an economic boom in years to come, but the country can break from the past only by providing real opportunity to all its people.

WHAT DO YOU THINK?

1. How has race been a form of caste in South Africa?
2. While apartheid is no longer law, why does racial inequality continue to shape South African society?
3. Does race operate as an element of caste in North America? Explain your answer.

Sources: Fredrickson (1981), Wren (1991), Hawthorne (1999), and Mabry and Masland (1999).

In India, the traditional caste system still guides people's choice of work, especially in rural areas. Below the four basic castes are the Harijans, people defined as outcasts or untouchables. These people perform jobs, such as cleaning the streets, defined as unclean for others of higher social position.

work, as priests, soldiers, barbers, leather workers, sweepers, and so on.

- Second, a caste system demands that people marry others of the same ranking. If people were to have "mixed" marriages with members of other castes, what rank would their children hold? Sociologists call this pattern of marrying within a social category *endogamous* marriage (*endo* stems from the Greek, meaning "within"). According to tradition—this practice is now rare and found only in remote rural areas—Indian parents select their children's marriage partners, often before the children reach their teens.

- Third, caste guides everyday life by keeping people in the company of "their own kind." Norms reinforce this practice by teaching, for example, that a "purer" person of a higher caste is "polluted" by contact with someone of lower standing.

- Fourth, caste systems rest on powerful cultural beliefs. Indian culture is built on the Hindu tradition that doing the caste's life work and accepting an arranged marriage are moral duties.

Caste and Agrarian Life

Caste systems are typical of agrarian societies because agriculture demands a lifelong routine of hard work. By teaching a sense of moral duty, a caste system ensures that people are disciplined for a lifetime of work and are willing to perform the same jobs as their parents. Thus, the caste system has hung on in rural areas of India. People living in the industrial cities of India have many more choices about work and marriage partners than people in rural areas.

Another country dominated by caste is South Africa, although the system of *apartheid*, or separation of the races, is no longer legal and is now in decline. The Thinking Globally box (on p. 243) takes a closer look.

YOUR TURN

Are there elements of caste in Canadian society? To what extent do parents pass on their social position to children? What about the idea that there are "women's" jobs and "men's" jobs? Where do Aboriginal people stand in our society?

THE CLASS SYSTEM

Because a modern economy must attract people to work in many occupations other than farming, it depends on developing people's talents in many diverse fields. This gives rise to a **class system,** *social stratification based on both birth and individual achievement.* Class systems are more open than caste systems, so people who gain schooling and skills may experience social mobility. As a result, class distinctions become blurred, and even blood relatives may have different social standings. Categorizing people according to their colour, sex, or social background comes to be seen as wrong in modern societies as all people gain political rights and, in principle, equal standing before the law. In addition, work is no longer fixed at birth but involves some personal choice. Greater individuality also translates into more freedom in selecting a marriage partner.

MERITOCRACY

The concept of **meritocracy** refers to *social stratification based on personal merit.* Because industrial societies need to develop a broad range of abilities beyond farming, stratification is based not just on the accident of birth but also on *merit* (from a Latin word meaning "worthy of praise"), which includes a person's knowledge, abilities, and effort. A rough measure of merit is a person's job and how well it is done. To increase meritocracy, industrial societies expand equality of opportunity and teach people to expect inequality of rewards based on individual performance.

In a pure meritocracy, social position would depend entirely on a person's ability and effort. Such a system would have ongoing social mobility, blurring social categories as individuals continuously move up or down in the system, depending on their latest performance. Caste societies define "merit" in terms of loyalty to the system—that is, dutifully performing whatever job comes with a person's birth. Caste systems waste human potential, but they are very orderly. A need for order is the reason industrial societies keep some elements of caste—such as letting wealth pass from generation to generation—rather than becoming complete meritocracies. A pure meritocracy would weaken families and other social groupings. After all, economic performance is not everything: Would we want to evaluate our family members solely on how successful they are in their jobs outside the home? Probably not. Class systems in industrial societies move towards meritocracy—to promote productivity and efficiency—but keep caste elements, such as family, to maintain order and social unity.

YOUR TURN

How much of your social position is owed to merit (i.e., personal ability and effort), and how much is owed to caste (i.e., passed on from your parents)?

STATUS CONSISTENCY

Status consistency is *the degree of consistency in a person's social standing across various dimensions of social inequality.* A caste system has limited social mobility and high status consistency, so the typical person has the same relative ranking with regard to wealth, power, and prestige. The greater mobility of class systems produces less status consistency. In Canada, for example, most university professors with advanced academic degrees (a Ph.D. and, in some fields, additional years of postdoctoral study) enjoy high social prestige but earn only average salaries. Low status consistency means that *classes* are much harder to define than *castes*.

ASCRIPTION AND ACHIEVEMENT: ENGLAND

The mix of caste and meritocracy in class systems is well illustrated by England, an industrial nation with a long agrarian history.

The Estate System

In the Middle Ages (from about 500 to about 1400), England had a castelike feudal system of three *estates* (Laslett, 1984).[1] The *first estate* was the clergy, who were thought to speak with the authority of God. Some clergy were local priests, who lived simple lives, but the highest church officials lived in palaces and presided over an organ-ization that owned much land, the major source of wealth; they also had a great deal of power to shape the political events of the day.

The *second estate* was a hereditary nobility that made up barely 5 percent of the population. The royal family—the king and queen at the top of the power structure—as well as nobles (including those titled as duke, marquess, earl, viscount, and baron) together owned most of the nation's land. Most of these men and women were wealthy and had no occupation; they had no need to work for an income. Well tended by servants, noble men used their leisure time to develop skills in horseback riding and warfare, and to cultivate refined tastes in art, music, and literature. To prevent vast landholdings from being divided by heirs when the nobles died, the English law of *primogeniture* (from the Latin meaning "firstborn") demanded that all land pass to the oldest son or other male relation. Younger sons had to find other means of support. Some became leaders in the church, where they would live as well as they were used to; others became military officers or judges or took up other professions considered honourable for gentlemen. In an age when no woman could inherit her father's property and few women had the opportunity to earn a living on their own, a noble daughter depended for her security on marrying well.

Below the clergy and the nobility, the vast majority of men and women formed the *third estate*, or commoners. Most commoners were serfs working land owned by the nobles or the church. Unlike members of the first or second estates, most had little schooling and were illiterate.

By the end of the eighteenth century, as the Industrial Revolution expanded England's economy, some commoners living in cities made enough money to challenge the nobility. More emphasis on meritocracy, the growing importance of money, and the expansion of schooling and legal rights eventually blurred social rankings and gave rise to a class system that remains more or less in place today.

Perhaps it is a sign of the times that, these days, traditional titles are put up for sale by nobles who need money. In 1996, for example, Earl Spencer (the brother of Princess Diana) sold one of his titles, Lord of Wimbledon, to raise the $300 000 he needed to redo the plumbing in one of his large homes (McKee, 1996).

England Today

England has a class system, but caste elements from England's past are still evident today. A small number of British families still holds considerable inherited wealth and enjoys the highest prestige, schooling at excellent universities, and political influence. A traditional monarch, Queen Elizabeth II, is

---

[1] The estate systems of the England, Sweden, and Finland placed nobility at the top, above the clergy and the commoners. The system in France placed the clergy at the top, above the nobility and the commoners.

In North American society, everyone's social position results from a mix of birth and individual achievement. The Wayans brothers, stars of both television and film, were born to a family with ten children in New York and rose to become among the highest-paid people in the country. Such a story is fairly common in the entertainment business, which is relatively open to new talent. Canada's Jim Carey, born to poor parents in Jackson's Point, Ontario (on Lake Simcoe), is enormously successful as a comedic actor—in the United States.

the United Kingdom's (and Canada's) head of state, and Parliament's House of Lords is composed of "peers," about half of whom are of noble birth; the House of Lords retains authority approximating that of the Canadian Senate, as well

as responsibility for legal judgments. (One of the peers is Conrad Black, who gave up Canadian citizenship in 1999 to become a baron, Lord Black of Crossharbour.) Control of government has rested, since the thirteenth century, in the House of Commons, where the prime minister and other leaders now reach their positions by achievement—winning an election—rather than by birth.

You can find a list of the richest people in Great Britain and other countries in London's *Sunday Times* at www.sunday-times.co.uk/richlist/.

Further down in the class hierarchy, roughly one-quarter of the British people now form the middle class. Many earn a comfortable income from a profession or business, and are likely to have investments in the form of stocks and bonds. Below the middle class, perhaps half of all Britons think of themselves as "working class," earning a modest income through manual labour. The remaining one-quarter of the British people make up the lower class, the poor who lack steady work or who work full time but are paid too little to live comfortably. Most lower-class Britons live in the nation's northern and western regions, which have become economically depressed by the closings of mines and factories.

Today's British class system has a mix of caste elements and meritocracy, producing a highly stratified society with some opportunity to move upwards or downwards. One result of the historical estate system is that social mobility occurs less often in the United Kingdom than it does in the United States (Kerckhoff, *et al.*, 1985). This more rigid system of inequality in the United Kingdom is reflected in the importance attached to accent. Distinctive patterns of speech develop in any society when people are set off from one another over many generations. People in the United States treat accent as a clue to where a person lives or grew up, easily identifying, for example, a midwestern twang or a southern drawl. In the United Kingdom, however, accent is a mark of social class, with upper-class people speaking "the Queen's English" but most people speaking "like commoners." So different are these accents that the British seem to be, as the saying goes, "a single people divided by a common language."

ANOTHER EXAMPLE: JAPAN

Social stratification in Japan also mixes caste and meritocracy. Japan is both the world's oldest continuously operating monarchy and a modern society where wealth follows individual achievement.

Feudal Japan

By the fifth century C.E., Japan was an agrarian society with a rigid caste system in which an imperial family ruled over nobles and commoners. The emperor ruled by divine right (meaning that he claimed that God intended him to rule), and his *shogun* (military leader) enforced the emperor's rule with the help of regional nobles or warlords.

Below the nobility were the *samurai*, a warrior caste whose name means "to serve." This second rank of Japanese society was made up of soldiers who learned martial arts and who lived by a code of honour based on absolute loyalty to their leaders.

As in Great Britain, most people in Japan at this time in history were commoners who worked very hard to live from day to day. Unlike their European counterparts, however,

Can you spot Great Britain's Prince William in this photo? He's just to the right of the centre in this wave at a rugby match. While he is part of a royal family that traces its ancestry for a thousand years, today's more egalitarian times encourage royals to try to act more like commoners in public.

Japanese commoners were not lowest in rank; below them were the *burakumin* (outcasts) looked down on by both lord and commoner. Like the lowest caste in India, these outcasts lived apart from others, performed the most distasteful work, and could not change their social standing.

Modern Japan

By the 1860s, the Japanese nobles realized that their traditional caste system would prevent the country from entering the modern industrial era. Besides, as in Britain, some nobles were happy to have their children marry wealthy commoners who had more money than they did. As Japan opened up to the larger world, the traditional caste system weakened. In 1871, the Japanese legally banned the social category of outcast, although today some people still look down on those whose ancestors held this rank. After Japan's defeat in World War II, the nobility lost their privileges; only the emperor remains as a symbol of Japan's traditions and he has little real power.

Social stratification in Japan is much different from the rigid caste system of centuries ago. Today, Japanese society consists of upper, upper-middle, lower-middle, and lower classes; the exact lines between these classes are unclear to most Japanese, and many people do move between classes over time. But because Japanese culture tends to respect tradition, family background is never far from the surface when sizing up someone's social standing. Officially, everyone is equal before the law but, in reality, many people still look at one another through the centuries-old lens of caste.

Finally, traditional ideas about gender continue to shape Japanese society. Legally, the two sexes are equal, but men dominate women in many ways. Because Japanese parents are more likely to send sons than daughters to college, there is a significant gender gap in education. With the recent economic downturn in Japan, many more women have entered the labour force. But most working women fill lower-level support positions in the corporate world, only rarely assuming leadership roles. In short, individual achievement in Japan's modern class system operates in the shadow of centuries of traditional male privilege (Norbeck, 1983; Brinton, 1988; French, 2002).

To review the lively debate in 2006 over whether a princess could be in line to become emperor of Japan, see http://news.bbc.co.uk/1/hi/world/asia-pacific/1656150.stm.

CLASSLESS SOCIETIES? THE FORMER SOVIET UNION

Nowhere in the world do we find a society without some degree of social inequality. Yet some nations, such as Russia, have claimed to be classless.

The Russian Revolution

The former Union of Soviet Socialist Republics was born out of a revolution in Russia in 1917. The Russian Revolution ended the feudal estate system ruled by nobles; farms, factories, and other productive property were transferred from private ownership to state control. The Russian Revolution was guided by the ideas of Karl Marx, who observed that private ownership of productive property is the basis of social classes (see Chapter 4, "Society"). When the state took control of the economy, Soviet officials boasted that they had created the first modern classless society.

After the collapse of the Soviet Union in 1991, that nation began a transition towards a market economy. Since then, some people have become quite rich, but others have lost their jobs as old, inefficient factories closed. As a result, the problem of poverty has become widespread, affecting perhaps one-third of the Russian people. Scenes like this one are all too common.

Critics, however, pointed out that, based on their jobs, the Soviet people actually were stratified into four unequal categories. At the top were *apparatchiks* (high government officials). Next came the Soviet intelligentsia, including lower government officials, college professors, scientists, physicians, and engineers. Below them were manual workers and, at the lowest level, the rural peasantry. In reality, the Soviet Union was not classless at all. But putting factories, farms, colleges, and hospitals under state control did create more economic equality—although with sharp differences in power—than in capitalist societies such as the United States.

The Modern Russian Federation

In 1985, Mikhail Gorbachev came to power in the Soviet Union with a new economic program known as *perestroika* (restructuring). Gorbachev saw that, while the Soviet system had reduced economic inequality, living standards were far behind those of other industrial nations. Gorbachev tried to generate economic growth by reducing the inefficient centralized control of the economy. Gorbachev's economic reforms turned into one of the most dramatic social movements in history. People in the Soviet Union and in other socialist countries of Eastern Europe blamed their poverty and their lack of basic freedoms on the repressive ruling class of Communist party officials. Beginning in 1989, people throughout Eastern Europe toppled their socialist governments and, in 1991, the Soviet Union itself collapsed, remaking itself as the Russian Federation.

The Soviet Union's story shows that social inequality involves more than economic resources. Soviet society did not have the extremes of wealth and poverty found in the United Kingdom, Japan, and the United States. But an elite class existed all the same, one based on political power rather than wealth.

What about social mobility in so-called classless societies? During the twentieth century, there was as much upwards social mobility in the Soviet Union as in the United States. Rapidly expanding industry and government drew many poor rural peasants into factories and offices. This trend illustrates what sociologists call **structural social mobility,** *a shift in the social position of large numbers of people owing more to changes in society itself than to individual efforts.* During the 1990s, the forces of structural social mobility in the new Russian Federation turned downwards. One indicator is that the average life span for Russian men dropped by eight years and for women by two years. Many factors are involved in this decline, including Russia's poor health care system, but the Russian people clearly have suffered in the turbulent period of economic change that began in 1991 (Bohlen, 1998; Gerber and Hout, 1998).

In the long run, closing inefficient state industries may improve the nation's economic performance. But in the short run, most citizens face hard times as living standards fall. As businesses return to private ownership, the gap between rich and poor has grown. Today, some Russians praise the recent changes while others hang on, patiently hoping for better times.

CHINA: EMERGING SOCIAL CLASSES

Sweeping political and economic change has affected not just the Russian Federation but also the People's Republic of China. After the Communist revolution in 1949, the state took control of all productive property. Communist party leader Mao Zedong declared all types of work to be equally important, so that, officially, social classes no longer existed. The new program greatly reduced economic inequality. But, as in the Soviet Union, social differences remained: the country was ruled by a political elite with enormous power and considerable privilege; below them were managers of large factories as

GLOBAL SNAPSHOT

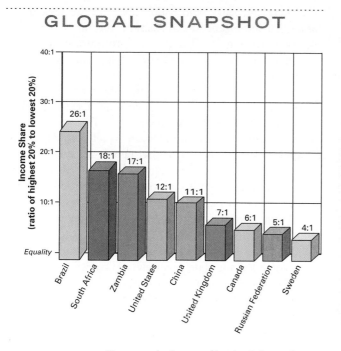

FIGURE 10-1   Economic Inequality in Selected Countries*

Many low- and middle-income countries have greater economic inequality than the United States. But the United States has more economic inequality than most high-income nations.

*These data are the most recent available, representing income share for various years between 1998 and 2003.

Sources: U.S. Census Bureau (2005) and World Bank (2005).

In recent decades, the government of China has permitted a market economy to operate in limited areas of the country. The result has been increased production and the emergence of a new business class with a lifestyle similar to that of wealthy people in North America.

well as skilled professionals; next came industrial workers; and, at the bottom, were rural peasants, who were not allowed to leave their villages and migrate to cities.

Further economic change came in 1978 when Mao died and Deng Xiaoping became China's leader. The state gradually loosened its hold on the economy, allowing a new class of business owners to emerge. Communist party leaders remain in control of the country and some have prospered, as they have joined the ranks of the small but wealthy elite who control new privately run industries. Much of this new economic growth has been concentrated in coastal areas, where living standards have soared far above those in China's rural interior.

Today, a new class system is emerging with a mix of the former political hierarchy and a new business hierarchy. Economic inequality in China has increased and, as Figure 10–1 shows, it is now about as great as in the United States—and substantially greater than in Canada and the United Kingdom. At this stage, scholars point to the new system's complexity and debate its likely future. But one lesson from China is clear: with new patterns of inequality emerging over time, social stratification is highly dynamic (Bian, 2002).

IDEOLOGY: THE POWER BEHIND STRATIFICATION

How do societies persist without sharing resources more equitably? The highly stratified British estate system and Japanese caste system each survived for centuries and, for 2000 years, people in India accepted the idea that they should be privileged or poor based on the accident of birth. A major reason that social hierarchies endure is **ideology,** *cultural beliefs that justify particular social arrangements, including patterns of inequality.* A belief—for example, the idea that rich people are smart and poor people are lazy—is ideological to the extent that it defines the rich as worthy and suggests that those who are less well off deserve their poverty.

Plato and Marx on Ideology

According to the Ancient Greek philosopher Plato (427–347 B.C.E.), every culture considers some type of inequality fair. Although Karl Marx understood this, he was far more critical of inequality than Plato. Marx criticized capitalist societies for defending wealth and power in the hands of a few as "a law of the marketplace." Capitalist law, he continued, defines the right to own property and ensures that money stays within the same families from one generation to the next. In short, Marx concluded, culture and institutions combine to support a society's elite, which is why established hierarchies last a long time.

Historical Patterns of Ideology

Ideology changes along with a society's economy and technology. Because agrarian societies depend on most people devoting themselves to lifelong labour, they develop caste systems that imbue performing the duties of a person's social position a moral responsibility. With the rise of industrial capitalism, an ideology of meritocracy arises, defining wealth and power as prizes to be won by those who perform the best. This change means that the poor—often the targets of charity under feudalism—are looked down on as personally undeserving. This harsh view is found in the ideas of the early sociologist Herbert Spencer, who modified the theories of Darwin on biological evolution; Spencer argued that society is a "jungle" with the "fittest" people rising to wealth and the "failures" sinking into miserable poverty.

History shows how difficult it is to change social stratification. However, challenges to the status quo always arise. The traditional idea that a woman's place is in the home, for example, has given way to increased economic opportunities for women in many societies today. The continuing progress towards racial equality in South Africa demonstrates widespread rejection of the ideology of apartheid. Social stratification, wherever it exists, can be analyzed from the theoretical perspectives of structural-functionalism, social conflict, and symbolic interactionism, to which we now turn.

The Functions of Social Stratification

Why does social stratification exist at all? One answer, consistent with the structural-functional approach, is that social inequality plays a vital part in the operation of society. This argument was set forth more than sixty years ago by Kingsley Davis and Wilbert Moore (1945).

THE DAVIS-MOORE THESIS

The **Davis-Moore thesis** states that *social stratification has beneficial consequences for the operation of a society.* How else, ask Davis and Moore, can we explain the fact that some form of social stratification has been found in every society? Davis

and Moore note that modern societies have hundreds of occupational positions of varying importance. Certain jobs—say, washing windows, cutting grass, or answering a telephone—are fairly easy and can be performed by almost anyone. Other jobs—such as designing new generations of computers or transplanting human organs—are difficult and demand the scarce talents of people with extensive and expensive training.

Therefore, Davis and Moore explain, the greater the functional importance of a position, the more rewards a society attaches to it. This strategy promotes productivity and efficiency because rewarding important work with income, prestige, power, and leisure encourages people to do these jobs and to work better, longer, and harder. In short, unequal rewards—the essence of social stratification—benefit society as a whole.

Davis and Moore claim that any society could be egalitarian, but only to the extent that people are willing to let *anyone* perform *any* job. Equality would also demand that someone who carries out a job poorly be rewarded the same as someone who performs it well. Such a system clearly would offer little incentive for people to try their best, reducing a society's productive efficiency.

The Davis-Moore thesis suggests the reason for stratification; it does not state precisely what rewards a society should give to any occupational position or just how unequal rewards should be. It merely points out that socioeconomic positions a society considers more important must carry enough reward to draw talented people away from less important work.

YOUR TURN

Use the Davis and Moore logic to explain why professors give grades from A to F. What would happen if they gave everyone the same grade? Explain.

Critical Review Although the Davis-Moore thesis is an important contribution to understanding social stratification, it has provoked criticism. Melvin Tumin (1953) wondered, first, how we assess the importance of a particular occupation. Perhaps the high rewards our society gives to physicians results partly from deliberate efforts by the medical profession to limit the supply of physicians and, thereby, increase the demand for their services. In Canada, the Canadian Medical Association controls the certification of physicians, but provincial governments control the number of positions in medical schools and the availability of residencies. Furthermore, do rewards actually reflect the contribution someone makes to society? Oprah Winfrey earns more in one day than the U.S. president earns all year. Would anyone argue that hosting a talk show is more important than leading a country? Before she left the corporate world for politics with a $150 000 income, Belinda Stronach was earning $12.5 million annually as president and CEO of Magna International. Then there are many cases such as that of Larry Ellison, the chief executive officer of Oracle who, even as the value of his company slid downwards, still earned US$700 million, an amount that would take a typical U.S. soldier almost 60 000 years to earn (Benjamin, 2002; Broder, 2002; Dunn, 2003). Do corporate executives deserve such megasalaries for their contributions to society? Take a look at the Applying Sociology box (pp. 252–53) for more on the topic of fair remuneration.

Second, Tumin claimed that Davis and Moore ignore how caste elements of social stratification can *prevent* the development of individual talent. Born to privilege, rich children have opportunities to develop their abilities, which is something many gifted poor children never have.

Third, living in a society that places so much emphasis on money, we tend to overestimate the importance of high-paying work; how much does someone who trades international currencies contribute to society? For the same reason, it is difficult for us to see the value of work that is not oriented towards making money, such as parenting, creative writing, playing music in a symphony, or just being a good friend to someone in need (Packard, 2002).

 Do corporate CEOs deserve their high salaries? The AFL-CIO offers a critical view at its website, where it tracks CEO salaries: www.aflcio.org/corporatewatch/paywatch/.

Societies differ in the importance they attach to both money and inequality. The Media Perspectives box (on p. 254) explains that European lifestyle goals differ from those of Americans. Where, one might ask, do Canadians fit in that continuum?

Finally, by suggesting that social stratification benefits all of society, the Davis-Moore thesis ignores the role of social inequality in promoting conflict and even revolution. This criticism leads us to the social-conflict approach, which provides a very different explanation for social inequality.

Stratification and Conflict

Social-conflict analysis argues that, rather than benefitting society as a whole, social stratification benefits some people and disadvantages others. This analysis draws heavily on the ideas of Karl Marx, with contributions from Max Weber.

KARL MARX: CLASS CONFLICT

Karl Marx, whose ideas are discussed fully in Chapter 4 ("Society"), explained that most people have one of two basic relationships to the means of economic production: they either own productive property or labour for others. Different productive roles arise from different social classes. In mediaeval Europe, the nobility and church officials owned the land on which peasants laboured as farmers. In industrial class systems, the capitalists (or the bourgeoisie) own the factories, which use the labour of workers (the proletarians). Marx lived during the nineteenth century, a time when a few industrialists in the United States were amassing great fortunes. Andrew Carnegie, J.P. Morgan,

John D. Rockefeller, and John Jacob Astor (one of the few very rich passengers to die on the *Titanic*) lived in fabulous mansions staffed by dozens of servants. Even by today's standards, their incomes were staggering. For example, Andrew Carnegie earned about US$20 million a year in 1900 (more than US$100 million in today's dollars), when the average American worker earned roughly US$500 a year (Baltzell, 1964; Pessen, 1990).

Marx explained that capitalist society *reproduces the class structure in each new generation.* This happens as families gain wealth and pass it down from generation to generation. But, he predicted, oppression and misery would eventually drive the working majority to come together to overthrow capitalism.

Critical Review Marx has had enormous influence on sociological thinking. But his revolutionary ideas—calling for the overthrow of capitalist society—also make his work highly controversial. One of the strongest criticisms of marxism is that it denies a central idea of the Davis-Moore thesis: that a system of unequal rewards is necessary to place talented people in the right jobs and to motivate them to work hard. Marx separated reward from performance; his egalitarian ideal was based on the principle "from each according to his ability; to each according to his needs" (Marx and Engels, 1972 [orig. 1848]:388). However, failure to reward individual performance may be precisely what caused the low productivity of the former Soviet Union and other socialist economies around the world. Defenders of Marxism respond to such criticism by asking why it is assumed that humanity is inherently selfish rather than social; individual rewards are not the only way to motivate people to perform their social roles (Clark, 1991; Fiske, 1991).

WHY NO MARXIST REVOLUTION?

Despite Marx's prediction, capitalism is still thriving. Why have industrial workers not overthrown capitalism? Ralf Dahrendorf (1959) suggested four reasons:

- *The fragmentation of the capitalist class.* Today, millions of stockholders, rather than single families, own most large companies. Day-to-day corporate operations are in the hands of a large class of managers, who may or may not be major stockholders. With stock widely held— about 50 percent of North American adults own stocks, some in the form of pension funds—more and more people have a direct stake in the capitalist system.

- *A higher standard of living.* As Chapter 16 ("The Economy and Work") explains, a century ago, most workers were in factories or on farms employed in **blue-collar occupations,** *lower-prestige jobs that involve mostly manual labour.* Today, most workers are engaged in **white-collar occupations,** *higher-prestige jobs that involve mostly mental activity.* These jobs are in sales,

APPLYING SOCIOLOGY

Salaries: Are the Rich Worth What They Earn?

According to the Davis-Moore thesis, rewards reflect an occupation's value to society. But are the talents of Julia Louis-Dreyfus, who earned about US$13 million a year as a sidekick on *Seinfeld*, worth almost as much as the efforts of all one hundred U.S. senators? When Roger Clemens played for the Toronto Blue Jays, was he worth as much as 35 or 40 of Canada's physicians or surgeons? In short, do earnings reflect the social importance of work? Salaries in industrial/capitalist societies, such as Canada, are the product of market forces. Defenders of the laws of supply and demand claim that the market impartially evaluates worth, rewarding each worker according to the supply of the talent in question and the public demand for it. According to this view, movie and television stars, top athletes, skilled professionals, and many business executives have rare talents that are much in demand; therefore, they may earn hundreds of times more than the typical worker.

According to the census of 2001, the average Canadian worker—employed full time, all year—earned $43 298; those with university certificates, diplomas and degrees earned twice as much as workers who did not graduate from high school: $61 156 and $32 240, respectively, for full-

Céline Dion is a multimillionaire who may earn as much as US$85 million for giving three concerts a year in Las Vegas.

time work. Cashiers, bartenders, and farmers made about $20 000 a year, actors about $36 000. Plumbers and fishers earned $40 000, while registered nurses earned $46 000, if they were lucky enough to be employed full-time. Crane operators and secondary school teachers earned about

$50 000, while engineers made $67 000. University professors and physicians with seven to ten years of schooling beyond the B.A. or B.Sc. earned $75 000 and $130 000, respectively (Statistics Canada, 2006b). Our members of parliament earned $150 000—more than the average physician—while the prime minister earned $260 000. Nonetheless, the earnings of physicians and parliamentarians pale in comparison with those of corporate executives, popular athletes, and entertainers.

Of course, celebrity salaries are the highest in the United States. Barry Bonds, with a 2006 salary of US$20 million, garners more than US$40 000 per hour playing baseball for the San Francisco Giants. And what about the US$100 000 Jim Carrey earns for every hour he spends making movies? Bill Cosby commands about US$100 000 per hour to take the stage, and Oprah Winfrey earns about US$200 000 for each hour she chats with guests before the television cameras. Mel Gibson landed a salary of US$25 million for filming *The Patriot*, and, at the start of the 2003 television season, the six actors in *Friends* were being paid US$1.2 million per episode (plus a percentage of profits). Understandably, many Canadians—among them Jim Carrey, Michael J. Fox, Mike

management, teaching, and other service fields. Most of today's white-collar workers do not think of themselves as an "industrial proletariat." Just as importantly, the average income in North America rose almost tenfold over the course of the twentieth century, even allowing for inflation, and the number of hours in the work week decreased. In short, most workers today are far better off than workers were a century ago, as a result of structural mobility. A rising standard of living means that people are more willing to accept the status quo.

- *More worker organizations.* Workers today have the right to form labour unions that make demands of management and to back up their demands with threats of work slowdowns and strikes. As a result, labour disputes are settled without threatening the capitalist system.

- *Greater legal protections.* Over the past century, North American governments have passed laws to make workplaces safer. In addition, pensions, employment insurance, disability grants, and social security now provide workers with greater financial security protection against penury.

Myers, Pamela Anderson, William Shatner, Tom Green, and Céline Dionne—have gone to the United States in search of greater opportunity and remuneration.

The top five executive salaries in Canada in 2002 include: $52 million to Frank Stronach as chair of the board of Magna International, $17 million to Travis Engen of Alcan, $12.6 million to Don Wright of the TD Bank, $12.5 million to Belinda Stronach as president and CEO of Magna International, and $12.3 million to Paul Tellier of the Canadian National Railway (*Report on Business*, 2003:147; globeinvestor, 2003).[1] Keeping in mind that the remuneration of American executives is often in the hundreds of millions of dollars, one might wonder if Canadian CEOs really deserve these incomes. On the other hand, who can deny the accomplishments of Frank Stronach—who "arrived in Canada from Austria in 1954 (as Frank Strohsack) with only his machinist papers and $200" and went on to establish an international giant in the auto parts industry (Newman, 1998: 117)? Clearly, Stronach and others like him have qualities that set them apart from the average Canadian.

Some critics claim that the market is not a good evaluator of occupational importance. The economy, they argue, is dominated by a small number of people who manipulate the system for their own benefit. In the 1980s, thirty-two of Canada's wealthiest families played "monopoly with the money of average Canadians" (Francis, 1986).

Peter C. Newman (1998) argues that this "old" establishment—based on inherited wealth, private schools, club contacts, and intermarriage—has been pushed aside by the "new" establishment, which anyone can join, comprised of hard-driving risk-takers, whose global networks are maintained through their cell phones or BlackBerries rather than posh country clubs. In this new world, you can be nobody one day and a very big somebody the next—and reverse the process just as quickly. Again, it is the rare individual who can tolerate the stress level of this way of life. Most of us take holidays for granted: these new business titans do not take real holidays at all. If they do travel for pleasure, it is with BlackBerry and computer in hand; they must remain connected.

On the negative side, corporate executives can pay themselves multi-million-dollar salaries and bonuses whether or not their companies do well. Gilbert Amelio, CEO of Apple Computer, laid off more than 4000 employees during 1996 and his company's stock price tumbled by almost 40 percent; yet he still paid himself more than US$23 million for his efforts. In Canada, Paul Stern of Northern Telecom Ltd. (now Nortel) was to have earned $5 million in 1992, despite serious mismanagement; his departure from the company, under a cloud, sent stock prices tumbling by almost 30 percent (Surtees, 1993). Newman notes that these were "monumental pay-packets that had little connection with the

success or failure of their enterprises" (1998:183).

A second problem with the idea that the market measures people's contributions to society is that many who make clear and significant contributions receive surprisingly little money. Tens of thousands of teachers, firefighters, and health care workers enhance the welfare of others every day for relatively small salaries. The average high school teacher would have to work for 460 years to earn as much as Amelio received in 1996. Using salary to measure social worth works only to the extent that market forces actually gauge one's societal contribution. Some people view market forces as the most accurate measure of occupational worth; others contend that lucrative activities may or may not be socially valuable. Thus, the market system remains controversial.

WHAT DO YOU THINK?

1. Do highly paid athletes and celebrities deserve their salaries? Why?
2. Assuming you have what it takes to do what Bill Gates or Frank Stronach has done, would you be willing to assume their stressful lifestyles?
3. Is it easy to become a millionaire in Canada? What about a billionaire?

[1] In 2002, 46 of Canada's top 50 CEOs were compensated to the tune of $5 to $52 million (*Report on Business*, 2003; globeinvestor, 2003).

A Counterpoint

Advocates of social-conflict analysis, however, counter that Marx's analysis of capitalism is still largely valid (Matthews, 1983; Brym, 1985; Smith, 1987; Clement, 1990; Wotherspoon and Satzewich, 1993). They offer this counterpoint:

1. **Wealth remains highly concentrated.** As Marx contended, wealth remains in the hands of the few. By the mid–1980s, Canada had six billionaire families, and another twenty-two worth $100 million or more, who control an inordinate amount of Canada's wealth

(Francis, 1986). By 2003, Canada's Thomson family ranked number 13 on *Forbes* magazine's list of the world's wealthiest people with an estimated worth of more than US$14 billion; by 2006, Forbes listed the family ninth wealthiest, worth US$19.6 billion. In particular, the concentration of wealth and ownership of newspapers, cable television, and other media by the Asper and Rogers families is a source of tremendous concern to critics of capitalist industrial society. Conrad Black sold his creation, the *National Post* to Asper's CanWest Global Communications—which

MEDIA PERSPECTIVES
Love of Leisure, and Europe's Reasons

Between mountains of suitcases and children racing each other with luggage trolleys at the airport of this Scandinavian capital [Copenhagen], Maibritt Ditlev, husband Anders and daughter Lotte in tow, remarked that her whole country seemed to be going on vacation. "In Europe we like our summer holidays," she said.... In fact, she works part time because she treasures time off. "We have a nice house and can afford to go on two family holidays a year—what would we need more money for?"

This image of a casual Western European work ethic tends to be viewed just short of scorn by the world's other wealthy economies. As Europeans like the Ditlevs happily continue to trade income for a slice of leisure time that would be unthinkable in the United States or Asia, the gloomy headlines about Europe's economic future multiply.

Europe, the standard criticism goes, has not matched the American expansion for most of the last decade and has even fallen behind Japan in recent quarters. Its citizens are on average almost 30 percent poorer than their counterparts on the other side of the Atlantic, according to the Organisation for Economic Co-operation and Development, a group of 30 countries committed to democracy and the market economy....

Is Europe, with the shortest work-weeks and longest holidays in the world, doomed to lag behind, a victim of its penchant for more leisure and a too generous welfare state? One response: If the answer is yes, then so what?...

Over the last half century, Western Europeans have gradually opted to work less and take longer vacations. They have put in place varying national versions of public universal health care, education, and retirement benefits. They have set up a complex web of minimum income legislation, including unemployment subsidies and disability benefits, and basic social welfare, in an effort to limit the risk of destitution....

As Joaquín Almunia, European commissioner for economic and monetary affairs, put it, for Europeans, economic growth is a tool. Not an end in itself.

"We are not in a race with the U.S.," he said. "Our goal is not to grow as fast as the U.S. or anybody else, but to do what we need to protect our economic and social model...."

The European Union faces challenges, including a stagnant aging population, chronic underemployment, and competitive pressures from the eight new Eastern European members and Asian growth markets like China and India....

But for all the bad publicity the European economy receives, it is not performing that poorly. The combined gross domestic product of the 15 members of the European Union before the expansion on May 1 lagged behind that of the United States by about one percentage point a year in the last decade, largely because the region's population expanded at less than half the pace of the United States'....

Polls show that Europeans are by and large happy to pay high taxes in return for social services, and anecdotal evidence suggests that the concept of well-being in Europe is less linked to material wealth than it is in the United States.

"Americans move from the 20,000 square foot house to the 30,000 square foot house to the 40,000 square foot house. It's a different mentality," said Kenneth S. Rogoff, an economist at Harvard University and former chief economist of the International Monetary Fund....

Still, some economists say Europe's social model is costing it dearly. In a society that prides itself on egalitarian values, too many people are unemployed or outside the labour market, doubly raiding public coffers by not paying taxes and often receiving benefits at the same time. The jobless rate in the European Union's 15 old members rose to 7.8 percent last year, compared with 6.1 percent in the United States....

A generous welfare state does not only have costs. Europe has less child poverty, a lower incidence of illiteracy, and a smaller prison population than the United States.... Europeans have a slightly higher life expectancy and can hope to spend more of their old age in good health than Americans....

"The main difference with the U.S. is that we spend more time enjoying life," said Jorgen Ronnest, director for international affairs at the Danish Employers' Confederation....

And if you look around, maybe we don't need more refrigerators and more cars...."

WHAT DO YOU THINK?

1. Based on this article, what are the major differences between the European and U.S. societies?
2. Do you agree with the European approach to life? Why?
3. Does Canada fit somewhere between the European and American models? Is it closer to Europe or to the United States?

Source: Adapted from Bennhold (2004).

also owns the *Montreal Gazette,* the *Ottawa Citizen,* the *Calgary Herald,* and the *Vancouver Sun,* among other Canadian newspapers. Rogers got its start in radio, but is now a major player in cable television, as well as internet, cellular telephone, and BlackBerry service; Rogers also owns *Maclean's* magazine. These three families have a large part of Canadian communications under their control.

2. **White-collar work offers little to workers**. As contemporary marxists see it, the white-collar revolution delivered little in the way of higher income or better working conditions over the factory jobs of a century ago. On the contrary, much white-collar work remains monotonous and routine, especially the low-level clerical jobs commonly held by women.

3. **Progress requires struggle**. Labour organizations may have advanced the interests of workers over the last half-century, but regular negotiation between workers and management hardly signals the end of social conflict. In fact, many of the concessions won by workers came about precisely through the class conflict Marx described. Moreover, workers still strive to gain concessions from capitalists and struggle to hold on to the advances already achieved.

4. **The law still favours the rich**. Workers have gained some legal protections over the course of the past century. Even so, the law still defends the overall distribution of wealth in Canada and the United States. Just as importantly, people with an average income cannot use the legal system to the same advantage as do the rich.

In sum, according to social-conflict theory, the fact that no socialist revolution has taken place in Canada or the United States hardly invalidates Marx's analysis of capitalism. As we shall see in Chapter 11 ("Social Class in Canada"), pronounced social inequality persists, as does social conflict—albeit less overtly and violently than in the nineteenth century.

Finally, some defenders of capitalism cite the collapse of communist regimes in Eastern Europe and the former Soviet Union as proof of the superiority of capitalism over socialism. Most analysts agree that socialism failed to meet the needs of the people it purported to serve, either in terms of raising living standards or ensuring personal freedoms. But, to be fair, socialism's failings do not excuse flaws in capitalism. Many critics maintain that capitalism in North America has yet to demonstrate its ability to address problems of public education and desperate poverty, especially among the urban underclass and Aboriginal peoples.

YOUR TURN

Applied to inequality in Canada, do you think Marx's analysis is accurate? Why?

MAX WEBER: CLASS, STATUS, AND POWER

Max Weber, whose approach to social analysis is described in Chapter 4 ("Society"), agreed with Karl Marx that social

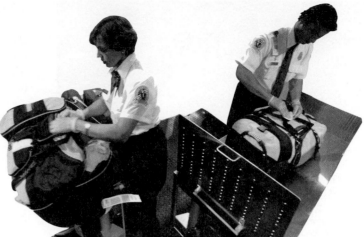

Most Canadian workers today (actually about 75%) have service jobs; instead of farming or working in a factory, they work with other people. Some analysts say that the spread of service work has made many people feel that they are "getting ahead" and, thereby, has reduced class conflict; others claim that many service jobs actually provide lower pay, fewer benefits, and less job security than factory jobs of the past. Which argument do you think is more correct? Why?

stratification causes social conflict, but he viewed Marx's economics-based model as simplistic. Instead, he claimed that social stratification involves three distinct dimensions of inequality. The first dimension is economic inequality—the issue so important to Marx—which Weber termed *class* position; Weber did not think of classes as well-defined categories but as a continuum ranging from high to low. Weber's second dimension is *status*, or social prestige, and the third is *power*.

The Socioeconomic Status Hierarchy

Marx viewed social prestige and power as simple reflections of economic position and did not treat them as distinct dimensions of inequality. But Weber noted that status consistency in modern societies is often quite low: a local official might exercise great power yet have little wealth or social prestige. Weber, then, portrays social stratification in industrial societies as a multidimensional ranking rather than a hierarchy of clearly defined classes. In line with Weber's thinking, sociologists use the term **socioeconomic status** to refer to *a composite ranking based on various dimensions of social inequality.*

Inequality in History

Weber claimed that each of his three dimensions of social inequality stands out at different points in the evolution of human societies. Status, or social prestige, is the main difference in agrarian societies, taking the form of honour. Members of these societies—whether nobles or servants—gain status by conforming to cultural norms that correspond to their rank. Industrialization and the development of capi-

The extent of social inequality in agrarian systems is greater than that found in industrial societies. One indication of the unchallenged power of rulers is the monumental structures built over years with the unpaid labour of common people. Although the Taj Mahal in India is among the world's most beautiful buildings, it is in fact the tomb of a single individual.

talism eliminate traditional rankings based on birth but create striking financial inequality. Thus, in an industrial society, the crucial difference between people is the economic dimension of class. Over time, industrial societies witness the growth of a bureaucratic state. Bigger government and the spread of all types of other organizations make power more important in the stratification system. Especially in socialist societies, where government regulates many aspects of life, high-ranking officials become the new ruling elite.

This historical analysis points to a final difference between Weber and Marx. Marx thought societies could eliminate social stratification by abolishing the private ownership of productive property that is the basis of capitalism. Weber doubted that overthrowing capitalism would significantly lessen social stratification. It might reduce economic differences, he reasoned, but socialism would increase inequality by expanding government and concentrating power in the hands of a political elite. Popular uprisings against socialist bureaucracies in Eastern Europe and the former Soviet Union support Weber's position.

Critical Review Weber's multidimensional view of social stratification has influenced sociologists greatly. But critics—particularly those who favour Marx's ideas—argue that, while social class boundaries may have blurred, industrial and post-industrial societies still show striking patterns of social inequality.

As we shall see in Chapter 11 ("Social Class in Canada"), income inequality has increased recently. While some people still favour Weber's multidimensional hierarchy, others think that, in light of this trend, Marx's view of the rich versus the poor is closer to the truth.

Stratification and Interaction

Because social stratification has to do with the way an entire society is organized, sociologists—including Marx and Weber—typically treat it as a macro-level issue. But a micro-level analysis of social stratification is also important because people's social standing affects their everyday interactions.

In most communities, people socialize primarily with others of more or less the same social standing. To some extent, this is because we tend to live near others like ourselves. In any public setting, such as a downtown shopping area, if you watch people for even a few minutes, you will see that couples or groups tend to contain individuals whose appearance and shopping habits are similar. People with very different social standing commonly keep their distance from one another. Well-dressed people walking down the street on their way to an expensive restaurant, for example, might move across the sidewalk or even cross the street to avoid getting close to those who appear to be homeless people.

Finally, just about everyone realizes that the way we dress, the car we drive or the bus we ride, and even the food and drink we order at the campus snack bar say something about our budget and personal tastes. Sociologists use the term **conspicuous consumption** to refer to *buying and using products because of the "statements" they make about social position.* Ignoring the water fountain in favour of paying for bottled water tells people you have extra money to spend. And no one needs a $100 000 automobile to get around, of course, but being seen in such a vehicle says "I have arrived" in more ways than one. In a *National Post* article about the twelve priciest homes in the United States, Vallis (2006) describes homes that sell in the range of ten to sixty million dollars. One is the three-story penthouse apartment in New York's "legendary Pierce Hotel": the asking price is seventy million U.S dollars for a home with a living room of 300 square metres (3,200 square feet) that was once the hotel's *ballroom.*

The Applying Theory table (on p. 257) summarizes the contributions of the three theoretical approaches to social stratification.

	Structural-Functional Approach	Social-Conflict Approach	Symbolic-Interaction Approach
What is the level of analysis?	Macro level	Macro level	Micro level
What is social stratification?	Stratification is a system of unequal rewards that benefits society as a whole.	Stratification is a division of a society's resources that benefits some and harms others.	Stratification is a factor that guides people's interaction in everyday life.
What is the reason for our social position?	Social position reflects personal talents and abilities in a competitive economy.	Social position reflects the way society divides resources.	The products we consume all make a "statement" about social position.
Are unequal rewards fair?	Yes. Unequal rewards boost economic production by encouraging people to work harder and try new ideas. Linking greater rewards to more important work is widely accepted.	No. Unequal rewards only serve to divide society, creating "haves" and "have-nots." There is widespread opposition to social inequality.	Maybe. People may or may not define inequality as fair. People may view their social position as a measure of self-worth, justifying inequality in terms of personal differences.

Stratification and Technology: A Global Perspective

We can weave together a number of observations made in this chapter to show that a society's technology affects its type of social stratification. This analysis draws on Gerhard Lenski's model of sociocultural evolution, detailed in Chapter 4 ("Society").

- *Hunter/gatherer societies.* With simple technology, hunter/gatherers produce only what is necessary for day-to-day living. Some people may produce more than others, but the group's survival depends on all sharing what they have. Thus, no categories of people are better off than others.

- *Horticultural, pastoral, and agrarian societies.* As technological advances create a surplus, social inequality increases. In horticultural and pastoral societies, a small elite controls most of the surplus. Large-scale agriculture is more productive still, and striking inequality—as great as at any time in history—places the nobility in an almost godlike position over the masses.

- *Industrial societies.* Industrialization turns the tide, pushing inequality downward. Prompted by the need to develop individual talents, meritocracy takes hold and weakens the power of the traditional elites. Industrial productivity also raises the standard of living of the historically poor majority. Specialized work demands schooling for all, sharply reducing illiteracy. A literate population, in turn, presses for a greater voice in political decision making, reducing inequality and lessening men's domination of women.

Over time, even wealth becomes somewhat less concentrated (contradicting Marx's prediction). In the 1920s, the richest 1 percent of the U.S. population owned about 40 percent of all wealth, a figure that fell to 30 percent by the 1980s (Williamson and Lindert, 1980; Beeghley, 1989). Such trends help explain why marxist revolutions occurred in *agrarian* societies—such as Russia (1917), Cuba (1959), and Nicaragua (1979)—where social inequality is most pronounced, rather than in industrial societies as Marx had predicted. However, in the United States, wealth inequality increased after 1990 and is once again about the same as it was in the 1920s (Keister, 2000). While at one time Canada appeared to have more billionaire families per capita than the United States—six compared to twelve (Francis, 1986)—it is likely that our overall pattern in the control of wealth is similar to that of the United States, though the gap between rich and poor is not as extreme.

Learn about the world's 587 billionaires in 2006, including 17 Canadians, at www.canadaka.net/modules.php?name=News&file=article&sid=488.

THE KUZNETS CURVE

In human history, then, technological advances first increase but then moderate the extent of social stratification. Greater inequality is functional for agrarian societies, but industrial societies benefit from a less inequitable system. This histori-

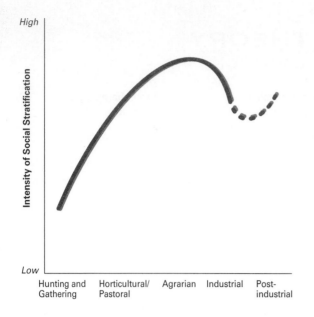

FIGURE 10-2 Social Stratification and Technological Development: The Kuznets Curve

The Kuznets curve shows that greater technological sophistication generally is accompanied by more pronounced social stratification. The trend reverses itself as industrial societies relax rigid, castelike distinctions in favour of greater opportunity and equality under the law. Political rights are more widely extended, and there is even some levelling of economic differences. However, the emergence of post-industrial society has brought an upturn in economic inequality, as indicated by the broken line added by author John Macionis.

Source: Created by John J. Macionis, based on Kuznets (1955) and Lenski (1966).

cal trend, recognized by Simon Kuznets (1955, 1966), the Harvard economist who was awarded a Nobel Prize in 1971, is illustrated by the Kuznets curve, shown in Figure 10–2 (above). Social inequality around the world generally supports the Kuznets curve. Global Map 10–1 (on p. 259)

The Centre on Budget and Policy Priorities has data and analysis of issues involving U.S. social inequality at www.cbpp.org.

shows that high-income nations that have passed through the industrial era (including the United States, Canada, and the nations of Western Europe) have somewhat less income inequality than nations in which a larger share of the labour force remains in farming (as is common in Latin America and Africa). Income inequality reflects not just technological development but also political and economic priorities. Of all high-income nations, the United States has the greatest income inequality.

And what of the future? Figure 10–2 shows that extending the trend described by Kuznets to the post-industrial era (the broken line) reveals increasing social inequality. As the Information Revolution moves ahead, North American society is experiencing greater economic inequal-

ity (see Chapter 11, "Social Class in Canada"), suggesting that the long-term trend may differ from what Kuznets observed fifty years ago (Nielsen and Alderson, 1997).

Social Stratification: Facts and Values

> The year was 2081 and everybody was finally equal. They weren't only equal before God and the law—they were equal in every way. Nobody was smarter than anybody else. Nobody was better looking than anybody else. Nobody was stronger or quicker than anybody else. All this equality was due to the 211th, 212th, and 213th Amendments to the Constitution and the unceasing vigilance of agents of the Handicapper General.

With these words, the novelist Kurt Vonnegut, Jr. (1968 [orig. 1961]:7) begins the story of "Harrison Bergeron," an imaginary account of a future United States in which all social inequality has been abolished. Vonnegut warns that, although attractive in principle, equality can be a dangerous concept in practice. His story describes a nightmare of social engineering in which every individual talent that makes one person different from another is systematically neutralized by the government.

To eliminate differences that make one person "better" than another, Vonnegut's state requires that physically attractive people wear masks that render them average looking, that intelligent people wear earphones that generate distracting noise, and that the best athletes and dancers be fitted with weights to make them as clumsy as everyone else. In short, while we may imagine that social equality would liberate people to make the most of their talents, Vonnegut concludes that a modern egalitarian society could exist only if everyone is reduced to the lowest common denominator.

Like Vonnegut's story, all of this chapter's explanations of social stratification involve value judgments. The Davis-Moore thesis states not only that social stratification is universal but also that it is necessary to make society highly productive. Class differences, from this point of view, reflect both variation in human abilities and the relative importance of different jobs. This makes complete equality undesirable because it could be achieved only in an inefficient society that cared little for developing individual talent and rewarding excellence.

Social-conflict analysis, advocated by Karl Marx, takes a much more positive view of equality. Marx thought that inequality is harmful because it causes both human suffering and conflict between haves and have-nots. As he saw it, social stratification springs from injustice and greed. As a result, Marx wanted people to share resources fairly.

WINDOW ON THE WORLD

GLOBAL MAP 10-1   Income Inequality in Global Perspective

Societies throughout the world differ in the rigidity and extent of their social stratification and their overall standard of living. This map highlights income inequality. Generally speaking, the United States stands out among high income nations (such as Great Britain, Sweden, Japan, and Australia) as having greater income inequality. The less economically developed countries of Latin America and Africa (including Colombia, Brazil, and the Central African Republic) as well as much of the Arab world, exhibit the most pronounced inequality of income. Is this pattern consistent with the Kuznets curve?

Source: Based on Gini coefficients obtained from World Bank (2005).

The Thinking It Through box (on p. 260) addresses the connection between intelligence and social class. This issue is among the most troublesome in social science, partly because of the difficulty in defining and measuring intelligence, but also because the idea that elites are somehow "better" than others challenges our democratic culture.

The next chapter ("Social Class in Canada") examines inequality in our own nation, highlighting recent economic polarization. Then, in Chapter 12 ("Global Stratification"), we survey social inequality throughout the world, explaining why some nations have so much more wealth than others. As you will learn, the study of social stratification at all levels involves a mix of facts and values about the shape of a just society.

THINKING IT THROUGH

The Bell Curve Debate: Are Rich People Really Smarter?

It is rare for a social science book to capture the attention of people throughout North America. But *The Bell Curve: Intelligence and Class Structure in American Life* (1994) by Richard J. Herrnstein and Charles Murray did this and more. The book ignited a firestorm of controversy over why social stratification divides North American society and, just as importantly, what should be done about it.

The Bell Curve is a long book that addresses many complex issues, but it makes eight major claims:

1. Something we can describe as "general intelligence" exists; people with more of it tend to be more successful in their careers than those with less.

2. At least half the variation in human intelligence is transmitted genetically from parents to children; the remaining variability derives from environmental factors that affect socialization.

3. During the past century—and especially since the Information Revolution began several decades ago—intelligence has become more necessary to perform the most important jobs.

4. At the same time, colleges and universities have shifted their admissions policies away from favouring children of inherited wealth to admitting young people with high grades in secondary school.

5. As a result of these changes in the workplace and on campus, North American society is now dominated by a "cognitive elite," people who are not only better educated but actually more intelligent.

6. As very intelligent people interact with others like themselves—both on the campus and in the workplace—the odds are high that they will pair up, marry, and have intelligent children, extending the "cognitive elite" into another generation.

7. A similar process is at work at the other end of the social ladder. Poor people who, on average, have lower intelligence have become socially segregated and tend to marry others like themselves, thereby passing along their more modest abilities to their children.

8. Herrnstein and Murray therefore conclude that, because membership in the affluent elite or the impoverished underclass is at least partly rooted in genetically inherited intelligence, we should not be surprised that the poor are more likely to have higher rates of crime and drug abuse. Further, we should expect that affirmative action will do little to help the poor.

Evaluating the claims made in *The Bell Curve* must begin with a hard look at the concept of intelligence. Critics of the book argue that most of what we call "intelligence" is the result not of genetic inheritance but of socialization. Intelligence tests, in other words, do not measure cognitive *ability* as much as they measure cognitive *performance*. Average IQ scores have been rising as the U.S. population becomes more educated. If schooling is so important to intelligence, then educational advantages alone would explain why rich children perform better on such tests.

Most researchers who study intelligence agree that genetics plays a part in children's intelligence, but most conclude that only 25 to 40 percent of intelligence is inherited—less than Herrnstein and Murray claim. Therefore, *The Bell Curve* misleads readers when it states that social stratification is a natural product of differences in inherited intelligence. Critics claim this book echoes the social Darwinism popular a century ago, which justified the great wealth of industrial tycoons as the "survival of the fittest."

Could it be that the more today's competitive society seems like a jungle, the more people think of stratification as a matter of nature rather than nurture? But even if it is flawed, *The Bell Curve* raises important issues. If some people are smarter than others, shouldn't we expect them to end up in higher social positions? Shouldn't we expect the people who rise to the top in most fields to be at least a little smarter than the rest of us? If this is true, is it fair? Finally, what can our society do to ensure that all people will have the opportunity to develop their abilities as fully as possible?

WHAT DO YOU THINK?

1. Do you think there is such a thing as "general intelligence"? Why?
2. Do you think that wealthy people, on average, are more intelligent than people of low social position? If so, how do you know which factor is the cause and which the effect?
3. Do you think social scientists should study issues such as differences in human intelligence if their results could justify social inequality? Why?

Sources: Herrnstein and Murray (1994), Jacoby and Glauberman (1995), Kohn (1996), and Arrow, *et al.* (2000).

10 MAKING THE GRADE

The following learning tools will help you see what you know, identify what you still need to learn, and expand your understanding beyond the text. You can also visit this text's Companion Website™ at www.pearsoned.ca/macionis to find useful practice tests.

KEY POINTS

What Is Social Stratification?

Social stratification, the ranking of categories of people in a hierarchy, is a trait of society, not just a result of individual differences, carries over from generation to generation, is universal but variable, and is supported by cultural beliefs.

Caste and Class Systems

Caste systems, which are typical of agrarian societies, are based on ascription (birth), permit little social mobility, and shape a person's entire life, including occupation and marriage. Class systems, which are typical of industrial societies, mix caste with meritocracy and allow some social mobility based on individual achievement. Both types of social stratification are supported by ideology—cultural values and beliefs—that defines certain kinds of inequality as just.

The Functions of Social Stratification

The Davis-Moore thesis states that social stratification is found in all societies because it promotes economic productivity. Disproportionate rewards attract the most able people to the most important jobs and encourage good performance. Critics of the Davis-Moore thesis note that it is difficult to assess the functional importance of any job fairly, stratification prevents many people from developing their abilities, and stratification benefits some at the expense of others, causing social conflict.

Stratification and Conflict

Karl Marx claimed that social stratification generates conflict. In industrial/capitalist societies, the capitalists or bourgeoisie own the means of production, seek profits, and dominate the proletarians, who provide labour in exchange for wages. The socialist revolution that Marx predicted has not occurred, at least in industrial societies such as the United States and Canada. Some sociologists consider this to be evidence that Marx was wrong, but others point out that our society still has striking social inequality and class conflict.

Max Weber identified three dimensions of social inequality: economic class, social status or prestige, and power. Because people's standing on the three dimensions may differ, stratification is not a matter of clear classes but takes the form of a multidimensional hierarchy.

Stratification and Interaction

In everyday life, people typically socialize with others of similar social standing. People may decide to dress in certain ways or buy certain products in order to increase their social standing in the eyes of others. Conspicuous consumption refers to buying and using products because of their association with social position.

Stratification and Technology: A Global Perspective

Through most of history, advancing technology has increased social stratification. Some reversal of this trend occurs in industrial societies, as shown by the Kuznets curve. Even so, post-industrial societies show some increase in economic inequality.

Social Stratification: Facts and Values

People's beliefs about social inequality reflect not just facts but also politics and values concerning how a society should be organized.

KEY CONCEPTS

social stratification (p. 241) a system by which a society ranks categories of people in a hierarchy

social mobility (p. 241) a change in position within the social hierarchy

caste system (p. 241) social stratification based on ascription (birth)

class system (p. 244) social stratification based on both birth and individual achievement

meritocracy (p. 244) social stratification based on personal merit

status consistency (p. 245) the degree of consistency in a person's social standing

across various dimensions of social inequality

structural social mobility (p. 248) a shift in the social position of large numbers of people owed more to changes in society itself than to individual efforts

ideology (249) cultural beliefs that justify particular social arrangements, including patterns of inequality

Davis-Moore thesis (p. 250) the assertion that social stratification is a universal pattern because it has beneficial consequences for the operation of a society

blue-collar occupations (p. 251) lower-prestige jobs that involve mostly manual labour

white-collar occupations (p. 251) higher-prestige jobs that involve mostly mental activity

socioeconomic status (p. 255) a composite ranking based on various dimensions of social inequality

conspicuous consumption (p. 256) buying and using products because of their "statements" about social position

APPLICATIONS & EXERCISES

1. Write down three examples of social stratification on your campus, and indicate what makes the students represented unequal. Does family background or individual talent seem to be more important in creating these social differences?

2. Sit down with parents, grandparents, or other relatives, and talk about how the social position of your own or someone else's family has changed over the last three generations. Has social mobility taken place? If so, describe the change. Was it caused by the effort of individuals or by changes in society itself?

3. The seven deadly sins (the human failings recognized by the Catholic Church during the Middle Ages) were pride, greed, envy, anger, lust, gluttony, and sloth. Why are these traits dangerous to an agrarian caste system? Are they a threat to a modern capitalist class system? Why?

PRENTICE HALL
mysoclab™
Where learning & the sociological imagination intersect.

To reinforce your understanding of this chapter, and to identify topics for further study, visit MySocLab at **www.pearsoned.ca/mysoclab/** for diagnostic tests and a multimedia ebook.

CHAPTER ELEVEN

Social Class in Canada

How are income and wealth divided within the Canadian population?

What factors place people in different social classes?

Why is the poverty rate higher among some categories of people than others?

Karen Moss, a twenty-two-year-old single mother, was packing up her belongings to move for the third time in seven months. Her dreams of improving her life with a college education were dashed when the Ontario government cut welfare payments by almost 22 percent in 1996. Then, Moss was receiving $957 per month—down from $1221—to support her son, Cameron, and herself.

Moss had also lost government funding for school. She had been doing very well in a retail management course at a local community college, but bureaucratic mix-ups and problems with getting a work placement forced her to discontinue her studies. "If it wasn't for the welfare cuts," Moss said, "I'd still be living in my old apartment and I'd be two semesters away from completing my course."

The cuts meant that Moss could no longer afford the $700 each month in rent for her one-bedroom apartment. She tried sharing an apartment with another single mother, and, when that didn't work, she moved in with her parents. But living in their small condominium was too cramped and stressful for Karen and her son. So once again she found herself looking for another place to live.

Cameron's father, also on welfare, did not help support their son. So Moss decided that the best thing to do was to try a fresh start in a new city. "I just want to get off welfare and get back on my feet. Once that happens, I'll look into trying to finish school," she said (Monsebraaten, 1996).

Canadians tend to think of Canada as a middle-class society, but in fact our society is highly stratified. The rich not only control most of the money, they also benefit from more schooling, they enjoy better health, and they consume a greater share of almost all goods and services than others do. On the other end of the socioeconomic spectrum, poor families struggle from day to day simply to make ends meet. This chapter will explain that the popular perception of Canada as a society with a bulging middle class and a uniformly high standard of living does not square with many important facts.

Dimensions of Social Inequality

Canada's egalitarian values suggest that we experience equality of opportunity and widespread upward mobility and that, at the very least, we provide a broad social safety net that catches those who fall through the cracks. We fail to recognize that, in reality, birth confers advantages and opportunities on some people that others who are less fortunate could never imagine.

Social inequality in Canada is not easily recognized because our primary groups—including family, neighbours, and friends—typically have the same social standing as we do. At work, we mix with others like ourselves. In effect, most of our daily interaction involve a narrow stratum of society, with only brief and impersonal encounters with people very different from ourselves. The mass media, even in their ads, project a largely middle-class picture of our social world, and recently governments have quoted statistics showing that Canadians have one of the highest standards of living in the world. The effect of these images of homogeneity is that the very rich and the very poor are largely invisible to the rest of us.

⟼ **YOUR TURN** ⟻

Why do you think Canada is generally perceived as a middle-class society in which most people have more or less equal social standing?

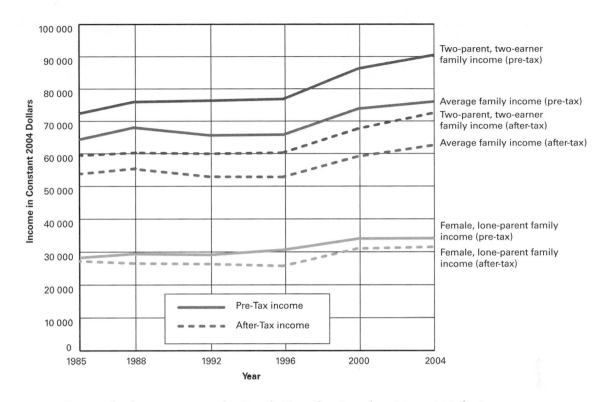

FIGURE 11-1   Pre- and After-tax Income by Family Type for Canada, 1985 to 2004*

*Prior to 1988, incomes rose rapidly. In 1961 and 1971, average income in constant 2004 dollars was $38 400 and $57 1000, respectively

Source: Calculations by L.M. Gerber based on Statistics Canada, catalogue no. 75-202-XIE.

When people do acknowledge their differences, they often talk of inequality as if it were determined by a single factor such as money. More accurately, however, social class in Canada has several dimensions. *Socioeconomic status*—examined in Chapter 10 ("Social Stratification")—amounts to a composite measure of social position that encompasses not only money but power, occupational prestige, and schooling.

INCOME

One important dimension of inequality involves **income,** *occupational wages or salaries, earnings from investments, and government transfer payments (e.g., welfare).* As revealed in Figure 11–1, average family income in Canada rose substantially between 1985 and 2004 (from $64 000 to $76 000 in constant 2004 dollars). Not revealed are the dramatic rise in real incomes in the preceding 25 years—up from $38 400 and $51 100 in 1961 and 1971, respectively (in 2004 dollars)—and the dip of $1100 in 1993 to $64 500 as the economy sank into a recession. Nonetheless, the increased buying power of the average family between 1996 and 2004 was most welcome.

Figure 11–1 provides more detailed information about the economic well-being of Canadian families—depicting pre- and after-tax income over time for three kinds of families. Note that two-parent, two-earner families have substantially higher incomes (pre- and after-tax) than the average family, and that the rise from 1996 was even sharper for them. An important contributor to rising income for the *average* family was the increase in dual-income families that began in the 1960s and 1970s. The sharper rise in the 1996 to 2004 period can be explained by the movement of women in these two-earner families into better paid and often professional jobs. The effect, in many cases, is the transformation of dual-income into dual-career families.

Pre-tax income in female, lone-parent families is *less* than half that of the average family. Because the proportionate tax bite is smaller at lower income levels, after-tax income in female lone-parent families is very close to half that of the average family—sometimes more, sometimes less. If you look carefully at the Figure 11–1, you will see a sharper increase—between 1996 and 2000—in after-tax income in female, lone-parent families, which narrows the gap between pre- and after-tax incomes. This is the result, at least in part, of an increase in the child tax credit.

Table 11–1 shows the distribution of income by quintiles (by fifths, or groups of 20%). Taking 2001 as the point of reference, the 20 percent of families with the highest earnings received 43.6 percent of all income—more than double their share if there were income equality—while the lowest-income quintile received only 5.2, or a quarter of its share. In short, the bulk of the nation's income is earned by a small proportion of families, while the rest of the population makes do with far less.

TABLE 11–1

Distribution of Family Income by Quintile in Canada, 1961–2001, and in the United States, 1990 and 2000

Quintile*	Canada					United States	
	1961	1971	1981	1991	2001	1990	2000
Lowest	6.6	5.6	6.4	6.4	5.2	3.9	4.3
Second	13.5	12.6	12.9	12.2	11.3	9.6	9.8
Middle	8.3	18.0	18.3	17.6	16.7	15.9	15.5
Fourth	23.4	23.7	24.1	23.9	23.3	24.0	22.3
Highest	38.4	40.0	38.4	40.0	43.6	46.6	47.4
Total	100.0	100.0	100.0	100.0	100.0	100.0	100.0

*Quintiles divide those with income into five equal categories. The distribution refers to the percentage of total income received in each category.

Sources: Fréchette (1988); Statistics Canada, catalogue no. 13-207; U.S. Bureau of the Census (2000), and Statistics Canada, 2001 Census, www.statcan.ca.

GLOBAL SNAPSHOT

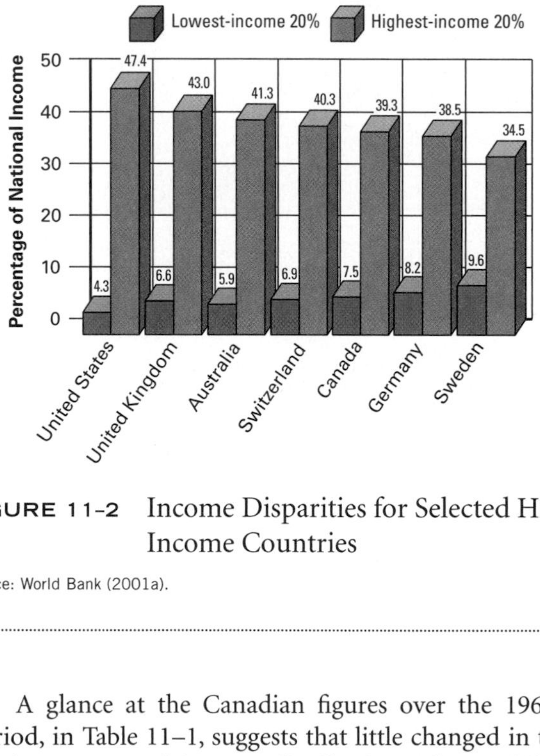

FIGURE 11–2   Income Disparities for Selected High-Income Countries

Source: World Bank (2001a).

when we discuss poverty, you will see that, in Canada, both the rich *and* the poor are getting richer.

A comparison of the Canadian and American figures in 1991/1990 and 2001/2000 in Table 11–1 suggests that, while Canada's income is more equitably distributed than that of the United States, our performance declined just as the Americans increased income equality. The most intriguing observations that you can make are the following: for Canada, between 1991 and 2001, the rich got richer and the poor got poorer; in the United States over the same decade, the rich got a little richer but *the poor also got richer.* In other words, during the 1990s, income disparity increased in Canada while it decreased in the United States.

World Bank data in Figure 11–2 paint a more positive picture of Canada's current record on income disparities. With 39.3 percent of income going to the highest-income quintile and 7.5 percent going to the lowest-income quintile, Canada's income distribution falls between that of Switzerland and Germany, and looks much better than that of the United States. Regrettably, other economic indicators—which point to increased income disparity in Canada—suggest that the World Bank data are out of line with those of our census. (Compare Figure 11–2 with Table 11–1.) More realistically, Canada should appear between the United States and the United Kingdom in Figure 11–2.

Canada Map 11–1 shows 2000 median incomes for Canada's census subdivisions, as well as for the country, provinces, and territories. This map reveals that median income is lowest in Newfoundland and Labrador, and Nunavut, and highest in the Yukon and Northwest Territories, ranging from $16 050 in Newfoundland and Labrador to $29 030 in the Northwest Territories. Ontario's median income, at $24 816, is the highest of the provinces, but is only about $2700 above the median income for Canada as a whole. Clearly, income disparity is not limited to Canadian individuals and families: it shows up as well among the provinces and territories.

A glance at the Canadian figures over the 1961–91 period, in Table 11–1, suggests that little changed in terms of the pattern of income distribution. That stability is discouraging considering Canada's economic growth and the expansion of our social welfare system over that period. It appears that, despite our efforts, we have failed to redistribute income to those who are less well off. More discouraging is the change between 1991 and 2001, which suggests that the top quintile gained income (40.0% to 43.6% of all income) at the expense of the poorest quintile (whose share dropped from 6.4% to 5.2%). On the basis of Table 11–1, one can conclude that, in Canada, the rich are getting richer while the poor are getting poorer. Later in this chapter,

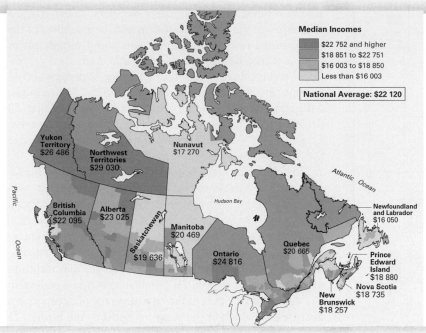

SEEING OURSELVES

CANADA MAP 11–1

Median Incomes by Province, Territory, and Census Subdivision, 2000

Source: Calculations by L.M. Gerber based on data retrieved in October 2003 from Statistics Canada online database, B2020, Profile Series.

Median Incomes

- $22 752 and higher
- $18 851 to $22 751
- $16 003 to $18 850
- Less than $16 003

National Average: $22 120

Yukon Territory $26 486
Northwest Territories $29 030
Nunavut $17 270
British Columbia $22 095
Alberta $23 025
Saskatchewan $19 636
Manitoba $20 469
Ontario $24 816
Quebec $20 665
Newfoundland and Labrador $16 050
Prince Edward Island $18 880
Nova Scotia $18 735
New Brunswick $18 257

Pacific Ocean
Atlantic Ocean
Hudson Bay

WEALTH

Income is but one component of **wealth,** *the total amount of money and other assets, minus outstanding debts.* Wealth in the form of stocks, bonds, real estate, and other privately owned property is distributed even less evenly than income. Paul Tellier, CEO of Bombardier, for example, has to declare his *income* to the Canada Revenue Agency, but not the value of his mansions or business holdings. It is the control of these kinds of assets that really sets the wealthy apart from the rest of us. When the political left talks of establishing a wealth tax and an inheritance tax, it is this component of wealth that it seeks to redistribute. Canada does not measure or tax wealth, but the United States does. The most recent American figures (for 2003) reveal that the richest 20 percent of families earn 48 percent of all income and own an astounding 84 percent of all wealth. In all likelihood, Canada's distribution of wealth differs little from that of the United States.

POWER

In Canadian society, as elsewhere, wealth stands as an important source of power. Major owners of corporate stock, for example, make decisions that create jobs for ordinary people or scale back operations, throwing people out of work. More broadly, the super-rich families who own most of the nation's wealth have a great deal of influence over the national political agenda (Clement, 1975; Francis, 1986). Chapter 17 ("Politics and Government") raises a question that has engaged sociologists for decades: Can a society maintain a political democracy if a small share of the population controls most of the wealth? Some analysts maintain that, while the rich may have some advantages, they do not dominate the political process. Others argue, as did Marx, that the political system represents the interests of the wealthy.

YOUR TURN

Everyone, regardless of social class, has the same right to vote. In which ways do the rich have more power to shape Canadian society than the rest of us?

OCCUPATIONAL PRESTIGE

Occupation is a major determinant of income, wealth, and power. In addition, it serves as a key source of social prestige, since we commonly evaluate one another according to the kind of work we do, respecting some while looking down on others. When we learned that Linda Cook is the president and CEO of Shell Canada in Calgary, we made numerous assumptions about her lifestyle, education, and income. Furthermore, we treated her with respect and listened closely to her opinions. Linda Cook recently moved to the Netherlands where she is with Royal Dutch/Shell. In 2006, she was ranked by Forbes as 56 among the world's 100 most powerful women. She wanted to get into the petroleum industry since her days of pumping gas as a teenager.

Find out about Linda Cook on the Forbes site: www.forbes.com/lists/2006/11/06women_Linda-Cook_PN4K.html.

For more than half a century, sociologists have measured the relative social prestige of various occupations (Counts, 1925; Blishen, 1958; Hodge, *et al.*, 1966; Blishen, *et al.*, 1987). Surveys asking respondents to rate occupations in terms of prestige produce a ranking that reflects both income and education. Physicians, lawyers, and engineers—all high on income and education—are ranked near the top on prestige, while cashiers and janitors are ranked near the

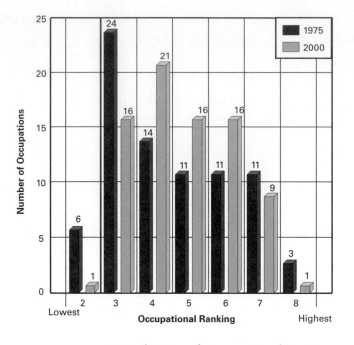

FIGURE 11-3 Distribution of Occupational Prestige, 1975 and 2000[3]

*Number of occupation titles rated at each level of prestige, from surveys of Kitchener-Waterloo, Ontario, 1975 and 2000.

Source: Goyder, John. "The Dynamics of Occupational Prestige: 1975–2000." *The Canadian Review of Sociology and Anthropology.* February Vol. 42, No. 1 (2005):1, 23.

bottom. In global perspective, occupational prestige rankings tend to be roughly the same in all industrial, high-income societies (Lin and Xie, 1988), including the United States, where physicians score 86 on the prestige scale and shoe shiners 09 (Macionis, 2007: 283). Almost everywhere, white-collar work that involves mental activity free from extensive supervision confers greater prestige than blue-collar occupations that require supervised, manual labour. There are exceptions to this pattern, however; for example, a blue-collar aircraft mechanic enjoys greater social prestige than a white-collar filing clerk.

Another study (Creese, *et al.*, 1991) ranked various occupational categories in Canada, applying the Blishen scale to data from the General Social Survey of 1986. In a ranking of 514 census occupations, physicians and surgeons come out at the top with a score of 101.3, while newspaper carriers and vendors scored 17.8. Collapsing occupations into broader categories makes certain patterns apparent. In the middle range of occupations, the Blishen scores are lower for women than for men, particularly in the various white- and blue-collar categories; this is where the *pink ghetto* jobs—lower status and poorly paid—are concentrated. Women and men have similar educational levels across occupational categories, with the few differences usually resulting from *higher* educational attainment

among women. However, the 1986 data reveal marked differences in the *income* of women and men: in most of the occupational categories, women earn about 60 percent of male income, but in the professional and semi-professional/technical categories, the figures are 72 percent and 84 percent, for women and men, respectively. Interestingly, self-employed professional women fare best, earning 88 percent of the income earned by their male counterparts. Chapter 13 ("Gender Stratification") deals with changes (i.e., improvements) in these figures over time.

In 2000, University of Waterloo professor John Goyder replicated a study of occupational prestige that was conducted in the Kitchener-Waterloo area of Ontario a quarter-century earlier. Noting that occupational prestige ratings done through the 1960s to 1980s were highly correlated (usually at the 0.99 level), Goyder (2005) decided to replicate the 1975 study to measure changes that intuition told him must have occurred. Both studies asked people, in face-to-face interviews, to rank a wide range of occupations. Because of changes in the economy between the studies, 13 obsolete job titles were dropped and 10 new ones were added; but 80 occupational categories were common to both studies.

Figure 11–3 reveals Goyder's findings that the distribution of rankings has changed dramatically. Fewer occupations are given either very low or very high rankings. By 2000, many more occupations were ranked in the middle ranges. The following examples illustrate the changes that underlie the graph: tool and die makers and autoworkers are *up* 12 points; fire fighters, police officers, and registered nurses are *up* 23, 13, and 10 points, respectively; while lawyers, members of Parliament, and physicists are *down* 15, 13, and 11 points, respectively. Physicians held up remarkably well, dropping less than one point from 93.6 to 92.7, while university professors dropped 5 points. Throughout the 1975 to 2000 period, many low- to moderate-prestige jobs have come to require added skills because of computers: truck drivers, farmers, secretaries, and nurses have to deal with new technology on the job. At the upper end of the scale, computers have had a different effect: "Internet and software packages help transform the common man and woman into instant experts with access to the latest research knowledge. The professions may have less prestige nowadays because the Internet has demystified their secret knowledge" (Goyder, 2005). Marshall McLuhan would have agreed with Goyder's analysis.

The Kitchener-Waterloo studies of 1975 and 2000 both addressed the gender dimension of occupational prestige. In

 each survey, random thirds were asked to rate job titles described as male-specified (e.g., "male accountant"), female-specified (e.g., "female accountant"), and gender neutral (e.g., "accountant") (Goyder, *et al.*, 2003; Goyder, 2005). In 1975, there was a

tendency to assign different rankings to male accountants and female accountants, for example, with greater prestige accruing to male workers. By 2000, that gender gap had disappeared (Goyder, *et al.*, 2003).

SCHOOLING

Education is an important determinant of labour force participation, occupation, and income, so it is highly valued in industrial societies. While industrial societies generally define schooling as everyone's right, the opportunity for formal education is not always equal. In Canada, traditionally, women did not pursue formal education as long as their male counterparts; however, in recent years, more than half of undergraduate degrees and community college diplomas have been earned by women, although they have not caught up with men in earning master's and doctoral degrees. While educational differences between men and women employed in similar jobs are minimal, overall, women have completed more years of schooling than men.

Schooling not only promotes personal development but also affects an individual's occupation and income. Individuals with higher levels of schooling are more likely to be in the labour force, to be employed rather than unemployed, and to earn higher incomes (Canada, 1992a). Perhaps the clearest indication of the link between education and income is the following: in 2000, the average income for people with less than high school graduation was $19 777; for those with university certificates, diplomas, or degrees, average income more than doubled, to $42 686.

Canadian Stratification: Merit and Caste

As we discussed in Chapter 10 ("Social Stratification"), the Canadian class system is partly a meritocracy in that social position reflects individual talent and effort. But it also has caste elements, because birth plays a part in what we become later in life.

ANCESTRY

Nothing affects social standing in Canada as much as our birth into a particular family, an event over which we have no control. Ancestry determines our point of entry into the system of social inequality. Some Canadian families, including the Reichmanns, Blacks, Aspers, Thomsons, Irvings, Nygards, and Stronachs, are known around the world. On a more modest scale, certain families in practically every Canadian community have wealth and power that have become well established over several generations. Being born to privilege or poverty sets the stage for future schooling, occupation, and income. While there are numerous rags-to-riches stories in Canada, many of the richest individuals—those with hundreds of millions of dollars in wealth—derived their fortunes primarily through inheri-

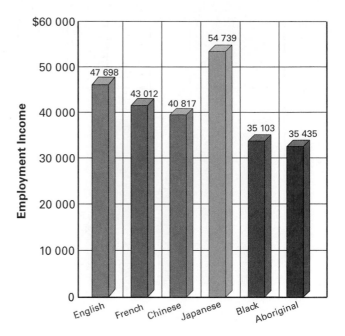

FIGURE 11-4   Average Employment Income in Canada for Selected Categories, 2001*

*Refers to median income earned by individuals working full time, all year.

Source: Calculations by L.M. Gerber based on Statistics Canada, Census 2001, catalogue numbers 97F0010XCD2001043, 97F0010XCB2001047, and 97F0011XCB2001055.

tance. By the same token, the legacy of poverty and the lack of opportunity that goes with it just as surely shape the future of those in need. The family, in short, transmits property, power, and possibilities from one generation to the next, contributing to the persistence of social stratification.

RACE AND ETHNICITY

While we think that Canadian society is largely egalitarian, race and ethnicity remain important determinants of social position. Elsewhere, you will learn that Canadians of Chinese and Japanese origins have higher levels of educational attainment than those of British and French origin, and that people who identify as Black are most active in the labour force and most likely to be employed. Aboriginal people lag behind in terms of educational attainment and employment rate. Figures 11–4 and 11–5 suggest that race and ethnicity have a bearing on income as well.

Figure 11–4 reveals that, among those who are employed *full time all year*, Canadians of Japanese origin have substantially higher average employment income than those of English and French origin. French and Chinese employment incomes are very similar and substantially higher than those of people who identify as Black or Aboriginal. Nonetheless, as low as Aboriginal income may appear to be, this represents a substantial improvement from 1991 to 2001 (compare with Macionis and Gerber, 2005:264). It is also worth noting that, while visible minorities in general (data not included) have lower average

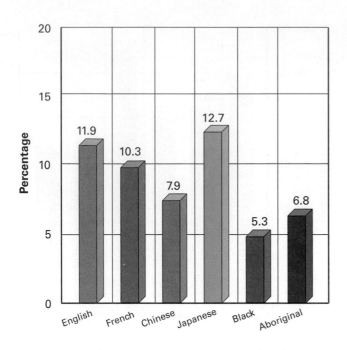

FIGURE 11-5 Percentage with Income of $60 000 or More for Selected Categories: Canada, 2001*

*These percentages refer to the proportion of each population fifteen years of age and over.

Source: Calculations by L.M. Gerber based on Statistics Canada, Census 2001, catalogue numbers 97F0010XCB2001043, 97F0010XCB2001047, and 97F0011XCB2001055.

employment incomes (for full-time employment) than the English or the French, the Japanese have exceptionally high incomes. The position of the Japanese as well as improvement in that of the Aboriginal population raise questions about racism or discrimination as the sole determinants of income inequality.

Figure 11–5 reveals income differences based on a different measure. The bars in the graph indicate the proportion of the population 15 years of age and over in each category with income of $60 000 or more. Note that, on this measure, the Japanese and the English are equal—followed by people of French, Chinese, Aboriginal, and Black origins, in that order. Once again, the attainment of high income by Aboriginal people has increased substantially—in fact more than doubled—during the 1990s.

Together, Figures 11–4 and 11–5 suggest that, while income is only one dimension of social class, race and ethnicity are clearly associated with differential placement in the socioeconomic hierarchy of Canada. On the other hand, it is clear that racism and discrimination only partly explain economic inequality. The Thinking about Diversity box (on p. 273) takes a look at social class distinctions *within* the Aboriginal community, providing a very different perspective on inequality.

GENDER

Women born into families of high social standing draw on many more social resources than men born into disadvantaged families. Yet, on average, women earn lower income, accumulate less wealth, enjoy lower occupational prestige, and rank lower in some aspects of educational achievement than men do. Later in the chapter, you will discover that women do not inherit the social position of their fathers to the extent that men do. You will also learn that households headed by women are many times more likely to be poor than are those headed by men. A full picture of the link between gender and social stratification is found in Chapter 13 ("Gender Stratification").

Clearly, who we are—in terms of family background, gender, race, and ethnicity—affects our placement in the socioeconomic hierarchy of Canada.

Social Classes in Canada

As Chapter 10 ("Social Stratification") explains, people living in rigid caste systems can tell anyone's social ranking at a glance. Assessing the social position in a more fluid class system, however, poses a number of challenges. Consider the joke about the fellow who orders a pizza, asking that it be cut into six slices because he isn't hungry enough to eat eight. While sociologists acknowledge extensive social inequality in North America, they have long debated precisely how to divide up this social hierarchy. Some who follow Karl Marx's thinking contend that there are two major classes; others suggest that North American society breaks down into as many as six categories. Still others align themselves with Max Weber, believing that people form a multidimensional status hierarchy, rather than clear-cut classes.

Defining classes in Canada is difficult owing to the relatively low level of status consistency. Especially towards the middle of the hierarchy, an individual's social standing on one dimension often contradicts that person's position on another (Tepperman, 1979; Gilbert and Kahl, 1987). A government official, for example, may control a multimillion-dollar budget yet earn a modest income. Similarly, members of the clergy typically enjoy ample prestige while possessing only moderate power and earning low pay. Or consider a lucky professional gambler or a gangster who may win little respect despite considerable wealth. The social mobility typical of class systems—again, most pronounced near the middle—means that social position often changes during one's lifetime, further blurring the lines between social classes.

Despite these problems of definition, it is useful to think of four general social classes in Canada: the upper class, the middle class, the working class, and the lower class. As we shall explain, however, some categories are more clear-cut than others.

THINKING ABOUT DIVERSITY:
RACE, CLASS, & GENDER
Social Class and Aboriginal Peoples

Many scholars and observers of the Canadian scene have characterized Aboriginal peoples as suffering from cultural dislocation, substance abuse, suicide, and poverty. Furthermore, the figures and tables throughout this text suggest that Aboriginal peoples lag behind the larger Canadian population in terms of education, labour force participation, and income. In other words, the general belief is that Aboriginal people—First Nations, non-Status Indians, Métis, and Inuit—live in relative poverty.

These observations apply to Aboriginal peoples in the *aggregate*. Indeed, Aboriginal peoples—on average—do fare poorly on a wide range of measures of social, economic, and physical health. Yet in an early publication, based on her analysis of 600 First Nations communities, Gerber (1979) pointed out the diversity among them. That diversity led her to develop a typology of reserve-based communities: Inert, Pluralistic, Municipal, and Integrative communities reveal very different responses to changing socioeconomic circumstances. Underlying this diversity are real differences in economic well-being. Where communities have acquired wealth, there is also individual diversity, as some individuals benefit more than others.

Wotherspoon and Satzewich (1993) observe the status of Aboriginal people from a marxist—or, rather, neo-marxist—perspective, noting that race, class, and gender relations enter into the picture. These variables, they argue, "intersect in complex ways to structure the social position of groups." The authors are quick to point out that, collectively, Aboriginal peoples "occupy disadvantaged positions within social and economic structures of Canada" and that, because they "share a structurally similar position," the assumption is that race and class converge—in other words, race equals class. While

the aggregate statistics support this assumption, Wotherspoon and Satzewich counter it with evidence that, in fact, Aboriginal people "are distributed across the range of class sites" (pp. 42–43). Some of that evidence comes from Gerber (1990), who provides an occupational breakdown of First Nations, non-Status Indians, Métis, and Inuit.

Aboriginal people are to be found in each of the marxist categories of proletariat, reserve army of labour, working class, petit bourgeoisie, and bourgeoisie. Thus, they span the range from street people to capitalists. However, while the media and the literature provide substantial analysis of Aboriginal communities and populations, they rarely focus on the Aboriginal capitalists (the petit bourgeoisie and the bourgeoisie), "those people who either own large sums of capital privately, or who control large sums of 'communally'- or Band-based capital" (Wotherspoon and Satzewich, 1993:64).

As expected, some Aboriginal-owned businesses are based on crafts, tourism, natural resources, construction, hunting, fishing, and farming; but others offer services in consulting and multimedia communications. Businesses are located on reserves and in major urban centres. The start-up capital for these ventures comes from land claim settlements, special funds from Indian and Northern Affairs Canada (INAC), or banks, some of which

To obtain more information about Aboriginal businesses, go to Aboriginal Business Canada at www.ic.gc.ca, or go directly to http://strategis.ic.gc.ca/epic/internet/inabc-eac.nsf/en/Home.

specifically serve Aboriginal people and businesses. Aboriginal businesses are newer and generally smaller than their mainstream counterparts, but many are multimillion-dollar ventures. In fact,

executive incomes put many Aboriginal individuals in Canada's upper-income categories. The federal government provides services for Aboriginal businesses through Indian and Northern Affairs Canada as well as through Industry Canada.

Frideres and Gadacz (2001: 93, 95) find that Aboriginal people lag behind Canadians in general on income, employment, and occupational attainment. On-reserve people fare the worst: the 1991 employment rate (i.e., percentage employed among people 15 years of age and over) for on-reserve Aboriginal people was 34.4 percent, compared with 67.9 percent among Canadians overall. In 1981, Aboriginal people earned 67 percent of the average income of Canadians in general; by 1991 Aboriginal earnings *dropped* to 60 percent of the Canadian average. At least during the 1981–91 period, the gap between the two groups got larger—and this "startling fact emerges despite the large and complex structures we have put in place to help Aboriginal people find a niche in our society and integrate into the economic structure."

On a more positive note, Figure 11–5 indicates that 6.8 percent of Aboriginal people who are employed full time earn more that $60 000 per year: this represents substantial improvement over the previous decade (the 1990s).

WHAT DO YOU THINK?

1. Were you aware that Aboriginal individuals are located throughout Canada's class structure?
2. Have you had personal contact with Aboriginal individuals, either in school or in your community? If so, how have those contacts affected your perceptions of Aboriginal peoples in general?
3. Why do Aboriginal individuals find it difficult to achieve equality in Canada?

THINKING IT THROUGH
Computers and Social Class

In the past decade or so, Canada ceased to be an industrial society and moved to the post-industrial phase. This means that the service sector has expanded to include a high proportion of knowledge-based industries, which in turn means that Canadians increasingly rely on information technology in a wide range of work environments. If computer literacy, in particular, is becoming the key to opportunity in Canada, then the question of who is comfortable with the technology is of considerable importance.

Schools throughout Canada—in rural or urban, affluent or poor communities—are gradually introducing computers into the classroom from the earliest grades; where available, special school networks and the internet have expanded horizons and revolutionized the learning process. But the number of computers available is usually limited, so that individual students often have little opportunity to put new skills into practice. The most adept students—often the boys—tend to monopolize the equipment, while the more reticent watch from the sidelines. As long as the supply of computers in the school is limited, additional exposure to computers in the home environment will play an important role in skill development. It is here that social class background has an impact.

John Goyder (1997) examined patterns of technology diffusion in Canada, comparing the presence of telephones in 1911 and personal computers (PCs) in 1994 in the homes of people in various occupational categories. Note that both of these technologies started off in offices and were later adopted in homes.

Goyder found that more affluent homes were more likely to have both telephones and computers. Home telephone subscribers in 1911, in Kingston, Ontario, were overwhelmingly in the professional and managerial categories: 96 percent of professionals had telephones at home, compared with 3 percent of those in skilled and semi-skilled trades. In 1994, PCs were more evenly distributed in the homes of various occupational categories. Among professionals (employed and self-employed), 61 percent had computers at home, compared with 24 percent of unskilled craft and farm labourers. Considering the expense of computers, the fact that about 25 percent of households in the four lowest occupational categories have PCs is remarkable and indicative of the centrality of computers in modern Canadian life. The absence of computers in the home of 39 percent of professionals may be a function of age: some older professionals have not adopted computers either in the office or at home.

Statistics Canada tracks changes in internet use by education and age of household head, specifying location of access (e.g., home, work, or school). Between 1997 and 2003, the proportion of households with home access headed by those with less than high school education increased from 3.9 to 31.6 percent. Among households with heads having university degrees, home access increased from 37.6 to 87.8 percent. The effect of the age of the household head has a similarly dramatic impact. Among households with heads under 35 years of age, internet access at home increased from 37.3 to 79.5 percent in the same five-year period. Among households with heads 65 years of age and over, home access increased from 5.3 to 24.9 percent. Clearly, both education and age of household head have dramatic effects on internet access at home (Statistics Canada, 2006b).

WHAT DO YOU THINK?

1. How important are computers in the home for preparing young people to succeed in school?
2. What differences have you observed between families with computers and those without?
3. Do primary and secondary schools have enough computers to meet the educational needs of their students?

In a society in which economic development is focused on knowledge-based industries, computer technology is being applied very widely, even in underground mining. Computer literacy is increasingly distinguishing the highly employable from those who face multiple barriers to satisfactory employment. If the children of the affluent have more exposure to computers at school, and that exposure is augmented by the presence of computers in the home, they are likely to perpetuate their parents' social class position. See the Thinking It Through box (above) for a closer look at the link between computers and social class.

THE UPPER CLASS

The upper class, perhaps 3 to 5 percent of the Canadian population, derives much of its income from inherited wealth, in the form of stocks and bonds, real estate, and other investments. And this income may be substantial. In January 1996, the *Financial Post* magazine profiled fifty of the richest individuals and families in Canada, each of them with a minimum net worth of $145 million and eight of them worth at least $1 billion. On the top at that time was Kenneth R. Thomson with a net worth of $8.2 *billion* (Hamilton, 1996). By 2003, *Forbes* listed him as the

People often distinguish between the "new" rich and those with "old" money. Men and women who suddenly begin to earn a high income tend to spend on "status symbols" because they enjoy the new thrill of high-roller living and want others to know of their success. Those who grow up surrounded by wealth, on the other hand, are used to a privileged way of life and are quieter about it. Thus, the conspicuous consumption of the lower-upper class (left) can differ dramatically from the more private pursuits and understatement of the upper-upper class (right).

thirteenth richest person in the world, with an estimated net worth of $14 billion (U.S.)—$18.3 billion Canadian (*Forbes*, 2003), and at the time of his death in 2006, the *Forbes* website listed him as ninth wealthiest, worth US$19.6 billion. The upper class thus comprises what Karl Marx termed *capitalists*, those who own or control most of the nation's productive property.

Despite this immense wealth, many members of the upper class work as top executives in large corporations, often earning salaries of $5 million or more: in 2002 Frank Stronach and Belinda Stronach of Magna Corporation were rewarded to the tune of $52 million and $12.5 million respectively, while Travis Engen of Alcan made $17 million (*Report on Business*, 2003:147). As corporate executives and as senior government officials, these privileged individuals further enhance their power to shape events in the nation—and the entire world.

Members of the upper class also attain the highest levels of education, typically in the most expensive and highly regarded schools and universities. Historically, though less so today, the upper class has been composed of people of British origin (Porter, 1965; Clement, 1975; Tepperman, 1979). In the mid–1990s, among the fifty most wealthy families or individuals noted above, about half were of British origin and the rest were a mix of Jewish, French, other European, and one Asian. Over the next decade or two, we can expect to find an increasing number of people of Asian ancestry represented in this highly select group.

Upper-Upper Class

The *upper-upper class*, often described as "high society" or "bluebloods," includes less than 1 percent of the Canadian population. Membership is usually the result of ascription or birth, as suggested by the old quip that the easiest way to break into "society" is to be born there. These families possess enormous wealth, primarily inherited rather than earned. For this reason, members of the upper-upper class are said to have *old money*. Set apart by their wealth, members of the upper-upper class live in a world of exclusive affiliations. They inhabit elite neighbourhoods, such as Forest Hill in Toronto or Westmount in Montreal. Schools extend this privileged environment. Their children typically attend private schools such as Upper Canada College with others of similar background, completing their formal education at high-prestige universities such as Cambridge, Oxford, or Harvard. In the historical pattern of European aristocrats, they study liberal arts rather than vocationally directed subjects.

Women of the upper-upper class often maintain a full schedule of volunteer work for charitable organizations. For example, women from Toronto's upper-crust neighbourhoods are the backbone of the Toronto Symphony and the National Ballet: old-money families support these organizations, offering their time as well as funds. While helping the larger community, such charitable activities also build networks that put these families at the centre of the nation's power elite (Ostrander, 1980, 1984).

Lower-Upper Class

The remaining 2 to 4 percent of the population that makes up the upper class falls into the *lower-upper class*. From the point of view of the average Canadian, such people seem every bit as privileged as the upper-upper class. The major difference, however, is that "lower-uppers" are the "working

For decades, farm families who worked hard could expect to fall within the middle class. But the trend towards large-scale agribusiness has put the future of the small family farm in doubt. While many young people in rural areas are turning away from farming towards other careers, some carry on, incorporating high technology into their farm management in their determined efforts to succeed. (Recall the discussion of the effect of new technologies on occupational prestige.)

rich" who depend on earnings rather than wealth as their primary source of income. Few people in this category inherit a vast fortune from their parents, although the majority do inherit some wealth.

Especially in the eyes of members of "society," those in the lower-upper class are merely the *nouveau riche*, people who can never savour the highest levels of prestige enjoyed by those with rich and famous grandparents. Thus, while the new rich typically live in expensive homes, they often find themselves excluded from the most prestigious clubs and associations maintained by families with old money.

Historically, the dream of great success has meant joining the ranks of the lower-upper class through exceptional accomplishment. The entrepreneurial individual who makes the right business moves with split-second timing, the athlete who accepts a million-dollar contract to play in the big leagues, the computer whiz who designs a new program that sets a standard for the industry—these are the lucky and talented achievers who reach the level of the lower-upper class. Their success stories fascinate us because this kind of upwards social mobility has long stood as a goal that, however unlikely, is still within the realm of the possible. A dual-earner family in which both wife and husband are professionals can make it into this lower-upper stratum of society. Members of the upper-upper class, in contrast, move in rarefied circles far from the everyday reality of the rest of us.

THE MIDDLE CLASS

Encompassing about 40 to 50 percent of the Canadian population, the middle class exerts tremendous influence on our culture. Television and other mass media usually portray middle-class people, and most commercial advertising is directed at the "average" consumer. The middle class encompasses far more racial and ethnic diversity than the upper class. While many upper-class people—especially upper-upper—know each other personally, such exclusiveness and familiarity do not characterize the middle class.

Upper-Middle Class

The top half of this large category is often termed the *upper-middle class*, based on above-average income in the range of $50 000 to $100 000 a year. Such income allows families in the upper-middle class to gradually accumulate considerable property—a comfortable house in a fairly expensive area, several automobiles, and some investments. Virtually all people in the upper-middle class receive university educations, and postgraduate degrees are common. Many go on to a high-prestige occupation (e.g., physician, engineer, lawyer, accountant, or business executive). Lacking the power of the upper class to influence national or international events, the upper-middle class often plays an important role in local political affairs.

Average-Middle Class

The rest of the middle class falls near the centre of our class structure. People in the *average-middle class* typically work in less prestigious white-collar occupations (as bank tellers, middle managers, and sales clerks) or in highly skilled blue-collar jobs (including electrical work and carpentry). Family income is sufficient to provide a secure, if modest, standard of living. Middle-class Canadians generally accumulate a small amount of wealth over the course of their working lives, and most will own a house. Middle-class men and women are likely to be high school graduates. If they do send their children to university, it is more likely to be the one closest to home to save on accommodation expenses. For a discussion of middle-class involvement in the Calgary Stampede, go to the Applying Sociology box (on p. 277).

THE WORKING CLASS

Including about one-third of the population, the *working class* (sometimes called the *lower-middle class*) refers to people who have lower incomes than those in the middle class and little or no accumulated wealth. In marxist terms, the working class forms the core of the industrial proletariat. The blue-collar occupations of the working class generally yield a family income that is somewhat below the national average, although unionized blue-collar workers can contribute to family incomes that are well above that level.

APPLYING SOCIOLOGY
Middle-Class Stampede?

Who participates in community festivals? Surely the Calgary Stampede, for example, draws a cross-section of the community and Canadians from a wide geographic area, into a generalized tension-release ritual. Without a doubt "yahoos" and "yippees" will be part of the spontaneous vocabulary of people everywhere. Right?

Visit the official website of the Calgary Stampede at http://calgary stampede.com.

Richard J. Ossenberg set out to show that, while homogeneous communities might give rise to generalized participation, complex urban centres such as Calgary would elicit differentiated or selective participation. His research involved "a systematic pub-crawl on two evenings of the weeklong Stampede" held every July. He expected to find that members of the middle class, who are more "sensitive to legal and other restrictive norms," might be most likely to respond to the relaxation of social controls with "festival-related aggressive/expressive behaviour" (1979:405).

Ossenberg had already carried out extensive analysis of Calgary bar behaviour as a way of discovering the social class structure in Calgary, so he knew which nine of the city's beer parlours and lounges would represent a cross-section of social classes. Those chosen for the study were close to the Stampede grounds: two were upper class, three were middle class, and four were lower class. The establishments are described as follows:

The upper-class establishments are usually patronized by the elite oil and ranching group as well as the *nouveau riche* and the occasional white-collar couple celebrating an anniversary. The middle-class bars are patronized by clerical workers, small business men, and generally middle-range employees of the larger local firms, with the occasional labourer drifting in. The lower-class bars are the clearest in definition. They are patronized by service personnel, labourers, winos, and deprived Indians as well as by members of newly arrived immigrant groups. (p. 406)

During the two evenings of observation, Ossenberg found that "only about one in ten of the tipplers at the lower-class establishments wore Western cowboy costume and most of those who did were completely ignored by the other patrons." The noise level was lower than usual, fights broke out less frequently, prostitutes were more in evidence, and patrons stuck to the normal pattern of men's parlour and "ladies and escorts" parlour, even though restrictions were lifted during the Stampede. And there were virtually no rodeo-related "yahoos" to be heard.

In the middle-class establishments (two cocktail lounges and one beer parlour in a posh hotel), 90 percent or more of the patrons were in cowboy or Western costume. In fact, the researchers were ridiculed for their lack of such attire. The noise levels were intolerable, "yippees" and "yahoos" filled the air, and back slapping and necking were the norm. Executives interacted freely with their secretaries, and tourists or strangers were readily accepted and even invited to house parties. Call girls, rather than street-walkers, made their appearances.

The two upper-middle–class cocktail lounges in Calgary's plush, reputable hotels presented a very different picture. About 25 percent of patrons were costumed, but the noisy celebration was missing. Here, as in the working-class bars, it was business as usual. The few costumed patrons who tried to liven up the scene soon left in disgust: "Let's blow this joint—it's like a graveyard" (p. 410).

Ossenberg concluded that Stampede week is "functional" for people who are inhibited in their daily lives and "look forward to the 'green light' of tolerated deviance during a community festival." Behaviour during such festivals reflects the social structure of the city but does not reinforce solidarity across class lines. It is, in effect, a "middle-class 'binge'."

Postscript In January 1996, Calgary had its first (annual) cowboy convention, in opulent surroundings. Here cowboys and cowgirls—the authentic and the wannabes—gathered to share cowboy lore, paraphernalia, and music, or simply to celebrate a way of life. So central is the horse to the cowboy lifestyle that—to the dismay of the hotel staff who had to clean up the plush carpets in their wake—several of the better-known horses were invited to mingle with their fans.

WHAT DO YOU THINK?

1. Have you ever been to the Calgary Stampede? Is it something you would enjoy—or does the festival not appeal to you? What kinds of people are attracted to it?
2. Are you surprised to learn that middle-class people are the most likely to get into the spirit of the Stampede?
3. Can you think of reasons for the lack of festivities in lower-class bars?

Source: Ossenberg (1979).

The life of this Newfoundland fisher has been changed drastically by the moratorium on cod fishing. How do you think different classes are affected by this type of change in the local economy?

Many working-class jobs provide little personal satisfaction, requiring discipline but rarely imagination, and subject workers to continual supervision. These jobs also provide fewer benefits, such as dental insurance and pension plans. University is less likely to be part of the experience of children of working-class parents. The many working-class families who own their own homes are likely to own them in lower-cost neighbourhoods.

THE LOWER CLASS

The 20 percent of our population with the lowest family income makes up the *lower class*. For these people, a lack of work and little income renders life unstable and insecure. The 1996 census placed 5.5 million Canadians, 19.7 percent of the population, as poor. The numbers had decreased by the 2001 census, so that 4.7 million people, or 16.2 percent of the population, were classified as poor. While some of these people are supported entirely by social benefits, others are among the *working poor*—those whose incomes from full-time jobs or multiple part-time jobs fall short of what is required to cover necessities such as food, shelter, and clothing. The working poor have low-prestige jobs that provide minimal income and little intrinsic satisfaction. Some have managed to complete high school, but university degrees and college diplomas are relatively rare. In fact, many lower-class men and women are functionally illiterate.

Lower-class families find themselves segregated into specific, less-desirable neighbourhoods—some of which are ethnically or racially distinct (Michelson, 1988:93). While there are many poor people in small towns and rural areas—where resource-based industries have collapsed or plants have closed, physical segregation of the poor is most starkly apparent in cities, where large numbers of poor people live in rental housing that is avoided by others.

Lower-class children quickly learn that many people consider them to be only marginal members of society. Observing their parents and other lower-status adults, they may conclude that their own futures hold little hope for breaking the cycle of poverty. Lower-class life, then, can generate self-defeating resignation among those cut off from the resources of an affluent society; welfare dependency, as a lifestyle, can be passed from one generation to the next. Some of the poor simply give up, but others—the working poor—go to great lengths to avoid going on welfare, often working at two or three jobs to make ends meet.

The policies of Conservative governments in Alberta and Ontario led to reductions in welfare payments and tighter eligibility requirements. Fewer people are on welfare but studies have yet to identify where the missing welfare recipients have gone or how they are managing to survive. Relatively low unemployment rates may account for some of the drop in welfare dependency.

The Difference Class Makes

Social stratification affects nearly every dimension of our lives. We will briefly examine some of the ways social standing is linked to our health, values, politics, and family life.

HEALTH

Health is closely related to social standing. Children born into poor families are three times more likely to die from disease, neglect, accidents, or violence during their first years of life than children born into privileged families. Among adults, people with above-average incomes are almost twice as likely as low-income people to describe their health as excellent. In addition, richer people live, on average, seven years longer because they eat more nutritious food, live in safer and less stressful environments, and receive better medical care (Lethbridge-Cejku and Vickerie, 2005).

VALUES AND ATTITUDES

Some cultural values vary from class to class. People with old money have an unusually strong sense of family history because their social position is based on wealth passed from generation to generation. Secure in their birthright privileges, people from the upper-upper class also favour understated manners and tastes; many *nouveau riche* engage in conspicuous consumption, using homes, cars, and even airplanes as status symbols to make a statement about their social position. Affluent people with greater education and financial security are also more tolerant of controversial behaviour such as homosexuality. Working-class people, who grow up in an atmosphere of greater supervision and discipline, and are less likely to attend college, tend to be less tolerant (Baltzell, 1979a; orig. 1958; Lareau, 2002; NORC, 2003).

FAMILY AND GENDER

Social class also shapes family life. Generally, lower-class families are somewhat larger than middle-class families because of earlier marriage and less career orientation on the part of women; labour force participation encourages women to limit family size. Also, working-class parents encourage children to conform to conventional norms and to respect authority figures. Parents of higher social standing pass on different cultural capital to their children, teaching them to express their individuality and imagination more freely. In both cases, parents are looking to the future; the odds are that less privileged children will have jobs that require them to follow rules and that more privileged children will have careers that require more creativity (Kohn, 1977; McLeod, 1995; Lareau, 2002).

The more money a family has, the more parents can develop their children's talents and abilities. One American study found that an affluent family earning US$105 000 a year will spend US$269 520 raising a child born in 2004 to the age of 18; middle-class parents with an annual income of US$55 500 will spend US$184 320; and a lower-income family, earning less than US$41 700, will spend US$133 370 (Lino, 2005). The Canadian figures might be higher because of the lower-value Canadian dollar but, whatever the exact numbers, raising children—with music lessons, sports activity, and higher education—is expensive here too. The bottom line is that privilege leads to privilege as family life reproduces the class structure in each new generation.

Class also shapes our world of relationships. In a classic study of married life, Elizabeth Bott (1971; orig. 1957) found that most working-class couples divide their responsibilities according to gender roles; middle-class couples, in contrast, are more egalitarian, sharing more activities and expressing greater intimacy. More recently, Karen Walker (1995) discovered that working-class friendships typically serve as sources of material assistance; middle-class friendships are likely to involve shared interests and leisure pursuits.

Social Mobility

Canadians have a dynamic society marked by significant social movement. Earning a university degree, landing a higher-paying job, or marrying someone who earns a good income contributes to *upward social mobility*; dropping out of school, losing a job, or becoming divorced (especially for women) may result in *downward social mobility*. Over the long term, social mobility is not so much a matter of changes in individuals as changes in society itself. In the first half of the twentieth century, for example, industrialization expanded the North American economy, pushing up living standards. Even people who were not good swimmers rode the rising tide of prosperity. More recently, *structural social mobility* in a downward direction has dealt many people economic setbacks.

Compared to high-income people, low-income people are half as likely to report good health and, on average, live about seven fewer years. The toll of low income—played out in inadequate nutrition, little medical care, and high stress—is easy to see on the faces of the poor, who look old before their time.

Sociologists distinguish between shorter- and longer-term changes in social position. **Intragenerational social mobility** is *a change in social position occurring during a person's lifetime*. **Intergenerational social mobility**, *upward or downward social mobility of children in relation to their parents*, is important because it usually reveals long-term changes in society, such as industrialization, that affect everyone.

SOCIAL MOBILITY IN CANADA

While the American dream may be attributed to people south of the border, Canadians share, to some extent, the belief that those who apply themselves can get ahead and that each new generation will do better than the last. Clearly, that is the hope of most of our immigrants. But how much social mobility is there in Canada?

Data from the 1986 General Social Survey revealed that Canadians have been a little more likely to experience upward than downward mobility (Creese, *et al.*, 1991). Compared with their fathers, 48 percent of women moved up, while 40 percent moved down; the comparable figures for men are 39 and 36 percent, respectively. Only 12 percent of women and 26 percent of men experienced no mobility

The mass media are full of suggestions that upward social mobility is within reach of everyone. Recent television shows, including *The Bachelor*, *The Bachelorette*, and *How to Marry a Millionaire* (*above*), spread the message that getting rich is as easy as saying "I do." How realistic is this claim?

at all, meaning that they ended up in the same occupational category as their fathers. Occupational inheritance (following in Dad's footsteps) occurs most commonly among men whose fathers are in the professional, white-collar, and farming categories. Specific occupational inheritance has been less common for women because of the types of occupations traditionally available to them.

While overall educational levels are increasing, class background continues to affect educational attainment: the higher the level of education and occupation of one's father, the more years of schooling one is likely to complete. Furthermore, a person's first job is *principally* affected by his or her level of education. Therefore, parental education and occupation have an impact on occupational status, not directly but through their effects on the educational attainment of the younger generation. Thus, a physician passes his occupation on to his child *if* he or she inspires that child to jump the educational hurdles required to gain admission to and complete medical school.

Education, then, is the key to occupational mobility in Canada. If family background has an impact, it is through its effect on schooling. But, as we saw earlier, francophones, visible minorities, and women have difficulty translating their educational accomplishments into higher-status, well-paid work.

Others have also noted the general lack of occupational inheritance in Canada. In a study of occupational mobility over four generations, Goyder and Curtis (1979) found that the occupations of great-grandfathers had no bearing whatsoever on those of their great-grandsons. Occupationally speaking, the descendants were all over the map. On the basis of their findings and those of others who have studied the extreme upper and lower ends of the spectrum, Goyder and Curtis conclude that the "two types of processes may well occur together: high overall three-generation mobility in the general population along with low three-generation mobility in poverty and elite groups" (p. 229). In other words, those at the very top and bottom of the socioeconomic ladder may experience substantial occupational inheritance, while those in the middle do not.

Historically, women have had less opportunity for upward mobility than men. As we shall see in Chapter 13 ("Gender Stratification"), the majority of working women hold clerical positions (e.g., secretaries) and low-paying service jobs (such as waiting tables). These jobs offer little chance for advancement, which effectively limits upward social or economic movement. Divorce also commonly results in downward social mobility for women—but not for men—as Chapter 18 ("Family") explains. Data reflecting income change during the 1980s and 1990s reveal a narrowing of the gap between the earnings of women and men, with the female-to-male income ratio increasing from about 60 to over 70 percent, for people working full time all year in 2000.

Poverty in Canada

Social stratification simultaneously creates haves and have-nots. Poverty, therefore, inevitably exists within all systems of social inequality. Sociologists employ the concept of poverty in two different ways, however. **Relative poverty,** which is by definition universal and inevitable, refers to *the deprivation of some people in relation to those who have more.* The richest and most egalitarian of societies have some members who live in relative poverty. Much more serious is **absolute poverty,** or *a deprivation of resources that is life-threatening.* Defined in this way, poverty is a pressing, but solvable, human problem. As the next chapter ("Global Stratification") explains, the global dimensions of absolute poverty place the lives of perhaps 800 million people—one in seven of the Earth's entire population—at risk. Even in affluent Canada, with its social safety net, families go hungry, live in inadequate housing, and endure poor health because of wrenching poverty.

THE EXTENT OF CANADIAN POVERTY

Poverty statistics are based on the "poverty line," also known as the "low-income cut-off." People who spend at least 55 percent of their pre-tax income on food, clothing, and shelter are considered to be below the poverty line. By that measure, a recent high of 15.7 percent of the population fell below the poverty line in 1995—in a recession period. By 2004, the proportion had dropped, fairly steadily, to 11.2 percent. It is this drop in the proportion of the population below the poverty line that gave rise to a little excitement at *The Globe and Mail*, where an editorial on April 1, 2006, claimed that "The poor, it seems, do not always get poorer. The number of low income families actually declined in 2004. And child poverty, despite alarming bulletins from the activists, isn't getting worse either" (p. A22). The editorial followed up on front page coverage—"Growth spurs decline in poverty" (Scoffield, 2006)—and a major analytical article with dramatic graphs (Mahoney, 2006) from the previous day.

In the past, Canada's lack of progress in eliminating poverty prompted a United Nations committee to sharply criticize the Canadian government "for allowing poverty and homelessness to persist at disturbing levels in one of the world's richest countries" (York, 1993:A1). At the time, about half of Canada's single mothers and a million children lived in poverty, and many Canadians depended on voluntary food banks to deal with hunger. While the proportion is now lower, the actual number is still large: in 2004, 865 000 Canadian children lived in poverty. Poverty means hunger, and many of the people at lower income levels are forced to rely on food banks and soup kitchens, both of which in Canada are run by voluntary organizations. The demand for food banks has increased substantially over the past few years to a point where, today, there are more than 650 food banks that feed more than 800 000 different people each month.

 For information about Canada's food banks and their annual Hunger Count, see www.cafb-acba.ca.

A 1998 United Nations report also criticized Canada for its poor response in dealing with human poverty. Canada placed tenth among seventeen industrialized nations—behind Sweden, the Netherlands, Germany, Norway, Italy, Finland, France, Japan, and Denmark—in "spreading around the wealth," reducing social inequality, and avoiding the immense social costs of impoverishment (Duffy and Mandel, 2001:79). The fact that so many people feel the need to resort to food banks, which function only because some people volunteer to staff them while others donate food, is particularly distressing in a country where we have the resources to alleviate poverty, if only we had the political will.

WHO ARE THE POOR?

While no single description covers all poor people, poverty is pronounced within certain segments of our population. Women, children, some visible minorities, and people living in rural areas are all at higher risk of being poor. Regional disparities in economic development and income are also in evidence, in that poverty is a particularly acute problem in the Atlantic provinces, Quebec, the territories, and the northern parts of the western provinces. With any combination of the above factors, the problem of poverty is especially serious.

Age

The burden of poverty falls heavily on Canadian children. In 2004, as presented in Figure 11–6, 12.8 percent of those under 18 years of age were living below the low-income cut-off. Child poverty rates rose from a low of 11.7 percent in 1989 to a high of 18.6 in 1996, before dropping off to 12.8 percent in 2004—mainly because of "the federal government's child tax benefit, which has been rising steadily over the past decade" (Scoffield, 2006). We have taken steps to eradicate child poverty—something that the Liberal party vowed to do during federal elections of 1993, 1997, and 2000. The Harper Conservative government's payment of $1200 per year per child under six will make another dent in Canada's child poverty rates, which should show up in statistics almost immediately.

Figure 11–6 reveals dramatic differences in poverty levels among children in different family types. Children in two-parent families are relatively unlikely to find themselves below the low-income cut-off (8.1% in 2004). In sharp contrast, 40 percent of children in female lone-parent families fell below the poverty line in 2004; the only bright spot in that statistic is its substantial decline from 59 percent in 1985—with a spike in the interim to 56 percent in 1996. While the situation of children in female lone-parent families has improved dramatically since 1996, the fact that 40 percent still fall below the poverty line is a scar on the face of our kinder, gentler society.

A generation ago, the elderly were at the greatest risk of poverty. In 1985, the poverty rates for women and men 65 years of age and over were 19.3 percent and 8.4 percent, respectively; by 2004, the rates had dropped to 7.3 percent and 3.5 percent. Figure 11–6 reveals that the situation of unattached individuals improved by about 5 percentage points from 1985 to 2004. In the meantime, *unattached* elderly people have seen their poverty level drop from 39 to 15.5 percent (to 17% for women and 11.6% for men). Clearly, better pension support from the government and employers has led to another success story in the elimination of poverty—but the movement of the baby boomers into the retirement years means that the *numbers* of elderly and poor elderly people will increase in the future. Simultaneously, we can expect a closing of the gap between the poverty rates of elderly men and women, as more women who have been employed and established careers reach retirement age.

Education

Education is another factor that determines the likelihood of having an income below the poverty line. People who have higher levels of education are less likely to be unemployed and more likely to have higher incomes. Not surprisingly, they are also less likely to fall below the poverty line: the incidence of poverty drops with each added level of education.

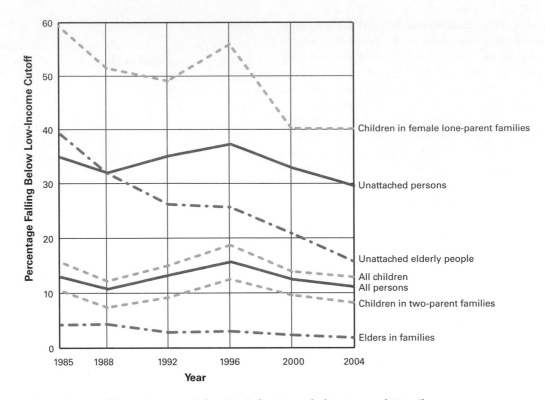

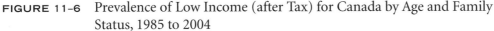

FIGURE 11-6   Prevalence of Low Income (after Tax) for Canada by Age and Family
Status, 1985 to 2004

Source: Statistics Canada, catalogue no. 75-202-X.

Race and Ethnicity

The likelihood of experiencing poverty is related to race and ethnicity in Canada, but the ranking of various categories is not necessarily what we might expect. A study based on 1986 census data offered some surprising results. Those of English origin are not all at the top of the income hierarchy; in fact, in a ranking of 60 ethnic and racial categories by average male income for those employed full time all year, those of English origin rank 25th (Gerber, 1990:79). The French, too, are near the middle. Canadians of Welsh and Scottish background appear in the top 15, along with those of Jewish and Japanese descent.

In the lowest 15 categories we find Black, West Indian, and Latin American people, some people of Asian origins, and Aboriginal peoples. The only categories that rank below Aboriginal peoples are groups that tend to be recent immigrants and possibly refugees (Chileans and other Latin Americans, Vietnamese, Haitians, Laotians, and Cambodians). While male income for those employed full time is only one indicator of economic well-being, the rank ordering by race or ethnicity is suggestive. We would expect to find that more of the individuals or families in the lowest 15 categories have incomes below the poverty line.

Further data analysis related to Figures 11–4 and 11–5 suggests that, despite improvements in recent years, some categories of people will continue to be poorer than others.

The proportion below the low-income cut-off in 2001 ranges from 9 percent or 10 percent for those of English, French or Japanese origins, to 25 percent of those of Chinese or Aboriginal origin, to 33 percent among those who identify as Black people.

Gender and Family Patterns

The disparity in male and female incomes and the fact that lone-parent families tend to be headed by females contribute to higher rates of poverty among women. Statistics Canada provides data that help account for the **feminization of poverty,** *the trend by which women represent an increasing proportion of the poor.* The effects of pay or employment inequity and family structure on the economic well-being of women are clear. Women are less likely to be employed: 63 percent of women 15 to 24 years of age are employed, as compared to 74 percent of men. Women who work full time all year are paid only 71.6 percent of male income. Further, women are more likely than men to be working part time.

Lone-parent families, which make up 14.5 percent of all families in 2001, tend to have lower incomes than two-parent families. Female-headed lone-parent families have

Information about women and the economy is presented on a website sponsored by the U.N. Platform for Action Committee in Manitoba at http://unpac.ca/economy/index2.html.

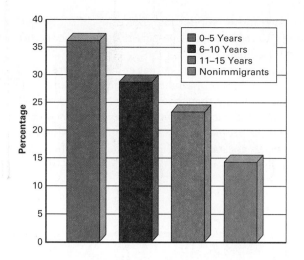

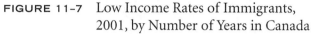

FIGURE 11-7   Low Income Rates of Immigrants, 2001, by Number of Years in Canada

Source: Adapted from Statistics Canada, *The Daily*, June 19, 2003, www.statcan.ca.

FIGURE 11-8   Average Family Income in Canada by Family Structure, 2001

Source: Adapted by L.M. Gerber from Statistics Canada, catalogue no. 97F0020XCB2001007.

the lowest average income, as shown in Figure 11–8, and the largest percentage falling below the official low-income cut-off. Of children living in female-headed lone-parent families, 45.4 percent live in poverty, as demonstrated in Figure 11–9.

It is clear, then, that lone-parent families have substantially lower incomes than two-parent families, and that female-headed lone-parent families are the most disadvantaged. Issues of pay equity, employment equity, and family structure combine to increase the incidence of poverty among women, thereby contributing to the feminization of poverty.

EXPLAINING POVERTY

The presence of 3.6 million poor people in one of the world's most affluent societies raises serious social and moral concerns. It also sparks considerable controversy within Canada—and from abroad. Many Canadians concur with the U.N. committees mentioned earlier, arguing that our government should take a much more active role in eradicating poverty. Others feel that the poor must bear responsibility for themselves. It is also possible to argue that *both* governments and the poor themselves need to contribute to the solution. The arguments underlying these approaches to the problem of poverty together frame a lively and pressing political debate.

One View: Blame the Poor

Proponents of one side of the issue hold the view that *the poor are primarily responsible for their own poverty*. In this land of immigration and once seemingly unlimited resources and opportunities, we have embraced the notion that people are largely responsible for their own social standing. This approach assumes that our society offers considerable opportunity for anyone able and willing to

take advantage of it. The poor, then, are those with fewer skills, less schooling, lower motivation, or, perhaps, a debilitating drug addiction—in sum, people who are somehow undeserving.

Anthropologist Oscar Lewis (1961) illustrates this approach in his studies of Latin American poverty. Lewis claims that the poor become entrapped in a *culture of poverty* that fosters resignation to one's plight. Socialized in this environment, children come to believe that there is little point in aspiring to a better life. The result is a self-perpetuating cycle of poverty. Edward Banfield (1974) adds the contention that, where there is intense poverty, there exists a distinctive lower-class subculture that denigrates and erodes personal achievement. One element of this subculture encourages living for the moment, rather than looking towards the future by engaging in hard work, saving, and other behaviour likely to promote upward social mobility. In Banfield's view, poor people who live largely for the moment perpetuate their own poverty; he defines this kind of behaviour as basically irresponsible, and he concludes that the poor reap more or less what they deserve.

Counterpoint: Blame Society

The other view of the issue is that *society is primarily responsible for poverty*. This alternative position, argued by William Ryan (1976), holds that society—not the poor—is responsible for poverty because of the way resources are distributed. In global context, societies that distribute wealth very disproportionately face a significant poverty problem. Societies that strive for more equality (such as Sweden and Japan) lack such extremes of social stratification. Poverty, Ryan insists, is not inevitable: the problem is simply a matter of low incomes, not personal deficiencies. Ryan interprets any lack of ambition on the part of poor

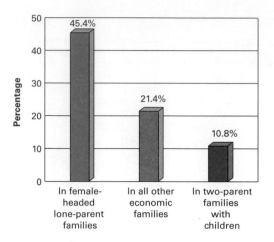

FIGURE 11-9 Percentage of Children under 18 Years of Age in Canada with Low Income by Family Structure, 2001

Source: Adapted by L.M. Gerber from Statistics Canada, catalogue no. 97F0020XCB2001007.

people as a *consequence* rather than a *cause* of their lack of opportunity. He therefore dismisses Banfield's analysis as little more than "blaming the victims" for their own suffering. In Ryan's view, social policies that empower the poor would give them real economic opportunity, and this should yield greater equality.

Critical Review Each of these explanations of poverty has won its share of public support, and each has advocates among government policy makers. Some, particularly on the right of the political spectrum, believe that society should strive to encourage equality of opportunity, but should otherwise adopt a laissez-faire attitude towards the poor. Others, on the political left, hold that society should actively reduce poverty by redistributing income more proportionately, providing a comprehensive daycare program like that of Quebec, or ensuring a guaranteed minimum income for every family.

Since the heads of many low-income families do not have jobs, their poverty is attributed to *not holding a job*. But the reasons that people do not work are a reflection on society as much as the individuals concerned. Middle-class women combine working and child-rearing, but doing so is much harder for poor women who cannot afford child care. Quebec is the exception with respect to child care, which is available at the phenomenal rate of $7 per day. In the rest of Canada, few employers provide child-care programs for their employees, and few low-income workers can afford to buy this service from the private sector. Where child-care subsidies are provided, parents may still find that, when all costs are considered, it is cheaper to stay at home and take care of one's own children. As noted above, the Harper Conservative government is providing $1200 per child annually to parents of children under six years of age, with

the intention of supporting choice in child care. Among those choices is that of one-parent staying at home to care for young children.

Most poor men report that either there are no jobs to be found, illness or disability has sidelined them, or, in the case of the elderly, they have retired. Overall, poor adults are poor not by choice, but because they know of no alternatives. These people may be among those for whom welfare (or social assistance) is a life-line. See the Thinking Critically box (on p 287) for a discussion of Canada's welfare dilemma.

YOUR TURN

When you talk about issues of income security and welfare with your friends or family, what are the main explanations of poverty that you hear?

THE WORKING POOR

Not all poor people are jobless. At various points in this chapter, tables and figures refer to salaries of people who work full time all year. Many of these salaries—for women, for certain occupations, and for people belonging to specific ethnic and racial categories—are low relative to the official poverty line. If these people, working full time, have incomes that are below the poverty line for individuals, what happens if they are single parents with two or three children? The working poor include the men and women who labour for at least fifty weeks of the year and yet cannot escape poverty; many people who involuntarily work part time are also included among the working poor. Such "working poverty" places the poor in a bind: their jobs provide low wages that barely allow them to make ends meet, but consume the time and energy needed to obtain training or schooling that might open new doors. People in this situation are often reluctant or simply unable to risk the jobs they do have in hopes of finding something better. Even with minimum wages of $6.50 to $8.50 in 2006 (depending on the province or territory), a full-time worker could not support a family above the official poverty line.

Clearly, individual ability and initiative play a part in shaping everyone's social position. On balance, though, the weight of sociological evidence points to society—not individual character traits—as the primary cause of poverty. This is because the poor are categories of people who contend with special barriers and limited opportunities.

HOMELESSNESS

Many low-income people in Canada cannot afford even basic housing. As a society, we have failed to ensure an adequate supply of affordable housing. In light of the enor-

African-American artist Henry Ossawa Tanner captured the humility and humanity of impoverished people in his painting *The Thankful Poor*. This insight is important in a society that tends to define poor people as morally unworthy and deserving of their bitter plight.

Henry Ossawa Tanner (1859–1973), *The Thankful Poor*. Private collection. Art Resource. New York.

mous wealth of our country and its purported commitment to providing opportunity and/or social safety nets for everyone, homelessness may be fairly described as a societal scar that demands an effective response.

Throughout Canada, thousands of people live on the streets, in various often temporary shelters, and even in our jails. The familiar stereotypes of homeless people—men sleeping in doorways and women carrying everything they own in a shopping bag—have been undermined by the reality of the "new" homeless: those thrown out of work by plant closings; people forced out of apartments by rising rents, condominium conversions, or "gentrification" (e.g., converting rooming houses into expensive single-family homes); and people unable to meet mortgage or rent payments because they must work for low wages. Clearly, no stereotype paints a complete picture of the homeless. But virtually all homeless people have one thing in common: poverty.

For that reason, the explanations of poverty already offered also apply to homelessness. One side of the debate places responsibility on personal traits of the homeless themselves. Perhaps one-third of homeless people are mentally ill; others are addicted to alcohol or other drugs. Some, for whatever reason, seem unable to cope in a complex and highly competitive society (Bassuk, 1984; Whitman, 1989). On the other side, advocates assert that homelessness results from *societal* factors, including a lack of low-income housing and the economic transition towards low-paying jobs (Kozol, 1988; Bohannon, 1991). Fully one-third of all homeless people are now entire families, and children are the fastest-growing category of the homeless. The closing of a plant, making it necessary for an

individual to take a poorly paid job at McDonald's, makes it very difficult to support a family.

No one disputes that a large proportion of homeless people have personal difficulties to some degree, although how much is cause and how much is effect is difficult to untangle. But structural changes in the Canadian economy coupled with declining government support for lower-income people have all contributed to homelessness. In the winter of 1995–96, the Toronto churches that provide emergency overnight accommodation for the homeless were finding that more *families* were appearing on their doorsteps. Some of these families were evicted by landlords when reduced welfare payments could no longer cover the rent. In the same winter (a record-setting one for cold in Toronto), at least two homeless people froze to death while huddled in their makeshift shelters. One man, who died under a highway ramp, did not even have shoes on his feet.

A comprehensive response to homelessness must consider both personal and societal dimensions of the problem. Increasing the supply of low-income housing (other than shelters) is one important step. In addition, low-income people must have the opportunity to earn the income necessary to pay for housing. Homelessness, however, is not only a housing problem—it is also a *human* problem. People who endure months or years of insecure living come to need various types of social services.

 A report by the U.S. Conference of Mayors on homelessness is found at http://usmayors.org/uscm/hungersurvey/2004/online report/HungerAndHomelessness Report2004.pdf.

The Media Perspectives box (on p. 288) provides you with insight into an attempt to make a census of the homeless in Toronto.

MEDIA PERSPECTIVES
Counting the Homeless in Toronto

The census of Canada, which counts and assesses the characteristics of our population, is carried out in the years ending in 1 (i.e., 1981 or 2001) and 6 (i.e., 1976 or 2006). Since almost all census forms are mailed to home addresses, homeless people fall through the cracks—just as they do for the General Social Survey, which asks much more detailed questions relating to overall well-being. As a result, we know very little about the numbers and characteristics of the homeless anywhere in Canada.

For the first time, on May 19, 2006, Toronto undertook a census of its homeless population—involving 1600 volunteers and 400 paid team leaders (earning $100 each), who covered the downtown core and outlying areas. *National Post* journalist, James Cowan (2006), reported on the survey, its methodology, and general reactions to the survey itself. A number of people—including some at the Scott Mission, which feeds the poor and homeless—were cynical about the whole process. While the volunteers generally were greeted warmly by the homeless themselves, some treated the project "with a mixture of skepticism and curiosity." For many of the homeless, though, it was the first time they had ever been asked, formally, about their opinions, needs, or identities. David Smith, executive director of the Scott Mission, noted that: "Asking someone directly what they think is a very affirming thing to do." On the other hand, he heard mainly negative

comments at the Scott—and nobody coming out to say, "Wow, this is an amazing thing."

The survey itself—which cost $90 000—was conducted as follows: "Working in three-to-four person groups, half of the teams were assigned to blanket the downtown core. Additional teams were sent to spots in Etobicoke, Scarborough, and North York where homeless people are believed to live, as well as 100 randomly selected locations," and 60 Toronto shelters (Cowan, 2006). High risk areas—like the Don Valley, and underneath bridges or the elevated Gardiner Expressway—were covered by city staff instead of volunteers. In the interests of quality control, 50 decoys (i.e., fake homeless people) were distributed across the survey area. Tracking the proportion of decoys who were interviewed would provide a measure of the survey's accuracy. Cowan noted one other thing: "Each homeless person who completed the survey received a $5 gift certificate for Tim Hortons, McDonald's, Pizza Pizza, or Country Style."

There were other *National Post* journalists at work that night. Peter Kuitenbrouwer (2006) sat the night out with Dave, Bonnie, and Cheryle, homeless people settled down at the corner of Bathurst and Queen West. He heard their life stories, and found out what Dave—father of four and drywaller, who became homeless after tearing the rotator cuff in his shoulder—thinks of the census: "I think it's a crock of s____." The obvious solution, accord-

ing to Dave and Bonnie, is more affordable housing. The three were in plain view and were clearly homeless with Cheryle lying on a blue sleeping bag fighting pneumonia, but they "never saw hide nor hair of a census-taker." Kuitenbrouwer therefore entitled his story "the uncounted ones."

In the meantime, Jacob Richler (2006) looked at the problem of over-counting—by posing as a homeless person himself, he answered the survey questions several times over: "'Have you already been interviewed tonight by someone wearing a name tag like this?' 'No,' I say, discretely patting the pocketful of $5 meal coupons I've been collecting at the rate of one per chat all night." Noting that people were asked if they identified themselves as "male / female / transgender / transsexual / other," Richler wondered what the City of Toronto meant by "other." Humour aside, it is clear that some homeless people were missed by the census takers and others were interviewed numerous times. The attempt to count every homeless person—once—clearly was flawed in execution.

WHAT DO YOU THINK?

1. Do you feel that this city census of the homeless is worthwhile or a waste of $90 000?
2. What kinds of questions would you have asked the homeless if you were co-ordinating these interviews?
3. Under what circumstances might you find yourself among the homeless? Can it happen to anyone?

⟷ ⟨ YOUR TURN ⟩ ⟷

Our society has been more generous with the "worthy" poor (such as elderly people) than with the "unworthy" poor (such as able-bodied people who, we assume, should take care of themselves). Why do you think we have not done more to reduce poverty among children, who surely fall into the "worthy" category?

Social stratification extends far beyond the borders of Canada. In fact, the most striking social inequality is found not within any one nation but in the different living standards from nation to nation around the world. In Chapter 12 ("Global Stratification"), we broaden our investigation of stratification by looking at global inequality.

THINKING CRITICALLY
The Welfare Dilemma

The predicament of Karen Moss, described at the beginning of this chapter, highlights a remarkable consensus in this country regarding welfare—nobody likes it. The political left criticizes it as an inadequate response to poverty; those on the right charge that it is hurting the people it allegedly helps and driving the country to bankruptcy; and the poor themselves find welfare a complex, confusing, and often degrading program.

Critics on the political right contend that, rather than alleviating poverty, welfare has actually *worsened* the problem for two reasons. First, it has eroded the traditional family by making living as a single person an attractive alternative to marriage. As the right sees it, welfare makes it economically beneficial for women to have children outside of marriage and is a key reason for the rapid rise in out-of-wedlock births among poor people. Second, the right-wing critique holds that government assistance undermines self-reliance among the poor and fosters dependency. Dependence on government handouts, argue critics, is the main reason that so many poor heads of households do not have steady, full-time jobs. Clearly, from the perspective of the right, welfare has strayed far from its original purpose of helping nonworking women with children make the transition to self-sufficiency—typically, after the death or divorce of a husband. Instead, dependence on welfare has become a way of life. Once trapped in dependency, poor women most often raise children who will themselves remain poor as adults.

The political left charges its opponents with using a double standard for assessing government social programs. Why, it asks, is there so much outrage at the thought of the government transferring money to poor mothers and children when most "welfare" goes to relatively rich people? From the perspective of the left, the amounts spent on welfare, while they are not negligible, pale in comparison with the tax write-offs received by more affluent people for the registered retirement savings plans (RRSPs) they buy each year. And what about the billions of dollars in tax write-offs for corporations, many of which are enjoying record profits? As the left sees it, "wealthfare" costs the country a great deal more than "welfare," even though public opinion supports the opposite view.

Critics claim that the political right—and much public opinion—distorts our understanding of the functions of social assistance. Images of irresponsible "welfare bums" mask the fact that most poor families who turn to public assistance are truly needy. Karen Moss received only $1221 a

 For insight into welfare programs of each province and territory, go to Canadian Social Research Links at www.canadian socialresearch.net/ welfare.htm.

month for herself and her son *before* the rates were cut, hardly enough to attract people to a "life of welfare dependency." Throughout Canada in recent years, the trend has been to slash welfare or social assistance rates as a deficit-reduction measure. Whatever the merits of social assistance, the political left faults it as a bandaid approach to the growing social problems of unemployment and poverty in Canada.

As for the charge that social assistance undermines families, the political left concedes that the proportion of single-parent families is rising, but disputes the argument that welfare is to blame. Rather, single parenting is a widespread cultural trend found at all class levels in most industrial societies. Therefore, leftist critics conclude, welfare or social assistance programs are not attacked because they have failed, but because they benefit poor people, a segment of the population long scorned as "undeserving." Our cultural tradition of equating wealth with virtue, and poverty with vice, allows rich people to display privilege as an indicator of ability—while poverty carries a negative stigma.

Many on the political right believe that welfare should be limited. Those on the left, in contrast, want to both improve and expand social assistance. Are there areas of common ground in this debate? The Conservative government of Ontario (under Mike Harris), as part of its welfare reform program, instituted "workfare," which makes income assistance contingent on able-bodied recipients performing useful work and participating in occupational training; the government of Alberta (under Ralph Klein) created a similar program. Ontario's "workfare" program, called "Ontario Works," still exists despite the fact that Dalton McGuinty has been Ontario's Liberal premier since 2003. Is this an indicator of "common ground" between left and right?

Visit the National Council of Welfare, which provides policy advice to politicians and statistical information on welfare recipients, at www.ncwcnbes. net/htmdocument/ principales/ mandat_e.htm.

WHAT DO YOU THINK?

1. Should provinces and territories slash their welfare budgets, without making efforts to recoup the tax write-offs that middle-class and wealthy people are awarded when they buy RRSPs? Is this just one more case of the poor being exploited because they are politically powerless?

2. Do you think welfare has become a way of life for many people, as the political right—and public opinion—asserts?

3. Do you feel that an expanded welfare program would lessen the extent of poverty in Canadian society? Why?

Social scientists debate the causes of poverty. Some cite the failings of individuals, such as lack of initiative or drug abuse, and others point to flaws of society, including a minimum wage that does not allow a full-time worker to support a family. Here, homeless people gather under a bridge in Hamburg, Germany.

11 MAKING THE GRADE

The following learning tools will help you see what you know, identify what you still need to learn, and expand your understanding beyond the text. You can also visit this text's Companion Website™ at www.pearsoned.ca/macionis to find useful practice tests.

KEY POINTS

Dimensions of Social Inequality

Social stratification in Canada involves inequality of income, wealth, power, and prestige. White-collar jobs generally offer greater income and prestige than blue-collar work. Many of the jobs typically held by women offer low social prestige or income. Schooling is also a resource that is distributed unequally on the basis of socioeconomic background, race, ethnicity, and to some extent gender.

Stratification in Canada: Merit and Caste

While Canadian society is partly a meritocracy, at birth children acquire the social position of their parents. Family ancestry, race and ethnicity, and gender all affect people's social standing.

Social Classes in Canada

The upper class (3 to 5% of the population) includes the richest and most powerful families. Most members of the

upper-upper class, those with old money, inherit their wealth; the lower-upper class, or the *nouveau riche* work at high-paying jobs. The middle class (40 to 50%) enjoys financial security, but only people of the upper-middle class have substantial wealth. With below-average incomes, most members of the working class or lower-middle class (one third) have blue-collar jobs, and only one-third of their children reach college. About 20 percent of the Canadian population belongs to the lower class; more than half of these people live below the government's poverty line.

The Difference Class Makes

People with above-average incomes have better health than those whose income is below average. Social class standing also shapes some values and political attitudes. Children born into families with higher social standing receive a great advantage in the form of cultural capital.

Social Mobility

Some social mobility occurs in Canada, as it does in other high-income countries. Typically, however, only small changes occur from one generation to the next. It is important to note that, today, there is as much downwards mobility as upwards mobility.

Poverty in Canada

The Canadian census of 2001 classifies 4.4 million people (14.4% of the population) as poor, while 15.6 percent of children are in that category (i.e., below the low-income cut-off).

The poor include those with limited education, some minorities, Aboriginal people, children, elderly people, and women. The *feminization of poverty* means that more poor families are headed by women. People who work full-time for subsistence wages are called "the working poor." The wealthiest families in Canada now earn more than ever. We now see improvement in economic well-being, after a period of decline in family income at the bottom of the scale, for various categories, such as unattached elders (those without families) and children in female, lone-parent families.

The *culture of poverty* thesis suggests that poverty is caused by shortcomings in the poor themselves. Others believe that poverty is caused by society's unequal distribution of jobs and wealth. The North American cultural emphasis on individual responsibility helps explain why welfare (social assistance) for the poor has long been controversial.

KEY CONCEPTS

income (p. 267) earnings from work or investments

wealth (p. 269) the total value of money and other assets, minus outstanding debts

intragenerational social mobility (p. 279) a change in social position occurring during a person's lifetime

intergenerational social mobility (p. 279) upward or downward social mobility of children in relation to their parents

relative poverty (p. 280) the deprivation of some people in relation to those who have more

absolute poverty (p. 280) a deprivation of resources that is life-threatening

feminization of poverty (p. 282) the trend of women making up an increasing proportion of the poor

APPLICATIONS & EXERCISES

1. Develop several questions that, taken together, will let you measure social class position. The trick is to decide what you think social class really means. Then try your questions on several adults, refining the questions as you proceed.

2. During an evening of television viewing, assess the social class of the characters you see on various programs. In each case, explain why you assign someone a particular social position. What patterns do you find?

3. Governor Arnold Schwarzenegger of California recently said, "In this country, it doesn't make any difference where you were born. It doesn't make any difference who your parents were. It doesn't make any difference if, like me, you couldn't even speak English until you were in your twenties. America gave me opportunities, and my immigrant dreams came true. I want other people to get the same chances I did, the same opportunities. And I believe they can." Do Canadians—and immigrants to Canada in particular—share this optimism about the opportunities available to newcomers? How many individuals can you name who came to Canada with very little only to rise to positions of wealth or high office?

PRENTICE HALL

Where learning & the sociological imagination intersect.

To reinforce your understanding of this chapter, and to identify topics for further study, visit MySocLab at **www.pearsoned.ca/mysoclab/** for diagnostic tests and a multimedia ebook.

12

Global Stratification

How much of the world's population lives in
absolute poverty?

Why are some of the world's countries so rich and
others so poor?

Are rich nations making global poverty
better or worse? How?

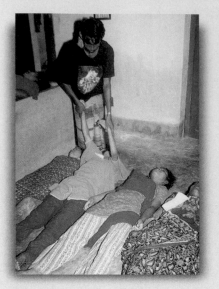

More than a thousand workers were busily sewing together polo shirts on the fourth floor of the garment factory in Narsingdi, a small town about 48 kilometres (30 miles) northeast of Bangladesh's capital city of Dhaka. The thumping of hundreds of sewing machines combined to produce a steady roar that never stopped throughout the long working day.

But in an instant everything changed—an electric gun a worker used to shoot spot remover gave off a spark, which ignited the flammable liquid. Suddenly, a work table burst into flames. Nearby workers rushed to smother the fire with shirts, but there was no stopping the blaze: in a room filled with combustible materials, the flames spread quickly.

The workers scrambled towards the narrow staircase that led to the street. At the bottom, however, the human wave pouring down the steep steps collided with a folding metal gate across the doorway that was kept locked to prevent workers from leaving during work hours. Panicked, the people turned, only to be pushed back by the hundreds behind them. In a single terrifying minute of screaming voices, thrusting legs, and pounding hearts, dozens were crushed and trampled. By the time the gates were opened and the fire put out, 52 garment workers lay dead.

Source: Based on Bearak (2001).

Tanveer Chowdhury manages the garment factory owned by his family where this fire took place. Speaking to reporters, he complained bitterly about the tragedy: "This fire has cost me $586 373, and that does not include $70 000 for machinery and $20 000 for furniture. I made commitments to meet deadlines, and I still have the deadlines. I am now paying for air freight at $10 a dozen when I should be shipping by sea at 87 cents a dozen." There was one other cost Chowdhury did not mention. To compensate families for the loss of their loved ones in the fire, he eventually agreed to pay $1952 per person (Bearak, 2001). In Bangladesh, life—like labour—is cheap.[1]

Garment factories like this one are big business in Bangladesh, where clothing makes up 75 percent of the country's total economic exports. Half of the garments shipped from Bangladesh end up in clothing stores in North America. The reason so much of the clothing we buy is made in poor countries like Bangladesh is simple economics: Bangladeshi garment workers labour for close to 12 hours a day, typically 7 days a week, yet earn between $400 and $500 a year, a pittance compared with wages in Canada or the United States.

These garment workers in Bangladesh are part of the roughly 1 billion of the world's people who work hard every day and yet remain poor. As this chapter explains, while poverty is a reality in Canada and other industrialized nations, the greatest social inequality is not *within* nations but *between* them (Goesling, 2001). We can understand the full dimensions of poverty only by exploring **global stratification,** *patterns of social inequality in the world as a whole.*

Global Stratification: An Overview

Chapter 11 ("Social Class in Canada") described social inequality in our country. In a global perspective, however, social stratification is far greater. Figure 12–1 divides the world's total income by fifths of the population. Recall from Figure 11–2 (on p. 268) that the richest 20 percent of the Canadian population earns close to 44 percent of the national income. The richest 20 percent of global population, however, receives about 80 percent of total world income. At the very top of the pyramid, the wealth of the world's richest person—Bill Gates in the United States, who was worth about $51 billion in 2005—is equivalent to the

---

[1] In this chapter, unless stated otherwise, all dollar amounts are in U.S. dollars.

total economic output of the world's 45 poorest *countries* (Miller and Newcomb, 2005; United Nations Development Programme, 2005). The poorest 20 percent of the Canadian population earns 5 percent of our total national income, but the poorest fifth of the world's people struggles to survive on just 1 percent of total world income. Canadians with income below the government's poverty line (i.e., the low-income cut-off) live *far* better than the majority of the Earth's people. People who earn an average income in a rich nation like Canada are extremely well-off by world standards.

A WORD ABOUT TERMINOLOGY

Classifying the world's 192 nations into categories ignores many striking differences. These nations have rich and varied histories, speak different languages, and take pride in distinctive cultures. However, various models have been developed that help distinguish countries on the basis of global stratification.

One such model, developed after World War II, labelled the rich industrial countries the "First World," less industrialized socialist countries the "Second World," and non-industrialized poor countries the "Third World." But the "three worlds" model is now less useful. For one thing, it was a product of Cold War politics by which the capitalist West (the First World) faced off against the socialist East (the Second World), while other nations (the Third World) remained more or less on the sidelines. But the sweeping changes in Eastern Europe and the collapse of the former Soviet Union mean that a distinctive Second World no longer exists. A second problem is that the "three worlds" model lumped together more than a hundred countries as the Third World. In reality, some relatively better-off nations of the Third World (such as Chile) have industrialized enough that they have fifteen times the per-person productivity of the poorest countries of the world (including Ethiopia).

These facts call for a modestly revised system of classification. Here, we define the fifty *high-income countries* as the richest nations with the highest overall standards of living. The world's eighty *middle-income countries* are not as rich; they are nations with a standard of living about average for the world as a whole. The remaining sixty *low-income countries* are nations with a low standard of living in which most people are poor. This model has two advantages over the older "three worlds" system. First, it focuses on economic development rather than whether societies are capitalist or socialist. Second, it gives a better picture of the relative economic development of various countries because it does not lump together all lower-income nations into a single Third World.

When ranking countries, keep in mind that there is *social* stratification within every nation. In Bangladesh, for example, members of the Chowdhury family, who own the garment factory where fire took the lives of 52 workers, earn as much as $1 million per year, which is several thousand times more than their workers earn. Of course, the full

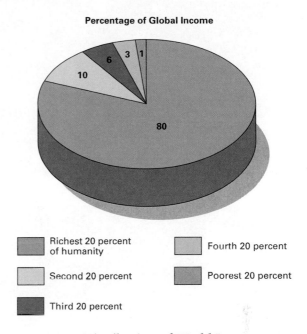

GLOBAL SNAPSHOT

Percentage of Global Income

Legend:
- Richest 20 percent of humanity
- Second 20 percent
- Third 20 percent
- Fourth 20 percent
- Poorest 20 percent

FIGURE 12-1   Distribution of World Income

Global income is very unequal, with the richest 20 percent of the world's people earning eighty times as much as the poorest 20 percent.

Sources: Calculated by John J. Macionis based on United Nations Development Programme (2000) and World Bank (2001a).

extent of global inequality is even greater, because the wealthiest people in rich countries like Canada live worlds apart from the poorest people in low-income nations such as Bangladesh, Haiti, or Sudan.

HIGH-INCOME COUNTRIES

In nations where the Industrial Revolution first took place more than two centuries ago, productivity increased more than a hundredfold. To understand the power of industrial and computer technology, consider that one small European nation, the Netherlands, is more productive than all the African nations south of the Sahara Desert; likewise, tiny South Korea outproduces India.

Global Map 12–1 shows that the high-income nations of the world cover roughly 25 percent of the Earth's land area, including parts of five continents, and they lie mostly in the northern hemisphere. They include the United States and Canada, the nations of Western Europe, Singapore, Hong Kong (now part of China), South Korea, and New Zealand. In 2005, the total population of these 50 nations was about 1.1 billion, or about 18 percent of the Earth's people. About three-quarters of the people in high-income countries live in or near cities. Production in rich nations is

Japan represents the world's high-income countries, in which industrial technology and economic expansion have produced material prosperity. The presence of market forces is evident in this view of downtown Tokyo (*above, left*). The Russian Federation represents the middle-income countries of the world. Industrial development and economic performance were sluggish under socialism; as a result, Moscow residents had to wait in long lines for their daily needs (*above, right*). The hope is that the introduction of a market system will raise living standards; in the short run Russian citizens must adjust to increasing economic inequality. Bangladesh (*left*) represents the world's low-income countries. As the photograph suggests, these nations have limited economic development and rapidly increasing populations. The result is widespread poverty.

capital-intensive; it is based on factories, big machinery, and advanced technology. Most of the largest corporations that design and market computers, as well as most computer users, are located in high-income countries. These countries control the world's financial markets, so daily events in the financial exchanges of New York, Europe, and Tokyo affect people throughout the world.

Significant cultural differences exist among high-income countries; for example, the nations of Europe recognize more than thirty official languages. But these societies have something in common: they all produce enough economic goods and services to enable their people to lead a comfortable life. *Per capita income* (that is, average income per person per year) ranges from about $10 000 annually (in Chile and South Africa) to more than $37 000 annually (in the United States and Norway). In fact, collectively, people in high-income countries enjoy 80 percent of the world's total income (World Bank, 2001a). Keep in mind that many low-income people live in high-income countries. The Thinking about Diversity box (on p. 297) profiles the striking poverty that exists along the southern border of the United States.

MIDDLE-INCOME COUNTRIES

Middle-income countries have a per capita income of between $2500 and $10 000, roughly the median for the world's nations. Taken together, middle-income countries span roughly 55 percent of the Earth's land area and include

about 4.5 billion people, or about 70 percent of humanity. Some countries, such as Russia, are far less crowded than others, such as El Salvador; but, compared to high-income countries, these societies are densely populated. Two-thirds of the people live in cities, and industrial jobs are common; the remaining one-third live in rural areas, where most are poor and lack access to schools, medical care, adequate housing, and even safe drinking water.

Looking at Global Map 12–1, we see that about eighty of the world's nations fall into the middle-income category. Among nations with higher average incomes are Mexico, Botswana, and Malaysia, where annual income is about $9000. At the lower end are Ecuador, Egypt, and Indonesia, with roughly $3000 annually in per capita income. Other middle-income nations include Peru and Brazil in South America and Namibia and Botswana in Africa. Recently, both India and China have entered the middle-income category, which now includes most of Asia. One cluster of middle-income countries includes those that once made up the Soviet Union and those of Eastern Europe. Formerly known as the "Second World," these countries had mostly socialist economies until popular revolts between 1989 and 1991 swept their governments aside. Since then, these nations have begun to introduce market systems, but so far the results have been uneven. Some, such as Poland, have improving economies, but living standards in others, such as Russia, have fallen.

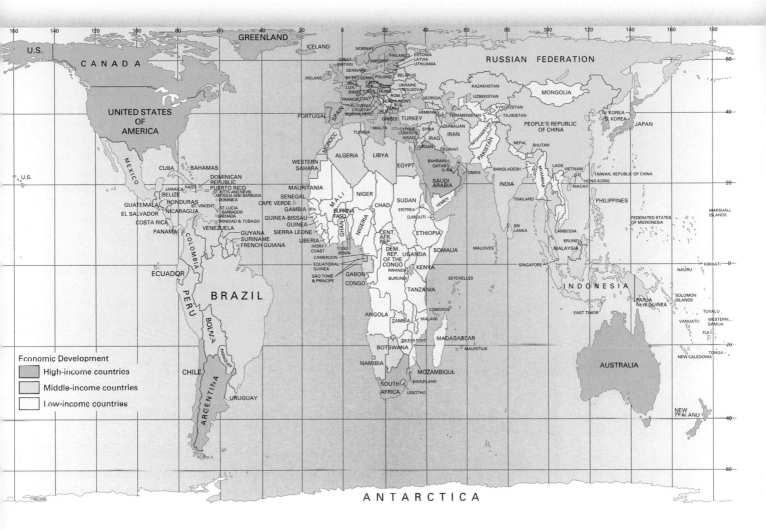

WINDOW ON THE WORLD

GLOBAL MAP 12-1   Economic Development in Global Perspective*

In *high-income countries* (including Chile, Argentina, South Africa, Israel, Saudi Arabia, Australia, and Japan), a highly productive economy provides people, on average, with material plenty. *Middle-income countries* (including most of Latin America and Asia) are less economically productive, with a standard of living about average for the world as a whole but far below that of the United States and Canada. These nations also have a significant share of poor people who are barely able to feed and house themselves. In the *low-income countries* of the world, poverty is severe and widespread. While small numbers of elites may live very well in the poorest nations, most people struggle to survive on a small fraction of the income common in North America.

*Data for this map are provided by the United Nations. Each country's economic productivity is measured in terms of its gross domestic product (GDP), which is the total value of all the goods and services produced by a country's economy within its borders in a given year. Dividing each country's GDP by the country's population yields the per capita, or per person, GDP, which allows us to compare the economic performance of countries of different population sizes.

High-income countries have a per capita GDP of more than $10 000. Many are far richer than this, however; the figure for the United States exceeds $37 000. Middle-income countries have a per capita GDP ranging from $2500 to $10 000. Low-income countries have a per capita GDP of less than $2500.

Figures used here reflect the purchasing power parities system, which the United Nations and the World Bank use as an estimate of what people can buy using their income in the local economy.

Source: Based on data from United Nations Development Programme (2005). Map projection from *Peters Atlas of the World* (1990).

Natural disasters worldwide are usually devastating for the poor. When Hurricane Katrina flooded the city of New Orleans in 2005, most of the population was evacuated, leaving behind those who were too old, too sick, or too poor to make their way to safety. This disaster revealed that, although the United States is a high-income nation, it contains more serious poverty than most people realize.

YOUR TURN

Most people from high-income countries who travel to middle- or low-income nations do so as tourists, but most who travel from middle- or low-income nations to high-income countries do so as immigrants. How would you explain this pattern?

LOW-INCOME COUNTRIES

Low-income countries, where the majority of people are very poor, are mostly agrarian societies with some industry. Many of these sixty nations, identified on Global Map 12–1, are found in Central and East Africa and in Asia. Low-income countries cover 20 percent of the planet's land area

and are home to 12 percent of its people. Population density is generally high, although greater in Asian countries, such as Bangladesh and Pakistan, than in Central African nations, such as Chad and the Democratic Republic of the Congo.

In poor countries, one-third of the people live in cities; most inhabit villages and farms as their ancestors have done for centuries. About half the world's people are farmers, most of whom follow cultural traditions. With limited industrial technology, they cannot be very productive, one reason that many suffer severe poverty. Hunger, disease, and unsafe housing shape the lives of the world's poorest people.

People living in affluent nations like ours find it hard to understand the scope of human need in much of the world. From time to time, televised pictures of famine in very poor countries, such as Ethiopia and Bangladesh, give us shocking glimpses of the poverty that makes every day a life-and-death struggle for many people in low-income nations. Behind these images lie cultural, historical, and economic forces that we shall explore in this chapter.

Global Wealth and Poverty

October 14, Manila, Philippines. What caught my eye was how clean she was—a girl no more than seven or eight years old. She was wearing a freshly laundered dress, and her hair was carefully combed. She stopped to watch us, following us with her eyes: camera-toting Americans stand out in this, one of the poorest neighbourhoods in the entire world.

Fed by methane from decomposing garbage, the fires never go out on Smokey Mountain, the vast garbage dump on the north side of Manila. Smoke covers the hills of refuse like a thick fog. But Smokey Mountain is more than a dump; it is a neighbourhood that is home to thousands of people. It is hard to imagine a setting more hostile to human life. Amid the smoke and the squalor, men and women do what they can to survive. They pick plastic bags from the garbage and wash them in the river, and they collect cardboard boxes or anything else they can sell. What chance do their children have, coming from families that earn only a few hundred dollars a year, with hardly any opportunity for schooling, year after year breathing this foul air? Against this backdrop of human tragedy, one lovely little girl has put on a fresh dress and gone out to play.

Now our taxi driver threads his way through heavy traffic as we head for the other side of Manila. The change is amazing: the smoke and smell of the dump give

THINKING ABOUT DIVERSITY:
RACE, CLASS, & GENDER
Las Colonias: "America's Third World"

We wanted to have something for ourselves," explains Olga Ruiz, who has lived in the border community of College Park, Texas, for eleven years. There is neither college nor park in College Park, nor does this dusty stretch of rural land have sewer lines or even running water. Yet this town is one of some 1800 settlements that have sprouted up in southern Texas along the 1930 kilometres (1200 miles) of the United States/Mexico border from El Paso down to Brownsville. Together, they are home to perhaps 700 000 people, a number expected to pass 1 million by 2010.

Many people speak of this area as *las colonias* (Spanish for "the colonies") or "America's Third World" because these desperately poor communities look much like their counterparts in Mexico and many other nations. But this is the United States, and almost all of the people living in *las colonias* are Hispanic Americans, 85 percent of them legal residents and more than half U.S. citizens.

Anastacia Ledsema, now 72 years old, moved to a *colonia* called Sparks more than 40 years ago. Born in Mexico, Ledsema married a Texas man, and

together they paid $200 for 0.10 hectare (a quarter-acre lot) in a new border community. For months, they camped out on their land. Step by step, they invested their labour and their money to build a modest house. Not until 1995 did their small community get running water—a service that had been promised by developers years before. When the water line finally did arrive, however, things changed more than they expected. "When we got water," recalls Ledsema, "that's when so many people came in." The population of Sparks quickly doubled to about 3000, overwhelming the water supply so that sometimes the faucet does not run at all.

The residents of all *las colonias* know that they are poor. Indeed, the census bureau recently declared the county surrounding one border community to be the poorest in the entire United States. Concerned over the lack of basic services here, Texas officials have banned any new settlements. But most of the people who move here—even those who start off sleeping in their cars or trucks—see these communities as the first step on the path to the American dream. Oscar Solis, a neighbourhood leader in Panorama Village, a community with a population of about 150, is proud to show visitors around the small but growing town. "All of this work we have done ourselves," he says with a smile, "to make our dreams come true."

WHAT DO YOU THINK?

1. Are you surprised that such poverty exists in the United States? Why?
2. Why do you think such communities get little attention from the mass media?
3. To what extent do you think people living in these communities will have their "dreams come true"? Explain.

Source: Based on Schaffer (2002)

way to neighbourhoods that could be in Miami or Los Angeles. A cluster of yachts floats on the bay in the distance. No more rutted streets; now we glide quietly along wide boulevards lined with trees and filled with expensive Japanese cars. We pass shopping plazas, upscale hotels, and high-rise office buildings. Every block or so we see the gated entrance to another exclusive residential community, with security guards standing watch. Here, in large, air-conditioned homes, the rich of Manila live—and many of the poor work. [John J. Macionis]

Low-income nations are home to some rich and many poor people. People who live with incomes of just a few hundred dollars a year suffer a greater burden of poverty than the poor of North America. This is not to suggest that poverty in Canada and the United States is a minor problem. In our rich countries, too little food, substandard housing, and limited access to the best medical care amount to a national tragedy. The recent discovery—by the media—of contaminated drinking water in about one hundred First Nation communities reveals another dimension in the gap between rich and poor.

GLOBAL SNAPSHOT

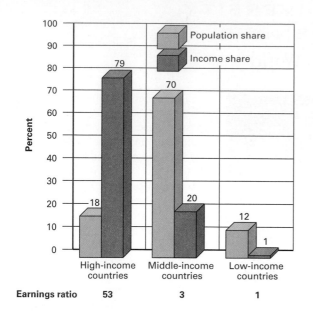

FIGURE 12-2   The Relative Share of Income and Population by Level of Economic Development

For every $1 earned by people in low-income countries, people in high-income countries earn $53.

Sources: Calculated by John J. Macionis based on United Nations Development Programme (2000) and World Bank (2001).

THE SEVERITY OF POVERTY

Poverty in poor countries is more severe than it is in rich countries. A key reason that the quality of life differs so much around the world is that economic productivity is lowest in precisely the regions where population growth is highest. Figure 12–2 shows the proportion of world population and global income for high-, middle-, and low-income countries. People in high-income countries are by far the most advantaged, with 79 percent of global income supporting just 18 percent of humanity. In middle-income nations, 70 percent of the world's people earn 20 percent of global income.

Table 12–1 shows the extent of wealth and well-being in specific countries around the world. The first column of figures gives gross domestic product for a number of high-, middle-, and low-income countries. (*Gross domestic product* (GDP) is the value of all the goods and services produced by a country's economy within its borders in a given year.) The United States, a large and highly productive nation, had a 2003 GDP of more than $10 trillion; Japan's GDP was more than $4 trillion; Canada's was about $1 trillion. A comparison of GDP figures shows that the world's richest nations are thousands of times more productive than the poorest countries.

TABLE 12–1

Wealth and Well-Being in Global Perspective, 2003

Country	Gross Domestic Product (GDP) (US$ billions)	GDP per Capita (PPP US$)*	Quality of Life Index
High-Income			
Norway	221	37 670	.963
Australia	522	29 632	.955
Sweden	302	26 750	.949
Canada	857	30 677	.949
United States	10 949	37 562	.944
Japan	4 301	27 967	.943
United Kingdom	1 795	27 147	.939
France	1 758	27 677	.938
South Korea	605	17 971	.901
Middle-Income			
Eastern Europe			
Russian Federation	433	9 230	.795
Romania	57	7 277	.792
Belarus	18	6 052	.786
Ukraine	50	5 491	.766
Latin America			
Mexico	626	9 168	.814
Brazil	492	7 790	.792
Venezuela	85	4 919	.772
Asia			
Malaysia	104	9 512	.796
Thailand	143	7 595	.778
People's Republic of China	1 417	5 003	.755
Middle East			
Iran	137	6 995	.736
Syria	22	3 576	.721
Africa			
Algeria	67	6 107	.722
Botswana	8	8 714	.565
Low-Income			
Latin America			
Haiti	3	1 742	.475
Asia			
Cambodia	4	2 078	.571
Pakistan	82	2 097	.527
Bangladesh	52	1 770	.520
Africa			
Guinea	4	2 097	.466
Ethiopia	7	711	.367
Central African Republic	1	1 089	.355
Niger	3	835	.281

*These data are purchasing power parity (PPP) calculations, which international organizations use to avoid currency rate distortion by showing the local purchasing power of each domestic currency.

Source: United Nations Development Programme (2005).

The second column in Table 12–1 divides GDP by entire population to give an estimate of what people can buy using their income in the local economy. The per capita GDP for rich countries, such as the United States, Sweden, Japan, and Canada, is very high, exceeding US$26 000. For middle-income countries, such as Mexico and the Russian Federation, the figures are in the US$7000 range. In the world's low-income countries, per capita GDP is just a few hundred dollars; in the Central African Republic or in Ethiopia, for example, a typical person labours all year to make what the average worker in the United States earns in a week.

The last column of Table 12–1 measures *quality of life*. This measurement, calculated by the United Nations, is based on income, education (extent of adult literacy and average years of schooling), and longevity (how long people typically live). Quality of life index values are decimals that fall between extremes of 1.0 (highest) and 0 (lowest). By this calculation, Norwegians enjoy the highest quality of life (at .963), with Canadians close behind (at .949). At the other extreme, people in the African nation of Niger have the lowest quality of life (at .281).

Relative versus Absolute Poverty

The distinction between relative and absolute poverty, made in Chapter 11 ("Social Class in Canada"), has an important application to global inequality. People living in rich countries generally focus on *relative poverty*, meaning that some people lack resources that are taken for granted by others. By definition, relative poverty exists in every society, rich or poor. More important in global perspective, however, is *absolute poverty*, a lack of resources that is life-threatening: human beings in absolute poverty lack the nutrition necessary for health and long-term survival. To be sure, some absolute poverty exists in North America. But such immediately life-threatening poverty strikes only a very small proportion of our population, such as the homeless. In low-income countries, by contrast, one-third or more of the people are in desperate need. The Media Perspectives box (on p. 301) explains the difficulty that the United Nations is having measuring the extent of serious poverty in the world.

Because absolute poverty is deadly, one global indicator of this problem is median age at death. Global Map 12–2 identifies the age by which half of all people born in a nation die. In rich societies, most people die after the age of 75; in poor countries, half of all deaths occur among children under the age of 10.

THE EXTENT OF POVERTY

Poverty in poor countries is more widespread than it is in North America. Chapter 11 ("Social Class in Canada") notes that, in 2004, the Canadian government officially classified 11.2 percent of the population as poor. In low-income countries, however, most people live no better than the poorest in Canada, and many are far worse off. As Global

Tens of millions of children fend for themselves every day on the streets of Latin America, where many fall victim to disease, drug abuse, and outright violence. What do you think must be done to put an end to scenes like this one in San Salvador, the capital city of El Salvador?

Map 12–2 shows, the high death rates in Africa are among children in Africa; absolute poverty is greatest there, where half the population is malnourished. In the world as a whole, at any given time, 15 percent of the people—about 1 billion—suffer from chronic hunger, which leaves them less able to work and puts them at high risk of disease (Kates, 1996; United Nations Development Programme, 2001). The typical adult in a rich nation like Canada consumes about 3500 calories a day, an excess that contributes to widespread obesity and related health problems. The typical adult in a low-income country not only does more physical labour but consumes just 2000 calories a day. The result is under-nourishment: too little food or not enough of the right kinds of food.

In the ten minutes it takes to read this section of the chapter, about 300 people in the world who are sick and weakened from hunger will die. This number amounts to about 40 000 people a day, or 15 million people each year. Clearly, easing world hunger is one of the most serious responsibilities facing humanity today.

POVERTY AND CHILDREN

Death comes early in poor societies, where families lack adequate food, safe water, secure housing, and access to medical care. Organizations fighting child poverty estimate that at least 100 million children living in cities in poor countries beg, steal, sell sex, or work for drug gangs to provide income for their families. Such a life almost always means dropping out of school and puts children at high risk of

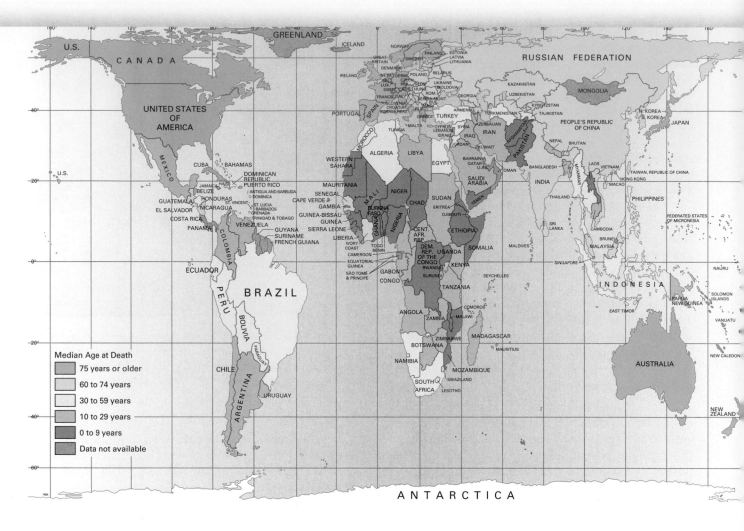

Median Age at Death

- 75 years or older
- 60 to 74 years
- 30 to 59 years
- 10 to 29 years
- 0 to 9 years
- Data not available

WINDOW ON THE WORLD

GLOBAL MAP 12–2   Median Age at Death in Global Perspective

This map identifies the age below which half of all deaths occur in any year. In the high-income countries of the world, including Canada, it is mostly the elderly who face death, that is, people aged 75 or older. In middle-income countries, including most of Latin America, most people die years or even decades earlier. In low-income countries, especially in Africa and parts of Asia, it is children who die, half of them never reaching their tenth birthday.

Sources: World Bank (1993), with updates by John J. Macionis; map projection from *Peters Atlas of the World* (1990).

disease and violence. Many girls, with little or no access to medical assistance, become pregnant—a case of children who cannot support themselves having children of their own.

Analysts estimate that another 100 million of the world's children leave their families altogether, sleeping and living on the streets as best they can. Roughly 50 million of these street children are found in Latin American cities, such as Mexico City and Rio de Janeiro, where half of all children grow up in poverty. Many of us know these cities as exotic travel destinations,

Read more about the lives of street children at www.hrw.org/children/street.htm.

but they are also home to thousands of street children living in makeshift huts, under bridges, or in alleyways (Ross, 1996; United Nations Development Programme, 2000; Collymore, 2002).

YOUR TURN

How do you think the experience of "childhood" as a stage of life differs in high- and low-income countries?

MEDIA PERSPECTIVES

Experts Wonder How To Measure Poverty

One of the United Nations' top goals is to cut in half the proportion of people living in extreme poverty by 2015.... Accurately monitoring poverty is essential for knowing whether the goal is achieved and whether antipoverty strategies are working.

But measuring poverty is difficult for a particular country, let alone the world.... Angelina Jolie challenged celebrities at the World Economic Forum in Davos, Switzerland,... to know "absolutely what they're talking about" when it comes to poverty, yet even experts would have trouble meeting her standard....

First, establishing a poverty line... involves an element of arbitrariness. For many poor families, not having enough money amounts to not having enough food. But there is no particular threshold level of income or expenditures above which people automatically become fully functioning, nourished members of society.

"Poverty lines are as much political as scientific constructions," said Angus Deaton, a Princeton economist and expert on economic development. In such places as different as the United States and India, the poverty line was initially set with reference to minimum standards of food consumption. Yet over time,... the poverty lines in both countries were adjusted to keep pace with overall price inflation, not the price of food or the share of food in the average family's budget....

The United Nations has set the line for extreme poverty at living on less than $1 a day. This threshold has obvious rhetorical appeal and surely qualifies as extreme poverty by any standard in developed [i.e., high-income] countries; it is also not far off the poverty line used by many of the

poorest countries themselves....

To convert the $1 poverty line into foreign currencies, the World Bank uses indices of "purchasing power parity." Simply put, these indices reflect the cost of buying a standard bundle of goods in each country.

While it is desirable to use purchasing indices, they are not available for all countries and are skewed towards... the wealthiest households, not the poorest, when they are available. Another problem is that the bundle of goods that poor families actually buy varies from country to country because of differences in tastes and availability....

Once the poverty line is set in local currency, the consumption of a representative sample of households much be compared with the line to determine the percent of people getting by on less than $1 a day. (Each household's consumption is spread equally among its members, another leap of faith.)

Again, this is harder than it sounds. The World Bank typically relies on whatever government surveys countries routinely produce.

But there is no uniform standard in the way countries collect and process their data.... Consider India, home to 33 percent of the world's poor—or 20 percent, depending on how the data are collected....

Perhaps the best one can hope for is consistency of measurement within countries to detect changes in poverty over time....

The Herculean measurement problems aside, careful research by Shaohua Chen and Martin Ravallion of the World Bank indicates that much progress has been made towards the goal of halving poverty in China and India. But, they found, little progress

has occurred in Latin America and Africa, and the former Soviet states are slipping into deeper poverty. Because China and India accounted for 60 percent of the world's poor in 1990, the goal of halving poverty may be achieved a decade from now, even while many regions see no progress....

An essential prerequisite is to improve poverty statistics and ensure their integrity. While the process of setting a poverty line is necessarily political, the task of measuring poverty should be insulated from political influences. The

The World Bank monitors and comments on poverty, including the development of poverty reduction strategies, at http//www.worldbank.org/poverty.

World Bank, however, is an inherently political institution.

Yet no other international body currently has the expertise or resources to monitor worldwide poverty....

This may not be a cause that celebrities are ready to line up for, but improving poverty data will put the world in a better position to monitor progress and evaluate poverty reduction strategies by the time the poverty line is moved up to $2 a day.

WHAT DO YOU THINK?

1. Why are poverty lines as much political as scientific?
2. Why is measuring poverty an important part of the effort to reduce poverty?
3. Do you think global poverty will be reduced by half within the next decade? Why?

Source: Adapted from Krueger (2005).

POVERTY AND WOMEN

In rich societies, much of the work women do is undervalued, underpaid, or overlooked entirely. In poor societies, women face even greater disadvantages. Most of the people who work in sweatshops (like the one described in the chapter opener) are women. To make matters worse, tradition keeps women out of many jobs in low-income nations;

in Bangladesh, for example, women work in garment factories because that society's conservative Muslim norms bar them from most other paid work and limit their opportunity for advanced schooling (Bearak, 2001). At the same

Visit the website of United Students against Sweatshops at www.studentsagainst sweatshops.org.

time, traditional norms in poor societies give women primary responsibility for

In rich nations, most parents expect their children to enjoy years of childhood, largely free from the responsibilities of adult life. This is not the case in poor nations across Latin America, Africa, and Asia. Poor families depend on whatever income their children can earn, and many children as young as six or seven work full days weaving or performing other kinds of manual labour. Child labour lies behind the low prices of many products imported for sale in this country.

child rearing and maintaining the household. Most women in poor countries receive little or no reproductive health care; limited access to birth control keeps women at home with their children, keeps the birth rate high, and limits the economic production of the country.

The United Nations estimates that, in poor countries, men own 90 percent of the land, a far greater gender disparity in wealth than is found in high-income nations. It is no surprise, then, that about 70 percent of the world's 1 billion people living near absolute poverty are women (Hymowitz, 1995).

SLAVERY

Poor societies have many problems in addition to hunger, including illiteracy, warfare, and even slavery. Upper Canada banned slavery in 1793, the British Empire in 1833, and the United States in 1865. But according to Anti-Slavery International, as many as 200 million men, women, and children (about 3% of humanity) still live in conditions that amount to slavery. Anti-Slavery International distinguishes four types of slavery:

- The first is *chattel slavery*, in which one person owns another. The number of chattel slaves is difficult to estimate because this practice is against the law almost everywhere. But the buying and selling of slaves still takes place in many countries in Asia, the Middle East, and especially Africa.

- A second, more common form of bondage is *child slavery*, in which desperately poor families send their children out into the streets to beg or steal or do whatever they can to survive. Perhaps 100 million children—many in the poorest countries of Latin America and Africa—fall into this category.

- Third, *debt bondage* is the practice by which employers pay workers wages, but not enough to cover the food and housing provided by the employer. Unable to settle their debts, workers cannot leave and are therefore slaves. Many workers in sweatshops in poor countries fall into this category.

- Fourth, *servile forms of marriage* may also amount to slavery. In India, Thailand, and some African nations, families marry off women against their will. Many end up as slaves working for their husband's family; some are forced into prostitution.

Finally, one additional form of slavery is *human trafficking*, the moving of men, women, and children from one place to another for the purpose of performing forced labour. Women or men are brought to a new country with the promise of a job and then forced to become prostitutes or farm labourers, or people adopt children from another country and then force them to work in sweatshops. Such activity is big business: next to trading in guns and drugs, trading in people brings the greatest profit to organized crime around the world (Orhant, 2002).

In 1948, the United Nations issued its Universal Declaration of Human Rights, Article 4 of which states: "No one shall be held in slavery or servitude; slavery and the slave trade shall be prohibited in all their forms." Nearly six decades later, this social evil persists. The Thinking Globally

 Read the U.N.'s Universal Declaration of Human Rights at www.unhchr.ch/udhr/lang/eng.htm.

box (on p. 303) describes the reality of one slave's life in Mauritania.

EXPLANATIONS OF GLOBAL POVERTY

What accounts for the severe and extensive poverty throughout much of the world? The rest of this chapter

THINKING GLOBALLY

"God Made Me To Be a Slave"

Fatma Mint Mamadou is a young woman living in North Africa's Islamic Republic of Mauritania. Asked her age, she pauses, smiles, and shakes her head. She has no idea when she was born. Nor can she read or write. What she knows is tending camels, herding sheep, hauling bags of water, sweeping, and serving tea to her owners. This young woman is one of perhaps 90 000 slaves in Mauritania.

In the central region of this nation, having dark brown skin almost always means being a slave to an Arab owner. Fatma accepts her situation; she has known nothing else. She explains in a matter-of-fact voice that she is a slave like her mother before her and her grandmother before that. "Just as God created a camel to be a camel," she shrugs, "he created me to be a slave."

Fatma, her mother, and her brothers and sisters live in a squatter settlement on the edge of Nouakchott, Mauritania's capital city. Their home is a hut 3 by 4 metres (9 by 12 feet) that they built from wood scraps and other materials found at construction sites. The roof is nothing more than a piece of cloth; there is no plumbing or furniture. The nearest water comes from a well a long way down the road.

In this region, slavery began 500 years ago. As Arab and Berber tribes raided local villages, they made slaves of the people, and so it has been for

Human slavery continues to exist in the twenty-first century.

dozens of generations ever since. In 1905, the French colonial rulers of Mauritania banned slavery. After the nation gained independence in 1961, the new government reaffirmed the ban. But such proclamations have done little to change strong traditions. Indeed, people like Fatma have no idea what "freedom to choose" means.

The next question is more personal: "Are you and other girls ever raped?" Again, Fatma hesitates. With no hint of emotion, she responds, "Of course, in the night the men come to breed us. Is that what you mean by 'rape'?"

WHAT DO YOU THINK?

1. How does tradition play a part in keeping some people in slavery?
2. Why do you think the world still tolerates slavery?
3. Explain the connection between slavery and poverty.

Source: Based on Burkett (1997).

---

weaves together explanations from the following facts about poor societies:

- *Technology.* About one-quarter of people in low-income countries farm the land using human muscle or animal power. With limited energy sources, economic production is modest.

- *Population growth.* As Chapter 22 ("Population, Urbanization, and Environment") explains, the poorest countries have the world's highest birth rates. Despite the death toll from poverty, the populations of many poor countries in Africa, for example, double every twenty-five years. In these countries, half the people are teenagers or younger. With so many people entering their childbearing years, a wave of population growth will roll into the future. In recent years, for example, the population of Chad has been swelling by 3.3 percent annually, so even with economic development, living standards have fallen.

- *Cultural patterns.* Poor societies are usually traditional. Holding on to long-established ways of life means resisting change—even changes that promise a higher

standard of living. The Applying Sociology box (on p. 304) explains how the responses of traditional people in India to their poverty differs from that of poor people in the United States.

- *Social stratification.* Low-income societies distribute their wealth very unequally. Chapter 10 ("Social Stratification") explained that social inequality is greater in agrarian societies than in industrial societies. In Brazil, for example, half of all farmland is owned by just 1 percent of the people (Bergamo and Camarotti, 1996).

- *Gender inequality.* Gender inequality in poor societies keeps women from holding jobs, which typically means they have many children. An expanding population, in turn, slows economic development. Many analysts conclude that raising living standards in much of the world depends on improving the social standing of women.

- *Global power relationships.* A final cause of global poverty lies in the relationships between/among the nations of the world. Historically, wealth flowed from poor societies to rich nations through **colonialism**, *the process by*

APPLYING SOCIOLOGY

"Happy Poverty" in India: Making Sense of a Strange Idea

While India has become a middle-income nation, its per capita GDP is just $2892, less than one-tenth that in the United States. For this reason, India is home to one-quarter of the world's hungry people. But most North Americans do not readily understand the reality of poverty in India. Many of the country's 1.1 billion people live in conditions far worse than those our society labels "poor." A traveller's first experience of Indian life can be shocking. Chennai (formerly, Madras), one of India's largest cities with 7 million inhabitants, seems chaotic to an outsider; streets choked with motorbikes, trucks, carts pulled by oxen, and waves of people. Along the roadway, vendors sit on burlap cloths selling fruits, vegetables,

and cooked food while people nearby talk, bathe, and sleep. While some people live well, Chennai is dotted with more than a thousand shanty settlements, home to half a million people from rural villages who have come in search of a better life.

Shantytowns are clusters of huts built with branches, leaves, and pieces of discarded cardboard and tin. These dwellings offer little privacy and lack refrigeration, running water, and bathrooms. A visitor from North America may feel uneasy in such an area, knowing that the poorest sections of our own inner cities seethe with frustration and sometimes explode with violence. The understanding of poverty among India's people differs from ours. No restless young men hang out at the corner, no drug dealers work the streets, and there is little danger of violence. In North America, poverty often means anger and isolation; in India, even shantytowns are organized around strong families—children, parents, and often grandparents—who offer a smile of welcome to a stranger.

For traditional Hindus in India, life is shaped by *dharma*, the concept of duty and destiny that teaches people to accept their fate, whatever it may be. Mother Teresa, who worked among the poorest of India's people, went to the heart of the cultural differences: "Americans have angry poverty," she explained. "In India, there is worse poverty, but it is a happy poverty."

Perhaps we should not describe anyone who clings to the edge of survival as happy. But poverty in India is eased by the strength and support of families and communities, a sense that life has a purpose, and by a world view that encourages each person to accept whatever life offers. As a result, a visitor may well come away from a first encounter with Indian poverty in confusion: "How can people be so poor, and yet apparently content, active, and *joyful?*"

WHAT DO YOU THINK?

1. What did Mother Teresa mean when she said that in parts of India there is "happy poverty"?
2. How might an experience like this in a very poor community change the way you think of being "rich"?
3. Do you know of any poor people who have attitudes towards poverty similar to these people in India? What would make people seem to accept being "poor"?

---

which some nations enrich themselves through political and economic control of other nations. The countries of Western Europe colonized much of Latin America beginning roughly 500 years ago. Such global exploitation allowed some nations to develop economically at the expense of other nations. While 130 former colonies gained their independence during the twentieth century, exploitation continues through **neocolonialism** (*neo* is

Greek for "new"), *a new form of global power relationships that involves not direct political control but economic exploitation by multinational corporations.* A **multinational corporation** is *a very large business that operates in many countries*; corporate leaders often impose their will on countries where they do business to create favourable economic conditions, just as colonizers did in the past (Bonanno, *et al.*, 2000).

Global Stratification: Theoretical Analysis

There are two major explanations for the unequal distribution of the world's wealth and power: *modernization theory* and *dependency theory*. Each theory suggests a different solution to the suffering of hungry people in much of the world.

MODERNIZATION THEORY

Modernization theory is *a model of economic and social development that explains global inequality in terms of technological and cultural differences between nations.* Modernization theory emerged in the 1950s, a time when U.S. society was fascinated by new developments in technology. To showcase the power of productive technology and also to counter the growing influence of the Soviet Union, U.S. policymakers drafted a market-based foreign policy that persists to this day.[1]

Historical Perspective

Until a few centuries ago, the entire world was poor, focusing on *subsistence*, or producing enough for family and community to survive. Because poverty has been the norm throughout human history, modernization theory claims that it is *affluence* that demands an explanation. Affluence came within reach of a growing share of people in Western Europe during the late Middle Ages as world exploration and trade expanded. Once the Industrial Revolution was under way, Western Europe and then North America were transformed. Industrial technology coupled with the spirit of capitalism created new wealth as never before. At first, this new wealth benefitted only a few. But industrial technology was so productive that, gradually, the living standard of even the poorest people began to improve. Absolute poverty, which had plagued humanity throughout history, was finally in decline.

During the twentieth century, the standard of living in high-income countries, where the Industrial Revolution began, jumped at least fourfold. Many middle-income nations in Asia and Latin America have industrialized, and they too have become richer. But with limited industrial technology, low-income countries have changed much less.

Modernization theory identifies *tradition* as the greatest barrier to economic development. In some societies, strong family systems and a reverence for the past discourage people from adopting new technologies that would raise their living standards. Even today, many people—from the North American Amish to Islamic people in rural regions of the Middle East and Asia, to the Semai of Malaysia—oppose technological advances as a threat to their family relationships, customs, and religious beliefs.

Max Weber (1958; orig. 1904–05) found that, at the end of the Middle Ages, Western Europe's cultural environment favoured change. As discussed in Chapter 4 ("Society"), Calvinists reshaped traditional Catholic beliefs to generate a way of life that promoted hard work and the accumulation of riches. Wealth—looked on with suspicion by the Catholic Church—became a sign of personal virtue, and the growing importance of individualism steadily replaced the traditional emphasis on family and community. Taken together, these new cultural patterns nurtured the Industrial Revolution.

Rostow's Stages of Modernization

Modernization theory holds that the door to affluence is open to all. As technological advances spread around the world, all societies should gradually industrialize. According to Walt W. Rostow (1960, 1978), modernization occurs in four stages:

1. *Traditional stage.* Socialized to honour the past, people in traditional societies cannot easily imagine how life can be very different. Therefore, they build their lives around families and local communities, following well-worn paths that allow for little individual freedom or change. Life is often spiritually rich but lacking in material goods. A century ago, much of the world was in this initial stage of economic development. Nations such as Bangladesh, Niger, and Somalia are still at the traditional stage and remain poor.

2. *Take-off stage.* As a society shakes off the grip of tradition, people start to use their talents and imagination, sparking economic growth. A market emerges as people produce goods not just for their own use but to trade with others for profit. Greater individualism, a willingness to take risks, and a desire for material goods also take hold, often at the expense of family ties, and time-honoured norms and values. Great Britain reached take-off by about 1800, the United States by 1820. Take-off in Canada occurred between 1890 and 1914 (Pomfret, 1981). Thailand, a middle-income country in eastern Asia, is now at this stage. Rich nations can help poor countries reach the take-off stage by supplying foreign aid, advanced technology, investment capital, and opportunities for schooling abroad.

3. *Drive to technological maturity.* During this stage, economic growth is a widely accepted idea that fuels a society's pursuit of higher living standards. A diversified

---

[1]This discussion of modernization theory draws on Rostow (1960, 1978), Bauer (1981), Berger (1986), Firebaugh (1996), and Firebaugh and Sandu (1998).

economy drives a population eager to enjoy the benefits of industrial technology. At the same time, however, people begin to realize—and sometimes regret—that industrialization is eroding traditional family and local community life. Great Britain reached this stage in about 1840, the United States by 1860, and Canada between 1914 and 1950. Mexico, Puerto Rico, and South Korea are among the nations now driving to technological maturity.

Absolute poverty is greatly reduced in nations in this stage of development. Cities swell with people who leave rural villages in search of economic opportunity. Specialization creates the wide range of jobs in the North American economy today. An increasing  focus on work makes relationships less personal. Growing individualism generates social movements demanding greater political rights. Societies approaching technological maturity also provide basic schooling for all their people and advanced training for some; the newly educated consider tradition to be backwards and push for further change. The social position of women steadily approaches that of men.

4. *High mass consumption.* Economic development steadily raises living standards as mass production stimulates mass consumption. Simply put, people soon learn to "need" the expanding array of goods that their society produces. The United States, Canada, Japan, and other rich nations moved into this stage by 1900. Now entering this level of economic development are two former British colonies that are prosperous small societies of Asia: Hong Kong and Singapore (independent since 1965).

YOUR TURN

Is the level of material consumption the only way, or the best way, to measure quality of life? Explain your answer.

The Role of Rich Nations

Modernization theory claims that high-income countries play four important roles in global economic development:

- *Controlling population.* Since population growth is greatest in the poorest societies, rising population can overtake economic advances. Rich nations can help limit population growth by exporting birth control technology and promoting its use. Once economic development is under way, birth rates should decline, as they have in industrialized nations, because children are no longer an economic asset.

- *Increasing food production.* Rich nations can export high-tech farming methods to poor nations to increase agricultural yields. Such techniques—collectively referred to as the Green Revolution—include new hybrid seeds, modern irrigation methods, chemical fertilizers, and pesticides for insect control.

- *Introducing industrial technology.* Rich nations can encourage economic growth in poor societies by introducing machinery and information technology, which raise productivity. Industrialization also shifts the labour force from farming to skilled industrial and service jobs.

- *Providing foreign aid.* Investment capital from rich nations can boost the prospects of poor societies trying to reach Rostow's take-off stage. Foreign aid can raise farm output by helping poor countries buy more fertilizer and build irrigation projects. In the same way, financial and technical assistance can help build power plants and factories to improve industrial output. Each year, the United States provides about $12 billion in foreign aid to developing countries: Canada gives about Cdn$3.6 billion. Neither country even approaches the 0.7 percent of GDP that the United Nations—and some vocal celebrities—would like to see.

Critical Review Modernization theory has many influential supporters among social scientists (Parsons, 1966; Moore, 1977, 1979; Bauer, 1981; Berger, 1986; Firebaugh and Beck, 1994; Firebaugh, 1996, 1999; Firebaugh and Sandu, 1998). For decades, it has shaped the foreign policies of the United States, Canada, and other rich nations. Supporters point to rapid economic development in Asia—including South Korea, Taiwan, Singapore, and Hong Kong—as proof that the affluence that accompanied industrialization in Western Europe and North America is within reach of other countries.

But modernization theory comes under fire from socialist countries (and left-leaning analysts in the West) as little more than a defence of capitalism. Its most serious flaw, according to critics, is that modernization simply has not occurred in many poor countries. The United Nations reported that living standards in a number of nations—including Haiti and Nicaragua in Latin America, and Sudan, Ghana, and Rwanda in Africa—were lower in the 1990s than they were in the 1960s (United Nations Development Programme, 1996).

A second criticism of modernization theory is that it fails to recognize how rich nations, which benefit from the status quo, often block paths to development for poor countries. Centuries ago, critics charge, rich countries industrialized from a position of global strength. Can we expect poor countries today to do so from a position of global weakness?

Third, modernization theory treats rich and poor societies as separate worlds, ignoring the ways in which international relations have affected all nations. Many countries in Latin America and Asia are still struggling to overcome the harm caused by colonialism, which boosted the fortunes of Europe.

Fourth, modernization theory holds up the world's most economically developed countries as the standard for judging the rest of humanity, revealing an ethnocentric bias. We should remember that our Western idea of "progress" has caused us to rush headlong into a competitive, materialistic way of life, which uses up the world's scarce resources and pollutes the natural environment.

Fifth, and finally, modernization theory suggests that the causes of global poverty lie almost entirely in the poor societies themselves. Critics see this analysis as little more than blaming the victims for their own problems. Instead, these critics argue, an analysis of global inequality should focus just as much on the behaviour of rich nations as it does on the behaviour of poor ones.

Concerns such as these reflect a second major approach to understanding global inequality: dependency theory.

DEPENDENCY THEORY

Dependency theory is *a model of economic and social development that explains global inequality in terms of the historical exploitation of poor nations by rich ones.* This analysis, which arose in the 1960s, puts the primary responsibility for global poverty on rich nations, which for centuries have systematically impoverished low-income countries and made them *dependent* on the rich ones. This destructive process continues today.

Historical Perspective

Everyone agrees that, before the Industrial Revolution, there was little affluence in the world. Dependency theory asserts, however, that people living in poor countries were actually better off economically in the past than their descendants are now. André Gunder Frank (1975), a noted supporter of this theory, argues that the colonial process that helped develop rich nations also led to the *under*development of poor societies.

Dependency theory is based on the idea that the economic positions of rich and poor nations of the world are linked and cannot be understood apart from each other. From this perspective, poor nations do not simply lag behind rich ones on the "path of progress"; rather, some nations became rich only because they impoverished others. Both are products of the global commerce that began five centuries ago.

The Importance of Colonialism

Late in the fifteenth century, Europeans began exploring the Americas, Africa, and Asia to establish colonies. They were so successful that, a century ago, England controlled about one-quarter of the world's land, boasting that "the sun never sets on the British Empire." Europeans and Africans engaged in a brutal form of human exploitation—the slave trade—from about 1500 until 1850. Even as the world was rejecting slavery, Europeans took control of most of the African continent, as Figure 12–3 shows. European powers dominated most of the continent until the early 1960s.

Modernization theory claims that corporations that build factories in low-income nations help people by providing them with jobs and higher wages than they had before; dependency theory views these factories as sweatshops that exploit workers. Following the dependency theory approach, these students are staging a protest at Gap and Nike stores in Boston.

Formal colonialism has almost disappeared from the world. The United States, itself originally a collection of small British colonies on the eastern seaboard of North America, soon pushed across the continent, purchased Alaska, and gained control of Haiti, Puerto Rico, Guam, the Philippines, the Hawaiian Islands, part of Panama, and Guantanamo Bay in Cuba. However, according to dependency theory, political liberation has not translated into economic independence. Far from it—the economic relationship between poor and rich nations, and the operation of multinational corporations, continue the colonial pattern of domination. This neocolonialism is the heart of the capitalist world economy.

Wallerstein's Capitalist World Economy

Immanuel Wallerstein (1974, 1979, 1983, 1984) explains global stratification using a model of the "capitalist world economy." Wallerstein's term "world economy" suggests that the prosperity of some nations and the poverty and dependency of other countries result from a global economic system. He traces the roots of the global economy to the beginning of colonization 500 years ago, when Europeans began gathering wealth from the rest of the world. Because the world economy is based in the high-income countries, it is capitalist in character.[1]

Wallerstein calls the rich nations the *core* of the world economy. Colonialism enriched this core by funnelling raw

---

[1]Based on Wallerstein's ideas, this section also draws on Frank (1980, 1981), Delacroix and Ragin (1981), Bergesen (1983), Dixon and Boswell (1996), and Kentor (1998).

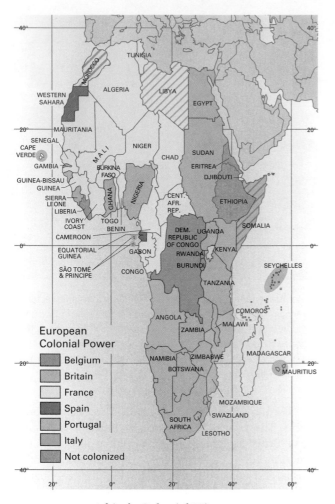

FIGURE 12-3 Africa's Colonial History

For more than a century, most of Africa was colonized by European nations, with France dominating in the northwest region of the continent and Great Britain dominating in the east and south.

materials from around the world to Western Europe, where they fuelled the Industrial Revolution. Today, multinational corporations operate profitably worldwide, channelling wealth to North America, Western Europe, Australia, and Japan. Low-income countries, on the other hand, represent the *periphery* of the world economy. Drawn into the world economy by colonial exploitation, poor nations continue to support rich ones by providing inexpensive labour and a vast market for industrial products. The remaining countries are considered the *semiperiphery* of the world economy; they include middle-income countries, such as Mexico and Brazil, that have closer ties to the global economic core.

According to Wallerstein, the world economy benefits rich societies by generating profits and harms the rest of the world by causing poverty. The world economy thus makes poor nations dependent on rich ones. This dependency involves three factors:

- *Narrow, export-oriented economies.* Poor nations produce only a few crops for export to rich countries. Examples

include coffee and fruit from Latin American nations, oil from Nigeria, hardwoods from the Philippines, and palm oil from Malaysia. Today's multinational corporations purchase raw materials cheaply in poor societies and transport them to core—and, increasing, semiperiphery—nations, where factories process them for profitable sale. As a result, poor nations develop few industries of their own.

- *Lack of industrial capacity.* Without an industrial base, poor societies face a double bind: they count on rich nations to buy their inexpensive raw materials and try to buy from them whatever expensive manufactured goods they can afford. In a classic example of this dependency, British colonial officials encouraged the people of India to raise cotton but prevented them from weaving their own cloth. Instead, the British shipped Indian cotton to their own textile mills in Birmingham and Manchester, manufactured the cloth, and shipped finished goods back to India, where the very people who harvested the cotton bought the garments. Dependency theorists claim that the Green Revolution—widely praised by modernization theorists—works the same way. Poor countries sell cheap raw materials to rich nations and then try to buy expensive fertilizers, pesticides, and machinery in return. Rich countries profit from this exchange more than poor nations.

- *Foreign debt.* Unequal trade patterns have plunged poor countries into debt to the core nations. Collectively, the poor nations of the world owe rich countries some $2.6 trillion; hundreds of billions of dollars are owed to the United States alone. Such staggering debt paralyzes a country, causing high unemployment and rampant inflation (World Bank, 2005).

The Role of Rich Nations

Modernization theory and dependency theory assign very different roles to rich nations. Modernization theory holds that rich countries *produce wealth* through capital investment and new technology. Dependency theory views global inequality in terms of how countries *distribute wealth*, arguing that rich nations have *over*developed themselves as they have *under*developed the rest of the world.

Dependency theorists dismiss the idea that programs developed by rich countries to control population and to boost agricultural and industrial output raise living standards in poor countries. Instead, they claim, such programs actually benefit rich nations and the ruling elites, not the poor majority, in low-income countries (Kentor, 2001).

Hunger activists Frances Moore Lappé and Joseph Collins (1986; Lappé, *et al.*, 2001) maintain that the capitalist culture of the United States encourages people to think of poverty as somehow inevitable. In this line of reasoning, poverty results from "natural" processes, including having too many children, and experiencing disasters such as droughts. But global poverty is far from inevitable; in their

As the world continues to grow richer, billions of people are being left behind. The shantytown of Cité Soleil near Port-au-Prince, the capital of Haiti, is built around an open sewer. What would you estimate life expectancy to be in such a place?

view, it results from deliberate policies. Lappé and Collins point out that the world already produces enough food to allow every person on the planet to become quite fat. Moreover, India and most of Africa actually *export* food, even though many of their own people go hungry.

According to Lappé and Collins, the contradiction of poverty amid plenty stems from rich nations' policy of producing food for profits, not people. That is, corporations in rich nations co-operate with elites in poor countries to grow and export profitable crops, such as coffee, thereby using land that could otherwise produce basics, such as beans and corn for local families. Governments of poor countries support the practice of growing for export because they need food profits to repay foreign debt. For Lappé and Collins, the capitalist corporate structure of the global economy is at the core of this vicious cycle.

YOUR TURN

Based on what you have read here and elsewhere, do you think that global hunger 50 years from now will be more or less serious? Explain your answer.

Critical Review The main idea of dependency theory is that no nation becomes rich or poor in isolation because a single global economy shapes the destiny of all nations. Pointing to continuing poverty in Latin America, Africa, and Asia, dependency theorists claim that development simply cannot proceed under the constraints now imposed by rich countries; rather, they call for radical reform of the entire world economy so that it operates in the interests of the majority of people.

Critics charge that dependency theory wrongly treats wealth as if no one gets richer without someone else getting poorer. Corporations, small business owners, and farmers can and do create new wealth through hard work and imaginative use of new technology. After all, they point out, the entire world's wealth has increased sixfold since 1950.

Second, critics say that dependency theory is wrong in blaming rich nations for global poverty because many of the world's poorest countries (e.g., Ethiopia) have had little contact with rich nations. On the contrary, a long history of trade with rich countries has dramatically improved the economies of many nations, including Sri Lanka, Singapore, and Hong Kong (all former British colonies), as well as South Korea and Japan. In short, say the critics, most evidence shows that foreign investment by rich nations encourages economic growth, as modernization theory claims, not economic decline, as dependency theorists claim (Vogel, 1991; Firebaugh, 1992).

Third, critics call dependency theory simplistic for pointing the finger at a single factor—capitalism—as the cause of global inequality (Worsley, 1990). Dependency theory views poor societies as passive victims and ignores factors inside these countries that contribute to their economic problems. Sociologists have long recognized the vital role of culture in shaping people's willingness to embrace or resist change. Under the rule of the ultratraditional Muslim Taliban, for example, Afghanistan became economically isolated, and its living standards sank to among the lowest in the world. Is it reasonable to blame capitalist nations for that country's stagnation?

Nor can rich societies be held responsible for the reckless behaviour of foreign leaders whose corruption and mili-

APPLYING THEORY
GLOBAL POVERTY

	Modernization Theory	Dependency Theory
Which theoretical approach is applied?	Structural-functional approach	Social-conflict approach
How did global poverty come about?	The whole world was poor until some countries developed industrial technology, which allowed mass production and created affluence.	Colonialism moved wealth from some countries to others, making some nations poor as it made other nations rich.
What are the main causes of global poverty today?	Traditional culture and a lack of productive technology.	Neocolonialism—the operation of multinational corporations in the global, capitalist economy.
Are rich countries part of the problem or part of the solution?	Rich countries are part of the solution, contributing new technology, advanced schooling, and foreign aid.	Rich countries are part of the problem, making poor countries economically dependent and in debt.

taristic campaigns impoverish their countries. Examples include the regimes of Ferdinand Marcos in the Philippines, François Duvalier in Haiti, Manuel Noriega in Panama, Mobutu Sese Seko in Zaire (now, Democratic Republic of the Congo), and Saddam Hussein in Iraq. Some leaders even use food supplies as weapons in internal political struggles, leaving the masses starving, as in the African nations of Ethiopia, Sudan, Somalia, and Zimbabwe. Likewise, many countries throughout the world have done little to improve the status of women or to control population growth.

Fourth, critics say that dependency theory is wrong to claim that global trade always makes rich nations richer and poor nations poorer. For example, in 2004 the United States had a trade deficit of $666 billion, meaning that it imports two-thirds of a trillion dollars more than it sells abroad. The single greatest debt was to China, whose profitable trade has now pushed that country into the ranks of middle-income countries (Crutsinger, 2005).

Fifth, critics fault dependency theory for offering only vague solutions to global poverty. Most dependency theorists urge poor nations to end all contact with rich countries, and some call for nationalizing foreign-owned industries. In other words, they charge, dependency theory is really an argument for some sort of world socialism. In light of the difficulties that socialist societies—even rich ones, such as the former Soviet Union—have had in meeting the needs of their own people, critics ask, should we really expect such a system to rescue the entire world from poverty?

---

[1]The Gross National Product (GNP) refers to the yearly value of goods and services produced by a country's citizens. Unlike the Gross Domestic Product, the GNP includes profits from capital invested abroad.

YOUR TURN

Which approach—modernization theory or dependency theory—do you find more convincing? Why?

The Applying Theory table (above) summarizes the main arguments of modernization theory and dependency theory.

Canada and Low-Income Countries

Canada's approach to development in low-income countries reveals tension between the modernization and dependency models on which it is based. In 1995, Canada spent Cdn$2.2 billion on aid to developing countries (0.29% of Gross National Product [GNP][1]), down from Cdn$3.2 billion (0.49% of GNP) in 1992. The 2003 federal budget called for increasing aid spending to Cdn$3.2 billion (0.26 % of GDP) in 2003 and set a goal of increasing this to Cdn$8 billion (0.40% of GDP) by 2015 (Partridge, 2003). An editorial in *The Globe and Mail* (2006) reports that the federal Conservative government will "add another $320 million to Ottawa's $3.6-billion–aid program for developing countries." Most Canadian aid is distributed through the Canadian International Development Agency (CIDA). In the past, CIDA has concentrated on encouraging industrial development, but it has recently started to emphasize self-sufficiency and improvement of the lives of the poor through enhancement of health care, housing, education, and agricultural methods. The involvement of women in development has also become a priority.

Canadians were shaken when—on Boxing Day, 2004—an earthquake in the Indian Ocean gave rise to a tsunami with disastrous consequences, including the loss of more than 150 000 lives, throughout coastal Asia. The Americans were there relatively quickly with hospital ships, aircraft carriers and helicopters. Canada's official response was slower. But the outpouring of generosity by the Canadian people was phenomenal: individuals, businesses, schools and other organizations donated tens of millions of dollars, much of which was eventually matched by the federal government. The flood of donations was so great that many organizations, like *Médecins sans frontiers*, received more money than they could deploy (Gregg, 2005). Eight months later, when Hurricane Katrina hit New Orleans, Canadians responded with generosity once again. In these days of instantaneous electronic communication—within Marshall McLuhan's global village—we see the images of disaster and respond. In the absence of such dramatic images, though, Canadians seem content that our government contributes only a small amount of foreign aid (roughly 0.28 percent of GDP), despite the fact that "something like 12 million people a year continue to die from treatable, preventable diseases" associated with poverty (*Globe and Mail*, 2005).

By the mid–1980s, Canada had responded to changing conditions in low-income countries "with increasingly sophisticated social, cultural, and economic programs for human development and self-reliance" (Tomlinson, 1991). But tension remains between the goals of eliminating poverty and creating an environment conducive to private-sector development and debt reduction through "economic structural adjustment" policies (Canada, 1987). Despite its humanitarian goals, much of Canada's aid continues to be linked to trade or the perceived potential for trade (that is, "tied aid"). While in this sense Canada's role is similar to that of the United States, some low-income countries are more comfortable accepting aid from Canada, which does not have the superpower status of the United States.

Nonetheless, aid from Canada is sometimes mixed with peacekeeping or military activity. Canada's current involvement in Afghanistan is, in effect, aid delivered through military force. Canada is contemplating stretching its commitments to intervene in Sudan to help the people of Darfur, who face what is widely recognized as genocide. This is another situation where aid cannot be delivered without military intervention. People

 Information about Canadian foreign aid initiatives is available at the CIDA website at www.acdi-cida.gc.ca.

who are opposed to Western military intervention everywhere else are pressing Canada and other countries to help Darfur (Wente, 2006). We are already involved in Darfur—helping to negotiate a fragile peace—but the Canadian government is under pressure to do more (Galloway, 2006).

In addition to its aid and trade involvements with low-income countries, Canada plays an active role in the generation and dissemination of knowledge in those societies.

Several Canadian universities are involved in overseas research and development projects, and most are involved in teaching foreign students who take their knowledge home. In 2001, Canada was host to 130 000 foreign students at all levels of education, from elementary to graduate school; 93 000, or 72 percent of these students, are enrolled at the postsecondary level. The overall figure reflects a 79 percent increase over 1995, which is attributable to economic growth in some of the countries the students come from and active recruitment on the part of our government (Canada, 2003). At this point, 55 percent of our foreign students come from South Korea, China, Japan, France, and Malaysia—countries that, one might say, are beneficiaries of Canada's educational activism. The Thinking it Through box (p. 312) describes one example of Canadian research and activism in the Yucatán.

YOUR TURN

Would you pay more for a cup of coffee to ensure that it was made using beans for which a farmer in a low-income country was paid a higher price? Why?

Global Stratification: Looking Ahead

Among the most important economic trends in recent decades is the development of a global economy. In North America, rising production and sales abroad bring profits to many corporations and their stockholders, especially those who already have substantial wealth. People who support the global economy claim that the expansion of trade results in benefits for all countries involved. For this reason, they endorse policies like the North American Free Trade Agreement. Critics of expanding globalization make other claims: factory jobs are lost in North American, as more manufacturing now takes place abroad where workers are underpaid and few laws ensure their safety in the workplace. In addition, expanding globalization places ever greater stress on the natural environment—often in low-income countries. But perhaps the greatest concern is the vast economic inequality that exists among the world's countries. The concentration of wealth in high-income countries, coupled with the grinding poverty in low-income nations, may well be the biggest problem facing humanity in the twenty-first century.

Both modernization theory and dependency theory offer some understanding of this urgent problem. In evaluating these theories, we must consider empirical evidence. Over the course of the twentieth century, living standards rose in most of the world. Even the economic output of the poorest 25 percent of the world's people almost tripled;

THINKING IT THROUGH
Seeking Livelihood Sustainability for Yucatán Farmers

Canadian rural sociologist Sally Humphries, of the University of Guelph, has devoted her career to enhancing sustainable agricultural development in the fragile tropical environments of Latin America. Some of her research (1993) has focused on the farmers of Mexico's Yucatán region, who have switched from traditional agriculture to intensive horticultural production for outside markets. Is it possible, Humphries asks, to maintain traditional systems in the face of market integration?

The traditional system, which *was* sustainable, evolved under conditions of low population pressure and, consequently, minimal environmental disruption. Traditional methods came under pressure when transportation links allowed a switch to delicate perishable crops, and tied the northern part of Yucatán to Mexican and world markets; at the same time, *profit* rather than *subsistence* became the goal.

Market integration resulted in more intensive use of the plots of land closest to water supplies (or irrigation;

in the past, cutting and burning of bush enriched the soil and prepared new plots for cultivation. To counter the soil depletion resulting from repeated use of the same plots—often with five or six plantings per year—farmers relied increasingly on purchased chemical fertilizers. Crop specialization, primarily in tomatoes, has left farmers vulnerable to losses owing to poor weather, pest attack, and plant diseases.

Agricultural intensification through irrigated vegetable growing has forced Yucatán farmers onto the "pesticide treadmill"—administering higher doses of chemicals, which lead to the destruction of natural pest predators, lowered pest resistance, and pest resurgence. The result has been an explosion of an uncontrollable, pesticide-resistant whitefly population—and environmental damage. Thus, while the decision to adopt vegetable production was rational in economic terms, giving rise to decades of income growth, it was less than rational in environmental terms.

Humphries concludes that, despite its benefits in providing work and

incomes above the regional norm, vegetable production in the northern Yucatán is nonsustainable under current technology. Her study points to the "difficulty of achieving the twin goal of economic and environmental sustainability." Those interested in traditional resource management must pay more attention to "the real life activities of producers and the implications of the market for traditional behaviour"—or, more succinctly, to the "decision-making and livelihood strategies" of farmers (p. 100).

WHAT DO YOU THINK?

1. What lessons should we take from this box regarding the relationship between economic and environmental concerns?
2. Is it possible to modernize farming without affecting the health of both people and the environment?
3. Is intervention by outside experts in traditional farming communities a good or a bad thing?

---

however, the economic output of the other 75 percent of the world's people increased about sixfold. By this measure, while all people are better off in *absolute* terms, there was almost twice as much *relative* economic inequality in the world in 2000 as there was in 1900. As Figure 12–4 suggests, the poorest of the world's people are being left behind.

Most of this economic polarization took place between 1900 and 1970. Since 1970, the degree of economic inequality worldwide has declined. In addition, at the turn of the millennium, there were only half the number of extremely poor people—those living on less than $1 per day—now than there were in 1970 (Schultz, 1998; Firebaugh, 1999, 2000; Sala-i-Martin, 2002). The greatest reduction in poverty has taken place in Asia, a region generally seen as an economic success story. In 1970, 75 percent of people

living on less than $1 a day were found in Asia; by 2000, that figure had fallen to 15 percent. Since then, both India and China have joined the ranks of middle-income nations (Sala-i-Martin, 2002; United Nations Development Programme, 2004).

Latin America represents a mixed case. During the 1970s, this region enjoyed significant economic growth; during the 1980s and 1990s, however, there was little overall improvement. Its share of people living on less than $1 a day was the same in 2000 (3%) as it was in 1970 (Sala-i-Martin, 2002).

Africa, especially the countries south of the Sahara Desert, represents a region of economic decline. There the extent of extreme poverty has become worse. In 1970, sub-Saharan Africa accounted for 11 percent of people living on

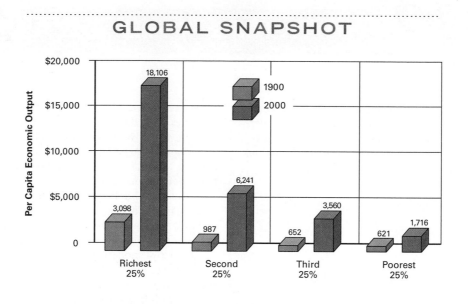

GLOBAL SNAPSHOT

FIGURE 12-4   The World's Increasing Economic Inequality

The gap between the richest and poorest people in the world is twice as big as it was a century ago.

Source: International Monetary Fund (2000).

less than $1 a day; by 2000, this share had risen to 66 percent (Sala-i-Martin, 2002).

These trends in economic performance have caused both modernization and dependency theorists to revise their views. Governments have played a large role in the economic growth that has occurred in Asia and elsewhere; this fact challenges modernization theory and its free-market approach to development. On the other hand, since the upheavals in the former Soviet Union and Eastern Europe, a global re-evaluation of socialism has been taking place. Because socialist nations have a record of decades of poor economic performance and political repression, many low-income nations are unwilling to follow the advice of dependency theory and place economic development entirely under government control.

While the world's future is uncertain, we have learned a great deal about global stratification. One insight offered by modernization theory is that poverty is partly a *problem of technology*. A higher standard of living for a surging world population depends on the ability of poor nations to raise their agricultural and industrial productivity. A second insight, derived from dependency theory, is that global inequality is also a *political issue*. Even with higher productivity, the human community must address crucial questions concerning how resources are distributed, both within societies and around the globe.

While economic development raises living standards, it also places greater strains on the natural environment. As nations such as India and China—with a combined population of 2.4 billion—become more affluent, their people will consume more energy and other resources and create more pollution. China has recently passed Japan to become the second largest consumer of oil, behind the United States.

Finally, the vast gulf that separates the world's richest and poorest people puts everyone at greater risk of war and terrorism as the poorest people challenge the social arrangements that threaten their existence (Lindauer and Weerapana, 2002). In the long run, we can achieve peace on this planet only by ensuring that all people enjoy a significant measure of dignity and security.

12 MAKING THE GRADE

The following learning tools will help you see what you know, identify what you still need to learn, and expand your understanding beyond the text. You can also visit this text's Companion Website™ at www.pearsoned.ca/macionis to find useful practice tests.

KEY POINTS

Global Stratification: An Overview

Around the world, social stratification is more pronounced than in North America. About 18 percent of the world's people live in industrialized, high-income countries such as the United States or Canada and receive 79 percent of all income. Another 70 percent of humanity lives in middle-income countries with significant industrialization, receiving about 20 percent of all income. About 12 percent of the world's people live in low-income countries with limited industrialization and earn only 1 percent of global income.

Global Wealth and Poverty

While relative poverty is found everywhere, low-income societies struggle with widespread absolute poverty. Worldwide, the lives of some 1 billion people are at risk because of poor nutrition. About 15 million people, most of them children, die annually from diseases caused by inadequate nutrition. Nearly everywhere in the world, women are more likely than men to live in poverty. Gender bias against women is greatest in poor agrarian societies. The poverty found in much of the world is a complex problem reflecting limited industrial technology, rapid population growth, traditional cultural patterns, internal social stratification, male domination, and global power relationships.

Global Stratification: Theoretical Analysis

Modernization theory maintains that successful development requires giving up cultural traditions that discourage the use of new technology. The modernization theorist Walt Rostow identifies four stages of development: the traditional stage, take-off, the drive to technological maturity, and high mass consumption. Arguing that rich societies hold the keys to creating wealth, modernization theory claims rich nations can help poor nations by providing population control programs, agricultural technology such as hybrid seeds and fertilizers that increase food production, industrial technology that includes machinery and information technology, and foreign aid to help pay for power plants and factories.

Critics of modernization theory say that rich nations do not spread economic development around the world. Further, they claim, because rich nations including the United States now control the global economy, today's poor nations cannot follow the same path to development taken by rich nations centuries ago.

Dependency theory claims that global wealth and poverty are the historical products of the capitalist world economy. The capitalist world economy emerged about 500 years ago with the spread of colonialism and continues today with the operation of multinational corporations.

Immanuel Wallerstein views the high-income countries as the advantaged "core" of the capitalist world economy; middle-income nations are the "semiperiphery," and poor societies form the global "periphery." Three key factors—export-oriented economies, a lack of industrial capacity, and foreign debt—make poor countries dependent on rich nations.

Critics of dependency theory argue that this approach overlooks the sixfold increase in the world's wealth since 1950 and note that the world's poorest societies have had weak, not strong, ties to rich countries.

Global Stratification: Looking Ahead

Both modernization theory and dependency theory offer useful insights into global inequality. Theorists from both approaches agree that there is an urgent need to address the various problems caused by worldwide poverty.

KEY CONCEPTS

global stratification (p. 292) patterns of social inequality in the world as a whole

colonialism (p. 303) the process by which some nations enrich themselves through political and economic control of other nations

neocolonialism (p. 304) a new form of global power relationships that involves not direct political control but economic exploitation by multinational corporations

multinational corporation (p. 304) a very large business that operates in many countries

modernization theory (p. 305) a model of economic and social development that explains global inequality in terms of technological and cultural differences between nations

dependency theory (p. 307) a model of economic and social development that explains global inequality in terms of the historical exploitation of poor nations by rich ones

APPLICATIONS & EXERCISES

1. Look through several issues of any current news or travel magazine, and notice any stories or advertising mentioning low-income countries (selling, say, coffee from Colombia or vacations to India for surgery). What picture of life in low-income countries does the advertising present? In light of what you have learned in this chapter, how accurate does this image seem to you?

2. Millions of students from abroad study on North American campuses. See if you can identify a woman and a man on your campus who was raised in a poor country. After explaining that you have been studying global stratification, ask if he or she is willing to share information about what life is like in his or her country. If so, ask about stratification as well as social position there.

3. Pick five of the global maps in this text (from p. xxii at the beginning of this book), and identify social traits of high-income countries and those of low-income countries. Try to use both modernization theory and dependency theory to explain the patterns you find.

PRENTICE HALL
mysoclab ™
Where learning & the sociological imagination intersect.

To reinforce your understanding of this chapter, and to identify topics for further study, visit MySocLab at **www.pearsoned.ca/mysoclab/** for diagnostic tests and a multimedia ebook.

13

CHAPTER THIRTEEN

Gender Stratification

How is gender a creation of society?

What difference does gender make
in people's lives?

Why is gender an important dimension of
social stratification?

In 1927, five women—each a well-known activist at the time—asked the Supreme Court of Canada to recognize women as "persons" so that they could be eligible for appointment to the Senate. The case is known as the *Persons Case*, and the women were Henrietta Muir Edwards, Nellie Mooney McClung, Louise Crummy McKinney, Emily Ferguson Murphy, and Irene Marryat Parlby. Collectively known as The Famous Five (or Valiant Five), they have statues erected in their honour in Calgary and on Parliament Hill in Ottawa and have their stories told in *100 Canadian Heroines* (Forster, 2004). You may be surprised to learn that the Supreme Court of Canada, in a unanimous ruling, declared in 1927 that the word "person" does *not* refer to women. After all, the *British North America Act* used the word "he" exclusively to refer to senators. The five women then went to London, England, to appeal to the Judicial Committee of the Privy Council—the final court of appeal for the British Empire at the time; in 1929, the Committee ruled that Canadian women *are* persons who could, therefore, serve in the Senate.

As a result, in 1930, Cairine Wilson was called by the governor general (not the prime minister, as is the case today) to become Canada's first woman senator. None of the Famous Five was made a senator.

If you think that the Privy Council ruling of 1929 confirmed equal rights for Canadian women in the broader sense, you would be wrong. It was not until 1940 that Quebec became the last province to grant women the right to vote—and that was not the end of the fight for gender equality. Astonishingly, women had to fight to get gender equality enshrined in the Canadian Charter of Rights and Freedoms in 1982. At a time when Prime Minister Trudeau and other politicians were willing to grant equality on the basis of race, ethnicity, age, disability, and religion, there were some who thought it would be unwise or even dangerous to add sex to the list, fearing demands for equal pay and abortion rights. The Advisory Council on the Status of Women was thwarted by the Liberals—specifically Lloyd Axworthy, the minister responsible for the status of women—in its attempt to hold a national conference on the proposed charter. Regional conferences were preferred by the government.

In defiance, through networking—on parliamentary telephones—three women (Doris Anderson, Pauline Jewett, and Flora MacDonald) were able to arrange for 1300 women from across Canada to gather in Ottawa for an ad hoc conference in February 1981. The women's conference was instrumental in getting sexual equality enshrined in our constitution—just as American women saw their Equal Rights Amendment go down to defeat (McKenzie, 1999: 123–25). Subsection 15(1) of the Canadian Charter of Rights and Freedoms (Canada, 1982) now provides that: "Every individual is equal before and under the law and has the right to the equal protection and equal benefit of the law without discrimination based on race, national or ethnic origin, colour, religion, sex, age, or mental or physical disability."

While sexual equality is now guaranteed by the Canadian Charter of Rights and Freedoms, women and men still lead different lives in Canada and throughout the world; in most respects, men are still in charge. Here, we explore the importance of gender as a major dimension of social stratification.

Gender and Inequality

Chapter 8 ("Sexuality and Society") explained the biological differences that divide the human population into categories of female and male. **Gender** refers to *the personal traits and social positions that members of a society attach to being female or male.* Gender operates as a dimension of social organization, shaping how we interact with others and how we think about ourselves. More importantly, gender also involves *hierarchy*, ranking men and women differently in terms of power, wealth, and other resources. This is why sociologists speak of **gender stratification,** *the unequal distribution of wealth, power, and privilege between men and women.* Gender, in short, affects the opportunities and constraints we face throughout our lives.

MALE/FEMALE DIFFERENCES

Many people think there is something "natural" about gender distinctions because biology does make one sex different from the other. But we must be careful not to think of social differences in biological terms. Until recently—1918 in Canada—women were denied the vote because it was assumed that women did not have enough intelligence or interest in politics to warrant enfranchisement. Such attitudes had nothing to do with biology; they reflected the *cultural* patterns of that time and place.

Another example is athletic performance. In 1925, most people—both women and men—believed that the best women runners could never compete with men in a marathon. Today, as Figure 13–1 shows, the gender gap has greatly narrowed, and the fastest women routinely post better times than the fastest men of decades past. Here again, most of the differences between men and women turn out to be socially created.

 For a multimedia presentation on "Pioneering Canadian Women in Sports," visit the CBC archives at http://archives.cbc.ca//300c. asp?id=1-41-714.

YOUR TURN

Do you think female and male athletes should compete on the same teams? Why? Do you think your gender affects your answer to this question?

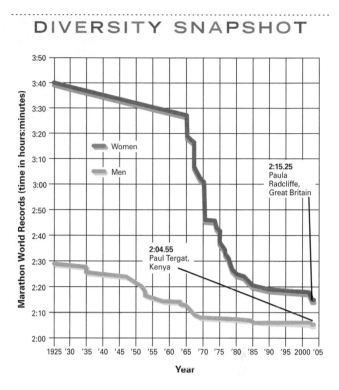

DIVERSITY SNAPSHOT

FIGURE 13-1   Men's and Women's Athletic Performance

Do men naturally outperform women in athletic competition? The answer is not obvious. Early in the twentieth century, men outpaced women by more than an hour in marathon races. But, as opportunities for women in athletics have increased, women have been closing the performance gap. Only ten minutes separate the current world marathon records for women and for men (both set in 2003).

Sources: *Christian Science Monitor,* © 1995. Christian Science Monitor and Marathonguide.com (2005). Adapted with permission of the *Christian Science Monitor.*

There are some differences in physical ability between the sexes. On average, males are 10 percent taller, 20 percent heavier, and 30 percent stronger, especially in their upper body (Ehrenreich, 1999). On the other hand, women outperform men in the ultimate game of life itself: life expectancies for women and men in Canada are 83.4 and 76.4 years, respectively (compared to 80.1 and 74.8 years in the United States).

In adolescence, males do a bit better in mathematics, and females show stronger verbal skills, differences that reflect both biology and socialization (Maccoby and Jacklin, 1974; Baker, *et al.,* 1980; Lengermann and Wallace, 1985; Tavris and Wade, 2001). However, research does not point to any difference in overall intelligence between males and females.

Biologically, then, men and women differ in limited ways; neither is naturally superior. But culture can define the two sexes very differently, as the global study of gender in the next section shows.

In every society, people assume that certain jobs, patterns of behaviour, and ways of dressing are "naturally" feminine while others are just as obviously masculine. But, in global perspective, we see remarkable variety in such social definitions. These men, Wodaabe pastoral nomads who live in Niger, are proud to engage in a display of beauty most people in our society would consider feminine.

GENDER IN GLOBAL PERSPECTIVE

The best way to see the cultural foundation of gender is by comparing one society to another. Three important studies highlight just how different "masculine" and "feminine" can be.

The Israeli Kibbutz

In Israel, collective settlements are called *kibbutzim*. The *kibbutz* (the singular form of the word) is an important setting for research because gender equality is one of its stated goals; men and women share in both work and decision making. In kibbutzim, both sexes share most everyday jobs: both men and women take care of children, cook and clean, repair buildings, and make day-to-day decisions concerning life in the kibbutz. Girls and boys are raised in the same way and, from the first weeks of life, children live together in dormitories. Women and men in kibbutzim have achieved remarkable—although not complete—social equality, evidence that cultures define what is feminine and what is masculine.

Margaret Mead's Research

The anthropologist Margaret Mead carried out ground-breaking research on gender. If gender is based on the biological differences between men and women, she reasoned, people everywhere should define "feminine" and "masculine" in the same way; if gender is cultural, these conceptions should vary. Mead studied three societies in New Guinea (1963; orig. 1935). In the mountainous home of the Arapesh, Mead observed men and women with remarkably similar attitudes and behaviour. Both sexes, she reported, were co-operative and sensitive to others—in short, what North American culture would label "feminine."

Moving south, Mead then studied the Mundugumor, whose head hunting and cannibalism stood in striking contrast to the gentle ways of the Arapesh. In this culture, both sexes were typically selfish and aggressive, traits North Americans define as more "masculine."

Finally, travelling west to the Tchambuli, Mead discovered a culture that, like our own, defines females and males differently. But, Mead reported, the Tchambuli *reversed* many of our notions of gender: females were dominant and rational, and males were submissive, emotional, and nurturing towards children. Based on her observations, Mead concluded that culture is the key to gender differences, because what one society defines as masculine another may see as feminine.

Some critics view Mead's findings as "too neat," as if she saw in these three societies just the patterns she was looking for. Deborah Gewertz (1981) challenged what she called Mead's "reversal hypothesis," pointing out that Tchambuli males are really the more aggressive sex. Gewertz explains that Mead visited the Tchambuli (who actually call themselves Chambri) during the 1930s, after they had lost much of their property in tribal wars; Mead had observed Chambri men rebuilding their homes: a temporary role only.

George Murdock's Research

In a broader study of more than two hundred pre-industrial societies, George Murdock (1937) found some global agreement about which tasks are feminine and which masculine. Hunting and warfare, Murdock concluded, generally fall to men, and home-centred tasks such as cooking and child care tend to be women's work. With their simple technology, pre-industrial societies apparently assign roles reflecting men's and women's physical characteristics. With greater size and strength, men hunt game and protect the group; because women bear children, they do most of the work in the home. But beyond this general pattern, Murdock found much variety. Consider agriculture: women did the farming in about the same number of societies as men; in most farming societies, the two sexes shared this work. When it came to many other tasks—from building shelters to tattooing the body—Murdock found that various societies were as likely to turn to one sex as the other.

YOUR TURN

Did you grow up in a home in which females and males had different jobs and responsibilities? How does this affect your view of gender?

IN SUM: GENDER AND CULTURE

Global comparisons show that, overall, societies do not consistently define tasks as either feminine or masculine. With industrialization, the importance of muscle power declines, further reducing gender differences (Nolan and Lenski, 2004). In sum, gender is too variable across cultures to be a simple expression of biology; what it means to be female and male is mostly a creation of society.

PATRIARCHY AND SEXISM

Although conceptions of gender vary, everywhere in the world we find some degree of **patriarchy** (literally, "the rule of fathers"), *a form of social organization in which males dominate females.* Despite mythical tales of societies run by female Amazons, **matriarchy,** *a form of social organization in which females dominate males,* has never been documented in human history. While some degree of patriarchy may be universal, women's power can rival that of men. During the 1700s and 1800s among the Seneca of North America, for example, women did the farming and controlled the food supply. Seneca men had to obtain women's support for their objectives (such as a military campaign), or women could simply withhold the necessary food (Freedman, 2002).

Around the world, as Global Map 13–1 shows, there is significant variation in the relative power and privilege of females and males. According to the United Nations gender development index, Norway, Australia, and Iceland give women the highest social standing; in contrast, women in the African nations of Niger, Burkina Faso, Mali, Sierra Leone, and Chad have the lowest social standing compared to that of men. Canada and the United States are also ranked high in terms of gender equality (United Nations Development Programme, 2005).

The justification for patriarchy is **sexism,** *the belief that one sex is innately superior to the other.* Sexism is not just a matter of individual attitudes; it is built into the institutions of society. *Institutional sexism* is found throughout the economy, with women concentrated in low-paying jobs. Similarly, the legal system has long excused violence against women, especially when committed by boyfriends, husbands, and fathers.

The Costs of Sexism

Sexism limits the talents and ambitions of the half of the human population who are women. While men benefit in some respects from sexism, their privilege comes at a high price. Masculinity in our culture encourages men to engage in many high-risk behaviours: using tobacco and alcohol, playing dangerous sports, and driving recklessly. As Marilyn French (1985) argues, patriarchy leads men to seek control, not only of women but also of themselves and their world. This is why masculinity is closely linked not only to accidents but also to suicide, violence, and stress-related diseases. The *Type A personality* (marked by chronic impatience, driving ambition, competitiveness, and free-floating hostility) is a recipe for heart disease and almost perfectly matches the behaviour that our culture considers masculine (Ehrenreich, 1983). The Thinking it Through box (on pp. 224–225 in Chapter 9) discusses hockey violence as an expression of "dangerous masculinity" and the Applying Sociology box (on p. 545 in Chapter 21) explores the Type A personality.

Finally, as men seek control over others, they lose opportunities for intimacy and trust. As one analyst put it, competition is supposed to "separate the men from the boys"; in practice, however, it separates men from men and everyone else (Raphael, 1988).

Is Patriarchy Inevitable?

In pre-industrial societies, women have little control over pregnancy and childbirth, which limits the scope of their lives. In those same societies, men's greater height and physical strength are highly valued resources. But industrialization and birth control technology give people choices about how to live. In societies like our own, biological differences offer little justification for patriarchy.

But males are dominant in Canada and elsewhere. Does this mean that patriarchy is inevitable? Some researchers claim that biological factors such as differences in hormones and slight differences in brain structure wire the two sexes with different motivations and behaviours—especially aggressiveness in males—making patriarchy difficult, perhaps even impossible, to eliminate (Goldberg, 1974; Rossi, 1985; Popenoe, 1993a; Udry, 2000). However, most sociologists believe that gender is socially constructed and *can* be changed. Just because no society has yet eliminated patriarchy does not mean that we must remain prisoners of the past.

To understand why patriarchy continues today, we next examine how gender is rooted and reproduced in society, a process that begins in childhood and continues throughout our lives.

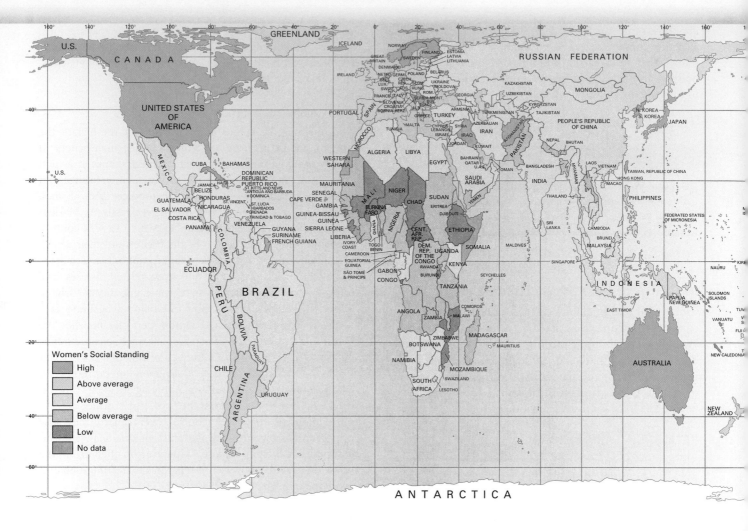

WINDOW ON THE WORLD

GLOBAL MAP 13–1   Women's Power in Global Perspective

Women's social standing in relation to men's varies around the world. In general, women live better in rich countries than in poor countries. Even so, some nations stand out: in Norway, Australia, and Iceland, women come closest to social equality with men.

Source: Data from Seager (2003).

Gender and Socialization

From birth until death, gender shapes human feelings, thoughts, and actions. Children quickly learn that their society considers females and males different kinds of people; by about age three, they begin to think of themselves in these terms.

In the past, women were described using such terms as "emotional," "passive," and "co-operative"; in contrast, men were described in opposing terms, such as "rational," "active," and "competitive." We have been taught to think of gender in terms of opposition—one sex being the opposite of the other—despite the fact that women and men have so much in common and research suggests that most young people develop personalities that are a mix of feminine and masculine traits (Bem, 1993).

Just as gender affects how we think of ourselves, so it teaches us how to behave. **Gender roles** (or sex roles) are *attitudes and activities that a society links to each sex.* A culture that defines males as ambitious and competitive encourages males to seek out positions of leadership and play team sports. To the extent that females are defined as deferential and emotional, they are expected to be supportive helpers and quick to show their feelings.

GENDER AND THE FAMILY

The first question people usually ask about a newborn—Is it a boy or a girl?—has great importance because the answer involves not just sex but the likely direction of the child's life. In fact, gender is at work even before the birth of a child because, especially in lower-income nations, parents hope their firstborn will be a boy rather than a girl.

Soon after birth, family members welcome infants into the "pink" world of girls or the "blue" world of boys (Bernard, 1981). Parents even send gender messages in the way they handle infants. One researcher at an English university presented an infant dressed as either a boy or a girl to a number of women; her subjects handled the "female" child tenderly, with frequent hugs and caresses, and treated the "male" child more roughly, often lifting him up high in the air or bouncing him on the knee (Bonner, 1984; Tavris and Wade, 2001). The lesson to children is clear: the female world revolves around co-operation and emotion, and the male world puts a premium on independence and action.

GENDER AND THE PEER GROUP

About the time they enter school, children begin to move outside the family and make friends with others of the same age. Considerable research shows that young children tend to form single-sex play groups (Martin and Fabes, 2001).

GENDER AND SCHOOLING

Even before children enter school, their reading tends to promote gender distinctions. A generation ago, the Royal Commission on the Status of Women (Canada, 1970) analyzed a selection of A multimedia presentation on the Royal Commission on the Status of Women is available from the cbc archives at http://archives.cbc.ca//300c.asp?id=1-73-86. children's texts and found that "versatile characters who have adventures are invariably males" (Mackie, 1983:185). Even math books represented males and females differently; for example, a problem focusing on the number of words typed per minute in 45 minutes referred to the typist as female. The royal commission concluded that "a woman's creative and intellectual potential is either underplayed or ignored in the education of children from their earliest years" (Canada, 1970:175). More recently, a growing awareness among authors, publishers, and teachers of the limiting effects of gender stereotypes on young people has led to changes. Today's books for children portray females and males in more balanced ways.

Through primary and secondary school, despite many efforts at change, classroom curricula may still encourage children to embrace traditional gender patterns. Young

Sex is a biological distinction that develops prior to birth. Gender is the meaning that a society attaches to being female or male. Gender differences are a matter of power, because what is defined as masculine typically has more importance than what is feminine. Infants begin to learn the importance of gender by the way parents treat them. Do you think this child is a girl or a boy? Why?

women are expected to excel in languages and social studies, young men in mathematics and sciences. In university, the pattern continues, with men and women tending towards different majors. Men are disproportionately represented in mathematics and the sciences, including physics, chemistry, and biology. Women cluster in the humanities (such as English), the fine arts (painting, music, dance, and drama), education courses, and the social sciences (including anthropology and sociology). New areas of study are also likely to be gender-typed: computer science, with its grounding in engineering, logic, and mathematics, attracts mostly men, while courses in gender studies tend to attract mostly women.

YOUR TURN

What is your declared or likely major? What proportion of students in your major is female or male? Is the pattern consistent with those described here?

Television crime programs such as *CSI* have male lead characters with women in supporting roles, largely to provide romantic interest. Can you think of other television shows that display this pattern? Are there others that have female leads? What about *Bones*?

GENDER AND THE MASS MEDIA

Since television first captured the public imagination in the 1950s, White males have held centre stage. Racial and ethnic minorities were all but absent from television until the early 1970s; only in the last few decades have programs featured women in prominent roles. Even when both sexes appear on camera, men generally play the brilliant detectives, fearless explorers, and skilled surgeons. Women, in contrast, play the less-capable characters and are often important primarily for their sexual attractiveness.

Change came slowly to advertising, which sells products by conforming to widely established cultural norms. Advertising presents the two genders, more often than not, in stereotypical ways. Historically, ads have shown women in the home, using cleaning products, serving foods, and trying out new appliances. Men, on the other hand, predominate in ads for cars, travel, banking services, industrial companies, and alcoholic beverages. The authoritative "voice-over" (the faceless voice that promotes products on television and radio) is almost always male (Davis, 1993).

A careful study of gender in advertising reveals some interesting patterns. Men are photographed to appear taller than women, implying male superiority. Women are more frequently presented lying down on sofas and beds or, like children, seated on the floor. The expressions and gestures of men exude competence and authority, whereas women are more likely to appear in childlike poses. Men focus on the products being advertised; women direct their interest to men, conveying support and submission (Erving Goffman, 1979; Cortese, 1999). See the Media Perspectives box (on p. 122 in Chapter 5) for further discussion of the treatment of minorities—including women—by the media.

Controversial images in current ads are presented at www.mediawatch.com.

Gender and Social Stratification

Gender affects more than thought and action. It also determines one's place in the social hierarchy. The reality of gender stratification can be seen most clearly in the world of work.

WORKING WOMEN AND MEN

In 1901, women made up 13 percent of Canada's paid workforce and earned half of men's income. By 1971, women had a labour force participation rate of 39.9 percent—meaning that 39.9 percent of women fifteen years of age and over were either employed or looking for work (i.e., unemployed); the comparable figure for men was 76.4 percent. By 2001, the female labour force participation rate was 61.1 percent—up 21.2 points; the male rate dropped slightly to 73.5 percent—down 2.9 points. Despite the substantial decrease in the gap between male and female employment participation rates, the female rate continues to be lower than that of men.

It is also possible to examine labour force participation rates by age. By looking at participation in the prime working years (i.e., 35 to 44 years of age) one is able to minimize the contaminating effects of prolonged schooling, child bearing and caring for pre-school children, disability, or retirement. If ever in your lifetime you are likely to be working, it is in that age range. Not surprisingly, in 1971 and 2001, the male labour force participation rates for those 35 to 44 years of age are 92.8 and 92.4, respectively. In contrast, the female labour force participation rate, for women 35 to 44 years of age, increased by 37.5 points between 1971 and 2001—from 43.9 to 81.4 percent—while the male rate remained essentially unchanged (Statistics Canada, 2001). In other words, in 1971, the majority of women were not in the labour force—*even in their prime working years.* By 2001, 4 out of 5 women in those middle years were working or looking for work. The most dramatic increase in participation had taken place in the age range for 35 to 44 years of age.

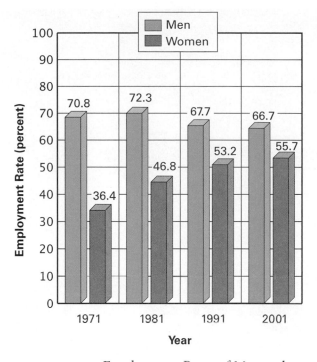

FIGURE 13-2   Employment Rates of Men and Women (15 Years of Age and over) in Canada, 1971 to 2001

Source: Compiled by L.M. Gerber based on data from Statistics Canada, catalogue no. 97F0012XCB2001003.

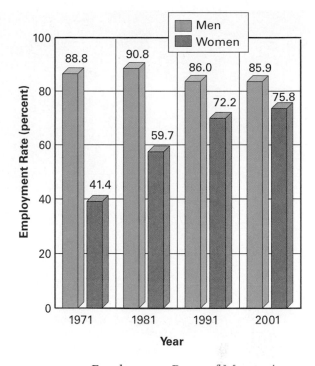

FIGURE 13-3   Employment Rates of Men and Women (35 to 44 Years of Age) in Canada, 1971 to 2001

Source: Compiled by L.M. Gerber based on data from Statistics Canada, catalogue no. 97F0012XCB2001003.

Figures 13–2 and 13–3 deal with trends in employment rates—that part of the labour force that is employed, rather than unemployed or looking for work, at specific points in time. Figure 13–2 reveals that the proportion of men aged 15 and over who are employed increased slightly between 1971 and 1981 before falling off to 66.7 percent in 2001. In contrast, women's employment rates start off low and rise steadily to 55.7 in 2001.

Focusing once again on the employment rates of people 35 to 44 years of age, we find higher levels for both men and women at each point in time (on Figure 13–3). Employment 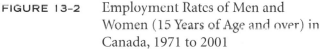 levels for men in these prime working years also rise slightly at first before dropping off (to 85.9%). Female employment, in the middle years, rises dramatically and consistently—from 41.4 percent to 75.8 percent—over a 30-year period. Under these circumstances, daycare (which we discuss later) becomes a critical social issue.

Factors that changed Canada's labour force include the decline of farming, the growth of cities, the post-industrial economy, shrinking family size, and a rising divorce rate—and the fact that 65 percent of married couples depend on two incomes (*Women in Canada*, 1995:65). Women working for income today are the rule rather than the exception, for they now represent almost half (47%) of our

 You can find information on labour force and participation rates (from 2001 to 2005) by sex and age group at www40.statcan.ca/l01/cst01/labor05.htm.

paid labour force. In the past, mothers with young children stayed at home: today they are very likely to continue working when their parental leave expires. In fact, many career women fail to take advantage of the full year of parental leave to which they are entitled. (*Parental leave* used to be called maternity leave; the term was changed when men began to leave work to care for infants.)

GENDER, OCCUPATIONS, AND INCOME

In the past, many jobs were done mainly by women—others mainly by men. During the past decade or two, we have seen considerable blurring of the distinctions between men's work and women's work. Women in unprecedented numbers are moving into business, finance, engineering, the sciences, medicine, and veterinary medicine—while a visit to a hospital or a nursing home reveals the presence of male nurses, who now make up 7 percent of the total. In 1982 and 1994 respectively, clerical occupations employed 34 and 27

 Select "Crossing the Bar," for a history of women's struggles to gain entrance into the legal profession in Ontario at http://library.lsuc.on.ca/GL/arch_museum.htm.

percent of all working women; by 2001, the figure had dropped to 14 percent. In this category are secretaries, typists,

In May 2006, Captain Nicola Goddard, twenty-six, was killed in a battle with the Taliban near Kandahar. She knew the risks of deployment to Afghanistan, yet was eager to take on the job for which she had been training for eight years. In both Canada and the United States, women comprise about 15 percent of the armed forces. Women became fully integrated in Canada's armed forces since gender equality was guaranteed, in 1982, by the Canadian Charter of Rights and Freedoms (except on submarines, until very recently). Unlike the United Kingdom and the United States, Canada allows women to serve in combat zones.

Belinda Stronach, former CEO and president of Magna International—the auto-parts manufacturer with more than US$12 billion in annual revenues—was named by *Fortune* as the second most powerful woman in business outside the United States. Given her influence on the international scene, it was no surprise to learn that she brought Stephen Harper and Peter MacKay together to effect the merger of the Canadian Alliance and the Progressive Conservatives in the fall of 2003—a move that would dramatically change Canada's political landscape (Dubé, 2003). Much has changed in the ensuing years: Stronach is now a Liberal MP under a Conservative minority government. But one thing is certain: Belinda Stronach will continue to make waves.

stenographers, and others whose efforts typically support the efforts of men. Not surprisingly, while in 1994 more than 80 percent of all such "pink-collar" jobholders were women, by 2001, the figure had dropped to 73 percent. The second largest category is service work, performed by over 17 percent of employed women. These jobs include waiting tables, hairdressing, house- or office-cleaning, and babysitting. Both categories of jobs—clerical and service—lie at the low end of the pay scale and offer limited opportunities for advancement.

Overall, gender stratification permeates the workplace, where men tend to hold occupational positions that confer more wealth and power than those typically held by women. On the other hand, change *is* occurring, however slowly. The Thinking it Through box (on pp. 328–31) takes a closer look at the complex interactions of gender, occupation, and income and deals with some of the factors that— along with discrimination and the "glass ceiling"—give rise to the gender gap.

HOUSEWORK: WOMEN'S "SECOND SHIFT"

In North America, we have always been of two minds about housework: we claim that it is essential to family life, but people get little reward for doing it (Bernard, 1981). Here, as around the world, taking care of the home and children has always been considered "women's work." With women's entry into the labour force, the amount of housework women do has gone down, but the *share* done by women has stayed the same. Figure 13–4 shows that, overall, women average 16.5 hours a week of housework, compared to 9.2 hours for men. As the figure shows, women in all categories do significantly more housework than men (Stapinski, 1998). Men do support the idea of women entering the paid labour force, and most count on the money women earn. But many men resist taking on a more equal share of household duties (Heath and Bourne, 1995; Harpster and Monk-Turner, 1998; Stratton, 2001). You may want to take another look at Global Map 6–1 (on p. 136) which deals with housework in a global perspective.

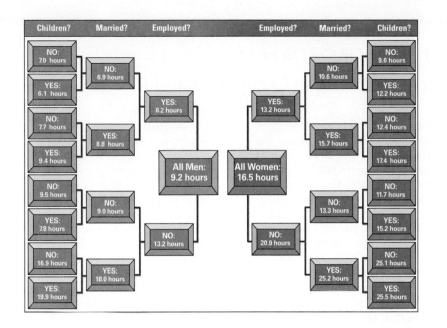

FIGURE 13-4   Housework: Who Does How Much?

Overall, women average 16.5 hours of housework per week, compared with 9.2 hours for men. This pattern holds whether people are employed or not, married or not, and parenting or not.

Source: Adapted from Stapinski (1998).

YOUR TURN

Consider the statements "He fathered the child" and "She mothered the child." How do they reflect the way gender shapes the meaning of parenting?

GENDER AND EDUCATION

In the past, our society considered schooling more necessary for men, who worked outside the home, than for women, who worked in the home. But times have changed. In Canada, in every year from 1999 to 2003, women earned more that 58 percent of all degrees, diplomas, and certificates granted throughout the country. Of the larger provinces, the only one that stood out was British Columbia which started off below average (at 57.8% female in 1999) and took the lead in 2003 (at 60.6% female).

 Learn about the evolution of the gender earnings gap among Canadian university graduates at www.statcan.ca/bsolc/english/bsolc?catno=11F0019MIE2004235.

Table 13–3 deals with educational attainment for men and women 15 years of age and over (which is the standard measure), and between 30 and 34 years of age. Data for the age range of 30 to 34 years are significant because they reflect recent changes in gender attainment patterns. Also, by 34 years of age, all candidates should have completed medical or graduate school. The first row in the table reveals that, for the adult population as a whole, women are more likely to have earned only a high school graduation certificate. Among people aged 30 to 34, women—but not men—have gone on to higher levels of certification. Within both age ranges, you can see that men are more likely to have trades certificates but, in the cohort of people aged 30 and 34, women are closing the gap. Both genders increased their trade certification levels, but the gap decreased from 6.3 points to 5.4.

In either age range, women are more likely than men to have college certification or bachelor's degrees. In each case, the women's advantage is greater between 30 and 34 years of age—reflecting gains made by the most recent cohorts of women. The proportions of men and women who are medical doctors increased in the cohort aged 30 to 34, with women almost achieving parity. The pattern for master's degrees is similar. Interestingly, while the proportion of women with Ph.D.s increased for the cohort aged 30 to 34, the proportion for men actually decreased. Considering these patterns, one can expect that the 2006 census will reveal that women in the cohort aged 30 to 34 will move ahead of men in attaining higher-level degrees.

Field of study also factors into the educational attainment picture. Among those 30 and 34 years of age with bachelor's degrees, men and women predominate in different fields of study. Men lead in engineering and the hard sciences (e.g., mathematics, physics, computer science) at 81 and 68 percent, respectively. Note that women are slower to move into engineering than these sciences. Women predominate most clearly in the health professions and education (at 82% and 70%, respectively), but also in fine arts (at 63%), the natural sciences (e.g., biology, nutrition, at 61%), the humanities (at 61%), and the social sciences (at 57%). In commerce or business administration, women make up 49.5 percent and in law they represent 48 percent. While the last two figures might surprise you, the fact that women make up 69 percent of those who have studied sociology will not.

THINKING IT THROUGH
Understanding the Gender Gap in Occupation and Income

Among people employed full-time all year, women earn 70 percent of male income. Generally speaking, we hear five explanations for this fact:

- Women choose occupations that are poorly paid (i.e., cashier rather than motor vehicle assembler).

- Women take time out from their jobs or careers to have children.

- Women are shut out of traditional male occupations, such as engineering.

- If women make it into these occupations at all, employers choose to pay them less.

- Women are less likely to be promoted.

Note that the last three explanations imply gender discrimination.

In an attempt to assess the merits of these five explanations, we can look at occupational and income data for women and men. We deal here with only thirty-three of the several hundred occupations in Canada. The occupations chosen range from upper to lower income—ranked by male income in 2000—and include a number to which you might aspire. Useful comparative statistics are calculated for you and presented in tables 13–1 and 13–2. Yes, the tables are difficult to read, but they contain a wealth of information extracted from Statistics Canada's massive census databases.

Before doing any analysis, we have to determine the nature of the data in each of the columns of tables 13–1 and 13–2—noting first that we deal here exclusively with workers who are employed full-time, all year. In Table 13–1, the first two columns refer to the distribution of male workers, by occupation, in 1995 and 2000. They reveal that in 1995, 2.6 percent of male full-time workers were truck drivers and, by 2000, their proportion had increased

to **2.98** percent. (**Bold** is used in the tables to indicate an increase over the five-year period.) Similarly, columns three and four, which deal with the occupational distribution of women, reveal that secretaries accounted for 7.79 percent of the female full-time workforce in 1995 and their proportion dropped to *5.9* percent by 2000. (*Italics* are used in the tables to indicate a decrease over time.) The last two columns provide the female-to-male ratios for 1995 and 2000. We can see that, for example, in 2000, **35.4** percent of specialist physicians and *38.2* percent of actors are women.

Table 13–2 deals specifically with the income gap between men and women. The first two columns reveal average incomes in 2000 for each of the thirty-three occupations by gender. Once again, we are dealing only with people who are employed full-time all year. The last two columns provide the female-to-male ratio in income; for example, the average income for female specialist physicians was 63.2 percent of male income in 1995, dropping off to *58.3* percent in 2000. Female actors earned 76.4 percent of male income n 1995 and **86.4** percent in 2000. Of the thirty-three occupations listed, female specialist physicians have the lowest earnings ratio relative to men: female nurses have the highest (*93.3*%), despite a drop from 97.1 percent.

Now that you know how to interpret these tables, we can look at the five explanations of the gender gap in income.

The first is that women choose jobs that are poorly paid. In 2000, women made up 80 to 98 percent of full-time cashiers, hairstylists/barbers, sewing machine operators, early childhood educators, secretaries, and registered nurses. Among the top five occupations in terms of income, the percentage of women varies from 14.5 to 35.4

percent. Whatever the decision-making process, women are indeed choosing to enter low-paying jobs, or at least choosing not to prepare for the high-paying jobs. Why, in the past, were women more likely to choose nurses' training, while men went to medical school? Currently, the majority of medical students in Canada are women, and many men have become nurses (comprising 7% of the full-time nursing workforce). Part of the answer lies in socialization. Girls learned that they were not "capable" of mastering the mathematics and science needed to get into medical school. Also, since most hoped to get married and raise families, it made little sense to plan for twelve or more years of postsecondary education.

The second explanation for the gender gap is that women take time off work or interrupt their careers to have children. If a young lawyer leaves her firm for six to ten years to have three children and raise them to school age, what happens to her career? Even if she only leaves work for three years of parental leave, she still takes a hit in terms of career continuity. As career-oriented women calculate the "costs" of having children, many decide to forgo motherhood altogether or to have only one child.

The third explanation for the gender gap is that gatekeepers exclude women from certain occupations. Steelworkers or truck drivers undoubtedly reacted with skepticism or even hostility when women first had the audacity to compete for their jobs; those in other male-dominated occupations undoubtedly resisted as well. But now the doors of engineering schools, medical schools, and veterinary colleges are wide open to women—and many such programs are 50, 60, or even 70 percent female today. Keep in mind, though, that many of the women working in these fields are younger

TABLE 13–1

Gender in Selected Occupations (Full-Time, All Year Workers), 1995 and 2000*

Occupation	Distribution by Occupation (%)[a]				Percentage Female by Occupation	
	Male Workers		Female Workers			
	1995	2000	1995	2000	1995	2000
all occupations					40.9	41.8
judges	0.03	0.03	0.01	0.01	23.1	24.4
specialist physicians	0.13	0.11	0.08	0.08	29.8	35.4
senior management	2.15	2.60	0.68	1.09	18.0	23.1
dentists	0.06	0.06	0.02	0.03	22.0	27.2
chemical engineers	0.14	0.13	0.03	0.03	11.6	14.5
university professors	0.57	0.47	0.29	0.27	26.1	29.5
human resources managers	0.31	0.26	0.36	0.50	44.9	58.1
pharmacists	0.16	0.16	0.24	0.24	51.4	52.3
police officers	1.03	0.90	0.19	0.22	11.4	15.2
chemists	0.15	0.16	0.09	0.12	29.1	35.3
fire-fighters	0.46	0.42	0.01	0.01	1.1	2.1
journalists	0.10	0.09	0.10	0.08	40.3	40.2
secondary school teachers	1.48	0.71	1.72	0.99	44.5	49.8
editors	0.06	0.07	0.08	0.11	47.5	51.7
elementary school teachers	0.82	0.40	4.16	2.24	77.8	80.2
physiotherapists	0.03	0.04	0.16	0.17	79.4	77.8
librarians	0.04	0.03	0.19	0.16	78.6	77.2
motor vehicle assemblers	0.78	0.69	0.37	0.35	24.6	26.7
registered nurses	0.18	0.20	3.56	3.51	93.0	92.5
social workers	0.17	0.15	0.63	0.70	72.4	76.6
heavy equipment operators	0.80	0.91	0.01	0.03	1.2	2.1
secretaries	0.08	0.08	7.79	5.90	98.5	98.1
actors	0.01	0.01	0.01	0.01	41.7	38.2
truck drivers	2.60	2.98	0.06	0.10	1.5	2.3
motor vehicle mechanics	1.94	1.84	0.02	0.03	0.8	1.3
chefs	0.25	0.32	0.07	0.09	17.2	17.2
farmers and farm managers	0.82	0.90	0.34	0.36	22.4	22.6
early childhood educators	0.02	0.04	0.90	1.21	96.2	95.9
bakers	0.24	0.21	0.25	0.26	42.0	47.2
sewing machine operators	0.06	0.05	0.95	0.83	92.2	91.8
hairstylists and barbers	0.14	0.13	0.76	0.73	78.5	80.0
farm workers	0.49	0.40	0.29	0.20	28.7	26.8
cashiers	0.20	0.18	1.63	1.49	84.6	85.3

* Values that have increased values appear in bold, decreased values in italics (1995 to 2000).

[a] The first four columns refer to the percentage of all full-time full-year workers in each of the 33 selected occupations for men and women in 1995 and 2000.

[b] The last two columns refer to the percentage female in each occupation.

Source: Calculations by L.M. Gerber based on Statistics Canada, Census 2001, Earnings of Canadians, catalogue no. 97F0019XCB2001060.

TABLE 13–2

Income by Gender in Selected Occupations (Full-time, All Year Workers), 1995, 2000

Occupation	Male Income[a] 2000	Female Income[a] 2000	Female/Male Income Ratio[b] 1995	2000
all occupations	$ 49 589	$ 34 999	71.0	70.6
judges	142 478	124 444	93.5	87.3
specialist physicians	126 790	73 946	63.2	58.3
senior management	116 392	70 845	59.8	60.9
dentists	113 265	67 279	54.8	59.4
chemical engineers	77 529	53 356	78.1	68.8
university professors	77 322	62 020	78.1	80.2
human resources managers	74 746	60 463	77.0	80.9
pharmacists	70 561	54 142	83.0	76.7
police officers	60 613	51 001	82.0	84.1
chemists	59 555	50 596	81.1	85.0
fire-fighters	56 556	46 305	73.7	81.9
journalists	54 341	43 857	81.4	80.7
secondary school teachers	52 865	48 350	88.8	91.5
editors	52 259	40 568	81.3	77.6
elementary school teachers	51 511	47 916	89.9	93.0
physiotherapists	51 223	46 301	88.5	90.4
librarians	51 138	46 815	96.9	91.5
motor vehicle assemblers	49 490	34 784	69.6	70.3
registered nurses	49 440	46 120	97.1	93.3
social workers	45 064	41 155	91.2	91.3
heavy equipment operators	41 648	37 192	88.3	89.3
secretaries	40 843	30 104	71.4	73.7
actors	40 810	35 251	76.4	86.4
truck drivers	38 511	31 204	82.6	81.0
motor vehicle mechanics	36 243	27 979	82.5	77.2
chefs	30 661	25 304	80.2	82.5
farmers and farm managers	29 053	21 596	71.3	74.3
early childhood educators	28 191	23 229	83.7	82.4
bakers	27 663	21 697	73.3	78.4
sewing machine operators	27 158	20 035	83.2	73.8
hairstylists and barbers	26 397	20 237	72.0	76.7
farm workers	23 692	19 293	74.8	81.4
cashiers	23 009	19 345	82.2	84.1

[a] The first two columns refer to average income for each of the 33 selected occupations—for men and women in 2000.
[b] The last two columns are women's income as a percentage of men's. Increased values appear in bold, decreased values in italics (1995 to 2000).

Source: Calculations by L.M. Gerber based on Statistics Canada, Census 2001, Earnings of Canadians, catalogue no. 97F0019XCB2001060.

than their male counterparts and therefore do not have the seniority or the experience that secure a high income.

The fourth explanation is that employers choose to pay women less. Perhaps the best way to poke a hole in that argument is to look at the income ratio for specialist physicians. In that prestigious occupation, women earned 63.2 percent of male income in 1995 before dropping to *58.3* percent in 2000. How can that happen? First, you should note that doctors in Canada do not have employers—perhaps 95 percent of them are in private practice (or in business), so there is no employer to pay the women less. Most physicians earn their income, and pay their office expenses, by billing government on a fee-for-service basis (i.e., every time they operate, deliver a baby, or take your blood pressure). If you look at the female-to-male ratio among specialist physicians, you will note that it increased by close to 6 points between 1995 and 2000. That means that *new* specialists are disproportionately *female*. They have had only a short time to establish their practice and gain the reputation that can bring them referrals from local family doctors. Income in many, if not most, other occupations is related to years of service; so, if women have recently increased their representation, they are *by definition* young relative to their male counterparts. Certainly, some employers may pay women less if they can get away with it, but one cannot discount or wish away the influence of age or seniority.

The last explanation is that women do not get promoted. The occupational category that most clearly reflects the results of promotion is senior management. Note first that senior management is a larger component of male *and* female full-time work in 2000, indicating change in the shape of the workforce. Then notice that the proportion of women increased by 5 points, from 1995 to 2000, so that women now make up almost a quarter of senior managers. Of course women face the "glass ceiling" (invisible but real) and discrimination in their quest for promotion, but the situation is changing, in part because there is a larger cadre of talented, career-oriented women from which to draw. These women need to put in their time before they qualify for promotion. Think for the moment about engineering firms, which have been criticized for the lack of female executives. Only recently have women entered engineering schools in significant numbers. If it takes men 15 years to move through the ranks to senior management levels, how long will it be before there is a pool of female engineers qualified for promotion to the top ranks? The point here is that discrimination—which accounts for about one-third of the gender gap in income (Fuller and Schoenberger, 1991)—is not the only explanation for the lack of women in the highest corporate ranks.

Warren Farrell, in *Why Men Earn More: The Startling Truth Behind the Pay Gap—and What Women Can Do About It* (2005), gives the following advice. If higher pay is your goal, you should "choose a field in technology or the hard sciences, not the arts or social sciences." Know that, in high-paying fields, you cannot "psychologically check out at the end of the day." You need to be willing to take risks, assume new and bigger responsibilities, work very long hours, put in more years of uninterrupted work with your current employer, relocate, and travel extensively on the job. More women today are willing to make these commitments and sacrifices—often forgoing marriage and children altogether. As women make these decisions and commitments, we will see more of them in the highest income brackets and at the top of the corporate world. But, dreams of gender equality notwithstanding, women may never equal men in their willingness to do what it takes to make it to the top.

WHAT DO YOU THINK?

1. A careful look at the data reveals that, for both women and men, the proportions of full-time workers involved in teaching (at university, secondary, and elementary levels) have declined, while the proportions of men *and* women working as truck drivers or in senior management have increased. Can you think of any reasons for these shifts?

2. Farrell points out that jobs with higher pay are often less fulfilling or emotionally satisfying (e.g., engineer versus child care professional). Are you willing to give up fulfillment to go for the higher pay? Does your gender affect your answer to this question?

3. In your opinion, which has the greater impact on women's income or promotion prospects: discrimination or value-based decisions? Explain your response.

TABLE 13–3

Educational Attainment by Gender (populations 15 and over, and 30 to 34 years of age), in Canada, Census 2001

	Population 15 Years and Older		Population 30 to 34 Years	
	Women	Men	Women	Men
High school graduation	24.1	21.9	21.1	22.1
Trades certificate	7.8	14.1	10.0	15.4
College certificate or diploma	17.3	12.5	24.0	17.6
Bachelor's degree	10.3	9.9	18.8	15.9
Medical degree	0.3	0.7	0.7	0.8
Master's degree	2.3	3.1	3.8	4.1
Doctorate (Ph.D.)	0.3	0.8	0.4	0.6

Source: Calculations by L.M. Gerber, based on Statistics Canada, Census 2001, *Education in Canada*, catalogue no. 95F0419XCB2001004.

GENDER AND POLITICS

Before 1918, women could not vote in federal elections. Until 1919, no women were allowed to sit in the House of Commons, and, until 1929, no women were allowed to sit in the Senate of Canada. It was not until 1940 that women could vote in all provincial elections—Quebec was the holdout; and not until 1982 were women granted equal protection and equal benefit of the law in the Canadian Charter of Rights and Freedoms. Table 13–4 cites benchmarks in women's gradual movement into Canadian politics and public life.

 Find out about the participation of Aboriginal women in Canadian politics at www.elections.ca/eca/eim/article_search/article.asp?id=26&lang=e&frmPageSize=&textonly=false.

Today, women are involved in all levels of politics in Canada. Still, the largest proportion of women politicians is found in the municipal arena. Women are also well represented on local school boards, where they can act on their normative and institutionalized "responsibility" for their children. Women face many barriers to participation in federal politics, especially if they have young families at home and live in different time zones from Ottawa, where they must spend a major portion of each year, or most of the year if they are cabinet ministers.

There are, however, signs of change. An increasing proportion of members of Parliament (MPs) are women. The Canadian Advisory Council on the Status of Women stated that, if the number of women in the House of Commons continued to increase at the rate it did between the 1984 and 1988 elections, in nine elections (or approximately 45 years), there would be equal numbers of men and women in the House. But while, by 1997, 20 percent of MPs were women, there was no change in the percentage after the 2000 election, suggesting that the expected increase in female representation had stalled. Surprisingly, the election of 2006, which resulted in a Conservative minority government under Stephen Harper, left us with the same level of representation by women, rather than a drop as some expected.

In 1989, the New Democratic Party became the first of Canada's major federal political parties to elect a woman leader: Audrey McLaughlin. In June 1993, Kim Campbell became Canada's first female prime minister by winning the leadership of the Progressive Conservative party when Brian Mulroney stepped down. From 1997 to 2003, Alexa McDonough was the only female party leader in the House of Commons. In the Liberal party, Sheila Copps was a star member of the federal cabinet, deputy prime minister for a term, and several times a contender for leadership of her party. Currently, several political women are in the news. Belinda Stronach, for instance, was instrumental in uniting the right—the Canadian Alliance and the Progressive Conservatives—before averting the collapse of Paul Martin's minority government by defecting to the Liberals.

YOUR TURN

Sweden, Norway, Finland, and Denmark have laws that require at least 25 percent of candidates for elected office to be women. Do you think Canada should adopt such a law? Why?

ARE WOMEN A MINORITY?

A *minority* is any category of people distinguished by physical or cultural difference that a society sets apart and subordinates. Given the economic disadvantage of being a woman in our society, it seems reasonable to say that Canadian women are a minority even though they outnumber men.[1]

---

[1]We use the term "minority" instead of "minority group" because, as explained in Chapter 7 ("Groups and Organizations"), women make up a *category*, not a group. People in a category share a status or identity but generally do not know one another or interact.

TABLE 13–4

Benchmarks for Women in Canadian Politics and Public Life

Year	Benchmark
1916	Women in Manitoba, Alberta, and Saskatchewan gain right to vote in provincial elections.
1917	Women with property permitted to hold office in Saskatchewan. Women in British Columbia and Ontario gain right to vote in provincial elections.
1918	Most women gain right to vote in federal elections.* Women in Nova Scotia gain right to vote in provincial elections.
1919	Women in New Brunswick gain right to vote in provincial elections.
1920	Uniform franchise established through the *Dominion Election Act*, making permanent the right of women to be elected to Parliament.
1921	Agnes Macphail is the first woman elected to the Canadian Parliament.
1922	Women in Prince Edward Island gain right to vote and to hold elected office.
1925	Women over age twenty-five gain right to vote in Newfoundland.
1929	Women are deemed "persons" and can therefore be appointed to the Senate after the British Privy Council overturns Supreme Court of Canada's 1928 *Persons Case* decision.
1930	First woman, Cairine Wilson, is appointed to the Senate.
1940	Women in Quebec gain right to vote in provincial elections, completing enfranchisement of most women in Canada.*
1957	Ellen Fairclough becomes the first woman federal cabinet minister.
1982	Activists Doris Anderson, Pauline Jewett, and Flora MacDonald help secure—for women—equal protection and equal benefit of the law under the Charter.
1983	Canadian *Human Rights Act* amended to prohibit sexual harassment and to ban discrimination on basis of pregnancy and family or marital status.
1984	Jeanne Sauvé is the first woman to be appointed as governor general.
1989	Audrey McLaughlin becomes the first woman to lead a federal Canadian political party.
1993	Kim Campbell becomes Canada's first woman prime minister.
1999	Adrienne Clarkson becomes the first governor general to belong to a visible minority (and the second woman).
2000	Beverley McLachlin is the first woman to be sworn in as Chief Justice of the Supreme Court of Canada.
2004	Ruby Dhalla and Yasmin Ratansi are the first Sikh woman and the first Muslim woman, respectively, to be elected as members of Parliament.
2004	Louise Arbour, a Supreme Court of Canada Justice, is appointed United Nations High Commissioner for Human Rights

*Exceptions are Chinese, Indo-Canadian, Japanese, Inuit, and First Nations women, who were excluded because of their race or ethnicity, rather than because they were women. Canadians of Chinese and Indian origins were enfranchised in 1947, and those of Japanese origin by 1948. Inuit men and women gained the right to vote in 1950, and First Nations men and women became enfranchised without losing their treaty status in 1960.

Source: Adapted from the Statistics Canada publication "Canada Year Book", Catalogue 11-402, 1992; *Canadian Global Almanac* 2005 (2004), McKenzie (1999).

Subjectively speaking, most White women do not think of themselves as members of a minority (Lengermann and Wallace, 1985). This is partly because, unlike racial and ethnic minorities, White women are well represented at all levels of the class structure, including the very top. Bear in mind, however, that, at every class level, women typically have less income, wealth, education, and power than men. Patriarchy makes women dependent on men—first their father and later their husband—for their social standing (Bernard, 1981).

MINORITY WOMEN: INTERSECTION THEORY

If women are defined as a minority, what about minority women? Are they doubly handicapped? This question lies at the heart of **intersection theory,** *the interplay of race, class, and gender, often resulting in multiple dimensions of disadvantage.* Research shows that disadvantages linked to gender and race often combine to produce especially low social standing (Ovadia, 2001). A First Nations woman, for example, is female, visible minority,[1] and subject to the

Indian Act—which results in multiple jeopardy (Gerber, 1995). Compared to the general Canadian population, as well as Inuit and Métis women and men, First Nations and non-Status Indian women have the lowest income.

American research reveals the same kinds of patterns. African-American women earn 61 percent as much as non-Hispanic White men, and Hispanic women earned 51 percent as much (U.S. Census Bureau, 2005). These differences reflect the lower positions of minority women in the occupational and educational hierarchies, confirming that, although gender has a powerful effect on our lives, it never operates alone. Class position, race, and ethnicity, and gender form a complex system of disadvantage for some and privilege for others (St. Jean and Feagin, 1998).

---

[1]While most Aboriginal people are racially distinct from the White majority and, thus, "visible," it is important to note that, for census purposes, they are not counted among visible minorities, owing to their special status in Canada.

MEDIA PERSPECTIVES
Powerful Canadian Women

Chief Justice for Canada Beverly McLachlin, the eldest of five children, grew up on a ranch in the foothills of the Alberta Rockies where she helped her mother cook for the ranch hands. As Chief Justice of the Supreme Court of Canada, she is arguably the most influential woman—if not person—in the country.

Most of us are vaguely aware of powerful or influential Canadian women in our collective past and present. Some of them are historical figures, such as the Famous Five, or Molly Brant, Emily Carr, Pauline Johnson, Agnes Macphail, Lucy Maud Montgomery, Laura Secord, or Harriet Tubman (Merritt, 1994; Forster, 2004). More recently, political activist Pauline Jewett joined the list of trailblazers (McKenzie, 1999).

Now, the *National Post* issues an annual report on Canada's most influential women, "The Power 50," and the Women's Executive Network annually recognizes one hundred of "Canada's Most Powerful Women." As Francis (2003) points out, any list of influential women is arbitrary and

 See the current list of the Women's Executive Network at www.wxnetwork.com/top100.html.

subjective. How do you choose fifty or one hundred when there is such a "wealth of talented Canadian women"? So much that is written about women in the workplace or gender stratification (e.g., this chapter) emphasizes the negative, focusing on the barriers faced by women—the effects of patriarchy, poverty, and the "glass ceiling." Here we will do an about-face and look at some of the stellar achievements of the women around us.

Chief Justice for Canada Beverly McLachlin, in addition to her legal training, has acquired an impressive number of honorary degrees "granted to acknowledge the incredible academic feats of a rancher's daughter who eventually reached the pinnacle of the Canadian judiciary system." Hers is an achieved, not ascribed, status—

without a whiff of inherited advantage or tokenism. On the other hand, her climb to the top was not always easy. Grateful to have come on the scene when our legal institutions were looking for female talent, she concedes that, at times, she was discouraged because "you felt you had to work harder with less opportunity and recognition" (Pratt, 2003).

There are many women who are the presidents, CEO's, or senior vice-presidents of major corporations, such as Linda Cook, CEO of Shell Canada; Linda Hasenfratz, CEO of Linamar Corp; Sherry Cooper, executive vice-president and global economic strategist, BMO Financial Group; Annette Verschuren, president of Home Depot Canada; Belinda Stronach, former president and CEO of Magna International; Anna Porter, co-founder, publisher and CEO of Key Porter Books; Heather Reisman, owner of Indigo, Chapters, and Coles; Kathy Sendall, senior vice-president of Petro-Canada; Lisa de Wilde, chair and CEO of TVOntario; Bonnie Fuller, editor-in-chief of *US Weekly*. It is worth noting that several of these companies are in such distinctly "masculine" fields as auto parts, oil and gas, and home improvement.

One of the most unlikely stories is that of Catherine McLeod-Seltzer and Eira Thomas, founders of Vancouver-based Stornoway Ventures. These

VIOLENCE AGAINST WOMEN

Perhaps the most wrenching kind of suffering that our society imposes on women is violence. As Chapter 9 ("Deviance") explained, official statistics paint criminal violence as overwhelmingly the actions of men—hardly surprising, since aggressiveness is a trait our culture defines as masculine. Furthermore, a great deal of "manly" violence is

 A United Nations report on violence against women and girls around the world can be found at www.unicef-icdc.org/publications/pdf/digest6e.pdf.

directed against women, which we also might expect because North American society devalues what is culturally defined as feminine.

A 1993 Statistics Canada survey found that 51 percent of Canadian women had experienced at least one instance of sexual or physical violence, about 25 percent of women were subject to violence at the hands of an intimate partner (Statistics Canada, 1994b). The most common location for gender-linked violence is the home. Richard Gelles (cited in Roesch, 1984) argues that, with the exception of the police

women already had "formidable reputations" in the prospecting world before they discovered two diamond-bearing rock formations on a remote tip of land in northern Nunavut. "'Exploration is in my blood,' Thomas says. 'It really is the thrill of the chase that I find rewarding'" (quoted in Hasselback, 2003). McLeod-Seltzer is equally in love with her work—and it is prospecting and mining we are talking about.

Then we have those women who change our way of thinking about the world around us. Jane Jacobs came to Canada from the United States where she had written the influential book *The Death and Life of Great American Cities*. Jacobs played a key role in stopping the Spadina Expressway, which many felt would have a devastating effect on downtown Toronto, and was an "urban planning activist" until her death in 2006. Her goal was to make cities liveable, and she had tremendous influence on local planners and politicians—making fans of Toronto mayor David Miller and NDP leader Jack Layton in the process (Evans, 2003).

Sheila Fraser, auditor general of Canada, has had immeasurable influence on the Canadian political scene during the past five years. Most notably, she was the one who uncovered and reported the mismanagement of funds in the Quebec sponsorship program (or Adscam). The Gomery inquiry into the sponsorship program, which was televised in English and French, lead to trials and convictions as well as the downfall of the Liberal government. The success of the Conservative government of Stephen Harper in heartland Quebec is directly attributable to Adscam. More recently, Sheila Fraser discovered that all is not well with the financing of Canada's gun registry; cost overruns were hidden from Parliament, and serious problems with the quality and accuracy of registry information were ignored. The gun registry fiasco will make it harder for the Liberals to regroup and regain the confidence of Canada's electorate. And the woman at the centre of this is the very powerful auditor general.

If we turn to the university scene, we find that at least four of Canada's major universities are headed by women: Heather Munroe-Blum, principal of McGill; Martha Piper, president of the University of British Columbia; Indira Samarasekera, president of the University of Alberta; and Lorna Marsden, president of York University. Each of these women has credentials galore, along with awards and honours for outstanding achievement. And each is incredibly influential. University presidents determine future directions in research, the nature of university/business liaisons, and, indirectly, social and economic policy. Most importantly, together they shape the educational experiences—and future prospects—of more than 150 000 students at any point in time.

Canada has had three women as governor general—all in the past twenty-five years. Each woman was chosen because of her accomplishments. Jeanne Sauvé, a successful journalist, then parliamentarian, and first woman Speaker of the House, was the first woman to be appointed to this position in 1984. Adrienne Clarkson (1999–2005) and Michaëlle Jean (appointed in 2005) have some things in common. Clarkson came to Canada as a refugee from China and made her name in broadcasting. As governor general, she spent Christmas or New Years with our troops in Kosovo, the Persian Gulf, or Afghanistan, and she travelled extensively throughout Canada giving people in the smallest and most remote communities a sense that they are special. Michaëlle Jean was born in Haiti and raised by a single mother in Montreal, and also made her name in broadcasting. She is keenly interested in immigrants, visible minorities, and the poor, wherever they are to be found in Canada. Both of these women also have strong ties to Aboriginal peoples.

These are only a few of the truly remarkable women who have made their marks on this country of ours. They stand as role models for all Canadians, but particularly for women.

WHAT DO YOU THINK?

1. Did you have any idea that there are hundreds of women like these in Canada?
2. How does it make you feel to read about these highly successful women? Does your own gender affect your reaction to this reading?
3. What is it that sets these women apart: special qualities, or special circumstances? Why?

---

and the military, the family is the most violent organization in the United States; there is no reason to think that the picture is any different in Canada. Both sexes suffer from family violence, although, by and large, women sustain more serious injuries than men do (Straus and Gelles, 1986; Shupe, *et al.*, 1987; Gelles and Cornell, 1990; Smolowe, 1994; Lupri, 2002). Chapter 18 ("Family") delves more deeply into the problem of family violence.

Violence against women also occurs in casual relationships. As Chapter 8 ("Sexuality and Society") explains, most sexual assaults (rapes) involve not strangers but men known—and often trusted—by women. (See the Applying Sociology box on p. 200 in Chapter 8.) Dianne F. Herman (2001) argues that the extent of abuse suggests that sexual violence is built into our way of life. All forms of violence against women—from the wolf whistles that intimidate women on city streets to a pinch in a crowded subway to physical assaults that occur at home—express what she calls a "rape culture" by which men try to dominate women. Sexual violence, then, is fundamentally about power rather

The basic insight of intersection theory is that various dimensions of social stratification—including race and gender—can add up to great disadvantages for some categories of people. Just as workers from visible minorities earn less than White workers, women earn less than men. Thus, women belonging to a visible minority confront a "double disadvantage" or experience "double jeopardy," ending up in low-paying jobs like this one.

than sex and should, therefore, be understood as a dimension of gender stratification (Nelson and Fleras, 1998).

In global perspective, violence against women is built into different cultures in different ways. One case in point is the practice of female genital mutilation, a painful and often dangerous surgical procedure performed in more than forty countries and known to occur in Canada and the United States, as shown in Global Map 13–2. The Thinking about Diversity box (on p. 338) highlights a case of genital mutilation that took place in California.

 For information on female genital mutilation, see www.who.int/mediacentre/factsheets/fs241/en/.

Violence by Women

Generally speaking, violence *by* women is off our radar screen—except when we are confronted with violent behaviour by gangs of girls (as in the 1997 murder of Reena Virk) or serial murder (as perpetrated by Karla Homolka and her husband Paul Bernardo). We are equally unaware of the fact that spousal abuse is committed by women against men (Lupri, 2003). Recently, the residents of Melfort, Saskatchewan (population 5500) learned that its girls are

not gentler than its boys: "It's the teenaged girls who start the majority of the fistfights, swarmings, and beatings." While members of Melfort's girl gangs report that "violence had become an ordinary part of their social scene," a national study reveals that, among twelve- to fifteen-year-olds, for every nine boys who engage in violent delinquency two girls do (Smith, 2004).

Violence against Men

If our way of life encourages violence against women, it may encourage even more violence against men. As noted in Chapter 9 ("Deviance"), in more than 80 percent of cases in which police make an arrest for a violent crime, including murder, robbery, and assault, the offender is a male. In addition, men are twice as likely as women to suffer serious assault, and three times more likely to fall victim to homicide. Lupri, who reports on numerous studies of spousal abuse including his own, finds "a consistent pattern in gender symmetry in woman-to-man and man-to-woman abuse" (2003:5).

Our culture tends to define masculinity in terms of aggression and violence—or "dangerous masculinity" (Atkinson, 2007). "Real men" work and play hard, speed on the highways, and let nothing stand in their way. A higher crime rate is one result. But even when no laws are broken, men's lives involve more stress and isolation than women's lives, which is one reason that the suicide rate for men is four times higher than for women. In addition, as noted earlier, men live, on average, about five fewer years than women.

Violence is not simply a matter of choices made by individuals. It is built into our way of life, with resulting harm to both men and women. In short, the way any culture constructs gender plays an important part in how violent or peaceful a society will be.

SEXUAL HARASSMENT

Sexual harassment refers to *comments, gestures, or physical contact of a sexual nature that are deliberate, repeated, and unwelcome.* During the 1990s, sexual harassment became an issue of national importance that rewrote the rules for workplace interaction between women and men. Most, but not all, victims of sexual harassment are women, for two main reasons. First, our culture encourages men to be sexually assertive and to see women in sexual terms. As a result, social interaction in the workplace, on campus, and elsewhere can easily take on sexual overtones. Second, most people in positions of power—including business executives, doctors, bureau chiefs, assembly-line supervisors, professors, and military officers—are men who oversee the work of women. Surveys carried out in widely different work settings show that half of the women respondents receive unwanted sexual attention (NORC, 2003).

Sexual harassment is sometimes obvious and direct: a supervisor may ask for sexual favours from an employee and make threats if the advances are refused. Courts have

WINDOW ON THE WORLD

GLOBAL MAP 13-2   Female Genital Mutilation in Global Perspective

Female genital mutilation is known to be performed in more than forty countries around the world. Across Africa, the practice is common and affects a majority of girls in the eastern African nations of Sudan, Ethiopia, and Somalia. In several Asian nations, including India, the practice is limited to a few ethnic minorities. In the United States, Canada, several European nations, and Australia, there are reports of the practice among some immigrants.

Source: Data from Seager (2003).

declared such *quid pro quo* sexual harassment to be a violation of civil rights. (The Latin phrase means "one thing in return for another.")

More often, however, sexual harassment is a matter of subtle behaviour—sexual teasing, off-colour jokes, the display of nudes—that may not even be *intended* to harass anyone. But by the *effect* standard favoured by many feminists, such actions add up to creating a *hostile environment.* Incidents of this kind are far more complex because they involve different perceptions of the same behaviour. For example, a man may think that, by repeatedly compliment-

ing a co-worker on her appearance, he is simply being friendly. The co-worker may believe that the man is thinking of her in sexual terms and is not taking her work seriously, an attitude that could harm her job performance and prospects for advancement.

PORNOGRAPHY

Chapter 8 ("Sexuality and Society") defined *pornography* as sexually explicit material that causes sexual arousal. It also underlies sexual violence. Defining pornography has long challenged scholars and lawmakers alike. Unable to set a

THINKING ABOUT DIVERSITY:
RACE, CLASS, & GENDER
Female Genital Mutilation: Violence in the Name of Morality

Meserak Ramsey, a woman born in Ethiopia and now working as a nurse in California, paid a visit to a friend's home. Soon after arriving, she noticed her friend's eighteen-month-old daughter huddled in the corner of a room in obvious distress. "What's wrong?" she asked.

Ramsey was shocked when the woman said her daughter had recently had a clitoridectomy, the surgical removal of the clitoris. This type of female genital mutilation—performed by a midwife, a tribal practitioner, or a doctor, and typically without anaesthesia—is common in Nigeria, Togo, Somalia, and Egypt, and is known to exist in certain cultural groups in other nations around the world.

Among members of highly patriarchal societies, husbands demand that their wives be virgins at marriage and remain sexually faithful thereafter. The point of female genital mutilation is to eliminate sexual feeling, which, people assume, makes the girl less likely to violate sexual norms and thus be more desirable to men. In about one-fifth of all cases, an even more severe procedure, called *infibulation*, is performed, in which the entire external genital area is removed and the surfaces are stitched together, leaving only a small hole for urination. Before marriage, a husband retains the right to open the wound and ensure himself of his bride's virginity.

How many women have undergone genital mutilation? Worldwide, esti-

These young women have just undergone female genital mutilation. What do you think should be done about this practice?

mates place the number at 135 million. In the United States, hundreds or even thousands of such procedures are performed every year; in Canada, there might be several hundred cases. Often, immigrant mothers and grandmothers who have themselves been mutilated insist that young girls in their family follow their example. Indeed, many immigrant women demand the procedure *because* their daughters now live in North America, where sexual mores are more lax.

"I don't have to worry about her now," the girl's mother explained to Meserak Ramsey. "She'll be a good girl."

Medically, the consequences of genital mutilation include more than

the loss of sexual pleasure. Pain is intense and can persist for years. There is also danger of infection, infertility, and even death. Ramsey knows this all too well: she herself underwent genital mutilation as a young girl. She is one of the lucky ones who has had few medical problems since. But the extent of her suffering is suggested by this story. She invited a young American couple to stay at her home. Late at night, she heard the woman cry out and burst into their room to investigate, only to learn that the couple was making love and the woman had just had an orgasm.

"I didn't understand," Ramsey recalls. "I thought that there must be something wrong with American girls. But now I know that there is something wrong with me." Or with a system that inflicts such injury in the name of traditional morality.

WHAT DO YOU THINK?

1. Is female genital mutilation a medical procedure or a means of social control? Explain your answer.
2. Can you think of other examples of physical mutilation imposed on women?
3. When immigrants come to Canada from countries with such practices, should they bring those aspects of their cultures with them? If you think not, how should we prevent these practices?

Sources: Based on Crossette (1995) and Boyle, *et al.* (2001).

single, specific standard to distinguish what is, and what is not, pornographic, the Supreme Court of Canada allows provinces/territories, and municipalities to decide what violates "community standards" of decency and lacks redeeming social value. But few doubt that pornography, loosely defined, is popular: X-rated videos, 900 telephone numbers offering sexual conversation, and a host of sexually explicit movies, magazines, and internet websites

together take in more than US$10 billion in sales each year in North America.

Traditionally, people have raised concerns about pornography as a *moral* issue. But pornography also plays a part in gender stratification. From this point of view, pornography is really a *power* issue because most pornography dehumanizes women, depicting them as the playthings of men. That is, pornography is really a power issue because

In the 1950s, Talcott Parsons proposed that sociologists interpret gender as a matter of *differences.* As he saw it, masculine men and feminine women formed strong families and made for an orderly society. In recent decades, however, social-conflict theory has reinterpreted gender as a matter of *inequality.* From this point of view, North American society places men in a position of dominance over women.

it fosters the notion that men should control both sexuality and women (Nelson and Robinson, 1999:355). In addition, there is widespread concern that pornography promotes violence against women by portraying them as weak and undeserving of respect. Men may show contempt for women defined this way by striking out against them. Surveys show that about half of American adults think that pornography encourages men to commit rape (NORC, 2003:235).

Like sexual harassment, pornography raises complex and conflicting issues. Despite the fact that some material may offend just about everybody, many support the rights of free speech and artistic expression. Pressure to restrict pornography has increased in recent decades, reflecting both the long-standing concern that pornography weakens morality as well as more recent concerns that it is demeaning and threatening to women.

YOUR TURN

The internet has made pornography more accessible; do you think it has become more acceptable as well? Why?

Theoretical Analysis of Gender

Why does gender exist in the first place? Each of sociology's two macro-level approaches, summarized in the Applying Theory table (on p. 341), offers insights about the importance of gender in social organization. We also consider feminist theoretical perspectives on gender, including those of postmodern feminists.

STRUCTURAL-FUNCTIONAL ANALYSIS

The structural-functional approach views society as a complex system of many separate but integrated parts. From this point of view, gender serves as a means to organize social life. As Chapter 4 ("Society") explained, members of hunter/gatherer societies had little power over the forces of biology. Lacking effective birth control, women were frequently pregnant, and the responsibilities of child care kept them close to home. At the same time, men's greater strength made them more suited for warfare and hunting game. Over the centuries, this sexual division of labour became institutionalized and largely taken for granted (Lengermann and Wallace, 1985; Freedman, 2002).

Industrial technology opens up a much greater range of cultural possibilities. With human muscles no longer the main energy source, the physical strength of men becomes less important. In addition, the ability to control reproduction gives women greater choices about how to live. Modern societies relax traditional gender roles as they become more meritocratic, because such rigid roles waste an enormous amount of human talent. Yet, because gender is deeply rooted in culture, change comes slowly.

Talcott Parsons: Gender and Complementarity

Talcott Parsons (1942, 1954, 1964; orig. 1951) argued that keeping some gender differences helps integrate society, at least in its traditional form. Gender forms a *complementary* set of roles that links men and women into family units and gives each sex responsibility for important tasks. Women take the lead in managing the household and raising children. Men connect the family to the larger world as they participate in the labour force. Therefore, gender plays an important part in socialization. Society teaches boys—presumably destined for the labour force—to be rational,

In the film *Iron Jawed Angels*, Hilary Swank portrays early women's rights activist Alice Paul, who worked tirelessly for passage of the Nineteenth Amendment to the Constitution giving women the right to vote. The United States was fighting World War I at the time, and there was little sympathy for what seemed to be radical ideas about gender. Alice Paul and others were taken to jail, where they began a hunger strike and refused to be force-fed (which explains the name of the movie). With the ratification of the Nineteenth Amendment, American women gained the right to vote in 1920.

self-assured, and competitive. Parsons called this complex of traits *instrumental* qualities. To prepare girls for child rearing, their socialization stresses *expressive* qualities, such as emotional responsiveness and sensitivity to others.

Society encourages gender conformity by instilling in men and women a fear that straying too far from accepted standards of masculinity or femininity will cause rejection by the other sex. In simple terms, women learn to reject nonmasculine men as sexually unattractive, and men learn to reject unfeminine women. In sum, gender integrates society both structurally—in terms of what people do, and morally—in terms of what they believe.

Critical Review Influential a half century ago, this approach has lost much of its standing today. First, functionalism assumes a singular vision of society that is not shared by everyone. Historically, many women have worked outside the home because of economic need, a fact not reflected in Parsons' conventional, middle-class view of family life. Second, Parsons' analysis ignores the personal strains and social costs of rigid, traditional gender roles. Third, in the eyes of those seeking sexual equality, what Parsons describes as gender "complementarity" amounts to little more than women submitting to male domination.

SOCIAL-CONFLICT ANALYSIS

From a social-conflict point of view, gender involves differences not just in behaviour but in power as well. Consider the striking similarity between the way ideas about gender benefit men, and the way oppression of racial and ethnic minorities benefits White people. Conventional ideas about gender do not make society operate smoothly; they create division and tension, with men seeking to protect their privileges as women challenge the status quo. As earlier chapters explain, the social-conflict approach draws heavily on the ideas of Karl Marx; yet, as far as gender is concerned, Marx was a product of his time: his writings focused almost entirely on men. His friend and collaborator Friedrich Engels, however, did develop a theory of gender stratification.

Friedrich Engels: Gender and Class

Looking back through history, Engels saw that, in hunter/gatherer societies, the activities of women and men, although different, had the same importance. A successful hunt brought men great prestige, but the vegetation gathered by women provided most of a group's food supply. As technological advances led to a productive surplus, however, social equality and communal sharing gave way to private property and, ultimately, a class hierarchy. With the rise of agriculture, men gained significant power over women. With surplus wealth to pass on to heirs, upper-class men wanted to be sure who their sons were, which led them to control the sexuality of women. The desire to control property brought about monogamous marriage and the family. Women were taught to remain virgins until marriage, to remain faithful to their husbands thereafter, and to build their lives around bearing and raising one man's children.

According to Engels (1902; orig. 1884), capitalism makes male domination even stronger. First, capitalism creates more wealth, which gives greater power to men as income earners and owners of property. Second, an expanding capitalist economy depends on turning people, especially women, into consumers who seek personal fulfilment through buying and using products. Third, society assigns women the task of maintaining the home to free men to work in factories. The double exploitation of capitalism, as Engels saw it, lies in paying men low wages for their labour and paying women no wages at all.

Critical Review Social-conflict analysis is critical of conventional ideas about gender, claiming that society would be better off if we minimized or even did away with this dimension of social structure. One problem with this approach is that it sees conventional families—supported by traditionalists as morally positive—as a social evil. Second, social-conflict analysis minimizes the extent to which women and men live together co-operatively, and often happily, in families. A third problem lies in the asser-

	Structural-Functional Approach	Social-Conflict Approach
What is the level of analysis?	Macro level	Macro level
What does gender mean?	Parsons described gender in terms of two complementary patterns of behaviour: masculine and feminine.	Engels described gender in terms of the power of one sex over the other.
Is gender helpful or harmful?	Helpful.	Harmful.
	Gender gives men and women distinctive roles and responsibilities that help society operate smoothly.	Gender limits people's personal development.
	Gender builds social unity as men and women come together to form families.	Gender divides society by giving power to men to control the lives of women.
		Capitalism makes patriarchy stronger.

tion that capitalism is the basis of gender stratification. In fact, agrarian societies are typically more patriarchal than industrial-capitalist societies. Although socialist nations—including China and the former Soviet Union—did move women into the workforce, by and large they provided women with very low pay in sex-segregated jobs (Rosendahl, 1997; Haney, 2002).

FEMINISM

Feminism is *the advocacy of social equality for women and men, in opposition to patriarchy and sexism.* The first wave of the feminist movement in Canada began in the mid–1800s as Canadian women were influenced by writing such as Mary Wollstonecraft's *A Vindication of the Rights of Women* (1792) and John Stuart Mill's *The Subjection of Women* (1869). The

 Find out more about the Persons Case by visiting the National Archives of Canada at www.archives.ca/05/0530_e. html.

primary objective of the early women's movement was securing the right to vote, which was achieved for federal elections in Canada by 1918 with the passage of the *Women's Franchise Act*. But other disadvantages persisted, prompting the rise of a second wave of feminism in the 1960s, which continues today.

Basic Feminist Ideas

Feminism views the personal experiences of women and men through the lens of gender. How we think of ourselves (*gender identity*), how we act (*gender roles*), and our sex's social standing (*gender stratification*) are all rooted in the operation of society. Although feminists disagree about many things, most support five general principles:

1. *Working to increase equality.* Feminist thinking is strongly political; it links ideas to action. Feminism is critical of the status quo, pushing for change towards social equality for women and men.

2. *Expanding human choice.* Feminists argue that cultural conceptions of gender divide the full range of human qualities into two opposing and limiting spheres: the female world of emotions and co-operation, and the male world of rationality and competition. As an alternative, feminists propose a "reintegration of humanity" by which all individuals can develop all human traits (French, 1985).

3. *Eliminating gender stratification.* Feminism opposes laws and cultural norms that limit the education, income, and job opportunities of women. For this reason, American feminists have long supported passage of the Equal Rights Amendment to the U.S. Constitution, which has yet to become law. In Canada, gender equality was guaranteed in the Canadian Charter of Rights and Freedoms (Canada, 1982) after a modern-day struggle over women's rights.

4. *Ending sexual violence.* Today's women's movement seeks to eliminate sexual violence. Feminists argue that patriarchy distorts the relationships between women and men, encouraging violence against women in the form of sexual assault (rape), domestic abuse, sexual harassment, and pornography (Dworkin, 1987; Freedman, 2002).

5. *Promoting sexual freedom.* Finally, feminism supports women's control over their sexuality and reproduction. Feminists support the free availability of birth control information.

GLOBAL SNAPSHOT

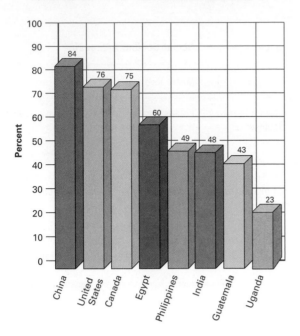

FIGURE 13-5   Use of Contraception by Married Women of Child-bearing Age

In the United States and Canada, most women of child-bearing age use contraception. In many low-income countries, however, most women do not have the opportunity to make this choice.

Source: United Nations Development Programme (2005).

As Figure 13–5 shows, about three-quarters of Canadian women of child-bearing age use contraception; the use of contraceptives is far less common in many low-income nations. In Canada, while information about birth control circulated from the early 1930s on, birth control became legal only in 1969 (Bishop, 1988). Most feminists also support a woman's right to choose whether to bear children or end a pregnancy, rather than allowing men—husbands, physicians, and legislators—to control their reproduction. Many feminists support gay people's efforts to end prejudice and discrimination in a mostly heterosexual culture (Ferree and Hess, 1995; Armstrong, 2002).

↔ YOUR TURN ↔

On your campus, do men's organizations (such as fraternities and athletic teams) enjoy special privileges? What about women's organizations?

Types of Feminism

Feminists agree on the importance of gender equality, but they disagree on how to achieve it: through liberal feminism, socialist feminism, or radical feminism (Stacey, 1983; Vogel, 1983; Ferree and Hess, 1995; Armstrong, 2002; Freedman, 2002).

Liberal Feminism

Liberal feminism is rooted in the classic liberal thinking that individuals should be free to develop their own talents and pursue their own interests. Liberal feminism accepts the basic organization of our society but seeks to expand the equality rights and opportunities of women. Liberal feminists also support reproductive freedom for all women. They respect the family as a social institution but seek changes, including more widely available parental leave and child care for parents who work. Given their belief in the rights of individuals, liberal feminists think that women should advance according to their own efforts, rather than working collectively for change. Both women and men, through their individual achievement, are capable of improving their lives—as long as society removes legal and cultural barriers.

Socialist Feminism

Socialist feminism evolved from the ideas of Karl Marx and Friedrich Engels. From this point of view, capitalism strengthens patriarchy by concentrating wealth and power in the hands of a small number of men. Socialist feminists do not think the reforms supported by liberal feminism go far enough. The family form created by capitalism must change if we are to replace "domestic slavery" with some collective means of carrying out housework and community-run child care. Replacing the traditional family can come about only through a socialist revolution that creates a state-centred economy to meet the needs of all. Such a basic transformation of society requires that women and men pursue their personal liberation not individually, as liberal feminists propose, but collectively.

Radical Feminism

Like socialist feminism, radical feminism finds liberal feminism inadequate. Radical feminists believe that patriarchy is so deeply rooted in society that even a socialist revolution would not end it. Instead, reaching the goal of gender equality means that society must eliminate gender itself. One possible way to achieve this goal is to use new reproductive technology (see Chapter 18, "Family") to separate women's bodies from the process of child bearing. With an end to motherhood, radical feminists reason, society could leave behind the entire family system, liberating women, men, and children from the oppression of family, gender, and sex itself (Dworkin, 1987). Thus, radical feminism envisions an egalitarian and gender-free society, a revolution more sweeping than the one sought by Marx.

Cultural and Postmodern Feminism

Canadians Nelson and Robinson (1999:101–111) identify several other variants of feminism, which differ from the liberal, socialist, and radical approaches outlined above.

Marxist feminism argues that one's position with respect to economic production determines all other aspects of social life: therefore, the entire structure of society must be changed to achieve gender equality.

Cultural feminism identifies "the suppression of distinctive or different female qualities, experiences, and values as the primary cause of women's subordination." Inclusive feminists reject a privileged White middle-class feminism that ignores the "experiences of differently raced, abled, and classed women."

And, lastly, *postmodern feminism* "rejects all statements of claim made by other branches of feminist thought," arguing that any theory "claiming to be fully explanatory is necessarily assuming a dominant and oppressive stance."

Clearly, all of the feminist approaches overlap to some extent so that specific authors may move among these approaches or blend them in one way or another.

Critical Review Feminism provokes criticism and resistance from both men and women who hold conventional ideas about gender. Some men oppose sexual equality for the same reason that many White people have historically opposed social equality for people from visible minorities: they do not want to give up their privileges. Other men and women, including those who are neither rich nor powerful, distrust a social movement—especially its radical expressions—that attacks the traditional family and rejects patterns that have guided male/female relations for centuries.

Men who have been socialized to value strength and dominance feel uneasy about feminist ideas of men as gentle and warm (Doyle, 1983). Similarly, some women whose lives centre on their husbands and children may think feminism does not value the social roles that give meaning to their lives. In general, resistance to feminism is strongest among women who have the least education and those who do not work outside the home (Marshall, 1985; Ferree and Hess, 1995).

Resistance to feminism is also found within academic circles. Some sociologists charge that feminism ignores a growing body of evidence that men and women do think and act in different ways, which may make complete gender equality impossible. Furthermore, say critics, with its drive

to increase women's presence in the workplace, feminism undervalues the crucial and unique contribution women make to the development of children, especially in the first years of life (Baydar and Brooks-Gunn, 1991; Popenoe, 1993a; Gibbs, 2001).

Finally, there is the question of how women should go about improving their social standing. Although a large majority of Canadians believes women should have equal rights, most also believe that women should advance individually, according to their abilities—rather than through collective action.

Opposition to feminism is primarily directed at its socialist and radical variants; otherwise, there is widespread support for the principles of liberal feminism. Moreover, we are seeing an unmistakable trend towards greater gender equality. In 1942, during World War II, when a Gallup poll asked Canadians "If women take the place of men in industry, should they be paid the same wages as men?" 89 percent of women and 78 percent of men agreed. By 1995, the idea of equal pay for equal work was supported by 98 percent of a representative sample of Canadians (Bibby, 1995:4).

Gender: Looking Ahead

Predictions about the future are always a matter of informed guesswork. Just as economists disagree about what the inflation rate will be a year from now, sociologists can offer only general observations about the likely future of gender and society. Change so far has been remarkable. A century ago, women were second-class citizens, without access to many jobs, barred from political office, and with no right to vote. While women remain socially disadvantaged, the movement towards equality has surged ahead. Two-thirds of those entering the workforce during the 1990s were women and, in most couples, both partners work. Today's economy depends on the earnings of women. Many factors have contributed to this change. Perhaps most importantly, industrialization and recent advances in computer technology have shifted the nature of work from physically demanding tasks that favour male strength to jobs that require thought and imagination: this change puts women and men on a more even footing. Also, because birth control technology has given us greater control over reproduction, women's lives are less constrained by unwanted pregnancies. Many women and men deliberately pursue social equality. For example, sexual harassment complaints in the workplace are now taken much more seriously than they were a generation ago. As more women assume positions of power in the corporate and political worlds, we can anticipate continuing social change in the twenty-first century.

THINKING ABOUT DIVERSITY:
RACE, CLASS, & GENDER
Canadian Women in Hockey: Going for Gold

At the turn of the century, Canadian women were involved in hockey, doing battle in long, flowing skirts that made them look like sisters of the cloth rather than members of a hockey team. In the 1930s, the Preston Rivulettes from what is now part of Cambridge, Ontario, recorded an incredible record of 348 wins to 2 losses! But World War II intervened, draining attention and energy away from hockey so that, by the 1950s, women's hockey had fizzled. The struggle to re-establish women's hockey—to get ice time, good equipment, sponsorships, public acceptance and support, media coverage, the attention of Don Cherry, and Olympic status—consumed the next forty to fifty years. In 1998, in Nagano, Japan, women's hockey was an official Olympic sport for the first time, and the world of Canadian women's hockey changed forever.

The game that originated in Canada had become part of our collective identity, and continues to be our most popular sport, is now played by women—legitimately! Many of the women on Team Canada grew up playing on boys' teams, while at least two, Manon Rheaume and Hayley Wickenheiser, have played in the professional male leagues. As a result of recent publicity and the decision to prohibit body-checking in women's hockey, parents in large numbers are now willing to enrol their young daughters in girls' hockey leagues. Girls' teams—which often play against boys' teams—are springing up throughout Canada, and girls' participation in hockey has almost quadrupled in the last decade to 25 000 players nationally.

Without doubt, the image of girls and women as hockey players is inconsistent with our societal expectations of femininity. Off the ice, most of these women—some of whom are mothers—conform to our cultural standards of feminine behaviour, dress, and makeup; however, when they don their protective hockey uniforms and helmets and step

The Canadian women's hockey team won gold—again—at the 2006 Winter Olympic Games in Turin, Italy.

out onto the ice, they enter a world in which they exhibit aggression, speed, and impressive skill: power skating, agility, and adroit handling of stick and puck become their tools.

This transformation from "woman" to "athlete" in a traditionally male or macho sport is not easy for the women themselves, nor is it easy for all members of the general public to accept. There are still people who feel strongly that women should stick to ballet, gymnastics, and synchronized swimming (another Canadian sporting development). Ambivalence is apparent in embarrassment on the part of some Team Canada members about the fact that their first world championship—in Ottawa in 1990—was won in pink and white uniforms. But, when the women's and men's hockey teams both won gold at the Salt Lake City Olympics of 2002, celebrations erupted throughout the country.

Olympic publicity has changed the lives of the women who play hockey for Team Canada. The quest for public awareness and support is over. Don Cherry's active support of women's hockey is now part of the public record. Major media in Canada all provided extensive coverage of the exploits and victories of Team Canada, women's style. The team members have agents and contracts for product endorsements. Sports Canada helps cover their expenses, and employers are willing to

give the athletes time off to prepare for championship or Olympic competition. These young women are now accustomed to being recognized on the street and being the subject of sometimes overwhelming media attention. The dramatic change in the status of women's hockey is exciting for female players across the country and for the Canadian public as a whole. In their own way, these women have stretched the limits of and changed the definition of femininity.

Postscript On January 16, 1998, as women's hockey was played for the first time at the Olympics, the CBC ran a full-length edition of *The National* about women's hockey in Canada and our Olympic team. Among other guests, two of the women who had played for the Preston Rivulettes in the 1930s and who would be watching Team Canada in Nagano, shared their thoughts on the dramatic changes in the world of women's hockey.

WHAT DO YOU THINK?

1. Did you know girls who played hockey when you were in high school? Did they seem like ordinary girls or were they different?

2. Would you encourage your own daughter to play hockey?

3. Read the Thinking it Through box about violence and crime in hockey (on po. 224–225 in Chapter 9). How does the link between hockey and "dangerous masculinity" reflect on Canada's support of women's hockey? Do you think women's hockey lacks appeal because of the absence of violence?

Sources: CBC (1998) and Smith (1997a, 1997b).

The following learning tools will help you see what you know, identify what you still need to learn, and expand your understanding beyond the text. You can also visit this text's Companion Website™ at www.pearsoned.ca/macionis to find useful practice tests.

KEY POINTS

Gender and Inequality

Gender refers to the meaning a culture attaches to being female or male. Because society gives men more power and other resources than it gives women, gender is an important dimension of social stratification. While some degree of gender stratification exists everywhere in the world, the degree of patriarchy varies from one society to another. Gender inequality also varies in any society over the course of history.

Gender and Socialization

Through the socialization process, gender becomes part of our personalities (gender identity) and our actions (gender roles). The major agents of socialization—family, peer groups, schools, and the mass media—reinforce cultural definitions of what is feminine and masculine.

Gender and Social Stratification

Gender stratification shapes the workplace. A majority of women are now in the paid labour force; however, they still predominate in clerical or service jobs. Unpaid housework remains a task performed mostly by women, whether or not they hold jobs outside the home. In comparisons of female and male workers who work full time, women earn 70 percent of male income. This disparity stems from differences in education, jobs, and family responsibilities, as well as from discrimination. Women are acquiring education in such traditional male fields as medicine, science and engineering and moving into related jobs in increasing numbers. One-quarter of senior management is composed of women. The number of women in politics has increased in recent decades, but representation in the House of Commons seems to have levelled off at 20 percent.

Intersection theory investigates the intersection of race, class, and gender, which often causes multiple disadvantages. Because women have a distinctive social identity and are disadvantaged, they are a minority, although most White women do not think of themselves that way. Minority women encounter greater social disadvantages than White women and earn much less than White men.

Violence against women and men is a widespread problem, linked to how society defines gender. Our society is also grappling with the issues of sexual harassment and pornography.

Theoretical Analysis of Gender

Structural-functional analysis suggests that in pre-industrial societies, distinctive roles for males and females reflect biological differences between the sexes. In industrial societies, marked gender inequality becomes dysfunctional and gradually decreases. Talcott Parsons claimed that complementary gender roles promote the social integration of families and society as a whole.

Social-conflict analysis views gender as a dimension of social inequality and conflict. Friedrich Engels tied gender stratification to the development of private property.

Feminism endorses the social equality of the sexes, and opposes patriarchy and sexism. Feminism also seeks to eliminate violence against women and to give women control over their reproduction. There are three main variants of feminist thinking: liberal feminism seeks equal opportunity for both sexes within the existing society; socialist feminism supports abolishing private property as the means to social equality; radical feminism seeks to create a gender-free society.

Gender: Looking Ahead

Industrialization and the development of computer technology have made the lives of women and men more alike over the past century. Because gender is deeply rooted in our way of life, change will be gradual, but efforts to increase gender equality continue.

KEY CONCEPTS

gender (p. 319) the personal traits and social positions that members of a society attach to being female or male

gender stratification (p. 319) the unequal distribution of wealth, power, and privilege between men and women

patriarchy (p. 321) a form of social organization in which males dominate females

matriarchy (p. 321) a form of social organization in which females dominate males

sexism (p. 321) the belief that one sex is innately superior to the other

gender roles (sex roles) (p. 322) attitudes and activities that a society links to each sex

intersection theory (p. 333) the interplay of race, class, and gender, often resulting in multiple dimensions of disadvantage

sexual harassment (p. 336) comments, gestures, or physical contact of a sexual nature that are deliberate, repeated, and unwelcome

feminism (p. 341) the advocacy of social equality for women and men, in opposition to patriarchy and sexism

APPLICATIONS & EXERCISES

1. Take a walk through a business area of your local community. Which businesses are frequented almost entirely by women? by men? by both men and women? Try to explain the patterns you find.
2. Watch several hours of children's television programming on a Saturday morning. Notice the advertising, which mostly sells toys and breakfast cereal. Keep track of the toys that are "gendered" (that is, aimed at one sex or the other). What traits do you associate with toys intended for boys and those intended for girls?
3. To what extent does being a male or a female affect your field of study and your career aspirations? Which do you think will be more important to you: family life or earning a high income? How will you balance those aspects of your life?

PRENTICE HALL
mysoclab
Where learning & the sociological imagination intersect.

To reinforce your understanding of this chapter, and to identify topics for further study, visit MySocLab at **www.pearsoned.ca/mysoclab/** for diagnostic tests and a multimedia ebook.

CHAPTER FOURTEEN

Race and Ethnicity

What are race and ethnicity, and how
are they created by society?

Why is Canada known as a nation of immigrants?

To what extent are race and ethnicity important
dimensions of social inequality today?

"When you're brought up with discrimination," says Barbara Carter of Dresden, Ontario, "you know what you can do and what you can't do. So you just abide by the rules and it's not that bad. We knew we couldn't go into the restaurants with our White girlfriends after school, so we just didn't go. I never understood, however, why there were two churches. There were two Baptist churches in town. One for the Whites and one for the Blacks."

"It was different for me," says Bruce. "I was a very bitter person when I was a teenager. At one time there was not one restaurant in town where I could get a cup of coffee. Towards the end of the war we had German prisoners of war around here. They were working in the sugar-beet fields under guard. The prisoners of war could go into the restaurants, but a Negro soldier in a Canadian army uniform couldn't. It was pretty bad. My aunt taught in a segregated school. The last one closed in the sixties.

"We went to Disney World a while ago," says Bruce. "We went to the Canadian pavilion. They have a movie about Canada there. It's a tremendous movie—all in the round. But do you know what? There is not one Black person in the whole movie. I was watching it and I thought, 'Wait a minute, where am I?' So I sat through it a second time to make sure. It's like we're a non-people. We weren't even in the crowd scenes."

Source: From *Welcome Home: Travels in Small-town Canada* by Stuart McLean. Copyright © Stuart McLaren, permission of Penguin Group (Canada), a Division of Pearson Penguin Canada Inc.

Globally, the pattern of inequality and conflict based on skin colour and culture is even more pronounced. Ukrainians, Moldavians, Azerbaijanis, and other ethnic peoples in Eastern Europe are struggling to recover their cultural identities after the collapse of the Soviet Union. In the Middle East, deep-rooted friction between Arabs and Jews continues in much the same way that Blacks and Whites strive to establish a just society in South Africa. In Rwanda, India, Sri Lanka, and elsewhere, racial and ethnic rifts frequently flare up into violent confrontation. Surely one of the greatest ironies of the human condition is that colour and culture—traits that are the roots of our greatest pride—are also those that most often foment hatred and violence and propel people into war. This chapter examines the meaning of race and ethnicity, explains how these social constructs have shaped human history, and suggests why they continue to play such a central part—for better or worse—in the world today.

The Social Meaning of Race and Ethnicity

Canadians and people elsewhere in the world frequently use the terms "race" and "ethnicity" imprecisely and interchangeably. For this reason, we begin with important definitions.

RACE

A **race** is *a socially constructed category of people who share biologically transmitted traits that members of a society consider important.* People may classify one another racially based on physical characteristics such as skin colour, facial features, hair texture, and body shape. Physical diversity appeared among our human ancestors as the result of living in different geographic regions of the world. In regions of intense heat, for example, humans developed darker skin, from the natural pigment melanin, as protection from the sun; in regions with moderate climates, people have lighter skin. Such differences are literally only skin deep because human beings the world over are members of a single biological species.

The striking variety of physical traits found today is also the product of migration; physical characteristics once common to a single place (such as light skin or curly hair) are now found in many lands. Mixture is especially pronounced in the Middle East, historically a crossroads of human migration. Greater physical uniformity characterizes more isolated people, such as the island-dwelling Japanese. But every population has some genetic mixture, and increasing contact among the world's people ensures even more blending of physical characteristics in the future.

Although we think of race in terms of biological elements, race is a socially constructed concept. At one level,

The range of biological variation in human beings is far greater than any system of racial classification allows. This fact is made obvious by trying to place all of the people pictured here into simple racial categories.

different categories of people "see" physical traits differently; for example, research shows that White people rate Black subjects as darker in skin tone than Black people do (Hill, 2002). Also, some people—especially biracial and multiracial people—define themselves and are defined by others differently, depending on the setting (Harris and Sim, 2002). More broadly, entire societies define physical traits differently. Typically, Canadians "see" fewer racial categories—commonly, Black, White, and Asian—than do Brazilians, who distinguish between *branca* (white), *parda* (brown), *morena* (brunette), *mulata* (mulatto), *preta* (black), and *amarela* (yellow) (Inciardi, *et al.*, 2000). In any society, definitions and meanings concerning race change over time; for example, in 1900, many North Americans viewed people of Irish and Italian ancestry as racially different, a practice that was rare by 1950 (Loveman, 1999). Today, the Canadian census allows people to describe themselves using any number of racial or ethnic terms—writing in up to four choices—so that our society now embraces a wide range of ethno-racial categories.

Racial and Ethnic Categories

Scientists invented the concept of "race" in the nineteenth century as they tried to organize the world's physical diversity, identifying three racial types. They called people with relatively light skin and fine hair *Caucasoid*, people with darker skin and coarse hair *Negroid*, and people with yellow or brown skin and distinctive folds on the eyelids *Mongoloid*. Sociologists consider such terms misleading at

best and harmful at worst. For one thing, no society contains biologically "pure" people. The skin colour of people we might call "Caucasoid" (or "Indo-European," "Caucasian," or, more commonly, "White") ranges from very light (typical in Scandinavia) to very dark (in southern India). The same variation exists among so-called "Negroid" ("African" or, more commonly, "Black") people and "Mongoloid" (that is, "Asian") people. In fact, many "white" people (say, in southern India) actually have darker skin than many "black" people (the Negroid Aborigines of Australia). Overall, the three racial categories differ in only 6 percent of their genes, less than the genetic variation *within* each category (Harris and Sim, 2002; American Sociological Association, 2003).

Why, then, do people make so much of race? With such categories, society ranks people in a hierarchy, which allows some people to feel that they are inherently better than others. Because racial ranking shapes access to wealth and prestige, societies may construct racial categories in extreme ways. Throughout much of the twentieth century, for example, many states in the American south labelled as "coloured" anyone with as little as one thirty-second African ancestry (that is, one African-American great-great-great-grandparent). Today, U.S. law leaves it up to parents to decide the race of a child. Even so, most Americans are still very sensitive to racial background. Canada has never measured race as one-quarter, one-eighth, or any other part. Nevertheless, race remains relevant: Aboriginal peoples have unique positions in Canadian society, with Status or

More people see themselves as multiracial than ever before. A well-known example is actress Halle Berry, whose mother is White and whose father is Black. Much more complicated is the ancestry of golf star Tiger Woods, who describes himself as one-eighth American Indian, one-quarter Thai, and one-quarter Chinese, as well as one-eighth White and one-quarter Black (White, cited in Macionis, 2007: 364).

Treaty Indians (First Nations) under the *Indian Act*; First Nations, non-status Indian, Inuit and Métis peoples under the *Canadian Charter of Rights and Freedoms*. We identify racial groups of immigrant background as visible minorities; and, officially at least, we celebrate multiculturalism and racial diversity as part of our Canadian identity.

YOUR TURN

How much interracial dating is there on your campus? How racially diverse are your school's student organizations and sports teams?

Whereas the United States has measured race—and ignored ethnicity—throughout its history, Canada has taken the opposite approach. While Canada has a long-standing interest in its ethnic composition, it was only in the 1996 census that an attempt was made to determine racial identification. In the past, attempts to determine the

size of our visible minority population were based on declared country of origin (or ancestry) and self-definition. If someone claimed to be of Jamaican origin, for example, it was assumed (often incorrectly) that he or she was Black. Similarly, and equally incorrectly at times, someone who declared British or U.S. origins was assumed to be White. Even First Nation members, whose precise numbers are known because of registration, are of mixed racial and ethnic ancestry. Therefore, past attempts to describe Canada in terms of racial composition were approximations only. Recently, the census has asked people to identify as Aboriginal, Black, and Visible Minority.

A Trend towards Mixture

Over many generations and throughout the Americas, the genetic traits from around the world have become mixed. Many dark- and light-skinned people have multi-racial ancestry. Whatever people may think, race is no black-and-white issue.

Today, people are more willing to define themselves as multiracial. When completing their 2000 census forms, almost 7 million Americans described themselves by checking two or more racial categories, while the official number of interracial births tripled over the past 20 years to about 5 percent of all births. In Canada, where we blend ethnic and racial categories and do not record births by race, 38 percent of the total population claims multiple origins. This is the case for 14 percent of those with Chinese background, 19 percent of East Indians, 38 percent of Japanese, 54 percent of North American Indians (i.e., Ojibwa and Cree would qualify as multiple origins), 62 percent of those who claim African (or Black) origins, and 77 percent of those claiming French origin.

ETHNICITY

Ethnicity is *a shared cultural heritage*. People define themselves or others as members of an *ethnic category* based on common ancestry, language, or religion that gives them a distinctive social identity. For certain purposes, as in dealing with ethnic categories that are undergoing change, it is important to distinguish between *objective* and *subjective* criteria (Isajiw, 1985). Objective criteria are traits such as ancestry, cultural practices, dress, religion, and language. Subjective criteria involve the internalization of a distinctive social identity, whereby people identify themselves or are perceived by others as belonging to a different group. Subjective ethnic identities may persist despite cultural assimilation, sometimes over many generations, without perpetuation of traditional ethnic culture (the objective components). For example, Canadian-born Finns continue to see themselves as "Finnish" though they do not speak the language, dance, sing, prepare foods, or go to sauna according to Finnish tradition. Whatever the degree of assimilation, ethnicity remains an important basis of social differentiation in Canada.

July 2000 saw approximately 4000 people of Finnish heritage and their partners descend on Toronto's Mel Lastman Square. They came from Canada, the United States, and Finland for a celebration of Finnish culture and traditions in the Finn Grand Fest 2000. Here, a young woman of Finnish ancestry tries on Lapland (Saami) hats with her boyfriend.

Her Excellency, The Right Honourable Michaëlle Jean was appointed governor general in 2005 to be Canada's representative for the Crown. As such, she reads the Throne Speech at the opening of each new Parliament, confers royal assent on all laws passed, and is Commander-in-Chief of our armed forces; she also officiates at ceremonial occasions, such as awarding the Order of Canada. Like her predecessor, Adrienne Clarkson, Michaëlle Jean comes from humble immigrant, visible minority roots. Born in Haiti and raised in Montreal by a single mother, she established herself in broadcasting and among the intellectual elite of Quebec. She has special interests in visible minorities, Aboriginal peoples, and the alleviation of poverty in Canada and abroad.

More than 5.2 million Canadians (18% of the population) claim languages other than French and English as their mother tongues. About half that number still speaks those languages at home. Furthermore, there are now more Catholics than Protestants in Canada, as Catholic French Canadians have been joined by immigrants from such traditionally Catholic areas as Italy, Poland, and Latin America. Canada's Jewish population (roughly 350 000 people) traces its ancestral ties to various countries, as do the Eastern Orthodox and Muslim people. (See Chapter 19, "Religion.")

Race and ethnicity, then, are quite different: one is biological, the other cultural. But the two sometimes go hand in hand. Japanese Canadians, for example, have distinctive physical traits and, for those who maintain their traditions, cultural attributes as well. But ethnic distinctiveness should not be viewed as racial. Jews may be described as a race but they are distinctive only in their religious beliefs and their history of persecution (Goldsby, 1977).

Finally, people can *change* their ethnicities by adopting a different way of life. Polish immigrants who discard their cultural background over time may cease to have a particular ethnicity. Someone of British ancestry might marry a German and become "more German" than his or her spouse. People of mixed Aboriginal and non-Aboriginal heritage may have blended into the dominant francophone or anglophone populations of their respective provinces or territories to the point where many are unaware of their mixed ancestry. From time to time, people actually renew

ethnic ties and identities after two or three generations, making serious efforts to return to their roots, be they Polish, Jewish, or Aboriginal.

MINORITIES

A **minority** is *any category of people distinguished by physical or cultural difference that a society sets apart and subordinates*. Minority standing can be based on race, ethnicity, or both. In recent years, the breadth of the term "minority" has expanded in meaning to include not only people with particular racial and ethnic traits but also people with physical disabilities and, as the previous chapter explained, women. Elderly people, gays, and lesbians can also be considered minorities.

Minorities have two major characteristics. One trait is that they share a *distinctive identity*. Because race is highly visible—and virtually impossible for a person to change, most minority men and women are keenly aware of their physical differences. The significance of ethnicity—which people can change—is more variable. In Canada, some people downplay their historic ethnicity, while others maintain their cultural traditions and lived in distinctive ethnic neighbourhoods. Some go so far as to insulate themselves

Recent research measuring student attitudes shows declining prejudice towards all racial and ethnic categories of the American population. Even so, attitudes towards Muslim and Arab Americans are the most negative, probably a result of publicity about global terrorism. Here, Arab Americans speak out against what they feel is the negative depiction of Arabs in the film *True Lies*.

from outside influences: Hasidic Jews in Montreal have been particularly successful in nurturing a lifestyle that separates them from their neighbours. The Hutterite people of the Prairies—who have the advantage of living in communal agricultural communities (or colonies)—manage even more effectively to minimize contact with the "outside."

A second characteristic of minorities is *subordination*. Chapter 11 ("Social Class in Canada") explained that minorities in Canada may have lower incomes and less occupational prestige than those of British or French origin, even if—as in the case of Black and Asian people—their levels of educational attainment are as high or higher. Thus, class, race, and ethnicity, as well as gender, are overlapping and reinforcing dimensions of social stratification.

Of course, not all members of any minority are disadvantaged. But even the greatest success rarely allows individuals to transcend their minority standing (Benjamin, 1991); that is, race or ethnicity often serves as a *master status* (described in Chapter 6, "Social Interaction in Everyday Life") that overshadows personal accomplishments.

The term "minority" suggests that these categories of people constitute a small proportion of a society's population. But this is not always the case. Black South Africans,

for example, form a numerical majority in their country, although they are grossly deprived of economic and political power by Whites. In Canada, women represent more than half the population but are still struggling to gain opportunities and privileges long enjoyed by men.

Prejudice

Prejudice is *a rigid and irrational generalization about an entire category of people.* Prejudice is irrational to the extent that people hold inflexible attitudes that are supported by little or no direct evidence. Further, prejudice leads people to characterize an entire category, the vast majority of whom they have never even met. Prejudice may target a particular social class, sex, sexual orientation, age, physical ability, religion, political affiliation, race, or ethnicity.

Prejudices are *pre*judgments that may be positive or negative. Our positive prejudices tend to exaggerate the virtues of people like ourselves, while our negative prejudices condemn those who differ from us. Negative prejudice runs along a continuum, ranging from mild aversion to outright hostility. Because attitudes are rooted in our culture, everyone has at least some measure of prejudice.

Take a test for prejudice at www.tolerance.org/hidden_bias/index.html.

STEREOTYPES

Prejudice often involves a **stereotype** (*stereo* is derived from Greek, meaning "hard" or "solid"), *a prejudicial view or description of some categories of people.* Many stereotypes involve emotions such as love and loyalty, generally towards members of ingroups, or hate and fear, generally towards outgroups; as a result, they are hard to change even in the face of contradictory evidence. For example, some people have a stereotypical understanding of the poor as lazy and irresponsible freeloaders who would rather rely on welfare than support themselves (Waxman, 1983). As was explained in Chapter 11 ("Social Class in Canada"), however, this stereotype distorts reality, since more than half of the poor people in Canada are children, working adults (including single mothers), or elderly people.

Stereotypes exist for virtually every racial and ethnic minority, and such attitudes can become deeply rooted in a society's culture. In Canada, many White people stereotype Aboriginal people and members of other visible minorities as lacking motivation to improve their own lives. Such attitudes assume that social disadvantage stems from personal deficiency. This stereotypical view ignores some key facts: most poor people in Canada are White, and most members of visible minorities work as hard as anyone else and are not poor. In this case, the bit of truth in the stereotype is that, proportionally, Aboriginal peoples and members of some other visible minorities are more likely than Whites to be poor. But by building a rigid attitude out of a few selected facts, stereotypes can grossly distort reality.

YOUR TURN

What factors might account for the trend towards less prejudice shown in this research? Consider factors in the country as a whole and also on campus.

Racism

A powerful and destructive form of prejudice, **racism** refers to *the belief that one racial category is innately superior or inferior to another.* Racism has pervaded world history.

 Racism can give rise to hate crimes. For more information, go to www.civilrights.org/issues/hate/.

The ancient Greeks, the peoples of India, and the Chinese were among the first to view people unlike themselves as inferior. Racism has also been widespread in Canadian history: at one point, the enslavement of people of African descent or of Aboriginal peoples (called *Panis* in New France) was supported by notions of their innate inferiority—as was the placement of Indian nations on reserves under paternalistic administration by British colonial officials.

Historically, the assertion that certain categories of people are *innately* inferior has provided a powerful justification for subjugation. By the end of the nineteenth century, European nations and the United States had forged vast colonial empires. Colonial exploitation often took the form of subjugating foreign peoples with the callous claim that they were somehow less human than the explorers who enslaved them. Canada never acquired external colonies, being one itself, but it did establish a system of *internal* colonialism involving "Indian" reserves.

Stanley Barrett, an anthropologist who did field research among various White supremists in Canada, notes that

> Racism constitutes an elaborate and systematic ideology; it acts as a conceptual tool to rationalize the division of the world's population into the privileged and the deprived. It is inherently a political phenomenon. It emerged with the advent of the colonization of the Third World by European nations, and thus coincided too with the development of capitalism. (1987:5–6)

In the twentieth century, racism was central to the Nazi regime in Germany. Nazi racial doctrine proclaimed a so-called Aryan race of blond-haired, blue-eyed Caucasians that was allegedly superior to all others and destined to rule the world. This racist ideology was used to justify the murder of anyone deemed inferior, including some 6 million European Jews and millions of Poles, gypsies, homosexuals, and people with physical and mental disabilities.

While some think of racism in Canada as a thing of the past, Fleras (2001) argues that it is an everyday reality for many Canadians: "a moving target that is difficult to pin down or control." Racism is simultaneously elusive and pervasive, and defies definition because Whites and minori-

Racial and ethnic stereotypes are deeply embedded in our culture and language. Many people speak of someone "gypping" another without realizing that this word insults European "gypsies"—properly called Roma, a category of people long pushed to the margins of European societies.

ties do not perceive it in the same way. Whites may think of racism as an "irrational aberration" in an otherwise benevolent society. Minorities, argues Fleras with a postmodern slant, experience a system in which "patterns of power and privilege are reproduced" so that they perpetuate "a racialized status quo" (pp. 81–82).

Although Canadians are by no means devoid of prejudice or racism, there is evidence that we are more tolerant of racial and ethnic minorities than are our American neighbours (Lipset, 1991:112). The fact that Toronto, in a very short period of time, went from being a city dominated by White Anglo-Saxon Protestants to one with many immigrants and visible minorities without major violence or disruption suggests a fair degree of social tolerance (Artibise and Stelter, 1988:244). Bibby (1995:52–54) reports that, between 1975 and 1995, Canadians became more aware of the fact that minorities are subject to discrimination (up about 10 points). Acceptance of interracial and interfaith marriage had increased by a similar amount: more than 80 percent approve of interracial marriage and 90 percent approve of interfaith marriage—remarkable levels in both cases.

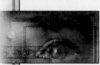

THINKING CRITICALLY
Does Race Affect Intelligence?

Are Asians more intelligent than Europeans? Is the typical European smarter than the average African? Assertions painting one category of people as more intellectually gifted than another have been common throughout history. Moreover, people have used such thinking to justify the privileges of an allegedly superior category or even to bar supposedly inferior people from entering a country.

The distribution of human intelligence forms a classic "bell curve" (see illustration). By convention, average intelligence is defined as an intelligence quotient (IQ) score of 100. Technically, an IQ score is mental age, as measured by a test, divided by age in years, with the result multiplied by 100; thus, an 8-year-old who performs like a 10-year-old has an IQ of 10 ÷ 8 = 1.2 × 100 = 120.

Philippe Rushton, a psychology professor at the University of Western Ontario, became the centre of academic controversy in 1989 when he claimed that—in terms of intelligence, conformity to the law, and sexual restraint—Asians are superior to Whites, who, in turn, are superior to Blacks. Other researchers and journalists were quick to point out the methodological flaws in his research, criticizing his basic assumptions, data collection, and causal inferences. So unacceptable were his assertions, in the context of political correctness, that some Canadians demanded his tenure at Western be revoked.

In a controversial study of intelligence and social inequality, Richard Herrnstein and Charles Murray (1994) argue that research evidence supports the conclusion that race is related to intelligence. Specifically, they place the IQ of people with European ancestry at 100. People of East Asian ancestry exceed that standard slightly, averaging 103; people of African descent fall below that standard, with an average IQ of 90. Of course, assertions of this kind fly in the face of our demo-

cratic and egalitarian beliefs, by implying that people of one racial type are inherently better than another. In response, some people charge that intelligence tests are invalid, while others question whether what we call "intelligence" has much real meaning.

Most social scientists acknowledge that IQ tests do measure something important that people think of as "intelligence," and they agree that some *individuals* have more intellectual aptitude than others. But they reject the notion that any *category* of people, on average, is smarter than any other. That is, categories of people may show small differences on intelligence tests, but the crucial question is *why*.

Thomas Sowell, an African-American social scientist, has demonstrated that most of the documented racial differences in intelligence are not the result of biology but people's environment. In some skilful sociological detective work, Sowell tracked down IQ scores for various racial and ethnic categories from early in the twentieth century. He found that, on average, immigrants from European nations such as Poland, Lithuania, Italy, and Greece, as well as from Asian countries including China and Japan, scored 10 to 15 points below the U.S. average. Sowell's critical discovery came next: people in these same categories *today* have IQ scores that are average or above average. Among Italian Americans, for example, average IQ jumped almost 10 points in 50 years; among Polish and Chinese

Americans, the rise was almost 20 points. Because genetic changes occur over thousands of years and these people largely married among themselves, biological factors simply cannot explain such a rise in IQ scores. Rather, the evidence points to changing cultural patterns. As immigrants settled in the United States, their new surroundings affected them in ways that improved their intellectual performance as measured in intelligence tests.

Sowell found that the same pattern applies to African Americans. African Americans living in the northern United States have historically outscored people living in the southern states on IQ tests by about 10 points. And among African Americans who migrated from the south to the north after 1940, IQ scores soon rose as they did among earlier immigrants. Thus, if environmental factors are the same for everyone, racial IQ differences largely disappear.

What disparities in IQ test scores do tell, according to Sowell, is that *cultural patterns* matter. Asians who score high on tests are no smarter than other people, but they may have been raised to value learning and to pursue excellence. For their part, African Americans are no less intelligent than anyone else, but they carry a legacy of disadvantage that can undermine self-confidence and discourage achievement.

WHAT DO YOU THINK?

1. If IQ scores reflect people's environments, are they valid measures of intelligence? Could they be harmful?
2. Why, according to Sowell, do some racial and ethnic categories show dramatic short-term gains in average IQ scores?
3. Do you think parents and schools influence children's IQ scores? If so, how?

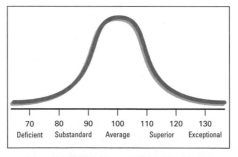

IQ: the distribution of intelligence

Sources: Knowles (1997), Herrnstein and Murray (1994), and Sowell (1994, 1995).

Overt racism in this country has subsided to some extent because of a more egalitarian culture and is "checked by the state in order to preserve social harmony and order" (Li, 1988:49). Racism persists, though in less open and direct forms, and research continues to document the injury and humiliation that racism causes to visible minorities (Ramcharan, 1982; Wotherspoon and Satzewich, 1993). As the Thinking Critically box (on p. 356) explains, however, racial differences in mental abilities are the result of environmental factors rather than biology.

More recently, racial conflict has intensified in Britain and Western European societies as Whites confront millions of immigrants from former colonies and refugees from strife-torn Eastern Europe. Several terrorist attacks in Europe served to exacerbate racial conflict. Similarly, in Canada, one can observe signs of increasing racial tensions during tough economic times (e.g., the early 1990s) and in response to political events abroad. Racism—in thought and deed—remains a serious social problem here and elsewhere.

THEORIES OF PREJUDICE

Where does prejudice come from? Social scientists provide several answers to this question, focusing on frustration, personality, culture, and social conflict.

Scapegoat Theory

Scapegoat theory holds that prejudice springs from frustration among people who are themselves disadvantaged (Dollard, et al., 1939). Take the case of a White woman frustrated by her low-paying job in a textile factory. Directing hostility at the powerful factory owners carries the obvious risk of being fired; instead, she may blame her low pay on the presence of minority co-workers. Her prejudice does not improve her situation, but it is a relatively safe way to express anger, and it may give her the comforting feeling that at least she is superior to someone. A **scapegoat,** then, is *a person or category of people, typically with little power, whom people unfairly blame for their own troubles.* Because they are usually "safe" targets, minorities are often used as scapegoats. The Nazis painted the Jews as responsible for all of Germany's ills in the 1930s. As a less extreme example, while our economy struggles to respond to corporate restructuring, globalization, and national debt, one hears rumblings among Canadians about lax immigration laws, and the immigrants and refugees who allegedly contribute to the shortage of jobs and the high costs of social welfare.

Authoritarian Personality Theory

T.W. Adorno and colleagues (1950) considered extreme prejudice a personality trait of certain individuals. This conclusion is supported by research showing that people who express strong prejudice towards one minority typically do so towards all minorities. These *authoritarian personalities* rigidly conform to conventional cultural values and see moral issues as clear-cut matters of right and wrong. People with authoritarian personalities also view

society as naturally competitive and hierarchical, with "better" people—like themselves—inevitably dominating those who are weaker, including all minorities.

Adorno also found that people tolerant towards one minority are likely to be accepting of all. They tend to be more flexible in their moral judgments and treat all people as equals. Adorno thought that people with little schooling and those raised by cold and demanding parents tend to develop authoritarian personalities. Filled with anger and anxiety as children, they grow into hostile, aggressive adults who seek out scapegoats.

Culture Theory

A third theory contends that, while extreme prejudice may be characteristic of certain people, some prejudice is found in everyone because it is embedded in culture. Belief in the social superiority of some categories of people—for example, the British and French or the hard-working and reliable people of northern and western European roots—still colours Canadian culture to some extent, despite Canada's multicultural policies and programs. Educational initiatives aim to broaden the traditionally Eurocentric attitudes by promoting appreciation of the culture and contributions of those of non-European backgrounds.

Emory Bogardus (1968) studied the effects of culturally rooted prejudices on interpersonal relationships for more than forty years. He devised the concept of *social distance* to assess how close or distant people feel in relation to members of various racial and ethnic categories. His research in the United States, which documented widespread agreement, found that Americans held the most positive views towards people of White English, Canadian, and Scottish background, even welcoming marriage with them. Attitudes were less favourable towards French, German, Swedish, and Dutch people, and the most negative prejudices targeted people of African and Asian descent.

When Canadians were asked to rank various racial and ethnic categories on the Bogardus scale (Mackie, 1974), the ranking was very similar—with British and American White Anglo-Saxon Protestants ranking first and second. Not only is there consistency within cultures but also between Canadian and American cultures, suggesting that such rankings are indeed normative.

According to Bogardus, then, prejudice is so widespread that we cannot explain it as merely a trait of a handful of people with authoritarian personalities, as Adorno suggests. Rather, Bogardus concludes, almost everyone expresses some bigotry because we live in a "culture of prejudice."

Conflict Theory

A fourth analysis views prejudice as the product of social conflict. According to this theory, powerful people use prejudice to justify their oppression of minorities. Canadians certainly did this with the Chinese labourers who were allowed to come to Canada to work—under appalling conditions—on the Canadian Pacific Railway in the 1870s

Lincoln MacCauley Alexander was born to immigrant parents in 1922 and grew up in Hamilton, Ontario. With a B.A. from McMaster University and a law degree from Osgoode Hall, Alexander practised law before entering federal politics as Canada's first Black MP. He was lieutenant-governor of Ontario from 1985 to 1991, and he has been chancellor of the University of Guelph since 1991. He is a Companion of the Order of Canada, and he has received honorary degrees from five universities and numerous outstanding-citizen awards. Hamilton's Lincoln Alexander Expressway is affectionately known as "The Linc." Throughout his career, he has sustained his interest in multicultural affairs.

and 1880s. Similarly, all elites benefit when prejudice divides workers along racial and ethnic lines, and discourages them from working together to advance their common interests (Geschwender, 1978; Olzak, 1989).

A different conflict-based argument, advanced by Shelby Steele (1990), is that minorities themselves cultivate a climate of race consciousness in order to win greater power and privileges. In raising *race consciousness*, Steele explains, minorities argue that they are victims and that White people are their victimizers. Because of their historic disadvantage, minorities claim that they are entitled to special considerations based on their race. While this strategy may yield short-term gains, Steele cautions that such policies are likely to spark a backlash from White people and others who condemn "special treatment" for anyone on the basis of race or ethnicity.

The Québécois have made precisely that kind of claim on the basis of past injustices and the threat of assimilation in an English-speaking North America. Some non-Quebecers feel that the wrongs of the past have now been redressed and that entrenching special status (that is, recognition as a "distinct society") in Canada's constitution is going too far. The Charlottetown Accord of 1992, along with many other matters, proposed such distinct society status for Quebec; the accord was rejected by Canadians in a referendum.

YOUR TURN

Which of these four theories of prejudice (scapegoat, authoritarian personality, culture, conflict) do you find most convincing? Why?

Discrimination

Closely related to prejudice is **discrimination,** *unequal treatment of various categories of people. Prejudice* refers to *attitudes,* but *discrimination* is a matter of *action.* Like prejudice, discrimination can be either positive—providing special advantages, or negative—creating obstacles, and ranges from subtle to blatant.

INSTITUTIONAL PREJUDICE AND DISCRIMINATION

We typically think of prejudice and discrimination as the hateful ideas or actions of specific people. But Stokely Carmichael and Charles Hamilton (1967) pointed out that far greater harm results from **institutional prejudice and discrimination,** *bias built into the operation of society's institutions,* including schools, hospitals, the police, and the workplace. For example, researchers have found that banks reject home mortgage applications from minorities at a higher rate than those from White people, even when income and quality of neighbourhood are held constant (Gotham, 1998). Anderson and Frideres describe the process as follows:

> Bureaucracies have the job of establishing regulations and priorities as well as qualifications for particular positions in our society. Only those individuals able to meet these initial qualifications will be able to participate in the ongoing institutional structure. For example, when Native people suggested that they be hired by the Department of Indian Affairs (with a staff of about 14 000), the response by the Minister of Indian Affairs was that placement was only possible for those belonging to a particular union, and having a particular position and level of seniority in the union. Unless these requirements were met, an Indian could not be hired, and if hired without these qualifications, the union would strike. (1981:208)

There was no need for the authors to point out that Aboriginal people were not members of the appropriate union. In the intervening decades, Aboriginal people have been accepted as and, indeed, encouraged to become employees in Indian Affairs.

PREJUDICE AND DISCRIMINATION: THE VICIOUS CIRCLE

Prejudice and discrimination reinforce each other. The Thomas theorem, discussed in Chapter 6 ("Social Interaction in Everyday Life"), offers a simple explanation of this fact: situations that are defined as real become real in their consequences (Thomas, 1966 [1931]:301). As Thomas recognized, stereotypes become real to people who believe them and sometimes even to those who are victimized by them. Prejudice on the part of White people towards people belonging to visible minorities does not produce *innate* inferiority, but it can produce *social* inferiority—pushing minorities into low-paying jobs, inferior schools, and racially segregated housing. Then, as White people see social disadvantage as evidence that minorities do not measure up, they begin a new round of prejudice and discrimination, giving rise to a vicious circle in which each perpetuates the other, as shown in Figure 14-1.

Majority and Minority: Patterns of Interaction

Sociologists describe patterns of interaction among racial and ethnic categories in a society in terms of four models: pluralism, assimilation, segregation, and genocide.

PLURALISM AND MULTICULTURALISM

Pluralism is *a state in which racial and ethnic minorities are distinct but have social parity.* In a pluralist society, categories of people are different but share resources more or less equally. The relationship between Quebec and the rest of Canada provides an example of pluralism in action. Aboriginal peoples, too, would like to acquire social and political parity or equality. While the United States considers itself to be pluralist—recently even multicultural Canada has an official policy of fostering multiculturalism, as discussed in Chapter 3 ("Culture").

Social diversity has long been a source of pride in Canada. Some argue that multiculturalism not only acknowledges but actually celebrates our differences and encourages the perpetuation of countless "ethnic villages," communities where people proudly maintain their cultural traditions. These ethnic communities—the components of our cultural mosaic—add variety and colour to our social landscape. The viability of these communities is affected by their levels of **institutional completeness,** *the complexity of community organizations that meet the needs of members.* Where communities are institutionally complete, members are able to live, shop, pray, and sometimes work within the boundaries of their culture. They might also have their own welfare and mutual aid societies, credit unions, newspapers, and radio stations. Breton (1964), who coined the term "institutional completeness," points out that the presence of these formal organizations encourages social relations within "ingroup" boundaries and minimizes "outgroup" contact.

Canada embraces the ideal of multiculturalism, recognition of cultural heterogeneity, and mutual respect among culturally diverse groups. Through policies of multiculturalism, Canada encourages people to participate fully in all aspects of Canadian life without feeling that it is necessary to

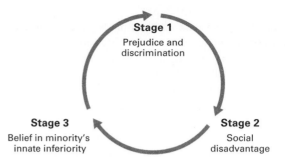

Stage 1: Prejudice and discrimination begin, often as an expression of ethnocentrism or an attempt to justify economic exploitation.

Stage 2: As a result of prejudice and discrimination, a minority is socially disadvantaged, occupying a low position in the system of social stratification.

Stage 3: This social disadvantage is then interpreted not as the result of earlier prejudice and discrimination but as evidence that the minority is innately inferior, unleashing renewed prejudice and discrimination by which the cycle repeats itself.

FIGURE 14-1   Prejudice and Discrimination: The Vicious Circle

Prejudice and discrimination can form a vicious, self-perpetuating circle.

give up their ethnic identities and cultural practices. The aim of multiculturalism is to promote unity through diversity and to enhance a Canadian identity that embraces differences. Canada began to use the term "multiculturalism" in the 1960s, in recognition of the diverse backgrounds of Canadians, and adopted multiculturalism as government policy by 1971. The Canadian *Multiculturalism Act* of 1988 sought "to recognize all Canadians as full and equal partners in Canadian society," and in 1991 this goal was given explicit support through the creation of a new Department of Multiculturalism and Citizenship (now Heritage Canada). Multicultural programs provide education, consultative support, and funding for a wide range of activities, including heritage-language training, race relations and cross-cultural understanding programs, the ethnic press, ethnic celebrations, policing and justice, and family violence programs.

For information about Heritage Canada programs to encourage multiculturalism and citizenship, visit www.canadianheritage.gc.ca, and for information on race relations, visit the Canadian Race Relations Foundation at www.crr.ca.

Not everyone approves of the official goal of multiculturalism. Critics argue that it discourages immigrant adaptation, and is divisive and detrimental to a shared and coherent Canadian identity. While Canadians prefer our cultural mosaic to the American melting pot—by a slim margin—and over 80 percent approve of interracial marriage (i.e., with Aboriginal, Asian, or Black people), 85 percent feel that immigrants have an obligation to learn Canadian ways (Bibby, 1995). Writer Neil Bissoondath, who feels that continued ethnic identification weakens the social fabric of Canada, met with hostility and caught the attention of the media when he made a plea to be accepted as an unhyphenated Canadian. Criticism of multiculturalism by this member of a visible minority led to cries of "traitor" or "sell out" from minority members and anger from mainstream defenders of the policy. Bissoondath (1994:5) feels that these reactions have "more than a little to do with the psychology of the True Believer, who sees Canada's multicultural policy as the only one possible."

In November 2004, Theo Van Gogh was murdered in the Netherlands for producing a film (*Submission, Part I*), which dealt with the mistreatment of women in the name of Islam. Van Gogh's co-producer, Ayaan Hirsi Ali—who had herself received death threats, came to Toronto a year after his death to help fight the adoption of sharia in Ontario. Sharia is a body of laws, based on Islamic teachings, for handling family matters. The Ontario government was considering the adoption of sharia to deal with matters of family law in the Muslim community in that province. This articulate, passionate, former Muslim woman argued that our adoption of sharia would take multiculturalism to its logical end, thereby authorizing discrimination against and mistreatment of women in one group of people (Fulford, 2005). In the end, Ontario did not give legal recognition to sharia: the arguments of Ali and other Muslim women were persuasive.

Questions about the impact of multiculturalism can be raised from other perspectives as well. Although they are not critical of multicultural policy, Reitz and Breton (1994) point out that Canada's cultural mosaic and the American melting pot result in only minimal differences in assimilation, economic integration, intermarriage, or tolerance of ethnic distinctiveness. Therefore, they argue, the perception that Canada's minorities retain their cultural identities more than minorities in the United States is largely an illusion.

ASSIMILATION

Assimilation is *the process by which minorities gradually adopt patterns of the dominant culture, thereby becoming more similar to the dominant group.* Assimilation involves changing modes of dress, values, religion, language, and friends. While the United States has been seen as a melting pot in which different nationalities fuse into a new way of life, this characterization is misleading. Rather than "melting" into some new cultural pattern, minorities have adopted the traits—the dress, the accent, and sometimes even the names—of the dominant culture established by the earliest settlers. Why? Assimilation is both the avenue to upward social mobility and the way to escape the prejudice and discrimination directed at visible foreigners (Newman, 1973).

The amount of assimilation varies by category. For example, Germans and Irish have "melted" more than Italians, and the Japanese more than the Chinese or Koreans. Supporters of multiculturalism, however, criticize the idea of assimilation for painting minorities as "the problem" and defining them—rather than elites—as the ones who need to do all the changing. In general, minorities

in the United States have adopted the English language. But recently the rapid growth of the Hispanic population has created areas where Spanish is the dominant language, has encouraged the study of Spanish as a second language, and—as a counterforce—has inspired a social movement seeking to establish English as the official language of the United States. In fact, as they experience pressure to become officially bilingual—English and Spanish—Americans look to Canada to assess the possible effects of such a policy. Many have concluded that the threat of Quebec separation clearly illustrates its dangers.

The fact that such ethnic enclaves still exist in the United States—where assimilation and the melting pot are the ideals—suggests that race and ethnicity endure as building blocks of American society (Glazer and Moynihan, 1970; Alba, 1985). In Canada, with its claim to be a colourful mosaic in which all the pieces make distinctive contributions, assimilation occurs as well. Immigrants learn to function in English and French, ancestral cultural practices fall into disuse, and people acquire a set of shared attitudes and values that can only be called Canadian. Despite our melting pot and mosaic ideals, the dynamics of assimilation and ethnic viability are similar in the United States and Canada (Reitz and Breton, 1994).

As a cultural process, assimilation involves changes in ethnicity—but not in race. For example, many North Americans of Japanese descent have discarded their traditional way of life but still have their racial identity. Even distinctive racial traits may diminish over generations as the result of **miscegenation,** *biological reproduction by partners of different racial categories.* While resistance to such biological mixing remains strong in some circles, miscegenation, often outside of marriage, has occurred throughout history. Canada's census data reveal racial as well as ethnic mixing by classifying people as either "single origin" or "multiple origin": see Table 14–1.

SEGREGATION

Segregation refers to *the physical and social separation of categories of people.* Some minorities, especially religious orders such as the Hutterites, voluntarily segregate themselves. The concentration of various ethnic and racial groups in Canada's cities results, at least in part, from voluntary action (that is, people want to live near people like themselves). Mostly, however, majorities segregate minorities involuntarily by excluding them (for example, the refusal of restaurant owners to serve Black Canadians, as in this chapter's opener). Various degrees of segregation characterize residential neighbourhoods, schools, workplaces, hospitals, and even cemeteries. While pluralism and multiculturalism foster distinctiveness without disadvantage, segregation enforces separation to the detriment of a minority.

South Africa's system of *apartheid* (described in Chapter 10, "Social Stratification") illustrates rigid and pervasive racial segregation, where Indigenous Africans were forced to

TABLE 14–1

The Top 25 Ethnic Origins in Canada, Showing Single- and Multiple-Origin Responses, 2001[*]

Ethnic Origin	Total Responses[a] %		Single Responses %		Multiple Responses %	
1. Canadian	11 682 680	39.4	6 748 135	36.9	4 934 550	43.5
2. English	5 978 875	20.2	1 479 520	8.1	4 499 355	39.7
3. French	4 668 410	15.8	1 060 755	5.8	3 607 655	31.8
4. Scottish	4 157 210	14.0	607 235	3.3	3 549 975	31.3
5. Irish	3 822 660	12.9	496 865	2.7	3 325 800	29.4
6. German	2 742 765	9.3	705 595	3.9	2 037 170	18.0
7. Aboriginal	1 365 065	4.6	565 040	3.1	800 200	7.1
8. Italian	1 270 370	4.3	726 275	4.0	544 090	4.8
9. Chinese	1 094 700	3.7	936 210	5.1	158 490	1.4
10. Ukrainian	1 071 060	3.6	326 200	1.8	744 860	6.6
11. Dutch (Netherlands)	923 310	3.1	316 220	1.7	607 090	5.4
12. Polish	817 085	2.8	260 415	1.4	556 670	4.9
13. East Indian	713 330	2.4	581 665	3.2	131 665	1.2
14. Norwegian	363 760	1.2	47 230	0.3	316 530	2.8
15. Portuguese	357 690	1.2	252 835	1.4	104 855	0.9
16. Welsh	350 365	1.2	28 445	0.2	321 925	2.8
17. Jewish	348 605	1.2	186 475	1.0	162 130	1.4
18. Russian	337 960	1.1	70 890	0.4	267 070	2.4
19. Filipino	327 545	1.1	266 140	1.5	61 410	0.5
20. Swedish	282 760	1.1	30 440	0.2	252 320	2.2
21. Hungarian (Magyar)	267 255	0.9	91 795	0.5	175 460	1.5
22. American (USA)	250 010	0.8	25 200	0.1	224 805	2.0
23. Greek	215 105	0.7	143 780	0.8	71 320	0.6
24. Spanish	213 100	0.7	66 545	0.4	146 555	1.3
25. Jamaican	211 725	0.7	138 180	0.8	73 545	0.6
Total Population	**29 639 035**	—	**18 307 540**	—	**11 331 490**	—

[*]The 1996 census asked people to indicate the ethnic or cultural groups to which their ancestors belong. A list of examples, including "Canadian," was provided, and respondents were asked to fill in up to four answers. The structure of this question produced a sevenfold increase in the number of people who identified themselves as single-origin "Canadian"—from 765 095 in 1991 to 5 326 995 in 1996. The number rose to 6 748 135 in 2001.

[a]The Total Responses column includes those individuals who claim each ethnic background as a single origin or as part of a multiple-origin response. The Single Response column includes those individuals whose parents share one ethnic background, while people with multiple origins might have, for example, Italian, English, and Scottish ancestry. Such hypothetical individuals would be counted three times in the Total or Multiple Responses columns.

Source: Calculations by L.M. Gerber from the Statistics Canada website http://www12.statcan.ca/english/census01/products/hightlights/ETO/Table1.cfm?Lang=E&T=501&GV=1&GID=0.

live on bantustans apart from other peoples. Apartheid was created by the European minority it served, and it was historically enforced through the use of brutal power (Fredrickson, 1981). South Africa has now ended official apartheid but, as yet, its basic racial structure has changed little. The nation remains essentially distinct societies that touch only when Black South Africans provide services for Whites or people of other colours. What Archbishop Desmond Tutu calls the "rainbow nation" has yet to emerge.

In the United States, too, racial segregation has a long history beginning with slavery and evolving into racially separated lodging, schooling, and transportation. Decisions such as the 1954 *Brown* case have reduced overt and *de jure*

The National Archives of Canada presents an online exhibition about the anti-slavery movement in Canada at www.collectionscanada.ca/anti-slavery/05310234_e.html.

(Latin, meaning "by law") discrimination; however, *de facto* ("in fact") segregation continues to this day in the form of countless neighbourhoods that are home to people of a single race. Research points to modest declines in racial segregation in the United States during recent decades (Farley, 1995).

Although Canadians might not want to think of themselves as practising segregation, we have done so historically and still do today. Early Black migrants—Loyalists in Nova Scotia and those brought via the Underground Railroad to Ontario—found themselves living in Africville (part of Halifax, Nova Scotia) or in small rural communities such as Buxton and Dawn in Ontario. The Thinking about Diversity box (on p. 362) explores this aspect of Canadian history. As a general rule, people in

Multimedia presentations from the CBC's archives document how Africville was uprooted in the 1960s: see http://archives.cbc.ca//300c.asp?id=1-69-96.

THINKING ABOUT DIVERSITY:
RACE, CLASS, & GENDER
Black Citizens of Canada: A History Ignored

When the average Canadian thinks about slavery, the image that comes to mind is likely that of plantation slavery in the Deep South. Few of us are aware that Canada has its own history of slavery and that about 3500 freed slaves came to Nova Scotia and New Brunswick as United Empire Loyalists. They had fought on the side of the British during the American Revolution as members of the Black Pioneers (also known as the Black Loyalists). We are also largely unaware of the 30 000 to 40 000 slaves who escaped and made it to Canada via the Underground Railroad between 1840 and 1865, when slavery was abolished in the United States.

Slaves were on the scene in the earliest settlements of New France. Olivier Le Jeune, who was brought here directly from Africa, was later sold in the first recorded slave sale in 1629. By 1759, there were 3604 slaves in New France—1132 Black people, the rest Aboriginal people. In 1793, under the leadership of John Graves Simcoe, Upper Canada became the first British colony to legislate the abolition of slavery.[1] While slavery remained legal in the rest of Canada until it was abolished throughout the British Empire in 1833, it had effectively died out by about 1810. Slavery was essentially unsuited to Canadian agriculture.

Fugitive slaves arrived in Ontario between the 1790s and 1860s. From about 1840, they used the Underground Railroad, an informal system of people and safe houses bringing escaped slaves to freedom in the northern United States and Canada. These former slaves formed scattered rural settlements across southern Ontario from Windsor to Barrie, where some farmed their own land while others hired themselves out as farm labourers. Some Black settlements, such as Buxton and Dawn, were thriving communities with their own schools, blacksmith shops, and other businesses.[2] Most of the residents of these communities and their descen-

Harriet Tubman, known as "Moses," had been assisted in her escape from slavery by workers on the Underground Railroad. She returned to Maryland a year later (1850) to free members of her family and then became one of the most active "conductors" on the Railroad, repeatedly risking her life to guide more than 300 slaves to freedom—many of them to Ontario, where she provided shelter for refugees in a rented house in St. Catharines.

dants eventually abandoned their rural homes and moved to the cities. Some, however, stayed behind. Descendants of the residents of Dawn still live in Dresden, Ontario.

Freed from slavery, Black people in Canada experienced economic hardship as well as prejudice and discrimination—suggesting that, despite our smugness, Canadians are not much more tolerant than Americans. Nevertheless, immigration from many parts of the world, including the Caribbean, has added to Canada's Black population, now comprising 574 000 individuals living mainly in southern Ontario and Montreal. At this time, there are three urban centres with significant Black populations: Halifax (3%), Montreal (4%), and Toronto (6%). More than half the Nova Scotians who belong to visible minorities identify themselves as Black and are descendants of Black Loyalists who came north at the time of the American Revolution.

Most live in Halifax where they have experienced their share of prejudice and discrimination. Nonetheless, since they are "old stock" Canadians rather than immigrants, their concerns and interests differ from those of Black people in other parts of the country.

The Black communities of Montreal are made up of immigrants and descendants who come from French-speaking countries such as Algeria and Haiti. But shared language has not resulted in easy or painless social and economic integration. Racism and discrimination are as likely to appear in Montreal as in Toronto, where many Black people encounter the combined barriers associated with recent immigration and visible minority status. Despite continued disadvantages, Black people have made important contributions to Canada's economic and cultural life. Current Governor General Michaëlle Jean was born in Haiti and had established a highly successful career in broadcasting before assuming her new position.

[1]When Governor Simcoe had dinner at the home of Mohawk leader and Loyalist Joseph Brant (Thayendanegea) in 1793, he was served by Brant's "Black slaves resplendent in scarlet uniforms with White ruffles, and with silver buckles on their shoes" (Walker, 1980:21).

[2]Dawn was founded in 1842 by Hiram Wilson and Josiah Henson. The latter, a "conductor" on the Underground Railroad who brought about a hundred slaves to freedom, is thought to be the model for Harriet Beecher Stowe's Uncle Tom in her anti-slavery novel *Uncle Tom's Cabin*.

WHAT DO YOU THINK?

1. Were you aware that we have so much slavery in our history?
2. How many examples of successful Black Canadians—in politics, music, athletics, or business—can you recall?
3. When you encounter Black Canadians, do you automatically think of them as immigrants?

Sources: McClain (1979), Walker (1980), Ducharme (1985), Winks (1988), Nader, *et al.* (1992), and Merrit (1993).

these communities did not receive the same kinds of land grants as other immigrants. They often attended segregated schools and were denied access to local services. Residential and social segregation were very real. The Thinking about Diversity box (on p. 362) deals with the experience of slavery in Canada's past.

The clearest example of segregation in Canada is found in our treatment of Aboriginal peoples, through the system of reserves for status Indians administered by Indian and Northern Affairs Canada. The overall effect has been one of extreme physical and social segregation, especially when reserves are located in remote areas. Prior to the late 1960s, most of the education of status Indian children took place in distant residential schools (far from their parents) or on these reserves. The physical and social segregation of the reserve system created barriers to integration with the mainstream—above and beyond those experienced by other Aboriginal people. (See the Thinking about Diversity box on residential schools on pp. 534–35 in Chapter 20.)

YOUR TURN

In your city or town, can you identify minority neighbourhoods? Which categories of people live there? To what degree is your community racially or ethnically segregated?

GENOCIDE

Genocide is *the systematic killing of one category of people by another.* This deadly form of racism and ethnocentrism violates nearly every recognized moral standard, yet it has occurred time and time again in human history. Genocide figured prominently in centuries of contact between Europeans and the original inhabitants of the Americas. From the sixteenth century on, as the Spanish, Portuguese, English, French, and Dutch forcibly established vast colonial empires, they decimated the Aboriginal populations of North, Central, and South America. Some Aboriginal peoples fell victim to calculated killing sprees; most succumbed to diseases brought by Europeans to which they had no natural immunities (Cottrell, 1979; Butterworth and Chance, 1981; Matthiessen, 1984; Sale, 1990; Dickason, 1997). The Beothuk (in what is now Newfoundland) who experienced the earliest contact with Europeans disap-

 See the Newfoundland and Labrador Heritage website for the history and culture of the Beothuk at www.heritage.nf. ca/aboriginal/beothuk.html.

peared completely by 1829. Feuding and open hunting season against the Beothuk, as well as tuberculosis, had taken their toll (Dickason, 1997).

Genocide also occurred in the twentieth century. Unimaginable horror befell Armenians—at the hands of Turks in 1915—and European Jews—in the 1930s and 1940s, as the Nazi regime seized control of much of Europe.

During Adolf Hitler's reign of terror, known as the Holocaust, the Nazis exterminated more than 6 million Jewish men, women, and children. Soviet dictator Josef Stalin murdered his country's people on an even greater scale, killing perhaps 28 million real and imagined enemies in the 1930s during his violent rule. Between 1975 and 1980, Pol Pot's Communist regime in Cambodia slaughtered anyone associated in any way with capitalist culture. Men and women able to speak a Western language and even individuals who wore eyeglasses, construed as a symbol of capitalist culture, were cut down. In all, some 2 million people (one-quarter of the population) perished in Cambodian "killing fields" (Shawcross, 1979).

More recently, the breakup of Yugoslavia resulted in conflict between ethnic Serbians and Albanians, based on 600 years of feuding. During the spring of 1999, an estimated 10 000 ethnic Albanians were victims of "ethnic cleansing" or mass murder by their Serbian neighbours. Bodies were burned, buried, and reburied in mass graves in attempts to conceal evidence of Serbian crimes. This is one of many troublespots to which Canadian Erin Mooney travelled, for her United Nations research into the experience of internal refugees created by ethnic cleansing (Mooney, 1995). In the winter of 2002, the Canadian commander, General Romeo Dallaire, led UN troops to prevent the genocide of Tutsis at the hands of Hutus in Rwanda. Unable to get the number of troops needed for the job—and defying UN orders to withdraw from Rwanda—Allaire witnessed the slaughter of 800 000 Tutsis in a 100-day reign of terror (Allen, 2002).

These four patterns of minority/majority interaction coexist in our society. We proudly point to patterns of pluralism (multiculturalism) and assimilation but only reluctantly acknowledge that our society has been built on segregation and genocide. The remainder of this chapter examines how these four patterns have shaped the history and present social standing of major racial and ethnic categories in Canada.

Race and Ethnicity in Canada

Thousands of years ago, the people we now call Aboriginal appeared on this continent. One theory is that they came over a land bridge that may have connected Alaska to Siberia. Of course, they might have come by sea. The first European explorers and settlers were met by more than fifty "founding" nations. The French and then the British established permanent settlements in the 1600s and 1700s, conveniently ignoring the Aboriginal nations and declaring themselves to be the two founding nations. Successive waves of immigration brought northern and then southern and eastern European people to our shores. More recently, in part as a result of changes in immigration laws, new Canadians have come from Asia, Africa, and the Caribbean. In addition, refugees have come to Canada in unprece-

TABLE 14–2

Ethnic Origins for Canada, the Provinces and Territories, 2001 (Rank Order by Percentage of Population)*

	NL	PE	NS	NB	QC	ON	MB	SK	AL	BC	YK	NW	NU
1.	**Canadian** (53.1)	**Canadian** (45.0)	**Canadian** (47.4)	**Canadian** (57.8)	**Canadien** (68.7)	**Canadian** (26.7)	*Canadian* (22.9)	**German** (28.6)	**Canadian** (27.7)	**English** (29.6)	**English** (27.1)	**NA Indian** (36.0)	**Inuit** (84.8)
2.	**English** (39.4)	**Scottish** (38.0)	**Scottish** (29.3)	**French** (26.9)	**French** (29.6)	*English* (24.0)	English (22.1)	**Canadian** (25.0)	**English** (25.6)	*Canadian* (24.3)	**Canadian** (26.8)	*Canadian* (19.6)	English (6.9)
3.	*Irish* (19.7)	**English** (28.7)	**English** (28.1)	*English* (23)	Irish (4.1)	*Scottish* (16.3)	*German* (18.2)	*English* (24.5)	German (19.6)	*Scottish* (15.0)	*NA Indian* (21.9)	*English* (16.6)	Scottish (5.5)
4.	Scottish	Irish	*Irish*	Irish	Italian	*Irish*	Scottish	*Scottish*	Scottish	Irish	*Irish*	Scottish	Canadian
5.	French	*French*	*French*	Scottish	English	French	Ukrainian	*Irish*	Irish	German	German	Irish	Irish
6.	NA Indian	German	German	German	Scottish	German	Irish	Ukrainian	French	Chinese	French	Inuit	French
7.	Inuit	Dutch	Dutch	Acadian	NA Indian	Italian	French	French	Ukrainian	French	Ukrainian	French	German
8.	German	Acadian	NA Indian	NA Indian	Québécois	Chinese	NA Indian	NA Indian	Dutch	E. Indian	Norwegian	German	NA Indian
9.	Métis	NA Indian	Welsh	Dutch	German	Dutch	Polish	Norwegian	NA Indian	Dutch	Norwegian	Métis	British
10.	Welsh	Welsh	Italian	Welsh	Jewish	E. Indian	Métis	Polish	Polish	Ukrainian	Dutch	Ukrainian	Ukrainian

*The first three ethnic categories for Canada and each province and territory include the percentage of population claiming each ethnic background (on the part of both parents, single origin—or just one parent, multiple origin).

Categories with more than 25 percent of the population appear in bold, while those with 15 to 25 percent appear in *italics*.

It is important to note that an individual with Scottish and Ukrainian background, for example, would be counted twice. The sum of the percentages therefore would be substantially more than 100.

Source: Calculations by L.M. Gerber from Statistics Canada, Census 2001, catalogue no. 97F0010XCB2001042.

---

dented numbers over the last decade. These inflows have completely transformed our socio-cultural landscape.

Table 14–1 shows the composition of Canada by ethnic origin for the 25 categories that are most represented in Canada, based on responses to census questions about ethnic origin. The category Total Responses includes people who have the same ancestry on both maternal and paternal sides (i.e., a single origin), as well as those who report mixed heritage (that is, multiple origins). Further columns report separate figures for people with a single origin and those with multiple origins. As a result of changes in the structure and wording of the census question on ethnic background, in 1996, we see a dramatic increase in the number of people claiming "Canadian" ancestry (see the note to Table 14–1). The proportion of the population claiming Canadian ethnicity or heritage increased from 3 percent in 1991 to 31 percent in 1996 to 39 percent in 2001—up 36 percentage points over the decade. What do you make of the fact that, while "Canadian" identification was increasing, 5.1 million fewer people declared themselves to be single-origin French? (You will get an answer when we turn our attention to the ethnic composition of the provinces and territories.)

Not surprisingly, considering their early settlement of this country, the largest ethnic categories in Canada (after those reporting Canadian ancestry) are English and French. Some 4.2, 3.8, and 2.7 million people are at least partly of Scottish, Irish, and German origin, respectively. People with Aboriginal, Italian, Chinese, or Ukrainian roots number more than 1 million each. Other ethnic categories among the top 25 drop off quickly in size—down to roughly 212 000 people of Jamaican origin. The results portray Canada as a country dominated by the British (mainly the English) and the French, but otherwise of remarkable diversity.

Comparing the numbers of people in each ethnic category reveals the extent of integration and intermarriage in Canada. While 1.5 million people claim English ancestry on both sides, more than three times that number (4.5 million) have some English ancestry. Among Canadians of German origin, three-quarters are of multiple origin; among those of Swedish origin, the figure is 89 percent. The majority of Aboriginal peoples (59%) have multiple origins as well. The newer immigrants, many of whom are visible minorities (Filipino, South Asian, or Jamaican), tend to have much lower proportions claiming multiple origins; however, these proportions are likely to increase over the next few decades. (Note that the choice of "Canadian" ancestry is also an indicator of cultural integration as people of many ethnic origins—including English for that matter—blend, economically and socially, at all levels of society.)

Table 14–2 shows the top 10 ethnic origins in the provinces and territories, revealing that ethnic and racial composition vary substantially from one part of the country to another. The proportion claiming "Canadian" background (either single- or multiple-origin) varies from 5 percent in Nunavut to 69 percent in Quebec. The frequency of the "Canadian" designation in the 2001 census makes it difficult to observe the traditional predominance of the British categories in the Maritimes or the European heritage of the western provinces. Another dramatic change is in the level of "French" identity in Quebec. In 1991, 75 percent of the Quebec population declared itself to be single-origin French. In 1996, only 41 percent declared either full or partial French ancestry and, by 2001, the level had dropped to 30 percent.

TABLE 14–3

Education, Employment, and Income among Selected Ethnic and Racial Categories, 2001

	English	French	Chinese	Japanese	Black	Aboriginal
Percentage with less than secondary school diploma*	34.9	30.6	30.2	18.4	28.2	48.0
Percentage with university degree*	12.4	16.2	27.3	27.8	12.7	4.4
Percentage employed*	52.2	57.7	54.3	56.5	62.4	49.7
Percentage employed full time all year*	33.5	35.5	31.6	31.4	34.3	25.6
Average employment income ($)**	47 698	43 012	40 817	54 739	35 103	35 435
Median income ($)	23 964	23 212	16 371	23 445	18 702	15 235

* Education and employment levels are calculated on the basis of population over 15 years of age.
** Average employment income, as calculated here, applies to workers employed full time, all year.

Source: Calculations by L.M. Gerber based on Statistics Canada, Census 2001, Catalogue numbers 97F0010XCB2001041, 97F0010XCB2001045, 97F0011XCB2001043, 97F0010XCB2001042, 97F0010XCB2001046, 97F0011XCB2001044, 97F0010XCB2001043, 97F0011XCB2001047, and 97F0011XCB2001055.

Recall that the first change, from 1991 to 1996, was a result of the suggestion that "Canadian" could be one of the write-in categories. The proportion of Quebecers identifying themselves as Canadian soared to 47 percent in 1996—the largest of any province or territory—and to 69 percent by 2001. Others who formerly identified themselves as "French" seem to have redefined themselves as "Québécois." From a national unity perspective, this should be something to celebrate. Right? But francophones fill out the *French* version of the census—where they indicate *Canadien* identity. The *habitant* of New France assumed the *Canadien* label long before the arrival of the British. Preliminary analysis of 2004 federal election results (by L.M. Gerber) reveals that in the electoral districts of Quebec, as percentage Canadien increases, so too does the percentage voting Bloc Québécois. Since areas that support the Bloc also vote Yes on sovereignty, one can safely assume that Canadian and *Canadien* are not synonymous. As francophones trade in "French" or "Québécois" for "*Canadien*" identity, they are not declaring solidarity with anglophones or those in other provinces who call themselves "Canadian."

Aboriginal peoples collectively appear among the top 10 ethnic categories in every province and territory. But they constitute the largest ethnic group only in Nunavut, where Inuit rank first (85%), and the Northwest Territories, where North American Indians rank first (36%) and Inuit sixth (11%). The Chinese rank eighth in Canada but appear among the top 10 only in Ontario and British Columbia. Despite the dramatic shift to "Canadian" identity across the country, diversity and regional variation in backgrounds are still apparent.

Canada's census in 1996 and 2001 attempted to measure the status of visible minorities status (as distinct from ethnicity or Aboriginal origins) to assess compliance with employment equity legislation. Respondents were asked to identify themselves as White, Chinese, South Asian, Black, Arab/West Asian, Filipino, Southeast Asian, Latin American, Japanese, Korean, or "Other." Black appeared as a choice among ethnic categories in the 1991 census, but now

is part of a more direct question aimed at identifying populations of visible minorities. See the Applying Sociology box (on p. 366) for further analysis.

SOCIAL STANDING

A great deal has been written about ethnic and racial inequality in Canada and its causes (Porter, 1965; Ramcharan, 1982; Gerber, 1983, 1990, 1996; Driedger, 1989; McAll, 1990; Wotherspoon and Satzewich, 1993; Frideres and Gadacz, 2001; Li, 2003; Frideres, 2005). The general consensus seems to be that the workings of our capitalist economy, along with racism, prejudice, and discrimination, contribute to socioeconomic inequality, with recent immigrants and visible minorities at the bottom of the scale. For a number of reasons, including a system of internal colonialism, Aboriginal peoples are the most severely disadvantaged in this regard.

Table 14–3 compares selected ethnic categories—English, French, Chinese, Japanese, Black, and Aboriginal—on a number of socioeconomic dimensions. Japanese Canadians have the lowest proportion without secondary school diplomas as well as the largest proportion with university degrees. Thus, they are the most highly educated of the categories. The Chinese are closer to the English and French in terms of high school graduation, but have a much higher proportion with university degrees. With a level of university attainment identical to that of the Japanese, the Chinese are the second best educated of the categories. Black Canadians are more likely to have completed secondary school than all categories except the Japanese and as likely to have university degrees as the English. This places them ahead of the English—but not the French—on educational attainment. At the other extreme, Aboriginal people are least likely to have earned secondary school diplomas as well as university degrees.

Turning to employment patterns, one notes that Blacks have the highest overall employment levels of all categories—and that they are as likely to be employed full time as any other category. The French and the Japanese are more likely to be employed than the English and the Chinese, while the

APPLYING SOCIOLOGY
Visible Minorities: Toronto, Vancouver, and Montreal

The 2001 census reveals that 4.0 million people (13.4% of Canada's population) identify themselves as members of visible minorities.[1] While the majority of these individuals are immigrants, increasing proportions are Canadian-born. Three census metropolitan areas (CMAs), namely Toronto, Vancouver, and Montreal, have attracted more than three-quarters of Canada's visible minority population. The mix of visible minorities is different in each city. Toronto is the most diverse: the 37 percent of the CMAs population comprised of visible minorities is 9 percent Chinese, 10 percent South Asian, and 7 percent Black. Vancouver's visible minority population (37% of the total) is almost entirely Asian, half of it Chinese. Montreal, with the smallest visible minority component (14%) is 4 percent Black and 10 percent mixed Asian.

The tendency of particular minorities to settle in specific neighbourhoods, where relatives or friends have already located, results in different concentrations in various parts of each CMA. Prior to the amalgamation of several municipalities into a larger Toronto (i.e., at the time of the 1991 census), Scarborough had the largest visible minority population (at 52%) in the country.[2] By 2001, with Scarborough no longer in existence, Burnaby (part of the Vancouver CMA) and Markham (in the Toronto CMA) took over as the areas with the largest visible minority composition. Burnaby, with a population that is 49 percent visible minority, is close to 40 percent Asian. Similarly, Markham (at 56% visible minority) is at least 45 percent Asian and 4 percent Black. Montreal Nord (24% visible minority) is 15 percent Black.

Toronto is the diversity capital of Canada with 37 percent of the country's population of visible minorities.

The fact that about 80 percent of Canada's immigrants in recent years have come from Asia, the Middle East, Africa, and the Caribbean has changed our understanding of the term "immigrant" (Li, 2003:44–45). While formally the term refers to anyone who came to Canada from another country, the "folk version" now tends to refer to people who appear foreign-looking—or those of different racial backgrounds. Even if they are born in Canada, members of visible minorities are likely to be labelled immigrants—and assumed to be the cause of urban problems. This social construction of "immigrants" as non-White and the source of problems is most likely to occur in Canada's major cities that are magnets to our more recent immigrants.

[1] Note that the statistics for visible minorities do not include Aboriginal peoples, whose inclusion would change the overall picture substantially. "Visible minorities" included in these figures are Black, South Asian, Filipino, Arab and West Asian, Latin American people, and Pacific Islanders.

[2] The five Scarborough electoral districts range from 43 to 85 percent visible minority. Scarborough Rouge River is the riding with the largest immigrant and visible minority components in Canada: at 67 and 85 percent, respectively (L.M. Gerber, 2006).

WHAT DO YOU THINK?

1. Have you had the experience of visiting—or living in—Toronto, Montreal, or Vancouver? How does the ethnic or racial diversity in those cities affect the lives of their residents?

2. When you think of "immigrants," who come to mind? Are people of German or Hungarian background included in your definition?

3. Under what circumstances might new immigrants move to smaller cities?

Sources: Chard and Renaud (2000), Li (2003), and calculations by L.M. Gerber based on Statistics Canada, Census 2001, catalogue no. 97F0010XCB2001004.

French and English are slightly more likely to be employed full time all year. Whereas Black Canadians are high on employment, including full-time employment, Aboriginal people are least likely to be employed, especially in full-time work. Looking at education and employment together, one can conclude that Blacks hold their own on education and excel in employment levels; Aboriginal people lag in terms of both educational attainment and employment levels.

In Canada, one would expect educational attainment and work force involvement to result in higher income. Not surprisingly, then, the Japanese—who excel on both measures of educational attainment—have the highest average incomes for full-time employment ($7041 more than the English, who come second). The French and Chinese are ranked third and fourth in terms of income earned for full-time employment, while Black and Aboriginal people lag far behind. In fact, Aboriginal people, who have the lowest levels of education by both measures in Table 14–3, have a slightly higher average income than Black people. In other words, for the Chinese and Blacks, educational attainment has not resulted in higher income for full-time work.

Median income—which is based on total income from all sources—provides further insight into economic well-being. The English, Japanese, and French respectively have the highest median incomes, while the Blacks come next. Chinese and Aboriginal individuals have the lowest median incomes. Explaining these income levels is not easy, but racism and discrimination play a part. Many immigrants enter the Canadian labour market at a lower entrance status than they occupied in their countries of origin (Ujimoto, 1979; Reitz, 1980; Li, 2003), and, like the Chinese, are not rewarded for high educational attainment. Aboriginal people face numerous barriers—in achieving higher education, in securing employment, and in earning decent incomes. To the extent that there is socioeconomic stratification in Canada based on race and ethnicity (Li, 1988; McAll, 1990), Aboriginal people are particularly disadvantaged (Gerber, 1990; Frideres and Gadacz, 2001).

SPECIAL STATUS SOCIETIES

On historical grounds, one might argue that people of British ancestry have special status within Canada. We have a British parliamentary system, the majority of Canadians speak English, and the dominant culture is Anglo-Saxon. In the past, admission to Canada itself, to the economic elite, and to the most exclusive clubs was controlled, for the most part, by Canadians of British descent. It could also be argued that the policy of multiculturalism gives special status to all of the ethnic and cultural minorities that contribute to the Canadian mosaic. Nonetheless, two categories stand out because they have unique relationships with the federal government and other Canadians: Aboriginal peoples and Québécois.

Aboriginal Peoples

"Aboriginal peoples" refers collectively to fifty-five or more sovereign peoples who occupied the North American continent before the arrival of European explorers and settlers. Aboriginal peoples include status Indians (or First Nations including the Cree, Ojibwa, Micmac, Blackfoot, Six Nations, and Haida), non-status Indians, Métis, and Inuit. (The census classifies status, or First Nation, and non-status Indians as North American Indian.) The Métis are a socio-cultural category of biracial descent—usually French and

Indian. The Inuit include the western Arctic Inuvialuit as well as three eastern Arctic Inuit cultures.

Registered or status Indians are registered with Indian and Northern Affairs Canada, which has responsibility for them under the *Indian Act*. In addition, there are many people who are biologically and culturally Indian but are not legally so, because their ancestors, for whatever reasons, did not enter into agreements with the Crown; they are referred to as non-status or non-registered Indians (Frideres and Gadacz, 2001: 24-31). Many individuals lost or gave up Indian status by acquiring a university education (in the early 1900s), in order to vote (prior to 1960, when Status Indians were granted the franchise), or by marriage (when a woman with Indian status married a man without). In 1985, Bill C-31 allowed people who had lost Indian status to reclaim it. More than 100 000 people, most of them women who had lost Treaty status by marrying out, took advantage of this opportunity.

The 2001 census identifies more than 976 000 individuals who claim Aboriginal ancestry: among them are 45 000 Inuit, 292 000 Métis, and 609 000 North American Indians (Treaty and non-Treaty). Since not all people acknowledge or are aware of their Aboriginal ancestors, these figures probably underestimate the number of people with Aboriginal ancestry. It is likely that more than 1.5 million Canadians have Aboriginal roots (Frideres, 1998:27).[1]

Registered Indians who live on reserves or settlements are the special responsibility of the Indian and Northern Affairs Canada. Their relationship with Ottawa over the years has been characterized as paternalistic and bureaucratic. For example, until the 1980s, children were often removed from their reserves and taken to boarding schools where they were punished for "talking Indian" among themselves, forced to speak English, and taught that their own languages and cultures were of no value. Removed from their homes and communities for ten months of the year and deprived of parent/child relationships, these children were not prepared to live effectively in either the Aboriginal or non-Aboriginal worlds. Christianity was imposed on communities and on children in boarding schools, and education beyond the level required for farming or raising livestock was discouraged. The effect of these measures was an erosion of the social, economic, and cultural fabric of community life. In January 1998, the federal government took the long overdue step of formally apologizing for the residential school experiences of Aboriginal youth, which often included physical and sexual

---

[1]A note about terminology: many of you are aware that use of the term "Indian" may be offensive to Aboriginal people. "Native," "Aboriginal," and "Indigenous" are useful collective terms—except when you need to differentiate among Indian, Métis, and Inuit. The term "First Nation" applies only to those who are status or registered Indians under the *Indian Act*. Likewise, the Assembly of First Nations includes only the chiefs of status-Indian communities. Non-registered Indians are not represented by the assembly or the responsibility of Indian and Northern Affairs Canada.

Canada's Aboriginal peoples have long been seeking self-determination—a struggle that has been more prominent in the media in recent years. Here protestors between Six Nations and Caledonia (southwest of Hamilton, Ontario) are trying to prevent the building of a subdivision on lands that Six Nations says it has never relinquished. Six Nations leaders and the government are negotiating a resolution to the conflict.

abuse. It would be 2005 before Ottawa announced $2 billion in compensation for individuals who had attended residential schools. An initial sum of $10 000 plus an additional $3000 per year will be paid to approximately 86 000 eligible people (CBC, 2005b). (For more on residential schools, see the Thinking about Diversity box on pp. 534–35 in Chapter 20.)

Because non-status Indians, the Métis, and the Inuit did not have reserves, they have escaped some of the negative effects of reserve life. Living in Canada's Arctic, the Inuit have not felt the same population pressures as Aboriginal peoples in the rest of the country. However, they have experienced the same gradual erosion of traditional patterns of life. Oil, gas, and uranium companies have degraded the fragile northern environment and reduced the game supply. Inuit families have moved into permanent settlements, both for employment and to meet the legal requirement of school attendance for their children. Consequently, extended families no longer establish year-round camps in traditional hunting grounds or teach their children the old survival skills that used to foster a sense of self-worth.

It is important to realize that there is a great deal of diversity among Aboriginal communities (Gerber, 1979), where individuals, communities, and organizations have made real strides in dealing with the problems they face. Where government policy once was based on the assumption that the "Indian problem" would solve itself through urban migration and assimilation, it is now recognized that communities on reserves and elsewhere are not only surviving but growing (Gerber, 1984). In addition, such high-profile Aboriginal leaders such as Ovid Mercredi, Matthew Coon Come, Phil Fontaine, Roberta Jamieson, and Paul Okalik have been effective in articulating their demands and thereby have gained public support for greater self-determination. (The Thinking about Diversity box on pp. 442–43 in

 For information about Aboriginal communities and national Aboriginal organizations in Canada, visit the Aboriginal Portal at www.aboriginalcanada.gc.ca/acp/site.nsf/en/index.html.

Chapter 17 looks at the issue of Aboriginal self-government.) National organizations such as the Assembly of First Nations, Inuit Tapiriit Kanatami, Native Council of Canada (now the Congress of Aboriginal Peoples), and Métis National Council were instrumental in negotiating recognition of the inherent right to self-government in the Charlottetown Accord—which was rejected in the 1992 federal referendum.

One dramatic result of the Aboriginal quest for self-government was the creation in 1999 of a new territory, Nunavut, which was carved out of the Northwest Territories. The new territorial government is controlled by the Inuit majority, with support from an established system of co-operatives and the Inuit Broadcasting Corporation. Political and administrative positions are bringing new employment prospects, potentially stimulating greater educational achievement and enhancing pride. Returning control of Inuit communities to Inuit hands will not alleviate

 Read more about Nunavut at www.gov.nu.ca/Nunavut.

problems overnight; the hope on the part of Inuit leaders, however, is that it will be one meaningful step towards dealing with a wide range of serious social problems. The Media Perspectives box (on p. 369) introduces you to the Aboriginal Peoples Television Network, which is available to all Canadians with cable or satellite service. It has tremendous potential to empower the Aboriginal community by providing it with the ability to communicate effectively with its members, wherever they live in Canada.

The Québécois: From New France to the Quiet Revolution and Beyond

The French presence in what is now Canada goes back to 1608, when the first permanent settlement in New France was established at Quebec City by Samuel de Champlain with twenty-eight settlers—eight of whom survived the first winter. France claimed a vast territory that extended west of

MEDIA PERSPECTIVES
The Aboriginal Peoples Television Network

Aboriginal peoples of Canada have something that has no parallel anywhere else in the world. They have their own television channel—the Aboriginal Peoples Television Network—that reaches every Canadian home with satellite or cable access. Importantly, the APTN does not have to rely on government grants or advertising for its survival: because of "mandatory carriage," it receives $0.25 per month from the satellite and cable fees of all Canadian subscribers. Thus, you and I enhance the network's independence (or autonomy) by subsidizing the APTN.

Karen Richards (2006), a University of Guelph graduate student, carried out an extensive study of the APTN—including its history, mandate, policies, and programming—framed by a postmodern orientation and analysis of empowerment. She also travelled to the APTN headquarters in Winnipeg to conduct semi-structured interviews with twenty-four staff members. These interviews were recorded on tape and then transcribed to print in a laborious, time-consuming process. The next stage involved content analysis in which Richards essentially counted the number of times certain concepts came up in the interviews. Then she recorded APTN broadcasts to get a sample of its programs through the week in all time slots—and did further content analysis based on the programming.

The staff at the APTN, Richards found, is very enthusiastic and feels empowered. Here are Aboriginal people making decisions about the content of newscasts and *Contact* (which deals with current issues)—or about coverage of the Ipperwash inquiry, elections, and the land dispute by Six Nations at Caledonia. Documentaries, children's shows, movies, and plays are all vetted and aired on a schedule determined by the staff. While most programs are in English, others in French and Aboriginal languages are also included (about 5 percent of census participants who identify themselves as Aboriginal speak Aboriginal languages at home). The staff at the APTN is largely Aboriginal, the few exceptions being experts with

Aboriginal Peoples Television Network

broadcasting experience brought in to mentor and train Aboriginal people to replace them.

One can make the argument that the APTN empowers both its staff and the Aboriginal community as a whole. There are hundreds of Aboriginal communities in Canada and about a million people in total who acknowledge some Aboriginal heritage. Among the latter, only 20 percent live on reserve. Others live in non-reserve, Métis, or Inuit settlements or in Canada's towns, cities, and metropolitan areas with the rest of us. In other words, the Aboriginal population is anything but homogeneous. Tremendous cultural diversity—stemming from fifty or more distinct linguistic and cultural heritages—and rural, small town, and urban residence mean that Aboriginal people differ among themselves just as other Canadians do. The power of broadcasting allows the APTN, potentially, to communicate with all of the Aboriginal individuals and communities in Canada. It also allows the APTN to change the way Aboriginal peoples are portrayed by the broadcasting medium as a whole. The APTN website (www.aptn.ca) encourages Aboriginal peoples and Canadians in general to respond to and comment on programs or issues of concern, so communication goes both ways.

Think, for a moment, about our discussion of media theorist, Marshal McLuhan in Chapter 1 ("The Sociological Perspective")—and try to imagine the impact of instant electronic communication—in this case APTN broadcasting—on the diverse and scattered Aboriginal population in Canada. McLuhan taught us that "the instantaneous world of electronic information media involves all of us, all at once" in a "global village" or "instantaneous happening." (See Chapter 1 "The Sociological Perspective.") This instant awareness explodes local boundaries,

which cease to exist, making each of us part of the global village. At the same time, the world implodes or collapses in on us as instantaneous communication comes at us from everywhere. Explosion and implosion occur simultaneously. Can you see how the APTN might explode the local boundaries that separate Cree, Ojibwa, Haida, Inuit, and Métis peoples? Being part of every other Aboriginal person's business draws people into a mini-global village as the larger pan-Aboriginal world collapses in on them. The transformation that McLuhan describes so graphically does not require every Aboriginal person to watch APTN; after all, the internet and the information age shape your grandmother's world—even if she herself knows nothing about computers.

On June 5, 2006, the APTN *National News* reported that former Prime Minister Paul Martin tabled a private member's bill in the House of Commons—in an attempt to get some of the elements of the Kelowna Accord onto the new Conservative government's agenda; Martin had negotiated the accord with Aboriginal leaders before his government was defeated. The newscast that evening also covered developments in the Six Nations land dispute near Caledonia. Neither of those stories made it onto the CBC *National* that night. Without the APTN, Aboriginal peoples would have been deprived of news that is vital to their interests. With the APTN, Aboriginal peoples are empowered by access to information. As Sir Francis Bacon once said, "Knowledge is power."

WHAT DO YOU THINK?

1. Have you ever watched anything on the Aboriginal Peoples Television Network?
2. How do you think the existence of APTN affects the lives of Aboriginal individuals?
3. How do you feel about the fact that your cable fees support APTN?

Source: Inspired by Richards (2006).

the Thirteen Colonies and down to Louisiana, encompassing most of southern Ontario and the Great Lakes region. But New France grew slowly because of a lack of interest on the part of France in supporting the tiny settlement or in sending more settlers to the area. The population grew from 8 in 1609 to just over 3000 in 1663—spread among Quebec City, Trois-Rivières, and Montreal—mainly because of an "extraordinary rate of child bearing" (Beaujot and McQuillan, 1982:4). Two centuries later, at the time of confederation, the French formed 31 percent of Canada's population of 3.5 million people. As a result of the size of the French population and its concentration in Quebec, the *British North America Act, 1867,* recognized the province's civil law tradition, Catholic schools, and language. Confederation was based on bilingualism and assumed that anglophone and francophone communities would coexist. English and French were to be the legislative and judicial languages in federal and Quebec institutions. Bilingualism was later strengthened and expanded by the *Official Languages Act, 1969,* which declared the equality of the two languages in Parliament and in the Canadian public service.

At confederation in 1867, Quebec encompassed a traditional society based on the seigneurial system of land tenure, in which *habitants* (tenant farmers) worked the lands of the *seigneurs* (landowners). In the political vacuum left by an ineffective provincial government, the Catholic Church took on itself the task of administering many aspects of Quebec society, including education, health care, and social welfare. The Catholic Church, which long dominated Quebec's major institutions, resisted change:

> Uninterested in questioning the established authorities and the excesses of industrialization, and wary of new ideas, the Quebec church was more concerned with maintaining its privileged position than with helping Quebecers enter the twentieth century. It extolled the virtues of rural life, cautioned against the evils of the city and the dangers of education, and preached the need to accept one's lot in life. (Latouche, 1988:1801)

Up to the 1980s, a British economic and industrial elite based in Montreal dominated the provincial economy. A clear linguistic class structure had developed with the unilingual English at the top, the unilingual French at the bottom, and bilingual people in the middle in supervisory positions. The unilingual French had few opportunities to better their social or financial standing, and even French-origin bilingual people could rise only so far. Individuals who moved to the cities to seek employment found that a linguistic ceiling restricted upward mobility.

Quebec's Quiet Revolution of the 1960s greatly diminished the political power and social influence of the Catholic Church, and began to challenge the economic domination of the British elites. Newly elected premier Jean Lesage chose to expand the role of the state in the economic, social, and cultural life of the province. The Lesage government established a department of education, encouraging the study of engineering, maths, sciences, and business especially by Catholics; nationalized Hydro-Québec to attract industry with the promise of cheap electricity; and took over the administration of Quebec's pension funds. These and other changes served to integrate Quebec into the North American economic structure (Coleman, 1984). Quebec was characterized by a rapidly growing working class, a declining birth rate—eliminating "the revenge of the cradle" as a tool for maintaining or improving the linguistic balance in Canada, and a decline in the influence of the Church.

French-Canadian society was becoming more like the rest of North America—urban, secular, and industrialized. As a result, language became the primary defining characteristic of Québécois society, and francophone Quebecers became even more aware of the relative numbers of French- and English-speaking people. They also realized that the continued existence of the small francophone minorities outside Quebec was threatened by assimilation. Reaching the conclusion that French language and culture could be protected only in the province of Quebec, many rejected their Canadian or French-Canadian identities and began to think of themselves as Québécois only. The desire to protect their distinct language and culture led them to seek institutional dominance in Quebec, and this in turn had profound implications for federal/provincial relations.

THE GROWING DEMAND FOR SOVEREIGNTY

The logical extension of a demand for institutional control was the demand for sovereignty. The late 1960s and 1970s saw an increase in Québécois nationalism and in support for the separatist movement. The sentiments that gave rise to the radical terrorist group Front de libération du Québec (FLQ) became more widespread and eventually paved the way for the 1976 election of the separatist Parti Québécois, led by René Lévesque. One of the first acts of this new government was to introduce Bill 101, making French the only official language of Quebec, including business and education. Francophones were no longer excluded from the economic elite. In addition, the children of immigrants from other countries or other provinces would be educated in French and assimilated into francophone culture (and eventually integrated into Québécois society.

In response to the election of a separatist government and the language laws, many anglophones and businesses, both large and small, left the province. From 1976 to 1981, Quebec's net loss through interprovincial migration was 156 000 people, double that of the previous five-year period.

 See CBC coverage of René Lévesque at http://archives. cbc.ca/300c.asp?id=1-73-870.

In a 1980 referendum on Quebec's "sovereignty association" with Canada, 60 percent of Quebecers voted No. The debate leading up the referendum was often divisive, especially in the city of Montreal. There, as elsewhere in the province, the referendum revealed a general pattern of increased support for sovereignty the further east one moved from Ontario (Gerber, 1992).

In 1982, under the Liberal government of Pierre Trudeau, Canada patriated its constitution and incorporated the Canadian Charter of Rights and Freedoms. The provincial government of Quebec did not agree to the conditions of patriation and did not sign the constitution at that point. Brian Mulroney and the Progressive Conservative party won the 1984 federal election with massive support in Quebec, in part because they promised amendments that would overcome Quebec's objections to the constitution.

For complex political reasons, the Meech Lake Accord of 1987, which included recognition of Quebec as a "distinct society," was not ratified by all the provincial legislatures (specifically Manitoba and Newfoundland) before its 1990 deadline. Among the reasons for public disenchantment with Meech was Quebec's 1988 sign law, which banned English from outdoor signs altogether. Anglophone Canadians perceived the sign law as a slap in the face. In turn, Quebecers saw the failure of the Meech Lake Accord as a symbol of rejection by English Canada. Such symbols, as Breton (1992) points out, can have a powerful political impact. Among other things, the failure of Meech spawned the separatist Bloc Québécois, a political party working at the federal level to promote the cause of separation.

The failure of Meech was followed by the rejection of the Charlottetown Accord by Canadians (including 55% of Quebecers) in the referendum of October 26, 1992. Support for the separatist Bloc Québécois and Parti Québécois grew, at least in part because of the repeated failures in constitutional accommodation as well as the economic pain associated with a prolonged recession. The success of the two separatist parties clearly reveals that the politics surrounding the quest for special status and related powers continues to have potentially explosive consequences for Canada. On October 30, 1995, Canadians were stunned by the razor-thin victory for the No

 The speech in which Brian Mulroney announced the Meech Lake accord to Parliament is available in text and audio form at www.nlc-bnc.ca/prime ministers/h4-4022-e.html.

side in Quebec's most recent referendum on sovereignty: 50.6 percent of Quebecers voted No and 49.4 percent voted Yes. Quebecers came dangerously close to giving its leaders the go-ahead to negotiate separation, which would have had incalculable costs for the country as a whole. The 1995 referendum alarm wakened federalist forces in Ottawa and Quebec City, reactivated the unity agenda, and again raised the question of what can be done to keep Canada whole (see the Thinking It Through box on p. 374). The Quebec election of 2003 produced a Liberal government under Jean Charest. Unlike his Parti Québécois predecessors, Charest reduced interprovincial tensions because of his willingness to work with the other premiers in a Canadian framework. After the Conservative unexpectedly won ten Quebec seats in the 2006 federal election, Prime Minister Harper made working with Premier Charest one of his top priorities.

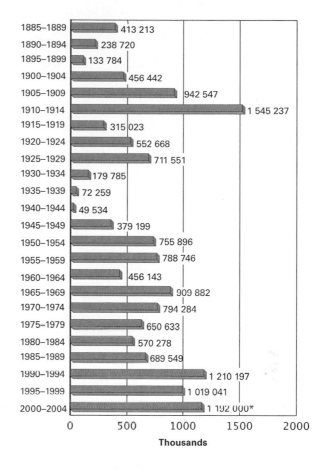

FIGURE 14-2   Immigration to Canada, 1885–1999

*Data for 2000–2004 are estimated.

Source: Created by L.M. Gerber based on statistics in Knowles (1997:206) and on Statistics Canada, Census 2001 Census 2001, catalogue no. 95F0358XCB2001004.

IMMIGRATION TO CANADA: A HUNDRED-YEAR PERSPECTIVE

Canada has been—and will remain—a land of immigrants. The ten-year period from 1905 to 1914 saw the arrival of 2.5 million people, making it the peak decade for Canadian immigration. (See Figure 14–2, which details our immigration history from 1885 to 1999.) At the height of immigration to Canada, in 1913, 1 in every 17 people was a newcomer—not just an immigrant, but someone who had arrived within the past year. In contrast, we now admit about 225 000 immigrants per year into a population of more than 31 million: 1 in every 140 people today is a newly arrived immigrant of the current year. Knowing the numbers of immigrants absorbed by the tiny Canadian population of the early 1900s should give us encouragement regarding Canada's ability to absorb the numbers arriving in recent years. Immigration increased from 1990–94 to 1995–99 and 2000–04—with more than a million individuals arriving in each of these periods.

Race and ethnicity retain their significance in part because of the continuous flow of immigrants into our

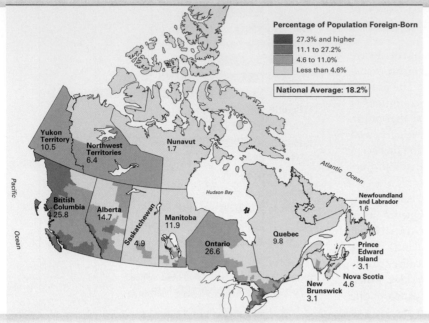

SEEING OURSELVES

CANADA MAP 14-1

Percentage of Population Foreign-Born for Canada, the Provinces, Territories, and Census Subdivision, 2001

Source: Calculations by L.M. Gerber based on the Statistics Canada Website http://statcan.ca/english/Pgdb/demo46a.htm.

Map labels:
Percentage of Population Foreign-Born
27.3% and higher
11.1 to 27.2%
4.6 to 11.0%
Less than 4.6%

National Average: 18.2%

Yukon Territory 10.5 · Northwest Territories 6.4 · Nunavut 1.7 · British Columbia 25.8 · Alberta 14.7 · Saskatchewan 4.9 · Manitoba 11.9 · Ontario 26.6 · Quebec 9.8 · Newfoundland and Labrador 1.6 · Prince Edward Island 3.1 · Nova Scotia 4.6 · New Brunswick 3.1 · Atlantic Ocean · Hudson Bay · Pacific Ocean

An advertising campaign to attract immigrants to western Canada is profiled at www.civilization.ca/hist/advertis/adindexe.html.

country. The first wave of immigration after confederation was driven by the desire to populate western Canada and to provide workers for the growing economy. This trend was encouraged by the controversial policies of Clifford Sifton, minister of the interior at about the turn of the twentieth century (Hiller, 2000).

During the Sifton years, Canada was still trying to promote immigration from Britain—in part out of political necessity. English Canadians assumed that the government would do everything it could to retain the British character of the country (Knowles, 1997). By setting up an immigration office in London, England, Sifton was able to increase the flow from Britain to the point where, by 1905, about a third of our immigrants came from there. But because Sifton was primarily interested in attracting good farmers to populate western Canada, he also started a trickle of Ukrainian immigration that would peak in 1913, when 22 363 individuals arrived from that country. These Ukrainians, along with a trickle of Doukhobors, Finns, Germans, and Scandinavians, were seen by many politicians and ordinary Canadians as ignorant, unassimilable aliens who would do irreparable damage to Canada (Knowles, 1997).

In the early 1900s, policy severely restricted immigration to Canada to White people of Anglo-Saxon origin. Southern and eastern Europeans, as well as Chinese, Japanese, and African American peoples, were discouraged from entering; for example, the *Chinese Immigration Act, 1923*, barred all but a select few Chinese from entering Canada. Despite these efforts, immigration soared—in part because politicians and businessmen believed that economic prosperity depended on continued population

growth. Immigration fell during World War I (1914–18), the Great Depression (1929–39), and World War II (1939–45). During a short boom in the 1920s, immigrants from Britain and Europe were admitted along with some Jews and Russian Mennonites. By 1931, however, Canada was to close her doors to refugees—especially Jewish refugees, in part because of widespread anti-Semitism.

After World War II there was mounting pressure to open the doors once again and accept large numbers of refugees. Once again, "old" Commonwealth countries and the United States were the initial source of regular immigrants (i.e., not refugees) needed to meet labour needs, settle unpopulated areas, and expand the internal market for goods. But by the 1950s, Germany, Italy, and the Netherlands had become important sources of immigrants, and immigration laws had been liberalized to allow more Asians, as well as Palestinian and Hungarian refugees. Further liberalization would occur under the Conservative government of John Diefenbaker, who foresaw a population of 40 million in the near future and argued that "Canada must populate or perish" (Knowles, 1997:146).

It was not until 1962 that Ellen Fairclough, Canada's first woman federal cabinet minister, put an end to our White Canada immigration policy. Education, and occupation and language skills replaced race or national origin as the criteria of admission. After the 1965 election, the Liberals formalized the selection criteria through what we call the *points system*, which allocates points to education, occupation, facility in English or French, age, and the demand for the applicant's skills in the Canadian labour market. The points system reduces reliance on the judgment of the individual immigration officer. More recently, Canada has experienced waves of immigration from the Caribbean and Asia

TABLE 14–4

Immigrant Population by Region of Birth, 1991–2001

Region	Number	Percentage
North, Central, and South America	167 440	9.1
Caribbean and Bermuda	84 005	4.6
Europe	357 845	19.5
Africa	139 770	7.6
Asia	1 066 230	58.2
Other	15 380	0.8
Total	1 830 670	100.0

Source: Adapted by L.M. Gerber from Statistics Canada, Census 2001, catalogue no. 95F0357XCB2001004.

TABLE 14–5

Top 10 Countries of Birth for Immigrants Arriving, 1991–2001

Country	Number	Percentage
China	197 360	10.8
India	156 120	8.5
Philippines	122 010	6.7
Hong Kong	118 385	6.5
Sri Lanka	62 590	3.4
Pakistan	57 990	3.2
Taiwan	53 755	2.9
United States	51 440	2.8
Iran	47 080	2.6
Poland	43 370	2.4
Other Countries	920 580	50.2
Total Immigrants	1 830 680	100.0

Source: Adapted by L.M. Gerber from Statistics Canada, Census 2001, catalogue no. 95F0357XCB2001004.

in the 1970s, from Central and South America in the 1980s, and from China and India in the 1990s. Hiller points out that "these repeated waves of immigration reinvigorated ethnic groups already resident in Canada, and reminded residents of their own ethnicity" (1991:173).

The *Immigration Act, 1976*, recognized three classes of people as eligible for landed immigrant status: *family class* (immediate family and dependent children, parents, and grandparents of Canadian citizens or landed immigrants), *humanitarian class* (refugees or persecuted and displaced persons), and *independent class* (those who apply as individuals and are admitted on the basis of the points system). These changes altered the countries of origin of the applicants, stimulated a greatly expanded flow of refugees, and increased applications by family members, who now outnumber independent applicants. In recent years, Canada has made a concerted effort to attract people who are experienced in business or who have significant amounts of money to invest.

The experience of Vietnamese refugees who came to Canada in the 1970s is explored through CBC archives at http://archives.cbc.ca/300c.asp?id=1-69-524.

Table 14–4 indicates the sources of immigrants to Canada from 1991 to 2001, by geographic region of birth. Asia is by far the major source region, sending us 58 percent of our immigrants, while Europe (the source of almost all immigration in the first half of the twentieth century) has dropped down to 19.5 percent. Table 14–5 reveals that China and India, which rank first and second, sent us almost 11 percent and 9 percent of our immigrants, respectively, between 1991 and 2001. During this period, 8 out of the top 10 birth countries for Canadian immigrants were Asian, including the Philippines, Hong Kong, Sri Lanka, Pakistan, Taiwan, and Iran. The only two non-Asian countries in the top 10 were the United States and Poland.

Most of the immigrants who have come to Canada in recent decades have gone to Ontario and British Columbia. As Canada Map 14–1 reveals, Alberta and Manitoba have also attracted immigrants, while the Atlantic provinces have not. Not surprisingly, the metropolitan areas of Toronto (44%) and Vancouver (38%) have the largest immigrant components; visible minorities made up about 37 percent of the populations of these two metropolitan areas. In Quebec, Montreal has attracted a significant immigrant component, whereas Quebec City has not. Recent immigration has clearly touched some parts of Canada more than others.

Race and Ethnicity: Looking Ahead

Immigration has contributed to the development of a country, which, though it started out Aboriginal, British, and French at confederation in 1867, is now quite rightly called multicultural. The characteristics of the newcomers have stimulated the continued, and often uneasy, awareness of race and ethnicity among Canadians. Their geographic distribution has contributed to regional diversity as people with different backgrounds found themselves concentrated in various parts of the country and in different cities, giving substance to the vision of Canada that former prime minister Joe Clark calls a "community of communities."

Canada is an experiment in multilayered pluralism—multilayered because the British, the French, the Aboriginal peoples, and other ethnic and racial minorities have different kinds of relationships with one another and with society as a whole. Each new wave of immigration adds to the complexity of the mosaic. Newly articulated demands and expectations on the part of the Québécois and the various Aboriginal peoples will contribute to the definition and redefinition of our unique country. Our survival as a country depends on our success in forging an identity out of diversity.

THINKING IT THROUGH
Distinct Societies and National Unity

Pluralism and diversity are so central to Canadian identity that they are enshrined in our constitution. The French language (official bilingualism and minority language rights), civil law (in Quebec), Catholic or denominational schooling, existing Aboriginal and Treaty rights, and the right to preserve and enhance our multicultural heritage are guaranteed by our constitution in the Canadian Charter of Rights and Freedoms (Canada, 1982). Freedom from the pressures of assimilation could be taken for granted in this country, yet some of us, anxious to ensure the viability of our own cultures, demand constitutional recognition as distinct societies.

The unwillingness or inability of Canadians throughout the country to respond positively to demands for such recognition by Quebec threatens the stability of our federation—as we learned so painfully on referendum day in October 1995, when the Québécois came within a hair's breadth of voting for sovereignty and separation. Because status as a distinct society is significant for both Quebec and Canada, the debate surrounding it receives a great deal of media attention. The concept or symbol of a "distinct society" could have explosive consequences (Breton, 1992). Applying the concept to Quebec, people elsewhere in Canada say, "But *of course* Quebec is a distinct society. It has its own language, legal system, political parties, and a vibrant French culture." Quebec leaders want to know why, if we accept Quebec's distinctiveness, we cannot agree to include that recognition in our constitution. The answer lies, in part, with the controversy surrounding the label itself.

Let's look at this concept. At one level, it implies that Quebec is *different*—and few would argue with that. (Aboriginal societies are different, too.) The controversy emerges with the argument that different or distinct implies *special* status. The notion that Quebec is not only different but perhaps *special* raises the issue of two classes of Canadians, one having special rights. It is this interpretation that raises the hackles of many Canadians and some provinces.

If we assume that the label "distinct society" is purely symbolic and merely implies the recognition of existing social and cultural differences, then putting it into the constitution would not have any significant effect. One way to restrict its potential impact on the constitution would be to define it carefully, so that the distinction implies no new powers, or no powers that substantially differentiate Quebec from the other provinces. However, to be acceptable to Quebec, "distinct society" must imply special powers, for it is through those that the Québécois hope to become "masters in their own house." To preserve and protect the small island of francophone culture, Quebec sovereigntists want unquestioned control over language (in business, education, social discourse, and government), immigration, employment, trade, natural resources, the economy, population policy and mobility, social services, and more. Since other provinces do not want all these powers, mainly because of funding concerns, granting them to Quebec would give that province special status.

Another aspect of Quebec's relationship with the rest of the country is threatening to other provinces. Many Québécois see confederation as joining together *two founding nations*, while other Canadians see it as joining *equal provinces*. Is Quebec now one of ten equal partners, or one of only two? Clearly, these are serious and potentially catastrophic clashes of vision.

In another attempt to circumvent the "distinct society" problem, Canada's premiers proposed constitutional recognition of Quebec's "unique characteristics" in the Calgary declaration of September 1997. Whatever words are used to describe different, special, or distinct status to imply enhanced autonomy, the impact is not neutral. The process itself is controversial and divisive and, even if we were able to deliver distinct society status, its implementation would generate its own strains.

The discussion is complicated by the less vocal but equally valid claim to status as distinct societies by Aboriginal peoples. The heated debate that erupts periodically around these powerful concepts is both inevitable and justifiable in the context of Canada's multidimensional pluralism.

Postscript In June 2003, the Liberals under Jean Charest defeated the Parti Québécois government of Bernard Landry in Quebec. This was highly significant for Canada because Jean Charest is willing to help the premiers of the other provinces make the country work better. Ever since the election of 1976, when René Lévesque led the separatist Parti Québécois to its first electoral victory, Quebec has been trying to enhance its sovereignty or increase its clout in Ottawa—even by threatening repeated referenda. When another Liberal, Robert Bourassa, was premier (1985–94), he could not play the role of a committed federalist but demanded further powers for Quebec and refused to work with the other premiers on shared problems. Jean Charest is determined to fix Quebec's economic problems by working within the existing Canadian framework. After its electoral breakthrough in Quebec in 2006, the new Conservative government under Stephen Harper set out to work with Charest on the fiscal imbalance and other federal/provincial irritants.

WHAT DO YOU THINK?

1. Francophones outside the province have been abandoned in Quebec's quest for greater autonomy and cultural protections. How might francophones in Ontario or Saskatchewan react to the granting of "distinct society" status to Quebec?
2. Aboriginal peoples claim distinctiveness and the right to self-determination as well. What are the implications of granting "distinct society" status to Quebec for the Aboriginal peoples in that province?
3. Should Canada grant special status to both Quebec and Aboriginal peoples?

14 MAKING THE GRADE

The following learning tools will help you see what you know, identify what you still need to learn, and expand your understanding beyond the text. You can also visit this text's Companion Website™ at www.pearsoned.ca/macionis to find useful practice tests.

KEY POINTS

The Social Meaning of Race and Ethnicity

Races are socially constructed categories by which societies set apart people with various physical traits. While scientists identified three broad categories—Caucasoids, Mongoloids, and Negroids, there are no pure races.

Ethnicity is based not on biology but on a shared cultural heritage. Just as people may or may not choose to emphasize their cultural distinctiveness, societies may or may not set categories of people apart because of their cultural heritage.

Minorities, including people of various races and ethnicities, are categories of people society sets apart, making them both distinct and disadvantaged.

Prejudice

Prejudice is a rigid and unfair generalization about a category of people. The social distance scale is one measure of prejudice. Racism, a destructive type of prejudice, asserts that one race is innately superior or inferior to another.

Discrimination

Discrimination is a pattern of action by which a person treats various categories of people unequally.

Majority and Minority: Patterns of Interaction

Pluralism means that racial and ethnic categories, although distinct, have equal social standing. Assimilation is a process by which minorities gradually adopt the patterns of the dominant culture. Segregation is the physical and social separation of categories of people. Genocide is the extermination of a category of people.

Race and Ethnicity in Canada

Aboriginal peoples, the earliest human inhabitants of the Americas, have endured genocide, segregation, and forced assimilation. Today, the social standing of Aboriginal peoples in Canada is well below the national average.

Blacks have a long history in Canada, as free Loyalists, as slaves prior to 1810, and later as escaped slaves coming to Canada via the Underground Railroad. The past two decades have seen increased immigration of Black peoples (from Africa, the Caribbean, and elsewhere), who have made their own cultural, economic, and political contributions to Canadian life.

Multiculturalism, a concept coined by Canada, is an essential part of our collective identity. While most Canadians feel that multiculturalism is a positive aspect of our lives, there are a few people who are highly critical of our multicultural policies.

The representation of racial and ethnic groups varies substantially from region to region and city to city in Canada, as does that of people who claim Canadian/*Canadien* ancestry.

The Québécois feel that French language and culture can be protected only within Quebec and that they need to have maximum control of their institutions—perhaps through separation—in order to achieve this.

Race and Ethnicity: Looking Ahead

Canada, which has historically accepted large numbers of immigrants, is currently receiving most of its immigrants from Asia, especially China and India. This will continue into the foreseeable future.

KEY CONCEPTS

race (p. 350) a socially constructed category of people who share biologically transmitted traits that members of a society consider important

ethnicity (p. 352) a shared cultural heritage

minority (p. 353) any category of people distinguished by physical or cultural difference that a society sets apart and subordinates

prejudice (p. 354) a rigid and irrational generalization about an entire category of people

stereotype (p. 354) an exaggerated description applied to every person in some category

racism (p. 355) the belief that one racial category is innately superior or inferior to another

scapegoat (p. 357) a person or category of people, typically with little power, whom people unfairly blame for their own troubles

discrimination (p. 358) unequal treatment of various categories of people

institutional prejudice and discrimination (p. 358) bias built into the operation of society's institutions

pluralism (p. 359) a state in which people of all races and ethnicities are distinct but have equal social standing

institutional completeness (p. 359) the complexity of community organizations that meet the needs of members

assimilation (p. 360) the process by which minorities gradually adopt patterns of the dominant culture

miscegenation (p. 360) biological reproduction by partners of different racial categories

segregation (p. 360) the physical and social separation of categories of people

genocide (p. 363) the systematic killing of one category of people by another

APPLICATIONS & EXERCISES

1. Give several of your friends or family members a quick quiz, asking them what share of the Canadian population is White, Black, Aboriginal, or Asian. Do they exaggerate the share of all minorities and understate the White proportion? Does your place of residence affect perceptions?

2. There are probably people on your campus or in your local community who are immigrants. Have you ever thought about asking such people about their homelands and their experiences since arriving in Canada? Most immigrants would be pleased to be asked and can provide a wonderful learning experience. If you are an immigrant yourself, how does your own experience differ from those of others?

3. Does the ethnic diversity of Canada affect what you eat? Check out your grocery stores, the restaurants in town, your favourite snacks. What is your conclusion?

PRENTICE HALL
mysoclab
Where learning & the sociological imagination intersect.

To reinforce your understanding of this chapter, and to identify topics for further study, visit MySocLab at **www.pearsoned.ca/mysoclab/** for diagnostic tests and a multimedia ebook.

CHAPTER FIFTEEN

Aging and the Elderly

What is the "greying" of Canada?

How is age a dimension of social inequality?

Why are elderly people devalued
in modern societies?

107 years young, she still loves to dance": that's the title of a *Globe and Mail* article describing Gladys Powers, a woman living in a nursing home in British Columbia who may be the last living female veteran of World War I. Powers is described as follows: "Born in London as a subject of Queen Victoria, she has lived in three centuries, survived two world wars and outlasted four husbands" (Hawthorn, 2006).

Gladys Winifred Stokes was born to a wealthy British family and, as a child, lived in the Ottoman Empire for four years with her family. By the time she was fourteen years old, she had lost both parents and her family fortune to her stepmother, ending up in the care of Church of England nuns. At eighteen she joined the war effort, ending up in the Women's Royal Air Force. As the war was ending, she met a tall, handsome soldier and moved with him to Canada as a war bride. When they decided to move from Calgary to Vancouver in 1914, they walked the railway track for lack of funds. On their month-long journey, they encountered a cougar: she assured her husband that the cougar would not attack because they were too skinny.

All her years have been eventful ones. After her fourth husband died, she lived alone in her home—until she was one hundred and three. Since moving into the Valhaven Home she has continued to be active as a regular in the daily exercise class. She uses a walker now, but that doesn't stop her from taking advantage of any opportunity to dance, thereby indulging one of her passions. Asked why she loves to dance, Powers replies, "You've got to have happiness in this world."

You have just been introduced to one of several fascinating elders you will meet in this chapter. Through their lives and as they aged, these individuals have been survivors—overcoming a range of challenges life has thrown at them. In their later years, they were among those who learned that social stratification is not just about class, gender, and race—it is also about age. While they overwhelmingly report that they are happy, older people face a number of disadvantages, including lower income, prejudice, and sometimes even abuse. These factors, along with deterioration in health, mean that, as Canada's population ages, increasing numbers of people face threats to their quality of life.

The Greying of Canada

A quiet but powerful revolution is reshaping Canada: the number of elderly people—women and men age 65 and over—is increasing more than twice as fast as the population as a whole. The effects of this "greying" of Canada (or population aging) are profound. Some statistics bring this change into sharp focus. The average annual growth of the youth population (from 1870 to 1990) was 1.2 percent, and that of persons older than 65 was double that rate, at 2.7 percent (Statistics Canada, 1992a). As a result of these opposing trends, 2001 census figures revealed that, in Canada, people older than 65 made up 13 percent of the whole population. When the results of the 2006 census are available, we should see increases in these trends.

In just over a century, the life expectancy of Canadians has doubled while their average number of children has declined by half. Figure 15–1 shows age/sex pyramids for the Canadian population, which reveal the percentages of males and females in each age category. The pyramids have shown and will continue to demonstrate dramatic shape changes with the tops becoming wider and the bottoms becoming narrower. Based on these trends one can predict that, by 2041, the proportion of the population aged 65 and over will have increased from 13 percent in 2001 to almost one-quarter of the whole population (23.8%) (McPherson, 2004: 6). Another way of measuring the aging of the Canadian population is by its median age, which has risen from 29.6 in 1981 to 37.6 in 2001.

Canada Map 15–1 shows the percentage of the population older than 65, by province, territory, and census subdivision. Note that the parts of Canada most inhabited by elderly people spread along our southern border and northward on the two coasts. Areas that are more than 16 percent elderly tend to be found in southern, rural Canada where the out-migration of young people accentuates the effect of declining birth rates. The parts of Canada in which Aboriginal people predominate remain relatively young.

What is prompting the aging of our society? Two factors stand out. The first is the baby boom that began in the late 1940s. After World War II, men and women enthusiastically settled into family life and the bearing of children. After 1965, the birth rate then took a sharp turn downward for the so-called baby bust; as a result, our population will become increasingly top heavy in the coming decades. As these trends continue, there comes a point at which population *decline* becomes a threat. Japan and several European countries already worry about the prospect of falling population counts, while Canada—which faces the same problem—promotes increased immigration as the solution.

Population decline usually threatens rich societies, but there is evidence that formerly communist countries "risk growing old before they become rich" (*The Economist*, 2006:50); the countries that are "going grey with worry" include 18 countries that, until recently, were part of the Soviet Union. The countries facing the greatest population decline by 2025 are Ukraine and Bulgaria; Russia faces a moderate loss, while Poland and Slovakia face minimal losses. Estonia is attempting, with some success, to increase its birth rate with generous parental leave and subsidized in-vitro fertilization but will not be able to reverse its population decline. The explanation offered by the World Bank is that women in these formerly communist countries have levels of education on par with their counterparts in rich countries.

 Check out internet services for people fifty and older at this portal: www.wiredseniors.com/ageofreason.

CANADA'S BIRTH RATE: GOING DOWN

The birth rate in Canada, in all but the baby-boom years, has been falling for more than a century. This is the usual trend as societies industrialize. Because children are more likely to survive into adulthood, couples bear fewer children. In addition, although children are an economic asset to farming families, they are an economic liability to families in industrial societies. In other words, children no longer add to their family's financial well-being but instead are a major expense. Finally, as more women achieve higher education, work outside the home, and commit to careers, they choose to have fewer children. This choice is made possible by advances in birth control technology during the past century.

LIFE EXPECTANCY: GOING UP

The past century has witnessed a remarkable 30-year increase in life expectancy. Females born in 1900 lived 50.2

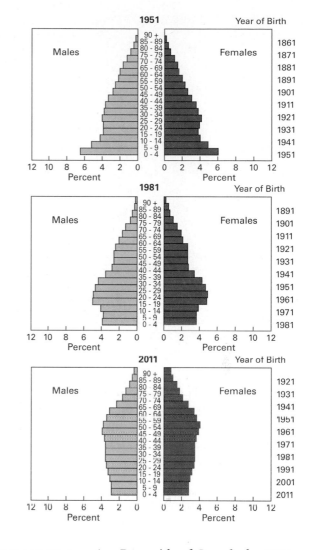

FIGURE 15-1   Age Pyramids of Canada for 1951, 1981, and 2011

Source: Adapted from the Statistics Canada publication "Report on the Demographic Situations in Canada", Catalogue 91-209, 1992.

years; males lived 47.2 years. In contrast, women now look forward to 83.4 years of life; men to 76.4 years. Our longer life spans are mainly the result of medical advances that virtually eliminated infectious diseases such as smallpox, diphtheria, and measles, which killed many young people in the past. More recent medical strides fend off cancer and heart disease, afflictions common to elderly people (Wall, 1980). The decline in mortality rates means that, of women born in 1950, only 5 percent will have died before becoming mothers; for every 100 women born in the 1800s, 40 died before giving birth to a child (Statistics Canada, 1992a). In addition, a rising standard of living has promoted the health of people of all ages. One clear indication of this change is that the fastest-growing segment of the entire population is people older than 85, who are already more than 20 times more numerous than they were at the beginning of the twentieth century. By 2041, about 15 percent of our elders

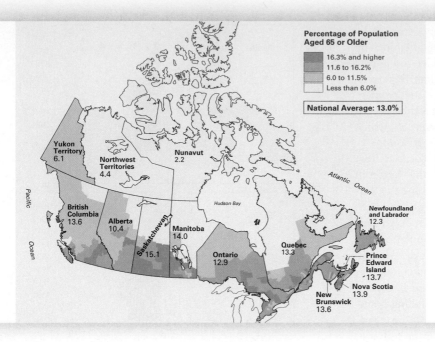

Percentage of the Population Aged 65 and Older for Canada, the Provinces, Territories, and Census Subdivision, 2001

Source: Calculations by L.M. Gerber, based on data retrieved from the Statistics Canada publication B20202, Profile Series, October 2003.

(people over 65) will be older than 80 years of age. Furthermore, the 2001 census "counted 3795 Canadians aged 100 or older... with women centenarians outnumbering men four to one" (McPherson, 2004: 5-6).

We can only begin to imagine the consequences of this massive increase in the elderly population. As elderly people retire from the labour force, they will add to the proportion of nonworking adults—which is already about 10 times greater than it was in 1900. The expanding elderly population will generate ever-greater demands for health care and other social services. Importantly, the ratio of elderly people to working-age adults—which analysts call the *old-age dependency ratio*—will almost double in the next 50 years. Pointing to "periodic fear-mongering by politicians and the media," McPherson argues that "we should not fear population aging, nor view it as a crisis." Instead, population aging should be viewed as a significant, but manageable challenge (2004: 9).

On the other hand, today's adults, especially women, differ in many important ways from previous generations. They will not be exactly like the people who are older than 65 today. Elderly people of the future will tend to have higher levels of education, fewer family responsibilities, better work experiences, more savings, and better health. Thus, predicting the use of social services (such as health care) on the basis of current use is very difficult (Statistics Canada, 1992b:144). Recall our discussion of poverty in Chapter 11 ("Social Class in Canada"): where you learned that, in recent years, Canada has made tremendous advances in alleviating poverty among elderly people. This in turn means that the elderly of the future will be less dependent on social services.

In recent years, older people have drawn heavily on the health care system. One study indicates that health care spending is 4.5 times greater for Canadians over 65, and 6.5 times greater for those over 75, than for those under 65 (Canada, 1991). Older Canadians make the greatest use of physicians, hospitals, and prescription drugs. As Chapter 21 ("Health and Medicine") explains, the costs of medical care have grown in recent years, a trend that shows no evidence of slowing. Unless steps are taken to address the real medical needs of millions of additional older people—at prices that Canadian taxpayers can afford, our society will face a monumental health care crisis in the coming years. While this is a widespread concern, there are analysts who argue that the situation is not as dismal as it seems, pointing out that today's seniors are healthier than any previous generation has been (Foot, 1998).

AN AGING SOCIETY: CULTURAL CHANGE

As the share of Canada's population that is older than 65 pushes upward, our way of life will change. In coming decades, interacting with elderly people will become commonplace. As the proportion of our population over 65 increases from 13 percent today to 17 percent by 2020 (or 1 for every 6 people) younger generations will inevitably have more contact with older people (Foot, 1998). Reduced age segregation, in turn, will lead to greater familiarity and shared understandings.

Will a "culture of aging" ever emerge? Probably not, for one key reason: elderly people collectively are too diverse. After all, the older Canadians represent an open category in which all of us, if we are lucky, end up. Thus, elderly people in Canada represent not just the two sexes but all cultures, classes, and races.

THINKING GLOBALLY

Can Too Many Be Too Old? A Report from Japan

With an average age of 41—compared to 38 in Canada, the population of Japan is among the oldest in the world. One cause of the aging Japanese population is a declining birth rate, which has fallen to just 1.3 children born for every woman. A second cause is increasing life expectancy. Girls born in Japan in 2004 can expect to live, on average, 85 years, and boys can expect to live 78 years.

Looking ahead, Japan's future population patterns alarm many people. First, the low birth rate means that Japan's population is now decreasing and will fall from 127 million today to about 110 million by 2050. Second, by 2050, half the Japanese population will be older than 53. This means that the country's labour force will shrink by millions of people, which could reduce the country's economic output and dramatically lower living standards. Third, the Japanese worry about how they will support their growing population of seniors. Today, there are three workers for every person over 65; by

2050, the old-age dependency ratio will fall to about one to one. This means that each person of working age will support one senior.

The importance of the Japanese case is that it is not unique. Other nations, including Italy and Spain, have populations almost as old as Japan's and, by 2050, they will face the same problems. Canada is among the "youngest" of the high-income countries but, in time, it will face the same problem.

WHAT DO YOU THINK?

1. Living longer is generally thought to be a good thing. What are some of the problems that come with an aging population?
2. When a nation's average age passes 50, what changes to popular culture might you expect?
3. How might immigration be a strategy to raise the old-age dependency ratio?

Source: Based on Porter (2004).

THE "YOUNG" OLD AND THE "OLD" OLD

Analysts sometimes distinguish between two cohorts of elderly people. The "younger" elderly, who are between 65 and 75 years of age, are typically autonomous, enjoy good health and financial security, and are likely to be living as couples. The "older" elderly, who have passed the age of 75, are more likely to be dependent on others because of health and money problems. Women outnumber men in both cohorts—owing to their greater longevity, a discrepancy that increases with advancing age: among the "oldest" old (those over the age of 85), about two-thirds are women.

While there are good reasons to be alert to population aging in Canada, there are scholars who argue that we have pressed the panic button fifteen years too early. The 2001 census suggests that the rate of growth in the elderly population has slowed down and will not pick up substantially until the first of the baby boomers hit retirement age (around 2010). Susan McDaniel, a demographer at the

University of Alberta, and David Foot, author of *Boom, Bust, and Echo*, agree that we have started worrying too early about the social costs of an elderly population now growing at a rate slower than anticipated (Mitchell, 1997). Foot adds that, when "all the surviving boomers are over 65, Canada's elderly as a percentage of its population will be about 22 percent, a level that will match, not exceed, the rest of the developed world" (1998:275). The implication is that other countries—mainly those of northern Europe—have already dealt with the issues that are causing panic here in Canada.

In what ways would colleges and universities change if more elders were to take part in campus life?

Jackrabbit (Herman Smith) Johannsen was born in Norway in 1875. Along with his skis, he left "an indelible mark on Canada: many kilometres of cross-country ski trails and jumps are directly attributable to him, and so are the thousands of skiers who have been inspired by his spirit of adventure and love for the Canadian winter." He promoted cross-country skiing through Quebec, Ontario, and parts of the United States. He was also responsible for introducing skiing to the Cree in northern Ontario—from whom he learned their language (his eighth) and who honoured him with the title Chief Jackrabbit. The Jackrabbit part stuck so well that many people never knew his Christian name. When asked, at 105 years of age, about his skiing, he said, "I'm steadier on skis with two poles to hold me up. But I'm not as good a skier as I was 100 years ago" (Norton, 1997). Johannsen died in 1987 at the age of 112.

Growing Old: Biology and Culture

Studying the greying of a society's population is the focus of **gerontology** (derived from the Greek word *geron*, meaning "an old person"), *the study of aging and elderly people.* Gerontologists—who work in many disciplines, including

medicine, psychology, and sociology—investigate not only how people change as they grow old but also the different ways in which societies around the world define old age. Given the rapid rate of growth in the aging population of North America, careers that deal with or involve study of the elderly are likely to expand as well.

BIOLOGICAL CHANGES

Aging amounts to a series of gradual, ongoing changes. How we think about life's transitions—whether we cheer our maturity or bemoan our physical decline—depends largely on whether our culture labels such changes as positive or negative. The youth-oriented way of life in Canada hails biological changes that occur early in life as positive. Through childhood and adolescence, we gain responsibility and look forward to expanded legal rights. But our culture

takes a dimmer view of the biological changes that unfold later in life. Few people receive congratulations for getting old. Rather, we commiserate with those entering old age and make jokes about aging to avoid the harsh conclusion that elderly people are on a slippery slope of physical and mental decline. We assume that, by about age 40, people cease growing *up* and begin growing *down*. How many people that you know have been "39" for a number of years?

Growing old does bring on certain physical problems. Grey hair, wrinkles, loss of height and weight, and an overall decline in strength and vitality all begin in middle age. After the age of 50, bones become more brittle so that injuries take longer to heal, and the odds of suffering from chronic illnesses (such as arthritis and diabetes) as well as life-threatening conditions (such as heart disease and cancer) rise steadily. The sensory abilities—taste, sight, touch, smell, and especially hearing—also become less keen with age (Treas, 1995; Segall and Chappell, 2000). One of the most troublesome problems of old age is a group of illnesses called *dementias*, which are characterized by progressive cognitive impairment, including the loss of abilities such as attention span, concentration, orientation, and memory. While dementias can result from several diseases that affect

 For more information about Alzheimer's, visit www.alzheimer.ca.

the brain, Alzheimer's is the best known and most common form of dementia (about 50% of dementia is Alzheimer's). Dementia is a serious and prevalent health problem among elderly Canadians, affecting between 5 and 10 percent of those older than 65, and approximately 20 percent of those over 80. The apparent increase in Alzheimer's is, almost entirely, the result of more people living past the age of 80 and more people living longer with the symptoms (McPherson, 2004: 425).

Without denying that health becomes more fragile with advancing age, the vast majority of older Canadians are neither discouraged nor disabled by their physical condition. Only about 1 in 10 seniors reports trouble walking, and fewer than 1 in 20 requires intensive care in a hospital or nursing home. No more than 1 percent of the elderly are bedridden. In a 1990 survey, less than 25 percent of people over the age of 55 characterized their health as "fair" or "poor," while about 75 percent described their overall condition as "good" or "excellent" (Keith and Landry, 1994:134). Not only are older Canadians in better health these days, but they are spending fewer days in the hospital as well. If these trends continue, older people will not be the drain on medical resources suggested by "apocalyptic demography" (Carrière, 2000).

Bear in mind, however, that patterns of well-being vary greatly within the elderly population. More health problems beset "older" elders past the age of 75. Moreover, because women typically live longer than men, women spend more of their lives suffering from chronic disabilities such as arthritis. In addition, well-to-do people are likely to live and work in a healthful and safe environment,

The reality of growing old is as much a matter of culture as it is of biology. In North America, being elderly often means being inactive; yet in many other countries, elders continue familiar and productive routines.

Visit the Canadian Association on Gerontology, which promotes the study of aging and improvement in the well-being of older people, at www.cagacg.ca.

a fact that pays benefits well into old age. Not surprisingly, happiness among elders is also related to health: "Senior men in good health living with a partner in good health were the most likely to report feeling happy," but, at the same time regardless of their partner's health, "over 90 percent of healthy senior men and women reported that they were happy" (Crompton and Kemeny, 2000).

Of course, since richer people can afford much more preventive medical care, indirectly, happiness levels depend on income. In one survey, 56 percent of men and 49 percent of women over 55 reported being very happy. Very few happy men (only 4%) or women (only 9%) had incomes of less than $10 000. The greatest proportion of very happy men (29%) fell into the highest income category (Keith and Landry, 1994:134).

PSYCHOLOGICAL CHANGES

Just as we tend to overstate the physical problems of aging, so it is easy to exaggerate the psychological changes that accompany growing old. Looking at intelligence over the life course, the conventional wisdom can be summed up in the simple rule "What goes up must come down" (Baltes and Schaie, 1974). If we measure skills like sensorimotor co-ordination (e.g., the ability to arrange objects to match a drawing), we do find a steady decline after midlife. The ability to learn new material and to think quickly also decline, although not until around age 70. But the ability to apply familiar ideas holds steady with advancing age, and the capacity for thoughtful reflection and spiritual growth actually increases (Baltes and Schaie, 1974; Metz and Miner, 1998).

We all wonder if we will think or feel differently as we get older. Gerontologists assure us that, for better or for worse, the answer is usually no. The only common personality change with advancing age is becoming more introspective. That is, people become more engaged with their own thoughts and emotions, and become less materialistic. Generally, therefore, two elderly people who were childhood friends would recognize in each other many of the same personality traits that distinguished them as youngsters (Neugarten, 1977; Wolfe, 1994).

AGING AND CULTURE

November 1, Kandy, Sri Lanka. Our little van struggles up the steep mountain incline. Breaks in the lush vegetation offer spectacular views that interrupt our conversation about growing old. "Then there are no old-age homes in your country?" I ask. "In Colombo and other cities, I am sure," our driver responds, "but not many. We are not like you Americans." "And how is that?" I counter, stiffening a bit. His eyes remain fixed on the road: "We would not leave our fathers and mothers to live alone." [John J. Macionis]

When do people grow old? How do younger people regard society's oldest members? How do elderly people view themselves? The answers people give to these questions vary from society to society, showing that, although aging is a biological process, it is also a matter of culture. How long and how well people live depend, first, on a society's technology and standard of living. Through most of human history, as the English philosopher Thomas Hobbes

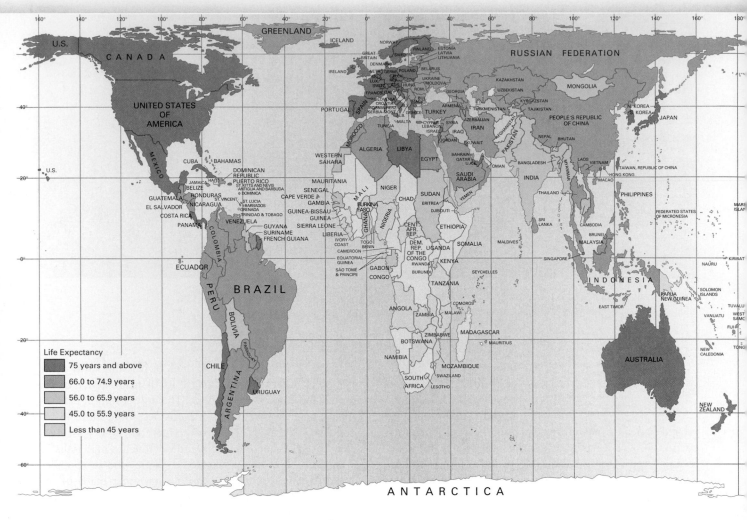

WINDOW ON THE WORLD

GLOBAL MAP 15–1 Life Expectancy in Global Perspective

Life expectancy shot upward over the course of the twentieth century in high-income countries, including Canada, the United States, Western Europe, Japan, and Australia. A newborn in Canada can now expect to live about 80 years. Our life expectancy would be greater still were it not for the high risk of death among infants born into poverty. Because poverty is the rule in much of the world, lives are correspondingly shorter, especially in parts of Africa, where life expectancy may be less than 40 years.

Source: Population Reference Bureau (2005).

(1588–1679) put it, people's lives were "nasty, brutish, and short"—although Hobbes himself made it to the ripe old age of 91. In his day, most people married and had children as teenagers, became middle-aged in their twenties, and died from various illnesses in their thirties and forties.

Many great men and women never reached what we would call old age at all. The English poet Keats died at age 26; Mozart, the Austrian composer, at 35. Among famous writers, none of the three Brontë sisters lived to the end of

her thirties, Edgar Allan Poe died at 40, Henry David Thoreau at 45, Oscar Wilde at 46, and Shakespeare at 52.

By about 1900, however, rising living standards and advancing medical technology in the United States and Western Europe had extended longevity to about age 50. As Global Map 15–1 shows, this is still the figure in many low-income countries today. In high-income

 For a report on aging in global perspective, go to www.census.gov/prod/2001pubs/p95-01-1.pdf.

APPLYING SOCIOLOGY
Aboriginal Elders: Cultural Custodians

For thousands of years, Aboriginal cultures have survived on Turtle Island (the Aboriginal name for North America), for the most part without written records. Their values, skills, knowledge, laws, and histories have been passed on orally from generation to generation—and elders play a pivotal role in that transmission. The result is that, where Aboriginal peoples strive to maintain cultural traditions, elders are held in high esteem.

Learn more about Sarah Abel, the highly respected Vuntut Gwitchin matriarch at www.oldcrow.yk.net/sarahen.htm

The 1993 Royal Commission on Aboriginal Peoples, in a massive report, published its findings on the social conditions of Aboriginal peoples throughout Canada. The following are some of the descriptions in the report that together define the position of elders—men and women—in Aboriginal societies and traditions. The Elders or Old Ones

*   Teach the "ancient wisdom about how to live, how to relate to the Creator, and how to coexist [with] brothers and sisters of the plant and animal world"
*   Have insight, wisdom, and authority
*   Have already walked a great distance on the path of life
*   Have received "the gifts of experience and knowledge"

Sarah Abel, 101 years old, lived in the isolated village of Old Crow above the Arctic Circle in the northern tip of the Yukon. Only at 100 years of age did she move out of the home in which she had raised seventeen children—on her own after her husband died of tuberculosis. She drove a dog sled, hunted moose and muskrat, and tanned her own hides; in other words, she did whatever had to be done. She had vivid memories of the past and told stories in person or on the CBC in her native tongue (Vuntut Gwitchin). As someone who had never touched alcohol, she worried a great deal about the social costs of alcohol abuse in her community (Brend, 1997). Sarah Abel died in August 1998 at the age of 102.

*   "Live their lives by example, according to the laws of the Creator"
*   Will recount stories and legends
*   Are good listeners
*   Apply spiritual understanding to community and family life
*   Are "a contemporary link to traditional knowledge"
*   See life as a sacred ceremony
*   "Play a critical role in the retention, renewal and celebration of Aboriginal languages"
*   Are the guardians of Aboriginal cultures
*   Can make important contributions in the classroom
*   Are teachers of the ethics of traditional justice
*   Mediate when conflicts arise
*   Lead the struggle for self-government
*   Take a holistic and spiritual approach to healing
*   Help youth find pride and strength in their Aboriginal identity

WHAT DO YOU THINK?

1. Could the rest of us learn something from the Aboriginal tradition of respect for the elderly?
2. Do you remember hearing stories of the old days from your grandparents and great grandparents?
3. Do you think older people can help youth deal with their problems?

Source: Based on the Royal Commission on Aboriginal Peoples (Canada 1996:107–43).

nations, however, increasing affluence has added almost 30 more years to the average life span.

Just as significant as longevity is the importance that societies attach to their older members. Most industrial societies push their elderly to the margins, as noted below. Canada, as a whole, is no exception. On the other hand, Aboriginal elders are highly respected, as revealed in the Applying Sociology box (above).

AGE STRATIFICATION: A GLOBAL SURVEY

Like race, ethnicity, and gender, age is a basis for social ranking. **Age stratification** is *the unequal distribution of wealth, power, and privilege among people at different stages of the life course.* Age stratification varies according to a society's level of technological development.

Hunter/Gatherer Societies

As Chapter 4 ("Society") explains, without the technology to produce a surplus of food, hunters and gatherers must be nomadic. This means that survival depends on physical strength and stamina. As members of these societies grow old (in this case, about age 30), they become less active and may even be considered an economic burden and, when food is in short supply, abandoned (Sheehan, 1976).

Pastoral, Horticultural, and Agrarian Societies

Once societies develop the technology to raise their own crops and animals, they produce a surplus. In such societies, some individuals build up considerable wealth over a lifetime. Of all age categories, the most privileged are typically older people, a pattern called **gerontocracy,** *a form of social organization in which older people have the most wealth, power, and prestige.* Old people, particularly men, are honoured and sometimes feared by their families, and they remain active leaders of society until they die. This respect for elders also explains the widespread practice of ancestor worship in agrarian societies.

Industrial and Post-industrial Societies

Industrialization pushes living standards upwards and advances medical technology, both of which increase human life expectancy. But although industrialization adds to the *quantity* of life, it can harm the *quality* of life for older people. Contrary to the practice in traditional societies, industrial societies give little power and prestige to elderly people. The reason is that, with industrialization, the prime source of wealth shifts from land—typically controlled by the oldest members of society—to businesses and other goods—(usually owned and managed by younger people. For all low-income nations, 76 percent of men and 44 percent of women over the age of 65 remain in the labour force; in high-income countries, these percentages are far smaller: 23 percent of men and 16 percent of women. The fact that older people move out of the paid labour force is one reason that the peak earning years among Canadian workers is about age 50, after which earnings decline.

In high-income countries, younger people move away from their parents to pursue their careers, depending less on their parents and more on their own earning power. In addition, because industrial, urban societies change rapidly, the skills, traditions, and life experiences that served the old may seem unimportant to the young. Finally, the tremendous productivity of industrial nations means that not all members of a society need to work, so most of the very old and the very young play nonproductive roles.

The long-term effect of all these factors transforms *elders* (a word with positive connotations) into *the elderly* (a term that carries far less prestige and turns people into a category). In post-industrial societies such as the United States and Canada, economic and political leaders are usually people between the ages of 40 and 60, who combine experience with up-to-date skills. Even as the U.S. population, on average, is getting older, the country's corporate executives are getting younger—declining from an average age of 59 in 1980 to 55 in 2005 (Herring, 2005). A similar trend is apparent here in Canada as the "old establishment" is replaced by the "new establishment" of business Titans (Newman, 1998). In rapidly changing sectors of the economy, especially the high-tech fields, many key executives are younger still, sometimes barely out of college or university. Industrial societies often give older people only marginal participation in the economy because they lack the knowledge and training demanded in a fast-changing marketplace.

An American study suggests that, despite overall trends, some occupations are dominated by older people. The average farmer is 55—the average age of the entire U.S. labour force is only 33—and more than one-third of today's farmers are over the age of 65. Older people also predominate in other traditional occupations, working as barbers, tailors, and shop clerks, and in jobs that involve minimal physical activity, such as night security guards (Yudelman and Kealy, 2000).

↔ YOUR TURN ↔

Our society is sometimes described as a "youth culture." Do you agree? Explain your answer.

Throughout the last century, Japan stood out as an exception to the rule that industrialization lowers the social standing of older people. Not only is the share of older people in Japan increasing as fast as anywhere in the world, but Japan's more traditional culture gives elders great importance. Most elders in Japan live with an adult daughter or son, and they play a significant role in family life. Elderly men in Japan are also more likely than their North American counterparts to stay in the labour force and, in many Japanese corporations, the oldest employees enjoy the greatest respect.

But Japan is becoming more like other industrial nations, where growing old means giving up some measure of social importance. In addition, a long economic downturn has left Japanese families less able to care for their older members, which may further weaken the traditional importance of elders (Yates, 1986; Ogawa and Retherford, 1997).

Transitions and Challenges of Aging

We confront change at each stage of life. Old age has its rewards but, of all stages of the life course, it presents the greatest challenges. Physical decline in old age is less serious than most younger people think. But even so, older people endure pain, limit their activities, increase their dependency on others, lose dear friends and relatives, and face up to their own mortality. Because our culture places such a high value on youthfulness, aging often leads to fear and self-doubt. One retired psychologist commented about old age: "Don't let the current hype about the joys of retirement fool you. They are not the best of times. It's just that the alternative is even worse" (Rubenstein, 1991).

FINDING MEANING

Chapter 5 ("Socialization") presented Erik Erikson's (1963; orig. 1950, 1980) theory that elderly people must resolve a tension of "integrity versus despair." No matter how much they still may be learning and achieving, older people recognize that their lives are nearing an end. As a result, elderly people spend more time reflecting on their past, remembering disappointments as well as accomplishments. Integrity, to Erikson, means assessing your life realistically; without such honesty, this stage of life may turn into a time of despair—a dead end with little positive meaning.

Negative myths about the health, happiness, and sexuality of older people abound (McPherson, 1990). Some elderly people share this dim view of their plight, but most have a more positive outlook. As Table 15–1 indicates, a large majority of senior men and women consider themselves to be happy—especially if these men and women and their partners are in good health. Those most likely to report happiness (96%) are men in good health with partners in good health; those least likely to report happiness (60%) are women in poor health with partners in poor health. Married elders have advantages over single ones in a number of areas, including morbidity (their rate of illness), mortality, and psychological well-being. Marriage appears to be particularly advantageous for elderly males because it unites them with a network of other people more easily than singlehood does (Nett, 1993).

Overall, research suggests that, while personal adjustments are necessary, the experience of growing old may provide cause for joy. However, a person's view does vary based on individual personality, family circumstances, social class, and financial position. People who adapt successfully to changes earlier in life can confidently look forward to deriving satisfaction and meaning from their lives later on. As Neugarten (1971) sees it, the key to successful aging lies is maintaining personal dignity and self-confidence while accepting growing old. She found that people with *integrated personalities* cope best with the challenges of growing old. In 2003, at least four new North American books tried to help older people—especially the retired—answer questions about the meaning of life. Some help elders achieve spiritual goals, while others stress making a continuing contribution to society through volunteering, or otherwise staying active and making a positive difference. With the proper outlook, old age provides the opportunity to develop wisdom, balance, gratitude, and self-awareness (Todd, 2003).

TABLE 15–1

Happiness Reported by Senior Men and Women by Health of Self and Spouse, 1996–97

	Percentage Who Are Happy	
	Older Men	Older Women
In good health		
Spouse in good health	96%	90%
Spouse in poor health	88	94
In poor health		
Spouse in good health	77	64
Spouse in poor health	64	60

Source: Adapted by L.M. Gerber from Crompton and Kemeny (2000:48).

SOCIAL ISOLATION

Being alone may provoke anxiety in people of any age; isolation, however, is most common among elderly people. Retirement closes off workplace social interaction, physical problems may limit mobility, and negative stereotypes depicting elderly people as "over the hill" may discourage younger people from close social contact with their elders.

The greatest cause of social isolation, however, is the inevitable death of significant others. Few human experiences affect people as profoundly as the death of a spouse. One study found that almost three-quarters of widows and widowers cited loneliness as their most serious problem (Lund, 1989). Widows and widowers must rebuild their lives in the absence of people with whom they may have spent most of their adult lives. Table 15–2 reveals that roughly three-quarters of men live with a spouse or partner, while this is true of only half of women aged 65 and older—and 39 percent of those aged 75 and older. Only about 1 in 5 older men lives alone, whereas this is true of half of women 75 years of age and older. Thus women, who typically outlive their husbands, are more likely to face isolation—as they more often live alone.

While some studies have found that elderly women suffer more mental health problems as a result of isolation (Nett, 1993), others have found that half of elderly widows *choose* to live in the homes they once shared with their husbands; in doing so, they rely on a wider range of social supports than men do (McDaniel, 1994). As illustrated in Figure 15–2, the 1995 General Social Survey revealed that elderly widows have close emotional ties to neighbours, in particular, as well as friends, other relatives, and their adult children (Bess, 2000). However, living alone—a valued dimension of autonomy—presumes the financial means to do so.

It may surprise you to learn that women who are widowed later in life (i.e., between the ages of 65 and 74) are three times more likely to live by themselves than women who were widowed before they were 65 (Bess, 2000:167). One reason may be that younger widows move in with their chil-

TABLE 15–2

Living Arrangements of Seniors: Canada, 2001*

| | Over 65 Years | | Over 75 Years | |
	Men	Women	Men	Women
Living with spouse[a]	78.6	52.4	73.5	38.7
Living with relatives	3.3	7.9	3.7	10.3
Living with non-relatives	1.4	1.4	1.4	1.2
Living alone	16.8	38.3	21.1	49.8

*Refers to seniors living in private households. Another 14 and 9 percent, respectively, of all men and women over 65 years of age live in other settings such as nursing homes and retirement residences.

[a]Refers to spouse or common-law partner.

Source: Calculations by L.M. Gerber based on Statistics Canada, Census 2001, catalogue no. 95F0315XCB2001004.

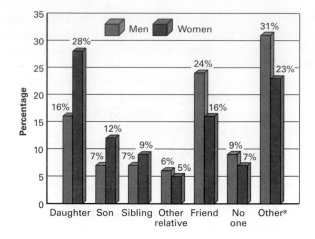

FIGURE 15–2   Sources of Emotional Support for Elderly Men and Women without Spouses, 1990*

*Includes persons without sons, daughters, siblings, etc.

[a]Includes neighbours, co-workers, clergy, doctors, professional counsellors, others, and "don't know." None of these specific sources exceeded 5 percent.

Source: Adapted from the Statistics Canada publication *General Social Survey analysis series*, Catalogue 89F00133, May 2003.

dren to help raise their grandchildren. Older widows may not be needed in child rearing and may not feel they have the energy. On the other hand, older widows who have grown accustomed to an empty nest and have created new lives for themselves without their adult children might be more reluctant to give up their independence by moving into a three-generation household. The formation of three-generation households is related to ethnicity as well. Recent immigrants, from Asia in particular, are more likely than other Canadians to have their parents or widowed mothers live in their homes (Gerber, 1983; Che-Alford and Hamm, 2000). Chinese-Canadians between 80 and 85 years of age are four times more likely to live with their adult children than are their non-Asian counterparts (McPherson, 2005: 216).

Some elderly people opt to live in housing specifically for them. Residences for older Canadians range from retirement communities offering many amenities and leisure activities to low-rent apartments for seniors, retirement homes (with dining rooms and housekeeping services) to nursing homes with full-time medical staff (McPherson, 2005: 219). The Media Perspectives box (on pp. 392–93) looks at some issues related to these residence options.

RETIREMENT

Work provides us not only with earnings but also with an important part of our personal identity. Therefore, retire-

See Help the Aged Canada, a nonprofit organization designed to assist elders in Canada and developing countries, at www.helptheaged.ca.

ment means not only a reduction in income but also less social prestige and perhaps some loss of purpose in life. Some organizations help ease this transition. Universities, for example, confer the title "professor emeritus" (*emeritus* is from the Latin, meaning "fully earned") or "professor emerita" (for women) on retired faculty members, who maintain many university privileges and often continue to publish and teach the occasional course. These highly experienced faculty members can be a

valuable resource not only to students but to younger professors as well (Parini, 2001).

Because older Canadians are socially diverse, there is no single formula for successful retirement. Part-time work occupies many people entering old age and provides some extra cash as well. Grandparenting is an enormous source of pleasure for many elders. Volunteer work is another path to rewarding activity, especially for those who have saved enough so that they do not have to work—one reason that volunteerism is increasing more among older people than in any other age category (Gardyn, 2000; Savishinsky, 2000; Shapiro, 2001).

Although retirement is a familiar idea, the concept developed only within the past century or so in high-income countries. High-income societies are so productive that not everyone needs to work; in addition, advanced technology places a premium on up-to-date skills. Therefore, retirement emerged as a strategy to permit younger workers—presumably, those with the most current knowledge and training—to have the largest presence in the labour force. A decade or so ago, it was common for people throughout Canada to retire at 65 years of age. Now people in a variety of occupations consider the possibility of early retirement. In high-income countries, private and public pension programs make it financially possible for older people to retire, an opportunity that does not exist for those living in low-income nations.

In Canada, retirement at age 65 is closely tied to the development of pension plans. This is the age, too, when mandatory retirement comes into effect for some workers. There has been an ongoing debate about whether mandatory retirement violates the individual's right to work (and freedom from age discrimination) as guaranteed under the Canadian Charter of Rights and Freedoms. But, while about half of the Canadian workforce has been subject to mandatory retirement regulations, only about 1 percent of the workforce would continue to work past 65, if given the choice (Tindale, 1991). Several provinces have already elim-

 For more on the ending of mandatory retirement, go to www.labour.gov.on.ca/english/news/m_mr.html and www.benefitsworld.com/aa/lgl/endingmandatoryretirement.asp.

inated mandatory retirement, with Ontario doing so most recently (on Dec. 12, 2006). Note that there has never been a law (federal or provincial) forcing mandatory retirement: instead there is a broad Canada-wide consensus, that 65 is the appropriate retirement age, which is reinforced by employers, unions, and pension plans.

In recent decades, with rapid transitions in the Canadian economy resulting from global economic restructuring, free trade agreements, and a general move to the political right, more and more people are being forced out of work or encouraged to take early retirement. Many of those who have been given the "golden handshake" in this era of unprecedented numbers of employee buyouts are embarking on brand new careers. Severance packages, which may be as high as two years' salary, are often used as the initial investment for the new venture (Lipovenko, 1996). In the last few years, with increasing threats of labour and skills shortages, we have reduced the emphasis on early retirement and taken steps to eliminate mandatory retirement.

AGING AND INCOME

On the whole, the image of elderly people as poverty-stricken is unfounded: the poverty rate among older Canadians has declined substantially since 1980. Among seniors who live with their spouses or other family members, poverty levels have declined from 18 percent in 1980 to 16.1 percent in 2001. In contrast, unattached elderly persons endured low income at levels of 68 percent and 42 percent in 1980 and 2001, respectively. Overall, however, 83 percent of older Canadians live above the low-income level, and some of them are affluent. Recall that the incidence of poverty among the elderly was discussed in considerable detail in Chapter 11 ("Social Class in Canada").

For most Canadians, retirement leads to a significant decline in income. For many, home mortgages and children's university expenses are paid off; yet the expenses for medical and dental care, household help, and home utilities typically rise. Many elderly people lack sufficient savings or pension benefits to be self-supporting; for this reason, various pension programs, including the Canada Pension Plan, are their greatest source of income. Because many retirees live with a fixed income, inflation tends to affect them more severely than it does younger working people. Women and members of visible minorities are especially likely to find that growing old means growing poorer.

As they become a larger share of the population in years to come, older people will probably play a larger part in popular culture. Clint Eastwood remains a mega-star at the age of seventy-five: he appears here with Hilary Swank on the set of *Million Dollar Baby*, the 2004 film that won an Oscar for Eastwood as director. Do you think this pattern is more typical of older men than of older women? Why?

Gender continues to shape the lives of people as they age. Elderly women are more likely to be poor than elderly men: in 2001, 46 percent of unattached elderly women and 33 percent of elderly men were poor. Income inequality among different ethnic and racial groups is also not blunted by growing old.

What is distinctive about the privation of the elderly, however, is that it is often hidden from view. Because of personal pride and a desire to maintain the dignity of independent living, many older people conceal financial problems even from their own families. It is often difficult for people who have supported their children for years to admit that they can no longer provide for themselves, even though it may be through no fault of their own.

CARE GIVING

In an aging society, the need for care giving is bound to increase. **Care giving** refers to *informal and unpaid care provided to a dependent person by family members, other relatives, or friends.* While parents provide care giving to children, the term is more often applied to the needs of elderly men and women. Indeed, today's middle-aged adults are called the "sandwich generation" because many will spend as much time caring for their aging parents as for their own children. Nelson and Robinson (1999: 466) point out that, more accurately, we should refer to the "sandwich phase" since it applies only to those who have care giving responsibility for their children and their parents simultaneously, and the situation is temporary.

MEDIA PERSPECTIVES

Aging in Retirement Residences and Nursing Homes

The aging of Canada's population has led to the rapid proliferation of retirement homes (some of them opulent) and nursing homes—or even whole towns, like Elliott Lake in northern Ontario, that reshape themselves into retirement communities. In each, older people live in settings designed to meet their special physical, social, and medical needs.

Retirement homes, with assisted living options, are of particular interest because they are a relatively new phenomenon. They differ from nursing homes in many ways—most significantly in their lack of public subsidy. In other words, the resident pays the full cost of his or her accommodation, meals, social activities, housekeeping, and nursing care. Physicians' services, on or off the premises, are covered by provincial health care plans. The cost of residence in a retirement home *with assisted living* may range from $3000 to $5000 per month or much more, making it accessible to more affluent seniors.

Note that most Canadians move into retirement residences before they need assistance with such daily living activities as eating, bathing, or getting out of bed; only a portion of residents require fully assisted living. Residents live as

individuals or couples in rooms, and share common areas (e.g., lounges, dining room, crafts room, library, gardens, exercise room). Accommodation costs may include meals, housekeeping, and transportation to, for example, concerts, wine country tours, or shopping at the mall. Seniors are encouraged to participate as actively as possible in a wide range of activities.

In an article for the *New York Times* entitled "Under One Roof, Aging Together Yet Alone," Jane Gross describes the assisted living setting as

a "dignified alternative" to the nursing home. She looks at a relatively posh assisted living facility called Atria Stratford in Stratford, Connecticut, finding that

Everyone complains about the food. Nobody wants to sit with the misfits. There are leaders and followers, social butterflies and loners, goody-goodies and trouble-makers. Friendships are intense and so are rivalries. Everybody knows everybody else's business.

The Care Givers

Surveys show that 80 percent of care giving to elders is provided by family members, in most cases by one person. Most care givers live close to the older person. In addition, 75 percent of all care giving is provided by women, most often daughters and wives. The gender norm is so strong that daughters-in-law are more likely than sons to care for an aging parent: "Regardless of what activities are included, research consistently finds that primary care givers are most likely to be women, in their roles as wives, daughters, or daughters-in-law" (Nelson and Robinson, 1999: 467). Also, "daughters or daughters-in-law tend to be the primary care-

givers, and elderly women, especially widows and divorcees, tend to be the recipients of more social support than men" (McPherson, 2004: 367).

About two-thirds of care givers are married, and one-third are also responsible for young children. When we add the fact that half of all care givers also have a part- or full-time job, it is clear that care giving is a responsibility over and above what most people already consider a full day's work. Half of all primary care givers spend more than 20 hours per week providing elder care. Canada's General Social Survey of 1996 reveals that, although care giving is not considered to be onerous, women are twice as likely as

She quotes public health professor Dr. Catherine Hawes, who described it as "high school all over again, without the expectations."

Life for the residents—overwhelmingly women with an average age of 85—is a humbling experience, involving loss of control, fear for the future, and loneliness in a group setting. People who are most impaired are ostracized by those who fear what they themselves may soon become. Complaints about food are commonplace, and memory loss leads to widespread suspicion. On the other hand, there is laughter, social interaction, friendship and, for some, love and marriage.

The situation in Canada's nursing homes is very similar, except for higher levels of physical and mental impairment. The newer nursing homes are anything but dark and dreary. Wings or floors are limited to twenty-eight residents who share common areas (e.g., lounges and dining rooms) and their own staff. You may be surprised to learn that this aspect of health care is provided mainly by private enterprise, and that a number of Ontario's nursing homes are owned by a Mennonite firm. Others cater to specific ethnic communities, though they must accept anyone who signs on to their waiting lists. Nursing homes are tightly regulated and subsidized by provincial governments to the point where anyone with a Canadian pension can afford the cost.

Medicare covers visits to physicians (on site or off) as well as prescription costs—as it does for all seniors. It may take up to two years on a waiting list to get into the nursing home of one's choice.

There's a modern dilemma facing retirement and nursing homes in Canada. In "Home for the Grey and Gay," Jo-Anne MacDonald looks into the housing experiences of aging gays and lesbians. Not long ago, gays feared growing old because they felt they had to go back into the closet in order to fit into a nursing home environment. Nursing homes were doing nothing to accommodate them. Recently, two of ten city-owned nursing homes in Toronto opened their doors to gay residents. They have changed their definition of "family members," added gay-themed movies to their film collections, given sensitivity training to staff and residents, encouraged conjugal visits, and declared themselves safe havens for "elderly gays, lesbians, bisexuals, and transgendered." Privately owned nursing homes are also seeking guidance in becoming gay-friendly. Soon, retirement homes—and some nursing homes—will have same-sex couples moving into single rooms or suites.

There are some 600 000 gays and lesbians in Canada who are over 45 years of age, with 80 000 of them living in Toronto. There is a condominium coming on stream in Toronto to cater to this older gay community. MacDonald's article does not point it out, but this would be an ideal setting for one floor designed as a retirement home (shared dining room and other facilities) with assisted living possibilities. Ideally, gays and lesbians—anywhere in Canada—will have a range of choices for accommodation and care as they age, where they are free to be themselves without risk of rejection, discrimination, or abuse. Some elderly gays, who grew up at a time when their relationships were illegal, must find this an astounding proposition.

WHAT DO YOU THINK?

1. Would you consider living in a retirement home, with assisted living options, before making the move to a nursing home? What are the advantages and disadvantages of doing so?
2. As your parents age, are you likely to accommodate them in your home, so that they will not need to move into a retirement or nursing home? Would they want to move in with you?
3. Why is it so important for retirement and nursing homes to rethink their approaches to gay residents?

Sources: Gross (2005) and MacDonald (2006).

---

men to report negative effects on their health. Men are less likely to feel burdened because women face our cultural expectation that care giving is "an integral part of the female role in our society" (Nelson and Robinson 1999: 468).

Elder Abuse

In Canada, we seem to awaken to social problems in stages: we became aware of child abuse during the 1960s, spousal abuse in the 1970s, and elder abuse in the 1980s. Abuse of older people takes many forms, from passive neglect to active torment, and includes verbal, emotional, financial, and physical harm. Most elderly people suffer from none of these, but research suggests that, in Canada, Europe, and the United States, the incidence of elder abuse and neglect ranges from 3 to 5 percent. Like other forms of family violence, abuse of the elderly often goes unreported because victims are reluctant to talk about their plight.

The Canadian Network for the Prevention of Elder Abuse defines *elder abuse* as harm to an older adult—that is, doing something that causes harm or distress or not doing something that is one's duty (such as providing food or medication). Most abuse occurs in relationships of trust linking the older person to family or service providers (e.g., lawyers, accountants, or nursing home staff). It can occur in the home or in institutions. Abuse, in the community or in institutions, is most likely to occur if care giving tasks are difficult and the care giver is otherwise stressed or lacking appropriate support from others. In Ontario, in recent years, hospital stays have been shortened by diverting patients (many of them elderly) to home care, either in the patient's own home or the home of a relative. While home care programs provide nursing and housekeeping support, "responsibility" for overall care is placed in the hands of family members. As a result of social policy, some care givers who are handed responsibility for frail and ill elders will find it highly stressful.

 For more information on elder abuse go to the Canadian Network for the Prevention of Elder Abuse at www.cnpea.ca.

AGEISM

In earlier chapters, we explained how ideology—including racism and sexism—serves to justify the social disadvantages of minorities. In a similar way, sociologists use the term **ageism** for *prejudice and discrimination against older people.* Elderly people are the primary targets of ageism, although middle-aged people can suffer as well. Examples of ageism include passing over qualified older job applicants in favour of younger workers or firing older workers first.

Like racism and sexism, ageism can be blatant (as when a university decides not to hire a sixty-year-old professor because of her age) or subtle (as when a nurse speaks to elderly patients in a condescending tone, as if they were children). Also like racism and sexism, ageism builds physical traits into stereotypes. In the case of elderly people, some people consider grey hair, wrinkled skin, and stooped posture signs of personal incompetence. Negative stereotypes portray older people as helpless, confused, unable to deal with change, and generally unhappy. Even "positive" images of sweet little old ladies and eccentric old gentlemen are stereotypes that gloss over individuality and ignore years of experience and accomplishment (Butler, 1975; Cohen, 2001). Sometimes ageism contains a bit of truth. Statistically speaking, older people are more likely than younger people to be mentally and physically impaired. But we slip into ageism when we make unfair generalizations about an entire category of people.

Betty Friedan (1993), a pioneer of today's feminist movement, argues that ageism is deeply rooted in our culture. Friedan points out that few elderly people appear in the mass media; only a small percentage of television shows, for example, feature main characters over 60. More generally, when most of us think about older people, it is often in negative terms. This older man *lacks* a job, that older woman has *lost* her vitality, and seniors *look back* to their youth. In short, says Friedan, we often treat being old as if it were a disease, marked by decline and deterioration, for which there is no cure. Even so, Friedan believes that older women and men are discovering that they still have a great deal to contribute. Advising small business owners, designing housing for the poor, teaching children to read—there are countless ways in which older people can help others and at the same time enhance their own lives.

YOUR TURN

On your campus, are the most popular faculty members younger instructors or older instructors? Does age play into a professor's student evaluations?

THE ELDERLY: A MINORITY?

Elderly people in Canada face social disadvantages. Does that mean that the elderly constitute are a minority in the same way as, say, Aboriginal people or women? Elderly Canadians appear to meet the definition of a minority because they have a clear social identity based on their age, and they are subject to prejudice and discrimination. But Gordon Streib (1968) argues that we should not think of elderly people as a minority. First, minority status is usually both permanent and exclusive. That is, a person is an Aboriginal person or a woman *for life* and cannot become part of the dominant category of White men. But being elderly is an *open* status because people are elderly for only part of their lives, and everyone who has the good fortune to live long enough grows old. Second, the elders at highest risk of being poor or otherwise disadvantaged fall into specific categories of people—women, Aboriginal peoples—who are at highest risk of being poor throughout the life course. As Streib sees it, it is not so much that the old grow poor as that the poor grow old. If so, older people are not a minority in the same sense as other categories. It might be better to say that elderly people are a part of our population that faces special challenges based on age.

Theoretical Analysis of Aging

We now apply sociology's theoretical approaches to gain insight into how society shapes the lives of elderly people. We consider structural-functional, symbolic-interaction, and social-conflict approaches in turn.

STRUCTURAL-FUNCTIONAL ANALYSIS: AGING AND DISENGAGEMENT

Drawing on the ideas of Talcott Parsons—an architect of the structural-functional approach—Elaine Cumming and William Henry (1961) explain that the physical decline and death that accompany aging can disrupt society. In response, society disengages elderly people, gradually transferring statuses and roles from older to younger people so that tasks are performed with minimal interruption. **Disengagement theory** is *the idea that society functions in an orderly way by disengaging people from positions of responsibility as they reach old age.* Based on both a developmental and functionalist perspective, disengagement theory assumes that change and adaptation are necessary for both the older individual and society (McPherson, 2004: 139). Disengagement ensures the orderly operation of society by removing aging people from productive roles before they are no longer able to perform them. Another benefit of disengagement in a rapidly changing society is that it makes room for young workers, who typically have the most up-to-date skills and training. Disengagement provides benefits to aging people as well. Although most sixty-year-olds wish to keep working, most begin to think about retirement and perhaps cut back a bit on their workloads. Exactly when people begin to disengage from their careers, of course, depends on their health, enjoyment of the job, and financial circumstances.

Retiring does not mean being inactive. Some people start a new career or a different job, while others pursue hobbies or engage in volunteer work. In general, people in their sixties start to think less about what they *have been doing* and begin to think more about what they *want to do* with the rest of their lives (Palmore, 1979; Schultz and Heckhausen, 1996; Voltz, 2000).

Critical Review Disengagement theory explains why rapidly changing high-income societies tend to define their oldest members as socially marginal. But there are several limitations to this approach. First, especially in recent years, many workers have found they cannot disengage from paid work because they need the income. Second, some elderly people, whether they are rich or poor, simply do not want to disengage from work they enjoy. Disengagement may also mean losing friends and social prestige. Third, it is not clear that the societal benefits of disengagement outweigh its social costs, which include the loss of human resources and the need to take care of people who might otherwise be able to support themselves. As the number of elderly people swells, finding ways to help them to remain independent is a high priority. Fourth, any rigid system of disengagement does not take account of the widely differing abilities of elderly people. Fifth, countries like Canada, with aging populations, *need* their older workers in the workforce. This concern leads us to the symbolic-interaction approach.

SYMBOLIC-INTERACTION ANALYSIS: AGING AND ACTIVITY

Drawing on the symbolic-interaction approach, **activity theory** is *the idea that a high level of activity increases personal satisfaction in old age.* Because everyone bases social identity on many roles, disengagement is bound to reduce satisfaction and meaning in the lives of older people. What aging people need is not to be pushed out of roles but to have many productive or recreational options. The importance of having choices is especially great for those aged 65 today, who can look forward to about 20 more years of life (Smart, 2001; Walsh, 2001). Activity theory does not reject the idea of job disengagement; it simply says that people need to find new roles to replace those they leave behind. Research confirms that elderly people who maintain a high activity level find the most satisfaction in their lives. Activity theory also recognizes that elderly people are

It is common for businesses to offer a "seniors discount" to people over 65 (or sometimes even 55). What is the reason for this practice? Would you prefer a policy of offering discounts to single parents with children, a category of people at higher risk of poverty? Why is that an unlikely move by businesses?

diverse, with highly variable interests, needs, and physical abilities. For this reason, the activities that people choose and the pace at which they pursue them are always an individual matter (Neugarten, 1977; Moen, *et al.*, 1992).

Critical Review Activity theory shifts the focus of analysis from the needs of society—as stated in disengagement theory—to the needs of elderly people themselves. It emphasizes the social diversity of aging and older people, and highlights the importance of choice in any government policy. A limitation of this approach is that it assumes that elders are both healthy and competent, which may not consistently be the case. Another problem with this approach is that it ignores the fact that many of the problems older people face—such as poverty—have more to do with society than with themselves. We turn now to the point of view of social-conflict theory.

SOCIAL-CONFLICT ANALYSIS: AGING AND INEQUALITY

A social-conflict analysis of aging is based on the idea that access to opportunities and social resources differs for people of different ages. For this reason, age is a dimension of social stratification. Middle-aged people enjoy the greatest power and the most opportunities and privileges, while

In many traditional societies, people express great respect not only for elders but also for their ancestors. Dani villagers in New Guinea mummified the body of this elder in a sitting position so that they could continue to honour him and feel his presence in their daily lives.

elderly people and children have a higher risk of poverty. Employers who replace older workers with younger men and women in order to keep wages low may not intend to discriminate against older people; however, to the extent that such policies have the effect of causing special harm to older workers, they amount to discrimination.

The social-conflict approach claims that our industrial-capitalist economy creates an age-based hierarchy. In line with Marxist thought, Steven Spitzer (1980) points out that a profit-oriented society devalues any category of people that is less productive. To the extent that older people do not work, our society labels them as mildly deviant.

Social-conflict analysis also draws attention to various dimensions of social inequality within the elderly population. Differences of class, race, ethnicity, and gender divide older people as they do everyone else. For this reason, some seniors have far greater economic security, access to better medical care, and more options for personal satisfaction in old age than younger people have. Likewise, elderly White people typically enjoy advantages denied to elders belonging to visible minorities. And women—an increasing majority as people age—suffer the social and economic disadvantages of both sexism and ageism.

Critical Review The social-conflict approach adds to our understanding of the aging process by highlighting age-based inequality and explaining how capitalism devalues elderly workers who are less productive. But critics claim that the real culprit is *industrialization*; as evidence, they point to the fact that elderly people are not better off under

a socialist system, as a Marxist analysis implies. Furthermore, the idea that either industrialization or capitalism necessarily causes older people to suffer is challenged by the long-term rise in income and well-being experienced by seniors in Canada and the United States.

Death and Dying

To every thing there is a season,
And a time for every purpose under heaven:
A time to be born and a time to die...

These well-known lines from the biblical book of Ecclesiastes state two basic truths about human existence: the fact of birth and the inevitability of death. Just as life varies throughout history and around the world, death has many faces. Death may occur at any age and be unexpected, but we conclude this chapter with a brief look at the changing character of death as the final stage in the process of growing old.

HISTORICAL PATTERNS OF DEATH

In the past, death was a familiar part of life. Many children died soon after birth, a fact that led many parents to delay naming children until they were one or two years old. For those fortunate enough to survive infancy, illness, accidents, and natural catastrophes made life uncertain at best. Sometimes food shortages forced societies to protect the majority by sacrificing the least productive members: *infanticide* is the killing of newborn infants, and *geronticide* is the killing of the elderly. Because death was commonplace, it was readily accepted.

As industrializing societies gradually learned more about health and medicine, death became less of an everyday experience. Fewer children died at birth, and accidents and disease took a smaller toll among adults. As a result, most people living in high-income societies today view dying as extraordinary, something that happens to the very old or to younger people in rare and tragic cases.

In 1900, about one-third of all deaths in North America occurred before the age of 5 and fully two-thirds before the age of 55. Today, by contrast, 85 percent of our population dies *after* the age of 55. Death and old age are closely linked in our culture.

THE MODERN SEPARATION OF LIFE AND DEATH

Now removed from everyday experience, death somehow seems unnatural. Social conditions prepared our ancestors to accept death, but modern society's youth culture and aggressive medical technology foster a desire for eternal youth and immortality. Death has become separated from life. Death is also *physically* removed from everyday activities. The clearest evidence of this is that few of us have ever seen a person die. Our ancestors typically died at home in the presence of family and friends, but most deaths today occur in impersonal settings such as hospitals and nursing homes. Even in hospitals, dying patients occupy a special part of the building, and hospital morgues are located well out of sight of patients and visitors alike (Ariès, 1974; Lee, 2002).

→ **YOUR TURN** ←

Ask members of your class if they have ever seen a person die. Does the response support the idea that modern society separates death from life?

ETHICAL ISSUES: CONFRONTING DEATH

In a society in which technology gives us the power to prolong life—or conversely to prolong the process of dying (McPherson, 2004: 434)—moral questions about when and how people should die are more pressing than ever. For example, the debate in 2005 surrounding the death of American Terri Schiavo, who had been kept alive by mechanical means for fifteen years, was not just about the fate of one woman; many people feel we need a better understanding of the right to die should be.

When Does Death Occur?

Perhaps the most basic question is the most difficult: Exactly how do we define death? Common sense suggests that life ceases when breathing and heartbeat stop. But the ability of medical personnel to resuscitate someone after a heart attack and artificially sustain breathing makes such definitions of death obsolete. Medical and legal experts continue to debate the meaning of death, but many now consider death an *irreversible* state involving no response to stimulation, no movement or breathing, no reflexes, and no indication of brain activity (Wall, 1980; Jones, 1998).

The Right To Die Debate

American Terri Schiavo remained alive without evidence of being conscious or responsive to her surroundings for fifteen years following a heart attack that cut off blood to her brain. Debate surrounding this case, which ended when her feeding tube was removed in 2005, shows that many people are less afraid of death than of the prospect of being kept alive at all costs. In other words, medical technology that can sustain life also threatens personal freedom by letting doctors or others rather than the dying person decide when life is to end. In response, people who support a movement for the right to die now seek control over their deaths just as they seek control over their lives (Ogden, 2001). After thoughtful discussion, patients, families, and physicians may decide not to take "heroic measures" to keep a person alive. Physicians and family members may decide to issue a "do not resuscitate" order, which will allow a patient to die. *Living wills*—documents stating which medical procedures an individual wants and does not want under specific conditions—are now widely used in Canada and the United States.

A more difficult issue involves mercy killing, or **euthanasia**—*assisting in the death of a person suffering from an incurable disease.* Euthanasia (from the Greek, meaning "a good death") poses an ethical dilemma because it involves not just refusing treatment but actively taking steps to end life. Some people see euthanasia as an act of kindness, while others consider it a form of murder. In Canada and the United States, euthanasia is illegal—even physician-assisted suicide for the elderly and those who are terminally ill—but the issue continues to be hotly debated. The Netherlands, in contrast, has the most permissive euthanasia law in the world; the Thinking Critically box (on p. 398) takes a closer look at it.

Canadians did their own soul-searching about euthanasia in the early 1990s. Sue Rodrigues had been diagnosed with the terminal illness amyotrophic lateral sclerosis (ALS, or Lou Gehrig's disease), that would lead to increasing disability and pain followed eventually by her death. Her situation was the subject of widespread media coverage because she applied to the courts—right to the Supreme Court of Canada—for permission to have assistance in committing suicide. The Supreme Court turned her down. Less than a year later, in February 1994, Rodrigues arranged for assisted suicide with her friend, a Canadian member of Parliament, Svend Robinson, at her side. Robinson had supported her through her court appeals and made it clear that he would be with her when she ended her life. The nature of the assistance Rodrigues required was never revealed and Robinson was not charged with a crime.

Should Canada hold the line on euthanasia or follow the lead of the Dutch? Supporters of the right to die maintain that, faced with unbearable suffering, an individual should be able to choose to live or die. And, if death is the choice, medical assistance should help people achieve a pain-free death (or death with dignity). On the other side of the debate, opponents fear that laws allowing physician-assisted suicide invite abuse. Pointing to the Netherlands, critics cite surveys indicating that, in most cases, the five conditions for physician-assisted suicide are not met. In particular, most physicians do not consult another doctor or even report the euthanasia to authorities. Of greater concern is the fact that, in about one-fifth of all physician-assisted suicides, the patient never explicitly asks to die. This is so even though half of these patients are conscious and capable of making decisions for themselves (Gillon, 1999). Such facts lead opponents to argue that legalizing physician-assisted suicide puts a nation on a slippery slope towards more and more euthanasia. How can we be sure, they ask, that ill people won't be pushed into accepting death by doctors who consider suicide the right choice for the terminally ill, or by family members who are weary of caring for them?

However the right to die debate turns out, Canadian society has entered a new era when it comes to dying. More often, individuals, family members, and medical personnel must face death not as a medical fact but as a negotiated outcome.

BEREAVEMENT

Elisabeth Kübler-Ross (1969) found that most people confront their own death in stages (see Chapter 5,

THINKING CRITICALLY

Death on Demand: Euthanasia in the Netherlands

Marcus Erich picked up the telephone and called his brother Arjen. In a quiet voice, thirty-two–year-old Marcus announced, "It's Friday at five o'clock." When the time came, Arjen was there, having driven to his brother's farmhouse an hour south of Amsterdam. They said their final goodbyes. Soon afterwards, Marcus's physician arrived. Marcus and the doctor spoke for a few moments, then the doctor prepared a "cocktail" of barbiturates and other drugs. As Marcus drank the mixture, he made a face, joking, "Can't you make this sweeter?" As the minutes passed, Marcus lay back and his eyes closed. But after half an hour, he was still breathing. At that point, according to their earlier agreement, the physician administered a lethal injection. Minutes later, Marcus's life came to an end.

Events like this take us to the heart of the belief that people have a right to die. Marcus Erich was dying from the virus that causes AIDS. For five years, his body had been wasting away, and he was suffering greatly, with no hope of recovery. He wanted his doctor to end his life, legally. Marcus lived in the Netherlands, a small nation that has gone further than any other in the world in allowing mercy killing, or euthanasia.

A 1981 Dutch law allows a physician to assist in a suicide if the following five conditions are met:

- The patient must make a voluntary, well-considered, and repeated request to a doctor for help in dying.
- The patient's suffering must be unbearable and without prospect of improvement.
- The doctor and the patient must discuss alternatives.
- The doctor must consult with at least one colleague who has access to the patient and the patient's medical records.
- The assisted suicide must be performed in accordance with sound medical practice.

Official records indicate that doctors end 3000 to 4000 lives every year in the Netherlands. But, because many cases are never reported, the actual number may be as much as double that.

WHAT DO YOU THINK?

1. What advantages and benefits do you see in the Dutch law permitting physician-assisted suicide?
2. What are the disadvantages or dangers of such a law?
3. Overall, do you support or oppose such a law? Explain your position.

Sources: Based on della Cava (1997) and Mauro (1997).

"Socialization"). Initially, individuals react with *denial*, followed by *anger;* then they try *negotiation*, hoping for divine intervention. Gradually, they fall into *resignation* and finally reach *acceptance.*

According to some researchers, bereavement follows the same pattern of stages. Those close to a dying person, for instance, may initially deny the reality of impending death and then, with time, gradually reach a point of acceptance. Other investigators, however, question any "linear stage" theory, arguing that bereavement is a personal and unpredictable process (Lund, *et al.*, 1986; Lund, 1989; Cutcliffe, 1998). What experts do agree on, however, is the fact that how family and friends view an impending death has an effect on the person who is dying. By accepting an approaching death, others help the dying person do the same; denying death isolates the dying person, who is unable to share feelings and experiences with others.

Many dying people find support in a *hospice.* Unlike a hospital, which is designed to cure disease, a hospice provides palliative care and helps people have a good death. These care centres for dying people try to minimize pain and suffering—either at the centre or at home—and encourage family members to stay close by. Most hospices also provide social support for family members experiencing bereavement (Foliart and Clausen, 2001).

Under the best of circumstances, bereavement often involves profound grief. Research documents show that bereavement is less intense for someone who accepts the death of a loved one and has brought satisfactory closure to the relationship. Such closure also allows family and friends to better comfort one another after death occurs.

Reaching closure is not possible when a death is unexpected. Especially in such cases, social disorientation may be profound and may last for years. One study of middle-aged women who had recently experienced the death of their husbands found that many felt they had lost not only a spouse but also their reason for living. In such circumstances, dealing successfully with bereavement requires the time and social support necessary to form a new sense of self and to recognize new life options (Atchley, 1983; Danforth and Glass, Jr., 2001). With the number of older people increasing so fast, understanding death and dying is taking on greater importance.

To learn more about palliative care in Canada, go to the Canadian Hospice Palliative Care Association at www.chpca.net.

Unlike a hospital, which tries to save and extend life, a hospice tries to give dying people greater comfort. The setting is, as much as possible, personal, and the dying person can have the companionship and support of family members.

Aging: Looking Ahead

This chapter has explored the greying of Canada and other high-income nations. By 2050, the elderly population of  this country will exceed the population of the entire nation in 1900—and 1 in 4 of seniors will be older than 85. In decades to come, then, Canadian society's oldest members will gain a far greater voice in everyday life. Younger people will find that careers relating to gerontology (the study of elderly people) are increasingly important.

With more elderly people living longer and longer, will our society have the support services to sustain them?

Remember that, as the needs of elderly people increase, a smaller share of younger people will be there to respond and to pay the bills for social services with their taxes. What about the spiralling medical costs of an aging society? As the baby boomers enter old age, some analysts paint a dooms-day picture, with desperate and dying elderly people every-where (Longino, 1994). In contrast, David Foot (1998: 275) argues that Europe has already learned to cope with propor-tions of elders greater than the 22 percent we expect to reach in Canada.

But there is also good news regarding the North American situation. For one thing, the health of tomorrow's elderly people (that is, today's middle-aged adults) is better than ever. Smoking and alcohol consumption are down and, as more people become aware of the national problem of obesity, they are eating more healthfully. Such trends suggest that tomorrow's older Canadians may well become more vigorous and independent. They also will enjoy the benefits of steadily advancing medical technology—although, as the Thinking It Through box (on p. 400) explains, the question of how much of a country's medical resources older people can claim is already being hotly debated.

Another positive sign is the growing financial strength of elderly people. While recent years have been stressful, it is likely that tomorrow's elders will be more affluent than ever before. The baby boomers will be the first generation of seniors with women who have been in the labour force most of their lives, a fact reflected in their substantial savings and pensions. At the same time, younger adults will face a mounting responsibility to care for aging parents. A falling birth rate coupled with a growing elderly population will demand that middle-aged people perform an increasing share of care giving for the very old.

Most of us need to learn more about caring for aging parents, which includes far more than meeting physical needs. More important lessons involve communicating, expressing love, and facing up to eventual death. In caring for our parents, we will also teach important lessons to our children, including the skills they will need, one day, to care for us.

THINKING IT THROUGH
Setting Limits: Must We "Pull the Plug" on Old Age?

As the elderly population of North America grows, as new technol-ogy gives us more power to prolong life, and as medical care gets increasingly expensive, many now wonder just how much old age we can afford. Currently, about half the average person's lifetime spending on medical care occurs during the final years of life, and the share is rising. Against the spiralling costs of prolonging life, we well may ask if what is medically possi-ble is morally desirable. In the decades to come, warns gerontologist Daniel Callahan (1987), a population of elderly people ready and eager to extend their lives will eventually force

continued

society either to pull the plug on old age, or shortchange everyone else.

To even raise this issue, Callahan admits, seems cold and heartless. But consider that the bill for health care of older people is doubling or quadrupling over time. This dramatic increase reflects the current policy of directing more and more medical resources to studying and treating the diseases and disabilities of old age. Callahan is writing about the American situation, but Canada must make similar decisions. The fact that almost all health care is publicly funded makes the problem here more acute: taxpayers have to pay the whole bill with no help from private wealth. So Callahan's case for limits applies to Canada every bit as much as it does to the United States:

- First, the more we spend on behalf of older people, the less we have to provide for others. With so many other demands, including child poverty, can we afford to spend more and more on the oldest members of our society?

- Second, a *longer* life does not necessarily mean a *better* life. Cost aside, does heart surgery that prolongs the life of an eighty-four–year-old woman a year or two necessarily improve the quality of her life? Cost considered, would those resources yield more "quality of life" if used, say, to give a ten-year-old child a kidney transplant? or to provide basic care and comfort to hundreds of low-income elders?

- Third, we need to reconsider our view of death as an enemy to be conquered at all costs. Rather, Callahan suggests, a more realistic position for an aging society is to treat death as a natural end to the life course. If we cannot make peace with death for our own well-being, then a society with limited resources must do it for the benefit of others.

But not everyone agrees. Shouldn't people who have worked all their lives and made our society what it is enjoy our generosity in their final years?

Would it be right to deny medical care to aging people?

In the twenty-first century, we face questions that few would have imagined even fifty years ago. Is peak longevity good for everyone? Is it even *possible* for everyone?

WHAT DO YOU THINK?

1. Should doctors and hospitals use a double standard, offering more complete care to the youngest people and more limited care to society's oldest members? Why or why not?
2. Do you think that a goal of the medical establishment should be to extend life at all costs? Explain your position.
3. How should society balance the health care needs of elderly people with all the needs of the rest of society (such as education, roads, public transit, clean water, and electricity), all of which are funded by the taxpayer?

Sources: Callahan (1987), Kapp (2001).

MAKING THE GRADE

The following learning tools will help you see what you know, identify what you still need to learn, and expand your understanding beyond the text. You can also visit this text's Companion Website™ at www.pearsoned.ca/macionis to find useful practice tests.

The Greying of Canada

The proportion of elderly people in Canada has risen from 4 percent in 1900 to about 13 percent today; by the middle of the twenty-first century, 25 percent of our society's members will be elderly.

Growing Old: Biology and Culture

Gerontology, the study of aging and elderly people, focuses on how people change in old age and on how various cultures define aging. Most younger people exaggerate the extent of disability among older people. Growing old is accompanied by a rising rate of disease and disability, but most seniors are healthy. Psychological research confirms that growing old does not result in overall loss of intelligence or radical changes in personality.

The age at which people are defined as old varies. Until several centuries ago, old age began as early as thirty. In poor societies today, where life expectancy is low, people become old at fifty or even forty. Worldwide, industrialization fosters a decline in the social standing of elderly people relative to younger people.

Transitions and Challenges of Aging

As people age, they face a number of problems, including social isolation brought on by retirement, physical disability, and the death of friends or a spouse. To deal with these issues, most elderly people enjoy the support of family members.

Since 1960, poverty among older people has declined. The aged poor include categories of people—such as single women and members of visible minorities—some of whom are at high risk of poverty at any age.

Most care giving for elderly people is performed by family members, typically women.

Ageism—prejudice and discrimination against old people—is used to justify age stratification. The fact that this category includes men and women of all races, ethnicities, and social classes suggests that older people collectively are not a minority.

Theoretical Analysis of Aging

Disengagement theory, based on the structural-functional approach, suggests that society helps elderly people disengage from positions of social responsibility before the onset of disability or death. This process provides for the orderly transfer of statuses and roles from the older to the younger generation.

Activity theory, based on the symbolic-interaction approach, claims that a high level of activity increases people's personal satisfaction in old age.

Age stratification is a focus of the social-conflict approach. A capitalist society's emphasis on economic efficiency leads to the devaluation of those who are less productive, including elderly people.

Death and Dying

Modern society has set death apart from everyday life. This avoidance of death also reflects the fact that most people in high-income societies die in old age. Recent trends suggest that people are confronting death more directly and seeking control over the process of dying.

Aging: Looking Ahead

As the proportion of older people increases, we face important questions about how to meet their needs. Medical costs are rising rapidly, but tomorrow's elderly people are likely to be more affluent than ever before.

KEY CONCEPTS

gerontology (p. 384) the study of aging and elderly people

age stratification (p. 387) the unequal distribution of wealth, power, and privilege among people at different stages of the life course

gerontocracy (p. 388) a form of social organization in which elderly people have the most wealth, power, and prestige

care giving (p. 391) informal and unpaid care provided to a dependent person by family members, other relatives, or friends

ageism (p. 394) prejudice and discrimination against older people

disengagement theory (p. 394) the idea that society functions in an orderly way by

disengaging people from positions of responsibility as they reach old age

activity theory (p. 395) the idea that a high level of activity increases personal satisfaction in old age

euthanasia (mercy killing) (p. 397) assisting in the death of a person suffering from an incurable disease

APPLICATIONS & EXERCISES

1. Ask several faculty nearing retirement about the practices and policies of your college or university for helping older faculty when they retire. Based on what you learn, decide whether retiring from an academic career is harder or easier than retiring from other kinds of work, and explain why.

2. Look through an issue of a popular magazine—say, *Maclean's* or *People*—and note pictures of men and women in news stories and advertising. What share of the pictures show elderly people? In what types of advertising are they featured?

3. Obtain a copy of a living will (try an online search), and try to respond to all the questions it asks. How does filling out this form affect your thinking about death?

PRENTICE HALL
mysoclab™
Where learning & the sociological imagination intersect.

To reinforce your understanding of this chapter, and to identify topics for further study, visit MySocLab at **www.pearsoned.ca/mysoclab/** for diagnostic tests and a multimedia ebook.

16

The Economy and Work

How does change in the economy reshape society?

What makes capitalist and socialist economies different?

Why have the types of jobs in Canada changed over the last fifty years?

"When you compare what my dad looked forward to against what I'm looking forward to, he expected that things would be better for us and that my children would have it better than I have. But there isn't that feeling any more." Ian Crump, a 45-year-old father of three, thus put three generations of experience in a nutshell. He was pondering the situation of the descendants of Kitty and Henry Neville Compton Crump at a family gathering at the old prairie homestead south of Regina. The family had felt the effects of the restructured economy, high taxes, and deficits that were contributing to a sense of economic malaise throughout Canada.

Ian's cousin Tom Crump went through an experience that clearly illustrates the changing job environment. As a hospital administrator in Vancouver, he had been preparing to lay off fifty people when his boss came in and announced that Crump himself would be the fifty-first. A senior position and seventeen years with the same employer proved to be no protection from ongoing economic upheaval and no base for launching his children into middle-class security. Downsizing and restructuring were leading to layoffs at all levels, including middle management, and breaking the link that once bound company and employee for a much longer period—possibly through the entire working life of the employee. Crump felt that "by the standards of his parents, the job was a brief interlude; by the expectations of his children, an eternity" (Greenspon, 1993).

The experiences of Ian Crump and his extended family were shared by many Canadians: early (forced) retirements, layoffs, part-time employment instead of the desired full-time work, periods of unemployment, a series of jobs rather than a secure long-term career. Factory closings, mergers, downsizing, restructuring, globalization, freelancing, outsourcing, two recessions in the past twenty years, and a jobless recovery have all contributed to economic insecurity. All of these changes, coupled with more working from a home office (often for multiple employers), mean that, increasingly, people can look forward to finding "work" rather than "jobs." The traditional pattern of working for decades for the same employer has been shaken to its core.

Here, we examine the economy as a social institution, explore the character of work today, and explain some of the consequences of the emerging global marketplace for Canadians. We will see that a good deal of the conventional wisdom about economic life no longer applies in the face of sweeping global changes. The economic upheaval described above is part of the recession experienced in Canada in the early 1990s. Our economy recovered well by the mid–2000s, but many of the workplace changes of the 1990s are with us still. In periods of economic stability or upheaval, sociologists debate how the economy ought to work, whose interests it ought to serve, and what companies and workers owe to each other.

The Economy: Historical Overview

The **economy** is *the social institution that organizes a society's production, distribution, and consumption of goods and services.* As an institution, the economy operates in a generally predictable manner. *Goods* are commodities ranging from necessities (food, clothing, shelter) to luxury items (cars, swimming pools, yachts). *Services* are activities that benefit others (for example, the work of priests, physicians, teachers, couriers, and software specialists). In Canada, more than in the United States, governments are involved in the distribution of a number of these services. We value goods and services because they ensure survival or because they make life easier or more interesting. Also, what people produce as workers and what they buy as consumers are important parts of social identity, as when we say, "He's a steelworker," or "She drives a Mercedes." The distribution of goods and services, then, shapes the lives of everyone in basic ways.

The complex economies that mark modern industrial and post-industrial societies are the product of centuries of technological innovation and social change. The following sections highlight three technological revolutions that reorganized the means of production and transformed social life.

THINKING ABOUT DIVERSITY:
RACE, CLASS, & GENDER
The French Canadians of Manchester, New Hampshire

In the 1870s, French-Canadian immigrants who had been forced out of impoverished farming areas by a scarcity of land found their way, in substantial numbers, from rural Quebec to the Amoskeag mills. The mill owners soon concluded that French Canadians were the ideal labour force, and Amoskeag proceeded to recruit them actively. Mill agents scanned the Quebec countryside for possible recruits, and advertisements in Quebec newspapers extolled the virtues of Amoskeag and Manchester.

French-Canadian workers were ideal in part because they had large families. Entire families, including children, were brought into the mills and could be counted on to draw kinfolk as well as their own large families. So numerous did they become that the mill bosses were forced to learn a little French. This large group was appreciated by management because it proved to be a "docile," "industrious," and "stable" labour force with a family-based structure that discouraged union involvement. Despite their numbers, however, not one French Canadian was promoted into the supervisory ranks—these positions were filled by native-born Americans or immigrants of British and northern European stock.

"Picking the cloth" after weaving, scene in a mode mill, Paterson, N.J.   © Underwood & Underwood, U-1595

The Amoskeag Manufacturing Company, once the largest textile factory in the world, was the pillar of economic life in Manchester, New Hampshire. From its founding in 1837 to its closing in 1935, the Amoskeag plant provided the major source of employment in Manchester and controlled the development of the city as a whole. When the company was initially founded, a community of young women from rural New England worked at the factory, living together in boarding houses with a 10 P.M. curfew and compulsory church attendance. Irish immigrant families, willing to work for lower wages, eventually replaced the mill girls.

Migration from Quebec to Manchester—a convenient stop on the railway linking Montreal and Boston—was so substantial that, by 1910, French Canadians made up 35 percent of the Amoskeag labour force and 38 percent of the population of Manchester. Some of the families that migrated to Manchester stayed only long enough to save some money before returning to their farms in Quebec. Others put down permanent roots and contributed a French flavour to life in the section of Manchester that is still called Little Canada.

WHAT DO YOU THINK?

1. What would have happened if the French Canadians who moved to Manchester and elsewhere in New England had gone to Ontario instead? What would Ontario look like today if, from the beginning, francophone migrants had gone west instead of south?
2. Why was Amoskeag so anxious to recruit workers from Quebec?
3. What does this story tell you about the migration patterns of families?

Source: Based on Hareven and Langenbach (1978).

THE AGRICULTURAL REVOLUTION

Members of the earliest human societies were hunters and gatherers living off the land. In these technologically simple societies, there was no distinct economy. Rather, production and consumption took place within the family. As Chapter 4 ("Society") explained, when people harnessed animals to plows, beginning some 5000 years ago, a new agricultural economy was created that was fifty times more productive than hunting and gathering. The resulting surplus meant that not everyone had to produce food, so many took on specialized work: making tools, raising animals, or building dwellings. Soon towns sprang up, linked by networks of traders dealing in food, animals, and other goods. These four factors—agricultural technology, job specialization, permanent settlements, and trade—made the economy a distinct social institution.

THE INDUSTRIAL REVOLUTION

By the mid-eighteenth century, a second technological revolution was under way, first in England and then in North America: the Industrial Revolution. The development of industry was even more powerful than the rise of agriculture in bringing change to the economy. Industrialization changed the economy in five fundamental ways:

The rise of a global economy means that more and more products originally produced in one country are now made and consumed around the world. What do you see as some of the good consequences of globalization? What about harmful consequences?

1. *New sources of energy.* Throughout history, "energy" had meant the muscle power of people or animals. But in 1765, English inventor James Watt introduced the steam engine, so that steam engines—a hundred times stronger than muscle power—soon drove heavy machinery.

2. *Centralization of work in factories.* Coal-fired steam-powered machines soon moved work from homes to factories, the centralized and impersonal workplaces housing the machines.

3. *Manufacturing and mass production.* Before the Industrial Revolution, most people grew or gathered raw materials (such as grain, wood, or wool). In an industrial economy, the focus shifts so that most people work to turn raw materials into a wide range of finished products (such as furniture and clothing).

4. *Specialization.* Before industrialization, people worked at home as artisans making products from start to finish. In the factory, a worker repeats a single task over and over, making only a small contribution to the finished product. Such specialization raises productivity but lowers the skill level of the average worker.

5. *Wage labour.* Instead of working for themselves, factory workers became wage labourers working for strangers, who often cared less for them than for the machines they operated.

The Industrial Revolution gradually raised the standard of living as countless new products and services fuelled an expanding marketplace. Yet the benefits of industrial technology were shared very unequally, especially at the begin-

ning. Some factory owners made vast fortunes, while the majority of industrial workers lived close to poverty. Women working in factories were among the most poorly paid; children, too, worked in factories or in coal mines for pennies a day. The Thinking about Diversity box (on p. 405) looks at the experience of francophone Canadians in an American textile factory.

THE INFORMATION REVOLUTION AND POST-INDUSTRIAL SOCIETY

By the middle of the twentieth century, the nature of production itself was changing once again. Canada was becoming a **post-industrial economy,** *a productive system based on service work and extensive use of information technology.* Automated machinery—and, more recently, robotics—reduced the role of human labour in factory production, while bureaucracy simultaneously expanded the ranks of clerical workers and managers.

Driving this change is a third technological breakthrough: the computer. Just as the Industrial Revolution did two-and-a-half centuries ago, the Information Revolution has introduced new kinds of products and new forms of communication and has altered the character of work. In general, there have been three significant changes:

1. *From tangible products to ideas.* The industrial era was defined by the production of goods; in the post-industrial era, people work with symbols. Computer programmers, graphic designers, financial analysts, advertising executives, architects, editors, and all sorts of consultants make up the labour force of the information age.

2. *From mechanical skills to literacy skills.* The Industrial Revolution required mechanical skills, but the Information Revolution requires literacy skills: speaking and writing well and, of course, knowing how to use a computer. People able to communicate effectively enjoy new opportunities; people without these skills face fewer opportunities.

3. *From factories to almost anywhere.* Industrial technology drew workers into factories located near power sources, but computer technology allows people to work almost anywhere. Laptop and wireless computers and cellphones now turn the home, a car, or even an airplane into a "virtual" office. In short, new information technology blurs the line between work and home life.

⟶ YOUR TURN ⟵

What are two advantages and two disadvantages of being able to work almost anywhere? Do you think the benefits of the "anywhere" office outweigh the downsides?

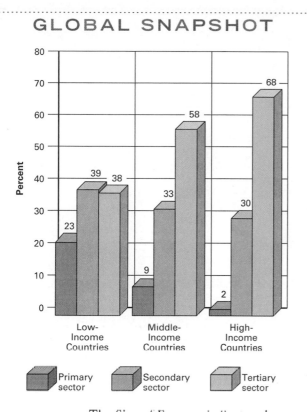

FIGURE 16-1   The Size of Economic Sectors by
Income Level of Country

As countries become richer, the primary sector of the economy
becomes smaller and the tertiary or service sector becomes larger.

Sources: Estimates based on United Nations Development Programme (2000) and World
Bank (2000).

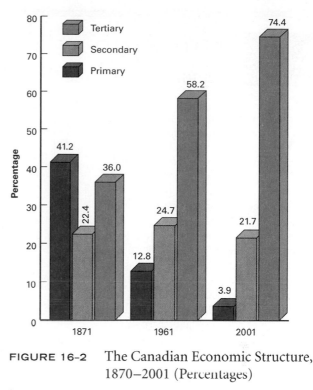

FIGURE 16-2   The Canadian Economic Structure,
1870–2001 (Percentages)

Sources: Adapted by L.M. Gerber from Watson (1988) and Statistics Canada, Census
2001, Catalogue number 97F0012XCB2001014.

SECTORS OF THE ECONOMY

The three revolutions just described reflect a shifting balance among the three sectors of a society's economy. The **primary sector** is *the part of the economy that draws raw materials from the natural environment.* The primary sector (agriculture, raising animals, fishing, forestry, and mining) is largest in low-income nations. Figure 16–1 shows that 23 percent of the labour force is employed in the primary sector in low-income countries, compared to 9 percent in middle-income nations and just 2 percent in high-income countries such as the United States. Figure 16–2 traces the decline of the primary sector in Canada from 41 percent of the labour force in 1871 to less than 4 percent in 2001. Note that the primary sector was larger in Canada in 1871, 1961, and 2001 than in low-, middle-, and high-income countries. In earlier years, this reflected the importance of farming—more recently, the continuing importance of oil, mining, and forestry.

The **secondary sector** is *the part of the economy that transforms raw materials into manufactured goods.* This sector, which grows quickly as societies industrialize, includes oper-

ations such as refining petroleum into gasoline and turning metals into tools and automobiles. The construction industries are also part of this secondary sector. The globalization of industry means that just about all the world's countries have a significant share of their workers in the secondary sector. Figure 16–1 shows that, at this point in time, the secondary sector employs a larger share of workers in low-income than in high-income countries. In Canada, as shown in Figure 16–2, Canada's secondary sector is small by world standards, but it has remained remarkably stable since 1870. Despite concerns about the effects of globalization, our manufacturing or goods-producing sector has not declined. On the other hand, our secondary sector is smaller than that of other countries—regardless of income level (see Figure 16–1). While Canada has lost manufacturing jobs to lower-wage countries in response to globalization, other manufacturing industries have been established to replace those jobs.

The "Thinking it Through" box (on p. 408) looks at the distribution of secondary sector employment—in terms of the percentage of the labour force employed in manufacturing—across Canada's provinces and territories.

The **tertiary sector** is *the part of the economy that involves services rather than goods.* Accounting for 38 percent of the labour force in low-income countries, the tertiary sector grows with industrialization and dominates the economies of middle-income countries (58% of the labour force) and high-income, post-industrial nations (68%). Three-quarters of the Canadian labour force is in

THINKING IT THROUGH
Regional Economic Disparities

Manufacturing industries in Canada are considered by some to be the real wealth-creating engine of our economy. Figure 16–3 shows the variation in the percentage of the Canadian labour force employed in manufacturing industries for different regions of Canada. Although one can debate the definition of "region" (Brodie, 1989), there is some justification for defining regions of Canada as units with institutional or political boundaries (Breton, 1981; Matthews, 1983). Furthermore, trying to measure regional disparities is easier if data (e.g., census data) are collected regularly for the units in question. For these reasons, throughout this box, regions are defined in terms of provinces and territories.

Despite consistent official efforts to promote regional development and to spread the manufacturing base more evenly throughout Canada, Ontario and Quebec remain the manufacturing core of the Canadian economy, with 23 to 25 percent of their workers involved. Another way of looking at the manufacturing clout of Ontario and Quebec is to note that, with 60 percent of the total Canadian population, they have 75 percent of the manufacturing jobs. Saskatchewan has the weakest manufacturing base of all the provinces—just above the level in the three territories. And British Columbia, for all its affluence, is still economically undiversified and overwhelmingly dependent on forestry (Marchak, 1986). In the context of the current oil boom, there is the danger that Albertans will become increasingly dependent on oil revenues to sustain the quality of life to which they have become accustomed.

Brym points out that two explanations have been offered for these regional disparities: the "mainstream" approach and the "radical" or political economy approach. The mainstream approach focuses on the geographic causes of diversity: distance from markets, physical barriers (such as

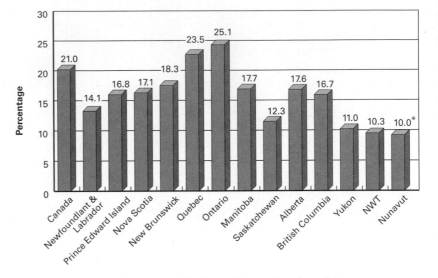

FIGURE 16–3   Percentage of Labour Force Employed in Manufacturing Industries for Canada, the Provinces, and the Territories, 2001

*Estimate provided for Nunavut, because of errors in the data.

Source: Calculations by L.M. Gerber, based on Statistics Canada, [online] at www.statcan.ca.

mountains), natural resources (generally in high demand), and population characteristics. From the radical, or political economy, perspective, inequities derive from human actions rather than nature, in that confederation allowed "powerful central Canadian economic interests to drain wealth from the weak peripheral or hinterland regions, such as the prairies and the maritimes" (Brym, 1986:8).

Some policies of federal, provincial/territorial, and municipal governments are designed to decrease economic disparities by attracting industry to disadvantaged regions or communities. This is done by facilitating rezoning and offering tax breaks and even subsidies that are more enticing than those of competing communities. Approaching the problem from another angle, the federal government has moved a number of its functions to parts of the country outside Ottawa.

Other policies accentuate the disparities by concentrating capital,

productive capacity, and jobs in a particular region. Population then flows to that region, which translates into political power (that is, increased representation in Parliament), and eventually into new policies that strengthen the economic centre. With half of Canada's population in the Windsor/Quebec City corridor, this trend is difficult to reverse.

WHAT DO YOU THINK?

1. Should governments take steps to reduce economic disparities throughout Canada—even if it means discouraging migration to areas with more job opportunities?

2. Why is it important, for regional economies, that manufacturing be spread more evenly throughout the country?

3. Since economic and political clout (and population) appear to be flowing naturally to urban Ontario and Quebec, should we not just allow the process to take its course?

WINDOW ON THE WO'RLD

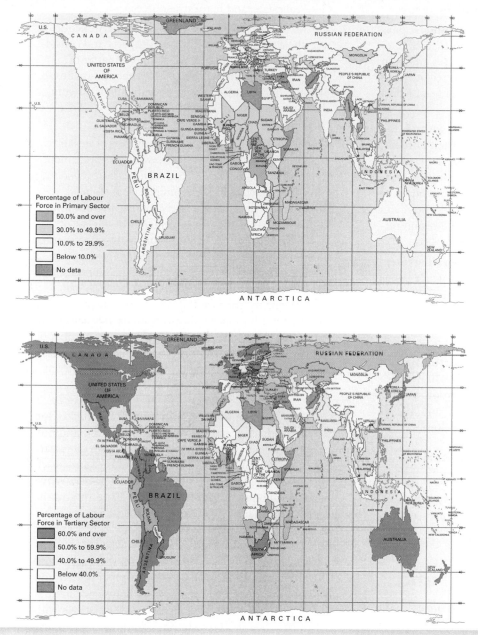

GLOBAL MAP 16–1

Agricultural Employment in Global Perspective

The primary sector of the economy is largest in the nations that are least developed: in the poor countries of Africa and Asia, up to half of all workers are farmers. This picture is altogether different in the world's most economically developed countries—including the United States, Canada, the United Kingdom, and Australia—which have only 2 percent of their work forces in agriculture.

Percentage of Labour Force in Primary Sector
- 50.0% and over
- 30.0% to 49.9%
- 10.0% to 29.9%
- Below 10.0%
- No data

GLOBAL MAP 16–2

Service-Sector Employment in Global Perspective

The tertiary sector of the economy becomes ever larger as a nation's income level rises. In the United States, Canada, Western Europe, Australia, and Japan, about two-thirds of the labour force performs service work.

Sources: Data from United Nations Development Programme (2000) and World Bank (2000, 2001); map projection from *Peters Atlas of the World* (1990).

Percentage of Labour Force in Tertiary Sector
- 60.0% and over
- 50.0% to 59.9%
- 40.0% to 49.9%
- Below 40.0%
- No data

service work, including secretarial and clerical work, food service, sales, law, health care, law enforcement, advertising, and teaching from preschool to university. This dramatic increase in the Canadian service sector was a result more of the shift in labour from the primary (extraction) sector than from the secondary (manufacturing) sector. Note that our tertiary sector is larger than that of other high-income countries: it's possible that only the United States—with 77 percent of its labour force in the service sector—has a larger tertiary component than Canada.

Another way to look at the economy within Canada is to compare different regions, as we do in the Thinking It Through box (on p. 408).

THE GLOBAL ECONOMY

New information technology is drawing people around the world closer together and creating a **global economy,** *expanding economic activity that crosses national borders.* The development of a global economy has five major consequences:

- **First, we see a global division of labour**. Different regions of the world specialize in one sector of economic activity. As Global Map 16–1 shows, agriculture represents about half the total economic output of the world's poorest countries. Global Map 16–2 indicates that most of the economic output of high-income countries, including

Canada, is in the service sector. The poorest nations, then, specialize in producing raw materials, while the richest nations specialize in the production of various services.

- **Second, an increasing number of products pass through more than one nation**. Look no further than your morning coffee: the beans may have been grown in Colombia and transported to Canada on a freighter registered in Liberia, made in Japan using steel from Korea and fuelled by oil from Venezuela.

- **Third, national governments no longer control the economic activity that takes place within their borders**. In fact, governments cannot even regulate the value of their national currencies because dollars, euros, pounds sterling, and yen are traded around the clock in financial markets in New York, Toronto, Tokyo, and elsewhere. Global markets are a network using satellite communications to link the world's businesses and markets.

- **Fourth, a small number of businesses, operating internationally, now controls a vast share of the world's economic activity**. A rough estimate is that the 600 largest companies account for half the entire world's economic output (Kidron and Segal, 1991; Gergen, 2002).

- **Fifth, and finally, globalization of the economy raises concerns about the rights and opportunities of workers**. Critics of this trend claim that North America is losing jobs—especially factory jobs—to low-income nations. Workers here face lower wages and higher unemployment, and most workers in low-income nations are paid extremely low wages. As a result, say critics, the global expansion of capitalism threatens the well-being of workers throughout the world.

The world is still divided into 192 politically distinct nations. But increasing international economic activity makes "nationhood" less significant than it was even a decade ago.

Economic Systems: Paths to Justice

Every society's economic system makes a statement about *justice* by determining who is entitled to what. Two general economic models are capitalism and socialism. No nation anywhere in the world has an economy that is completely one or the other; capitalism and socialism represent two ends of a continuum along which all real-world economies can be located. We now look, in turn, at these two models.

CAPITALISM

Capitalism is *an economic system in which natural resources and the means of producing goods and services are privately owned*. An ideal capitalist economy has three distinctive features:

1. *Private ownership of property*. In a capitalist economy, individuals can own almost anything. The more capi-

talistic an economy is, the more private ownership there is of wealth-producing property, such as factories, real estate, and natural resources.

2. *Pursuit of personal profit*. A capitalist society encourages the accumulation of private property and considers the profit motive natural—simply a matter of doing business. The Scottish philosopher Adam Smith (1723–1790) claimed that, from individuals pursuing their self-interest, an entire society prospers (1937; orig. 1776).

3. *Competition and consumer choice*. A purely capitalist economy is a free-market system with no government interference (sometimes called a *laissez-faire economy*, from the French words meaning "leave it alone"). Adam Smith stated that a freely competitive economy regulates itself by the "invisible hand" of the law of supply and demand. Consumers regulate a free-market economy, Smith explained, by selecting the goods and services offering the greatest value. As producers compete for the customer's business, they provide the highest-quality goods at the lowest possible prices. In Smith's time-honoured phrase, from narrow self-interest comes the "greatest good for the greatest number of people." Government control of an economy distorts market forces by reducing the quantity and quality of goods; in the process, it shortchanges consumers.

Justice in a capitalist system amounts to freedom of the marketplace, where a person can produce, invest, and buy according to individual self-interest. Tim Horton can create a chain of doughnut shops, Grandma can invest in Nortel, and shoppers can spend at The Bay or on E-bay. While Canada is a capitalist society, the guiding hand of government plays an extensive role in economic affairs. In other words, ours is a capitalist system with socialist leanings. Through taxation and various regulatory agencies, governments influence what companies produce, the quality and cost of merchandise, the products that are imported and exported, and how we consume or conserve natural resources. (The recent softwood lumber negotiations with the United States provide a dramatic example.) Government also defines and determines the extent of "Canadian content" and otherwise determines what we will see on television or hear on the radio. The federal government, and some provincial governments, own and operate a number of businesses, including the Canadian Broadcasting Corporation, Via Rail, Atomic Energy of Canada, and Hydro-Québec. Governments regulate securities, step in to prevent the collapse of businesses (such as Algoma Steel), mandate minimum wages, enforce workplace safety standards, regulate corporate mergers, provide farm price supports, and administer employment insurance, welfare, and pensions. Not surprisingly, federal, provincial/territorial, and municipal governments employ 5 percent of Canada's labour force in public administration.

Capitalism still thrives in Hong Kong (*left*), evident in streets choked with advertising and shoppers. Socialism is more the rule in China's capital Beijing (*right*), a city dominated by government buildings rather than a downtown business district.

SOCIALISM

Socialism is *an economic system in which natural resources and the means of producing goods and services are collectively owned.* In its ideal form, a socialist economy rejects each of the three characteristics of capitalism just described in favour of three opposite features:

1. *Collective ownership of property.* A socialist economy limits rights to private property, especially property used to generate income. Government controls such property and makes housing and other goods available to all, not just to the people with the most money.

2. *Pursuit of collective goals.* The individualistic pursuit of profit goes against the collective orientation of socialism. What capitalism celebrates as the "entrepreneurial spirit," socialism condemns as greed; individuals are urged to work for the common good of all.

3. *Government control of the economy.* Socialism rejects capitalism's laissez-faire approach in favour of a *centrally controlled* or *command economy* operated by the government. Commercial advertising therefore has only a small role in socialist economies.

Justice in a socialist context means not competing to gain wealth but meeting everyone's basic needs in a roughly equal manner. From a socialist point of view, the common capitalist practice of giving workers as little in pay and benefits as possible to boost company earnings is putting profits before people, and is unjust. Cuba, China, and some two dozen other nations in Asia, Africa, and Latin America model their economies on socialism, placing almost all wealth-generating property under state control (McColm, *et al.*, 1991; Freedom House, 2005). The extent of world socialism has declined in recent years as the countries in Eastern Europe and the former Soviet Union now gear their economies towards a market system.

Many people think of *socialism* and *communism* as the same thing, but they are not. **Communism** is *a hypothetical economic and political system in which all members of a society are socially equal.* Karl Marx viewed socialism as one important step on the path towards the ideal of a communist society that abolishes all class divisions. In many socialist societies today, the dominant political party describes itself as communist, but the communist goal has not been achieved in any society. Why? For one thing, social stratification involves differences in power as well as wealth. Socialist societies have reduced economic differences by regulating people's range of choices. In the process, government did not "wither away," as Marx imagined it would; rather, government has grown, giving socialist political elites enormous power and privilege. Marx might have agreed that a communist society is a *utopia* (from Greek words meaning "no place"), an ideal society. Yet Marx considered communism a worthy goal and might well have objected to so-called Marxist societies such as North Korea, China, and Cuba for falling short of the promise of communism.

WELFARE CAPITALISM AND STATE CAPITALISM

Many nations of Western Europe, including Sweden, Finland, France, and Italy, have market-based economies but also offer broad social welfare programs. Analysts call this third type of economic system **welfare capitalism,** *an economic and political system that combines a mostly market-based economy with extensive social welfare programs.* Canada falls between Europe and the United States in its embrace of these programs. Under welfare capitalism, the government owns some of the largest industries and services, such as transportation, the mass media, and health care. In Sweden and Italy, about 12 percent of economic production is "nationalized," or state-controlled. Most industry is left in private hands, although it is subject to extensive government regulation. High taxation—aimed especially at the rich—

Societies with mostly capitalist economies are very productive, providing a high overall standard of living. At the same time, however, these societies distribute income and wealth very unequally. In what social classes do you think people express the most, and the least, support for the mostly capitalist economies of the United States and Canada?

funds a wide range of social welfare programs, including universal health care and child care (Olsen, 1996).

Yet another blend of capitalism and socialism is **state capitalism,** *an economic and political system in which companies are privately owned but co-operate closely with the government.* State capitalism is the rule among the nations along the Pacific Rim. Japan, South Korea, and Singapore are all capitalist countries, but their governments work in partnership with large companies, supplying financial assistance and controlling foreign imports to help their businesses compete in world markets (Gerlach, 1992).

RELATIVE ADVANTAGES OF CAPITALISM AND SOCIALISM

Which economic system works best? Comparing economic models is difficult because all countries mix capitalism and socialism to varying degrees. In addition, nations differ in cultural attitudes towards work, access to natural resources, levels of technological development, and patterns of trade. Despite such complicating factors, some crude comparisons are revealing.

One key dimension of economic performance is productivity. A commonly used measure of economic output, introduced in Chapter 12 ("Global Stratification"), is *gross domestic product* (GDP), the total value of all goods and services produced annually. Per capita (per person) GDP allows us to compare the economic performance of nations of different population sizes. The output of mostly capitalist countries at the end of the 1980s varied somewhat, but averaging the figures for the United States, Canada, and the nations of Western Europe yielded a per capita GDP of about US$13 500. The comparable figure for the mostly socialist former Soviet Union and nations of Eastern Europe was about US$5000. This means that the mostly capitalist countries outproduced the mostly socialist

nations by a ratio of 2.7 to 1 (United Nations Development Programme, 1990). A recent comparison of socialist North Korea (per capita GDP of US$1000) and capitalist South Korea (US$18 000) provides an even sharper contrast (Omestad, 2003).

The distribution of resources within a population is another important measure of how well an economic system works. A comparative study of Europe in the mid–1970s, when that region was split between mostly capitalist and mostly socialist countries, compared the earnings of the richest 5 percent of the population and the poorest 5 percent (Wiles, 1977): societies with mostly capitalist economies had a ratio of 10 to 1; the ratio for socialist countries was about 5 to 1. In other words, capitalist economies support a higher overall standard of living, but with greater income inequality. Said another way, socialist economies create more economic equality but with a lower overall living standard.

Personal Freedom

One additional consideration in evaluating capitalism and socialism is the personal freedom each gives its people. Capitalism emphasizes *freedom to* pursue personal self-interest. Capitalism, after all, depends on the freedom of producers and consumers to interact, with little interference by the state. Socialism, by contrast, emphasizes *freedom from* basic want. The goal of equality requires the state to regulate the economy, which in turn limits the personal choices and opportunities for citizens. No system has yet been able to offer both political freedom and economic equality. In the capitalist United States, the political system guarantees many personal freedoms, but these freedoms are not worth as much to a poor person as to a rich one. By contrast, China or Cuba has more economic equality, but people do not have as much freedom to speak out or travel within or outside of the country.

Global comparisons indicate that mostly socialist economies generate greater economic equality, although living standards remain relatively low. Mostly capitalist economies, by contrast, generate more economic inequality but have relatively high living standards. As the Russian Federation has moved from socialism towards capitalism, there is widespread evidence of increasing economic inequality, including the building of large mansions by those who have become rich. This complex is being built by a business tycoon in the suburbs of the Russian capital, an area coming to be known as "the Beverly Hills of Moscow."

CHANGES IN SOCIALIST COUNTRIES

In 1989 and 1990, the nations of Eastern Europe, which had been seized by the Soviet Union at the end of World War II, overthrew their socialist regimes. These nations—including the German Democratic Republic (or East Germany), Czechoslovakia, Hungary, Romania, and Bulgaria—are moving towards capitalist market systems after decades of state-controlled economies. In 1991, the Soviet Union itself formally dissolved, and the new Russian Federation has introduced some free-market principles. Within a decade, three-quarters of former Soviet government enterprises were partly or entirely in private hands (Montaigne, 2001).

There were many reasons for these sweeping changes. First, the capitalist economies far outproduced their socialist counterparts. The socialist economies were successful in achieving economic equality, but living standards were low compared to those of Western Europe. Second, Soviet socialism was heavy-handed, rigidly controlling the media and restricting individual freedoms. In short, socialism did away with *economic* elites, as Karl Marx predicted, but, as Max Weber foresaw, socialism increased the power of *political* elites.

So far, the market reforms in Eastern Europe are proceeding unevenly. Some nations (i.e., the Czech Republic, Slovakia, Poland, and the Baltic states of Latvia, Estonia, and Lithuania) are doing relatively well, but others (i.e., Romania, Bulgaria, and the Russian Federation) have been buffeted by price increases and falling living standards. Officials hope that expanding production will eventually bring a turnaround. However, the introduction of a market economy has brought with it an increase in economic inequality (Buraway, 1997; World Bank, 2005).

Work in the Post-industrial Economy

Change is not restricted to the socialist world; the economy of Canada has also changed dramatically during the last century. The Industrial Revolution transformed the Canadian workforce a century ago; further changes are taking place today. In 2001, 16.7 million Canadians were in the labour force, representing two-thirds of those over the age of 15. As has been the case historically, a larger proportion of men (73.3%) than women (60.7%) are in the labour force. But the gender gap in labour force participation has diminished in recent decades: the figure for males has increased very little since 1980, but the female rate is up from 46.7 percent. It is important to note that the labour force includes those who are employed as well as those who are looking for work (in other words, the unemployed).

According to the census of 2001, labour force participation varies substantially among selected racial and ethnic categories. Combining the employed and unemployed in Figure 16-4, reveals that the highest level of labour-force participation is highest among Blacks (at 70.5%). The remaining categories are ranked as follows: French (67.2%); Aboriginal (61.4%); Japanese (60.2%); Chinese (59.3%): and English (55.9%). The 2001 data represent a drop of 5 points for Blacks since 1986 as well as an increase of 11 points for Aboriginals (Macionis and Gerber, 2005: 392). Clearly, race is not a barrier to participation in the labour force in Canada, but further discussion below reveals that participation is only part of the picture.

THE DECLINE OF AGRICULTURAL WORK

At the beginning of the twentieth century, about 35 percent of the Canadian labour force was engaged in farming. By 1961, this proportion had fallen to almost 13 percent and, by 2001, to less than 4 percent. Still, because today's agriculture involves more machinery and fewer people, it is more productive than ever. A century ago, a typical farmer could feed 5 people; today, one farmer feeds 75. This dramatic rise in productivity also reflects new types of crops, pesticides that promote higher yields, greater energy consumption, and other advances in farming techniques. The average Canadian farm has more than doubled in size from about 100 hectares (250 acres) in 1950 to about 240 hectares (600 acres) today.

This process signals the eclipse of "family" farms, which are declining in number and produce only a small part of our agricultural yield; more and more production is carried out by corporate agribusinesses (Bakker and Winson, 1993). But, more productive or not, this transformation has

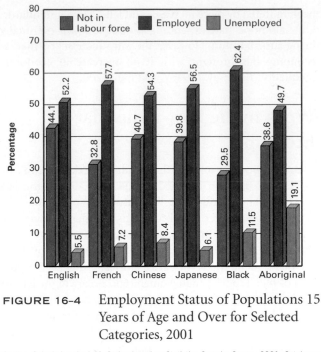

FIGURE 16–4   Employment Status of Populations 15 Years of Age and Over for Selected Categories, 2001

Source: Calculations by L.M. Gerber based on Statistics Canada, Census 2001, Catalogue numbers 97F0010XCB2001042, 97F0010XCB2001046, and 97F0011XCB2001044.

brought painful adjustments for farming communities throughout Canada, as a way of life is lost. The rest of us are affected indirectly by this change: prices have generally been kept low by the rising productivity of agribusiness, although a growing proportion of people are concerned about the effect of widespread use of pesticides and chemicals on crops. One of the goals of genetic modification is to limit the need for such chemicals. Organic farming, which is increasing in production and in popularity with consumers, is a response to both pesticide proliferation and genetic modification.

FROM FACTORY WORK TO SERVICE WORK

A century ago, industrialization swelled the ranks of blue-collar workers. By 1950, however, a white-collar revolution had moved a majority of workers into service occupations. By 2001, 75 percent of the Canadian labour force worked in the service sector, and the vast majority of new jobs were being created in this sector. As Chapter 11 ("Social Class in Canada") explains, the expansion of service work is one reason many people call Canada a middle-class society. But much service work—including sales and clerical positions and jobs in hospitals and restaurants—pays much less than former factory jobs. This means that many of the jobs in today's post-industrial society provide only a modest standard of living.

THE DUAL LABOUR MARKET

Sociologists see the jobs in today's economy falling into two categories. The **primary labour market** offers *jobs that provide extensive benefits to workers.* This segment of the

labour market includes professions such as medicine, engineering, and law, as well as upper-management positions. These are jobs that people think of as *careers*, interesting work that provides high income, job security, and opportunity for advancement.

Few of these advantages apply to work in the **secondary labour market**, *jobs that provide minimal benefits to workers.* This segment of the labour force is employed on low-skilled, blue-collar assembly lines (where workers are not unionized) and in low-level service-sector jobs, including clerical positions. Workers in the secondary labour market receive lower income, have less job security and fewer benefits, and find less satisfaction in their work. Women and other minorities are overly represented in the secondary labour market workforce (Nelson, 1994; Kalleberg, *et al.*, 2000). Another term used to describe some of these workers is the *reserve army of labour*, the part of the labour force that is last hired during expansion and first fired when the economy contracts. These problems are especially serious for women, other minorities, and particularly Aboriginal workers, who tend to be overrepresented in this segment of the labour force (Gerber, 1990; Wotherspoon and Satzewich, 1993). Frideres and Gadacz (2001:98) point out that Aboriginal people often work in seasonal and part-time jobs with little security: even highly skilled Aboriginal workers employed by mining exploration companies face discrimination, lower wages, and relatively poor working conditions.

LABOUR UNIONS

Labour unions are *worker organizations that seek to improve wages and working conditions through various strategies, including negotiations and strikes.* In Canada, union membership has been remarkably stable over the last twenty years at just over one-third of the labour force, peaking at 35.1 percent in 1983. The involvement of women increased slightly, while that of men decreased to the point where, in 1997, women constituted 45 percent of union membership in Canada. The involvement of Canadian workers in international unions has dropped dramatically, while national unions have grown (Glenday, 2001:18–19). The highest level of union membership is found in government or public administration, at over 70 percent; the manufacturing and service sectors are both about the one-third mark, while mining and the trades lag behind. Most of the new service-sector jobs being created today are not unionized.

There is substantial interprovincial variation in levels of unionization. In Newfoundland and Labrador, 55.1 percent of the labour force is unionized; at the other end of the spectrum, Alberta is at 26.6 percent (Statistics Canada, 1990). The other relatively highly unionized provinces are British Columbia, Ontario, and especially Quebec. The differences are not entirely the result of the economic structures of the various provinces, for even within the same industry there can be substantial variation: the level of

To visit the Canadian Labour Congress, the national voice of the labour movement, representing 2.5 million unionized workers, go to www.clc-ctc.ca.

unionization within the construction industry, for example, varies from 81 percent in Quebec to 25 percent in Prince Edward Island. In the years 1998 to 2002, collective agreements have achieved annual wage increases of 1.7 to 3.3 percent in all industries for Canada as a whole. Some of the largest increases were in federal and provincial/territorial administration.

In global perspective, union membership in industrialized countries varies substantially—from a low of 16 percent of the workforce in the United States to about one-third in Canada, Switzerland, and Japan, half in Great Britain, and a high of more than 90 percent in Denmark and Sweden. Clearly, some cultures are more receptive to unions than others; those with social-democratic values tend to have higher levels of unionization. The United States, with its pro-capitalist values, has never been particularly supportive of the union movement. In the twenty-first century, Canadian unions face new challenges in the face of flatter organizational structures (less room for promotion), downsizing, and outsourcing as corporations attempt to remain competitive in a global environment. Instead of focusing on wage increases, unions now struggle to ensure job security. Trade unions will negotiate for reductions in working time, restrictions on overtime, voluntary early retirement, improved training for job transfer, and an end to subcontracting (Glenday, 2001:33).

YOUR TURN

Are you planning to work in a unionized environment? What are the advantages and disadvantages of union involvement?

PROFESSIONS

All kinds of jobs today are called *professional*—we hear of professional tennis players, professional house cleaners, and even professional exterminators. As distinct from *amateur* (from the Latin for "lover," meaning someone who acts out of love for the activity itself), a professional does some task for a living. But, to be more accurate, a **profession** is *a prestigious white-collar occupation that requires extensive formal education*. People performing this kind of work make a profession (a public declaration) of their willingness to work according to certain principles. Professions include the ministry, medicine, law, academia, architecture, engineering, accountancy, and social work. An occupation is considered to be a profession to the extent that it demonstrates the following four characteristics (Goode, 1960; Ritzer and Walczak, 1990):

- *Theoretical knowledge*. Professionals have a theoretical understanding of their field rather than mere technical training. Anyone can master first-aid skills, for example,

but physicians have a theoretical understanding of human health. In this sense, tennis players, house cleaners, and exterminators do not qualify as "professionals" in this sense.

- *Self-regulating practice*. Many professionals, like physicians and lawyers, are self-employed in private practice rather than working for a company. Professionals oversee their own work and observe a code of ethics. Most professionals belong to associations that determine educational qualifications, license members to practice, and set standards.

- *Authority over clients*. Because of their expertise, professionals are sought out by clients, who value their advice and follow their directions.

- *Community orientation rather than self-interest*. The traditional professing of duty states an intention to serve others rather than merely to seek income; this is most clearly the case in the ministry.

In almost all cases, professional work requires not just a university degree but also a graduate degree. Many occupations that do not qualify as true professions nonetheless seek to *professionalize* their services. Claiming professional standing often begins by renaming the work to suggest special, theoretical knowledge, moving the field away from its original, lesser reputation. Stockroom workers become "inventory supply managers," and exterminators are reborn as "insect control specialists."

As noted above, interested parties may also form a professional association that certifies their skills. This organization then licenses its members, writes a code of ethics, and emphasizes the work's importance in the community through public relations. To win public acceptance, a professional association may also establish schools or other training facilities and perhaps start a professional journal (Abbott, 1988). Not all occupations try to claim professional status. Some *paraprofessionals*, including paralegals and medical technicians, possess specialized skills but lack the extensive theoretical education required of full professionals.

Because of Canada's proximity to the United States, it faces the lost of its professional and otherwise highly educated workforce in a process referred to as the brain drain. As the Media Perspectives box (on pp. 416–17) indicates, we have only recently countered this trend with brain gain.

SELF-EMPLOYMENT

Self-employment—*earning a living without working for a large organization*—was once commonplace in North America. Families owned and operated farms, and self-employed workers in the cities owned shops and other small businesses or sold their skills on the open market. C. Wright Mills (1951) estimated that, in the early nineteenth century, about 80 percent of the American labour force was self-employed; with the onset of the Industrial Revolution that picture changed dramatically. Self-employment plummeted

MEDIA PERSPECTIVES
Brain Drain: Brain Gain

Columnist and author Jeffrey Simpson applied sociological methods to his work when he prepared his book, *Star-Spangled Canadians: Canadians Living the American Dream* (2000). His research involved historical and statistical analyses and, most importantly, in-depth interviews with Canadians who live and work in the United States. His book appeared at a time of increasing concern about the so-called brain drain.

Simpson points out that immigration to the United States is nothing new for Canadians. In fact, historical flows were much larger than the relative trickle today: "Canada's population of 30 million might today be 40 or 50 million had so many Canadians not migrated to the United States, or had so many immigrants to Canada stayed put rather than passing through Canada en route to their eventual destination: the United States" (p. 2). The current concern about the brain drain stems from the fact that today's minor flow, facilitated by the free trade agreement, consists of highly skilled and educated people lured south by the promise of expanded opportunities and higher incomes: "They are, in a sense, NAFTA's children" (p. 142).

Interviews Simpson conducted across the country revealed that the overwhelming reason for moving to the United States was opportunity—not higher income or lower taxes. For some, such as the 2000 to 5000

nurses who have left Canada each year since 1992, it is simply a matter of finding employment. That many others left for the same reason can be deduced from the fact that, for university graduates (in 1997), unemployment rates were 2 percent and 4.6 percent for the United States and Canada, respectively. With the U.S. economy growing much faster than Canada's, there were simply more and better jobs south of the border. In fact, during the 1990s, many American corporations—most notably Microsoft—began aggressively recruiting on Canadian campuses, especially at the University of Waterloo.

For other Canadian expatriates, opportunity meant better research facilities, state-of-the-art equipment, the ability to work at the "cutting edge" of one's field, greater challenges, larger audiences, a greater critical mass of colleagues, or, more simply, a range and scale of options that cannot be matched in Canada. We are losing our innovators and our entrepreneurs in part because American culture celebrates success while ours does not. Those interviewed by Simpson sense that "Americans recognize, honour, and thrive on success, whereas Canadians are more likely to think that a successful person, economically speaking, got there by mysterious means, might have a skeleton or two lurking in the closet, or somehow doesn't quite deserve to be there" (p. 156).

In summary, the brain drain numbers are not large when one compares today's migration to historic levels or even to the already reduced levels of the 1950s and 1960s. The important distinction is that recent emigrants do not come from all walks of life, as did their earlier counterparts: the emigrant of the 1990s was more highly skilled and educated, and more likely to be a professional—specifically, part of the knowledge-based economy.

Although 250 000 or more immigrants reach Canada each year—many of them highly educated and holding professional credentials, they cannot necessarily step into the shoes of those who have left. Among recent emigrants are people who were recruited by American companies and universities precisely because they excel in their fields. The ideal, according to Simpson, is to create an environment that continues to attract immigrants (including Americans) while simultaneously slowing the brain drain to the south. In an effort to do just that, the federal government established a program to create up to 2000 Canada Research Chairs that would allow our universities to attract and retain internationally renowned researchers.

More recently, Canada has succeeded in attracting highly qualified people from the United States. Saskatchewan had been losing about 20 000 people a year—"many of them young and recently educated"—but

to one-third, one-fifth, and lower in both Canada and the United States.

In 2001, close to 15 percent of Canada's workers were self-employed (compared to 7.5 percent of American workers) with the highest levels of self-employment to be found in fishing, trapping, and agriculture. Analysis related to that of Figure 16-4, indicates substantial variation in self-employment levels among selected racial and ethnic categories. Workers of English (15%), Chinese and Japanese (14%) origins are most

likely to be self employed, followed by those of French (12%), Black (11%), and Aboriginal (8%) heritage.

Professionals such as lawyers, physicians, architects, accountants, and dentists have always been well represented among the self-employed because their schooling and skills have high market value. But most self-employed workers in Canada have been small business owners, plumbers, carpenters, freelance writers, editors, artists, and long-distance truck drivers. Increasingly, women are joining the

managed a unique brain gain in the fall of 2004. Ingrid Pickering and Graham George, professors of molecular environmental science and geological science, moved with their children from sunny warm California to snowy cold Saskatoon: "Both were offered prestigious Canada Research Chairs at the University of Saskatchewan and came to Saskatoon specifically to continue their research using the new $174-million synchrotron light source that has been built on the edge of the university campus" (MacGregor, 2004). The extravagant tool, which is essential to their work, is the "most modern light-beam in the world," the Canadian Light Source. Two other key players came to Saskatoon from Chicago and Grenoble, France. A top notch facility with cutting-edge technology is attracting top notch people. Equally significant, in terms of attracting the brightest scientific minds and keeping bright graduates from leaving Canada, is the Institute for Quantum Computing at the University of Waterloo (Janigan, 2006).

A front page story of *The Globe and Mail* recently proclaimed that the University of British Columbia "scored a major academic coup, snagging an American Nobel Prize winner with a promise to pump $12 million over the next five years towards the professor's passion to improve the teaching of science" (Matas, 2006). Professor Carl Weiman, who is leaving the University of Colorado at Boulder, is a Nobel laureate (in 2001) as part of a team proving "the existence of a form of matter predicted by Albert Einstein called the Bose-Einstein condensate."

He is now most interested in educational reform, and the University of British Columbia offered him the opportunity to pursue that passion.

Canada has initiated a brain gain—bringing talented Canadians back home and luring others from the United States and overseas—by creating Canada Research Chairs, the Canadian Institutes of Health Research with a budget of $700 million, and the Canadian Foundation for Innovation to allow for the purchase of the latest in research equipment. As a result, more of the brightest and best are staying or moving here: "For the first time in 30 years, more doctors are returning to Canada than leaving the country for so-called greener pastures in the United States or overseas" (Ubelacker, 2005). The Canadian Institute for Health Information reported that, in 2004, for the first time since it began collecting data in 1969, more physicians returned to Canada (317) than left (262). Despite a gradual decline in the number leaving since the mid–1960s and despite a gradual increase in the total number of doctors throughout Canada, it is no easier to find a family doctor or get access to specialists. Population growth has kept pace with the supply of physicians. To complicate matters, physicians who have experienced burnout are opting for reduced hours and others are retiring—while medical schools are graduating fewer doctors than in the past. As a result, meeting the health care demands of an aging population will be a challenge.

On the whole, more Canadians and Americans are moving back and forth across the border these days:

nonetheless, "the number of people relocating south of the border remains significantly higher than the number heading north" (Greenaway, 2006a). The number of Canadians moving to the United States reached a high of 21 900 in 2005, while more than 8000 Americans moved north to Canada. Clearly, migrants are following opportunities in both directions, but 60 percent of Canadians move south under the employment category while 57 percent of Americans moving to Canada come under the family class. The level of cross-border migration suggests that neither Canadians nor Americans expect to lose in terms of quality of life. Despite greater optimism about the economy here, Canadians continue to move south in record numbers. On the other hand, Canada is no longer losing out in terms of excellence: we have moderated the brain drain with brain gain.

WHAT DO YOU THINK?

1. Do you know anyone who has moved to the United States because of job opportunities there?
2. Would you consider moving to the United States if the right job became available? Why?
3. What additional steps do you think Canada could take to keep highly qualified Canadians here and to attract more well educated immigrants from the United States and elsewhere?

Sources: Based mainly on Simpson (2000); also MacGregor (2004), Ubelacker (2005), Greenaway (2006a), Janigan (2006), and Matas (2006).

---

ranks of the self-employed—mainly, though not exclusively, in white-collar or professional occupations and small business (Gardner, 2000); but 65 percent of self-employed Canadians are still men.

Analysis of enumeration areas in Burlington, Ontario (Gerber, Statistics Canada Microdata, 1991), reveals that, in one-quarter of the areas, 15 to 18 percent of working men—but only 6 percent of women—were self-employed. The areas where larger proportions of men and women were self-

The Canada Small Business Centres network provides information and links to federal and provincial/territorial programs and services for small businesses at www.cbsc.org.

employed tended to have higher levels of at-home work, home ownership, university degrees, and incomes—and more people who were married. By and large, self-employed people in Burlington are not marginal to the mainstream economy: they are numerous, well educated, and relatively affluent. Undoubtedly, computers have facilitated the move to self-employment from home offices.

D'Arcy Moses, of Cree and Dene descent, is from the Deh Cho region of the Northwest Territories. Incorporating Aboriginal themes and issues in his carvings and fashion creations—many in fur and hide—Moses is a popular and highly successful designer working out of Montreal.

 For more information on D'Arcy Moses and other fur designers, go to www.furcouncil.com/english/news/031105a.htm.

Our society has always painted an appealing picture of working independently or establishing one's own small business: no time clocks to punch and no one looking over your shoulder. For those excluded from organizations by prejudice or discrimination, self-employment has served as a strategy to increase economic opportunity (Evans, 1989). Further, self-employment holds the potential of earning a great deal of money. But, for all its advantages, self-employment presents workers with special problems. Many are vulnerable to fluctuations in the economy: during the recession of the early 1990s, small businesses filed for bankruptcy in alarming numbers. Another common problem is that, unless they buy expensive insurance, self-employed people lack the pension, employment insurance, parental leave and health care benefits provided to employees of large organizations. Furthermore, self-employed people who work from home offices are isolated from meaningful contact with co-workers.

TABLE 16–1

Employment among Canadians 25 to 44 Years Old by Sex and Educational Attainment, 2001

Level of Education	Both Sexes	Men	Women
Total	80.8	85.7	75.8
Less than grade 9	50.2	59.8	37.6
Some secondary school	68.0	76.5	57.1
High school graduate	79.6	86.2	73.0
Some postsecondary	77.2	82.4	72.2
Postsecondary certificate or diploma	85.2	89.2	81.2
University degree	85.3	89.1	81.8

Source: Compiled by L.M. Gerber, from the Statistics Canada publication "Women in Canada: Work Chapter Updates", Catalogue 89F00133, May 2003.

UNDEREMPLOYMENT

Underemployment is employment that uses less than a person's full credentials, talents, or abilities. It is a serious problem in Canada that affects many categories of workers and is increasingly recognized as the "gap between usable knowledge and its actual use in employment" (Livingstone, 2001:144). Many part-time workers are in that position involuntarily because full-time employment is unavailable to them. Younger workers, many of whom have university degrees, find themselves underemployed, as "almost 50 percent of university graduates in Canada find themselves in jobs that do not require university-level credentials" (Côté and Allahar, 2001:258; Kelly, *et al.*, 2000). Women who hit the "glass ceiling" and immigrants whose credentials are not recognized in Canada are also among the underemployed. For every person who is underemployed, Canada loses the potential value of his or her human capital. As a society, we do not take full advantage of the skills and knowledge of our citizens.

Although people with higher levels of education are, by definition, more susceptible to underemployment, it is important to keep in mind that level of education is a major predictor of employment itself. Table 16–1 shows that, with each increase in educational attainment (except some postsecondary), employment goes up for both women and men. In assessing the underemployment of people with university certification, one might ask if, after a period in entry-level positions, those with these credentials are more rapidly promoted.

UNEMPLOYMENT

Some unemployment is found in every society. Few young people entering the labour force find a job immediately. Some older workers leave the workforce temporarily while seeking a new job, to have children, or because of a strike; others suffer from long-term illnesses. And others who are illiterate or without skills find themselves locked out of the job market. Although people may be quick to blame themselves if they find themselves out of work, unemployment is not just a personal problem; it is also a product of the economy itself. Capable and willing workers lose their jobs when economic recession occurs, if occupations become obsolete, or as factories close in the face of rising foreign competition. Even Stelco in Hamilton, Ontario, Canada's largest steel producer, was in danger of collapse in 2003. Mergers and downsizing can also lead to the dismissal of employees from all levels of an organization. The emerging post-industrial economy has shattered the job security of workers in many traditional blue-collar occupations as well (Kasarda, 1983).

In capitalist societies such as Canada, the unemployment rate rarely dips below 5 percent of the labour force. Public officials view this level of unemployment as natural, and sometimes even describe it as "full" employment; unemployment becomes a publicly acknowledged problem only when the unemployment rate exceeds 7 or 8 percent (Albrecht, 1983). In principle, predominantly socialist societies consider work to be each person's right and obligation, so the government may create jobs to keep the unemployment rate low. In practice, however, unemployment is as great a problem in these societies.

Canada's unemployment rate rose to over 11 percent in 1992 and 1993, before dropping to 9.5 percent in 1995 and to 8.1 percent by December 1997. By 2000 and 2005, our unemployment rate had dropped further to 7.4 percent and 6.8 percent, respectively. While there have been substantial gains in the numbers employed since the recession of the early 1990s, economic restructuring meant that hundreds of thousands of old jobs were lost as new ones were created. Many people who failed to make the transition from old to new jobs were casualties of this employment shift.

Part-time work currently accounts for 18 percent of all employment. In 1994, 5.4 percent of all workers (compared to 2.3% in 1981) were "involuntary part-timers," or people who have been unable to find full-time employment (Wells, 1996). In 2001 and 2005, of all workers were employed 18.3 and 18.1 percent, respectively, were part-time workers (11% of male and 27% of female workers in both years). Some women, even physicians and other professionals, work part-time by choice for a wide range of reasons, including family responsibilities, but others do so involuntarily. Thus, some, but not all, of this part-time work can be classified as underemployment.

The national unemployment rate tells only part of the story, for unemployment in provinces such as Prince Edward Island and Newfoundland and Labrador may approach twice the national rate. While Canada Map 16–1 reveals the regional pattern in unemployment rates, it is worth noting that cities or metropolitan areas have widely divergent rates: unemployment in Chicoutimi-Jonquière is roughly three times that of Toronto.

Unemployment rates differ for various segments of the Canadian population. As revealed in Figure 16-4 (p. 414), in 2001, the lowest unemployment rates were found among the Japanese (6.1%), English (6.5%) and French (7.2%). Those of Chinese (8.4%) and Black (11.5) origins experienced somewhat higher rates of unemployment, while Aboriginal people fared much worse (at 19.1%). Unemployment among Black Canadians is down 3 points from 1991, but among Aboriginal people it is up 7 points. Note that these rates refer to the standard unemployment rates measured as a percentage of the labour force that is unemployed and actively looking for work, and that Aboriginal people are more active in the labour force now than in 1991 (up 9 points). This means that part of the increase in unemployment (a negative factor) is due to increased labour force participation (a positive factor). It is clear, however, that Aboriginal people are doubly disadvantaged when it comes to economic integration. In part, this is the result of a history of internal colonialism, de facto segregation, rural isolation, lower levels of educational attainment, and cultural dislocation (Gerber, 1990; Wotherspoon and Satzewich, 1993; Frideres and Gadacz, 2001).

Official unemployment statistics, based on monthly national surveys, generally understate unemployment for two reasons. First, to be counted among the unemployed, a person must be actively seeking work. Especially during economic recessions, many people become discouraged after failing to find a job and stop looking; these "discouraged" workers are not counted among the unemployed. Further, many people who are unable to find jobs for which they are qualified take "lesser" employment while seeking new positions in their fields. Such people are included among the employed, although they too might better be described as underemployed. Official statistics also overlook the fact that some people who are out of work receive income from odd jobs, unreported work, or illegal activity.

To find out about unemployment benefits in Canada, go to www.canadabenefits.gc.ca/faeclist.jsp?catid—2&geo=5&lang-en.

THE UNDERGROUND ECONOMY

Government requires all businesses and individual workers to periodically report on their economic activity, especially earnings. Not reporting income received makes a transaction part of the **underground economy,** *economic activity involving income or the exchange of goods and services that is not reported to the government as required by law.* On a small scale, evidence of the underground economy can be found everywhere: teenagers baby-sit for neighbours; a family makes some extra money by holding a garage sale without reporting the income to the government. Of course, far more of the underground

Read about the global underground economy in forced labour for illegal activities and other forms of economic slavery at http://news.bbc.co.uk/2/hi/europe/4534393.stm/.

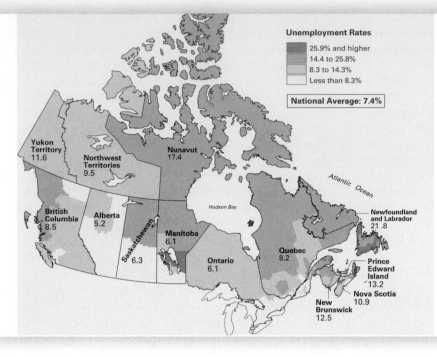

Unemployment Rates by Province, Territory, and Census Subdivision, 2001

Source: Calculations by L.M. Gerber from the Statistics Canada CANSIM database http://cansim2.statcan.ca, Table 183-0003.

economy is attributable to criminal activity such as illegal drug sales, prostitution, bribery, theft, illegal gambling, and loan sharking.

But the single largest segment of the underground economy involves "honest" people who fail to accurately report their legally obtained income on income tax forms. Self-employed people, such as various tradespeople or owners of small businesses, may understate their incomes; waiters, waitresses, and other service workers may not report the full amount of their tips received in cash. Even relatively small omissions and misrepresentations on individual income tax returns add up to billions of dollars in the underground economy (Simon and Witte, 1982; Dalglish, 1993).

In Canada, the underground economy accounted for some 15 to 20 percent of economic activity in 1990, up from about 10 percent a decade earlier (Dalglish, 1993:20). A survey by the Canadian Home Builders' Association estimated that 55 percent of all renovations in 1992 were done "under the table," with cash payment that was undeclared as income. Statistics Canada suggests that underground activity accounts for only 3.5 percent of GDP. While estimates of the magnitude of the problem vary widely, the existence and growth of the underground economy is not disputed.

This sudden increase in underground economic activity has been attributed to high tax levels in general and, in particular, to the imposition of the Goods and Services Tax (GST) in 1991. The effect of taxing services, for the first time, was to greatly increase the demand for cash payments for under the table services. One indication of this trend is a

57 percent increase, between 1991 and 1992, in the use of hard cash rather than credit cards or cheques (Dalglish, 1993). Although the GST has been reduced by 1 percentage point (and may be reduced again), the tax situation remains essentially unchanged, so there is little reason to expect a decrease in the size of the underground economy.

YOUR TURN

In what ways have you been part of the underground economy? Do you think avoiding taxes on any earned income is wrong? What do you think of babysitting or garage sales as sources of undeclared income?

NEW INFORMATION TECHNOLOGY AND WORK

Another workplace issue is the increasing role of computers and other new information technology. The Information Revolution is changing what people do in a number of ways (Rule and Brantley, 1992; Vallas and Beck, 1996):

1. **Computers are deskilling labour**. Just as industrial machinery replaced the craft and trade masters of an earlier era, computers now threaten the skills of managers. More business operations are based not on executive decisions but on computer modelling. In other words, a machine decides whether to place an order, stock a dress in a certain size and colour, or approve a loan application.

Working through Cyberspace

The 1998 Winter Olympic Games in Nagano, Japan, gave IBM an opportunity to showcase its latest technology by transmitting, worldwide, millions of megabytes of data from the games to television viewers, radio listeners, newspaper readers, and internet surfers. Now, IBM (1998) makes the same technology available to business organizations that are involved in "e-business" or internet-based commerce.

Business has become increasingly dependent on computers linked by intranets, extranets, and the World Wide Web. The number of people connected to the web is expected to increase to 1.5 billion by 2007 (Computer Industry Almanac Inc., 2002). In Canada alone, private and public sales online increased 27 percent between 2001 and 2002 to reach a total of $13.7 billion (Statistics Canada, 2003b). But the web is not limited to commercial transactions. Employees of a Vancouver firm can work—on data analysis, design, reports, or problem solving as part of an interactive group—from a home office in Winnipeg, Munich, or Helsinki. Work has invaded cyberspace—the McLuhanesque world that is free of the limitations of time and space.

Inco's Stobie mine in Sudbury, Ontario, is taking miners out of the underground tunnels and seating them at surface computer terminals from which they run automated drill rigs and scoop trams in various locations (Robinson, 1998). Robo-operator Stan Holloway—who spent fifteen years in Inco's dangerous, dreary, diesel-fumed tunnels—is grateful to be comfortably seated, operating million-dollar scoop trams with a joystick and foot pedals and observing the otherwise back-breaking job through miniature cameras and microphones mounted on the machines. Inco turned to this kind of high-tech mining in order to remain competitive at this particular mine, which has thirty to forty years' worth of low-grade ore left at the site. To remain in operation, Stobie must compete with mines that have high-grade ore and low labour costs. In Russia, a miner makes about $850 per year; Sudbury miners are employed at $85 000 to $100 000 per year. Robo-trams and drill rigs do a lot of dangerous and dirty work but displace large numbers of highly paid miners. Only a few miners will make the transition from hard manual labour to robo-operator.

Finance Canada (1997) points out that many Canadian industries—beyond software, electronics, and aviation—are leaders in the development and adoption of new technology. New methods of inventory management are changing retailing and the skills needed by personnel, and satellite-generated images are used in resource exploration and development. So pervasive is this change that knowledge-based technology is now the major stimulus to economic growth and job creation. In the past decade, employment growth has been closely linked to intensity of information technology:

- employment has increased substantially (12%) in areas of high information-technology intensity,

- employment has increased moderately (8%) in areas of medium intensity, and

- employment has declined (–9%) in sectors that make minimal use of information technology (Statistics Canada, 2003b).

Canada's Research in Motion made staying connected much easier for today's busy executive with its invention of the BlackBerry. Newman's Titans (or "new" establishment) are connected at all hours with counterparts around the world. Unlike the family dynasties of the "old" establishment—bound by private school, country club, and intermarriage, the "Titans of the Info Age are joined more by their cellphones than by any sense of belonging" (Newman, 1998:4). Their networks need to be aggressively managed, and the BlackBerry makes it possible to phone, transmit e-mail, and even read attached documents while on the go—even on rare extended weekends or holidays.

WHAT DO YOU THINK?

1. Is your future work likely to be confined to a nine-to-five weekday schedule or will you be continuously connected to the "office" and co-workers by cellphone, laptop, and BlackBerry?

2. Do you know people whose jobs have been transformed by the new technology? What kinds of jobs were involved?

3. How has the Information Revolution affected family life in Canada?

2. **Computers are making work more abstract.** Most industrial workers have a hands-on relationship with their products. Post-industrial workers use symbols to perform abstract tasks, such as making a company more profitable or making software more user-friendly.

3. **Computers limit workplace interaction.** As workers spend more time at computer terminals, they become increasingly isolated from other workers.

4. **Computers increase employers' control of workers.** Computers allow supervisors to monitor

Unemployment means not having a job and the income it provides. But it also means not having the respect that comes from being self-reliant in a society that expects people to take care of themselves. How does the sociological perspective help us to understand being out of work as more than a personal problem?

In today's corporate world, computers are changing the nature of work just as factories did more than a century ago. In what ways is computer-based work different from factory work? In what ways is it the same?

employees' output continuously, whether they work at computer terminals or on assembly lines.

5. **Computers allow companies to relocate work**. Because computer technology allows information to flow almost anywhere instantly, the symbolic work in today's economy may not take place where we might think. We have all had the experience of calling a business (say, a hotel or a toy store) located in our own town only to find that we are talking to a person at a computer workstation or call centre thousands of kilometres away, perhaps in another country. (See the Thinking Globally box on p. 421 for further insight on this issue.)

Such changes remind us that technology is not socially neutral. Rather, it changes the relationships between people in the workplace, shapes the way we work, and often alters the balance of power between employers and employees. Understandably, then, people welcome some aspects of the Information Revolution and oppose others.

Corporations

At the core of today's capitalist economies lies the **corporation,** *an organization with a legal existence including rights and liabilities apart from those of its members.* By incorporating, an organization becomes a legal entity, able to enter into contracts and own property. Incorporation, which arose about a century ago, protects the personal wealth of owners and top executives from lawsuits that might arise from busi-

ness debts or harm to consumers. Most large corporations operating in Canada are public, that is, owned by potentially thousands of shareholders, including other corporations, rather than private, where ownership is limited to a single person or family. This dispersion of corporate ownership has spread wealth by making more people small-scale capitalists. Ralf Dahrendorf (1959) adds that the day-to-day operation of a public corporation is the task of white-collar executives who are responsible to the shareholders. Nonetheless, a great deal of corporate stock is owned by a small number of the corporation's top executives and directors, who, in Canada, have been members of a very small number of families (Clement, 1975; Francis, 1986); these major shareholders comprise a small economic elite, which owns and operates the richest and most powerful Canadian businesses. Although a "new" establishment has taken over from the old family dynasties (Newman, 1998) and a significant proportion of the population now owns stock—often in retirement savings plans or pension funds—Canada still has an economic elite. Ultimately, the proliferation of corporations has not substantially changed how large businesses operate or affected the distribution of wealth in Canada.

ECONOMIC CONCENTRATION

Profit-making corporations range in size from one-person businesses to veritable giants, such as Loblaw Companies (134 000 employees) and Onex Corp. (138 000 employees) (*Globe and Mail, The*, 2006b:66). Many of Canada's corporations are small, with less than $100 000 in assets, but the largest corporations dominate the Canadian economy and periodically expand their empires through mergers and buyouts of smaller firms. In a pattern that differs from that of the United States, Canada's banks and other financial institutions are well represented among the top corporations in terms of revenue and profits. The attempted merger, announced in January 1998, of the Royal Bank and the Bank of Montreal would have enhanced the position of the new bank within Canada—and placed it among the top twenty-five banks in the world. Their hopes were dashed when the federal government failed to approve the merger for fear that it would reduce competition in service to the public.

Canada's problem of corporate concentration stems from

- The inordinate wealth and power of specific individuals, families, and corporations
- Interlocking directorships that bind otherwise diverse corporations
- Geographic centralization of investment in Ontario and Quebec, and
- The tendency of corporations to expand or diversify by merging or buying existing firms instead of developing new productive capacity

This last problem was exacerbated by the 1989 free trade agreement with the United States, as evidenced by a $20-billion boom in acquisitions and mergers in the first few months of that year (Bronson, 1993:204). This trend has been referred to as "paper entrepreneurship," which does nothing to contribute to Canada's wealth: "The pie remains the same size, but the pieces are cut differently" (Francis, 1986:229).

Table 16–2 ranks, by profits, the top 60 companies in Canada from *The Globe and Mail*'s Top 1000 for 2006. At the top of the list are 4 companies with more than $3 billion in profits: the bottom 4 (ranked 57 to 60) have profits in the $300 to 350 million range. Revenue in these top companies ranges from just under $1 to $33 billion, but the rankings of the top 60—by revenue—range from $1 to $150 billion. Because of differences in expenses, rankings by revenue and profits are not highly correlated. For example, Precision Drilling Trust is ranked 18 on profits but only 135 on revenue: but it is a very big corporation by either measure. Note that all of these Top 1000 companies trade on Canadian stock markets and many of them pay dividends to shareholders who share their profits. Taxes paid to federal and provincial/territorial governments are also based on profits. And of course the revenues of these companies pay the salaries of millions of employees.

By taking a close look at the data in Table 16–2, you will make some interesting observations. The top 60 corporations employ a very large number of people—ranging from 151 500 at George Weston, Ltd. to 15 at Canadian Oils Sands Trust. There are 4 corporations with "Trust" in their names; these are a new phenomenon in Canada, the basic principle being that shareholders own the income stream, but not the assets (e.g., buildings, equipment, mines) of the

corporations. Since essentially these trusts shuffle money, they require relatively few employees. On the other hand, the range of employees at these trusts (15 to 6500) suggests that there are some reporting irregularities here: the 6500 could include company employees in general, rather than just the employees managing the revenue in the trust.

Among the top 60 companies there are 6 banks and 6 insurance companies, 5 management firms, and 3 telephone companies. The banks are there because, as noted above, our major banks are very large. (The United States has hundreds of small and often local banks.) Research in Motion (of BlackBerry fame) is classified as a technology firm. The only retailers that made it into the top 60 are Sears, Shoppers Drug Mart, and Canadian Tire. On the other hand, there are 14 oil companies, 2 pipelines, 4 mining companies, 2 gold companies (precious metals), and 2 steel producers. The companies ranked 61 to 100 include more oil companies as well as firms involved in forestry and food production.[1] Clearly, money, finance, oil, and natural resources in general contribute massively to the Canadian economy.

There are many corporations—just as large—that do not appear on this list because they are not traded on Canadian stock exchanges. Some of those corporations are private companies owned by families (i.e., the Irvings of New Brunswick) or groups of investors, with no publicly traded shares. Others are foreign-owned subsidiaries such as General Motors and Honda, which are traded on American and Japanese exchanges.

One of the obvious conclusions to be drawn from Table 16–2 is that oil production is a major component of the Canadian economy, including foreign trade. Lately, the Alberta oil sands—with reserves close to those of Saudi Arabia—have been the source of much of that oil. Because we are an oil superpower and our economy depends on the extraction and export of oil—specifically from the oil sands, our production of greenhouse gases continues to climb. This in turn makes it extremely difficult for us to meet our commitments under the Kyoto Protocol.

← → YOUR TURN ← →

Do you think a corporation's being very big benefits the public by making the organization efficient? Or does being very big make a corporation so strong that it doesn't need to be accountable to the public? Explain your position.

---

[1]Number 140 on the list (ranked by profits) is a company called Extendicare, which reported $95 million in profits and almost $2 billion in revenue. Extendicare owns and operates retirement homes (with assisted living options) and Paramed, which provides homecare (housekeeping and nursing) to elderly people, disabled people, and patients released from hospital.

TABLE 16–2

Canada's Top Corporations Ranked by Profits, 2006[1]

Rank	Company	Revenue (Cdn$000s)	Number of Employees	Rank	Company	Revenue (Cdn$000s)	Number of Employees
1.	EnCana Corp.	16 899 960*	4 196	31.	Canadian Natural Resources	n.a.	2 897
2.	Royal Bank of Canada	29 403 000	60 012	32.	Inco Ltd.	5 457 500*	11 707
3.	Manulife Financial	32 187 000	42 000	33.	Onex Corp.	n.a.	138 000
4.	Bank of Nova Scotia	18 332 000	46 631	34.	National Bank of Canada	5 320 000	16 993
5.	Imperial Oil	26 936 000	5 096	35.	Fording Canadian Coal	1 881 000	2 901
6.	Bank of Montreal	15 138 000	33 785	36.	Canadian Oil Sands Trust	2 039 000	15
7.	Toronto-Dominion Bank	18 665 000	50 991	37.	ING Canada Inc.	4 446 000	6 500
8.	Bell Canada	17 294 000	55 000	38.	Magna International	26 990 140*	82 000
9.	Manufacturers Life Insurance	20 574 000	19 700	39.	Sears Canada	6 238 000	41 107
10.	Shell Canada	14 394 000	4 564	40.	Loblaw Cos.	n.a.	134 000
11.	Brookfield Asset Management	5 596 740*	23 500	41.	Ipsco Inc.	3 620 902*	2 500
12.	Husky Energy	10 328 000	3 032	42.	Telus Corp.	8 201 000	29 819
13.	BCE Inc.	19 150 000	60 000	43.	George Weston Ltd.	n.a.	151 500
14.	Sun Life Financial	21 871 000	14 338	44.	IGM Financial	2 348 000	3 320
15.	Petro-Canada	17 673 000	4 816	45.	Potash Corp. of Saskatchewan	4 628 078*	4 879
16.	Great-West Lifeco	23 883 000	19 000	46.	Penn West Energy	1 919 000	730
17.	Power Financial	26 280 000	20 100	47.	Enbridge Inc.	8 697 000	4 500
18.	Precision Drilling Trust	1 283 000	6 500	48.	Canadian Pacific Railway	4 446 000	15 675
19.	Canadian National Railway	7 252 000	21 540	49.	Canada Life Financial	6 046 000	3 800
20.	Talisman Energy	9 649 000	2 138	50.	Barrick Gold	2 970 060*	7 400
21.	Brascade Corp.	1 597 012*	22 000	51.	HSBC Bank Canada	2 487 000	6 325
22.	Tech Cominco	4 570 000	7 103	52.	Research in Motion	2 515 760*	4 784
23.	Great-West Life Assurance	18 380 000	12 000	53.	Enerplus Resources Fund	1 452 000	566
24.	Suncor Energy	10 561 000	5 152	54.	Shopper's Drug Mart	7 151 000	37 000
25.	TransCanada PipeLines	6 890 000	2 350	55.	Gerdau Ameristeel	4 708 080*	7 200
26.	TransCanada Corp.	6 879 000	2 375	56.	ARC Energy Trust	1 084 000	375
27.	Nexen Inc.	4 846 000	3 282	57.	Goldcorp Inc.	1 069 229*	4 337
28.	Thomson Corp.	10 288 420*	40 000	58.	Agrium Inc.	3 918 780*	4 719
29.	Falconbridge Ltd.	9 668 920*	14 500	59.	Canadian Tire Corp.	7 775 000	50 000
30.	Power Corp.	26 738 000	24 769	60.	Pengrowth Energy Trust	1 176 000	308

[1]All corporations listed here trade publicly on the Canadian stock exchange. Privately held companies or those traded on foreign exchanges are not included here, even though they may be larger than the ones listed.

*Revenue for corporations reporting in US$ were converted to Cdn$ at the rate of 1.18.

Source: *The Globe and Mail*, Report on Business "The Top 1000" (July/August 2006). Reprinted by permission from *The Globe and Mail*

CONGLOMERATES AND CORPORATE LINKAGES

The largest businesses are **conglomerates**, *giant corporations composed of many smaller corporations.* A conglomerate emerges as a corporation enters new markets, spins off new companies, or takes over other companies. Forging a conglomerate is also a way to diversify a company, so that new products can provide a hedge against declining profits in the original market. Sometimes these mergers are extremely diverse, as illustrated by New Brunswick's Irving empire (Francis, 1986:16). The Irving group of companies is big by anybody's standards. It includes the country's largest shipyard and drydock facilities. Irving Oil is one of Canada's 10 largest oil companies, with 3000 service stations in Atlantic Canada and the Ottawa Valley; it has the country's largest

refinery, as well as untold holdings in oil and gas discoveries in western Canada. Irving's forestry business is world-scale, including half a dozen pulp and paper mills and sawmills, and title to 0.6 million hectares (1.5 million acres) of timberlands in New Brunswick and Maine, an area equivalent to the size of Prince Edward Island. Included as well are fleets of ships, trucks, buses, and railway cars; most of the media in the province; stores selling cars, food, hardware, drugs, and construction materials; and factories producing everything from pre-fabricated housing to concrete, steel, and hundreds more products. It is hard to get an exact picture of the scope of the Irving empire. None of the companies is publicly owned, and the Irvings fiercely protect their privacy through a complicated and impenetrable corporate structure.

While the Information Revolution is centred in high-income countries such as Canada, the effects of high technology are becoming evident even in low-income nations. Do you think the expansion of information technology will change the lives of rural people such as these peasants in Vietnam? If so, how?

In the 1980s, Beatrice Foods, then a Canadian company, was another corporate umbrella, containing more than 50 smaller corporations that manufacture such well-known products as Hunt's foods, Tropicana fruit juices, La Choy foods, Orville Redenbacher popcorn, Max Factor cosmetics, Playtex clothing, and Samsonite luggage. But Beatrice has long since been purchased by Parmalat of Milan, Italy, and lost its diversified umbrella function. Toronto-based George Weston Limited is another corporate umbrella but more clearly in the food sector, as it owns, among other companies, Loblaws, Zehrs, Provigo, Fortinos, and Interbake Foods (which supplies most of the Girl Guide cookies to Canada and the United States).

Corporations are not only linked in conglomerates, but also through interlocking directorates, social networks of people serving simultaneously on the boards of directors of many corporations. These connections give corporations access to insider information about each other's products and marketing strategies (Clement, 1975; Marlios, 1975; Herman, 1981; Scott and Griff, 1985). Peter Bentley of Vancouver-based Canfor Corporation, for example, sat on more than a dozen "blue ribbon boards," had "titled Europeans on his boards and has served on theirs," and "entered into countless partnerships with English and German firms" (Francis, 1986:193–94).

Corporations are also linked by owning each other's stock. For example, in today's global economy, many companies invest heavily in other corporations commonly regarded as their competitors. In the automobile industry, Ford owns a significant share of Mazda, General Motors is a major investor in Isuzu, and DaimlerChrysler is part owner of Mitsubishi. Corporations are also linked by extremely wealthy families who own their stock (Clement, 1975). Among the Canadian families who have had large and varied corporate holdings in Canada are the Irving, McCain, Molson, Steinberg, Bronfman, Eaton, Desmarais, Richardson, Mannix, Belzberg, and Bentley families. With business interests in common, these families know each other and interact socially. Gwen Moore (1979) has described how social networks (discussed in Chapter 7, "Groups and Organizations") informally link members of the corporate elite. In other words, corporate executives travel in many of the same social circles, allowing them to exchange valuable information. Such networks enhance not only the economic clout of big businesses, but also expand the influence of corporate leaders in political, social, and charitable organizations (Clement, 1975; Useem, 1979; Francis, 1986).

Peter C. Newman, columnist and author, argues that the picture outlined above is outdated. Some of the families named are not just "old" establishment: they go back further to the "Jurassic Canadian Establishment." In his third volume on the Canadian establishment, *Titans: How the New Canadian Establishment Seized Power* (1998), Newman argues that Canada's economy is in the hands of a new breed of entrepreneurs. Gone are the days of old family control through family dynasties based on exclusive club memberships, inherited wealth, interlocking directorships, contacts, and intermarriage. The new establishment, a meritocracy, is based on "what one can do" rather than on "whom one knows." The vertical structure of Canadian business has been transformed into a broader one "where nobody really can prevent someone popping up almost anywhere in the scene" (Newman, quoting John Evans, p. 18).

Where the "old" establishment was linked by club membership, the new one is based on networks that are sustained by cellphones, the internet, and transcontinental flights. The creative spark that gives birth to great

THINKING GLOBALLY
The Free Market or Government Intervention?

The market or government intervention? Each is a means of economic decision making, determining what products and services companies produce and what people will consume. So important is this process that the degree to which the market or government directs the economy affects how nations define themselves, choose their allies, and identify their enemies.

Historically, the United States has relied on the market—the "invisible hand" of supply and demand—for most economic decisions. Canada has a tradition of greater government involvement in the economy in terms of both control and ownership. The North American Free Trade Agreement (NAFTA) pushes Canada in the direction of reduced government interference in the economy.[1]

Nevertheless, for the most part, both the United States and Canada allow the market to move prices for products upwards or downwards according to the supply of sellers and the demand of buyers. The market thus co-ordinates the efforts of countless people, each of whom—to return to Adam Smith's insight—is motivated only by self-interest.

Defenders also praise the market for discouraging racial and ethnic prejudice. Though you might restrict your social contacts, in theory at least, you can trade with whomever offers the best deal. As the economists Milton and Rose Friedman (1980) remind us, a more-or-less freely operating market system provides capitalist countries with the highest standards of living; in effect, they argue, the market has produced economic prosperity.

But others point to the contributions government makes to the economy in Canada and, to a lesser extent, in the United States. Government steps in to carry out tasks that no one would do for profit: even Adam Smith, for example, looked to government to defend the country against external enemies. Government also plays a role in constructing and maintaining public projects such as roads and utilities, as well as medical care, education, social security, public housing other social services, safety and environmental regulation, and workers compensation for injuries. While Canada is privatizing many of these services, our government still plays a substantial role in the economy—a role that is supported by high levels of taxation.

High taxation and the proliferation of government services and regulation go hand in hand with our widely embraced philosophies of collectivism and egalitarianism. According to Gairdner (1990:3), these policies allow the central government to "control and engineer the condition of society" in an attempt to ensure equality of outcome for all. The effect of this social engineering is to break down traditional values such as "the primacy of honesty, freedom and hard work; respect for society, authority and private

---

enterprises is "hard to define and impossible to reproduce," Newman states; no longer can "the essential life force that creates and sustains family fortune... be passed on to the eldest son through genes" (p. 24). The result is that control of Canada's corporate world is slipping away from the old dynasties into the hands of an aggressive, global elite of the new economy.

CORPORATIONS AND THE GLOBAL ECONOMY

Corporations have grown in size and power so fast that they account for most of the world's economic activity. In the process, the largest corporations, centred in the United States, Canada, Japan, and Western Europe, have spilled across national borders and now view the entire world as one vast marketplace. Such *multinational corporations* produce and market products in many different nations. Canada's Nortel, Magna International, and Alcan are among the huge corporations that earn much—and in some cases, most—of their profits outside their own countries. Because most of the planet's resources and people are found in low-income countries, multinationals spread their operations around the world to gain access to raw materials, inexpensive labour, and vast markets. Multinational corporations recognize that poor countries contain most of the world's resources and people, who will work for attractively low wages. A manufacturing worker in Mexico, whose average hourly wage is $2.21, labours for almost two weeks to earn what a worker in Canada, the United States, or Japan (about $17 per hour) earns in a single day.

As Chapter 12 ("Global Stratification") explained, the impact of multinationals on poor countries is controversial. Modernization theorists claim that multinationals, by unleashing the great productive power of capitalism, raise living standards in poor nations, offering them tax revenue, new jobs, and advanced technology that together accelerate economic growth (Berger, 1986; Firebaugh and Beck, 1994; Firebaugh and Sandu, 1998). Dependency theorists counter that multinationals make global inequality worse, blocking the development of local industries and pushing poor countries to make goods for export, rather than food and other products for local people. From this standpoint, multinationals make poor nations poorer and increasingly dependent on rich nations (Wallerstein, 1979; Walton and Ragin, 1990; Dixon and Boswell, 1996; Kentor, 1998).

property; and all related matters built upon these values." Gairdner and other supporters of free markets believe that minimal state regulation best serves the public interest.

But not everyone views the market as a positive force. For one thing, critics point out, the market has little incentive to produce anything that is not profitable. That is why few private companies set out to meet the needs of poor people since, by definition, they have little money to spend. Some analysts are critical of a free-wheeling capitalist market economy, which by its nature erodes or threatens essential public services (Barlow and Campbell, 1991; Hurtig, 1991; Shields and McBride, 1994). For them, American ownership of the Canadian economy, corporate power and control, and NAFTA (which pushes us into the embrace of American capitalism) threaten Canadian values, our national identity, and the quality of life of all our citizens. In fact, since Canada is essentially an economic union, diminishing federal involvement in the economy and in the provision of social services may even threaten national

unity. Such critics look to government to curb what they see as the market system's self-destructive tendencies. Government takes a strong regulatory role, intervening in the market to control inflation (by setting interest rates), to protect the well-being of workers (by imposing workplace safety standards), and to benefit consumers (by mandating standards for product quality). Even so, advocates of a stronger role for government point out that the power of corporations in Canadian society is so great that the government still cannot effectively challenge the capitalist elite.

Critics also support government's role in curbing the market's tendency to magnify social stratification. Since market economics concentrate income and wealth in the hands of a few, a government system of taxation that applies higher rates to the rich counters this tendency in the name of social justice.

For a number of reasons then, the market operating alone does not serve the public interest. While Canadians are largely supportive of the market, they also see benefits to the public

through government involvement in the economy. In fact, government assists not only individual citizens but business itself by providing investment capital, constructing infrastructure, and shielding companies from foreign competition. Yet in Canada and around the world, people continue to debate the optimal balance of market forces and government decision making.

[1]One notable exception to this trend is the treatment of Canada's poultry, egg, and milk marketing boards, which require trade barriers for their survival. NAFTA's five-member dispute panel—in a "smashing victory" for Canada—voted unanimously to allow Ottawa to maintain high border tariffs indefinitely, in spite of the NAFTA agreement to phase out tariffs between the United States and Canada over eighteen months (Fagan, 1996).

WHAT DO YOU THINK?

1. How do visions of the market and government intervention in the economy fuel the debate during elections in Canada?
2. Why do defenders of the free market assert that "the government that governs best is the government that governs least"?
3. Does your family feel that income tax rates in Canada are too high? too low? Why?

Modernization theory hails the market as the key to progress and affluence for all the world's people, and dependency theory calls for replacing market systems with government-based economic policies. The Thinking Globally box (on pp. 426–27) takes a closer look at the issue of market versus government economies.

The Economy: Looking Ahead

Social institutions are organizational strategies by which societies meet various needs of their members. But, as we have seen, the Canadian economy only partly succeeds in this respect. Though highly productive, our economy distributes its products in a highly unequal fashion. Moreover, as we move into the new century, economic transformations in our society and the world present us with new opportunities and challenges. One of these challenges, the "brain drain" of Canadian professionals to the United States, is described in the Media Perspectives box (on pp. 416–17).

As this chapter highlights, the Information Revolution is driving much of this change. In the post-industrial era, the share of the Canadian labour force involved in the service (or tertiary) sector has increased dramatically to 74 percent. Increasingly, the broad range of workers involved in this sector (e.g., hairdressers, physicians, researchers, tax consultants, computer programmers) are highly skilled and educated people. Most of them (such as teachers from primary to university levels) find that, with each passing year, information technology is more integral to their work.

As we look to the coming years, our society must face up to the fact that millions of men and women lack the language and computer skills needed to participate in a post-industrial economy. Can we afford to consign these workers and their families to the margins of society? How can the government, schools, and families prepare young people to perform the kind of work their society makes available to them?

A second transformation that will define this century is the emergence of a global economy. Two centuries ago, the ups and downs of a local economy reflected events and trends within a single town. One century ago, local communities throughout the country had become interconnected so that prosperity in once place depended on producing goods demanded by people elsewhere. We have entered this century with powerful economic connections on the global level. It now makes little sense to speak of a national economy: what Saskatchewan farmers produce and sell may be affected more by what transpires in the wheat-growing region of Russia than by events in their own provincial capital. In short, Canadian workers and business owners are not only generating new products and services, but are doing so in response to factors and forces that are distant and unseen.

Finally, change is causing analysts around the world to rethink conventional economic models. The emerging global system shows that socialist economies are less productive than their capitalist counterparts, one important reason for the recent collapse of socialist regimes in Eastern Europe and the former Soviet Union. But capitalism, too, has seen marked changes, especially an increasing involvement of government in the economy. Moreover, productive enterprises have outgrown national boundaries with the emergence of multinational corporations. The world's societies are becoming increasingly interconnected, as illustrated by the European Union and free trade agreements in the Americas.

What will be the long-term effects of all these changes? Two conclusions seem inescapable: the economic future of Canada and other nations will be played out in a global arena, and we must face up to the issue of global inequality. Whether the world economy ultimately reduces or deepens the disparity between rich and poor societies may well steer our planet towards peace or war.

16 MAKING THE GRADE

The following learning tools will help you see what you know, identify what you still need to learn, and expand your understanding beyond the text. You can also visit this text's Companion Website™ at www.pearsoned.ca/macionis to find useful practice tests.

KEY *P*OINTS

The Economy: Historical Overview

The economy is the major social institution through which a society produces, distributes, and consumes goods and services. In technologically simple societies, the economy is part of family life. Agrarian societies show some productive specialization. Industrialization rapidly expands the economy through greater specialization and new energy sources that power machines in large factories. The post-industrial economy is characterized by a shift from producing goods to providing services. Just as the Industrial Revolution propelled the industrial economy of the past, the Information Revolution is now advancing the post-industrial economy.

The primary sector of the economy, which generates raw materials, is the largest sector in low-income countries. In all nations, the secondary (manufacturing) sector represents about one-third of the economy. The tertiary (service) sector dominates the economy in high-income countries.

The expanding global economy now produces and consumes products and services across national boundaries. Today, the 600 largest corporations, operating internationally, account for most of the world's economic output.

Economic Systems: Paths to Justice

Capitalism is based on the private ownership of productive property and the pursuit of profit in a competitive marketplace. Socialism is grounded in the collective ownership of productive property through government control of the economy. While the Canadian economy is predominantly capitalist, government is broadly involved in economic life. Government plays a greater role in the welfare capitalist economies of some Western European nations (such as Sweden), and the state capitalism of many Asian nations (such as Japan).

Capitalism is very productive, providing a high average standard of living. A capitalist system allows the freedom to act according to self-interest. Socialism is less productive but generates greater economic equality and offers everyone freedom from basic want.

Work in the Post-industrial Economy

Agricultural work has declined in Canada during the past century. Blue-collar employment is also reduced and now involves only one-quarter of the labour force. Today, two-thirds of Canadian workers have white-collar service jobs.

A profession is a special category of white-collar work based on theoretical knowledge, occupational autonomy, authority over clients, and a claim to serve the community. Today, 15 percent of Canada's workers are self-employed. While professionals fall into this category, most self-employed workers are small business owners—such as farmers, fishers, plumbers, carpenters, or artists.

Capitalist societies tend to maintain an unemployment rate of at least 5 percent. Socialist societies, too, struggle with high unemployment.

The underground economy represents perhaps 15 to 20 percent of the economic activity in Canada, including most criminal business as well as legal income unreported for taxation.

Corporations

Corporations form the core of the Canadian economy. The largest corporations, which are conglomerates, account for most corporate assets and profits. Multinational corporations have grown in number and size during the past century. The consequences for global economic development are a matter of continuing controversy.

The Economy: Looking Ahead

In the future, our society must prepare more people to perform the type of work being created by the Information Revolution. In addition, the expanding global economy means we produce and consume in response to distant factors and forces in other parts of the world.

KEY CONCEPTS

economy (p. 404) the social institution that organizes a society's production, distribution, and consumption of goods and services

post-industrial economy (p. 406) a productive system based on service work and high technology

primary sector (p. 407) the part of the economy that draws raw materials from the natural environment

secondary sector (p. 407) the part of the economy that transforms raw materials into manufactured goods

tertiary sector (p. 407) the part of the economy that involves services rather than goods

global economy (p. 408) expanding economic activity that crosses national borders

capitalism (p. 410) an economic system in which natural resources and the means of producing goods and services are privately owned

socialism (p. 411) an economic system in which natural resources and the means of producing goods and services are collectively owned

communism (p. 411) a hypothetical economic and political system in which all members of a society are socially equal

welfare capitalism (p. 411) an economic and political system that combines a mostly market-based economy with extensive social welfare programs

state capitalism (p. 412) an economic and political system in which companies are privately owned but cooperate closely with the government

primary labour market (p. 414) jobs that provide extensive benefits to workers

secondary labour market (p. 414) jobs that provide minimal benefits to workers

labour unions (p. 414) organizations of workers that seek to improve wages and working conditions through various strategies, including negotiations and strikes

profession (p. 415) a prestigious white-collar occupation that requires extensive formal education

self-employment (p. 415) earning a living without working for a large organization

underground economy (p. 419) economic activity involving income not reported to the government as required by law

corporation (p. 422) an organization with a legal existence, including rights and liabilities, separate from that of its members

conglomerate (p. 424) a giant corporation composed of many smaller corporations

APPLICATIONS & EXERCISES

1. Do some research to learn about the economy of your province/territory or community, including the type of work people do and the unemployment rate. You will find a wealth of information and will be able to profile your own community through Statistics Canada's website (www.statcan.ca).

2. Visit a discount store such as Wal-Mart or Zellers and do a little fieldwork in an area of the store that interests you. Pick ten products and see where each is made. Do the results support the existence of a global economy?

3. How are computers changing university and college campuses, the nature of the learning experience, and contact between students and faculty?

PRENTICE HALL
mysoclab™
Where learning & the sociological imagination intersect.

To reinforce your understanding of this chapter, and to identify topics for further study, visit MySocLab at **www.pearsoned.ca/mysoclab/** for diagnostic tests and a multimedia ebook.

CHAPTER SEVENTEEN

Politics and Government

How do political systems vary around the world?

Is Canada truly democratic?

Does politics matter in your life?

At the end of January 2005, people poured into the streets throughout Iraq to select the people who now serve as their leaders. The idea of electing leaders was new and exciting for many of the voters; for decades the country had been ruled by a dictator who tolerated no political opposition. But not everybody was lining up to vote. An organized movement opposed both the elections and the presence of U.S. coalition forces in their country. To keep citizens from the polls, they threatened that the streets would run with the blood if anyone dared to vote. At a time when suicide bombings and other attacks happen every day, people have good reason to take such warnings seriously. Others, including many Sunni Muslims, did not wish to take part in an election that seemed likely to elect mostly Shiite Muslims, which would limit the Sunnis' power (Wines, 2005).

Despite these concerns, about 60 percent of eligible Iraqi voters went to the polls. In fact, Iraq's voter turnout matched Canada's and exceeded that of the United States in recent elections. Can Iraq boast that it is well on the road to becoming a democracy? Or are Canada and the United States not as democratic as we like to think?

Questions about who has the power to make decisions in any society lead us to the issue of politics. Formally, **politics** (or, the polity) is *the social institution that distributes power, sets a society's goals, and makes decisions.* The fact that millions of people in North America do not take part in elections—even without the threats to voters, such as those in Iraq—suggests that we face considerable voter apathy. Do Canadians and Americans who fail to vote not care—or does each feel that an individual vote makes no difference?

Power and Authority

The sociologist Max Weber (1978; orig. 1921) claimed that every society is based on **power,** which he defined as *the ability to achieve desired ends despite resistance from others.* The use of power is the business of **government,** *a formal organization that directs the political life of a society.* Governments demand compliance on the part of a population; yet Weber noted that most governments do not openly threaten their people. Most of the time, people respect, or at least accept, their society's political system. No government, Weber asserted, is likely to keep its power for very long if compliance comes *only* from the threat of brute force, because there could never be enough police to watch everyone—and who would watch the police? Every government,

therefore, tries to make itself seem legitimate in the eyes of its citizens. This brings us to Weber's concept of **authority,** *power that people perceive as legitimate rather than coercive.* How do governments transform raw power into more stable authority? Weber pointed to three ways: traditional authority; rational-legal authority; and charismatic authority.

TRADITIONAL AUTHORITY

Pre-industrial societies, observed Weber, rely on **traditional authority,** *power legitimized by respect for long-established cultural patterns.* Woven into a population's collective memory, traditional authority means that people accept a system, usually one of hereditary leadership, simply because it has always been that way. In centuries past, Chinese emperors were legitimized by tradition, as were nobles in mediaeval Europe. The power of tradition can be so strong that, for better or worse, people typically come to view traditional rulers as almost godlike.

Traditional authority declines as societies industrialize. Hannah Arendt (1963) points out that traditional authority remains strong only as long as everyone shares the same beliefs and way of life. Modern scientific thinking, the specialization demanded by industrial production, and the social change and cultural diversity brought on by immigration all combine to weaken tradition. Therefore, no Canadian prime minister or American president would claim to rule by the grace of God, as many rulers in the ancient world did. Canada still has a monarch, Queen Elizabeth II, as its head of state, although today's more democratic culture has shifted real power to commoners popularly elected to office. On the recommendation of our prime minister, the queen appoints the governor general, whose job description includes many ceremonial functions such as opening Parliament. Despite this minimal role, many Canadians are uncomfortable with any attachment to the monarchy. The recent decline in prestige suffered by the British monarchy contributed to Canada's move from deference to defiance—the Canadian revolution in attitudes described by Peter C. Newman (1995).

Traditional authority also supports *patriarchy*, the domination of women by men. This traditional form of power is still widespread, although it is increasingly challenged. Less controversial is the traditional authority parents have over their children. As children, most of us can remember challenging a parent's demand by asking "Why?" only to hear the response "Because I said so!" Answering this way, the parent makes clear that the demand is not open for debate; to respond otherwise would ignore the parent's traditional authority over the child and put the two on an equal footing.

RATIONAL-LEGAL AUTHORITY

Weber defined **rational-legal authority** (sometimes called bureaucratic authority) as *power legitimized by legally enacted rules and regulations*. Rational-legal authority is power legitimized in the operation of lawful government. As Chapter 7 ("Groups and Organizations") explains, Weber viewed bureaucracy as the type of organization that dominates in rational-thinking, modern societies. The same rational world view that promotes bureaucracy also erodes traditional customs and practices. Instead of looking to the past, members of today's high-income societies seek justice through formally enacted laws.

Rationally enacted rules also guide the use of power in everyday life. The authority of deans and classroom teachers, for example, rests on the offices they hold in bureaucratic colleges and universities. The police, too, depend on rational-legal authority. In contrast to traditional authority, rational-legal authority comes not from family background but from a position in government organization. A traditional monarch rules for life, but modern presidents or prime ministers accept and give up power according to law, which shows that their authority lies in the office, not in the person.

YOUR TURN

Why do we call police and others who exercise rational authority "officers"?

The death of Pierre Elliott Trudeau in 2000, though not unexpected, resulted in an unprecedented outpouring of emotion and tributes from Canadians across the country. No one—not even his sons—could have foreseen the public reaction to the death of our charismatic, infuriating, flamboyant, enigmatic former prime minister. Whatever our individual feelings about this exceptional man, it is clear that he has become part of our collective definition of what it means to be Canadian—on both national and global scales.

CHARISMATIC AUTHORITY

Finally, Weber pointed out that power can turn into authority through charisma. **Charismatic authority** is *power legitimized by extraordinary personal abilities that inspire devotion and obedience.* Unlike traditional and rational-legal authority, charismatic authority depends less on a person's ancestry or office, and more on individual personality. Charismatic leaders have surfaced throughout history, using their personal skills to turn an audience into followers. Often they make their own rules and challenge the status quo. Examples of charismatic leaders can be as different as Jesus of Nazareth and Adolf Hitler. The fact that they and others—such as India's liberator Mahatma Gandhi and American civil rights leader Martin Luther King, Jr.—succeeded in transforming the society around them explains why charismatic people are almost always highly controversial.

The prospects of politicians in Canada rise or fall according to their degree of personal charisma. Among our more charismatic prime ministers, John Diefenbaker (1957–63) and Pierre Elliott Trudeau (1968–79, 1980–84) were able to inspire Canadians with oratory and a vision of Canada. The fervour that accompanied Trudeau into his first term of office, dubbed Trudeaumania, is a phenomenon that has not been matched since. Tommy Douglas, René Lévesque, and Lucien Bouchard were also charismatic leaders.

MEDIA   To learn about Mohandas K. (Mahatma) Gandhi, visit www.gandhiinstitute.org and about Martin Luther King, go to www.lib.lsu.edu/hum/mlk.

In 2005, just 28 of the world's 192 nations were political monarchies in which a single family passes power from generation to generation. Here, the African nation of Swaziland celebrates the coronation of a young king. While Canada is a monarchy, ours is a constitutional monarchy where democratically elected leaders exercise the real power.

Because charismatic authority flows from a single individual, the leader's death creates a crisis for the movement the leader has created. For the movement to survive, Max Weber explained, what must happen is the **routinization of charisma,** *the transformation of charismatic authority into some combination of traditional and bureaucratic authority.* After the death of Jesus, followers institutionalized his teachings, creating a church built on tradition and bureaucracy. Routinized in this way, the Roman Catholic Church has lasted for 2000 years and, in 2005, elected its 266th leader, Pope Benedict XVI.

Politics in Global Perspective

Political systems have changed over the course of history. Technologically simple hunter/gatherer societies, once found all over the planet, operated like large families without formal governments. Leadership generally fell to a man with unusual strength, hunting skill, or personal charisma. But with few resources, such leaders might control their own people but could never rule a large area (Nolan and Lenski, 2004).

Agrarian societies are larger, with specialized jobs and a material surplus. In these societies, a small elite gains control of most of the wealth and power, moving politics from the family to become a social institution in its own right. This is the point in history when leaders start to claim a divine right to rule, gaining some measure of Weber's traditional authority. Leaders may also benefit from rational-legal authority to the extent that their rule is supported by law.

As societies grow even bigger, politics takes the form of a national government, or *political state.* But the effectiveness of a political state depends on the available technology.

Centuries ago, armies moved slowly on foot, and communication over even short distances was uncertain. For this reason, the early political empires—such as Mesopotamia in what is now Iraq about 5000 years ago—took the form of many small *city-states.* More complex technology brings about the larger-scale system of *nation-states.* Currently, the world has 192 independent nation-states, each with a somewhat distinctive political system. Generally, however, they fall into four categories: monarchy, democracy, authoritarianism, and totalitarianism.

MONARCHY

Monarchy (with Latin and Greek roots meaning "one ruler") is *a political system in which a single family rules from generation to generation.* Monarchy is commonly found in ancient agrarian societies: the Bible, for example, tells of great kings such as David and Solomon, and the Rome empire was ruled by a succession of families, supported by military might. In the world today, twenty-eight nations have royal families, some of which trace their ancestry back for centuries.[1] In Weber's terms, then, monarchy is legitimized by tradition.

During the Middle Ages, *absolute monarchs* in much of the world claimed a monopoly of power based on divine right. Today, claims of divine right are rare, although monarchs in a number of nations (including Kuwait, Saudi Arabia, and Bahrain) still exercise almost absolute control over their people. With industrialization, monarchs

---

[1]Monarchies are in Europe (Sweden, Norway, Denmark, the United Kingdom, the Netherlands, Liechtenstein, Luxembourg, Belgium, Spain, and Monaco), in the Middle East (Jordan, Saudi Arabia, Oman, Qatar, Bahrain, and Kuwait), in Africa (Lesotho, Swaziland, and Morocco), and in Asia (Brunei, Samoa, Tonga, Thailand, Malaysia, Cambodia, Nepal, Bhutan, and Japan).

gradually lose authority in favour of elected officials. All the European nations with royal families today are *constitutional monarchies*, meaning that their monarchs are little more than symbolic heads of state; actual governing is the responsibility of elected officials, led by a prime minister and guided by a constitution. In these nations, nobility formally reigns, but elected officials actually rule.

DEMOCRACY

The historical trend in the modern world is towards **democracy,** *a political system that gives power to the people as a whole.* More accurately, a system of *representative democracy* puts authority in the hands of leaders chosen by the people who, from time to time, compete for office in elections. Democratic governments spend moneys, gathered through taxes and other means, to meet the needs of society and business. The size of government expenditure in several countries, including Canada, is shown in Figure 17–1. Most high-income industrialized countries of the world claim to be democratic, including those that still have royal families. Industrialization and democratic government go together because both require a literate populace. Also, the traditional legitimization of power in an agrarian monarchy gives way, with industrialization, to rational-legal authority. Thus, democracy and rational-legal authority are linked just as monarchy and traditional authority are.

But countries such as Canada are not truly democratic for two reasons. First, there is the lack of public accountability of the bureaucracy. All democratic political systems rely on the work of large numbers of bureaucratic officials, as described in Chapter 7 ("Groups and Organizations"). The actual task of public administration in Canada involves close to 1 million people as federal, provincial/territorial, and municipal employees, making government Canada's largest employer. These bureaucrats are not elected and, therefore, are not directly accountable to Canadians.

The second reason Canada is not truly democratic is economic inequality. In a highly stratified society, the rich will have far more political clout than the poor and will be more likely to vote. Moreover, given the even greater resources and political influence of large organizations, especially multinational corporations, how can we think our "democratic" system responds to—or even hears—the voices of its citizens? Government has moved to reduce the ability of large corporations to affect election outcomes: corporations in Canada are now limited to donations of no more than $1000 to political parties or leadership candidates—whereas individuals can contribute more than $5000.

All governments spend money, but those in democratic countries are authorized to generate revenues through a variety of taxes and other means in order to meet the needs of society. Figure 17–1 measures the size of government in terms of its expenditures. Note that, while Canada is in the middle, its expenditures (as a percentage of the Gross Domestic Product) are much closer the United States than to the European countries of Sweden, Denmark and France.

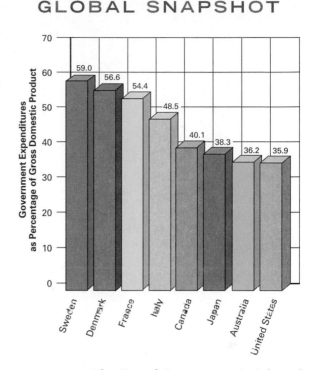

GLOBAL SNAPSHOT

FIGURE 17-1   The Size of Government in Selected Democracies, 2003

Government expenditure accounts for a smaller share of economic output in the United States than in other high-income countries. Canada is closer to the United States than to the European countries on this measure.

Source: U.S. Census Bureau (2004).

In addition, democratic countries provide their citizens with many rights and freedoms. Global Map 17–1 shows one assessment of the extent of political freedom around the world. According to Freedom House, an organization that tracks political trends, 89 of the world's 192 nations were free, respecting many civil liberties, in 2005. This represents a gain for freedom: just 76 nations were free a decade earlier by the same measure (Freedom House, 2005).

How does Canada as a democracy compare to the United States? In an article entitled "Who Owns Democracy?" Carroll (2006) examines the ideological message that "democracy is good, the democracy found in English-speaking countries is best, and American democracy is the best of the best" (p. 277). Political analysts have been known to compare American values (outside the South) with Canadian political values (outside Quebec) and find virtually no difference. Carroll makes the intriguing observation that the Methodists and Baptists of the American South best embody the democratic ideals of the American Revolution. The revolution led to the erosion of traditional authority, encouraged citizens to think for themselves, and gave rise to a passion for equality. Evangelical

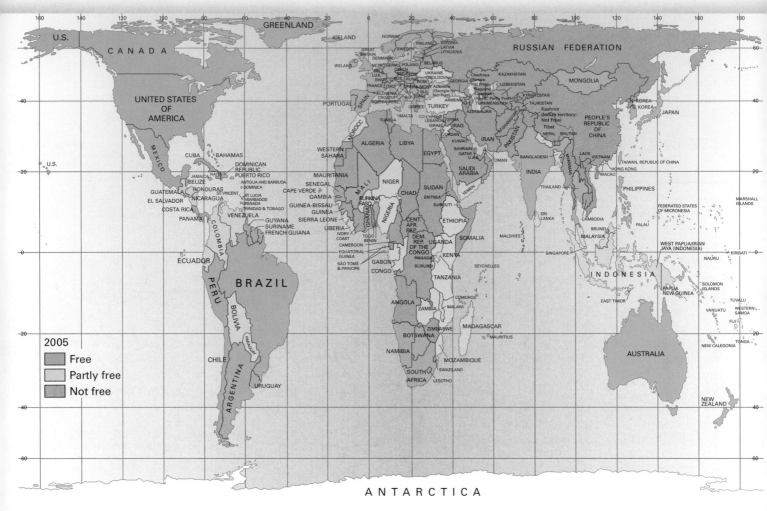

WINDOW ON THE WORLD

GLOBAL MAP 17–1 Political Freedom in Global Perspective

In 2005, a total of 89 of the world's 192 nations (containing 44% of all people), were politically "free": that is, they offered their citizens extensive political rights and civil liberties. Another 54 countries, which included 19 percent of the world's people, were "partly free," with more limited rights and liberties. The remaining 49 nations (home to 37% of humanity) fall into the category of "not free." In these countries, government sharply restricts individual initiative. Between 1980 and 2005, democracy made significant gains, largely in Latin America and Eastern Europe. In Asia, India (containing 1 billion people) returned to the "free" category in 1999. In 2000, Mexico joined the ranks of nations considered "free" for the first time.

Source: Freedom House (2005).

Christians, more than any other religion, embraced those values, allowing local autonomy and minimizing formal educational requirements for the ministry. Dropping the most distinctively democratic part of the United States out of the comparison allows academics to continue a forty-year debate about the differences, or absence of differences, in Canadian and American political values—without reaching a conclusion.

Democracy and Freedom: Capitalist and Socialist Approaches

Despite internal problems, rich capitalist nations such as Canada and the United States claim to be democracies. Of course, socialist countries such as Cuba and China make the same claim. This curious fact suggests that we need to look more closely at political economy, the interplay of politics and economics.

The political life of the United States, Canada, and the European Union is largely shaped by the economic principles of capitalism, described in Chapter 16 ("The Economy and Work"). The pursuit of profit within a market system requires that "freedom" be defined in terms of people's right to act in their own self-interest; therefore, the capitalist approach to political freedom translates into personal liberty, the freedom to act in whatever ways maximize personal profit or other advantage. From this point of view, "democracy" means that individuals have the right to select their leaders from among those running for office. However, capitalist societies are marked by a striking inequality of income and wealth. If everyone acts according to self-interest, the inevitable result is that some people have much more power to get their way than others. It is this elite that dominates the economic and political life of the society.

By contrast, socialist systems claim they are democratic because their economies meet everyone's basic needs for housing, schooling, work, and medical care. Despite being a much poorer country than the United States, Cuba provides basic medical care to its entire population regardless of ability to pay.[1] Critics of socialism point out that the extensive government regulation of social life in these countries is oppressive. The socialist governments of China and Cuba, for example, do not allow their people to move freely within or across their borders and tolerate no organized political opposition, freedom of speech, or freedom of the press.

These contrasting approaches to democracy and freedom raise an important question. Can economic equality and political liberty go together? To foster economic equality, socialism limits the choices of individuals. Capitalism, on the other hand, provides broad political liberties, which in practice mean little to the poor.

← → YOUR TURN ← →

In your opinion, what is the most important way in which people can be "free"? Are civil liberties or economic security more important? Explain your answer.

AUTHORITARIANISM

Some nations prevent their people from having a voice in politics. **Authoritarianism** is *a political system that denies the people participation in government.* An authoritarian government is indifferent to people's needs, offers them no voice in selecting leaders, and uses force in response to dissent or opposition. The absolute monarchies in Saudi Arabia and Bahrain are authoritarian, as is the military dictatorship in Ethiopia. Usually, people resist heavy-handed government. But not always: the Thinking Globally box (on p. 438) looks at the "soft" authoritarianism that thrives in the small Asian nation of Singapore.

TOTALITARIANISM

The most intensely controlled political form is **totalitarianism,** *a highly centralized political system that extensively regulates people's lives.* Totalitarianism emerged in the twentieth century as technological advances gave governments the ability to control their populations very rigidly. The Vietnamese government closely monitors the activities of not just visitors but all its citizens. Similarly, the government of North Korea uses surveillance equipment and powerful computers to control its people by collecting and storing information about them. Totalitarian governments span the political spectrum from fascist (including Nazi Germany) to communist (including North Korea). In all cases, however, one party claims total control of the society and permits no opposition.

Although some totalitarian governments claim to represent the will of the people, most seek to bend people to the will of the government. As the term itself implies, such governments have a *total* concentration of power, allowing no organized opposition. By denying citizens the right to assemble and controlling access to information, these governments create an atmosphere of isolation and fear. In the former Soviet Union, for example, the public had no access to telephone directories, copying equipment, fax machines, or even accurate city maps. Socialization in totalitarian societies is intensely political, with the goal of obedience and commitment to the system. In North Korea, one of the world's most totalitarian states, pictures of leaders and political messages are everywhere, reminding citizens that they owe total allegiance to the state. Government-controlled schools and mass media present only official versions of events.

A GLOBAL POLITICAL SYSTEM?

Chapter 16 ("The Economy and Work") described the emergence of a global economy, in which large corporations operate with little regard to national boundaries. Is globalization changing politics in the same way? On one level, the answer is No. While most of the world's economic activity is international, the planet remains divided into nation-states, just as it has been for centuries. The United Nations, founded in 1945, was a small step towards global government, but to date its political role in the world has been limited. The European Union is essentially an economic coalition, but it is attempting to forge some level of political integration as well—with countries taking turns presiding over Europe for six-month periods: economic and political integration have met with active resistance on many fronts.

---

[1]Canada has universal health care, for our democracy is a capitalist system tinged with socialism, but our health care system is for *essential* medical services; such non-essentials as cosmetic surgery, optometry, prescription drugs, some immunization and diagnostic techniques, and dental care are typically paid by private insurance (for those with employee or private health plans) or out of pocket (by the less fortunate).

THINKING GLOBALLY

"Soft" Authoritarianism or Planned Prosperity? A Report from Singapore

Singapore is on the tip of the Malay peninsula and has a population of 4.3 million. To many of its people, the tiny nation seems an Asian paradise. Surrounded by poor societies grappling with rapidly growing populations, rising crime rates, and dirty, sprawling cities—Singapore stands apart with its affluence, cleanliness, and safety. Visitors from abroad sometimes say it seems more of a theme park than a country.

Since gaining its independence from Malaysia in 1965, Singapore has startled the world with its economic development and its high per capita income. It has scarcely any social problems such as crime, slums, unemployment, or children living in poverty. There are hardly any traffic jams, and you won't find graffiti on subway cars or litter in the streets.

The key to Singapore's orderly environment is the ever-present government, which actively promotes traditional morality and regulates just about everything. The state owns and manages most of the country's housing and has a hand in many businesses. It provides tax breaks for family planning and for the completion of additional years of schooling. To limit traffic, the government slaps hefty surcharges on cars, pushing the price of a basic sedan up to about US$40 000.

Singapore has tough anticrime laws that mandate death by hanging for drug dealing, and permit police to hold a person suspected of a crime without charge or trial. The government has outlawed some religious groups (including Jehovah's Witnesses) and bans pornography outright. To keep the city clean, the state forbids smoking in public, bans eating on its subways, imposes stiff fines for littering, and even regulates the use of chewing gum.

In economic terms, Singapore does not fit the familiar categories. Government control of many businesses, including television stations, telephone service, airlines, and taxis, seems socialist; yet, unlike most socialist enterprises, these businesses operate efficiently and very profitably. Singapore's capitalist culture applauds economic growth, although the government cautions people against being too materialistic. Hundreds of multinational corporations are based here.

Singapore's political climate is as unusual as its economy. Freedom House (2005) characterizes Singapore as "partly free." The law provides for elections of political leaders, but one party—the People's Action party—has dominated the political process since independence and controls almost all the seats in the country's parliament.

Singapore is not a democratic country in the conventional sense. But most people in this prospering nation are quite happy with their way of life. Singapore's political system offers a simple bargain: government demands loyalty from its people; in return, it gives them security and prosperity. Critics charge that this system amounts to a "soft" authoritarianism that controls people's lives and stifles political dissent. But most of the people of Singapore know the struggles of living elsewhere and, for now at least, consider the trade-off a good one.

WHAT DO YOU THINK?

1. What aspects of political life in Singapore described here do you like? Why?
2. What aspects of political life in Singapore described here do you not like? Why?
3. Would you say that Singapore offers a better life than ours? Why or why not?

But there is another level on which politics has become a global process. For some analysts, multinational corporations have created a new political order because of their enormous power to shape events throughout the world. In other words, politics is dissolving into business as corporations grow larger than governments. Also, the Information Revolution has moved national politics onto the world stage. E-mail, text messaging, and cellphones mean that few countries can conduct their political affairs in complete isolation.

Finally, several thousand *nongovernmental organizations* seek to advance global issues, such as human rights (e.g., Amnesty International, Human Rights Watch) or an ecologically sustainable world (e.g., Greenpeace, David Suzuki Foundation). Such organizations will continue to play a key part in expanding the global political culture.

Information about and links to nongovernmental organizations can be found at www.ngo.org.

In sum, just as individual nations are losing control of their own economies, governments cannot fully manage the political events occurring within their borders.

Politics in Canada

Canada's national existence comes from the other side of the political upheaval that gave birth to the United States. Seymour Martin Lipset points out that: "The United States is the country of the revolution, Canada of the counterrevolution"; the Americans sought "a form of rule derived from the people and stressing individualism," while Canadians desired "free institutions within a strong monarchical state" (1991:1). "Life, liberty, and the pursuit of happiness" are the goals of our neighbours to the south; Canada chose "peace, order, and good government."

Part of the impetus for confederation was economic, but the leaders in various parts of what was to become Canada were watching nervously, fearing economic and political absorption, if not military conquest, by the increasingly populous and aggressive United States. The colonies that formed Canada came together somewhat reluctantly: Newfoundlanders initially rejected confederation in an 1869 election, and the people of Nova Scotia would have done the same had they been asked to vote on the issue. Nowhere did political union occur without vigorous debate and passionate opposition. Table 17–1 reveals that Canada was formed in bits and pieces from 1867 to 1949, when Newfoundlanders did vote Yes to confederation in a referendum.

Because the provinces joined Canada at different times and through various kinds of agreements, they have never had uniform relationships with the federal government. The north, without provincial status, is comprised of territories controlled by the federal government. Furthermore, Quebec was seen as unique from the beginning because of its French-speaking Catholic majority. Canada is a rather loose confederation in that important powers were left in provincial hands. Questions of federal/provincial jurisdiction—the centralization or decentralization of power—have been with us since 1867 and may never be fully resolved. Canada's provincial structure, its geographic size and diversity, and its immigration and settlement history add important regional dimensions to our collective identity and to Canadian politics. The presence of Quebec, the only entity with a French-speaking majority in North America, adds to our Canadian experience in terms of identity, federal/provincial relations, and unity. Our existence as a "fragile federation" (Marsden and Harvey, 1979), ever mindful of the factors that divide and unite us, is expressed in our periodic constitutional navel gazing.

Canadians are represented in Parliament by the Senate, an appointed body with 105 seats apportioned on a regional

TABLE 17–1

Dates of Entry into Confederation

Province or Territory	Date
New Brunswick	July 1, 1867
Nova Scotia	July 1, 1867
Ontario	July 1, 1867
Quebec	July 1, 1867
Manitoba	July 15, 1870
Northwest Territories[a]	July 15, 1870
British Columbia	July 20, 1871
Prince Edward Island	July 1, 1873
Yukon Territory	June 13, 1898
Alberta	September 1, 1905
Saskatchewan	September 1, 1905
Newfoundland[b]	March 31, 1949
Nunavut[c]	April 1, 1999

[a]Rupert's Land and the North-Western Territories (including central-to-northern Ontario and Quebec, the area west to British Columbia, and north to the Arctic) was purchased from the Hudson's Bay Company in 1870. A small portion became Manitoba; the remainder, known as the North-West Territories, was governed from Ottawa. Not until the early twentieth century were northern Ontario, northern Quebec, Alberta, Saskatchewan, and the Yukon Territory transferred from the Northwest Territories.

[b]Newfoundland was officially renamed Newfoundland and Labrador in 2001.

[c]Nunavut is a federal territory carved out of lands in the eastern Northwest Territories.

Sources: Adapted from Waite (1988); Hall (1999); and *Canadian Global Almanac 2003* (2003).

basis to the Maritimes, Ontario, Quebec, and western provinces,[1] and the House of Commons, with 308 seats distributed roughly on the basis of population. Quebec and Ontario together elect 59 percent (181) of the 308 members of parliament (MPs), so they have a decisive impact on which party wins the most seats, and who becomes prime

The parliamentary website offers information at www.parl.gc.ca.

minister. Also, the predominance of MPs from Ontario and Quebec reduces the likelihood that Parliament will pass legislation contrary to the interests of central Canada. The unhappiness of the peripheral provinces with the political clout of central Canada at both House of Commons and Senate levels was behind the quest, by the Reform Party in the early 1990s, for a *Triple-E Senate* (that is equal, effective, and elected). Equal Senate representation for all provinces could counter Quebec/Ontario dominance in the House.

[1]There are twenty-four seats in the Senate for each of the regions named, plus six for Newfoundland and Labrador, and one each for the Yukon, Northwest Territories, and Nunavut.

THINKING ABOUT DIVERSITY: RACE, CLASS, & GENDER

Aboriginal Self-Government

Canada's Aboriginal peoples are not treated like other Canadians—for good historical reasons. The first European explorers and settlers encountered at least fifty-five *founding nations* (Dickason, 1997), distinct linguistic and cultural societies that were self-governing in their traditional territories with formal alliances among tribes. The Six Nations Confederacy (Haudenosaunee) had an elaborate constitution and *federal* structure. Fifty hereditary peace chiefs met yearly to deal with common problems and to make new laws: "The laws and decisions of the Confederacy were passed on by word of mouth and recorded in wampum, arguably the world's oldest constitution, predating the American Constitution by 200 years" (Nader, *et al.*, 1992). Some elements of this constitution were included in the federal structures of both the United States and Canada.

The First Nations taught the explorers and early settlers to survive on this harsh continent, introducing them to corn, squash, beans, potatoes, and tobacco. The fur trade depended on Aboriginal expertise, labour, and the canoe, the design of which has not been improved (Nader, *et al.*, 1992). If the Six Nations Confederacy, with its widespread reputation for military prowess, had not sided with the British

against the French in the 1750s and with the British and the Loyalists during the American Revolution in 1777, Canada might now be either French or part of the United States. During the American attack on Canada in 1812, the British concluded that "Amerindian support was vital to the preservation of Britain's remaining North American colonies" (Dickason, 1992:217).

As settlers flowed into Canada, former fur trade partners and military allies found themselves in conflict over land. To acquire lands occupied by Aboriginal peoples and to avoid the kind of resistance to settlement that occurred in the United States, numerous treaties were negotiated—from the pre-confederation period in the Maritimes through to 1921 in the Northwest Territories. The descendants of those who signed treaties are sometimes called Treaty Indians: they are subject to the *Indian Act* and remain the responsibility of Indian and Northern Affairs Canada.

The terms of the treaties varied over time and across the country (Frideres and Gadacz, 2001), but most commonly they involved the surrender of lands in exchange for reserves and other guarantees (e.g. fishing and hunting rights). Interpretation of the treaties has been subject to consider-

able debate – but more important, in light of the current quest for self-government, is the question of whether the existence of treaties implies recognition of sovereignty. Aboriginal people believe that they were sovereign prior to the treaties and that the treaties did not extinguish that sovereignty.

Section 25 of our Charter of Rights and Freedoms (1982) recognizes and affirms the existing aboriginal and treaty rights of native peoples, including Indian, Inuit, and Métis. In 1987, when the Meech Lake Accord was negotiated in an effort to have Quebec sign on to the Constitution, the Aboriginal request for recognition of the right to self-government was ignored altogether. In response, a Cree member of the Manitoba Legislative Assembly, Elijah Harper, took steps to scuttle "Meech" just before its ratification deadline in 1990.

Representatives of four Native organizations participated in the next round of constitutional negotiation, with the result that the Charlottetown Accord of August 1992 recognized the *inherent* right to self-government: "The Aboriginal peoples of Canada, being the first peoples to govern this land, have the right to promote their languages, cultures and traditions and to ensure the integrity of their societies, and their governments constitute

CULTURE, ECONOMICS, AND POLITICS

Unlike Americans, who embrace individualism wholeheartedly, Canadians endorse it with ambivalence. Our individualism is tempered by a sense of communal responsibility, recognition of legitimate group interests, and the realization that we are, in the words of former Prime Minister Joe Clark, a "community of communities." When the Trudeau government gave us the Charter in 1982, analysts pointed out that we had moved closer to embracing the individualism of the United States:

The Canadian Charter of Rights and Freedoms is not the American Bill of Rights. It preserves the principle of parliamentary supremacy and places less emphasis on individual, as distinct from group, rights than does the American document. But the Charter brings Canada much closer to the American stress on protection of the individual and acceptance of judicial supremacy with its accompanying encouragement to litigiousness (the tendency to sue) than is true of other parliamentary countries. (Lipset, 1991:3)

one of three orders of government in Canada."[1] The defeat of this accord in the referendum of October 26, 1992, was a bitter disappointment to some Aboriginal negotiators.

In the meantime, many Aboriginal communities are managing their own affairs. The Royal Commission on Aboriginal Peoples (Canada, 1996b) declared that the right of Aboriginal peoples to govern themselves predates confederation, has a basis in Canadian law, and is already protected in our constitution. Some formal self-government agreements have been negotiated between various Aboriginal peoples, the federal government, and their respective provinces or territories.

In a dramatic development, the Northwest Territories decided in a 1992 referendum to carve a new territory out of its eastern region. Nunavut, with one-fifth of Canada's land mass and a population that is 80 percent Inuit, became a distinct entity with its own territorial government in 1999. The territorial assembly is a public government and not self-government as the Assembly of First Nations would define it.[2] The development of Nunavut is enhanced by the existence of the Aboriginal Peoples Television Network, successful co-operatives, experienced Inuit businesspeople, and sophisticated leadership. But the Inuit still face formidable challenges as they assume the tasks of territorial government.

During the Quebec separatist debate, the Grand Council of the Crees, in a report entitled *Sovereign Injustice* (1995), concluded that Quebec has no

right to secede from Canada or to forcibly include the Cree and their territories in a sovereign Quebec. When Quebec held its sovereignty referendum in October 1995, the Cree conducted their own, in which they almost unanimously chose *not* to be part of an independent Quebec. Combined with their referendum, a Grand Council report (1995), based on extensive research into international and Canadian law and precedent, signal that others cannot continue to make decisions for the Cree.

In 2003, Minister of Indian Affairs Robert Nault found himself at loggerheads with the Assembly of First Nations over his attempt to modernize the *Indian Act*. The purpose of the proposed "First Nations Governance Act" was to provide communities with modern tools of governance, allowing them to assume substantial new powers while being accountable to their members. Despite consultation with First Nation communities regarding the proposed changes, the Assembly and its leader Matthew Coon Come argued that, once again foreign laws and administrative practices were being forced on First Nations. The government withdrew the proposed Act. If the principle of the inherent right to self-government were taken seriously, the First Nations, Métis, and Inuit themselves would design and implement any new governance acts.

In 2005, Alberta's Lubicon Cree Band sent representatives to the United Nations Commission on Human Rights in Geneva to ask for help in

resolving a "long-standing land-rights dispute" (*Globe and Mail, The*, 2005). In 1990, the commission had criticized Canada's handling of the dispute as the Band fought for a reserve that Ottawa had promised to create in 1939. You may wonder why one of Canada's First Nations would be turning to the United Nations: in fact, the international body has declared that all peoples have the right to self-determination.

[1]Use of the word "inherent" is important because it implies that the right to self-government is neither granted by the Canadian government nor subject to repeal. Instead, the right is based on Aboriginal status and granted by the Creator. In 1984, the Canadian Parliament recognized that the right to Aboriginal self-government is inherent.

[2]The territorial government of Nunavut is a *public* government serving all of its residents, Inuit and non-Inuit alike. *Ethnic* government applies to the Inuit alone, on the lands set aside in a separate land claim agreement.

WHAT DO YOU THINK?

1. Do you think that *all* Aboriginal peoples should have the right to self-determination as the United Nations declares?
2. Were you aware of the role of Aboriginal peoples in the exploration and settlement of Canada, as well as in keeping Canada British and independent of the United States?
3. How should Ottawa respond to Aboriginal land claims in populated areas such as southern Ontario or Quebec? What would you think if you owned some of the disputed land?

In accordance with our emphasis on the collectivity, Canadians endorse a broadly interventionist government. Although in recent years Canadians have been increasingly worried about the costs of government activity, they nonetheless expect government to deal with national defence, law and order, international relations, radio and television broadcasting, stabilization of the economy, regional development, pensions, employment insurance, welfare, transportation, education (right up through university), medical care, culture and heritage, and environmental and safety standards. The federal government also

has a special responsibility toward Aboriginal peoples, which, as outlined in the Thinking about Diversity box (on pp. 440–441) points out, has been undergoing changes of a political nature. In fact, to the extent that we can articulate a "Canadian" identity, it is based on some of the government services that make us a tolerant and caring society. The widespread anxiety about free trade with the United States arose partly from the fear of job loss, but also from the fear that resulting pressures to harmonize with our powerful neighbour would threaten our cultural and social welfare programs, in particular, our medicare system.

Some Canadian voters vote for particular candidates, but many remain loyal to the same political party from election to election. Party affiliation is often shown through lawn signs—which may be subject to sabotage, as was this one in the election of 2000.

Government is more involved in the daily lives of its citizens in Canada than in the United States, but this does not mean that Canadians are in complete agreement regarding the appropriateness of that involvement. Some people feel that governments should take a more activist role in areas such as child care, job creation, minority rights, employment or pay equity, and environmental protection. Others feel that government already does far too much, at too great expense, and that it should be withdrawing many of its programs and encouraging privatization of services where feasible. These differences in perspective are in part a function of socioeconomic status and regional subculture, and are reflected in the policies and platforms of Canada's political parties.

POLITICAL PARTIES

Since about the time of confederation, Canadians have joined to form **political parties,** *organizations operating within the political system that seek control of the government.* Although we take political parties for granted today as part of a democracy, the party system had tentative beginnings here—and was hotly debated in the United States, where George Washington and Benjamin Franklin, among others, feared that parties would tear their fledgling nation apart.

The two political parties that Canadians have known since the 1860s trace their roots to the period after 1840, when the United Provinces of Upper and Lower Canada came into being. In fact, a Liberal-Conservative coalition of factions under Sir George-Étienne Cartier and Sir John A. Macdonald provided sufficient political stability to allow for the negotiation of confederation. The first House of Commons had, among others, Tory (Conservative) and Grit (Liberal) factions, which, by 1867, were beginning to align themselves with specific sets of policies and supporters. The Tories were "firmly protectionist, expansionist, and

pro-business," while the Grits were "anti-railroad, anti-protectionist, and pro-agrarian" (Van Loon and Whittington, 1981:326–27). After World War I, a number of minor parties appeared on the scene, the most long-lived of which was the anti-capitalism Co-operative Commonwealth Federation, which became the New Democratic Party after 1961.

In recent decades, about twenty different parties have registered at the federal level alone—some of them surviving only long enough to contest one election. While each of these parties fielded candidates in ridings across the country, only the Progressive Conservative, Liberal, New Democratic, and Social Credit parties elected MPs over extended periods of time. The newest parties turned Canadian politics upside down in the federal election of 1993, and nothing has been the same since: in that year, the Bloc Québécois and the Reform Party entered Canada's political arena and gave regionalism—in Quebec and western Canada—a new face. By 2000, after failing in its attempt to merge with the Progressive Conservatives, Reform changed its name to the Canadian Reform Conservative Alliance (Canadian Alliance, for short). Faced with the prospect of electoral annihilation by a Liberal Party led by Paul Martin, the two parties made a last-ditch effort to merge in the fall of 2003. The result was the Conservative Party of Canada, with a new leader (Stephen Harper), ready to contest the federal election of 2004. The Conservatives lost the 2004 election but won in 2006, forming a minority government.

Functions of Political Parties

Political parties in Canada and elsewhere have the following key societal functions:

1. *Promoting political pluralism.* Political parties create centres of power independent of the government. This is why totalitarian governments routinely quash all political parties, save their own.

2. *Increasing political involvement.* Ideally, parties draw people into the political process by articulating various points of view on controversial issues. By encouraging public debate, political campaigns help make government more responsive to the people.

3. *Selection of political candidates and leaders.* Political parties nominate candidates to run for office: in nomination meetings for each constituency, local party members choose the candidates who will run for office in the next election. When national or provincial parties select new leaders, riding associations elect the delegates who go to the leadership conventions—except among parties (e.g., the new Conservative party) that forego conventions and have party members vote individually for their leaders.

4. *Forging political coalitions.* While parties can divide a society, they often forge broad coalitions among people

Left			Middle		Right	
Communist Party of Canada	New Democratic Party	Bloc Québécois	Liberal Party of Canada		Conservative Party of Canada	Christian Heritage Party

FIGURE 17-2   Selected Canadian Political Parties on a Left–Right Continuum

interested in specific issues. Party platforms usually incorporate a wide range of proposals to appeal to many people, making victory at the polls more likely. Many nations have dozens of narrowly based political parties. Canada has had two dominant federal parties fairly consistently since confederation—until the 1993 election introduced its two new challengers.

5. *Maintaining political stability.* By maintaining relatively consistent positions on a number of issues, the major parties promote political stability. For this reason, of course, those who seek radical change in Canada may criticize political parties in general.

Parties and the Political Spectrum

Political ideology is commonly viewed in terms of the political spectrum, a continuum ranging from communism on the left to extreme conservatism on the right. The *political left* in Canada, as represented by the New Democrats (NDP), can be described as anticapitalist (or anti big business), egalitarian, collectivist, and interventionist. It supports a broad safety net of social welfare programs, including universal child care, education, and medicare. Government or public ownership and regulation of major industries, unionization, inheritance taxes, and progressive taxation (that is, rates that increase with income) are also among its policies. The left opposes free trade with the United States and Mexico, because of its presumed negative effects on employment and social programs. It is also opposed to globalization, is in favour of the Kyoto Accord, and is environmentally sensitive.

As one might expect, those on the *political right* espouse a different set of values and goals. They are in favour of private enterprise, big business, and free markets. Competitiveness, globalization, restructuring, deficit reduction, and privatization of Crown corporations are laudable goals in the eyes of the right, as are private property rights, tax exemptions for capital gains, and free trade. Those on the right generally feel that, while government expenditures on social programs are necessary, they should be restricted by people's ability to pay for them. These values are consistent with *fiscal* conservatism. The Canadian Alliance endorsed an additional set of values referred to as *social* conservatism: many of these (including anti-abortion and anti-gay policies) are consistent with the values of fundamentalist Christians. Policies referred to as *family values* are the cornerstone of social conservatism, which also embraces some American-style individual rights, such as unfettered gun ownership. For

the most part, the new Conservative party has had to steer clear of social conservatism in order to broaden its electoral support. Now that it is competitive in Quebec, as of the election of 2006, it has to tread even more carefully.

Many Canadians conclude that there are no ideological differences among our major political parties—at least not between the Liberals and the old Progressive Conservatives. William Christian (1983) disagrees, noting that there are some very clear and consistent ideological strains that have characterized our parties over time. Our parties and their ideological orientations are the result of our unique political history and European roots, so that they are very different from the Democratic and Republican parties of the United States. Furthermore, the ideological *mix* in our parties makes it difficult to accurately place them on a left–right continuum. For example, there were "Red" and "Pink" (meaning socialist) Tories in the Progressive Conservative party. Whereas the stance of the Canadian Alliance was unambiguously on the right, the new Conservative party includes those Red and Pink Tories.

Placing Canadian parties on a left–right continuum, as in Figure 17–2, is done with some hesitation, since most parties are "mixed bags," and there is always some movement in party positions. Our major parties moved a little to the right a decade ago, in response to developments in the United States and widespread anxiety about government deficits and debt.

For a comprehensive set of links to political parties in Canada, maintained by a private citizen, go to http://home.ican.net/~alexng/can.html.

VOTER APATHY

In both Canada and the United States, citizens are less likely to vote today than they were a century ago. In the 2000 U.S. presidential election, which turned on a few hundred votes, only half of all registered voters went to the polls. In 2004, participation rose to 60 percent, still lower than in almost all other high-income countries. In Canada, where 70 to 90 percent of eligible voters turned out in all but four elections since 1867, the last four federal elections had much lower voter turnout: 67.0 percent in 1997, 61.2 percent in 2000, 60.9 percent in 2004, and 64.7 percent in 2006.

Who is and is not likely to vote? Women are slightly more likely than men to cast a ballot; people older than 65 are much more likely to vote than young adults; and some ethnic and racial minorities are less likely to exercise their franchise than others. Generally speaking, people with a bigger stake in society—homeowners; parents with young

About 60 to 65 percent of eligible voters actually voted in recent federal elections. Will increasing cynicism about politics and politicians reduce turnout even further?

children; people with more schooling, good jobs, and higher income—are more likely to vote. Of course, we should expect some nonvoting because, at any given time, thousands of people are sick or away from home or have recently moved to a new neighbourhood. In addition, an inability to read and write discourages voting among adults with limited literacy, and those with physical disabilities that limit mobility may have difficulty getting to the polls.

Elections Canada has gone to great lengths to reach out to young voters and to facilitate voting on the part of those who are way from home or unable to get to the polls. Now, once an election has been called, you can vote ahead of time in the electoral office in your riding—or you can arrange to vote in another riding or by a mail-in ballot from abroad. If you are ill, or unable to drive or walk, there are election workers who will bring a ballot to your own home at your convenience.

YOUR TURN

Why do you think so many young people do not vote? Have you voted in the past and do you plan to vote in future elections? What about your friends?

Of course, there are many people, including young adults, who can make it to the polls but choose not to because of *indifference* or *alienation*. Some people fail to see the relevance of voting—What's in it for me?—or to see it as one's civic duty. Others have lost faith in politicians—because of scandal or failed election promises—and the political process itself. The recent dip in turnout is also

related to the competitiveness of the electoral process. If elections in your riding are won by large margins, as they often are in Canada, it's hard to see the effect of your single vote. We have also gone through a period in Canada when the Liberals were assured of victory because of vote-splitting on the right between Reform (later, Alliance) and the Progressive Conservatives. If there is no party that can defeat the Liberals, then neither liberals nor conservatives feel a pressing need to turn out to vote (Pammett and LeDuc, 2004). By 2006, the new Conservative Party under Stephen Harper looked as if it had a chance to form a minority government—and voter turnout increased from 61 percent to 65 percent. A more competitive election resulted in higher voter turnout.

Party Support

Although some Canadians support one political party throughout their lives, and may even come from families that have supported the same party for generations, most of us are considerably more fickle. As a result of changes in party platforms, leaders, dominant issues, the economy, as well as personal social or geographic mobility, there are people who have voted for three or more parties at various points in their lives. It is also common for Canadians to vote for different parties at the federal and provincial levels, even when the elections are only weeks or months apart. Many observers of the Quebec political scene argue that the Québécois hedge their bets by voting for a separatist party (Parti Québécois) at the provincial level and the Liberals or Conservatives federally, or the Bloc Québécois federally and the Liberals provincially. As strange as it might seem to an outside observer, this kind of split voting can be the result of cool calculation rather than confusion on the part of the voter.

 You can look at election results for your own riding (even at the polling station or level) as well as the provinces and Canada by going to www.elections.ca.

Recently there have been dramatic changes in political alignment in this country, as Figure 17–3 reveals. In 1993, we turned away from a long-term three-party system to embrace a mix including strong regional parties and, in 1997, we confirmed the regional pattern of support (Frizzell and Pammett, 1997). As Figure 17–3 shows, the 1993 election saw the near-collapse of the Progressive Conservative and New Democratic parties, coupled with the sudden appearance of the Bloc Québécois and the Reform party. The 1997 and 2000 results, with minor changes, suggest that Reform/Alliance and the Bloc had staying power. By 2004, the Alliance and the Progressive Conservatives had merged to form the new Conservative Party of Canada (CPC)—which garnered 30 percent of the popular vote and began its breakthrough into Ontario and points east. In 2006, Stephen Harper's CPC won 36.3 percent of the vote Canada-wide, beating the seemingly invincible Liberals by 6 percentage points and 21 seats. One might describe the current party system as "three plus one," since three parties again dominate the country, except in Quebec where the Bloc maintains its base.

The federal election of 1988 revealed varying levels of support throughout the country for Progressive Conservatives, Liberals, and New Democrats. See Figure 17–4. People in Saskatchewan, British Columbia, and the Yukon were most likely to vote for the NDP, while the Liberals fared well in the Maritimes. Conservative support in Alberta was traditional, while that in Quebec was based on the policies and personal appeal of Prime Minister Brian Mulroney.

The 1993 election results present a very different picture. Half of the votes in Quebec went to the new Bloc Québécois at the expense of the Progressive Conservatives and, to a lesser extent, the NDP. Preston Manning's Reform Party, with roots in Alberta, succeeded there, but also made substantial inroads into British Columbia, Saskatchewan, Manitoba, and even Ontario. The concentration of Bloc seats in Quebec and Reform seats in British Columbia and Alberta accentuates the regional aspect of this pivotal election. Patterns of party support in the elections of 1997 and 2000 were very similar to those of 1993, despite the fact that (by 2000) Preston Manning's Reform Party had reshaped itself into of Stockwell Day's Canadian Alliance.

Just before the 2004 federal election (results not shown), the Progressive Conservatives and the Canadian Alliance finally merged under the leadership of Stephen Harper, becoming the Conservative Party of Canada. The new party was unable to attract the level of support of the combined Progressive Conservative and Canadian Alliance parties in 2000—nonetheless, its 31.5 percent of the popular vote was enough to give the new CPC twenty-four seats—or that elusive breakthrough—in Ontario. By 2006, Paul Martin's Liberal government was limping badly, suffering the effects of indecision and the sponsorship scandal in Quebec (known as Adscam). In its second election, the new Conservative party gained strength across the country (except in Manitoba) and made huge gains in Quebec (8.8% to 24.6% of the vote). The result was a minority Conservative government (124 of the 308 seats) with 40 seats in Ontario (up from 24) and ten in Quebec (up from 0).

We know a great deal about party support in various parts of the country. We also know what kinds of ridings (in terms of social and economic composition) support the major political parties. Analysis of the effects of riding characteristics on levels of party support (Gerber, 2006b)—in Canada's 308 ridings—reveals that ridings with large immigrant or visible minority components support the Liberals (rejecting the Bloc in Quebec); those with higher average incomes support the Conservatives (rejecting the Bloc and NDP); and, after controlling for income,[1] more highly educated ridings support the NDP. This ecological (i.e., riding-level) analysis is consistent with the findings of individual level research revealing that ethnicity and social class are important determinants of voting behaviour.

In the United States, there is a sharp urban-rural divide in voting patterns—with urban areas voting for the Democrats and rural areas voting Republican. Looking at

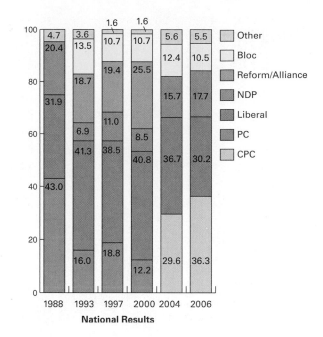

FIGURE 17-3   Support for Canada's Federal Political Parties, Canada, 1988, 1993, 1997, 2000, 2004, and 2006 (by Percentage of Votes)

Source: Calculated by L.M. Gerber from the Report of the Chief Electoral Officer, 1988, 1993, 1997, 2000, 2004, and 2006 (www.elections.ca).

an electoral map of Canada might lead you to the same conclusion: all of the blue (CPC) ridings are outside our three largest urban areas. However, while "the ethnically diverse metropolitan areas of Toronto, Montreal, and Vancouver failed to elect any Conservatives, voting behaviour in smaller cities across the country suggests that, in the absence of diversity, there is no rural-urban divide" (Gerber, 2006b). This means that, in the federal election of 2006, the Conservatives gained ground in all types of ridings. They failed to win seats, despite increased support, in the multicultural ridings of our three major cities because the Liberal lead is so great.[2] In smaller cities, including Quebec City, the Conservatives were much more successful.

POLITICAL SOCIALIZATION

Pierre Trudeau, Brian Mulroney, and now Stephen Harper are among the prime ministers of Canada who raised young

---

[1]Recall, in Chapter 2 ("Sociological Investigation" p. 33), that we examine the relationship between residential density and delinquency rate. Until we control for income level, it looks as though high residential density causes delinquency, whereas both variables are affected by income (or are the result of low income).

[2]The Scarborough area of Toronto is recognized as the most ethnically diverse part of the world. The Scarborough ridings are as much as 66.8 percent immigrant and 84.6 percent visible minority. With Liberal support (in 2004) as high as 75.6 percent, you can see why even a gain of 15 percent in Conservative support (in 2006) would not result in a CPC win (Gerber, 2006b).

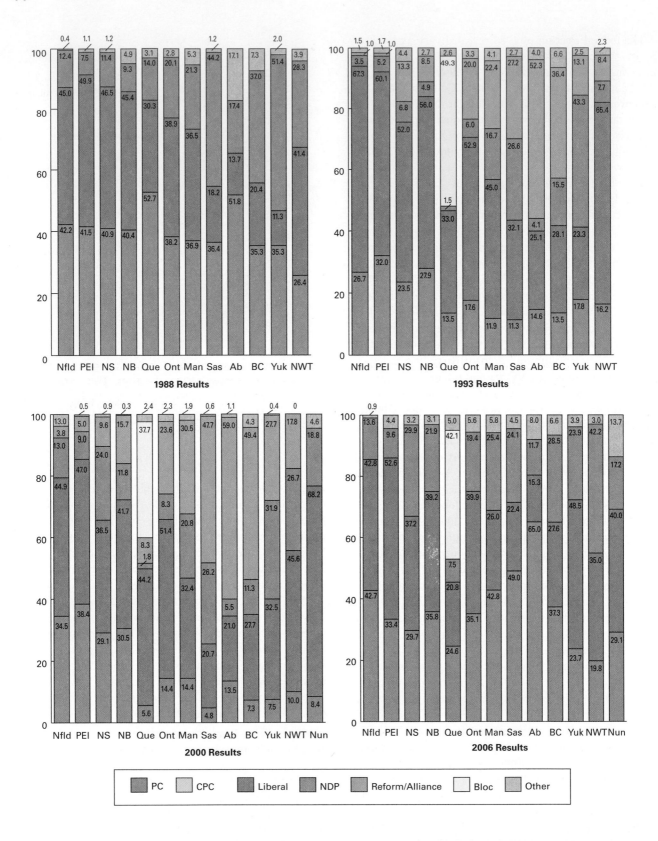

FIGURE 17-4   Support for Canada's Political Parties, by Province and Territory, in Selected Federal Elections: Percentage of Votes in the Elections of 1988, 1993, 2000, and 2006

Source: Calculated by L.M. Gerber from the Report of the Chief Electoral Officer, 1988, 1993, 2000, and 2006 (www.elections.ca).

Since Pierre Trudeau dazzled us with his diving, skiing, dancing, and white-water canoeing, we have been conscious of the physical fitness of our prime ministers. For the election of 1993, Jean Chrétien needed to prove he was not yesterday's man, too old for the job, or in poor health; these concerns fell by the wayside when Canadians saw images of Chrétien water-skiing—on *one* ski. As Prime Minister Chrétien fought off leadership rivals and prepared for election 2000, he again displayed his physical prowess—on the ski slopes. His opponent, Stockwell Day, injected athletic competition by jet skiing, running, roller-blading, doing karate kicks, and generally showing off his muscular build. After then, neither Paul Martin nor Stephen Harper used the fitness card in his prime-ministerial bid.

children at 24 Sussex Drive and Harrington Lake (the official residences of the prime minister). While all three of them would shield their children from many aspects of political life, their children undoubtedly learned the basic tenets of liberalism and conservatism from their parents. These families are unusual in their intense involvement in politics; as a result of more intimate exposure, one would expect their children to be very aware of politics and to have clear party affiliations. Justin Trudeau and Ben Mulroney are already celebrities and may well run for office in a few years.

Political attitudes, like other elements of culture, are acquired through the socialization process. Of the major agents of socialization shaping our political views—the family, the schools, and the mass media—the family is in a position to exert the earliest influence. The family is a powerful agent of socialization; not surprisingly, then, children typically come to share many opinions held by their parents. Because neighbourhoods and schools tend to be relatively homogeneous in socioeconomic terms, a child's initial peer groups are likely to reinforce ideas about the world learned at home. In Canada, many children express a partisan preference by grade 4, and by grade 8 a majority do so (Van Loon and Whittington, 1981:122). Children are more likely to learn about politics if their families are actively involved, if there is a great deal of political talk in the household, and if their families are of higher socioeconomic status. Also, male children absorb political information and identify political symbols at an earlier age than their female counterparts.

As described in Chapter 20 ("Education"), schools teach the culture's dominant political values, one of them being respect for authority. Canadian school children learn to recognize political symbols, such as the flag, the prime minister, and the queen, and, like children elsewhere, start off with positive feelings about these political icons. Interestingly, in the early 1980s, children in grades 4 and 5 overwhelmingly chose the queen as their favourite political figure (over the prime minister or governor general), and not until grade 8 did a majority (53%) realize that the prime minister is more powerful than

the queen (Van Loon and Whittington, 1981:121). The picture today is very different because politicians, the media, and schools have downplayed the role of the monarchy—despite the fact that Queen Elizabeth is still our head of state. In fact, very few schools offer anything like the formal civics classes found in American schools: our political socialization appears to be both more subtle and more informal.

The mass media, too, convey values and opinions pertaining to politics. Conservatives sometimes charge the Canadian media with having a left-wing agenda, while critics on the left complain that what is packaged as "news" really amounts to support for the status quo. Specific newspapers are frequently identified as having liberal or conservative sympathies, and some of the francophone media in Quebec have been labelled separatist. Although it is not clear that they convert their readers or viewers at a basic philosophical level, there is little doubt that the media are active players in the day-to-day conduct of politics and that their involvement has changed the way politics is done. Good sound bites and catchy phrases are gold to a politician, especially when uttered in time for the evening news. Advertising consumes a major part of election campaign budgets, and image takes precedence over substance. (See the Media Perspectives box on p. 448 for a closer look at the effects of media coverage on politics and election outcomes.)

 For access to political news that doesn't always make a splash in major media, visit www.tompaine.com/newsworthy/.

The image projected on nightly television can help to make or break a political career, as our former short-term prime ministers Joe Clark, John Turner, and Kim Campbell learned. During election campaigns, Canadian politicians (e.g. Trudeau, Chrétien, and Day) have engaged in displays of athleticism for the media; by contrast, some U.S. presidential candidates displayed their religiosity. Bill Clinton tried to deflect attention from his first-term sexual troubles by providing for photo opportunities of the devout family man: he was photographed emerging from church—family Bible

MEDIA PERSPECTIVES
Who Decides? The Impacts of Modern Communications

Parliamentary democracy in Canada involves political parties, party discipline, equal representation (in theory, at least), local constituencies (where the candidate with the most votes wins), a prime minister, cabinet (chosen by the prime minister), and the Senate (appointed by prime ministers, present and past). In the wings, the Prime Minister's Office controls physical access as well as the flow of information to the prime minister. The net effect of these interacting components, with imperfections at each level of representation, is a system in which our prime minister—given a majority government—has more power in decision making and implementation than the U.S. president.

In the past, newspapers and the radio reported on the activities of our elected officials, undoubtedly affecting future electoral outcomes, but the speed with which news led to opinion change and to effective pressure on parliamentarians and their leaders was limited. Because politicians were "in the know" and we were not, Canadians relied on and deferred to the political elite.

Today there is almost constant communication between politicians and the voter. Television, satellite transmission, the telephone, improved transporta-tion, the internet, e-mail, almost continu-ous opinion polling, and the potential for electronic voting ensure that the general public can be more quickly and completely informed about what is going on and that politicians can more quickly take the pulse of the public. In addition, bloggers have joined the ranks of those seeking to influence both politicians and public opinion.

Electronic or televised town halls do not always turn out as expected. The Reform party made an early attempt to establish its platform through an ultra-democratic process of electronic consul-tation with party members. Preston Manning soon learned that consensus is more difficult to achieve over cyberspace than in a crowded convention, where participants are subject to persuasion. Former Liberal Prime Minister Jean Chrétien had a disappointing experience with a televised town hall when the situ-ation became confrontational. Both of these experiments in communicative democracy were abandoned.

Politicians are very sensitive to public opinion and wary of offending potential voters. They are still subject to all of the traditional influences and constraints, but their responses to these must be tempered by their new instant and intimate relationship with the public. We know about Oka, Manitoba floods, ice storm disasters, helicopter purchases and cancellations, progress on same-sex marriage legislation, or conflict over lands claimed by First Nations *as events unfold*. We watch our political leaders and judge them— instantly and continually.

More active citizen participation— through discussions, public meetings, electronic town hall meetings, radio and television talk shows, letters to the editor, e-mail, referenda, blogs, and public opinion polls—serves to keep politicians on their toes. Some people applaud this spirit of active participa-tion. After all, in a democratic system government *should* be aware of and responsive to public opinion, even as it changes between elections. Clearly, these "activists" counter the influence of big business, lobbyists, or senior bureau-crats. On the other hand, governments are elected by millions of voters on the basis of campaign promises. In that light, should less representative individ-uals influence our politicians on an ongoing basis? Should events of the day and shifting public moods divert govern-ment action? Some argue that this kind of give and take between politicians and the general public enhances the demo-cratic process, while others argue that

under his arm, wife and daughter by his side. In the 2000 pres-idential election, George Bush and Al Gore openly claimed to be born-again Christians. Joe Lieberman (a conservative Jew) told Americans that, when Gore called to offer him the candi-dacy for vice president, the two men prayed together on the phone. We do have Canadian politicians who are Christian fundamentalists: Preston Manning and Stockwell Day (former leaders of Reform and the Canadian Alliance) are prominent examples. Both Manning and Day believe that reli-gion and politics *should* mix but had to tone down their reli-giosity because—as Prime Minister Stephen Harper also learned—at the national level in Canada, overt religious expression does not play well in the media.

Also during elections, televised debates between the leaders of political parties—the "acid test of image manage-ment" (Attallah, 2004: 275)—are mandatory in today's political climate and can have a significant impact on the voters' impressions of the party leaders. Early in the campaign, the eleven candidates vying for the leadership of the Liberal party were assessed for fluency in French and English—and only five of them passed the test (Clark, 2006). Without that fluency, party leaders cannot partici-pate effectively in those all-important debates.

As we saw in Chapter 2 ("Sociological Investigation"), opinion polls are particularly worrisome to some observers of the political scene. The timing of polls, sample size, and the wording of questions have dramatic effects on outcomes: for example, including the name of the Green Party in a question on party preference inflates the number choosing that response to almost double its actual vote yield (Marzolini, 2004). And, when the elec-torate is volatile and voters are waiting to make their deci-sions at the last minute, polls from different firms can vary wildly. Do polls reflect or shape public opinion?

Hillwatch, a government rela-tions firm, offers links to reports on current Canadian polls at www.hillwatch.com/ pollingstation/pollingstation.htm.

the effects, which are increasingly real and immediate, are actually ones of distortion. Comedian Rick Mercer revealed the frivolous side of constant polling and referenda when he collected more than 1 million Canadian signatures on his online petition to have Canadian Alliance leader Stockwell Day change his name to "Doris."

The most dramatic illustration of the power of the media to shape public opinion and bring down a government was that of the Quebec sponsorship scandal. In November 2004, Canada's Auditor General Sheila Fraser reported that advertising and sponsorship contracts—which were instituted by the Chrétien government in the wake of the 1995 referendum to increase the federal presence in the province—constituted gross mismanagement. Fraser concluded that "as much as $100 million of the $250 million program budget had been siphoned off to private firms and individuals through various illegitimate schemes, including overbilling, artificial invoices, fictitious contracts, and blatant payments" (Mancuso, et al., 2006). When he took over from Chrétien as Liberal leader and prime minister, Paul Martin commissioned Mr. Justice Gomery to investigate the sponsorship program in order to determine how much money had disappeared, how it was mishandled, and who was responsible.

For more than six months, Canadians were able to watch events unfold on television—first in English and then in French, when the inquiry was moved to Quebec. Politicians, bureaucrats, business executives, and administrative assistants were grilled daily—on our television screens—about their knowledge of or involvement in the mismanagement of taxpayers' money. Canadians found out that some ad agencies were given large sums of money for promotional work that was never done and that high-level government officials were aware of the mismanagement or personally involved. The most damning revelation for the Liberal government was that money intended for the promotion of Canada within Quebec (i.e., by sponsoring sports and cultural events) made its way into Quebec Liberal coffers—to be used for campaign purposes. So serious are these infractions, that several men have since been convicted of crimes. If Canadians were angry, Quebecers were furious: the implication of the sponsorship program itself was that their loyalty could be bought by paper flags and advertisements in public venues.

What about the political fallout? As we geared up for the election of 2006, Paul Martin's Liberal government tried desperately to hold off an election until after the publication of the second Gomery report. The first was damning, and the second was to talk about how to prevent such debacles in the future. In the end, the government was defeated in the late fall with an election date of January 23, 2006. Unfortunately for the Liberal government, Adscam and government corruption were on the top of many minds—especially in Quebec. It's impossible to measure the impact of the sponsorship scandal and the televised inquiry, but Stephen Harper's Conservatives increased their share of the popular vote from 29.6 to 36.3 percent—and their seat count from 99 to 124—between 2004 and 2006. This was enough to give them a minority government and to break the Liberal lock on government that was created when the right splintered in 1993. In comparison, the election results in Quebec astounded everyone: Conservative support rose from 8.8 to 24.6 percent while the party's seats increased from 0 to 10. The Conservatives, rather than the Liberals, are now Quebec's alternative to the Bloc Québécois.

WHAT DO YOU THINK?

1. Is your awareness of politics affected by the fact that politicians are on the internet? Do bloggers contribute to your political awareness and attitudes?
2. Do you ever watch such programs as *Air Farce* and *This Hour has 22 Minutes*? To what extent do these shows keep you up to date on current events?
3. Were you aware of the impact of the sponsorship scandal on the election of 2006? Do you think it is likely to be long lasting? Why?

YOUR TURN

If it looks as though your party is losing support at the last minute, are you more likely to get out and vote? Will you vote for the party that is dropping in popularity or the one to which others seem to be turning?

Other agents of political socialization are the many organizations to which people belong. Some of these are professional, ethnic, or voluntary associations, unions, or special-interest organizations such as women's or environmental groups. From time to time, churches attempt to mobilize their members behind a particular cause, such as fighting abortion or arranging for the sponsorship of refugees. Seniors clubs, formed initially to encourage social interaction among elders, might find themselves marching on Ottawa to protest the de-indexing of pensions. Political parties themselves would normally recruit people already inclined to be political activists; once they are party members, people may increase their participation levels, political knowledge and sophistication, and partisanship. Some of these organizations are founded for political purposes; others with a wide range of nonpolitical goals become political only as a result of circumstances.

POLITICAL PARTICIPATION

Needless to say, socialization does not increase *everyone's* political involvement or enthusiasm for our system of government: significant segments of our population learn that the political system responds little, if at all, to their needs. Indifference or even hostility towards the political system is evident among those who are disadvantaged and feel powerless to remedy the situation. In other cases, those who become committed and actively involved in political action may turn away, disillusioned, when they see how the political system actually works. In fact, as the Spicer Commission reported in 1991, Canadians have become increasingly cynical about politicians and the political process in general. According to some observers, this is part of a general change in attitude involving Canadians in a move from deference to numerous elites to active defiance (Newman, 1995; Nevitte, 1996).

Lester Milbrath (1966) proposed a typology reflecting a *hierarchy of participation* in electoral politics. He classified individual participation as falling into *gladiatorial*, *transitional*, and *spectator* roles. At the gladiatorial level, participants are actually involved in the political fray, as in attending strategy meetings or running for political office. In a transitional role, one might contact a politician, contribute time to a campaign, or give money to a political party. As a spectator, one might express interest in politics, expose oneself to political information, and vote—then sit back to watch the returns on television.

According to a 1974 survey, at most 5 percent of Canadians are involved at Milbrath's gladiatorial level. Another 40 percent participate at the transitional level, most commonly attending a rally or an all-candidates meeting, and trying to influence the votes of friends or co-workers. Only 5 percent have never voted in a federal election, while 80 to 90 percent engage in informal discussion about elections and follow the campaign to some extent through the media. While people are a little less inclined to vote in provincial than federal elections, other types of participation seem to be similar at both levels of government (Van Loon and Whittington, 1981). Considering the voter apathy discussed above, one might expect that, in recent elections participation at gladiatorial, transitional, and spectator levels has declined along with turnout. In federal elections of the last three decades, 60 to 76 percent of eligible voters came out to the polls—compared with 50 to 60 percent in the United States. Turnout for provincial elections is generally a little lower and, in municipal elections, is lower still. To the extent that elections constitute spectator sport, turnout improves if it is a good race.

Canadians participated at every stage of the constitutional negotiations leading to the defeat of the Charlottetown Accord in 1992. After the defeat of the Meech Lake Accord, public demands for wider involvement in constitutional discussions led to the creation of the Spicer Commission in 1990, which conducted town halls and home meetings, and offered a toll-free phone line. In the end more than 400 000 Canadians participated in the sometimes painful, intensely introspective debate about our constitution.

The Participation of Women

As Chapter 13 ("Gender Stratification") discussed, the movement for women to vote began in Canada in the 1880s. But, since it had to function simultaneously at the provincial and federal levels, it was subject to all "the regional conflicts and divisions that characterized other Canadian social movements" (Bashevkin, 1993:4). Despite divisions that were especially damaging to this movement, women in Canada finally acquired the right to vote at the federal level in 1918. Manitoba was the first province to extend the vote to women (1916), while Quebec was the last (1940). The extension of the vote to women set the scene for a series of political firsts. Agnes Macphail quickly ran for and won federal political office (1921), but she had to deal with numerous obstacles—including people who said, "We can't have a woman." It was not until 1957 that Canada had its first female federal cabinet minister, Ellen Fairclough; and it was 1984 before women were given portfolios other than those deemed most "suited" to women, such as health, education, or the status of women. Prime Minister Brian Mulroney broke this pattern at the federal level by appointing Pat Carney to international trade, Barbara McDougall to junior finance, and Kim Campbell to the justice portfolio (Bashevkin, 1993:88). In 1989, Audrey McLaughlin became the first federal party leader (of the NDP), and Kim Campbell's leadership win in 1993 automatically made her Canada's first female prime minister. Although, in ideological and practical terms, the New Democratic Party has been most persistent in the promotion of women, these firsts involve all three of the major parties.

Despite these highly visible firsts, women are still under-represented in politics. Women tend to be the support staff of a political party rather than its candidates. As one moves higher within a party's hierarchy, one finds the representation of women becoming smaller. Most female candidates run for minor parties or in ridings where wins are unlikely. As well, the proportion of females running for office and winning is greatest at the municipal level, somewhat lower at the provincial level, and lower still at the federal level.

There has been a steady increase in the number of women elected at the federal level in recent years, from 5 percent winning in the 1980 election, to 10 percent in 1984, 13 percent in 1988, 18 percent in 1993, and 21 percent in 1997 and 2000. These figures are high compared with the United States, Britain, and France, which have legislatures that are about 6 percent female, but low when compared with Finland, Sweden, Norway, and Denmark, where 32 to 38 percent of their legislatures are female (Bashevkin, 1993). The 2006 federal election sent 64 women to Ottawa (20.8% of the 308 MPs): female representation is 11.3 percent in the Conservative caucus, 20.4 percent for the Liberals, 33.3 percent for the Bloc, and 41.4 percent for the New Democrats (i.e., the elected MPs of each party) (Canada, 2006). It is worth noting that overall female representation has not improved since 1997.

Nellie McClung (*left*), Manitoba-born teacher, author, and activist, was welcomed in many settings as an effective and humorous speaker. She fought for women's suffrage, prohibition, factory safety, and many other reforms. She was one of the chief activists in the *Persons Case*, which involved a court battle to have women legally recognized as persons. Because of her efforts and those of her colleagues, women were given the right to vote (in 1918), to sit in the House of Commons (1919), and to be appointed to the Senate (in 1929) (Hallett, 1988).

Agnes Macphail (*right*) was the first woman elected to the House of Commons in 1921, the first federal election in which women could vote. Like her friend, Nellie McClung, Macphail was a teacher. She was involved in the agricultural co-operative movement of Ontario, various feminist causes, and prison investigation and reform. She founded the Elizabeth Fry Society of Canada and was the first woman appointed to Canada's delegation to the United Nations. Macphail was largely responsible for Ontario's first pay-equity legislation in 1951 (Black, 1988).

Among the barriers to women's participation are socialization, lack of financing or contacts, and the electoral system itself. To the extent that gender stereotypes contribute to resistance on the part of voters and reluctance on the part of potential female candidates, the appearance (even though temporary) of Kim Campbell in the prime minister's office and of Sheila Copps as deputy prime minister may have expanded horizons. All of our parties are aware of the need to include women among cabinet ministers. An additional, rarely noted, barrier is the geographic size of Canada. Members of parliament have to spend much of the year in Ottawa, away from their families. While the House is sitting, MPs commute weekly—sometimes crossing two or three time zones to get to work. Considering our cultural expectations in child-care and other family responsibilities, it is not surprising that few women commit to careers in federal politics. Small countries (i.e., Finland, Norway, Sweden, and Denmark) do not require such extended commutes for parliamentarians; neither do Canada's provinces or municipalities.

Theoretical Analysis of Power in Society

Sociologists have long debated how power is spread throughout society. Power is a very difficult topic to study because decision making is complex and often takes place behind closed doors. Despite this difficulty, researchers have developed three competing models of power.

THE PLURALIST MODEL: THE PEOPLE RULE

The **pluralist model,** closely linked to structural-functional theory, is *an analysis of politics that sees power as spread among many competing interest groups.* Pluralists claim that politics is an arena of negotiation. With limited resources, no organization can expect to realize all its goals. Organizations therefore operate as *veto groups*, realizing some success but mostly keeping opponents from achieving all their ends. The political process relies heavily on creating alliances and compromises among numerous interest groups so that policies gain wide support. In short, pluralists see power as spread widely throughout society, with all people having at least some voice in the political system (Dahl, 1961, 1982; Rothman and Black, 1998).

In *The Vertical Mosaic: An Analysis of Social Class and Power in Canada* (1965)—a Canadian classic—John Porter addresses the question of who makes major decisions, or exercises power, in Canada. On the basis of extensive research, he concludes that there are competing elites at the top of five major organizational clusters: economic, political, bureaucratic, labour, and ideological (that is, church, education, and media). Of the five, the economic or corporate elite and the bureaucratic elite are the most powerful. While there is competition among these elites because of the opposing interests of their respective institutions, Porter points out that these powerful and wealthy elites are also highly integrated. To keep the system working, they are willing to accommodate one another. As a result, Canada has what one might call *co-operative pluralism.*

THE POWER ELITE MODEL: A FEW PEOPLE RULE

The **power elite model** is *an analysis of politics that views power as concentrated among the rich.* This second approach is closely allied with the social-conflict paradigm in sociology. The term "power elite" is a lasting contribution of C. Wright Mills (1956), who argued that the upper class holds the bulk

	Pluralist Model	Power Elite Model	Political Economy Model
Which theoretical approach is applied?	Structural-functional approach	Social-conflict approach	Social-conflict approach
How is power spread throughout society?	Power is spread widely so that all groups have some voice.	Power is concentrated in the hands of top political and business leaders.	Power is directed by the operation of the capitalist economy.
Is Canada a democracy?	Yes. Power is spread widely enough to make the country a democracy.	No. Power is too concentrated for the country to be a democracy.	No. The capitalist economy sets political decision making, so the country is not a democracy.

of society's wealth, enjoys most of its prestige, and exercises the lion's share of power. Mills claimed that the power elite stands atop the three major sectors of society—the economy, the government, and the military. Thus, the power elite includes the "super rich" (executives and large stockholders of major corporations), top officials in government, and the highest ranking officers in the military. Further, Mills explained, these elites move from one sector to another, consolidating their power as they go. It is not unusual for national political leaders to enter public life from powerful and highly paid positions in business. For example, Brian Mulroney was a labour lawyer and then vice president of Iron Ore Company of Canada before becoming prime minister. Since he left political office, he has returned to Montreal to practise corporate law and sits on many boards for influential corporations. Paul Martin was the owner and CEO of Canadian Steamship Lines (Deneault, 2006) as he was about to become our prime minister; in order to avoid future conflict of interest, he passed the company on to his sons.

In the 1970s, Wallace Clement (1975) argued that Canada is ruled by an economic or corporate elite that is becoming increasingly powerful. The members of this group are likely to have upper-class origins and to have a vested interest in maintaining the capitalist system. As a result of the dense networks that bind the economic, political, and bureaucratic elites, they are blending into one group dominated by the corporate elite. Clement rejects the pluralist model, noting that the state and private capital are complementary and mutually dependent. In effect, the state and the capitalists act as one. Power elite theorists challenge the claim that Canada is a political democracy. They maintain that the concentration of wealth and power is simply too great for the average person's voice to be heard. They reject the pluralist idea that various centres of power serve as checks and balances on one another. Instead, the power elite model maintains that those at the top encounter no real opposition.

On the other hand, even the most powerful members of our society do not always get their way. As long as ordinary people continue to form political associations or express themselves in the context of various interest groups, our society will retain a substantial degree of pluralism. There are numerous examples of situations where Québécois, Aboriginal peoples, environmentalists, labour unions, or feminists have won concessions and inspired policy changes that are anathema to big business (e.g., Kyoto). The Charlottetown Accord was defeated in a referendum in 1992, despite support by major political parties, big business, and the media, because grassroots opposition and the Reform party mobilized the "No" supporters and staged an upset victory.

THE MARXIST MODEL: THE SYSTEM IS BIASED

A third approach to understanding politics is the **Marxist political economy model,** *an analysis that explains politics in terms of the operation of a society's economic system.* The power elite model focuses on the enormous wealth and power of certain individuals; the Marxist model goes further and sees bias rooted in a country's institutions, especially its economy. As noted in Chapter 4 ("Society"), Karl Marx claimed that a society's economic system (capitalist or socialist) shapes its political system. Therefore, the power elites do not simply appear out of nowhere; they are creations of capitalism itself. From this point of view, reforming the political system—say, by limiting the amount of money that rich people can contribute to political candidates—is unlikely to bring about true democracy. The problem does not lie in the *people* who exercise great power or the *people* who don't vote; the problem is rooted in the *system* itself, what Marxists call the "political economy of capitalism." In other words, as long as a country has a mostly capitalist economy—as does Canada—the majority of people will be shut out of politics, just as they are exploited in the workplace.

The Applying Theory table (on p. 452) summarizes the three models of power and the political system. Which of these three models applies to Canada? Over the years, research has shown support for each one. In the end, how you think our political system ought to work is as much a matter of political values as of scientific fact.

Power beyond the Rules

In politics, there is always disagreement over a society's goals and the means to achieve them. A political system tries to resolve these controversies within a system of rules. But political activity sometimes breaks the rules or tries to do away with the entire system.

REVOLUTION

Political revolution is *the overthrow of one political system in order to establish another.* Reform involves change *within* a system, through modification of the law or, in the extreme case, a *coup d'état* (in French, literally, "stroke of the state"), in which one leader topples another. Revolution involves change in the type of system itself. No political system is immune to revolution, nor does revolution produce any one kind of government. America's Revolutionary War (1775–81) replaced colonial rule by the British monarchy with a representative democracy. French revolutionaries in 1789 also overthrew a monarch, only to set the stage for the return of monarchy in the person of Napoleon. In 1917, the Russian Revolution replaced monarchy with a socialist government built on the ideas of Karl Marx. In 1991, a second Russian revolution dismantled the socialist Soviet Union, and the nation was reborn as the Russian Federation, which has been moving towards a market system although it has yet to provide a greater political voice for its people.

Closer to home, one sees revolutionary potential in Quebec's quest for greater autonomy. In the referendum on October 30, 1995, 49.4 percent of the people of Quebec voted Yes to Quebec becoming sovereign. Had a few more people voted Yes, they would have set in motion a process that would dismantle Canada as presently constituted and force the creation of two or more new and very different political entities.

Despite their striking variety, revolutions share a number of traits (de Tocqueville, 1955; orig. 1856; Skocpol, 1979; Tilly, 1986):

1. *Rising expectations.* Common sense suggests that revolution would be more likely when people are severely deprived, but history shows that most revolutions occur when people's lives are improving. Rising expectations, rather than bitterness and despair, make revolutions more likely.

2. *Unresponsive government.* Revolutions become more likely when a government is unwilling to reform itself, especially when demands for reform by powerful segments of society are ignored.

3. *Radical leadership by intellectuals.* The English philosopher Thomas Hobbes (1588–1679) claimed that intellectuals provide the justification for revolution, and universities are often the centre of political change. Students played a critical role in China's prodemocracy movement and the uprisings in Eastern Europe.

4. *Establishing a new legitimacy.* Overthrowing a political system is not easy, but ensuring a revolution's long-term success is harder still. Some revolutionary movements are held together mostly by hatred of the past regime and fall apart once new leaders are installed.

Revolutionaries must also guard against counterrevolutionary drives led by overthrown leaders. This explains the speed and ruthlessness with which victorious revolutionaries typically dispose of former leaders.

Scientific analysis cannot declare that a revolution is good or bad. The full consequences of such an upheaval depend on personal values and typically become evident only after many years. Fifteen years after its revolution, the future of the former Soviet Union remains uncertain.

TERRORISM

On September 11, 2001, terrorists hijacked four commercial airliners: one crashed in a wooded area; the other three were flown into public buildings full of people. The attack killed more than 3000 innocent people representing 68 nations and including 25 Canadians, injured many thousands more, completely destroyed the twin towers of the World Trade Center in New York City, and seriously damaged the Pentagon in Washington, D.C. Not since the attack on Pearl Harbor at the outbreak of World War II had the United States suffered such a blow. Indeed, these events were the most serious terrorist acts recorded in North America. As the Thinking Critically box (on p. 456–57) observes, these events also had implications for the relationship between Canada and the United States.

Terrorism refers to *acts of violence or the threat of violence used as a political strategy by an individual or a group.* Like revolution, terrorism is a political act beyond the rules of established political systems. According to Paul Johnson (1981), terrorism has four distinguishing characteristics. First, terrorists try to paint violence as a legitimate political tactic, even though such acts are condemned by virtually every nation. Terrorists also bypass, or are excluded from, established channels of political negotiation. Therefore, terrorism is a weaker organization's strategy against a stronger enemy.

The violence of terrorism has become commonplace in international politics in recent decades. In 2004, there were 651 acts of terrorism worldwide, which claimed 1907 lives and injured 6704 people. Most of those killed were in the Middle East, linked to either the conflict between Israel and

Increasing security in a time of danger generally means reducing freedom. As part of the ongoing war on terrorism, security teams are far more evident in public places. In what ways does increased police surveillance threaten our freedoms?

the Palestinians or the conflict in Iraq. But many nations were involved, including Spain and Russia, where the bloodiest attacks of the year occurred (U.S. Department of State, 2005).

In Canada, the Front de libération du Québec (FLQ), which may have comprised fewer than 30 people, used terrorism to promote its goal of an independent, socialist Quebec. From 1963 to 1971, it was involved in 200 or more bombings of increasing seriousness. In 1970, its members kidnapped James Cross, the British trade commissioner, and Pierre Laporte, a Quebec cabinet minister, whom they subsequently murdered. As was its intent, the FLQ caught the attention of the country.

To find out what the Canadian Intelligence Security Service has to say about terrorist groups active in Canada, go to www.csis-scrs.gc.ca/en/priorities/terrorism.asp.

Second, Johnson asserts that terrorism is used not just by groups but also by governments against their own people. *State terrorism* is the use of violence, generally without support of law, by government officials as a way to control the population. State terrorism is lawful in some authoritarian and totalitarian states, which survive by creating widespread fear and intimidation. Saddam Hussein, for example, relied on secret police and state terror to protect his power in Iraq.

Third, democratic societies reject terrorism in principle, but they are especially vulnerable to terrorists because they give extensive civil liberties to their people and have less extensive police networks. This susceptibility helps to explain the tendency of democratic governments to suspend civil liberties if they fear attack, as was done in 1970 when, in response to the murder of Pierre Laporte by the FLQ, Pierre Trudeau invoked the *War Measures Act* and arrested more than 450 people, many of whom were suspected of being FLQ members and sympathizers. Since the 2001 terrorist attacks in the United States, we have had new civil rights concerns. Individuals, some of them Canadian, have been held without being charged in the

United States: Syrian-born Canadian Maher Arar in 2002 was deported, on information from the RCMP, by U.S. authorities to Syria, where he was imprisoned and tortured for more than a year before being returned to Canada. In 2006, a public inquiry exonerated Arar and held the RCMP responsible for giving inaccurate information to the U.S. authorities. Other Arab or Muslim Canadians, or those belonging to other visible minorities, have been subject to what looks like racial profiling as they are singled out for prolonged searches and questioning *en route* to the United States. Canadian author Rohinton Mistry is one of many to report such harassment.

Fourth, and finally, terrorism is always a matter of definition. Governments claim the right to maintain order, even by force, and may label opposition groups that use violence as "terrorists." Political differences may explain why one person's "terrorist" is another's "freedom fighter" (Jenkins, 2003). This is illustrated well by Che Guevara, by the Irish Republican Army, and by the Palestinian/Israeli conflict.

While hostage taking and outright killing provoke anger, taking action against terrorists poses challenges. Because most terrorist groups are shadowy organizations with no formal connection to any established state, identifying the parties responsible may be difficult. In addition, any military response risks confrontation with other governments. Yet, as terrorism expert Brian Jenkins warns, the failure to respond "encourages other terrorist groups, who begin to realize that this can be a pretty cheap way to wage war" (quoted in Whitaker, 1985:29).

YOUR TURN

Do you think you will live to see a world free from terrorism? Why or why not?

WAR AND PEACE

Perhaps the most critical political issue is **war,** *organized, armed conflict among the people of two or more nations, directed by their governments.* War is as old as humanity, but understanding it is crucial today because humanity now has weapons that can destroy the entire planet. Many people think of war as an extraordinary occurrence; yet for almost all of the twentieth century, nations somewhere on Earth were in violent conflict. Most wars are localized, while others, like the two world wars, are widespread. Canada's involvement in several of these wars cost Canadian lives: 60 661 Canadians were killed in World War I, 42 042 in World War II, and 312 in the Korean War. In the Vietnam War, some Canadian individuals signed up to fight in the American forces, but Canada's official role involved serving on truce commissions and supplying medical or technical assistance. Since Vietnam, Canada has generally been involved in the world's troublespots, such as Rwanda and Bosnia, as a peacekeeper. We are now moving into a more open combat role in Afghanistan, and need to recognize that most of our peacekeeping has been accomplished with weapons.

The Causes of War

Wars occur so often that we might think there is something natural about armed confrontation. But there is no evidence that human beings must wage war under any particular circumstances. On the contrary, governments around the world usually have to force their people to go to war. Like all forms of social behaviour, warfare is a product of *society* that is more common in some places than others. The Semai of Malaysia, among the most peace-loving of the world's peoples, rarely resort to violence; in contrast, the Y[[No mapping for (238) \'b9]]?nomamö of Venezuela and Brazil are quick to wage war. If society holds the key to war or peace, under what circumstances do humans go to battle? Quincy Wright (1987) cites five factors that promote war:

1. *Perceived threats.* Societies mobilize in response to a perceived threat to their people, territory, or culture. Leaders in the United States and the United Kingdom justified the recent military campaign to disarm Iraq, for example, by stressing the threat that Saddam Hussein posed to their countries.

2. *Social problems.* When internal problems generate widespread frustration at home, a society's leaders may divert public attention by attacking an external "enemy" as a form of scapegoating. While American leaders claimed that the war in Iraq was a matter of national security, there is little doubt that the onset of the war diverted attention from the struggling national economy and boosted the popularity of President Bush.

3. *Political objectives.* Poor nations, such as Vietnam, have used wars to end foreign domination. On the other hand, powerful countries, such as the United States,

There is an old saying that all is fair in love and war, but wars (like relationships) are actually carried out according to rules. The recent war on terrorism has raised questions about the rights of captured enemy combatants, most of whom are not soldiers in any nation's army. Should the prisoners held at the U.S. base in Guantanamo Bay, Cuba, be treated according to the rules of war as spelled out in the United Nations Geneva Convention? Should they have access to the American courts, as American citizens do?

may benefit from a periodic show of force to increase global political standing. (Recall the deployments of troops in Somalia, Haiti, Bosnia, Afghanistan, and Iraq.)

4. *Moral objectives.* Nations rarely claim that they are going to war to gain wealth and power. Instead, their leaders infuse military campaigns with moral urgency. By calling the 2003 invasion of Iraq "Operation Iraqi Freedom," U.S. leaders tried to portray the mission as a morally justified war of liberation from an evil tyrant.

5. *The absence of alternatives.* A fifth factor promoting war is the absence of alternatives. While the goal of the United Nations is to maintain international peace by finding alternatives to war, the organization has had limited success in preventing conflict between nations.

Is Terrorism a New Kind of War?

After the terrorist attacks on September 11, 2001, U.S. government officials spoke of terrorism as a new kind of war. War has historically followed certain patterns: it is played out according to some basic rules, the warring parties are known to each other, and the objectives of the warring parties—which generally involve control of territory—are clearly stated. Terrorism breaks from these patterns. The identity of terrorist individuals and organizations may not be known, those involved may deny their responsibility, and their goals may be unclear. The 2001 terrorist attacks against the United States were not attempts to defeat the nation militarily or to

THINKING CRITICALLY

After 9/11: Managing Our Relationship with the United States

On the day when two passenger planes were flown into the twin towers of the World Trade Center in New York ordinary Canadians reacted with horror and compassion. In the immediate aftermath, Canadians throughout the country—in particular in tiny Gander, Newfoundland and Labrador—opened their hearts and homes to airline passengers diverted from flight paths to American airports. Three days later, about 100 000 people gathered on Parliament Hill to pay their respects to the victims of terrorism in New York. There seemed to be widespread empathy for our neighbours to the south, along with a sense of shared vulnerability as we faced the unprecedented attack on North American soil.

Before long, a different perspective on the events of September 11, 2001, began to emerge. We feared a loss of sovereignty or independence in the face of pressure to agree to a common perimeter for defence and border control. Pressure to harmonize our immigration policy with that of the Americans gave rise to images of racial profiling, which is not consistent with Canadian values. And latent anti-Americanism, which helps us maintain our distinctiveness from our giant neighbour, seemed to rise to the surface, manifesting itself as the notion that the Americans brought the terrorist attacks on themselves. The attacks, it was argued, were a response to provocation—either American foreign policy in the Middle East and elsewhere or Western (i.e., American) indifference to global inequality. The sense that the terrorist attacks were an attack on all of us was replaced with one that—despite the symbolism of the *World* Trade Center—made the United States the villain and the attack understandable, if not justifiable. Prime Minister Chrétien had an opportunity, in his first message of condolence, to influence public opinion and counter this interpretation of events. He did not. It was in this context that President Bush failed to list Canada among America's friends in his speech to Congress.

It was with reluctance that Canada joined the "war on terror" in Afghanistan where, tragically, we have lost soldiers to combat, as well as American friendly fire. Our role has actually expanded over time. In late 2003, maintaining a precarious peace in Kabul was the job at hand but, more recently, we have assumed leadership in clearing southern Afghanistan of Taliban insurgents. It is in this action that more Canadian soldiers have been killed, including our first female officer.

When U.S. president George W. Bush turned his attention to Iraq on the grounds that it produced and used weapons of mass destruction against its own people and allegedly supported suicide bombers by making payments to their families, he looked to Canada for military support. Canada's leadership dug in its heels and actively resisted direct involvement in Iraq. We had every right to say No to participation in Iraq, but there was no need for Canadian officials to insult George Bush (calling him a "moron" and a "failed statesman") or the American people ("Damn Americans! I hate the bastards!"). Such comments did nothing to heal a relationship with Americans that was fraying at the edges. Sadly, we were aggravating the Americans when, in fact, we *were* contributing to the war in Iraq, albeit indirectly: Canada had ships patrolling the Gulf in a supportive role, soldiers

---

secure territory. They were carried out by people representing not a country but a cause. In short, they were expressions of anger and hatred, an effort to destabilize the country and create widespread fear.

Conventional warfare is symmetrical, with two nations sending their armies into battle. By contrast, terrorism is an unconventional form of warfare, an asymmetrical conflict in which a small number of attackers uses terror and their own willingness to die to level the playing field against a much more powerful enemy. Although the terrorists may be ruthless, the nation under attack must exercise restraint in its response to terrorism because little may be known about the identity and location of those responsible. It is for this reason that the United States has had limited success in ending the insurgency in Iraq.

The Costs and Causes of Militarism

The cost of armed conflict extends far beyond battlefield casualties. Together, the world's nations spend almost US$1 trillion annually (US$159 for every person on the planet) for military purposes. Spending this much diverts resources from the desperate struggle for survival by hundreds of millions of poor people. Defence is the U.S. government's second largest expenditure (after social security), accounting for 20 percent of all federal spending: in 2004, it amounted to US$414 billion; the war on terrorism and the Iraq War have only pushed this number higher.

In recent years, the United States has emerged as the world's only superpower, with more military might than the next nine countries combined (Gergen, 2002). For decades, military spending went up as a result of the *arms race*

fighting within British and American units, and senior military personnel involved in the Iraq war at the decision-making level.

There are many Canadians who argue that we must nurture our relationship with the Americans for two very important reasons. Our military strength has been eroded to the point where, more than ever, we are dependent on the United States for our defence. In addition, the United States is our major trading partner: in excess of 85 percent of our exports go to the United States, with about $2 billion in trade going back and forth across our common border *every day*. Since the implementation of our free trade agreements, our trade *surplus*—exports minus imports—has increased steadily to $133 billion in 2001. In short, we are militarily and economically dependent on our giant neighbour.

Canadians and Americans shared fallout from the terrorist attacks of September 11, 2001, as well as SARS, West Nile disease, mad cow disease, and the power outage of 2003. We cannot close our borders and effectively isolate ourselves from each other. The Bush administration came under pressure as a result of several decisions Canada made in 2003: our steps towards legalization of same-sex marriage, our decriminalization of marijuana use, and our sale of cheaper prescription drugs to Americans. Since the same-sex marriage issue is hotly debated in the United States, our example is hard to ignore. The marijuana issue, in turn, is accentuated by the flow of our homegrown pot to American users. Lest you think this is a minor concern, take note of the fact that marijuana is big business in Canada—second only to the cattle industry among our agricultural producers. *Conservatively* estimated, our pot production is valued at $7 billion, compared to $7.8 billion in cattle; as with our other exports, 85 percent of our high-grade marijuana is exported to the United States (Turner, 2003). Recently, more and more American individuals and even municipalities have been buying their prescription drugs from Canada, in most cases for less than half the price in the United States. Some of those drugs are brand-name drugs sold to Canada at lower prices, only to be sold back to Americans; others are generic drugs produced in Canada in defiance of American patent laws. Busloads of Americans cross the border to pick up their prescription drugs while others use the internet to place their orders.

Some of the most biting criticism of U.S. policy on Iraq comes from Americans themselves—and much of it is aired on CNN. In the eyes of those critics, Canada was right to stay out of the war in Iraq. There are also many Americans who think Canada is "cool" for its stand on same-sex marriage, marijuana, or prescription-drug price controls. Nonetheless, the Bush administration, which faced each of these controversies on its own turf, has been understandably exasperated with those unco-operative Canadians up north. Prime Minister Harper seems to be healing some of the wounds in our relationship with the United States, but he has to be mindful of public opinion at home which, at least in the present climate, doesn't allow him to get too cosy with President Bush.

WHAT DO YOU THINK?

1. How would Canadians and the Canadian government have reacted if the attacks on September 11, 2001, had been directed against Toronto's CN Tower and commercial core?

2. Should the fact that Canadian and American economies are highly integrated mean that we should work together on security issues? What are the consequences of not co-operating on security?

3. If the United States had had a Democratic president at the time of the 2001 terrorist attacks, would events have unfolded very differently? Would Canada's reaction have been different?

---

between the United States and the Soviet Union, which dropped out of the race after its collapse in 1991. But some analysts (i.e., those who support power elite theory) link high military spending to the domination of U.S. society by a **military-industrial complex,** *the close association of the federal government, the military, and defence industries.* The roots of militarism, then, lie not just in external threats to American security but also in its institutional structures (Marullo, 1987; Barnes, 2002).

A final reason for continuing militarism is regional conflict. During the 1990s, for example, localized wars broke out in Bosnia, Chechnya, and Zambia: tensions continue to run high between Israelis and Palestinians, and have only in recent years cooled between Catholic and Protestant militants in Ireland. Even limited wars have the potential to grow and draw in other countries. India and Pakistan—both nuclear powers—moved to the brink of war in 2002. In 2006, the announcement by North Korea that it had detonated a nuclear weapon raised tensions in Asia and around the world. And Iran continues to develop nuclear technology, raising fears that this nation may soon have an atomic bomb.

Nuclear Weapons

Despite the easing of superpower tensions, the world still contains 20 000 nuclear warheads, representing a destructive power of 5 tonnes of TNT for every person on the planet. If even a small fraction of this stockpile is used in war, life as we know it could end on much of the Earth. Albert Einstein, whose genius contributed to the development of nuclear weapons, reflected in a telegram (24 May 1946): "The unleashed power of the atom has changed everything *save our modes of thinking*, and we thus drift towards unparalleled catastrophe." In short, nuclear weapons make unrestrained war unthinkable in a world not yet capable of peace.

In recent years, the world has become aware of the death and mutilation caused by millions of land mines placed in the ground during wartime and left there afterwards. Civilians—many of them children—maimed by land mines receive treatment in this clinic in Kabul, Afghanistan.

The United States, the Russian Federation, the United Kingdom, France, China, Israel, India, Pakistan, and North Korea all have nuclear weapons. The danger of catastrophic war increases with **nuclear proliferation,** *the acquisition of nuclear weapons technology by more and more nations.* While a few nations stopped the development of nuclear weapons—Argentina and Brazil halted work in 1990, and South Africa dismantled its arsenal in 1991—by 2025 as many as 50 nations could have the ability to fight a nuclear war. Such a trend makes even the smallest regional conflict very dangerous to the entire planet.

Mass Media and War

The Iraq War was the first war in which television crews travelled "embedded" with U.S. and U.K. troops, reporting as the campaign unfolded. The mass media provided ongoing and detailed reports of events; cable television made available live coverage of the war 24 hours a day, 7 days a week. Media outlets critical of the war—especially the Arab news channel Al-Jazeera—tended to report the slow pace of the conflict, the casualties to coalition forces, and the deaths and injuries suffered by Iraqi civilians—information that would increase pressure to end the war. Media outlets supportive of the war—including most news organizations in the United States—tended to report the rapid pace of the war and the casualties to Saddam Hussein's forces and to downplay harm to Iraqi civilians as minimal and unintended. In sum, the power of the mass media to provide selective information to a worldwide audience means that television and other media are almost as important to the outcome of a conflict as the military that are doing the actual fighting.

Pursuing Peace

How can the world reduce the dangers of war? Here are the most recent approaches to peace:

1. *Deterrence.* The logic of the arms race linked security to a "balance of terror" between the superpowers. The principle of *mutual assured destruction* means that the side launching a first-strike nuclear attack against the other will face greater retaliation. This deterrence policy kept the peace during more than fifty years of the Cold War between the United States and the Soviet Union. But this strategy fuelled an enormously expensive arms race and had little effect on nuclear proliferation, which represents a growing threat to peace. Deterrence also does little to stop terrorism or to prevent war started by a powerful nation (such as the United States) against a weaker foe (such as the Taliban's regime in Afghanistan or Saddam Hussein's Iraq).

2. *High-technology defence.* If technology created the weapons, perhaps it can also protect us from them. Such is the claim of the *strategic defence initiative.* Under this strategy, satellites and ground installations would destroy enemy missiles soon after they were launched. Critics claim that the system, which they refer to as "Star Wars," would be, at best, a leaky umbrella. Others worry that building such a system will spark another massive arms race.

3. *Diplomacy and disarmament.* Some analysts believe that the best path to peace is diplomacy rather than technology (Dedrick and Yinger, 1990). Teams of diplomats working together can increase security by reducing, rather than building, weapons stockpiles. But disarmament has limitations. No nation wants to be weakened by letting down its defences. Successful diplomacy depends on everyone involved making efforts to resolve a common problem (Fisher and Ury, 1988). Although the United States and the Soviet Union succeeded in negotiating arms reduction agreements, the world now faces increasing threats from other nations such as North Korea.

4. *Resolving underlying conflict.* In the end, reducing the dangers of war may depend on resolving underlying conflicts by promoting a more just world. Poverty, hunger, and illiteracy are all root causes of war. Perhaps the world needs to reconsider the wisdom of spending thousands of times as much money on militarism as we do on efforts to find peaceful solutions (Sivard, 1988; Kaplan and Schaffer, 2001).

THINKING IT THROUGH

Reforming Canada's Political System: Throwing out the Baby with the Bathwater

Canada's political system can be described as a parliamentary democracy and a constitutional monarchy, with Queen Elizabeth II as our head of state. Prior to confederation, French Canadians were already resisting our ties to the British Empire and the monarchy. As Canada became more multicultural and less British, others argued that we should abolish the monarchy—and become a republic with a president. Undercurrents of the debate over the monarchy are detectable much of the time.

Canada's Senate is criticized harshly because the prime minister *appoints* senators, who serve until they are seventy-five. Since it is not elected, the Senate lacks the legitimacy to flex its muscles to counter the House of Commons—where 59 percent of the members come from the populous provinces of Ontario and Quebec. When the Reform party emerged to run in the 1993 federal election, one of the main planks in its platform was senate reform: its Triple-E Senate would be *equal, elected,* and *effective.* Each province, regardless of population, would elect the same number of senators. A watered-down version of senate reform was included in the Charlottetown Accord, which was defeated by referendum in 1992.

The third element of our political system that comes under attack is the one by which we elect our members of Parliament. Under our system of 308 mini-elections at the riding (or electoral district) level, regional parties win a disproportionate number of seats; conversely, parties with support spread evenly throughout the country may win relatively few seats. A dramatic instance of this occurred in 1993, when 16 percent of Canada's voters supported the Progressive Conservatives and 18.7 percent supported Reform; despite the similarity in popular vote, the Conservatives won 2 seats (0.7%) while Reform won 52 (17.6%). The reason is that Reform was concentrated in western Canada—in specific ridings—while Conservative support was spread fairly evenly throughout Canada. In our *first-past-the-post electoral system*, the party with the most votes in any one of our ridings wins the seat. Regional or riding level concentration of party support increases the chances of winning seats.

The most commonly advocated alternative is a system of *proportional representation*, in which the number of seats won mirrors the popular vote. In Election 2000, for example, the Liberals won 101 of 103 Ontario seats (98%) with 49.5 percent of the popular vote; the Canadian Alliance won 2 seats (1.9%) with 19.1 percent of the Ontario vote. Proportional representation would have given the Liberals 51 seats and the Alliance 20. If the Alliance had been rewarded with 20 Ontario seats and 2 of the 32 Atlantic seats, western voters would not have felt that "their" party, once again, had been shut out in the east. Under proportional representation, the Liberals would have had fewer Ontario seats, but more throughout the western provinces, so that the regional bases of political parties would be weakened. Throughout Canada, the Liberals would have won 123 of 301 seats instead of the 172 that they won in 2000 under the first-past-the-post system. Under proportional representation, we would not have had a majority Liberal government. In fact, in a multi-party system like ours, majority governments would be less common under proportional representation.

So what do we lose, apart from majority governments, if we adopt proportional representation? The answer is simple: our MPs would be the babies thrown out with the bathwater. Our MPs, who usually live in their ridings, are the ones to whom we go with our problems and for whom some of us volunteer during and between elections. MPs are also the ones who act as hosts if their constituents appear in Ottawa, and who watch out for the interests of their ridings as the House of Commons goes about its business. Under proportional representation, we could no longer say that Medicine Hat is an Alliance riding or Joliette is a Bloc Québécois riding—because there would *be* no ridings for which to tally the votes! The relationship between people and their government representatives would be very different.

Some Canadians advocate abolition of the monarchy, Senate reform, and proportional representation to reform our polity. But, to accomplish any one of these, we would need to amend our constitution. Since any of these would constitute major change, consent of the House of Commons, the Senate, and the legislatures of all ten provinces would be required. Furthermore, we would turn to a referendum to seek public approval. The likelihood that any amendment would make it over these hurdles is small. If you were a prime minister doing rather well under the current set of rules, would *you* be eager to initiate constitutional change?

WHAT DO YOU THINK?

1. Is our political system as democratic as it should be? Explain your answer.
2. Are you bothered by the fact that Canada is a constitutional monarchy?
3. Would it matter to you if we went to proportional representation and lost the relationship between our MPs and their constituencies?

Politics: Looking Ahead

Change in political systems is ongoing. Several problems and trends are likely to be important as the twenty-first century unfolds. One troublesome problem in Canada and the United States is the inconsistency between our democratic ideals and our low turnout at the polls. Perhaps, as conservative pluralist theorists say, many people do not bother to vote because they are content with their lives. On the other hand, liberal power elite theorists may be right in their view that people withdraw from a system that concentrates wealth and power in the hands of so few people. Or perhaps, as radical Marxist critics claim, people find that our political system gives little real choice, limiting options and policies to those that support our capitalist economy. In any case, the current high level of apathy indicates that significant political reform is needed. The Thinking It Through box (on p. 459) takes a look at proposed reforms of the Canadian political system.

A second issue is the global rethinking of political models. The Cold War between the United States and the Soviet Union encouraged people to think of politics in terms of the two opposing models, capitalism and socialism. Today, however, people are more likely to consider a broader range of political systems that links government to the economy in various ways. "Welfare capitalism" as found in Sweden, or "state capitalism" as found in Japan and South Korea, are just two possibilities. In all cases, promoting the broadest democratic participation is an important goal.

Third, we still face the danger of war in many parts of the world. Even as the United States and the Russian Federation dismantle some warheads, vast stockpiles of nuclear weapons remain, and nuclear technology continues to spread around the world. In addition, new superpowers are likely to arise—China and India are likely candidates, and regional conflicts and terrorism are likely to continue. We can only hope—and vote!—for leaders who will find nonviolent solutions to the age-old problems that provoke war, putting us on the road to world peace.

17 MAKING THE GRADE

The following learning tools will help you see what you know, identify what you still need to learn, and expand your understanding beyond the text. You can also visit this text's Companion Website™ at www.pearsoned.ca/macionis to find useful practice tests.

KEY POINTS

Power and Authority

Politics is the major social institution by which a society distributes power and organizes decision making. Max Weber explained that raw power is transformed into authority by tradition, rationally enacted rules and regulations, or the personal charisma of a leader.

Politics in Global Perspective

Monarchy, based on traditional authority, is common in preindustrial societies. While constitutional monarchies persist in some industrial nations, industrialization favours democracy based on rational-legal authority and extensive bureaucracy.

Authoritarian political regimes deny people participation in government. Totalitarian political systems go even further, rigidly regulating people's everyday lives.

There are 192 politically independent nation-states in the world. A political trend, however, is the growing wealth and power of multinational corporations that operate around the world. In an age of computers and other new information technology, governments can no longer control the flow of information across their boundaries or all events within them.

Politics in Canada

The government of Canada is based on an elected House of Commons and an appointed Senate. Because representation in the House of Commons is based (roughly) on population, Quebec and Ontario together have 59 percent of the seats. This weighting in favour of central Canada is a source of concern for the other provinces.

Canada has traditionally had three major political parties at the federal level. The Progressive Conservative party leaned to the right on social and economic issues, the Liberal party is closer to the centre, and the New Democratic party is further to the left. Since each of the parties—including the new Conservative Party of Canada—is a bit of a mixture, accurate placement on a left–right continuum is difficult.

One of the major political struggles going on in Canada involves the centralization versus the decentralization of power, or provincial versus federal power.

Canadian government takes an active role in the daily lives of its citizens and our political culture supports widespread intervention in social and economic spheres.

Aboriginal self-government is a current issue that has deep historic roots. Since Parliament recognized the inherent right to Aboriginal self-government in 1984, many Aboriginal peoples have negotiated or are negotiating self-government under a wide range of agreements.

Theoretical Analysis of Power in Society

The pluralist model holds that political power is spread widely in the United States; the power elite model takes an opposing view, arguing that power is concentrated in a small, wealthy segment of the population. The Marxist political economy view claims that our political agenda is determined by our capitalist economy, meaning that true democracy is impossible.

Power beyond the Rules

Revolution radically transforms a political system. Terrorism, another nonconventional political tactic, employs violence in the pursuit of political goals and is widely used by groups against a much more powerful enemy. Terrorism is emerging as a new form of asymmetrical warfare.

War and Peace

War is armed conflict directed by governments. The development and spread of nuclear weapons have increased the threat of global catastrophe. World peace ultimately depends on resolving the tensions and conflicts that fuel militarism.

Politics: Looking Ahead

Canada and the United States claim to be democratic but fail to involve almost half their adult populations in political processes. Addressing the problem of political apathy is an important challenge for the decades ahead. In addition, the world's nations must face up to the dangers of war, especially the spread of nuclear technology used to make weapons that threaten the entire planet.

 **KEY CONCEPTS**

politics (p. 432) the social institution that distributes power, sets a society's goals, and makes decisions

power (p. 432) the ability to achieve desired ends despite resistance from others

government (p. 432) a formal organization that directs the political life of a society

authority (p. 432) power that people perceive as legitimate rather than coercive

traditional authority (p. 432) power legitimized by respect for long-established cultural patterns

rational-legal authority (bureaucratic authority) (p. 433) power legitimized by legally enacted rules and regulations

charismatic authority (p. 433) power legitimized by extraordinary personal abilities that inspire devotion and obedience

routinization of charisma (p. 434) the transformation of charismatic authority into some combination of traditional and bureaucratic authority

monarchy (p. 434) a political system in which a single family rules from generation to generation

democracy (p. 435) a political system that gives power to the people as a whole

authoritarianism (p. 437) a political system that denies the people participation in government

totalitarianism (p. 437) a highly centralized political system that extensively regulates people's lives

political party (p. 442) an organizations operating within the political system that seeks control of the government

pluralist model (p. 451) an analysis of politics that sees power as spread among many competing interest groups

power elite model (p. 451) an analysis of politics that sees power as concentrated among the rich

Marxist political economy model (p. 452) an analysis that explains politics in terms of the operation of a society's economic system

political revolution (p. 453) the overthrow of one political system in order to establish another

terrorism (p. 453) acts of violence or the threat of violence used as a political strategy by an individual or a group

war (p. 455) organized, armed conflict among the people of two or more nations, directed by their governments

military-industrial complex (p. 457) the close association of the federal government, the military, and defence industries

nuclear proliferation (p. 458) the acquisition of nuclear weapons technology by more and more nations

APPLICATIONS & EXERCISES

1. Talk to your friends and classmates about their attitudes towards politics? Are they interested, and do they vote? Why? If not, ask if they expect to take more of an interest as they grow older, get jobs, and form families.
2. The internet provides enormous organizational potential, linking people who share an interest in some political issue.

Visit website www.womennet.ca/, the goal of which is to provide a cyberspace community for women. Do you think such sites will make a difference in Canadian politics?
3. Along with several other people, make a list of leaders you think are or were charismatic. Discuss why someone is on the list. Do you think personal charisma is something more than "being good on television"? If so, precisely what is it?

PRENTICE HALL **mysoclab** Where learning & the sociological imagination intersect.

To reinforce your understanding of this chapter, and to identify topics for further study, visit MySocLab at **www.pearsoned.ca/mysoclab/** for diagnostic tests and a multimedia ebook.

18

CHAPTER EIGHTEEN

Family

What is a family?

How are Canadian families changing?

Why is child care a controversial issue?

When you see a woman pushing a stroller, does it cross your mind that you might be watching a lesbian mother? By some estimates, 10 percent of women are lesbians—and 20 to 30 percent of those lesbians are mothers. In the early 1990s, gaining recognition and acceptance as mothers (that is, as legitimate, good mothers) was not easy—especially for lesbian mothers who left heterosexual relationships and tried to gain custody of their children.

Many of these women chose not to contest custody in court because they feared defeat by a homophobic legal system. Instead, they hoped for liberal access rights. They had learned that there was an informal distinction between "good" and "bad" lesbian mothers. The "good" ones were those "who live quiet, discreet lives, who promise that they will raise their children to be heterosexual, [and] who appear to the outside world to be heterosexual single parents"—in other words, those who are completely secretive about being a lesbian. The "bad" ones were the women "who are politically active, who attend gay and lesbian demonstrations, and who view their lesbianism as one aspect of an entire challenge to society" (Arnup, 1995: 331)—that is, those who have "come out" (are public about being a lesbian).

Knowing the criteria the courts considered in determining "the best interests of the child," lesbian mothers faced difficult choices. Most tried to appear as "straight" as possible in court to increase the chances of gaining custody, rather than be open about being a lesbian: "Such women have met with harsh criticism from some elements of the lesbian community, however, for sustaining an oppressive familial ideology, rather than standing up for their rights as open and proud lesbian mothers" (p. 333).

When they gained custody of their children, lesbian mothers had to decide whether to be open about their unusual family situations—in the community, at school, at church. Now that Canada has legalized same-sex marriage, changed its formal definition of marriage, and opened the door to adoption by gay or lesbian couples, we can expect profound—though not instant—impacts on our society's acceptance of families with lesbian or gay parents.

In Canada, the state of the family is a hot topic. Indeed, a rising chorus of voices charges that families in Canada are fast becoming an endangered species. And some hard facts back up their case. The marriage rate within Canada is decreasing, while the divorce rate has increased. The proportion of Canadians 15 years of age and older who have ever been divorced doubled between 1975 and 1995—from 7 to 14 percent (Bibby, 1995:6). Marital breakdown, coupled with the increase in the number of children born to unmarried women, means that half of Canadian children born today will live with a single parent for some time before reaching age 18. Not surprisingly, the proportion of Canadian children living in poverty remains a persistent problem. Taken together, these facts suggest a basic truth: families in Canada and in other industrial societies are changing dramatically.

Not long ago, the cultural ideal of the family consisted of a working husband, a homemaker wife, and their young children. Today, fewer people embrace this singular vision of the family, and, at any given time, only a minority of Canadian households fit that description.

This chapter highlights important changes in family life and offers some insights into these trends. Yet, changing family patterns are nothing new to this country. A century ago, concern over the decline of the family swept the nation as the Industrial Revolution propelled men from farms to factories. Today, of course, many of the same concerns surround the women whose careers increasingly draw them away from home. In short, changes in other social institutions, especially the economy, are—for better or worse—affecting marriage and family life.

The Canadian census describes a married or cohabiting couple as a family—but have you noticed that "the couple next door" becomes "the family next door" only with the arrival of the first child? That all-important child is the reason for this first "family" portrait.

Photo Credit: Julie Johnson.

The Family: Basic Concepts

The **family** is *a social institution found in all societies that unites people in co-operative groups to care for one another, including any children.* Family ties are also called **kinship,** *a social bond based on common ancestry, marriage, or adoption.* All societies contain families, but exactly who people call their kin has varied through history and varies today from one culture to another.

A family changes as a child grows up and leaves the family into which he or she was born—to form a family of his or her own. Here, as in other countries, families form around **marriage,** *a legal relationship, usually involving economic co-operation, sexual activity, and child bearing.* The traditional belief is that people should marry before having children; this expectation is embedded in the word *matrimony,* which in Latin means "the condition of motherhood." Today in Canada, children are born to single women as well as to common-law and married couples—and many children are being raised by same-sex couples. In addition, more couples are remaining childless. In effect, child bearing will be the central focus of fewer marriages.

Just as we have changed our definition of marriage, we are changing our understanding of "family." Census 2001 defined families as married or common-law couples with or without children, or a lone parent of any marital status with at least one child living at home. Most significantly, in 2001 a couple living common-law might be of opposite or same sex. For the 2006 census, a *married* couple might be of opposite or same sex. We have come a long way from the days when only a married couple with children was considered a "family."

Some couples choose to adopt a child. The Thinking about Diversity box (on p. 468) explores the growing trend of international adoption: Canadian couples choosing a child from a different country and, perhaps, different cultural, ethnic, and racial background.

Families: Global Variations

How closely related do people have to be in order to be part of a family? In pre-industrial societies, people commonly recognize the **extended family,** *a family consisting of parents and children as well as other kin.* This large group is sometimes called the *consanguine family* because it includes everyone with "shared blood." With industrialization, however, increasing social mobility and geographic migration give rise to the **nuclear family,** *a family composed of one or two parents and their children.* The nuclear family is also called the *conjugal family,* meaning "based on marriage." While many people in our society think of kinship in terms of extended families, most people carry out daily routines within a nuclear family.

MARRIAGE PATTERNS

Cultural norms, and often laws, identify people as suitable or unsuitable marriage partners. Some marital norms promote **endogamy,** *marriage between people of the same social category.* Endogamy limits potential partners to people of the same age, race, religion, or social class. By contrast, **exogamy** is *marriage between people of different social categories.* In rural areas of India, for example, people are expected to marry someone of the same caste (endogamy) but from a different village (exogamy). The reason for endogamy is that people of similar position pass along their standing to their offspring, maintaining the traditional social hierarchy. Exogamy, on the other hand, links communities, encouraging alliances and the spread of culture.

In high-income nations, laws permit only **monogamy** (from the Greek, meaning "one union"), *marriage that unites two partners.* Global Map 18–1 shows that monogamy is the rule throughout North and South America as well as Europe. Many countries in Africa and southern Asia permit **polygamy** (from the Greek, meaning

Families come in many forms, and celebrity couples represent them all. After living together, Ashton Kutcher, age twenty-seven, and Demi Moore, age forty-two, were recently married (*left*). They live with her three children from a previous marriage, who refer to Kutcher as "My Other Dad." Rosie O'Donnell and Kelli Carpenter (*right*) married in San Francisco in 2004, but their marriage licence was later revoked by the California Supreme Court. They live with O'Donnell's three adopted children.

"many unions"), *marriage that unites a person with two or more spouses.* Polygamy has two forms. By far the more common form is **polygyny** (from the Greek, meaning "many women"), *marriage that unites one man and two or more women.* For example, Islamic nations in the Middle East and Africa permit men up to four wives. Even so, most Islamic families are monogamous because few men can afford to support several wives and even more children.

Read the background to a documentary on a polygamous community in British Columbia at www.cbc.ca/fifth/bustupin bountiful/.

Polyandry (from the Greek, meaning "many men" or "many husbands") is *marriage that unites one woman and two or more men.* This extremely rare pattern exists in Tibet, a mountainous land where agriculture is difficult. There, polyandry discourages the division of land into parcels too small to support a family and divides the work of farming among many men.

Most of the world's societies have at some time permitted more than one marital pattern. Even so, most marriages have been monogamous (Murdock, 1965; orig. 1949). This historical preference for monogamy reflects two facts of life: supporting several spouses is very expensive, and the number of men and women in most societies is roughly equal.

YOUR TURN

Given the high level of divorce in Canada, is "serial monogamy" a better description of our marriage system than "monogamy"? Explain your position.

RESIDENTIAL PATTERNS

Just as societies regulate mate selection, they also designate where a couple lives. In pre-industrial societies, most newly-weds live with one set of parents who offer them protection, support, and assistance. Most common is the norm of **patrilocality** (Greek for "place of the father"), *a residential pattern in which a married couple lives with or near the husband's family.* But some societies, such as the Six Nations (Haudenosaunee), favour **matrilocality** (meaning "place of the mother"), *a residential pattern in which a married couple lives with or near the wife's family.* Societies that engage in frequent local warfare tend towards patrilocality, so sons are close to home to offer protection. On the other hand, societies that engage only in distant warfare may be either patrilocal or matrilocal, depending on whether its sons or daughters have greater economic value (Ember and Ember, 1971, 1991).

Industrial societies show yet another pattern. Finances permitting, they favour **neolocality** (from the Greek, meaning "new place"), *a residential pattern in which a married couple lives apart from both sets of parents.*

PATTERNS OF DESCENT

Descent refers to *the system by which members of a society trace kinship over generations.* Most pre-industrial societies trace kinship through either the father's side or the mother's side of the family. **Patrilineal descent,** the more common pattern, is *a system tracing kinship through men.* In this pattern, children are related to others only through their fathers, so that fathers pass property on to their sons. Patrilineal descent characterizes most pastoral and agrarian

WINDOW ON THE WORLD

GLOBAL MAP 18-1   Marital Form in Global Perspective

Monogamy is the only legal form of marriage throughout the western hemisphere and in much of the rest of the world. In most African nations and in southern Asia, however, polygamy is permitted by law.

Source: *Peters Atlas of the World* (1990).

societies, in which men produce the most valued resources. Less common is **matrilineal descent,** *a system tracing kinship through women.* Matrilineal descent, in which mothers pass property to their daughters, is found more frequently in horticultural societies, where women are the main food producers. Industrial societies with greater gender equality recognize **bilateral descent** ("two-sided descent"), *a system tracing kinship through both men and women.* In this pattern, children recognize people on both the father's side and the mother's side as relatives.

The "Thinking about Diversity" box (on p. 468) deals with international adoption which creates problems in both tracing lineage and maintaining contact between children and their biological families.

YOUR TURN

Based on this discussion, how would you explain the practice of a woman taking her husband's name after marriage?

THINKING ABOUT DIVERSITY: RACE, CLASS, & GENDER
International Adoption

The rate of international adoption by Canadians has increased rapidly from 10 per year in 1970 to roughly 2000 per year from 42 different countries in the 2000s.

Visit Citizenship and Immigration Canada for information and assistance to people seeking to adopt internationally at www.cic.gc.ca/english/sponsor/adopt-1.html.

Citizenship and Immigration Canada, which offers assistance in adopting from abroad on its website, suggests that you should start the sponsorship process even before you find a child.

In the past, childless Canadian couples adopted the children of unwed mothers. Abortion was illegal and infrequent, and women who bore and raised children outside marriage were stigmatized. Now, abortion is legal and relatively available, and women who give birth outside marriage are increasingly likely to keep their babies. In a way that became controversial, many Aboriginal children were adopted by non-Aboriginal couples; now, social workers place available children with relatives, foster homes, or adoptive parents within the Aboriginal community. As a result of these changes,

between 1980 and 1990, adoptions of children born in Canada declined almost 50 percent.

So childless couples have turned to international adoption. What does the future hold for these families? Often, the adopted child's cultural heritage differs from that of the adoptive family. For instance, Vietnamese boatlifts in 1971 unleashed the largest wave of international adoptions since the end of the Korean War in the 1950s. China's one-child policy, established in the 1980s, has led many Chinese couples to give daughters up for adoption, so that they can try again for a son to carry on the family name. Currently, about half of Canadian foreign adoptions are from China, where, because of the money involved, orphanages prefer foreign over Chinese couples—despite policies that favour domestic adoption.

Research in Canada by Westhues and Cohen (1994) indicates that most of these adoptions are successful, in terms of self-esteem, degree of integration into the adoptive family, peer relations, and the children's comfort with their personal ethnic background. The unfolding stories of these adoptions and the children's adjustment to

Canadian society will continue to hold great interest for Canadian researchers in the years to come.

There is another alternative to foreign adoption. Throughout Canada are 60 000 to 80 000 children under the age of 18 who are in government care. Instead of being adopted, these children are bounced among foster homes until they are "aged out of the system" at 19. When governments spend on media campaigns to increase awareness of these children, adoption rates spike, but government officials are reluctant to treat children as commodities.

WHAT DO YOU THINK?

1. Are international adoptions a good solution to Canada's lack of "adoptable" children?
2. Do you know people who have adopted children from abroad? How have these adoptions worked out?
3. What do you think of Madonna's adoption of one-year-old David Banda from Malawi?

Sources: Fulton (1995), Westhues and Cohen (1994), Mason (2006), and York (2006).

PATTERNS OF AUTHORITY

Worldwide, polygyny, patrilocality, and patrilineal descent are dominant and reflect the global pattern of patriarchy. But in industrial societies, more egalitarian family patterns evolve, especially as the share of women in the labour force increases. Even in North America, however, men are still typically heads of households, and most children are given their fathers' surnames. In Quebec, where married women keep their birth names, children may get the mother's or father's surname, or both, with the option of choosing one later on.

Theoretical Analysis of the Family

As in earlier chapters, the three major theoretical approaches offer a range of insights about the family. We can use all three to gain a deeper understanding of family life.

FUNCTIONS OF THE FAMILY: STRUCTURAL-FUNCTIONAL ANALYSIS

According to the structural-functional approach, the family performs many vital tasks. In fact, the family operates as the backbone of society.

The family is a basic building block of society because it performs important functions, such as conferring social position and regulating sexual activity. To most members, the family, at least in ideal terms, is where individuals enjoy the feeling of belonging and find emotional support. Marc Chagall conveyed the promise of marriage in his painting, *To My Wife*.

Marc Chagall (1887–1985), painting, *To My Wife*, 1933–44. Georges Pompidou Centre, Paris. The Bridgeman Art Library, London. © 2003 Artists Rights Society (ARS), New York/ADAGP, Paris.

1. *Socialization.* As explained in Chapter 5 ("Socialization"), the family is the first and most important setting for child rearing. Ideally, parents help children become well-integrated, contributing members of society (Parsons and Bales, 1955). Of course, family socialization continues throughout life. Adults change within marriage and, as any parent knows, mothers and fathers learn as much from their children as their children learn from them.

2. *Regulation of sexual activity.* Every culture regulates sexual activity in the interest of maintaining kinship organization and property rights. The **incest taboo** is *a norm forbidding sexual relations or marriage between certain relatives.* While the incest taboo exists in every society, exactly which relatives cannot marry varies from one culture to another. The matrilineal Dinee (or Navajo), for example, forbid marrying any relative of one's mother. Our bilateral society applies the incest taboo to both sides of the family but limits it to close relatives, including parents, grandparents, siblings, aunts, and uncles. But even brother/sister, but not parent/child, marriages existed among the ancient Egyptian, Incan, and Hawaiian nobility (Murdock, 1965; orig. 1949). Reproduction between close relatives of any species can result in mental and physical damage to offspring. Yet only human beings observe an incest taboo, a fact suggesting that the key reason for controlling incest is social. Why? First, the incest taboo limits sexual competition in families by restricting sex to spouses. Second, because kinship defines people's rights and obligations towards one another, reproduction among close relatives would hopelessly confuse kinship ties and threaten social order. Third, forcing people to marry outside their immediate families creates ties within the larger society.

3. *Social placement.* Families are not needed for people to reproduce, but they help maintain social organization. Parents pass their own social identities—in terms of race, ethnicity, religion, and social class—to their children at birth.

4. *Material and emotional security.* Many people view the family as a "haven in a heartless world," offering physical protection, emotional support, and financial assistance. Perhaps this is why people living in families tend to be happier, healthier, and wealthier than people living alone (Goldstein and Kenney, 2001).

Critical Review Structural-functional analysis explains why society, at least as we know it, is built on families. But this approach glosses over the diversity of family life and ignores the role of other social institutions (such as government) in meeting the same human needs. Finally, structural-functionalism overlooks negative aspects of family life, including patriarchy and family violence.

YOUR TURN

To understand what your family means to you, make a list of all the benefits of family life, and then try to find an alternative source (such as friends, clubs, or government) for each one.

Women have long been taught to see marriage as the key to a happy life. Social-conflict theory, however, points to the fact that marriage often means a lifetime sentence of unpaid domestic labour. Susan Pyzow's painting, *Bridal Bouquet,* makes the point.

© Susan Pyzow, *Bridal Bouquet,* watercolour on paper, 10 × 13.5 in. Studio SPM Inc.

INEQUALITY AND THE FAMILY: SOCIAL-CONFLICT AND FEMINIST ANALYSIS

Like the structural-functional approach, the social-conflict approach, including feminist analysis, considers the family as central to our way of life. But rather than focusing on ways that kinship benefits society, this approach points out how the family perpetuates social inequality.

1. *Property and inheritance.* Friedrich Engels (1902; orig. 1884) traced the origin of the family to men's need, especially in the upper classes, to identify heirs so that they could hand down property to their sons. Families thus concentrate wealth and reproduce the class structure in each new generation.

2. *Patriarchy.* Feminists link the family to patriarchy. To know their heirs, men must control the sexuality of women. Families therefore transform women into the sexual and economic property of men. A century ago in Canada, the earnings of wives belonged to their husbands and, today, women still bear most of the responsibility for child rearing and housework.

3. *Racial and ethnic inequality.* Racial and ethnic categories persist over generations because most people marry others like themselves. Endogamous marriage supports racial and ethnic hierarchies.

Critical Review Social-conflict and feminist analysis shows another side of family life: its role in social stratification. Engels criticized the family as supporting capitalism. But noncapitalist societies also have families and family problems. The family may be linked to social inequality, as Engels argued, but the family carries out societal functions not easily accomplished by other means.

Constructing Family Life: Micro-Level Analysis

Both structural-functional and social-conflict analyses view the family as a structural system. By contrast, micro-level analysis explores how individuals shape and experience family life.

SYMBOLIC-INTERACTION ANALYSIS

Ideally, family living offers an opportunity for *intimacy,* a word with Latin roots meaning "sharing fear." As family members share many activities over time, they build emotional bonds. Of course, the fact that parents act as authority figures often limits their closeness to younger children. Only as children approach adulthood do kinship ties open up to include sharing confidences with greater intimacy (Macionis, 1978).

Social-Exchange Analysis

Social-exchange analysis, another micro-level approach, describes courtship and marriage as forms of negotiation (Blau, 1964). Dating allows each person to assess the advantages and disadvantages of a potential spouse. In essence, exchange analysts suggest, people "shop around" for partners to make the best "deal" they can.

In patriarchal societies, gender roles dictate the elements of exchange. Men bring wealth and power to the marriage marketplace, and women bring beauty, health, and the ability to bear children (and dowries in some societies). The importance of beauty explains women's traditional concern with their appearance. But as women have joined the labour force, they are less dependent on men to support them, and so the terms of exchange are converging for men and women.

↔ **YOUR TURN** ←

Thinking about the "marriage marketplace," why do you think women have traditionally been less willing than men to reveal their age?

APPLYING THEORY

FAMILY

	Structural-Functional Approach	Social-Conflict and Feminist Approach	Symbolic-Interaction Approach
What is the level of analysis?	Macro level	Macro level	Micro level
What is the importance of the family for society?	The family performs vital tasks, including socializing the young and providing emotional and financial support for members. The family helps regulate sexual activity.	The family perpetuates social inequality by handing down wealth from one generation to the next. The family supports patriarchy as well as racial and ethnic inequality.	The reality of family life is constructed by members in their interaction. Courtship typically brings together people who offer the same level of advantages.

Critical Review Micro-level analysis balances structural-functional and social-conflict visions of the family as an institutional system. Both the interaction and exchange viewpoints focus on the individual experience of family life. However, micro-level analysis misses the bigger picture: family life is similar for people in the same social and economic categories.

The Applying Theory table (above) summarizes what we can learn by applying each of the theoretical approaches to family life.

Stages of Family Life

The family is a dynamic institution, with marked changes throughout life. New families begin with courtship and evolve as the new partners settle into the realities of married life. Next, for most couples at least, come the years spent developing careers and raising children, leading to the later years of marriage after the children have left home to form families of their own. We will look briefly at each of these four stages.

COURTSHIP

November 2, Kandy, Sri Lanka. Winding through the rain forest of this beautiful island, our van driver, Harry, recounts how he met his wife. Actually, he explains, it was more of an arrangement: the two families were both Buddhist and of the same caste. "We got along well, right from the start," recalls Harry. "We had the same background. I suppose she or I could have said No. But love marriages happen in the city, not in the village where I grew up." [John J. Macionis]

In rural Sri Lanka, as in rural areas of low- and middle-income countries throughout the world, most people consider courtship too important to be left to the young (Stone, 1977). *Arranged marriages* are alliances between extended families of similar social standing and usually involve an exchange not just of children but also of wealth and favours. Romantic love has little to do with marriage, and parents may make such arrangements when their children are very young. A century ago in Sri Lanka and India, for example, half of all girls married before reaching age fifteen (Mayo, 1927; Mace and Mace, 1960). As the Thinking Globally box (on p. 473) explains, child marriage is still found in parts of the world.

Because traditional societies are more culturally homogeneous, almost all young men and women have been well socialized to be good spouses. Therefore, parents can arrange marriages with little thought about whether the two individuals involved are *personally* compatible because they know that the partners will be *culturally* compatible.

Industrialization erodes the importance of extended families and weakens tradition. Young people in industrial societies choose their own mates and delay marriage until they have gained the financial security needed to live apart from their parents and the experience needed to select a suitable partner. During this time, dating sharpens courtship skills and allows sexual experimentation.

Arranged marriages are becoming more common *in Canada*, particularly among Chinese and Southeast Asian families. Roughly 60 000 Canadians marry overseas annually and file international spousal sponsorship applications. In all too many cases, these marriages—contracted for up to $25 000—are terminated once the foreign partner achieves permanent residency in Canada (Jiménez, 2006).

 Check out how people use the internet to find partners at www.syl.com.

"Son, you're all grown up now. You owe me two hundred and fourteen thousand dollars."

Romantic Love

Our culture celebrates *romantic love*—affection and sexual passion for another person—as the basis for marriage. We find it hard to imagine marriage without love, and popular culture—from fairy tales like *Cinderella* to today's television sitcoms and dramas—portrays love as the key to a successful marriage. Our society's emphasis on romance motivates young people to "leave the nest" to form new families of their own, and physical passion helps new couples through the difficult adjustments of living together. On the other hand, because feelings change over time, romantic love is a less stable foundation for marriage than social and economic considerations—which is one reason the divorce rate is much higher in Canada than in countries with arranged marriages. But even in our country, sociologists point out, society aims Cupid's arrow more than we like to think. Most people fall in love with others of the same race, of comparable age, and of similar social class. Our society "arranges" marriages by encouraging **homogamy** (literally, "like marrying like"), *marriage between people with the same social characteristics.*

YOUR TURN

How similar are your parents (or you and your boyfriend/girlfriend) in terms of age, social class background, race, ethnicity, and education?

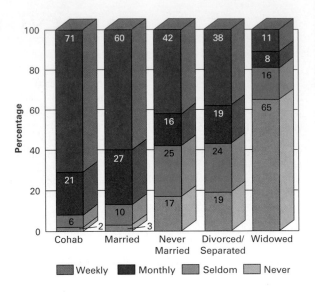

FIGURE 18–1   Sexual Activity by Marital Status

Source: Bibby (1995:66).

SETTLING IN: IDEAL AND REAL MARRIAGE

Our culture gives the young an idealized, "happily ever after" picture of marriage. Such optimism can lead to disappointment, especially for women, who are taught to view marriage as the key to happiness. Also, romantic love involves a good deal of fantasy: we fall in love with others not always as they are but as we want them to be.

Sexuality, too, can be a source of disappointment. In the romantic haze of falling in love, people may see marriage as an endless sexual honeymoon, only to face the sobering realization that sex becomes less than an all-consuming passion. Although the frequency of marital sex does decline over time, about two in three married people report that they are satisfied with the sexual dimension of their relationships. In general, couples with the best sexual relationships experience the most satisfaction in their marriages. Sex may not be the key to marital bliss but, more often than not, good sex and good relationships go together (Blumstein and Schwartz, 1983; Laumann, *et al.*, 1994). About 60 percent of married couples say that they are having sex weekly (Bibby, 1995:66). Figure 18–1 indicates sexual activity by marital status.

Infidelity—*sexual activity outside marriage*—is another area in which the reality of marriage does not coincide with our cultural ideal. We strongly support traditional marriage vows "to forsake all others." In a survey, for example, 3 out of 4 adults said that extramarital sex is "always wrong," and only 4 percent believed that it was never wrong (Bibby, 1983). Even so, 17 percent of men and 9 percent of women indicated that they had been sexually unfaithful to their partners at least once (*Gallup Sexual Life Style Survey*, 1988). Moreover, increased rates of premarital sex may suggest even greater weakening of the bonds of fidelity within marriage (Herold, 1984:13).

THINKING GLOBALLY

Early to Wed: A Report from Rural India

Sumitra Jogi cries as her wedding is about to begin. Are they tears of joy? Not exactly. This "bride" is an eleven-month-old squirming in the arms of her mother. The groom? A boy of six.

In a remote, rural village in India's western state of Rajasthan, two families gather at midnight to celebrate a traditional wedding ritual. It is May 2: in Hindu tradition, an especially good day to marry. Sumitra's father smiles as the ceremony begins; her mother cradles the infant, who has fallen asleep. The groom, dressed in a special costume with a red and gold turban on his head, gently reaches up and grasps the baby's hand. Then, as the ceremony reaches its conclusion, the young boy leads the child and mother around the wedding fire three-and-a-half times, as the audience beams at the couple's first steps together as husband and wife.

Child weddings are illegal in India but, in the rural regions, traditions are strong and marriage laws are hard to enforce. As a result, thousands of children marry each year. "In rural Rajasthan," explains one social welfare worker, "all the girls are married by age fourteen. These are poor, illiterate families, and they don't want to keep girls past their first menstrual cycle." For the immediate future, Sumitra Jogi will remain with her parents. But in eight or ten years, a second ceremony will send her to live with her husband's

The two-year-old girl on the left is breastfeeding during her wedding ceremony in a small village in the state of Rajasthan, India; her new husband is eight years old. Although outlawed, such arranged marriages involving children are still known to take place in traditional, remote areas of India.

family, and her married life will begin. If the responsibilities of marriage lie years in the future, why do families push their children to marry at such an early age? Parents of girls know that the younger the bride, the smaller the dowry offered to the groom's family. Then, too, when girls marry this young, there is no question about their virginity, which raises their value on the marriage market. Arranged marriages are an alliance between families. No one thinks about love or the fact that the children are too young to understand what is taking place (Anderson, 1995).

WHAT DO YOU THINK?

1. Why are arranged marriages common in very traditional regions?
2. List several advantages and disadvantages of arranged marriages from the point of view of the families involved. Do you think the advantages outweigh the disadvantages? Why or why not?
3. Can you point to ways in which mate selection in the Canada is "arranged" by society?

YOUR TURN

Try to make sense of the discrepancy in these Canadian figures relating to partners (not necessarily spouses): 33 and 35 percent of men and women, respectively, have been cheated on by a partner; on the other hand, 10 and 5 percent of men and women, respectively, would cheat on their partners if there was no chance of getting caught (Bricker and Wright, 2005:214–15). Go figure.

CHILD REARING

Despite the substantial demands children make on the time and energy of parents, almost all Canadians include at least one child in their conception of the ideal family. The smaller families of today represent a marked change from

two centuries ago, when eight children was average! Big families pay off in pre-industrial societies because children perform needed labour. Indeed, people generally regard having children as a wife's duty and, without reliable birth-control technology, child bearing is a regular event. Of course, a high death rate in pre-industrial societies prevents many children from reaching adulthood; as late as 1900, a substantial minority of children born in Canada died in infancy or early childhood (*Canada Year Book*, 1994).

Economically speaking, industrialization transforms children from a vital asset to a burdensome liability. Today, the expense of raising a child is substantial, especially if it involves university education. This helps to explain the steady drop in family size during the twentieth century to

 For expert advice, links, and networks for Canadians with questions about parenting, see www.canadianparents.com.

slightly more than 1 child per family in Canada today. The trend towards smaller families also holds for all other industrial societies. But the picture differs sharply in low-income countries in Latin America, Asia, and especially Africa, where many women have few alternatives to bearing and raising children. In such societies, 4 to 6 children is the norm.

Parenting is expensive, and a lifetime commitment. As society affords its members greater choice in family life, more people opt to delay childbirth or to remain childless. Women also put off having children until they are older, so that they are giving birth three or four years later than they did in 1970. The majority of Canadian parents would like to put more time and energy into child rearing but, unless we are willing to accept a lower standard of living, economic realities demand that most parents pursue careers outside the home. Thus, the child-rearing patterns we have described reflect ways of coming to terms with economic change.

As Chapter 13 ("Gender Stratification") explained, most women with young children now work for income. In 2001, 72.6 percent of women aged 25 to 34 (married or living common-law) were employed; therefore, most mothers with children under 18 worked for income outside the home. But while women and men share the burden of earning income, women continue to bear the traditional responsibility for raising children and doing housework. Many men in our society are eager parents, but most resist sharing responsibility for household tasks that our culture historically has defined as women's work. Nevertheless, Canada's General Social Survey reveals that participation by men is steadily increasing. There are now more stay-at-home dads (up from 4 to 11 percent since 1986) and more dads taking parental leave (Fitzpatrick, 2006). Parental leave policies vary among provinces and territories. In Ontario, for example, parents have a full year of parental leave which can be used by either parent or shared by both—six months each perhaps.

Ultimately, as more women join men in the labour force, parents have less time for parenting. Children of working parents spend most of the day at school or in daycare and many school-age youngsters are *latchkey kids* who fend for themselves after school. (The Media Perspectives box on pp. 486–87 explores related issues.) Traditionalists in the debates on "family values" caution that mothers often work at the expense of children, who receive less parenting. Progressives counter that such criticism ignores the role of fathers in parenting and unfairly faults women for seeking equal opportunity in the world of work.

Considering the changes in parenting and child-care practices over the past 20 years, it is reassuring to learn that  9 in 10 Canadian teens give their moms a grade of A or B with 50 percent giving them an A; two in three dads get A or B, with 29 percent getting an A (Bricker and Wright, 2005: 172). Taking into account the normal tensions between parents and teenagers, this is indeed a good parental report card.

THE FAMILY IN LATER LIFE

Increasing life expectancy in Canada means that, barring divorce, couples are likely to remain married for a long time. By about age fifty, *most* have completed the task of raising children, so the remaining years of marriage bring a return to living with only one's spouse. Like the birth of children, their departure requires adjustments to the "empty nest," although the marital relationship—bringing mutual understanding and companionship—often becomes closer and more satisfying in midlife.

Personal contact with children usually continues, since most older adults live a short distance from at least one of their children. Moreover, many Canadians are grandparents, who help their daughters and sons with child care and a host of other responsibilities. On the other hand, recent developments have created new intergenerational challenges for Canadian families: the transition to adulthood has been extended, so that, increasingly, "midlife parenthood comprises prolonged periods of co-residence with grown young adults" (Mitchell, 2000:80). Mitchell found that, according to the 1995 General Social Survey, 27 percent of adults aged 19 to 35 had left home and returned for periods of four months or more. The termination of a job or a relationship, financial considerations, and the need to complete schooling are among the reasons for returning. Some of those who returned for financial reasons could afford to live on their own—but not at their parents' standard of living. The "crowded nest" is common to many families for the reasons outlined above, but another factor is a three-year delay in marriage for both women and men since the mid 1970s—from 24 to 27 years of age for women, and 26 to 29 for men (Boyd and Norris, 2000).

Significantly, older adults can find themselves returning to child rearing: "more than 55 000 grandparents in Canada are raising their grandchildren—on their own" (Vallis, 2005). Since many grandparents take over child rearing to avoid foster care, they are raising at-risk children just when they might expect rest and relaxation. Social workers consider grandparents to be the first line of defence when parents, often single mothers, are incapable of raising their children (perhaps because of substance abuse or mental illness). These relationships are not always easy. Imagine raising a teenager when you are in your sixties or seventies.

The other side of the coin, explained in Chapter 15 ("Aging and the Elderly"), is that more adults in midlife must care for aging parents. The "empty nest" may be filled by a parent coming to live in the home (Che-Alford and Hamm, 2000); regardless, parents living to eighty and beyond require practical, emotional, and financial care that can be more taxing than raising young children (Cranwick, 2000). The oldest of the baby boomers—now sixty—are often called the "sandwich generation" because they will spend as many years caring for their aging parents as they did for their own offspring.

The final, and surely the most difficult, transition in married life comes with the death of a spouse. Wives typically outlive their husbands because of women's longer life expectancy and the fact that wives are usually younger than husbands to begin with. Wives can therefore expect to spend a significant period of their lives as widows. Bereavement and loneliness accompanying the death of a spouse are extremely difficult, and the experience may be worse for widowers, who usually have fewer friends than widows and may be unskilled at cooking and housework.

Recently, increased numbers of married or common-law couples—some of them same-sex couples—have not had children. They face the same problems of aging and bereavement that single or unmarried adults do—without the supportive networks that children and grandchildren might have provided.

Canadian Families: Class, Race, and Gender

Dimensions of inequality—social class, ethnicity and race, and gender—are powerful forces that shape marriage and family life. This discussion addresses each factor in turn, but bear in mind that they overlap in our lives.

SOCIAL CLASS

Social class determines both a family's financial security and its range of opportunities. Interviewing working-class women, Lillian Rubin (1976) found that wives thought a good husband was one who held a steady job, did not drink too much, and was not violent. Rubin's middle-class respondents, in contrast, never mentioned such things; these women simply *assumed* that a husband would provide a safe and secure home. Their ideal husband was someone they could talk to easily, sharing feelings and experiences.

There is even a link—with a twist—between social class and the willingness of men to help with housework. Canada's General Social Survey reveals that only in dual-earner families where the woman earns more than $100 000 do men and women do the same amount of housework: 1.6 hours per day (Fitzpatrick, 2006).

Clearly, women's and men's aspirations for marriage—and what they get—are linked to social class. Much the same holds for children; boys and girls lucky enough to be born into more affluent families enjoy better mental and physical health, develop more self-confidence, and go on to greater achievement than children born to poor parents (Duncan, *et al.*, 1998; Corak, 2000; deBrouker and Lavallée, 2000).

ETHNICITY AND RACE

As Chapter 14 ("Race and Ethnicity") reveals, ethnicity and race are powerful social forces that can affect family life. Keep in mind, however, that the families of any racial or ethnic category do not fit particular stereotypes.

Aboriginal Families in Canada

There are more than seven hundred Aboriginal communities in Canada: about six hundred First Nation (status Indian) reserves, and dozens of non-status Indian, Inuit, and Métis villages and settlements. Over the past few decades, increasing numbers of First Nation members are living off reserve—currently about half of the population. While Calgary, Edmonton, Saskatoon, and Winnipeg have substantial Aboriginal populations, residence in the major cities of Montreal, Vancouver, and Toronto is also increasing (Gerber, 1995). Given this diversity, it is impossible to discuss the family patterns of Aboriginal peoples as a homogeneous group.

Aboriginal people are often among the most economically deprived members of our society, and suffer discrimination and prejudice, resulting in high rates of unemployment, inadequate housing, and family instability. One researcher notes that: "under these circumstances, identification with traditional cultures suffers, and their central familistic values of kin solidarity, respect for elders, and the welfare of children have been weakened" (Nett, 1993:101). Moreover, because of their political and economic subordination by Europeans, the family norms of many Aboriginal people have been threatened.

Throughout the early 1900s, most Aboriginal people lived on reserves or with extended families in isolated regions. Child care was the responsibility of the extended family, and highly respected elders taught the young their languages and traditions. Christian missionaries, who had made concerted efforts to assimilate and Christianize Aboriginal peoples, took children away from their families to church-run residential schools to teach them another language, religion, and culture, and to despise their own. With adults and children separated and pursuing different paths, traditional family values began to erode: elders lost their authority, extended families lost their responsibilities for nurturing and caretaking, and young people raised outside normal family settings failed to learn parenting skills to apply later on when raising their own children. In addition, resettlement programs broke up whole communities and diminished family ties even further. The federal government has only in recent years recognized and apologized for "the tragedy of residential schools" (Fleras, 2001: 294) that have done so much damage to Aboriginal family and community life. By 2006, individuals who had suffered sexual and psychological abuse in the residential school system were offered financial compensation.

The intervention of the state and the churches in Aboriginal family life has other manifestations deriving from the lack of recognition of the role played by the extended family in providing for children when parents die or are incapacitated (Wotherspoon and Satzewich, 1993:88). From the 1950s until the mid–1970s, under the auspices of social workers employed by various Children's Aid Societies, children were taken away from parents who

TABLE 18–1

Approval of Intergroup Marriage, 1975 through 1995

	1975	1980	1985	1990	1995
Whites and Aboriginal partners	75%	80%	83%	84%	84%
Whites and Asians (Oriental)	66	75	78	82	83
Whites and East Indians/Pakistanis	58	66	72	77	80
Whites and Blacks	57	64	72	79	81
Protestants and Roman Catholics	86	88	89	90	92
Protestants and Jews	80	84	84	86	90
Roman Catholics and Jews	78	81	82	85	89

Source: Bibby (1995:54).

were no longer functioning as adequate parents because of poverty, unemployment, prejudice, alcohol abuse, and a variety of other social conditions. Many of these children were placed in non-Aboriginal foster homes, where they lost contact with their remaining traditions and culture; others were adopted by non-Aboriginal families in Canada and even in the United States. Having observed the severe adjustment problems of many of these children, authorities now focus on keeping children with their families whenever possible or placing them with other Aboriginal families when it is necessary to remove them (Baker, 1991).

In 2001, 38 percent of the First Nations population—about 212 000 people—lived off reserve. There are another 333 000 people who identify themselves as Aboriginal (i.e., non-status Indian, Métis, and Inuit). Some of these people—especially northern Inuit, Métis, and First Nations where reserves are rare—live in small settlements with their families, but the majority live in Canada's urban and metropolitan centres. That puts the urban Aboriginal population at about the half million mark, and raises questions about the quality of family life in Canada's cities. Many Aboriginal individuals, who migrate to urban areas, do so as isolated individuals in search of employment opportunities, housing, schooling or training, or better access to welfare. Others go to join members of their extended families, often living with them during transition (Gerber, 1976). There are also Aboriginal people—a small number—whose urban family lives are similar to those of the White middle class: "they live in single-family units as married adults with children; they have full-time employment; and they live in acceptable housing"; they have attained "a level of education, health, and well-being possessed by the vast majority of non-Aboriginal citizens of Canada" (Frideres and Gadacz, 2001: 156).

Racial and Ethnic Minority Families

Canada's diversity—the result of its immigration history—is reflected in family forms as well. Policies favouring family class immigration (that is, family reunification through the sponsorship of close family members) ensured a continuing stream of newcomers with strong subcultural identities and values (Li, 1996). As a result we include a wide variety of family patterns in Canadian society.

Conversely, there are family values and practices that are common to many of these minorities. Traditional values often include religion, authoritarian or permissive parenting styles, cultural guidelines for marriage and courtship including arranged marriage, scripted gender relations and nonmainstream notions of gender equality, prohibitions on dating or drinking, and emphasis on family rather than the individual (Fleras, 2001: 181–82). In addition, immigrant families—for example, Italians and Chinese—are more likely to keep their elderly parents/grandparents at home (Gerber, 1983). Intergenerational conflict is common in immigrant families as young people, who attend public schools, challenge the cultural values of their parents. They want the freedom to hang out with their peers and participate in party and dating scenes. Teenagers tend to feel that the constraints of their families and ethnic communities are unduly strict. You may believe that the dominant White Anglo-Saxon Protestant community is "prejudiced" and opposed to intermarriage, but some of Canada's ethnic and racial minorities push endogamy on their children. Even Finnish immigrants have been known to resist the marriage of their children to people of non-Finn heritage. In that light, recent trends in intermarriage and related attitudes are worth a look.

MIXED MARRIAGE

Most spouses have similar social backgrounds with regard to class, race, and ethnicity, but over the course of the past century, ethnicity has mattered less and less. Thus, a man of German/French ancestry might marry a woman of Irish/English background. To get a sense of the extent of ethnic and racial mixing on Canada, take another look at the "Thinking about Diversity" box (on p. 468 in Chapter 5).

Race remains a formidable consideration, however. In 2001, Canadians of African, Arab, Asian, and Aboriginal descent represented about 17 percent of the entire population. Roughly 17 percent of marriages would be mixed, if people ignored race altogether in choosing marriage partners. The actual proportion is not as large, attesting to the continuing importance of race in social relations. Nonetheless, the number of racially mixed marriages will continue to increase as visible minorities comprise more of the overall population. Table 18–1 shows that Canadians have become more accepting of intergroup marriage over time. The vast majority (80% to 92%) of Canadian adults approve of intermarriage across various racial and religious lines (Bibby, 1995:54). It will be some time before the extent of racial intermarriage mirrors this level of acceptance.

Two of twenty cousins in the Gerber family married across racial lines (i.e., 10 percent). But that is only one family. How many interracial marriages are there among your relatives or acquaintances?

GENDER

Jessie Bernard (1982; orig. 1973) said that every marriage is actually *two* different relationships: a woman's marriage and a man's marriage. The reason is that few marriages are composed of two equal partners. Patriarchy has weakened, but most people still expect men to be older and taller than their wives and to have more important, better-paying jobs. The persistence of the notion of man-as-breadwinner and wife-as-homemaker was illustrated in a study of steelworkers and their wives in Hamilton, Ontario. In 1979–80, when the Women Back into Stelco Committee launched a successful discrimination complaint with the Ontario Human Rights Commission, the introduction of female co-workers into the masculine world of dangerous manual labour and big machinery was resisted by the steelworkers. Detailed interviews revealed that steelmaking was seen as men's work and was linked to the notion that men must be breadwinners. This attitude was tied to men's "deeper sense of responsibility to provide for their families" (Livingstone and Luxton, 1995:187).

Such patriarchal values are associated with the persistent notion that marriage is more beneficial to women than to men (Bernard, 1982; orig. 1973). The positive stereotype of the carefree bachelor contrasts sharply with the negative image of the lonely spinster. This image is rooted in a traditional view that women are fulfilled only by being wives and mothers. However, according to Bernard, married women have poorer mental health, less happiness, and more passive attitudes towards life than single women. Married men, on the other hand, generally live longer, are better off mentally, and report being happier than single men. These differences suggest why, after divorce, men are more eager than women to remarry. Bernard concluded that there is no better assurance of long life, health, and happiness for a man than a woman well socialized to devote her life to taking care of him and providing the security of a well-ordered home. She was quick to add that marriage *could* be healthful for women if husbands did not dominate wives and expect them to do almost all the housework.

Do you think that this gendered picture of marriage from the early 1980s is completely out-dated? How?

Transitions and Problems in Family Life

The newspaper columnist Ann Landers once remarked that 1 marriage in 20 is wonderful, 5 in 20 are good, 10 in 20 are tolerable, and the remaining 4 are "pure hell." Families can be a source of joy but, for some, the reality falls far short of the ideal.

DIVORCE

Our society strongly supports marriage, and 9 out of 10 people marry at some point. But many of today's marriages eventually unravel. Figure 18–2 shows a ninefold increase in the Canadian divorce rate from 1968 to 1988, followed by gradual decline thereafter. Before 1968, divorces were granted only if one of the spouses was proven to have committed adultery; at that time, the divorce rate was 40 per 100 000 people. Note that, despite the peak, the divorce rate in the late 1970s is not too different from that in the 2000s: the rate dropped to 222 divorces per 100 000 people in 2003.

Divorce rates in Canada and the United States rose and dropped off again in a similar pattern—though the United States still has the highest divorce rate in the world (50 percent higher than Canada's). Many researchers have tried to explain today's relatively high divorce rates (Furstenberg and Cherlin, 1991; Etzioni, 1993; Popenoe, 1999; Greenspan, 2001):

1. **Individualism is on the rise**. Today's family members spend less time together. We have become more individualistic and more concerned about personal happiness and earning income than about the well-being of family and children.

2. **Romantic love fades**. Because our culture bases marriage on romantic love, relationships may fail as sexual passion fades. Many people end a marriage in favour of a new relationship that promises renewed excitement and romance.

3. **Women are less dependent on men**. Women's increasing participation in the labour force has reduced wives' financial dependence on husbands. Therefore, women find it easier to leave unhappy marriages.

4. **Many of today's marriages are stressful**. With both partners working outside the home in most cases, jobs leave less time and energy for family life. This makes raising children harder than ever. Children do stabilize some marriages, but divorce is most common during the early years of marriage, when many couples have young children.

5. **Divorce is socially acceptable**. Divorce no longer carries the powerful stigma it did several generations ago. Family and friends are now less likely to discourage couples in conflict from divorcing.

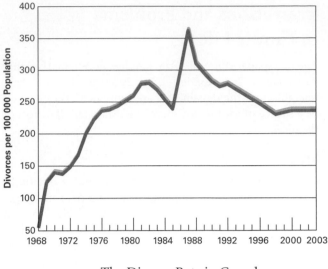

FIGURE 18-2   The Divorce Rate in Canada, 1968–2003

Sources: Compiled by L.M. Gerber from Statistics Canada, 1991, catalogue nos. 82-003S17 and 84-213, and Statistics Canada, CANSIM table 053-0002.

6. **Legally, a divorce is easier to get.** The *Divorce Act, 1968,* allowed for divorce in circumstances beyond adultery—if one of the spouses had committed a matrimonial offence (such as adultery, or emotional or physical cruelty), if one spouse had deserted, or if the spouses had lived apart for at least three years. In 1985, the Act was rewritten, making "marriage breakdown" the only reason for divorce. Marriage breakdown includes separation of at least one year, adultery, and physical and mental cruelty.

Who Divorces?

At greatest risk of divorce are young spouses—especially those who marry after a brief courtship—who lack money and emotional maturity. The chance of divorce also rises if the couple marries after an unexpected pregnancy, or if one or both partners use alcohol or drugs. People whose parents divorced also have a higher divorce rate themselves. Researchers suggest that a role-modelling effect is at work: children who see parents go through divorce are more likely to consider divorce themselves (Amato, 2001). Finally, people who are not religious are more likely to divorce than those who have strong religious beliefs.

Divorce is also more common when both partners have successful careers, perhaps because of the strains of a two-career marriage, or perhaps because financially secure people do not feel they have to stay in an unhappy home. Finally, those who divorce once are more likely to divorce again, probably because high-risk factors follow them from one marriage to another (Glenn and Shelton, 1985).

Canada Map 18–1 takes a look at divorce levels throughout the country. For Canada as a whole, 7.9 percent of the

Divorce may be a solution for a couple in an unhappy marriage, but it can be a problem for children who experience the withdrawal of a parent from their social world. In what ways can divorce be harmful to children? Is there a positive side to divorce? How might separating parents better prepare their children for the transition of parental divorce?

↔ YOUR TURN ↔

Celebrities are notorious for multiple marriages and divorces. Do you know couples who have been married and divorced several times?

population 15 years of age and older was divorced in 2001. Quebec and Yukon have the highest levels, Nunavut and Newfoundland and Labrador, the lowest. Divorce is pronounced where religious values are weaker and where people are more likely to move often, thereby distancing themselves from the support of family and friends. People in Yukon fit both of those descriptions, forming the largest proportion claiming "no religion" and substantial migration into and out of the territory in response to changes in the resource industries. While very few Quebecers claim no religion, the province did experience rapid secularization during the Quiet Revolution, so that their attachment to the Catholic Church is relatively weak. The Quiet Revolution also involved rural-urban migration and social mobility, both of which weaken ties to old communities and networks.

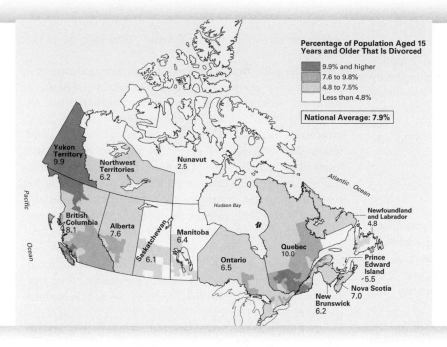

Percentage of Population Aged 15 Years and Older That Is Divorced

- 9.9% and higher
- 7.6 to 9.8%
- 4.8 to 7.5%
- Less than 4.8%

National Average: 7.9%

Yukon Territory 9.9
Northwest Territories 6.2
Nunavut 2.5
British Columbia 8.1
Alberta 7.6
Saskatchewan 6.1
Manitoba 6.4
Ontario 6.5
Quebec 10.0
Newfoundland and Labrador 4.8
Prince Edward Island 5.5
Nova Scotia 7.0
New Brunswick 6.2
Atlantic Ocean
Hudson Bay
Pacific Ocean

SEEING OURSELVES

CANADA MAP 18–1

Percentage of Population Aged 15 Years and Older That Is Divorced by Province, Territory, and Census Subdivision, 2001

Source: Calculations by L.M. Gerber based on data from the Statistics Canada website http://www.statcan.ca/english/census96/oct14/mar1.htm.

Divorce and Children

Because mothers often gain custody of children but fathers typically earn more income, the well-being of children after a divorce often depends on fathers making court-ordered child support payments. Yet, in any given year, half the children legally entitled to support receive only partial payments or no payments at all. Too many "deadbeat dads" fail to support their youngsters—sometimes moving to another province to escape the system. In response, the courts can now require employers to withhold money from the earnings of fathers who fail to pay.

The effects of divorce on children go beyond financial support. Divorce can tear young people from familiar surroundings, entangle them in bitter feuding, and distance them from a parent they love. Most serious of all, many children blame themselves for their parents' breakup. Divorce changes the course of their lives, often resulting in emotional and behavioural problems, and raising the risk of dropping out of school or getting into trouble with the law. Many experts counter that divorce is better for children than families torn by tension and violence. In any case, parents should remember that, if they consider divorce, more than their own well-being is at stake (Wallerstein and Blakeslee, 1989; Popenoe, 1993; Amato and Sobolewski, 2001).

For the past two decades, Canada's divorce courts have, when possible, favoured joint custody—which deals not with access but with decision making about children. Now, the results of the experiment with joint custody can be seen. When parents are able to put children first and avoid confrontation, joint custody can work very well. But, too often, *every* decision made about their children results in fights and recriminations between high-conflict parents—with "seriously traumatized children" caught in the middle. Furthermore, some fathers with joint custody agreements mistakenly assume that they should have their children half of the time. There are good reasons for revisiting the joint custody question, but it may not happen because powerful forces are aligned on both sides of the debate (Makin, 2006).

REMARRIAGE

Four out of five people who divorce remarry, most within five years. Thus, almost half of all marriages are now remarriages for at least one partner. Men, who benefit more from wedlock, are more likely than women to remarry. Remarriage often creates *blended families*, composed of children and some combination of biological parents and stepparents. With brothers, sisters, half siblings, a stepparent—not to mention a biological parent who might live elsewhere and be married to someone else with other children, young people in blended families face the challenge of defining many new relationships and deciding just who is part of the nuclear family. Parents often have trouble defining responsibility for household work among people unsure of their relations to each other. When the custody of children is an issue, ex-spouses can be an unwelcome presence for people in a new marriage. Although blended families require that members adjust to their new circumstances, they offer both young and old the chance to relax rigid family roles (Furstenberg and Cherlin, 2001; McLanahan, 2002).

YOUR TURN

A girl who has been an only child becomes part of a blended family and suddenly has two older brothers. What adjustments might she have to make?

FAMILY VIOLENCE

The ideal family is a source of pleasure and support. However, the disturbing reality of many homes is **family violence,** *emotional, physical, or sexual abuse of one family member by another.* The sociologist Richard J. Gelles calls the family "the most violent group in society with the exception of the police and the military" (quoted in Roesch, 1984:75).

Violence against Women

The common stereotype of a violent partner is a lower-class man who now and then drinks too much, loses control, and beats up his wife. In reality, although financial problems and unemployment do make the problem worse, violence against women in the home is perpetrated by men of all social classes, races, and ethnicities. Furthermore, this violence often occurs at random. Family brutality frequently goes unreported to police, but researchers estimate that 20 percent of couples (1 in 5) endure at least some violence each year. Many of these couples experience serious incidents of violence, including kicking, biting, and punching (Lupri, 1988: 170–71). Almost 30 percent of women who are murdered—as opposed to 6 percent of men—are killed by spouses, ex-spouses, or unmarried partners (Lupri, 1988). In 1989, 119 women in Canada were murdered by former husbands or partners (Begin, 1991). Overall, women are more likely to be injured by a family member than they are to be mugged or sexually assaulted by a stranger or injured in an automobile accident.

Physically abused women have traditionally had few options. They may want to leave home, but many—especially those with children and without much money—have nowhere to go. Most wives are also committed to their marriages and believe—however unrealistically—that they can help an abusive husband change. Some, unable to understand a husband's violence, blame themselves. Others, raised in violent families, consider assault to be part of family life. Most abused women see no way out of the family violence that makes fear the centre of their lives. In one study, researchers found that one-quarter of women who had entered a metropolitan hospital after attempting suicide had been a victim of family violence (Stark and Flitcraft, 1979).

In 1990, Canada's solicitor general attempted to address the problem of crime and abuse against women by producing *Woman Alone,* a book of prevention advice. But this document ignored the situations that most frequently expose women to danger—domestic and private settings where they are threatened by men they know. One reason for this misjudgment is that victimization studies ask about "crime" and "many victims do not perceive their partners' violent

The National Clearinghouse on Family Violence offers research and resources to address family violence: see www.hc-sc.gc.ca/hppb/familyviolence.

actions as crimes in the legal sense" (DeKeseredy, *et al.,* 1995:479).

In the past, the law regarded domestic violence as a private family matter. Now, even without separation or divorce, a woman can obtain court protection from an abusive spouse. "Stalker" legislation, introduced in 1993, protects women and children who are being threatened and followed. Some medical personnel are also more aware today of the tell-tale signs of spousal violence and are more likely to report such cases to police than they were in the past. Communities throughout North America are establishing shelters that provide counselling as well as temporary housing for women and children driven from their homes by violence. Some people who abuse their partners are also joining self-help groups in an effort to understand and control their own behaviour. In various ways, then, our society is beginning to help families with this serious problem.

It is important to understand that, when men and women are asked how often they engage in a range of violent acts against their partners (i.e., as methods of conflict resolution, so that sexual assault is not included), men are almost as likely to be victims of domestic violence as women (Lupri, 2002). While Canada, quite rightly, has mobilized to assist women and children, there is no attempt to help the male victims who also suffer severe loss of self-esteem. For more on the topic of spousal violence see the Thinking it Through box (on p. 481).

Violence against Children

Family violence also victimizes children. Perhaps 4 percent of all youngsters suffer abuse each year, including several hundred who die as a result. Child abuse entails more than physical injury because abusive adults misuse power and trust to undermine a child's emotional well-being. Child abuse is most common among the youngest and most vulnerable children (Straus and Gelles, 1986; Van Biema, 1994; Besharov and Laumann, 1996). Many abused children suffer in silence, believing that they are to blame for their own victimization. Abuse, compounded by years of guilt, can leave lasting emotional scars that prevent people abused as children from forming healthy relationships as adults.

In 1996, children were reported missing in Canada at a rate of 1 every 9 minutes—more than 56 000 in that year. An alarming 78 percent of these youngsters are runaways; 57 percent of the runaways are girls; and the runaways are getting younger. Too many of these youngsters leave home because of abuse (psychological, sexual, or physical) and neglect. In the recession of the early 1990s, more of these children left home because their parents said they could not afford to keep them, thereby repeating a pattern that appeared during the recession of the early 1980s. These numbers are described as an alarming sign of the increasing disintegration of the family (Mitchell, 1998).

THINKING IT THROUGH
Spousal Violence in Canada

A report on Family Violence in Canada reveals that an "estimated 7 percent of women and 6 percent of men in a current or previous spousal relationship encountered spousal violence during the five years up to and including 2004" (Statistics Canada, 2005). Spousal violence rates were highest among young couples (aged 15 to 24), in relationships of three years or less, and among people who were separated and in common-law relationships.

Figure 18–3 indicates the rates of spousal violence experienced by women and men over the five year periods ending in 1999 and 2004. Rates are provided for people who are currently in unions, for those who are no longer in those unions, and for both categories combined. Although about three-quarters of the violence took place during the marital or common-law union, some of it occurred after they had separated. Of course violence may be the main reason for separation.

The data indicate that "the nature and consequences of spousal violence were more severe for women than for men" and women were more than twice as likely to be injured as men. Women were much more likely to fear for their lives and suffer more than 10 violent episodes. Heavy drinking and the presence of emotional abuse were associated with higher rates of spousal abuse as well. Furthermore, separation had an affect: "one-third (34%) of women who experienced violence during their relationship said that the violence increased in severity or frequency after separation." Nearly one-quarter (23%) of female victims reported that the most serious form of violence experienced was being beaten, choked, or threatened by having a gun or knife used against them. This was the case for 15 percent of male victims. The report on family violence notes the following:

About 44% of female victims of spousal violence indicated that they suffered injury because of the violence, more than twice the proportion of 19% among male victims. In addition, 13% of female victims sought medical attention, compared with only 2% of male victims. Over one-third of women victims said that the violence was reported to the police—compared to 17% of men victims. In addition, 38% of women who reported to the police also sought a restraining order, more than twice the proportion of men.

Clearly, spousal violence is a major concern in Canada. We are more aware of violence perpetrated by men against women, because the consequences are generally more severe, but men also experience spousal abuse.

Postscript Since 1960, there have been about 2000 solved homicide/suicides, where the perpetrator takes his or her own life after the homicide: "About three-quarters of victims of homicide/suicides were killed by a family member.... Over half (57%) of family homicide/suicides involved spouses, and, of these incidents, virtually all (97%) involved female victims killed by a male spouse."

WHAT DO YOU THINK?

1. Were you aware that men are also the victims of spousal abuse?
2. What are the effects of spousal violence on children?
3. What can the legal system or the police do to reduce family violence?

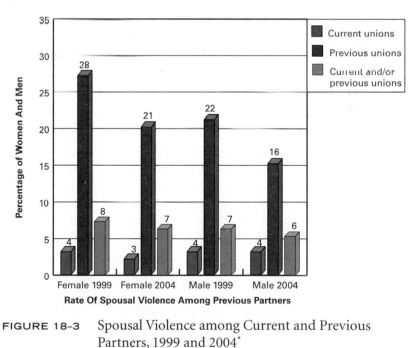

FIGURE 18-3   Spousal Violence among Current and Previous Partners, 1999 and 2004*

*Unions include common-law partners.

Source: From Statistics Canada, *The Daily*, Thursday, 14 July 2005.

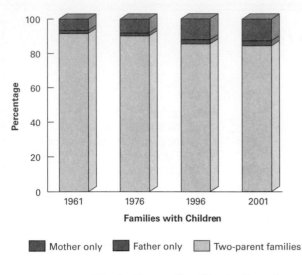

FIGURE 18-4 Single-Parent Families in Canada, 1961, 1976, 1996, and 2001

Sources: Compiled by L.M. Gerber from Statistics Canada, catalogue nos. 91-522 and 97F0005XCB2001006.

About 90 percent of child abusers are men, but they conform to no simple stereotype. Most abusers, however, share one trait: having been abused themselves as children. Research shows that violent behaviour in close relationships is learned. In families, then, violence begets violence (Gwartney-Gibbs, *et al.*, 1987; Widom, 1996).

Elder Abuse

Another form of family violence that society was slow to recognize is elder abuse. Parents are living longer and the costs, in terms of time and money, of care giving into old age can be the cause of considerable stress for the "sandwich generation," which is simultaneously caring for parents and children. Of course, the frail elderly are vulnerable to abuse (physical, psychological, and financial) because of failing mental and physical abilities. For more on elder abuse, which is under-reported because of shame and dependence, see Chapter 15, "Aging and the Elderly" (pp. 391–92).

Alternative Family Forms

Most families in the United States are composed of married couples raising children. But, in Canada, couples (married and common-law combined) with children under 25 living at home represent only 44 percent of all families—down from 49 and 55 percent in 1991 and 1981 respectively. Other family forms have become common.

ONE-PARENT FAMILIES

As Figure 18–4 indicates, in 1961, 8.4 percent of Canadian families with children were headed by a single parent and

In recent years, the proportion of young people who cohabit—that is, live together without being married—has risen sharply. This trend contributes to the debate over what is and is not a family. Do you consider a cohabiting couple to be a family? Why?

91.6 percent were husband/wife families. By 2001, single-parent families had risen to 15.6 percent. The proportion of one-parent families is growing, and almost 12 percent of children in Canada now live in these families. One-parent families—about four times more likely to be headed by women than men—may result from divorce, the inability to find a suitable husband, unplanned pregnancy, or an unmarried woman's decision to have a child.

Unmarried women—many of whom are career women—may opt to have children through *in vitro* fertilization or adoption, often foreign adoption. Why would an unmarried woman take such steps?

Single parenthood increases a woman's risk of poverty because it limits her ability to work and to further her education. The converse is also true: poverty raises the odds that a young woman will become a single mother (Trent, 1994).

TABLE 18–2

Low Income among Families with Children under 18*

Family Structure	Percentage Low-Income
Female lone-parent families	65.6
Male lone-parent families	22.2
Common-law couples	18.8
Married couple families	13.8
All families	12.6

*Of all families, 70.8 percent include married couples, 13.7 percent common-law couples, 12.6 percent female lone parents, and 2.9 percent male lone parents. Many of the married and common-law couples have had no children at all, or have no children living at home.

Source: Compiled by L.M. Gerber on the basis of Statistics Canada, Census 2001, Cat. No. 97F0020XCB2001006.

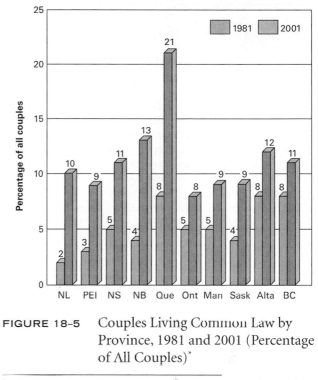

FIGURE 18-5   Couples Living Common Law by Province, 1981 and 2001 (Percentage of All Couples)*

*Includes married and common-law couples with and without children.

Sources: Statistics Canada, catalogue Nos. 93-312 and 93-320, cited in Stout (1994:9); calculations by L.M. Gerber based on Statistics Canada, Census 2001, catalogue no. 97F0005XCB2001006.

Considerable research shows that growing up in a one-parent family usually disadvantages children. Some studies indicate that, because a father and a mother each make distinctive contributions to a child's social development, it is unrealistic to expect one parent alone to do as good a job. But the most serious problem among families with one parent—especially if that parent is a woman—is poverty. An astounding 65.6 percent of female lone-parent families with children under 18 fall below the low-income cut-off: see Table 18–2. On average, a child growing up in a single-parent family starts out poorer, gets less schooling, and ends up with a lower income as an adult. Such children are also more likely to be single parents themselves (Popenoe, 1993b; Blankenhorn, 1995; Wu, 1996; Duncan, *et al.*, 1998; Kantrowitz and Wingert, 2001; McLanahan, 2002).

COHABITATION

Cohabitation is *the sharing of a household by an unmarried couple.* A generation ago, widespread use of terms such as "shacking up" and "living in sin" reflected disapproval of the arrangement. In global perspective, cohabitation is common in Sweden and other Nordic societies as a long-term form of family life, with or without children. But it is rare in more traditional and Catholic nations such as Italy. As Canadian society has grown more accepting, the proportion of couples cohabiting has increased from 8 percent in 1981 to 16.4 percent in 2001. Figure 18–5 shows the increase in cohabitation over this period by province. Quebec stands out clearly as the province with the most dramatic increase in common-law living. In the Applying Sociology box (on p. 484) we take a closer look at the phenomenon in Canada from a sociological perspective.

GAY AND LESBIAN COUPLES

In 1989, Denmark became the first country to legalize same-sex marriage, thereby extending to gay and lesbian couples the legal advantages of inheritance, taxation, and joint property ownership. Norway (1993), Sweden (1995), the Netherlands (2001), Belgium (2003) and Spain (2005) followed suit. Fifteen other European countries now recognize gay civil partnerships (Knox, 2004).

In the United States, the states of Vermont, Connecticut, and Hawaii, as well as a number of major cities, including San Francisco and New York, have passed laws giving limited marital benefits to gay and lesbian couples. Still, the U.S. Congress passed a law in 1996 defining marriage as joining one man and one woman and, until 2004, gay marriage remained illegal in all fifty states. In 2004, the supreme court of Massachusetts ruled that gay and lesbian couples had a right to marry, and legal marriages began in May of that year. That decision prompted officials in San Francisco and other U.S. cities to perform thousands of marriages for gay and lesbian couples, despite state laws banning such unions. Courts later declared those marriages to be illegal. In the November 2004 elections, voters in thirteen states passed ballot measures changing their state constitutions to recognize only marriages between one man and one woman. Even though they were barred from legal marriage, many gay men and especially lesbians formed long-term, committed partnerships and families.

As described in Chapter 8 ("Sexuality and Society"), the situation in Canada is quite different. In 1998, British Columbia gave separating same-sex parents equal privileges and obligations with respect to their children. In 1995, gay

APPLYING SOCIOLOGY
Cohabitation among Canadians

Zheng Wu (2000) has used a number of data sources—the Canadian census of various years and the General Social Surveys of 1990 and 1995—to study cohabitation. He assumes that the increase in cohabitation over the past few decades indicates a change in the norms that regulate the behaviour of families and their members.

Normative change tends to occur slowly, over long periods of time, in response to massive social and structural change. These changes challenge established lifestyles and values, forcing the development of normative solutions. Marriage and fertility trends—and ultimately cohabitation, as an alternative to marriage—are affected by economic factors, to be sure, but they also vary by language, religion, and region. Although Quebec was once Canada's most conservative province, it now stands out as the most liberal on social and welfare issues. Despite its Catholic roots, fertility and marriage rates are low—and cohabita-

tion levels are high. Other factors affecting levels of cohabitation are referred to as age, cohort, and period effects (the effects of being born into a particular age cohort at a specific point in time).

In 1981, 8 percent of all couples were cohabiting or living common-law. By 2001, the figure had increased to 16.4 percent—representing 1.2 million common-law couples. These couples are to be found disproportionately in Quebec and in Aboriginal communities. In 1981, cohabitation peaked among those 20 to 24 years of age (8.2%); the next highest level was 7.6 percent among those aged 25 to 29. By 1996, the peak had moved up one age category to those aged 25 to 29 (with 16.9% cohabiting); for those aged 30 to 34, the figure was 14.1 percent.

Wu also looked at the factors that were associated with approval of premarital sex and cohabitation. Among the factors that predicted higher levels of approval of both were education, Catholicism, church atten-

dance, being Canadian-born, being single, and living in Quebec. Within Canada, actual rates of cohabitation are increasing, as is approval of this alternative family form. Also, people are increasingly likely to have children within such unions. Nonetheless, cohabitation is inherently unstable. About 30 percent of these unions last for no more than 3 years, and only 1 in 20 lasts for 15 years. On the bright side, the reason for dissolving half of all cohabitations is the marriage of the two partners.

WHAT DO YOU THINK?

1. How likely are you, or your friends, to cohabit or live common-law?
2. How would your family, neighbours, or church react if you were to live common-law?
3. Should common-law couples marry when they have children?

Source: Based on Wu (2000).

---

and lesbian couples in Ontario won the right to adopt the biological children of their partners under the "stepparent adoption clause" of the *Child and Family Services Act*. In June 2003, after marriage laws were struck down by courts in Ontario, British Columbia, and Quebec, the federal government announced it would submit legislation allowing same-sex marriages to the Supreme Court for review. In 2005, same-sex marriage became legal in Canada. When the 2006 census results are tabulated (a process that takes three to four years), we will know how many gays and lesbians have married since 2003 and 2005. In the meantime, we can be sure that the legalization of same-sex marriage has completely changed the situation described in the opener to this chapter.

The first same-sex couple to marry legally in Canada offers news, legal updates, and resources for same-sex partners at www.samesexmarriage.ca.

SINGLEHOOD

In the past, at least 9 out of 10 Canadians married, so "singlehood" was seen as a transitory stage in life. Here we are talking about legal marital status—not "being single" because someone is temporarily without a girl/boyfriend. Since Canada treats common-law relationships like marriages, one could think of "true" singlehood as being outside marriage or common-law relationships. Nonetheless, since common-law relationships tend to be short-lived (see the Applying Sociology box above), and young women still dream of marriage and a wedding, it is worth looking at changes in the proportion of our population that never marries.

Most striking is the rising number of single young women. Throughout North America in 1960, 1 in 4 women aged 20 to 24 was single; by 1990, the proportion was nearing two-thirds. By 2003, the figure in the United States had soared to 74 percent; in Canada, the 2001 census revealed an astounding 88.5 percent. Underlying this is a recent change in the average age of marriage for men and women (up three years in each case), so that delayed marriage is a major factor. Women are going to college, university, and even graduate school in greater numbers, participating in the labour force, and establishing careers. Many are marrying later, or living common-law, and having children later, while others chose to forgo marriage and children altogether.

By midlife, women who have not married confront a lack of available men. Because our culture expects a woman to "marry up," the older a woman is, the more education she has, and the better her job, the more difficulty she has finding a suitable husband. Since most first marriages take place when a person is in the late twenties or thirties, Table 18–3 sets the pattern for the future. Note that, in each of the cohorts above 55 years of age, over 90 percent of men and women got married—some 30 to 65 years before.

As an aside, you might think back to the earlier observation that marriage is most beneficial to men: women aged 85 to 89 are 33 percent more likely to have never married. Therefore, it appears that *single women live longer* than their married peers.

It is in the cohort for people aged 45 to 49—who married in the early 1980s—that we see a sudden increase in the proportion of women and men who never married. The cohort for people aged 35 to 39 is also past the normal age of first marriage, so the figures of 32.7 and 24 percent, respectively, indicate a meaningful trend. Younger couples really are less likely to marry.

Does this mean that more young men and women are living alone and lonely? Of course not! Many of them live common-law, while others have meaningful, loving relationships that do not involve cohabitation. But, there are more women (and men) who are opting for independence outside marriage or common-law relationships.

New Reproductive Technology and the Family

Recent medical advances involving *new reproductive technology* are also changing families. In 1978, England's Louise Brown became the world's first "test-tube" baby. Since then, tens of thousands of children have been conceived this way. A decade from now, 2 or 3 percent of the children in high-income nations may result from new reproductive technologies. Test-tube babies are the product of *in vitro* fertilization, in which doctors unite a woman's egg and a man's sperm "in glass" (usually not a test tube but a shallow dish) rather than in a woman's body. Doctors then either implant the resulting embryo in the womb of the woman who is to bear the child, or freeze it for use at a later time.

At present, new reproductive technologies help some couples who cannot conceive by conventional means. These techniques may eventually help reduce the incidence of

TABLE 18–3

Singlehood across Generations (Percentage Never Married, by Selected Age Cohorts) 2001

Age (in Years)	Men	Women
85 to 89	6.2	8.3
75 to 79	6.2	6.1
65 to 69	6.6	5.7
55 to 59	8.3	7.0
45 to 49	16.2	12.5
35 to 39	32.7	24.0
25 to 29	71.5	57.6
20 to 24	94.9	88.5

Source: Calculations by L.M. Gerber based on Statistics Canada, Census 2001, Catalogue No. 95F0407XCB2001004.

birth defects. Genetic screening of sperm and eggs allows medical specialists to increase the odds of having a healthy baby. But new reproductive technology also raises difficult and troubling questions. When one woman carries an embryo formed from the egg of another, who is the mother? When a couple divorces, which spouse is entitled to decide what is to be done with frozen embryos? Should parents use genetic screening to select the physical traits of their child? Such questions remind us that technology changes faster than our ability to understand the consequences of its use (Cohen, 1998; Nock, *et al.*, 1999).

The Family: Looking Ahead

Family life in Canada will continue to change—and with change comes controversy. Here, as in the United States, advocates of "traditional family values" line up against those who support greater personal choice—to wed or not to wed, divorce, abortion, single parenthood. No doubt, the traditional family is threatened.

First, the divorce rate is likely to remain high, even in the face of evidence that marital breakup harms children. Today's marriages are about as durable as they were a century ago, when many were cut short by death. The difference is that now more couples *choose* to end marriages that fail to live up to their expectations. Thus, although the divorce rate has declined since 1990, it is unlikely to return to the low rates that marked the early decades of the twentieth century.

Second, family life in the twenty-first century will be more diverse than ever. Cohabiting couples, one-parent families, gay and lesbian families, and blended families are all on the rise. Most families are still based on marriage, and most married couples still have children. But the diversity of family forms implies a trend towards more personal choice.

MEDIA PERSPECTIVES
The Controversy over Child Care

anadians were first promised an affordable universal daycare system in the federal election campaign of 1993—the first won by the Liberals under the leadership of Jean Chrétien—but it failed to appear on the political landscape until the elections of 2004 and 2006. During this period, the political right had been reunited under Stephen Harper's Conservative Party of Canada and Paul Martin's Liberal government was reeling under the impact of the sponsorship scandal in Quebec. These two factors contributed to the election of a Liberal minority government in 2004 and a Conservative minority government in 2006. Two vastly different models of child care were to be front and centre by the election of 2006.

In the platform for the election of 2004, the Liberals promised to spend $5 billion on child care—but "only $91 million would be spent in 2004 and $93 million in 2005" (Clarkson, 2004: 44). Lawyer and former hockey player Ken Dryden, who won a seat in the 2004 election, was given the portfolio of minister of social development; he was entrusted with the task of developing and promoting the government's child care initiative, which would emphasize early childhood learning. He took his proposal into the 2006 election.

Child care in a regulated daycare centre in Canada can cost more than $1000 per month for an infant and $800 per month for a toddler: let's call it $850/month, or $10 000 per year. It would cost the government roughly the same amount per space because it too has to meet staffing and facility regulations, and cover capital costs for creating the spaces. At that rate, the government could cover 9100 spaces in 2004. Assuming that parents will keep their infants home for the first year, and half-day kindergarten kicks in for four- and five-year-olds, there are 1.4 million children who are theoretically eligible for these 9100 "universal" spaces. It was never clear if "universal and affordable" meant parents would pay a nominal amount like the $7 per day paid in Quebec. In that case, the Liberal budget might cover 11 000 spaces. *If* the provinces and territories were to contribute matching funds, the total might go up to 22 000 spaces—*for 1.4 million* eligible children. The biggest problem here is creating the required number of spaces with the funding promised by the Liberal government—without increasing the amount paid by parents.

Enter the Conservative Party of Canada with its child care benefit of $100 per month ($1200 per year) for each child under six years of age. This means that $2.5 billion *every year* will

be going into the pockets of all parents of young children—to be taxed in the hands of the lower-income parent—for them to use for regulated daycare, nannies, sitters down the street, or relatives assuming child-care functions. Most importantly, for lower-income families with two or three children under six, the money might make it possible for one of the parents to stay at home instead of working part-time or full-time at some menial job. The Conservative plan also allows for financial and tax incentives to encourage communities and organizations to create daycare spaces (e.g., workplace daycare in large corporations or office buildings). This plan provides for the creation of new daycare spaces, while giving all parents more choice in their child-care arrangements.

Quebec has a child-care plan in place that seems, at least in part, to be the model for the Liberal plan. An extensive daycare system, in which parents pay $7 per day for care, has made it more feasible for mothers of young children to enter or return to the labour force (Peritz, 2006). Table 18–4 shows that employment among women aged 25 to 34—prime years for raising young children—increased dramatically from 1981 to 1991, then surpassed that of women elsewhere in Canada by 2001. A study of daycare in two small communities on the Ottawa River

Third, men will play a limited role in child rearing. In the 1950s, a decade that many people view as the "golden age" of families, men began to withdraw from active parenting (Snell, 1990; Stacey, 1990). In recent years, a small countertrend—the stay-at-home dad—is evident, with some older and highly educated fathers staying at home with young children, many using computer technology to continue their work. But the stay-at-home dad represents a small fraction of

 Visit a website for stay-at-home fathers at www.slowlane.com.

fathers with young children. In the end, high divorce rates and the increase in single motherhood are weakening children's ties to fathers and increasing children's risk of poverty.

Fourth, families will continue to feel the effects of economic changes. In many homes, both household partners work, reducing marriage and family to the interaction

(Albanese, 2006) looks at the ripple effects of $7 a day child care (whether in home care or a larger facility). Albanese argues that allowing mothers to go to work, and in some cases get off welfare, and placing children into daycare (of either type) decreased financial pressures at home and helped children acquire social and language skills that they were not learning at home.

In Alberta, which has a booming economy and a shortage of workers of all types, employment of women of prime child-rearing age went from above average in 1981 to below average in 2001. Noting the same trend specifically among mothers with partners and preschool children, Brethour (2006) attempts to account for the exodus of women—even career women—from their jobs. He points out that daycare is inadequate but attributes the disappearance of job-holding women to Alberta's prosperity. In other words, salaries are so high in Alberta that more families do well on the earnings of a single breadwinner. As baby boomers retire, Canada as a whole will face labour shortages of crisis proportions. When that happens, universal daycare will be essential to keep the economy from collapsing.

So what is the best approach to child care? Quebec's best-known pediatrician, *le bon Dr. Chicoine*, argues—on the basis of attachment theory—that parents and babies need time to bond before children are sent to daycare (Wente, 2006). Children older than two or two-and-a-half benefit from the

TABLE 18–4

Employment among Married Women (25 to 34 Years of Age) for Canada, Quebec, Ontario, and Alberta: 1981, 1991, 2001*

	Percentage Employed		
	1981	**1991**	**2001**
Canada	55.8	68.5	72.6
Quebec	50.5	66.5	74.1
Ontario	61.5	71.0	72.8
Alberta	57.5	69.9	71.6

*Married includes women in common-law unions.

Source: Calculations by L.M. Gerber from Statistics Canada, Catalogue No. 97F0012XCB2001001.

socialization it offers, but he recommends daycare in moderation rather than the 60 hours per week, 52 weeks a year that is common in Quebec. He is particularly concerned about the mothers in blue-collar families who have no choice but to return to work as quickly as possible, arguing that they really need a way to stay home. Those, of course, are the mothers who might benefit from the Conservatives' child benefit of $100 per month.

An article in *The Globe and Mail* entitled "Mr. Harper's child-proof political strategy" (Adams, 2006) notes that, from a political perspective, the Conservatives' child care benefit is brilliant. It is very popular among several categories of people: 64 percent of parents with children under six favour the $1200 benefit—especially those in Quebec where they already have a

daycare program and the cheques cover much of the $7/day cost. Adams argues that, without institutional child-care supports, many women who would like to work cannot, and that children who get a head start (early childhood education) have an advantage when they start school. A sense of fairness, he says, will eventually lead us to "a national, public child-care infrastructure."

WHAT DO YOU THINK?

1. Which is fairer: $1200 per child under six to enhance choice, or a subsidized daycare program that allows women to work and pursue careers?
2. Which approach would appeal most to feminists? Why?
3. Which approach would you want for your own children? Why?

of weary men and women who try to fit a little "quality time" with their children into an already full schedule. The long-term effects of the two-career couple on families as we have known them are likely to be mixed. Dual-career families—and single motherhood—require alternatives in child care as discussed in the Media Perspectives box (on pp. 486–87).

Fifth and finally, the importance of new reproductive technology will increase. Ethical concerns about whether

what *can* be done *should* be done will surely slow these developments, but new forms of reproduction will continue to alter the traditional experience of parenthood.

Despite the changes and controversies that have shaken the family, most people still report being happy as partners and parents. Therefore, marriage and family life are likely to remain foundations of our society for generations to come.

MAKING THE GRADE

The following learning tools will help you see what you know, identify what you still need to learn, and expand your understanding beyond the text. You can also visit this text's Companion Website™ at www.pearsoned.ca/macionis to find useful practice tests.

KEY POINTS

The Family: Basic Concepts

All societies are built on kinship. Family forms vary across cultures and over time.

Families: Global Variations

In industrialized societies, marriage is monogamous. Many pre-industrial societies, however, permit polygamy, of which there are two types: polygyny and polyandry. In global perspective, patrilocality is most common, but industrial societies favour neolocality and a few societies have matrilocal residence. Industrial societies use bilateral descent, and pre-industrial societies are either patrilineal or matrilineal.

Theoretical Analysis of the Family

Structural-functional analysis identifies major family functions: socialization of the young, regulation of sexual activity, social placement, and provision of material and emotional support. Social-conflict theories, including feminist analysis, explore how the family perpetuates social inequality by transmitting divisions based on class, ethnicity, race, and gender. Micro-level analysis highlights the diversity of family life.

Stages of Family Life

Courtship leads to the formation of new families. Romantic love is central to mate selection in North America and Europe but not in much of the rest of the world. Even in Canada, romantic love usually joins people with similar social backgrounds.

The vast majority of married couples have children, although family size has decreased over time. The main reason for this decline is industrialization, which transforms children into economic liabilities, encourages women to gain an education and join the labour force, and reduces infant mortality. Married life changes as children leave home to form families of their own. Many middle-aged couples care for aging

parents, and many older couples are active grandparents. The final transition in marriage begins with the death of a spouse, usually the husband.

Canadian Families: Class, Race, and Gender

Families differ according to social class, race, and ethnicity. Some immigrant families, for example, are more likely than others to maintain extended kinship ties. Poor families are most likely to be headed by single women. Among all categories of people, well-to-do families enjoy the most options and the greatest financial security.

Gender affects family dynamics since husbands dominate in most marriages. Research suggests that marriage provides more benefits for men than for women.

Transitions and Problems in Family Life

The divorce rate today is ten times what it was a century ago; nearly four in ten current marriages will end in divorce. Most people who divorce—especially men—remarry, often forming blended families that include children from previous marriages. Family violence, which most seriously victimizes women and children, is all too common. Most adults who abuse family members were themselves abused as children.

Alternative Family Forms

Our society's family life is becoming more varied. Lone-parent families, cohabitation, gay and lesbian couples, and single-hood have proliferated in recent years. While Canadian law only recently recognized same-sex marriages, many gay men and lesbians form long-lasting relationships and, increasingly, are raising children.

New Reproductive Technology and the Family

New reproductive technology is changing conventional ideas of parenthood. This technology makes parenthood possible for couples who cannot conceive children in the usual way, but it also raises ethnical questions about the extent to which parents can "design" their children.

The Family: Looking Ahead

In the near future, divorce rates are likely to remain high and families will continue to be diverse. Fathers are likely to continue to play a limited role in the lives of many children.

KEY CONCEPTS

family (p. 465) a social institution found in all societies that unites people in co-operative groups to care for one another, including any children

kinship (p. 465) a social bond based on common ancestry, marriage, or adoption

marriage (p. 465) a legal relationship, usually involving economic co-operation, sexual activity, and child bearing

extended family (consanguine family) (p. 465) a family consisting of parents and children as well as other kin

nuclear family (conjugal family) (p. 465) a family composed of one or two parents and their children

endogamy (p. 465) marriage between people of the same social category

exogamy (p. 465) marriage between people of different social categories

monogamy (p. 465) marriage that unites two partners

polygamy (p. 465) marriage that unites a person with two or more spouses

polygyny (p. 466) marriage that unites one man and two or more women

polyandry (p. 466) marriage that unites one woman and two or more men

patrilocality (p. 466) a residential pattern in which a married couple lives with or near the husband's family

matrilocality (p. 466) a residential pattern in which a married couple lives with or near the wife's family

neolocality (p. 466) a residential pattern in which a married couple lives apart from both sets of parents

descent (p. 466) the system by which members of a society trace kinship over generations

patrilineal descent (p. 466) a system tracing kinship through men

matrilineal descent (p. 467) a system tracing kinship through women

bilateral descent (p. 467) a system tracing kinship through both men and women

incest taboo (p. 469) a norm forbidding sexual relations or marriage between certain relatives

homogamy (p. 472) marriage between people with the same social characteristics

infidelity (p. 472) sexual activity outside marriage

family violence (p. 480) emotional, physical, or sexual abuse of one family member by another

cohabitation (p. 483) the sharing of a household by an unmarried couple

APPLICATIONS & EXERCISES

1. Parents and grandparents can be a wonderful source of information about changes in marriage and the family. Ask them at what ages they married, what their married lives have been like, and what changes in family life today stand out for them. Compare the answers of two or more relatives. Are they very different?

2. Relationships with various family members differ. With which family member—mother, father, brother, sister—do you most readily share confidences? Who in your family would be the last to know? Why? Which family member would you turn to first in a crisis, and why?

3. A recent survey found that just one-third of families eat dinner together often. Are family meals part of your routine? What other regular family rituals do you participate in? Do members of your family feel that they spend enough time together?

PRENTICE HALL
mysoclab™
Where learning & the sociological imagination intersect.

To reinforce your understanding of this chapter, and to identify topics for further study, visit MySocLab at **www.pearsoned.ca/mysoclab/** for diagnostic tests and a multimedia ebook.

CHAPTER NINETEEN

Religion

How religious are Canadians?

What are the effects of religion on social behaviour?

How do religions in the East and the West differ?

"Make Jesus your CEO." These are words that you might hear at the Carruthers Creek Community Church in Ajax, Ontario, described as "the $3.8 million, [4273 square metre] building looks more like a large, modern high school/community centre complex than one of [Toronto's] growing number of U.S.–style evangelical megachurches" (Lachaine, 2006). The church draws 900 grandparents, parents, children, *and teens* each Sunday to its distinctly unchurchy services. Congregants arrive to the sounds of soul funk wafting through the lobby and stop for a coffee under the Carruthers Creek Coffee Company logo. Children run around the huge gym before their Sunday school classes, while teens cluster in the fellowship room, complete with dance floor. Everything is done to make congregants and newcomers—of any age—feel welcome.

The service is a mix of conventional and popular: "the real show begins upon entry into the chapel. The lights are dim in the concert-quality theatre" with stained glass projected on the side walls and a removable wooden cross at centre stage. Musical gear—electric and acoustic guitars, mammoth drum kit, keyboards, and an electric bass—stands ready to accompany two singers, one a teenaged girl with an alternative look, the other a middle-aged man in sweater and gold necklace: "their harmonies send shivers down the spine [and] could easily be played on rock radio: angsty, obscure lyrics combined with modern melody" (Lachaine, 2006). Thirty-year-old Pastor Thompson, in untucked shirt and jeans, delivers "his shoot-from-the-hip plainspeak in an urgent whisper, as though he's sharing the word of God with you and only you in the back room of a crowded bar. The audience is hushed and rapt for his entire 40-minute sermon" (Lachaine, 2006).

How, you might ask, does *this* church thrive when others are struggling to survive?

This chapter begins by explaining religion from a sociological point of view. We then explore the changing face of religious belief throughout history and around the world, and examine the vital and sometimes controversial place of religion in today's society.

Religion: Basic Concepts

The French sociologist Emile Durkheim stated that religion involves "things that surpass the limits of our knowledge" (1965 [1915]:62). We define most objects, events, or experiences as **profane** (from the Latin, meaning "outside the temple"), *an ordinary element of everyday life*. But we also consider some things **sacred,** *set apart as extraordinary, inspiring awe and reverence.* Setting the sacred apart from the profane is the essence of all religious belief. **Religion,** then, is *a social institution involving beliefs and practices based on recognizing the sacred.*

There is great diversity in matters of faith, and nothing is sacred to everyone on Earth. Although people regard most books as profane, Jews believe the Torah (the first five books of the Hebrew Bible, or Old Testament) is sacred, in the same way that Christians revere the Old and New Testaments of the Bible and Muslims exalt the Qur'an (Koran).

But no matter how a community of believers draws religious lines, Durkheim (1965; orig. 1915) explained, people understand profane things in terms of their everyday usefulness. We log on to the internet with our computer or turn a key to start our car. What is sacred we reverently set apart from everyday life, giving it a revered or holy aura. Marking the boundary between the sacred and the profane, for example, Muslims remove their shoes before entering a mosque, to avoid defiling a sacred place with soles that have touched the profane ground outside. The sacred is embodied in **ritual,** or *formal, ceremonial behaviour.* Holy communion is the central ritual of Christianity; to the Christian faithful, the wafer and wine consumed during communion are never treated in a profane way as food but as the sacred symbols of the body and blood of Jesus Christ.

RELIGION AND SOCIOLOGY

Because religion deals with ideas that transcend everyday experience, neither common sense nor sociology can prove or disprove religious doctrine. Religion is a matter of **faith,** *belief based on conviction rather than scientific evidence.* The New Testament of the Bible defines "faith" as "the conviction of things not seen" (Hebrews 11:1) and urges Christians to "walk by faith, not by sight" (2 Corinthians 5:7). Some people with strong faith may be disturbed by the thought of sociologists turning a scientific eye on what they hold sacred. However, a sociological study of religion is no threat to anyone's faith. Sociologists study religion just as they study the family—to understand religious experiences around the world and how religion is tied to other social institutions. They make no judgments that a specific religion is right or wrong; rather, scientific sociology takes a more worldly approach, asking why religions take a particular form in one society or another and how religious activity affects society as a whole.

Find online resources for the study of religion at www.princeton.edu/~csrelig/links/links.html.

Theoretical Analysis of Religion

Sociologists apply the major theoretical approaches to the study of religion just as they do to any other topic. Each approach provides distinctive insights into the way religion shapes social life.

FUNCTIONS OF RELIGION: STRUCTURAL-FUNCTIONAL ANALYSIS

According to Durkheim (1965; orig. 1915), society has a life and power of its own beyond the life of any individual. In other words, society itself is godlike, shaping the lives of its members and living on beyond them. Practising religion, people celebrate the awesome power of their society. No wonder people around the world transform certain everyday objects into sacred symbols of their collective life. Members of technologically simple societies do this with a **totem,** *an object in the natural world collectively defined as sacred.* The totem—perhaps an animal or an elaborate work of art—becomes the centrepiece of ritual, symbolizing the power of society over the individual. In our society, the flag is treated with respect: it is not used in a profane way (say, as a tablecloth) or allowed to touch the ground.

Regularly taking part in religious rituals sharpens the distinction between the sacred and the profane. The wafer used in the Christian ritual of holy communion is not associated with the everyday sense of food; rather, it is a sacred symbol of the body of Christ.

Durkheim identified three major functions of religion that contribute to the operation of society:

*   *Social cohesion.* Religion unites people through shared symbolism, values, and norms. Religious thought and ritual establish rules of fair play, organizing our social life.

*   *Social control.* Every society uses religious ideas to promote conformity. By defining their god as a "judge," many religions encourage people to obey cultural norms. Religion can also be used to back up the power of political systems. In the Middle Ages, royalty claimed to rule by "divine right," so that obedience was seen as doing God's will. Few political leaders in the western world make this claim but many publicly ask for God's blessing, implying that their efforts are right and just. Many American politicians are open about their religious beliefs: their counterparts among Canada's parliamentarians quietly attend prayer breakfasts without drawing attention to themselves.

*   *Providing meaning and purpose.* Religious belief offers the comforting sense that our brief lives serve some greater purpose. Strengthened by such beliefs, people are less likely to despair in the face of change or even tragedy. For this reason, we mark major life course transitions (i.e., birth, marriage, and death) with religious observances.

Critical Review In Durkheim's structural-functional analysis, religion represents the collective life of society. The major weakness of this approach is that it downplays religion's dysfunctions, especially the fact that strongly held beliefs can generate social conflict. Many nations march to war under the banner of their gods and, today, terrorists have claimed that their god motivates their actions. A study

Religion is founded on the concept of the sacred—that which is set apart as extraordinary and which demands our submission. Bowing, kneeling, or prostrating oneself are all ways of symbolically surrendering to a higher power. These Buddhist pilgrims are making their way to a holy place on Mount Kallas in western Tibet.

of conflict in the world would probably show that religious beliefs have provoked more violence than, say, differences of social class.

CONSTRUCTING THE SACRED: SYMBOLIC-INTERACTION ANALYSIS

From a symbolic-interaction point of view, religion—like all of society—is socially constructed (although perhaps with divine inspiration). Through various rituals, from daily prayers to such annual religious observances as Easter or Passover, people sharpen the distinction between the sacred and the profane. Peter Berger (1967:35–36) claims that placing our small, brief lives within some "cosmic frame of reference" gives us the appearance of "ultimate security and permanence."

Marriage is a good example. If two people look on marriage as merely a contract, they can walk away whenever they want to. Their bond makes far stronger claims on them when it is defined as "holy" matrimony, which is surely one

reason that the divorce rate is lower among people with strong religious beliefs. More generally, whenever human beings face uncertainty or life-threatening situations—such as illness, natural disaster, terrorist attack, or war—we turn to our sacred symbols.

Critical Review Using the symbolic-interaction approach, people use religion to give everyday life sacred meaning. Berger adds that the ability of the sacred to give special meaning to society depends on ignoring the fact that it is socially constructed. After all, how much strength could we gain from beliefs if we saw them merely as strategies for coping with tragedy? Also, this micro-level analysis ignores religion's link to social inequality, to which we now turn.

INEQUALITY AND RELIGION: SOCIAL-CONFLICT ANALYSIS

The social-conflict approach highlights religion's support of social inequality. Karl Marx claimed that religion serves ruling elites by legitimizing the status quo and diverting people's attention from social inequities. Today, the British monarch is the formal head of the Church of England, illustrating the close ties between religious and political elites. In that light, working for political change would mean opposing the church and, by implication, God. Religion also encourages people to endure without complaint social problems of this world while they look hopefully to a "better world to come." In a well-known statement, Marx dismissed religion as "the sigh of the oppressed creature, the sentiment of a heartless world, and the soul of soulless conditions. It is the opium of the people" (1964 [1848]:27).

Religion and social inequality are also linked through gender. Virtually all the world's major religions are patriarchal, as explored in the Thinking about Diversity box (on p. 496).

Critical Review Social-conflict analysis reveals the power of religion to support social inequality. Yet religion also promotes change towards equality. For example, nineteenth-century religious groups in the United States played an important part in the movement to abolish slavery. In the 1950s and 1960s, religious organizations and their leaders were the core of the civil rights movement. In the 1960s and 1970s, many clergy opposed the Vietnam War, and, today, many support progressive causes such as feminism and gay rights.

⟷ **YOUR TURN** ⟷

Can you think of examples of nations using the idea of "converting heathens" to justify controlling other societies? Explain.

APPLYING THEORY

RELIGION

	Structural-Functional Approach	Symbolic-Interaction Approach	Social-Conflict Approach
What is the level of analysis?	Macro level	Micro level	Macro level
What is the importance of religion for society?	Religion performs vital tasks, including uniting people and controlling behaviour.	Religion strengthens marriage by giving it (and family life) sacred meaning.	Religion supports social inequality by claiming that the social order is just.
	Religion gives life meaning and purpose.	People often turn to sacred symbols for comfort when facing danger and uncertainty.	Religion turns attention from problems in this world to a "better world to come."

The Applying Theory table (above) summarizes the three theoretical approaches to understanding religion.

Religion and Social Change

Religion is not just the conservative force portrayed by Karl Marx. At some points in history, as Max Weber (1958; orig. 1904–05) explained, religion has promoted dramatic social change.

MAX WEBER: PROTESTANTISM AND CAPITALISM

Max Weber argued that particular religious ideas set into motion a wave of change that brought about the Industrial Revolution in Western Europe. The rise of industrial capitalism was encouraged by Calvinism, a movement within the Protestant Reformation. As Chapter 4 ("Society") explains in detail, John Calvin (1509–1564) was a leader in the Protestant Reformation who preached the doctrine of predestination. According to Calvin, an all-powerful and all-knowing God had selected some people for salvation but condemned most to eternal damnation. Each individual's fate, sealed before birth and known only to God, was either eternal glory or endless hellfire. Driven by anxiety over their fate, Calvinists understandably looked for signs of God's favour in this world and came to see prosperity as a sign of divine blessing. Religious conviction and a rigid devotion to duty led Calvinists to work all the time, and many amassed great wealth. But money was not for selfish spending or for sharing with the poor, whose plight they saw as a mark of God's rejection. As agents of God's work on Earth, Calvinists believed that they best fulfilled their "calling" by reinvesting profits and achieving ever-greater success in the process. All the while, Calvinists lived thrifty lives and adopted technological advances, which laid the groundwork for the rise of industrial capitalism. In time, the religious fervour that motivated early Calvinists weakened, leaving a profane "Protestant work ethic." To Max Weber, industrial capitalism itself arose as a "disenchanted" religion, further showing the power of religion to alter the shape of society.

LIBERATION THEOLOGY

Historically, Christianity has reached out to oppressed people, urging all to a stronger faith in a better life to come. In recent decades, however, some church leaders and theologians have taken a decidedly political approach and endorsed **liberation theology,** *the combining of Christian principles with political activism, often Marxist in character.* This social movement started in the 1960s in Latin America's Roman Catholic Church. Today, Christian activists continue to help people in poor nations liberate themselves from abysmal poverty. Their message is simple: social oppression runs counter to Christian morality, so, as a matter of faith and justice, Christians must promote greater social equality.

Pope Benedict XVI, like Pope John Paul II before him, condemns liberation theology for distorting traditional church doctrine with left-wing politics. Nevertheless, the liberation theology movement has gained strength in the poorest countries of Latin America, where many people's Christian faith drives them to improve conditions for the poor and oppressed (Neuhouser, 1989; Williams, 2002).

Types of Religious Organizations

Sociologists categorize the hundreds of different religious organizations found in North America along a continuum, with *churches* at one end and *sects* at the other. We can describe any actual religious organization in relation to these two ideal types by locating it on a church/sect continuum.

THINKING ABOUT DIVERSITY:
RACE, CLASS, & GENDER

Religion and Patriarchy: Does God Favour Males?

Why do two-thirds of adults in the United States say they think of God as "father" rather than "mother" (NORC, 2003: 146)? It is probably because most North Americans link godly traits, such as wisdom and power, to men. Just about all the world's religions tend to favour males, a fact evident in passages from their sacred writings.

The Qur'an (Koran), the sacred text of Islam, declares that men are to dominate women:

> Men are in charge of women.... Hence good women are obedient.... As for those whose rebelliousness you fear, admonish them, banish them from your bed, and scourge them. (quoted in Kaufman, 1976:163)

Christianity, the major religion of the Western world, also supports patriarchy. Many Christians revere Mary, the mother of Jesus, but the New Testament also includes the following passages:

> A man... is the image and glory of God; but woman is the glory of man. For man was not made from woman, but woman from man. Neither was man created for woman, but woman for man. (1 Corinthians 11:7–9)
>
> As in all the churches of the saints, the women should keep silence in the churches. For they are not permitted to speak, but should be subordinate, as even the law says. If there is anything they desire to know, let them ask their husbands at home. For it is shameful for a woman to speak in church. (1 Corinthians 14:33–35)
>
> Wives, be subject to your husbands, as to the Lord. For the

husband is the head of the wife as Christ is the head of the church.... As the church is subject to Christ, so let wives also be subject in everything to their husbands. (Ephesians 5:22–24)

> Let a woman learn in silence with all submissiveness. I permit no woman to teach or to have authority over men; she is to keep silent. For Adam was formed first, then Eve; and Adam was not deceived, but the woman was deceived and became a transgressor. Yet woman will be saved through bearing children, if she continues in faith and love and holiness, with modesty. (1 Timothy 2:11–15)

Judaism also has traditionally supported patriarchy. Male Orthodox Jews say the following words in daily prayer:

> Blessed art thou, O Lord our God, King of the Universe, that I was not born a gentile.
>
> Blessed art thou, O Lord our God, King of the Universe, that I was not born a slave.
>
> Blessed art thou, O Lord our God, King of the Universe, that I was not born a woman.

Many patriarchal religions also exclude women from the clergy. Today, Islam and the Roman Catholic Church ban women from the priesthood, as do about half of Protestant denominations. But a growing number of Protestant religious organizations, including the Church of England, ordain women. Orthodox Judaism upholds the traditional prohibition against women serving as rabbis, but Reform and Conservative Judaism look to both men and women as spiritual leaders.

Feminists argue that, unless traditional ideas of gender are removed from our understanding of God, women will never be equal to men in the church. The theologian Mary Daly puts the matter bluntly: "If God is male, then male is God" (quoted in Woodward, 1989:58).

WHAT DO YOU THINK?

1. Are you or other members of your family affiliated with a religious organization? If so, what evidence of patriarchy do you see in this religion?
2. Why do you think many religions encourage people to think of God as male?
3. Can you think of God in terms that do not include gender? Explain your answer.

CHURCH

Drawing on the ideas of his teacher Max Weber, Ernst Troeltsch (1931) defined a **church** as *a type of religious organization that is well integrated into the larger society.* Churchlike organizations usually persist for centuries and include generations of the same families. Churches have well-established rules and regulations, and expect leaders to be formally trained and ordained. Although concerned with the sacred, a church accepts the ways of the profane world. Church members think of their god in intellectual terms (say, as a force for good) and favour abstract moral standards (e.g., "treat others as you wish to be treated yourself"—a rule common to the world's major religions and cultures) over specific rules for day-to-day living. By teaching morality in safely abstract terms, church leaders avoid social controversy. For example, many congregations celebrate the unity of all peoples but say little about their own lack of racial diversity; by downplaying this type of conflict, a church makes peace with the status quo (Troeltsch, 1931).

A church may operate with or apart from the state. As its name implies, a **state church** is *a church formally allied with the state.* State churches have existed throughout human history. For centuries, Roman Catholicism was the official religion of the Roman Empire, and Confucianism was the official religion of China until early in the twentieth century. Today, the Anglican church is the official church of England; Islam the official religion of Morocco, Pakistan, and Iran; and Judaism the official religion of Israel. State churches count everyone in the society as a member, which sharply limits tolerance of religious differences.

By contrast, a **denomination,** is *a church, independent of the state, that recognizes religious pluralism.* Denominations exist in nations, including Canada, that formally separate church and state. Canada has dozens of Christian denominations (including Catholic, United Church, Anglican, Baptist, Lutheran, and Presbyterian) as well as various categories of Judaism, Islam, and other traditions. Although members of any denomination hold to their own doctrine, they recognize the right of others to have different beliefs.

SECT

The second general religious form is the **sect,** *a type of religious organization that stands apart from the larger society.* Sect members have rigid religious convictions and deny the beliefs of others. A church tries to appeal to everyone—the term "catholic," for instance, also means "universal"—but a sect instead forms an exclusive group. To members of a sect, religion is not just one aspect of life but a firm plan for how to live. In extreme cases, members of a sect withdraw completely from society in order to practice their religion without interference. The Hutterites and Old Order Mennonites are examples of Canadian sects that have remained isolated from the mainstream. Since our culture views religious tolerance as a virtue, members of sects are sometimes accused of being narrow-minded in their insistence that they alone have the true faith (Stark and Bainbridge, 1979).

In organizational terms, sects are less formal than churches. Sect members may be highly spontaneous and emotional in worship, compared to members of churches, who tend to listen passively to their leaders. Sects also reject the intellectualized religion of churches, stressing instead the personal experience of divine power. Rodney Stark (1985:314) contrasts a church's vision of a distant God ("Our Father, who art in Heaven") with a sect's more immediate God ("Lord, bless this poor sinner kneeling before you now").

Churches and sects also have different patterns of leadership. The more churchlike an organization, the more likely that its leaders are formally trained and ordained. Sectlike organizations, which celebrate the personal presence of God, expect their leaders to exhibit divine inspiration in the form of **charisma** (from the Greek, meaning "divine favour"), *extraordinary personal qualities that can infuse people with emotion and turn them into followers.* Sects generally form as breakaway groups from established religious organizations (Stark and Bainbridge, 1979). Their psychic intensity and informal structure make them less stable than churches, and many sects blossom only to disappear soon after. The sects that do endure typically become more like churches, with declining emphasis on charismatic leadership as they become more bureaucratic.

To sustain their membership, many sects actively recruit, or *proselytize,* new members; for example, members of Jehovah's Witnesses go door to door to share their faith with others in the hope of attracting new members. Sects value highly the experience of *conversion,* a personal transformation or religious rebirth. Finally, churches and sects differ in their social composition. Because they are more closely tied to the world, well-established churches tend to include people of higher social standing. Sects attract more disadvantaged people. A sect's openness to new members and its promise of salvation and personal fulfilment appeal to people who feel they are social outsiders.

CULT

A **cult** is *a religious organization that is largely outside a society's cultural traditions.* Most sects spin off from conventional religious organizations. A cult, however, typically forms around a highly charismatic leader who offers a compelling message about a new and very different way of life. As many as 5000 cults exist in North America (Marquand and Wood, 1997). Because some cult principles or practices are unconventional, the popular view is that they are deviant or even evil. The suicides in 1997 in California of 39 members of Heaven's Gate cult—people who claimed that dying was a doorway to a higher existence, perhaps in the company of aliens from outer space— confirmed the negative image the public holds of most cults. The suicides of 53 members (in Switzerland and Quebec) of the Order of the Solar Temple in 1994, and of 5

In global perspective, the range of religious activity is truly astonishing. Members of this Southeast Asian cult show their devotion to God by suspending themselves in the air using ropes and sharp hooks that pierce their skin.

Animism is widespread among Aboriginal peoples, who live respectfully within the natural world on which they depend for their survival. These Aleut kayakers live in Eklutna, a village north of Anchorage, Alaska, which has been inhabited by people with much the same way of life for almost 500 years. Animists see a divine force present not only in themselves but in everything around them.

more members in 1997—in the belief that death on Earth would allow transit to another planet where their lives would continue—also contributed to the notion that cult members are insane (Shupe, 1995; Gleick, 1997).

This charge is unfair because there is nothing basically wrong with this kind of religious organization. Many long-standing religions—including Christianity, Islam, and Judaism—began as cults. Of course, few cults exist for very long. One reason is that they are even more at odds with the larger society than sects. Many cults demand that members not only accept their doctrine but also adopt a radically new lifestyle. This is why people sometimes accuse cults of brainwashing their members, although research suggests that most people who join cults experience no psychological harm (Kilbourne, 1983; Williams, 2002).

YOUR TURN

Over time a sect or cult can become an established religious organization (or church). Under what conditions might such a transformation occur?

Religion in History

Like other social institutions, religion shows marked variation according to time and place. Let us look at several ways in which religion has changed over the course of history.

RELIGION IN PRE-INDUSTRIAL SOCIETIES

Early hunters and gatherers practised **animism** (from the Latin, meaning "the breath of life"), *the belief that elements of the natural world are conscious life forms that affect humanity.* Animistic people view forests, oceans, mountains, and even the wind as spiritual forces. Many Aboriginal societies in North America are animistic, which explains their reverence for the natural environment.

To learn more about traditions of the Kwakiutl people of Canada's northwest coast, visit www.mala.bc.ca/www/discover/educate/posters/lauriec.htm.

Belief in a single divine power responsible for creating the world began with pastoral and horticultural societies, which first appeared 10 000 to 12 000 years ago. The conception of God as a "shepherd" arose because Christianity, Judaism, and Islam had their beginnings among pastoral peoples. Religion gains importance in agrarian societies, which develop a specialized priesthood in charge of religious organizations. The central role of religion is seen in the huge cathedrals that dominated the towns of mediaeval Europe.

RELIGION IN INDUSTRIAL SOCIETIES

The Industrial Revolution introduced a growing emphasis on science. More and more, people looked to doctors and scientists for the knowledge and comfort they used to get from priests. But religion persists in industrial societies because science is powerless to address issues of ultimate meaning in human life. In other words, learning *how* the world works is a matter for scientists, but *why* we and the rest of the universe exist at all is a question of faith.

World Religions

The diversity of religions in the world is almost as wide-ranging as the diversity of culture itself. Many of the thousands of different religions are found in just one place and have few followers. But there are a number of *world religions*, which are widely known and have millions of adherents. We briefly describe six world religions, which together claim 4 billion believers—two-thirds of humanity.

 Learn more about different religions at www.adherents.com.

CHRISTIANITY

Christianity is the most widespread world religion, with 2 billion followers, almost one-third of the world's people. Most Christians live in Europe or the Americas; more than 85 percent of the people in the United States and Canada identify with Christianity. As shown in Global Map 19–1, people who think of themselves as Christian represent a large share of the population in many world regions, with the notable exceptions of northern Africa and Asia. European colonization spread Christianity throughout much of the world over the past 500 years. Its dominance in the West is shown by the fact that our calendar numbers years from the birth of Christ (from the Greek for "anointed one," a translation of the Hebrew word for "Messiah").

As noted earlier, Christianity began as a cult, drawing elements from Judaism, a much older religion. Like many cults, Christianity was built on the personal charisma of a leader, Jesus of Nazareth, who preached a message of personal salvation. Jesus did not directly challenge the political power of his day, the Roman Empire—telling his followers to "render therefore to Caesar things that are Caesar's" (Matthew 22:21)—but his message was revolutionary all the same, promising that faith and love would triumph over sin and death.

Christianity is one example of **monotheism,** *belief in a single divine power.* As a new religion it differed from the Roman Empire's traditional **polytheism,** *belief in many gods.* Yet Christianity views the Supreme Being as a sacred Trinity: God the Creator; Jesus Christ, Son of God and Redeemer; and the Holy Spirit, a Christian's personal experience of God's presence.

The claim that Jesus was divine rests on beliefs relating to his virgin birth and of his final days on Earth. Brought to trial as a threat to established political leaders, Jesus was tried in Jerusalem and sentenced to death by crucifixion, a common means of execution at the time. This explains why the cross of the crucifixion became a sacred Christian symbol. According to Christian belief, three days after his execution, Jesus arose from the dead, showing that he was the Son of God.

Jesus' followers, especially his twelve closest associates,

YOUR TURN

Dan Brown's book, *The Da Vinci Code,* the subsequent movie, and Kathy Reich's book, *Cross Bones,* question Christ's virgin birth and death/resurrection. Why are the two books and the film so controversial?

known as the apostles, spread Christianity throughout the Mediterranean region. At first, the Roman Empire persecuted Christians. But, by the fourth century, the empire had adopted Christianity as a state church—the official religion of what became known as the Holy Roman Empire. Christianity took various forms, including the Roman Catholic Church and the Orthodox church, based in Constantinople (now Istanbul, Turkey); towards the end of the Middle Ages, the Protestant Reformation in Europe gave rise to hundreds of new denominations.

In Canada today, numerous denominations—the United and Anglican Churches are the two largest—command sizeable followings: 10 percent and 7 percent of Canada's population, where Roman Catholics predominate at 43 percent.

ISLAM

Islam has about 1.2 billion followers, which is almost one-fifth of humanity. Followers of Islam are called Muslims. In 2001, Muslims made up 2 percent of Canada's population. While we tend to associate Islam with Arabs in the Middle

 "The Spirit of Islam," an exhibition by the Museum of Anthropology at the University of British Columbia, explores Islamic spirituality through its exquisite calligraphy: see www.moa.ubc.ca/spiritofislam.

East, where a majority of the people is Muslim, in fact most of the world's Muslims live elsewhere. Global Map 19–2 shows that most people in northern Africa and Indonesia are Muslims; in addition, large concentrations of Muslims are found in western Asia in Pakistan, India, Bangladesh, and the southern republics of the former Soviet Union. Because Muslims have a higher birth rate than followers of any other major religion, it is possible that Islam could become the world's dominant religion by the end of this century.

Islam is the word of God as revealed to Muhammad, who was born in the city of Mecca (now in Saudi Arabia) about the year 570. To Muslims, Muhammad is a prophet, not a divine being as Jesus is to Christians. The text of the Qur'an (Koran), which is sacred to Muslims, is the word of Allah (Arabic for "God") as transmitted through Muhammad, Allah's messenger. In Arabic, the word *islam* means both "submission" and "peace," and the Qur'an urges

WINDOW ON THE WORLD

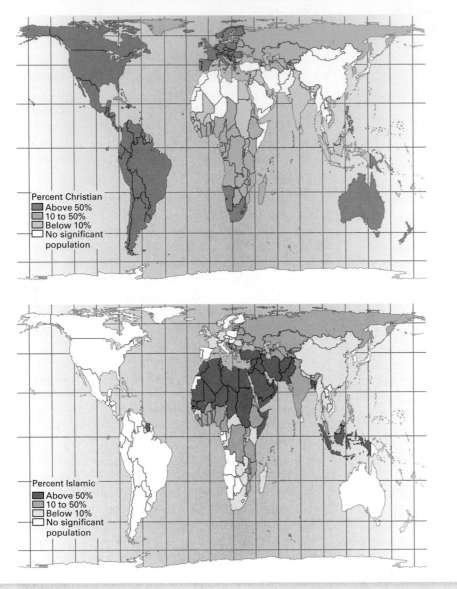

Percent Christian
- Above 50%
- 10 to 50%
- Below 10%
- No significant population

GLOBAL MAP 19–1

Christianity in Global Perspective

Source: *Peters Atlas of the World* (1990).

Percent Islamic
- Above 50%
- 10 to 50%
- Below 10%
- No significant population

GLOBAL MAP 19–2

Islam in Global Perspective

Source: *Peters Atlas of the World* (1990).

submission to Allah as the path to inner peace. Muslims express this personal devotion in a ritual of prayers five times each day.

After the death of Muhammad, Islam spread rapidly. While divisions arose among Muslims, all accept the Five Pillars of Islam: recognizing Allah as the one, true God and Muhammad as God's messenger; ritual prayer; giving alms to the poor; fasting during the month of Ramadan; and making a pilgrimage at least once in a lifetime to the Sacred House of Allah in Mecca (Weeks, 1988; El-Attar, 1991). Like Christianity, Islam holds people accountable to God for their

deeds on Earth. Those who live obediently will be rewarded in heaven, and evildoers will suffer unending punishment.

Muslims are also required to defend their faith, which has led to calls for holy wars against unbelievers, in roughly the same way that mediaeval Christians fought in the Crusades. Recent decades have witnessed a rise in militancy and anti-Western feeling in much of the Muslim world, where many people see the United States as both militarily threatening and representing a way of life that they view as materialistic and immoral. Westerners—who typically know little about Islam and may stereotype all Muslims in terms of the terrorist actions of a few—respond with confusion and sometimes hostility (Eck, 2001; Ryan, 2001).

Many outsiders view Muslim women as among the world's most socially oppressed people. There are differences among Muslim nations in terms of rights given to women: Tunisia allows women far more opportunities than, say, Saudi Arabia, which does not allow women to drive a car or to vote—except, recently, in municipal elections (Ganley, 1998). It is true that many Muslim women lack the personal freedoms enjoyed by Muslim men, yet most accept the mandates of their religion and find security in a system that guides the behaviour of both women and men (Peterson, 1996). Defenders of Islam also point out that patriarchy was well established in the Middle East long before the birth of Muhammad and that Islam actually improved the social position of women by requiring husbands to deal justly with their wives. For example, Islam permits a man to have up to four wives, but it requires men to have only one wife if having more would cause him to treat any woman unjustly (Qur'an, "The Women," v. 3).

JUDAISM

In terms of numbers, Judaism's 15 million followers worldwide make it something less than a world religion. The followers of Judaism are referred to as Jews, who make up a majority of the population of only one country, Israel. But Judaism is of special importance to us because the largest concentration of Jews (6 million people) is found in North America. Jews look to the past as a source of guidance in the present and for the future. Judaism has deep historical roots that extend 4000 years before the birth of Christ to the ancient societies of Mesopotamia (located in what is now Iraq). At that time, Jews were animistic; but this belief changed after Jacob (grandson of Abraham, the earliest great ancestor) led his people to Egypt. Jews survived centuries of slavery in Egypt until, in the thirteenth century B.C.E., Moses, the adopted son of an Egyptian princess, was called by God to lead the Jews from bondage. This exodus (this word's Latin and Greek roots mean "a marching out") from Egypt is remembered by Jews today in the annual ritual of Passover. Once liberated, the Jews became monotheistic, recognizing a single, all-powerful God.

A distinctive concept of Judaism is the *covenant*, a special relationship with God by which the Jews became God's "chosen people." The covenant implies a duty to observe God's law, especially the Ten Commandments as revealed to Moses on Mount Sinai. Jews regard the Old Testament of the Bible as both a record of their history and a statement of the obligations of Jewish life. Of special importance are the Bible's first five books (Genesis, Exodus, Leviticus, Numbers, and Deuteronomy), called the *Torah* (a word meaning "teaching" and "law"). In contrast to Christianity's central concern with personal salvation, Judaism emphasizes moral behaviour in this world.

Many religions promote literacy because they demand that followers study sacred texts. As part of their upbringing, most Islamic parents teach their children lessons from the Qur'an (Koran); later, the children will do the same for a new generation of believers.

Judaism has three main denominations. Orthodox Jews (including more than 1 million people in North America) strictly observe traditional beliefs and practices, wear traditional dress, segregate men and women at religious services, and eat only kosher foods. Such traditional practices set off Orthodox Jews from the larger society, making them sect-like. In the mid–nineteenth century, many Jews wanted to join in with the larger society, which led to the formation of the more churchlike Reform Judaism (now including more than 1.3 million people in North America). A third segment, Conservative Judaism (with about 2 million adherents in North America), has established a middle ground between the other two denominations.

Whatever the denomination, Jews share a cultural history of oppression as a result of prejudice and discrimination. A collective memory of centuries of slavery in Egypt, conquest by Rome, and persecution in Europe has shaped the Jewish identity. It was Jews in Venice, Italy, who first lived in an urban ghetto (this word comes, perhaps, from the Italian *borghetto*, meaning "settlement outside of the city walls"), and this residential segregation soon spread to other parts of Europe. Jewish immigration to North America began in the mid–1600s. The early immigrants who prospered were assimilated into largely Christian communities. But as larger numbers arrived at the end of the nineteenth century, prejudice and discrimination against Jews—commonly termed *anti-Semitism*—increased. In Canada, Jews

 Visit "Open Hearts, Closed Doors," a virtual museum that tells the stories of Jewish war orphans who came to Canada after World War II at www. virtualmuseum.ca/Exhibitions/orphans/english.

were not allowed to work in certain institutions, and others maintained quotas: for instance, there were quotas on the number of

Jewish students who were to be admitted to universities (Abella, 1989). During World War II, German Jewish refugees were refused admittance to Canada (Abella and Troper, 1982) when anti-Semitism reached a vicious peak and the Nazi regime in Germany systematically annihilated six million Jews.

Today, the social standing of Jews is well above average. The University of Toronto, in its *National Report '97*, announced the endowment of two chairs in Jewish studies, an innovative and comprehensive program that reflects the belief that "the study of Jewish culture and history is critical to the understanding of Western civilization" and highly relevant to a "young, multicultural country like Canada." Still, many Jews are concerned about the future of their religion because in the United States and Canada, only half the children growing up in Jewish households are learning Jewish culture and ritual, and more than half marry non-Jews (Eisen, 1983; Dershowitz, 1997; Van Biema, 1997; Keister, 2003).

HINDUISM

Hinduism is the oldest of all the world religions, originating in the Indus River valley about 4500 years ago. Today, there are about 800 million Hindus, which is 12 percent of the world's people. Global Map 19–3 shows that Hinduism remains an Eastern religion, mostly practised in India and Pakistan, but with a significant presence in southern Africa and Indonesia. Note, though, that these countries also have sizeable Muslim populations. Over the centuries, Hinduism and the culture of India have blended so that now one is not easily described apart from the other. This connection also explains why Hinduism—unlike Christianity, Islam, and Judaism—has not diffused widely to other nations. But with 1.5 million followers in North America, Hinduism is an important contributor to our cultural diversity.

Hinduism differs from most other religions in that it is not linked to the life of any single person. In addition, Hinduism envisions God as a universal moral force rather than a specific entity. For this reason, Hinduism (like other Eastern religions, as we shall show shortly) is sometimes described as an "ethical religion." Hindu beliefs and practices vary widely, but all Hindus believe that they have moral responsibilities, called *dharma*. Dharma, for example, calls people to observe the traditional caste system, described in Chapter 10 ("Social Stratification").

Another Hindu principle, *karma,* involves a belief in the spiritual progress of the human soul. To a Hindu, each action has spiritual consequences, and proper living results in moral development. Karma works through *reincarnation*, a cycle of death and rebirth by which a person is reborn into a spiritual

state corresponding to the moral quality of a previous life. Unlike Christianity and Islam, Hinduism recognizes no ultimate judgment at the hands of a supreme god. But in the ongoing cycle of rebirth, it may be said that people get what they deserve. For those who reach *moksha*, the state of spiritual perfection, the soul will no longer be reborn.

The case of Hinduism shows that not all religions can be neatly labelled as monotheistic or polytheistic. Hinduism is monotheistic in so far as it views the universe as a single moral system; yet Hindus see this moral force at work in every element of nature. Hindus connect to this moral force through their private meditation and rituals, which vary from village to village across the vast nation of India. Many also participate in public events, such as the *Kumbh Mela*, which every twelve years brings some 20 million pilgrims to bathe in the purifying waters of the sacred Ganges River. (The ashes of Mahatma Gandhi, an Indian Hindu with worldwide renown for his pacifism, were spread over the Ganges.)

Hinduism is not well understood in North America, although elements of Hindu thought have entered the "New Age" movement. Almost 2 million people in North America have Indian ancestry and the number of immigrants from India is rising; in Canada, the Indian community is comprised almost equally of Hindus and Sikhs. The Hindu and Sikh religions are similar in many respects—the belief in karma and rebirth, and their roots in India—but diverse in others. Importantly, their adherents form distinct communities in Canada.

BUDDHISM

About 2500 years ago, the rich culture of India gave rise to Buddhism. Today, some 350 million people (5% of humanity) are Buddhists, and almost all live in Asia. As shown in Global Map 19–4, Buddhists are a majority of the population in Myanmar (Burma), Thailand, Cambodia, and Japan. Buddhism is also widespread in India and China. Canada's Buddhist population is about the same size as the Hindu and Sikh populations: each of the three comprises about 1 percent of our population.

Buddhism has much in common with Hinduism: it recognizes no god of judgment, sees each daily action as having spiritual consequences, and believes in reincarnation. But like Christianity, Buddhism has its origins in the life of one person. Siddhartha Gautama was born to a high-caste family in Nepal in 563 B.C.E. Even as a young man, he was deeply spiritual. At the age of twenty-nine, he experienced a personal transformation, which led him to years of travel and meditation. By the end of this journey, he achieved what Buddhists describe as *bodhi*, or enlightenment. By gaining an understanding of the essence of life, Gautama became the Buddha (a Sanskrit word meaning "enlightened one"). Drawn by his personal charisma, followers spread the Buddha's teachings (the *dhamma*) throughout India. In the third century B.C.E., India's ruler became a Buddhist and sent missionaries throughout Asia, transforming Buddhism into a world religion.

WINDOW ON THE WORLD

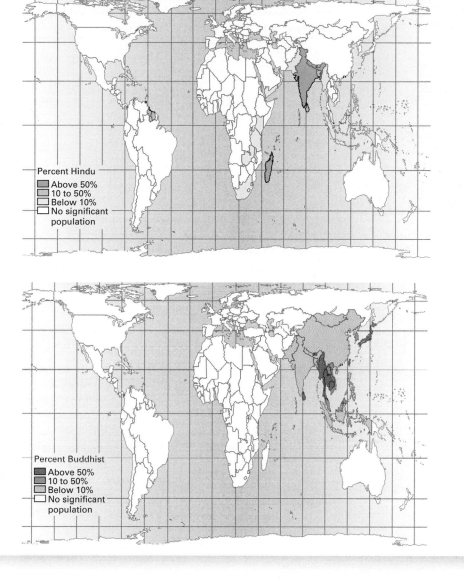

GLOBAL MAP 19–3

Hinduism in Global Perspective

Source: *Peters Atlas of the World* (1990).

GLOBAL MAP 19–4

Buddhism in Global Perspective

Source: *Peters Atlas of the World* (1990).

Buddhists believe that much of life involves suffering. This idea is rooted in the Buddha's own travels in a very poor society. But, the Buddha claimed, the solution to suffering is not wealth. On the contrary, a concern with money holds back spiritual development. Instead, the Buddha taught that we must use meditation to move beyond selfish concerns and desires. Only by quieting the mind can people connect with the power of the larger universe—the goal described as *nirvana*, a state of enlightenment and peace (Thomas, 1975; Van Biema, 1997; Eck, 2001).

CONFUCIANISM

From about 200 B.C.E. until the beginning of the twentieth century, Confucianism was a state church, the official reli-

gion of China. After the 1949 revolution, the communist government of the emergent People's Republic of China repressed all religious expression. But even today, hundreds of millions of Chinese are influenced by Confucianism. China is still home to Confucian thought, although Chinese immigration has spread this religion to other nations in Southeast Asia. Perhaps 100 000 followers of Confucius live in North America.

Confucius, whose Chinese name was K'ung-fu-tzu (i.e., Master K'ung), lived between 551 and 479 B.C.E. Like the Buddha, Confucius was deeply moved by people's suffering. The Buddha's response was sectlike—a spiritual withdrawal from the world. Confucius took a more churchlike approach, instructing his followers to engage

Great Britain's Prince Charles greets his guest, the Dalai Lama, the religious and political leader of the Tibetan people. The Dalai Lama, the best-known Buddhist teacher in the world, received the Nobel Peace Prize in 1989 for his efforts to liberate his people from Chinese control through nonviolent means.

TABLE 19–1

Religious Affiliation for Canada's Largest Religions, Percentage of Population in 2001

Religion	Percentage
Roman Catholic	43.2
United Church	9.6
Anglican	6.9
Baptist	2.5
Lutheran	2.0
Muslim	2.0
Presbyterian	1.4
Pentecostal	1.2
Jewish	1.1
Buddhist	1.0
Hindu	1.0
Sikh	0.9
Greek Orthodox	0.7
Mennonite	0.6
Jehovah's Witnesses	0.5
No Religion	16.2

Source: Adapted by L.M. Gerber from Statistics Canada, Census 2001, Highlight tables at www.statcan.ca.

the world according to a code of moral conduct. In the same way that Hinduism became part of the Indian way of life, Confucianism became linked to the traditional culture of China. A central idea of Confucianism is *jen*, meaning "humaneness." In practice, this means that always placing moral principle above self-interest, looking to tradition for guidance in how to live. In the family, Confucius taught, each must be loyal and considerate. For their part, families must remember their duties towards the larger community. In this model, layers of moral obligation unite society as a whole.

Of all world religions, Confucianism stands out as lacking a clear sense of the sacred. Perhaps Durkheim would have said that Confucianism is the celebration of the sacred character of society itself. Others might call Confucianism less a religion than a model of disciplined living. However you look at it, Confucianism shares with religion a body of beliefs and practices that seek moral goodness and social harmony (Schmidt, 1980; McGuire, 1987; Ellwood, 2000).

RELIGION: EAST AND WEST

You may already have noticed two general differences between the belief systems of Eastern and Western societies. First, religions that arose in the West (Christianity, Islam, Judaism) have a clear focus on God. Eastern religions (Hinduism, Buddhism, Confucianism), however, tend to be ethical codes; they make less clear-cut distinctions between the sacred and the profane.

Second, followers of Western religions join together in congregations, worshipping together in a special place at a regular time. Followers of Eastern religions, by contrast, express their religion in their daily lives. Temples do exist, but they are used by individuals rather than groups according to no special schedule. In a country like Japan, temples are as likely to be filled with tourists as with worshipers.

These two differences are important, but they do not overshadow a common element of all religions: a call to move beyond selfish everyday concerns in pursuit of a higher moral purpose. Religions may take different paths to this goal, but they all encourage a spiritual sense that there is more to life than what we see around us.

The Ontario Consultants on Religious Tolerance offer an extensive library on different faiths and on controversial religious topics (from abortion to homosexuality to female clergy) at www.religioustolerance.org.

Religion in Canada

Given that Canada is often depicted as a *secular*, or nonreligious, society, it may surprise some of you to learn that 84 percent of Canadians tell pollsters that they believe in God. Furthermore, 67 percent say that "my religious faith is very important to my day-to-day life," and 69 percent believe in the resurrection of Jesus Christ (Bricker and Wright, 2005). Pointing to significant decline in religious service attendance (Bibby 1995: 2004), scholars continue to debate the extent and depth of our religiosity. While some claim that religion remains central to our way of life, others conclude that the decline of the traditional family and the growing importance of science are weakening religious faith.

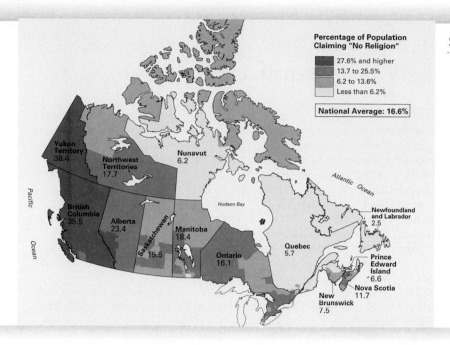

Percentage of Population
Claiming "No Religion"

27.6% and higher
13.7 to 25.5%
6.2 to 13.6%
Less than 6.2%

National Average: 16.6%

Yukon Territory 38.4
Northwest Territories 17.7
Nunavut 6.2
British Columbia 35.5
Alberta 23.4
Saskatchewan 15.5
Manitoba 18.4
Ontario 16.1
Quebec 5.7
Newfoundland and Labrador 2.5
Prince Edward Island 6.6
Nova Scotia 11.7
New Brunswick 7.5

Pacific Ocean
Atlantic Ocean
Hudson Bay

SEEING OURSELVES
CANADA MAP 19-1

Canadians Claiming "No Religion" (by Province, Territory, and Census Subdivision), 2001

Source: Calculations by L.M. Gerber based on data from Statistics Canada, "Religions in Canada," Catalogue No. 93-319.

RELIGIOUS AFFILIATION

The Canadian census shows that 84 percent of us—compared to 85 percent of Americans—identify with a religion. The same proportion of Canadians claims belief in God (Bibby, 2004a). We are 78 percent Christian (Catholic and Protestant), the largest non-Christian category being Muslim (2% of the population). Canada Map 19-1 shows the distribution of people claiming "no religion" across Canada, increasing from east to west to over 35 percent in British Columbia and the Yukon.

RELIGIOSITY

Religiosity is *the importance of religion in a person's life.* Exactly how religious we are depends on precisely how the concept is operationalized. Clearly, the question "How religious are we?" has no easy answer: weekly attendance at religious services is down to 20 percent of the Canadian population, yet 84 percent of us say we believe in God—and 45 percent of us pray daily (Bricker and Wright, 2005:80, 84).

If asked, most of you would assume that Americans are much more religious than Canadians. Right? Certainly that's what the media would lead us to expect. In the 1940s, weekly church attendance in Canada "was over 60% while U.S. attendance was closer to 40%. Now U.S. attendance is still around 40%, while ours is half that" (Bricker and Wright, 2005:80). Actually, NORC (2003) puts the current American figure at 30 percent. If you were to measure religiosity by church attendance, 20 percent weekly attendance would suggest that religion in Canada is almost dead and 30 percent in the United States places American religion just behind Canada's on that downward spiral. But 81 percent of Canadians told Ipsos-Reid pollsters that "you

don't need to go to church to be a good Christian" (Bricker and Wright:80). In other words, Canadians measure religiosity by more than attendance at church services.

The fact that 84 percent of us (and 85% of Americans) identify with a religion may mean little—but the fact that 45 percent of us (and 56% of Americans) pray daily is *highly*

Take the "What's your spiritual type?" quiz at www.beliefnet.com/section/quiz/index.asp?sectionID=&surveyID=27.

significant. People who pray daily take their religion very seriously—even if they do not attend services—so, depending on the measure you use, you could argue for religious decline or renaissance in Canada. For more on this topic, go to the Applying Sociology box (on p. 506).

On another level, religion *appears* to be much more important to Americans than to Canadians. American politicians—Bill Clinton, Al Gore, George Bush, to name a few—make frequent references to God and their own religious practices; prayer breakfasts are common. Although Canadian politicians are known to have prayer breakfasts from time to time, they generally downplay their religious beliefs—as Stephen Harper did when he tried to broaden

Read "Religion in Canada: Its Development and Contemporary Situation" at www.as.wvu.edu/coll03/relst/are/o'toole.html.

the appeal of the new Conservative party. Part of the difference in appearances stems from the fact that Canadians are more private about their faith (Lachaine, 2006). For example, it was only after the death of Pierre Elliott Trudeau that we learned he was a devout Roman Catholic (Krauss, 2003); according to Margaret Trudeau, he spent his last days talking about his death and resurrection, which he believed would reunite him with his son Michel and his parents (Bibby, 2004b:127).

APPLYING SOCIOLOGY
Religion in Canada: Decline or Renaissance?

Reginald Bibby (1995) points out that, for the overall population of Canada, weekly attendance at religious services dropped off dramatically (from 60% to 25%) between 1945 and 1995. The decline has been particularly dramatic for Roman Catholics in Quebec and mainline Protestant churches (United, Anglican, Presbyterian, and Lutheran) in the rest of the country. In 1995, weekly attendance was least common in Quebec and British Columbia (19% and 21%, respectively) and highest in the Atlantic region (38%). By 2000, weekly attendance had dropped to 22 percent (Bibby, 2004a), or 20 percent according to Ipsos-Reid polling (Bricker and Wright, 2005)—compared to 30 percent among Americans (NORC, 2003).

Michael Adams (2003, 2005), president of the polling firm Environics, carried out extensive research comparing values and social trends in Canada and the United States—revealing, through very sophisticated analysis, increasing divergence of values. Adams notes religious revival and fervour in the United States, a decline in religiosity (i.e., secularization) in Canada—and even different purposes and meanings of Canadian and American religiosity. In *Fire and Ice* (2003:186), Adams argues that, in Canada, religion is perceived as a means of "confronting the mysterious aspects of our lives" and honouring "the great imponderables of existence." In the United States, religion is the "source of strong moralist narratives and strict rules for personal conduct, [the] end of dialogue, not its beginning." Religion, as the Americans know it, is clearly dead in Canada.

In two recent books, *Restless Churches* (2004a) and *Restless Gods* (2004b), Reginald Bibby argues that the secularization thesis has been over-

stated and that there is real potential for significant religious renaissance or renewal in Canada. On the basis of longitudinal research on religion in Canada, Bibby notes that, despite declining attendance, 84 percent of Canadians identify with a religion. In addition, 81 percent believe God exists, 73 percent have spiritual needs, 68 percent believe in life after death, 47 percent have experienced God's presence, and 47 percent pray at least weekly. In a neat analysis of "Religious Nones" (the 16 percent who declare no religion), Bibby reveals that membership in the "None" category is often temporary; furthermore, significant proportions believe in God, sometimes pray or attend church, and would consider more involvement in religious groups under certain conditions.

From Bibby's perspective, the mainline Christian churches (the Christian monopoly) can be optimistic. Very few people switch religious identities—and, if they do, they switch from one of the small religions (e.g., Jewish or Muslim) to Christianity (i.e., assimilation). People are also unlikely to switch between Christian categories. The "growth" of fundamentalist or evangelical churches is no widespread revival, as they have been singularly unsuccessful in gaining converts. Their growth stems from their ability to retain children and geographically mobile members. Fundamentalists made up 8 percent of the Canadian population from 1871 to 2001, meaning their church growth kept pace with population growth. Since evangelical churches have the highest attendance levels, and their members are more public about their faith than other Canadians (on television and in person), they are highly visible and thus *appear* to be taking over. If the Catholic and mainline Protestant

churches can figure out how to gather their own "dropouts" back into the fold *and* hold on to their children, they can generate a renaissance.

To project future attendance, Frank Jones (2000) uses data from the National Longitudinal Survey of Children and Youth (1994–95) to look at religious observance among Canadian children under age twelve. He found that 23 percent of Canada's children attend religious services weekly—a level that is consistent with that in the total population—and 36 percent attend at least once a month. Jones points out that regular attendance among children varies by age, sex, region, and religious affiliation. Children in Atlantic Canada had the highest weekly or monthly attendance rate (52%), those in Quebec, the lowest (19%). If the mainline Christian churches could hold on to these children (and later *their* children), a modest revival would be under way.

Three recent polls pegged adult weekly attendance rates at 30 percent, 26 percent, and 27 percent, bringing us very close to the American 30 percent noted above. Bibby concludes: "Think of it: one in four Canadian adults in services on any given weekend… some five million people— plus lots of kids. There is no other group activity in Canada that begins to compare with such a level of involvement" (2004a:23).

WHAT DO YOU THINK?

1. Were you under the impression that the fundamentalists or evangelicals were taking over?
2. Are you surprised to learn that American weekly attendance rates are currently only slightly higher than ours?
3. Do you see any signs of religious revival among the people you know?

YOUR TURN

Would our society be better or worse if Canadians were more religious? Explain your answer.

RELIGION: CLASS AND ETHNICITY

Religious affiliation is related to a number of other factors, including social class, ethnicity, and race.

Social Class

Historically, Canada has been stratified along religious lines. By and large, Protestants with high social standing are people of northern European background. Members of the Anglican Church, and later the other establishment Protestant churches, have long been among Canada's most affluent, powerful people. Anglophone political and economic dominance, and traditional Catholic doctrine, kept Catholics in Quebec subordinate and poor.

Jews in Canada command unexpectedly high social standing, considering that they often contend with anti-Semitism; the reason for this achievement is mostly cultural, since Jewish tradition places great value on education and achievement. While a large proportion of Jews began life in North America in poverty, many—but certainly not all—improved their social position over time while ensuring the success of subsequent generations.

Although income is only one dimension of social class, the ranking of various religious categories by income in Table 19–2 shows that stratification along religious lines is still with us. Jews have the highest average income, while members of the United Church, Anglicans, Presbyterians, and Lutherans also earn above-average incomes. Members of all other religions, including Christian fundamentalists and Roman Catholics, fall below the Canadian average. Despite massive changes in Canada's population after World War II, the old relationship between religion and economic well-being persists.

Ethnicity

Throughout the world, religion is tied to ethnicity, mostly because a single religion stands out in specific countries or geographic regions. Islam predominates in the Arab societies of the Middle East, Hinduism is fused with the culture of India, and Confucianism runs deep in Chinese society. Christianity and Judaism do not follow this pattern; while these religions are mostly Western, Christians and Jews are found all over the world.

Religion and national identity come together in Canada as well. We have, for example, Anglo-Saxon Protestants, Irish Catholics, Russian Jews, and Greek Orthodox adherents. This linking of nation and creed results from the influx of immigrants from nations with a single major religion, or from societies where large numbers of a particular religious group emigrated, perhaps to escape persecution. Still, nearly every ethnic category displays some religious diversity. People of English ancestry, for instance, may be Protestants, Roman Catholics, Jews, or followers of other religions.

TABLE 19–2

Average Income by Selected Religious Affiliations, 1991

Religion	Average Income
Jewish	$34 488
United	24 096
Anglican	24 088
Presbyterian	23 668
No religion	22 536
Lutheran	22 365
Roman Catholic	20 523
Baptist	20 311
Greek Orthodox	17 863
Mennonite	17 691
Pentecostal	16 756
Jehovah's Witness	15 509
Canadian average	21 524

Source: Analysis by L.M. Gerber from Statistics Canada 1991 Census, Individual Public Use Microdata.

Religion in a Changing Society

All social institutions evolve over time. Just as the economy, politics, and the family have changed over the course of the past century, so has our religious life.

SECULARIZATION

Secularization is *the historical decline in the importance of the supernatural and the sacred.* Secularization (from Latin, meaning "the present age") is commonly associated with modern, technologically advanced societies in which science is the major way of understanding.

Secularization was at the core of the Quiet Revolution in Quebec during the 1960s. The Catholic Church—which had administered welfare, health care, and education in addition to dealing with the spiritual needs of Quebec society—lost influence on the religious front, while giving up its social service involvement to the provincial government. Today, Canadians are more likely to experience the transitions of birth, illness, and death in the presence of physicians (with scientific knowledge) than of religious leaders (whose knowledge is based on faith). This shift alone suggests that religion's relevance to our everyday lives has declined. Harvey Cox explains:

The world looks less and less to religious rules and rituals for its morality or its meanings. For some, religion provides a hobby, for others a mark of national or ethnic identification, for still others an aesthetic delight. For relatively few does it provide an inclusive and commanding system of personal and cosmic values and explanations (1971 [orig. 1965]:3).

If Cox is right, should we expect religion to disappear some day? Most sociologists say no. As noted above, the vast majority of people in Canada and the United States still say they believe in God, and about half of us claim to pray each day. In addition, 84 or 85 percent of Canadians and Americans claim a religious identification or affiliation. Canadian society is not on the road to complete secularization. While church attendance has declined, other measures of our beliefs suggest that religion is alive and well—or even undergoing a renaissance (Bibby, 2004a, 2004b).

Whether religious change is good or bad is open to debate. Conservatives tend to see any weakening of religion as a mark of moral decline. Progressives view secularization as liberation from the all-encompassing belief systems of the past, giving people more choice in their beliefs. Secularization has also helped bring the practices of some religious organizations—such as ordaining only men—into line with widespread social attitudes that support greater gender equality.

According to the secularization thesis, religion should weaken in high-income nations as people enjoy higher living standards and greater security. A global perspective shows that this thesis holds for the countries of Western Europe, where most measures of religiosity have declined and are now low. But in the United States—the richest country of all—religion remains strong and may even be getting stronger. Canada, which falls between Europe and the United States on so many measures, may be closer to the Americans on the religious front than many of us realize.

CIVIL RELIGION

One dimension of secularization is the rise of **civil religion** (Robert Bellah, 1975), *a quasi-religious loyalty binding individuals in a basically secular society.* In other words, while some dimensions of formal religion are weakening, our patriotism and citizenship retain many religious qualities. Canada is a case in point. Just as religion presents a blueprint for leading a good life, a vast majority of people in Canada believe that their political, economic, and medical systems exemplify what is good, and that life in Canada is the best in the world. Civil religion also involves a wide range of rituals, from rising to sing the national anthem at sporting events to holding elections or hearing the Speech from the Throne. At such events, the Canadian flag—like the Christian cross or the Jewish Star of David—serves as a sacred symbol of our national identity that we treat with reverence. Civil religion is not a specific religious doctrine. It does, however, incorporate many elements of traditional religion into the political system of a secular society.

"NEW AGE" SEEKERS: SPIRITUALITY WITHOUT FORMAL RELIGION

December 29, Machu Picchu, Peru. We are ending the first day exploring this magnificent city built by the Inca people high in the Andes Mountains. Lucas, a local shaman, or religious leader, is leading a group of twelve travelers in a ceremony of thanks. He kneels on the dirt floor of the small stone building and places offerings—corn and beans, sugar, plants of all colours, and even bits of gold and silver—in front of him as gifts to Mother Earth as he prays for harmony, joy, and the will to do good for one another. His words and the magic of the setting make the ceremony very moving. [John J. Macionis]

In recent decades, an increasing number of people are seeking spiritual development outside of established religious organizations, leading some analysts to conclude that we are becoming a *postdenomination society.* In simple terms, more people seem to be spiritual seekers, believing in a vital spiritual dimension to human existence that they pursue more or less separately from membership in any formal denomination.

What exactly is the difference between this focus on spirituality and a traditional concern with religion? One analysis (Cimino and Lattin, 1999:62) comments that spirituality is

> the search for... a religion of the heart, not the head. It's a religious expression that downplays doctrine and dogma, and revels in direct experience of the divine—whether it's called the "holy spirit" or "divine consciousness" or "true self." It's practical and personal, more about stress reduction than salvation, more therapeutic than theological. It's about feeling good rather than being good. It's as much about the body as the soul.

Millions North Americans take part in a spirituality movement referred to as "New Age"; its adherents are called seekers. The anthropologist and spiritual teacher Hank Wesselman (2001:39–42) identifies five core values that define this approach:

- **Seekers believe in a higher power.** There exists a higher power, a vital force that is within all things and all people. Humans, then, are partly divine.
- **Seekers believe we're all connected.** Everything and everyone is interconnected as part of a universal divine pattern.
- **Seekers believe in a spirit world.** The physical world is not all there is; a more important spiritual reality (or "spirit world") also exists.
- **Seekers want to experience the spirit world.** Spiritual development means gaining the ability to experience the

New Age "seekers" are people in pursuit of spiritual growth, often using the age-old technique of meditation. The goal of this activity is to quiet the mind so that, by moving away from everyday concerns, one can hear an inner, divine voice. Countless people attest to the spiritual value of meditation; it has also been linked to improved physical health.

spirit world. Many seekers come to understand that helpers and teachers who dwell in the spirit world can and do touch their lives.

- **Seekers pursue transcendence**. Various techniques (such as yoga, meditation, and prayer) give people an increasing ability to rise above the immediate physical world (i.e., through the experience of "transcendence"), which is seen as the larger purpose of life.

From a traditional point of view, this New Age concern with spirituality may seem more like psychology than religion (Tucker, 2002). Yet, like civil religion, it is a new form of religious interest in the modern world.

YOUR TURN

Can you see elements of both Western and Eastern religions in New Age spirituality? Explain.

RELIGIOUS REVIVAL: "GOOD OLE-TIME RELIGION"

At the same time New Age spirituality is becoming more popular, a great deal of change has been going on in the world of organized religion. In the United States, membership in liberal mainstream denominations (such as Episcopalian and Presbyterian) has declined steadily since 1960. During the same period, affiliation with more conservative religious organizations (including the Mormons, the Seventh-day Adventists, and especially Christian sects) has risen steadily. In Canada, between 1981 and 1991,

Presbyterian membership decreased by 22 percent, United Church by 18 percent, Anglican and Lutheran by 10 percent, and Baptist by 5 percent. In the meantime, most of the smaller, often evangelical, denominations grew significantly. Secularization itself may be self-limiting so that, as churchlike organizations become more worldly, people abandon them in favour of sectlike religious communities that offer a more intense religious experience (Stark and Bainbridge, 1981). More recently, Bibby (2004a, 2004b) notes the potential for religious renaissance not only among fundamentalist but also mainstream churches.

RELIGIOUS FUNDAMENTALISM

Fundamentalism is *a conservative religious doctrine that opposes intellectualism and worldly accommodation in favour of restoring traditional, otherworldly religion*. In the United States, fundamentalism has made the greatest gains among Protestants; Southern Baptists, for example, are the largest religious community in that country. But fundamentalism has also grown among Jews (i.e., Orthodox) and Catholics (i.e., Opus Dei).

Canada has fundamentalists, or evangelicals, among Baptists and Lutherans; Pentecostals are evangelical, as are most of the megachurches (like the one discussed in the opener to this chapter) that have popped up all over the country. The Peoples' Church in Toronto, with a congregation of almost 3000, is an example of an *old* evangelical megachurch; it already had a congregation of 2000 or more in the 1960s. An interesting thing about evangelical churches is that they made up 8 percent of our population in 1871, 8 percent in 1951, and 8 percent in 2001 (Bibby,

2004a:39). As you can see in the Applying Sociology box (on p. 506), their secret is being able to hold onto their children. Their numbers have grown in proportion to the increase in Canada's population.

In response to what they see as the growing influence of science and the weakening of the conventional family, religious fundamentalists defend what they call "traditional values." As they see it, liberal churches are simply too open to compromise and change. Religious fundamentalism is distinctive in five ways (Hunter, 1983, 1985, 1987):

- **Fundamentalists take the words of sacred texts literally.** Fundamentalists insist on a literal reading of sacred texts such as the Bible to counter what they see as excessive intellectualism among more liberal religious organizations. For example, fundamentalist Christians believe that God created the world in seven days precisely as described in the biblical book of Genesis.

- **Fundamentalists reject religious pluralism.** Fundamentalists believe that tolerance and relativism water down personal faith; therefore, they maintain that their religious beliefs are true and other beliefs are not.

- **Fundamentalists pursue the personal experience of God's presence.** In contrast to the worldliness and intellectualism of other religious organizations, fundamentalism seeks a return to "good old-time religion" and spiritual revival. To fundamentalist Christians, being "born again" and having a personal relationship with Jesus Christ should be evident in a person's everyday life.

- **Fundamentalists oppose "secular humanism."** Fundamentalists think accommodation to the changing world weakens religious faith. They reject "secular humanism," our society's tendency to look to scientific experts rather than God for guidance about how to live. There is nothing new in this tension between science and religion; it has existed for several centuries, as the Thinking it Through box (on p. 512) explains.

- **Many fundamentalists endorse conservative political goals.** Although fundamentalism tends to back away from worldly concerns, some fundamentalist leaders have entered politics to oppose what they call the "liberal agenda," including feminism and gay rights. Fundamentalists oppose abortion and gay marriages, support the traditional two-parent family, seek a return to prayer in schools, and criticize the mass media for colouring stories with a liberal bias. In Canada, these were elements of the "hidden agenda" that the Canadian Alliance was accused of carrying into the federal elections of 2004 and 2006.

Opponents regard fundamentalism as rigid and self-righteous. But many people find in fundamentalism, with its greater religious certainty and emphasis on the emotional experience of God's presence, an appealing alternative to the more intellectual, tolerant, and worldly "mainstream" denominations (Marquand, 1997).

Which religions are fundamentalist? In recent years, the world has become familiar with an extreme form of fundamentalist Islam that is intolerant of other beliefs and even supports violence against Western cultures and people. In North America, the term is most correctly applied to conservative Christian organizations in the evangelical tradition, including Pentecostals, Southern Baptists, Seventh-day Adventists, and Assemblies of God.

THE ELECTRONIC CHURCH

In contrast to small village congregations of years past, some religious organizations—especially fundamentalist ones—have become electronic churches featuring "prime-time preachers" (Hadden and Swain, 1981). Electronic religion in the United States has propelled Oral Roberts, Pat Robertson, and others to greater prominence than all but a few clergy in the past. Canadian "televangelists" David Mainse and Terry Winter, true to the "Canadian personality," are relatively low-key and have exhibited fewer public "sins" (Bibby, 1987:34–36). In Canada, about 5 percent of the national television audience regularly tunes in to religious television. Moreover, the majority of people who watch religious programs on television are also regular churchgoers—with almost 80 percent church attendance either weekly (68%) or monthly (11%). Recently, an increasing number of religious organizations are using computer technology to spread their message, a trend that Pope John Paul II termed the "new evangelism." The Media Perspectives box (on p. 511) deals in part with finding God online.

Visit the Monastery of Christ in the Desert at www.christdesert.org.

Looking Ahead: Religion in the Twenty-First Century

The popularity of media ministries, the rapid growth of religious fundamentalism, and the continuing adherence of millions more people to mainstream churches show that religion will remain a major institution of modern society. Moreover, high levels of immigration from many religious countries (Asia, Africa, the Caribbean, and elsewhere) will intensify and diversify the religious character of Canadian society in the decades to come.

In addition, the pace of social change is accelerating. As the world becomes more complex, rapid change seems to outstrip our capacity to make sense of it all. But, rather than undermining religion, this process fires the religious imagination of people who seek a sense of religious community and ultimate meaning in life. Tensions between the spiritual realm of religion and the secular world of science and

MEDIA PERSPECTIVES
Check the Media: Religion is Hot!

Six hundred years ago in mediaeval Europe, face-to-face contact was required for transmitting religious ideas: clerics gathered in universities or monasteries to study, later transmitting their knowledge to the masses attending religious services. Bibles and other sacred texts, hand copied by monks, were rare, until Johann Gutenberg, a German inventor, built a movable-type press and published the first printed book—a Bible—in 1456. Within fifty years, millions of books were in print across Europe, most of them about religious matters. Printing of the Bible, the Qur'an (Koran), and other religious texts put the word of God into the hands of virtually anyone—not just the clergy, religious leaders, or scholars. Without printed Bibles, the Protestant Reformation would not have occurred.

In the twentieth century, radio (beginning in the 1920s) and television (after 1950) extended the reach of religious leaders, who founded "media congregations" no longer confined to buildings. There was a time when *100 Huntley Street* was a radio program aired only in Toronto; now it is the flagship show for the Crossroads Television System, founded by evangelist David Mainse, which broadcasts religious and family programming from its headquarters in Burlington, Ontario. This is only one of the many radio and television stations that air religious programming throughout Canada. Many listeners and viewers attend services regularly, but others may have no religious affiliation,

or mobility problems that make it impossible for them to attend services in person. In short, electronic communication has created what Marshall McLuhan might have called a "church without walls," allowing "live" programming to enter our homes though instant communication.

Today, we have access to a wide range of books (e.g., *Restless Gods* as well as *Restless Churches* by Canadian sociologist, Reginald Bibby) and magazines dealing with religion. Newspapers keep tabs on religious developments—like the spread of evangelical megachurches, the decline of religion in a secular not-American Canada, or the decline of organized religion with the persistence of faith or spirituality. In fact, a pervasive newspaper debate revolves around whether religion is in decline or renaissance. One of the most watched movies of 2004 was Mel Gibson's *Passion of the Christ*, which portrays the final days before and the crucifixion of Jesus. And Dan Brown's books, *The Da Vinci Code* and *Angels & Demons*, have sold millions of copies worldwide in multiple languages—despite the fact that the Catholic Church, Opus Dei, and other religious leaders oppose them. Kathy Reich's *Cross Bones* picks up on a similar theme. However disturbing these books might be to the Christian establishment, they deal with basic religious issues.

It takes only a few minutes online to discover that religion is alive and well on the internet. You can find electronic Bibles, a proverb a day, and

prophecies, as well as announcements of events, products, publications, and conventions. Chat groups, university or college courses, monthly magazines, and prayer groups provide opportunities for active religious participation. Today, hundreds of thousands of websites offer messages from established churches, obscure cults, and New Age organizations.

With more information out there than ever before, some analysts anticipate a new postdenominational age in which religious ideas are no longer bound by particular organizations. Electronic information technology may also usher in an age of "cyberchurches." Television has already shown that it can transmit the personal charisma and spiritual message of religious leaders to ever-larger audiences. Perhaps the internet will create "virtual" congregations, larger than any before.

WHAT DO YOU THINK?

1. More and more religious organizations are using the internet to spread their messages. Do you think this will strengthen or weaken religion?
2. Are you attuned to media coverage of religious issues? Is it because you are religious or spiritual? Are you just curious?
3. Have you read *The Da Vinci Code*? Why?

Source: Based on Ramo (1996), Bibby (2004a, 2004b), Adams (2005), Casey (2006) and Lachaine (2006).

technology will surely continue—as suggested in the Thinking It Through box (on p. 512).

But science is simply unable to provide answers to the most basic human questions about the purpose of our lives.

Moreover, new technology that can begin and sustain life confronts us with vexing moral dilemmas as never before. Against this backdrop of uncertainty, it is little wonder that many people rely on their faith for assurance and hope.

THINKING IT THROUGH
Does Science Threaten Religion?

About 400 years ago, the Italian physicist and astronomer Galileo (1564–1642) helped start the Scientific Revolution with some startling discoveries: dropping objects from the leaning Tower of Pisa, he derived laws of gravity; making his own telescope, he observed the stars and found that Earth orbited the sun. Galileo was challenged by the Roman Catholic Church, which had preached for centuries that Earth stood motionless at the centre of the universe. Galileo made matters worse by responding that religious leaders had no business talking about matters of science. Soon he found his work banned and himself under house arrest. As Galileo's treatment shows, from the start, science has had an uneasy relationship with religion.

Galileo would have been an eager observer of the famous "Scopes monkey trial," when science and religion clashed over the issue of creation. In 1925, the state of Tennessee put a small-town science teacher named John Thomas Scopes on trial for teaching Darwinian evolution in the local high school. Charles Darwin's master work, *On the Origin of Species*, states that humanity evolved from lower forms of life over billions of years. But this theory counters the biblical account of creation found in Genesis, which states that "God created the heavens and the earth," introducing life on the third day and, on the fifth and sixth days, animal life—including human beings fashioned in God's own image. Tennessee state law forbade teaching "any theory that denies the story of the Divine

Creation of man as taught in the Bible" and, in particular, the idea that "man descended from a lower order of animals." Scopes was found guilty and fined $100. His conviction was reversed on appeal, but the Tennessee law stayed on the books until 1967. A year later in *Epperson* v. *Arkansas*, the U.S. Supreme Court struck down all such laws as unconstitutional government support of religion.

Today—almost four centuries after Galileo was silenced—people still debate the apparently conflicting claims of science and religion. A third of American adults believe that the Bible is the literal word of God and reject any scientific findings that run counter to it (NORC, 2003:157). But a middle ground is emerging: half of Americans now accept the Bible as a book of truths inspired by God without being correct in a literal, scientific sense. That is, science and religion are different ways of understanding different questions.

While Galileo and Darwin devoted their lives to investigating *how* the natural world works, religion deals with *why* we and the natural world exist in

the first place. In 1992, a Vatican commission concluded that the church's silencing of Galileo was wrong. Most scientific and religious leaders now agree that science and religion represent important but different truths. Many also believe that today's rush to scientific discovery leaves our world in greater need of the moral guidance provided by religion.

But what do students think about religion, science, and the meaning of life? A survey of students at one small east coast university and one large urban campus in Ontario found that most students consider themselves to be religious (58%) and scientific (64%) (Campbell, 2005). Most also find themselves disagreeing with family or friends over religious and scientific issues (61% and 57%, respectively), while 84 percent think—often or sometimes—about the meaning of life. Significantly, 88 percent indicate that it is possible to be both religious and scientific. So questions of religion, science, and the meaning of life matter to students—and they can integrate all three in their lives.

WHAT DO YOU THINK?

1. Can a religious individual be an objective scientist?
2. Does the sociological study of religion challenge one's faith? Why?
3. Many people think scientific discovery is changing our lives too fast. Do you agree? Why?

Sources: Based on Gould (1981), Huchingson (1994), Applebome (1996) and Campbell (2005).

19 MAKING THE GRADE

The following learning tools will help you see what you know, identify what you still need to learn, and expand your understanding beyond the text. You can also visit this text's Companion Website™ at www.pearsoned.ca/macionis to find useful practice tests.

KEY *P*OINTS

Religion: Basic Concepts

Religion is a major social institution based on setting the sacred apart from the profane. Religion is grounded in faith rather than scientific evidence, and people express their religious beliefs through various rituals. Sociologists study how religion is linked to other social patterns but make no claims about the truth of any religious belief.

Theoretical Analysis of Religion

Durkheim explained that, through religion, we celebrate the power of our society. His structural-functional analysis suggests that religion promotes social cohesion and conformity, and gives meaning and purpose to life.

Using the symbolic-interaction approach, Peter Berger explains that we socially construct religious beliefs in the same way that we build all the reality we experience. We are especially likely to seek religious meaning when faced with life's uncertainties and disruptions.

Social-conflict analyst Karl Marx claimed that religion justifies the status quo. In this way, religion supports inequality and discourages change towards a more just and equal society.

Religion and Social Change

Max Weber argued, in opposition to Marx, that religion can encourage social change. He showed how Calvinism contributed to the rise of industrial capitalism. Liberation theology, a fusion of Christian principles and political activism, tries to encourage social change.

Types of Religious Organizations

Churches are religious organizations well integrated into their society. They fall into two categories: state churches and denominations.

Sects are the result of religious division and are marked by charismatic leadership and suspicion of the larger society.

Cults are religious organizations based on new and unconventional beliefs and practices.

Religion in History

Technologically simple societies were generally animistic, with religion existing only as a part of family life. In more complex agrarian or pastoral societies, religion emerges as a distinct social institution.

World Religions

Followers of six world religions—Christianity, Islam, Judaism, Hinduism, Buddhism, and Confucianism—represent three-quarters of all humanity. Western religions (Christianity, Islam, Judaism) share a focus on God and have well-defined congregations; Eastern religions (Hinduism, Buddhism, and Confucianism) tend to be ethical codes largely fused with the broader culture.

Religion in Canada

Canada can be described as an increasingly secular but still religious society. The operationalization of "religiosity" affects the picture. In Canada, 84 percent of adults identify with a religion, 45 percent pray daily, but only 20 percent attend religious services weekly. There is a debate in Canada dealing with the decline or revival of organized religion.

Religion in a Changing Society

Secularization is the historical decline in the importance of the supernatural and the sacred. Although some indicators of religiosity (like membership in mainstream churches) have declined throughout North America, others (membership in sects) have increased. Religious identification, belief in god and at least weekly prayer are almost equally common in Canada and the United States. Secularization is not bringing and end to religion. Nonetheless, in a more secular society, civil religion may take the form of quasi-religious patriotism that ties people to their society.

Spiritual seekers are part of the growing New Age movement that pursues spiritual development outside conventional religious organizations. Seekers believe in a higher power that links everything; they use meditation and prayer to move beyond the physical world to experience the spiritual world.

Also on the rise, worldwide, is fundamentalism, which opposes religious accommodation to the world. Fundamentalists take the words of religious texts literally and reject religious diversity as they pursue the personal experience of god's presence. In Canada, Christian evangelicals have long comprised about 8 percent of the population.

Religion: Looking Ahead

Some of the continuing appeal of religion lies in the inability of science to address timeless questions about the ultimate meaning of human existence.

KEY CONCEPTS

profane (p. 492) an ordinary element of everyday life

sacred (p. 492) set apart as extraordinary, inspiring awe and reverence

religion (p. 492) a social institution involving beliefs and practices based on recognizing the sacred

ritual (p. 493) formal, ceremonial behaviour

faith (p. 493) belief based on conviction rather than scientific evidence

totem (p. 493) an object in the natural world collectively defined as sacred

liberation theology (p. 495) the combining of Christian principles with political activism, often Marxist in character

church (p. 497) a type of religious organization that is well integrated into the larger society

state church (p. 497) a church formally allied with the state

denomination (p. 497) a church, independent of the state, that recognizes religious pluralism

sect (p. 497) a type of religious organization that stands apart from the larger society

charisma (p. 497) extraordinary personal qualities that can infuse people with emotion and turn them into followers

cult (p. 497) a religious organization that is largely outside a society's cultural traditions

animism (p. 498) the belief that elements of the natural world are conscious life forms that affect humanity

monotheism (p. 499) belief in a single divine power

polytheism (p. 499) belief in many gods

religiosity (p. 505) the importance of religion in a person's life

secularization (p. 507) the historical decline in the importance of the supernatural and the sacred

civil religion (p. 508) a quasi-religious loyalty binding individuals in a basically secular society

fundamentalism (p. 509) a conservative religious doctrine that opposes intellectualism and worldly accommodation in favour of restoring traditional, otherworldly religion

APPLICATIONS & EXERCISES

1. Some colleges are very religious; others are very secular. Investigate the place of religion on your campus. Is your school affiliated with a religious organization? Was it ever? Is there a chaplain or other religious official? See if you can learn from campus sources what share of students regularly attend any religious service.

2. Develop five questions that might be used on a questionnaire or in an interview to measure how religious people are. Present them to several people. Use the results to show that how religious people appear to be depends on exactly what questions you ask them.

3. Is religion getting weaker? To evaluate the claim that our society is undergoing secularization, go to the library or local newspaper office and obtain an issue of your local newspaper published 50 years ago and, if possible, one published 100 years ago. Compare the amount of attention to religious issues then and now.

PRENTICE HALL
mysoclab™
Where learning & the sociological imagination intersect.

To reinforce your understanding of this chapter, and to identify topics for further study, visit MySocLab at **www.pearsoned.ca/mysoclab/** for diagnostic tests and a multimedia ebook.

CHAPTER TWENTY

Education

How does economic development affect
a country's schools?

Why do we have serious problems in our schools?

Why is education an important dimension
of social inequality?

"If you're an Indian in your twenties living on a reserve, you need to leave *right now*." When *Globe and Mail* columnist John Ibbitson (2006) opened with those words, he raised many hackles—notably of readers, Aboriginal and non-Aboriginal, who oppose the forces of assimilation.

Ibbitson reached this conclusion after reading a study by Michael Mendelson of educational achievement among Aboriginal Canadians between the ages of 20 and 24: "those status Indians, non-status Indians, Métis, and Inuit who should just be completing their education." Among Canadians in general, 16 percent of those aged 20 to 24 have not completed high school. For status Indians living on reserve, that number is *58 percent*—or 3.6 times the Canadian rate, and there were no signs of improvement from the 1996 to 2001 census. The efforts made to improve educational outcomes on reserve have not worked; so, Ibbitson asserts, education systems have "utterly failed to rescue the latest generation of on-reserve [Aboriginal] Canadians."

There is a brighter side to this story. Young urban Aboriginal people have twice the high school completion rates of those on reserve, and Aboriginal students "who do finish high school have the same postsecondary completion rates as the general population." Furthermore, urban Aboriginal people have average incomes that are 80 percent of the average income of Torontonians, 77 percent of the average income of Montrealers, and 75 percent of the average income of Ottawa residents. However controversial Ibbitson's advice, one can see why he advises Aboriginal young people on reserves to "Pack your bags, say goodbye to your family and friends and get out of there.... Move to Toronto or Ottawa or Montreal. Find a job, any job, then get yourself back in school."

Most young people in Canada dream of higher education as the passport to good jobs. But, especially for people growing up in low-income, low-education families, the odds of getting to college or university are small. Who goes to on to postsecondary education in Canada? What is the impact of higher education on the type of job you get or the money you make later? This chapter answers these questions by focusing on **education**, *the social institution through which society provides its members with important knowledge, including basic facts, job skills, and cultural norms and values.* In high-income countries such as Canada, education is largely a matter of **schooling**, *formal instruction under the direction of specially trained teachers.*

Education: A Global Survey

Currently, Canadian young people spend most of their first eighteen years in school, but, in our distant past, the privilege of schooling was limited to a small elite. In the 1830s in Upper Canada, only half of the children attended school—and for an average of twelve months in total (Johnson, 1968:27). In low-income countries today—as in Upper Canada—the vast majority of people receive little or no schooling.

SCHOOLING AND ECONOMIC DEVELOPMENT

The extent of schooling in any society is tied to its economic development. In low- and middle-income countries—which are home to most of the world's people—families and communities teach young people important knowledge and skills. Formal schooling, and especially learning that is not directly connected to survival, is available mainly to wealthy people who do not need to work. After all, the Greek root of the word *school* means "leisure." In ancient Greece, famous teachers such as Socrates, Plato, and Aristotle taught aristocratic, upper-class men. The same was true in ancient China, where the famous philosopher K'ung-fu-tzu (Confucius) shared his wisdom with a privileged few.

In many low-income nations, girls are as likely to work as to attend school. In Afghanistan, under the strict rule of the Taliban, girls were all but absent from school. By the beginning of 2002, however, the picture was changing. Here we see girls at the Manu Chera school for girls in central Kabul completing a classroom assignment.

Today, the limited schooling that takes place in lower-income countries reflects the national culture. In Iran, for example, schooling is closely tied to Islam. Similarly, schooling in Bangladesh, Zimbabwe, and Nicaragua has been shaped by the distinctive cultural traditions of these nations. All lower-income countries have one trait in common when it comes to schooling: there is not very much of it. In the world's poorest nations (including several in Central Africa), only half of all children ever get to school; worldwide, only half of all children ever get to the secondary grades. As a result, about one-third of the world's people cannot read or write. Global Map 20–1 shows the extent of illiteracy around the world, and the following national comparisons illustrate the link between the extent of schooling and economic development.

SCHOOLING IN INDIA

India has recently become a middle-income country, but people there still earn only about 8 percent of U.S. average income, and most poor families depend on the earnings of children. Even though India has outlawed child labour, many children continue to work in factories weaving rugs or making handicrafts—up to 60 hours per week, which greatly limits their chances for schooling. Today, 81 percent of children in India complete primary school, typically in crowded schoolrooms where one teacher may face as many as 60 children (twice as many as in Canada). Less than half of Indian children go on to secondary school, and very few acquire postsecondary education. As a result, 39 percent of India's people can neither read nor write.

Patriarchy also shapes Indian education. Indian parents are joyful at the birth of a boy, because he and his future wife will both contribute income to the family. But there are economic costs to raising a girl: parents must provide a dowry (a gift of wealth to the groom's family) and, after her marriage, a daughter's work benefits her husband's family.

Therefore, as many Indians see less reason to invest in the schooling of girls, only 30 percent of girls (compared to 45% of boys) reach the secondary grades. So what do the girls do while the boys are in school? Most of the children working in Indian factories are girls—a family's way of benefitting from their daughters while they can (United Nations Development Programme, 1995).

SCHOOLING IN JAPAN

Schooling has not always been part of the Japanese way of life. Before industrialization brought mandatory education in 1872, only a privileged few attended school. Today, Japan's educational system is widely praised for producing some of the world's highest achievers. The early grades concentrate on transmitting Japanese traditions, especially a sense of obligation to family. Starting in their early teens, students take a series of difficult and highly competitive examinations. Scores on these written tests decide the future of all Japanese students.

More men and women graduate from high school in Japan (96%) than in Canada or the United States. But these competitive examinations allow just half of high school graduates—compared to 55 percent and 67 percent in Canada and the United States, respectively—to go on to postsecondary studies. Understandably, Japanese students and their parents take entrance examinations very seriously, and about half the students attend "cram schools" to prepare for them. Japanese schooling produces impressive results. In a number of fields, notably mathematics and science, Japanese students outperform students in every other high-income country.

SCHOOLING IN THE UNITED KINGDOM

During the Middle Ages, schooling was a privilege of the British nobility, who studied classical subjects, having little concern for the practical skills needed to earn a living. But

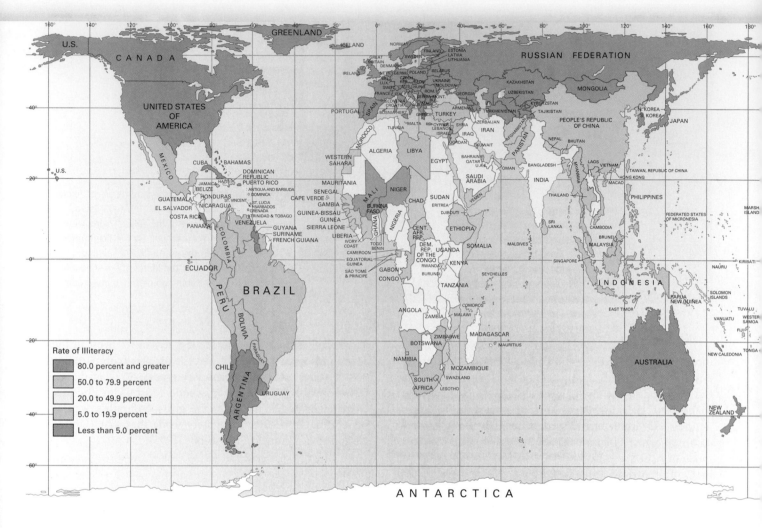

WINDOW ON THE WORLD

GLOBAL MAP 20-1 Illiteracy in Global Perspective

Reading and writing skills are widespread in high-income countries, where illiteracy rates generally are below 5 percent. In much of Latin America, however, illiteracy is more common, one consequence of limited economic development. In 22 nations—16 of them in Africa—illiteracy is the rule rather than the exception; there, people rely on the oral tradition of face-to-face communication rather than the written word.

Source: United Nations Development Programme (2005); map projection from *Peters Atlas of the World* (1990).

as the Industrial Revolution created a need for an educated labour force and, as working-class people demanded access to schools, a rising proportion of the population entered the classroom. The law now requires every child to attend school until age sixteen (a year longer in the Scottish system). Traditional class differences still affect schooling in the United Kingdom, with most wealthy families sending their children to *public schools*, which North Americans would refer to as private boarding schools. These elite schools enrol about 7 percent of British students and teach not only academic subjects but also the special patterns of speech, mannerisms, and social graces of the British upper class. Because these academies are very expensive, non-elite students in the United Kingdom attend state-supported day schools (Ambler and Neathery, 1999).

The UK has tried to reduce the importance of social background in schooling by expanding the university system and by linking admission to competitive entrance examinations. For those who score the highest, the government pays most of the costs. But many well-to-do children who do not score very well still manage to get in to Oxford or Cambridge, the most prestigious of its universities. Many "Oxbridge" graduates go on to positions at the top of the British power elite: more than two-thirds of the highest-ranking members of the government, for example, have "Oxbridge" degrees (Sampson, 1982; Gamble, *et al.*, 1993).

These brief sketches of schooling in India, Japan, and Britain show the crucial importance of economic development. In poor countries, many children—especially girls—work rather than go to school. Rich nations enact mandatory education laws to prepare an industrial workforce as well as to satisfy demands for greater equality. But a nation's history and culture still matter, as we see in the intense competition of Japanese schools, the traditional social stratification that shapes schools in the UK, and, in the next section, the practical emphasis found in Canadian schools.

SCHOOLING IN CANADA

Initial developments in education in what would later become Canada took place in the early French settlements, where the three Rs—in this case, reading, 'riting, and religion—were taught in church-controlled schools (Johnson, 1968). By 1636, the Jesuits had established a "*collège*" that eventually became Laval University, which claims to be North America's oldest institution of higher education. By 1668, a trade or vocational school had been established in St. Joachim. In the Maritimes, an Anglican academy established in 1785 became the University of New Brunswick in 1859. The earliest primary schools in Upper Canada, which were established in the 1780s, began receiving government funding in 1792. Elitist boarding schools started in 1807 were the first step in establishing a secondary school system.

Prior to confederation in 1867, governments in Canada had already created separate Catholic and Protestant school systems, embraced universal education and teacher training, and put texts and curricula under the control of a department of education. In 1883, Toronto became the second North American city to establish kindergarten within the school system and, by about 1920, Canada had compulsory education to the end of elementary school or

 Half a century of controversy over the role of religion in Canadian public schools is surveyed at http://archives.cbc.ca/300c.asp?id=1-69-97.

the age of sixteen in most provinces. (In the United States, all states had compulsory education by 1918.) In this period, secondary schools were being established and expanded across Canada. The principle of mass education had been firmly entrenched, partly in response to the requirements of the Industrial Revolution for a literate and skilled workforce.

It is important to note that *official* literacy and *functional* literacy are not the same. Although Canada claims to have minimal illiteracy by international standards, educators and others have long voiced concerns about the extent to which

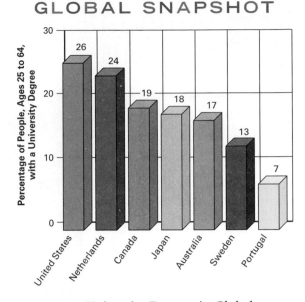

Percentage of People, Ages 25 to 64, with a University Degree

United States: 26
Netherlands: 24
Canada: 19
Japan: 18
Australia: 17
Sweden: 13
Portugal: 7

FIGURE 20-1 University Degrees in Global Perspective

Source: U.S. Census Bureau (2000).

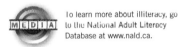 To learn more about illiteracy, go to the National Adult Literacy Database at www.nald.ca.

Canadians have the literacy and numeracy skills required to cope with daily living and work—to say nothing of academic pursuits. **Functional illiteracy** is *a lack of the reading and writing skills needed for everyday living.* Our Thinking it Through box (on p. 522) takes a close look at functional illiteracy in Canada.

The percentage of the population age 15 and older with university degrees rose from 6.4 percent in 1976 to 9.6 percent in 1986 and 13.3 percent in 1996. By 2001, 15.2 percent of adults had university degrees. In other words, over a 25-year period, the proportion of people over 15 with university degrees increased by 141 percent, or almost 1.5 times.

In Canada, the school reformers of the late 1800s were concerned that the "classical curriculum did not reflect the realities of the new economic order. Education, thus, came to be viewed as an essential precondition for national economic growth" (Gilbert, 1989:105). Wide participation and universality were important goals. Canada also has a policy of universal, publicly supported primary and secondary schooling, including that in the separate Catholic system. Canada has 273 publicly funded postsecondary institutions, 69 of which are classified as universities; tuition fees at our universities cover up to 30 percent of the costs, while government subsidies and fundraising account for the rest.

Canada ranks second to the United States and well above the average of 14 other high-income countries in the proportion of 20- to 24-year-olds enrolled in postsecondary education. We rank above the United States and below only Sweden in terms of public expenditures on education: 8 percent of our gross national product (Canada, 1992a). Figure 20–1 indicates, however, that Canada falls substantially behind

THINKING IT THROUGH

Functional Illiteracy: Must We Rethink Education?

Imagine being unable to read the labels on cans of food, the instructions for assembling a child's toy, the dosage on a medicine bottle, or even the information on your own paycheque. These are some of the debilitating experiences of functional illiteracy, reading and writing skills inadequate for carrying out everyday responsibilities.

According to the National Literacy Secretariat, only 63 percent of Canadians have sufficient literacy and numeracy skills to deal adequately with everyday tasks; an additional 22 percent have some problems; and about 15 percent have difficulty recognizing familiar words or doing simple addition and subtraction (Montigny, 1994:322). By 1994, another literacy survey revealed that the percentages in the two lower categories had increased to 25 percent and 22 percent, respectively. Canadians are not alone in this respect, though, for it is estimated that about 1 in 4 adults in the United States is functionally illiterate, and that the proportions are higher among the elderly and visible minorities.

Functional illiteracy is a complex social problem, caused partly by an educational system that passes children from one grade to the next whether they learn or not. Community indifference and parents who offer little encouragement to learn language skills also contribute.

Functional illiteracy costs the North American economy more than $100 billion a year, through decreased productivity (by workers who perform their jobs improperly) and increased accidents (by people unable to understand written instructions). It also reflects the costs of supporting those

Jacques Demers, former coach in the National Hockey League, admits in a biography, *En toutes lettres* (meaning "all spelled out" in English), that he is illiterate.

unable to read and write well enough to find work—possibly ending up on public assistance or in prison.

Correcting this national problem requires one approach for young people and another for adults. To stop functional illiteracy before it happens, the public must demand that children not graduate until they have learned basic language skills. For adults, the answer begins with diagnosis—a difficult task since many feel shame at their plight and avoid disclosure. Once such people are identified, however, effective adult education programs are required.

It should be noted that, in some cases, illiteracy is not an inability to read at all, but an inability to read in English or French. In all the countries participating in the International Adult Literacy Survey, immigrants are disproportionately represented in the lower literacy levels in the languages of the host countries (National Literacy

Secretariat, 2006). Canada has an active program teaching English as a second language to the constantly replenished body of immigrant schoolchildren and adults.

In November 2005, we learned that Jacques Demers never learned to read or write. Despite his handicap Demers led the Montreal Canadiens "to an unlikely Stanley Cup title in 1993. He also coached the Quebec Nordiques, the St. Louis Blues, the Detroit Red Wings, and the Tampa Bay Lightning" (CBC Sports, 2005). For all these positions, he managed to hide his disability from everyone but his wife. Demers explains that he did not learn to read or write in school: he grew up in an abusive home where his father routinely beat him and his mother, and he was so anxious all the time that he could not sleep or focus in school. When asked why he revealed his illiteracy at this point, he explained that he now feels free or liberated. Also, he wants parents to understand the damage done to children by abuse. Illiteracy is one of the potential disabilities caused by violence in the home.

WHAT DO YOU THINK?

1. Do you know anyone who is illiterate? How does it affect his or her life?
2. What does it take to succeed despite illiteracy? How could Demers have hidden this disability until now?
3. Do you see the lack of functional illiteracy as a significant social problem?

Sources: Based on Kozol (1980, 1985), Montigny (1994), National Literacy Secretariat (2006), CBC Sports (2005).

both the United States and the Netherlands in terms of the proportion of population aged 25 to 64 with university degrees.

Besides trying to make schooling more widely accessible, Canadian society has long favoured *practical* learning,

that is, education that has a direct bearing on people's lives, and especially on their occupations. The educational philosopher John Dewey (1859–1952) advanced the idea that children would readily learn information and skills they found useful. Rejecting the traditional emphasis on teaching a fixed body of knowledge to each generation of students, Dewey (1968; orig. 1938) endorsed progressive education that reflected people's changing concerns and needs. With the Quiet Revolution in Quebec in the 1960s, the classical education favoured by the religious elite was replaced by a system encouraging the study of business, engineering, and science.

Despite the overall trend towards applied or practical fields, Canada lags behind a number of other countries in terms of the proportion of its degrees awarded in engineering. In fact, in Canada the proportion of degrees granted in engineering—to men and women—is less than half that of Belgium, Portugal, Finland, Japan, Sweden, Germany, and Denmark (Oderkirk, 1993:10). The rapid pace of technological change in recent years shows up in a decline in the number of degrees granted in the social sciences, arts, and humanities, coupled with increases in

 Statistics Canada provides data on education at www.statcan.ca; click on Census, then "Search by topic," then "Education in Canada."

the areas of engineering, mathematics, and science. From 1994 to 1998—a very short period of time—the proportion of degrees granted in engineering and applied sciences increased from 7.1 to 7.5 percent; women earned 18.4 and 21.1 percent of those degrees in the two years, respectively. Similarly, the proportion of degrees granted in mathematics and physical sciences increased between 1994 and 1998 from 5.4 to 5.8 percent—with 29.9 and 31.2 percent, in those years respectively, being earned by women. Therefore, there is a clear but gradual shift towards engineering, mathematics, and science, coupled with increased representation of women.

The Functions of Schooling

Structural-functional analysis looks at ways in which formal education supports the operation and stability of society. We look briefly at five ways that this happens.

SOCIALIZATION

Technologically simple societies transmit their ways of life informally from parents to children. As societies become more technologically complex, young people need information and skills that family members can no longer provide. Other social institutions, specifically a formal education system, therefore play a greater role in socialization. In industrial societies, schooling requires specially trained personnel to convey the knowledge needed for adult roles.

In primary school, children learn basic language and mathematical skills. Secondary school builds on this foundation and, for many, college or university allows further specialization. In addition, schools transmit cultural values and norms. Sometimes the operation of the classroom itself serves to teach important cultural lessons. Where, in the United States, spelling bees and classroom drills are intended to foster competitive individualism, in Canada there is more emphasis on activities that encourage co-operation, sharing, and team effort. Competitiveness is

Educators have long debated the proper manner in which to educate children with disabilities. On the one hand, such children may benefit from distinctive facilities and specially trained teachers. On the other hand, they are less likely to be stigmatized as "different" if included in regular classroom settings. What do you consider to be the ramifications of the "special education" versus "inclusive education" debate for the classroom experience of all children, not only those who have disabilities?

actually discouraged in many Canadian classrooms because of potential damaging effects on the self-esteem of those who cannot compete successfully.

Nor is the political component of education as aggressively promoted in Canada as it is in other countries. For example, the American political system and way of doing business are commonly championed in the classroom, and rituals such as saluting the flag and singing "The Star-Spangled Banner" foster patriotism. While Canadian children do sing "O Canada," provincial and territorial educational systems place less emphasis on Canadian history or the workings of our political system than do American systems—and a consciousness of military purpose or presence is almost completely lacking here. Instead of espousing a unified cultural identity, our classrooms try to encourage respect for the many cultures that make up the Canadian mosaic.

CULTURAL INNOVATION

The faculty at colleges and universities create culture as well as pass it on to students. Research in the sciences, the social sciences, the humanities, and the fine arts leads to discovery and change in our way of life. For example, medical research at major universities has helped increase life expectancy, just as research by sociologists and psychologists helps us learn how to better enjoy our lives so we can take advantage of our longevity. Marshall McLuhan foresaw the radical cultural transformation and innovation that would accompany the use of the electronic media—specifically television and the computer—in education. Suddenly, he predicted, there would be classrooms without walls: teaching, educational content, and links with the wider world would change irrevocably. His insight is now our reality.

SOCIAL INTEGRATION

Schooling helps to forge a mass of people into a unified society. This integrative function is especially important in nations characterized by great social diversity. As we saw in Chapter 3 ("Culture"), Canada has had a long experience with the challenges of multiculturalism and linguistic dualism, and has tried—not always successfully—to foster Canadian nationalism while accommodating a wide variety of interest groups. As a result, our educational policies have been sensitive to the problems of maintaining equality of access and unity in the face of diversity. We have been reluctant to push a national identity because of Quebec's sensitivities and our embrace of the mosaic model (Jaenen, 1981).

Societies in the Americas, Africa, and Asia similarly strive to foster social integration through schooling. Normally, schools try to meet this challenge by establishing a common language to encourage broad communication and to forge a national identity. Of course, some ethnic minorities resist state-sponsored schooling precisely for this reason. In Canada, Hutterites, a culturally distinctive people, teach their children within their colonies; they use the Alberta provincial curriculum and speak in English for part of the day, but continue to speak their German dialect within their communities. Québécois perceive a threat to their distinct culture, resent the need to learn English for economic survival, and insist on full provincial control of education; Quebec has declared itself a unilingual province and, only under special circumstances, can a child be educated in English there. Aboriginal peoples in Canada have been struggling as well to establish greater control of their own schools. In each of the above cases, the peoples in question resist formal schooling in the language of the majority because of very real threats to linguistic and cultural survival.

While there is understandable resistance to majority-controlled schooling by certain segments of the population, the striking cultural diversity of our country increases the importance of formal education as a path to social integration. The expansion of educational facilities and the enactment of mandatory education laws coincided with the arrival of hundreds of thousands of immigrants from a wide variety of origins who somehow had to be transformed into Canadians. Even today, formal education plays a major role in integrating disparate groups, as immigrants from Asia (roughly 50 percent of recent immigrants), the Caribbean, Eastern Europe, and Latin America, as well as roughly 30 000 refugees a year blend their traditions with the existing cultural mix. Although our school systems seek to provide all of them with the linguistic and other skills needed for employment and daily life, Canada has not insisted that they give up their various identities completely.

The retention of other identities is assisted, where there are concentrations of people with shared backgrounds, through our heritage language programs, which provide formal education in traditional languages for children from ethnic minorities. These programs sometimes attract other students, so that, somewhere in Canada, young people of British or Ukrainian ancestry are studying Japanese or Italian. Furthermore, since our country is officially bilingual and since bilingualism is needed for certain types of jobs, specifically those in government service, we have French immersion schooling throughout the country. About 3.5 percent of Canada's primary and secondary school students are enrolled in second language or French immersion programs. Across the provinces and territories, immersion enrolments vary from 1.6 and 1.8 percent, respectively, in Nova Scotia and the Northwest Territories to 6.3 and 6.6 percent, respectively, in New Brunswick and Prince Edward Island.

SOCIAL PLACEMENT

Formal education helps young people assume culturally approved statuses and perform roles that contribute to the ongoing life of society. Ideally, schools accomplish this by identifying and developing aptitudes and abilities—and evaluating each student's performance in terms of achievement rather than social background. In principle, teachers encourage the "best and the brightest" to pursue the most challenging and advanced studies, and the rest to pursue educational programs and occupations suited to their talents. Thus, schooling enhances meritocracy by making personal merit a foundation of future social position.

Meritocracy has always had special significance to people who begin life with social disadvantages based on ascribed traits such as sex, race, ethnicity, and social class. For this reason, schooling is the major avenue of upward social mobility in Canada.

LATENT FUNCTIONS OF SCHOOLING

Schooling also serves several less widely recognized functions. It provides child care for the growing number of one-parent and two-career families. In addition, schooling occupies thousands of young people in their teens and twenties who would otherwise be competing for limited opportunities in the job market. High schools, colleges, and universities also bring together people of marriageable age. Finally, schools establish networks that serve as a valuable career resource throughout life.

Critical Review Structural-functional analysis stresses ways in which formal education supports the operation of a

Graduation is an important event in the lives of an increasing number of Canadians. Young people who have reached this stage can expect to find better jobs and earn higher incomes than the peers they left behind.

modern society. However, this approach overlooks how the classroom behaviour of teachers and students can vary from one setting to another, a focus of the symbolic-interaction approach discussed next. In addition, structural-functional analysis fails to address the problems of our educational system and the ways in which it helps to reproduce the class structure in each generation, which is the focus of social-conflict analysis discussed later.

Schooling and Social Interaction

The basic idea of the symbolic-interaction approach is that people create the reality they experience in their day-to-day interaction. We use this approach to explain how stereotypes can shape what goes on in the classroom.

THE SELF-FULFILLING PROPHECY

Chapter 6 ("Social Interaction in Everyday Life") presented the Thomas theorem, which states that situations people define as real become real in their consequences. Put another way, people who expect others to act in certain ways often encourage that very behaviour. Doing so, people set up a *self-fulfilling prophecy*.

Jane Elliott, an elementary school teacher in the White community of Riceville, Iowa, carried out a simple experiment that showed how a self-fulfilling prophecy can take place in the classroom. In 1968, Elliot was teaching a fourth-grade class when Dr. Martin Luther King Jr. was assassinated. Her students were puzzled and asked why a national hero had been brutally shot. Elliott responded by asking her White students what they thought about Black people, and

she was stunned to find out that they held many powerful and negative stereotypes. To illustrate the harmful effects of such stereotypes, Elliott performed a classroom experiment. Noting that almost all of the children had blue or brown eyes, she told the children that those with brown eyes were smarter and worked harder than children with blue eyes. To facilitate identification, pieces of brown- or blue-coloured cloth were pinned to every student's collar.

Elliott recalls the effect of this "lesson" on student behaviour: "It was just horrifying how quickly they became what I told them they were." Within half an hour, Elliot continued, a blue-eyed girl named Carol had changed from a "brilliant, carefree, excited little girl to a frightened, timid, uncertain, almost-person." Not surprisingly, in the hours that followed, the brown-eyed students came to life, speaking up more and performing better than they had done before. The prophecy was fulfilled: because the brown-eyed children thought they were superior, they became superior in their classroom performance—as well as "arrogant, ugly and domineering" towards the blue-eyed children. For their part, the blue-eyed children began underperforming, becoming the inferior people they believed themselves to be.

At the end of the day, Elliott explained their experience. She applied the lesson to race, pointing out that, if White children thought they were superior to Black children, they would expect to do better in school, just as many Black children who live in the shadow of the same stereotypes would underperform in school. The children also realized that the society that teaches these stereotypes and hatred encourages the kind of violence that ended the life of Dr. King (Kral, 2000).

Sociological research has documented the fact that young children living in low-income communities typically learn in classrooms with a low budget and large class size (*left*) that do not provide for high technology and other instructional materials. Children from high-income communities—some of whom attend private schools—enjoy classroom experiences with fewer students per teacher and the latest learning technology (*right*).

Critical Review The symbolic-interaction approach explains how we all build reality in our everyday interactions with others. When school officials define some students as "gifted," for example, we can expect teachers to treat them differently and the students themselves to behave differently as a result of having been labelled in this way. If students and teachers come to believe that one race is academically superior to another, the ensuing behaviour will be a self-fulfilling prophecy. One limitation of this approach is that people do not make up beliefs about superiority and inferiority; rather, these beliefs are built into a society's system of social inequality, which brings us to the social-conflict approach.

Schooling and Social Inequality

Social-conflict analysis explains how schooling both causes and perpetuates social inequality. In this way, it can explain how stereotypes of "good" and "bad" students described in the symbolic-interaction discussion arise in the first place. In addition, a social-conflict approach challenges the structural-functional idea that schooling develops everybody's talents and abilities by noting that schooling contributes to social stratification.

Traditionally, schooling was deemed more important for males than for females. The gender gap in education decreased in recent decades—at least in terms of numbers—but women still predominate in the arts and social sciences, while men pursue mathematics and engineering. Throughout Canada, efforts have been made to provide gender-neutral texts and library materials and to remove materials that perpetuate negative stereotypes or are offen-

sive to ethnic, racial, and religious minorities. Schools are also attempting to incorporate multicultural programs and materials into their curricula to increase tolerance and understanding among youngsters of different backgrounds. The intent, in part, is to eradicate stereotypes and to raise the aspiration levels of those who felt excluded by the system.

Social class background is also an important determinant of familiarity with computers, which is increasingly vital to education and employment. Home computer ownership rises (from below 30%) to well over 60 percent in the homes of those who are university educated, who have incomes of $70 000 or more, and who are professionals (Forcese, 1997:124; Goyder, 1997: 70). Children from these families have an advantage as they progress through the educational system.

Regional variation in affluence and economic structure give rise to marked differences in educational attainment. Canada Map 20–1 indicates the proportions of provincial and territorial populations, 15 years or older, that have acquired a university degree. The levels range from 7.5 percent in Nunavut to 17.3 percent in Ontario. The Yukon and British Columbia are also above average in educational attainment. Note that, since there are no universities located in the territories, the Yukon attracts much of its university-educated population from elsewhere to take jobs in government, natural resources, defence, and research.

It is also the case that affluence affects the extent to which Canadians take advantage of educational opportunities. Along with gender, social class is a strong predictor of aspirations to attend university (Porter, *et al.*, 1982): in fact, one is much more likely to attend university or college if one's parents are white-collar workers with postsecondary education (Guppy and Arai, 1993; Corak, 2000; de Broucker and Lavallée, 2000).

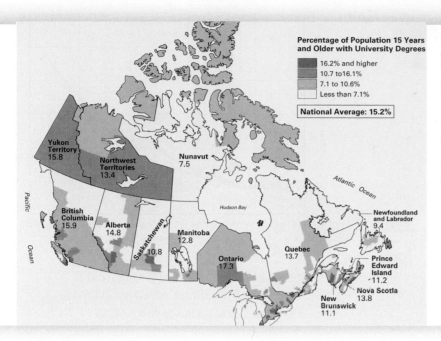

SEEING OURSELVES
CANADA MAP 20-1

Population 15 Years or Older with University Degree (Percentages by Province, Territory, and Census Subdivision), 2001

Source: Calculations by L.M. Gerber based on the Statistics Canada website, http://www.statcan.ca/english/Pgdb/educ41a.htm.

Percentage of Population 15 Years and Older with University Degrees

- 16.2% and higher
- 10.7 to16.1%
- 7.1 to 10.6%
- Less than 7.1%

National Average: 15.2%

Yukon Territory 15.8
Northwest Territories 13.4
Nunavut 7.5
British Columbia 15.9
Alberta 14.8
Saskatchewan 10.8
Manitoba 12.8
Ontario 17.3
Quebec 13.7
Newfoundland and Labrador 9.4
Prince Edward Island 11.2
Nova Scotia 13.8
New Brunswick 11.1

Atlantic Ocean
Hudson Bay
Pacific Ocean

SOCIAL CONTROL

Social-conflict analysis asserts that schooling acts as a means of social control, reinforcing acceptance of the status quo. In various, often subtle ways, schools reproduce the status hierarchy, although this process is not always evident to students or even to teachers. Bowles and Gintis (1976) point out that public education grew exponentially in the late nineteenth century when capitalists were seeking a docile, disciplined, and literate workforce. Mandatory education laws ensured that schools would teach immigrants the English language,[1] as well as cultural values that support capitalism. Compliance, punctuality, and discipline were—and still are—part of what is called the **hidden curriculum**, *subtle presentations of political or cultural ideas in the classroom.*

STANDARDIZED TESTING

Here is a question of the kind traditionally used to measure the intelligence and academic ability of school-age children.

```
Painter is to painting as _____ is
to sonnet.

Answers: (a) driver (b) poet (c) priest
(d) carpenter
```

The correct answer is (b) poet: a painter creates a painting as a *poet* creates a sonnet. This question purports to measure logical reasoning, but demonstrating this skill depends on knowing what each term means. Unless students are familiar with sonnets as a form of written verse, they are unlikely to answer the question correctly. An upper middle-class student of European descent is likely to have more of the experiences rewarded by such tests. (The same person might not score as well on an intelligence test devised by an Cree or an Inuk.) Controversy surrounds such tests, for they reflect our society's dominant culture, thereby placing the members of minorities at a disadvantage. Children from less affluent backgrounds are also at a disadvantage because they face "tests of intelligence and cognitive skills weighted in favour of middle- and upper-class children" (Porter, *et al.*, 1982:9). The motivations and attitudes transmitted by affluent parents also help children on these tests.

Educational specialists claim that biases of these kinds have been eliminated from standardized tests, since testing organizations carefully study response patterns and drop any question that favours one category of students over another. Critics, however, maintain that some bias based on class, race, or ethnicity is inherent in any formal testing, because questions inevitably reflect our society's dominant culture and thereby put minorities at a disadvantage (Owen, 1985; Crouse and Trusheim, 1988; Putka, 1990).

STREAMING AND SOCIAL INEQUALITY

Many Canadian schools practise **streaming**, *the assigning of students to different types of educational programs.* Streaming (also called tracking or ability grouping) is also a common practice in many other industrial societies, including the United States, Germany, Great Britain, France, and Japan. The educational justification for streaming is to give students the kind of schooling appropriate to individual aptitude. For a variety of reasons, including innate ability and level of

---

[1]Until Quebec passed Bill 101 in 1977, making French the sole official language in Quebec as well as the language of business, francophones had to be fluently bilingual to succeed economically. Even in Quebec, English was the language of business.

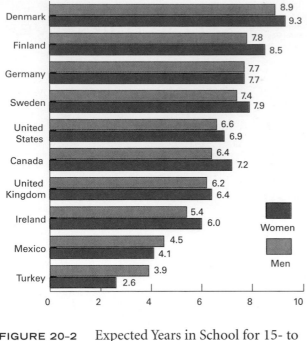

FIGURE 20-2 Expected Years in School for 15- to 29-Year-Olds in Selected OECD Countries (2003)

Source: Compiled by L.M. Gerber from Organisation for Economic Cooperation and Development Education database, Table C4.1a (2003) at www.oecd.org.

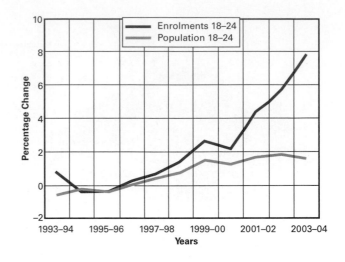

FIGURE 20-3 Proportion of Young Adults Attending University, 2005

Source: Statistics Canada, *The Daily*, October 11, 2005.

motivation, some students are capable of more challenging work than others. Young people also differ in their interests, with some drawn to languages, while others seek training in art or science. Given this diversity of talent and focus, no single program would serve all individuals well.

Critics see streaming as a thinly veiled strategy to perpetuate privilege. Research shows that social background has as much to do with streaming as personal aptitude. Students from affluent families generally do well in school and on tests and, so, are placed in university-bound streams (with the best teachers), while students from poor families end up in programs that curb their aspirations and prepare them for lower-level jobs. Streaming, therefore, effectively segregates students—academically and socially—into different worlds.

In light of these criticisms, many schools are now cautious about streaming. Recent initiatives in Ontario aimed at destreaming were met with opposition from school boards and teachers as well as from parents, who are concerned that their university-bound children will receive lower-quality education in destreamed classrooms.

Without streaming, less academically inclined children may be unable to compete with their classmates, and teachers face the difficult task of teaching students of differing abilities in one class; but these problems are not insurmountable. Rigid streaming, on the other hand, has a powerful impact on student learning and self-concept.

Young people in higher streams tend to see themselves as bright and able, whereas those in lower streams end up with less ambition and lower self-esteem (Bowles and Gintis, 1976; Oakes, 1985; Kilgore, 1991; Kozol, 1992).

ACCESS TO HIGHER EDUCATION

In industrial societies, since lawyers, physicians, or professors cannot pass credentials on to their children, higher education is the path to occupational achievement. Figure 20–2 shows the number of years 15- to 29-year-olds are expected to spend in school in selected countries within the Organisation for Economic Cooperation and Development. At the top of the list, you will find industrialized European countries whose young people stay in school until they are, on average, 22 to 24 years of age: in all but Germany, women stay in school a little longer. In the United States and Canada, young people attend until they are 21 or 22 years of age, but the gender gap—which favours women—is wider in Canada. In the United Kingdom and Ireland, they stay to 20 or 21 years of age, and in Mexico and Turkey—where the gender gap favours males—they stay to 18 or 19 years of age, on average. These data suggest that only in Denmark and Finland can we expect the *average* young person to complete university.

Enrolment in postsecondary education has risen dramatically since World War II and in recent decades. Between 1988 and 1994, while Canada's population grew by 8.8 percent, full-time postsecondary enrolment grew by 18.1 percent (Statistics Canada, 1996). That trend has continued to the present: "Enrolment at Canadian universities recorded its strongest increase in 28 years during the academic year 2003–04, due to a rise in the number of students aged 18 to 24, Ontario's double cohort, and a record gain in students from other countries" (Statistics

Canada, 2005a). (See Figure 20–3.) University enrolment was 990 400 in 2003–04, up 6.1 percent from the previous year and 20.4 percent from 1997–98, with enrolment hitting record highs for six consecutive years. Figure 20–3 indicates that the proportions of young adults enrolled in university have increased dramatically since fall 1993.

There are many reasons why most people in Canada do not attend and graduate from university or college. Some high-school students enter the labour force right away; others cannot afford further education because of the costs of tuition and deferred income. Vast distances between homes and the nearest university or college are also major deterrents. In addition, many high school students have been convinced that they cannot succeed at the postsecondary level. In one respect at least, we have moved closer to the goal of equal access to higher education in Canada: as noted earlier, women are now more likely than men to attend university. Low or moderate family income, however, remains a formidable barrier to enrolment: young people with lower family incomes or fathers in blue-collar occupations are much less likely to go to university (Wotherspoon, 1991; Corak, 2000). Most universities provide financial assistance to students in the form of bursaries and scholarships, and governments make loans available to those of limited means. Nevertheless, many people cannot afford the remaining costs. The problem has been accentuated in recent years, as cutbacks in government funding have forced tuition increases. See the Applying Sociology box (on p. 534) for further discussion of factors affecting educational attainment.

Figure 20–4 shows that, according to the census of 2001, the Black community in Canada had educational attainment levels similar to those of English origin: the percentages (of those over 15 years of age) with high school certification and university degrees are almost identical. While observing that those who claim French origins have higher levels of educational attainment than either English or Black people, you should keep in mind that many francophones identify themselves as *Canadien*—and that they, in turn, have substantially lower levels of attainment. (Those who call themselves French rather than *Canadien* or Québécois appear to stand apart.) People of Chinese and Japanese origins have less than 12 percent of their populations with high school certification only—in part because so many go on to attain university degrees. At roughly double the rate of the English or French, 27 and 28 percent of Chinese and Japanese Canadians have university degrees. The visible minorities in general—at 24 percent—have higher levels of university completion than the Canadian population as a whole. This is the result of our immigration selection procedures and the "points system" which takes educational background into account. Furthermore, among the visible minorities, there are groups like the Chinese and Japanese who have especially high educational aspirations for their Canadian-born children.

The pattern of educational attainment among Aboriginal people (Figure 20–4) is of special interest. A

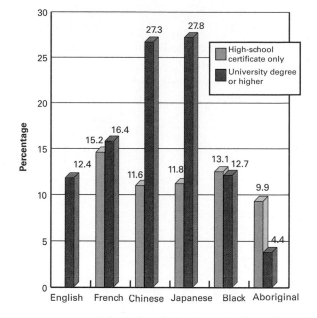

FIGURE 20-4   Educational Attainment for Selected Categories, 2001[*]

*Percentages based on populations 15 years of age or older.

Source: Source: Calculations by L. M. Gerber based on Statistics Canada, Census 2001, Catalogue numbers 97F0010XCB2001041, 97F0010XCB2001045, and 97F0011XCB2001043.

For a multimedia presentation on Canada's residential schools, go to http://archives.cbc.ca/300c.asp?id=1-70-692.

relatively small proportion of Aboriginal people have high school certification: in this case, it is because their children drop out before completing high school. As noted in the opener to this chapter, this is especially true for those living on reserve. While only 4.4 percent of Aboriginal people (15 years of age and older) have university degrees, this represents more than a doubling between 1991 and 2001. In order to change the attainment level for the whole population over 15—in a ten year period—the increase in university attendance and completion has to be dramatic. The effects of this change will become even more apparent in future censuses. Further background on the experiences of Aboriginal children in residential schools is provided in the Thinking about Diversity box (on pp. 532–33).

Higher education, whether from university or college, expands career opportunities and increases earnings. Figure 20–5 shows that employment among 25- to 44-year-olds increases with educational attainment. This is especially true for women. Labour-force participation for the population aged 15 and over (not shown) reveals even more dramatic increases. Once again, women experience the greater effect, with labour-force participation increasing fourfold from the lowest to the highest levels of education.

Table 20–1 deals with the average earnings of people aged 15 and older by educational attainment. In Canada and each of the provinces and territories, average incomes rise

TABLE 20–1

Average Earnings of the Population 15 Years and over by Highest Level of Schooling, Provinces and Territories, 2001*

	Canada	NL	PEI	NS	NB	Que	Ont	Man	Sask	Alb	BC	Yuk	NWT	Nun
All levels	$31 757	$24 165	$22 303	$26 632	$24 971	$29 385	$35 185	$27 178	$25 691	$32 603	$31 544	$31 526	$36 645	$28 215
Less than high school graduation certificate	21 230	15 922	15 058	18 251	17 074	20 553	22 691	19 201	18 288	22 196	21 971	19 265	20 428	14 772
High school graduation certificate and/or some post-secondary	25 477	16 860	18 236	20 553	20 395	24 071	27 606	22 921	21 780	25 789	25 671	25 753	31 603	26 722
Trades certificate or diploma	32 743	26 118	24 090	27 595	27 694	27 535	36 843	29 357	28 755	37 443	34 196	33 352	42 712	32 454
College certificate or diploma	32 736	28 196	25 613	26 930	27 178	28 742	36 309	29 351	27 742	33 572	33 159	33 817	42 245	39 113
University certificate, diploma, or degree	48 648	41 942	37 063	41 146	40 375	45 834	53 525	41 856	40 279	50 069	44 066	45 982	56 892	58 992

*These figures refer to earned income or employment income.

Source: Compiled by L.M. Gerber, based on Statistics Canada, Census 2001, Highlight Tables, Earnings of Canadians, www.statcan.ca.

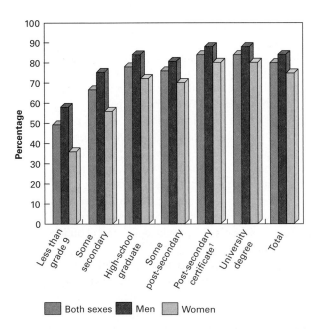

Both sexes   **Men**   **Women**

FIGURE 20-5   Employment of 25- to 44-Year-Olds by Educational Attainment and Sex, 2001

[1]Post-secondary certificate or diploma includes trades certificates.

Sources: Calculations by L.M. Gerber based on Statistics Canada, catalogue no. 89F0133XIE.

steadily with higher levels of education, except for those holding a trades or college certificate; thus, incomes at least double from the lowest to highest educational categories. Throughout the country, the largest increases show up among those who have earned university certificates, diplomas, or degrees. Among the provinces, university graduates have the highest average earnings in Ontario and Alberta. However, the highest incomes for this category are to be found in the Northwest Territories and Nunavut ($57 000 and $59 000): to be expected, since university graduates in the territories are normally highly paid professionals from elsewhere working in government, mining, exploration, and defence.

Obtaining a university degree, as opposed to a college diploma, also decreases the likelihood of unemployment two years after graduation; as one progresses from bachelor's through master's and doctoral degrees, the likelihood of being unemployed is further reduced (Canada, 1992a:40). Many people find schooling to be its own reward, but the income figures shown here indicate that schooling is also a sound investment in financial terms, increasing income by hundreds of thousands of dollars over a person's working life.

PRIVILEGE AND PERSONAL MERIT

If, as social-conflict analysis suggests, attending university is a rite of passage for affluent men and women, then

APPLYING THEORY
EDUCATION

	Structural-Functional Approach	Symbolic-Interaction Approach	Social-Conflict Approach
What is the level of analysis?	Macro level	Micro level	Macro level
What is the importance of education for society?	Schooling performs many vital tasks for the operation of society, including socializing the young and encouraging discovery and invention to improve our lives. Schooling helps unite a diverse society by teaching shared norms and values.	Teachers' expectations can affect self-image and academic performance.	Schooling maintains social inequality through unequal schooling for rich and poor. Within individual schools, streaming places privileged children into advanced or university-oriented programs.

schooling transforms social privilege into personal merit. But given the North American cultural emphasis on individual achievement, we tend to see credentials as "badges of ability," as Sennett and Cobb (1973) put it, rather than as symbols of family affluence. When we congratulate the typical new graduate, we often overlook the social resources that made this achievement possible. In the same way, we are quick to condemn the high school dropout as personally deficient, with little thought for the social circumstances that surround that person's life. See the Applying Sociology box (on p. 534) for an exploration of educational attainment.

Critical Review Social-conflict analysis links formal education and social inequality, and shows how schooling transforms privilege into personal worthiness, and social disadvantage into personal deficiency. However, critics claim that social-conflict analysis minimizes the extent to which schooling provides upward social mobility for talented men and women—especially those from modest backgrounds. Further, despite the claims of many conflict theorists that schooling supports the status quo, "politically correct" educational curricula are challenging patterns of social inequality on many fronts.

The Applying Theory table (above) provides an overview of education from the perspectives of the symbolic interaction, structural functional, and social conflict approaches.

Problems in Schools

Canadians have long debated the quality of education, but, over the past decades, the debate has intensified.

SCHOOL DISCIPLINE

Canadians and Americans alike believe that schools should inculcate personal discipline and that the job is not being done properly. The U.S. government estimates that several hundred thousand students and at least one thousand teachers are physically assaulted on school grounds every year. This violence at school is blamed on poverty-stricken urban environments that breed drug use as well as violence on the street and at home. All too often, violence in American communities and schools involves the use of guns.

Canada's school discipline problems are not of the same type or magnitude, but there have been many

 For the results of a survey of programs to prevent violence at school, see ww2.psepc-sppcc. gc.ca/publications/corrections/ 199502_e.asp.

instances of assault on students and teachers; students have been found at school with knives—most often in specific schools prone to violence—but rarely with guns. At the postsecondary level, the 1989 killing of 14 female engineering students—at Montreal's l'École Polytechnique—shocked Canadians. More recently (September 2006), a woman was killed in a shooting rampage at Montreal's Dawson College, which left the shooter dead and 19 other people injured. Such incidents drive home the realization that, even within our schools, we are not immune to deadly violence.

More commonly, however, the discipline problems in our schools involve students who display disdain for learning, are rude to their teachers or challenge their authority, skip classes, disrupt the classroom, or otherwise interfere with the formal education of themselves and others. "When I was young," parents will say, "we did what the teacher told us." Selective memory notwithstanding, there undoubtedly has been a gradual decline in classroom discipline over the past few decades related to larger societal trends. In teach-

THINKING ABOUT DIVERSITY:
RACE, CLASS, & GENDER

Aboriginal Education: The Legacy of Canada's Residential Schools

Around the turn of the last century, Canada's federal government paid churches to expand their residential schools for Indian and Inuit children. The intent was to "civilize" and assimilate the children by stamping out their own languages and cultures—replacing them with English or French, rudimentary reading and arithmetic, and agricultural and domestic skills.

Only recently have we become aware of the damaging consequences of the residential school experience. Removed from their communities and families, the children were ill-prepared for life in the mainstream or for a return to their own communities. Inadequate and, in effect, damaging educational practices were accompanied in many of these schools by verbal, physical, and sexual abuse. By the time the residential schools were phased out in the early 1960s, several generations of First Nation and Inuit youngsters had paid a very heavy price.

Vicki English-Currie describes her experience in a residential school—in this case, the Roman Catholic Indian Residential School at Brocket, Alberta—to which she was taken at the tender age of seven. There the missionaries assumed total responsibility for and control over her life. She experienced the transition from home to residential school as one of total shock, enormous setback, and "the beginning of a lifetime of cultural tragedy." In this setting, her formal education was overshadowed by accumulating "stress, anger, fear, and hostility."

English-Currie was excited to go to school because she idolized the Grey nuns. When her mother dropped her off at the school door, a nun pushed her into her room with her bag and closed the door – introducing her to the violence she would experience at school. For English-Currie, this was "the beginning of an education of oppression and the end to family life [which was to leave the children] undereducated, in poverty, and dependent upon the false charity of the Indian agent and the mission schools." The pictures in their textbooks were of White, middle-class professionals—never traditional leaders of their own peoples: "As a result the students' self-esteem, self-determination, self-worth, pride, and confidence slowly dwindled into a desire to be white" when, at the time, "Indian people were not allowed by law to leave the reserve to attend higher educational institutions." They were told that Indian religion was heathen and that Indian culture and language were savage, the result being that the children felt degraded and insignificant (English-Currie, 1993:114–16).

Because Aboriginal students were thought to be cognitively deficient, the core subjects of math, reading, and writing were not the major focus of their education. Therefore, when the government closed the residential schools in the early 1960s, Aboriginal youngsters were unprepared to cope with integrated provincial and territorial schools. Finding themselves two or three grades behind their peers, Aboriginal youth dropped out.

---

ers' college, discussion of educational theory and the finer points of pedagogy do nothing to prepare would-be teachers for their first field placements, where the most pressing question is how to maintain *control* in the classroom. Teachers, who are trained to teach but find that their energies are diverted into policing students, experience frustration and disillusionment on the job.

DROPPING OUT

If many students are disruptive in class, others are not there at all. The problem of dropping out—quitting school before completing a high school diploma—leaves young people, many of whom are disadvantaged to begin with, ill-equipped for the world of work and at high risk for poverty. In a report entitled *Leaving School*, which compares school leavers and high school graduates, Gilbert and colleagues (1993) note that leavers are more likely

- to be from single-parent or no-parent households
- to have parents with lower educational attainment
- to be married and to have dependent children (especially the women)
- to have lower grade averages
- to have failed a grade in elementary school
- to have worked more than 20 hours per week during their final school year
- to use alcohol (regularly) and drugs

Young people who drop out of school in a credential-based society are more likely to end up unemployed or in low-paying jobs. Faced with this reality, as many as a quarter of school-leavers return to the classroom at a later time.

Statistics Canada (2005b) notes that our high school dropout rates have been declining since the early 1990s—

The youngsters who were educated in residential schools suffered the long-term consequences of being separated from their families and communities, and of being wrenched from familiar cultural surroundings and thrust into an alien world where they felt unwelcome. These same youngsters, raised outside normal families, were the ones who soon faced parenthood, for which they were ill prepared.

While 60 percent of on-reserve First Nations children now attend schools operated by their First Nation, the transition to high school—usually to an integrated provincial or territorial school—is still painful. As a result, the majority of Aboriginal youth do not graduate. The Royal Commission on Aboriginal Peoples points out that these youngsters "'leave the school system without the requisite skills for employment [and] without the language and cultural knowledge of their people'" (quoted in Schissel and Wotherspoon, 2003:59).

In a survey of Aboriginal school children, Schissel and Wotherspoon found that when high school students are asked about barriers to learning, they mention poverty, housing problems, and violence—but racism tops the list. Although Aboriginal students express an overwhelming desire to

attend university, their aspirations do not translate into reality. The authors conclude that all schools—particularly isolated rural and northern schools—need to help students understand the nature of postsecondary education, the availability of funding, and the reality of rural/urban transition.

The importance of education to the employment prospects of Aboriginal people is clear. Tait (2000) notes that, in 1996, the unemployment rate for young Aboriginal adults, without high school, was 40 percent; for those with a university degree, it was 9 percent. Fortunately, there has been considerable improvement in Aboriginal educational achievement over the past decade: the proportions of college and university grads have doubled. By 1996, only 45 percent of young Aboriginal adults had failed to complete high school (compared to 60 percent in 1986); college completion had risen from 15 to 20 percent; and the earning of university degrees increased from 2 to 4 percent. Aboriginal people living in Canada's largest cities lead the way with respect to educational attainment, whereas those living on reserve improved least—as noted in the opener to this chapter. Better education and employment prospects among Aboriginal

peoples will stimulate further educational achievement and boost the transmission of intellectual capital to future generations.

An editorial in the *National Post* (May 1, 2006) reported that our government agreed to compensate the victim's of "Canada's shameful residential school program." More than 80 000 individuals "who were taken from their homes and forced to attend the church-run schools meant to assimilate them into the White culture" are eligible for compensation up to $10 000, plus $3000 for each year of attendance. This constitutes clear recognition of the devastating legacy of Canada's residential school system.

WHAT DO YOU THINK?

1. What would your life be like if your parents had attended residential school?
2. Do you have Aboriginal students on your campus? If so, do you now have a better understanding of the barriers they have overcome?
3. Should we do more than provide financial compensation to those who suffered physical and sexual abuse in residential schools?

especially in the Atlantic provinces. The decline was greater for young women than men, and in urban centres rather than small towns and rural areas. "The high school dropout rate is defined as the proportion of young people aged 20 to 24 who are not attending school, and who have not graduated from high school": by this measure, the dropout rate for 1990–91 was 16.7 percent—declining to 9.8 percent by 2004–05. Since employers are less likely to hire high school dropouts, their unemployment rate (at 19.4%) is double that of others in this age group.

While progress at the national level is encouraging, Newfoundland and Labrador and Prince Edward Island are the stars. Their rates dropped from the highest in the country (20%) in the early 1990s to 8 or 10 percent by 2004–05, placing them among the regions with the lowest dropout rates. Quebec and the Prairie provinces have rates above 10 percent in recent years, but these represent a

decline from 16 percent to 17 percent, respectively, in the early 1900s.

Dropping out is more common in rural areas and small towns rather than in urban areas—especially in Quebec, Manitoba, and Alberta. Although rates for both have declined by 2004–05, they remain 12.2 percent for young men and 7.2 percent for young women. Interestingly, the American dropout rate—which is measured for 16- to 24-year-olds—is currently 10.7 percent: very close to Canada's 9.8 percent.

ACADEMIC STANDARDS

Canada and the United States share a growing concern with the quality of schooling or, more pointedly, with the quality of publicly funded schooling. In 1983 in the United States, the National Commission on Excellence in Education prepared *A Nation at Risk*, a comprehensive report on the

APPLYING SOCIOLOGY
Explaining Educational Attainment

Over several decades, Canada has witnessed a marked increase in the number of children raised in lone-parent or blended/stepparent families. Frederick and Boyd (2000) used data from the 1994 General Social Survey to look at the impact of family structure on high school completion. They found that adults (aged 22 to 44), who had lived with both biological parents at age 15, were more likely to have completed high school than those from lone-parent families (80%) or blended families (71%), or stepparent families (70%).

Looking at the interaction of parental education and family structure, Frederick and Boyd found that 94 percent of those who grew up with two biological parents who had completed high school were more likely to do so themselves. Where parents had not completed high school, graduation rates dropped off dramatically—to 71 percent and 59 percent, respectively, for those who had lived with both biological parents or a lone parent at age 15. Clearly, parental education and family structure both have significant effects.

Using Canadian data from the 1994 International Adult Literacy Survey, de Broucker and Lavallée (2000) assessed the role of "inherited intellectual capital" in the acquisition of postsecondary education. Most adults aged 26 to 35 have at least as much education as their parents. Not surprisingly, young adults whose parents had postsecondary education were more likely to earn postsecondary diplomas or degrees.

Fathers' occupations also have an effect: fathers with high-status occupations have children with higher educational attainment. The literacy survey suggests that one way of passing on intellectual capital is to provide books and read to one's children: parents with university degrees, regardless of income, are much more likely to have the habit of reading to their children, contributing to an environment that is conducive to learning.

Supportive parents can help their children achieve amazing things. Five Canadian women—Dina, Ada, Rita, Linda, and Cindy Maxwell—received their undergraduate degrees from Harvard, "where faculty and staff still talk about the Maxwell sisters from New Brunswick" because of the goodwill they generated there. Daughters of a physician from Ghana and a Canadian nurse, they attended Harvard on scholarships, loans, and parental contributions—and went on to study medicine (Cindy and Linda) and the law (Rita, Ada, and Dina). These impressive young women

explain that "their father's stern but positive guidance, combined with their mother's warm and protective support, made them the women they are today" (Reinhart and Armstrong, 2006).

For years, the top-achieving students in the Toronto public school system have been Asian—especially Chinese and increasingly South Asian: "for all the hardships faced by new immigrants, their kids are the brightest of the bright" (Wente, 2006). Immigrant and first-generation children, disproportionately, are the valedictorians and—at the other extreme—the dropouts. Canadian-born youngsters are in the middle of the pack. In the United States as well as Canada, educational achievement by students of Asian ancestry is described as "stunning." Cultural capital, which is formed at home, makes ethnicity more important than any other factor—socioeconomic background, curriculum, or family structure—as a determinant of educational attainment.

WHAT DO YOU THINK?

1. Can something as simple as reading to children affect academic aspirations and achievements? Why?
2. Living with both biological parents who are educated affects the educational attainment of children? Why?
3. Why do students of Asian backgrounds do so well in Canadian schools?

---

quality of American schools. The report noted that "nearly 40 percent of seventeen-year-olds cannot draw inferences from written material; only one-fifth can write a persuasive essay; and only one-third can solve mathematical problems requiring several steps" (1983:9). Furthermore, scores on the Scholastic Aptitude Test have declined steadily since the early 1960s. Few observers of the North American scene doubt that schooling has suffered a setback. *A Nation at Risk*

also noted with alarm the extent of functional illiteracy. Roughly 1 in 8 children in the United States completes secondary school without learning to read or write very well. The Thinking it Through box (on p. 522) makes it clear that functional illiteracy is a major problem in Canada as well. The practice of passing youngsters to the next grade, despite reading and writing deficits, contributes to this problem.

Canadians express concerns about the quality of our educational experience, in part because of observations about the skills (or lack thereof) of graduates, but also because of the lack of fit between these skills and the demands of the labour market, as indicated by unemployment levels. Concerns were heightened in 1992, when Canadian students appeared to do poorly in international mathematics tests involving a number of countries (including Japan). Barlow and Robertson (1994) assert that the results were misleading because they compared the performance of elite groups of students in some countries with a more broadly based Canadian cohort. However, media, special reports, and the business community were quick to criticize the public school systems, thereby capitalizing on public disaffection and manipulating public opinion against schools (Barlow and Robertson, 1994). The provincial and territorial governments, being responsible for education, were quick to join in the criticism of schools and the search for solutions. Using the test scores in the international study of performance in mathematics, some argued for a radical restructuring of education in Canada. Among the suggested solutions to our problems were many that are consistent with the political right and corporate interests:

- national testing and standards to measure the quality of the "product"—that is, students

- downsizing for greater efficiency so there are fewer school boards and teachers

- vouchers to allow students and families to shop for their schools

- privatization to create schools run by the private sector

- partnerships between corporations and schools or universities

- corporate sponsorship of various programs, often involving overt advertising within schools, and

- harmonization with educational practices in the United States.

HOME SCHOOLING

Home schooling is gaining popularity in North America, where about 2 percent of school-age children are educated at home. Home schooling is more popular in the United States than in Canada, where it is most prevalent in Alberta. It is legal in Canada and is used by many families stationed abroad (e.g., in the military). Why do parents undertake the enormous challenge of schooling their own children? Some twenty years ago, most of the parents who pioneered home schooling did so in order to give their children a strongly religious upbringing. Today, however, many simply do not believe that public schools are doing a good job and think they can do better. To benefit their children, they are willing to forgo careers, alter work schedules, and relearn algebra or other necessary subjects. Many belong to groups in which parents pool their efforts, specializing in what each knows best.

Currently, our society is debating many strategies for improving education. Some parents have kept their children out of formal education altogether, believing their youngsters can learn more at home, using information available not only in books, but also in cyberspace.

Advocates of home schooling point out that, given the poor performance of many public schools, no one should be surprised that a growing number of parents are willing to step in to teach their own children. In addition, this system works: on average, students who learn at home outperform those who learn in school. One critic argues that home schooling "takes some of the most affluent and articulate parents out of the system. These are the parents who know how to get things done with administrators" (Chris Lubienski, quoted in Cloud and Morse, 2001:48). The Media Perspectives box (on p. 536), with its emphasis on cyber-school, or online learning, has real implications for home schooling—as long as parents are not traditional in orientation.

 Check out resources for home schooling in Canada at www.flora.org/homeschool-ca/.

YOUR TURN

Have you considered a career in teaching? If so, why? If not, what could be done to make the field more appealing to you?

EDUCATION AND THE WORLD OF WORK

The province of New Brunswick has taken a novel approach to education in its utilitarian role of preparing people to participate in a changing and, it is hoped, expanding labour market. While former premier Frank McKenna actively recruited businesses to establish in or relocate to New

MEDIA PERSPECTIVES
Welcome to Cyber-School

The wired planet has no boundaries and no monopolies of knowledge. The affairs of the world are now dependent upon the highest information of which man is capable.... The boundaries between the world of affairs and the community of learning have ceased to exist. The workaday world now demands encyclopedic wisdom.... Under these conditions, the old forms of specialized jobs has lost meaning. It was meaningful at very low speeds, but it has now been assumed into patterns of electric speeds. This change of pace from production-line to online computer programming has been ignored, just as the shift from hardware to software accelerates, making the old categories meaningless. (McLuhan and Nevitt, quoted in Benedetti and DeHart, 1996:172)

Education is responding to the arrival of computer-literate children and the demands of a drastically altered, knowledge-based economy by integrating computers and the internet throughout the education system—from kindergarten to Ph.D. The goal at primary and secondary levels is to have computers in every classroom; universities and colleges are placing more emphasis on computer-based, interactive, self-directed learning in the context of global electronic information flow. Much of the computer access is arranged for the classroom or on-campus labs, but students are also logging on to school or campus websites from home. On some campuses in Canada, it is compulsory for each student to have a computer and modem at home; everywhere, students are given email addresses

with their registration packages. Some private schools and colleges or university programs require laptops in class. Expanded and more technologically sophisticated distance-learning options and even virtual universities are being developed.

At the John D. Bracco School in northeast Edmonton, a third of the student body "skips classes." The students in question are studying from home via the school's home page. "We've pushed the walls of the school into the community," says principal Ron Bradley, who heads up the online program called LearnNet. The school walls now embrace students from all over Alberta and as far away as Sri Lanka and Holland. The program started in grades 7 to 9 at John D. Bracco (later in grades 10 to 12) and extended down to grade 2 at Kirkness School. The reasons for choosing LearnNet are varied, including the desire for home schooling, a family move to a remote area, or a student's attention deficit disorder. Internet-based learning has expanded the reach of John D. Bracco teachers into a geographically unbounded community (Gooderham, 1997).

Examples of computer-based learning and research abound. In Hamilton, Ontario, students of Scott Park High School have created YouthNet, an internet-based student project, and YouthNet Mail, a homework hotline and voting system for students to rank their favourite movies, music, and computer games. A retired teacher in Summerland, British Columbia, created an internet-based project called Global THINK; participants include about a thousand B.C. students along with others from as far away as Ontario and Alaska (Foss, 1997). SchoolNet is available in Ontario.

At the university level we see computer conferencing, online courses, multimedia distance education, and more complex virtual universities. Undergraduate and graduate students are relying increasingly on the internet as a means of communication and a source of information. For example, Statistics Canada data and publications increasingly are available only on the internet or on CD-ROM: its publication *The Daily*, among many other products, no longer appears on paper at all. Federal election results are available online.

Academic journals in the sciences and social sciences are also becoming available online. Most recently, purely electronic journals—several in sociology—have appeared. The researcher conducts computer analyses, writes a paper through word processing, submits the paper electronically, has it sent to reviewers via the internet, and then sees it published in electronic form. Throughout this process, pen may never be set to paper. Access to information as well as the production and dissemination of knowledge have changed profoundly and irrevocably.

WHAT DO YOU THINK?

1. What are the advantages or disadvantages of the virtual university? Would you be able to function effectively in that context?
2. Home schooling, which is common in Alberta, can be highly traditional, or technologically advanced and internet-based. What are the advantages or disadvantages of home schooling?
3. Are you at the point in your studies where you do almost all of your reading beyond your text and your studying online?

Brunswick, some of his province's schools made a special, complementary offer. Their graduates would enter the workforce with "guaranteed" skills: if an employer found them wanting, they could return for upgrading at the

schools' expense. Strategic spending on education has helped to decrease the overall dropout rate in New Brunswick as well. An appropriately educated, bilingual workforce is one of the factors allowing Moncton, New

THINKING CRITICALLY
Is Political Correctness Undermining Education?

Are you PC? Is your teacher? What about this textbook? The last decade has seen a heightened level of political debate on the university campus. About 1980, *political correctness* became popular as a way to refer to thinking and acting in accordance with liberal political principles. To be "politically correct" (PC), at least as opponents see it, implies that truth is less a matter of scientific evidence than having the right kind of politics. Surveying today's campus scene, James Davison Hunter (1991:211) concludes: "The cultural ethos of the modern university clearly favours a progressivist agenda," including support for feminism, gay rights, and various other movements towards social equality.

To some people, political correctness threatens the traditional open-mindedness of the university—at its worst transforming professors into political activists and teaching into indoctrination. Moreover, political correctness may have a chilling effect in the classroom, making students wary of expressing opinions about controversial issues (say, homosexuality or racial differences in measured intelligence) for fear of offending others who might, in turn, charge them with "homophobia" or "racism."

Professors, too, feel the pressure to be politically correct: Douglas Massey (1995) points out that a number of

well-known researchers have been ostracized by their peers for publishing the results of research that is scientifically solid but that advances "unpopular notions" about race and gender.

But not everyone thinks PC is a problem. Many students and faculty defend a politically engaged campus on moral grounds. As they see it, there is much injustice in the world that cries out for redress. Richard Rorty (1994), for example, applauds the fact that some academic departments have become "sanctuaries for left-wing political views," because activist colleagues are "doing a great deal of good for people who have gotten a raw deal," namely, women, Black people, gay men, and lesbians. By focusing on marginalized people, he continues, the politically engaged campus will help to make society "much more decent, more tolerant, and more civilized."

Keep in mind, too, that political correctness can be easily exaggerated. While it is probably fair to characterize academia (and sociologists, overall) as politically liberal or left-wing, virtually every campus includes faculty, administrators, and students who continue to espouse a wide range of political opinions. Further, charges of political correctness in academia are nothing new. Just sixty years ago, for example, a majority of American states sought to keep teachers in check by requiring that they sign a loyalty oath before

permitting them to speak in the classroom (Hunter, 1991).

Quite literally, the perception of political correctness can affect the discussion of Canada/United States relations—or the Middle East since the 2001 terrorist attacks in the United States. Picture someone in a Canadian university classroom arguing that the United States is right to demand extra payments on our exports that are supported by Canadian government subsidies, or that President Bush was right to invade Iraq, or that Israelis have every right to retaliate against Palestinian suicide bombers. In all likelihood, these opinions will not be expressed at all because those who hold these views have been told they are not PC.

WHAT DO YOU THINK?

1. Overall, do you think that academia has a political bias? What is the bias?
2. How should teachers, or textbooks, present explicitly political stands on controversial issues?
3. Have you or other students remained silent during class discussions for fear of sounding "politically incorrect"? Has a course or reading ever led you to change attitudes you came to see as narrow minded?

Brunswick, to entice a wide range of companies to relocate there. Moncton is attracting international attention, and was chosen in 1993 as one of the top five "Best Cities for Business" (*Report on Business Magazine*, 1993:55). Advanced telecommunications technology is one of the factors allowing many companies to move to an area without a large population base.

A large study, *Making the Match* (Evers, *et al.*, 1993), involving twenty companies and five universities, was designed to assess the skill development experiences of Canadian university students and graduates, as well as the fit

between these skills and the needs of corporations. The skills most in demand and shortest in supply were not technical skills (such as using a computer) but a skill composite: the ability to integrate and use information, adapt to change, take reasonable risks, and conceptualize the future. Leadership and conflict management skills are also scarce. The educational system must develop technical skills in its students as well as use innovative approaches to foster the skills needed by industry. Interestingly, there is a link between these skills and the educational "aims and objectives" espoused by many of Canada's colleges and universities.

Education: Looking Ahead

As a society, Canada is undergoing a series of changes with implications for our educational systems. First, we are dealing with increasing diversity as a result of steady immigration, cultural pluralism—partly in response to our policy of multiculturalism, ethnic nationalism—most visibly among Québécois and Aboriginal peoples, as well as continuing regional and class divisions. In this context, the educational system is required to promote equality of access, participation, and outcome—as well as to play an integrative role, in part by fostering a Canadian identity that overrides our differences.

Second, Canada is experiencing technological change involving the expanded use of computers and robots, which in turn has an impact on organizational patterns (e.g., the possibility of working at home while electronically hooked up to the office). The promise of this new technology goes beyond helping students to learn basic skills: computers actually may improve the overall quality of learning. Interacting with computers prompts students to be more active and allows them to progress at their own pace. For students with disabilities who cannot write using a pencil, computers permit easier self-expression. Using computers in schools, in some cases as early as kindergarten, also appears to increase learning speed and retention of information.

The numerous benefits of computers should not blind us to their limitations, however. Computers will never bring to the educational process the personal insight or imagination of a motivated humane teacher. While the jury may be out on whether computers have improved teaching, there is no doubt they have proliferated in the classroom. Computers have become central to the experience of students in many classes, from kindergarten to university. In some Canadian universities, all students are required to have computers and modems and, in some programs, they are required to bring laptop computers to class. This type of requirement presents the danger of a new source of inequality in access to knowledge.

And third, we face a shrinking world of shifting political alliances, economic restructuring, multinational corporations, and global competition—wherein we strive to maintain our quality of life. In so far as education is responsible for the development of skills relevant to the labour market, our schools must foster in students both technical skills and an ability to be innovative, flexible, and analytical.

Education is intricately involved with change as a catalyst, an adaptive mechanism, and a force for maintaining tradition and continuity. (See the Thinking Critically box on p. 537.) It is simultaneously an explosive irritant and one of the ingredients in the glue that binds us together.

20 MAKING THE GRADE

The following learning tools will help you see what you know, identify what you still need to learn, and expand your understanding beyond the text. You can also visit this text's Companion Website™ at www.pearsoned.ca/macionis to find useful practice tests.

KEY POINTS

Education: A Global Survey

Education is the major social institution for transmitting knowledge and skills, as well as teaching cultural norms and values. In pre-industrial societies, education occurs informally within the family; industrial societies develop formal systems of schooling to educate their children. Most developed societies undertake compulsory mass education, reflecting both democratic political ideals and the needs of the industrial-capitalist economy.

The Functions of Schooling

Structural-functional analysis highlights major functions of schooling, including socialization, cultural innovation, social integration, and the placement of people in the social hierarchy. Latent functions of schooling include providing child care and building social networks.

Schooling and Social Interaction

The symbolic-interaction approach helps us understand that stereotypes can have important consequences for how people act. If students think they are academically superior, they are likely to perform better; students who think they are inferior are likely to perform less well.

Schooling and Social Inequality

Social-conflict analysis links schooling to the hierarchy involving class, race, and gender. Formal education also serves as a means of generating conformity to produce obedient adult workers. The use of standardized achievement tests is controversial. Some people see them as a reasonable measure of academic aptitude and learning, but others say they are culturally biased tools that may lead to labelling less privileged students as personally deficient. Streaming or tracking is another controversial issue. Some people see streaming as a way to provide appropriate instruction for students with different interests and aptitudes; others say that tracking gives privileged youngsters a richer education.

Problems in Schools

Many people are critical of public schooling. Lack of discipline and questionable standards are seen as problems. In addition, young women and men drop out of high school, thereby placing themselves at high risk of unemployment and poverty. Declining academic standards are reflected in lower than average scores on academic achievement tests and functional illiteracy among a significant proportion of high school graduates.

Education: Looking Ahead

Canada's education system is faced with the task of integrating people of many backgrounds and fostering a Canadian identify—without destroying our diversity.

The Information Revolution is changing education through the increasing use of computers and requiring students to prepare for work requiring new skill sets.

KEY CONCEPTS

education (p. 518) the social institution through which society provides its members with important knowledge, including basic facts, job skills, and cultural norms and values

schooling (p. 518) formal instruction under the direction of specially trained teachers

functional illiteracy (p. 521) a lack of the reading and writing skills needed for everyday living

hidden curriculum (p. 527) subtle presentations of political or cultural ideas in the classroom

streaming (tracking, or ability grouping) (p. 527) assigning students to different types of educational programs

APPLICATIONS & EXERCISES

1. Think back to your secondary school. Does it have a streaming policy? Does a student's social background affect his or her stream?

2. Talk to friends and classmates who are planning to become teachers. What motivates them? How do they see their future roles?

3. To explore the role of new information technology in reshaping education, visit Athabasca University at www.athabascau.ca. What do you see as the advantages and disadvantages of this type of schooling?

PRENTICE HALL
mysoclab™
Where learning & the sociological imagination intersect.

To reinforce your understanding of this chapter, and to identify topics for further study, visit MySocLab at **www.pearsoned.ca/mysoclab/** for diagnostic tests and a multimedia ebook.

Health and Medicine

How is health a social issue?

Which Canadians have the best health?

Why is there an obesity epidemic
in North America?

Stephanie says she cannot remember a time in her life when she was not on a diet. The sixteen-year-old, who lives in Gimli, Manitoba, shakes her head. "It's, like, I can't do anything about it. I know I don't look good. My mom says I shouldn't eat so much; the nurse at school says the same thing. "'Why can't I ever lose any weight?'"

Stephanie does have a weight problem. Although she stands just 160 cm (63 inches) tall, she weighs 109 kilograms (240 pounds). Doctors would call her morbidly obese, and the longer she remains so heavy, the greater her odds of serious disease and even death at a young age.

She is not alone. In a society where fast food has become a national dish and people use the word "supersize" as a verb, too many of us are getting fat. Not some people—but *most* people are overweight. Being overweight is not just a matter of looks. It is a critical health issue, putting obese people at high risk for heart disease, stroke, and diabetes. Each year, about 300 000 people in North America die early from diseases related to being overweight.

It is easy to dismiss being overweight as a personal flaw. The choices we make do matter, but we are up against biological factors and, more importantly, *powerful cultural forces.* North Americans are confronted with unhealthy fast food at every turn. Our national consumption of hamburgers, potato chips, sugar-rich soft drinks, pizza, and candy bars rises every year. The tendency to eat fast food, even in family settings, is accentuated by our lifestyles: single-parent and dual career families—combined with hectic schedules of sport, music and dance lessons—leave precious little time for home-cooked meals at the dining-room table.

What Is Health?

The World Health Organization defines **health** as *a state of complete physical, mental, and social well-being* (1946:3).

 Learn more about the World Health Organization, the first director-general of which, Dr. Chisholm, was a Canadian, at www.who.int/en/.

This definition underscores the major theme of this chapter that health is not just a matter of personal choice, nor it is only a biological issue. Patterns of well-being and illness are rooted in the organization of society.

HEALTH AND SOCIETY

Society shapes people's health in four major ways:

1. **Cultural patterns define health.** Standards of health vary from place to place. A century ago, yaws, a conta-

gious skin disease, was so common in sub-Saharan Africa that people there considered it normal (Dubos, 1980; orig. 1965). In North America, a rich diet is so common that most adults and about one-quarter of all children are overweight. "Health," therefore, is sometimes a matter of having the same disease as your neighbours (Pinhey, et al, 1997). What people see as healthful also reflects what they think is morally good. Men may think a competitive or aggressive approach to life is "healthy" or natural, because it fits with our norms of masculinity—but the resulting stress contributes to heart disease and many other illnesses (as noted in the Applying Sociology box on p. 543). "Dangerous masculinity" may result in accidents and assault, specifically in sports such as hockey (see the Thinking It Through box on p. 224–25 in Chapter 9, "Deviance"). People who object to homosexuality on moral grounds call this sexual orientation "sick," even though it is natural from a biological point of view. In these ways, ideas about health can act as a form of social control, encouraging conformity to cultural norms.

2. **Cultural standards of health change over time.** In the early twentieth century, some doctors warned women not to go to university because higher education strained the female brain. Others claimed that masturbation was a threat to health. We know now that both of these ideas are false. On the other hand, fifty years ago, few doctors understood the dangers of cigarette smoking or too much sun exposure, practices that we now recognize as dangerous health risks. We are only

APPLYING SOCIOLOGY
Masculinity: A Threat to Health?

Doctors call it "coronary-prone behaviour." Psychologists call it the "Type A personality." Almost everyone recognizes it as a North American concept of masculinity. This combination of attitudes and behaviour, common among men in our society, includes chronic impatience ("C'mon! Get outta my way!"); uncontrolled ambition ("I've gotta have it.... I *need* that!"); and free-floating hostility ("Why are so many people *such idiots*?").

This pattern, although normal from a cultural point of view, is one major reason that men who are driven to succeed are at high risk of heart disease. By acting out the Type A personality, such men may get the job done, but set in motion complex biochemical processes that are very hard on the human heart.

Here are a few questions to help you assess your own degree of risk or that of someone important to you:

1. **Do you believe you have to be aggressive to succeed?** Do you believe that "nice guys finish last"? If your answer to these questions is

Yes, for your heart's sake, try to remove hostility from your life. One starting point is to eliminate profanity from your speech. Try replacing aggression with compassion, which can be surprisingly effective in dealing with other people. Medically speaking, compassion and humour—rather than irritation and aggravation—will improve your health.

2. **How well do you handle uncertainty and opposition?** Do you have moments when you fume "Why won't the waiter take my order?" or "This customer just doesn't get it!" We all like to know what's going on, and we like others to agree with us. But the world often doesn't work this way. Accepting uncertainty and

opposition makes us more mature and certainly healthier.

3. **Are you uncomfortable showing positive emotions?** Many men think giving and accepting love—from women, from children, and from other men—is a sign of weakness. But the medical truth is that love supports health and anger damages it.

As human beings, we have a great deal of choice about how to live. Think about the choices you make, and reflect on how our society's idea of masculinity often makes men hard on others, including those they love, and—just as importantly—hard on themselves.

WHAT DO YOU THINK?

1. Is masculinity harmful to health? Explain your answer.
2. Do you think some types of masculinity contribute to alcohol abuse, accidents, or suicide?
3. How can sociology play a part in changing men's aggressive behaviour for the better?

Sources: Based on Friedman and Rosenman (1974) and Levine (1990).

---

now beginning to recognize the extent to which the high salt (or sodium) content of prepared foods is a major contributor to high blood pressure. Even patterns of basic hygiene change over time. Today, 75 percent of adults report bathing every day; back in 1950, only 30 percent said the same (Gallup, 2000).

3. **A society's technology affects people's health.** The three leading causes of death in North America a century ago were all contagious diseases. Today, improved living standards and advancements in medical technology have sharply reduced the number of deaths from infectious disease, leaving cancer and heart disease to account for over half of all deaths in Canada today. Poor sanitation and inadequate medical resources in poor societies today give rise to the infectious diseases that are common in those countries. Industrialization does raise living standards and improve health, but it also

creates new health threats—by overtaxing the world's resources and creating pollution.

4. **Social inequality affects people's health.** All societies distribute resources unequally. In Canada, despite **universal medical coverage**, *a system in which the costs of essential medical services are covered by the state*, the rich have far better physical and mental health than the poor. They also live longer.

Health: A Global Survey

The impact of social factors on human well-being is apparent in the improved health associated with economic development and advanced technology. Differences in societal development are also reflected in the striking differences in health around the world.

HEALTH IN HISTORY

With only simple technology, our ancestors could do little to improve health. Hunters and gatherers faced frequent food shortages, which sometimes forced mothers to abandon their children. Those lucky enough to survive infancy were still vulnerable to injury and illness, so half died by the age of 20 and few lived to the age of 40 (Nolan and Lenski, 2004).

As societies developed agriculture, food became more plentiful. Yet social inequality also increased: elites enjoyed better health than peasants and slaves, who lived in crowded unsanitary shelters and often went hungry. In the growing cities of mediaeval Europe, human waste and other refuse piled up in the streets, spreading infectious diseases, so that plagues periodically wiped out entire towns (Mumford, 1961).

HEALTH IN LOW-INCOME COUNTRIES

In much of the world, severe poverty cuts decades off the life expectancy enjoyed in rich countries. People in most parts of Africa, for example, have life expectancies of barely 50, meaning that, in the poorest countries, *infant mortality*—the death rate among children under one year of age—is high and many children die before reaching their teens.

The World Health Organization reports that 1 billion people around the world—about 1 person in 6—suffer from serious illness because of poverty. Bad health can result both from eating a single type of food or, more commonly, from having too little to eat. Malnutrition kills people of all ages, especially children. In low-income countries, sanitation is also a killer. Safe drinking water is as hard to come by as a balanced diet, and bad water carries a number of infectious diseases, including influenza, pneumonia, and tuberculosis, which are widespread killers in poor societies today. To make matters worse, medical personnel are few and far between; as a result, the world's poorest people—many of whom live in Central Africa—never see a physician.

In poor nations with minimal medical care, 10 percent of children die within a year of birth. In some countries, half the children never reach adulthood. For those who do grow up, illness and poverty form a vicious cycle: poverty breeds disease, which in turn undermines the ability to work. When medical technology does control infectious disease, the populations of poor nations rise. Without resources to ensure the well-being of the people they have now, poor societies can ill afford population increases. Therefore, programs that lower death rates in poor countries will succeed only if they are coupled with programs that reduce birth rates.

HEALTH IN HIGH-INCOME COUNTRIES

By 1800, as the Industrial Revolution took hold, factory jobs in the cities attracted people from all over the countryside in England and Europe. Cities quickly became over-crowded, a condition that made the already poor sanitation worse. Factories fouled the air with smoke, which few recognized as a health threat until well into the twentieth century. Accidents in the workplace were common.

Industrialization did gradually improve health in Western Europe and North America by providing better nutrition and safer housing for most people. After 1850, medical advances began to control infectious diseases. In 1854, for example, Dr. John Snow mapped the street addresses of London's cholera victims and found they had all drunk contaminated water from the same well. Not long afterwards, scientists linked cholera to a specific bacterium and developed a vaccine against the deadly disease. Armed with scientific knowledge, early activists campaigned against age-old practices such as discharging raw sewage into the same rivers used for drinking water. By the early twentieth century, death rates from infectious diseases had fallen sharply. The leading killers in 1900—influenza and pneumonia—account for just a small percentage of deaths today in high-income countries such as Canada and the United States. It is now chronic illnesses—such as heart disease, cancer, and stroke—that cause most deaths, usually in old age.

Health in Canada

In the spring and summer of 2003, Canada experienced three acute health crises that required the response of federal and provincial or territorial health authorities. Later, during 2005 and early 2006, Canadians were forced to respond to the threat of pandemic disease. The Thinking It Through box (on p. 545) takes a closer look at these health crises. Apart from such crises, Canadians enjoy health that is good by world standards—mainly because Canada is a rich country. Despite our affluence, though, some categories of people are better off than others.

WHO IS HEALTHY? AGE, GENDER, CLASS, AND RACE

Social epidemiology is *the study of health and disease as distributed throughout a society's population.* Just as early social epidemiologists, like Dr. John Snow, traced the spread of epidemic diseases, researchers today examine the connection between health and our physical and social environments. Patterns of health can be viewed in terms of age, gender, social class, and race.

For information on nutrition and health, go to www.hc-sc.gc.ca/fn-an/index_e.html.

AGE AND GENDER

Death is now rare among Canadian young people, with two notable exceptions: increases in mortality resulting from accidents and, more recently, from the sexually transmitted acquired immune deficiency syndrome (AIDS) (discussed in detail, below). Nonetheless, socio-cultural environments still affect the present and future health of youngsters: Canada's

THINKING IT THROUGH
SARS, West Nile, Mad Cow, and Bird Flu

In March 2003, two cases of atypical pneumonia in Toronto were identified as severe acute respiratory syndrome, better known as SARS. Suddenly, Canada was part of a global network that eventually would include 31 countries with suspected or probable SARS cases. The adequacy of federal and provincial responses to this new public health menace was questioned openly. We were faced with a two-pronged threat—importation of new cases from abroad and spread from the medical facilities that were caring for active SARS cases—and, initially, coped badly on both fronts.

Tourism in Toronto, and Canada as a whole, was dealt a crippling blow when the World Health Organization issued a travel advisory discouraging non-essential visits to Toronto. Conferences were cancelled and individuals from around the world changed travel plans. Some residents of Toronto began to avoid public places, Chinese restaurants and businesses in particular, as several SARS patients were of Chinese ancestry. Hundreds of other residents were "voluntarily" quarantined in their homes. Until it became clear that new cases arose almost exclusively in hospitals—and not from casual contact on the subway—there was a great deal of anxiety in Toronto. Six months later, with only one active case remaining, people going into doctors' offices, clinics, and hospitals were still washing their hands thoroughly and signing forms. By August 25, 2003, 438 cases of SARS (251 probable, 187 suspected, and 38 deaths) had been identified.

Next, we had to deal with one case of "mad cow" disease from an Alberta farm. A slaughtered cow had appeared ill when it arrived at the abattoir, but a delay of several months in testing its brain tissues meant that the task of tracking down its bovine contacts, feed sources, and offspring were especially complicated. Thousands of cattle linked in any way to the one identified case were slaughtered and tested for bovine spongiform encephalopathy (BSE), which had decimated herds in Europe in the previous decade. New regulations mandated that certain tissues (e.g., brain) be kept out of animal or human foods and that diseased carcasses not be used for animal feed.

Whereas loyal Canadians, including politicians, continued to eat beef, our cattle industry was devastated by American steps to close the border to Canadian beef and cattle. Since beef is our leading agricultural product and since 80 percent is exported to the United States, the Canadian economy reeled once again. In the fall of 2003, farmers had to decide what to do with thousands of cattle that had not been slaughtered and/or exported. Unable to feed them through the coming winter, farmers burned excess healthy cattle. It would take two years for a gradual easing of restrictions to eliminate the ban. Fortunately, none of the infected cattle identified in Canada or the U.S. entered the human food chain where it would have threatened people with the ultimately fatal Creutzfeldt-Jakob disease.

The West Nile scare in the summer of 2003 had a happier outcome. First reported in Canada among Ontario crows and blue jays in 2001, West Nile virus was confirmed in humans only in the summer and fall of 2002, with 3 confirmed cases, 14 suspected cases, and 1 death in Ontario. Canadians braced themselves for many more cases—but, perhaps because of mosquito control measures and diligent application of mosquito repellent, the number of Ontario cases in 2003 was limited to 2. Elsewhere, the numbers were similarly small—2 in the Atlantic provinces, 6 in Manitoba, and 1 each in Saskatchewan, Alberta, and British Columbia. Of course, there were many sub-clinical cases of West Nile infection, since the vast majority of infected people are symptom free. Nonetheless, Canada responded appropriately to limit the spread of a potentially deadly disease.

In 2005, we became aware of the threat of bird (or avian) flu, a much-hyped pandemic said to be "long overdue" with the potential to kill millions worldwide. Starting in Asia, the flu gradually appeared in pockets in Europe and even North America. A virus called H5N1 was infecting chickens—and people who handled the birds were falling ill and dying. Because those with mild symptoms were never diagnosed, it seemed that half the people who caught the flu (from birds) were dying. The World Health Organization declared that *human-to-human* transmission of something like H5N1 is inevitable and here in North America we started producing and stockpiling antiviral medications (e.g., Tamiflu and Relenza). More ominously, we are debating who should get the limited supply of antivirals. Front-line responders like doctors and firefighters were obvious choices, but how do you value babies, young adults, or elderly people? Who do we need to save to ensure that Canadian society survives in the event of pandemic influenza?

WHAT DO YOU THINK?

1. Did the Canadian government handle each of these crises well?
2. Should government decide who gets antivirals or should individuals be able to buy their own supplies?
3. Do the media blow these health crises out of proportion? Explain your answer.

Sources: Canada (2006b, 2006c), Fumento (2006), and Kirkey (2006).

TABLE 21–1

Self-Reported Health: Canadian Women and Men by Age, 1975 to 1995

| | Percentage Reporting "Excellent" or "Good" Health | | | |
| | 1975 | | 1995 | |
	Women	Men	Women	Men
All adults	73	84	80	85
18 to 34	84	94	84	94
35 to 54	76	87	84	85
55 and older	58	66	63	68

Source: Adapted by L.M. Gerber from Bibby (1995:86).

TABLE 21–2

Mortality and Life Expectancy, First Nations and All Canadians, 1960 and 2001[*]

| | 1960 | | 2001 | |
	First Nations	Canadian	First Nations	Canadian
Crude death rate[a]	10.9	8.0	9.2	6.0
Infant mortality rate[b]	79.0	27.3	13.0	8.0
Male life expectancy[c]	59.7	68.5	68.0	74.0
Female life expectancy	63.5	74.3	71.3	80.0

[*]First Nations data are for registered Status Indians on or off reserve, including the territories where most First Nations do not have reserves. Data do not include Inuit, Métis, or non-Status Indians.

[a] Deaths per 1000 population.
[b] Deaths of children in first year of life per 1000 live births.
[c] Age to which a person can expect to live, calculated at time of birth.

Source: Adapted by L.M. Gerber from Frideres and Gadacz (2001:66)

 For a report on the factors contributing to youth obesity, go to www.statcan.ca/Daily/English/031103/d031103a.htm.

children, who are subject to poor diet, lack of exercise, and secondhand smoke, are the obesity and the heart patients of tomorrow.

Measures of self-reported health over two decades (Bibby, 1995) reveal that, by 1995, Canadian women were increasingly likely to report "excellent" or "good" health, as shown in Table 2–1. Though reported well-being drops off with age, for both genders, women fared better in 1995 than in 1975. In 1975, reported well-being among women declined after age 35; in 1995, the decline shows up only after age 55. The explanation for the gender gap in well-being after age 55 is that women live longer than men—5 years on average—and therefore spend more time in the stage of life when health is on the decline.

SOCIAL CLASS AND RACE

Infant mortality is twice as high for disadvantaged children as for children born into privileged families. While the health of the richest children in Canada is the best in the world, our poorest children—Aboriginal children in particular—are as vulnerable to disease as those in the low-income countries of the world. Infant mortality rates for First Nations have dropped dramatically since 1960, as shown in Table 21–2, but are still 1.6 times those of the Canadian population. Think about that for a moment: the infant mortality rate for First Nations is almost double that of *all* Canadians—rich and poor, not just affluent Canadians. This suggests double jeopardy: these babies die especially frequently because they are poor and status-Indian. Equally disturbing is the fact that post-neonatal death rates (infants aged one month to one year) "are more than three times higher for Indians"—note *three times higher*. These rates reflect the poverty, poor housing, and other environmental conditions affecting First Nation families (Frideres and Gadacz, 2001:71).

These data do not differentiate rates for on-reserve and off-reserve residents: were they to do so, we would find that on-reserve infant mortality rates would be much higher. Surveys

indicate that "residents of rural and remote communities have poorer health than people who live in urban centres" and that "the farther a community is from a large urban centre, the poorer the health of the residents" (McPherson, 2004:413). On this basis, one could say that reserve-based First Nations—most of whom live outside urban centres—suffer triple jeopardy: they become ill and die at younger ages because they are poor, status-Indian, and rural.

Researchers tell us that adults in high-income families overwhelmingly report that their health is excellent or very good, but fewer than half in low-income families say the same. Health and social status are strongly related in terms of the incidence of disease or longevity. Affluent people, with more social capital, are healthier because "they have more knowledge power (from education), more purchasing power (from income) and more employment power (from prestige and access to networks)" (McPherson, 2004:412). Having a higher income boosts health by improving nutrition and access to better health care, and by allowing safer and less stressful surroundings (Krueger, *et al.*, 2003; Lethbridge-Cejku and Vickerie, 2005).

General health and life expectancy tend to be higher for immigrants than for those born in Canada. The "healthy immigrant effect" is most apparent "among recent immigrants because healthier people are more likely to emigrate, and because health requirements in the *Immigration Act* screen out people with serious medical conditions" (McPherson, 2004:412). The longer immigrants lived in Canada, the more their health status approached the norm. Over time, the poverty that characterizes many ethnic groups or visible minorities takes its toll on health: "Immigrants make less use of health services, especially mental and preventive health services, than the Canadian-born population" (p. 413).

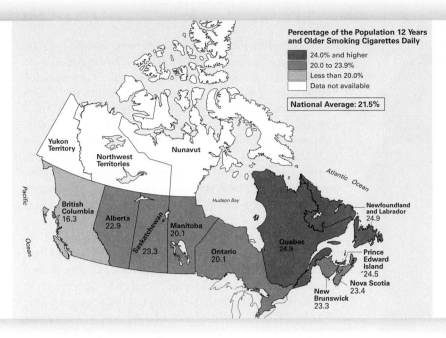

SEEING OURSELVES

CANADA MAP 21–1

Percentage of the Population 12 Years
and Older Smoking Cigarettes Daily,
2000–2001

Source: Data compiled by L.M. Gerber from the Statistics Canada
website, http://www.statcan.ca/english/Pgdb/health07a.htm.

CIGARETTE SMOKING

Cigarette smoking tops the list of preventable hazards to health. It was only after World War I that smoking became popular in Canada. Despite growing evidence of its dangers, smoking remained fashionable. Recently, among adults—but not among young people smoking has fallen out of favour and is considered a mild form of social deviance. As concern about the health effects of smoking grew, consumption of cigarettes fell from its peak in 1960, when almost 45 percent of Canadian adults smoked. By 2000–01, only 21.5 percent of Canadians were smokers: Canada Map 21–1 shows levels ranging from 16.3 percent in British Columbia to 24.9 percent in Quebec and in Newfoundland and Labrador. These figures represent a drop in smoking from 24.3 percent in 1994–95 to 21.5 percent for Canada as a whole, and a drop from 29.1 percent to 24.9 percent in Quebec.

Despite the addictive quality of nicotine and the difficulty of quitting, it is surprising to learn that 24 percent of the people who were smoking in 1994–95 had quit by 2000–01. The percentage of Canadians who quit ranged from 24 to 26 percent in all of the provinces except Prince Edward Island, British Columbia, and Alberta, where the quitting rates were much lower (21%, 20%, and 16%, respectively).

Cigarettes have taken a growing toll on women's health. Lung cancer now competes with breast cancer as a leading cause of death among Canadian women. Worse yet, smoking is estimated to be responsible for one-quarter of deaths of men and women between 35 and 84 years of age. Smokers endure frequent minor illnesses, such as influenza, and pregnant women who smoke increase the likelihood of spontaneous abortion (miscarriage), prenatal death, and babies with a low birth weight. Even nonsmokers exposed to secondhand cigarette smoke have a higher risk of smoking-related diseases.

The tobacco industry maintained for years that, because the precise link between cigarettes and disease was not specified, the health effects of smoking remained "an open question." Nonetheless, laws mandating smoke-free environments are spreading rapidly. By 1997, the tobacco industry had conceded that cigarette smoking is harmful to health and agreed to end marketing strategies that target youngsters. In 1998, Canada took steps to restrict advertising and the sponsorship of sporting and cultural events by the tobacco industry. The tobacco industry has increased its focus on world markets, especially in low-income countries where there is less regulation of tobacco products. In many countries, especially in Asia, a large majority of men smoke. Worldwide, more than 1 billion adults smoke (about 30% of the total), consuming some 6 trillion cigarettes annually—and smoking is on the rise. The good news on this front is that, about ten years after quitting, an ex-smoker's health is almost as good as that of someone who never smoked at all.

YOUR TURN

Researchers report that the less schooling people have, the more likely they are to smoke. Why do you think this is the case?

EATING DISORDERS

An **eating disorder** is *an intense form of dieting or other unhealthy method of weight control driven by the desire to be very thin.* One eating disorder, anorexia nervosa, is characterized by dieting to the point of starvation; another is bulimia, which involves binge eating followed by induced

Mary-Kate Olsen (*right*) with her twin sister Ashley Olsen, is among the many young women celebrities who have struggled with an eating disorder. To what extent do you think the mass media are responsible for encouraging young women to be so thin that some even put their lives at risk? Explain your view.

YOUR TURN

In the fall of 2006, the European fashion industry took steps to keep dangerously thin models off the runways. Do you think this is justified?

vomiting to avoid weight gain. Eating disorders have a significant cultural component: 95 percent of people who suffer from anorexia nervosa or bulimia are women, mostly from affluent White families. Our culture equates slenderness with being successful and attractive. Conversely, we tend to stereotype overweight women and, to a lesser extent, men as lazy, sloppy, and even stupid (Levine, 1987). Research shows that most young women believe that "guys like thin girls," being thin is critical to physical attractiveness, and they are not as thin as men would like. In fact, most of them want to be even thinner than the men want them to be. Men, in contrast, express more satisfaction with their body shape (Fallon and Rozin, 1985). Because few achieve our culture's unrealistic standards of beauty, many women develop low self-images. Our idealized image of beauty leads many young women to diet to the point of risking their health and even their lives.

OBESITY

Eating disorders such as anorexia nervosa and bulimia are not the biggest eating-related problem in North America. At the other end of the scale, literally, we have the increasing problem of obesity. The Canadian Community Health Survey, which directly measures the heights and weights of respondents, found that obesity rates for adults and children rose substantially over the past 25 years. Between 1978–79 and 2004, obesity rates among children aged 2 to 17 rose from 3 percent to 8 percent, while over the same time period adult rates rose from 14 percent to 23 percent, the latter representing 5.5 million adult Canadians (Statistics Canada, 2005c).

Obesity is an intractable problem: once people are overweight they are more likely to gain further weight than to take it off. The National Population Health Survey revealed that, over an eight-year period, one-quarter of the Canadians who had been overweight at the beginning were obese by 2002–03, while only 10 percent dropped to normal weight. Women, younger men, and the poor were most likely to become obese. Not surprisingly, if parents are obese, children are at greater risk of obesity as well (Statistics Canada, 2005d). Unfortunately, being overweight limits physical activity and raises the risk of debilitating diseases like heart disease, stroke, and diabetes.

What are the social causes of obesity? One factor is that more people have jobs that keep them sitting at desks or in front of computer screens—rather than engaging in the type of physical labour that was common a century ago. Even when we are not on the job, much of the work around the house is done by machines. Children spend more of their time sitting as well—watching television or playing video games. Then, of course, there is diet. The typical North American is eating more salty and fatty food than ever before. And meals are getting bigger. The U.S. Department of Agriculture recently reported that, in 2000, the typical adult consumed 140 more pounds (64 kilograms) of food in a year than was true just a decade earlier. Comparing old and new editions of cookbooks, recipes that used to say they would feed six now say they will feed four. The odds of being overweight go up among people with lower incomes partly because stores in low-income communities offer a greater selection of low-cost, high-fat foods, and fewer healthful fruits and vegetables (Hellmich, 2002).

YOUR TURN

Calculate your *body mass index*: [weight in pounds ÷ (height in inches)^2] × 703. A body mass index of 18.5 to 24.9 is normal, 25.0 to 29.9 is considered overweight, 30.0 and above is obese. Where does your body mass index fall? Were you surprised by the results?

SEXUALLY TRANSMITTED DISEASES

Sexual activity, though both pleasurable and vital to the continuation of our species, can transmit more than fifty kinds of *sexually transmitted diseases* (STDs). Because our culture associates sex with sin, some people regard these diseases not only as illnesses but also as marks of immorality. Sexually transmitted diseases grabbed national attention during the Sexual Revolution of the 1960s, when infection rates rose as people began sexual activity earlier and with a greater number of partners. The rise in sexually transmitted diseases is an exception to the general decline of infectious diseases during the twentieth century. By the late 1980s, the rising dangers of sexually transmitted diseases—especially AIDS—generated a sexual counter-revolution as people moved away from casual sex (Kain, 1987; Laumann, et al., 1994). The following sections briefly describe several common STDs.

Gonorrhea and Syphilis

Gonorrhoea and syphilis, among the oldest known diseases, are caused by microscopic organisms that are almost always transmitted by sexual contact. Untreated, gonorrhoea causes sterility; syphilis damages major organs and can result in blindness, mental disorders, and death. Recent increases in rates of infection of both gonorrhoea and syphilis are attributed to failure to use safer sex methods. Health Canada reports that rates of gonorrhoea infection rose more than 40 percent in the past five years—after consistently declining over the previous 20 years. Unfortunately, drug-resistant strains of the disease are also on the upswing. Cases of syphilis were rare in Canada in the 1990s but, between 1997 and 2003, the number of cases quadrupled. Localized outbreaks have been reported in Vancouver, Calgary, Toronto, Ottawa, and Montreal, many within the sex trade and the gay community.

Genital Herpes

Genital herpes is a virus that infects at least 45 million adolescents and adults in the United States (1 in 5). Canadian data are not available because physicians are not required to report cases. Although far less dangerous than gonorrhoea and syphilis, herpes is incurable. People with genital herpes may not have any symptoms, or they may experience periodic, painful blisters on the genitals accompanied by fever and headache. Although not fatal to adults, genital herpes in pregnant women can be transmitted during a vaginal delivery, and it can be deadly to a newborn; for this reason, women with active infections are typically delivered by caesarean section (Sobel, 2001).

For Health Canada information on STDs, go to www.hc-sc.gc.ca/dc-ma/sti-its/index_e.html.

Acquired Immune Deficiency Syndrome (AIDS)

The most serious of all sexually transmitted diseases is acquired immune deficiency syndrome (AIDS). Identified in 1981, it is incurable and almost always fatal, although, with new medication, some people are living with the disease for more than 20 years. AIDS is caused by the human immunodeficiency virus (HIV), which attacks white blood cells, weakens the immune system, and makes people vulnerable to a wide range of diseases that eventually cause death. Officials recorded roughly 43 000 new cases of AIDS in the United States in 2003. Canada reported roughly 400; compared to the 1800 new cases reported in 1993, we seem to be doing very well—but keep in mind that these figures refer to AIDS cases only. Thousands more people—in fact, roughly 58 000—carry the HIV virus, which is often undiagnosed and even unsuspected by the carriers themselves.

The first AIDS case in Canada was reported by the Laboratory Centre for Disease Control in February 1982. By December 1993, there had been 6187 reported deaths from AIDS in Canada, and another 2896 people documented as living with AIDS. By December 2002 these numbers had risen to 12 674 reported deaths due to AIDS, 19 213 people diagnosed with AIDS, and 52 640 people diagnosed with HIV. It is important to note that, since the late 1990s, Canada's widespread education campaign has led to changes in sexual practices and drug and intravenous use, with resulting declines in rates of new HIV infection and deaths from AIDS. Annual HIV infections reached a high of 1804 in 1994 and deaths from AIDS reached a high of 1481 in 1995, before dropping to 428 (HIV) and 158 (AIDS) in 2001 (Canada, 2003d:61, 40, 11). The rapid decline in AIDS diagnoses and deaths seems to have reassured people to the extent that many have abandoned safer-sex practices.

Figure 21–1(a) compares the infection routes for AIDS cases in Canada of 1979–99 with those of 2005. Note that the proportions of cases derived from male homosexual contact, intravenous drug use, and blood clotting agent decreased by 2005. Proportionately more cases in 2005 came from contact in a country where HIV is endemic (common) and from sexual contact with a person at risk. At the same time, the proportion attributed to heterosexual contact doubled—from 7.9 percent to 16.8 percent (Gandhi, 2006). The point here is that you do not need to be gay, a drug user, or in the sex trade to be at risk for AIDS.

Figure 21–1(b) reveals that the relationship between AIDS and ethnic background in Canada changed dramatically between 1979–99 and 2005. The proportion of White people with AIDS dropped from 84 percent to 60 percent, while the proportions Black, Aboriginal, and Asian/Arab increased. The proportion of Aboriginal people with AIDS increased six times—from 2.7 percent to 16.4 percent of the cases (Gandhi, 2006).

Women account for 8 percent of all AIDS cases reported in Canada. From 1982 to 1984, 20 women were diagnosed with AIDS; between 1988 and 1989, 157 women had contracted the disease. By June 2001, 1437 cases of AIDS among women had been reported; 16 percent of all cases reported in 2001 involved females (up from 5.6% of cases reported before 1990). As of December 1999, there

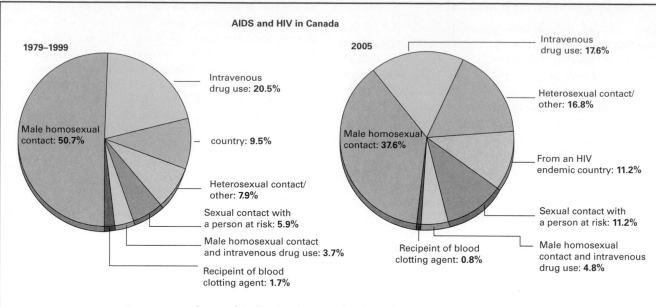

AIDS and HIV in Canada

1979–1999

Male homosexual contact: **50.7%**

Intravenous drug use: **20.5%**

country: **9.5%**

Heterosexual contact/other: **7.9%**

Sexual contact with a person at risk: **5.9%**

Male homosexual contact and intravenous drug use: **3.7%**

Recipeint of blood clotting agent: **1.7%**

2005

Male homosexual contact: **37.6%**

Intravenous drug use: **17.6%**

Heterosexual contact/other: **16.8%**

From an HIV endemic country: **11.2%**

Sexual contact with a person at risk: **11.2%**

Male homosexual contact and intravenous drug use: **4.8%**

Recipeint of blood clotting agent: **0.8%**

FIGURE 21-1(a)   Percentage Share of Infection Routes in Canada, 1979–99 Compared to 2005

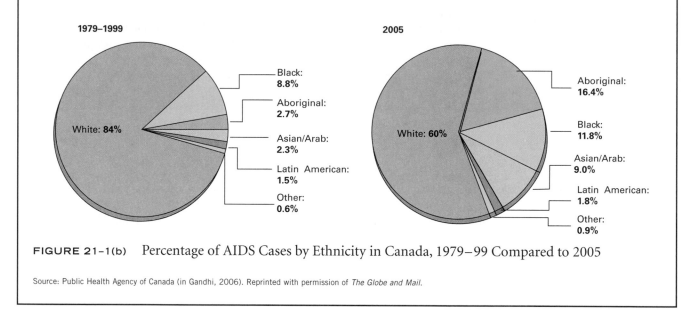

1979–1999

White: **84%**

Black: **8.8%**

Aboriginal: **2.7%**

Asian/Arab: **2.3%**

Latin American: **1.5%**

Other: **0.6%**

2005

White: **60%**

Aboriginal: **16.4%**

Black: **11.8%**

Asian/Arab: **9.0%**

Latin American: **1.8%**

Other: **0.9%**

FIGURE 21-1(b)   Percentage of AIDS Cases by Ethnicity in Canada, 1979–99 Compared to 2005

Source: Public Health Agency of Canada (in Gandhi, 2006). Reprinted with permission of *The Globe and Mail.*

were 185 children under age 15 diagnosed with AIDS; 83 percent of them had contracted AIDS from their mothers before or around the time of birth.

As noted above, another disturbing trend is the spread within the Aboriginal community. While the overall increase in AIDS cases has levelled off, the incidence within the Aboriginal population has been increasing steadily. The proportion of Aboriginal people among AIDS cases increased from 1.5 percent before 1986 to 17.6 percent in 2005. Injection drug use is responsible for 64 percent of AIDS cases among Aboriginal women and 28 percent among Aboriginal men (Canada, 2006b; Gandhi, 2006).

Globally, HIV infects some 40 million people—half of them under the age of 25—and the number is rising rapidly. The global AIDS death toll now exceeds 20 million; around

the world each day, 8700 people die of AIDS and 14 000 more are infected with HIV. As Global Map 21–1 shows, Africa—especially south of the Sahara—has the highest HIV infection rate and accounts for 66 percent of all world cases. A recent United Nations study found that, across much of sub-Saharan Africa, 15-year-olds face a 50/50 chance of becoming infected with HIV. The risk is especially high for girls, not only because HIV is transmitted more easily from men to women but also because many African cultures expect women to be submissive to men. According to some analysts, the AIDS crisis now threatens the political and economic security of Africa, which in turn affects the entire world (Ashford, 2002; United Nations, 2004).

On being infected with HIV, people display no symptoms at all, so most are unaware of their condition.

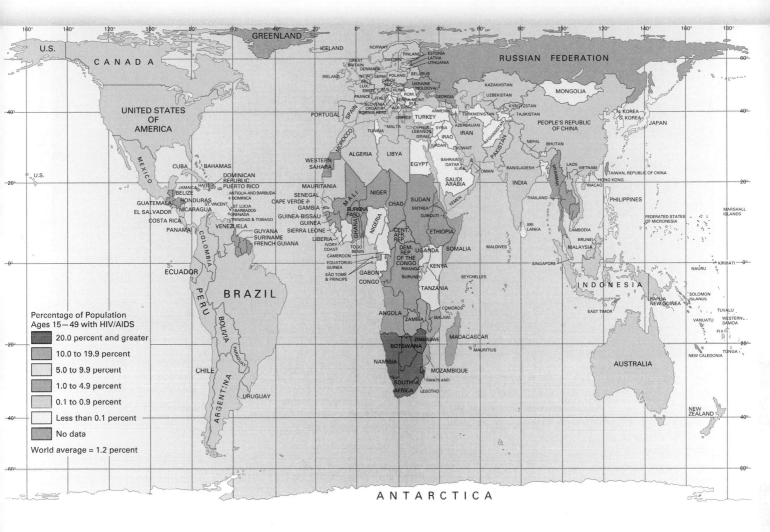

WINDOW ON THE WORLD

GLOBAL MAP 21-1   HIV/AIDS Infection of Adults in Global Perspective

Of all global HIV infections, 64 percent are in sub-Saharan Africa. In countries such as Botswana and Swaziland, more than one-third of people between the ages of 15 and 49 are infected with HIV/AIDS. This very high infection rate reflects the prevalence of other sexually transmitted diseases and infrequent use of condoms, two factors that promote transmission of HIV. All of Southeast Asia accounts for about 17 percent of global HIV infections. In Cambodia, 2 to 3 percent of people aged 15 to 49 are now infected. All of North and South America taken together account for 8 percent of global HIV infections. By world standards, the incidence of infection in predominantly Muslim nations is extremely low.

Sources: Population Reference Bureau (2003, 2005); and United Nations (2004); map projection from *Peters Atlas of the World* (1990).

For United Nations efforts to combat AIDS, go to www.unaids.org/en/.

Symptoms of AIDS may not appear for a year or longer but, during this time, an infected person may infect others. Within 5 years, one-third of infected people develop full-blown AIDS; half develop AIDS within 10 years, and almost all become sick within 20 years. In low-income countries, the progression of this illness is much more rapid than elsewhere.

HIV is infectious but not contagious. That is, HIV is transmitted from person to person through blood, semen, or breast milk but not through casual contact such as shaking hands, hugging, sharing towels or dishes, swimming together, or even by coughing and sneezing. The risk of transmitting the virus through saliva (as in kissing) is extremely low. The chance of transmitting HIV through sexual activity is greatly reduced by the use of latex

Stephen Lewis, former Canadian Ambassador to the United Nations and UNICEF director, is now the United Nations Special Envoy for HIV/AIDS in Africa. An inspiring speaker who easily moves audiences as he describes the devastation wrought by AIDS in Africa, he tells of speaking to local crowds made up of orphans and their grandmothers–with the parent generation missing altogether. He played an active role in the International AIDS Conference in Toronto (August 2006) and has established the Stephen Lewis Foundation to provide grassroots care for women and children with AIDS as well as orphans and their care-giver grandmothers.

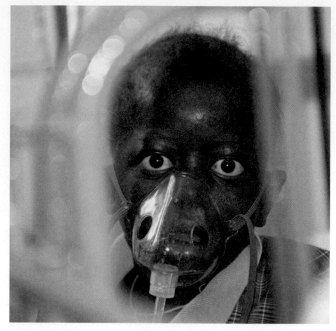

In the African nation of Kenya, there are about 500 deaths from AIDS every day. In parts of sub-Saharan Africa, the epidemic is so great that half of all children will become infected with HIV. This young Nairobi child, who already has AIDS, is fighting for his life.

condoms. However, abstinence or an exclusive relationship with an uninfected person are the only sure ways to avoid infection.

Some specific behaviours do put people at high risk of HIV infection. The first is *anal sex*, which can cause rectal bleeding, allowing easy transmission of HIV from one person to another. *Sharing needles* to inject drugs is a second high-risk behaviour, which in turn makes sex with an intravenous drug user very risky. Intravenous drug use is more common among poor people in North America, Aboriginal and Black people among them. *Using any drug*, including alcohol, also increases the risk of HIV infection to the extent that it impairs judgment. In other words, even people who understand what places them at risk of infection may act less responsibly if they are under the influence of alcohol, marijuana, or some other drug.

The American and Canadian governments responded slowly to the AIDS crisis, largely because the earliest people to be infected—gay men and intravenous drug users—were widely viewed as deviant. But funds allocated for AIDS research have increased rapidly to US$19 billion annually in the United States. In 2004, the Canadian government announced that "federal HIV/AIDS funding would increase to $84 million from $42.2 million annually over five years." Critics argue that Canada should be spending $100 million or $200 million on prevention alone (Gandhi, 2006). Researchers have identified some drugs, including protease inhibitors, that suppress the symptoms of the disease. Nevertheless, educational programs remain the most effective weapon against AIDS, since prevention is the only way to stop a disease that so far has no cure.

ETHICAL ISSUES SURROUNDING DEATH

Now that technological advances are giving human beings the power to draw the line separating life and death, we must decide how and when to do so. In other words, questions about the use of medical technology have added an ethical dimension to health and illness.

When Does Death Occur?

Common sense suggests that life ceases when breathing and heartbeat stop. But the ability to replace a heart and artificially sustain respiration makes that definition of death obsolete. As discussed in Chapter 15 ("Aging and the Elderly"), medical and legal experts now define death as an *irreversible state* involving no response to stimulation, no movement or breathing, no reflexes, and no indication of brain activity (Ladd, 1979; Wall, 1980; Jones, 1998).

Do People Have a Right to Die?

Today, medical personnel, family members, and patients themselves face the agonizing burden of deciding when a terminally ill person should die. In 1992, the Parliament of Canada abolished attempted suicide as a crime but retained the prohibition against assisting a suicide. Individuals periodically challenge this law, as did Sue Rodriguez, a British Columbia woman with Lou Gehrig's disease, as discussed in Chapter 15 ("Aging and the Elderly"). Rodriguez eventually would have been unable to swallow, to speak, to walk, or even to turn over without assistance. She would have needed a respirator to breathe. As her condition worsened, she would be less able to end her own life. She wanted permission for a doctor, at a given time in the future, to set up an intravenous tube filled with a lethal dose of medication. Her case spawned both widespread support and fervent opposition from churches, right-to-life activists, and provincial and federal governments (Wood, 1993). In 1993, the Supreme Court of Canada ruled that the state's interest in protecting the sanctity of life took precedence over the individual's right to a dignified death. In the end, Rodriguez was helped to die by an anonymous physician and her friend, maverick MP Svend Robinson.

Normally, the first responsibility of physicians and hospitals is to protect a patient's life. Even so, a mentally competent person in the process of dying may refuse medical treatment or even nutrition. Moreover, laws require hospitals, nursing homes, and other medical facilities to honour the desires of a patient made earlier in the form of a living will. Thus, we do make decisions regarding when and how death will occur.

What about Mercy Killing?

As discussed in Chapter 15 ("Aging and the Elderly"), mercy killing is the common term for *euthanasia*, assisting in the death of a person suffering from an incurable disease. Euthanasia (from the Greek, meaning "a good death") poses an ethical dilemma, being at once an act of kindness and a form of killing. Support for a patient's right to die (that is, passive euthanasia) is growing in North America. But assisting in the death of another person (active euthanasia) still provokes controversy and may violate the law.

In October 1993, Saskatchewan farmer Robert Latimer killed his badly disabled daughter Tracy by carbon monoxide poisoning. He felt that his daughter's life of constant pain was not worth living: he killed her because he loved her. A groundswell of public sentiment, both supportive and hostile, erupted. Latimer was convicted of second-degree murder in 1995 and given a one-year prison sentence. Although convicted, he was released from prison and confined to his farm. In 1998, an appeal court convicted Latimer of murder, with a mandatory life sentence (25 years imprisonment, without parole for 10 years). In January 2001, the Supreme Court of Canada turned down his appeal

Nancy Morrison, a Halifax physician, was charged with murdering a terminally ill cancer patient in November 1996. The judge threw out the charges, but the case reignited heated debate on the morality of mercy killing.

for a new trial and ruled that he should serve at least 10 years in prison (Beltrame, 2001). The Court would not consider compassionate grounds for a more lenient sentence.

The debate on euthanasia usually centres on the following issues. Those who categorically view life—even with suffering and disability—as preferable to death, reject both passive and active euthanasia. People who recognize circumstances under which death is preferable to life endorse passive or perhaps active euthanasia, but they face the practical problem of determining just when life should be ended. (See the Thinking Critically box in Chapter 15 on p. 396.)

The Medical Establishment

Medicine is *the social institution that focuses on fighting disease and improving health.* Through most of human history, health care was the responsibility of individuals and their families. Medicine emerges as a social institution only as societies become more productive and people take on specialized work. Members of agrarian societies today still turn to various traditional health practitioners, including herbalists and acupuncturists, who play a central part in improving health. In industrial societies, medical care falls

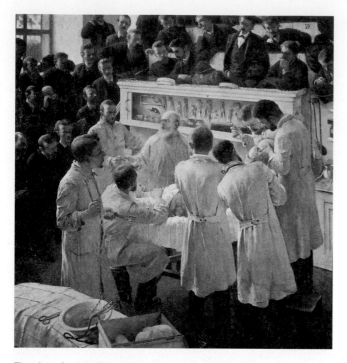

The rise of scientific medicine during the nineteenth century resulted in new skills and technology for treating many common ailments that had afflicted humanity for centuries. At the same time, however, scientific medicine pushed forms of health care involving women to the margins and placed medicine under the control of men living in cities. We see this pattern in the A.F. Seligmann painting *General Hospital*, showing an obviously all-male medical school class in Vienna in 1880.

mainly to specially trained and licensed professionals, from anaesthesiologists to X-ray technicians.

THE RISE OF SCIENTIFIC MEDICINE

In colonial North America, doctors, herbalists, druggists, midwives, and ministers all engaged in various forms of healing arts. But not all did so effectively: unsanitary instruments, lack of anaesthesia, and simple ignorance made surgery a terrible ordeal in which doctors probably killed as many patients as they saved. Gradually, however, specialists learned more about human anatomy, physiology, and biochemistry. Early in the nineteenth century, medical societies appeared in Canada as doctors established themselves as self-regulating professionals (Blishen, 1991). Formal colleges of medicine offered training in the field. The increase in the number of medical schools paralleled the growth in the number of hospitals (Stevens, 1971). Medical societies required those who wished to practice or teach medical skills to obtain licences, and these organizations enforced conformity to specific medical standards.

The establishment in 1865 of the General Council of Medical Education and Registration in Upper Canada signified acceptance of the scientific model of medicine, and widely publicized the medical successes of its members to further improve its own image. Scientific researchers were touted for tracing the cause of life-threatening illnesses to bacteria and viruses, and also for developing vaccines to prevent disease (Blishen, 1991).

Still, alternative approaches to health care, such as regulating nutrition, also had many defenders. Of course, conventional doctors criticized these alternative approaches to health care. They established the Canadian Medical Association in 1867. With control of the certification process, the association was able to define what constituted medical practice. Thus, doctors, through the provincial colleges, could determine what the various "paramedical" occupations could and could not do. Before long, the practice of medicine was limited mainly to those with a medical degree. In the process, both the prestige and income of physicians rose dramatically.

Other practitioners, such as naturopaths, herbal healers, and midwives held to their traditional roles, but at a high cost: all have been relegated to fringe areas of the medical profession. With far less social prestige and income than physicians, such professionals now have a small, if devoted, following in Canada (Blishen, 1991; Nancarrow Clarke, 1996). Treatment by chiropractors is now partially covered by provincial health insurance, and midwives have recently been legally recognized as birth attendants in Ontario (Rajhathy and Roulard, 1994:40). Further, more than one-third of North Americans use some form of "complementary" medicine (Eisenberg, et al., 1993).

The rise of scientific medicine, taught in expensive, urban medical schools, also changed the social profile of doctors. There is and has long been an overrepresentation of medical students from higher-level social backgrounds (Blishen, 1991). Traditionally, medicine is a male-dominated profession, as women were long considered unfit to practice medicine (Starr, 1982; Huet-Cox, 1984; Nancarrow Clarke, 1996). While in 1992 more than 80 percent of physicians were men and some 97 percent of nurses were women, younger cohorts are changing these male/female ratios dramatically, as noted below.

HOLISTIC MEDICINE

In recent years, the scientific model of medicine has been tempered by the more traditional model of **holistic medicine,** *an approach to health care that emphasizes the prevention of illness and takes into account a person's entire physical and social environment.* Holistic practitioners agree on the need for drugs, surgery, artificial organs, and high technology, but they emphasize treatment of the whole person, rather than symptoms, and focus on health, rather than disease. Holistic practitioners treat patients as people in the context of lifestyle and environmental factors. Holistic medicine favours an *active* approach to *health*, rather than a reactive approach to *illness*—shifting responsibility for health—promoting behaviour to us as patients. In addition, holistic practitioners generally provide their personal treatment in homes, rather than in hospitals or offices (Gordon, 1980; Patterson, 1998).

YOUR TURN

How much responsibility should you take for your own health? In what ways can a society improve the health of its population?

PAYING FOR MEDICAL CARE: A GLOBAL SURVEY

As medicine has come to rely on high technology, the costs of providing medical care have skyrocketed. Countries throughout the world use various strategies to meet these costs.

MEDICINE IN SOCIALIST NATIONS

In nations with mostly socialist economies, government provides medical care directly to the people. These countries hold that all citizens have the right to basic medical care—paid for by the government using public funds. The state owns and operates medical facilities and pays salaries to doctors and other medical care workers, who are government employees.

China, an industrializing but still mostly agrarian nation, faces the immense task of providing for the health of more than 1 billion people. China has experimented with private medicine, but the government controls most medical care. China's "barefoot" doctors, roughly comparable to our paramedics, bring some modern methods of medical care to millions of farm workers in rural villages. Otherwise, traditional healing arts, including acupuncture and the use of medicinal herbs, are still widely practised in China. The Chinese approach to health is based on a holistic concern for the interplay of mind and body (Kaptchuk, 1985).

The Russian Federation is transforming a state-dominated economy into more of a market system. For this reason, medical care is currently in transition. Nonetheless, the idea that everyone has a right to basic medical care remains widespread. As in China, people do not choose a physician but report to a local government-operated health facility. Physicians have much lower incomes than medical doctors in North America, earning about the same salary as skilled industrial workers. Interestingly, about 70 percent of Russian doctors are women, compared to 30 percent in Canada. In recent years, the Russian Federation has suffered setbacks in health care and a falling standard of living. A rising demand for medical care has strained a bureaucratic system that, at best, provides highly standardized and impersonal care. The optimistic view is that, as market reforms proceed, both living standards and the quality of medical services will improve. In Russia's uncertain times, what does seem certain is that inequality in medical care will increase (Specter, 1995; Landsberg, 1998).

MEDICINE IN CAPITALIST NATIONS

Capitalist countries are inclined to have people pay for medical care out of their own pockets. However, because

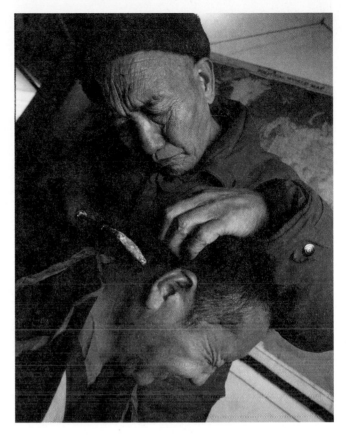

Traditional healers work to improve people's health throughout the world, especially in low income nations. Here, a Chinese practitioner treats a patient by burning rolled herbs into his scalp.

high cost puts medical care beyond the reach of many people, government programs underwrite much of the expense.

In 1891, Sweden began a mandatory, comprehensive system of government medical care. Citizens pay for this program with their taxes, which are among the highest in the world. Typically, physicians are government employees, and most hospitals are government-managed. Because this medical system resembles that found in socialist societies, Sweden's system is called **socialized medicine,** *a medical care system in which the government owns and operates most medical facilities and employs most physicians.*

In 1948, Great Britain also established socialized medicine by creating a dual system of medical service. All British citizens are entitled to medical care provided by the National Health Service, but those who can afford to may go to doctors and hospitals that operate privately. Physicians in Japan also have private practices, but a combination of government programs and private insurance pays their patients' medical costs.

As shown in Figure 21–2, the Japanese approach medical care much as Europeans do and Canada does, with most medical expenses paid through government.

The United States stands alone among industrialized nations in having no universal, government-sponsored

GLOBAL SNAPSHOT

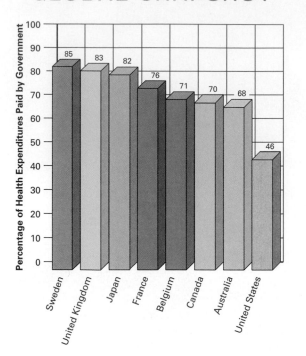

FIGURE 21-2   Extent of Socialized Medicine in
Selected Countries

Of all high-income countries, the United States has the smallest
percentage of government-provided medical care. Canada's record
is similar to that of Belgium and Australia.

Sources: U.S. Census Bureau (2004) and World Bank (2005).

program of medical care. The United States has a **direct fee
system,** *a medical care system in which patients pay directly
for the services of physicians and hospitals.* Europeans look to
government to fund about 80 percent of their medical costs
(paid for through taxation), but the U.S. government pays
just 46 percent of medical costs (U.S. Census Bureau, 2004).
In the United States, rich people can purchase the best
medical care in the world; yet, the poor are worse off than
their counterparts in Canada and Europe. This difference
explains the relatively high death rates among both infants
and adults in the United States (United Nations
Development Programme, 2005). Why does the United
States have no national medical care program? Because its
culture stresses self-reliance, government intervention is
limited. Political support for a national medical program
has not been strong, even among labour unions, which have
concentrated on winning medical care benefits from
employers. Further, the American Medical Association and
the health insurance industry have strongly and consistently
opposed national medical care (Starr, 1982).

Expenditure for medical care in the United States
increased dramatically from US$12 billion in 1950 to more
than US$1.5 trillion in 2002. This sum amounts to more
than US$4000 per person—more than any other nation in
the world spends for medical care. Who pays the medical
bills? The answer is a combination of private and public
insurance programs, plus health maintenance organizations, which provide medical services and preventive care
for subscribers. In all, 84 percent of Americans have some
medical care coverage, either private or public. But most
health plans do not provide full coverage, so serious illness
threatens even middle-class people with financial hardship:
about 16 percent of Americans have no medical insurance
at all. In Canada, to avoid the loss of savings and income to
the ravages of disease, we have contemplated the institution
of coverage for catastrophic drug costs—such as those
involved in the treatment of some cancers and AIDS.
Canadian medicare still lacks universal public insurance for
prescription drugs (or "pharmacare").

MEDICINE IN CANADA

Canadians have universal medical coverage administered
through provincial and territorial governments. The
Canadian government pays doctors and hospitals—who
operate privately or independently—for the services they
provide, according to a schedule of fees set annually by
governments in consultation with professional medical
associations. Thus, Canada has government-funded and
-regulated medical care but, because practitioners operate
privately, our medicare system is not socialized medicine. In
effect, it is socialized medical insurance. (See the Media
Perspectives box on p. 558–58 for further details.)

Canada's system of universal medicare has a long
history, with seeds before confederation. By 1884, Canada's
Public Health Act required the establishment of health
boards and sanitary regulations at the local level. In 1919,
Prime Minister Mackenzie King introduced the idea of
universal health care as part of the Liberal party platform,
but it was not until 1972 that all provinces were part of a
federal program providing comprehensive medical insurance—eleven years after such a program was first introduced in Saskatchewan by New Democratic Premier
Tommy Douglas.[1] Canada's law was shaped by recommen-
dations of a Royal Commission on Health Services, which
reported in 1964 under Mr. Justice Emmett Hall of the
Supreme Court of Canada. The law was based on four basic
premises (Nancarrow Clarke, 1996:256):

* *Universality.* All residents of Canada would be eligible on
  equal terms, regardless of such differences as previous

---

[1]Actor Kiefer Sutherland is the son of actor Shirley Douglas, and the grandson of Tommy Douglas. In 2004, Tommy Douglas was voted "The Greatest
Canadian" (in a CBC contest) for his role in bringing health care to Canada.

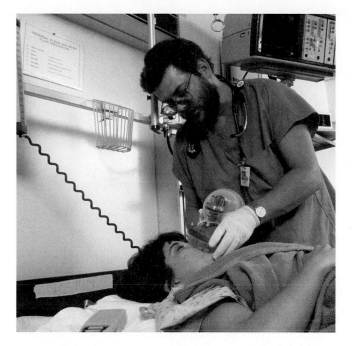

One strategy for dealing with a shortage of nurses is to recruit more men into the profession. Anyone visiting a Canadian hospital today will notice a significant number of men on nursing staffs.

health records, age, income, membership, or other considerations.

- *Portability.* The benefits were to be portable from province to province or territory.

- *Comprehensive coverage.* The benefits were to include all necessary medical services and certain surgical services performed by a dental surgeon in hospital.

- *Administration.* The plan was to be run on a nonprofit basis

For a look at Tommy Douglas's campaign to establish medicare in Canada, see http://archives. cbc.ca/300c.asp?IDCat=73&ID Dos=90&IDLan=1&IDMenu=73.

Canada's system has the advantage of providing care for everyone at a total cost that is significantly lower than that needed to operate the non-universal medical system in the United States. Health expenditures, as a percentage of GDP, peaked in 1993 at 9.9 percent, dropping to 8.9 percent by 1997, mainly because of a growing economy. By 2000, Canada's health expenditures had risen to $95 billion, or 9.3 percent of GDP. In contrast, American health care expenditures represent at least 13 percent of GDP.

YOUR TURN

Do you know which medical services are and are not covered by your provincial or territorial medicare program?

TABLE 21-3

The Representation of Canadian Women in Medicine by Age, 2003

Age*	Percentage Female	
	All Physicians	Specialists
Under 35	50.9	43.6
35–44	40.5	35.4
45–54	31.0	26.8
55–64	17.2	15.3
65+	9.8	7.9
Unknown	27.9	30.0
Total	30.4	25.3

*Excludes physicians older than 80 years of age.

Source: Calculations by L.M. Gerber based on the Canadian Medical Association Masterfile, January 2003.

THE SHORTAGE OF NURSES

Another important issue in medical care is the shortage of nurses across North America and, in fact, the world. Canada and the United States combined have some 2.5 million registered nurses, but about 7 percent of available jobs are unfilled. The main cause of the shortage is that fewer people are entering the nursing profession. During the past decade, enrolments in nursing programs have dropped, even as the need for nurses—driven by population aging—increases. Why this decline? Today's young women have a wide range of occupational choices, so that fewer are drawn to the traditionally female occupation of nursing. This fact is evident in the rising median age of working nurses, which is now 44. Another reason is that many nurses are unhappy with working conditions, citing heavy patient loads, too much required overtime, a stressful working environment, and a lack of recognition and respect from supervisors, physicians, and hospital managers. Most nurses say they would not recommend the field to others, and many are leaving the field for other jobs.

Drastic cutbacks in funding by the Liberal government in

To learn more about the exodus of Canadian nurses to the United States, see www.nurseweek. com/news/features/00-07/canada. html, and for more information on shortage of nurses, see www. maoknowledgedepol.ca/ strengthening_nursing/rar_the_ nursing_shortage.asp.

the 1990s led hospitals to cut staff, which in turn caused many more nurses to look to the United States for employment opportunities—and much higher salaries. American hospitals actively recruit Canadian nurses, often providing generous signing bonuses. As a result, Canada loses 15 nurses to the United States for every American nurse who comes north.

CANADIAN WOMEN IN MEDICINE

Gone are the days when physicians were almost always male: today, 30 percent are women. As shown in Table 21–3, among physicians under 35 years of age, women represent half of all physicians, and an astounding 44 percent of specialists. The

MEDIA PERSPECTIVES
Two-Tiered Health Care: Threat, Fact, or Fiction?

In the fall of 2000, Canadians found themselves involved in a federal election campaign, one that took a number of unexpected turns and resulted with a third majority Liberal government. Central to the Liberal campaign—and much of the media coverage—was the attempt to instil fear in eastern Canada of Stockwell Day and his Canadian Alliance. Day and his Alliance candidates, according to the Liberals, were "social conservatives" who, through a "hidden agenda" would force their religious beliefs about abortion, capital punishment, and homosexuality on the whole country. Even more damaging was the allegation that they would introduce "two-tiered medicine" resulting in separate systems of medical care for the rich and the poor. They would accomplish this by allowing *private* clinics to deliver health care.

In the weeks that followed, the Liberals, the New Democrats, and the media refused to acknowledge a reality that Stockwell Day was unable to articulate clearly. The reality is that the funding of Canada's universal medicare is public, yet its *delivery* is almost

Mr. Justice Emmett M. Hall (1898–1995) had a distinguished legal career leading to his appointment to the Supreme Court of Canada, from which he retired in 1973 at the age of seventy-five. Beyond his legal role, Hall helped to develop public medical care in Saskatchewan—before going on to design a system of universal health care for all of Canada, which was implemented in 1967. As the designer of our national medicare program, Hall created a social institution that is dear to our hearts and central to our Canadian identity.

entirely private. It was not in the interests of the Liberals, the New Democrats, or the media to clarify this issue—even when, two years later, Liberal senator Michael Kirby was making exactly the same point—that public funding and private delivery are the norm in Canada. The media did pick up on Kirby's Senate Committee recommendation that "all Canadians have timely access to medically necessary health services regardless of their ability to pay." In the federal election of 2006, "wait-time guarantees" were front and centre, but neither the media nor the politicians pointed out that guaranteed services delivered by the private sector.

In an academic report entitled "Getting What We Pay For: Myths and Realities about Financing Canada's Health Care System," Raisa Deber (2000) points out the distinction between financing and delivery. She also claims that our failure to distinguish between finance and delivery makes it difficult to diagnose the problems in our system—a point echoed by Senator Kirby's committee. We call our

---

presence of so many women in specialties means that women are willing to undertake two to six extra years of residency, often postponing child bearing until their thirties, or forgoing it altogether. Table 21–2 does not give the gender breakdown for residents, but the trend suggests that women predominate among residents and especially current medical students, with some medical schools such as McMaster's graduating classes that are overwhelmingly female (73% in 1999).

Many young women doctors—especially residents in emergency and on hospital wards—have to correct the impression that they are nurses. The stereotypical image of doctor as male is still with us—  remember that cultural lag requires time. But young people growing up today are increasingly exposed to women physicians in real life and in the mass media. As a result, twenty or thirty years from now, the stereotypical physician may well be female. By contrast, the appearance of male nurses on our hospital wards is not reflected yet in the mass media.

Theoretical Analysis of Health and Medicine

Each of sociology's major theoretical approaches helps us organize and interpret facts and issues concerning human health.

STRUCTURAL-FUNCTIONAL ANALYSIS: ROLE THEORY

Talcott Parsons (1951) viewed medicine as society's strategy to keep its members healthy. According to this model, illness is dysfunctional because it undermines people's abilities to perform their roles.

The Sick Role

Society responds to sickness not only by providing medical care but also by affording people a **sick role,** *patterns of*

medicare system *public* because the government ensures its universality by paying most of the bills. Yet Canadians have failed to recognize that almost all of the delivery is *private*. Most of our hospitals are private, nonprofit organizations, run by independent boards. Nursing homes and home care providers are also private organizations. Physicians in Canada are not government employees but private practitioners or people in business. They bill governments for services rendered but have to pay rent, staff salaries, and equipment costs from their revenues.

As long as there is a single payer—the government—and individuals cannot pay to jump a queue for medical services, we do not have a two-tier system with superior services for the wealthy. Some Canadians have to be sent to the United States for cancer treatment in private clinics when services here are not available, but that does not signify unequal access—because Canadian governments pay their expenses. If private clinics, as opposed to hospitals, in Alberta are allowed to do hip surgery and the government picks up the tab, then once again, this is not two-tiered service.

In Canada, part of the debate about universality revolves around insured and uninsured services. Public funding does not cover all components of medical care: dentistry, cosmetic surgery, eye care (i.e., glasses, laser surgery), and drugs are among the services left to private insurance or payment by the individual. In fact, in Canada, public expenditure on health care is only 70 percent of the total cost, compared to 88 percent in Belgium and 83 percent in the United Kingdom (Deber, 2000). *The Canada Health Act* protects only publicly "insured" services from queue jumping on the part of those willing to pay out of pocket or through private insurance. Uninsured services are funded and delivered entirely within the private sphere.

On August 23, 2006, both the *National Post* and *The Globe and Mail* covered the election of Dr. Brian Day as president of the Canadian Medical Association. This is significant because Dr. Day is the co-founder of a private, state-of-the-art surgical centre that operates outside Canada's publicly funded system. In other words, it is both *privately* funded and *privately* delivered: patients pay for its services personally or through their private insurance. The concern of some is that Day will use his one-year presidency to push for further privatization of health care—that is, increased private delivery that is not funded by government insurance (Greenaway, 2006b; Picard, 2006).

This brings a new dimension to the public/private debate about health care. Day says that he supports medicare and that his private clinic simply aids in the timely delivery of quality care. The Quebec Supreme court recently ruled that it is unconstitutional to stop someone from paying privately for care if waiting for a public service is too long. Since provincial and territorial governments limit the number of procedures (e.g., hip surgeries) they will or can afford to cover, we may not be able to give "wait-time" guarantees without considering the option of private funding.

WHAT DO YOU THINK?

1. What do you think of the argument that private delivery, if publicly funded, does not constitute a two-tier system of health care?
2. Do you think taxpayers should pick up the tab for a broader range of health care services (e.g., drugs or cosmetic surgery)?
3. Why is health care a political issue in Canada?

---

behaviour defined as appropriate for people who are ill. According to Parsons, the sick role releases people from normal obligations such as going to work or attending classes. To prevent abuse of this privilege, however, people cannot simply claim to be ill; they must "look the part" and, in serious cases, get the help of a medical expert. After assuming the sick role, the patient must want to get better and must do whatever is needed to regain good health, including co-operating with health professionals.

The Physician's Role

Physicians evaluate people's claims of sickness and help restore the sick to normal routines. To do this, physicians use their specialized knowledge and expect patients to co-operate with them, providing necessary information and following "doctor's orders" to complete the treatment.

Critical Review   Parsons's analysis links illness and medicine to the broader organization of society. Others have extended the concept of the sick role to some non-illness situations such as pregnancy (Myers and Grasmick, 1989). One limitation of the concept of the sick role is that it applies to acute conditions (e.g., flu or a broken leg) better than to chronic illnesses, which may not be reversible (e.g., heart disease). In addition, a sick person's ability to assume the sick role (i.e., to take time from work to regain health) depends on the patient's resources; many working poor, for example, cannot afford to assume a sick role. Finally, illness is not entirely dysfunctional; it can have some positive consequences. Sometimes, a person who experiences a grave illness finds the opportunity to re-evaluate his or her life and gains a better sense of what is truly important (Myers, 2000; Ehrenreich, 2001). Finally, critics point out that Parsons's analysis gives doctors, rather than patients, the primary responsibility for health. A more prevention-oriented approach gives each of us as individuals the responsibility to pursue health.

SYMBOLIC-INTERACTION ANALYSIS: THE MEANING OF HEALTH

According to the symbolic-interaction approach, society is less a grand system than a complex and changing reality. In this model, health and medical care are socially constructed by people in everyday interaction.

The Social Construction of Illness

If both health and illness are socially constructed, people in a poor society may view hunger and malnutrition as normal. Similarly, many members of our own society give little thought to the harmful effects of a rich diet. Our response to illness also is based on social definitions that may or may not square with medical facts. People with AIDS may be forced to deal with fear and prejudice that has no medical basis. Likewise, students may pay no attention to signs of real illness on the eve of a vacation but head for the infirmary hours before a midterm examination with a case of the sniffles. In short, health is less an objective fact than a negotiated outcome. How people define a medical situation may actually affect how they feel. Medical experts marvel at *psychosomatic* disorders (a fusion of Greek words for "mind" and "body"), when state of mind guides physical sensations (Hamrick, et al., 1986). Applying sociologist W.I. Thomas's theorem (presented in Chapter 6, "Social Interaction in Everyday Life"), we can say that once health or illness is defined as real, it can become real in its consequences.

The Social Construction of Treatment

Also in Chapter 6, we used Erving Goffman's *dramaturgical* approach to explain how physicians tailor their physical surroundings (their offices) and their behaviour (the presentation of self) so that others see them as competent and in charge. Sociologist Joan Emerson (1970) further illustrates this process of reality construction in her analysis of a gynaecological examination carried out by a male doctor. This situation is vulnerable to misinterpretation, since a man's touching of a woman's genitals is conventionally viewed as a sexual act and, possibly, an assault. To ensure that people define the situation as impersonal and professional, the medical staff wear uniforms and furnish the examination room with nothing but medical equipment. The doctor's manner and overall performance are designed to make the patient feel that, to him, examining the genital area is no different from treating any other part of the body. A female nurse is usually present during the examination, not only to assist the physician but also to avoid any impression that a man and a woman are "alone together." Managing situational definitions in this way is only rarely taught in medical

schools. The oversight is unfortunate because, as Emerson's analysis shows, understanding how people construct reality in the examination room is as important as mastering the medical skills required for treatment.

How might sociological insights help doctors improve their relationships with patients and perhaps even reduce the likelihood of being sued?

Critical Review The symbolic-interaction approach reveals that what people view as healthful or harmful depends on numerous factors that are not, strictly speaking, medical. This approach also shows that, in any medical procedure, both patient and medical staff engage in a subtle process of reality construction. Critics fault the symbolic-interaction approach for implying that there are no objective standards of well-being. Certain physical conditions—arthritis, paralysis, blindness—define interpersonal relations, regardless of how we view those conditions.

SOCIAL-CONFLICT ANALYSIS: HEALTH AND INEQUALITY

Social-conflict analysis points out the connection between health and social inequality and, taking a cue from Karl Marx, ties medicine to the operation of capitalism. Researchers have focused on three main issues: access to medical care, the effects of the profit motive, and the politics of medicine.

Access to Care

Health is important to everyone. Yet, by requiring individuals to pay for medical care, capitalist societies allow the richest people to have the best health. The access problem is most serious in the United States because it has no universal medical care system. Conflict theorists argue that capitalist medical care provides excellent medical care for the rich but not for the rest of the population. Most of the 46 million Americans who lack medical coverage (16% of the population) have moderate to low incomes.

The Profit Motive

Some conflict analysts go further, arguing that the real problem is not access to medical care but the character of capitalist medicine itself. The profit motive turns physicians, hospitals, nursing homes, home care, and the pharmaceutical industry into multibillion-dollar corporations. The quest for higher profits encourages physicians to recommend unnecessary tests and surgery, and to rely too

APPLYING THEORY

HEALTH

	Structural-Functional Approach	Symbolic-Interaction Approach	Social-Conflict Approach
What is the level of analysis?	Macro level	Micro level	Macro level
How is health related to society?	Illness is dysfunctional for society because it prevents people from carrying out their daily roles. The sick role releases people who are ill from responsibilities while they try to get well.	Societies define "health" and "illness" differently according to their living standards. How people define their own health affects how they actually feel (psychosomatic conditions).	Health is linked to social inequality, with rich people having more access to care than poor people. Capitalist medical care places the drive for profits over the needs of people, treating symptoms rather than addressing poverty as a cause of illness.

much on drugs, rather than focusing on the improvement of people's lifestyles. In Canada, where medical insurance is socialized, the profit motive is attenuated but not eliminated. Pharmaceuticals, dentistry, nursing homes and home care services are almost entirely in the private sector. Also, since physicians are in private practice their earnings are determined by the extent of their billings relative to their expenses (which would include the costs of office space, equipment, receptionists or nurses, professional fees, insurance and continuing education).

Medicine as Politics

Although science declares itself politically neutral, scientific medicine frequently takes sides on important social issues. The American medical establishment, for example, has always strongly opposed government medical care programs. The history of medicine itself shows how racial and sexual discrimination have been supported by "scientific" opinions about, say, the inferiority of women (Leavitt, 1984). Consider the diagnosis of "hysteria," a term that has its origins in the Greek word *hyster*, meaning "uterus." In choosing this word to describe a wild, emotional state, the medical profession suggested that being a woman is somehow the same as being irrational. Even today, according to conflict theory, scientific medicine explains illness exclusively in terms of bacteria and viruses, ignoring the damaging effects of poverty. In effect, scientific medicine hides the bias in our medical system by transforming this social issue into simple biology.

Recently, physicians and politicians have been engaged in an unusual medicalization issue—the medicinal use of marijuana—where *politicians* are seeking to influence appropriate medical intervention. Along with moves to decriminalize marijuana, Canada's federal government is allowing physicians to prescribe and dispense it to patients for control of pain, nausea, and other symptoms, especially among terminally ill patients. Doctors, in turn, are reluctant because marijuana has not gone through the normal, rigorous clinical trials that establish efficacy and safety. In the end, some physicians will co-operate, while others will not—just as some refuse to prescribe birth control because of their personal beliefs.

 Get information about medicinal use of marijuana in Canada at www.drugwise-droguesois-fute.hc-sc.gc.ca/law-loi/medical_e.asp.

Critical Review Social-conflict analysis provides still another view of the relationships among health, medicine, and society. According to this approach, social inequality is the reason some people have better health than others. The most common objection to the conflict approach is that it minimizes the gains in health brought about by scientific medicine and higher living standards. Moreover, it is the profit motive that drives the horrendously expensive process for research, development, and clinical trial required to bring to market life-saving or life-enhancing drugs—such as those to relieve HIV/AIDS. Governments, as a general rule, do not underwrite such expensive and risky endeavours.

In sum, sociology's three major theoretical approaches explain why health and medicine are social issues. The Applying Theory table (above) sums up what they teach us.

The renowned French scientist Louis Pasteur (1822–1895), who spent much of his life studying how bacteria cause disease, said just before he died that health depends less on bacteria than on the social environment in which the bacteria are found (quoted in Gordon, 1980:7). Explaining Pasteur's insight is sociology's contribution to human health.

Health and Medicine: Looking Ahead

In the early 1900s, deaths from infectious diseases like diphtheria and measles were common. Because scientists had yet to develop penicillin and other antibiotics, even a small wound might become infected, and a simple infection from a minor wound was sometimes life threatening. A century later, most of us—at least most young people—take good health and long life for granted. Although the obesity epidemic is cause for concern, it seems reasonable to expect improvements in health to continue during the twenty-first century. Another encouraging trend is that more people are taking responsibility for their own health. Every one of us can live better and longer if we avoid tobacco, eat healthful meals, drink alcohol in moderation, and exercise regularly.

Yet certain health problems will continue to plague Canadian society in the decades to come. With no cure in sight, it seems likely that the AIDS epidemic will persist for some time. At this point, the only way to steer clear of contracting HIV is to make a decision to avoid all of the risky behaviours noted in this chapter. Furthermore, the changing social profile of people with AIDS—which increasingly afflicts the poor—reminds us that Canada falls short in addressing the health of marginalized members of our society.

Repeating a pattern seen in earlier chapters, we find that problems of health are far greater in poor societies of the world than they are in Canada. The good news is that life expectancy for the world as a whole has been rising—from 48 years in 1950 to 67 years today—and the biggest gains have been made in low-income countries (Population Reference Bureau, 2005). But in much of Latin America, Asia, and especially Africa, hundreds of millions of adults and children lack adequate food, safe water, and needed medical attention. Improving health in the world's poorest societies remains a critical challenge in the twenty-first century. In 2003, Prime Minister Chrétien and President Bush pledged significant funding to counter HIV and AIDS in Africa. When rock singer Bono appeared at the Liberal convention that was to elect Paul Martin as the party leader in November 2003, he made it clear that he would hold the new prime minister to the promise of his predecessor. The US$19 billion allocated annually by the United States and the $42 to $84 million (increasing over five years) allocated by Canada for AIDS research and treatment is a reflection of those pledges. But Bono and other critics argue that Canada's contribution should be much greater.

High-income countries are likely to continue to grapple with soaring costs and ethical issues of increasingly technological and genetic solutions to medical challenges. The Thinking Critically box (on p. 563) explores issues related to genetic research.

From a policy perspective, the World Health Organization and governments worldwide have to prepare for the possibility of pandemic influenza (of bird or some other origin)—which many analysts argue is not just a possibility but inevitable. Practical problems, such as producing massive quantities of antiviral medications, and ethical questions, such as who is to get the antivirals, loom large in our future.

Most of the challenges to health and medical care that we face in the future are the result of knowing too little—but it is also possible to know too much. The Thinking Critically box (on p. 563) asks if we really want to look into the genetic crystal ball. That question, deceptively simple on one level, introduces numerous ethical issues (e.g. "genetic privacy" and "designer children"). Where we have been concerned, primarily, with what we can do, the future will raise questions of what we *ought* to do with unprecedented knowledge.

THINKING CRITICALLY

The Genetic Crystal Ball: Do We Really Want To Look?

The liquid in the laboratory test tube seems ordinary enough, like a syrupy form of water. But this liquid is one of the greatest medical breakthroughs of all time; it may even hold the key to life itself. The liquid is deoxyribonucleic acid, or DNA, the spiralling molecule found in cells of the human body that contains the blueprint for making each one of us human as well as different from every other person. The human body is

 Find out more about the Human Genome Project at www.ornl.gov/sci/techresources/Human_Genome/home.shtml.

composed of some 100 trillion cells, most of which contain a nucleus of twenty-three pairs of chromosomes (one of each pair comes from each parent). Each chromosome is packed with DNA, in segments called genes. Genes guide the production of protein, the building block of the human body.

If genetics sounds complicated (and it is), the social implications of genetic knowledge are even more complex. Scientists discovered the structure of the DNA molecule in 1952 and in recent years they have made great gains in "mapping" the human genome. Charting the genetic landscape may lead to understanding how each bit of DNA shapes our being. But do we really want to turn the key to unlock the secrets of life itself? What do we do with this knowledge once we have it?

In the Human Genome Project, many scientists see a chance to prevent certain illnesses before they even begin. Research already has identified genetic abnormalities that cause some forms of cancer, sickle-cell anemia, muscular dystrophy, Huntington's disease, cystic fibrosis,

Scientists are learning more and more about the genetic factors that prompt the eventual development of serious diseases. If offered the opportunity, would you want to undergo genetic screening that would predict the long-term future of your own health?

and other crippling and deadly afflictions. In the future, genetic screening—a scientific "crystal ball"—could let people know their medical destiny and allow doctors to manipulate segments of DNA to prevent diseases before they appear.

But many people urge caution in such research, warning that genetic information can easily be abused. At its worst, genetic mapping opens the door to Nazi-like efforts to breed a "super race." In 1994, China began to regulate marriage and childbirth to prevent "new births of inferior quality." It seems inevitable that some parents will want to use genetic testing to evaluate the health, or even the eye and hair colour, of their future children; this technology may give them the opportunity to abort a fetus because it

falls short of their standards or to create "designer children."

Then there are issues of "genetic privacy." What is scientifically possible is not always morally desirable.[*] Society is already struggling with questions about the proper use of our expanding knowledge of human genetics. Is it possible that a person could request a genetic evaluation of a prospective partner before agreeing to marry? Might a life insurance company demand genetic testing before issuing a policy? Could an employer screen job applicants to weed out those whose future illnesses might drain the company's medical care funds? Such ethical dilemmas will only multiply as genetic research moves forward in the years to come.

WHAT DO YOU THINK?

1. Traditional wedding vows join couples "in sickness and in health." Do you have a right to know the future health of your intended partner before tying the knot? Why?
2. Do you think parents should be able to genetically "design" their children? Why?
3. Should people who are possible or probable carriers of serious gene-based diseases be required to undergo genetic screening when they contemplate having children?

Sources: Thompson (1999) and Golden and Lemonick (2000).

---

[*] Many Indigenous peoples have objected to having their genetic material added to the Human Genome Project without their consent. In part, they are concerned about the ways in which these materials might be used in the future.

MAKING THE GRADE

The following learning tools will help you see what you know, identify what you still need to learn, and expand your understanding beyond the text. You can also visit this text's Companion Website™ at www.pearsoned.ca/macionis to find useful practice tests.

KEY POINTS

What Is Health?

Health is a social issue because personal well-being depends on a society's technology and its distribution of resources. A society's culture shapes definitions of health and patterns of medical care.

Health: A Global Survey

Historically, human health was poor by today's standards. Health improved dramatically in Western Europe and North America in the nineteenth century, first because of industrialization and later because of medical advances. A century ago, infectious diseases were leading killers; today, most people in high-income countries die in old age of chronic illnesses such as heart disease, cancer, or stroke.

Poor nations suffer from inadequate sanitation, hunger, and other problems linked to poverty. Life expectancy is about 20 years less than in the United States; in the poorest nations, half the children do not survive to adulthood.

Health in Canada

More than three-quarters of Canadian children born today will live to at least age 65. Throughout life, Canadian men report better health than women (though the gender gap closed between 1975 and 1995) and people of high social position enjoy better health than the poor.

Current issues in Canadian health care include cigarette smoking, which is the greatest preventable cause of death, the obesity epidemic, the recent increase in sexually transmitted diseases, potential pandemics, and ethical dilemmas associated with the right to die.

The Medical Establishment

Health care was historically a family concern but has become the responsibility of trained specialists. The model of scientific medicine is the foundation of the Canadian medical establishment—although alternative medicine is regaining some ground.

Socialist nations define medical care as a right that governments offer equally to everyone. Capitalist nations view medical care as a commodity to be purchased, although most capitalist governments support medical care through socialized medicine or national health insurance. The United States is the only high-income nation with no comprehensive medical care program. Canada has a hybrid system, in which public funding by governments provides universal medical care that is delivered almost entirely by the private sector.

Theoretical Analysis of Health and Medicine

A major part of the structural-functional analysis of health is the sick role, which excuses the ill person from routine social responsibilities. The symbolic-interaction approach investigates how health and medical treatments are largely matters of socially constructed definitions. Social-conflict analysis focuses on the inequitable distribution of health and medical care.

Health and Medicine: Looking Ahead

Health has improved in Canada during the past century. Future improvements are also likely, especially if people take greater responsibility for their own health, and if we improve health care delivery to the poor (including isolated Aboriginal communities).

We will continue to deal with HIV/AIDS in Canada and in Africa. Canada needs to plan an appropriate response to pandemic influenza, which world health experts say is unavoidable.

KEY CONCEPTS

health (p. 542) a state of complete physical, mental, and social well-being

universal medical coverage (p. 543) a system in which the costs of essential medical services are covered by the state

social epidemiology (p. 544) the study of how health and disease are distributed throughout a society's population

eating disorder (p. 547) an intense form of dieting or other unhealthy method of weight control driven by the desire to be very thin

medicine (p. 553) the social institution that focuses on fighting disease and improving health

holistic medicine (p. 554) an approach to health care that emphasizes the prevention of illness and takes into account a person's entire physical and social environment

socialized medicine (p. 555) a medical care system in which the government owns and operates most medical facilities and employs most physicians

direct fee system (p. 556) a medical care system in which patients pay directly for the services of physicians and hospitals

sick role (p. 558) patterns of behaviour defined as appropriate for people who are ill

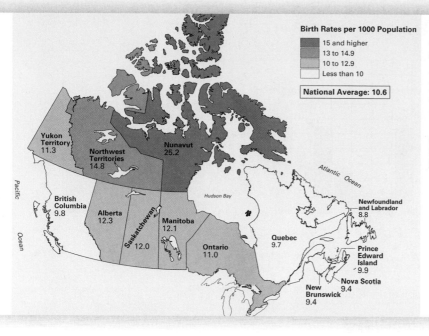

Birth Rates per 1000 Population

- 15 and higher
- 13 to 14.9
- 10 to 12.9
- Less than 10

National Average: 10.6

Yukon Territory 11.3

Northwest Territories 14.8

Nunavut 25.2

British Columbia 9.8

Alberta 12.3

Saskatchewan 12.0

Manitoba 12.1

Ontario 11.0

Quebec 9.7

Newfoundland and Labrador 8.8

Prince Edward Island 9.9

Nova Scotia 9.4

New Brunswick 9.4

Pacific Ocean

Atlantic Ocean

Hudson Bay

SEEING OURSELVES

CANADA MAP 22–1

Birth Rates per 1000 Population, by Province and Territory, 2002–2003 (July 1–June 30)

Source: Calculations by L.M. Gerber based on the Statistics Canada publication "Annual Demographic Statistics," 1996, Catalogue 91-213, April 1997.

300 million before it spiked upward at about 1750. Now 74 million people are added to the planet's population each year; in 2005, the total was 6.5 billion.

The causes and consequences of this drama are the basis of **demography**, *the study of human population.* Demography (from Greek, meaning "description of people") is a cousin of sociology that analyzes the size and composition of a population, and studies how and why people move from place to place. Demographers collect statistics and raise important questions about the effects of population change. The following sections present basic demographic concepts.

To find data on Canadian demography, click "Population and demography" under "Statistics by Subject" on the Statistics Canada website www.statcan.ca.

FERTILITY

The study of human population begins with the number of people born. **Fertility** is *the incidence of child bearing in a country's population.* During her child-bearing years, from the onset of menstruation (typically in her early teens) to menopause (usually in her forties), a woman is capable of bearing more than 20 children; but *fecundity,* or maximum possible child bearing, is sharply reduced by health, cultural norms, finances, and personal choice. Demographers often measure fertility using the **crude birth rate,** *the number of live births in a given year for every thousand people in a population.* This birth rate is "crude" because it is based on the entire population, not just women in their child-bearing years. Making comparisons using crude birth rates can be misleading because one society may have a higher proportion of women of child-bearing age than another—as a result of the baby boom for example. But it is easy to calculate and serves as a good indicator of a society's overall fertility. A crude birth rate is calculated by dividing the number of live births in a given year by a society's total population, and multiplying the result by 1000. For example, in Canada in 2002–03 there were 331 522 live births in a population of 31.6 million: therefore, there were 10.9 live births for every 1000 people, for a crude birth rate of 10.5.

Figure 22–1 (a) shows that, in global perspective, the crude birth rate of North Americans is low. Canada Map 22–1 reveals that fertility within Canada varies dramatically, from a low of 8.8 per 1000 population in Newfoundland and Labrador to 25.2 in Nunavut. The low in Newfoundland and Labrador is the result of steady out-migration of young people of child-bearing age. Quebec's relatively low fertility rate is the result of the Quiet Revolution of the 1960s, when francophones threw off their poor, rural, Catholic past and embraced a secular, urban future, where educated women entered the labour force. The women of Quebec incurred new opportunity costs (promotion or seniority) if they took time off work to have children; as a result, their birth rate declined and has remained low to the present.

There is a peculiar snag in Ontario's birth records. Over the past decade, an estimated 30 000 births have gone unrecorded—for babies who died shortly after birth. Unlike infant deaths, births are not recorded automatically but require parents to file an application for a birth certificate. In Ontario, local municipalities charge an application fee between $10 and $35 for a birth certificate. Parents might not think to apply for a birth certificate for a baby who died within minutes or days of birth, especially if no one tells them it is their responsibility; a high fee (e.g., $35 in Toronto) provides a further disincentive. As a result, in Ontario deaths are counted accurately while births are undercounted. This distorts population counts in Canada's largest province as well as population projections for the entire country (Abraham, 2006).

GLOBAL SNAPSHOT

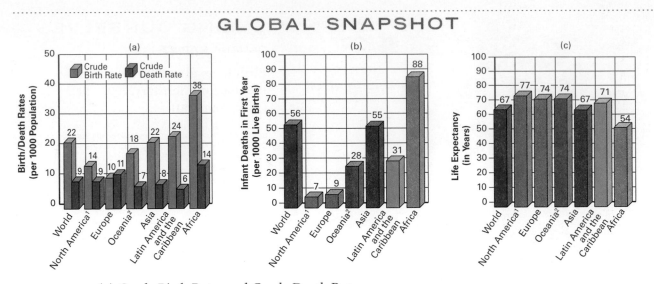

FIGURE 22-1 (a) Crude Birth Rates and Crude Death Rates, (b) Infant Mortality Rates, and (c) Life Expectancy around the World, 2004

By world standards, North America has low birth and death rates, very low infant mortality rates, and high life expectancy.

[1]United States and Canada.

[2]Australia, New Zealand, and South Pacific Islands.

Source: Population Reference Bureau (2005).

YOUR TURN

Can you point to specific ways in which your life would be different if you had five or six brothers and sisters, compared to none, one, or two?

MORTALITY

Population size is also affected by **mortality,** *the incidence of death in a society's population.* To measure mortality, demographers use a **crude death rate,** *the number of deaths in a given year for every thousand people in a population.* The crude death rate is calculated as the number of deaths in a year divided by the total population, multiplied by 1000. In 2001, Canada's crude death rate was 7.5 per 1000 population. This rate, low by world standards, is lower than that of the United States (8.7 in 2001).

A third, widely used demographic measure is the **infant mortality rate,** *the number of deaths among infants in the first year of life for each thousand live births in a given year.* As described in Chapter 21 ("Health and Medicine"), this rate is derived from dividing the number of deaths of children under one year of age by the number of live births during the same year and multiplying the result by 1000. In 2001, Canada's infant mortality rate was 5.0 per 1000 live births. This is lower than the U.S. rate (6.8), but above that of most European and

Scandinavian countries or Japan (3.9). Like other demographic variables, this rate conceals considerable variation among segments of the Canadian population. For example, infant mortality rates are higher among the poor, in isolated communities, and among Aboriginal peoples. Nonetheless, infant mortality offers a good general measure of overall quality of life and is, therefore, used as one indicator of socioeconomic development. Figure 22–1 (b) shows that infant mortality in North America is low by world standards.

Societies with low infant mortality rates have high **life expectancy,** *the average life span of a society's population.* Canadian males born in 2001 can expect to live 77 years, while females can expect to live to 82—one or two years longer than their counterparts in the United States. Life expectancy in rich, industrialized countries is about 20 years longer than it is in poorer societies (see Figure 22–1 (c)).

MIGRATION

Population size is also affected by **migration,** *the movement of people into and out of a specified territory.* Movement into an area, or *immigration,* is measured as an *in-migration rate,* calculated as the number of people entering an area for every 1000 people in the population. Movement out of an area, or *emigration,* is measured in terms of an *out-migration rate,* the number leaving for every 1000 people. Both types of migration usually occur at once; the difference is the *net* migration rate.

Fertility in Canada has fallen during the past century and is now quite low. But some categories of our population have much higher fertility rates. The Hutterites of Alberta and the Amish in the United States provide examples: it is common for such couples to have five, six, or more children.

All nations experience internal migration, that is, movement within their borders from one region to another. Within Canada, Ontario, British Columbia, and Alberta fairly consistently gain population at the expense of other provinces or territories. Migration is sometimes voluntary, as when people leave a small town and move to a larger city. In such cases, push/pull factors are typically at work: a lack of jobs pushes people to move, and more opportunity pulls them elsewhere. Migration can also be involuntary, such as the forcible transport of 10 million Africans to the western hemisphere as slaves, or the relocation of Aboriginal people from their ancestral lands into towns or onto reserves.

POPULATION GROWTH

Fertility, mortality, and migration all affect the size of a society's population. In general, rich nations (such as Canada) grow as much from immigration as from natural increase; poor nations (such as Pakistan) grow almost entirely from natural increase. Demographers derive the *natural growth rate* of a population by subtracting the crude death rate from the crude birth rate. The natural growth rate of the Canadian population in 2002–03 was 3.3 per 1000 (the crude birth rate of 10.5 minus the crude death rate of 7.2), or 0.33 percent annually. Global Map 22–1 shows that population growth in Canada and other high-income nations is well below the world average of 1.2 percent. The highest growth region in the world is Africa (at 2.3%). A handy rule of thumb for estimating population growth is to divide a society's population growth rate into the number 70; this yields the *doubling time* in years. Thus, an annual growth rate of 2 percent (found in parts of Latin America) doubles a population in 33 years, and a 3 percent growth rate (found in some countries in Africa) drops the doubling time to just 23 years. Rapid population growth in the poorest

YOUR TURN

Saudi Arabia's current population growth rate is 2.7 percent. At this rate, how long will it take the Saudi population to double?

countries is deeply troubling because these countries can barely support the populations they have now.

POPULATION COMPOSITION

Demographers also study the makeup of a society's population at a given point in time. One variable is the **sex ratio,** *the number of males for every 100 females in a nation's population.* In 2001, the sex ratio in Canada was 98.1, or 98 males for every 100 females. Sex ratios are usually below 100 because, on average, women outlive men. In India, however, the sex ratio is 106, because many parents value sons more than daughters and may either abort a female fetus or, after birth, give more care to a male infant, raising the odds that he will live.

A more complex measure is the **age-sex pyramid,** *a graphic representation of the age and sex of a population.* Figure 22–2 presents the age-sex pyramids for Canada in 1971, 1981, and 2001. The left side indicates the distribution of males of different ages, while the right side shows the corresponding distribution of females. The rough pyramidal shape of these figures results from higher mortality as people age. Also note that after about age 30, women increasingly outnumber men in Canada. The bulge that moves up the pyramid from 1971 to 1991 represents the *baby boom* from the mid–1940s to 1970. The contraction just below age 20 on the 1981 pyramid shows that the baby boom was followed by a *baby bust* as the birth rate dipped from 28.2 in 1955 to a low of 12.7 in 1996. The bulges in the

WINDOW ON THE WORLD

GLOBAL MAP 22-1   Population Growth in Global Perspective

The richest countries of the world—including the United States, Canada, and European nations—have growth rates below 1 percent. The nations of Latin America and Asia typically have growth rates around 1.5 percent. Africa has an overall growth rate of 2.3 percent, despite only small increases in countries with a high rate of AIDS. In global perspective, we see that a society's standard of living is closely related to its rate of population growth; population is rising fastest in the world regions that can least afford to support more people.

Source: Population Reference Bureau (2005); map projection from *Peters Atlas of the World* (1990).

three pyramids in Figure 22–2 reveal the upward motion of the baby boom generation over a 30-year period.

History and Theory of Population Growth

In the past, people wanted large families because human labour was the key to productivity. In addition, until rubber condoms were invented 150 years ago, the prevention of pregnancy was uncertain at best. But high death rates from infectious diseases put a constant brake on population growth. A major demographic shift began about 1750 as the world's population turned upward, reaching the 1 billion mark by 1800. This benchmark—which took all of human history to reach—was repeated 130 years later in 1930, when the Earth's population reached 2 billion people. In other words, population was increasing and the *rate* of

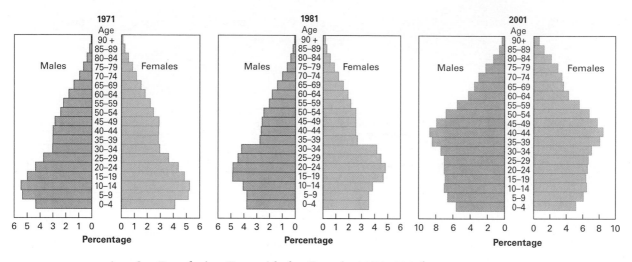

FIGURE 22-2   Age-Sex Population Pyramids for Canada, 1971–2001*

*Note that, in 1971, the baby boom shows up among people aged 5 to 19; by 2001, the baby boom is among people aged 30 to 50.

Source: Adapted by L.M. Gerber from the Statistics Canada publication "Age, Sex and Marital Status (data products: nation series: 1991 Census of Population)," 1991, Catalogue 93-310, July 1992.

growth was accelerating. Global population reached 3 billion by 1962 (just 32 years after the second billion) and 4 billion by 1974 (only 12 years afterwards). The rate of world population increase has stabilized recently, but our planet passed the 5 billion mark in 1987 and the 6 billion mark in 1999. In no previous century did the world's population even double. In the twentieth century, it quadrupled.

Currently, the world is adding about 74 million people each year; 96 percent of this increase is in poor countries. Experts predict that Earth's population will reach between 8 billion and 9 billion by 2050 (O'Neill and Balk, 2001). Given the world's troubles feeding the present population, such an increase is a matter of urgent concern.

MALTHUSIAN THEORY

The sudden population growth 250 years ago sparked the development of demography. Thomas Robert Malthus (1766–1834), an English economist and clergyman, warned that population increase would soon lead to social chaos. Malthus (1926; orig. 1798) calculated that population would increase in what mathematicians call a *geometric progression* (e.g., 2, 4, 8, 16, 32, and so on). At such a rate, Malthus concluded, world population would soon soar out of control. Food production would also increase, Malthus explained, but only in *arithmetic progression* (e.g., 2, 3, 4, 5, 6, and so on) because, even with new agricultural technology, farmland is limited. Thus, Malthus presented a distressing vision of the future: people reproducing beyond what the planet could feed, leading ultimately to widespread starvation and war over what resources were available.

Malthus recognized that artificial birth control or abstinence might change his prediction. But he found one morally wrong and the other quite impractical. Because, in Malthus's mind, famine and war stalked humanity, he was justly known as "the dismal parson."

Critical Review   Fortunately, Malthus's prediction was flawed. By 1850, the European birth rate began to drop, partly because children were becoming an economic liability rather than an asset and partly because people began using artificial birth control. Also, Malthus underestimated human ingenuity: modern irrigation techniques, fertilizers, and pesticides increased farm production far more than he could have imagined. Some criticized Malthus for ignoring the role of social inequality in world abundance and famine. Karl Marx (1967; orig. 1867), for example, objected to viewing suffering as a "law of nature" rather than the curse of capitalism. More recently, "critical demographers" have claimed that saying poverty is caused by high birth rates in low-income countries amounts to blaming the victims; on the contrary, they see global inequality as the real issue (Horton, 1999; Kuumba, 1999).

Still, Malthus offers an important lesson. Habitable land, clean water, and fresh air are limited resources, and greater economic productivity have taken a heavy toll on the natural environment. In addition, medical advances have lowered death rates, pushing up world population. Common sense tells us that no level of population growth can go on forever. People everywhere must become aware of the dangers of population increase.

DEMOGRAPHIC TRANSITION THEORY

A more complex analysis of population change is **demographic transition theory,** *the thesis that population patterns reflect a society's level of technological development.* Figure 22–3 shows the demographic consequences at four levels of technological development.

Stage 1:   pre-industrial, agrarian societies have high birth rates because of the economic value of children and the absence of birth control. Death rates are

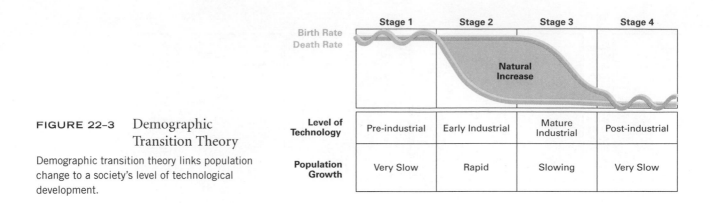

FIGURE 22–3 Demographic Transition Theory

Demographic transition theory links population change to a society's level of technological development.

also high because of low living standards and limited medical technology. Outbreaks of disease neutralize births, so population rises and falls with only a modest overall increase. This was the case for thousands of years in Europe before the Industrial Revolution.

Stage 2: the onset of industrialization, brings a demographic transition as death rates fall with increasing food supplies and scientific medicine. But birth rates remain high, resulting in rapid population growth. It was during Europe's Stage 2 that Malthus formulated his ideas, which accounts for his pessimistic view of the future. The world's poorest countries today are in this high-growth stage.

Stage 3: a mature industrial economy, brings a drop in the birth rate, curbing population growth once again. Fertility falls because most children survive to adulthood and because high living standards make raising children expensive. In short, affluence transforms children from economic assets into economic liabilities. Smaller families, made possible by effective birth control, are also favoured by women working outside the home. As birth rates follow death rates downwards, population growth slows further.

Stage 4: corresponds to a post-industrial economy in which the demographic transition is complete. The birth rate keeps falling, partly because dual-income couples gradually become the norm and partly because the cost of raising children continues to increase. This trend, linked to steady death rates, means that population grows only very slowly or even decreases. This is the case today in Japan, Europe, and the United States.

Critical Review Demographic transition theory suggests that the key to population control lies in technology. Instead of the runaway population increase feared by Malthus, this theory sees technology slowing growth and spreading material resources.

Demographic transition theory is linked to modernization theory, one approach to global development discussed in Chapter 12 ("Global Stratification"). Modernization theorists are optimistic that poor countries will solve their population problems as they industrialize.

But critics, notably dependency theorists, strongly disagree. Unless there is a redistribution of global resources, they maintain, our planet will become increasingly divided into industrialized "haves," enjoying low population growth, and non-industrialized "have-nots," struggling in vain to feed more and more people.

GLOBAL POPULATION TODAY: A BRIEF SURVEY

What can we say about population in today's world? Drawing on the discussion so far, we can identify important patterns and reach several conclusions.

The Low-Growth North

When the Industrial Revolution began in the northern hemisphere, the population increase in Western Europe and North America was a high 3 percent annually. But, in the centuries since, the growth rate has steadily declined, and in 1970, it fell below 1 percent. According to demographic transition theory, as our post-industrial society settles into Stage 4, our birth rate is less than the replacement level of 2.1 children per woman, a point demographers term **zero population growth**—*the level of reproduction that maintains population in a steady state*. More than 60 nations, almost all of them rich, are at or below the point of zero population growth.

 To find out more about population growth, go to www.populationconnection.org.

Factors holding down population in these post-industrial societies include a high proportion of men and women in the labour force, the rising costs of raising children, trends towards later marriage and singlehood, and widespread use of contraceptives and abortion. In high-income nations, then, population increase is not the pressing problem that it is in poor countries. On the contrary, many governments in high-income countries are concerned about a future problem of *underpopulation* because declining population may be difficult to reverse and because the

THINKING GLOBALLY

Empowering Women: The Key to Controlling Population Growth

Sohad Ahmad lives with her husband in a farming village 80 kilometres (50 miles) south of Cairo, Egypt's capital. Ahmad lives a poor life, like hundreds of millions of other women in the world; yet, her situation differs in an important respect: she has had only two children and will have no more.

Why do Ahmad and her husband reject the conventional wisdom that children are an economic asset? One part of the answer is that Egypt's growing population has already created such a demand for land that Ahmad's family could not afford more even if they had the children to farm it. But the main reason is that she does not want her life defined only by child bearing. Like Ahmad, more women in Egypt are taking control of their fertility and seeking educational and economic opportunities. For this reason, Egypt has made great progress in reducing its annual population growth from 3.0 percent just ten years ago to 2.0 percent today.

With its focus on raising the standing of women, the 1994 Cairo population conference broke new ground. Past

population control programs have tried simply to make birth control technology available to women. This effort is vital, since only half the world's married women use effective birth control. But even with birth control available, the population continues to expand in societies that define women's primary responsibility as raising children. Dr. Nafis Sadik, an Egyptian woman who heads the United Nations efforts at population control, sums up the new approach to lowering birth rates this way: *give women more life choices, and they will have fewer children.*

In other words, women who have access to schooling and jobs, who can

decide when and whether to marry, and who bear children as a matter of choice will limit their own fertility. Schooling must be available to older women, too, Dr. Sadik adds, because elders exercise great influence in local communities. Evidence from countries around the world is that raising the social standing of women and controlling population go hand in hand.

WHAT DO YOU THINK?

1. Why do many analysts claim that controlling population depends on expanding women's choices?
2. What specific laws or programs can you suggest that might reduce child bearing?
3. Is population control an issue for people in rich countries as well as those in poor countries? Why?

Sources: Ashford (1995), Axinn and Barber (2001), and Population Reference Bureau (2005).

---

swelling ranks of elderly people need to look to fewer and fewer young people for support (McDonald, 2001; Kent and Mather, 2002).

YOUR TURN

What effect do you think our country's high level of immigration—which typically brings young people—will have on our ability to support more and more older people?

The High-Growth South

Population is a critical problem in poor nations of the southern hemisphere. No nation of the world lacks industrial technology entirely; demographic transition theory's

Stage 1 applies today to remote rural areas of low-income nations. But much of Latin America, Africa, and Asia is at Stage 2, with a mix of agrarian and industrial economies. Advanced medical technology, supplied by high-income countries, has sharply reduced death rates, but birth rates remain high. This is why poor countries now account for two-thirds of Earth's people and 96 percent of global population increase.

Read about population control focused on youth in Asia at www.asia-initiative.org.

In low-income countries throughout the world, birth rates have fallen from an average of about 6 children per woman in 1950 to about 3 today. But fertility this high will continue to intensify global poverty. At a 1994 global population conference in Cairo, delegates from 180 nations agreed that a key element in controlling world population growth was improving the status of women. The Thinking Globally box (above) takes a closer look. In much of the world, mortality is falling. To limit population growth,

This street scene in Calcutta, India, conveys the vision of the future found in the work of Thomas Robert Malthus, who feared that population increase would overwhelm the world's resources. Demographic transition theory offers a more hopeful outcome.

people—especially in poor countries—must control births as successfully as they fend off deaths.

Urbanization: The Growth of Cities

October 8, Hong Kong. The cable train grinds to the top of Victoria Peak, where we behold one of the world's most spectacular vistas: the city of Hong Kong at night! A million bright, colourful lights ring the harbour as ships, ferries, and traditional Chinese junks churn by. Few places match Hong Kong for sheer energy. This small city is as economically productive as the state of Wisconsin or the nation of Finland. We could sit here for hours entranced by the spectacle of Hong Kong. [John J. Macionis]

For most of human history, the sights and sounds of great cities such as Hong Kong, Rio de Janeiro, and Los Angeles were simply unimaginable. Our distant ancestors lived in small, nomadic groups, moving as they depleted vegetation or hunted migratory game. The tiny settlements that marked the emergence of civilization in the Middle East some 10 000 years ago held only a small fraction of the Earth's population. Today the largest three or four cities of the world hold as many people as the entire planet did then.

Urbanization is *the concentration of population into cities*. Urbanization redistributes and concentrates population within a society and transforms many patterns of social life. We will trace these changes in terms of three urban revolutions: the emergence of cities 12 000 years ago, the development of industrial cities after 1750, and the explosive growth of cities in low-income countries today.

THE EVOLUTION OF CITIES

Cities are a relatively new development in human history. Only about 10 000 years ago did our ancestors begin founding permanent settlements, which paved the way for the *first urban revolution*.

The First Cities

As explained in Chapter 4 ("Society"), hunting and gathering forced people to move much of the time; however, once our ancestors discovered how to domesticate animals and cultivate crops, they were able to stay in one place. Raising their own food also created a material surplus, which freed some people from food production and allowed them to build shelters, make tools, weave cloth, and take part in religious rituals. The emergence of cities led to both specialization and higher living standards.

The first city was Jericho, which lies to the north of the Dead Sea in what is now the West Bank. When first settled some 10 000 years ago, it was home to only 600 people. But, as the centuries passed, cities grew to tens of thousands of people and became the centres of vast empires. By 3000 B.C.E., Egyptian cities flourished, as did cities in China about 2000 B.C.E. and in Central and South America about 1500 B.C.E.. In North America, however, only a few Indigenous peoples in North America formed settlements; widespread urbanization did not occur until the arrival of European settlers in the seventeenth century.

Pre-industrial European Cities

European cities date back some 5000 years to the Greeks and later the Romans, both of whom created great empires and founded cities across Europe, including Vienna, Paris, and London. With the fall of the Roman Empire, the so-called Dark Ages began as people withdrew within defensive walled settlements and warlords battled for territory. Only in the eleventh century did Europe become more peaceful; trade flourished once again, allowing cities to grow. Mediaeval cities were quite different from those familiar to us today. Beneath towering cathedrals, the narrow and winding streets of such cities as London, Brussels, and Florence teemed with merchants, artisans, priests, peddlers, jugglers, nobles, and servants. Guilds such as bakers, carpenters, and metalworkers often clustered together in distinct sections or quarters. Ethnicity also defined communities as residents tried to keep out people who differed from themselves: the term "ghetto" (from the Italian *borghetto*, meaning "outside the city walls") was first used to describe the neighbourhood in Venice into which Jews were segregated.

Industrial European Cities

As the Middle Ages came to a close, steadily increasing commerce enriched a new urban middle class, or *bourgeoisie* (French, meaning "townspeople"). With more and more money, the bourgeoisie soon rivalled the hereditary nobility. By about 1750, the Industrial Revolution triggered a second *urban revolution*, first in Europe and then in North America. Factories unleashed tremendous productive power, causing cities to grow bigger than ever before. London, the largest European city, reached 550 000 people by 1700 and exploded to 6.5 million by 1900 (Weber, 1963; orig. 1899; Chandler and Fox, 1974).

Cities not only grew but changed shape as well. Older winding streets gave way to broad, straight boulevards to handle the increasing flow of commercial traffic. Steam and electric trolleys soon crisscrossed expanding cities. Because land was now a commodity to be bought and sold, developers divided cities into regular-sized lots (Mumford, 1961). The centre of the city was no longer the cathedral but a bustling central business district filled with banks, retail stores, and tall office buildings. With a new focus on business, cities became more crowded and impersonal. Crime rates rose. Especially at the outset, a few industrialists lived in grand style, but most men, women, and children barely survived by working in factories.

Organized efforts by workers to improve their lives eventually brought changes to the workplace, better housing, and the right to vote. Public services such as water, sewerage, and electricity further improved urban living. Today some urbanites still live in poverty, but a rising standard of living has partly fulfilled the city's historical promise of a better life.

THE GROWTH OF NORTH AMERICAN CITIES

Indigenous peoples who occupied North America before Europeans arrived were mostly migratory peoples, who seldom made permanent settlements—the Iroquois village in what became Montreal being one exception. Villages and towns like those in Europe sprang up as a product of colonization: the Spanish made a settlement at St. Augustine, Florida, in 1565; Samuel de Champlain founded Port Royal for the French in what is now Nova Scotia in 1605; the English founded Jamestown, Virginia, in 1607; and

Champlain founded a trading post at what is now Quebec City in 1608. New Amsterdam, later called New York, was established by the Dutch in 1624, Montreal was founded by Maisonneuve in 1642, Halifax was founded in 1749 by the British to counter the French influence in North America, and York (now Toronto) was founded in 1793. These tentative intrusions onto Indigenous peoples lands were accompanied by an expanded fur trade, an invasion of rural settlers, colonial expansion, and a struggle for control over lands involving Indian nations and British and French military and colonists—all of which led to massive immigration and gradual urbanization.

By 2000, the United States had 200 cities with a population of more than 100 000, while Canada had 40 cities of that size. Each country now has more than three-quarters of its total population living in urban areas. How North America became so urban is explained in the brief history that follows.

Settlement in North America to 1850

New York and Boston started out as tiny villages in a vast wilderness. Dutch New Amsterdam at the top of Manhattan Island (1624) and English Boston (1630) developed along the lines of mediaeval towns of Europe, with narrow, winding streets that still curve through lower Manhattan and downtown Boston. New Amsterdam was walled on its north side, the site of New York's Wall Street. Boston, the largest colonial settlement, had a population of only 7000 in 1700. Economic growth soon transformed these quiet villages into thriving towns with wide streets, usually built on a grid pattern.

When York (now, Toronto) was founded in 1793 by John Graves Simcoe, commander of the Queen's Rangers and later the first lieutenant-governor of Upper Canada, Montreal was already a bustling city of more than 5500. In Upper Canada there were only about 15 settler families between Burlington Bay and the Bay of Quinte—a distance of 200 kilometres (Benn, 1993). Simcoe's intent was to move the capital from its vulnerable location at Newark (now Niagara-on-the-Lake) to one from which an American invasion could more easily be repelled. He also wanted to establish a civilian community and a naval base at York. The map in Figure 22–4 shows York Harbour, the location of the Garrison (now called Fort York), and the settlement. The gridlike settlement is near the area where Toronto's St. Lawrence Market stands today (Benn, 1993). The north/south lines above Queen Street mark the parcels of land that Simcoe granted to some of his regimental comrades and others in an effort to entice them to settle in York as a local aristocracy (which became the "Family Compact"). The lines separating their land allotments are major north/south arteries in Toronto.

As the first settlements grew, North America remained overwhelmingly rural. In 1790, the first U.S. census counted a national population of 4 million, a scant 5 percent of

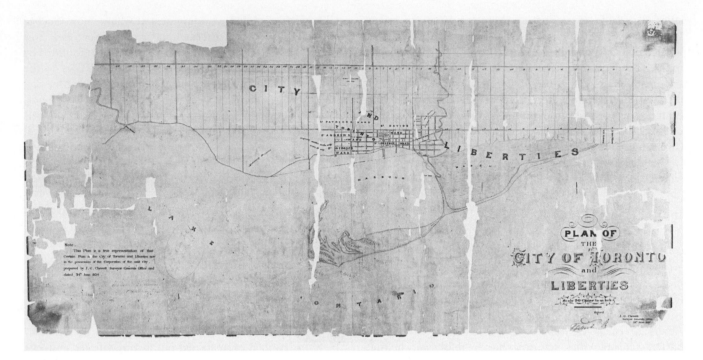

FIGURE 22-4 Map of York (Toronto), 1793

York was designed on a grid pattern as a temporary capital for Upper Canada. It was located on a protected bay where it could be shielded from potential attack by Americans.

TABLE 22-1

The Urban Population of Canada, 1871–2001

Year	Population (000s)	Percentage Urban
1871	3 689	19.6
1881	4 325	25.7
1891	4 833	31.8
1901	5 371	37.5
1911	7 207	45.4
1921	8 788	49.5
1931	10 377	52.7
1941	11 507	54.5
1951	14 009	62.9
1961	18 238	69.6
1971	21 568	76.1
1981	24 343	75.7
1991	27 297	76.6
1996	28 847	77.9
2001	30 007	79.7

Sources: Adapted by L.M. Gerber from Artibise and Stelter (1988) and the Statistics Canada publication "Population and Dwelling Counts-Urban Areas (data products; population and dwelling counts: 1991 Census of Population)", 1991, Catalogue 93-305, June 1992.

States and Canada essentially disappeared by 1940 and, today, both countries are 80 percent urban. Table 22–1 shows Canada's population growth and levels of urbanization from 1871 to 2001.

Urban Expansion

Early in the nineteenth century, towns sprang up across North America—somewhat later in Canada than in the United States. Waterways, new roads, and railway lines encouraged this growth. British Columbia agreed to join confederation in 1871 on condition that a transcontinental railway be completed. The last spike was not driven until 1885, but the Canadian Pacific Railway gave a powerful boost to settlement and economic development, especially in towns and cities located along the railway. Calgary, for example, was incorporated as a town in 1884 and, by 1893, with a population of about 4000, it became a city. Harbours, too remained significant; Halifax harbour required extensive repair after a tragic explosion in 1917, plans for which are shown in Figure 22–5.

By 1920 and 1931, respectively, U.S. and Canadian censuses revealed that more than 50 percent of their populations were living in cities. To some, increased urbanization constituted progress towards better living, but others mourned the gradual passing of traditional agrarian life. Over time, rural/urban tensions grew more pronounced, with adversaries trading negative stereotypes that pitted "ignorant country cousins" against "shady city slickers" (Callow, 1969).

whom lived in cities. By confederation in 1867 in Canada, the U.S. population of about 40 million was 20 percent urban, while Canada's population of about 3 million was almost as urban at 18 percent. The vast majority of people in both countries lived on farms and small villages. The small gap between the level of urbanization in the United

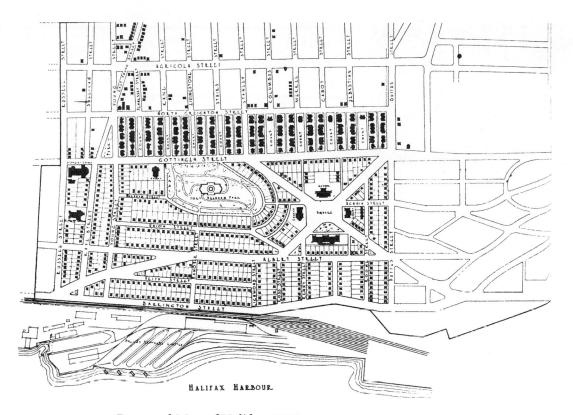

FIGURE 22-5   Proposed Map of Halifax, 1917

In 1917, Halifax was the scene of Canada's worst disaster: 1600 people were killed, more than 9000 were injured, and thousands left homeless when a French munitions ship and Belgian relief vessel collided in Halifax Harbour—setting off further explosions and multiple fires in the city. Thomas Adams, a British planner then living in Canada, proposed an amazing feat of restoration: a plan for central Halifax that dispensed with the grid pattern and included diagonal and gently curving streets to emphasize vistas and greenery (Sewell, 1993; Kitz, 1989). Robert MacNeil's novel *Burden of Desire* (1992) is a love story based on the Halifax disaster and the inspiration for the Canadian/American feature-length film of the same name.

Source: Sewell (1993).

The Metropolitan Era

Dizzying growth and concentration of population by the 1940s marked the coming of the **metropolis,** *a large city that socially and economically dominates the surrounding area.* The current Canadian definition of a Census Metropolitan Area is for a population of at least 100 000 spread out among one or more municipalities with economic and commuting ties. These metropolises have become the manufacturing, commercial, and residential centres of North America.

By the 1880s, industrial technology was producing steel girders and mechanical elevators so that builders were raising structures ten storeys above the ground. And this, of course, was only the beginning. In 1975, Toronto's CN Tower was completed: at 553.3 metres, it is still the world's tallest free-standing structure on land. City centres contain these kinds of monuments as well as clusters of soaring buildings of glass, concrete, and steel, while public transit and roadways allow for lower-density city sprawl that stretches for kilometres. Canada has 25 Census Metropolitan Areas, as shown on Table 22–2, ranging in population size from Toronto at more than 5 million to Thunder Bay, Ontario, at 125 700.

YOUR TURN

Do you think of city streets as a place for socializing or simply as routes to some destination? Does your home town or city ban traffic from certain streets to create pedestrian areas?

SUBURBS AND CENTRAL CITIES

Just as central cities flourished a century ago, we have recently witnessed the expansion of **suburbs,** *urban areas beyond the political boundaries of a city.* The first suburbanites were well-to-do but, by the late 1940s, less wealthy people also came to view a single-family house on its own piece of leafy suburban ground as the ideal lifestyle. The mobility provided by increasingly affordable automobiles

A century ago, as this scene from the film *Gangs of New York* suggests, people living in cities used the streets for most of their daily activities. Today, by contrast, the idea of "living on the streets" is associated with the poor and homeless. Why do you think street life is less valued today than it was in the past?

TABLE 22–2

Population of Census Metropolitan Areas in Canada, 1956 and 2001*

	Population (000s)	
	1956	**2001**
Calgary, AB	201.0	969.6
Chicoutimi, QC	90.9	158.8
Edmonton, AB	254.8	954.1
Halifax, NS	164.2	359.1
Hamilton, ON	338.2	680.0
Kitchener, ON	128.7	431.2
London, ON	154.4	425.2
Montreal, QC	1745.0	3511.4
Oshawa, ON	62.8	304.6
Ottawa–Hull, ON/QC	345.4	1108.5
Québec, QC	311.6	694.0
Regina, SK	89.7	198.3
St. Catharines–Niagara, ON	85.0	391.9
St. John's, NL	79.1	176.4
Saint John, NB	86.0	127.3
Saskatoon, SK	72.8	231.5
Sherbrooke, QC	61.8	155.0
Sudbury, ON	97.9	157.0
Thunder Bay, ON	N.A.	125.7
Toronto, ON	1502.2	4907.0
Trois-Rivières, QC	75.4	141.2
Vancouver, BC	665.0	2099.4
Victoria, BC	133.8	319.4
Windsor, ON	185.8	313.7
Winnipeg, MB	412.2	684.3

*A Census Metropolitan Area is defined by Statistics Canada as a large urban area (with at least 100 000 population) together with neighbouring urban and rural areas that has a high degree of social and economic integration.

Source: Adapted from the Statistics Canada publication "Population and Dwelling Counts-Urban Areas" 1991 Census of Population)," 1991, Catalogue 93-305, June 1992.

made this dream come true for more and more people. After World War II, men and women eagerly returned to family life, igniting the baby boom. Since central cities offered little space for new housing construction, suburbs blossomed almost overnight.

Today, more than half of Canada's urbanites live in municipalities outside central cities, or in newer central cities, like those on the Prairies, which are largely suburban in style. As a result of the overall flight to the suburbs by young families and the fact that more people are living alone in their downtown homes, vigorous construction in the central cities has not stopped the decline in some central city populations (Michelson, 1988:86). As population decentralized, businesses also began to migrate to the suburbs. Older people today can recall trips downtown to shop, but, by the 1970s, the suburban mall had replaced main street as the centre of retail trade. Manufacturing interests, too, moved to the suburbs, where there was relief from high taxes, escalating property costs, and traffic congestion. The result was financial difficulty for the older central cities owing to reduced tax revenue.

In 1953, in response to this disparity between the core of the city and outlying areas, Ontario created "Metropolitan Toronto" by combining the central city of Toronto with twelve of its suburbs. The province had to impose the solution initially, as none of the municipalities was enamoured of the prospect. But, as a result of the success of Metropolitan Toronto, other urban regions in Canada have followed suit.[1] The benefits of this model of urban development are clear when we compare Canada's situation to that of the United States. Since American cities rarely adopt a metropolitan-type government, they tend to suffer much more from decaying inner cities: "Canadian metropolitan areas suffer fewer of the glaring contrasts in welfare, infrastructure, and supportive services differentiating American central cities and suburbs" (Michelson, 1988:97).

When several adjacent metropolitan regions get so large that they bump up against each other and form a continuous urban area, they form what is called a **megalopolis,** *a vast urban region containing a number of cities and their surrounding suburbs.* Gottmann (1961) first coined the term "megalopolis" in reference to the area between and including Boston and Washington. An equivalent area in Canada, known as the Golden Horseshoe, stretches from Oshawa in the east, through Toronto, and west to St. Catharines; the Windsor–Quebec City corridor forms

---

[1]Note that the creation of the new city of Toronto in 1997 through the amalgamation of six cities—into the Greater Toronto Area—is distinct from the creation of a metropolitan area.

Many small towns have gained population through migration from cities. This "rural rebound" has been most pronounced in towns that offer spectacular natural beauty and recreational attractions, such as mountains, lakes, and ski areas. There are times when people living in the scenic town of Banff, Alberta, cannot find a parking space.

another, looser version. The political and economic dominance of these regions is quite apparent from the fact that the Golden Horseshoe alone contains about one-third of Canada's population, while the larger Windsor–Quebec City corridor contains about half.

Urbanism as a Way of Life

Early sociologists in Europe and the United States focused their attention on the rise of cities and the differences between rural and urban life. We briefly present their accounts of urbanism as a way of life.

FERDINAND TÖNNIES: *GEMEINSCHAFT* AND *GESELLSCHAFT*

In the late nineteenth century, the German sociologist Ferdinand Tönnies (1855–1937) studied how life in the new industrial metropolis differed from life in rural villages. From this contrast, he developed two concepts that have become a lasting part of sociology's terminology. Tönnies (1963; orig. 1887) used the German word ***Gemeinschaft*** (meaning roughly "community") to refer to *a type of social organization in which people are closely tied by kinship and tradition*. The *Gemeinschaft* of the rural village joins people in what amounts to a single primary group.

By and large, argued Tönnies, *Gemeinschaft* is absent in the modern city. On the contrary, urbanization creates ***Gesellschaft*** (a German word meaning roughly "association"), *a type of social organization in which people come together only on the basis of individual self-interest*. In the *Gesellschaft* way of life, individuals are motivated by their own needs rather than by a desire to help improve the well-being of everyone. City dwellers display little sense of community or common identity, and look to others mainly when they need something. Tönnies saw in urbanization a weakening of close, long-lasting social relations in favour of the brief and impersonal ties—or secondary relationships—typical of business.

EMILE DURKHEIM: MECHANICAL AND ORGANIC SOLIDARITY

The French sociologist Emile Durkheim (see Chapter 4, "Society") agreed with much of Tönnies' thinking about cities. However, Durkheim countered that urbanites do not lack social bonds; they simply organize social life differently from the ways rural people do. Durkheim described traditional, rural life as *mechanical solidarity*, social bonds based on common sentiments and shared moral values. With its emphasis on tradition, Durkheim's concept of mechanical solidarity bears a striking similarity to Tönnies' *Gemeinschaft*. Urbanization erodes mechanical solidarity, Durkheim explained, but it also generates a new type of bonding, which he called *organic* solidarity, social bonds based on specialization and interdependence. This concept, which parallels Tönnies' *Gesellschaft*, reveals an important difference between the two thinkers. Both thought the growth of industrial cities weakened tradition, but Durkheim optimistically pointed to a new kind of solidarity. Where people had been joined by *likeness*, Durkheim now saw them joined by *difference*. For Durkheim, urban society offered more individual choice, moral tolerance, and personal privacy than people find in rural villages. In sum, for Durkheim, something is lost in the process of urbanization, but much is gained.

Peasant Dance (*above*), by Pieter Breughel the Elder, conveys the essential unity of rural life forged by generations of kinship and neighbourhood. By contrast, Ernest Fiene's *Nocturne* (*left*) communicates the impersonality common to urban areas. Taken together, these paintings capture Tönnies' distinction between *Gemeinschaft* and *Gesellschaft*.

Pieter Breughel the Elder (c. 1525/30–1569), *Peasant Dance*, c. 1565, Kunsthistorisches Museum, Vienna/Superstock.

Ernest Fiene (1894–1965), *Nocturne*. Photograph © Christie's Images.

GEORG SIMMEL: THE BLASÉ URBANITE

The German sociologist Georg Simmel (1858–1918) offered a microanalysis of cities, studying how urban life shapes individual experience. According to Simmel (1964; orig. 1905), individuals perceive the city as a crush of people, objects, and events. To prevent being overwhelmed by all this stimulation, urbanites develop a *blasé attitude*, tuning out much of what goes on around them. Such detachment does not mean that city dwellers lack compassion for others; they simply keep their distance as a survival strategy so they can focus their time and energy on those who really matter to them.

THE CHICAGO SCHOOL: ROBERT PARK AND LOUIS WIRTH

In the 1920 and 1930s, sociologists in the United States— there were no sociology departments in Canada yet—joined the study of rapidly growing cities. Robert Park, a leader of the first U.S. sociology program at the University of Chicago, sought to add a street-level perspective by getting out and studying real cities: "I suspect that I have actually covered more ground, tramping about in cities in different parts of the world, than any other living man" (1950:viii). Walking the streets, Park found the city to be an organized mosaic of distinctive ethnic communities, commercial centres, and industrial districts. Over time, he observed these "natural areas" develop and change in relation to one another. To Park, the city was a living organism, a human kaleidoscope.

Another major figure in the Chicago School of urban sociology was Louis Wirth (1897–1952). Wirth (1938) is best known for blending the ideas of Tönnies, Durkheim, Simmel, and Park into a comprehensive theory of urban life. Wirth began by defining the city as a setting with a large, dense, and socially diverse population, traits that result in an impersonal, superficial, and transitory way of life. Living among millions of others, urbanites come into contact with many more people than residents of rural areas. So, when city people notice others at all, they usually know them not in terms of *who they are* but *what they do*— as, for instance, the bus driver, florist, or grocery store clerk. Specialized urban relationships are pleasant for all concerned, but we should remember that self-interest rather than friendship is usually the main reason for the interaction.

Finally, limited social involvement coupled with great social diversity make city dwellers more tolerant than rural villagers. Rural communities often jealously enforce their narrow traditions, but the heterogeneous population of a city rarely shares any single code of moral conduct (Wilson, 1985, 1995).

Critical Review In both Europe and the United States, early sociologists presented a mixed view of urban living. Rapid urbanization troubled Tönnies, and Wirth saw personal ties and traditional morality lost in the anonymous rush of the city. Durkheim and Park emphasized urbanism's posi-

THINKING ABOUT DIVERSITY:
RACE, CLASS, & GENDER
Census 2001: Minorities a Major Presence in Canada's Largest Metropolitan Areas

According to the results of the 2001 census, immigrants and visible minorities are a major presence in Canada's largest cities. So marked is this concentration of minorities, that Scarborough (now part of Toronto) has been recognized by the World Health Organization as the world's most ethno-racially diverse community (McKenzie, 2007).

New immigrants typically settle in Toronto, Vancouver, and Montreal, where they join the "old" immigrants (i.e., those who have not moved on to other parts of Canada), thereby adding to the proportion of foreign-born people in each of the cities. Keep in mind that immigrants have come to Canada for six decades or more — initially from Europe, then from Asia and other parts of the world. Similarly, visible minorities are not necessarily immigrants, as 30 percent are born in Canada. This is why the percentage of immigrants and percentage of visible minority in Table 22–3 do not match.

Immigrants overwhelmingly arrive in Canada through Toronto, Montreal, and Vancouver. Since they find their own ethnic communities established in these cities, they are likely to stay there, at least for a while. Gradually, immigrants move on to other parts of Canada — including other metropolitan areas in Table 22–3 (excluding Quebec City). Calgary and Hamilton are over 20 percent immigrant. Canada's visible minorities have congregated in Toronto and Vancouver specifically. Since they are among more recent immigrants, they have not had as much time to spread out throughout the country. Nonetheless, they are well-represented in Calgary, Edmonton, and Winnipeg.

TABLE 22–3

Ethno-Racial Diversity in Canada's Ten Largest Metropolitan Areas: 2001

Metropolitan Area	Population	Percentage Aboriginal	Percentage Immigrant	Percentage Visible Minority
Toronto, ON	4 647 955	1.0	43.7	36.8
Montreal, QC	3 380 645	1.5	18.4	13.6
Vancouver, BC	1 967 475	2.7	37.5	36.9
Ottawa–Hull, ON/QC	1 050 755	3.2	17.6	14.1
Calgary, AB	943 310	3.6	20.9	17.5
Edmonton, AB	927 020	6.0	17.8	17.8
Quebec, QC	673 105	1.5	2.9	1.6
Winnipeg, MB	661 730	9.5	16.5	12.5
Hamilton, ON	655 055	2.0	23.6	9.8
London, ON	427 215	2.3	18.8	9.0
Canada	29 639 030	4.5	18.4	13.4

Source: Compiled by L.M. Gerber from Statistics Canada, Census 2001, catalogue numbers 97F0010XCB2001044 and 97F0010XCB2001001.

Aboriginal peoples, because of their special history and relationship with Canada, are not considered to be visible minorities. They, too, are unevenly represented in Canada's largest metropolitan areas. While 4.5 percent of Canada's population claims Aboriginal origins, this is true of 9.5 and 6.0 percent, respectively, of the populations of Winnipeg and Calgary.

As suggested above, the concentration of immigrants and visible minorities is even more pronounced than Table 22–3 suggests. The five electoral districts of Scarborough are 51 to 69 percent immigrant and 43 to *85* percent visible minority—giving rise to its designation by the World Health Organization as the world's most

diverse community. Not surprisingly, since multicultural districts are known to vote Liberal, the Scarborough ridings exhibited the highest levels of support for the Liberal party in the federal elections of 2004 and 2006 (Gerber, 2006a, 2006b).

WHAT DO YOU THINK?

1. Why do immigrants and minorities gravitate to some communities and not others?
2. How does ethno-racial diversity contribute to city life?
3. What are some specific challenges faced by cities with large populations of new immigrants?

tive face, pointing to more personal freedom and greater personal choice.

One problem with all these views is that they paint urbanism in broad strokes that overlook the effects of class, race, and gender. There are many kinds of urbanites—rich and poor, Black and White, anglophone and francophone, women and men—all leading distinctive lives. As the Thinking about Diversity box (on p. 583) explains, the proportions of immigrants, visible minorities, and Aboriginal people in Canada's largest metropolitan areas increased rapidly over the past two decades.

URBAN ECOLOGY

Sociologists—especially members of the Chicago School—developed **urban ecology,** *the study of the link between the physical and social dimensions of cities.* For example, why are cities located where they are? The first cities emerged in fertile regions where the ecology favoured raising crops. Pre-industrial people, concerned with defence, built their cities on mountains (i.e., ancient Athens was perched on an outcropping of rock) or surrounded by water (i.e., Paris and Mexico City were founded on islands). With the coming of the Industrial Revolution, economic considerations situated all the major U.S. cities near rivers and natural harbours that facilitated trade.

Urban ecologists also study the physical design of cities. In 1925, Ernest W. Burgess, a student and colleague of Robert Park's, described land use in Chicago in terms of *concentric zones.* City centres, Burgess observed, are business districts bordered by a ring of factories, followed by residential rings with housing that becomes more expensive the farther it is from the noise and pollution of the city's centre. Homer Hoyt (1939) refined Burgess's observations, noting that distinctive districts sometimes form *wedge-shaped sectors.* For example, one fashionable area may develop next to another, or an industrial district may extend outward from a city's centre along a train or trolley line. Chauncy Harris and Edward Ullman (1945) added yet another insight: as cities decentralize, they lose their single-centre form in favour of a *multicentred model.* As cities grow, residential areas, industrial parks, and shopping districts typically push away from one another. Few people wish to live close to industrial areas, for example, so the city becomes a mosaic of distinct districts.

Social area analysis investigates what people in particular neighbourhoods have in common. Three factors seem to explain most of the variation: family patterns, social class, and race and ethnicity (Shevky and Bell, 1955; Johnston, 1976). Families with children look for areas with single-family homes or large apartments and good schools. The rich seek high-prestige neighbourhoods, often in the central city near cultural attractions. People with a common race or ethnic heritage may cluster in distinctive communities.

Brian Berry and Philip Rees (1969) tie together many of these insights. They explain that distinct family types tend to settle in the concentric zones described by Burgess. Specifically, households with few children tend to cluster towards the city's centre, and those with more children live farther away. Social class differences are primarily responsible for the sector-shaped districts described by Hoyt—for instance, the rich occupy one side of the tracks, and the poor, the other. And racial and ethnic neighbourhoods are found at various points throughout the city, consistent with Harris and Ullman's multicentred model.

URBAN POLITICAL ECONOMY

As urban problems—rioting, crime, poverty, and unemployment—proliferated, most visibly in the United States, some analysts turned away from the ecological approach to a social-conflict understanding of city life. *Urban political economy* is influenced by the thinking of Karl Marx, although the scene of social conflict shifts from the workplace to the city (Lindstrom, 1995).

The ecological approach of the Chicago School saw the city as a "natural" organism, with particular districts and neighbourhoods developing according to an internal logic. Political economists disagree, claiming that city life is defined mostly by people with power: corporate leaders and the political elite. In Canada, U.S. multinational corporations, foreign investors, and the global capitalist system are seen as important players as well. These powerholders make the economic and political decisions that determine the location, size, shape, and character of major cities. For example, deindustrialization of the Maritime provinces, and shifts in political and economic clout up the St. Lawrence River to Montreal and then to Toronto caused an inordinate concentration of capital, industry, population, and political power in southern Quebec and Ontario. This relatively small area—and Metropolitan Toronto in particular—emerged as the core to the peripheral areas, or hinterland, of the country. The industrialized core dominates weaker areas, rural and urban, that are dependent on natural resources. This relationship accounts for regional inequalities, regionalism, and even threats to national unity (Matthews, 1983; Brym, 1986; Goyder, 1990; Hiller, 2000).

Critical Review The urban political economy paradigm has gained much attention in recent years. For one thing, compared to the older urban ecology approach, the political economy view seems better able to address the harsh realities of urban life. But analysis based on the political economy perspective has been largely limited to capitalist societies in the modern era. Capitalism and industrialization are assumed to cause the problems of urban life, while the environment and physical structure of cities are ignored.

Jane Jacobs (1961, 1970, 1984), a highly esteemed expert on urban development and urban life, argues that urban social problems are the result of economic stagnation, but sustaining economic development is not a simple function of the availability of capital and political will. Cities are vital

For information about the works and influence of Jane Jacobs, go to http://bss.sfsu.edu/pamuk/urban/.

to developing economies, but conditions including environment, population growth, economic differentiation, and a crucial mix of industries are required to sustain economic health. Jacobs, who was keenly interested in neighbourhoods—all kinds of them (Kelly, 2006), asserted that cities should be built for people.

Urbanization in Poor Nations

Twice in its history, the world has experienced a revolutionary expansion of cities. The first urban revolution began about 10 000 years ago with the first urban settlements and continued until permanent settlements were in place on several continents. About 1750, the second took off; it lasted for two centuries as the Industrial Revolution spurred rapid urban growth of in Europe and North America.

A third urban revolution is now under way. Today, approximately 75 percent of people in industrial societies are already city dwellers. But extreme urban growth is occurring in low income nations. In 1950, about 25 percent

For an interactive map that demonstrates changes to global urban growth since 1950, visit http://news.bbc.co.uk/1/shared/spl/hi/world/06/urbanisation/html/urbanisation.stm.

of the people in poor countries lived in cities; in 2005, the figure was close to 50 percent. In 1950, only 7 cities in the world had populations over 5 million, and only 2 of these were in low-income countries. By 2005, 49 cities had passed this mark, and 32 of them were in less developed nations (Brockerhoff, 2000; GeoHive, 2005).

This third urban revolution is taking place, according to demographic transition theory, because many poor nations have entered the high-growth Stage 2. Falling death rates have fuelled population increases in Latin America, Asia, and especially Africa. For urban areas, the rate of increase is *twice* as high because in addition to natural increase, millions of people leave the countryside each year in search of jobs, health care, education, and conveniences such as running water and electricity.

Cities offer more opportunities than rural areas, but they provide no quick fix for the massive problems of escalating population and grinding poverty. Many cities in low-income nations, such as Mexico City, Cairo, Calcutta, and Manila, are simply unable to meet the basic needs of their populations. All these cities are surrounded by wretched shantytowns—settlements of makeshift homes built from discarded materials. In some places, city dumps are home to thousands of poor people, who pick through piles of waste hoping to find enough food to make it through another day.

Environment and Society

Population growth and urbanization have come at a high price. Never before in history have human beings placed

Jane Jacobs, a writer and activist, was born in the United States, where she wrote her influential book *The Death and Life of Great American Cities* (1961). In 1969 with her architect husband and two sons, who were eligible for drafting into the U.S. military, she moved to Toronto; there, she continued writing and played an active role in urban planning. Jacobs who argued that cities should be built for people, not cars. A Toronto icon since her involvement in the movement to stop the Spadina Expressway, Jacobs died in 2006, at the age of 89.

such demands on the planet. This disturbing development brings us to the final section of this chapter: the interplay between the natural environment and society. Like demography, **ecology** is another cousin of sociology, formally defined as *the study of the interaction of living organisms and the natural environment.* Ecology rests on the research of natural scientists as well as social scientists. In this text, we focus on the aspects of ecology that involve familiar sociological concepts and issues.

The **natural environment** is *Earth's surface and atmosphere, including living organisms, air, water, soil, and other resources necessary to sustain life.* Like every other species, humans depend on the natural environment to survive. Yet with our capacity for culture, humans stand apart from other species; we alone take deliberate action to remake the world according to our own interests and desires, for better and for worse. Why is the environment of interest to sociologists? Simply because environmental problems—from pollution to acid rain to global warming—do not arise from the natural world operating on its own. Rather, as we shall explain, such issues result from the organized patterns of collective living, so they are *social* problems (Marx, 1994).

THE GLOBAL DIMENSION

The study of the natural environment requires a global perspective. The reason is simple: regardless of political divisions among nations, the planet is a single **ecosystem,** *a*

Sociological insight helps us see that environmental problems do not simply "happen." Rather, the state of the natural environment reflects the ways in which social life is organized. The greater the technological power of a society, the greater that society's ability to threaten the natural environment.

system composed of the interaction of all living organisms and their natural environment. The Greek meaning of *eco* is "house," reminding us that this planet is our home and that all living things and their natural environment are interrelated. A change in any part of the natural environment ripples throughout the entire global ecosystem.

Consider, from an ecological point of view, our love of hamburgers. North Americans have created a huge demand for beef, which has greatly expanded the ranching industry in Brazil, Costa Rica, and other Latin American nations. To produce the lean meat sought by fast-food corporations, cattle in Latin America feed on grass, which requires a great deal of land. Latin American ranchers acquire grazing land by clearing thousands of hectares of forest—vital to maintaining Earth's atmosphere—each year.

TECHNOLOGY AND THE ENVIRONMENTAL DEFICIT

Members of hunter/gatherer societies with simple technology, described in Chapter 4 ("Society"), hardly affect the environment because they are small in number and use simple technologies that do not harm their environment. On the contrary, nature affects their lives as they follow the migration of game, watch the rhythm of the seasons, and suffer from natural catastrophes such as fires, floods, droughts, and storms.

Societies at intermediate stages of technological development have greater effects on the environment. Such societies are both larger and richer. But the environmental impact of horticulture (small-scale farming), pastoralism (the herding of animals), and even agriculture (the use of animal-drawn plows) is limited because people still rely on muscle power for producing food and other goods.

The Industrial Revolution greatly increased human impacts on the natural environment. Muscle power gave way to engines that burn fossil fuels: coal at first and then oil. Such machinery affects the environment in at least two ways: we consume more natural resources, and we release more pollutants into the atmosphere. Even more significantly, armed with industrial technology, we are able to bend nature to our will, tunnelling through mountains, damming rivers, irrigating deserts, and drilling for oil in the Arctic and on the ocean floor. This explains why people in high-income nations, who represent just 18 percent of humanity, now use 80 percent of the world's energy (Miller, 1992; York, *et al.*, 2002).

The environmental impact of industrial technology goes beyond energy consumption. Higher living standards and the demand for more products increase the problem of solid waste, since people ultimately throw away most of what they produce, as well as pollution, since industrial production generates smoke and other toxic substances.

People have long recognized the material benefits of industrial technology, but only a century after the Industrial Revolution did they begin to see the long-term effects on the natural environment. Today, we realize that the technological power to make our lives better can also put the lives of future generations at risk, and there is widespread debate about how to address these issues. Evidence is mounting that we are running up an **environmental deficit,** *profound long-term harm to the natural environment caused by humanity's focus on short-term material affluence* (Bormann, 1990). This concept is important for three reasons. First, it reminds us that environmental concerns are *sociological,* reflecting societies' priorities about how people should live. Second, it suggests that much environmental damage to air, land, and water is *unintended.* By focusing on the short-term benefits of, say, cutting down forests, strip mining, or using throwaway packaging, we fail to see their long-term environmental effects. Third, in some respects, the environmental deficit is *reversible.* We have created environmental problems but can also undo many of them.

CULTURE: GROWTH AND LIMITS

Whether we recognize environmental dangers and decide to do something about them is a cultural matter. Thus, along with technology, culture has powerful environmental consequences.

The Logic of Growth

One of the core values of North Americans is *material comfort,* the belief that money and the things it buys enrich our lives. We also believe in the idea of *progress,* thinking the future will be better than the present. In addition, we look to science to make our lives easier and more rewarding. In simple terms, "having things is good," "life gets better," and "people are clever." Taken together, such cultural values form the *logic of growth.* This is closely related to the modernization theory of development.

YOUR TURN

Can you point to ways in which the mass media and our popular culture (music, films, and television) encourage people to support the logic of growth?

An optimistic view of the world, the logic of growth holds that more powerful technology has improved our lives and new discoveries will continue to do so in the future. For high-income nations, the logic of growth has been the driving force behind settling the wilderness, building towns and roads, pursuing material wealth, and consumerism. However, our pursuit of such progress can lead to unexpected problems, including strain on the environment. The logic of growth responds by arguing that people—in particular, scientists and other technology experts—will find a way out of any problem that growth places in our path. For example, if the world runs short of oil, our experts will come up with hydrogen, solar, or nuclear engines, or some other as yet unknown technology to meet the world's energy needs.

Critics, such as dependency theorists and environmentalists, counter that the logic of growth is flawed because it assumes that natural resources such as oil, clean air, fresh water, and topsoil will always be plentiful. We can and will exhaust these *finite* resources if we continue to pursue growth at any cost. Echoing Malthus, environmentalists warn that, if we call on Earth to support increasing numbers of people, we will surely deplete finite resources, destroying the environment—and ourselves—in the process.

The Limits to Growth

If we cannot invent our way out of the problems created by the logic of growth, perhaps we need another way of thinking about the world. Environmentalists counter by pointing out that growth must have limits. Stated simply, the *limits to growth thesis* is that humanity must put in place policies to control the growth of population, production, and use of resources in order to avoid environmental collapse. *The Limits to Growth*, a controversial book that was influential in supporting the environmental movement (Meadows, *et al.*, 1972), calculated the planet's available resources, rates of population growth, amount of land available for cultivation, levels of industrial and food production, and amount of pollutants released into the atmosphere. The authors concede that any long-range predictions are speculative, and some critics think they are plain wrong (Simon, 1981). But right or wrong, the conclusions of the study call for serious consideration. First, the authors claim that we are quickly consuming Earth's finite resources: supplies of oil, natural gas, and other energy sources are already falling sharply and will continue to drop, a little faster or slower depending on the conservation policies of high-income

nations and the speed with which middle- and low-income nations industrialize. Within the next hundred years, resources will run out and cripple industrial output, which will also cause a decline in food production.

This limits to growth theory shares Malthus's pessimism about the future. People who accept it doubt that current patterns of life are sustainable for even another century. If so, we face a fundamental choice: either we make voluntary changes in how we live, or widespread hunger and conflict will *force* change on us.

 MEDIA View aerial photos of environmental damage, as well as related topics, at www.sprol.com.

YOUR TURN

Are you willing to pay higher prices for products such as hybrid cars or things made with recycled materials that are better for the environment? Why?

SOLID WASTE: THE DISPOSABLE SOCIETY

Throughout North America, people generate a massive amount of solid waste—about 0.7 billion kilograms (1.5 billion pounds) *each and every day*. Figure 22–6 shows the average composition of a typical community's garbage. As a rich nation of people who value convenience, Canada has become a *disposable society*. We consume vast numbers of products, many of which have throwaway packaging. For example, fast food is served with cardboard, plastic, and foam containers that we throw away within minutes. Countless other products, from film to fishhooks, are elaborately packaged to make the products more attractive to the customer and to discourage tampering and theft. Manufacturers market soft drinks, beer, and fruit juices in aluminum cans, glass jars, and plastic containers, which not only consume finite resources but also generate mountains of solid waste. Then there are countless items intentionally designed to be disposable: pens, razors, flashlights, batteries, even cameras. Other products, from light bulbs to automobiles, are designed to have a limited useful life and then become unwanted junk. As Connett (1991) points out, even the words we use to describe what we throw away—*waste, litter, trash, refuse, garbage, rubbish*—show how little we value what we cannot immediately use.

In North America, each of us consumes 50 times more steel, 170 times more newspaper, 250 times more gasoline, and 300 times more plastic each year than the typical person in a low-income country, such as Haiti (Miller, 1992). This high level of consumption means not only that we use a disproportionate share of the planet's natural resources but also that we generate most of the world's refuse.

We say that we "throw things away" but 80 percent of our solid waste never goes "away"; rather, it ends up in

FIGURE 22-6   Composition of Community Trash

We throw away a wide range of material, with paper the single largest part of our garbage.

Source: U.S. Environmental Protection Agency (2005) (or Based on Franklin Associates (1986) and Corley, *et al.* (1993)).

Water, vital to life, is in short supply. The state of Gujarat, in western India, has experienced a decade-long drought. In the village of Natwarghad, people crowd together, lowering pots into the local well, taking what little water is left.

landfills, which are, literally, filling up. Material in landfills can pollute groundwater, as well as soil, air, and surface waters. Although in most places, laws now regulate what can be discarded in a landfill, too many dumps contain hazardous materials that are polluting water both above and below the ground. In addition, what goes into landfills all too often stays there, sometimes for centuries. Tens of millions of tires, diapers, and other items we bury in landfills each year do not decompose at all, but remain as an unwelcome legacy for future generations.

Environmentalists argue that we should address the problem of solid waste by doing what many of our grandparents did: turn "waste" into a resource. One way to do this is through *recycling*, reusing things we would otherwise discard. Many products, such as plastic bags and containers, can be reused around the home; spectacles, lightly used clothing, furniture, and household goods can be donated for others to use. Most Canadian cities have recycling programs for residents to get rid of unwanted glass, cans, and paper. A few, like Guelph, Ontario, collect dry and wet waste (plus diapers) and convert the wet, organic waste into fertile soil. Toronto has been sending its waste to Michigan—in 400 trucks a day along Highway 401—since the failure of its controversial plan to take its garbage, by train, to the former Adams Mine near Kirkland Lake. Michigan is backing out of its agreement to absorb Toronto's residential waste, and the nearby Regional Municipality of Halton may come to the rescue. Halton has already been approved as the site of a waste incineration plant, and is looking at the possibility of building a larger plant to accommodate Toronto's waste.

To learn more about Halton's present and proposed waste management plans, including a green cart program for organic waste, go to www.halton.ca/PPW/waste.

WATER AND AIR

Oceans, lakes, and streams are the lifeblood of the global ecosystem. Humans depend on water for drinking, bathing, cooking, recreation, and a host of other activities. Through the *hydrologic cycle*, Earth naturally recycles water and refreshes the land. The process begins as heat from the sun causes Earth's water, 97 percent of which is in the oceans, to evaporate and form clouds. Because water evaporates at lower temperatures than most pollutants, the water vapour that rises from the seas is relatively pure, leaving various contaminants behind. Water then falls to Earth as rain, which drains into streams and rivers and, finally, returns to the sea. Two major concerns about water for humans, then, are supply and pollution.

Water Supply

Only about 1 percent of Earth's water is suitable for drinking. It is not surprising, then, that for thousands of years, water rights have figured prominently in laws around the world. Today, some regions of the world, especially the tropics, enjoy plentiful fresh water, using a small share of the available supply. However, high demand, coupled with modest reserves, makes water supply a matter of concern in central North America and much of Asia, where people look to rivers rather than rainfall for their water. In China, deep aquifers are dropping rapidly. In the Middle East, water supply is reaching a critical level. Iran is rationing water in its capital city. In Egypt, the Nile River provides just one-sixth as much water per person as it did in 1900. Across northern Africa and the Middle East, as many as 1 billion people may lack the water they need for irrigation and drinking by 2025.

Rising population and the development of more complex technology have greatly increased the world's appetite for water. The global consumption of water—now estimated at 4 billion cubic feet per year—has tripled since 1950 and is rising steadily. As a result, even in those parts of the world that receive plenty of rainfall, people are using groundwater faster than it can be replenished naturally. In the Tamil Nadu region of southern India, for example, so much groundwater is being used that the water table has fallen 30 metres (100 feet) over the last several decades. Mexico City—which has sprawled to some 3625 square kilometres (1400 square miles)—has pumped so much water from its underground aquifer that the city has sunk 9 metres (30 feet) during the past century and continues to drop about 5 centimetres (2 inches) per year. Farther north in the United States, the Ogallala aquifer, which lies below seven states from South Dakota to Texas, is now dropping by about 46 centimetres (18 inches) a year, raising fears that it will run dry within several decades.

In Canada, where fresh water supplies—though diminishing—are adequate for the time being, we worry that we will become the fresh water supplier for other countries. If we were to export water to the United States for commercial purposes, the North American Free Trade Agreement would require us to keep the tap open, even as our own supplies are threatened. In light of such developments, we must face the reality that water is a valuable, finite resource. Greater conservation of water by individuals—the average North American consumes about 38 million litres (10 million gallons) in a lifetime—is part of the answer. However, households around the world account for just 10 percent of water use. It is even more crucial that we curb water consumption by industry, which uses 20 percent of the global total, and by farming, which consumes 70 percent of the total for irrigation.

Water Pollution

In large cities from Mexico City to Cairo to Shanghai, many people have no choice but to drink contaminated water. Infectious diseases like typhoid, cholera, and dysentery—all caused by waterborne micro-organisms—spread rapidly through these populations. Besides ensuring ample *supplies*

Read and see Dr Jim Byrne's work at Lethbridge University on degradation of Canada's water resources at www. innovationalberta.com/article. php?articleid=574.

of water, then, we must protect the *quality* of water. Water quality in North America is generally good by global standards. However, even here the problem of water pollution is steadily growing. According to the Sierra Club, an environmental organization, rivers and streams absorb some 230 million kilograms (500 million pounds) of toxic waste each year. This pollution results not just from intentional dumping but also in runoff containing agricultural fertilizers, factory farm or feedlot pollutants, lawn chemicals, and contaminants from landfill sites.

According to the Sierra Club, Conservative prime ministers and Republican presidents have had the best environmental records: "When Brian Mulroney was recently declared the 'greenest prime minister' in Canadian history, there was disbelief that a right-winger could be so honoured" (Hamilton, 2006). The Sierra Club chose Mulroney for the award because he worked effectively with U.S. president, Ronald Reagan in fighting acid rain. Tory prime ministers and environment ministers have had the greenest records—along with Republican American president, Richard Nixon. The administration of George W. Bush has "outperformed the Canadian Liberal government in fighting pollution." For more on Canadian and American records in environmental protection, see the Media Perspectives box (on p. 591).

A special problem is *acid precipitation* (rain or snow made acidic by air pollution), which destroys plant and animal life. Acid precipitation begins with power plants burning fossil fuels (oil and coal) to generate electricity; this burning releases sulphuric and nitrous oxides into the air. As the wind sweeps these gases into the atmosphere, they react with the air to form sulphuric and nitric acids, which turns atmospheric moisture acidic. This is a case where one type of pollution causes another: air pollution from industrial and hospital smokestacks contaminates water in lakes and streams that collect acid precipitation. Acid precipitation is truly a global phenomenon

See and read about the dramatic changes to the Sudbury environment at www.sudburysoilsstudy. com/EN/overview/background.asp.

because the regions that suffer the harmful effects may be distant from the original pollution. For instance, British power plants have produced acid rain that has devastated forests and fish in Norway and Sweden, up to 1600 kilometres (1000 miles) to the northeast. In Canada, the Inco smokestacks in Sudbury, Ontario, once destroyed vegetation for hundreds of kilometres, including the fish habitat of Killarney Provincial Park lakes. Now, pollution controls in the smokestacks have allowed for the gradual revival of vegetation in the Sudbury area, in what is now known to be one of Canada's environmental success stories.

Air Pollution

Because we are surrounded by air, we are more aware of air pollution than contaminated water. One of the unexpected consequences of industrial technology, especially the factory and the motor vehicle, has been a decline in air quality. In London in the mid–twentieth century, factory smokestacks, automobiles, and coal fires used to heat homes all added to what was probably the worst urban air quality of the last century. What some English people jokingly called "pea soup" fogs were in reality a deadly mix of pollutants. In the worst episode, over five extremely cold days in December 1952 when coal use soared, an especially thick haze that hung over London killed thousands of people.

Air quality improved in the final decades of the twentieth century. High-income nations passed laws that banned high-pollution heating, including the coal fires that choked London in the 1950s. Scientists devised ways to make factories as well as automobiles and trucks operate more cleanly. If people in rich countries can breathe a bit more easily than they once did, the problem of air pollution in poor societies is becoming more serious. One reason is that people in low-income countries still rely on wood, coal, peat, and other "dirty" fuels for cooking fires and to heat their homes. And nations eager to encourage short-term industrial development may pay little attention to the longer-term dangers of air pollution. As a result, many cities in Latin America, Eastern Europe, and Asia are plagued by air pollution as bad as London's pea soup fogs.

RAIN FORESTS

A **rainforest** is *a region of dense forestation, located close to the equator.* The largest tropical rain forests are in South America (notably Brazil), west-central Africa, and Southeast Asia. In all, the world's rain forests cover some 2 billion acres, or 7 percent of Earth's total land surface.

Like other global resources, rain forests are falling victim to the needs and appetites of the surging world population. As noted earlier, to meet the demand for beef, ranchers in Latin America burn forested areas to increase their supply of grazing land. We are also losing rain forests to the hardwood trade. People in rich nations pay high prices for mahogany and other woods because, as the environmentalist Norman Myers (1984b:88) puts it, they have "a penchant for parquet floors, fine furniture, fancy paneling, weekend yachts, and high-grade coffins." Under such economic pressure, the world's rain forests are now just half their original size, and they continue to shrink by about 1 percent (65 000 square miles) annually, which amounts to about an acre every second. Unless we stop this loss, the rain forests will vanish before the end of this century, and with them will go protection for Earth's biodiversity and climate.

 For more information about rainforests, visit www.rain forestweb.org.

Canada has the world's largest remaining coastal lowland temperate rainforest at Clayoquot Sound on Vancouver Island. A grassroots environmental group founded in 1979, Friends of Clayoquot Sound, has lobbied governments to change forest policy and deal with First Nations rights there. Nuu-Chah-Nulth live, hunt, and fish in the Clayoquot area; they have dedicated Meares Island as a Tribal Park, hosted festivals and blockades, and worked with the Friends to change global attitudes to ancient temperate rainforests. The largest civil disobedience action in Canadian history—the Clayoquot Sound protest from July to October 1993—resulted in the arrest of 800 people, the loss of $10 million in European and American contracts by the forest products company MacMillan Bloedel (taken over by U.S.-based Weyerhauser in 2000), and a government task force on a Clayoquot Sound sustainable development strategy. As a result, social justice for First Nations became an integral part of the wilderness and eco-forestry movements (Langer, 1996). Furthermore, the forest industry agreed to adjust its cutting practices in the temperate rainforest.

Global Warming

Why are rainforests so important? One reason is that they cleanse the atmosphere of carbon dioxide. Since the beginning of the Industrial Revolution, the amount of carbon dioxide produced by humans, mostly from factories and automobiles, has risen sharply. Much of this carbon dioxide is absorbed by the oceans, but plants—notably trees—also take in carbon dioxide and expel oxygen. This is why rainforests are vital to maintaining the chemical balance of the atmosphere. The problem is that production of carbon dioxide is rising while the amount of plant life on Earth is shrinking. To make matters worse, rainforests are being destroyed mostly by burning, which releases even more carbon dioxide into the atmosphere. Experts estimate that the atmospheric concentration of carbon dioxide is now 20 to 30 percent higher than it was 150 years ago (Revkin, 2002).

High above Earth, carbon dioxide acts like the glass roof of a greenhouse, letting heat from the sun pass through to the surface while preventing much of it from radiating away from the planet. The result of this greenhouse effect, ecologists say, is **global warming,** *a rise in Earth's average temperature due to an increasing concentration of carbon dioxide in the atmosphere.* Over the past century, the global temperature has risen about 1°F to an average of 15°C (59°F). Scientists warn that it could rise by 5°F to 10°F during this century, which would melt vast areas of the polar ice caps and raise sea levels to cover low-lying land around the world. Were this to happen, water could cover all of Bangladesh, for example, and much of the coastal United States. On the other hand, some of the most productive agricultural regions of central North America could become arid.

MEDIA PERSPECTIVES
Environmentally Friendly Canada, Eh!

Many Canadians believe that we have come a long way on the environmental front. After all, we have recycling programs; some cities even have wet/dry systems that convert organic waste to compost. And Canada turns tires—banned from landfill sites for decades—into an asphalt additive or into the bouncy flooring material for the Disney World exhibit *Honey, I Shrunk the Kids* and Hamilton Harbour's water playground in Ontario. We have environmental reviews for major resource developments, regulations governing the disposal of pollutants into waterways or the air, international agreements on emissions reduction, a wonderful system of national and provincial parks, and an environmentally sensitive public.

Canada has an environmental movement whose activities are quick to draw public attention to the clear-cutting of forests in British Columbia or over fishing in Atlantic coastal waters. First Nations, such as Walpole Island (Ontario) are attempting to achieve sustainable development (Jacobs, 1992; Nin.da.waab.jig, 1992), and organizations such as the Wendaban Stewardship Authority are being created to blend Aboriginal and non-Aboriginal environmental knowledge and to co-manage timber, land, and resource development in the Temagami area (Shute and Knight, 1995). Surely we can be forgiven if we are a little smug about our environmental record?

Looks can be deceiving, though! Behind the scenes, federal and provincial governments have cut their own environmental budgets. In Ontario, environmental laws were weakened, enforcement budgets cut, and regulatory powers taken away (Fine, 1997). So lax is the enforcement of regulations that Ontario ranks fourth among North America's polluters, behind Ohio, Texas, Indiana, and Pennsylvania. By 1997, Ontario Hydro's nuclear energy program was in serious difficulty and the utility began to deactivate some of its plants amid daunting safety and pollution concerns (Mittelstaedt,

1997). As 1998 rolled in, Toronto was debating the merits of its household recycling program: it is extremely costly and ineffective in ensuring the reuse of materials, and some of the Blue Box deposits were actually ending up in landfill sites.

Decisions regarding environmental issues are inherently political—and controversial. Having failed to live up to its earlier promises regarding emission targets, Canada was expected to set new ones at the 1997 environmental summit in Kyoto to deal with carbon emissions and the threat to global warming. The Vancouver-based David Suzuki Foundation took out full-page newspaper ads aimed at stopping the global warming plague. In Alberta, tear-mongering reached a fever pitch because the proposed emission targets would reduce the demand for oil and natural gas, which would be catastrophic for that province's economy. Premier Ralph Klein, the resource industries, and the Alberta public were up in arms—and Prime Minister Chrétien felt pressured to accommodate them (Bercuson and Cooper, 1997).

When the Kyoto agreement was revisited in November 2000, Canada's commitment to reduce global carbon emissions remained in question. In that round, Canada proposed achieving our reduction goals by "protecting" forests (here and abroad) and buying "credits" from countries that had succeeded in reducing emissions. Notably, the federal government had no plans for Canadians to actually reduce our own emissions. Nonetheless, Canada ratified the Kyoto accord in 2002, only to have the Harper Conservative government pull back in 2006—promising reductions though technological innovation and a clean air act put before the House in October 2006.

By this time, we had learned from the David Suzuki Foundation and others, that Canada has the *worst* record in meeting its Kyoto targets— below the United States, Japan, and

Visit the Suzuki Foundation to read its position on climate change and the Kyoto Accord at www.davidsuzuki. org/Climate_ Change/.

New Zealand. Instead of declining, Canada's greenhouse gas emissions had *increased by 32 percent* over 1990 levels; American emissions had increased, too, but only by 22 percent. Two very big reasons for our inability to meet our Kyoto target are the Alberta tar sands (a large part of our economy) and our reliance on cars and trucks to move people and products around this vast country.

Canadians have other environmental concerns. The shipment of hazardous or toxic waste from the United States into Canada quintupled between 1993 and 1999 (to 663 000 tonnes), while the reverse flow, from Canada into the United States, remained relatively stable. Ontario and Quebec are the main recipients of this hazardous waste. Most U.S. states have increased regulations and restrictions, and Mexico has banned toxic imports altogether—while Canada's regulations remain lax (Hogue, 2000).

Canadian governments are engaged in a high-wire act. Environmentalists at home and abroad exert considerable pressure on Canadian politicians to protect our natural environment. Businesses, workers, and agencies in the resource sector are equally persuasive in their demands for reduced restrictions. The people who design and implement our environmental policies and programs do so in the face of relentless cross-pressures.

WHAT DO YOU THINK?

1. Would you be willing to pay more for fuel, reduce the use of your car, turn the thermostat down in the winter and up in the summer, and take public transit whenever possible to help reduce greenhouse gases?
2. Are you an environmentalist in action, in theory, or not at all?
3. Is the threat of global warming real or overblown? Explain your reasoning.

Members of small, simple societies, such as the Tan't Batu in the Philippines, live in harmony with nature; they do not have the technological means to greatly affect their forest homeland and may hold extensive knowledge of its living components. Although we in complex societies like to think of ourselves as superior to such people, the truth is that there is much we can—and must—learn from them.

Not all scientists share this vision of future global warming. Some point out that global temperature changes have been taking place throughout history, apparently with little or nothing to do with rainforests. Higher concentra-

 Read concerned scientists' information about global warming at www.ucsusa.org/ global_warming/science/ global-warming-faq.html.

tions of carbon dioxide in the atmosphere might speed up plant growth since plants thrive on this

gas, and this increase would correct the imbalance and push Earth's temperature down once again. But a consensus is building that global warming is a problem that threatens the future of all of us (McDonald, 1999; Kerr, 2005).

YOUR TURN

How do you think global warming could affect you personally?

DECLINING BIODIVERSITY

Clearing rainforests also reduces Earth's biodiversity because rainforests are home to almost half the planet's living species. On Earth, there are as many as 30 million species of animals, plants, and micro-organisms. Several dozen unique species of plants and animals cease to exist every day. Given the vast numbers of living species, why should we be concerned by the loss of a few? Environmentalists give four reasons:

- First, our planet's biodiversity provides a varied source of human food. Using agricultural high technology, scientists can "splice" familiar crops with more exotic plant life, making food more bountiful as well as more resistant to insects and disease. Thus, biodiversity helps feed our planet's rapidly increasing population.

- Second, Earth's biodiversity is a vital genetic resource used by medical and pharmaceutical researchers to produce hundreds of new compounds each year that cure disease and improve our lives. For example, Canadian children have a good chance of surviving leukemia, a disease that was a killer two generations ago, because of a compound derived from a tropical flower called the rosy periwinkle. The oral birth control pill, used by tens of millions of women in North America, is another product of plant research with the Mexican forest yam.

- Third, with the loss of any species of life—whether it is the magnificent California condor, the famed Chinese panda, the spotted owl, or even a single species of ant—the beauty and complexity of our natural environment are diminished. And there are clear warning signs of such loss: three-quarters of the world's 9000 species of birds are declining in number.

- Finally, unlike pollution, the extinction of any species is irreversible and final. An important ethical question, then, is whether we who live today have the right to impoverish the world for those who live tomorrow (Myers, 1991; Wilson, 1991; Brown, *et al.*, 1993).

ENVIRONMENTAL RACISM

Conflict theory has given rise to the concept of **environmental racism,** *the pattern by which environmental*

 The Heinz Center publishes analyses of society's effect on the natural environment at www.heinzctr.org/ publications.htm.

hazards are greatest for poor people, especially minorities. Historically, factories that spewed pollution stood

near neighbourhoods of the poor and visible minorities. Why? In part, the poor themselves were drawn to factories in search of work, and their low incomes often meant they could afford housing only in undesirable neighbourhoods. Sometimes the only housing that fit their budgets stood in the very shadow of the plants and mills where they worked.

Nobody wants a factory or dump nearby, but the poor have little power to resist. Through the years, the most serious environmental hazards have been located not near the neighbourhoods of the affluent but near those of the vulnerable and powerless. In Canada, Aboriginal communities are frequently affected. Uranium mines have contaminated ground and surface water in many areas where Aboriginal peoples live and hunt. Clear-cutting of forests and flooding for power generation have contaminated water and destroyed natural habitat in the James Bay region of Quebec, where Cree, in a 1975 land agreement with Canada, had been guaranteed long-term hunting and fishing rights. Lubicon Cree in north-central Alberta have been fighting since 1930 for recognition of their rights and settlement of their land claim, and to stop the province of Alberta from selling timber and natural gas rights on their land. The proposal in 2000 to transport Toronto's garbage to the Adams Mine would have resulted in contamination of groundwater in Kirkland Lake and First Nations lands. And in October 2005, Kashechewan, a First Nation community of 1700 in Northern Ontario, was evacuated because of widespread illness caused by contaminated drinking water. Subsequently, we learned that about half of the reserve communities in Canada have inadequate water treatment plants.

Looking Ahead: Towards a Sustainable Society and World

The demographic analysis presented in this chapter points to some disturbing trends. We see, first, that Earth's population has reached record levels because birth rates remain high in poor nations and death rates have fallen just about everywhere. Reducing fertility will remain a pressing need throughout this century. Even with some recent decline in the rate of population increase, the nightmare Thomas Malthus described is still a real possibility, as the Thinking It Through box (on p. 594) explains.

Further, population growth remains greatest in the poorest countries of the world, those without the means to support their present populations, much less future ones. Supporting 74 million additional people on our planet each year, 70 million of whom are in low-income countries, will require a global commitment to provide not only food but housing, schools, and employment as well. The well-being of the entire world may ultimately depend on resolving the economic and social problems of poor, overly populated countries and bridging the widening gulf between "have" and "have-not" nations.

Urbanization is continuing, especially in poor countries where people migrate to cities in the hope of finding a better life. But the sheer numbers of people who live in the emerging global supercities—such as Mexico City, Mexico; São Paulo, Brazil; Kinshasa, Congo; Mumbai, India; and Manila, Philippines—have created urban problems on a massive scale.

Around the world, humanity is facing a serious environmental challenge. Part of this problem is population increase, which is greatest in poor countries. But another part is the high levels of consumption in rich nations such as our own. By increasing the planet's environmental deficit, our present way of life is borrowing against the well-being of our children and their children. Globally, members of rich societies, who currently consume so much of Earth's resources, are mortgaging the future security of the poor countries of the world.

The answer, in principle, is to create an **ecologically sustainable culture,** *a way of life that meets the needs of the present generation without threatening the environmental legacy of future generations.* Sustainable living depends on three strategies. First, the world

To read more about population increase, the environment, and global inequality, go to www.peopleandplanet.net.

needs *to bring population growth under control.* The current population of 6.5 billion is already straining the natural environment. Clearly, the higher the world's population climbs, the more difficult environmental problems will become. Even if the recent slowing of population growth continues, the world will have 8 billion people by 2050. Few analysts think that the planet can support this many people; most argue that we must hold the line at about 7 billion, and some argue that we must *decrease* population in the coming decades (Smail, 2007).

A second strategy is *to conserve finite resources.* This means meeting our needs with a responsible eye towards the future by using resources efficiently, seeking alternative sources of energy, and, in some cases, learning to live with less. And, a third strategy is *to reduce waste.* Whenever possible, using less is the best solution, with recycling programs as part of the answer.

Making these strategies work depends on a more basic change in the way we think about ourselves and our world. Our *egocentric* outlook sets self-interest as the standard for how to live, but a sustainable environment demands an *ecocentric* outlook that helps us see how the present is tied to the future and why everyone must work together. Most nations in the southern half of the world are *underdeveloped,* unable to meet the basic needs of their people. At the same time, most countries in the northern half of the world are *overdeveloped,* using more resources than the planet can sustain over time. The changes needed to create a sustainable ecosystem will not come easily, and they will be costly. But the price of not responding to the growing environmental deficit will certainly be greater (Kellert and Bormann, 1991; Brown, *et al.,* 1993; Population Action International, 2000).

Finally, consider that the great dinosaurs dominated this planet for some 160 million years and then perished forever. Humanity is far younger, having existed for a mere 250 000 years. Compared to the rather dim-witted

THINKING IT THROUGH
Apocalypse: Will People Overwhelm the Planet?

Are you worried about the world's increasing population? Think about this: by the time you finish reading this box, more than 1000 people will have been added to our planet. By this time tomorrow, global population will have risen by more than 200 000. Currently, as Table 22–4 shows, there are 4 births for every 2 deaths on the planet, pushing the world's population upwards by 74 million annually. Put another way, global population growth amounts to adding another Egypt to the world each year.

It is no wonder that many demographers and environmentalists are deeply concerned about the future. The 2 billion people we have added since 1974 exceed the planet's total population in 1900. Might Thomas Robert Malthus, who predicted that overpopulation would push the world into war and suffering, be right after all? Lester Brown and other *neo-Malthusians* predict a coming apocalypse if we do not change our ways. Brown (1995) admits that Malthus failed to imagine how much technology—especially fertilizers and altering of plant genetics—could boost the planet's agricultural output. But Brown maintains that Earth's rising population is rapidly outstripping its finite resources. Families in many poor countries can find little firewood; members of rich

countries are depleting the oil reserves; everyone is draining the supply of clean water and poisoning the planet with waste. Some analysts argue that we have already passed the capacity of the Earth to "carry" our population, and we need to hold the line or even reduce global population to ensure the long-term survival of humanity.

But other analysts, the *anti-Malthusians*, sharply disagree. Julian Simon (1995) points out that, two centuries after Malthus predicted catastrophe, Earth supports almost six times as many people who, on average, live longer, healthier lives than ever before. With more advanced technology, people have devised ways to increase productivity and limit population increase. As Simon sees it, this is

cause for celebration. Human ingenuity has consistently proved the doomsayers wrong. And Simon is betting it will continue to do so.

WHAT DO YOU THINK?

1. Where do you place your bet? Do you think Earth can support 8 or 10 billion people? Explain your reasoning.
2. About 96 percent of current population growth is in poor countries. What does this mean for the future of rich nations? for the future of poor ones?
3. What should people in high-income countries do to ensure the future of children everywhere?

TABLE 22–4

Global Population Increase

	Births	Deaths	Net Increase
Per year	130 013 274	56 130 242	73 883 032
Per month	10 834 440	4 677 520	6 156 919
Per day	356 201	153 781	202 419
Per hour	14 842	6 408	8 434
Per minute	247	107	141
Per second	4.1	1.8	2.3

Sources: Based in part on Brown (1995), Simon (1995), Scanlon (2001), and Smail (2007).

dinosaurs, our species has the gift of great intelligence. But how will we use this ability? What are the chances that our species will continue to flourish 160 million years—or even thousands of years—from now? The answer depends on the choices that will be made by one of the 30 million species living on Earth: human beings.

22 MAKING THE GRADE

The following learning tools will help you see what you know, identify what you still need to learn, and expand your understanding beyond the text. You can also visit this text's Companion Website™ at www.pearsoned.ca/macionis to find useful practice tests.

KEY POINTS

Demography: The Study of Population

Fertility and mortality, measured as crude birth rates and crude death rates, are major factors affecting population size. In global terms, North American and European population growth rates are low. Immigration as a major contributor has special importance to the historical growth of Canada and the United States. Demographers use age-sex pyramids to show graphically the composition of a population and to project population trends. *Sex ratio* refers to a society's balance of females and males.

History and Theory of Population Growth

Historically, world population grew slowly because high birth rates were largely offset by high death rates. About 1750, a demographic transition began as world population rose sharply, mostly from falling death rates. Thomas Robert Malthus warned that population growth would outpace food production and the result would be social calamity. Demographic transition theory, however, contends that technological advances gradually slow population increase. World population is expected to reach between 8 billion and 9 billion by 2050. Most of this increase will take place in poor societies.

Urbanization: The Growth of Cities

The first urban revolution began with the appearance of cities about 10 000 years ago. By about 2000 years ago, cities had emerged in most regions of the world except North America. Pre-industrial cities have low-rise buildings; narrow, winding streets; and personal social ties.

A second urban revolution began about 1750 as the Industrial Revolution spurred rapid urban growth in Europe. The physical form of cities changed as planners created wide, regular streets to allow for easier trade and technology allowed for taller structures. The emphasis on commerce and the increasing size of cities made urban life more anonymous.

Urbanism came to North America with Europeans, who settled in towns along the Atlantic coastline. By 1850, hundreds of new cities had been founded across to the Pacific. By 1920, a majority of the North American population lived in urban areas, and the largest metropolises were home to millions of people. About 1950, cities began to decentralize with the growth of suburbs and edge cities. Nationally, Sunbelt cities—but not the older Snowbelt cities—are increasing in size and population.

Urbanism as a Way of Life

Rapid urbanization in Europe during the nineteenth century led early sociologists to contrast rural and urban life. Ferdinand Tönnies built his analysis on the concepts of *Gemeinschaft* and *Gesellschaft*, and Emile Durkheim used similar concepts of mechanical solidarity and organic solidarity. Georg Simmel claimed that the overstimulation of city life produced a blasé attitude in urbanites.

At the University of Chicago, Robert Park claimed that cities permit greater social freedom. Louis Wirth saw large, dense, heterogeneous populations creating an impersonal and self-interested, though tolerant, way of life. Other researchers have explored urban ecology and urban political economy.

Urbanization in Poor Nations

A third urban revolution is now occurring in low-income countries. Today, most of the world's largest cities are found in poor nations.

Environment and Society

The state of the environment is a social issue because it reflects how human beings organize social life. Societies increase the environmental deficit by focusing on short-term benefits and ignoring the long-term consequences brought on by their way of life. The more complex a society's technology, the greater its capacity to alter the natural environment.

The "logic of growth" thesis supports economic development, claiming that people can solve environmental problems as they arise. The opposing "limits to growth" thesis states that societies must curb development to prevent eventual environmental collapse.

Environmental issues that affect societies include disposing of solid waste and protecting the quality of air and water. The supply of clean water is already low in some parts of the world. Rainforests help remove carbon dioxide from the atmosphere and are home to a large share of this planet's living species. Under pressure from commercial interests, the world's rainforests are now half their original size and are shrinking by about 1 percent annually. *Environmental racism* refers to the pattern by which the poor, especially minorities and Aboriginal peoples, suffer most from environmental hazards.

Looking Ahead: Towards a Sustainable Society and World

To achieve a sustainable environment that does not threaten the well-being of future generations, we must control world population, conserve finite resources, and reduce waste and pollution.

KEY CONCEPTS

demography (p. 569) the study of human population

fertility (p. 569) the incidence of child bearing in a country's population

crude birth rate (p. 569) the number of live births in a given year for every 1000 people in a population

mortality (p. 570) the incidence of death in a country's population

crude death rate (p. 570) the number of deaths in a given year for every 1000 people in a population

infant mortality rate (p. 570) the number of deaths among infants under one year of age for each 1000 live births in a given year

life expectancy (p. 570) the average life span of a country's population

migration (p. 570) the movement of people into and out of a specified territory

sex ratio (p. 571) the number of males for every 100 females in a nation's population

age-sex pyramid (p. 571) a graphic representation of the age and sex of a population

demographic transition theory (p. 573) the thesis that population patterns reflect a society's level of technological development

zero population growth (p. 574) the level of reproduction that maintains population in a steady state

urbanization (p. 576) the concentration of population into cities

metropolis (p. 579) a large city that socially and economically dominates an urban area

suburbs (p. 579) urban areas beyond the political boundaries of a city

megalopolis (p. 580) a vast urban region containing a number of cities and their surrounding suburbs

Gemeinschaft (p. 581) a type of social organization in which people are closely tied by kinship and tradition

Gesellschaft (p. 581) a type of social organization in which people come together only on the basis of individual self-interest

urban ecology (p. 584) the study of the link between the physical and social dimensions of cities

ecology (p. 585) the study of the interaction of living organisms and the natural environment

natural environment (p. 585) Earth's surface and atmosphere, including living organisms, air, water, soil, and other resources necessary to sustain life

ecosystem (p. 585) a system composed of the interaction of all living organisms and their natural environment

environmental deficit (p. 586) profound long-term harm to the natural environment caused by humanity's focus on short-term material affluence

rainforest (p. 590) a region of dense forestation, located close to the equator

global warming (p. 590) a rise in Earth's average temperature resulting from an increasing concentration of carbon dioxide in the atmosphere

environmental racism (p. 592) the pattern by which environmental hazards are greatest for poor people, especially minorities

ecologically sustainable culture (p. 593) a way of life that meets the needs of the present generation without threatening the environmental legacy of future generations

APPLICATIONS & EXERCISES

1. Here is an illustration of the problem of runaway growth (Milbrath, 1989:10): "A pond has a single water lily growing on it. The lily doubles in size each day. In 30 days, it covers the entire pond. On which day does it cover half the pond?" When you realize the answer, discuss the implications of this example for population increase.

2. Draw a mental map of a city familiar to you with as much detail of specific places, districts, roads, and transporta-

tion facilities as you can. Compare your map to a real one or, better yet, a map drawn by someone else. Try to account for the differences.

3. As an interesting exercise, carry a plastic bag around for a single day and collect in it everything you want to throw away. Most people are surprised to find that the average North American discards close to 2.25 kilograms (5 pounds) of paper, metal, plastic, and other materials daily. Over a lifetime, that's about 50 tonnes.

PRENTICE HALL
mysoclab™
Where learning & the sociological imagination intersect.

To reinforce your understanding of this chapter, and to identify topics for further study, visit MySocLab at **www.pearsoned.ca/mysoclab/** for diagnostic tests and a multimedia ebook.

The summer of 1990 was pivotal for Canada's First Nations: after Elijah Harper and Oka, the relationship between Aboriginal peoples and other Canadians would never be the same. The Meech Lake Accord was to be ratified by each of the provinces by June 23, to allow amendments to the constitution that would satisfy Quebec—and, thereafter, block constitutional changes sought by Aboriginal leaders. Newfoundland was poised to vote and Manitoba was going through the procedural steps for ratification. The snag came in the form of Elijah Harper (a Cree Member of the Legislative Assembly) who, through dramatic delay tactics, prevented ratification by the Manitoba legislature—thereby "killing" the accord.

In the meantime, the town of Oka, Quebec, was ensuring its international visibility by proposing to expand a golf course onto lands that the people of Kanesatake considered to be a sacred burial ground. A barricade erected across a rural road in response to this threat gave rise to a five-month armed confrontation between the residents of Kanesatake, aided by Mohawk Warriors, on one side and the Quebec police and, later on, the Canadian forces on the other.

The significance of these events lay not in the fact that Aboriginal peoples and their leaders were taking decisive action to defend their interests—but in the fact that their struggle had captured the attention of the media, the general public, and Aboriginal individuals throughout the country. Suddenly, there was an outpouring of support for Elijah Harper and the people of Kanesatake in the form of letters, donations of food and money, marches, a run to bring a peace feather from British Columbia to Oka, a peace camp at Oka, and the barricade of the Mercier Bridge into Montreal by the people of Kahnawake. Daily, if not hourly, coverage of the Manitoba legislature and the tense, armed confrontation at Oka hypnotized Canadians and mobilized Aboriginal peoples in support of a cause. A growing sense of solidarity emerged as Aboriginal individuals everywhere watched events unfold. Many people who had paid little attention to their Aboriginal roots were suddenly intensely interested, proud, and somehow empowered by this new sense of movement and common cause. Raised consciousness and forged bonds had profound effects on relations among Aboriginal peoples, other Canadians, and governments. A social movement was born.

For most of the past century, sociologists focused on established social patterns such as the family and social stratification. They paid little attention to collective behaviour, considering most of it unusual or deviant. But numerous social movements that burst on the scene during the tumultuous 1960s changed all that. As this chapter explains, a **social movement** is *organized activity that encourages or discourages social change.* Social movements are the most important type of **collective behaviour,** *activity involving a large number of people, often spontaneous, and usually in violation of established norms.* Other forms of collective behaviour—also controversial and sometimes provoking change—are mobs, riots, and crowds; rumour and gossip; public opinion; fashions and fads; panic and mass hysteria.

Studying Collective Behaviour

Collective behaviour is difficult for sociologists to study for three reasons:

- **Collective behaviour is diverse.** Collective behaviour involves a wide range of human action. At first glance, it is difficult to see what disasters have in common with fads, rumours, and mob behaviour.

- **Collective behaviour is hard to explain.** Some rumours—such as the claim in 2004 that electing Stephen Harper's Conservatives would allow him to implement a "hidden agenda"—have consequences. Other rumours die out without impact. Why does one rumour catch on but others do not?

- **Much collective behaviour is transitory.** Sociologists have long studied social institutions such as the family because they are continuing parts of society. Disasters, rumours, and fads, however, come and go quickly.

Some researchers point out that these problems apply not just to collective behaviour but to most forms of human behaviour (Aguirre and Quarantelli, 1983). In addition, collective behaviour is not always so surprising; anyone can predict that crowds will form at sporting events and music festivals, and sociologists can study these gatherings at first hand or record them on videotape to study later. Researchers can even anticipate some natural disasters, such as tornadoes or hurricanes, and be ready to study how people respond to such events (Miller, 1985).

As a result of their efforts, sociologists now know a great deal about collective behaviour. The most basic lesson is that all collective behaviour involves the action of some **collectivity,** *a large number of people whose minimal interaction occurs in the absence of well-defined and conventional norms.* Collectivities are of two types. A *localized collectivity* refers to people physically close to one another, as in the case of crowds and riots. A *dispersed collectivity*, or *mass behaviour,* involves people who influence one another despite being spread over a large area. Examples of this type of collective behaviour include rumours, public opinion, and fashion.

Be sure to keep in mind how collectivities differ from the already familiar concept of *social groups* (see Chapter 7, "Groups and Organizations"). Here are three key differences:

- **People who are part of collectivities have little or no social interaction.** People in social groups interact frequently and directly. People in mobs or other localized collectivities interact very little. Most people taking part in dispersed collectivities, such as a fad, do not interact at all.

- **Collectivities have no clear social boundaries.** Social group members share a sense of identity, but people engaged in collective behaviour usually do not. People in a local crowd may have the same object of their attention, such as someone on a ledge threatening to jump, but they feel little sense of unity. Individuals involved in dispersed collectivities, such as the people who spread a rumour about the possibility of a military draft, have almost no awareness of shared membership. To give another example, people may share concerns over many issues, but usually it is difficult to say exactly who falls within the ranks of, say, the environmental or the feminist movement.

- **Collectivities generate weak and unconventional norms.** Conventional cultural norms usually regulate the behaviour of people in groups. Some collectivities, such as people travelling together on an airplane, do observe conventional norms, but their interaction is usually limited to polite small talk with respect for the privacy of others sitting nearby. Other collectivities—such as excited fans after a game who take to the streets drinking and overturning cars—behave according to no clear guidelines (Weller and Quarantelli, 1973; Turner and Killian, 1993).

Localized Collectivities: Crowds

One major form of collective behaviour is the **crowd,** *a temporary gathering of people who share a common focus of attention and who influence one another.* Most of our ancestors never saw a large crowd: in mediaeval Europe, for example, about the only time large numbers of people gathered in one place was when armies faced off on the battlefield (Laslettt, 1984). Today, however, crowds of 25 000 or more are common at rock concerts, sporting events, and even the registration halls of large universities.

YOUR TURN

Do you think people go to athletic games or musical events in part because they enjoy the experience of being in a large crowd? Explain your answer.

All crowds are not alike. Herbert Blumer (1969) identified four categories of crowds:

- A *casual crowd* is a loose collection of people who interact little, if at all. People lying on a beach or people who rush to the scene of an automobile accident have only a passing awareness of one another.

- A *conventional crowd* results from deliberate planning, as illustrated by a country auction, a college lecture, or a celebrity's funeral. In each case, the behaviour of people involved follows a clear set of norms.

- An *expressive crowd* forms around an event with emotional appeal, such as a religious revival, a NASCAR race, or the New Year's Eve celebration in New York City's Times Square. Excitement is the main reason people join

It's September 2005: More than 5000 students and alumni have descended on Kingston, Ontario, for homecoming at Queen's University. The Aberdeen Street parties have been getting wilder over the past few years; this one turned into a riot, resulting in several overturned cars, other property damage, and more than 100 charges for liquor and other offences. The following year Queen's incorporated the photo into a poster implying that several thousand onlookers were also idiots.

expressive crowds, which makes this spontaneous experience exhilarating for those involved.

- An *acting crowd* is a collectivity motivated by an intense, single-minded purpose, such as an audience rushing the doors of a concert hall or fleeing from a mall after hearing gunshots. Acting crowds are set in motion by powerful emotions, which can sometimes trigger mob violence.

Any crowd can change from one type to another. In 2001, for example, a conventional crowd of more than 10 000 fans filed into a soccer stadium in Johannesburg, South Africa, to watch a match between two rival teams. After a goal was scored, the crowd erupted, and people began to push towards the field. Within seconds, an acting crowd had formed, and a stampede began, which ended up crushing 47 people to death (Nessman, 2001).

Deliberate action by a crowd is not simply the product of rising emotions. Participants in *protest crowds*—a fifth category we can add to Blumer's list—may stage marches, boycotts, sit-ins, and strikes for political purposes (McPhail and Wohlstein, 1983). The antiwar demonstrations that have taken place on many campuses and in many large cities since the beginning of the Iraq War are examples of protest crowds. Sometimes protest crowds have the low-level energy characteristic of a conventional crowd; at other times, people become emotional enough to form an acting crowd.

MOBS AND RIOTS

When an acting crowd turns violent, the result may be the birth of a **mob,** *a highly emotional crowd that pursues a violent or destructive goal.* Despite, or perhaps because of, their intense emotions, mobs tend to dissipate quickly. How long a mob continues to exist depends on its precise goals and whether its leadership tries to inflame or calm the crowd.

Lynching is one of the most notorious examples of mob behaviour. The term is derived from Charles Lynch, of colonial Virginia, who tried to enforce law and order in his community before there were formal police and courts; the word "lynch" soon came to mean violence and murder carried out beyond the law. Lynching in the United States has always been coloured by race. After the Civil War, lynch mobs terrorized newly freed slaves. Any Black person who challenged White superiority risked being hanged or burned alive by hateful White men. Lynch mobs—typically composed of poor White men who felt threatened by competition from freed slaves—reached their peak between 1880 and 1930; police recorded some 5000 lynchings in that period, though many more undoubtedly occurred. Like public executions, lynchings were popular events, attracting hundreds of spectators. Sometimes victims were killed quickly, but others were tortured before being put to death. Most of these killings took place in the American Deep South, where the farming economy depended on a cheap and obedient labour force. On the western frontier, lynch mobs targeted people of Mexican and Asian descent. In about 25 percent of reported lynchings, White mobs killed other White men. Lynching women was rare; only about 100 such cases are known, almost all involving Black women (White, 1969; orig. 1929; Grant, 1975; Lacayo, 2000).

A highly energized crowd with no particular purpose is a **riot,** *a social eruption that is highly emotional, violent, and undirected.* Unlike the action of a mob, a riot usually has no clear goal, except perhaps to express dissatisfaction. The cause of most riots is some long-standing anger or grievance; violent action is ignited by some minor incident that

What explains the behaviour of crowds? People once thought a crowd takes on a "mind of its own"; now, it is more correct to say that people are brought together by some shared interest. In the case of this protest crowd in Quebec City, the participants are demanding that the province not cut funding to education or raise tuition fees. Exactly what happens next, however, depends on many factors that unfold as the protest proceeds.

causes people to start destroying property and harming other persons (Smelser, 1962; Rosenfeld, 1997).

In October 2003, a crowd turned to rioting when a Montreal club announced the cancellation of a concert: the punk rock band that was to appear that night had been turned back at the border. In the few minutes before police arrived, angry young people smashed store windows, set fire to a number of cars, and overturned others. Whereas a mob action usually ends when a specific violent goal has been achieved or decisively prevented, a riot tends to disperse only as participants run out of steam or as community leaders or police gradually bring them under control.

Riots often serve as collective expressions of social injustice. Industrial workers, for example, have rioted to vent rage at their working conditions, and race riots have occurred with striking regularity. In Vancouver in 1907, in response to steady migration from China of what seemed to be unfairly competitive cheap labour and a sudden influx of more than 8000 Japanese, a riot broke out, during which local people lashed out violently against Japanese residents and looted their businesses. In Los Angeles in 1992, the acquittal of police officers involved in the beating of African-American motorist Rodney King set off an explosive riot. Violence and fires killed more than 50 people, injured thousands, and destroyed property worth hundreds of millions of dollars. These riots were followed almost immediately by race riots on the streets of Toronto.

Riots are not always fired by hate. They can also stem from positive feelings, such as the celebration of the 1993 Stanley Cup victory in Montreal, which turned into a night of looting and violence. Days later, in anticipation of further violence, the Montreal Canadiens were protected during their victory parade by hundreds of police officers and the riot squad. Similar occurrences have happened elsewhere in Canada after sporting events. In the fall of 1995, another "party" turned into a riot at the Queen's University homecoming (Doolittle, 2005).

CROWDS, MOBS, AND SOCIAL CHANGE

Ordinary people can gain power by acting collectively. Historically, because crowds have been able to effect social change, they have also provoked controversy. Defenders of the established social order fear "the mob." In countries around the world, elites know that the masses, when well organized, pose a threat to their power; however, the collective action condemned by some people is supported by others as rightful protest. In 1839, 53 Africans rose up and seized the ship *Amistad* off the coast of Cuba to prevent them from landing in the Americas and being sold into slavery. Were these men a vicious mob? Not according to the U.S. Supreme Court, which ruled that the men were fighting for their freedom and were entitled to release.

Moreover, crowds share no single political cast: some call for change—others resist it. Judeans rallying to the Sermon on the Mount by Jesus of Nazareth, traditional weavers destroying new industrial machines that were threatening their jobs, masses of marchers carrying banners and shouting slogans for or against abortion—these and countless other cases across the centuries show that crowds can challenge or support their society (Rudé, 1964; Canetti, 1978; Tarrow, 1994).

EXPLAINING CROWD BEHAVIOUR

What accounts for the behaviour of crowds? Social scientists have developed three explanations: contagion theory, convergence theory, and emergent norm theory.

Contagion Theory

An early explanation of collective behaviour was offered by the French sociologist Gustave Le Bon (1841–1931). According to Le Bon's *contagion theory* (1960; orig. 1895),

The 2003 meeting of the World Trade Organization in Seattle, Washington, was the occasion for protests by those opposed to the expanding global marketplace. Try to apply contagion, convergence, or emergent norm theory to an event such as this one. Which approach seems to make the most sense to you? Why?

crowds exert a hypnotic influence over their members. Shielded by the anonymity found in large numbers, people forget about personal responsibility and give in to the contagious emotions of the crowd. A crowd thereby assumes a life of its own, stirring up emotions and driving people towards irrational, even violent, action.

Critical Review Le Bon's idea that crowds provide anonymity and can generate strong emotions is surely true. Yet, as Clark McPhail (1991) points out, a considerable body of research shows that "the madding crowd" does not take on a life of its own; its actions result from the policies and decisions made by specific individuals. In the case of the 2003 nightclub fire in Rhode Island, which killed 97 people, the high death toll did not result simply from the crowd "going wild" and becoming trapped inside the flaming building; later investigation showed that the band had used dangerous fireworks onstage, flames ignited flammable sound-proofing material on the ceiling, and the room had no sprinkler system. As a result, fire engulfed the entire building in minutes, before many people realized what was happening (Apuzzo, 2003; Forliti, 2003).

While collective behaviour may involve strong emotions, such feelings may not be irrational, as contagion theory suggests. Emotions, as well as action, can reflect real fear—as in the nightclub fire—or result from a sense of injustice.

Convergence Theory

Convergence theory holds that crowd behaviour comes not from the crowd itself but from the particular people who join in. From this point of view, a crowd is a convergence of like-minded individuals. Contagion theory states that crowds cause people to act in a certain way; convergence theory says the opposite, claiming that people who wish to act in a certain way come together to form crowds. In recent years, the crowds that formed at demonstrations opposing the Iraq War, for example, did not cause participants to become antiwar. On the contrary, participants came together because of their political attitudes.

Critical Review By linking crowds to broader social forces, convergence theory rejects Le Bon's claim that crowd behaviour is irrational in favour of the view that people in crowds express existing beliefs and values. But in fairness to Le Bon, people sometimes do things in a crowd that they would not have the courage to do alone, because crowds can spread responsibility among many people. In addition, crowds can intensify an emotion simply by creating a critical mass of like-minded people.

EMERGENT NORM THEORY

Ralph Turner and Lewis Killian (1993) developed the *emergent norm theory* of crowd dynamics. These researchers admit that social behaviour is never entirely predictable but, if similar interests draw people into a crowd, distinctive patterns of behaviour may emerge.

According to Turner and Killian, crowds begin as collectivities containing people with mixed interests and motives. Especially in the case of expressive, acting, and protest crowds, norms may be vague and changing. Consider how many Iraqi citizens began looting government buildings after U.S. troops toppled Saddam Hussein; over time, while some citizens continued to steal anything they could carry, others tried to stop the lawlessness. In short, people in crowds make their own rules as they go along.

Critical Review Emergent norm theory represents a middle ground approach to crowd dynamics. Turner and Killian (1993) explain that crowd behaviour is neither as irrational as contagion theory suggests nor as deliberate as convergence theory implies. Certainly, crowd behaviour reflects the desires of participants, but it is also guided by norms that emerge as the situation unfolds.

Decision making does play a role in crowd behaviour, although people watching from the sidelines may not realize it. Frightened people clogging the exits of a burning nightclub, for example, may appear to be victims of irrational panic but, from their point of view, fleeing a rapidly spreading fire makes a lot of sense. Emergent norm theory points out that people in a crowd take on different roles. Some step forward as leaders; others become lieutenants, rank-and-file followers, inactive bystanders, and even opponents (Weller and Quarantelli, 1973; Zurcher and Snow, 1981).

Dispersed Collectivities: Mass Behaviour

It is not just people clustered together in crowds who take part in collective behaviour. **Mass behaviour** refers to *collective behaviour among people spread over a wide geographic area.*

RUMOUR AND GOSSIP

A common type of mass behaviour is **rumour,** *unconfirmed information that people spread informally, often by word of mouth.* People pass along rumours through face-to-face

 To track the truth about internet rumours, visit www.nonprofit.net/hoax.

communication, of course, but today's modern technology—including telephones, the mass media, e-mail, and the internet—spreads rumours faster and farther than ever before. Rumour has three main characteristics:

- **Rumour thrives in a climate of uncertainty.** Rumours arise when people lack clear and certain information about an important issue. The fact that no one really knew Conservative leader Stephen Harper or his intentions helps to explain why rumours were flying in the months before the 2004 federal election, which delivered a minority Liberal government.

- **Rumour is unstable.** People change rumours as they pass them along, usually giving them "spin" that serves their own interests. The Liberals had one slant on the "hidden agenda" rumour: the Conservatives had another perspective.

- **Rumour is difficult to stop.** The number of people aware of a rumour increases very quickly because each person spreads information to many others. Rumours go away eventually but, in general, the only way to control them is for a believable source to issue a clear and convincing statement of the facts. Winning the 2006 election, allowed Prime Minister Harper to show that there was no "hidden agenda" after all.

Rumour can trigger the formation of crowds or other collective behaviour. For this reason, officials establish a rumour-control centre during a crisis in order to manage information. Yet some rumours persist for generations, perhaps because people enjoy them. The Thinking Critically box (on p. 606) gives a classic example.

Gossip is *rumour about people's personal affairs.* Charles Horton Cooley (1962; orig. 1909) explained that rumour involves some issue many people care about, but gossip interests only a small circle of people who know a particular person. This is why rumours spread widely but gossip tends to be localized.

Communities use gossip as a means of social control, using praise and blame to encourage people to conform to local norms. Also, people gossip about others to raise their own standing as social "insiders" or to put other people down (Baumgartner, 1998; Nicholson, 2001). Yet no community wants gossip to get so out of control that no one knows what to believe: people who gossip too much are criticized as "busybodies."

PUBLIC OPINION AND PROPAGANDA

Another form of highly dispersed collective behaviour is **public opinion,** *widespread attitudes about controversial issues.* Exactly who is, or is not, included in any "public" depends on the issue involved. Over the years in Canada, "publics" have formed over issues such as water fluoridation, greenhouse gases, the killing of seal pups, gun control, Quebec separatism, immigration, health care, same-sex marriage, and even the constitution. As this list indicates, public issues are important matters about which people disagree. On any given issue, anywhere, some 10 percent of people will offer no opinion because of ignorance or apathy. Over time, public interest rises and falls; for example, interest in women's rights in Canada was strong during the decades of the movement to secure votes for women but declined after the right was won—federally in 1918, and provincially when Quebec became the last province to extend the vote to women in 1940 (see Chapter 13, "Gender Stratification"). Since the 1960s, a second wave of feminism has created a public with strong opinions on gender issues.

On any issue, not everyone's opinion carries the same clout. Some categories of people have more social influence than others because they are wealthier, more powerful, or better educated. Many special-interest groups shape public policy even though they represent only a small fraction of the population. In general, privileged people make use of their affluence, prestige, and social contacts to promote their opinions more effectively than others.

Political leaders, special-interest groups, and businesses all seek to influence public tastes and attitudes by using **propaganda,** *information presented with the intention of shaping public opinion.* Although the term has negative connotations, propaganda is not necessarily false. A thin line separates information from propaganda: the difference depends mostly on the presenter's intention. We offer *information* to enlighten others; we use *propaganda* to sway an audience towards some viewpoint. Political speeches, commercial advertising, and even some university lectures may disseminate propaganda with the goal of making people think or act in some specific way. Input from Canada's business community during the 1987 debate over

THINKING CRITICALLY
The Rumour Mill: Paul Is Dead!

One of the best-known rock groups of the twentieth century was the Beatles—Paul McCartney, John Lennon, George Harrison, and Ringo Starr—whose music caused a cultural revolution in the 1960s. However, today's young people may not know the rumour that circulated about Paul McCartney at the height of the group's popularity (Rosnow and Fine, 1976; Kapferer, 1992).

On October 12, 1969, a young man telephoned a Detroit disk jockey to say that he had discovered the following "evidence" that Paul McCartney was dead:

1. At the end of the song "Strawberry Fields Forever" on the *Magical Mystery Tour* album, if you filter out the background noise, you will hear a voice saying, "I buried Paul!"

2. The phrase "Number 9, Number 9, Number 9" from the song "Revolution 9" on *The Beatles* (commonly known as "The White Album"), when played backwards, seems to say, "Turn me on, dead man!"

Two days later, the University of Michigan student newspaper ran a story entitled "McCartney Is Dead: Further Clues Found." It sent millions of Beatles fans racing for their albums to look for them:

3. A picture inside the *Magical Mystery Tour* album shows John, George, and Ringo wearing red carnations, but Paul is wearing a black flower.

4. The cover of the *Sergeant Pepper's Lonely Hearts Club Band* album shows a grave with yellow flowers arranged in the shape of Paul's bass guitar.

5. On the inside of that album, McCartney wears an armpatch with the letters "OPD." Is this the initials of some police department or confirmation that Paul had been "officially pronounced dead"?

6. On the back cover of the same album, three Beatles are facing forward but McCartney has his back to the camera.

7. On the album cover of *Abbey Road*, John Lennon is clothed as a clergyman, Ringo Starr wears an undertaker's black tie, and George Harrison is clad in workman's attire as if ready to dig a grave. For his part, McCartney is barefoot, which is how Tibetan ritual says to prepare a corpse for burial.

8. Also on the cover of *Abbey Road*, John Lennon's Volkswagen appears behind Paul with the licence plate "28 IF," as if to say that McCartney would be *28 if* he were alive.

Rumour had it that McCartney had died of head injuries suffered in an automobile accident in November 1966 and that, after the accident, record company executives had secretly replaced Paul with a double.

Of course, McCartney is very much alive. He still jokes about the "Paul is dead" episode, and few doubt that he dreamed up some of the details of his own "death," with a little help from his friends. But the story has a serious side, showing how quickly rumours can arise and how they spread in a climate of mistrust: in the late 1960s, many young people were quite ready to believe that the media and other powerful interests were concealing McCartney's death.

Back in 1969, McCartney himself denied the rumour in a *Life* magazine interview. But thousands of suspicious readers noticed that, on the other side of the page with McCartney's picture was an ad for an automobile: holding this page up to the light, the car lay across McCartney's chest and blocked his head. Another clue!

WHAT DO YOU THINK?

1. What types of rumours have circulated recently on your campus?
2. What made them begin? What made them go away?
3. Overall, do you think rumours are helpful, harmful, or harmless? Why?

---

free trade with the United States was denounced by opponents as propaganda, as were all of the pronouncements of the three major federal political parties during the 1992 referendum on the Charlottetown Accord.

One way to legitimize propaganda is to show that it is consistent with public opinion, as measured by pollsters. In August 2006, headlines in *The Globe and Mail* implied that Canadians were outraged by Prime Minister Stephen Harper's decision to stand by Israel in its response to attacks by Hezbollah. On the basis of a Globe/CTV poll, most Canadians believe that Harper supports Israel to please U.S. President Bush. Suspecting that the findings might be the result of question design, Western Standard/Compas conducted its own poll with very different results (Steel, 2006). The results of the two polls are presented in Figure 23–1. A glance reveals that the Western Standard/Compas poll (in part (a)) and Globe/CTV poll (in part (b)) presented respondents with different response

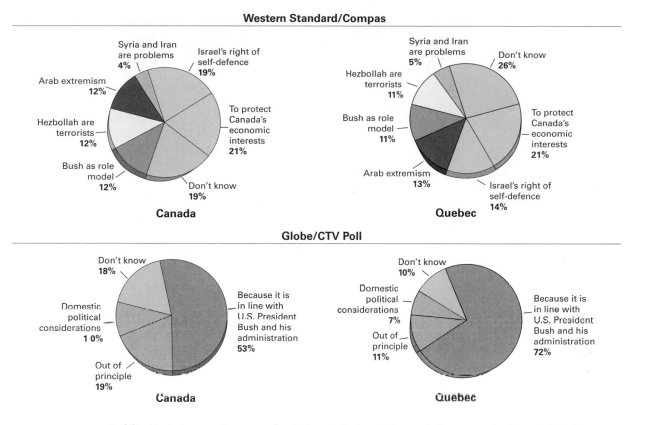

FIGURE 23-1   Public Opinion on Reasons for Prime Minister Harper's Support for Israel, 2006

Source: From *The Western Standard*, August 28, 2006: 26.

options. With only "out of principle" and "domestic considerations" as alternative options, the majority of Globe/CTV respondents (53% of Canadians and 72% of Quebecers) said that Harper chose to support Israel in order to be "in line with U.S. President George W. Bush and his administration." Given a number of more specific options—such as "Israel's right of self-defence" or protection of "Canada's economic interests," Western Standard/Compas respondents were much *less* likely to cite the Bush factor (12% of Canadians and 11% of Quebecers). It should be no surprise to learn that Globe/CTV is pro-Liberal in its leanings, while Western Standard/Compas is pro-Conservative: the design of their respective questions had clear impacts on the results. We hope this example will lead you to ask about the actual wording of the question when you read that an overwhelming majority of people have expressed some opinion—especially when the issue is controversial.

YOUR TURN

Have you ever taken a course in which the information presented by the professor, one of the readings, or a film seemed to be propaganda? What made it seem that way? Ask some of your classmates if they agree with you.

FASHIONS AND FADS

Fashions and fads also involve people spread over a large area. A **fashion** is *a social pattern favoured by a large number of people.* People's tastes in clothing, music, and automobiles, as well as ideas about politics, change often, going in and out of fashion. In pre-industrial societies, clothing and personal appearance change very little, reflecting traditional *style.* Women and men, the rich and the poor, lawyers and carpenters wear distinctive clothes and hairstyles that reflect their occupations and social standing (Lofland, 1973; Crane, 2000). In industrial societies, however, established style gives way to changing fashion. For one thing, modern people care less about tradition and are often eager to try out new lifestyles. Higher rates of social mobility also cause people to use their appearance to make a statement about themselves.

The German sociologist Georg Simmel (1971; orig. 1904) explained that rich people are usually the trendsetters, because they attract lots of attention and they have the money to spend on luxuries. As the U.S. sociologist Thorstein Veblen (1953; orig. 1899) put it, fashion involves *conspicuous consumption* as people buy expensive products—from bottled water to Hummers—not because they need such things but simply to show off their wealth. Ordinary people who want to look wealthy are eager to buy less expensive copies of items made fashionable by the rich.

A recent fad is the wearing of colourful plastic bracelets to express support for various organizations and causes, including efforts to find a cure for AIDS, breast cancer, and other diseases.

In this way, a fashion moves downwards through the class structure. Eventually, a fashion loses its prestige when too many average people share a "look," so the rich move on to something new. Fashions, in short, are born at the top of the social hierarchy, rise to mass popularity in department stores, and soon are forgotten by almost everyone.

Since the 1960s, however, there has been a reversal of this pattern in the United States, and many fashions favoured by rich people are drawn from people of lower social position. This pattern began with blue jeans, which have long been worn by people doing manual labour. During the civil rights and antiwar movements of the 1960s, jeans became popular among college students who wanted to identify with working people. Today, cargo pants and other emblems of the hip-hop culture allow even the most affluent entertainers and celebrities to mimic the styles that began among the inner-city poor. Even rich and famous people may identify with their ordinary roots: in one of her songs, Jennifer Lopez sings, "Don't be fooled by the rocks that I've got, I'm still, I'm still Jenny from the block."

A **fad** is *an unconventional social pattern that people embrace briefly but enthusiastically.* Fads, sometimes called *crazes,* are common in high-income societies, where many people have the money to spend on amusing, if often frivolous, products. During the 1950s, two young Californians produced a brightly coloured plastic hoop, a version of a toy popular in Australia, that you can swing around your waist by gyrating the hips. The "hula hoop" became a national craze. In less than a year, hula hoops all but vanished, reappearing sporadically. Pokémon cards are another example of the rise and fall of a fad (Aguirre, *et al.* 1988).

How do fads differ from fashions? Fads capture the public imagination but quickly burn out. Because fashions reflect basic cultural values like individuality and sexual attractiveness, they tend to stay around for a while. Therefore, a fashion—but rarely a fad—becomes a more lasting part of popular culture. Streaking, for instance, was a fad that came out of nowhere and soon vanished; blue jeans, on the other hand, originated in the rough mining camps of the gold rush in the 1870s and are still popular today.

PANIC AND MASS HYSTERIA

A **panic** is *a form of collective behaviour in which people in one place react to a threat or other stimulus with irrational, frantic, and often self-destructive behaviour.* The classic illustration of a panic is people streaming towards the exits of a crowded theatre after someone yells, "Fire!" As they flee, they may trample one another or block the exits so that few actually escape. Closely related to panic is **mass hysteria** (or moral panic), *a form of dispersed collective behaviour in which people react to a real or imagined event with irrational and even frantic fear.* Whether the cause of the hysteria is real or not, a large number of people take it very seriously. Parents' fears that their children may become infected with HIV by a schoolmate who has AIDS may stir as much hysteria in a community as the very real danger of an approaching hurricane. Moreover, actions of people in the grip of mass hysteria generally make the situation worse. At an extreme, mass hysteria leads to chaotic flight and sends crowds into panic. People who see others overcome by fear may become more afraid themselves, as hysteria feeds on itself.

During the evening before Hallowe'en in 1938, CBS radio broadcast a typical program of dance music. Suddenly, a voice interrupted with a "special report" of explosions on the surface of the planet Mars and, soon after, the crash landing of a mysterious cylinder near a farmhouse in New Jersey. This was a theatrical dramatization by Orson Welles of H.G. Wells's novel *War of the Worlds* (Cantril, *et al.*, 1947; Koch, 1970). The program then switched to an "on-the-scene reporter" who presented a chilling account of giant monsters equipped with death-ray weapons emerging from a spaceship. An "eminent astronomer" informed the audience that Martians had begun a full-scale invasion of Earth. Back then, most North Americans relied on radio for factual news. There was an announcement to clarify that the broadcast was fiction, but about 1 million of the 10 million listeners in the United States and Canada missed the announcement and believed that the play was real. By the time the show was over, thousands were hysterical, gathering in the streets to spread news of the "invasion," while others flooded telephone switchboards with warnings to friends and relatives. Many simply jumped into their cars and fled.

To hear the 1938 radio broadcast that started a national panic, go to www.waroftheworlds.org.

Sociologists classify disasters into three types. Hurricane Katrina, which brought massive flooding to New Orleans, is an example of a natural disaster (*left*). The 1989 grounding of the tanker *Exxon Valdez*, which spilled 41.6 million litres (11 million gallons) of crude oil off the coast of Alaska, was a technological disaster (*centre*). The slaughter of 800 000 people in Rwanda between April and June 1994 is an example of intentional disaster (*right*).

As illustrated, the mass media may contribute to hysteria or panic. Diseases, disasters, and deadly crime all get intense coverage by television and other media, which hope to gain audience. Erich Goode (2000:549) points out that "The mass media *thrive* on scares; contributing to moral panics is the media's stock in trade." Look at the role of the mass media in spreading our panic regarding the "inevitable" bird flu pandemic: intensive coverage for several months, then nothing—despite the fact that it remains equally inevitable.

DISASTERS

A **disaster** is *an event, generally unexpected, that causes extensive harm to people and damage to property.* Disasters are of three types.[1] The first is the *natural disaster*, such as a flood, hurricane, earthquake, forest fire, or tsunami. A second type is the *technological disaster*, which is widely regarded as an *accident* but is more accurately a failure to control technology. The massive oil spill from the *Exxon Valdez* tanker running aground off the coast of Alaska in 1989 and the nuclear explosion at the Chernobyl power plant in Ukraine in 1986 were both technological disasters. A third type of disaster is the *intentional disaster*, in which organized groups deliberately harm others. War, terrorist attacks, and

 Read a detailed report of the Rwandan massacres at www.cbc.ca/news/background/rwanda/.

genocide, such as the massacres in Yugoslavia in 1992–95 and Rwanda in 1994, are examples of intentional disasters.

Kai Erikson (1976, 1994, 2005b) has investigated dozens of disasters of all types. From his investigations of floods, nuclear contamination, oil spills, and genocide, Erikson reached three major conclusions about the social consequences of disasters. First, we all know that disasters harm people and destroy property; but what most people don't realize is that disasters also cause serious damage to the human community. The Saguenay flood of 1996 killed seven, levelled an entire neighbourhood, and forced the evacuation of 16 000 people. When a dam bursts or overflows, as in this case, however rapid and effective the assistance from outside—people are paralyzed by the loss of family members, friends, and an entire way of life. A decade later, parts of the community have never been rebuilt. We may know when disasters start, Erikson points out, but we cannot know when they will finally end. Often, when disasters strike, it is the poor that suffer the most. This lesson was made clear when Hurricane Katrina struck New Orleans in 2005: one year later, the middle-class and affluent neighbourhoods are returning to normal, while the poor Black neighbourhoods look very much as Katrina left them.

---

[1]The first two types are based on Erikson (2005b). The third type is added by author John Macionis.

APPLYING SOCIOLOGY
A Never-Ending Disaster

It was just after dawn on March 1, 1954, and the air was already warm on Utrik Island, a small bit of coral and volcanic rock in the South Pacific that is one of the Marshall Islands. The island was home to 159 people who lived by fishing, much as their ancestors have done for centuries. The Utrik people knew only a little about the outside world: a missionary from the United States taught the local children, and two dozen military personnel lived at a small American weather station with an airstrip that received one plane each week.

At 6:45 A.M., the western sky suddenly lit up brighter than anyone had ever seen and, seconds later, a rumble like a massive earthquake rolled across the island. Some of the islanders thought the world was coming to an end. Their world—at least as they had known it—had changed forever.

About 250 kilometres (160 miles) to the west, on Bikini Island, the United States military had just detonated an atomic bomb, a huge device with a thousand times the power of the bomb used in 1945 to destroy the Japanese city of Hiroshima. The enormous blast vaporized Bikini Island and sent a massive cloud of dust and radiation into the atmosphere. The military expected winds to take the cloud north into an open area of the ocean, but the cloud blew east instead. By noon, the radiation cloud engulfed a Japanese fishing boat ironically called the *Lucky Dragon*, exposing the 23 people on board to a dose of radiation that would

eventually sicken or kill them all. By late afternoon, the deadly cloud reached Utrik Island.

The cloud was made up of coral and rock dust, all that was left of Bikini Island. The dust fell softly on Utrik Island, and children who remembered pictures of snow shown to them by their missionary teacher ran out to play in the white powder that was piling up everywhere. No one realized that it was contaminated with deadly radiation.

Three and a half days later, the U.S. military landed planes on Utrik

Island and informed all the people that they would have to leave immediately, bringing nothing with them. For three months, the islanders were held on another military base, and then they were taken home. Many of the people who were on the island that fateful morning died young, typically from cancer or some other disease associated with radiation exposure. But, even today, those who survived consider themselves and their island poisoned by the radiation, and they believe that the poison will never go away.

The radiation may or may not still be in the islanders' bodies, but it has worked its way deep into their culture. More than 50 years after the atomic bomb exploded, people on Utrik still talk about the morning that "everything changed." The damage from this disaster turns out to be much more than medical: it is a social transformation that has left the people with a deep belief that they are all sick, that life will never be the same, and that people could have prevented the disaster but did not.

WHAT DO YOU THINK?

1. In what sense is a disaster like this one never really over?
2. In what ways did the atomic bomb test change the culture of the Utrik people?
3. The U.S. government never formally took responsibility for what happened. What do you think it should do now?

Source: Based on K.T. Erikson (2005b).

Second, Erikson explains that the social damage is more serious when an event involves some toxic substance, as is common with technological disasters. After the catastrophic explosion and radiation leak in 1986 at the Chernobyl nuclear plant, people in Ukraine were exposed to a dangerous substance that they feared and over which they had no control. The Applying Sociology box (above) explores a similar example, which is still affecting people on Utrik Island and their descendants more than 50 years after it occurred.

Third, the social damage is most serious when the disaster is caused by the actions of other people. This can happen through negligence or carelessness (in the case of technological disasters) or through wilful action (in the case of intentional disasters). Our belief that "other people will do us no harm" is a basic foundation of social life, Erikson claims. But when others act carelessly (as in the 1984 pesticide gas leak in Bhopal, India) or intentionally in ways that harm us (as in genocide or terrorism), those who survive typically lose their trust in others to a degree that may never go away.

Social Movements

As noted at the outset of this chapter, a *social movement* is an organized activity that encourages or discourages social change. Social movements are among the most important types of collective behaviour because they often have lasting effects on the shape of our society. Social movements are common in the modern world, but this was not always the case. Pre-industrial societies are tightly bound by tradition, making social movements extremely rare.

The many subcultures and countercultures found in industrial and post-industrial societies encourage social movements. In North America and Europe, significant public issues are likely to give rise to social movements favouring change and to countermovements resisting it. In recent decades in Canada, for example, the gay rights movement has won the right to same-sex marriage—not just formal domestic partnerships, as is the case in other jurisdictions that support same-sex unions. In response, a countermovement has also formed to try to turn back the clock on gay unions.

The early history of the gay rights movement in Canada is profiled in film and audio excerpts at http://archives.cbc.ca/300c.asp?id=1-69-599.

Prior to the 1980s there were three major dynamic sources of social change in Canada: class relations, regional identity, and the bilingual and multicultural nature of our society (Marsden and Harvey, 1979:4). Since then, many of Canada's social movements have arisen from one of four sources:

- Quebec, where the francophone majority seeking to reshape its relationship with the rest of the country or, possibly, to establish its sovereignty
- regional interests responding to economic and political inequities and numerous cultural differences
- Aboriginal peoples struggling to gain recognition of the inherent right to self-government, and
- Ethnic and racial minorities attempting to participate as equals within the larger society without completely losing their identities

With the patriation of our constitution in 1982 and the incorporation of the Canadian Charter of Rights and Freedoms (Canada, 1982), we have entered a new era. Numerous issues have been brought to the forefront, claiming Charter protection and inspiring social movements and various degrees of social change. Earlier movements, of women or gays and lesbians, gained momentum and reached many goals in this period. Others, mobilized around the human rights of refugees and permanent residents (previously called landed immigrants), are in full force. A smaller movement endorsing euthanasia and the right to die seems to gain momentum periodically in response to the plight of specific individuals, such as Sue Rodriguez (see Chapter 15, "Confronting Death" and Chapter 21, "Do We Have the Right To Die?"). Beyond these social issues, Canada also has an active environmental movement.

TYPES OF SOCIAL MOVEMENTS

Sociologists classify social movements according to several variables (Aberle, 1966; Cameron, 1966; Blumer, 1969). One variable asks, *Who is changed?* Some movements target selected people, and others try to change everyone. A second variable asks, *How much change?* Some movements seek only limited change in our lives, and others pursue radical transformation of society. Combining these variables results in four types of social movements, shown in Figure 23–2:

- *Alternative social movements* are the least threatening to the status quo because they seek limited change in only some narrow segment of the population. Planned Parenthood, for example, encourages individuals of child-bearing age to take the consequences of sexual activity more seriously by practising birth control.

- *Redemptive social movements* also have a selective focus, but they seek radical change in those they engage. Alcoholics Anonymous, for example, is an organization that helps alcoholics to achieve a sober life.

- *Reformative social movements*, which generally work within the existing political system, seek only limited social change but encompass the entire society. They can be progressive (promoting a new social pattern) or reactionary (countermovements trying to preserve the status quo or to return to past social patterns). In the ongoing debate about abortion in Canada, both the anti-abortion and pro-choice organizations are reformative social movements. Right-wing movements such as the Western Guard, the National Citizens Coalition, and the Ku Klux Klan are examples of reactionary countermovements.

- *Revolutionary social movements* are the most extreme. They seek basic transformation of a society. Sometimes pursuing specific goals, sometimes spinning utopian dreams, these social movements reject existing social institutions as flawed while promoting radically new alternatives. The nationalist or sovereigntist (i.e., separatist) movement in Quebec is revolutionary because it seeks, at the very least, a radical restructuring of federal institutions to give Quebec more political and economic autonomy; failing that, Quebec nationalists would argue, the need to protect their distinct society requires the establishment of an independent state and the complete overthrow of existing institutions. As with the social conservative movement, the creation of the federal Bloc Québécois and the provincial Parti Québécois lend legitimacy to a revolutionary and potentially separatist movement by incorporating it within Canada's political structure. Few other nations would pass this test of tolerance.

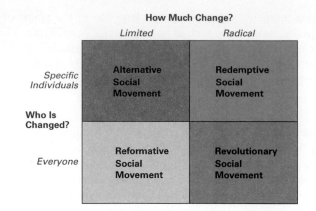

How Much Change?

FIGURE 23-2 Four Types of Social Movements

There are four types of social movements based on who is changed and how great the change is.

Source: Based on Aberle (1966).

YOUR TURN

Have you ever taken part in a social movement or witnessed one in action? If so, which of the four types best describes that movement?

CLAIMS MAKING

In 1981, the Centers for Disease Control and Prevention began to track a strange disease that was killing people, most of them homosexual men. It was a deadly disease, but there was little public attention and few stories in the mass media. Only about five years later did the public become aware of the rising number of deaths and begin to think of the disease as a serious social threat. The disease came to be known as acquired immune deficiency syndrome (AIDS) (see Chapter 21, "Health and Medicine").

The change in public thinking about AIDS was the result of **claims making,** *the process of trying to convince the public and public officials of the importance of joining a social movement to address a particular issue.* In other words, for a social movement to form, some issue has to be defined as a problem that demands public attention. Usually, claims making begins with a small number of people. In the case of AIDS, the gay community in large cities—notably San Francisco, New York, and Toronto—mobilized to convince people of the dangers posed by this deadly disease. Over time, if the mass media give an issue attention and public officials speak out on behalf of the problem, the social movement gains strength. Considerable public attention has now been given to AIDS, and there is ongoing research aimed at finding a cure for this deadly disease.

The process of claims making goes on all the time. Two highly diverse examples are the Aboriginal rights movement relating to land claims, social justice, and quality of life; and

the movement to ban the use of cellular telephones in automobiles relating to the thousands of automobile accidents each year in North America related to the use of phones while driving. Some jurisdictions in North American and Europe have passed laws about this practice, and debate continues in others (McVeigh, *et al.*, 2003; Macionis, 2005). The Media Perspectives box (on p. 613) explores the movement to ban cellphone use by car drivers, from a global perspective.

EXPLAINING SOCIAL MOVEMENTS

Because social movements are intentional and long-lasting, sociologists find this type of collective behaviour easier to explain than brief episodes of mob behaviour or mass hysteria. Several theories to explain social movements have gained importance.

Deprivation Theory

Deprivation theory holds that social movements seeking change arise among people who feel deprived. People who feel they lack enough income, safe working conditions, basic political rights, or plain human dignity may organize a social movement to bring about a more just state of affairs (Morrison, 1978; Rose, 1982).

The rise of the Ku Klux Klan and the passage of Jim Crow laws by White people intent on enforcing segregation in the southern United States after the Civil War illustrate deprivation theory. With the end of slavery, White landowners lost a source of free labour and poorer White people lost the claim that they were socially superior to African Americans. This

For information on hate groups in North America, visit www.splcenter.org/intel/history.jsp.

change produced a sense of deprivation, prompting White people to try to keep all "coloured" people "in their place" (Dollard, *et al.*, 1939). African Americans' deprivation was far greater, of course, but, as a minority in a racist society, they had little opportunity to organize. During the twentieth century, however, African Americans did organize successfully in pursuit of racial equality.

As Chapter 7 ("Groups and Organizations") explained, deprivation is a relative concept. Regardless of anyone's absolute amount of money and power, people feel either good or bad about their situation only by comparing themselves to some other category of people. **Relative deprivation,** then, is *a perceived disadvantage arising from some specific comparison* (Stouffer, *et al.*, 1949; Merton, 1968).

Alexis de Tocqueville's study of the French Revolution offers a classic illustration of relative deprivation (1955; orig. 1856). Why did rebellion occur in progressive France where feudalism was breaking down, rather than in more traditional Germany, where peasants were much worse off? Tocqueville's answer was that, as bad as their conditions were, German peasants had known nothing but feudal servitude and, therefore, had no basis for feeling deprived. French peasants, by contrast, had seen improvements in their lives that made

"Car Phone Danger Too Great to Ignore"

That's the title of the lead editorial in the Toronto *Star* (2006a). Think for a moment. Would that have been the subject of an editorial in 1996?

A decade ago, very few people had cellphones. Those that were available were huge, chunky beasts in comparison to the tiny ones available today. Car phones were even larger and actually installed in cars and trucks. Since then, people rather than vehicles have become increasingly wired. Teens and powerful business tycoons are equally dependent on their computers, cellphones, and BlackBerries to keep in touch—in *constant* touch. Many business people and professionals are available 24 hours, 7 days a week, even on holiday. The international business set needs BlackBerries or cellphones that are functional anywhere in the world, and high-quality internet access is one of the first requirements of their hotels.

In the past few years, there have been media reports in North America and Europe detailing the dangers of cellphone use while driving, and

attributing untold numbers of traffic fatalities to cellphone-distracted drivers. So effective has been the movement to ban cellphone use by drivers, that many countries, some Canadian provinces, and some American states have banned them—except, perhaps, for hands-free devices.

About 50 countries have laws banning or restricting cellphone use by drivers, among them Australia, Germany, France, the Netherlands, Sweden, Switzerland, and Lithuania. California is expected to sign a ban into law very soon after conducting a study that identified cellphones as "the most common cause of distracted-driving accidents in every year since 2001." New York, New Jersey, and Connecticut have banned hand-held cellphones already. Here in Canada, Newfoundland and Labrador banned cellphone use by drivers in 2002; Alberta and other provinces are considering the same move.

The *Star* editorial notes that Ontario is disinclined to take this step. Premier Dalton McGuinty says "We can't have a

law for everything" and the Ontario Ministry of Transportation identifies cellphone use as only one of several possible driver distractions rather than the Number 1 risk. In a move that should support the anti-cellphone movement in Ontario, the *Star* notes:

Clearly, it is time Ontario adopted a law on cellphone use on our roads. As a first step to a possible total ban, McGuinty's government should immediately follow the lead of many jurisdictions in the world and punish drivers who use hand-held phones with hefty fines and demerit points.

WHAT DO YOU THINK?

1. Should drivers be allowed to use cellphones?
2. Have you ever been distracted by your cellphone while driving?
3. In October 2006, a private members bill in Ontario proposes to ban cellphone use for teenage drivers only. Would this ban be fair? Why?

them eager for more change. Consequently, the French—but not the Germans—felt relative deprivation. As Tocqueville saw it, increasing freedom and prosperity did not satisfy people as much as it sparked their desire for an even better life.

Closer to home, Tocqueville's insight helps explain patterns of rioting during the 1960s. Protest riots involving African Americans took place not in the southern United States, where many Black people lived in miserable poverty, but in Detroit, where the auto industry was booming, Black unemployment was low, and Black home ownership was the highest in the country (Thernstrom and Thernstrom, 1998).

Critical Review Deprivation theory challenges our common sense assumption that the worst-off people are the most likely to organize for change. People do not organize simply because they suffer in an absolute sense; rather, social movements arise out of a sense of *relative* deprivation. Both Tocqueville and Marx—as different as they were

in many ways—agreed on the importance of relative deprivation in the formation of social movements.

But most people experience some discontent all the time, so deprivation theory leaves us wondering why social movements arise among some categories of people and not others. A second problem is that deprivation theory suffers from circular reasoning: we assume that deprivation causes social movements but, often, the only evidence of deprivation is the social movement itself (Jenkins and Perrow, 1977). A third limitation is that this approach focuses on the cause of a social movement and tells us little about what happens after movements take form (McAdam, *et al.*, 1988).

Mass Society Theory

William Kornhauser's *mass society theory* (1959) argues that socially isolated people seek out social movements as a way to gain a sense of belonging and importance. From this point of view, social movements are most likely to arise in

Mass society theory suggests that people join social movements in order to gain a sense of meaning and purpose in their lives. How well do you think this theory explains the behaviour of people in this prolife (anti-abortion) demonstration? Why?

impersonal, *mass* societies. This theory points out the *personal* as well as the *political* consequences of social movements that offer a sense of community to people otherwise adrift in society (Melucci, 1989). It follows, says Kornhauser, that categories of people with weak social ties are those most eager to join a social movement. People who are well-integrated socially, by contrast, are unlikely to seek membership in a social movement. Kornhauser concludes that activists tend to be psychologically vulnerable people who eagerly join groups and can be manipulated by group leaders. For this reason, Kornhauser claims, social movements are rarely very democratic.

Critical Review To Kornhauser's credit, his theory focuses on both the kind of society that produces social movements and the kinds of people who join them. But one criticism is that there is no clear standard for measuring the extent to which we live in a "mass society," so his thesis is difficult to test. A second criticism is that explaining social movements in terms of people hungry to belong ignores the social justice issues that movements address. Put otherwise, mass society theory suggests that flawed people— rather than a flawed society—are responsible for social movements.

What does research show about mass society theory? The record is mixed. Research by Piven and Cloward (1977) supports Kornhauser's approach—finding that a breakdown of routine social patterns encourages poor people to form social movements. Also, a study of the New Mexico State Penitentiary found that, when prison programs that promoted social ties among inmates were suspended, inmates were more likely to protest their conditions (Useem, 1997). But other studies cast doubt on this approach. Some researchers conclude that the Nazi movement in Germany did not draw heavily from socially

isolated people (Lipset, 1963; Oberschall, 1973). Similarly, many of the people who took part in urban riots during the 1960s had strong ties to their communities (Sears and McConahay, 1973). Evidence also suggests that most young people who join religious movements have fairly normal family ties (Wright and Piper, 1986). Finally, researchers who have examined the biographies of 1960s political activists find evidence of deep and continuing commitment to political goals rather than isolation from society (McAdam, 1988, 1989; Whalen and Flacks, 1989).

Structural Strain Theory

One of the most influential theories about social movements was developed by Neil Smelser (1962). His *structural strain theory* identifies six factors that encourage the development of social movements. Smelser's theory also suggests which factors encourage unorganized mobs or riots and which encourage highly organized social movements. The prodemocracy movement that transformed Eastern Europe in the late 1980s illustrates the factors in Smelser's theory:

- *Structural conduciveness.* Social movements begin to emerge when people come to think their society has some serious problems. In Eastern Europe, these problems included low living standards and political repression by national governments.

- *Structural strain.* People begin to experience relative deprivation when society fails to meet their expectations. Eastern Europeans joined the prodemocracy movement because they compared their living standards to the higher ones in Western Europe; they also knew that their standard of living was lower than socialist propaganda had for years led them to expect.

- *Growth and spread of an explanation.* Forming a well-organized social movement requires a clear statement of not just the problem but also its causes and solutions. If people are confused about why they are suffering, they will probably express their dissatisfaction in an unorganized way through rioting. In the case of Eastern Europe, intellectuals played a key role in the prodemocracy movement by pointing out economic and political flaws in the socialist system and proposing strategies to increase democracy.

- *Precipitating factors.* Discontent may exist for a long time before some specific event sparks collective action. Such an event occurred in 1985 when Mikhail Gorbachev came to power in the Soviet Union and began his program of *perestroika* (restructuring). As Moscow relaxed its rigid control over Eastern Europe, people there saw a historic opportunity to reorganize political and economic life and claim greater freedom.

- *Mobilization for action.* Once people share a concern about some public issue, they are ready to take action—to distribute leaflets, stage protest rallies, and build alliances with sympathetic organizations. The initial success of the Solidarity movement in Poland—helped by the Reagan administration in the United States and by Pope John Paul II in the Vatican—mobilized people throughout Eastern Europe to press for change. The rate of change became faster and faster. What had taken a decade in Poland required only months in Hungary and only weeks in other Eastern European nations.

- *Lack of social control.* The success of any social movement depends, in large part, on the response of political officials, police, and the military. Sometimes the state moves swiftly to crush a social movement, as happened in the case of prodemocracy forces in the People's Republic of China. But Gorbachev adopted a policy of nonintervention in Eastern Europe, opening the door for change. Ironically, the movements that began in Eastern Europe soon spread to the Soviet Union itself, ending the historic domination of the Communist party in 1991 and producing a new political confederation.

Critical Review Smelser's analysis explains how various factors help or hurt the development of social movements. Structural strain theory also explains why people may respond to their problems either by forming organized social movements or through spontaneous mob action. Yet Smelser's theory contains some of the same circularity of argument found in Kornhauser's analysis. A social movement is caused by strain, says Smelser, but the only evidence of underlying strain is often the social movement itself. Finally, structural strain theory is incomplete, overlooking the important role that resources such as the mass media or international alliances play in the success or failure of a social movement (Jenkins and Perrow, 1977; McCarthy and Zald, 1977; Olzak and West, 1991). Canada's Aboriginal peoples have been particularly adept at gaining

media coverage and winning support for their cause in the United States, Europe, the United Nations, and the Canadian public.

Resource Mobilization Theory

Resource mobilization theory points out that no social movement is likely to succeed—or even get off the ground—without substantial resources, including money, human labour, office and communications equipment, access to the mass media, and a positive public image. In short, any social movement rises or falls on how well it attracts resources, mobilizes people, and forges alliances.

Outsiders can be just as important as insiders in affecting the outcome of a social movement. Because socially disadvantaged people, by definition, lack the money, contacts, leadership skills, and organizational know-how that a successful movement requires, sympathetic outsiders fill the resource gap. In North America, well-to-do White people, including college students, joined the Black civil rights movement in the 1960s, and many affluent men have joined women as leaders of the women's movement.

Resources connecting people are also vital. The 1989 prodemocracy movement in China was fuelled by students, whose location on campuses clustered together in Beijing allowed them to build networks and recruit new members (Zhao, 1998). More recently, the internet and cellphones are important resources that help organizations link hundreds of thousands of people in one country or around the world. Prior to the Iraq War, for example, two individuals using their computers were able to get 120 000 people in 190 countries to sign a petition opposing the war.

The availability of organizing ideas online has helped many social movements to grow over time. "Take Back the Night," for example, is an annual occasion for rallies in North America at which people speak out in opposition to violence against women, children, and families.

 For more about Take Back the Night, go to www.campus outreachservices.com/resources/ tbtnhistory.htm.

Using online resources, even a small number of people can plan and carry out an effective political event (Valocchi, 1996; Passy and Giugni, 2001; Packer, 2003).

Critical Review Resource mobilization theory recognizes that resources as well as discontent are necessary to the success of a social movement. Research confirms the importance of forging alliances to gaining resources and notes that movements with few resources may, in desperation, turn to violence to call attention to their cause (Grant and Wallace, 1991; Jenkins, *et al.*, 2003). Critics of this theory counter that "outside" people and resources are not always needed to ensure a movement's success. They argue that even relatively powerless segments of a population can promote change if they are able to organize effectively and have strongly committed members (Donnelly and Majka, 1998). Aldon Morris (1981) adds that the success of the

Social movements are often given great energy by powerful visual images, which is one key idea of culture theory. During World War II, the photo of six soldiers raising the U.S. flag on the tiny Pacific island of Iwo Jima (*left*) increased morale at home and, later, was the inspiration for a memorial sculpture. Some 25 years later, the photo of children running from a napalm strike by U.S. planes on My Lai village in South Vietnam (*right*) made headline news. The girl in the middle of the picture had ripped the flaming clothes from her body. This photo strengthened the social movement in North America against the war in Vietnam.

civil rights movement of the 1950s and 1960s was the result of Black people drawing mostly on their own skills and resources. A second problem with this theory is that it overstates the extent to which powerful people are willing to challenge the status quo. Some rich White people did provide valuable resources to the Black civil rights movement but, probably more often, elites were indifferent or opposed to significant change (McAdam, 1982, 1983; Pichardo, 1995).

Culture Theory

In recent years, sociologists have developed *culture theory*, the recognition that social movements depend not only on material resources and the structure of political power but also on cultural symbols. That is, people in any particular situation are likely to mobilize to form a social movement only to the extent that they develop "shared understandings of the world that legitimate and motivate collective action" (McAdam, *et al.*, 1996:6; see also Williams, 2002).

In part, mobilization depends on a sense of injustice, as suggested by deprivation theory; in addition, people must come to believe that they are not able to respond to their situation effectively by acting alone. Social movements gain strength as they develop symbols and a sense of community that both build strong feelings and direct energy into organized action. Media images of the burning World Trade Center towers after the terrorist attacks of September 11, 2001, helped mobilize people to support the "war against terrorism." Photos of gay couples celebrat-

 The standoff at Oka is captured in CBC documentary footage at http://archives.cbc.ca/300c.asp?id=1-71-99.

ing their weddings have helped fuel both the gay rights movement and the countermovement trying to prevent the expansion of gay marriage. Likewise, images of First Nation barricades at Oka, Caledonia, and other places fuel their rights movement and agitate those who feel that Canada's Aboriginal peoples are a pampered lot who deserve no special treatment.

Critical Review A strength of culture theory is reminding us that social movements depend not just on material resources but also on cultural symbols. At the same time, powerful symbols—such as the flag and ideas about patriotism and respecting our leaders—help support the status quo. How and when symbols turn people from supporting the system towards protest against it are questions in need of further research.

Political Economy Theory

Marxist *political economy theory* also has something to say about social movements. From this point of view, social movements arise within capitalist societies because the capitalist economic system fails to meet the needs of the majority of people. Despite great economic productivity, Canadian society struggles to deal with separatism in Quebec, an ailing—and hotly debated—health care system, pro- and anti-Kyoto factions, and unrelenting poverty, especially in Aboriginal communities.

Critical Review A strength of political economy theory is its macro-level approach. Other theories explain the rise of social movements in terms of traits of individuals (such as

SUMMING UP

Theories of Social Movements

Deprivation Theory	People experiencing relative deprivation begin social movements. The social movement is a means of seeking change that brings participants greater benefits. Social movements are especially likely when rising expectations are frustrated.
Mass Society Theory	People who lack established social ties are mobilized into social movements. Periods of social breakdown are likely to spawn social movements. The social movement gives members a sense of belonging and social participation.
Structural Strain Theory	People come together because of their shared concern about the inability of society to operate as they believe it should. The growth of a social movement reflects many factors, including a belief in its legitimacy and some precipitating event that provokes action.
Resource Mobilization Theory	People may join for all the reasons noted above and also because of social ties to existing members. But the success or failure of a social movement depends largely on the resources available to it. Also important is the extent of opposition within the larger society.
Culture Theory	People are drawn to a social movement by cultural symbols that define some cause as just. The movement itself usually becomes a symbol of power and justice.
Political Economy Theory	People unite to address the societal ills caused by capitalism, including unemployment, poverty, and lack of health care. Social movements are necessary because a capitalist economy inevitably fails to meet people's basic needs.
New Social Movements Theory	People who join social movements are motivated by quality of life, not necessarily economic concerns. Mobilization is national or international in scope. New social movements arise in response to the expansion of the mass media and new information technology.

weak social ties or a sense of relative deprivation) or traits of movements (such as their available resources); this approach focuses on the institutional structures of society itself (i.e., the economic and political systems). This approach does explain social movements concerned with economic issues, but it is less helpful in understanding the recent rise of social movements concerned with such non-economic issues as obesity, animal rights, or the state of the natural environment.

New Social Movements Theory

A final theoretical approach addresses what are often called "new" social movements. *New social movements theory* suggests that recent social movements in the post-industrial societies of North America and Western Europe have a new focus in three ways (McAdam, *et al.*, 1988; Pakulski, 1993).

First, long-established social movements, such as those led by labour organizations, are concerned mostly with economic issues. New social movements, however, tend to focus on improving our social and physical surroundings. The environmental movement, for example, is trying to reduce global warming and address other environmental dangers, such as loss of biodiversity.

Second, most of today's social movements are international, focusing on global ecology, the social standing of women and gay people, animal rights, and opposition to war worldwide. In other words, as the process of globalization links the world's nations, social movements are becoming global.

Third, most social movements of the past drew strong support from working class people, but new social movements that focus on non-economic issues usually draw support from the middle and upper-middle classes. As discussed in Chapter 17 ("Politics and Government"), many affluent people tend to be conservative on economic issues because they have wealth to protect, but liberal on social issues partly as a result of extensive education. In rich nations, the number of highly educated professionals—the people who are most likely to support new social movements—is increasing, a fact that suggests these movements will grow (Jenkins and Wallace, 1996; Rose, 1997).

Critical Review One strength of new social movements theory is recognizing that social movements have become international along with the global economy. This theory also highlights the power of the mass media and new information technology to unite people around the world in pursuit of political goals. However, critics claim that this approach exaggerates the differences between past and present social movements. The women's movement today, for example, focuses on many of the same issues—workplace conditions and pay—that have concerned women and labour organizations for decades.

Each of the seven theories presented here offers some explanation for the emergence of social movements. The Summing Up table (above) outlines them all.

STAGES IN SOCIAL MOVEMENTS

Despite the many differences that set one social movement apart from another, all unfold in roughly the same way, as shown in Figure 23–3. Researchers have identified four different stages in the life of the typical social movement (Blumer, 1969; Mauss, 1975; Tilly, 1978). The last is decline, which may occur for any of five reasons.

Stage 1: **Emergence.** Social movements are driven by the perception that all is not well. Some, such as the civil rights and women's movements, are born of widespread dissatisfaction. Others emerge only as a small vanguard increases public awareness of some issue, as gay activists did with respect to the threat posed by AIDS. In 1998, when Jean Charest left federal politics to lead the Quebec Liberals, an underlying social movement seemed to be emerging, creating the conditions for effective charismatic leadership on his part. The raising of the Canadian flag in front of city hall in Quebec City in April 1998—for the first time since the failure of the Meech Lake Accord in 1990—was a visible symbol of a growing willingness among francophones to embrace a dual Québécois/Canadian identity. Opinion polls at the time suggested a surge of proCanadian sentiment and a reluctance to choose between the two identities. Recently, reaction to the sponsorship scandal may have turned back the clock.

Stage 2: **Coalescence.** After emerging, a social movement must define itself clearly and develop a strategy for "going public." Leaders must determine policies, select tactics, build morale, and recruit new members. At this stage, the movement may engage in collective action, such as rallies or demonstrations, to attract media attention and public notice. The movement may also form alliances with other organizations to gain necessary resources.

Stage 3: **Bureaucratization.** To become an established political force, a social movement must assume bureaucratic traits (described in Chapter 7, "Groups and Organizations"). As it becomes routinized, a social movement depends less on the charisma and talents of a few leaders, instead relying more on a capable staff. When social movements do not become established in this way, they risk dissolving. For example, many activist organizations on university campuses during the late 1960s were energized by a single charismatic leader and, consequently, did not last long. On the other hand, the National Action Committee on the Status of Women,

despite changing leadership, is well established and offers a steady voice on behalf of feminists in Canada. Canada's environmental movement has reached the bureaucratization stage in that we have an environmental ministry and a wide range of environmental organizations.

Stage 4: **Decline.** Eventually, most social movements lose their influence. Frederick Miller (1983) suggests four reasons why this may occur:

If members have met their goals, decline may simply signal success. For example, the women's enfranchisement movement declined after it won the right for women to vote in Canada and the United States. Such clear-cut successes are rare, since few social movements have a single goal. More commonly, winning one victory leads to new campaigns. Because gender issues extend far beyond voting, the women's movement has recast itself time and again.

A social movement may fade owing to organizational factors, such as poor leadership, loss of interest among members, insufficient funds, or repression by authorities. Some people lose interest when the excitement of early efforts is replaced by formal routines. Fragmentation by internal conflicts over goals and tactics is another common problem. Political parties with radical goals like those of the Parti Québécois—formed in 1968 with sovereignty as its central aim—can lose some of their more committed and activist members when they have to modify their platforms, however temporarily, to govern or to ensure re-election, as in 1984 for the Parti Québécois.

A social movement can fall apart if the established power structure, through offers of money, prestige, and other rewards, diverts leaders from their goals. *Co-optation* (that is, selling out) is one facet of the iron law of oligarchy (discussed in Chapter 7, "Groups and Organizations"). Organizational leaders may use their positions to enrich themselves or may simply move on to mainstream careers once initial goals are met. The former poverty activist and head of the Daily Bread food bank in Toronto, Gerard Kennedy, for example, entered politics, becoming a Liberal cabinet minister in Ontario and a political "insider"; he then spent much of 2006 as a candidate for the leadership of the federal Liberal party. By contrast, some people leave lucrative or high-prestige occupations to become activists: Cat Stevens, a rock star in the 1970s, became a Muslim, changed his name to Yusuf Islam, and now promotes his religion. Stephen Lewis left Ontario politics, where he was Opposition leader, to be an activist and is now United Nations Special Envoy on HIV/AIDS to Africa.

A social movement can collapse because of repression. Officials may crush a social movement by frightening away participants, discouraging new recruits, and even imprisoning leaders. In general, the more revolutionary the social movement, the more officials try to repress it. In Canada in the 1960s, the FLQ—a revolutionary movement aiming for

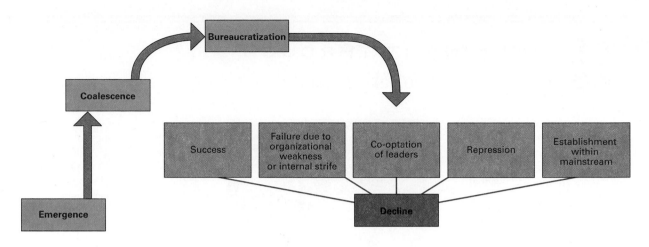

FIGURE 23-3   Stages in the Lives of Social Movements

Social movements typically go through four stages before declining; decline may occur for any of five reasons.

an independent socialist Quebec—used bombs, kidnapping, and murder to promote its cause. In response, Prime Minister Trudeau invoked the *War Measures Act* in peacetime to suspend civil liberties and facilitate the arrest of FLQ members and sympathizers. By 1971, the FLQ had folded.

Another reason, beyond those noted by Miller, is that a social movement may "go mainstream." Some movements become an accepted part of the system—typically after realizing some of their goals—to the point where they no longer challenge the status quo. The Canadian and American labour movements are now well-established parts of mainstream society: the leaders control large organizations and vast sums of money so they now have more in common with the business tycoons they once opposed than with rank and file workers. Until 1990, the government of South Africa, for example, banned the African National Congress (ANC), which was then a political organization seeking to overthrow the state-supported system of apartheid. Even suspected members of the ANC were subject to arrest. In 1990, the government lifted the decades-old ban and released ANC leader Nelson Mandela from prison; in 1994, Mandela became president of South Africa, by then a country moving away from apartheid.

SOCIAL MOVEMENTS AND SOCIAL CHANGE

Social movements exist to encourage—or to resist—social change. Whatever the intention, their success varies from case to case. Gender equality, still only a partially realized goal, has been advanced by the actions of numerous women's groups in Canada and elsewhere. The gay rights movement has made tremendous strides in the last two decades—notably same-sex marriage—and will undoubtedly press on to advance new goals. Environmentalists, as

well, have experienced major successes and have changed public awareness dramatically.

Sometimes we overlook the success of past social movements and take for granted the changes that other people struggled so hard to win. Beginning a century ago, workers' movements fought to end child labour in factories, limit working hours, make the workplace safer, and establish the right to bargain collectively with employers. And women today have greater legal rights and economic opportunities won by earlier generations of women. Thus, social change is both the cause and the consequence of social movements.

Social Movements: Looking Ahead

Especially since the turbulent decade of the 1960s—a decade marked by widespread social protests—Canadian society has been pushed and pulled by many social movements and countermovements. Sometimes tension explodes into violence, as with the Oka standoff described at the beginning of this chapter. In other cases, the struggles are more restrained, as with the mobilization for and against gay and lesbian rights or Quebec independence (see the Thinking It Through box on p. 620). Yet people on all sides of controversial issues agree that many of this nation's most pressing problems—national unity, regionalism, poverty—remain unresolved. In the meantime, new issues have moved to centre stage.

Social movements have always been part of our society, although their focus, tactics, and intensity change with time. There is little doubt, therefore, that social movements will continue to shape our way of life. Indeed, for three reasons, their scope is likely to increase. First, protest should increase as women and other historically excluded cate-

THINKING IT THROUGH
Are You Willing To Take a Stand?

Are you satisfied with our society as it is? Indeed, despite the fact that 92 percent of Canadians claim to be "very happy" or "pretty happy," there are many things that people would change about our way of life. Pessimism about our society is widespread. About 70 percent of Canadians believe that, in financial terms, the lot of the average person is getting worse. Only a quarter of us have "a great deal" or "quite a bit" of confidence, respectively, in our federal and provincial leaders. We feel that the rich, corporations, and politicians have too much power, and that politicians are paid too much. We fear crime. And 85 percent of us believe that the "courts do not deal harshly enough with criminals" (Bibby, 1995).

When asked if people who commit crimes with handguns should face minimum 10-year sentences, 58 percent of Canadians agree. Up to 60 percent of Canadians do not trust politicians; 46 percent worry that they would not be able to meet expenses if they were to become critically ill; and 40 percent feel stressed because life is beyond control and the world is changing too fast (Bricker and Wright, 2005).

But are we willing to take a stand to bring about social change? How many of us are willing to serve on a picket line or barricade, march in protest or in a Gay Pride parade, vote against our preferred party in the House of Commons, or tie ourselves to a tree to stop clear-cutting? Certainly, there are good reasons to avoid political controversy. Any time we challenge the system—whether on campus, at work, or in the larger political arena—we risk making enemies, losing a job, or perhaps even sustaining physical injury. Challenging the status quo, by definition, means stepping on powerful

A rally in Montreal, October 1995, to encourage Quebecers to vote No in the sovereignty referendum.

toes. For Canadians, who, traditionally, have deferred to authority more readily than Americans, such challenges in themselves may seem to question basic values.

While it may be the case that only a small percentage of Canadians are willing to take a stand publicly on specific issues, there have been some highly visible and well-publicized instances of Canadians joining in collective action to address social problems. For example, in October 1995, three days before the referendum on sovereignty in Quebec, an estimated 150 000 Canadians gathered at a massive No rally in Montreal, many who had travelled from elsewhere in Canada, to express their solidarity with the people of Quebec. Despite the fact that airlines and buses offered cut

rates (fare subsidies, in effect), participation required families to disrupt their routines and people to take time off from work or school. Some analysts felt that the outpouring of support from the rest of Canada touched Quebecers and may have helped to bring about the photo finish in favour of the No side. Others pointed out that many Quebecers were outraged by outside interference in their affairs. In any case, Quebec's chief electoral officer declared that the politicians and corporations who organized the rally acted in contravention of Quebec's referendum laws and, therefore, behaved illegally.

Some may argue, in light of cultural values emphasizing the responsibility of individuals for their own well-being, that collective action is no remedy for social ills. Sociology, of course, poses a counterpoint to this cultural individualism. As C. Wright Mills (1959) pointed out decades ago, many of the problems we encounter as individuals are caused by the structure of society. Mills maintained that solutions to many of life's challenges depend on collective effort—that is, on people willing to join together to take a stand for their beliefs.

WHAT DO YOU THINK?

1. Does the reluctance of Canadians to address problems through collective action mean that they are basically satisfied with their lives and their society?

2. Have you ever participated in a political demonstration? What were its goals? What did it accomplish?

3. Identify ways that life today has been affected by people who took a stand in the past. Think about race and ethnic relations, the environment, the status of women, and conditions of employment.

gories of people gain a greater political voice; thus, the twenty-first century should be marked by more social movements here at home. Second, at a global level, anyone with a satellite dish, personal computer, or fax machine can stay abreast of political events, often as they happen. Finally, new technology and the emerging global economy mean that social movements are now uniting people throughout the entire world—or throughout Marshall McLuhan's global village. Since many problems are global in scope, only international co-operation can solve them.

MAKING THE GRADE

The following learning tools will help you see what you know, identify what you still need to learn, and expand your understanding beyond the text. You can also visit this text's Companion Website™ at www.pearsoned.ca/macionis to find useful practice tests.

KEY POINTS

Studying Collective Behaviour

Collective behaviour differs from group behaviour in that it involves limited social interaction within vague social boundaries, usually guided by weak and often unconventional norms.

Localized Collectivities: Crowds

Crowds, an important type of collective behaviour, take various forms: casual crowds, conventional crowds, expressive crowds, acting crowds, and protest crowds. Crowds that become emotionally intense can create violent mobs and riots. Mobs pursue a specific goal; rioting involves unfocused destruction. Crowd behaviour can threaten the status quo, which is why crowds have figured heavily in social change throughout history.

Contagion theory views crowds as anonymous, suggestible, and swayed by rising emotions. Convergence theory states that crowd behaviour reflects the desires people bring to them. Emergent norm theory suggests that crowds develop their own behavioural norms.

Dispersed Collectivities: Mass Behaviour

One form of mass behaviour is rumour, which thrives in a climate of uncertainty. Rumour involves public issues, while gossip deals with personal issues.

Public opinion consists of people's positions on important, controversial issues. Public attitudes change over time and at any point on any given issue, some people hold no opinion at all.

People living in industrial societies use fashion as a source of social prestige. A fad is more unconventional than a fashion; while people may follow a fad with enthusiasm, it usually goes away in a short time.

A panic (in a local area) or mass hysteria (across an entire society) are types of collective behaviour in which people respond to a significant event, real or imagined, with irrational, frantic, and often self-destructive actions.

Disasters are generally unexpected events that cause great harm to many people. Disasters are of three types: natural disasters (flood or earthquake), technological disasters (oil spill or nuclear plant accident), and intentional disasters (terrorist attack or genocide).

Social Movements

Social movements try to promote or discourage change. Sociologists classify social movements according to the range of people they try to involve and the extent of change they try to accomplish.

Social movements engage in claims making to try to convince people that a particular issue should be a matter of public attention.

According to deprivation theory, social movements arise as people feel deprived in relation to some standard of well-being. Mass society theory holds that people join social movements to gain a sense of belonging and moral direction. Structural strain theory states that a social movement develops as the result of six factors and that clearly stated grievances encourage the formation of social movements; undirected anger, by contrast, promotes rioting. Resource mobilization theory ties the success or failure of a social movement to the availability of resources such as money, human labour, and alliances with other organizations. Culture theory notes the importance of symbols as well as material resources to the success of a social movement. The political economy approach claims that social movements arise within capitalist societies that fail to meet the needs of a majority of people. New social movements theory focuses on quality-of-life issues that are usually international in scope.

A typical social movement proceeds through consecutive stages: emergence (defining the public issue), coalescence (entering the public arena), bureaucratization (becoming formally organized), and decline (from failure or, sometimes, success).

Social Movements: Looking Ahead

Social movements have had a major effect on Canadian society, especially since the 1960s. With technology linking people as never before, it is likely that social movements, many of them international in scope, will be more common in the future.

KEY CONCEPTS

social movement (p. 600) organized activity that encourages or discourages social change

collective behaviour (p. 600) activity involving a large number of people that is unplanned, often controversial, and sometimes dangerous.

collectivity (p. 601) a large number of people whose minimal interaction occurs in the absence of well-defined and conventional norms

crowd (p. 601) a temporary gathering of people who share a common focus of attention and who influence one another

mob (p. 602) a highly emotional crowd that pursues a violent or destructive goal

riot (p. 602) a social eruption that is highly emotional, violent, and undirected

mass behaviour (p. 605) collective behaviour among people spread over a wide geographic area

rumour (p. 605) unconfirmed information that people spread informally, often by word of mouth

gossip (p. 605) rumour about people's personal affairs

public opinion (p. 605) widespread attitudes about controversial issues

propaganda (p. 605) information presented with the intention of shaping public opinion

fashion (p. 607) a social pattern favoured by a large number of people

fad (p. 608) an unconventional social pattern that people embrace briefly but enthusiastically

panic (p. 608) a form of collective behaviour in which people in one place react to a threat or other stimulus with irrational, frantic, and often self-destructive behaviour

mass hysteria (moral panic) (p. 608) a form of dispersed collective behaviour in which people react to a real or imagined event with irrational and even frantic fear

disaster (p. 608) an event, generally unexpected, that causes extensive harm to people and damage to property

claims making (p. 612) the process of trying to convince the public and public officials of the importance of joining a social movement to address a particular issue

relative deprivation (p. 612) a perceived disadvantage arising from some specific comparison

APPLICATIONS & EXERCISES

1. With ten friends, try this experiment. One person writes down a detailed "rumour" about someone important and then whispers it to the second person, who whispers it to the third, and so on. The last person to hear the rumour writes it down again. Compare the two written versions of the rumour. Are you surprised by the results of your experiment? Why?

2. With other members of the class, identify recent fad products. What makes people want them? Why do people lose interest in them so quickly?

3. What social movements are represented by organizations on your campus? Invite the leaders of several to describe their groups' goals and strategies to your class.

PRENTICE HALL

mysoclab

Where learning & the sociological imagination intersect.

To reinforce your understanding of this chapter, and to identify topics for further study, visit MySocLab at **www.pearsoned.ca/mysoclab/** for diagnostic tests and a multimedia ebook.

Social Change:
Traditional, Modern, and
Postmodern Societies

Why do societies change?

How does modern society shape people's lives?

What do sociologists say is good and
bad about today's society?

Firelight flickers in the gathering darkness as Kanhonk sits, as he has does at the end of the day, ready to begin an evening of animated talk and story telling. Kanhonk is chief of the Kaiapo, about 7000 people indigenous to the Xingu River area of Brazil's Amazon rainforest. This is the hour when Kaiapo celebrate their heritage: because Kaiapo are a traditional people with no written language, the elders rely on evenings by the fire to teach their culture and instruct the grandchildren. In the past, evenings like this were filled with tales of brave Kaiapo warriors fighting off their neighbours or Portuguese traders in pursuit of slaves and gold.

As the minutes pass, only a few older villagers assemble for the evening ritual. "It is the Big Ghost," one man grumbles, to explain the poor turnout. The Big Ghost has indeed descended on them, its bluish glow spilling from windows of homes throughout the village. The Kaiapo children—and many adults as well—are watching television. Installing a satellite dish in the village several years ago has had greater consequences than anyone imagined. In the end, what their enemies failed to do with weapons, the Kaiapo may well do to themselves with prime time programming.

Kaiapo are among 230 000 Indigenous peoples who inhabit Brazil. They stand out because of their striking body paint and ornate ceremonial dress. Recently, they have become rich from gold mining and the harvesting of mahogany trees. Now they must decide if their newfound fortune is a blessing or a curse. To some, affluence means the opportunity to learn about the outside world through travel and television. Others, like Chief Kanhonk, are not so sure.

Sitting by the fire, he thinks aloud, "I have been saying that people must buy useful things like knives and fishing hooks. Television does not fill the stomach. It only shows our children and grandchildren White people's things." The oldest priest, Bebtopup, nods in agreement: "The night is the time the old people teach the young people. Television has stolen the night" (Simons, 2007).

The story about television in Kaiapo society raises profound questions about the causes and consequences of change. Kaiapo villagers may be edging towards modernity, but does a higher standard of living necessarily improve their way of life? The drama that is changing Kaiapo life is being played out around the globe as more and more traditional cultures are being transformed by the materialism and affluence of rich societies.

 Learn more about Kayapó, and other Indigenous peoples, at www.socioambiental.org/pib/epienglish/kayapo/kayapo.shtm.

Within Canada, people are grappling with similar issues—and the influence of television in particular. In Nunavut, Inuit were concerned about the damaging effects of television programming that originates in the United States and southern Canada. With financial assistance from the federal government, they created the Inuit Broadcasting Corporation (**www.inuitbroadcasting.ca**), which produces news, documentaries, children's programs (including cartoons and puppet shows), and talk shows that deal with issues of relevance to Inuit—in their own language,

Inuktitut. Unlike the Kaiapo, through their own broadcasting, Inuit have been able to mitigate some of the intrusive and damaging impacts of television on their culture. More recently, all Canadians have had access to the Aboriginal Peoples Television Network (**www.aptn.ca**) by cable and satellite. In January 2001, the network increased its international content from 10 to 30 percent to include more programming about Indigenous peoples around the world.

This chapter examines social change as a process with both positive and negative consequences. Of particular interest to us are *modernity*, changes brought about by the Industrial Revolution, and *postmodernity*, recent transformations sparked by the Information Revolution and the post-industrial economy. Whatever the consequences, one thing is clear—the rate of change has never been faster than it is today.

What Is Social Change?

In earlier chapters, we examined relatively fixed or *static* social patterns, including status and role, social stratification, and social institutions. We also looked at the *dynamic* forces that have shaped our way of life, ranging from innovations in technology to the growth of bureaucracy and the expansion of cities. These are all dimensions of **social change,** *the transformation of culture and social institutions over time.* The process of social change has four major characteristics:

1. **Social change happens all the time**. "Nothing is constant except death and taxes" goes the old saying. Yet even our experience with death has changed dramatically as life expectancy doubled over the course of a century. In 1900, people paid little or no taxes on their earnings; over the course of the twentieth century, taxes increased dramatically, along with the size and scope of government. In short, just about everything is subject to the twists and turns of change. Still, some societies change faster than others. As Chapter 4 ("Society") explained, hunter/gatherer societies change quite slowly; by contrast, members of today's high-income societies experience significant change within a single lifetime.

YOUR TURN

What are the three most important changes that have occurred during your lifetime? Explain your answer.

It is also true that, in a given society, some cultural elements change faster than others. William Ogburn's (1964) theory of *cultural lag* (see Chapter 3, "Culture")

states that material culture usually changes faster than nonmaterial culture; that is, things change faster than ideas and attitudes. For example, the genetic technology that allows scientists to alter and perhaps even to create life has developed more rapidly than our ethical standards for deciding when and how to use it.

2. **Social change is sometimes intentional but often unplanned**. Industrial societies actively promote many kinds of change. For example, scientists seek more efficient forms of energy, and advertisers try to convince us that life is incomplete without this or that new gadget. Yet rarely can anyone envision all the consequences of the changes that are set in motion. In 1900, when people relied on horses for transportation, many people looked ahead to motorized vehicles that would carry them in a single day distances that took them weeks or months. But no one could see how much the mobility provided by automobiles would alter people's lives, scattering family members, threatening the environment, and reshaping cities and suburbs. Nor could automotive pioneers have predicted that more than 42 000 people would die each year as a result of car accidents in North America.

3. **Social change is controversial**. The history of the automobile shows that social change brings both good and bad consequences. Capitalists welcomed the Industrial Revolution because new technology increased productivity and swelled profits. However, workers feared that machines would make their skills obsolete and resisted the push towards "progress." Today, as in the past, changing patterns of social interaction between Black people and White people, women and men, and homosexuals and heterosexuals are welcomed by some people and opposed by others.

4. **Some changes matter more than others**. Some changes (such as clothing fads) have only passing significance; others (such as the invention of computers) may change the entire world. Will the Information Revolution turn out to be as important as the Industrial Revolution? Like the automobile and television, the computer has both positive and negative effects, providing new kinds of jobs while eliminating old ones, isolating people in offices while linking people in global electronic networks, offering vast amounts of information while threatening personal privacy.

Causes of Social Change

Social change has many causes. In a world linked by sophisticated communication and transportation technology, change in one place often sets off change elsewhere.

CULTURE AND CHANGE

Chapter 3 ("Culture") identified three important sources of cultural change. First, *invention* produces new objects,

These young boys are performing in a break-dance competition in Chengdu, China, in 2005. Hip-hop music, dress style, and dancing have become popular in China, a clear case of cultural diffusion. Cultural patterns move from place to place, but not always with the same meaning. How might Chinese youth understand hip-hop and break dancing differently from the young African Americans who originated it?

ideas, and social patterns. Rocket propulsion research, which began in the 1940s, has produced spacecraft that reach towards the stars. Today we take such technology for granted; during this century, a significant number of people may well travel in space.

Second, *discovery* occurs when people take note of existing elements of the world. Medical advances, for example, offer a growing understanding of the human body. Beyond the direct effects on human health, medical discoveries have stretched life expectancy, setting in motion the "greying" of society (see Chapter 15, "Aging and the Elderly").

Third, *diffusion* creates change as products, people, and information spread from one society to another. Ralph Linton (1937b) recognized that many familiar elements of our culture came from other lands. Cloth used to make our clothing, for example, was developed in Asia, the mechanical clocks we see all around us were invented in mediaeval Europe, and the coins we carry in our pockets were first used in Turkey.

In general, material things diffuse more easily than cultural ideas. That is, new breakthroughs, such as the science of cloning, occur faster than our understanding of when—and even whether—they are morally desirable.

CONFLICT AND CHANGE

Tension and conflict in a society also produce change. Karl Marx saw class conflict as the engine that drives societies

from one historical era to another (see Chapter 4, "Society," and Chapter 10, "Social Stratification"). In industrial-capitalist societies, he maintained, the struggle between capitalists and workers pushes society towards a socialist system of production. In the hundred or more years since Marx's death, this model has proved simplistic. Yet Marx correctly foresaw that social conflict arising from inequality—involving not just class but also race and gender—would force changes in every society, including our own, to improve the lives of working people.

IDEAS AND CHANGE

Max Weber also contributed to our understanding of social change. Although Weber agreed that conflict could bring about change, he traced the roots of most social change to ideas. For example, people with charisma, such as Martin Luther King, Jr., can carry a message that sometimes changes the world.

Weber also highlighted the importance of ideas by showing how the religious beliefs of early Protestants set the stage for the spread of industrial capitalism (see Chapter 4, "Society"). The fact that industrial capitalism developed primarily in areas of Western Europe where the Protestant work ethic was strong proved to Weber (1958; orig. 1904–05) the power of ideas to bring about change.

Ideas also direct social movements. Chapter 23 ("Collective Behaviour and Social Movements") explained how change occurs when people join together in the pursuit of a common goal, such as cleaning up the environment or improving the lives of oppressed people.

DEMOGRAPHIC CHANGE

Population growth places escalating demands on the natural environment, while altering cultural patterns. While Canada enjoys a bounty of physical space, urbanization and industrialization have changed our way of life and will continue to do so. More than three-quarters of Canadians live in cities, which cover only a small percentage of the land surface.

Profound change is also taking place as our population, collectively speaking, grows older. As Chapter 15 ("Aging and the Elderly") explains, in 2001, more than 13 percent of Canadians were over 65—more than double the proportion of the population in 1901. Statistics Canada estimates that, by the year 2031, seniors will account for almost *one-quarter* of the population. Medical research and health care services will increasingly focus on elderly people, and life will change in countless additional ways as homes and household products are redesigned to meet the needs of older consumers.

Migration within and among societies is another demographic factor that promotes change. Since the early 1800s, millions of immigrants have come to Canada, initially to fish or participate in the fur trade or to establish farming homesteads—more recently, to seek a better life in the growing urban areas. Immigrants to Canada's urban centres were joined by a steady flow of migrants from rural Canada, where high fertility and changes in the structure of agriculture resulted in surplus population. As a result of immigration and rural/urban migration, Canada's urban population grew from 18 percent of the total population in 1871 to 80 percent by 2001. In just 130 years, Canada was transformed from a nation of settlers to an urban-industrial society with one of the world's largest economies.

Modernity

A central concept in the study of social change is **modernity**, *social patterns resulting from industrialization.* In everyday usage, *modernity* (its Latin root means "lately") refers to the present in relation to the past. Sociologists include in this catchall concept all of the social patterns set in motion by the Industrial Revolution, which began in Western Europe in the 1750s. **Modernization**, then, is *the process of social change begun by industrialization.* The time- line inside the front cover of the text highlights important events that mark the emergence of modernity.

Peter Berger (1977), in his influential study of social change, identified four major characteristics of modernization:

- *The decline of small, traditional communities.* Modernity involves "the progressive weakening, if not destruction, of the... relatively cohesive communities in which human beings have found solidarity and meaning throughout most of history" (Berger, 1977:72). For thousands of years, in the camps of hunter/gatherers and in the rural villages of Europe and North America, people lived in small communities where social life revolved around family and neighbourhood. Such traditional worlds gave each person a well-defined place that, although limiting range of choice, offered a strong sense of identity, belonging, and purpose.

Canada has a land mass of close to 10 million square kilometres—second in size to Russia—with a population density of only 2.8 persons per square kilometre. Since about 80 percent of our population lives within 160 kilo- metres of the U.S. border, there is a great deal of space through which to scatter other communities. Small, iso- lated communities—many with fewer than a hundred members, and many of them Aboriginal—still exist in Canada, but they are now home to only a small percent- age of the overall Canadian population. Even so, cars, telephones, television, and the internet give most remote rural families the pulse of the larger society and connect them to the entire world.

- *The expansion of personal choice.* Members of traditional, pre-industrial societies view their lives as shaped by forces beyond human control—gods, spirits, or simply fate. As the power of tradition weakens, people come to see their lives as an unending series of options, a process Berger calls *individualization.* Canadians, for example,

may choose a lifestyle—or even adopt one after another, showing an openness to change. Indeed, a common belief in our modern culture is that people *should* take control of their lives.

- *Increasing social diversity.* In pre-industrial societies, strong family ties and powerful religious beliefs enforce conformity and discourage diversity and change. Modernization promotes a more rational, scientific world view as tradition loses its hold and people gain more and more individual choice. The growth of cities, the expansion of impersonal bureaucracy, and the social mix of people from various backgrounds combine to foster diversity of belief and behaviour.

- *Orientation towards the future and a growing awareness of time.* Premodern people focus on the past, but people in modern societies think more about the future. Modern people are not only forward-looking but optimistic that new inventions and discoveries will improve their lives. Modern people also organize their daily routines down to the very minute. With the introduction of mechanical clocks in the late Middle Ages, Europeans began to think not in terms of sunlight and seasons but in terms of days, hours, and minutes. Preoccupied with personal gain, modern people demand precise measurement of time and are likely to agree that "time is money." Berger points out that one good indicator of a society's degree of modern- ization is the extent to which people wear wristwatches.

Finally, recall that modernization touched off the development of sociology itself. As Chapter 1 ("The Sociological Perspective") explained, the discipline origi nated in the wake of the Industrial Revolution in Western Europe, where social change was proceeding most rapidly. Early European and U.S. sociologists tried to analyze the rise of modern society and its consequences, good and bad, for human beings.

FERDINAND TÖNNIES: THE LOSS OF COMMUNITY

The German sociologist Ferdinand Tönnies (1855–1937) produced a lasting account of modernization in his theory of *Gemeinschaft* and *Gesellschaft* (see Chapter 22, "Population, Urbanization, and Environment"). Like Peter Berger, whose work he influenced, Tönnies (1963; orig. 1887) viewed modernization as the progressive loss of *Gemeinschaft,* or human community. As Tönnies saw it, the Industrial Revolution weakened the social fabric of family and tradition by introduc- ing a businesslike emphasis on facts, efficiency, and money. European and North American societies gradually became rootless and impersonal as people came to associate mostly on the basis of self-interest—the state Tönnies termed *Gesellschaft.*

For a short biography of Tönnies, visit the Gallery of Sociologists at www. TheSociologyPage.com.

Early in the twentieth century, much of Canada approxi- mated Tönnies' concept of *Gemeinschaft.* For generations,

In response to the accelerating pace of change in the nineteenth century, Paul Gauguin left his native France for the South Seas where he was captivated by a simpler and seemingly timeless way of life. He romanticized this environment in his painting, *Nave Nave Moe (Sacred Spring)*.

Paul Gauguin, French (1848–1903), *Nave Nave Moe (Sacred Spring)*, 1894. Hermitage, St. Petersburg, Russia. Oil on canvas, 73 × 98 cm. © The Bridgeman Art Library International Ltd.

families lived in small villages and towns, bound together in a hard working, slow moving way of life. Telephones (invented in 1876) were rare; it wasn't until 1915 that someone placed the first coast-to-coast call. Living without television—not widespread until after 1950, families entertained themselves, often gathering with friends in the evening to share stories, sorrows, or song. Without rapid transportation—Henry Ford's assembly line began in 1908, but cars became commonplace only after World War II, many people viewed their own home town as their entire world. Inevitable tensions and conflicts divided these communities of the past. But, according to Tönnies, because of the traditional spirit of *Gemeinschaft*, people were "essentially united in spite of all separating factors" (1963 [1887]:65).

Modernity turns societies inside out so that, as Tönnies put it, people are "essentially separated in spite of uniting factors" (1963 [1887]:65). This is the world of *Gesellschaft*, where, especially in large cities, most people live among strangers and ignore the people they pass on the street. Trust is hard to come by in a mobile and anonymous society where people tend to put their personal needs ahead of group loyalty and, increasingly, adults believe "you can't be too careful" in dealing with others. No wonder researchers conclude that, even as we become more affluent, the social health of modern societies has declined (Myers, 2000).

Our high level of geographic mobility is one important cause of a sense of rootlessness. Over one year, about 1 in 6 individuals changes his or her place of residence. Close to half of all Canadians move over a five-year interval; 7 percent of the population moves from outside the province/territory or the country, while 23 percent moves within the same municipality. Table 24–1 shows that people between the ages of 15 and 29 are the most mobile, with

56.0 percent having moved within the last five years. The relatively high level of mobility in the youngest age category in the table (5- to 14-year-olds) probably results from the search for more suitable accommodation by the 30- to 44-year-old parents of these children. In Canada's General Social Survey (1985), the most frequently stated reasons for moving were to purchase or build a home, to live in a larger home, to live in a better neighbourhood, to live near work, and to establish an independent household. Each of these top-ranked reasons is consistent with movement among 30- to 44-year-olds, who are leaving the homes of their parents, getting married, having children, and moving to larger homes to accommodate their children.

Critical Review Tönnies' theory of *Gemeinschaft* and *Gesellschaft* is the most widely cited model of modernization. The theory's strength lies in combining various dimensions of change: growing population, the rise of cities, and increasing impersonality in social interaction. But modern life, though often impersonal, still has some degree of *Gemeinschaft*. Even in a world of strangers, modern friendships can be strong and lasting. Some analysts also think that Tönnies favoured—perhaps even romanticized—traditional societies while overlooking bonds of family, neighbourhood, and friendship that continue to flourish in modern societies.

EMILE DURKHEIM: THE DIVISION OF LABOUR

The French sociologist Emile Durkheim (whose work is discussed in Chapter 4, "Society"), shared Tönnies' interest in the profound social changes that resulted from the Industrial Revolution. For Durkheim (1964; orig. 1893),

SOCIOLOGY @ WORK   modernization is defined by an increasing *division of labour*, or specialized economic activity. Every member of a traditional society performs more or less the same daily round of activities; modern societies function by having people perform highly specific roles.

Durkheim explained that pre-industrial societies are held together by *mechanical solidarity*, or shared moral sentiments; in other words, members of pre-industrial societies view everyone as basically alike, doing the same kind of work and belonging together. Durkheim's concept of mechanical solidarity is virtually the same as Tönnies' *Gemeinschaft*. With modernization, the division of labour becomes more and more pronounced. To Durkheim, this change means less mechanical solidarity but more of another kind of tie: *organic solidarity*, or mutual dependency between people engaged in specialized work. Put simply, modern societies are held together not by likeness but by difference: all of us must depend on others to meet most of our needs. Organic solidarity corresponds to Tönnies' concept of *Gesellschaft*.

Despite obvious similarities in their thinking, Durkheim and Tönnies viewed modernity somewhat differently. To Tönnies, modern *Gesellschaft* amounts to the loss of social solidarity, because modern people lose the "natural" and "organic" bonds of the rural village, leaving only the "artificial" and "mechanical" ties of the big industrial city. Durkheim had a different view of modernity, even reversing Tönnies' language to bring home the point. Durkheim labelled modern society "organic," arguing that modern society is no less natural than any other, and he described traditional societies as "mechanical" because they are so regimented. Durkheim viewed modernization not as the *loss* of community but as a change from community based on bonds of likeness (kinship and neighbourhood) to community based on economic interdependence (the division of labour). Durkheim's view of modernity is thus both more complex and more positive than Tönnies' view.

Critical Review Durkheim's work, which resembles that of Tönnies, is a highly influential analysis of modernity. Of the two, Durkheim was more optimistic; still, he feared that modern societies might become so diverse that they would collapse into *anomie*, a condition in which norms and values are so weak and inconsistent that society provides little moral guidance to individuals. Living with weak moral norms, modern people can become egocentric, placing their own needs above those of others and finding little purpose in life.

Evidence supports Durkheim's contention that anomie plagues modern societies. Suicide rates, which Durkheim considered a prime index of anomie, have risen over the past century in both Canada and the United States; in Canada, the rates have doubled. Suicide rates are especially high in Aboriginal communities, which are still experiencing rapid social change.

TABLE 24-1

Canadian Mobility by Age Group (Percentage Changing Residence over a Five-Year Period)

Age Group	1996–2001
5–14 years	45.1
15–29 years	56.0
30–44 years	54.2
45–64 years	29.2
65 years and over	19.4
Total	43.3

Source: Calculations by L.M. Gerber from Statistics Canada, 2001 Census Tables, www.statcan.ca.

Even though modernization is associated with numerous indicators of stress or distress, shared norms and values are still strong enough to give the majority of people a sense of meaning and purpose. Whatever the hazards of anomie, most people seem to value the personal freedom modern society gives us.

MAX WEBER: RATIONALIZATION

For Max Weber (also discussed in Chapter 4, "Society"), modernity meant replacing a traditional world view with a rational way of thinking. In pre-industrial societies, Weber explained, tradition acts as a constant brake on change: to traditional people, "truth" is roughly the same as "what has always been" (1978 [1921]:36). To modern people, however, "truth" is the result of rational calculation. Because they value efficiency and have little reverence for the past, modern people adopt whatever social patterns allow them to achieve their goals.

Echoing Tönnies and Durkheim, who held that industrialization weakens tradition, Weber declared modern society to be "disenchanted." The unquestioned truths of an earlier time had been challenged by rational thinking. In short, modern society turns away from the gods. Throughout his life, Weber studied various modern "types"—the capitalist, the scientist, the bureaucrat—all of whom share the detached world view that Weber believed was coming to dominate humanity.

Critical Review Compared with Tönnies and especially Durkheim, Weber was critical of modern society. He knew that science could produce technological and organizational wonders but worried that science was turning us away from more basic questions about the meaning and purpose of human existence. Weber feared that rationalization, especially in bureaucracies, would erode the human spirit with endless rules and regulations. Some of Weber's critics think that the alienation he attributed to bureaucracy actually stemmed from social inequality. That criticism leads us to the ideas of Karl Marx.

George Tooker's 1950 painting *The Subway* depicts a common problem of modern life: weakening social ties and eroding traditions create a generic humanity in which everyone is alike yet each person is an anxious stranger in the midst of others.

George Tooker, *The Subway,* 1950, egg tempera on gesso panel, 18⅛ × 36⅛ inches, Whitney Museum of American Art, New York. Purchased with funds from the Juliana Force Purchase Award, 50.23. Photograph © 2000 Whitney Museum of American Art.

YOUR TURN

Looking at Weber's three "modern types" shown in the drawing on the next page, state in your own words what they have in common. What social traits would you expect all of them to lack?

KARL MARX: CAPITALISM

For Karl Marx, modern society was synonymous with capitalism; he saw the Industrial Revolution as primarily a *capitalist revolution.* Marx traced the emergence of the bourgeoisie in mediaeval Europe to the expansion of commerce. The bourgeoisie gradually displaced the feudal aristocracy as the Industrial Revolution gave it a powerful new productive system. Marx agreed that modernity weakened small communities (as described by Tönnies), sharpened the division of labour (as noted by Durkheim), and fostered a rational world view (as Weber claimed). But he saw all these simply as conditions necessary for capitalism to flourish. Capitalism, according to Marx, draws population from farms and small towns into an ever-expanding market system centred in cities; specialization is needed for efficient factories; and rationality is exemplified by the capitalists' endless pursuit of profit.

For more on Durkheim, Weber, and Marx, visit the Gallery of Sociologists at www. TheSociologyPage.com.

Earlier chapters have painted Marx as a spirited critic of capitalist society, but his vision of modernity also includes a good bit of optimism. Unlike Weber, who viewed modern society as an "iron cage" of bureaucracy, Marx believed that social conflict in capitalist societies would sow seeds of revolutionary change, leading to an egalitarian socialism. Such a society, as he saw it, would harness the wonders of industrial technology to enrich people's lives and also rid the world of social classes, the source of social conflict and so much suffering. Although Marx was an outspoken critic of modern society, he nevertheless imagined a future of human freedom, creativity, and community.

Critical Review Marx's theory of modernization is a complex theory of capitalism. But he underestimated the dominance of bureaucracy in modern societies. In socialist societies in particular, the stifling effects of bureaucracy turned out to be as bad as, or even worse than, the dehumanizing aspects of capitalism. The upheavals in Eastern Europe and the former Soviet Union in the late 1980s and early 1990s reveal the depth of popular opposition to oppressive state bureaucracies.

YOUR TURN

Of the four theorists just discussed—Tönnies, Durkheim, Weber, and Marx—who was the most optimistic about modern society? Who was the most pessimistic? Explain your responses.

Theoretical Analysis of Modernity

The rise of modernity is a complex process involving many dimensions of change, as described in previous chapters and summarized in the first Summing Up table (on p. 634). How can we make sense of so many changes going on all at once? Sociologists have developed two broad explanations of modern society, one guided by the structural-functional approach and one based on social-conflict theory.

Max Weber maintained that the distinctive character of modern society was its rational world view. Virtually all of Weber's work on modernity centred on types of people he considered typical of their age: the scientist, the capitalist, and the bureaucrat. Each is rational to the core: the scientist is committed to the orderly discovery of truth, the capitalist to the orderly pursuit of profit, and the bureaucrat to orderly conformity to a system of rules.

STRUCTURAL-FUNCTIONAL THEORY: MODERNITY AS MASS SOCIETY

One broad approach—drawing on the ideas of Ferdinand Tonnies, Emile Durkheim, and Max Weber—understands modernization as the emergence of *mass society* (Kornhauser, 1959; Nisbet, 1966, 1969; Berger, *et al.*, 1974; Pearson, 1993). A **mass society** is *a society in which prosperity and bureaucracy have weakened traditional social ties.* A mass society is highly productive; on average, people have more income than ever. At the same time, it is marked by weak kinship and impersonal neighbourhoods, so individuals often feel socially isolated. Although many people have material plenty, they are spiritually weak and often experience moral uncertainty about how to live.

The Mass Scale of Modern Life

Mass society theory argues, first, that the scale of modern life has greatly increased. Before the Industrial Revolution, Europe and North America formed a mosaic of countless rural villages and small towns. In these small communities, which inspired Tönnies' concept of *Gemeinschaft*, people lived out their lives surrounded by kin and guided by a shared heritage. Gossip was an informal yet highly effective way to ensure conformity to community standards. These small communities, with their strong moral values and their low tolerance of social diversity, exemplified the state of mechanical solidarity described by Durkheim. For example, before 1690, English law demanded that everyone participate regularly in the Christian ritual of Holy Communion (Laslett, 1984); later, among the New England colonies, only Rhode Island tolerated religious dissent. In general, because

social differences were repressed in favour of conformity to established norms, subcultures and countercultures were few, and change proceeded slowly.

Increasing population, the growth of cities, and specialized economic activity driven by the Industrial Revolution gradually altered this pattern. People came to know one another by their jobs (e.g., as "the doctor" or "the bank clerk") rather than by their kinship group or hometown. People looked on most others simply as strangers. The face-to-face communication of the village was eventually replaced by the impersonal mass media: newspapers, radio, television, and computer networks. Large organizations steadily assumed more and more responsibility for seeing to the daily tasks that had once been carried out by family, friends, and neighbours; public education drew more and more people to schools; police, lawyers, and courts supervised a formal justice system. Even charity became the work of faceless bureaucrats working for various social welfare agencies.

Geographic mobility and exposure to diverse ways of life all weaken traditional values. People become more tolerant of social diversity, defending individual rights and freedom of choice. Treating people differently because of race, sex, or religion is defined as backwards and unjust. In the process, minorities at the margins of society gradually gain greater power and broader participation in public life.

The mass media give rise to a national culture that may wash over traditional differences that set off one region from another, as one analyst put it: "Even in Baton Rouge, La., the local kids don't say 'y'all' any more; they say 'you guys,' just like on TV" (Gibbs, 2000:42). In this way, mass society theorists fear, transforming people of various backgrounds into a generic mass may end up dehumanizing everyone.

SUMMING UP

Traditional and Modern Societies: The Big Picture

Elements of Society	Traditional Societies	Modern Societies
Cultural Patterns		
Values	Homogeneous; sacred character; few subcultures and countercultures	Heterogeneous; secular character; many subcultures and countercultures
Norms	Great moral significance; little tolerance of diversity	Variable moral significance; high tolerance of diversity
Time orientation	Present linked to past	Present linked to future
Technology	Pre-industrial; human and animal energy	Industrial; advanced energy sources
Social Structure		
Status and role	Few statuses, most ascribed; few specialized roles	Many statuses, some ascribed and some achieved; many specialized roles
Relationships	Typically primary; little anonymity or privacy	Typically secondary; much anonymity and privacy
Communication	Face to face	Face-to-face communication supplemented by mass media
Social control	Informal gossip	Formal police and legal system
Social stratification	Rigid patterns of social inequality; little mobility	Fluid patterns of social inequality; high mobility
Gender patterns	Pronounced patriarchy; women's lives centred on the home	Declining patriarchy; increasing number of women in the paid labour force
Settlement patterns	Small scale; population typically small and widely dispersed in rural villages and small towns	Large scale; population typically large and concentrated in cities
Social Institutions		
Economy	Based on agriculture; much manufacturing in the home; little white-collar work	Based on industrial mass production; factories become centres of production; increasing white-collar work
State	Small-scale government; little state intervention in society	Large-scale government; much state intervention in society
Family	Extended family as the primary means of socialization and economic production	Nuclear family retains some socialization functions but is more a unit of consumption than of production
Religion	Religion guides world view; little religious pluralism	Religion weakens with the rise of science; extensive religious pluralism
Education	Formal schooling limited to elites	Basic schooling becomes universal, with growing proportion receiving advanced education
Health	High birth and death rates; short life expectancy because of low standard of living and simple medical technology	Low birth and death rates; longer life expectancy because of higher standard of living and sophisticated medical technology
Social Change	Slow; change evident over many generations	Rapid; change evident within a single generation

YOUR TURN

Can you give five examples of "mass culture" that are the same throughout Canada? What elements of culture tend to be distinctive from region to region?

The Ever-Expanding State

In the small-scale pre-industrial societies of Europe, government amounted to little more than a local noble. A royal family formally reigned over an entire nation but, without efficient transportation or communication, even absolute monarchs had far less power than today's political leaders. Technological innovation allowed government to expand, and the centralized state grew in size and importance. At the time of confederation in 1867, federal and provincial governments had limited functions. Since then, government in Canada has entered more and more areas of social life—establishing publicly owned enterprises in the areas of transportation, communication, and natural resources; regulating wages and working conditions; establishing standards for products of all kinds; educating the population; delivering medical care; protecting the environment; and providing financial assistance to ill, disabled, aged, and unemployed Canadians. To pay for such programs, taxes have soared, so that today's average worker labours for six months a year just to pay for the broad array of services the government provides.

In a mass society, power resides in large bureaucracies, leaving people in local communities little control over their lives. For example, government officials mandate that local schools must have a standardized educational program, local products must be government-certified, and every citizen must maintain extensive tax records. While such regulations may protect people and advance social equality, they also force us to deal more and more with nameless officials in distant and often unresponsive bureaucracies, and they undermine the autonomy of families and local communities.

Critical Review The growing scale of modern life certainly has positive aspects, but at the price of losing some of our cultural heritage. Modern societies increase individual rights, tolerate greater social differences, and raise standards of living (Inglehart and Baker, 2000). But they are prone to what Weber feared most—excessive bureaucracy—as well as Tönnies' self-centredness and Durkheim's anomie. Modern society's size, complexity, and tolerance of diversity all but doom traditional values and family patterns, leaving individuals isolated, powerless, and materialistic. As Chapter 17 ("Politics and Government") noted, voter apathy is a serious problem in the United States and more recently in Canada despite the differences in our political systems. But should we be surprised that individuals in vast, impersonal societies think no one person can make much of a difference?

Critics sometimes say that mass society theory romanticizes the past. They remind us that many people in small towns were actually eager to set out for a higher standard of living in cities. Moreover, mass society theory ignores problems of social inequality. Critics say this theory attracts conservatives who defend conventional morality and overlook the historical inequality of women and other minorities.

SOCIAL-CONFLICT THEORY: MODERNITY AS CLASS SOCIETY

The second interpretation of modernity derives largely from the ideas of Karl Marx. From a social-conflict perspec-

tive, modernity takes the form of a **class society**, *a capitalist society with pronounced social stratification*. That is, although agreeing that modern societies have expanded to a mass scale, this approach views the heart of modernization as an expanding capitalist economy, marked by inequality (Habermas, 1970; Polenberg, 1980; Blumberg, 1981; Harrington, 1984; Buechler, 2000).

Capitalism

Class society theory follows Marx in claiming that the increasing scale of social life in modern society results from the growth and greed unleashed by capitalism. Because a capitalist economy pursues ever-greater profits, both production and consumption steadily increase. According to Marx, capitalism rests on "naked self-interest" (Marx and Engels, 1972 [1848]:337). This self-centredness weakens the social ties that once united small communities. Capitalism also treats people as commodities: a source of labour and a market for capitalist products.

Capitalism supports science, not just as the key to greater productivity but as an ideology that justifies the status quo. That is, modern societies encourage people to view human well-being as a technical puzzle to be solved by engineers and other experts rather than through the pursuit of social justice. For example, a capitalist culture seeks to improve health through scientific medicine rather than by eliminating poverty, which is a core cause of poor health.

Business also raises the banner of scientific logic, trying to increase profits through greater efficiency. As Chapter 16 ("The Economy and Work") explains, today's capitalist corporations have reached enormous size and control unimaginable wealth as a result of "going global" as multinationals. From the class society point of view, the expanding scale of life is less a function of *Gesellschaft* than the inevitable and destructive consequence of capitalism.

Persistent Inequality

Modernity has gradually eroded the rigid categories that set nobles apart from commoners in pre-industrial societies. But class society theory maintains that elites persist—albeit now as capitalist millionaires rather than as nobles born to wealth and power. Canada has more billionaire families per capita than the United States: in the early 1980s Canada had six, while the United States, with an economy twelve times larger, had only double that number (Francis, 1986). Furthermore, the distribution of family income is skewed in Canada: from 1951 to 2001, with minor fluctuations, families in the top 20 percent earned about 40 percent of all income while the lowest fifth earned just over 6 percent of all income. When measured in terms of individual income, the pattern is accentuated, with the top quintile earning 46.5 percent of income and the lowest quintile earning 3.4 percent (Statistics Canada, catalogue no. 13-207-XPB).

What of the state? Mass society theorists contend that the state works to increase equality and combat social prob-

Social-conflict theory sees modernity not as a mass society but as a class society in which some categories of people are second-class citizens. This six-year-old boy waits for his mother to finish cooking a simple dinner outside their trailer on the Navajo Reservation near Window Rock, Arizona. The family lives without electricity or running water—a situation shared by thousands of other Dinee (Navajo) families. In both the United States and Canada, Aboriginal peoples are among the last to experience the benefits of modernity.

lems. Marx was skeptical that the state could accomplish more than minor reforms because, as he saw it, the real power lies in the hands of capitalists who control the economy. Other class society theorists add that, to the extent that working people and visible minorities enjoy greater political rights and a higher standard of living today, these changes are the fruits of political struggle, not expressions of government goodwill. Therefore, they conclude, despite our pretensions of democracy, power still rests primarily in the hands of those with wealth and influence.

Critical Review Class society theory dismisses Durkheim's argument that people in modern societies suffer from anomie, claiming instead that they suffer from alienation and powerlessness. Not surprisingly, then, the class society interpretation of modernity enjoys widespread support among liberals and radicals who favour greater equality and call for extensive regulation or the abolition of the capitalist marketplace.

A basic criticism of class society theory is that it overlooks the increasing prosperity of modern societies and the fact that discrimination based on race, ethnicity, and gender is now illegal and is widely viewed as a social problem. In addition, most people in North America—especially in the United States—are not committed to an egalitarian society, preferring a system of unequal rewards that reflects personal differences in talent and effort. Based on the failure of socialism in such countries as the Soviet Union, Eastern Europe, and China to generate a high standard of living, few observers think that a centralized economy would cure the ills of modernity. Many of the problems in predominantly capitalist societies—from unemployment, hunger, and industrial pollution to unresponsive government—are also found in socialist nations.

The second Summing Up table (on p. 637) contrasts these two interpretations of modernity. Mass society theory focuses on the increasing scale of life and the growth of government; class society theory stresses the expansion of capitalism and the persistence of inequality.

MODERNITY AND THE INDIVIDUAL

Both mass society and class society theories look at the broad societal changes that have taken place since the Industrial Revolution. But from these macro-level approaches we can also draw micro-level insights into how modernity shapes individual lives.

Mass Society: Problems of Identity

Modernity liberated individuals from the small, tightly knit communities of the past. Most people in modern societies, therefore, have privacy and freedom to express their individuality. Mass society theory suggests, however, that extensive social diversity, isolation, and rapid social change make it difficult for many people to establish any coherent identity at all (Wheelis, 1958; Riesman, 1970; orig. 1950; Berger, *et* al., 1974). Canadians have had considerable difficulty articulating a national identity—and, indirectly, personal identities—to the point where Lipset (1991:42) states that national identity "is the quintessential Canadian issue." Proximity to the United States, regional tensions, ethnic and cultural diversity, bilingualism, and rapid social change make clear self-definition more difficult for Canadians (Taras, *et al.*, 1993; Hiller, 2006).

Chapter 5 ("Socialization") explained that a person's personality is largely a product of one's social experiences. The small, homogeneous, and slowly changing societies of the past provided a firm if narrow foundation for building a meaningful identity. For example, the Hutterite communi-

SUMMING UP

Two Interpretations of Modernity

	Mass Society	Class Society
Process of modernization	Industrialization; growth of bureaucracy	Rise of capitalism
Effects of modernization	Increasing scale of life; rise of the state and other formal organizations	Expansion of the capitalist economy; persistence of social inequality

ties that still flourish in Canada's Prairie provinces, especially in Alberta, teach young men and women "correct" ways to think and behave—and most learn to embrace this life as "natural" and right. Everything is shared—property, work, meals—in these tiny communal societies that have perpetuated the Hutterite way of life, largely unchanged for more than 400 years. Under these circumstances, which contrast sharply with those of modern mass society, it is relatively easy to establish a coherent and secure sense of personal identity.

Mass societies, with their characteristic diversity and rapid change, provide only shifting sands on which to build a personal identity. Left to make their own life decisions, many people—especially those with greater affluence—confront a bewildering range of options. Autonomy has little value without standards for making choices; in a tolerant mass society, people may find one path no more compelling than the next. Not surprisingly, many people shuttle from one identity to another, changing their lifestyle, relationships, and even religion in search of an elusive "true" self. Beset by the widespread "relativism" of modern societies, people without a moral compass lack the security and certainty once provided by tradition.

For David Riesman (1970; orig. 1950), modernization brings changes in **social character**, *personality patterns common to members of a particular society.* Pre-industrial societies promote what Riesman terms **tradition-directedness**, *rigid conformity to time-honoured ways of living.* Members of traditional societies model their lives on what has gone before so that what is "good" is equivalent to "what has always been."

Tradition-directedness corresponds to Tönnies' *Gemeinschaft* and Durkheim's mechanical solidarity. Culturally conservative, tradition-directed people think and act alike. Unlike the conformity found in modern societies, this uniformity is not an attempt to mimic one another. Instead, people are alike because everyone draws on the same solid cultural foundation. Hutterite women and men exemplify tradition-directedness; in Hutterite culture, tradition ties everyone to ancestors and descendants in an unbroken chain of communal living "as ordained by God."

Members of diverse and rapidly changing societies think of a tradition-directed personality as deviant because it seems so rigid. Modern people, by and large, prize personal flexibility and sensitivity to others. Riesman calls this type of social character **other-directedness**, *a receptiveness to the latest trends and fashions, often expressed in the practice of imitating others.* Because their socialization occurs within societies that are continuously in flux, other-directed people develop fluid identities marked by superficiality, inconsistency, and change. They try on different roles and identities, sometimes like so many pieces of new clothing, and engage in various "performances" as they move from setting to setting (Goffman, 1959). In a traditional society, such "shiftiness" marks a person as untrustworthy but, in a modern society, the ability to fit in virtually anywhere is a valued personal trait (Wheelis, 1958). In societies that value the up-to-date rather than the traditional, people anxiously solicit the approval of others, looking to members of their own generation rather than to elders as significant role models. "Peer pressure" can be irresistible to people with no enduring standards to guide them.

Modern society urges individuals to be true to themselves. But when social surroundings change so rapidly, how can people develop the self to which they should be true? This problem is at the root of the identity crisis so widespread in industrial societies today. "Who am I?" is a question that many of us struggle to answer. In truth, this problem is not so much psychological as sociological, reflecting the inherent instability of modern mass society.

YOUR TURN

Would you call yourself more tradition-directed or more other-directed? Where do you turn for standards in making choices about how to live?

Class Society: Problems of Powerlessness

Class society theory paints a different picture of modernity's effects on individuals. This approach maintains that persistent social inequality undermines modern society's

The Canadian Revolution through the Information Revolution: The Point of No Return

Journalist and author Jeffrey Simpson opens his book *Faultlines* (1993) with the following passage:

Canada's traditional political culture in the 1980s cracked like river ice in spring. No single current produced the crack-up; it arose from the confluence of powerful new economic, demographic and political factors and the resurgence of older currents. By the early 1990s, a country that had always been at heart a political arrangement—for it had never been a cultural union or a natural economic entity—found its govern- mental institutions discredited and indebted, its national parties widely reviled, its political leaders mocked, its Constitution the source of divi- sion rather than pride, its economy battered by pressures from abroad, its habitual optimism dimmed.

The relative stability of the past, based on elite accommodation, brokerage politics, and deference to authority, had been shattered. Peter C. Newman traced the radical transformation of Canada's political, social, cultural, and

economic landscape in *The Canadian Revolution, 1985–1995: From Deference to Defiance* (1995). Political scientist Neil Nevitte used the World Values Survey to reveal changes in Canadian values during the volatile 1980s, in his book *The Decline of Deference* (1996). These authors agree that Canada and Canadians have changed profoundly.

Through the 1980s and early 1990s, Canadians lost faith in many of the country's major institutions: organ- ized religion, marriage, the Canada Pension Plan, the monarchy, political parties, the Red Cross, the military and peacekeepers, the Grey Cup, Canada Post, the railways, Ontario Hydro, banks, and corporations. Canadians are less inclined to believe in the inevitability of progress, in the ability of governments to solve our problems, or in corporations as the basis for investment or long-term careers.

Refusing to defer to traditional leadership and authority, Canadians turned inwards for solutions to their problems, seeking information and making decisions—often in defiance of the elite. For example, a majority said No to the Charlottetown Accord and No

to the Conservatives in the 1993 federal election—reducing them from 169 seats to 2. The Québécois were saying No to the separatist leadership of Quebec, and to perpetual economic and political turmoil based on the "neverendum referendum." Influential pollster Allan Gregg (1998) notes that, through the 1980s and 1990s, Canadians have gone from being *the most* deferential people in the Western world to seeking new rights and taking decision making away from leaders.

Marshall McLuhan predicted the radical transformation of Canadian society in the 1960s and early 1970s (Bendetti and DeHart, 1996) as the result of the development of the elec- tronic media. Television was invading homes and classrooms during that period, and computers—room-sized monstrosities at the time—were chang- ing information processing. We moved into a world of instantaneous all-at- onceness: "Time, in a sense, has ceased as space has vanished... [W]e now live in a global village of our own making, a simultaneous happening... created by instant electronic informa- tion movement" (quoted in Bendetti and DeHart, 1996:40). McLuhan

---

promise of individual freedom. For some people, modernity serves up great privilege but, for many, everyday life means coping with economic uncertainty and a growing sense of powerlessness (Newman, 1993; Ehrenreich, 2001).

For racial and ethnic minorities—particularly most Aboriginal peoples—the problem of relative disadvantage looms even larger. Similarly, although women participate more broadly in modern societies, they continue to run up against traditional barriers of sexism. This approach rejects the claim by mass society theory that people suffer from too much freedom. According to class society theory, our society still denies a majority of people full participation in social life.

As Chapter 12 ("Global Stratification") explained, the expanding scope of world capitalism has placed more of Earth's population under the influence of multinational corporations. As a result, about three-quarters of the world's income is concentrated in the high-income nations, where only 18 percent of its people live. Is it any wonder, class society theorists ask, that people in poor nations seek greater power to shape their own lives? The problem of widespread powerlessness led Herbert Marcuse (1964) to challenge Max Weber's statement that modern society is rational. Marcuse condemned modern society as irrational for failing to meet the needs of so many people. Modern capitalist societies

foresaw the walls coming down between families, nations, and economies as people became intensely involved in the affairs of everyone else—everywhere. He predicted that electronic data would become indispensable to all decision making in business, politics, and education; education would be completely transformed; students from around the world would develop a sense of unity; people would forge personal identities in the context of the new simultaneous world; violence would escalate in the quest for identity and people (even children) would kill to feel real; privacy would be a thing of the past; and one could be superhuman and nobody simultaneously.

As early as 1971, McLuhan said that the "wired planet has no boundaries and no monopolies of knowledge," that specialized jobs had lost meaning, and that we might return to a "cottage economy" again because one could run the world's largest factory from a kitchen computer. *Individuals* now have instant access to information, data, or knowledge, at the same time that these are available to the traditional elites—decision makers and leaders in business, government, education, or religion. Deference to these traditional authorities is difficult to maintain under these conditions. Knowledge is power, and knowledge—through the electronic media—is available to the masses.

Peter C. Newman also sees the electronic media as a central force for social change:

The invisible hand of technology had provided citizens with the ammunition for their Revolution. The advent of saturation television coverage of real-time news events, such as the raw footage of the Aboriginal standoff at Oka, Quebec, left politicians with no place to hide. The new rules expected open covenants be openly negotiated. But by the decade's end, television, which had been the dominant technological force at the beginning of the decade, was being supplanted by the computer. A full-scale rout of authority was guaranteed by the advent of the power of the internet. Unregulated access to unlimited, cheap information meant the computer channel that was signing up thousands of Canadian recruits daily had changed their world—and ours—by dramatically empowering its users. (1995:xxi)

Information technology is so central to the transformation we have experienced that a new basis for social class appears to be evolving. In the post-industrial world, control of "the means of production"—using Marxist terms—means access to information, primarily through the use of computers. Affluent families are more likely to have computers, and children who grow up using computers have a head start as they further develop their computer skills at school. Growth in employment is taking place almost entirely in the knowledge-based sector. The result is a new privileged class made up of superbly educated, computer literate men and women (Newman, 1995; also Forcese, 1997; Goyder, 1997).

A *Globe and Mail* editorial (May 1, 2006b) illustrates the information revolution in its discussion of Wikipedia: "the wildly popular online encyclopedia that has turned conventional wisdom about reference sources on its head." Where experts or authorities once wrote encyclopaedia entries, *anyone* can contribute or modify items in Wikipedia. By making all of us potential authors or editors, the revolutionary Wikipedia "puts a question mark over the whole idea that information must move from credentialed producer to passive consumer."

WHAT DO YOU THINK?

1. Is the above an accurate description of the transformation of the last two decades?
2. Do you consult Wikipedia? Do you check information you find there in other sources? Is it a reliable reference in your opinion?
3. Is the Information Revolution good or bad for society?

produce unparalleled wealth, but poverty remains the daily plight of more than 1 billion people. Marcuse adds that technological advances further reduce people's control over their own lives. Sophisticated technology gives a great deal of power to a small core of specialists—not the majority of people—who now dominate the discussion of issues such as computing, energy production, and medical care. Countering the common view that technology *solves* the world's problems, Marcuse argues that science *causes* them. In sum, class society theory asserts that people suffer because modern, scientific societies concentrate both wealth and power in the hands of a privileged few.

MODERNITY AND PROGRESS

In modern societies, most people expect—and applaud—social change. People link modernity to the idea of *progress* (from Latin, meaning "moving forward"), a state of continual improvement. In contrast, we denigrate stability as a form of stagnation. This chapter began by describing Kaiapo villagers in Brazil, for whom affluence has broadened opportunities but weakened traditional heritage. Among Kaiapo, social change, with all its beneficial and detrimental consequences, is too complex simply to equate with progress. More precisely, whether we see a given change as progress depends on our values. A rising standard

Mass society theory relates feelings of anxiety and lack of meaning in the modern world to rapid social change that washes away tradition. This notion of modern emptiness is captured in the photo on the left. *Class society theory*, by contrast, ties such feelings to social inequality, by which some categories of people are made into second-class citizens or not made citizens at all, an idea expressed in the photo on the right.

of living historically among Canadians has helped to make lives longer and more comfortable: North Americans have considerable confidence in science to continue to improve our lives.

Social change is both complex and controversial. Modern society's recognition of basic human rights is valued by most people. The assertion that individuals have rights simply by virtue of their humanity is a distinctly modern idea that can be found in the Canadian Charter of Rights and Freedoms, the American Declaration of Independence, and the United Nations' Declaration of Human Rights. But, as Chapter 3 ("Culture") explained, we now have something of a "culture of rights" that often overlooks the duties and obligations we have to one another. In principle, almost everyone in our society supports the idea that individuals should have considerable autonomy in shaping their own lives. Yet, as people exercise their freedom of choice, they inevitably challenge social patterns cherished by those who maintain more traditional ways of life. For example, people may choose not to marry, to live with someone without marrying, or to enter into a same-sex partnership or marriage. To those who support individual choice, such changes symbolize progress; to those who value traditional family patterns, however, these developments signal societal decay.

New technology, too, provokes controversy. Rapid transportation and efficient communication have improved our lives in many respects, but complex technology has also weakened traditional attachments to home towns and even to families. Industrial technology has also unleashed an unprecedented threat to the natural environment and, in the form of nuclear weapons, endangered humanity itself. Today we wonder about the impacts of computer technology. We have instant access to people around the world but are cut off from our neighbours. We have more information than ever before, but our personal privacy is threatened as never before. In short, we know that social change comes faster all the time, but we may see a particular change as progress or a step backwards—as good or bad for society. For more on the transformation of Canadian society by the information revolution see the Media Perspectives box (on pp. 638–39).

MODERNITY: GLOBAL VARIATION

October 1, Kobe, Japan. Riding the computer-controlled monorail high above the streets of Kobe or the 320-kilometre-per-hour bullet train to Tokyo, we see Japan as the society of the future; its people are in love with high technology. Yet the Japanese remain strikingly traditional in other respects: few corporate executives and almost no senior politicians are women, young people still show seniors great respect, and public orderliness contrasts with the chaos of many U.S. cities. [John J. Macionis]

Japan is a nation at once traditional and modern. This contradiction reminds us that, although it is useful to contrast traditional and modern societies, the old and the new often co-exist in unexpected ways. In today's China, ancient

Confucian principles are mixed with contemporary socialist thinking. In Saudi Arabia and Qatar, the embrace of modern technology is mixed with respect for the ancient principles of Islam. Likewise, in Mexico and much of Latin America, people observe centuries-old Christian rituals even as they struggle to move ahead economically. In short, combinations of traditional and modern are far from unusual; rather, they are found throughout the world. The Media Perspectives box (on pp. 638–39) considers Canadians in flux, in part through the electronic revolution Marshall McLuhan predicted.

Postmodernity

If modernity was the product of the Industrial Revolution, is the Information Revolution creating a postmodern era? A number of scholars think so, and they use the term **postmodernity** to refer to *social patterns characteristic of post-industrial societies.* Precisely what postmodernism is remains a matter of debate. The term has been used for decades in literary, philosophical, and even architectural circles. It moved into sociology on a wave of social criticism that has been building since the spread of left-leaning politics in the 1960s. While there are many variants of postmodern thinking, all share the following five themes (Hall and Neitz, 1993; Inglehart, 1997; Rudel and Gerson, 1999):

1. **In important respects, modernity has failed.** The promise of modernity was a life free from want. As postmodernist critics see it, however, the twentieth century was unsuccessful in solving social problems like poverty because many people still lack financial security.

2. **The bright light of "progress" is fading.** Modern people look to the future, expecting that their lives will improve in significant ways. Members and even leaders of postmodern societies, however, are less confident about what the future holds. The strong optimism that carried society into the modern era more than a century ago has given way to stark pessimism; most Canadians believe that life is getting worse (Bibby, 1995:8).

3. **Science no longer holds the answers.** The defining trait of the modern era was a scientific outlook and a confident belief that technology would make life better. But postmodern critics argue that science has not solved many old problems (such as poor health) and has even created new problems (such as pollution, declining natural resources, and the "inevitable" flu pandemic). Postmodernist thinkers discredit science, claiming that it implies a singular truth. On the contrary, they maintain, there is no one truth. This means that objective reality does not exist; rather, many realities result from social construction.

4. **Cultural debates are intensifying.** Now that more people have all the material things they really need, ideas are taking on more importance. In this sense, postmodernity is also a postmaterialist era, in which more careers involve working with symbols and in which issues such as social justice, the environment, and animal rights command more and more public attention.

5. **Social institutions are changing.** Just as industrialization brought a sweeping transformation to social institutions, the rise of a post-industrial society is remaking society all over again. For example, the postmodern family no longer conforms to any single pattern—as individuals are choosing among many new family forms.

Critical Review Analysts who claim that high-income societies are entering a postmodern era criticize modernity for failing to meet human needs. In defence of modernity, there have been marked increases in longevity and living standards over the course of the past century. Even if we accept postmodernist views that science is bankrupt and progress is a sham, what are the alternatives? There are those who would argue that Canada and the United States have taken two different paths into modernity, while others argue that the differences have been overplayed (see the Thinking Critically box on pp. 642–43).

Looking Ahead: Modernization and our Global Future

In the Thinking Globally box in Chapter 1 (on p. 9), we imagined the entire world reduced to a village of 1000 people. About 180 residents of this "global village" come from high-income countries. Another 180 people are so poor that their lives are at risk. The tragic plight of the world's poor shows that the world is in desperate need of change. Chapter 12 ("Global Stratification") presented two competing views of why 1 billion people around the world are poor. *Modernization theory* claims that, in the past, the entire world was poor and that technological change, especially the Industrial Revolution, enhanced human productivity and raised living standards in many nations. From this point of view, the solution to global poverty is to promote technological development around the world.

For reasons suggested earlier, however, global modernization may be difficult. Recall that David Riesman portrayed pre-industrial people as *tradition-directed* and likely to resist change. So modernization theorists advocate that the world's rich societies help poor countries to grow economically. Industrial nations can speed development by exporting technology to poor regions, welcoming students from these countries, and providing foreign aid to stimulate economic growth.

A review of modernization theory in Chapter 12 points to some success with policies in Latin America and to greater success in the small Asian countries of Taiwan, South Korea, Singapore, and Hong Kong (now part of China). But jump-starting development in the poorest countries of the world poses greater challenges. And, even where dramatic change

THINKING CRITICALLY

We're Different, Eh?

There are many Canadians who believe that, in important ways, we differ from the Americans. Michael Adams, in *Fire and Ice* (2003), argues that the Americans are retrenching—they defer to authority, believe father is the master of the house and embrace fundamentalist religion, while Canadians are moving in a different direction. Others argue that we are becoming more like Americans: globalization, the dominance of the American media, and the free trade agreement have led to homogeneity or value convergence.

Is the United States a nation in decline? Clearly, by some measures, it is thriving. Between 1960 and 1995, for example, the nation's economic output tripled and median family income, controlled for inflation, climbed by more than one-third. During the same time span, the official poverty rate dropped by half. By 2004, infant mortality had declined further, life expectancy had increased—and poverty among elderly people had been greatly reduced. High school dropout rates declined and college completion rates improved. And Americans continue to volunteer and give to charity much more generously than do Canadians.

Nonetheless, other indicators paint a more disturbing picture of American life. Between 1960 and 1995, violent crime shot up fourfold; the number of children born to single mothers as well as the number of children supported by welfare rose more than fivefold; the divorce rate doubled; and teen suicide tripled. Television viewing increased dramatically, and academic achievement, as measured by test scores, had declined. By 2004, child abuse had increased fourfold, average weekly wages had declined in real dollars, and the income gap between rich and poor had widened. Voter turnout declined steadily. Between 1970 and 2004, the proportion of Americans without health care coverage increased from 10 percent to 16 percent.

Bennett (1993) argues that decline in the United States is primarily moral—a matter of weakening individual character. Americans are less concerned about what they owe to others (i.e., moral obligation), less inclined to sacrifice for the common good, less concerned about social conformity and respectability, and less restrained in sexual matters. American social institutions—families, churches, schools, and neighbourhoods—have been responsible for building individual character. Compassion, tolerance, honesty, and respect for authority are taught by these now-enfeebled social institutions: the result of their decline is "social regression."

If asked, many Canadians would raise similar concerns regarding our society. In the mid–1990s, we were not confident about our economy, at least with respect to job creation and job security. Taking inflation into account, our average family income declined after 1989—recovering fully only by

has occurred, modernization involves a trade-off. Traditional people, such as Brazil's Kaiapo, may gain wealth through economic development, but they lose their cultural identity and values as they are drawn into a global "McCulture" based on Western materialism, pop music, trendy clothes, and fast food. One Brazilian anthropologist expressed hope for the future of the Kaiapo: "At least they quickly understood the consequences of watching television.... Now [they] can make a choice" (Simons, 2007).

But not everyone thinks that modernization is really an option. According to a second approach to global stratification, *dependency theory*, today's poor societies have little ability to modernize, even if they want to. From this point of view, the major barrier to economic development is not traditionalism but the global domination of rich capitalist societies. Dependency theory asserts that rich nations achieved their modernization at the expense of poor ones, plundering poor nations' natural resources and exploiting their human labour. Even today, the world's poorest countries remain locked in a disadvantageous economic relationship with rich nations, dependent on wealthy countries to buy their raw materials and in return provide them with whatever manufactured products they can afford. According to this view, continuing ties with rich societies only perpetuates current patterns of global inequality.

Whichever approach you find more convincing, keep in mind that change in North America is no longer separate from change in the rest of the world. At the beginning of the twentieth century, most people in today's high-income countries lived in relatively small settlements with limited awareness of the larger world. Today, a century later, the entire world has become one huge village because the lives of all people are increasingly linked.

The last century witnessed unprecedented human achievement. Yet solutions to many problems of human existence—including finding meaning in life, resolving conflicts between nations, and eliminating poverty—have eluded us. To this list of pressing matters new concerns have been added, such as controlling population growth and establishing an environmentally sustainable society. In the next hundred years, we must be prepared to tackle such problems with imagination, compassion, and determination. Our growing understanding of human society gives us reason to be hopeful that we can get the job done.

1998. Despite our improving economy, about 15 percent of Canadian families, especially Aboriginal families, continue to fall below the poverty line. Violent crime and homicide rates increased initially and then declined through the late 1990s and early 2000s, yet Canadians are increasingly fearful about their safety. We are cynical about politicians and worried about the quality of our schools and the survival of the family as we know it. Our political will to ensure universal and timely access to medical care is even in question. Voter turnout is declining here too, among young people in particular. Like Americans, we live in an age of entitlement rather than of duty, of individual rights rather than responsibility for one's community. To many observers, it seems as though we are simply a few steps behind the United States with respect to the growth of social problems.

Despite these changes, Canadians seem to have retained certain moral and social values. While we are less likely to attend religious services, 84 percent of us believe in God and 45 percent pray daily. Honesty and reliability are "very important" to about 90 percent of Canadians, and family life to

86 percent. Cultural, racial, and religious intermarriage is approved by 80 to 90 percent of Canadians, suggesting that we have become quite tolerant. And, recently, we have legalized same-sex marriage. Furthermore, our level of social compassion has remained quite high, as evidenced by our beliefs that people who are poor deserve adequate income and medical care (84% and 96%, respectively). If ours has become a more cynical and dangerous society, it is clear that we have not rejected our basic social values. Keep in mind, though, that professing such beliefs and values is not the same as putting them into action.

Anti-American sentiment is out in the open today, but it seems that much of it is directed against the government, President Bush, and the Iraq war—not against Americans themselves. Close to a million Canadian adults favour our becoming part of the United States, while many more support political and economic union. Of employed Canadians, 19 percent (24% in British Columbia and Quebec) would prefer to work and live in the United States, and 70 percent support our participation in the North American Free Trade

Agreement. Only 15 percent of Canadians say they are "anti-American" at heart while 70 percent agree that "I value and respect the United States and its citizens" (Bricker and Wright, 2005). Furthermore, we have no qualms about immersing ourselves in American culture—its books, magazines, movies, and television programs—thereby failing to support Canadian culture through our choices.

We may define ourselves as "*not* American" and disagree with many things that Americans do, but—despite differences in attitudes and values—deep down, the average Canadian is not *anti*-American.

WHAT DO YOU THINK?

1. Are Canadians morally superior to Americans? How?
2. Would you consider working and living in the United States? Do you have family friends and relatives doing so?
3. How do we get the impression that Canadians are anti-American?

Sources: Bennett (1993), Sauvé (1994), Bibby (1995), Adams (2003), and Bricker and Wright (2005).

24 MAKING THE GRADE

The following learning tools will help you see what you know, identify what you still need to learn, and expand your understanding beyond the text. You can also visit this text's Companion Website™ at www.pearsone.ca/macionis to find useful practice tests.

KEY POINTS

What Is Social Change?

Every society changes all the time, sometimes faster, sometimes slower. Social change often generates controversy.

Causes of Social Change

Social change takes many forms: invention produces new objects and ideas; discovery gives us a fresh awareness of things in the world; diffusion spreads objects or ideas from one place to another. Causes of social change include social conflict (Marx) and ideas (Weber), as well as migration and other demographic factors.

Modernity

Modernity refers to the social consequences of industrialization, which include the erosion of traditional communities, expanding personal choice, increasingly diverse beliefs, and a focus on the future.

Ferdinand Tönnies described modernization as the transition from *Gemeinschaft* to *Gesellschaft,* with the decline of traditional community and the rise of individualism.

Emile Durkheim saw modernization as a society's expanding division of labour. Mechanical solidarity, based on shared activities and beliefs, is gradually replaced by organic solidarity, in which specialization makes people interdependent.

Max Weber saw modernity as the decline of tradition and rise of rationality. Weber feared the dehumanizing effects of rational organization.

Karl Marx saw modernity as the triumph of capitalism over feudalism. Capitalism creates social conflict, which Marx claimed would bring about revolutionary change towards an egalitarian socialist society.

Theoretical Analysis of Modernity

According to mass society theory, modernity increases the scale of life, enlarging the role of government and other formal organizations in carrying out tasks previously performed by families in local communities. Cultural diversity and rapid social change make it difficult for people in modern societies to develop stable identities and to find meaning in their lives.

According to class society theory, modernity involves the rise of capitalism. By concentrating wealth in the hands of a few, modern capitalist societies generate widespread feelings of powerlessness.

Social change is too complex and controversial simply to be equated with social progress.

Postmodernity

Postmodernity refers to the cultural traits of post-industrial societies. Postmodern criticism of society centers on the failure of modernity, and specifically science, to fulfil its promise of prosperity and well-being.

Looking Ahead: Modernization and Our Global Future

Modernization theory links global poverty to the power of tradition. Rich nations can help poor countries develop their economies.

Dependency theory explains global poverty as the product of the world economic system. The operation of multinational corporations makes poor nations economically dependent on rich nations.

KEY CONCEPTS

social change (p. 627) the transformation of culture and social institutions over time

modernity (p. 629) social patterns resulting from industrialization

modernization (p. 629) the process of social change begun by industrialization

mass society (p. 633) a society in which prosperity and bureaucracy have weakened traditional social ties

class society (p. 635) a capitalist society with pronounced social stratification

social character (p. 637) personality patterns common to members of a particular society

tradition-directedness (p. 637) rigid conformity to time-honoured ways of living

other-directedness (p. 637) openness to the latest trends and fashions, often expressed by imitating others

postmodernity (p. 641) social patterns characteristic of post-industrial societies

APPLICATIONS & EXERCISES

1. Ask an elderly relative or friend to name the most important social changes during his or her lifetime. Do you think your world will change as much during your lifetime?
2. Ask your friends and classmates to make five predictions about Canadian society in the year 2050, when you will be elderly. Compare notes. On what issues is there agreement?
3. Consider modern society as described by Tönnies, Durkheim, Weber, and Marx—then look at Canada as it exists today. List the characteristics of Canadian society under each of the theorists to determine which one describes our country most accurately.

PRENTICE HALL

mysoclab™
Where learning & the sociological imagination intersect.

To reinforce your understanding of this chapter, and to identify topics for further study, visit MySocLab at **www.pearsoned.ca/mysoclab/** for diagnostic tests and a multimedia ebook.

GLOSSARY

abortion (p. 197) the deliberate termination of a pregnancy

absolute poverty (p. 280) a deprivation of resources that is life-threatening

achieved status (p. 133) a social position a person takes on voluntarily that reflects personal ability and effort

activity theory (p. 395) the idea that a high level of activity increases personal satisfaction in old age

age-sex pyramid (p. 571) a graphic representation of the age and sex of a population

age stratification (p. 387) the unequal distribution of wealth, power, and privilege among people at different stages of the life course

ageism (p. 394) prejudice and discrimination against older people

agriculture (p. 86) large-scale cultivation using plows harnessed to animals or more powerful energy sources

alienation (p. 93) the experience of isolation and misery resulting from powerlessness

animism (p. 498) the belief that elements of the natural world are conscious life forms that affect humanity

anomie (p. 99) Durkheim's term for a condition in which society provides little moral guidance to individuals

anticipatory socialization (p. 120) learning that helps a person achieve a desired position

ascribed status (p. 133) a social position a person receives at birth or takes on involuntarily later in life

asexuality (p. 193) a lack of sexual attraction to people of either sex

assimilation (p. 360) the process by which minorities gradually adopt patterns of the dominant culture

authoritarianism (p. 437) a political system that denies the people participation in government

authority (p. 432) power that people perceive as legitimate rather than coercive

beliefs (p. 64) specific statements that people hold to be true

bilateral descent (p. 467) a system tracing kinship through both men and women

bisexuality (p. 193) sexual attraction to people of both sexes

blue-collar occupations (p. 251) lower-prestige jobs that involve mostly manual labour

bureaucracy (p. 165) an organizational model rationally designed to perform tasks efficiently

bureaucratic inertia (p. 169) the tendency of bureaucratic organizations to perpetuate themselves

bureaucratic ritualism (p. 169) a focus on rules and regulations to the point of undermining an organization's goals

capitalism (p. 410) an economic system in which natural resources and the means of producing goods and services are privately owned

capitalists (p. 90) people who own and operate factories and other businesses in pursuit of profits

care giving (p. 391) informal and unpaid care provided to a dependent person by family members, other relatives, or friends

caste system (p. 241) social stratification based on ascription (birth)

cause and effect (p. 32) a relationship in which change in one variable (the independent variable) causes change in another (the dependent variable)

charisma (p. 497) extraordinary personal qualities that can infuse people with emotion and turn them into followers

charismatic authority (p. 433) power legitimized by extraordinary personal abilities that inspire devotion and obedience

church (p. 497) a type of religious organization that is well integrated into the larger society

civil religion (p. 508) a quasi-religious loyalty binding individuals in a basically secular society

claims making (p. 612) the process of trying to convince the public and public officials of the importance of joining a social movement to address a particular issue

class conflict (or struggle) (p. 92) conflict between entire classes over the distribution of a society's wealth and power

class consciousness (p. 92) Marx's term for workers' recognition of themselves as a class unified in opposition to capitalists and ultimately to capitalism itself

class society (p. 635) a capitalist society with pronounced social stratification

class system (p. 244) social stratification based on both birth and individual achievement

cohabitation (p. 483) the sharing of a household by an unmarried couple

cohort (p. 125) a category of people with something in common, usually their age

collective behaviour (p. 600) activity involving a large number of people that is unplanned, often controversial, and sometimes dangerous.

collectivity (p. 601) a large number of people whose minimal interaction occurs in the absence of well-defined and conventional norms

colonialism (p. 303) the process by which some nations enrich themselves through political and economic control of other nations

communism (p. 411) a hypothetical economic and political system in which all members of a society are socially equal

community-based corrections (p. 232) correctional programs operating within society at large rather than behind prison walls

concept (p. 31) a mental construct that represents some part of the world in a simplified form

concrete operational stage (p. 112) Piaget's term for the level of human development at which individuals first see causal connections in their surroundings

conglomerate (p. 424) a giant corporation composed of many smaller corporations

conspicuous consumption (p. 256) buying and using products because of their "statements" about social position

control (p. 32) holding constant all variables except one in order to see clearly the effect of that variable

corporate crime (p. 219) the illegal actions of a corporation or people acting on its behalf

corporation (p. 422) an organization with a legal existence, including rights and liabilities, separate from that of its members

correlation (p. 32) a relationship in which two (or more) variables change together

counterculture (p. 72) cultural patterns that strongly oppose those widely accepted within a society

crime (p. 210) the violation of a society's formally enacted criminal law

crimes against property (property crimes) (p. 223) crimes that involve theft of property belonging to others

criminal justice system (p. 210) a formal response by police, courts, and prison officials to alleged violations of the law

criminal recidivism (p. 232) later offences committed by people previously convicted of crimes

critical sociology (p. 36) the study of society that focuses on the need for social change

crowd (p. 601) a temporary gathering of people who share a common focus of attention and who influence one another

crude birth rate (p. 569) the number of live births in a given year for every 1000 people in a population

crude death rate (p. 570) the number of deaths in a given year for every 1000 people in a population

cult (p. 497) a religious organization that is largely outside a society's cultural traditions

cultural integration (p. 73) the close relationships among various elements of a cultural system

cultural lag (p. 73the fact that some cultural elements change more quickly than others, disrupting a cultural system

cultural relativism (p. 74) the practice of judging a culture by its own standards

cultural transmission (p. 62) the process by which one generation passes culture to the next

cultural universals (p. 76) traits that are part of every known culture

culture (p. 56) the values, beliefs, behaviour, and material objects that together form a people's way of life

culture shock (p. 57) personal disorientation when experiencing an unfamiliar way of life

Davis-Moore thesis (p. 250) the assertion that social stratification is a universal pattern because it has beneficial consequences for the operation of a society

deductive logical thought (p. 49) reasoning that transforms general theory into specific hypotheses suitable for testing

democracy (p. 435) a political system that gives power to the people as a whole

demographic transition theory (p. 572) the thesis that population patterns reflect a society's level of technological development

demography (p. 569) the study of human population

denomination (p. 497) a church, independent of the state, that recognizes religious pluralism

dependency theory (p. 307) a model of economic and social development that explains global inequality in terms of the historical exploitation of poor nations by rich ones

dependent variable (p. 32) a variable that is changed by another (independent) variable

descent (p. 466) the system by which members of a society trace kinship over generations

deterrence (p. 230) the attempt to discourage criminality through the use of punishment

deviance (p. 210) the recognized violation of cultural norms

direct fee system (p. 556) a medical care system in which patients pay directly for the services of physicians and hospitals

disaster (p. 608) an event, generally unexpected, that causes extensive harm to people and damage to property

discrimination (p. 358) unequal treatment of various categories of people

disengagement theory (p. 394) the idea that society functions in an orderly way by disengaging people from positions of responsibility as they reach old age

division of labour (p. 99) specialized economic activity

dramaturgical analysis (p. 138) Erving Goffman's term for the study of social interaction in terms of theatrical performance

dyad (p. 160) a social group with two members

eating disorder (p. 547) an intense form of dieting or other unhealthy method of weight control driven by the desire to be very thin

ecologically sustainable culture (p. 593) a way of life that meets the needs of the present generation without threatening the environmental legacy of future generations

ecology (p. 585) the study of the interaction of living organisms and the natural environment

economy (p. 404) the social institution that organizes a society's production, distribution, and consumption of goods and services

ecosystem (p. 585) a system composed of the interaction of all living organisms and their natural environment

education (p. 518) the social institution through which society provides its members with important knowledge, including basic facts, job skills, and cultural norms and values

ego (p. 111) Freud's term for a person's conscious efforts to balance innate pleasure-seeking drives with the demands of society

empirical evidence (p. 30) information we can verify with our senses

endogamy (p. 465) marriage between people of the same social category

environmental deficit (p. 586) profound long-term harm to the natural environment caused by humanity's focus on short-term material affluence

environmental racism (p. 592) the pattern by which environmental hazards are greatest for poor people, especially minorities

ethnicity (p. 352) a shared cultural heritage

ethnocentrism (p. 73) the practice of judging another culture by the standards of one's own culture

ethnomethodology (p. 137) Harold Garfinkel's term for the study of the way people make sense of their everyday surroundings

Eurocentrism (p. 71) the dominance of European (especially English) cultural patterns

euthanasia (mercy killing) (p. 397) assisting in the death of a person suffering from an incurable disease

exogamy (p. 465) marriage between people of different social categories

experiment (p. 41) a research method for investigating cause and effect under highly controlled conditions

expressive leadership (p. 156) group leadership that focuses on the group's well-being

extended family (consanguine family) (p. 465) a family consisting of parents and children as well as other kin

fad (p. 608) an unconventional social pattern that people embrace briefly but enthusiastically

faith (p. 493) belief based on conviction rather than scientific evidence

false consciousness (p. 91) Marx's term for explanations of social problems as the shortcomings of individuals rather than as the flaws of society

family (p. 465) a social institution found in all societies that unites people in co-operative groups to care for one another, including any children

family violence (p. 480) emotional, physical, or sexual abuse of one family member by another

fashion (p. 607) a social pattern favoured by a large number of people

feminism (p. 341) the advocacy of social equality for women and men, in opposition to patriarchy and sexism

feminization of poverty (p. 282) the trend of women making up an increasing proportion of the poor

fertility (p. 569) the incidence of child bearing in a country's population

folkways (p. 67) norms for routine or casual interaction

formal operational stage (p. 112) Piaget's term for the level of human development at which individuals think abstractly and critically

formal organization (p. 163) a large secondary group organized to achieve its goals efficiently

functional illiteracy (p. 521) a lack of the reading and writing skills needed for everyday living

fundamentalism (p. 509) a conservative religious doctrine that opposes intellectualism and worldly accommodation in favour of restoring traditional, otherworldly religion

Gemeinschaft (p. 581) a type of social organization in which people are closely tied by kinship and tradition

gender (pp. 36, 319) the personal traits and social positions that members of a society attach to being female or male

gender-conflict approach (p. 17) a point of view that focuses on inequality and conflict between women and men

gender identity (p. 186) traits that females and males, guided by their culture, incorporate into their personality

gender roles (sex roles) (p. 322) attitudes and activities that a society links to each sex

gender stratification (p. 319) the unequal distribution of wealth, power, and privilege between men and women

generalized other (p. 115) George Herbert Mead's term for widespread cultural norms and values we use as a reference in evaluating ourselves

genocide (p. 363) the systematic killing of one category of people by another

gerontocracy (p. 388) a form of social organization in which elderly people have the most wealth, power, and prestige

gerontology (p. 384) the study of aging and elderly people

Gesellschaft (p. 581) a type of social organization in which people come together only on the basis of individual self-interest

global economy (p. 408) expanding economic activity that crosses national borders

global perspective (p. 6) the study of the larger world and our society's place in it

global stratification (p. 292) patterns of social inequality in the world as a whole

global warming (p. 590) a rise in Earth's average temperature resulting from an increasing concentration of carbon dioxide in the atmosphere

gossip (p. 605) rumour about people's personal affairs

government (p. 432) a formal organization that directs the political life of a society

groupthink (p. 159) the tendency of group members to conform, resulting in a narrow view of some issue

hate crime (p. 221) a criminal act against a person or a person's property by an offender motivated by racial or other bias

Hawthorne effect (p. 41) a change in a subject's behaviour caused simply by the awareness of being studied

health (p. 542) a state of complete physical, mental, and social well-being

heterosexism (p. 203) a view that labels anyone who is not heterosexual as "queer"

heterosexuality (p. 193) sexual attraction to someone of the other sex

hidden curriculum (p. 527) subtle presentations of political or cultural ideas in the classroom

high culture (p. 70) cultural patterns that distinguish a society's elite

high-income countries (p. 7) nations with the highest overall standards of living

holistic medicine (p. 554) an approach to health care that emphasizes the prevention of illness and takes into account a person's entire physical and social environment

homogamy (p. 472) marriage between people with the same social characteristics

homophobia (p. 195) discomfort over close personal interaction with people thought to be gay, lesbian, or bisexual

homosexuality (p. 193) sexual attraction to someone of the same sex

horticulture (p. 86) the use of hand tools to raise crops

hunting and gathering (p. 85) the use of simple tools to hunt animals and gather vegetation

hypothesis (p. 41) a statement of a possible relationship between two (or more) variables

id (p. 111) Freud's term for the human being's basic drives

ideal culture (p. 68) *social patterns mandated by cultural values and norms*

ideal type (p. 94) an abstract statement of the essential characteristics of any social phenomenon

ideology (249) cultural beliefs that justify particular social arrangements, including patterns of inequality

in-group (p. 160) a social group towards which a member feels respect and loyalty

incest taboo (pp. 187, 469) a norm forbidding sexual relations or marriage between certain relatives

income (p. 267) earnings from work or investments

independent variable (p. 32) a variable that causes change in another (dependent) variable

inductive logical thought (p. 49) reasoning that transforms specific observations into general theory

industrialism (p. 87) the production of goods using advanced sources of energy to drive large machinery

infant mortality rate (p. 570) the number of deaths among infants under one year of age for each 1000 live births in a given year

infidelity (p. 472) sexual activity outside marriage

institutional completeness (p. 359) the complexity of community organizations that meet the needs of members

institutional prejudice and discrimination (p. 358) bias built into the operation of society's institutions

instrumental leadership (p. 156) group leadership that focuses on the completion of tasks

intergenerational social mobility (p. 279) upward or downward social mobility of children in relation to their parents

interpretive sociology (p. 34) the study of society that focuses on the meanings people attach to their social world

intersection theory (p. 333) the interplay of race, class, and gender, often resulting in multiple dimensions of disadvantage

intersexual people (p. 185) people whose bodies, including genitals, have both female and male characteristics

interview (p. 43) a series of questions a researcher asks respondents in person

intragenerational social mobility (p.279) a change in social position occurring during a person's lifetime

kinship (p. 465) a social bond based on common ancestry, marriage, or adoption

labelling theory (p. 215) the idea that deviance and conformity result not so much from what people do as from how others respond to those actions

labour unions (p. 414) organizations of workers that seek to improve wages and working conditions through various strategies, including negotiations and strikes

language (p. 62) a system of symbols that allows people to communicate with one another

latent functions (p. 15) the unrecognized and unintended consequences of any social pattern

liberation theology (p. 493) the combining of Christian principles with political activism, often Marxist in character

life expectancy (p. 570) the average life span of a country's population

looking-glass self (p. 114) Cooley's term for a self-image based on how we think others see us

low-income countries (p. 7) nations with a low standard of living in which most people are poor

macro-level orientation (p. 18) a broad focus on social structures that shape society as a whole

manifest functions (p. 15) the recognized and intended consequences of any social pattern

marriage (p. 465) a legal relationship, usually involving economic co-operation, sexual activity, and child bearing

Marxist political economy model (p. 452) an analysis that explains politics in terms of the operation of a society's economic system

mass behaviour (p. 605) collective behaviour among people spread over a wide geographic area

mass hysteria (moral panic) (p. 608) a form of dispersed collective behaviour in which people react to a real or imagined event with irrational and even frantic fear

mass media (p. 120) the means for delivering impersonal communications to a vast audience

mass society (p. 633) a society in which prosperity and bureaucracy have weakened traditional social ties

master status (p. 133) a status that has special importance for social identity, often shaping a person's entire life

material culture (p. 56) the physical things created by members of a society

matriarchy (p. 321) a form of social organization in which females dominate males

matrilineal descent (p. 467) a system tracing kinship through women

matrilocality (p. 466) a residential pattern in which a married couple lives with or near the wife's family

measurement (p. 31) a procedure for determining the value of a variable in a specific case

mechanical solidarity (p. 99) Durkheim's term for social bonds, based on common sentiments and shared moral values, that are strong among members of pre-industrial societies

medicalization of deviance (p. 216) the transformation of moral and legal deviance into a medical condition

medicine (p. 553) the social institution that focuses on fighting disease and improving health

megalopolis (p. 580) a vast urban region containing a number of cities and their surrounding suburbs

meritocracy (p. 244) social stratification based on personal merit

metropolis (p. 579) a large city that socially and economically dominates an urban area

micro-level orientation (p. 18) a close-up focus on social interaction in specific situations

middle-income countries (p. 7) nations with a standard of living about average for the world as a whole

migration (p. 570) the movement of people into and out of a specified territory

military-industrial complex (p. 457) the close association of the federal government, the military, and defence industries

minority (p. 353) any category of people distinguished by physical or cultural difference that a society sets apart and subordinates

miscegenation (p. 360) biological reproduction by partners of different racial categories

mob (p. 602) a highly emotional crowd that pursues a violent or destructive goal

modernity (p. 629) social patterns resulting from industrialization

modernization (p. 629) the process of social change begun by industrialization

modernization theory (p. 305) a model of economic and social development that explains global inequality in terms of technological and cultural differences between nations

monarchy (p. 434) a political system in which a single family rules from generation to generation

monogamy (p. 465) marriage that unites two partners

monotheism (p. 499) belief in a single divine power

mores (p. 67) norms that are widely observed and have great moral significance

mortality (p. 570) the incidence of death in a country's population

multiculturalism (p. 71) an educational program recognizing the cultural diversity of the United States and promoting the equality of all cultural traditions

multinational corporation (p. 304) a very large business that operates in many countries

natural environment (p. 585) Earth's surface and atmosphere, including living organisms, air, water, soil, and other resources necessary to sustain life

neocolonialism (p. 304) a new form of global power relationships that involves not direct political control but economic exploitation by multinational corporations

neolocality (p. 466) a residential pattern in which a married couple lives apart from both sets of parents

network (p. 161) a web of weak social ties

nonmaterial culture (p. 56) the ideas created by members of a society

nonverbal communication (p. 139) communication using body movements, gestures, and facial expressions rather than speech

norms (p. 67) rules and expectations by which a society guides the behaviour of its members

nuclear family (conjugal family) (p. 465) a family composed of one or two parents and their children

nuclear proliferation (p. 458) the acquisition of nuclear weapons technology by more and more nations

objectivity (p. 33) personal neutrality in conducting research

oligarchy (p. 170) the rule of the many by the few

operationalize a variable (p. 31) specifying exactly what is to be measured before assigning a value to a variable

organic solidarity (p. 99) Durkheim's term for social bonds, based on specialization and interdependence, that are strong among members of industrial societies

organizational environment (p. 166) factors outside an organization that affect its operation

organized crime (p. 220) a business supplying illegal goods or services

other-directedness (p. 637) openness to the latest trends and fashions, often expressed by imitating others

out-group (p. 160) a social group towards which a person feels a sense of competition or opposition

panic (p. 608) a form of collective behaviour in which people in one place react to a threat or other stimulus with irrational, frantic, and often self-destructive behaviour

participant observation (p. 44) a research method in which investigators systematically observe people while joining them in their routine activities

pastoralism (p. 86) the domestication of animals

patriarchy (p. 321) a form of social organization in which males dominate females

patrilineal descent (p. 466) a system tracing kinship through men

patrilocality (p. 466) a residential pattern in which a married couple lives with or near the husband's family

peer group (p. 120) a social group whose members have interests, social position, and age in common

personal space (p. 141) the surrounding area over which a person makes some claim to privacy

personality (p. 108) a person's fairly consistent patterns of acting, thinking, and feeling

plea bargaining (p. 226) a legal negotiation in which a prosecutor reduces a charge in exchange for a defendant's guilty plea

pluralism (p. 359) a state in which people of all races and ethnicities are distinct but have equal social standing

pluralist model (p. 451) an analysis of politics that sees power as spread among many competing interest groups

political party (p. 442) an organizations operating within the political system that seeks control of the government

political revolution (p. 453) the overthrow of one political system in order to establish another

politics (p. 432) the social institution that distributes power, sets a society's goals, and makes decisions

polyandry (p. 466) marriage that unites one woman and two or more men

polygamy (p. 465) marriage that unites a person with two or more spouses

polygyny (p. 466) marriage that unites one man and two or more women

polytheism (p. 499) belief in many gods

popular culture (p. 70) cultural patterns that are widespread among a society's population

population (p. 42) the people who are the focus of research

pornography (p. 197) sexually explicit material intended to cause sexual arousal

positivism (p. 13) a way of understanding based on science

post-industrial economy (p. 406) a productive system based on service work and high technology

post-industrialism (p. 88) technology that supports an information-based economy

postmodernism (p. 19) an approach that is critical of modernism, with a mistrust of grand theories and ideologies

postmodernity (p. 641) social patterns characteristic of post-industrial societies

power (p. 432) the ability to achieve desired ends despite resistance from others

power elite model (p. 451) an analysis of politics that sees power as concentrated among the rich

prejudice (p. 354) a rigid and irrational generalization about an entire category of people

preoperational stage (p. 112) Piaget's term for the level of human development at which individuals first use language and other symbols

presentation of self (p. 138) Erving Goffman's term for a person's efforts to create specific impressions in the minds of others

primary group (p. 155) a small social group whose members share personal and lasting relationships

primary labour market (p. 414) jobs that provide extensive benefits to workers

primary sector (p. 407) the part of the economy that draws raw materials from the natural environment

primary sex characteristics (p. 185) the genitals, organs used for reproduction

profane (p. 492) an ordinary element of everyday life

profession (p. 415) a prestigious white-collar occupation that requires extensive formal education

proletarians (p. 90) people who sell their labour for wages

propaganda (p. 605) information presented with the intention of shaping public opinion

prostitution (p. 197) the selling of sexual services

public opinion (p. 605) widespread attitudes about controversial issues

queer theory (p. 203) a growing body of research findings that challenges the heterosexual bias in Western society

questionnaire (p. 43) a series of written questions a researcher presents to subjects

race (p. 350) a socially constructed category of people who share biologically transmitted traits that members of a society consider important

race-conflict approach (p. 18) a point of view that focuses on inequality and conflict between people of different racial and ethnic categories

racism (p. 355) the belief that one racial category is innately superior or inferior to another

rainforest (p. 590) a region of dense forestation, located close to the equator

rational-legal authority (bureaucratic authority) (p. 433) power legitimized by legally enacted rules and regulations

rationality (p. 94) a way of thinking that emphasizes deliberate, matter-of-fact calculation of the most efficient way to accomplish a particular task

rationalization of society (p. 95) Weber's term for the historical change from tradition to rationality as the main mode of human thought

real culture (p. 68) actual social patterns that only approximate cultural expectations

reference group (p. 159) a social group that serves as a point of reference in making evaluations and decisions

rehabilitation (p. 230) a program for reforming the offender to prevent later offences

relative deprivation (p. 612) a perceived disadvantage arising from some specific comparison

relative poverty (p. 280) the deprivation of some people in relation to those who have more

reliability (p. 31) consistency in measurement

religion (p. 492) a social institution involving beliefs and practices based on recognizing the sacred

religiosity (p. 505) the importance of religion in a person's life

replication (p. 34) repetition of research by other investigators

research method (p. 40) a systematic plan for doing research

resocialization (p. 126) efforts to effect radical change in an inmate's personality by carefully controlling the environment

retribution (p. 230) an act of moral vengeance by which society makes the offender suffer as much as the suffering caused by the crime

riot (p. 602) a social eruption that is highly emotional, violent, and undirected

ritual (p. 493) formal, ceremonial behaviour

role (p. 134) behaviour expected of someone who holds a particular status

role conflict (p. 135) conflict among the roles connected to two or more statuses

role set (p. 135) a number of roles attached to a single status

role strain (p. 135) tension among the roles connected to a single status

routinization of charisma (p. 434) the transformation of charismatic authority into some combination of traditional and bureaucratic authority

rumour (p. 605) unconfirmed information that people spread informally, often by word of mouth

sacred (p. 492) set apart as extraordinary, inspiring awe and reverence

sample (p. 42) a part of a population that represents the whole

Sapir-Whorf thesis (p. 64) the idea that people see and understand the world through the cultural lens of language

scapegoat (p. 357) a person or category of people, typically with little power, whom people unfairly blame for their own troubles

schooling (p. 518) formal instruction under the direction of specially trained teachers

science (p. 30) a logical system that bases knowledge on direct, systematic observation

scientific management (p. 170) Frederick Taylor's term for the application of scientific principles to the operation of a business or other large organization

scientific sociology (p. 31) the study of society based on systematic observation of social behaviour

secondary analysis (p. 46) a research method in which a researcher utilizes data collected by others

secondary group (p. 155) a large and impersonal social group whose members pursue a specific goal or activity

secondary labour market (p. 414) jobs that provide minimal benefits to workers

secondary sector (p. 407) the part of the economy that transforms raw materials into manufactured goods

secondary sex characteristics (p. 185) bodily development, apart from the genitals, that distinguishes biologically mature females and males

sect (p. 497) a type of religious organization that stands apart from the larger society

secularization (p. 507) the historical decline in the importance of the supernatural and the sacred

segregation (p. 360) the physical and social separation of categories of people

self (p. 113) George Herbert Mead's term for the part of an individual's personality composed of self-awareness and self-image

self-employment (p. 415) earning a living without working for a large organization

sensorimotor stage (p. 112) Piaget's term for the level of human development at which individuals experience the world only through their senses

sex (p. 185) the biological distinction between females and males

sex ratio (p. 571) the number of males for every 100 females in a nation's population

sexism (p. 321) the belief that one sex is innately superior to the other

sexual harassment (p. 336) comments, gestures, or physical contact of a sexual nature that are deliberate, repeated, and unwelcome

sexual orientation (p. 193) a person's romantic and emotional attraction to another person

sick role (p. 558) patterns of behaviour defined as appropriate for people who are ill

significant others (p. 115) people, such as parents, who have special importance for socialization

social change (p. 627) the transformation of culture and social institutions over time

social character (p. 637) personality patterns common to members of a particular society

social conflict (p. 90) the struggle between segments of society over valued resources

social-conflict approach (p. 16) a framework for building theory that sees society as an arena of inequality that generates conflict and change

social construction of reality (p. 136) the process by which people creatively shape reality through social interaction

social control (pp. 68, 210) attempts by society to regulate people's thoughts and behaviour

social dysfunction (p. 15) any social pattern that may disrupt the operation of society

social epidemiology (p. 544) the study of how health and disease are distributed throughout a society's population

social functions (p. 15) the consequences of any social pattern for the operation of society as a whole

social group (p. 154) two or more people who identify and interact with one another

social institutions (p. 91) the major spheres of social life, or societal subsystems, organized to meet human needs

social interaction (p. 132) the process by which people act and react in relation to others

social mobility (p. 241) a change in position within the social hierarchy

social movement (p. 600) organized activity that encourages or discourages social change

social stratification (p. 241) a system by which a society ranks categories of people in a hierarchy

social structure (p. 15) any relatively stable pattern of social behaviour

socialism (p. 411) an economic system in which natural resources and the means of producing goods and services are collectively owned

socialization (p. 108) the lifelong social experience by which people develop their human potential and learn culture

socialized medicine (p. 555) a medical care system in which the government owns and operates most medical facilities and employs most physicians

societal protection (p. 230) rendering an offender incapable of further offences temporarily through imprisonment or permanently by execution

society (p. 84) people who interact in a defined territory and share a culture

sociobiology (p. 77) a theoretical approach that explores ways in which human biology affects how we create culture

sociocultural evolution (p. 84) Lenski's term for the changes that occur as a society gains new technology

socioeconomic status (p. 255) a composite ranking based on various dimensions of social inequality

sociological perspective (p. 2) the special point of view of sociology that sees general patterns of society in the lives of particular people

sociology (p. 2) the systematic study of human society

spurious correlation (p. 32) an apparent but false relationship between two (or more) variables that is caused by some other variable

state capitalism (p. 412) an economic and political system in which companies are privately owned but cooperate closely with the government

state church (p. 497) a church formally allied with the state

status consistency (p. 245) the degree of consistency in a person's social standing across various dimensions of social inequality

status set (p. 132) all the statuses a person holds at a given time

status (p. 132) a social position that a person holds

stereotype (p. 354) an exaggerated description applied to every person in some category

stigma (p. 216) a powerfully negative label that greatly changes a person's self-concept and social identity

streaming (tracking, or ability grouping) (p. 527) assigning students to different types of educational programs

structural-functional approach (p. 15) a framework for building theory that sees society as a complex system whose parts work together to promote solidarity and stability

structural social mobility (p. 248) a shift in the social position of large numbers of people owed more to changes in society itself than to individual efforts

subculture (p. 71) cultural patterns that set apart some segment of a society's population

suburbs (p. 579) urban areas beyond the political boundaries of a city

superego (p. 111) Freud's term for the cultural values and norms internalized by an individual

survey (p. 42) a research method in which subjects respond to a series of statements or questions in a questionnaire or an interview

symbol (p. 60) anything that carries a particular meaning recognized by people who share a culture

symbolic-interaction approach (p. 18) a framework for building theory that sees society as the product of the everyday interactions of individuals

technology (p. 69) knowledge that people use to make a way of life in their surroundings

terrorism (p. 453) acts of violence or the threat of violence used as a political strategy by an individual or a group

tertiary sector (p. 407) the part of the economy that involves services rather than goods

theoretical approach (theoretical paradigm) (p. 4) a basic image of society that guides thinking and research

theory (p. 14) a statement of how and why specific facts are related

Thomas theorem (p. 137) W.I. Thomas's statement that situations that are defined as real are real in their consequences

total institution (p. 126) a setting in which people are isolated from the rest of society and manipulated by an administrative staff

totalitarianism (p. 437) a highly centralized political system that extensively regulates people's lives

totem (p. 493) an object in the natural world collectively defined as sacred

tradition (p. 94) values and beliefs passed from generation to generation

traditional authority (p. 432) power legitimized by respect for long-established cultural patterns

tradition-directedness (p. 637) rigid conformity to time-honoured ways of living

transsexuals (p. 185) people who feel they are one sex even though biologically they are the other

triad (p. 161) a social group with three members

underground economy (p. 419) economic activity involving income not reported to the government as required by law

universal medical coverage (p. 543) a system in which the costs of essential medical services are covered by the state

urban ecology (p. 584) the study of the link between the physical and social dimensions of cities

urbanization (p. 576) the concentration of population into cities

validity (p. 31) actually measuring exactly what you intend to measure

values (p. 64) culturally defined standards that people use to decide what is desirable, good, and beautiful, and that serve as broad guidelines for social living

variable (p. 31) a concept whose value changes from case to case

victimless crimes (p. 223) violations of law in which there are no obvious victims

violent crimes (p. 223) crimes against people that involve violence or the threat of violence

war (p. 455) organized, armed conflict among the people of two or more nations, directed by their governments

wealth (p. 269) the total value of money and other assets, minus outstanding debts

welfare capitalism (p. 411) an economic and political system that combines a mostly market-based economy with extensive social welfare programs

white-collar crime (p. 219) crime committed by people of high social position in the course of their occupation

white-collar occupations (p. 251) higher-prestige jobs that involve mostly mental activity

zero population growth (p. 574) the level of reproduction that maintains population in a steady state

REFERENCES

ABBOTT, ANDREW. *The System of Professions: An Essay on the Division of Expert Labor.* Chicago, IL: University of Chicago Press, 1988.

ABELLA, IRVING. *A Coat of Many Colours: Two Centuries of Jewish Life in Canada.* Toronto: Lester and Orpen Dennys, 1989.

ABELLA, IRVING, and HAROLD TROPER. *None Is Too Many: Canada and the Jews in Europe, 1933–1948.* Toronto: Lester and Orpen Dennys, 1982.

ABERLE, DAVID F. *The Peyote Religion Among the Navaho.* Chicago, IL: Aldine, 1966.

ABLEY, MARK. "Losing our Languages." *National Post* (February 14, 2006):A18.

ABRAHAM, CAROLYN. "Red tape denied baby Sonja her brief life." *The Globe and Mail* (July 22, 2006):A1.

ADAMS, MICHAEL. *Fire and Ice: The United States, Canada and the Myth of Converging Values.* Toronto: Penguin Canada, 2003.

——. "My Canada doesn't include religiosity." *The Globe and Mail* (January 10, 2005):A13.

——. "Mr. Harper's child-proof political strategy." *The Globe and Mail* (May 2. 2006):A15.

ADORNO, THEODOR W., ELSE, FRANKEL-BRUNSWICK, DANIEL J. LEVINSON, and R. NEVITT SANFORD. *The Authoritarian Personality.* New York: Harper & Brothers, 1950.

AGUIRRE, BENIGNO E., and E.L. QUARANTELLI. "Methodological, Ideological, and Conceptual-Theoretical Criticisms of Collective Behavior: A Critical Evaluation and Implications for Future Study." *Sociological Focus.* Vol. 16, No. 3 (August 1983):195–216.

AGUIRRE, BENIGNO E., E.L. QUARANTELLI, and JORGE L. MENDOZA. "The Collective Behavior of Fads: Characteristics, Effects, and Career of Streaking." *American Sociological Review.* Vol. 53, No. 4 (August 1988):569–84.

AKERS, RONALD L., MARVIN D. KROHN, LONN LANZA-KADUCE, and MARCIA RADOSEVICH. "Social Learning and Deviant Behavior." *American Sociological Review.* Vol. 44, No. 4 (August 1979):636–55.

ALBA, RICHARD D. *Italian Americans: Into the Twilight of Ethnicity.* Englewood Cliffs, NJ: Prentice Hall, 1985.

ALBANESE PATRIZIA. "Small Town, Big Benefits: The Ripple Effect of $7/Day Child Care." *The Canadian Review of Sociology and Anthropology.* 43(2) (2006):125–40.

ALBAS, DANIEL, and CHERYL ALBAS. "Studying Students Studying: Perspectives, Identities and Activities." In Mary Lorenz Dietz, Robert Prus, and William Shaffir, eds. *Doing Everyday Life: Ethnography as Human Lived Experience.* Mississauga, ON: Copp Clark Longman, 1994.

ALBRECHT, WILLIAM P., JR. *Economics.* 3d ed. Englewood Cliffs, NJ: Prentice Hall, 1983.

ALLAN, EMILIE ANDERSEN, and DARRELL J. STEFFENSMEIER. "Youth, Under-employment, and Property Crime: Differential Effects of Job Availability and Job Quality on Juvenile and Young Adult Arrest Rates." *American Sociological Review.* Vol. 54, No. 1 (February 1989):107–23.

ALLEN, TERRY, The General and the Genocide: General Romeo Dallaire, 2002. [Online] Available www.thirdworldtraveler.com/Heroes/Gen_Romeo_Dallaire. html.

ALLEN, THOMAS B., and CHARLES O. HYMAN. *We Americans: Celebrating a Nation, Its People, and Its Past.* Washington, DC: National Geographic, 1999.

AMATO, PAUL R. "What Children Learn from Divorce." *Population Today.* Vol. 29, No. 1 (January 2001):1, 4.

AMATO, PAUL R., and JULIANA M. SOBOLEWSKI. "The Effects of Divorce and Marital Discord on Adult Children's Psychological Well-Being." *American Sociological Review.* Vol. 66, No. 6 (December 2001):900–21.

AMBLER, JOHN S., and JODY NEATHERY. "Education Policy and Equality: Some Evidence from Europe." *Social Science Quarterly.* Vol. 80, No. 3 (September 1999):437–56.

AMERICAN MEDICAL ASSOCIATION. Executive Summary of Media Violence Survey Analysis, 1996. [Online] Available http://www.ama-assn.org/ad-com/releases/1996/mvan1909.htm.

AMERICAN SOCIOLOGICAL ASSOCIATION. "Code of Ethics." Washington, DC: American Sociological Association, 1997.

——. *The Importance of Collecting Data and Doing Social Scientific Research on Race.* Washington, DC: American Sociological Association, 2003.

AMNESTY INTERNATIONAL. "The Death Penalty: List of Abolitionist and Retentionist Countries.". [Online] Available on April 3, 2000, at http://www. amnesty.org/ailib/intcam/dp/abrelist.htm.

AMNESTY INTERNATIONAL. "Abolitionist and Retentionist Countries." [Online] Available on June 4, 2005, at http://web.amnesty.org/pages/deathpenalty-countries-eng.

ANDERSON, ALAN B., and JAMES S. FRIDERES. *Ethnicity in Canada: Theoretical Perspectives.* Toronto: Butterworths, 1981.

ANDERSON, DORIS. *The Unfinished Revolution.* Toronto: Doubleday Books, 1991.

ANDERSON, ELIJAH. "The Code of the Streets." *Atlantic Monthly.* Vol. 273 (May 1994):81–94.

——. "The Ideologically Driven Critique." *American Journal of Sociology.* Vol. 197, No. 6 (May 2002):1533–50.

ANDERSON, JOHN WARD. "Early to Wed: The Child Brides of India." *Washington Post* (May 24, 1995):A27, A30.

ANDERSON, JOHN WARD, and MOLLY MOORE. "World's Poorest Women Suffer in Common." *Columbus Dispatch* (April 11, 1993):4G.

ANG, IEN. *Watching* Dallas: *Soap Opera and the Melodramatic Imagination.* London, UK: Methuen, 1985.

ANGIER, NATALIE. "Sexual identity predominates: Case of boy raised as girl underscores importance of prenatal events, MDs say." *The Globe and Mail* (March 14, 1997):A1.

AMERICAN PSYCHOLOGICAL ASSOCIATION. *Violence and Youth: Psychology's Response.* Washington, DC: American Psychological Association, 1993.

APPLEBOME, PETER. "70 Years After Scopes Trial, Creation Debate Lives." *New York Times* (March 10, 1996):1, 10.

APUZZO, ALAN. "R.I. Official: Club Owners Not Helpful." [Online] Available February 24, 2003, at http://news.yahoo.com.

ARENDT, HANNAH. *Between Past and Future: Six Exercises in Political Thought.* Cleveland, OH: Meridian Books, 1963.

ARIÈS, PHILIPPE. *Centuries of Childhood: A Social History of Family Life.* New York: Vintage Books, 1965.

ARMSTRONG, JANE. "RCMP Scour Second Site." *The Globe and Mail* (July 21, 2003):A1.

ARMSTRONG, ELISABETH. *The Retreat from Organization: U.S. Feminism Reconceptualized.* Albany, NY: State University of New York Press, 2002.

ARNUP, KATHERINE. " 'We Are Family': Lesbian Mothers in Canada." In E.D. Nelson and B.W. Robinson, eds. *Gender in the 1990s: Images, Realities and Issues.* Scarborough, ON: Nelson Canada, 1995. pp. 330–45.

ARROW, KENNETH, SAMUEL BOWLES, and STEVEN DURLAUF. *Meritocracy and Economic Inequality.* Princeton, NJ: Princeton University Press, 2000.

ARTIBISE, ALAN F.J. "Canada as an Urban Nation", *Daedalus* 117, Fall, 1988.

ARTIBISE, ALAN F.J., and GIL STELTER. "Urbanization." In *The Canadian Encyclopedia.* 2d ed. Edmonton: Hurtig Publishers, 1988. pp. 2235–36.

ASCH, SOLOMON. *Social Psychology.* Englewood Cliffs, NJ: Prentice Hall, 1952.

ASHFORD, LORI S. "New Perspectives on Population: Lessons from Cairo." *Population Bulletin.* Vol. 50, No. 1 (March 1995).

ATCHLEY, ROBERT C. "Retirement as a Social Institution." *Annual Review of Sociology.* Vol. 8. Palo Alto, CA: Annual Reviews, 1982. pp. 263–87.

ATKINSON, MICHAEL. "It's Still Part of the Game: Masculinity, Crime and Victimization in Ice Hockey." In L. Fuller (ed.) *Sport, Rhetoric, Gender and Violence: Historical Perspectives and Media Representations.* New York: Palgrave MacMillan, 2007.

ATTALLAH, PAUL. "Television and the Canadian Federal Election of 2004." In Jon H. Pammett and Christopher Dornan (eds.) *The Canadian General Election of 2004.* Toronto: The Dundurn Group, 2004. pp. 264–89.

ATWOOD, MARGARET. "True Trash." In *Wilderness Tips.* Toronto: McClelland & Stewart, 1991. pp.1–30.

AXINN, WILLIAM G., and JENNIFER S. BARBER. "Mass Education and Fertility Transition." *American Sociological Review.* Vol. 66, No. 4 (August 2001): 481–505.

BADETS, JANE, and LINDA HOWATSON-LEO. "Recent Immigrants in the Workforce." In Statistics Canada, *Canadian Social Trends. Volume 3.* Toronto: Thompson Educational Publishing, 2000.

BAKALAR, NICHOLAS. "Reactions: Go On, Laugh Your Heart Out." *New York Times* (March 8, 2005). [Online] Available March 11, 2005, at http://www.nytimes. com/2005/03/08/health/08reac.html.

BAKER, MARY ANNE, CATHERINE WHITE BERHEIDE, FAY ROSS GRECKEL, LINDA CARSTARPHEN GUGIN, MARCIA J. LIPETZ, and MARCIA TEXLER SEGAL. *Women Today: A Multidisciplinary Approach to Women's Studies.* Monterey, CA: Brooks/Cole, 1980.

BAKER, MAUREEN. In Lorne Tepperman and R. Jack Richardson, eds. *The Social World: An Introduction to Sociology.* Toronto: McGraw Hill Ryerson, 1991. pp. 353–81.

BAKER, PATRICIA S., WILLIAM C. YOELS, JEFFREY M. CLAIR, and RICHARD M. ALLMAN. "Laughter in the Triadic Geriatric Encounters: A Transcript-Based Analysis." In Rebecca J. Erikson and Beverly Cuthbertson-Johnson, eds., *Social Perspectives on Emotion.* Vol. 4. Greenwich, CT: JAI Press, 1997: 179–207.

BAKKER, J.I. (HANS). "Wilhelm Dilthey: Classical Sociological Theorist." *Quarterly Journal of Ideology: A Critique of Conventional Wisdom.* Vol. 22, No. 1–2 (1999).

BAKKER, J.I. (HANS), and T.R.A. (THEO) BAKKER. "The Club DJ: A Semiotic and Interactionist Analysis." *Symbolic Interaction* Vol. 29, No. 1 (2006):71–82.

BAKKER, J.I. (HANS), and ANTHONY WINSON. "Rural Sociology." In Peter S. Li and B. Singh Bolaria, eds. *Contemporary Sociology: Critical Perspectives.* Toronto: Copp Clark Pitman, 1993. pp. 500–17.

BALDUS, BERND, and VERNA TRIBE. "The Development of Perceptions and Evaluations of Social Inequality Among Public School Children." *Canadian Review of Sociology and Anthropology.* Vol. 15, No. 1 (1978):50–60.

BALTES, PAUL B., and K. WARNER SCHAIE. "The Myth of the Twilight Years." *Psychology Today.* Vol. 7, No. 10 (March 1974):35–39.

BALTZELL, E. DIGBY. *The Protestant Establishment: Aristocracy and Caste in America.* New York: Vintage Books, 1964.

——. *Philadelphia Gentlemen: The Making of a National Upper Class.* Philadelphia, PA: University of Pennsylvania Press, 1979; orig. 1958.

BANFIELD, EDWARD C. *The Unheavenly City Revisited.* Boston: Little, Brown, 1974.

BARASH, DAVID. *The Whispering Within.* New York: Penguin Books, 1981.

BARLOW, MAUDE, and BRUCE CAMPBELL. *Take Back the Nation.* Toronto: Key Porter Books, 1991.

BARLOW, MAUDE, and HEATHER-JANE ROBERTSON. *Class Warfare: The Assault on Canada's Schools.* Toronto: Key Porter, 1994.

BARNES, JULIAN E. "War Profiteering." *U.S. News & World Report* (May 13, 2002b):20–24.

——. "Unequal Education." *U.S. News & World Report* (March 22, 2004):66–75.

BARRETT, STANLEY R. *Is God a Racist? The Right Wing in Canada.* Toronto: University of Toronto Press, 1987.

BARON, JAMES N., MICHAEL T. HANNAN, and M. DIANE BURTON. "Building the Iron Cage: Determinants of Managerial Intensity in the Early Years of Organizations." *American Sociological Review.* Vol. 64, No. 4 (August 1999):527–47.

BAROVICK, HARRIET. "Tongues That Go out of Style." *Time* (June 10, 2002):22.

BASHEVKIN, SYLVIA B. *Toeing the Lines: Women and Party Politics in Canada.* 2d ed. Toronto: Oxford University Press, 1993.

BASSETT, ISABEL. *The Bassett Report: Career Success and Canadian Women.* Toronto: Collins, 1985.

BASSUK, ELLEN J. "The Homelessness Problem." *Scientific American.* Vol. 251, No. 1 (July 1984):40–45.

BAUER, P.T. *Equality, the Third World, and Economic Delusion.* Cambridge, MA: Harvard University Press, 1981.

BAUMGARTNER, M.P. "Introduction: The Moral Voice of the Community." *Sociological Focus.* Vol. 31, No. 2 (May 1998):105–17.

BAYDAR, NAZLI, and JEANNE BROOKS-GUNN. "Effect of Maternal Employment and Child-Care Arrangements on Preschoolers' Cognitive and Behavioral Outcomes: Evidence from Children from the National Longitudinal Survey of Youth." *Developmental Psychology.* Vol. 27 (1991):932–35.

BBC. "The Paul McCartney Death Clues," March 9, 2000 [Online] Available at http://www.bbc.co.uk/h2g2/guide/A277328.

BEARAK, BARRY. "Lives Held Cheap in Bangladesh Sweatshops." *New York Times* (April 15, 2001):A1, A12.

BEAUJOT, RODERIC, and KEVIN MCQUILLAN. *Growth and Dualism: The Demographic Development of Canadian Society.* Toronto: Gage, 1982.

BECKER, HOWARD S. *Outside: Studies in the Sociology of Deviance.* New York: Free Press, 1966.

BEDARD, PAUL. "Washington Whispers." *U.S. News & World Report* (March 25, 2002):2.

BEEGHLEY, LEONARD. *The Structure of Social Stratification in the United States.* Needham Heights, MA: Allyn & Bacon, 1989.

BEGIN, PATRICIA. *Violence Against Women: Current Response* (Catalogue No. 1391B67). Ottawa: Ministry of Supply and Services, September 1991.

BEGLEY, SHARON. "Gray Matters." *Newsweek* (March 7, 1995):48–54.

——. "How to Beat the Heat." *Newsweek* (December 8, 1997):34–38.

BELL, DANIEL. *The Coming of Post-Industrial Society: A Venture in Social Forecasting.* New York: Basic Books, 1973.

BELLAH, ROBERT N. *The Broken Covenant.* New York: Seabury Press, 1975.

BELLAH, ROBERT N., RICHARD MADSEN, WILLIAM M. SULLIVAN, ANN SWIDLER, and STEVEN M. TIPTON. *Habits of the Heart: Individualism and Commitment in American Life.* New York: Harper & Row, 1985.

BELLE, MARILYN, and KEVIN MCQUILLAN. "Births Outside Marriage: A Growing Alternative." In Statistics Canada, *Canadian Social Trends. Volume 3.* Toronto: Thompson Educational Publishing, 2000.

BELTRAME, JULIAN. "Latimer's Last Chances for Earlier Release Appear Slim." *Maclean's* (January 29, 2001).

BEM, SANDRA LIPSITZ. *The Lenses of Gender: Transforming the Debate on Sexual Inequality.* New Haven, CT: Yale University Press, 1993.

BENEDETTI, PAUL, and NANCY DEHART, EDS. *On McLuhan: Forward Through the Rearview Mirror.* Scarborough, ON: Prentice Hall, 1996.

BENEDICT, RUTH. "Continuities and Discontinuities in Cultural Conditioning." *Psychiatry.* Vol. 1 (May 1938):161–67.

BENJAMIN, LOIS. *The Black Elite: Facing the Color Line in the Twilight of the Twentieth Century.* Chicago, IL: Nelson-Hall, 1991.

BENJAMIN, MATTHEW. "Suite Deals." *U.S. News & World Report* (April 29, 2002): 32–34.

BENN, CARL. *Historic Fort York, 1793–1993.* Toronto: Natural Heritage, 1993.

BENNETT, WILLIAM J. "Quantifying America's Decline." *Wall Street Journal* (March 15, 1993).

BENOKRAITIS, NIJOLE, and JOE FEAGIN. *Modern Sexism: Blatant, Subtle, and Overt Discrimination.* 2d ed. Englewood Cliffs, NJ: Prentice Hall, 1995.

BERCUSON, DAVID, and BARRY COOPER. "A New Tax on Energy Is Unacceptable." *The Globe and Mail* (November 8, 1997):D2.

BERGAMO, MONICA, and GERSON CAMAROTTI. "Brazil's Landless Millions." *World Press Review.* Vol. 43, No. 7 (July 1996):46–47.

BERGER, PETER L. *Invitation to Sociology.* New York: Anchor Books, 1963.

——. *The Sacred Canopy: Elements of a Sociological Theory of Religion.* Garden City, NY: Doubleday, 1967.

——. *The Capitalist Revolution: Fifty Propositions About Prosperity, Equality, and Liberty.* New York: Basic Books, 1986.

——. *Redeeming Laughter: The Comic Dimension of Human Experience.* Berlin: Walter de Gruyter, 1997.

BERGER, PETER, BRIGITTE BERGER, and HANSFRIED KELLNER. *The Homeless Mind: Modernization and Consciousness.* New York: Vintage Books, 1974.

BERGER, PETER L., and HANSFRIED KELLNER. *Sociology Reinterpreted: An Essay on Method and Vocation.* Garden City, NY: Anchor Books, 1981.

BERGESEN, ALBERT, ED. *Crises in the World-System.* Beverly Hills, CA: Sage, 1983.

BERNARD, JESSIE. *The Female World.* New York: Free Press, 1981.

——. *The Future of Marriage.* New Haven, CT: Yale University Press, 1982; orig. 1973.

BERNSTEIN, NINA. "On Frontier of Cyberspace, Data Is Money, and a Threat." *New York Times* (June 12, 1997):A1, B14–15.

BERRY, BRIAN L., and PHILIP H. REES. "The Factorial Ecology of Calcutta." *American Journal of Sociology.* Vol. 74, No. 5 (March 1969):445–91.

BERTEAU, CELESTE. "Disconnected Intimacy: AOL Instant Messenger Use among Kenyon College Students." Senior thesis. Kenyon College, 2005.

BESHAROV, DOUGLAS J., and LISA A. LAUMANN. "Child Abuse Reporting." *Society.* Vol. 34, No. 4 (May/June 1996):40–46.

BESS, IRWIN. "Widows Living Alone." In Statistics Canada, *Canadian Social Trends. Volume 3.* Toronto: Thompson Educational Publishing, 2000. pp. 165–69.

BEST, RAPHAELA. *We've All Got Scars: What Boys and Girls Learn in Elementary School.* Bloomington: Indiana University Press, 1983.

BIAN, YANJIE. "Chinese Social Stratification and Social Mobility." *Annual Review of Sociology.* Vol. 28 (2002):91–116.

BIBBY, REGINALD W. "The Moral Mosaic: Sexuality in Canada 80s." *Social Indicators Research.* Vol. 13 (1983):171–84.

——. *Fragmented Gods: The Poverty and Potential of Religion in Canada.* Toronto: Irwin, 1987.

——. *The Bibby Report: Social Trends Canadian Style.* Toronto: Stoddart, 1995.

——. *Canada's Teens: Today, Yesterday and Tomorrow.* Toronto: Stoddart, 2001.

——. *Restless Churches: How Canada's Churches Can Contribute to the Emerging Religious Renaissance.* Toronto: Novalis. 2004a.

——. *Restless Gods: The Renaissance of Religion in Canada.* Toronto: Novalis, 2004b.

BIBBY, REGINALD W., and DONALD C. POSTERSKI. *The Emerging Generation: An Inside Look at Canada's Teenagers.* Toronto: Irwin Publishing, 1985.

BISHOP, MARY F. "Birth Control." In *The Canadian Encyclopedia.* 2d ed. Vol. 1. Edmonton: Hurtig Publishers, 1988:231–32.

BISSOONDATH, NEIL. *Selling Illusions: The Cult of Multiculturalism in Canada.* Toronto: Penguin Books, 1994.

BLACK, NAOMI. "Agnes MacPhail." In *The Canadian Encyclopedia.* 2d ed. Vol. 2. Edmonton: Hurtig Publishers, 1988. p. 1281.

BLACKWOOD, EVELYN, and SASKIA WIERINGA, EDS. *Female Desires: Same-Sex Relations and Transgender Practices across Cultures.* New York: Columbia University Press, 1999.

BLANKENHORN, DAVID. *Fatherless America: Confronting Our Most Urgent Social Problem.* New York: HarperCollins, 1995.

BLAU, JUDITH R., and PETER M. BLAU. "The Cost of Inequality: Metropolitan Structure and Violent Crime." *American Sociological Review.* Vol. 47, No. 1 (February 1982):114–29.

BLAU, PETER M. *Exchange and Power in Social Life.* New York: Wiley, 1964.

——. *Inequality and Heterogeneity: A Primitive Theory of Social Structure.* New York: Free Press, 1977.

BLAU, PETER M., TERRY C. BLUM, and JOSEPH E. SCHWARTZ. "Heterogeneity and Intermarriage." *American Sociological Review.* Vol. 47, No. 1 (February 1982):45–62.

BLISHEN, BERNARD R. "The Construction and Use of an Occupational Class Scale." *Canadian Journal of Economics and Political Science.* Vol. XXIV (1958):519–25.

——. *Doctors in Canada.* Toronto: University of Toronto Press, 1991.

BLISHEN, BERNARD R., W. CARROLL, and C. MOORE. "The 1981 Socio-Economic Index for Occupations in Canada." *Canadian Review of Sociology and Anthropology.* Vol. 24 (1987):465–88.

BLUMBERG, ABRAHAM S. *Criminal Justice.* Chicago, IL: Quadrangle Books, 1970.

BLUMBERG, PAUL. *Inequality in an Age of Decline.* New York: Oxford University Press, 1981.

BLUMER, HERBERT G. "Collective Behavior." In Alfred McClung Lee, ed. *Principles of Sociology.* 3d ed. New York: Barnes & Noble Books, 1969. pp. 65–121.

BLUMSTEIN, PHILIP, and PEPPER SCHWARTZ. *American Couples.* New York: William Morrow, 1983.

BOBO, LAWRENCE, and VINCENT L. HUTCHINGS. "Perceptions of Racial Group Competition: Extending Blumer's Theory of Group Position to a Multiracial Social Context." *American Sociological Review.* Vol. 61, No. 6 (December 1996):951–72.

BOGARDUS, EMORY S. "Comparing Racial Distance in Ethiopia, South Africa, and the United States." *Sociology and Social Research.* Vol. 52, No. 2 (January 1968):149–56.

BOHANNAN, CECIL. "The Economic Correlates of Homelessness in Sixty Cities." *Social Science Quarterly.* Vol. 72, No. 4 (December 1991):817–25.

BOHLEN, CELESTINE. "Facing Oblivion, Rust-Belt Giants Top Russian List of Vexing Crises." *New York Times* (November 8, 1998):1, 6.

BONANNO, ALESSANDRO, DOUGLAS H. CONSTANCE, and HEATHER LORENZ. "Powers and Limits of Transnational Corporations: The Case of ADM." *Rural Sociology.* Vol. 65, No. 3 (September 2000):440–60.

BONILLA-SANTIAGO, GLORIA. "A Portrait of Hispanic Women in the United States." In Sara E. Rix, ed. *The American Woman, 1990–91: A Status Report.* New York: Norton, 1990. pp. 249–57.

BONNER, JANE. Research presented in "The Two Brains." Public Broadcasting System telecast, 1984.

BORITCH, HELEN. *Fallen Women: Female Crime and Criminal Justice in Canada.* Toronto: ITP Nelson, 1997.

BORMANN, F. HERBERT. "The Global Environmental Deficit." *BioScience.* Vol. 40 (1990):74.

BOTT, ELIZABETH. *Family and Social Network.* New York: Free Press, 1971; orig. 1957.

BOULDING, ELISE. *The Underside of History.* Boulder, CO: Westview Press, 1976.

BOWLES, SAMUEL, and HERBERT GINTIS. *Schooling in Capitalist America: Educational Reform and the Contradictions of Economic Life.* New York: Basic Books, 1976.

BOYD, MONICA, and NORRIS, DOUG. "Crowded Nest? Young Adults at Home." *Canadian Social Trends.* Vol. 3. Toronto: Thompson, 2000. pp. 161–64.

BOYER, DEBRA. "Male Prostitution and Homosexual Identity." *Journal of Homosexuality.* Vol. 17, Nos. 1–2 (1989):151–84.

BOYLE, ELIZABETH HEGER, FORTUNATA SONGORA, and GAIL FOSS. "International Discourse and Local Politics: Anti-Female-Genital-Cutting Laws in Egypt, Tanzania, and the United States." *Social Problems.* Vol. 48, No. 4 (November 2001):524–44.

BOZINOFF, LORNE, and PETER MacINTOSH. "Vast Majority of Canadians Believe in God and Heaven." Toronto: Gallup Report, August 30, 1990.

BREND, YVETTE. "Why History Lives in Old Crow." *The Globe and Mail* (November 11, 1997):A2.

BRETHOUR, PATRICK. "The Boardroom or Romper Room?" *The Globe and Mail* (May 1, 2006):A1.

BRETON, RAYMOND. "Institutional Completeness of Ethnic Communities and the Personal Relations of Immigrants." *American Journal of Sociology.* Vol. 70 (1964):193–205.

——. "Ethnic Stratification Viewed from Three Theoretical Perspectives." In James E. Curtis and William G. Scott, eds. *Social Stratification: Canada.* 2d ed. Scarborough, ON: Prentice Hall, 1979:270–94.

——. "Regionalism in Canada." In David Cameron, ed. *Regionalism and Supranationalism.* Montreal: Institute for Research on Public Policy, 1981.

——. *Why Meech Failed: Lessons for Canadian Constitutionmaking.* Toronto: C.D. Howe Institute, 1992.

BRICKER, DARRELL, and JOHN WRIGHT. *What Canadians Think... about Almost Everything.* Toronto: Doubleday Canada, 2005.

BRINTON, MARY C. "The Social-Institutional Bases of Gender Stratification: Japan as an Illustrative Case." *American Journal of Sociology.* Vol. 94, No. 2 (September 1988):300–34.

BROCKERHOFF, MARTIN P. "An Urbanizing World." *Population Bulletin.* Vol. 55, No. 3 (September 2000):1–44.

BRODIE, JANINE. "The Political Economy of Regionalism." In Wallace Clement and Glen Williams, eds. *The New Canadian Political Economy.* Montreal: McGill-Queen's University Press, 1989. pp. 138–59.

BRODER, DAVID S. "Stock Options Belong in the Line of Fire." *Columbus Dispatch* (April 21, 2002):G3.

BROOKS, DAVID. *Bobos in Paradise: The New Upper Class and How They Got There.* New York: Simon & Schuster, 2000.

BROWN, LESTER R. "Reassessing the Earth's Population." *Society.* Vol. 32, No. 4 (May/June 1995):7–10.

BROWN, LESTER R., ET AL., EDS. *State of the World 1993: A Worldwatch Institute Report on Progress Toward a Sustainable Society.* New York: Norton, 1993.

BROWN, MARY ELLEN, ED. *Television and Women's Culture: The Politics of the Popular.* Newbury Park, CA: Sage, 1990.

BRYM, ROBERT J. "The Canadian Capitalist Class, 1965–1985." In Robert J. Brym, ed. *The Structures of the Canadian Capitalist Class.* Toronto: Garamond, 1985:1–20.

BRYM, ROBERT J., ED. *Regionalism in Canada.* Toronto: Irwin, 1986.

BRYM, ROBERT J., and BONNIE J. FOX. *From Culture to Power: The Sociology of English Canada.* Don Mills, ON: Oxford University Press, 1989.

BURAWAY, MICHAEL. "Review Essay: The Soviet Descent into Capitalism." *American Journal of Sociology.* Vol. 102, No. 5 (March 1997):1430–44.

BUECHLER, STEVEN M. *Social Movements in Advanced Capitalism: The Political Economy and Cultural Construction of Social Activism.* New York: Oxford University Press, 2000.

BURKETT, ELINOR. "God Created Me to Be a Slave." *New York Times Magazine* (October 12, 1997):56–60.

BUTLER, ROBERT N. *Why Survive? Being Old in America.* New York: Harper & Row, 1975.

BUTTERWORTH, DOUGLAS, and JOHN K. CHANCE. *Latin American Urbanization.* Cambridge: Cambridge University Press, 1981.

CAFB. Canadian Association of Food Banks. Annual Report. 2004. [Online] Available at http://www.cafb-acba.ca/documents/04annual_report.pdf.

CALLAHAN, DANIEL. *Setting Limits: Medical Goals in an Aging Society.* New York: Simon & Schuster, 1987.

CALLOW, A.B., JR., ED. *American Urban History.* New York: Oxford University Press, 1969.

CAME, BARRY. "Coming of Age: As He Turns 18, Prince William Is Showing an Independent Streak." *Maclean's* (May 22, 2000):14.

CAMERON, WILLIAM BRUCE. *Modern Social Movements: A Sociological Outline.* New York: Random House, 1966.

CAMPBELL. ROBERT A. "Students' Views on the Relationship between Religion and Science: Analyses of Results from a Comparative Survey." *The Canadian Review of Sociology and Anthropology* 42(3) (August, 2005):249–66.

CANADA. Royal Commission on the Status of Women in Canada. *Report of the Royal Commission on the Status of Women in Canada.* Ottawa: Information Canada, 1970.

——. *Canadian Charter of Rights and Freedoms,* enacted as Part I of the *Constitution Act, 1982,* being Schedule B to the *Canada Act, 1982* (U.K.), 1982, c.11.

——. Canadian International Development Agency. *Sharing Our Future: Canadian International Development Assistance.* Ottawa: Ministry of Supply and Services Canada, 1987.

——. *Demographic Aging: The Economic Consequences.* Ottawa: Ministry of Supply and Services, 1991.

——. Secretary of State Canada. *Profile of Higher Education in Canada* (S2-196/1991). Ottawa: Ministry of Supply and Services, 1992.

——. Royal Commission on Aboriginal Peoples. *Ethical Guidelines for Research.* 8 pp. Ottawa: Supply and Services Canada, 1993a.

——. House of Commons. Standing Committee on Communications and Culture. *Television Violence: Fraying our Social Fabric.* Issue No. 6. Ottawa: Supply and Services Canada, 1993b.

——. Royal Commission on Aboriginal Peoples. *Choosing Life: Special Report on Suicide among Aboriginal People.* Ottawa: Minister of Supply and Services Canada, 1995.

——. *Report of the Royal Commission on Aboriginal Peoples: Perspectives and Realities.* Vol. 4. Ottawa: Minister of Supply and Services Canada, 1996a.

——. Final report of the Royal Commission on Aboriginal Peoples. 6 Vols. Ottawa: Ministry of Indian Affairs and Northern Development, 1996b.

——. *The Economic and Fiscal Update.* Ottawa: Department of Finance, October 1997.

——. Advisory Council on Suicide Prevention. *Acting on What We Know: Preventing Youth Suicide in First Nations.* Ottawa: Health Canada, 2003a. [Online] Available at hhttp://www.hc-sc.gc.ca/fnihb-dgspni/fnihb/cp/publications/preventing_youth_suicide.htm.

——. Social Sciences and Humanities Research Council of Canada. Tri-Council Policy Statement: Ethical Conduct for Research Involving Humans. 2003b (includes updates to 2005). [Online] Available at http://www.pre.ethics.gc.ca/english/policystatement/policystatement.cfm.

——. Citizenship and Immigration Canada. Priorities, Planning, and Research Branch. "Foreign Students in Canada, 1980–2001," January 2003c. [Online] Available at http://www.cic.gc.ca/english/srr/research/foreign-students/students.html#_Toc32910764.

——. Health Canada. *HIV and AIDS in Canada: Surveillance Report to December 31, 2002,* Division of HIC/AIDS Epidemiology and Surveillance, Centre for Infectious Disease Prevention and Control, Health Canada, 2003d. [Online] Available at http://www.hc-sc.gc.ca/pphb-dgspsp/publicat/aids-sida/ haic-vsac1202/index.html.

——. Correctional Service Canada. 2006a. [Online] Available at http://www.csc-scc.gc.ca.

——. Health Canada. 2006b. [Online] Available at http://www.hc-sc.gc.ca.

——. Canada Food Inspection Agency. 2006c. [Online] Available at http://www.inspection.gc.ca.

CANADA'S 125TH ANNIVERSARY YEARBOOK. Ottawa: Minister of Supply and Services, 1992.

CANADA YEAR BOOK. Ottawa: Statistics Canada, 1994.

CANADIAN GLOBAL ALMANAC 1993: A BOOK OF FACTS. John Robert Colombo, ed. Toronto: Macmillan, 1992.

CANADIAN GLOBAL ALMANAC 2003. Toronto: Wiley & Sons, 2002.

CANADIAN GLOBAL ALMANAC. Toronto: Wiley & Sons, 2005.

CANETTI, ELIAS. *Crowds and Power.* New York: Seabury Press, 1978.

CANTOR, MURIAL G., and SUZANNE PINGREE. *The Soap Opera.* Beverly Hills, CA: Sage, 1983.

CANTRIL, HADLEY, HAZEL GAUDET, and HERTA HERZOG. *Invasion from Mars: A Study in the Psychology of Panic.* Princeton, NJ: Princeton University Press, 1947.

CARMICHAEL, STOKELY, and CHARLES V. HAMILTON. *Black Power: The Politics of Liberation in America.* New York: Vintage Books, 1967.

CARROLL, JAMES R. "Congress Is Told of Coal-Dust Fraud UMW; Senator from Minnesota Rebukes Industry." *Louisville Courier Journal* (May 27, 1999):1A.

CARRIÉRE, YVES. "Population and Hospital Days: Will There Be a Problem?" In Ellen M. Gee and Gloria M. Gutman, *The Overselling of Population Aging: Apocalyptic Demography, Intergenerational Challenges, and Social Policy.* Don Mills, ON: Oxford University Press, 2000. pp. 26–44.

CARRIGAN, D. OWEN. *Crime and Punishment in Canada: A History.* Toronto: McClelland & Stewart, 1991.

CARROLL, MICHAEL P. "Who Owns Democracy? Explaining the Long-running Debate over Canadian/American Value Differences." *The Canadian Review of Sociology and Anthropology* 42(3) (2005):267–82.

CASEY, QUENTIN. "Organized religion in decline, but faith is not." *National Post* (May 3, 2006):A2.

CBC. *The National Magazine.* January 16, 1998.

CBC. "SEC accuses Conrad Black of Fraud." 2004. [Online] Available at http://www.cbc.ca/story/business/national/2004/11/15/blacksec_041115.html.

——. "Conrad Black: Lager-heir to London lord." 2005a. [Online] Available at http://www.cbc.ca/news/background/black_conrad/.

——. Residential School Package. News Online. Available on Novermber 23, 2005.

——. Carla Robinson. 2006. [Online] Available at http://www.cbc.ca/programguide/personality/?personality=Robinson%2C+Carla&program=Absolutely+Canadian.

CBC SPORTS. "Former NHL coach Jacques Demers admits he's illiterate." 2005. [Online] Available at .

CENTER FOR THE STUDY OF SPORT IN SOCIETY. *1997 Racial Report Card: A Study in the NBA, NFL, and Major League Baseball.* Boston: Northeastern University, 1998.

CHANDLER, TERTIUS, and GERALD FOX. *3000 Years of Urban History.* New York: Academic Press, 1974.

CHAGNON, NAPOLEON A. *Ynomamö: The Fierce People.* 4th ed. Austin, TX: Holt, Rinehart and Winston, 1992.

CHARD, JENNIFER, and VIVIENNE RENAUD. "Visible Minorities in Toronto, Vancouver, and Montréal." In Statistics Canada, *Canadian Social Trends. Volume 3.* Toronto: Thompson Educational Publishing, 2000.

CHAUNCEY, GEORGE. *Gay New York: Gender, Urban Culture, and the Making of the Gay Male World, 1890–1940.* New York: Basic Books, 1994.

CHE-ALFORD, JANET, and BRIAN HAMM. "Under One Roof: Three Generations Living Together." *Canadian Social Trends. Volume 3.* Toronto: Thompson Educational Publishing, 2000. pp. 161–64.

CHRISTIAN, WILLIAM. "Innis, Harold Adams." In *The Canadian Encyclopedia.* 2d ed. Vol. 1. Edmonton: Hurtig, 1988. p. 1069.

CIMINO, RICHARD, and DON LATTIN. "Choosing My Religion." *American Demographics.* Vol. 21, No. 4 (April 1999):60–65.

CLARK, CAMPBELL. "Six Liberal contenders don't pass as bilingual." *The Globe and Mail* (May 15, 2006):A1.

CLARK, CURTIS B. "Geriatric Abuse: Out of the Closet." In *The Tragedy of Elder Abuse: The Problem and the Response.* Hearings before the Select Committee on Aging, House of Representatives (July 1, 1986):49–50.

CLARK, MARGARET S., ED. *Prosocial Behavior.* Newbury Park, CA: Sage, 1991.

CLARKSON, STEPHEN. "Disaster and Recovery: Paul Martin as Political Lazarus." In Jon H. Pammett and Christopher Dornan (eds.) *The Canadian General Election of 2004.* Toronto: The Dundurn Group, 2004. pp. 28–65.

CLEMENT, WALLACE. *The Canadian Corporate Elite: Economic Power in Canada.* Toronto: McClelland & Stewart, 1975.

——. "Comparative Class Analysis: Locating Canada in a North American and Nordic Context." *Canadian Review of Sociology and Anthropology.* Vol. 27, No. 4 (1990).

COWAN, JAMES. "Toronto asks its $90,000 question." *National Post* (April 20, 2006):1.

CLOUD, JOHN, and JODIE MORSE. "Home Sweet School." *Time* (August 27, 2001):46–54.

CLUFF, JULIE, ALISON HUNTER, and RONALD HINCH. "Feminist Perspectives on Serial Murder: A Critical Analysis." Homicide Studies. Vol. 1, No. 3:291–308.

COHEN, ADAM. "Test-Tube Tug-of-War." *Time* (April 6, 1998):65.

COHEN, ALBERT K. *Delinquent Boys: The Culture of the Gang.* New York: Free Press, 1971; orig. 1955.

COHEN, ELIAS. "The Complex Nature of Ageism: What Is It? Who Does It? Who Perceives It?" *Gerontologist.* Vol. 41, No. 5 (October 2001):576–78.

COLAPINTO, JOHN. *As Nature Made Him: The Boy Who Was Raised as a Girl.* Toronto: HarperCollins, 2000.

COLEMAN, WILLIAM D. *The Independence Movement in Quebec, 1945–1980.* Toronto: University of Toronto Press, 1984.

COLLYMORE, YVETTE. "Migrant Street Children on the Rise in Central America." *Population Today.* Vol. 30, No. 2 (February/March 2002):1, 4.

COLTON, HELEN. *The Gift of Touch: How Physical Contact Improves Communication, Pleasure, and Health.* New York: Seaview/Putnam, 1983.

COMTE, AUGUSTE. *Auguste Comte and Positivism: The Essential Writings.* Gertrud Lenzer, ed. New York: Harper Torchbooks, 1975.

COMPUTER INDUSTRY ALMANAC INC. "Internet Users Will Top 1 Billion in 2005" (press release), March 12, 2002. [Online] Available at http://www.c-i-a.com.

CONNETT, PAUL H. "The Disposable Society." In F. Herbert Bormann and Stephen R. Kellert, eds. *Ecology, Economics, and Ethics: The Broken Circle.* New Haven, CT: Yale University Press, 1991. pp. 99–122.

COOLEY, CHARLES HORTON. *Social Organization.* New York: Schocken Books, 1962; orig. 1909.

——. *Human Nature and the Social Order.* New York: Schocken Books, 1964; orig. 1902.

CORAK, MILES. "Getting Ahead: Does Your Parents' Income Count?" In *Canadian Social Trends. Volume 3.* Toronto: Thompson Educational Publishing, 2000.

CORBEIL, JEAN-PIERRE. "Sport Participation in Canada." In Statistics Canada, *Canadian Social Trends. Volume 3.* Toronto: Thompson Educational Publishing, 2000a.

CORLEY, ROBERT N., O. LEE REED, PETER J. SHEDD, and JERE W. MOREHEAD. *The Legal and Regulatory Environment of Business.* 9th ed. New York: McGraw-Hill, 1993.

CORTESE, ANTHONY J. *Provocateur: Images of Women and Minorities in Advertising.* Lanham, MD: Rowman & Littlefield, 1999.

CÔTÉ, JAMES E., and ANTON L. ALLAHAR. "Youth: The Disinherited Generation." In Dan Glenday and Ann Duffy, eds. *Canadian Society: Meeting the Challenges of the Twenty-First Century.* Toronto: Oxford University Press, 2001.

COTTRELL, JOHN, and THE EDITORS OF TIME-LIFE. *The Great Cities: Mexico City.* Amsterdam: 1979.

COUNTS, G.S. "The Social Status of Occupations: A Problem in Vocational Guidance." *School Review.* Vol. 33 (January 1925):16–27.

COWGILL, DONALD, and LOWELL HOLMES. *Aging and Modernization.* New York: Appleton-Century-Crofts, 1972.

COWLEY, GEOFFREY. "The Prescription That Kills." *Newsweek* (July 17, 1995): 54.

COX, HARVEY. *The Secular City.* Rev. ed. New York: Macmillan, 1971; orig. 1965.

CRANE, DIANA. *Fashion and Its Social Agenda: Class, Gender, and Identity in Clothing.* Chicago: University of Chicago Press, 2000.

CRANWICK, KELLY. "Canada's Caregivers." *Canadian Social Trends.* Vol. 3. Toronto: Thompson, 2000. pp. 121–25.

CREESE, GILLIAN, NEIL GUPPY, and MARTIN MEISSNER. *Ups and Downs on the Ladder of Success.* Ottawa: Statistics Canada, 1991.

CROSSETTE, BARBARA. "Female Genital Mutilation by Immigrants Is Becoming Cause for Concern in the U.S." *New York Times International* (December 10, 1995):11.

CROUSE, JAMES, and DALE TRUSHEIM. *The Case Against the SAT.* Chicago, IL: University of Chicago Press, 1988.

CRUTSINGER, MARTIN. "Trade Deficit Hits $665.9 Billion in 2004." [Online] Available March 16, 2005, at http://news.yahoo.com.

CTV. "Jews most likely target of hate crimes: survey." 2004. [Online] Available at .

——. "Gomery Report: Key Players." 2005. [Online] Available at http://www.ctv.ca/servlet/ArticleNews/story/CTVNews/20051031/gomeryreport_sponsorshipplayers_20051031/20051031/.

CUMMING, ELAINE, and WILLIAM E. HENRY. *Growing Old: The Process of Disengagement.* New York: Basic Books, 1961.

CURRIE, ELLIOTT. *Confronting Crime: An American Challenge.* New York: Pantheon Books, 1985.

CURTIS, JAMES E., DOUGLAS E. BAER, and EDWARD G. GRABB. "Nations of Joiners: Explaining Voluntary Association Membership in Democratic Societies." *American Sociological Review.* Vol. 66, No. 6 (December 2001):783–805.

CURTISS, SUSAN. *Genie: A Psycholinguistic Study of a Modern-Day "Wild Child."* New York: Academic Press, 1977.

CUTCLIFFE, JOHN R. "Hope, Counseling, and Complicated Bereavement Reactions." *Journal of Advanced Nursing.* Vol. 28, No. 4 (October 1998):754–62.

DAHL, ROBERT A. *Who Governs?* New Haven, CT: Yale University Press, 1961.

——. *Dilemmas of Pluralist Democracy: Autonomy vs. Control.* New Haven, CT: Yale University Press, 1982.

DAHRENDORF, RALF. *Class and Class Conflict in Industrial Society.* Stanford, CA: Stanford University Press, 1959.

DALGLISH, BRENDA. "Cheaters." *Maclean's* (August 9, 1993):18–21.

DANFORTH, MARION M., and J. CONRAD GLASS JR. "Listen to My Words, Give Meaning to My Sorrow: A Study in Cognitive Constructs in Middle-Aged Bereaved Widows." *Death Studies.* Vol. 25, No. 6 (September 2001):413–30.

DARROCH, JACQUELINE E., JENNIFER J. FROST, SUSHEELA SINGH, and STUDY TEAM. "Teenage Sexual and Reproductive Behavior in Developed Countries: Can More Progress Be Made?" Occasional Paper No. 3. November 2001. [Online] Available May 30, 2005, at http://www.guttmacher.org/pubs/eurosynth_rpt.pdf.

DARWIN, CHARLES. *On the Origin of Species.* London, UK: Penguin, 1968; orig. 1859.

DAVIDSON, JULIA O'CONNELL. *Prostitution, Power, and Freedom.* Ann Arbor, MI: University of Michigan Press, 1998.

DAVIES, CHRISTIE. *Ethnic Humor Around the World: A Comparative Analysis.* Bloomington: Indiana University Press, 1990.

DAVIES, MARK, and DENISE B. KANDEL. "Parental and Peer Influences on Adolescents' Educational Plans: Some Further Evidence." *American Journal of Sociology.* Vol. 87, No. 2 (September 1981):363–87.

DAVIS, DONALD M. Cited in "T.V. Is a Blonde, Blonde World." *American Demographics,* special issue: Women Change Places. Ithaca, NY, 1993.

DAVIS, KINGSLEY. "Extreme Social Isolation of a Child." *American Journal of Sociology.* Vol. 45, No. 4 (January 1940):554–65.

——. "Final Note on a Case of Extreme Isolation." *American Journal of Sociology.* Vol. 52, No. 5 (March 1947):432–37.

——. "Sexual Behavior." In Robert K. Merton and Robert Nisbet, eds. *Contemporary Social Problems.* 3d ed. New York: Harcourt Brace Jovanovich, 1971:313–60.

DAVIS, KINGSLEY, and WILBERT MOORE. "Some Principles of Stratification." *American Sociological Review.* Vol. 10, No. 2 (April 1945):242–49.

DE BROUKER, PATRICE, and LAVAL LAVALLÉE. "Getting Ahead: Does Your Parents' Education Count?" In Statistics Canada, *Canadian Social Trends. Volume 3.* Toronto: Thompson Educational Publishing, 2000.

DEBER, RAISA. "Getting What We Pay For: Myths and Realities about Financing Canada's Health Care System." *Dialogue on Health Reform.* University of Toronto. 2000. [Online] Available at http://www.utoronto.ca/hlthadmn/dhr/.

DEDRICK, DENNIS K., and RICHARD E. YINGER. "MAD, SDI, and the Nuclear Arms Race." Manuscript in development. Georgetown College, 1990.

DEKESEREDY, WALTER S., and RONALD HINCH. *Woman Abuse: Sociological Perspectives.* Toronto: Thompson Educational Publishing, 1991.

DEKESEREDY, WALTER S., RONALD HINCH, HYMAN BURSHTYN, and CHARLES GORDON. "Taking Woman Abuse Seriously: A Critical Response to the Solicitor General of Canada's Crime Prevention Advice." In E.D. Nelson and B.W. Robinson, eds. *Gender in the 1990s: Images, Realities, and Issues.* Scarborough, ON: Nelson Canada, 1995. pp. 478–89.

DELACROIX, JACQUES, and CHARLES C. RAGIN. "Structural Blockage: A Crossnational Study of Economic Dependency, State Efficacy, and Underdevelopment." *American Journal of Sociology.* Vol. 86, No. 6 (May 1981):1311–47.

DELLA CAVA, MARCO R. "For Dutch, It's as Easy as Asking a Doctor." *USA Today* (January 7, 1997):4A.

DENEAULT, ALAIN. *Paul Martin and his Companies.* Vancouver: Talonbooks, 2006.

DEPEW, ROBERT. "Policing Native Communities: Some Principles and Issues in Organizational Theory." *Canadian Journal of Criminology.* Vol. 34 (1992).

DERBER, CHARLES. *The Wilding of America: Money, Mayhem, and the New American Dream.* 3rd ed. New York: Worth, 2004.

DERSHOWITZ, ALAN. *The Vanishing American Jew.* Boston: Little, Brown, 1997.

DE TOCQUEVILLE, ALEXIS. *The Old Regime and the French Revolution.* Stuart Gilbert, trans. Garden City, NY: Anchor/Doubleday Books, 1955; orig. 1856.

DEUTSCHER, IRWIN. *Making a Difference: The Practice of Sociology.* New Brunswick, NJ: Transaction, 1999.

DEWEY, JOHN. *Experience and Education.* New York: Collier Books, 1968; orig. 1938.

DIAMOND, MILTON. "Sexual Identity, Monozygotic Twins Reared in Discordant Sex Roles and a BBC Follow-Up." *Archives of Sexual Behavior.* Vol. 11, No. 2 (April 1982):181–86.

DICKASON, OLIVE PATRICIA. *Canada's First Nations: A History of Founding Peoples from the Earliest Times.* Toronto: McClelland & Stewart, 1992.

——. *Canada's First Nations: A History of Founding Peoples from Earliest Times.* 2d ed. Toronto: Oxford University Press, 1997.

DIXON, WILLIAM J., and TERRY BOSWELL. "Dependency, Disarticulation, and Denominator Effects: Another Look at Foreign Capital Penetration." *American Journal of Sociology.* Vol. 102, No. 2 (September 1996):543–62.

DOLLARD, JOHN, NEAL E. MILLER, LEONARD W. DOOD, OH MOWER, and ROBERT R. SEARS. *Frustration and Aggression.* New Haven, CT: Yale University Press, 1939.

DONOVAN, VIRGINIA K., and RONNIE LITTENBERG. "Psychology of Women: Feminist Therapy." In Barbara Haber, ed. *The Women's Annual 1981: The Year in Review.* Boston, MA: G.K. Hall, 1982. pp. 211–35.

DONNELLY, PATRICK G., and THEO J. MAJKA. "Residents' Efforts at Neighborhood Stabilization: Facing the Challenges of Inner-City Neighborhoods." *Sociological Forum.* Vol. 13, No. 2 (June 1998):189–213.

DOOLITTLE, ROBYN. "Queen's may not be very amused." *The Toronto Star* (September 26, 2005):A16.

DOYLE, JAMES A. *The Male Experience.* Dubuque, IA: Wm. C. Brown, 1983.

DRYBURGH, HEATHER. "Teenage Pregnancy" *Health Reports.* Vol. 12, No. 1 (October 1, 2003). Statistics Canada Catalogue 82-003. [Online] Available at http://www.statcan.ca/english/kits/preg/preg3.htm.

DUBÉ, FRANCINE. "Magna's Political Matchmaker." *National Post* (October 18, 2003):A1.

DU BOIS, W.E.B. *The Philadelphia Negro: A Social Study.* New York: Schocken Books, 1967; orig. 1899.

DUBOS, RENÉ. *Man Adapting.* New Haven, CT: Yale University Press, 1980; orig. 1965.

DUCHARME, MICHELLE. "The History of Guelph's Black Community." *The Ontarion* (March 26, 1985):7. Archival Collections: University of Guelph Library.

DUFFY, ANN, and NANCY MANDELL. "The Growth in Poverty and Social Inequality: Losing Faith in Social Justice." In Dan Glenday and Ann Duffy, *Canadian Society: Meeting the Challenges of the Twenty-First Century.* Toronto: Oxford University Press Canada, 2001.

DUNCAN, GREG J., W. JEAN YEUNG, JEANNE BROOKS-GUNN, and JUDITH R. SMITH. "How Much Does Childhood Poverty Affect the Life Chances of Children?" *American Sociological Review.* Vol. 63, No. 3 (June 1998):406–23.

DUNLOP, GARFIELD. *Hansard.* Ontario. December 1, 2003:236.

DUNN, LUCIA F. "Is Combat Pay Effective? Evidence from Operation Desert Storm." *Social Science Quarterly.* Vol. 84, No. 2 (June 2003):344–58.

DURKHEIM, EMILE. *The Division of Labor in Society.* New York: Free Press, 1964a; orig. 1895.

——. *The Rules of Sociological Method.* New York: Free Press, 1964b; orig. 1893.

——. *The Elementary Forms of Religious Life.* New York: Free Press, 1965; orig. 1915.

——. *Suicide.* New York: Free Press, 1966; orig. 1897.

——. *Sociology and Philosophy.* New York: Free Press, 1974; orig. 1924.

DURNING, ALAN THEIN. "Supporting Indigenous Peoples." In Lester R. Brown et al., eds. *State of the World 1993: A Worldwatch Institute Report on Progress Toward a Sustainable Society.* New York: Norton, 1993:80–100.

DWORKIN, ANDREA. *Intercourse.* New York: Free Press, 1987.

EBOH, CAMILLUS. "Nigerian Woman Loses Appeal against Stoning Death." [Online] Available August 19, 2002, at http://news.yahoo.com.

ECK, DIANA L. *A New Religious America: How a "Christian Country" Has Become the World's Most Religiously Diverse Nation.* San Francisco, CA: HarperSanFrancisco, 2001.

EDITORIAL. *The Globe and Mail* (January 7, 2005).

——. *The Globe and Mail* (May 2, 2006a).

——. "Car Phone Danger Too Great to Ignore." *Toronto Star* (August 30, 2006b):A20.

——. *National Post* (May 1, 2006c).

——. *The Globe and Mail* (May 1, 2006d).

EDWARDS, DAVID V. *The American Political Experience.* 3d ed. Englewood Cliffs, NJ: Prentice Hall, 1985.

EDWARDS, PETER. "Boot Campers Get Cool Welcome." *Toronto Star* (August 1, 1997):A1.

EHRENREICH, BARBARA. *The Hearts of Men: American Dreams and the Flight from Commitment.* Garden City, NY: Anchor Books, 1983.

——. "The Real Truth About the Female Body." *Time.* Vol. 153, No. 9 (March 15, 1999):56–65.

——. *Nickel and Dimed: On (Not) Getting By in America.* New York: Henry Holt, 2001.

EICHLER, MARGRIT. *Nonsexist Research Methods: A Practical Guide.* Winchester, MA: Unwin Hyman, 1988.

EISEN, ARNOLD M. *The Chosen People in America: A Study of Jewish Religious Ideology.* Bloomington: Indiana University Press, 1983.

EISENBERG, DAVID M., ET AL. "Unconventional Medicine in the United States: Prevalence, Costs and Patterns of Use." *New England Journal of Medicine.* Vol. 328, No. 4 (1993):246–52.

EKMAN, PAUL. "Biological and Cultural Contributions to Body and Facial Movements in the Expression of Emotions." In A. Rorty, ed. *Explaining Emotions.* Berkeley: University of California Press, 1980a. pp. 73–101.

——. *Face of Man: Universal Expression in a New Guinea Village.* New York: Garland Press, 1980b.

EKMAN, P., and FRIESEN, W.V. *Unmasking the face.* Englewood Cliffs, NJ: Prentice Hall, 1975.

EL-ATTAR, MOHAMED. Personal communication with John J. Macionis. 1991.

ELIAS, ROBERT. *The Politics of Victimization: Victims, Victimology and Human Rights.* New York: Oxford University Press, 1986.

ELLISON, CHRISTOPHER G., JOHN P. BARTKOWSKI, and MICHELLE L. SEGAL. "Do Conservative Protestant Parents Spank More Often? Further Evidence from the National Survey of Families and Households." *Social Science Quarterly.* Vol. 77, No. 3 (September 1996):663–73.

ELLWOOD, ROBERT S. "East Asian Religions in Today's America." In Jacob Neusner, ed. *World Religions in America: An Introduction.* Louisville, KY: Westminster John Knox Press, 2000:154–71.

ELMER-DEWITT, PHILIP. "First Nation in Cyberspace." *Time.* Vol. 142, No. 24 (December 6, 1993):62–64.

——. "Battle for the Internet." *Time.* Vol. 144, No. 4 (July 25, 1994):50–56.

EMBER, MELVIN, and CAROL R. EMBER. "The Conditions Favoring Matrilocal Versus Patrilocal Residence." *American Anthropologist.* Vol. 73, No. 3 (June 1971):571–94.

——. *Anthropology.* 6th ed. Englewood Cliffs, NJ: Prentice Hall, 1991.

EMERSON, JOAN P. "Behavior in Private Places: Sustaining Definitions of Reality in Gynecological Examinations." In H.P. Dreitzel, ed. *Recent Sociology.* Vol. 2. New York: Collier, 1970. pp 74–97.

ENGELS, FRIEDRICH. *The Origin of the Family.* Chicago, IL: Charles H. Kerr & Company, 1902; orig. 1884.

ENGLISH-CURRIE, VICKI. "An Education of Oppression." In Jeanne Perreault and Sylvia Vance (eds.) *Writing the Circle.* Edmonton: NeWest Press, 1993.

ERIKSON, ERIK H. *Childhood and Society.* New York: Norton, 1963; orig. 1950.

——. *Identity and the Life Cycle.* New York: Norton, 1980.

ERIKSON, KAI T. *Everything in Its Path: Destruction of Community in the Buffalo Creek Flood.* New York: Simon & Schuster, 1976.

——. *A New Species of Trouble: Explorations in Disaster, Trauma, and Community.* New York: Norton, 1994.

—— *Wayward Puritans: A Study in the Sociology of Deviance.* New York: Wiley, 2005a; orig. 1966.

——. Lecture delivered at Kenyon College, Gambier, Ohio, February 7, 2005b.

ESTES, RICHARD J. "The Commercial Sexual Exploitation of Children in the U.S., Canada, and Mexico." Reported in "Study Explores Sexual Exploitation." [Online] Available September 10, 2001, at http://news.yahoo.com.

ETZIONI, AMITAI. *A Comparative Analysis of Complex Organization: On Power, Involvement, and Their Correlates.* Rev. and enlarged ed. New York: Free Press, 1975.

——. "How to Make Marriage Matter." *Time.* Vol. 142, No. 10 (September 6, 1993):76.

EVANS, MARK. "A beacon in the urban jungle." *National Post* (March 8, 2003):PW6.

EVANS, M.D.R. "Immigrant Entrepreneurship: Effects of Ethnic Market Size and Isolated Labor Pool." *American Sociological Review.* Vol. 54, No. 6 (December 1989):950–62.

EVERS, FREDERICK T., JAMES C. RUSH, JASNA A. KRMPOTIC, and JOANNE DUNCAN-ROBINSON. *Making the Match. Phase II (Final Technical Report).* Universities of Guelph and Western Ontario, 1993.

FAGAN, DREW. "Canada Triumphs in Tariff Battle." *The Globe and Mail* (July 16, 1996):A1.

FALK, GERHARD. Personal communication with John J. Macionis. 1987.

FALLON, A.E., and P. ROZIN. "Sex Differences in Perception of Desirable Body Shape." *Journal of Abnormal Psychology.* Vol. 94, No. 1 (1985):100–5.

FARLEY, CHRISTOPHER JOHN. "Winning the Right to Fly." *Time.* Vol. 146, No. 9 (August 28, 1995):62–64.

FARRELL, WARREN. *Why Men Earn More.* New York: American Management Association, 2005.

FEAGIN, JOE R., and VERA HERNÁN. *Liberation Sociology.* Boulder, CO: Westview Press, 2001.

FELLMAN, BRUCE. "Taking the Measure of Children's T.V." *Yale Alumni Magazine* (April 1995):46–51.

FERNANDEZ, ROBERTO M., and NANCY WEINBERG. "Sifting and Sorting: Personal Contacts and Hiring in a Retail Bank." *American Sociological Review.* Vol. 62, No. 6 (December 1997):883–902.

FERREE, MYRA MARX, and BETH B. HESS. *Controversy and Coalition: The New Feminist Movement across Four Decades of Change.* 3rd ed. New York: Routledge, 1995.

FIFE, SANDY. "The Total Quality Muddle." *The Globe and Mail: Report on Business* (November 1992):64–74.

FINANCIAL POST 500, THE. Toronto: The National Post, 2003.

FINKELSTEIN, NEAL W., and RON HASKINS. "Kindergarten Children Prefer Same-Color Peers." *Child Development.* Vol. 54, No. 2 (April 1983):502–08.

FIREBAUGH, GLENN. "Growth Effects of Foreign and Domestic Investment." *American Journal of Sociology.* Vol. 98, No. 1 (July 1992):105–30.

——. "Does Foreign Capital Harm Poor Nations? New Estimates Based on Dixon and Boswell's Measures of Capital Penetration." *American Journal of Sociology.* Vol. 102, No. 2 (September 1996):563–75.

——. "Empirics of World Income Inequality." *American Journal of Sociology.* Vol. 104, No. 6 (May 1999):1597–1630.

——. "The Trend in Between-Nation Income Inequality." *Annual Review of Sociology.* Vol. 26 (2000):323–39.

FIREBAUGH, GLENN, and FRANK D. BECK. "Does Economic Growth Benefit the Masses? Growth, Dependence, and Welfare in the Third World." *American Sociological Review.* Vol. 59, No. 5 (October 1994):631–53.

FIREBAUGH, GLENN, and DUMITRU SANDU. "Who Supports Marketization and Democratization in Post-Communist Romania?" *Sociological Forum.* Vol. 13, No. 3 (September 1998):521–41.

FISCHER, CLAUDE S., *ET AL. Networks and Places: Social Relations in the Urban Setting.* New York: Free Press, 1977.

FISCHER, CLAUDE W. *The Urban Experience.* 2d ed. New York: Harcourt Brace Jovanovich, 1984.

FISHER, ELIZABETH. *Woman's Creation: Sexual Evolution and the Shaping of Society.* Garden City, NY: Anchor/Doubleday, 1979.

FISHER, ROGER, and WILLIAM URY. "Getting to YES." In William M. Evan and Stephen Hilgartner, eds. *The Arms Race and Nuclear War.* Englewood Cliffs, NJ: Prentice Hall, 1988. pp. 261–68.

FISKE, ALAN PAIGE. "The Cultural Relativity of Selfish Individualism: Anthropological Evidence That Humans Are Inherently Sociable." In Margaret S. Clark, ed. *Prosocial Behavior.* Newbury Park, CA.: Sage, 1991. pp. 176–214.

FITZGERALD, JIM. "Martha Stewart Enjoys Comforts of Home." [Online] Available March 6, 2005, at http://news.yahoo.com.

FITZPATRICK, MEAGAN. "Housework begins to sink in with men." *National Post* (July 20, 2006):A12.

FOLIART, DONNE F., and MARGARET CLAUSEN. "Bereavement Practices among California Hospices: Results of a Statewide Survey." *Death Studies.* Vol. 25, No. 5 (July 2001):461–68.

FORTH, AMY. "R.I. Nightclub Fire Kills at Least 39." [Online] Available February 21, 2003, at http://news.yahoo.com.

FLAHERTY, MICHAEL G. "A Formal Approach to the Study of Amusement in Social Interaction." *Studies in Symbolic Interaction.* Vol. 5. New York: JAI Press, 1984. pp. 71–82.

——. "Two Conceptions of the Social Situation: Some Implications of Humor." *The Sociological Quarterly.* Vol. 31, No. 1 (Spring 1990).

FLERAS, AUGIE. *Social Problems in Canada: Conditions, Constructions, and Challenges.* Toronto: Pearson Education Canada, 2001.

FLETCHER, JOSEPH. *The Ethics of Genetic Control: Ending Reproductive Roulette.* Garden City, New York: Anchor/Doubleday, 1974.

FLORIDA, RICHARD, and MARTIN KENNEY. "Transplanted Organizations: The Transfer of Japanese Industrial Organization to the U.S." *American Sociological Review.* Vol. 56, No. 3 (June 1991):381–98.

FOOT, DAVID K. *Boom, Bust and Echo 2000: Profiting from the Demographic Shift in the New Millennium.* Toronto: Macfarlane Walter & Ross, 1998.

FORBES. "World's Richest People." [Online] Available February 27, 2003 at http://www.forbes.com/lists.

FORCESE, DENNIS. *The Canadian Class Structure.* 4th ed. Toronto: McGraw-Hill Ryerson, 1997.

FORD, CLELLAN S., and FRANK A. BEACH. *Patterns of Sexual Behavior.* New York: Harper & Row, 1951.

FORSTER, MERNA. *100 Canadian Heroines: Famous and Forgotten Faces.* Toronto: The Dundurn Group, 2004.

FOUCAULT, MICHEL. *The History of Sexuality: An Introduction.* Vol. 1. Robert Hurley, trans. New York: Vintage, 1990; orig. 1978.

——. *Power/Knowledge.* ed. Colin Gordon. New York: Pantheon Books, 1980.

FRANCIS, DIANE. *Controlling Interest: Who Owns Canada?* Toronto: Macmillan, 1986.

——. *Bre-X: The Inside Story.* Toronto: Key Porter Books, 1997.\

——. "Canadian women raise the bar." *National Post* (March 8, 2003):PW1.

FRANK, ANDRÉ GUNDER. *On Capitalist Underdevelopment.* Bombay: Oxford University Press, 1975.

——. *Crisis: In the World Economy.* New York: Holmes & Meier, 1980.

——. *Reflections on the World Economic Crisis.* New York: Monthly Review Press, 1981.

FRANKLIN ASSOCIATES. *Characterization of Municipal Solid Waste in the United States, 1960–2000.* Prairie Village, KS: Franklin Associates, 1986.

FRÉCHETTE, PIERRE. "Income Distribution." *The Canadian Encyclopedia.* 2d ed. Vol. 2. Edmonton: Hurtig Publishers, 1988. pp. 1051–1052.

FREDERICK, JUDITH A., and MONICA BOYD. "The Impact of Family Structure on High School Completion." In Statistics Canada, *Canadian Social Trends. Volume 3.* Toronto: Thompson Educational Publishing, 2000.

FREDRICKSON, GEORGE M. *White Supremacy: A Comparative Study in American and South African History.* New York: Oxford University Press, 1981.

FREEDMAN, ESTELLE B. *No Turning Back: The History of Feminism and the Future of Women*. New York: Ballantine Books, 2002.

FREEDOM HOUSE. *Freedom in the World 2005*. [Online] Available July 11, 2005, at http://www.freedomhouse.org.

FRENCH, HOWARD W. "Teaching Japan's Salarymen to Be Their Own Men." *New York Times* (November 27, 2002):A4.

FRENCH, MARILYN. *Beyond Power: On Women, Men, and Morals*. New York: Summit Books, 1985.

FRETZ, WINFIELD. *The Waterloo Mennonites: A Community in Paradox*. Waterloo, ON: Wilfrid Laurier Press, 1989.

FRIDERES, JAMES S. *Aboriginal Peoples in Canada: Contemporary Conflicts*. 5th ed. Scarborough, ON: Prentice Hall/Allyn and Bacon Canada, 1998.

FRIDERES, JAMES S. "Ethnogenesis: Immigrants to Ethnics and the Development of a Rainbow Class Structure." *Canadian Issues* (Spring, 2005):58–60.

FRIDERES, JAMES S., and RENÉ GADACZ. *Aboriginal Peoples in Canada: Contemporary Conflicts*. Toronto: Prentice Hall, 2001.

FRIEDAN, BETTY. *The Fountain of Age*. New York: Simon and Schuster, 1993.

FRIEDMAN, MEYER, and RAY H. ROSENMAN. *Type A Behavior and Your Heart*. New York: Fawcett Crest, 1974.

FRIEDMAN, MILTON, and ROSE FRIEDMAN. *Free to Choose: A Personal Statement*. New York: Harcourt Brace Jovanovich, 1980.

FRIZZELL, ALAN, and JON H. PAMMETT, EDS. *The Canadian General Election of 1997*. Toronto: Dundurn Press, 1997.

FULFORD, ROBERT. "Multiculturalism's eloquent enemy." *National Post* (August, 15, 2005):A16.

FULLER, REX, and RICHARD SCHOENBERGER. "The Gender Salary Gap: Do Academic Achievement, Intern Experience, and College Major Make a Difference?" *Social Science Quarterly*. Vol. 72, No. 4 (December 1991):715–26.

FULTON, E. KAYE. "Bringing Home Baby." *Maclean's* (May 21, 1995):34–42.

FUMENTO, MICHAEL. "Don't Ruffle Your Feathers." *National Post* (March 17, 2006):A19.

FURSTENBERG, FRANK F., JR., and ANDREW CHERLIN. *Divided Families: What Happens to Children When Parents Part*. Cambridge, MA: Harvard University Press, 1991.

——. "Children's Adjustment to Divorce." In Bonnie J. Fox, ed., *Family Patterns, Gender Relations*. 2nd ed. New York: Oxford University Press, 2001.

GAGNÉ, PATRICIA, RICHARD TEWKSBURY, and DEANNA McGAUGHEY. "Coming Out and Crossing Over: Identity Formation and Proclamation in a Transgender Community." *Gender and Society*. Vol. 11, No. 4 (August 1997):478–508.

GALLOWAY, GLORIA. "MPs debate doing more in Darfur." *The Globe and Mail* (May 2, 2006):A11.

GALLUP ORGANIZATION. Data reported in "Americans and Homosexual Civil Unions." *Society*. Vol. 40, No. 1 (December 2002):2.

GAMBLE, ANDREW, STEVE LUDLAM, and DAVID BAKER. "Britain's Ruling Class." *The Economist*. Vol. 326, No. 7795 (January 23, 1993):10.

GAMSON, WILLIAM A. "Beyond the Science-versus-Advocacy Distinction." *Contemporary Sociology*. Vol. 28, No. 1 (January 1999):23–26.

GANDHI, UNNATI. "The War on AIDS hits home." *The Globe and Mail* (August 8, 2006):A4.

GANLEY, ELAINE. "Among Islamic Countries, Women's Roles Vary Greatly." *Washington Times* (April 15, 1998):A13.

GANS, HERBERT J. *People and Plans: Essays on Urban Problems and Solutions*. New York: Basic Books, 1968.

——. *Deciding What's News: A Study of CBS Evening News, NBC Nightly News, Newsweek and Time*. New York: Vintage Books, 1980.

GAIRDNER, WILLIAM D. *The Trouble With Canada*. Toronto: Stoddart Publishing, 1990.

GARDNER, ARTHUR. "Their Own Boss: The Self-Employed in Canada." In Statistics Canada, *Canadian Social Trends. Volume 3*. Toronto: Thompson Educational Publishing, 2000.

GARDYN, REBECCA. "Retirement Redefined." *American Demographics*. Vol. 22, No. 11 (November 2000):52–57.

GARFINKEL, HAROLD. "Conditions of Successful Degradation Ceremonies." *American Journal of Sociology*. Vol. 61, No. 2 (March 1956):420–24.

——. *Studies in Ethnomethodology*. Cambridge: Polity Press, 1967.

GEERTZ, CLIFFORD. "Common Sense as a Cultural System." *The Antioch Review*. Vol. 33, No. 1 (Spring 1975):5–26.

GELLES, RICHARD J., and CLAIRE PEDRICK CORNELL. *Intimate Violence in Families*. 2d ed. Newbury Park, CA: Sage, 1990.

GEOHIVE. "Agglomerations." [Online] Available October 3, 2005, at http://www.geohive.com/charts/city_million.php.

GEORGE, SUSAN. *How the Other Half Dies: The Real Reasons for World Hunger*. Totowa, NJ: Rowman & Allanheld, 1977.

GERBER, LINDA M. *Minority Survival: Community Characteristics and Out-Migration from Indian Communities Across Canada*. Toronto: University of Toronto Press, 1976.

——. "The Development of Canadian Indian Communities: A Two-Dimensional Typology Reflecting Strategies of Adaptation to the Outside World." *Canadian Review of Sociology and Anthropology*. Vol. 16, No. 4 (1979):123–50.

——. "Ethnicity Still Matters: Socio-Demographic Profiles of the Ethnic Elderly in Ontario." *Canadian Ethnic Studies*. Vol. XV, No. 3 (1983):60–80.

——. "Community Characteristics and Out-Migration from Canadian Indian Communities: Path Analyses." *Canadian Review of Sociology and Anthropology*. Vol. 21 (1984):145–65.

——. "The Federal Election of 1968: Social Class Composition and Party Support in the Electoral Districts of Ontario." *Canadian Review of Sociology and Anthropology*. Vol. 23, No. 1 (1986):118–35.

——. "Multiple Jeopardy: A Socio-economic Comparison of Men and Women among the Indian, Métis and Inuit Peoples of Canada." *Canadian Ethnic Studies*. Vol. XXII, No. 3 (1990):69–84.

——. "Referendum Results: Defining New Boundaries for an Independent Quebec." *Canadian Ethnic Studies*. Vol. XXIV, No. 2 (1992):22–34.

——. "Indian, Métis, and Inuit Women and Men: Multiple Jeopardy in a Canadian Context." In E.D. Nelson and B.W. Robinson, eds. *Gender in the 1990s: Images, Realities, and Issues*. Scarborough, ON: Nelson Canada, 1995. pp. 466–77.

GERBER, LINDA M. "The ethnic and immigrant composition of ridings and party support in the Canadian federal election of 2004." *Canadian Ethnic Studies* (2006a)

——. "Urban Diversity: Riding Composition and Party Support in the Canadian Federal Election of 2004." *The Canadian Journal of Urban Research* (2006b) 15(2):105–18.

GERBER, MARTIN. Personal communications with L.M. Gerber. 2006.

GERBER, THEODORE P., and MICHAEL HOUT. "More Shock than Therapy: Market Transition, Employment, and Income in Russia, 1991–1995." *American Journal of Sociology*. Vol. 104, No. 1 (July 1998):1–50.

GERGEN, DAVID. "King of the World." *U.S. News & World Report* (February 25, 2002):84.

GERLACH, MICHAEL L. *The Social Organization of Japanese Business*. Berkeley and Los Angeles, CA: University of California Press, 1992.

GERSTEL, NAOMI. "Divorce and Stigma." *Social Problems*. Vol. 43, No. 2 (April 1987):172–86.

GERTH, H.H., and C. WRIGHT MILLS, EDS. *From Max Weber: Essays in Sociology*. New York: Oxford University Press, 1946.

GESCHWENDER, JAMES A. *Racial Stratification in America*. Dubuque, Iowa: Wm. C. Brown, 1978.

GEWERTZ, DEBORAH. "A Historical Reconsideration of Female Dominance Among the Chambri of Papua New Guinea." *American Ethnologist*. Vol. 8, No. 1 (1981):94–106.

GIBBS, NANCY. "The Pulse of America along the River." *Time* (July 10, 2000):42–46.

——. "What Kids (Really) Need." *Time* (April 30, 2001):48–49.

GILBERT, DENNIS, and JOSEPH A. KAHL. *The American Class Structure: A New Synthesis*. 3d ed. Homewood, IL: The Dorsey Press, 1987.

GILBERT, NEIL. "Realities and Mythologies of Rape." *Society*. Vol. 29, No. 4 (May–June 1992):4–10.

GILBERT, S.N. "The Forgotten Purpose and Future Promise of University Education." *Canadian Journal of Community Mental Health*. Vol. 8, No. 2 (1989):103–22.

GILBERT, SID, LYNN BARR, WARREN CLARK, MATTHEW BLUE, and DEBORAH SUNTER. *Leaving School: Results from a National Survey Comparing School Leavers and High School Graduates 18 to 20 Years of Age*. Catalogue No. LM-294-07-93E. Ottawa: Queen's Printer, 1993.

GILLIGAN, CAROL. *In a Different Voice: Psychological Theory and Women's Development*. Cambridge, MA: Harvard University Press, 1982.

——. *Making Connections: The Relational Worlds of Adolescent Girls at Emma Willard School*. Cambridge, MA: Harvard University Press, 1990.

GILLON, RAANAN. "Euthanasia in the Netherlands: Down the Slippery Slope?" *Journal of Medical Ethics*. Vol. 25, No. 1 (February 1999):3–4.

GINSBURG, FAYE, and ANNA LOWENHAUPT TSING, EDS. *Uncertain Terms: Negotiating Gender in American Culture*. Boston:, MA Beacon Press, 1990.

GIOVANNINI, MAUREEN. "Female Anthropologist and Male Informant: Gender Conflict in a Sicilian Town." In John J. Macionis and Nijole V. Benokraitis, eds. *Seeing Ourselves: Classic, Contemporary, and Cross-Cultural Readings in Sociology*. 2d ed. Englewood Cliffs, NJ: Prentice Hall, 1992. pp. 27–32.

GLAZER, NATHAN, and DANIEL P. MOYNIHAN. *Beyond the Melting Pot*. 2d ed. Cambridge, MA: MIT Press, 1970.

GLEICK, ELIZABETH. "The Marker We've Been Waiting For." *Time*. Vol. 149, No. 14 (April 7, 1997):28–42.

GLENDAY, DAN. "Off the Ropes: New Challenges and Strengths Facing Trade Unions in Canada." In Dan Glenday and Ann Duffy, eds. *Canadian Society: Meeting the Challenges of the Twenty-First Century*. Toronto: Oxford University Press, 2001.

GLENN, NORVAL D., and BETH ANN SHELTON. "Regional Differences in Divorce in the United States." *Journal of Marriage and the Family*. Vol. 47, No. 3 (August 1985):641–52.

GLOBE AND MAIL, THE. "Canadian aboriginals ask UN for help in land battle". (October 17, 2005):A8.

GLOBEINVESTOR. "50 best paid executives." 2003. [Online] Available at www.globevestor.com/series/top1000/tables/executives/2003/.

GLUECK, SHELDON, and ELEANOR GLUECK. *Unraveling Juvenile Delinquency*. New York: Commonwealth Fund, 1950.

GOESLING, BRIAN. "Changing Income Inequalities within and between Nations: New Evidence." *American Sociological Review*. Vol. 66, No. 5 (October 2001):745–61.

GOFFMAN, ERVING. *The Presentation of Self in Everyday Life*. Garden City, NY: Anchor Books, 1959.

——. *Asylums: Essays on the Social Situation of Mental Patients and Other Inmates*. Garden City, NY: Anchor Books, 1961.

——. *Stigma: Notes on the Management of Spoiled Identity*. Englewood Cliffs, NJ: Prentice Hall, 1963.

——. *Interactional Ritual: Essays on Face to Face Behavior*. Garden City, NY: Anchor Books, 1967.

——. *Gender Advertisements*. New York: Harper Colophon, 1979.

GOLDBERG, BERNARD. *Bias: A CBS Insider Exposes How the Media Distort the News*. Washington, DC: Regnery, 2002.

GOLDBERG, STEVEN. *The Inevitability of Patriarchy*. New York: William Morrow, 1974.

GOLDEN, FREDERIC, and MICHAEL D. LEMONICK. "The Race Is Over." *Time* (July 3, 2000):18 23.

GOLDFARB, JEFFREY C. *Beyond Glasnost: The Post-Totalitarian Mind*. Chicago, IL: University of Chicago Press, 1989.

GOLDSBY, RICHARD A. *Race and Races*. 2d ed. New York: Macmillan, 1977.

GOLDSMITH, H.H. "Genetic Influences on Personality from Infancy." *Child Development*. Vol. 54, No. 2 (April 1983):331–35.

GOLDSTEIN, JOSHUA R., and CATHERINE T. KENNEY. "Marriage Delayed or Marriage Forgone? New Cohort Forecasts of First Marriage for U.S. Women." *American Sociological Review*. Vol. 66, No. 4 (August 2001):506–19.

GOODE, ERICH. "No Need to Panic? A Bumper Crop of Books on Moral Panics." *Sociological Forum*. Vol. 15, No. 3 (September 2000):543–52.

GOODE, WILLIAM J. "Encroachment, Charlatanism, and the Emerging Profession: Psychology, Sociology and Medicine." *American Sociological Review*. Vol. 25, No. 6 (December 1960):902–14.

GORDON, JAMES S. "The Paradigm of Holistic Medicine." In Arthur C. Hastings *et al.*, eds. *Health for the Whole Person: The Complete Guide to Holistic Medicine*. Boulder, CO: Westview Press, 1980. pp. 3–27.

GORDON, SOL, and CRAIG W. SNYDER. *Personal Issues in Human Sexuality: A Guidebook for Better Sexual Health*. 2d ed. Boston: Allyn & Bacon, 1989.

GORMAN, CHRISTINE. "Stressed-Out Kids." *Time* (December 25, 2000):168.

GOTHAM, KEVIN FOX. "Race, Mortgage Lending, and Loan Rejections in a U.S. City." *Sociological Focus*. Vol. 31, No. 4 (October 1998):391–405.

GOTTFREDSON, MICHAEL R., and TRAVIS HIRSCHI. "National Crime Control Policies." *Society*. Vol. 32, No. 2 (January–February 1995):30–36.

GOTTMANN, JEAN. *Megalopolis*. New York: Twentieth Century Fund, 1961.

GOULD, STEPHEN J. "Evolution as Fact and Theory." *Discover* (May 1981):35–37.

GOYDER, JOHN. *Technology and Society: A Canadian Perspective*. Peterborough, ON: Broadview Press, 1997.

——. *Essentials of Canadian Sociology*. Toronto: McClelland & Stewart, 1990.

——. "The Dynamics of Occupational Prestige: 1975–2000.". Vol. 42, No. 1 (2005):1, 23.

GOYDER, JOHN C., and JAMES E. CURTIS. "Occupational Mobility in Canada over Four Generations." In James E. Curtis and William G. Scott, eds. *Social Stratification: Canada*. 2d ed. Scarborough, ON: Prentice Hall, 1979.

GOYDER, JOHN,, and . "The Allocation of Male and Female Occupational Prestige in an Ontario Urban Area: A Quarter-Century Replication.". Vol. 40, No. 4 (2003):417.

GRAND COUNCIL OF THE CREES. *Sovereign Injustice: Forcible Inclusion of the James Bay Crees and Cree Territory into a Sovereign Quebec*. Nemaska, Quebec: the Grand Council, 1995.

GRANDIN, ELAINE, *ET AL*. "Couple Violence and Psychological Distress," *Canadian Journal of Public Health*, Vol. 89(1), 1998:43–47.

GRANT, DON SHERMAN, II, and MICHAEL WALLACE. "Why Do Strikes Turn Violent?" *American Journal of Sociology*. Vol. 96, No. 5 (March 1991):1117–50.

GRANT, DONALD L. *The Anti-Lynching Movement*. San Francisco: R and E Research Associates, 1975.

GREEN, GARY PAUL, LEANN M. TIGGES, and DANIEL DIAZ. "Racial and Ethnic Differences in Job-Search Strategies in Atlanta, Boston, and Los Angeles." *Social Science Quarterly*. Vol. 80, No. 2 (June 1999):263–90.

GREENAWAY, NORMA. "Canada losing more than it's gaining." *National Post* (July 4, 2006a):A4.

——. "Physicians signal frustration, elect private-care chief." *National Post* (August 23, 2006b):A6.

GREENBERG, DAVID F. *The Construction of Homosexuality*. Chicago, IL: University of Chicago Press, 1988.

GREEN PARTY. "The Gomery Report." 2005. [Online] Available at .

GREENSPAN, STANLEY I. *The Four-Thirds Solution: Solving the Child-Care Crisis in America*. Cambridge, MA: Perseus, 2001.

GREENSPON, EDWARD. "The Incredible Shrinking Middle Class." *The Globe and Mail* (July 31, 1993):D1.

GREGG, ALLAN R. "Brave New Epoque." *Maclean's* (April 6, 1998):56–60.

——. "What tsunamis tell us about our changed world." *The Globe and Mail* (January 7, 2005):A15.

GROSS, JANE. "Under One Roof, Aging Together Yet Alone." *The New York Times* (January 30, 2005).

GUPPY, NEIL, and A. BRUCE ARAI. "Who Benefits from Higher Education? Differences by Sex, Social Class, and Ethnic Background." In James E. Curtis, Edward Grabb, and Neil Guppy, eds. *Social Inequality in Canada: Patterns, Problems, Policies*. 2d ed. Scarborough, ON: Prentice Hall, 1993. pp. 214–32.

GWARTNEY-GIBBS, PATRICIA A., JEAN STOCKARD, and SUSANNE BOHMER. "Learning Courtship Agression: The Influence of Parents, Peers, and Personal Experiences." *Family Relations*. Vol. 36, No. 3 (July 1987):276–82.

GWYNNE, S.C., and JOHN F. DICKERSON. "Lost in the E-Mail." *Time*. Vol. 149, No. 15 (April 21, 1997):88–90.

HABERMANN, CLYDE. "For Disabled, It's Hooray for Hollywood." *The New York Times* (January 28, 2005).

HABERMAS, JÜRGEN. *Toward a Rational Society: Student Protest, Science, and Politics*. Jeremy J. Shapiro, trans. Boston, MA: Beacon Press, 1970.

HADDEN, JEFFREY K., and CHARLES E. SWAIN. *Prime Time Preachers: The Rising Power of Televangelism*. Reading, MA: Addison-Wesley, 1981.

HAFNER, KATIE. "Making Sense of the Internet." *Newsweek*. (October 24, 1994):46–48.

HAGAN, JACQUELINE MARIA. "Social Networks, Gender, and Immigrant Incorporation: Resources and Restraints." *American Sociological Review*. Vol. 63, No. 1 (February 1998):55–67.

HAGAN, JOHN, and PATRICIA PARKER. "White-Collar Crime and Punishment: The Class Structure and Legal Sanctioning of Securities Violations." *American Sociological Review*. Vol. 50, No. 3 (June 1985):302–16.

HAIG, ROBIN ANDREW. *The Anatomy of Humor: Biopsychosocial and Therapeutic Perspectives*. Springfield, IL: Charles C. Thomas, 1988.

HALBERSTAM, DAVID. *The Reckoning*. New York: Avon Books, 1986.

HALL, DAVID J. "North-West Territories, 1870–1905." In *The Canadian Encyclopedia: Year 2000 Edition*. Toronto: McClelland & Stewart, 1999. p. 1657.

HALL, JOHN R., and MARY JO NEITZ. *Culture: Sociological Perspectives*. Englewood Cliffs, NJ: Prentice Hall, 1993.

HALLETT, M.E. "Nellie McClung." In *The Canadian Encyclopedia*. 2d ed. Vol. 2. Edmonton: Hurtig Publishers, 1988. p. 1257.

HAMER, DEAN, and PETER COPELAND. *The Science of Desire: The Search for the Gay Gene and the Biology of Behavior*. New York: Simon & Schuster, 1994.

HAMILTON, ANITA. "Speeders, Say Cheese." *Time* (September 17, 2001):32.

HAMILTON, DWIGHT. "50 Richest Canadians: It's So Much Better to Be Rich." *The Financial Post Magazine* (January 1996):14–28.

HAMILTON, GRAEME. "Tory blue has shades of green." *National Post* (April 20, 2006).

HAMILTON, RICHARD F. "*The Communist Manifesto* at 150." *Society*. Vol. 38, No. 2 (January/February 2001):75–80.

HAMRICK, MICHAEL H., DAVID J. ANSPAUGH, and GENE EZELL. *Health*. Columbus, OH: Merrill, 1986.

HANDGUN CONTROL, INC. 1998. [Online] Available at http://www.handguncontrol.org.

HANEY, CRAIG, CURTIS BANKS, and PHILIP ZIMBARDO. "Interpersonal Dynamics in a Simulated Prison." *International Journal of Criminology and Penology*. Vol. 1 (1973):69–97.

HANEY, LYNNE. "After the Fall: East European Women since the Collapse of State Socialism." *Contexts*. Vol. 1, No. 3 (Fall 2002):27–36.

HANNIGAN, JOHN A. "Sociology and the Environment." In Robert J. Brym, *New Society: Sociology for the 21st Century*. Toronto: Harcourt Brace, 1995.

HAREVEN, TAMARA K. "The Life Course and Aging in Historical Perspective." In Tamara K. Hareven and Kathleen J. Adams, eds. *Aging and Life Course Transitions: An Interdisciplinary Perspective*. New York: Guilford Press, 1982:1–26.

HAREVEN, TAMARA K., and RANDOLPH LANGENBACH. *Amoskeag: Life and Work in an American Factory City*. New York: Pantheon Books, 1978.

HARPSTER, PAULA, and ELIZABETH MONK-TURNER. "Why Men Do Housework: A Test of Gender Production and the Relative Resources Model." *Sociological Focus*. Vol. 31, No. 1 (February 1998):45–59.

HARRIS, DAVID R., and JEREMIAH JOSEPH SIM. "Who Is Multiracial? Assessing the Complexity of Lived Race." Vol. 67, No. 4 (August 2002):614–27.

HASSELBACK, DREW. "The queens of diamonds." *National Post*. (March 8, 2003):PW3.

HARLOW, HARRY F., and MARGARET KUENNE HARLOW. "Social Deprivation in Monkeys." *Scientific American.* Vol. 207 (November 1962):137–46.

HARRINGTON, MICHAEL. *The New American Poverty.* New York: Penguin Books, 1984.

HARRIS, CHAUNCEY D., and EDWARD L. ULLMAN. "The Nature of Cities." *The Annals.* Vol. 242 (November 1945):7–17.

HARRIS, MARVIN. *Cultural Anthropology.* 2d ed. New York: Harper & Row, 1987.

HAWTHORNE, PETER. "South Africa's Makeover." *Time.* Vol. 154, No. 2 (July 12, 1999).

HAWTHORN, TOM. "107 years young, she still loves to dance". *The Globe and Mail* (May 10, 2006):A3.

HEATH, JULIA A., and W. DAVID BOURNE. "Husbands and Housework: Parity or Parody?" *Social Science Quarterly.* Vol. 76, No. 1 (March 1995):195–202.

HELGESEN, SALLY. *The Female Advantage: Women's Ways of Leadership.* New York: Doubleday, 1990.

HELIN, DAVID W. "When Slogans Go Wrong." *American Demographics.* Vol. 14, No. 2 (February 1992):14.

HELMES-HAYES, R. *A Quarter-Century of Sociology and the University of Toronto, 1963–1988.* Toronto: Canadian Scholars' Press, 1988.

HELLMICH, NANCI. "Environment, Economics Partly to Blame." *USA Today* (October 9, 2002):9D.

HENLEY, NANCY, MYKOL HAMILTON, and BARRIE THORNE. "Womanspeak and Manspeak: Sex Differences in Communication, Verbal and Nonverbal." In John J. Macionis and Nijole V. Benokraitis, eds. *Seeing Ourselves: Classic, Contemporary, and Cross-Cultural Readings in Sociology.* 2d ed. Englewood Cliffs, NJ: Prentice Hall, 1992:10–15.

HERMAN, DIANNE. "The Rape Culture." In John J. Macionis and Nijole V. Benokraitis, eds. *Seeing Ourselves: Classic, Contemporary, and Cross-Cultural Readings in Sociology.* 5th ed. Upper Saddle River, NJ: Prentice Hall, 2001.

HERMAN, EDWARD S. *Corporate Control, Corporate Power: A Twentieth Century Fund Study.* New York: Cambridge University Press, 1981.

HERPERTZ, SABINE C., and HENNING SASS. "Emotional Deficiency and Psychopathy." *Behavioral Sciences and the Law.* Vol. 18, No. 5 (September/October 2000):567–80.

HEROLD, E.S. *Sexual Behaviour of Canadian Young People.* Markham, ON: Fitzhenry and Whiteside, 1984.

HERRING, HUBERT B. "An Aging Nation Is Choosing Younger Bosses." *New York Times* (February 20, 2005). [Online] Available April 12, 2005, at http://www.researchnavigator.com/.

HERRNSTEIN, RICHARD J., and CHARLES MURRAY. *The Bell Curve: Intelligence and Class Structure in American Life.* New York: Free Press, 1994.

HERZOG, BRAD. "A Man of His Words." *Cornell Alumni Magazine.* Vol. 106, No. 4 (January/February 2004):58–63.

HESS, BETH B. "Breaking and Entering the Establishment: Committing Social Change and Confronting the Backlash." *Social Problems.* Vol. 46, No. 1 (February 1999):1–12.

HIGHWAY, TOMSON. *Kiss of the Fur Queen.* Toronto: Doubleday, 1999.

HILL, MARK E. "Race of the Interviewer and Perception of Skin Color: Evidence from the Multi-City Study of Urban Inequality." *American Sociological Review.* Vol. 67, No. 1 (February 2002):99–108.

HILLER, HARRY H. *Canadian Society: A Macro Analysis.* 5th ed. Toronto, ON: Pearson Prentice Hall, 2006.

HIRSCHI, TRAVIS. *Causes of Delinquency.* Berkeley: University of California Press, 1969.

HOCHSCHILD, ARLIE RUSSELL. "Emotion Work, Feeling Rules, and Social Structure." *American Journal of Sociology.* Vol. 85, No. 3 (November 1979): 551–75.

——. *The Managed Heart.* Berkeley, CA: University of California Press, 1983.

HODGE, ROBERT W., DONALD J. TREIMAN, and PETER H. ROSSI. "A Comparative Study of Occupational Prestige." In Reinhard Bendix and Seymour Martin Lipset, eds. *Class, Status, and Power: Social Stratification in Comparative Perspective.* 2d ed. New York: Free Press, 1966. pp. 309–21.

HOERR, JOHN. "The Payoff from Teamwork." *Business Week.* No. 3114 (July 10, 1989):56–62.

HOGUE, CHERYL. "U.S. Exports of Hazardous Waste to Canada Continue to Rise." *Chemical and Engineering News* (November 13, 2000):26.

HOPE, TRINA L., HAROLD G. GRASMICK, and LAURA J. POINTON. "The Family in Gottfredson and Hrischi's General Theory of Crime: Structure, Parenting, and Self-Control." *Sociological Focus.* Vol. 36, No. 4 (November 2003): 291–311.

HORTON, HAYWARD DERRICK. "Critical Demography: The Paradigm of the Future?" *Sociological Forum.* Vol. 14, No. 3 (September 1999):363–67.

HOWLETT, KAREN, *ET AL.* "Enron Deception Aided by CIBC: U.S. Report." *The Globe and Mail* (July 29, 2003).A1.

HOYT, HOMER. *The Structure and Growth of Residential Neighborhoods in American Cities.* Washington, DC: Federal Housing Administration, 1939.

HUET-COX, ROCIO. "Medical Education: New Wine in Old Wine Skins." In Victor W. Sidel and Ruth Sidel, eds. *Reforming Medicine: Lessons of the Last Quarter Century.* New York: Pantheon Books, 1984:129–49.

HUFFMAN, KAREN. *Psychology in Action.* New York: Wiley, 2000.

HUFFMAN, MATT L., STEVEN C. VELASCO, and WILLIAM T. BIELBY. "Where Sex Composition Matters Most: Comparing the Effects of Job Versus Occupational Sex Composition of Earnings." *Sociological Focus.* Vol. 29, No. 3 (August 1996):189–207.

HUMAN RIGHTS WATCH. "Children's Rights: Child Labor." 2004. [Online] Available August 29, 2005, at http://www.hrw.org/children/labor.htm.

HUMPHREYS, ADRIAN. "First Gay Marriage Legal, for Now." *National Post* (January 15, 2001):A1.

——. "He Is No Longer an Unknown Child." *National Post* (November 7, 2002):3.

HUMPHRIES, SALLY. "The Intensification of Traditional Agriculture among Yucatec Maya Farmers: Facing up to the Dilemma of Livelihood Sustainability." *Human Ecology.* Vol. 21, No. 1 (1993):87–102.

HUNTER, JAMES DAVISON. *American Evangelicalism: Conservative Religion and the Quandary of Modernity.* New Brunswick, NJ: Rutgers University Press, 1983.

——. "Conservative Protestantism." In Philip E. Hammond, ed. *The Sacred in a Secular Age.* Berkeley, CA: University of California Press, 1985. pp. 50–66.

——. *Evangelicalism: The Coming Generation.* Chicago, IL: University of Chicago Press, 1987.

——. *Culture Wars: The Struggle to Define America.* New York: Basic Books, 1991.

HURTADO, SYLVIA, ALEXANDER W. AUSTIN, WILLIAM S. KORN, and KATHRYN M. MAHONEY. *The American Freshman: National Norms for Fall 2004.* Los Angeles: UCLA Higher Education Research Institute, 2004.

HURTIG, MEL. *The Betrayal of Canada.* Toronto: Stoddart Publishing, 1991.

——. *A New and Better Canada: Principles and Policies of a New Canadian Political Party.* Toronto: Stoddart, 1992.

HUTCHINGSON, JAMES E. "Science and Religion." *The Herald* (Dade County, Florida) (December 25, 1994):1M, 6M.

HYMOWITZ, CAROL. "World's Poorest Women Advance by Entrepreneurship." *Wall Street Journal* (September 9, 1995):B1.

HYMOWITZ, KAY S. "Kids Today Are Growing Up Way Too Fast." *Wall Street Journal* (October 28, 1998):A22.

IBBITSON, JOHN. "A bleak choice for young Indians." *The Globe and Mail* (August 3, 2006):A4.

IBM. "Focus on E-business." *The Globe and Mail* (January 28, 1998):Section C.

IDE, THOMAS R., and ARTHUR J. CORDELL. "Automating Work." *Society.* Vol. 31, No. 6 (September–October 1994):65–71.

INCIARDI, JAMES A. *Elements of Criminal Justice.* 2nd ed. New York: Oxford University Press, 2000.

INCIARDI, JAMES A., HILARY L. SURRATT, and PAULO R. TELLES. *Sex, Drugs, and HIV/AIDS in Brazil.* Boulder, CO: Westview Press, 2000.

INGLEHART, RONALD. *Modernization and Postmodernization: Cultural, Economic, and Political Change in 43 Societies.* Princeton, NJ: Princeton University Press, 1997.

INGLEHART, RONALD, and WAYNE E. BAKER. "Modernization, Cultural Change, and the Persistence of Traditional Values." *American Sociological Review.* Vol. 65, No. 1 (February 2000):19–51.

INGLEHART, RONALD, and CHRISTIAN WELZEL. *Modernization, Cultural Change and Democracy.* New York: Cambridge University Press, 2005.

INNIS, HAROLD A. *The Fur Trade in Canada.* Toronto: University of Toronto Press, 1930.

INTERNATIONAL MONETARY FUND. *World Economic Outlook.* April 2000. [Online] Available http://www.imf.org/external/pubs/ft/weo/2000/01/index.htm.

INTERNATIONAL TELECOMMUNICATION UNION. *World Telecommunication Development Report.* Data cited in World Bank, *2005 World Development Indicators.* Washington, DC: World Bank, 2005.

INTERNET WORLD STATS. Various pages. 2006. [Online] Available at http://www.internetworldstats.com.

ISAJIW, WSEVELOD W. "Definitions of Ethnicity." In Rita M. Bienvenue and Jay E. Goldstein, eds. *Ethnicity and Ethnic Relations in Canada.* 2d ed. Toronto: Butterworths, 1985. pp. 5–18.

JACOBS, DAVID. "Inequality and Police Strength." *American Sociological Review.* Vol. 44, No. 6 (December 1979):913–25.

JACOBS, DEAN. "Walpole Island: Sustainable Development." In Diane Engelstad and John Bird, eds. *Nation to Nation: Aboriginal Sovereignty and the Future of Canada.* Concord, ON: House of Anansi Press, 1992. pp. 179–85.

JACOBS, JANE. *The Death and Life of Great American Cities.* New York: Random House, 1961.

——. *The Economy of Cities.* New York: Vintage Books, 1970.

——. *Cities and the Wealth of Nations.* Toronto: Random House, 1984.

JACOBY, RUSSELL, and NAOMI GLAUBERMAN, EDS. *The Bell Curve Debate.* New York: Random House, 1995.

JAENEN, CORNELIUS. "Mutilated Multiculturalism." In J. Donald Wilson, ed. *Canadian Education in the 1980s.* Calgary, AB: Detselig Enterprises, 1981.

JANIS, IRVING. *Victims of Groupthink.* Boston: Houghton Mifflin, 1972.

——. *Crucial Decisions: Leadership in Policymaking and Crisis Management.* New York: Free Press, 1989.

JANNIGAN, MARY. "How can we be innovative enough to keep our best brains?" *The Globe and Mail*, January 2, 2006: A5.

JENKINS, J. CRAIG. *Images of Terror: What We Can and Can't Know about Terrorism*. Hawthorne, NY: Aldine de Gruyter, 2003.

JENKINS, J. CRAIG, and CHARLES PERROW. "Insurgency of the Powerless: Farm Worker Movements (1946–1972)." American Sociological Review. Vol. 42, No. 2 (April 1977):249–68.

JENKINS, J. CRAIG, and MICHAEL WALLACE. "The Generalized Action Potential of Protest Movements: The New Class, Social Trends, and Political Exclusion Explanations." *Sociological Forum*. Vol. 11, No. 2 (June 1996):183–207.

JIMÉNEZ, MARINA. "Arranged marriages becoming more common, officials say." *The Globe and Mail* (May 11, 2006):A12.

JOHNSON, CATHRYN. "Gender, Legitimate Authority, and Leader-Subordinate Conversations." *American Sociological Review*. Vol. 59, No. 1 (February 1994):122–35.

JOHNSON, F. HENRY. *A Brief History of Canadian Education*. Toronto: McGraw-Hill, 1968.

JOHNSON, HOLLY. *Dangerous Domains: Violence Against Women in Canada*. Toronto: Nelson Canada, 1996.

JOHNSON, PAUL. "The Seven Deadly Sins of Terrorism." In Benjamin Netanyahu, ed. *International Terrorism*. New Brunswick, NJ: Transaction Books, 1981. pp. 12–22.

JOHNSTON, R.J. "Residential Area Characteristics." In D. T. Herbert and R. J. Johnston, eds. *Social Areas in Cities. Vol. 1: Spatial Processes and Form*. New York: Wiley, 1976. pp. 193–235.

JONES, D. GARETH. "Brain Death." *Journal of Medical Ethics*. Vol. 24, No. 4 (August 1998):237–43.

JONES, FRANK. "Are Children Going to Religious Services?" In Statistics Canada, *Canadian Social Trends. Volume 3*. Toronto: Thompson Educational Publishing, 2000.

JONES, JUDY. "More Miners Will Be Offered Free X-Rays; Federal Agency Wants to Monitor Black-Lung Cases." *Louisville Courier Journal* (May 13, 1999):1A.

JORDAN, ELLEN, and ANGELA COWAN. "Warrior Narratives in the Kindergarten Classroom: Renegotiating the Social Contract?" *Gender and Society*. Vol. 9, No. 6 (December 1995):727–43.

KAIN, EDWARD L. "A Note on the Integration of AIDS into the Sociology of Human Sexuality." *Teaching Sociology*. Vol. 15, No. 4 (July 1987):320–23.

KAIN, EDWARD L., and SHANNON HART. "AIDS and the Family: A Content Analysis of Media Coverage." Presented to National Council on Family Relations, Atlanta, GA, 1987.

KALISH, CAROL B. "International Crime Rates." Bureau of Justice Statistics Special Report, May. Washington, DC: U.S. Government Printing Office, 1988.

KALLEBERG, ARNE L., BARBARA F. RESKIN, and KEN HUDSON. "Bad Jobs in America: Standard and Nonstandard Employment Relations and Job Quality in the United States." *American Sociological Review*. Vol. 65, No 2 (April 2000): 256–78.

KALLEN, EVELYN. *Ethnicity and Human Rights in Canada*. Don Mills, ON: Oxford University Press, 2003.

KAMINER, WENDY. "Volunteers: Who Knows What's in It for Them." *Ms.* (December 1984):93–94, 96, 126–28.

KANTER, ROSABETH MOSS. *Men and Women of the Corporation*. New York: Basic Books, 1977.

KANTER, ROSABETH MOSS, and BARRY A. STEIN. "The Gender Pioneers: Women in an Industrial Sales Force." In R.M. Kanter and B.A. Stein, eds. *Life in Organizations*. New York: Basic Books, 1979. pp. 134–60.

KANTROWITZ, BARBARA. "Mothers on Their Own." *Newsweek* (December 23, 1985):66–67.

KANTROWITZ, BARBARA, and PAT WINGERT. "Unmarried with Children." *Newsweek* (May 28, 2001):46–52.

———. "What's at Stake." *Newsweek* (January 27, 2003):30–37.

KAPFERER, JEAN-NOEL. "How Rumors Are Born." *Society*. Vol. 29, No. 5 (July–August 1992):53–60.

KAPLAN, DAVID E., and MICHAEL SCHAFFER. "Losing the Psywar." *U.S. News & World Report* (October 8, 2001):46.

KAPTCHUK, TED. "The Holistic Logic of Chinese Medicine." In Shepard Bliss et al., eds. *The New Holistic Health Handbook*. Lexington, MA: The Steven Greene Press/Penguin Books, 1985:41.

KASARDA, JOHN D. "Entry-Level Jobs, Mobility and Urban Minority Employment." *Urban Affairs Quarterly*. Vol. 19, No. 1 (September 1983):21–40.

KATES, ROBERT W. "Ending Hunger: Current Status and Future Prospects." *Consequences*. Vol. 2, No. 2 (1996):3–11.

KAY, PAUL, and WILLETT KEMPTON. "What Is the Sapir–Whorf Hypothesis?" *American Anthropologist*. Vol. 86, No. 1 (March 1984):65–79.

KEISTER, LISA A. "Religion and Wealth: The Role of Religious Affiliation and Participation in Early Adult Asset Accumulation." *Social Forces*. Vol. 82, No. 1 (September 2003):175–207.

KEISTER, LISA A., and STEPHANIE MOLLER. "Wealth Inequality in the United States." *Annual Review of Sociology*. Vol. 26 (2000):63–81.

KEITH, JULIE, and LAURA LANDRY. "Well-being of Older Canadians." In Craig McKie and Keith Thompson, eds. *Canadian Social Trends*. Toronto: Thompson Educational Publishing, 1994.

KELLER, HELEN. *The Story of My Life*. New York: Doubleday, Page, 1903.

KELLERT, STEPHEN R., and F. HERBERT BORMANN. "Closing the Circle: Weaving Strands Among Ecology, Economics, and Ethics." In F. Herbert Bormann and Stephen R. Kellert, eds. *Ecology, Economics, and Ethics: The Broken Circle*. New Haven, CT: Yale University Press, 1991. pp. 205–10.

KELLY, DEIRDRE. "The places that mattered to Jane Jacobs." *The Globe and Mail* (April 29, 2006):M3.

KEMP, ALICE ABEL, and SHELLEY COVERMAN. "Marginal Jobs or Marginal Workers: Identifying Sex Differences in Low-Skill Occupations." *Sociological Focus*. Vol. 22, No. 1 (February 1989):19–37.

KENT, MARY M., and MARK MATHER. "What Drives U.S. Population Growth?" *Population Bulletin*. Vol. 57, No. 4 (December 2002):3–40.

KENTOR, JEFFREY. "The Long-Term Effects of Foreign Investment Dependence on Economic Growth, 1940–1990." *American Journal of Sociology*. Vol. 103, No. 4 (January 1998):1024–46.

KERCKHOFF, ALAN C., RICHARD T. CAMPBELL, and IDEE WINFIELD-LAIRD. "Social Mobility in Great Britain and the United States." *American Journal of Sociology*. Vol. 91, No. 2 (September 1985):281–308.

KERR, RICHARD A. "Climate Models Heat Up." *Science Now* (January 26, 2005):1–3.

KIDRON, MICHAEL, and RONALD SEGAL. *The New State of the World Atlas*. New York: Simon & Schuster, 1991.

KILBOURNE, BROCK K. "The Conway and Siegelman Claims Against Religious Cults: An Assessment of Their Data." *Journal for the Scientific Study of Religion*. Vol. 22, No. 4 (December 1983):380–85.

KILGORE, SALLY B. "The Organizational Context of Tracking in Schools." *American Sociological Review*. Vol. 56, No. 2 (April 1991):189–203.

KING, KATHLEEN PIKER, and DENNIS E. CLAYSON. "The Differential Perceptions of Male and Female Deviants." *Sociological Focus*. Vol. 21, No. 2 (April 1988):153–64.

KINSEY, ALFRED, ET AL. *Sexual Behavior in the Human Male*. Philadelphia: Saunders, 1948.

———. *Sexual Behavior in the Human Female*. Philadelphia: Saunders, 1953.

KINSMAN, GARY. *The Regulation of Desire: Homo and Hetero Sexualities*. Montreal: Black Rose Books, 1996.

KIRKEY, SHARON. "Should Pandemic vaccine skip kids, elderly?" *National Post* (May 12, 2006):A1.

KITTRIE, NICHOLAS N. *The Right to Be Different: Deviance and Enforced Therapy*. Baltimore, MD: Johns Hopkins University Press, 1971.

KITZ, JANET E. *Shattered City: The Halifax Explosion and the Road to Recovery*. Halifax, NS: Nimbus Publishing Limited, 1989.

KLEIN, DANIEL B., and CHARLOTTA STERN. "How Politically Diverse Are the Social Sciences and Humanities? Survey Evidence from Six Fields." National Association of Scholars 2004. [Online] Available January 13, 2005, at http://www.nas.org/aa/klein_launch.htm.

KLUCKHOHN, CLYDE. "As an Anthropologist Views It." In Albert Deuth, ed. *Sex Habits of American Men*. New York: Prentice Hall, 1948.

KNOWLES, VALERIE. *Strangers at Our Gates: Canadian Immigration and Immigration Policy, 1540–1990*. Toronto: Dundurn, 1997.

KNOX, NOELLE. "European Gay Union Trends Influence U.S. Debate." *USA Today* (July 14, 2004):5A.

KOCH, HOWARD. *The Panic Broadcast: Portrait of an Event*. Boston: Little, Brown, 1970.

KOCHANEK, KENNETH D., ET AL. "Deaths: Final Data for 2002." *National Vital Statistics Report*. Vol. 53, No. 5 (October 12, 2004). Hyattsville, MD: National Center for Health Statistics.

KOHLBERG, LAWRENCE. *The Psychology of Moral Development: The Nature and Validity of Moral Stages*. New York: Harper & Row, 1981.

KOHLBERG, LAWRENCE, and CAROL GILLIGAN. "The Adolescent as Philosopher: The Discovery of Self in a Postconventional World." *Daedalus*. Vol. 100 (Fall 1971):1051–86.

KOHN, MELVIN L. *Class and Conformity: A Study in Values*. 2d ed. Homewood, IL: Dorsey Press, 1977.

———. "The 'Bell Curve' from the Perspective of Research on Social Structure and Personality." *Sociological Forum*. Vol. 11, No. 2 (1996):395.

KOMAROVSKY, MIRRA. "Cultural Contradictions and Sex Roles: The Masculine Case." *American Journal of Sociology*. Vol. 78, No. 4 (January 1973):873–84.

KORNHAUSER, WILLIAM. *The Politics of Mass Society*. New York: Free Press, 1959.

KOZOL, JONATHAN. *Prisoners of Silence: Breaking the Bonds of Adult Illiteracy in the United States*. New York: Continuum, 1980.

———. *Illiterate America*. Garden City, NY: Doubleday, 1985.

———. *Rachel and Her Children: Homeless Families in America*. New York: Crown Publishers, 1988.

——. *Savage Inequalities: Children in America's Schools.* New York: Harper Perennial, 1992.

KRAL, BRIGITTA. "The Eyes of Jane Elliott." *Horizon Magazine.* 2000. [Online] Available June 8, 2005, at http://www.horizonmag.com/4/jane-elliott. asp.

KRAUSS, CLIFFORD. "In God We Trust... Canadians Aren't So Sure." *New York Times* (March 26, 2003). [Online] Available at http://www.nytimes.com /2003/03/26/international/americas/26LETT.html?ex=1049718839&ei=1& en=7b6d16eaa7fa6364.

KRUEGER, ALAN B. "U.N. Aims To Cut Poverty in Half As Experts Wonder How To Measure It." *The New York Times.* February 3, 2005.

KRUEGER, PATRICK M., RICHARD G. ROGERS, ROBERT A. HUMMER, FELICIA B. LeCLERE, and STEPHANIE A. BOND HUIE. "Socioeconomic Status and Age: The Effect of Income Sources and Portfolios on U.S. Adult Maturity." *Sociological Forum.* Vol. 18, No. 3 (September 2003):465–82.

KRUKS, GABRIEL N. "Gay and Lesbian Homeless/Street Youth: Special Issues and Concerns." *Journal of Adolescent Health.* Special Issue. No. 12 (1991): 515–18.

KÜBLER-ROSS, ELISABETH. *On Death and Dying.* New York: Macmillan, 1969.

KUITENBROUWER, PETER. "The uncounted ones." *National Post* (April 20, 2006):A15.

KUUMBA, M. BAHATI. "A Cross-Cultural Race/Class/Gender Critique of Contemporary Population Policy: The Impact of Globalization." *Sociological Forum.* Vol. 14, No. 3 (March 1999):447–63.

KUZNETS, SIMON. "Economic Growth and Income Inequality." *The American Economic Review.* Vol. XLV, No. 1 (March 1955):1–28.

——. *Modern Economic Growth: Rate, Structure, and Spread.* New Haven, CT: Yale University Press, 1966.

LACAYO, RICHARD. "Blood at the Root." *Time* (April 10, 2000):122–23.

LACHAINE, PIERRE. "Make Jesus your CEO." *National Post* (March 25, 2006):TO12.

LADD, JOHN. "The Definition of Death and the Right to Die." In John Ladd, ed. *Ethical Issues Relating to Life and Death.* New York: Oxford University Press, 1979. pp. 118–45.

LANDSBERG, MITCHELL. "Health Disaster Brings Early Death in Russia." *Washington Times* (March 15, 1998):A8.

LANE, DAVID. "Social Stratification and Class." In Erik P. Hoffman and Robbin F. Laird, eds. *The Soviet Polity in the Modern Era.* New York: Aldine, 1984. pp. 563–605.

LANGBEIN, LAURA I., and ROSEANA BESS. "Sports in School: Source of Amity or Antipathy?" *Social Science Quarterly.* Vol. 83, No. 2 (June 2002):436–54.

LANGER, VALERIE. "It Happened Suddenly (Over a Long Period of Time): A Clayoquot History." 1996. [Online] Available at http://www.ancient rainforest.org/history.htm.

LAPCHICK, RICHARD. *The 2004 Racial and Gender Report Cards.* Institute for Diversity and Ethics in Sport, University of Central Florida. 2005. [Online] Available July 6, 2005, at http://www.bus.ucf.edu/sport/cgi-bin/site/ sitew.cgi?page=/news/index.htx.

LAPPÉ, FRANCES MOORE, and JOSEPH COLLINS. *World Hunger: Twelve Myths.* New York: Grove Press/Food First Books, 1986.

LAPPÉ, FRANCES MOORE, JOSEPH COLLINS, and PETER ROSSET. *World Hunger: Twelve Myths.* 2nd ed. New York: Grove Press, 1998.

LAPRAIRIE, CAROL P. "Community Types, Crime and Police Services on Canadian Indian Reserves." *Journal of Research in Crime and Delinquency.* Vol. 25, No. 4 (1988):375–91.

LAREAU, ANNETTE. "Invisible Inequality: Social Class and Childrearing in Black Families and White Families." *American Sociological Review.* Vol. 67, No. 5 (October 2002):747–76.

LASLETT, PETER. *The World We Have Lost: England Before the Industrial Age.* 3d ed. New York: Charles Scribner's Sons, 1984.

LaROSSA, RALPH, and DONALD C. REITZES. "Two? Two and One-Half? Thirty Months? Chronometrical Childhood in Early Twentieth-Century America." *Sociological Forum.* Vol. 166, No. 3 (September 2001):385–407.

LATOUCHE, DANIEL. "Québec." In *The Canadian Encyclopedia.* 2d ed. Vol. 3. Edmonton: Hurtig Publishers, 1988. pp. 1793–802.

LAUMANN, EDWARD O., JOHN H. GAGNON, ROBERT T. MICHAEL, and STUART MICHAELS. *The Social Organization of Sexuality: Sexual Practices in the United States.* Chicago, IL: University of Chicago Press, 1994.

LAVELLE, MARIANNE. "Payback Time." *U.S. News & World Report* (March 11, 2002):36–40.

LAVIN, DANIELLE, and DOUGLAS W. MAYNARD. "Standardization vs. Rapport: Respondent Laughter and Interviewer Reaction during Telephone Surveys." *American Sociological Review.* Vol. 66, No. 3 (June 2001):453–79.

LEAVITT, JUDITH WALZER. "Women and Health in America: An Overview." In Judith Walzer Leavitt, ed. *Women and Health in America.* Madison: University of Wisconsin Press, 1984. pp. 3–7.

LE BON, GUSTAVE. *The Crowd: A Study of the Popular Mind.* New York: Viking Press, 1960; orig. 1895.

LEE, FELICIA R. "Long Buried, Death Goes Public Again." *New York Times* (2002). [Online] Available November 2, 2002, at http://www.researchnavigator. com.

LEMERT, EDWIN M. *Social Pathology.* New York: McGraw-Hill, 1951.

——. *Human Deviance, Social Problems, and Social Control.* 2d ed. Englewood Cliffs, NJ: Prentice Hall, 1972.

LEMONICK, MICHAEL D. "The Search for a Murder Gene." *Time* (January 20, 2003):100.

LENGERMANN, PATRICIA MADOO, and RUTH A. WALLACE. *Gender in America: Social Control and Social Change.* Englewood Cliffs, NJ: Prentice Hall, 1985.

LENSKI, GERHARD E. *Power and Privilege: A Theory of Social Stratification.* New York: McGraw-Hill, 1966.

LENSKI, GERHARD, PATRICK NOLAN, and JEAN LENSKI. *Human Societies: An Introduction to Macrosociology.* 7th ed. New York: McGraw-Hill, 1995.

LENTON, RHONDA L. "Homicide in Canada and the U.S.A.: A Critique of the Hagan Thesis." In Alexander Himelfarb and James Richardson, eds. *Sociology for Canadians.* 2d ed. Toronto: McGraw-Hill Ryerson, 1989.

——. "Techniques of Child Discipline and Abuse by Parents." *Canadian Review of Sociology and Anthropology,* Vol. 7, No. 2 (1990):157–85.

LEONARD, EILEEN B. *Women, Crime, and Society: A Critique of Theoretical Criminology.* New York: Longman, 1982.

LETHBRIDGE-CEJKU, MARGARET, and JACKLINE VICKERIE. *Summary Health Statistics for U.S. Adults: National Health Interview Survey, 2003.* Vital and Health Statistics, Series 10, No. 225. Hyattsville, MD: National Center for Health Statistics, 2005.

LeVAY, SIMON. *The Sexual Brain.* Cambridge, MA: MIT Press, 1993.

LEVER, JANET. "Sex Differences in the Complexity of Children's Play and Games." *American Sociological Review.* Vol. 43, No. 4 (August 1978):471–83.

LEVINE, MICHAEL P. *Student Eating Disorders: Anorexia Nervosa and Bulimia.* Washington, DC: National Educational Association, 1987.

——. "Reducing Hostility Can Prevent Heart Disease." *Mount Vernon* (Ohio) *News* (August 7, 1990):4A.

LEVINSON, DANIEL J., WITH CHARLOTTE N. DARROW, EDWARD B. KLEIN, MARIA H. LEVINSON, and BRAXTON McKEE. *The Seasons of a Man's Life.* New York: Alfred A. Knopf, 1978.

LEWIS, OSCAR. *The Children of Sanchez.* New York: Random House, 1961.

LI, PETER S. *Ethnic Inequality in a Class Society.* Toronto: Wall and Thompson, 1988.

——. *The Making of Post-War Canada.* Toronto: Oxford University Press, 1996.

——. *Destination Canada: Immigration Debates and Issues.* Toronto: Oxford University Press Canada, 2003.

LIAZOS, ALEXANDER. "The Poverty of the Sociology of Deviance: Nuts, Sluts and Perverts." *Social Problems.* Vol. 20, No. 1 (Summer 1972):103–20.

LICHTER, S. ROBERT, STANLEY ROTHMAN, and LINDA R. ROTHMAN. *The Media Elite: America's New Powerbrokers.* Bethesda, MD: Adler & Adler, 1986.

LIN, NAN, KAREN COOK, and RONALD S. BURT, EDS. *Social Capital: Theory and Research.* Hawthorne, N.Y.: Aldine de Gruyter, 2001.

LIN, NAN, and WEN XIE. "Occupational Prestige in Urban China." *American Journal of Sociology.* Vol. 93, No. 4 (January 1988):793–832.

LINDAUER, DAVID L., and AKILA WEERAPANA. "Relief for Poor Nations." *Society.* Vol. 39, No. 3 (March/April 2002):54–58.

LINDSTROM, BONNIE. "Chicago's Post-Industrial Suburbs." *Sociological Focus.* Vol. 28, No. 4 (October 1995):399–412.

LINO, MARK. *Expenditures on Children by Families, 2004.* U.S. Department of Agriculture, Center for Nutrition Policy and Promotion. Miscellaneous Publication No. 1528–2004. Washington, DC: U.S. Government Printing Office, 2005.

LINTON, RALPH. "One Hundred Percent American." *The American Mercury.* Vol. 40, No. 160 (April 1937):427–29.

——. *The Study of Man.* New York: D. Appleton-Century, 1937.

LIPOVENKO, DOROTHY. "Golden Handshakes Launch New Careers." *The Globe and Mail* (January 29, 1996):A1, A6.

LIPSET, SEYMOUR MARTIN. *Political Man: The Social Bases of Politics.* Garden City, NY: Anchor/Doubleday, 1963.

——. *Canada and the United States.* Charles F. Donan and John H. Sigler, eds. Englewood Cliffs, NJ: Prentice Hall, 1985.

——. *Continental Divide: The Values and Institutions of the United States and Canada.* New York: Routledge, 1991.

LISKA, ALLEN E., and BARBARA D. WARNER. "Functions of Crime: A Paradoxical Process." *American Journal of Sociology.* Vol. 96, No. 6 (May 1991):1441–63.

LITTLE, CRAIG, and ANDREA RANKIN. "Why Do They Start It? Explaining Reported Early-Teen Sexual Activity." *Sociological Forum.* Vol. 16, No. 4 (December 2001):703–29.

LIVERNASH, ROBERT, and ERIC RODENBURG. "Population Change, Resources, and the Environment." *Population Bulletin.* Vol. 53, No. 1 (March 1998).

LIVINGSTONE, DAVID W. "Public Education at the Crossroads: Confronting Underemployment in a Knowledge Society." In Dan Glenday and Ann Duffy, eds. *Canadian Society: Meeting the Challenges of the Twenty-First Century.* Toronto: Oxford University Press, 2001.

LIVINGSTONE, D.W., and MEG LUXTON. "Gender Consciousness at Work: Modification of the Male Breadwinner Norm Among Steelworkers and Their Spouses." In E.D. Nelson and B.W. Robinson, eds. *Gender in the 1990s:*

Images, Realities, and Issues. Scarborough, ON: Nelson Canada, 1995. pp. 172–200.

LOFLAND, LYN. *A World of Strangers.* New York: Basic Books, 1973.

LONGINO, CHARLES F., JR. "Myths of an Aging America." *American Demographics.* Vol. 16, No. 8 (August 1994):36–42.

LORD, WALTER. *A Night to Remember.* Rev. ed. New York: Holt, Rinehart & Winston, 1976.

LORENZ, FREDERICK O., and BRENT T. BRUTON. "Experiments in Surveys: Linking Mass Class Questionnaires to Introductory Research Methods." *Teaching Sociology.* Vol. 24, No. 3 (July 1996):264–71.

LOVEMAN, MARA. "Is 'Race' Essential?" *American Sociological Review.* Vol. 64, No. 6 (December 1999):890–98.

LOY, PAMELA HEWITT, and LEA P. STEWART. "The Extent and Effects of Sexual Harassment of Working Women." *Sociological Focus.* Vol. 17, No. 1 (January 1984):31–43.

LUKER, KRISTEN. *Abortion and the Politics of Motherhood.* Berkeley: University of California Press, 1984.

LUND, DALE A. "Conclusions about Bereavement in Later Life and Implica-tions for Interventions and Future Research." In Dale A. Lund, ed. *Older Bereaved Spouses: Research With Practical Applications.* London, UK: Taylor-Francis-Hemisphere, 1989. pp. 217–31.

LUND, DALE A., MICHAEL S. CASERTA, and MARGARET F. DIMOND. "Gender Differences Through Two Years of Bereavement Among the Elderly." *The Gerontologist.* Vol. 26, No. 3 (1986):314–20.

LUNMAN, KIM. "National Response Needed, Cauchon Maintains." *The Globe and Mail* (June 11, 2003):A4.

LUPRI, EUGENE. "Male Violence in the Home." In Craig McKie and K. Thompson, eds. *Social Trends in Canada.* Toronto: Thompson Educational Publishers, 1988. pp. 170–72.

——. "Intimate Violence: Male Abuse." Unpublished manuscript. University of Calgary, 2002.

LUXTON, MEG. *More Than a Labour of Love.* Toronto: Women's Press, 1980.

LYALL, SARAH, and ROBIN POGREBIN. "Desperately Seeking Diana." *The Globe and Mail* (September 11, 1997).

LYND, ROBERT S. *Knowledge For What? The Place of Social Science in American Culture.* Princeton, NJ: Princeton University Press, 1967.

MABRY, MARCUS, and TOM MASLAND. "The Man after Mandela." *Newsweek* (June 7, 1999):54–55.

MACCOBY, ELEANOR EMMONS, and CAROL NAGY JACKLIN. *The Psychology of Sex Differences.* Palo Alto, CA: Stanford University Press, 1974.

MACE, DAVID, and VERA MACE. *Marriage East and West.* Garden City, NY: Doubleday (Dolphin), 1960.

MACIONIS, JOHN J. "Intimacy: Structure and Process in Interpersonal Relationships." *Alternative Lifestyles.* Vol. 1, No. 1 (February 1978a):113–30.

——. "A Sociological Analysis of Humor." Presentation to the Texas Junior College Teachers Association, Houston, 1987.

——. *Social Problems.* 2nd ed. Upper Saddle River, NJ: Prentice Hall, 2005.

——. *Sociology, Eleventh Edition.* Upper Saddle River, NJ: Pearson Prentice Hall, 2007.

MACIONIS, JOHN J., and LINDA M. GERBER. *Sociology* (5th Canadian ed.) Toronto: Pearson/Prentice Hall Canada, 2005.

MACIONIS, JOHN J., and VINCENT R. PARRILLO. *Cities and Urban Life.* Upper Saddle River, NJ: Prentice Hall, 1998.

——. *Cities and Urban Life.* 3rd ed. Upper Saddle River, NJ: Prentice Hall, 2004.

MADDOX, SETMA. "Organizational Culture and Leadership Style: Factors Affecting Self-Managed Work Team Performance." Paper presented at the annual meeting of the Southwest Social Science Association, Dallas, Texas, February 1994.

MAHONEY, JILL. "Web skeptics take note: The sky hasn't fallen." *The Globe and Mail* (January 26, 2006a):A8.

——. "Canadians happier in the bedroom than Americans". *The Globe and Mail* (April 20, 2006b):A3.

——. "Single mother has more money, less cash." *The Globe and Mail* (March 31, 2006c):A8.

MAKIN, KIRK. "Gay Marriage Is Legalized." *The Globe and Mail* (June 11, 2003):A1

——. "Split decisions." *The Globe and Mail* (July 29, 2006):F1.

MALTHUS, THOMAS ROBERT. *First Essay on Population 1798.* London, UK: Macmillan, 1926; orig. 1798.

MANCUSO, MAUREEN, MICHAEL M. ATKINSON, ANDRÉ BLAIS, IAN GREENE, and NEIL NEVITTE. *A Question of Ethics: Canadians Speak Out.* Don Mills, ON: Oxford University Press, 2006.

MARCHAK, PATRICIA. "The Rise and Fall of the Peripheral State: The Case of British Columbia." In Robert J. Brym, ed. *Regionalism in Canada.* Toronto: Irwin, 1986. pp. 123–60.

MARCUSE, HERBERT. *One-Dimensional Man.* Boston: Beacon Press, 1964.

MARE, ROBERT D. "Five Decades of Educational Assortative Mating." *American Sociological Review.* Vol. 56, No. 1 (February 1991):15–32.

MARKOFF, JOHN. "Remember Big Brother? Now He's a Company Man." *New York Times* (March 31, 1991):7.

MARLIOS, PETER. "Interlocking Directorates and the Control of Corporations: The Theory of Bank Control." *Social Science Quarterly.* Vol. 56, No. 3 (December 1975):425–39.

MARQUAND, ROBERT. "Worship Shift: Americans Seek Feeling of 'Awe.'" *Christian Science Monitor* (May 28, 1997):1, 8.

MARQUAND, ROBERT, and DANIEL B. WOOD. "Rise in Cults as Millennium Approaches." *Christian Science Monitor* (March 28, 1997):1, 18.

MARSDEN, LORNA R., and EDWARD B. HARVEY. *Fragile Federation: Social Change in Canada.* Toronto: McGraw-Hill Ryerson, 1979.

MARSHALL, SUSAN E. "Ladies Against Women: Mobilization Dilemmas of Antifeminist Movements." *Social Problems.* Vol. 32, No. 4 (April 1985): 348–62.

MARTIN, CAROL LYNN, and RICHARD A. FABES. Research cited in Marianne Szegedy-Maszak, "The Power of Gender." *U.S. News & World Report* (June 4, 2001):52.

MARTIN, RICHARD C. *Islam: A Cultural Perspective.* Englewood Cliffs, NJ: Prentice Hall, 1982.

MARTIN, SANDRA. "Reining in the Space Cowboys." *The Globe and Mail* (April 19, 2000):R1, R2.

MARULLO, SAM. "The Functions and Dysfunctions of Preparations for Fighting Nuclear War." *Sociological Focus.* Vol. 20, No. 2 (April 1987):135–53.

MARX, KARL. Excerpt from "A Contribution to the Critique of Political Economy." In Karl Marx and Friedrich Engels, *Marx and Engels: Basic Writings on Politics and Philosophy.* Lewis S. Feurer, ed. Garden City, NY: Anchor Books, 1959. pp. 42–46.

——. *Karl Marx: Early Writings.* T.B. Bottomore, ed. New York: McGraw-Hill, 1964a.

——. *Karl Marx: Selected Writings in Sociology and Social Philosophy.* T.B. Bottomore, trans. New York: McGraw-Hill, 1964b; orig. 1848.

——. *Capital.* Friedrich Engels, ed. New York: International Publishers, 1967; orig. 1867.

MARX, KARL, and FRIEDRICH ENGELS. "Manifesto of the Communist Party." In Robert C. Tucker, ed. *The Marx-Engels Reader.* New York: Norton, 1972; orig. 1848. pp. 331–62.

——. *The Marx-Engels Reader.* 2nd ed. Robert C. Tucker, ed. New York: Norton, 1978; orig. 1859.

MARX, LEO. "The Environment and the 'Two Cultures' Divide." In James Rodger Fleming and Henry A. Gemery, eds. *Science, Technology, and the Environment: Multidisciplinary Perspectives.* Akron, OH: University of Akron Press, 1994. pp 3–21.

MARZOLINI, MICHAEL. "Public Opinion Polling and the 2004 Election." In Jon H. Pammett and Christopher Dornan (eds.) *The Canadian General Election of 2004.* Toronto: The Dundurn Group, 2004. pp. 290–313.

MASON, GARY. "Looking to adopt? There's no place like home." *The Globe and Mail* (June 1, 2006):A8.

MASSEY, DOUGLAS S. Review of *The Bell Curve: Intelligence and Class Structure in American Life* by Richard J. Herrnstein and Charles Murray. *American Journal of Sociology.* Vol. 101, No. 3 (November 1995):747–53.

MATAS, ROBERT. "UBC scores academic coup by luring Nobel physicist." *The Globe and Mail* (March 20, 2006):A1.

MATHEWS, T.J., and BRADY E. HAMILTON. "Trend Analysis of the Sex Ratio at Birth in the United States." *National Vital Statistics Reports.* Vol. 53, No. 20 (June 14, 2005). Hyattsville, MD: National Center for Health Statistics.

MATTHEWS, RALPH. "*There's No Better Place Than Here*": *Social Change in Three Newfoundland Communities.* Toronto: Peter Martin Associates, 1976.

——. *The Creation of Regional Dependency.* Toronto: University of Toronto Press, 1983.

MATTHIESSEN, PETER. *Indian Country.* New York: Viking Press, 1984.

MAURO, TONY. "Ruling Likely Will Add Fuel to Already Divisive Debate." *USA Today* (January 7, 1997):1A, 2A.

MAUSS, ARMAND L. *Social Problems of Social Movements.* Philadelphia: Lippincott, 1975.

MAYO, KATHERINE. *Mother India.* New York: Harcourt, Brace, 1927.

McADAM, DOUG. *Political Process and the Development of Black Insurgency, 1930–1970.* Chicago, IL: University of Chicago Press, 1982.

——. "Tactical Innovation and the Pace of Insurgency." *American Sociological Review.* Vol. 48, No. 6 (December 1983):735–54.

——. *Freedom Summer.* New York: Oxford University Press, 1988.

——. "The Biographical Consequences of Activism." *American Sociological Review.* Vol. 54, No. 5 (October 1989):744–60.

McADAM, DOUG, JOHN D. McCARTHY, and MAYER N. ZALD. "Social Movements." In Neil J. Smelser, ed. *Handbook of Sociology.* Newbury Park, CA: Sage, 1988. pp. 695–737.

McADAM, DOUG, JOHN D. McCARTHY, and MAYER N. ZALD. EDS. *Comparative Perspectives on Social Movements: Political Opportunities, Mobilizing Structures, and Cultural Framings.* New York: Cambridge University Press, 1996.

McALL, CHRISTOPHER. *Class, Ethnicity and Social Inequality.* Montreal and Kingston: McGill-Queen's University Press, 1990.

McBROOM, WILLIAM H., and FRED W. REED. "Recent Trends in Conservatism: Evidence of Non-Unitary Patterns." *Sociological Focus.* Vol. 23, No. 4 (October 1990):355–65.

McCARTHY, JOHN D., and MAYER N. ZALD. "Resource Mobilization and Social Movements: A Partial Theory." *American Journal of Sociology.* Vol. 82, No. 6 (May 1977):1212–41.

McCLAIN, PAULA DENISE. *Alienation and Resistance: The Political Behaviour of Afro-Canadians.* Palo Alto, CA: R&E Research Associates, 1979.

McCOLM, R. BRUCE, D. BRICKER, J. FINN, J. KARL, D.W. PAYNE, J.E. RYAN, and G. ZARYCKY. *Freedom in the World: Political Rights and Civil Liberties, 1990–1991.* New York: Freedom House, 1991.

McDANIEL, SUSAN. "Emotional Support and Family Contacts of Older Canadians." In Craig McKie and Keith Thompson, eds. *Canadian Social Trends. Volume 2.* Toronto: Thompson Educational Publishing, 1994. pp. 129–32.

MacDONALD, JO-ANNE. "Home for the Grey and Gay." *National Post* (August 15, 2005).

McDONALD, KIM. A. "Debate over How to Gauge Global Warming Heats Up Meeting of Climatologists." *Chronicle of Higher Education.* Vol. XLV, No. 22 (February 5, 1999):A17.

McDONALD, LYNN. *The Women Founders of the Social Sciences.* Ottawa: Carleton University Press, 1994.

McDONALD, TERRY. *Hill Times Index of the 37th House of Commons* (January 19, 2001).

MACGREGOR, ROY. "Why in the world did you move here from California?" *The Globe and Mail.* (December 28, 2004):A2.

McGUIRE, MEREDITH B. *Religion: The Social Context.* 2d ed. Belmont, CA: Wadsworth, 1987.

MacKAY, JUDITH. *The Penguin Atlas of Human Sexual Behavior.* New York: Penguin Group, 2000.

McKEE, VICTORIA. "Blue Blood and the Color of Money." *New York Times* (June 9, 1996):49–50.

MacKENZIE, BETSY. "Therapeutic Abortion in Canada." In Craig McKie and Keith Thompson, eds. *Canadian Social Trends.* Toronto: Thompson Educational Publishing, 1990.

McKENZIE, JUDITH. *Pauline Jewett: A Passion for Canada.* Montreal and Kingston: McGill-Queen's University Press, 1999.

McKENZIE, JUDITH I. "The Inner Suburbs of the Greater Toronto Area." In *Health, Governance, and Citizenship in Four Canadian Cities,* ed. Karen B. Murray. Vancouver: University of British Columbia Press, 2006.

MACKIE, MARLENE. "Ethnic Stereotypes and Prejudice: Alberta Indians, Hutterites and Ukrainians." *Canadian Ethnic Studies.* Vol. x (1974):118–29.

——. *Exploring Gender Relations: A Canadian Perspective.* Toronto: Butterworths, 1983.

McLANAHAN, SARA. "Life without Father: What Happens to the Children?" *Contexts.* Vol. 1, No. 1 (Spring 2002):35–44.

McLEAN, STUART. *Welcome Home: Travels in Smalltown Canada.* Toronto: Viking, 1992.

MACLEAN'S/CTV POLL, 1994. January 2, 1995. Cited in Rathus, Spencer A., Jeffrey S. Nevid, Lois Fischner-Rathus, and Edward S. Herold. *Human Sexuality in a World of Diversity.* Canadian Edition. Toronto: Pearson Canada, 2004. p. 424.

McLEOD, JANE D., and MICHAEL J. SHANAHAN. "Poverty, Parenting, and Children's Mental Health." *American Sociological Review.* Vol. 58, No. 3 (June 1993):351–66.

McLEOD, JAY. *Ain't No Makin' It: Aspirations and Attainment in a Low-Income Neighborhood.* Boulder, CO: Westview Press, 1995.

McLUHAN, MARSHALL. *The Gutenberg Galaxy.* New York: New American Library, 1969.

MacNEIL, ROBERT. *Burden of Desire.* New York: Harcourt Brace & Company, 1992.

McPHAIL, CLARK. *The Myth of the Madding Crowd.* New York: Aldine, 1991.

McPHAIL, CLARK, and RONALD T. WOHLSTEIN. "Individual and Collective Behaviors Within Gatherings, Demonstrations, and Riots." *Annual Review of Sociology.* Vol. 9. Palo Alto, CA: Annual Reviews, 1983. pp. 579–600.

McPHERSON, BARRY D. *Aging as a Social Process: An Introduction to Individual and Population Aging.* 2d ed. Toronto: Butterworths, 1990.

——. *Aging as a Social Process: Canadian Perspectives.* 4th ed. Don Mills, ON: Oxford University Press, 2004.

McRAE, SUSAN. *Cross-Class Families: A Study of Wives' Occupational Superiority.* New York: Oxford University Press, 1986.

MEAD, GEORGE HERBERT. *Mind, Self, and Society.* Charles W. Morris, ed. Chicago, IL: University of Chicago Press, 1962; orig. 1934.

MEAD, MARGARET. *Sex and Temperament in Three Primitive Societies.* New York: William Morrow, 1963; orig. 1935.

MEADOWS, DONELLA H., DENNIS L. MEADOWS, JORGAN RANDERS, and WILLIAM W. BEHRENS, III. *The Limits to Growth: A Report on the Club of Rome's Project on the Predicament of Mankind.* New York: Universe, 1972.

MELTZER, BERNARD N. "Mead's Social Psychology." In Jerome G. Manis and Bernard N. Meltzer, eds. *Symbolic Interaction: A Reader in Social Psychology.* 3d ed. Needham Heights, MA: Allyn & Bacon, 1978.

MELUCCI, ALBERTO. *Nomads of the Present: Social Movements and Individual Needs in Contemporary Society.* Philadelphia, PA: Temple University Press, 1989.

MENZIES, KEN. *The People-Serving Society.* Manuscript draft. University of Guelph. [n.d.]

MERRIT, SUSAN E. *Her Story: Women from Canada's Past.* St. Catharines, ON: Vanwell Publishing, 1993.

MERTON, ROBERT K. "Social Structure and Anomie." *American Sociological Review.* Vol. 3, No. 6 (October 1938):672–82.

——. *Social Theory and Social Structure.* New York: Free Press, 1968.

MESSING, PHILIP. "City Crime Plummets." *New York Post* (September 5, 2003). [Online] Available at http://www.nypost.com/news/regionalnews/5020.htm.

METZ, MICHAEL E., and MICHAEL H. MINER. "Psychosexual and Psychosocial Aspects of Male Aging and Sexual Health." *Canadian Journal of Human Sexuality.* Vol. 7, No. 3 (Summer 1998):245–60.

MICHELS, ROBERT. *Political Parties.* Glencoe, IL: Free Press, 1949; orig. 1911.

MICHELSON, WILLIAM. "Urbanization and Urbanism." In James Curtis and Lorne Tepperman, eds. *Understanding Canadian Society.* Toronto: McGraw-Hill Ryerson, 1988:73–104.

MILBRATH, LESTER W. *Political Participation: How and Why Do People Get Involved in Politics.* Chicago, IL: Rand McNally, 1966.

——. *Envisioning a Sustainable Society: Learning Our Way Out.* Albany: State University of New York Press, 1989.

MILGRAM, STANLEY. "Behavioral Study of Obedience." *Journal of Abnormal and Social Psychology.* Vol. 67, No. 4 (1963):371–78.

——. "Group Pressure and Action Against a Person." *Journal of Abnormal and Social Psychology.* Vol. 69, No. 2 (August 1964):137–43.

——. "Some Conditions of Obedience and Disobedience to Authority." *Human Relations.* Vol. 18 (February 1965):57–76.

——. "The Small World Problem." *Psychology Today* (May 1967):60–67.

MILLER, ARTHUR G. *The Obedience Experiments: A Case of Controversy in Social Science.* New York: Praeger, 1986.

MILLER, DAVID L. *Introduction to Collective Behavior.* Belmont, CA: Wadsworth, 1985.

MILLER, FREDERICK D. "The End of SDS and the Emergence of Weatherman: Demise Through Success." In Jo Freeman, ed. *Social Movements of the Sixties and Seventies.* New York: Longman, 1983. pp. 279–97.

MILLER, G. TYLER, JR. *Living in the Environment: An Introduction to Environmental Science.* Belmont, CA: Wadsworth, 1992.

MILLER, MARK. "Under Cover, in the Closet." *Newsweek* (January 14, 1991):25.

MILLER, MATTHEW, and PETER NEWCOMB, EDS. "The Forbes 400." *Forbes* (Special issue, October 10, 2005).

MILLER, WILLIAM J., and RICK A. MATTHEWS. "Youth Employment, Differential Association, and Juvenile Delinquency." *Sociological Focus.* Vol. 34, No. 3 (August 2001):251–68.

MILLS, C. WRIGHT. *White Collar: The American Middle Classes.* New York: Oxford University Press, 1951.

——. *The Power Elite.* New York: Oxford University Press, 1956.

——. *The Sociological Imagination.* New York: Oxford University Press, 1959.

MIRACLE, TINA S., ANDREW W. MIRACLE, and ROY F. BAUMEISTER. *Human Sexuality: Meeting Your Basic Needs.* Upper Saddle River, NJ: Prentice Hall, 2003.

MITCHELL, ALANNA. "Greying of Canada Oversold Notion." *The Globe and Mail* (July 30, 1997):A4.

——. "More Children Running Away Younger, Statscan Says." *The Globe and Mail* (February 13, 1998):A3.

MITCHELL, BARBARA A. "The Refilled 'Nest.'" In Ellen M. Gee and Gloria M. Gutman, eds. *The Overselling of Population Aging: Apocalyptic Demography, Intergenerational Challenges, and Social Policy.* Don Mills, ON: Oxford University Press, 2000.

MITTELSTAEDT, MARTIN. "Change Unavoidable for Ontario Hydro." *The Globe and Mail* (August 18, 1997):A1.

MOEN, PHYLLIS, DONNA DEMPSTER-McCLAIN, and ROBIN M. WILLIAMS. "Successful Aging: A Life-Course Perspective on Women's Multiple Roles and Health." *American Journal of Sociology.* Vol. 97, No. 6 (May 1992):1612–38.

MONSEBRAATEN, LAURIE. "Struggling On in Wake of Cuts." *Toronto Star* (May 5, 1996): F6.

MONTAIGNE, FEN. "Russia Rising." *National Geographic.* Vol. 200, No. 5 (September 2001):2–31.

MONTIGNY, GILLES. "Reading Skills." In Craig McKie and Keith Thompson, eds. *Canadian Social Trends: A Canadian Studies Reader. Volume 2.* Toronto: Thompson Educational Publishing, 1994. pp. 111–19.

MOONEY, ERIN. "Presence, *ergo* Protection? UNPROFOR, UNHCR, and the ICRC in Croatia and Bosnia and Herzegovina." *International Journal of Refugee Law* 7/3 (1995).

MOORE, GWEN. "The Structure of a National Elite Network." *American Sociological Review.* Vol. 44, No. 5 (October 1979):673–92.

——. "Gender and Informal Networks in State Government." *Social Science Quarterly.* Vol. 73, No. 1 (March 1992):46–61.

MOORE, WILBERT E. "Modernization as Rationalization: Processes and Restraints." In Manning Nash, ed. *Essays on Economic Development and Cultural Change in Honor of Bert F. Hoselitz.* Chicago, IL: University of Chicago Press, 1977. pp. 29–42.

——. *World Modernization: The Limits of Convergence.* New York: Elsevier, 1979.

MORRIS, ALDON. "Black Southern Sit-In Movement: An Analysis of Internal Organization." *American Sociological Review.* Vol. 46, No. 6 (December 1981):744–67.

MORRISON, DENTON E. "Some Notes Toward Theory on Relative Deprivation, Social Movements, and Social Change." In Louis E. Genevie, ed. *Collective Behavior and Social Movements.* Itasca, IL: Peacock, 1978. pp. 202–9.

MUHTADIE, LUMA. "The Jewel in Its Crown: CBC Beats Foes at Coronation." *The Globe and Mail* (June 2, 2003):A3.

MUMFORD, LEWIS. *The City in History: Its Origins, Its Transformations, and Its Prospects.* New York: Harcourt, Brace & World, 1961.

MURDOCK, GEORGE PETER. "Comparative Data on the Division of Labor by Sex." *Social Forces.* Vol. 15, No. 4 (May 1937):551–53.

——. "The Common Denominator of Cultures." In Ralph Linton, ed. *The Science of Man in World Crisis.* New York: Columbia University Press, 1945. pp. 123–42.

——. *Social Structure.* New York: Free Press, 1965; orig. 1949.

MURRAY, STEPHEN O., and WILL ROSCOE, EDS. *Boy-Wives and Female-Husbands: Studies of African Homosexualities.* New York: St. Martin's Press, 1998.

MYERS, DAVID G. *The American Paradox: Spiritual Hunger in an Age of Plenty.* New Haven, CT: Yale University Press, 2000.

MYERS, NORMAN. "Humanity's Growth." In Sir Edmund Hillary, ed., *Ecology 2000: The Changing Face of the Earth.* New York: Beaufort Books, 1984. pp. 16–35.

——. "Biological Diversity and Global Security." In F. Herbert Bormann and Stephen R. Kellert, eds. *Ecology, Economics, and Ethics: The Broken Circle.* New Haven, CT: Yale University Press, 1991. pp. 11–25.

MYERS, SHEILA, and HAROLD G. GRASMICK. "The Social Rights and Responsibilities of Pregnant Women: An Application of Parsons' Sick Role Model." Paper presented to Southwestern Sociological Association, Little Rock, AR, March 1989.

NADER, RALPH, NADIA MILLERON, and DUFF CONACHER. *Canada Firsts.* Toronto: McClelland & Stewart, 1992.

NANCARROW CLARKE, JUANNE. *It's Cancer: The Personal Experiences of Women Who Have Received a Cancer Diagnosis.* Toronto: IPI, 1985.

——. *Health, Illness & Medicine in Canada.* 2d ed. Toronto: McClelland & Stewart, 1996.

——. "Media Portrayal of Disease from the Medical, Political Economy and Life Style Perspectives." *Qualitative Health Research.* Vol. 1, No. 3 (1991):287–308.

NATIONAL COMMISSION ON EXCELLENCE IN EDUCATION. *A Nation at Risk.* Washington, DC: U.S. Government Printing Office, 1983.

NATIONAL LITERACY SECRETARIAT. International Adult Literary Survey, 2006. [Online] Available at http://www.nald.ca/.

NEILL, SHIRLEY. "Unionization in Canada." In Craig McKie and Keith Thompson, eds. *Canadian Social Trends.* Toronto: Thompson Educational Publishing, 1990.

NELSON, E.D., and AUGIE FLERAS. *Social Problems in Canada: Issues and Challenges.* 2d ed. Scarborough, ON: Prentice Hall, 1998.

NELSON, E.D., and BARRY W. ROBINSON. *Gender in Canada.* Scarborough, ON: Prentice Hall, 1999.

NELSON, JOEL I. "Work and Benefits: The Multiple Problems of Service Sector Employment." *Social Problems.* Vol. 42, No. 2 (May 1994):240–55.

NESSMAN, RAVI. "Stampede at Soccer Match Kills 47." [Online]. Available April 11, 2001, at http://news.yahoo.com.

NETT, EMILY M. *Canadian Families: Past and Present.* 2d ed. Toronto: Butterworths, 1993.

NEUGARTEN, BERNICE L. "Grow Old with Me. The Best Is Yet to Be." *Psychology Today.* Vol. 5 (December 1971):45–48, 79, 81.

——. "Personality and the Aging Process." *The Gerontologist.* Vol. 12, No. 1 (Spring 1972):9–15.

——. "Personality and Aging." In James E. Birren and K. Warner Schaie, eds. *Handbook of the Psychology of Aging.* New York: Van Nostrand Reinhold, 1977. pp. 626–49.

NEUHOUSER, KEVIN. "The Radicalization of the Brazilian Catholic Church in Comparative Perspective." *American Sociological Review.* Vol. 54, No. 2 (April 1989):233–44.

NEUMAN, W. LAURENCE. *Social Research Methods: Qualitative and Quantitative Approaches.* 3d ed.; Boston: Allyn & Bacon, 1997;. 4th ed. 2000.

NEVITTE, NEIL. *The Decline of Deference.* Peterborough, ON: Broadview Press, 1996.

NEWMAN, KATHERINE S. *Declining Fortunes: The Withering of the American Dream.* New York: Basic Books, 1993.

NEWMAN, PETER C. *The Canadian Revolution, 1985–1995: From Deference to Defiance.* Toronto: Penguin Books, 1995.

——. *Titans: How the New Canadian Establishment Seized Power.* Toronto: Penguin, 1998.

NEWMAN, WILLIAM M. *American Pluralism: A Study of Minority Groups and Social Theory.* New York: Harper & Row, 1973.

NFO CFGROUP. "Public Divided About Definition of Marriage." [Online] Available September 5, 2003 at http://www.nfocfgroup.com/news/news.html#news_items.

NICHOLSON, NIGEL. "Evolved to Chat: The New Word on Gossip." *Psychology Today* (May/June 2001):41–45.

NIELSEN, FRANCOIS, and ARTHUR S. ALDERSON. "The Kuznets Curve: The Great U-Turn: Income Inequality in U.S. Counties, 1970 to 1990." *American Sociological Review.* Vol. 62, No. 1 (February 1997):12–33.

NIKIFORUK, ANDREW. "When Water Kills." *Maclean's* (June 12, 2000).

NIN.DA.WAAB.JIG. Walpole Island Heritage Centre. "Walpole Island in 2005: A View from the Future." In Diane Engelstad and John Bird, eds. *Nation to Nation: Aboriginal Sovereignty and the Future of Canada.* Concord, ON: House of Anansi Press, 1992. pp. 186–96.

NISBET, ROBERT A. *The Sociological Tradition.* New York: Basic Books, 1966.

——. *The Quest for Community.* New York: Oxford University Press, 1969.

——. "Sociology as an Art Form." *In Tradition and Revolt: Historical and Sociological Essays.* New York: Vintage Books, 1970.

NOCK, STEVEN L., JAMES D. WRIGHT, and LAURA SANCHEZ. "America's Divorce Problem." *Society.* Vol. 36, No. 4 (May/June 1999):43–52.

NOLAN, PATRICK, and GERHARD LENSKI. *Human Societies: An Introduction to Macrosociology.* 9th ed. Boulder, CO: Paradigm, 2004.

NORBECK, EDWARD. "Class Structure." In *Kodansha Encyclopedia of Japan.* Tokyo: Kodansha, 1983. pp. 322–25.

NORC. *General Social Surveys, 1972–1998: Cumulative Codebook.* Chicago, IL: National Opinion Research Center, 1999.

——. *General Social Surveys, 1972–2002: Cumulative Codebook.* Chicago, IL: National Opinion Research Center, 2003.

NORTON, PHILLIP. "Jackrabbit Johannsen: The Pioneer of Skiing in Canada." *Canadian Geographic* (April/May 1997):18–23.

NULAND, SHERWIN B. "The Hazards of Hospitalization." *Wall Street Journal* (December 2, 1999):A22.

OBERSCHALL, ANTHONY. *Social Conflict and Social Movements.* Englewood Cliffs, NJ: Prentice Hall, 1973.

ODERKIRK, JILLIAN. "Education Achievement: An International Comparison." *Canadian Social Trends* (Autumn 1993):8–12.

OGAWA, NAOHIRO, and ROBERT D. RETHERFORD. "Shifting Costs of Caring for the Elderly Back to Families in Japan: Will It Work?" *Population and Development Review.* Vol. 23, No. 1 (March 1997):59–95.

OGBURN, WILLIAM F. *On Culture and Social Change.* Chicago, IL: University of Chicago Press, 1964.

OGDEN, RUSSEL D. "Nonphysician-Assisted Suicide: The Technological Imperative of the Deathing Counterculture." *Death Studies.* Vol. 25, No. 5 (July 2001):387–402.

O'HARROW, ROBERT, JR. "ID Theft Scam Hits D.C. Area Residents." [Online] Available February 21, 2005, at http://news.yahoo.com/.

OLSEN, GREGG M. "Re-Modeling Sweden: The Rise and Demise of the Compromise in a Global Economy." *Social Problems.* Vol. 43, No. 1 (February 1996):1–20.

OLZAK, SUSAN. "Labor Unrest, Immigration, and Ethnic Conflict in Urban America, 1880–1914." *American Journal of Sociology.* Vol. 94, No. 6 (May 1989):1303–33.

OLZAK, SUSAN, and ELIZABETH WEST. "Ethnic Conflict and the Rise and Fall of Ethnic Newspapers." *American Sociological Review.* Vol. 56, No. 4 (August 1991):458–74.

OMESTAD, THOMAS. "A Balance of Terror." *U.S. News & World Report* (February 3, 2003):33–35.

O'NEILL, BRIAN, and DEBORAH BALK. "World Population Futures." *Population Bulletin.* Vol. 56, No. 3 (September 2001):3–40.

ONTARIO. *The Report of the Commission on Systemic Racism in the Ontario Criminal Justice System.* Toronto: Queen's Printer for Ontario, 1996.

——. *Words That Count Women Out/In.* Toronto: Ontario Women's Directorate, 1992.

ORHANT, MELANIE. "Human Trafficking Exposed." *Population Today.* Vol. 30, No. 1 (January 2002):1, 4.

ORLANSKY, MICHAEL D., and WILLIAM L. HEWARD *Voices: Interviews with Handicapped People.* Columbus, OH: Merrill, 1981.

OSGOOD, D. WAYNE, JANET K. WILSON, PATRICK M. O'MALLEY, JERALD G. BACHMAN, and LLOYD D. JOHNSTON. "Routine Activities and Individual Deviant Behavior." *American Sociological Review.* Vol. 61, No. 4 (August 1996):635–55.

OSSENBERG, RICHARD J. "Social Class and Bar Behavior during an Urban Festival." In James E. Curtis and William G. Scott, eds. *Social Stratification: Canada.* 2d ed. Scarborough, ON: Prentice Hall, 1979.

OSTRANDER, SUSAN A. "Upper Class Women: The Feminine Side of Privilege." *Qualitative Sociology.* Vol. 3, No. 1 (Spring 1980):23–44.

——. *Women of the Upper Class.* Philadelphia, PA: Temple University Press, 1984.

OUCHI, WILLIAM. *Theory Z: How American Business Can Meet the Japanese Challenge.* Reading, MA: Addison-Wesley, 1981.

OVADIA, SETH. "Race, Class, and Gender Differences in High School Seniors' Values: Applying Intersection Theory in Empirical Analysis." *Social Science Quarterly.* Vol. 82, No. 2 (June 2001):341–56.

OWEN, DAVID. *None of the Above: Behind the Myth of Scholastic Aptitude.* Boston: Houghton Mifflin, 1985.

PACKER, GEORGE. "Smart-Mobbing the War." *New York Times Magazine* (March 9, 2003):46–49.

PAKULSKI, JAN. "Mass Social Movements and Social Class." *International Sociology.* Vol. 8, No. 2 (June 1993):131–58.

PALMORE, ERDMAN. "Predictors of Successful Aging." *The Gerontologist.* Vol. 19, No. 5 (October 1979):427–31.

PAMMETT, JON H., and LAWRENCE LEDUC. "Behind the Turnout Decline." In Jon H. Pammett and Christopher Dornan (eds.) *The Canadian General Election of 2004.* Toronto: The Dundurn Group, 2004. pp. 338–60.

PARENTI, MICHAEL. *Inventing Reality: The Politics of the Mass Media.* New York: St. Martin's Press, 1986.

PARINI, JAY. "The Meaning of Emeritus." *Dartmouth Alumni Magazine* (July/August 2001):40–43.

PARK, ROBERT E. *Race and Culture.* Glencoe, IL: Free Press, 1950.

PARSONS, TALCOTT. "Age and Sex in the Social Structure of the United States." *American Sociological Review.* Vol. 7, No. 4 (August 1942):604–16.

——. *Essays in Sociological Theory.* New York: Free Press, 1954.

——. *The Social System.* New York: Free Press, 1964; orig. 1951.

——. *Societies: Evolutionary and Comparative Perspectives.* Englewood Cliffs, NJ: Prentice Hall, 1966.

PARSONS, TALCOTT, and ROBERT F. BALES, EDS. *Family, Socialization and Interaction Process.* New York: Free Press, 1955.

PARTRIDGE, JOHN. "Balanced Foreign Aid Policy Urged." *The Globe and Mail* (October 8, 2003). [Online] Available at http://www.globeinvestor.com/servlet/ArticleNews/story/LAC/20031008/RCONFERENCE.

PASSY, FLORENCE, and MARCO GIUGNI. "Social Networks and Individual Perceptions: Explaining Differential Participation in Social Movements." *Sociological Forum.* Vol. 16, No. 1 (March 2001):123–53.

PATTERSON, ELISSA F. "The Philosophy and Physics of Holistic Health Care: Spiritual Healing as a Workable Interpretation." *Journal of Advanced Nursing.* Vol. 27, No. 2 (February 1998):287–93.

PEARSON, DAVID E. "Post-Mass Culture." *Society.* Vol. 30, No. 5 (July–August 1993):17–22.

PERITZ, INGRID. "Sex-Change Soldier Hails Canada's Liberal Attitudes." *The Globe and Mail* (February 22, 2000):A1.

——. "Public daycare helps fuel Quebec work force." *The Globe and Mail* (May 1, 2006):A4.

PERRUCCI, ROBERT. "Inventing Social Justice: SSSP and the Twenty-First Century." *Social Problems.* Vol. 48, No. 2 (May 2001):159–67.

PERSELL, CAROLINE HODGES. *Education and Inequality: A Theoretical and Empirical Synthesis.* New York: Free Press, 1977.

PESSEN, EDWARD. *Riches, Class, and Power: America Before the Civil War.* New Brunswick, NJ: Transaction Books, 1990.

PETERS ATLAS OF THE WORLD. New York: Harper & Row, 1990.

PETERSEN, TROND, ISHAK SAPORTA, and MARC-DAVID L. SEIDEL. "Offering a Job: Meritocracy and Social Networks." *American Journal of Sociology.* Vol. 106, No. 3 (November 2000):763–816.

PETERSON, SCOTT. "Women Live on Own Terms behind the Veil." *Christian Science Monitor* (July 31, 1996):1, 10.

PEVERE, GEOFF, and GREIG DYMOND. *Mondo Canuck: A Canadian Pop Culture Odyssey.* Scarborough, ON: Prentice Hall Canada, 1996.

PHILADELPHIA, DESA. "Rookie Teacher, Age 50." *Time* (April 9, 2001):66–68.

——. "Tastier, Plusher—and Fast." *Time* (September 30, 2002):57.

PHILP, MARGARET. "Aboriginal Languages Nearing Extinction: Expert." *The Globe and Mail* (May 13, 2000):A7.

PICARD, ANDRÉ. "Future CMA head says he supports medicare." *The Globe and Mail* (August 23, 2006):A5.

PICHARDO, NELSON A. "The Power Elite and Elite-Driven Countermovements: The Associated Farmers of California During the 1930s." *Sociological Forum.* Vol. 10, No. 1 (March 1995):21–49.

PINCHOT, GIFFORD, and ELIZABETH PINCHOT. *The End of Bureaucracy and the Rise of the Intelligent Organization.* San Francisco, CA: Berrett-Koehler, 1993.

PINHEY, THOMAS K., DONALD H. RUBINSTEIN, and RICHARD S. COLFAX. "Overweight and Happiness: The Reflected Self-Appraisal Hypothesis Reconsidered." *Social Science Quarterly.* Vol. 78, No. 3 (September 1997):747–55.

PINKER, STEVEN. *The Language Instinct.* New York: Morrow, 1994.

——. "Are Your Genes to Blame?" *Time* (January 20, 2003):98–100.

PIVEN, FRANCES FOX, and RICHARD A. CLOWARD. *Poor People's Movements: Why They Succeed, How They Fail.* New York: Pantheon Books, 1977.

PODOLNY, JOEL M., and JAMES N. BARON. "Resources and Relationships: Social Networks and Mobility in the Workplace." *American Sociological Review.* Vol. 62, No. 5 (October 1997):673–93.

POLENBERG, RICHARD. *One Nation Divisible: Class, Race, and Ethnicity in the United States Since 1938.* New York: Pelican Books, 1980.

POMFRET, RICHARD. *The Economic Development of Canada.* Toronto: Methuen, 1981.

POPENOE, DAVID. "Parental Androgyny." *Society.* Vol. 30, No. 6 (September/October 1993a):5–11.

——. "American Family Decline, 1960–1990: A Review and Appraisal." *Journal of Marriage and the Family.* Vol. 55, No. 3 (August 1993b):527–55.

——. "Can the Nuclear Family Be Revived?" *Society.* Vol. 36, No. 5 (July/August 1999):28–30.

POPULATION ACTION INTERNATIONAL. *People in the Balance: Population and Resources at the Turn of the Millennium.* Washington, DC: Population Action International, 2000.

POPULATION REFERENCE BUREAU. *2005 World Population Data Sheet.* Washington, DC: Population Reference Bureau, 2005.

PORTER, EDUARDO. "Old, in the Way, and Hard at Work." *New York Times* (August 29, 2004). [Online] Available April 15, 2005, at http://www.researchnavigator.com.

PORTER, JOHN. *The Vertical Mosaic: An Analysis of Social Class and Power in Canada.* Toronto: University of Toronto Press, 1965.

PORTER, JOHN, MARION PORTER, and BERNARD R. BLISHEN. *Stations and Callings.* Toronto: Methuen, 1982.

POWELL, CHRIS, and GEORGE E. C. PATON, EDS. *Humour in Society: Resistance and Control.* New York: St. Martin's Press, 1988.

PRATT, LAURA. "Madame Chief Justice: Passing judgment." *National Post* (March 8, 2003):PW1.

PRESS, ANDREA L. Review of *Enlightened Racism: "The Cosby Show," Audiences, and the Myth of the American Dream,* by Sut Jhally and Justin Lewis. *American Journal of Sociology.* Vol. 99, No. 1 (July 1993):219–21.

PRICEWATERHOUSECOOPERS. "Filmed Entertainment Industry in Canada the Fastest Growing in World," September 13, 2003. [Online] Available at http://www.pwcglobal.com/extweb/ncpressrelease.nsf/docid/B8AC0264872F898085256D9B00634DB6.

PRIMEGGIA, SALVATORE, and JOSEPH A. VARACALLI. "Southern Italian Comedy: Old to New World." In Joseph V. Scelsa, Salvatore J. LaGumina, and Lydio Tomasi, eds. *Italian Americans in Transition.* New York: The American Italian Historical Association, 1990. pp. 241–52.

PRUS, ROBERT. "Approaching the Study of Human Group Life: Symbolic Interaction and Ethnographic Inquiry." In Mary Lorenz Dietz, Robert Prus, and William Shaffir, eds. *Doing Everyday Life: Ethnography as Human Lived Experience.* Mississauga, ON: Copp Clark Longman, 1994.

PUTKA, GARY. "SAT to Become a Better Gauge." *Wall Street Journal* (November 1, 1990):B1.

QUINNEY, RICHARD. *Class, State and Crime: On the Theory and Practice of Criminal Justice.* New York: David McKay, 1977.

RADEMACHER, ERIC W. "The Effect of Question Wording on College Students." *The Pittsburgh Undergraduate Review.* Vol. 8, No. 1 (Spring 1992):45–81.

RAJHATHY, JUDITH, and DAVID ROULARD. "Victory for Health Freedom." *Health Naturally* (June/July 1994).

RAMCHARAN, SUBHAS. *Racism: Nonwhites in Canada.* Toronto: Butterworths, 1982.

RAMO, JOSHUA COOPER. "Finding God on the Web." *Time* (December 16, 1996):60–67.

RAPHAEL, RAY. *The Men from the Boys: Rites of Passage in Male America.* Lincoln, NE, and London, UK: University of Nebraska Press, 1988.

RECKLESS, WALTER C., and SIMON DINITZ. "Pioneering with Self-Concept as a Vulnerability Factor in Delinquency." *Journal of Criminal Law, Criminology, and Police Science.* Vol. 58, No. 4 (December 1967):515–23.

REID, SUE TITUS. *Crime and Criminology.* 6th ed. Fort Worth, TX: Holt, Rinehart & Winston, 1991.

REIMAN, JEFFREY H. *The Rich Get Richer and the Poor Get Prison: Ideology, Class, and Criminal Justice.* 3d ed. New York: John Wiley & Sons, 1990.

REINHART, ANTHONY, and JANE ARMSTRONG. "One by one, sisters earn Harvard honours." *The Globe and Mail* (June 26, 2006):A1.

REITZ, JEFFREY G. *The Survival of Ethnic Groups.* Toronto: McGraw-Hill Ryerson, 1980.

REITZ, JEFFREY G., and RAYMOND BRETON. *The Illusion of Difference: Realities of Ethnicity in Canada and the United States.* Toronto: C.D. Howe Institute, 1994.

REPORT ON BUSINESS. "The Top 1000: Canada's Power Book." Vol. 20, No. 1. *The Globe and Mail* (July 2003):73–154.

——. "THE TOP 1000." *The Globe and Mail* (July/August 2006): 65.

REPORT ON BUSINESS MAGAZINE. The Globe and Mail. (August 1993):55.

RESKIN, BARBARA F., and DEBRA BRANCH MCBRIER. "Why Not Ascription? Organizations' Employment of Male and Female Managers." *American Sociological Review*. Vol. 65, No. 2 (April 2000):210–33.

REVKIN, ANDREW C. "Can Global Warming Be Studied Too Much?" *New York Times* (December 3, 2002):D1, D4.

RICHARDS, KAREN. *The Aboriginal Peoples Television Network: An Institutional Model of Empowerment*. MA thesis. Department of Sociology. Guelph: University of Guelph, 2006.

RICHLER, JACOB. "Last night, I walked in another's mismatched shoes." *National Post* (April 20, 2006):A15.

RIDGEWAY, CECILIA L. *The Dynamics of Small Groups*. New York: St. Martin's Press, 1983.

RIESMAN, DAVID. *The Lonely Crowd: A Study of the Changing American Character*. New Haven, CT: Yale University Press, 1970; orig. 1950.

RITZER, GEORGE. *The McDonaldization of Society: An Investigation into the Changing Character of Contemporary Social Life*. Thousand Oaks, CA: Pine Forge Press, 1993.

——. *The McDonaldization Thesis: Explorations and Extensions*. Thousand Oaks, CA: Sage, 1998.

——. "The Globalization of McDonaldization." *Spark* (February 2000):8–9.

RITZER, GEORGE, and DAVID WALCZAK. *Working: Conflict and Change*. 4th ed. Englewood Cliffs, NJ: Prentice Hall, 1990.

ROBINSON, ALLAN. "Inco Sends in the Robo-Miners." *The Globe and Mail* (January 3, 1998):B1.

ROESCH, ROBERTA. "Violent Families." *Parents*. Vol. 59, No. 9 (September 1984):74–76, 150–52.

ROETHLISBERGER, F.J., and WILLIAM J. DICKSON. *Management and the Worker*. Cambridge, MA: Harvard University Press, 1939.

RORTY, RICHARD. "The Unpatriotic Academy." *New York Times* (February 13, 1994):15.

ROSE, FRED. "Toward a Class-Cultural Theory of Social Movements: Reinterpreting New Social Movements." *Sociological Forum*. Vol. 12, No. 3 (September 1997):461–94.

ROSE, JERRY D. *Outbreaks*. New York: Free Press, 1982.

ROSENDAHL, MONA. *Inside the Revolution: Everyday Life in Socialist Cuba*. Ithaca, NY: Cornell University Press, 1997.

ROSNOW, RALPH L., and GARY ALAN FINE. *Rumor and Gossip: The Social Psychology of Hearsay*. New York: Elsevier, 1976.

ROSS, JOHN. "To Die in the Street: Mexico City's Homeless Population Boom as Economic Crisis Shakes Social Protections." *SSSP Newsletter*. Vol. 27, No. 2 (Summer 1996):14–15.

ROSSI, ALICE S. "Gender and Parenthood." In Alice S. Rossi, ed. *Gender and the Life Course*. New York: Aldine, 1985:161–91.

ROSTOW, WALT W. *The Stages of Economic Growth: A Non-Communist Manifesto*. Cambridge: Cambridge University Press, 1960.

——. *The World Economy: History and Prospect*. Austin: University of Texas Press, 1978.

ROTHMAN, STANLEY, and AMY E. BLACK. "Who Rules Now? American Elites in the 1990s." *Society*. Vol. 35, No. 6 (September/October 1998):17–20.

ROTHMAN, STANLEY, STEPHEN POWERS, and DAVID ROTHMAN. "Feminism in Films." *Society*. Vol. 30, No. 3 (March–April 1993):66–72.

RUBENSTEIN, ELI A. "The Not So Golden Years." *Newsweek* (October 7, 1991):13.

RUBIN, KEN. "Privacy." In *The Canadian Encyclopedia*. 2d ed. Vol. 3. Edmonton: Hurtig Publishers, 1988. p. 1761.

RUBIN, LILLIAN BRESLOW. *Worlds of Pain: Life in the Working-Class Family*. New York: Basic Books, 1976.

RUDÉ, GEORGE. *The Crowd in History: A Study of Popular Disturbances in France and England, 1730–1848*. New York: Wiley, 1964.

RUDEL, THOMAS K., and JUDITH M. GERSON. "Postmodernism, Institutional Change, and Academic Workers: A Sociology of Knowledge." *Social Science Quarterly*. Vol. 80, No. 2 (June 1999):213–28.

RULE, JAMES, and PETER BRANTLEY. "Computerized Surveillance in the Workplace: Forms and Delusions." *Sociological Forum*. Vol. 7, No. 3 (September 1992):405–23.

RYAN, PATRICK J. "The Roots of Muslim Anger." *America* (November 26, 2001):8–16.

RYAN, WILLIAM. *Blaming the Victim*. Rev. ed. New York: Vintage Books, 1976.

RYMER, RUSS. *Genie*. New York: HarperPerennial, 1994.

SAGAN, CARL. *The Dragons of Eden*. New York: Ballantine, 1977.

SAINT JEAN, YANICK, and JOE R. FEAGIN. *Double Burden: Black Women and Everyday Racism*. Armonk, NY: Sharpe, 1998.

SALA-I-MARTIN, XAVIER. "The World Distribution of Income." Working Paper No. 8933. Cambridge, Mass.: National Bureau of Economic Research, 2002.

SALE, KIRKPATRICK. *The Conquest of Paradise: Christopher Columbus and the Columbian Legacy*. New York: Alfred A. Knopf, 1990.

SAMPSON, ANTHONY. *The Changing Anatomy of Britain*. New York: Random House, 1982.

SANSOM, WILLIAM. *A Contest of Ladies*. London, UK: Hogarth, 1956.

SAPIR, EDWARD. "The Status of Linguistics as a Science." *Language*. Vol. 5 (1929):207–14.

——. *Selected Writings of Edward Sapir in Language, Culture, and Personality*. David G. Mandelbaum, ed. Berkeley: University of California Press, 1949.

SAUVÉ, ROGER. *Borderlines: What Canadians and Americans Should—but Don't—Know About Each Other*. Whitby, ON: McGraw-Hill Ryerson, 1994.

SAVISHINSKY, JOEL S. *Breaking the Watch: The Meanings of Retirement in America*. Ithaca, N.Y.: Cornell University Press, 2000.

SCANLON, STEPHAN J. "Food Availability and Access in Less Industrialized Societies: A Test and Interpretation of Neo-Malthusian and Technoecological Theories." *Sociological Forum*. Vol. 16, No. 2 (June 2001):231–62.

SCHAFFER, MICHAEL. "American Dreamers." *U.S. News & World Report* (August 26, 2002):12–16.

SCHEFF, THOMAS J. *Being Mentally Ill: A Sociological Theory*. 2d ed. New York: Aldine, 1984.

SCHELLENBERG, KATHRYN. "Policing the Police: Technological Surveillance and the Predilection for Leniency." *Criminal Justice and Behavior* (1995).

——. "Taking It or Leaving It: Instability and Turnover in a High-Tech Firm." *Work and Occupations*. Vol. 23, No. 2 (1996):190–213.

SCHLOSSER, ERIC. *Fast-Food Nation: The Dark Side of the All-American Meal*. New York: Perennial, 2002.

SCHMIDT, ROGER. *Exploring Religion*. Belmont, CA: Wadsworth, 1980.

SCHOFER, EVAN, and MARION FOURCADE-GOURINCHAS. "The Structural Contexts of Civil Engagement: Voluntary Association Membership in Comparative Perspective." *American Sociological Review*. Vol. 66, No. 6 (December 2001): 806–28.

SCOFFIELD, HEATHER. "Growth spurs decline in poverty." *The Globe and Mail* (March 31, 2006):A1.

SCHULTZ, T. PAUL. "Inequality in the Distribution of Personal Income in the World: How It Is Changing and Why." *Journal of Population Economics*. Vol. 11, No. 2 (1998):307–44.

SCOTT, D.B. "Lean Machine." *Report on Business Magazine, The Globe and Mail* (November 1992):90–99.

SCOTT, HANNAH. *The Female Serial Killer: A Well-Kept Secret of the "Gentler Sex."* Master's thesis. University of Guelph, 1992.

SCOTT, JOHN, and CATHERINE GRIFF. *Directors of Industry: The British Corporate Network, 1904–1976*. New York: Blackwell, 1985.

SEAGER, JONI. *The Penguin Atlas of Women in the World*. 3rd ed. New York: Penguin Putnam, 2003.

SEARS, DAVID O., and JOHN B. MCCONAHAY. *The Politics of Violence: The New Urban Blacks and the Watts Riot*. Boston: Houghton Mifflin, 1973.

SEGALL, ALEXANDER, and NEENA L. CHAPPELL. *Health and Health Care in Canada*. Toronto: Prentice Hall, 2000.

SENNETT, RICHARD. *The Corrosion of Character: The Personal Consequences of Work in the New Capitalism*. New York: Norton, 1998.

SENNETT, RICHARD, and JONATHAN COBB. *The Hidden Injuries of Class*. New York: Vintage Books, 1973.

SEWELL, JOHN. *The Shape of the City: Toronto Struggles with Modern Planning*. Toronto: University of Toronto Press, 1993.

SHAPIRO, JOSEPH P. "Back to Work, on Mission." *U.S. News & World Report* (June 4, 2001).

SHAWCROSS, WILLIAM. *Sideshow: Kissinger, Nixon and the Destruction of Cambodia*. New York: Pocket Books, 1979.

SHEEHAN, TOM. "Senior Esteem as a Factor in Socioeconomic Complexity." *The Gerontologist*. Vol. 16, No. 5 (October 1976):433–40.

SHELDON, WILLIAM H., EMIL M. HARTL, and EUGENE MCDERMOTT. *Varieties of Delinquent Youth*. New York: Harper, 1949.

SHELEY, JAMES F., JOSHUA ZHANG, CHARLES J. BRODY, and JAMES D. WRIGHT. "Gang Organization, Gang Criminal Activity, and Individual Gang Members' Criminal Behavior." *Social Science Quarterly*. Vol. 76, No. 1 (March 1995):53–68.

SHERMAN, LAWRENCE W., and DOUGLAS A. SMITH. "Crime, Punishment, and Stake in Conformity: Legal and Informal Control of Domestic Violence." *American Sociological Review*. Vol. 57, No. 5 (October 1992):680–90.

SHEVKY, ESHREF, and WENDELL BELL. *Social Area Analysis*. Stanford, CA: Stanford University Press, 1955.

SHIELDS, JOHN, and STEPHEN MCBRIDE. "Dismantling a Nation: The Canadian Political Economy and Continental Free Trade." In Les Samuelson, ed. *Power and Resistance: Critical Thinking About Canadian Social Issues*. Halifax, NS: Fernwood Publishing, 1994. pp. 227–60.

SHIPLEY, JOSEPH T. *Dictionary of Word Origins*. Totowa, NJ: Roman & Allanheld, 1985.

SHIVELY, JOELLEN. "Cowboys and Indians: Perceptions of Western Films Among American Indians and Anglos." *American Sociological Review*. Vol. 57, No. 6 (December 1992):725–34.

SHUPE, ANSON, WILLIAM A. STACEY, and LONNIE R. HAZLEWOOD. *Violent Men, Violent Couples: The Dynamics of Domestic Violence*. Lexington, MA: Lexington Books, 1987.

SHUPE, ANSON. *In the Name of All That's Holy: A Theory of Clergy Malfeasance*. Westport, CT: Praeger, 1995.

SHUTE, JEREMY J., and DAVID B. KNIGHT. "Obtaining an Understanding of Environmental Knowledge: Wendaban Stewardship Authority." *The Canadian Geographer.* Vol. 39, No. 2 (1995):101–11.

SIMMEL, GEORG. *The Sociology of Georg Simmel.* Kurt Wolff, ed. New York: Free Press, 1950. pp. 118–69.

——. "The Metropolis and Mental Life." In Kurt Wolff, ed. *The Sociology of Georg Simmel.* New York: Free Press, 1964:409–24; orig. 1905.

——. "Fashion." In Donald N. Levine, ed. *Georg Simmel: On Individuality and Social Forms.* Chicago, IL: University of Chicago Press, 1971; orig. 1904.

SIMON, CARL P., and ANN D. WITTE. *Beating the System: The Underground Economy.* Boston: Auburn House, 1982.

SIMON, JULIAN. *The Ultimate Resource.* Princeton, NJ: Princeton University Press, 1981.

SIMON, JULIAN. "More People, Greater Wealth, More Resources, Healthier Environment." In Theodore D. Goldfarb, ed., *Taking Sides: Clashing Views on Controversial Environmental Issues.* 6th ed. Guilford, CT: Dushkin, 1995.

SIMON, RITA J., and N. SHARMA. "Women and Crime: Does the American Experience Generalize?" In F. Adler and R.J. Simon, eds. *Criminology of Deviant Women.* Boston: Houghton Mifflin, 1979.

SIMONS, CAROL. "Japan's Kyoiku Mamas." In John J. Macionis and Nijole V. Benokraitis, eds. *Seeing Ourselves: Classic, Contemporary, and Cross-Cultural Readings in Sociology.* Englewood Cliffs, NJ: Prentice Hall, 1989. pp. 281–86.

SIMONS, MARLISE. "The Price of Modernization: The Case of Brazil's Kaiapo Indians." In John J. Macionis and Nijole V. Benokraitis, eds., *Seeing Ourselves: Classic, Contemporary, and Cross-Cultural Readings in Sociology.* 7th ed. Upper Saddle River, NJ: Prentice Hall, 2007.

SIMPSON, GEORGE EATON, and J. MILTON YINGER. *Racial and Cultural Minorities: An Analysis of Prejudice and Discrimination.* 4th ed. New York: Harper & Row, 1972.

SIMPSON, JEFFREY. *Faultlines: Struggling for a Canadian Vision.* Toronto: HarperCollins, 1993.

——. *Star-Spangled Canadians: Canadians Living the American Dream.* Toronto: Harper Collins, 2000.

SINGER, JEROME L., and DOROTHY G. SINGER. "Psychologists Look at Television: Cognitive, Developmental, Personality, and Social Policy Implications." *American Psychologist.* Vol. 38, No. 7 (July 1983):826–34.

SIVARD, RUTH LEGER. *World Military and Social Expenditures, 1987–88.* 12th ed. Washington, DC: World Priorities, 1988.

SKELTON, CHAD. "Decide Military's Role, Ottawa Told." *The Globe and Mail* (August 12, 1997):A4.

SKOCPOL, THEDA. *States and Social Revolutions: A Comparative Analysis of France, Russia, and China.* Cambridge, UK: Cambridge University Press, 1979.

SMAIL, J. KENNETH. "Let's *Reduce* Global Population!" In John J. Macionis and Nijole V. Benokraitis, eds., *Seeing Ourselves: Classic, Contemporary, and Cross-Cultural Readings in Sociology.* 7th ed. Upper Saddle River, NJ: Prentice Hall, 2007.

SMART, TIM. "Not Acting Their Age." *U.S. News & World Report* (June 4, 2001): 54–60.

SMELSER, NEIL J. *Theory of Collective Behavior.* New York: Free Press, 1962.

SMITH, ADAM. *An Inquiry into the Nature and Causes of the Wealth of Nations.* New York: The Modern Library, 1937; orig. 1776.

SMITH, DAN. *The Seventh Fire: The Struggle for Aboriginal Self-Government.* Toronto: Key Porter, 1993.

SMITH, DOROTHY E. "Women, the Family and Corporate Capitalism." In M. Stephenson, ed. *Women in Canada.* Don Mills, ON: General Publishing, 1977. pp. 32–48.

——. "Women's Inequality and the Family." Department of Sociology, Ontario Institute for Studies in Education, Mimeograph, 1979.

——. "Women, Class and the Family." In R. Miliband and J. Saville, eds. *The Socialist Register.* London, UK: Merlin Press, 1983.

——. *The Everyday World as Problematic: A Feminist Sociology.* Toronto: University of Toronto Press, 1987.

SMITH, DOUGLAS A. "Police Response to Interpersonal Violence: Defining the Parameters of Legal Control." *Social Forces.* Vol. 65, No. 3 (March 1987):767–82.

SMITH, DOUGLAS A., and PATRICK R. GARTIN. "Specifying Specific Deterrence: The Influence of Arrest on Future Criminal Activity." *American Sociological Review.* Vol. 54, No. 1 (February 1989):94–105.

SMITH, DOUGLAS A., and CHRISTY A. VISHER. "Street-Level Justice: Situational Determinants of Police Arrest Decisions." *Social Problems.* Vol. 29, No. 2 (December 1981):167–77.

SMITH, GRAEME. "What is wrong with the girls of Melfort?" *Globe and Mail* (June 12, 2004): F3.

SMITH, GWEN. "The Home Team." *Maclean's* (April 17, 1997a):68.

——. "She Shoots; She Scores!" *Elm Street* (November/December 1997b):32.

SMITH, ROBERT ELLIS. *Privacy: How to Protect What's Left of It.* Garden City, NY: Anchor/Doubleday, 1979.

SMITH-LOVIN, LYNN, and CHARLES BRODY. "Interruptions in Group Discussions: The Effects of Gender and Group Composition." *American Journal of Sociology.* Vol. 54, No. 3 (June 1989):424–35.

SMOLOWE, JILL. "When Violence Hits Home." *Time.* Vol. 144, No. 1 (July 4, 1994):18–25.

SNELL, MARILYN BERLIN. "The Purge of Nurture." *New Perspectives Quarterly.* Vol. 7, No. 1 (Winter 1990):1–2.

SNIDERMAN, PAUL M., DAVID A. NORTHRUP, JOSEPH F. FLETCHER, PETER H. RUSSELL, and PHILIP E. TETLOCK. "Psychological and Cultural Foundations of Prejudice: The Case of Anti-Semitism in Quebec." *Canadian Review of Sociology and Anthropology.* Vol. 30, No. 2 (May 1993):242–70.

SOBEL, RACHEL K. "Herpes Tests Give Answers You Might Need to Know." *U.S. News & World Report* (June 18, 2001):53.

SOCIETY OF OBSTETRICIANS AND GYNAECOLOGISTS OF CANADA. 2006. [Online] Available at http://www.sexualityandu.ca.

SOUTH, SCOTT J., and STEVEN F. MESSNER. "Structural Determinants of Intergroup Association: Interracial Marriage and Crime." *American Journal of Sociology.* Vol. 91, No. 6 (May 1986):1409–30.

SOWELL, THOMAS. *Race and Culture.* New York: Basic Books, 1994.

——. "Ethnicity and IQ." In Steven Fraser, ed. *The Bell Curve Wars: Race, Intelligence and the Future of America.* New York: Basic Books, 1995:70–79.

——. *Migrations and Cultures: A World View.* New York: Basic Books, 1996.

SPECTER, MICHAEL. "Plunging Life Expectancy Puzzles Russia." *New York Times* (August 2, 1995):A1, A2.

——. "Moscow on the Make." *New York Times Magazine* (June 1, 1997):48–55, 72, 75, 80, 84.

SPEER, JAMES A. "The New Christian Right and Its Parent Company: A Study in Political Contrasts." In David G. Bromley and Anson Shupe, eds. *New Christian Politics.* Macon, GA: Mercer University Press, 1984. pp. 19–40.

SPITZER, STEVEN. "Toward a Marxian Theory of Deviance." In Delos H. Kelly, ed. *Criminal Behavior: Readings in Criminology.* New York: St. Martin's Press, 1980:175–91.

STACEY, JUDITH. *Patriarchy and Socialist Revolution in China.* Berkeley, CA: University of California Press, 1983.

STACEY, JUDITH. *Brave New Families: Stories of Domestic Upheaval in Late Twentieth-Century America.* New York: Basic Books, 1990.

STACK, STEVEN, IRA WASSERMAN, and ROGER KERN. "Adult Social Bonds and the Use of Internet Pornography." *Social Science Quarterly.* Vol. 85, No. 1 (March 2004):75–88.

STAPINSKI, HELENE. "Let's Talk Dirty." *American Demographics.* Vol. 20, No. 11 (November 1998):50–56.

STARK, EVAN, and ANN FLITCRAFT. "Domestic Violence and Female Suicide Attempts." Presentation to American Public Health Association, New York, 1979.

STARK, RODNEY. *Sociology.* Belmont, CA: Wadsworth, 1985.

STARK, RODNEY, and WILLIAM SIMS BAINBRIDGE. "Of Churches, Sects, and Cults: Preliminary Concepts for a Theory of Religious Movements." *Journal for the Scientific Study of Religion.* Vol. 18, No. 2 (June 1979):117–31.

STARR, PAUL. *The Social Transformation of American Medicine.* New York: Basic Books, 1982.

STATISTICS CANADA. *Perspectives on Labour and Income.* Catalogue No. 71-202. Ottawa: Statistics Canada, 1990.

——. *Report on the Demographic Situation in Canada,* Catalogue No. 91-209. Ottawa: Statistics Canada, 1992a.

——. *Lone-Parent Families in Canada.* Catalogue No. 89-522E. Ottawa: Statistics Canada, 1992b.

——. *Juristat Service Bulletin.* Catalogue No. 85-002. Ottawa: Statistics Canada, 1994a.

——. *Violence Against Women Survey.* Ottawa: Minister of Industry, Science and Technology, 1994b.

——. "Social Indicators." *Canadian Social Trends* (Spring 1996).

——. "2001 Census: Age and Sex," *The Daily,* July 16, 2002a. [Online] Available at http://www.statcan.ca/Daily/English/020716/td020716.htm.

——. "Profile of Canadian Families and Households: Diversification Continues," 2001 Census Analysis Series, Catalogue no. 96F0030XIE2001003, October 22, 2002b. [Online] Available at www12.statcan.ca/english/census01/products/analytic/companion/fam/contents.cfm.

——. "Average Hours per Week of Television Watching, Fall 2001," Canadian Statistics, December 2, 2002c. [Online] Available at http://www.statcan.ca/english/Pgdb/arts23.htm.

——. "Television Viewing," *The Daily,* December 2, 2002d. [Online] Available at http://www.statcan.ca/Daily/English/021202/d021202a.htm.

——. "Homicides, 2002." *The Daily,* October 1, 2003a. [Online] Available at http://www.statcan.ca/Daily/English/031001/d031001a.htm.

——. "Electronic Commerce and Technology," *The Daily,* April 2, 2003b. [Online] Available at http://www.statcan.ca/Daily/English/030402/td030402.htm.

——. *Building on our Competencies. Canadian Results of the International Adult Literacy and Skills Survey.* Catalogue no. 89-617-X1E. Ottawa: Ministry of Industry, 2003c.

——. "Pilot survey of hate crime." *The Daily.* June 1, 2004. [Online] Available at .

——. "Family violence in Canada: A statistical profile." *The Daily.* July 14, 2005. [Online] Available at http://www.statcan.ca/Daily/English/050714/td050714.htm.

——. "University enrolment." *The Daily.* October 11, 2005a. [Online] Available at http://www.statcan.ca/Daily/English/051011/d051011b.htm.

——. "Education Matters: Trends in dropout rates among the provinces." *The Daily.* December 16, 2005b. [Online] Available at http://www. statcan.ca/Daily/English/051011/d051011b.htm.

——. "National Population Health Survey—Obesity: A growing issue." *The Daily.* April 7, 2005c. [Online] Available at http://www.statcan.ca/ Daily/English/050407/d050407a.htm.

——. "Canadian Community Health Survey: Obesity among children and adults." *The Daily.* July 6, 2005d. [Online] Available at http://www.statcan. ca/Daily/English/050706/d050706a.htm.

——. CANSIM. 2006a. [Online] Table.

——. *Crimes by Type of Offence.* 2006b. [Online] Available at http://www40. statcan.ca/l01/cst01/legal02.htm.

——. Employment income by occupation. 2006c. [Online] Available at Catalogue No. 97F0019XCB2001003.

——. Canadian Statistics. "Characteristics of household Internet users." 2006d. [Online] Available at http://www40.statcan.ca/l01/cst01/comm10a.htm.

——. Income by highest level of educational attainment. 2006e. [Online] Catalogue No. 97F0020XCB2001003.

STEELE, SHELBY. *The Content of Our Character: A New Vision of Race in America.* New York: St. Martin's Press, 1990.

STEVENS, ROSEMARY. *American Medicine and the Public Interest.* New Haven, CT: Yale University Press, 1971.

STONE, LAWRENCE. *The Family, Sex and Marriage in England, 1500–1800.* New York: Harper & Row, 1977.

STORMS, MICHAEL D. "Theories of Sexual Orientation." *Journal of Personality and Social Psychology.* Vol. 38, No. 5 (May 1980):783–92.

STOUFFER, SAMUEL A., ARTHUR A. LUMSDAINE, MARION HARPER LUMSDAINE, ROBIN M. WILLIAMS, JR., M. BREWSTER SMITH, IRVING L. JANIS, SHIRLEY A. STAR, and LEONARD S. COTTRELL, JR. *The American Soldier.* Volume 1 *Adjustment During Army Life.* Princeton, NJ: Princeton University Press, 1949.

STRATTON, LESLIE S. "Why Does More Housework Lower Women's Wages? Testing Hypotheses Involving Job Effort and Hours Flexibility." *Social Sciences Quarterly.* Vol. 82, No. 1 (March 2001):67–76.

STRAUS, MURRAY A., and RICHARD J. GELLES. "Societal Change and Change in Family Violence from 1975 to 1985 as Revealed by Two National Surveys." *Journal of Marriage and the Family.* Vol. 48, No. 4 (August 1986):465–79.

STREIB, GORDON F. "Are the Aged a Minority Group?" In Bernice L. Neugarten, ed. *Middle Age and Aging: A Reader in Social Psychology.* Chicago, IL: University of Chicago Press, 1968. pp. 35–46.

SULLIVAN, BARBARA. "McDonald's Sees India as Golden Opportunity." *Chicago Tribune* (April 5, 1995):B1.

SUMNER, WILLIAM GRAHAM. *Folkways.* New York: Dover, 1959; orig. 1906.

SURTEES, LAWRENCE. "Northern Telecom: The Morning After." *The Globe and Mail* (July 5, 1993): B1, B4.

SUTHERLAND, EDWIN H. "White Collar Criminality." *American Sociological Review.* Vol. 5, No. 1 (February 1940):1–12.

SUTHERLAND, EDWIN H., and DONALD R. CRESSEY. *Criminology.* 10th ed. Philadelphia, PA: J.B. Lippincott, 1978.

SZASZ, THOMAS S. *The Manufacture of Madness: A Comparative Study of the Inquisition and the Mental Health Movement.* New York: Dell, 1961.

——. *The Myth of Mental Illness: Foundations of a Theory of Personal Conduct.* New York: Harper & Row, 1970; orig. 1961.

——. "Cleansing the Modern Heart." *Society.* Vol. 40, No. 4 (May/June 2003):52–59.

——. "Protecting Patients against Psychiatric Intervention." *Society.* Vol. 41, No. 3 (March/April 2004):7–10.

TAIT, HEATHER. "Educational Achievement of Young Aboriginal Adults." In Statistics Canada, *Canadian Social Trends. Volume 3.* Toronto: Thompson Educational Publishing, 2000.

TAJFEL, HENRI. "Social Psychology of Intergroup Relations." *Annual Review of Psychology.* Palo Alto, CA: Annual Reviews, 1982. pp. 1–39.

TANNAHILL, REAY. *Sex in History.* Chelsea, Mich.: Scarborough House Publishers, 1992.

TANNEN, DEBORAH. *Talking from 9 to 5: How Women's and Men's Conversational Styles Affect Who Gets Heard, Who Gets Credit, and What Gets Done at Work.* New York: Wm. Morrow, 1994.

TARAS, DAVID, BEVERLY RASPORICH, and ELI MANDEL. *A Passion for Identity: An Introduction to Canadian Studies.* Scarborough, ON: Nelson, 1993.

TARROW, SIDNEY. *Social Movements, Collective Action and Politics.* New York: Cambridge University Press, 1994.

TAVRIS, CAROL, and CAROL WADE. *Psychology in Perspective.* 3rd ed. Upper Saddle River, NJ: Prentice Hall, 2001.

TAYLOR, FREDERICK WINSLOW. *The Principles of Scientific Management.* New York: Harper Bros., 1911.

TEPPERMAN, LORNE. "Status Inconsistency in the Toronto Elite of the 1920s." In James Curtis and William G. Scott. *Social Stratification: Canada.* 2d ed. Scarborough, ON: Prentice Hall, 1979.

TEWKSBURY, RICHARD, and PATRICIA GAGNÉ. "Transgenderists: Products of Nonnormative Intersections of Sex, Gender, and Sexuality." *Journal of Men's Studies.* Vol. 5, No. 2 (November 1996):105–29.

THERNSTROM, ABIGAIL, and STEPHAN THERNSTROM. "American Apartheid? Don't Believe It." *Wall Street Journal* (March 2, 1998):A18.

THOMAS, EDWARD J. *The Life of Buddha as Legend and History.* London, UK: Routledge & Kegan Paul, 1975.

THOMAS, EVAN, JOHN BARRY, and MELINDA LIU. "Ground Zero." *Newsweek* (May 25, 1998):28–32A.

THOMAS, W.I. "The Relation of Research to the Social Process." In Morris Janowitz, ed. *W.I. Thomas on Social Organization and Social Personality.* Chicago, IL: University of Chicago Press, 1966; orig. 1931. pp. 289–305.

THOMAS, W.I., and F. ZNANIECKI. *The Polish Peasant in Europe and America.* New York: Octagon Books, 1971; orig 1919.

THOMPSON, DICK. "Gene Maverick." *Time* (January 11, 1999):54–55.

THORNBERRY, TERRANCE, and MARGARET FARNSWORTH. "Social Correlates of Criminal Involvement: Further Evidence on the Relationship Between Social Status and Criminal Behavior." *American Sociological Review.* Vol. 47, No. 4 (August 1982):505–18.

THORNE, BARRIE, CHERIS KRAMARAE, and NANCY HENLEY, EDS. *Language, Gender and Society.* Rowley, MA: Newbury House, 1983.

TIERNEY, JOHN. "Adultescent." *The New York Times* (December 26, 2004).

TILLY, CHARLES. *From Mobilization to Revolution.* Reading, MA: Addison-Wesley, 1978.

——. "Does Modernization Breed Revolution?" In Jack A. Goldstone, ed. *Revolutions: Theoretical, Comparative, and Historical Studies.* New York: Harcourt Brace Jovanovich, 1986:47–57.

TINDALE, JOSEPH A. "Older Workers in an Aging Workforce." Ottawa: Statistics Canada, 1991.

TITTLE, CHARLES R., WAYNE J. VILLEMEZ, and DOUGLAS A. SMITH. "The Myth of Social Class and Criminality: An Empirical Assessment of the Empirical Evidence." *American Sociological Review.* Vol. 43, No. 5 (October 1978):643–56.

TODD, DOUGLAS. "Giving Old Age Meaning." *National Post* (July 28, 2003):A11.

TÖNNIES, FERDINAND. *Community and Society (Gemeinschaft und Gesellschaft).* New York: Harper & Row, 1963; orig. 1887.

TOFANI, LORETTA. "AIDS Ravages a Continent, and Sweeps a Family." *Philadelphia Inquirer* (March 24, 1991):1, 15–A.

TOLSON, JAY. "The Trouble with Elites." *The Wilson Quarterly.* Vol. XIX, No. 1 (Winter 1995):6–8.

TOMLINSON, BRIAN. "Development in the 1990s: Critical Reflections on Canada's Economic Relations with the Third World." In Jamie Swift and Brian Tomlinson, eds. *Conflicts of Interest: Canada and the Third World.* Toronto: between the lines, 1991.

TORRES, LISA, and MATT L. HUFFMAN. "Social Networks and Job Search Outcomes among Male and Female Professional, Technical, and Managerial Workers." *Sociological Focus.* Vol. 35, No. 1 (February 2002):25–42.

TREAS, JUDITH. "Socialist Organization and Economic Development in China: Latent Consequences for the Aged." *The Gerontologist.* Vol. 19, No. 1 (February 1979):34–43.

——. "Older Americans in the 1990s and Beyond." *Population Bulletin.* Vol. 50, No. 2 (May 1995). Washington, DC: Population Reference Bureau.

TRENT, KATHERINE. "Family Context and Adolescents' Expectations About Marriage, Fertility, and Nonmarital Childbearing." *Social Science Quarterly.* Vol. 75, No. 2 (June 1994):319–39.

TROELTSCH, ERNST. *The Social Teaching of the Christian Churches.* New York: Macmillan, 1931.

TUMIN, MELVIN M. "Some Principles of Stratification: A Critical Analysis." *American Sociological Review.* Vol. 18, No. 4 (August 1953):387–94.

——. *Social Stratification: The Forms and Functions of Inequality.* 2d ed. Englewood Cliffs, NJ: Prentice Hall, 1985.

TUCKER, JAMES. "New Age Religion and the Cult of the Self." *Society.* Vol. 39, No. 2 (February 2002):46–51.

TURCOTTE, PIERRE, and ALAIN BÉLANGER. "Moving in Together: The Formation of First Common-Law Unions." In *Canadian Social Trends: Volume 3.* Toronto: Thompson Educational Publishing, 2000. pp. 105–08.

TURNER, JONATHAN. *On the Origins of Human Emotions: A Sociological Inquiry into the Evolution of Human Emotions.* Stanford, CA: Stanford University Press, 2000.

TURNER, RALPH H., and LEWIS M. KILLIAN. *Collective Behavior.* 2d ed. Englewood Cliffs, NJ: Prentice Hall, 1972; 3d ed. 1987; 4th ed. 1993.

UBELACKER, SHERYL. "Finally, more doctors returning to Canada than leaving." *The Globe and Mail.* (August 25, 2005):A13.

UDRY, J. RICHARD. "Biological Limitations of Gender Construction." *American Sociological Review.* Vol. 65, No. 3 (June 2000):443–57.

UGGEN, CHRISTOPHER. "Ex-Offenders and the Conformist Alternative: A Job-Quality Model of Work and Crime." *Social Problems.* Vol. 46, No. 1 (February 1999):127–51.

UJIMOTO, K. VICTOR. "Postwar Japanese Immigrants in British Columbia: Japanese Culture and Job Transferability." In Jean Leonard Elliott, ed. *Two Nations, Many Cultures: Ethnic Groups in Canada*. Scarborough, ON: Prentice Hall, 1979.

UNESCO. Data reported in "Tower of Babel Is Tumbling Down—Slowly." *U.S. News & World Report* (July 2, 2001):9.

UNITED NATIONS. *The World's Women, 2000: Trends and Statistics*. New York: United Nations, 2000.

——. *AIDS Epidemic Update*. December 2004. [Online] Available September 28, 2005, at http://www.unaids.org/.

UNITED NATIONS DEVELOPMENT PROGRAMME. *Human Development Report 1990*. New York: Oxford University Press, 1990.

——. *Human Development Report 1995*. New York: Oxford University Press, 1995.

——. *Human Development Report 1996*. New York: Oxford University Press, 1996.

——. *Human Development Report 2000*. New York: Oxford University Press, 2000.

——. *Human Development Report 2001*. New York: Oxford University Press, 2001.

——. *Human Development Report 2004*. New York: Oxford University Press, 2004.

——. *Human Development Report 2005*. New York: Oxford University Press, 2005.

UPTHEGROVE, TAYNA R., VINCENT J. ROSCIGNO, and CAMILLE ZUBRINSKY CHARLES. "Big Money Collegiate Sports: Racial Concentration, Contradictory Pressures, and Academic Performance." *Social Science Quarterly*. Vol. 80, No. 4 (December 1999):718–37.

U.S. CENSUS BUREAU. *International Data Base*. [Online] Available February 24, 2000 at http://www.census.gov/ipc/.

——. *Fertility of American Women: June 2002*. Current Population Reports, P20-548. Washington, DC: U.S. Government Printing Office, 2003.

——. *Income, Poverty, and Health Insurance Coverage in the United States, 2003*. Current Population Reports (P60-226). Washington, DC: U.S. Government Printing Office, 2004.

——. *Income, Poverty, and Health Insurance Coverage in the United States: 2004*. Current Population Reports (P60-229). Washington, DC: U.S. Government Printing Office, 2005.

U.S. DEPARTMENT OF STATE. "Remarks on Release of 'Country Reports on Terrorism' for 2004." Washington, DC (April 27, 2005). [Online] Available September 26, 2005, at http://www.state.gov/s/ct/rls/rm/45279.htm.

U.S. ENVIRONMENTAL PROTECTION AGENCY. "Municipal Solid Waste." May 17, 2005. [Online] Available October 3, 2005, at http://www.epa.gov/msw/facts.htm.

USEEM, MICHAEL. "The Social Organization of the Corporate Business Elite and Participation of Corporate Directors in the Governance of American Institutions." *American Sociological Review*. Vol. 44, No. 4 (August 1979):553–72.

VALDEZ, A. "In the Hood: Street Gangs Discover White-Collar Crime." *Police*. Vol. 21, No. 5 (May 1997):49–50, 56.

VALLAS, STEPHEN P., and JOHN P. BECK. "The Transformation of Work Revisited: The Limits of Flexibility in American Manufacturing." *Social Problems*. Vol. 43, No. 3 (August 1996):339–61.

VALLEE, F.G. "Porter, John Arthur." In *The Canadian Encyclopedia*. 2d ed. Edmonton: Hurtig Publishers, 1988: 1726.

VALLIS, MARY. "When grandkids don't leave." *National Post* (October 8, 2005):A1.

——. "Opulence at Home." *National Post* (May 6, 2006):A3.

VALOCCHI, STEVE. "The Emergence of the Integrationist Ideology in the Civil Rights Movement." *Social Problems*. Vol. 43, No. 1 (February 1996):116–30.

VAN BIEMA, DAVID. "Parents Who Kill." *Time*. Vol. 144, No. 20 (November 14, 1994):50–51.

——. "Buddhism in America." *Time*. Vol. 150, No. 15 (October 13, 1997):71–81.

VAN LOON, RICHARD J., and MICHAEL S. WHITTINGTON. *The Canadian Political System: Environment, Structure and Process*. 3d ed. Toronto: McGraw-Hill Ryerson, 1981.

VEBLEN, THORSTEIN. *The Theory of the Leisure Class*. New York: The New American Library, 1953; orig. 1899.

VOGEL, EZRA F. *The Four Little Dragons: The Spread of Industrialization in East Asia*. Cambridge, MA: Harvard University Press, 1991.

VOGEL, LISE. *Marxism and the Oppression of Women: Toward a Unitary Theory*. New Brunswick, NJ: Rutgers University Press, 1983.

VOLD, GEORGE B., and THOMAS J. BERNARD. *Theoretical Criminology*. 3d ed. New York: Oxford University Press, 1986.

VONNEGUT, KURT, JR. "Harrison Bergeron." In *Welcome to the Monkey House*. New York: Delacorte Press/Seymour Lawrence, 1968; orig. 1961. pp. 7–13

VOWELL, SARAH. "Canuck Yuks." *Salon*, January 27, 1999. [Online] Available http://www.salon.com/ent/music/vowe/1999/01/27vowe.html.

WALDIE, PAUL, and KAREN HOWLETT. "Reports Reveal Tight Grip of Ebbers on WorldCom." *The Globe and Mail* (June 11, 2003):B1, B7.

WALKER, JAMES W. ST. G. *A History of Blacks in Canada*. Ottawa: Ministry of Supply and Services Canada, 1980.

WALKER, KAREN. " 'Always There for Me': Friendship Patterns and Expectations among Middle- and Working-Class Men and Women." *Sociological Forum*. Vol. 10, No. 2 (June 1995):273–96.

WALL, THOMAS F. *Medical Ethics: Basic Moral Issues*. Washington, DC: University Press of America, 1980.

WALLERSTEIN, IMMANUEL. *The Modern World-System: Capitalist Agriculture and the Origins of the European World-Economy in the Sixteenth Century*. New York: Academic Press, 1974.

——. *The Capitalist World-Economy*. New York: Cambridge University Press, 1979.

——. "Crises: The World Economy, the Movements, and the Ideologies." In Albert Bergesen, ed. *Crises in the World-System*. Beverly Hills, CA: Sage, 1983:21–36.

——. *The Politics of the World Economy: The States, the Movements, and the Civilizations*. Cambridge: Cambridge University Press, 1984.

WALLERSTEIN, JUDITH S., and SANDRA BLAKESLEE. *Second Chances: Men, Women, and Children a Decade After Divorce*. New York: Ticknor & Fields, 1989.

WALSH, MARY WILLIAMS. "No Time to Put Your Feet Up as Retirement Comes in Stages." *New York Times* (April 15, 2001):1, 18.

WALTON, JOHN, and CHARLES RAGIN. "Global and National Sources of Political Protest: Third World Responses to the Debt Crisis." *American Sociological Review*. Vol. 55, No. 6 (December 1990):876–90.

WARR, MARK, and CHRISTOPHER G. ELLISON. "Rethinking Social Reactions to Crime: Personal and Altruistic Fear in Family Households." *American Journal of Sociology*. Vol. 106, No. 3 (November 2000):551–78.

WATSON, WILLIAM. "Economy." In *The Canadian Encyclopedia*. 2d ed. Edmonton: Hurtig Publishers. 1988: 652–56.

WATTS, DUNCAN J. "Networks, Dynamics, and the Small-World Phenomenon." *American Journal of Sociology*. Vol. 105, No. 2 (September 1999):493–527.

WEBER, ADNA FERRIN. *The Growth of Cities*. New York: Columbia University Press, 1963; orig. 1899.

WEBER, MAX. *The Protestant Ethic and the Spirit of Capitalism*. New York: Charles Scribner's Sons, 1958; orig. 1904–05.

——. *Economy and Society*. G. Roth and C. Wittich, eds. Berkeley: University of California Press, 1978; orig. 1921.

WEEKS, JOHN R. "The Demography of Islamic Nations." *Population Bulletin*. Vol. 43, No. 4 (December 1988). Washington, DC: Population Reference Bureau.

WEITZMAN, LENORE J. *The Divorce Revolution: The Unexpected Social and Economic Consequences for Women and Children in America*. New York: Free Press, 1985.

——. "The Economic Consequences of Divorce Are Still Unequal: Comment on Peterson." *American Sociological Review*. Vol. 61, No. 3 (June 1996):537–38.

WELLER, JACK M., and E.L. QUARANTELLI. "Neglected Characteristics of Collective Behavior." *American Journal of Sociology*. Vol. 79, No. 3 (November 1973):665–85.

WELLMAN, BARRY. "The Community Question: Intimate Networks of East Yorkers." *American Journal of Sociology*. Vol. 84, No. 5 (March 1979):1201–31.

WELLMAN, BARRY, and MILENA GULIA. "Net-Surfers Don't Ride Alone: Virtual Communities as Communities." In Barry Wellman, ed. *Networks in the Global Village: Life in Contemporary Communities*. Boulder, CO: Westview Press, 1999. pp. 331–66.

WELLS, JENNIFER. "Jobs." *Maclean's* (March 11, 1996):12–16.

WENDELL, SUSAN. "Toward a Feminist Theory of Disability." In E.D. Nelson and B.W. Robinson, eds. *Gender in the 1990's: Images, Realities, and Issues*. Toronto: Nelson Canada, 1995. pp. 455–56.

WENTE, MARGARET. "Never again? Who are we kidding?" *The Globe and Mail* (May 11, 2006a):A21.

——. "The baby and the bath water." *The Globe and Mail* (April 22, 2006b):A21.

——. "A+ for cultural capital." *The Globe and Mail* (June 27, 2006c):A15.

WESSELMAN, HANK. *Visionseeker: Shared Wisdom from the Place of Refuge*. Carlsbad, CA: Hay House, 2001.

WESTHUES, ANNE, and JOYCE S. COHEN. "International Adoption in Canada: Predictions of Well-Being." In *Child Welfare in Canada: Research and Policy Implications*, ed. Joe Hudson and Burt Galaway. Toronto: Thompson Educational Publishing, 1994.

WHALEN, JACK, and RICHARD FLACKS. *Beyond the Barricades: The Sixties Generation Grows Up*. Philadelphia: Temple University Press, 1989.

WHEELIS, ALLEN. *The Quest for Identity*. New York: Norton, 1958.

WHITAKER, MARK. "Ten Ways to Fight Terrorism." *Newsweek* (July 1, 1985):26–29.

WHITE, RALPH, and RONALD LIPPITT. "Leader Behavior and Member Reaction in Three 'Social Climates.' " In Dorwin Cartwright and Alvin Zander, eds. *Group Dynamics*. Evanston, IL: Row, Peterson, 1953. pp. 586–611.

WHITE, WALTER. *Rope and Faggot.* New York: Arno Press and New York Times, 1969; orig. 1929.

WHITMAN, DAVID. "Shattering Myths about the Homeless." *U.S. News & World Report* (March 20, 1989):26, 28.

WHITNELL, TIM. "MD Wants Tabloids Banned." *The Burlington Post* (September 7, 1997):1.

WHORF, BENJAMIN LEE. "The Relation of Habitual Thought and Behavior to Language." In *Language, Thought, and Reality.* Cambridge, MA: Technology Press of MIT; New York: Wiley, 1956:134–59; orig. 1941.

WHYTE, DONALD R., and FRANK G. VALLEE. "Sociology." In *The Canadian Encyclopedia.* 2d ed. Edmonton: Hurtig Publishers, 1988. pp. 2035–36.

WHYTE, WILLIAM FOOTE. *Street Corner Society.* 3d ed. Chicago, IL: University of Chicago Press, 1981; orig. 1943.

WIDOM, CATHY SPATZ. "Childhood Sexual Abuse and Its Criminal Consequences." *Society.* Vol. 33, No. 4 (May/June 1996):47–53.

WILDAVSKY, BEN. "Small World, Isn't It?" *U.S. News & World Report* (April 1, 2002):68.

WILES, P.J.D. *Economic Institutions Compared.* New York: Halsted Press, 1977.

WILKINS, R., and O.B. ADAMS. *Healthfulness of Life: A Unified View of Mortality, Institutionalization, and Non-institutionalized Disability in Canada.* Montreal: The Institute for Research on Public Policy, 1983. p. 126.

WILLIAMS, PETER W. *America's Religions: From Their Origins to the Twenty-First Century.* Urbana: University of Illinois Press, 2002.

WILLIAMS, ROBIN M., JR. *American Society: A Sociological Interpretation.* 3rd ed. New York: Knopf, 1970.

WILLIAMS, T. *The Impact of Television: A Natural Experiment in Three Communities.* New York: Academic Press, 1986.

WILLIAMSON, JEFFREY G., and PETER H. LINDERT. *American Inequality: A Macroeconomic History.* New York: Academic Press, 1980.

WILSON, BARBARA. "National Television Violence Study." Reported in Julia Duin, "Study Finds Cartoon Heroes Initiate Too Much Violence." *Washington Times* (April 17, 1998).A4.

WILSON, EDWARD O. "Biodiversity, Prosperity, and Value." In F. Herbert Bormann and Stephen R. Kellert, eds. *Ecology, Economics, and Ethics: The Broken Circle.* New Haven, CT: Yale University Press, 1991. pp. 3–10.

WILSON, ROBERT R. "Playing and Being Played: Experiencing West Edmonton Mall." In Lynne van Luven and Priscilla L. Walton, eds. *Pop Can: Popular Culture in Canada.* Scarborough, ON: Prentice Hall, 1999. pp. 82–90.

WILSON, THOMAS C. "Urbanism and Tolerance: A Test of Some Hypotheses Drawn from Wirth and Stouffer." *American Sociological Review.* Vol. 50, No. 1 (February 1985):117–23.

——. "Urbanism and Unconventionality: The Case of Sexual Behavior." *Social Science Quarterly.* Vol. 76, No. 2 (June 1995):346–63.

WINES, MICHAEL. "Democracy Has to Start Somewhere." *New York Times* (February 6, 2005). [Online] Available April 24, 2005, at http://www.research navigator.com/.

WINKS, ROBIN W. "Slavery". In *The Canadian Encyclopedia.* 2d ed. Edmonton: Hurtig Publishers, 1988: 2010–11.

WINSLOW, DONNA. *The Canadian Airborne Regiment in Somalia. A Socio-cultural Inquiry.* Ottawa: Commission of Inquiry into the Deployment of Canadian Forces to Somalia, 1997.

WIRTH, LOUIS. "Urbanism as a Way of Life." *American Journal of Sociology.* Vol. 44, No. 1 (July 1938):1–24.

WOLFE, DAVID B. "Targeting the Mature Mind." *American Demographics.* Vol. 16, No. 3 (March 1994):32–36.

WOLFF, LEE, and DOROTA GEISSEL. "Street Prostitution in Canada." In Statistics Canada, *Canadian Social Trends. Volume 3.* Toronto: Thompson Educational Publishing, 2000.

WOLFGANG, MARVIN E., TERRENCE P. THORNBERRY, and ROBERT M. FIGLIO. *From Boy to Man, From Delinquency to Crime.* Chicago, IL: University of Chicago Press, 1987.

WOMEN IN CANADA: A STATISTICAL REPORT. 3d ed. Catalogue No. 89-503E. Ottawa: Statistics Canada, 1995.

WOOD, DANIELL. "Death Wish: Would You Choose an Assisted Suicide?" *Chatelaine* (July 25–29, 1993):94.

WOODWARD, KENNETH L. "Feminism and the Churches." *Newsweek.* Vol. 13, No. 7 (February 13, 1989):58–61.

WORLD BANK. *World Development Report 1993.* New York: Oxford University Press, 1993.

——. *Entering the 21st Century: World Development Report 1999/2000.* New York: Oxford University Press, 2000.

——. *World Development Report 2000/2001.* Washington, DC: The World Bank, 2001a.

——. *World Development Indicators 2001.* Washington, DC: The World Bank, 2001b.

——. *2005 World Development Indicators.* Washington, DC: World Bank, 2005.

WORLD HEALTH ORGANIZATION. *Constitution of the World Health Organization.* New York: World Health Organization Interim Commission, 1946.

WORLD VALUES SURVEY, 1990–1993. Ann Arbor, MI: Inter-university Consortium for Political and Social Research, 1994.

WORLD VALUES SURVEY. "Latest Publications: Predict 2005—FIGURE." 2004. [Online] Available April 25, 2005, at http://www.worldvaluessurvey.com/library/index.html.

WORSLEY, PETER. "Models of the World System." In Mike Featherstone, ed. *Global Culture: Nationalism, Globalization, and Modernity.* Newbury Park, CA: Sage, 1990. pp. 83–95.

WORTHINGTON, PETER. Interview with Clifford Olsen. *Saturday Night* (July/August 1993).

WOTHERSPOON, TERRY. "Transforming Canada's Education System: The Impact on Educational Inequalities, Opportunities and Benefits." In B. Singh Bolaria, ed. *Social Issues and Contradictions in Canadian Society.* Toronto: Harcourt Brace Jovanovich, 1991. pp. 448–63.

WOTHERSPOON, TERRY, and VIC SATZEWICH. *First Nations: Race, Class, and Gender Relations.* Scarborough, ON: Nelson, 1993.

WREN, CHRISTOPHER S. "In Soweto-by-the-Sea, Misery Lives on as Apartheid Fades." *New York Times* (June 9, 1991):1, 7.

WRIGHT, RICHARD A. *In Defense of Prisons.* Westport, CT: Greenwood Press, 1994.

WRIGHT, ROBERT. "The Man Who Invented the Web." *Time,* Canadian Edition (May 19, 1997):44.

WRIGHT, STUART A., and ELIZABETH S. PIPER. "Families and Cults: Familial Factors Related to Youth Leaving or Remaining in Deviant Religious Groups." *Journal of Marriage and the Family.* Vol. 48, No. 1 (February 1986):15–25.

WU, LAWRENCE L. "Effects of Family Instability, Income, and Income Instability on the Risk of a Premarital Birth." *American Sociological Review.* Vol. 61, No. 3 (June 1996):386–406.

WU, ZHENG. *Cohabitation: An Alternative Form of Family Living.* Don Mills, ON: Oxford University Press, 2000.

YATES, RONALD E. "Growing Old in Japan. They Ask Gods for a Way Out." *Philadelphia Inquirer* (August 14, 1986):3A.

YEATTS, DALE E. "Creating the High Performance Self-Managed Work Team: A Review of Theoretical Perspectives." Paper presented at the annual meeting of the Southwest Social Science Association, Dallas, February 1994.

YOELS, WILLIAM C., and JEFFREY MICHAEL CLAIR. "Laughter in the Clinic: Humor in Social Organization." *Symbolic Interaction.* Vol. 18, No. 1 (1995):39–58.

YORK, GEOFFREY. "UN Body Chastises Canada on Poverty." *The Globe and Mail* (June 25, 1993):A1–2.

——. "Locals unwelcome at Chinese orphanages: Agencies favour overseas adoptions." *The Globe and Mail* (July 24, 2006):A3.

YORK, RICHARD, EUGENE A. ROSA, and THOMAS DEITZ. "Bridging Environmental Science with Environmental Policy: Plasticity of Population, Affluence, and Technology." *Social Science Quarterly.* Vol. 83, No. 1 (March 2002):18–34.

YUDELMAN, MONTAGUE, and LAURA J. M. KEALY. "The Graying of Farmers." *Population Today.* Vol. 28, No. 4 (May/June, 2000):6.

ZHAO, DINGXIN. "Ecologies of Social Movements: Student Mobilization during the 1989 Prodemocracy Movement in Beijing." *American Journal of Sociology.* Vol. 103, No. 6 (May 1998):1493–1529.

ZIMBARDO, PHILIP G. "Pathology of Imprisonment." *Society.* Vol. 9 (April 1972):4–8.

ZURCHER, LOUIS A., and DAVID A. SNOW. "Collective Behavior and Social Movements." In Morris Rosenberg and Ralph Turner, eds. *Social Psychology: Sociological Perspectives.* New York: Basic Books, 1981:447–82.

PHOTO CREDITS

Roncen Patrick/Corbis/Sygma; p. 291, Peter Charlesworth; p. 292, Getty Images, Inc.—Agence France Presse; p. 294 (top left) Martin Benjamin/The Image Works, (top right) Peter Turnley/Corbis/Bettmann, (bottom) Pablo Bartholomew/Getty Images, Inc.—Liaison; p. 296, Smiley N. Pool/Dallas Mornning News/Corbis/Bettmann; p. 297, David Butow/Redux Pictures; p. 299, Yuri Cortez/ Agence France Presse/Getty Images; p. 302, (left) Joe McDonald/Corbis/Bettmann, (centre and right) Robert van der Hilst/Corbis/Bettmann; p. 303, Malcolm Linton/Getty Images, Inc.—Liaison; p. 304, Steve Maines/Stock Boston; p. 307, Robert van der Hilst/The Image Works; p. 309, Mark Edwards/Still Pictures/Peter Arnold, Inc.

Chapter 13: Page 316, (left) Bob Daemmrich/The Image Works, (centre) Corbis Royalty Free, (right) Joe Bator/Corbis/Bettmann; p. 317, Gideon Mendel/Corbis/Bettmann; p. 318, © Barrett&MacKay Photo; p. 320, Angela Fisher/Carol Beckwith/Robert Estall Photo Agency; p. 323, Nancy Richmond/The Image Works; p. 324, CBS TV/Picture Desk, Inc./Kobal Collection; p. 326, (left) courtesy Canadian Forces, (right) Jake Wright; p. 334, CP Photo/Jonathan Hayward; p. 336, David Grossman/The Image Works; p. 338, Kuenzig/laif/Aurora Photos; p. 339, Willinger/Hulton Archive/Getty Images Inc.—Hulton Archive Photos; p. 340, HBO/Picture Desk, Inc./Kobal Collection; p. 344, CP Photo/Paul Chiasson.

Chapter 14: Page 348, (left) Marcia Keegan, Corbis/Bettmann, (centre) Carole Bellaiche/Corbis/Sygma, (right) Kevin Fleming/Corbis/Bettmann; p. 349, David R. Frazier Photolibrary, Inc.; p. 350, Black Cultural Centre for Nova Scotia; p. 351, (top left) Joel Gordon/Joel Gordon Photography, (top center) Leong Ka Tai, (top right) Owen Franken/Corbis/Bettmann, (bottom left) Charles O'Rear/Corbis/Bettmann, (bottom center) Paul W. Liebhardt, (bottom right) Lisi Dennis/Lisl Dennis; p. 352, AP Wide World Photos; p. 353, (left) Linda Gerber, (right) Sergent Éric Jolin, Rideau Hall; p. 369, Paul Conklin/PhotoEdit; p. 355, Peter Turnley/Corbis; p. 358, Lincoln MacCauley Alexander; p. 362, Culver Pictures Inc., p. 366, EPA Photo/EPA/Warren Toda; p. 368, CP Photo/Nathan Denette; p. 369, logo courtesy of APTN.

Chapter 15: Page 378, (left) Karen Kasmauski/Corbis/Bettmann, (centre) UN/DPI, (right) AP Wide World Photos; p. 379, Ariel Skelley/Corbis/Bettmann; p. 380, Jean Konda-Witte/Abbotsford Times; p. 383, Tom Wagner/Corbis/SABA Press Photos, Inc.; p. 384, Michael Drummond, Photographer; p. 385, (left) Michael Newman/PhotoEdit, (right) © John Garrett/Corbis, p. 387, *The Whitehorse Star*/Cathie Archbould; p. 391, Meric W. Wallace/Warner Bros/Bureau L.A. Collections/Corbis/Bettmann; p. 392, CP Photo/John Mahoney; p. 395, Laima Druskis/Pearson Education/PH College; p. 396, Chris Rainier/Corbis/Bettmann; p. 399, Spencer Grant/Stock Boston.

Chapter 16: Page 402, (left) Jonathan Blair/Corbis/Bettmann, (centre) Beawiharta/Reuters/Corbis/Bettmann, (right) Jim Pickerell/The Stock Connection; p. 403, Mark Wilson/Getty Images, Inc.—Liaison; p. 404, Marko Shark; p. 405, Underwood & Underwood/Library of Congress; p. 406, Sven-Olof Lindblad/Photo Researchers, Inc.; p. 411, (left) Bellavia/REA/Corbis/SABA Press Photos, Inc., (right) John Bryson/Corbis/Sygma; p. 412, Alamy Images; p. 413, Gamma Press USA, Inc.; p. 418, Christopher Morris; p. 422, (left) Joel Stettenheim/CORBIS, (right) Matthew Borkoski/Index Stock Imagery, Inc.; p. 425, Chris Brown/Corbis/SABA Press Photos, Inc.

Chapter 17: Page 430, (left) Paul Fusco/Magnum Photos, Inc., (centre) Toby Talbot/AP Wide World Photos, (right) Jason Reed/Reuters/Corbis/Reuters America LLC; p. 431, CP Photo/Nathan Denette; p. 432, AP Wide World Photos; p. 433, The official portrait of the Right Honourable Pierre Elliot Trudeau by Myfanwy Spencer Pavelic/© House of Commons/By Myfanwy Spencer Pavelic; p. 434, Durand/SIPA Press; p. 438, David Ball/Index Stock Imagery, Inc.; p. 442, Winnipeg Free Press /Joe Bryksa; p. 444, Elections Canada; p. 447, (left) CP Photo/Clement Allard, (right) CP Photo/Adrian Wyld; p. 451, (left and right) National Archives of Canada; p. 454, Sarnia Observer/Glenn Ogilvie; p. 455, AP Wide World Photos; p. 458, Joe McNally, Life Magazine © TimePix.

Chapter 18: Page 462, (left) Corbis Royalty Free, (centre) Corbis Royalty Free, (right) Owen Franken/Corbis/Bettmann; p. 464, Toronto Sun/Craig Robertson; p. 465, Julie Johnson; p. 466, (left) Getty Images, (right) AP Wide World Photos; p. 469, The Bridgeman Art Library International; p. 470, Paul Marcus/Studio SPM, Inc.; p. 473, AP Wide World Photos; p. 478, Mark J. Barrett/Creative Eye/MIRA.com; p. 482, Bill Bachmann/The Image Works

Chapter 19: Page 490, (left) Bojan Brecelj/Corbis/Bettmann, (centre) Mashkov Yuri/ITAR-TASS/Corbis/Bettmann, (right) Friedrich Stark/Das Fotoarchiv/Peter Arnold, Inc.; p. 491, Jason Reed/Reuters/Corbis/ Reuters America LLC; p. 492, © *National Post*/Brent Foster; p. 493, Michael Newman/PhotoEdit; p. 494, Galen Rowell/ Peter Arnold, Inc.; p. 496, © David Rubinger/Bettmann/CORBIS—All Rights Reserved; p. 498 (left) © Doranne Jacobson/International Images, (right) Ian Berry/Magnum Photos, Inc.; p. 501, Annie Griffiths Belt/NGS Image Collection; p. 504, AP Wide World Photos; p. 509, Philip North-Coombes/Getty Images Inc.—Stone Allstock; p. 512, © Gary Braasch/Bettmann/CORBIS—All rights reserved.

Chapter 20: Page 516, (left) Lynsey Addario/Corbis/Bettmann, (centre) UN/DPI, (right) Louise Gubb/Corbis/SABA Press Photos, Inc.; p. 517, Paul Barton/Corbis/Bettmann; p. 518, Artic Photo/ B+C Alexander; p. 519, AP Wide World Photos; p. 522, courtesy Orizon; p. 523, Bob Daemmrich Photography, Inc.; p. 525, www.slidefarm.com; p. 526 (left) Michael Newman/PhotoEdit, (right) Getty Images, Inc.; p. 534, First Light; p. 535, First Light.

Chapter 21: Page 540, (left) Gregory Primo Gottman, (centre) Richard T. Nowitz/Corbis/Bettmann, (right) Gideon Mendel/Corbis/Bettmann; p. 541, AP Wide World Photos; p. 542, Martin Parr/Magnum Photos, Inc.; p. 543, Steve Prezant/Corbis/Stock Market; p. 548, © Lucy Nicholson/Bettmann/ CORBIS—All Rights Reserved; p. 552 (left) The Stephen Lewis Foundation © 2006, (right) George Mulala/Peter Arnold, Inc.; p. 553, CP Photo/Andrew Vaughan; p. 554, Adalbert Franz Seligmann, *Allgemeines Krankenhaus* (General Hospital), 19th Century Painting, canvas/Erich Lessing/Art Resource, NY; p. 555, Galen Rowell/Mountain Light Photography, Inc.; p. 557, Billy E. Barnes/PhotoEdit; p. 558, Copyright The Supreme Court of Canada, The Supreme Court of Canada Collection; p. 563, Steve Murez/Black Star.

Chapter 22: Page 566, (left) Dinodia/The Image Works, (centre) Lester Lefkowitz/ Corbis/Bettmann, (right) David Austen/Woodfin Camp & Associates; p. 567, Wilfried Krecichwost/Zefa/Corbis Zefa Collection; p. 568, Ontario Ministry of Agriculture and Food; p. 571, David and Peter Turnley/Corbis/Bettmann; p. 575, Lauren Goodsmith/ The Image Works; p. 576, AP Wide World Photos; p. 580, Mario Tursi /Miramax /Dimension Films /The Kobal Collection; p. 581, First Light/Ron Watts; p. 585, Toronto Star/Dick Lock; p. 586, James King Holmes/Science Photo Library/Photo Researchers, Inc.; p. 588, Dave Amit/Reuters/Landov LLC; p. 589, Corporate Knights; p. 592, Eric Pasquier/Corbis/Sygma.

Chapter 23: Page 598, (left) Bobby Yip/Reuters/Corbis/Reuters America LLC, (centre) A. Ramey/PhotoEdit, (right) Fabrizio Bensch/Reuters/ Corbis/Reuters America LLC; p. 599, AP Wide World Photos; p. 600, CP Photo/Shaney Komulainen; p. 602, The Kingston Whig-Standard; p. 603, Canapress, CP Photo; p. 604, © David Butow/Corbis SABA; p. 606, Sabina Dowell; p. 608, © Joel Gordon 2005—All rights reserved; p. 609 (left) Rick Wilking/Reuters/Corbis/Bettmann; (centre) Al Grillo/Peter Arnold, Inc.; (right) AP Wide World Photos; p. 610, CORBIS—NY; p. 614, CP Photo/ Tom Hanson; p. 616 (left) Corbis/Bettmann, (right) Huynh Cong "Nick" Ut/AP Wide World Photos; p. 620, Reuters/Peter Jones.

Chapter 24: Page 624, (left) Joe McDonald/Joe McDonald, (centre) Ed Kashi/Corbis/ Bettmann, (right) B.S.P.I./Corbis/Bettmann; p. 625, Robert Essel NYC/Corbis/Bettmann; p. 626, Mauri Rautkari/World Wide Fund for Nature; p. 628, China Images/Getty Images, Inc.; p. 636, Eric Draper/AP Wide World Photos; p. 640 (left) Ed Pritchard/Getty Images Inc.—Stone Allstock, (right) Mark Richards/PhotoEdit.

NAME INDEX

SUBJECT INDEX

Note: Entries for tables, figures, and notes are followed by *t*, *f*, and *n*, respectively.